**2018**

# International Student Handbook

**2018**

CollegeBoard

# International Student Handbook

**31st Edition**

The College Board, New York

**The College Board**

The College Board is a mission-driven not-for-profit organization that connects students to college success and opportunity. Founded in 1900, the College Board was created to expand access to higher education. Today, the membership association is made up of over 6,000 of the world's leading educational institutions and is dedicated to promoting excellence and equity in education. Each year, the College Board helps more than seven million students prepare for a successful transition to college through programs and services in college readiness and college success — including the SAT® and the Advanced Placement Program®. The organization also serves the education community through research and advocacy on behalf of students, educators, and schools.

For further information, visit www.collegeboard.org.

Editorial inquiries concerning this book should be directed to Guidance Publications, The College Board, 250 Vesey Street, New York, NY 10281; or telephone 800-323-7155.

Copies of this book are available from your local bookseller or may be ordered from College Board Publications, P.O. Box 7500, London, KY 40742-7500. The book may also be ordered online through the College Board Store at www.collegeboard.org. The price is $31.99.

ISBN: 978-1-4573-0925-0

Printed in the United States of America

Distributed by Macmillan. For information on bulk purchase, please contact Macmillan Corporate and Premium Sales Department at 800-221-7945, ext. 5442.

JAN 0 2 2018

# Contents

# Preface

The importance of international educational exchange in promoting understanding across national, cultural, religious and racial borders cannot be underestimated. Hundreds of thousands of students who study overseas each year create a global citizenry that is culturally aware and respectful of people of different backgrounds. These benefits translate into a more understanding and peaceful world society. Individually, students are enriched and draw lifetime benefits from the opportunity to learn a discipline in a different cultural context, acquire or perfect a foreign language, be immersed in and learn from another culture, and teach one's culture to others.

The United States has an unparalleled system of higher education in terms of the number of institutions and the variety and quality of their programs of study. There are more than 3,900 universities offering bachelor's and associate degrees in more than 1,200 subject areas. The sheer size and diversity of the U.S. higher education system can make the task of finding the institution that is right for you seem daunting. The process of researching, selecting and applying to colleges and universities in the United States is difficult and time-consuming, but it is well worth the investment.

It is important for students to find the institution that will best meet their educational, professional and personal needs. With this in mind, the objective of the *College Board International Student Handbook* is to provide international students with up-to-date, objective and thorough information to help them make informed decisions about their education. The undergraduate institutions described in this book are fully accredited by agencies recognized by the U.S. Department of Education and encourage international student enrollment.

The book is designed to be used in conjunction with the *College Board College Handbook* and the *College Board Book of Majors*, as well as the wide array of resources available on the Internet, in order to find the college or university that best fits a student's needs. Nearly all colleges and universities have websites, which are listed in this publication. The College Board encourages you to explore our own website (bigfuture.org) where students can conduct a college search, register for the SAT® and SAT Subject Tests™, and learn about materials to prepare for the exams.

We would like to acknowledge those who worked on the *International Student Handbook*, especially the following nine admission professionals who provided their expertise.

Stephanie Balmer, Dean of Admissions, Dickinson College, Carlisle, Pa.

Jeff Brenzel, Dean of Undergraduate Admissions, Yale University, New Haven, CT.

Peter Briggs, Director, Office for International Students and Scholars, Michigan State University, East Lansing, Mich.

Ken Bus, Director, International Students Program, Glendale Community College, Ariz.

Joseph DeCrosta, Director of International Programs, Duquesne University, Pittsburgh, Pa.

David Dillman, Executive Director of Transfer and International Student Admission, Austin College, Sherman, Texas

Jennifer Fondiller, Dean of Admissions and Financial Aid, Barnard College, New York, NY

Ann Gogerty, Senior International Admissions Counselor, Iowa State University, Ames, Iowa

Mark G. Reid, Executive Director of International Admission, University of Miami, Coral Gables, Fla.

This publication is the result of the cooperation between College Board International and the College Board's Guidance Publications department; government agencies involved with international educational exchange; EducationUSA advisers; and international admission officers at U.S. colleges and universities. The college data are based primarily on information supplied by the colleges themselves in response to the College Board's Annual Survey of Colleges 2017, with some data supplied by federal and state agencies. Data collection, management and verification was directed by Chris Hagan, with the guidance of Joe Williams. Jenny Xie, Randy Peery, Kayla Tompkins, David Christ, Karen Villa, Jessica Shaddy, Ivonne Lester, Kelsey Cross, and Blake Bralley compiled, edited and verified the data. Technical support was provided by Assar Tarazi, Susan Redick, Priyanka Sabapathy, and Srinivas Bachu. Tom Vanderberg was responsible for the overall editorial direction of this book.

We wish to give special acknowledgment to Renée Gernand, who recently retired. It is with sincere appreciation that we thank her for the leadership and service she gave to both the College Board and to the entire higher education community.

All these professionals share a common belief that the proper placement of and service to international students at U.S. campuses are critical to the development of mutual understanding through the exchange process. As stated by the Bureau of Educational and Cultural Affairs, U.S. Department of State: "The doors of U.S. educational institutions are open to all qualified students from around the world. The United States is proud of an educational system that attracts students and scholars from across the globe."

*College Board International*
The College Board

# Part I:
# Applying to college in the United States

# Planning calendar for U.S. study

## Two years before admission...

For admission in August or September, begin two years in advance.

### September

- If you have access to the Internet, visit the College Board's websites at bigfuture.org. These sites are rich with information on colleges, careers and scholarships.

- Find out about sources of U.S. college information in your country — libraries, advising centers, U.S. educational organizations or commissions, and the Internet. The U.S. Department of State sponsors a network of EducationUSA advising centers in more than 170 countries to provide students with free, up-to-date information and help to apply for degree programs at American colleges and universities. A listing of these centers is located in Part III of this book.

- Review the sections in this book on choosing and comparing colleges. Use the College Search on the BigFuture™ website (https://bigfuture.collegeboard.org) to find colleges and universities that have the features you want. Once you have a manageable list, use this book to get essential international student information about each of those colleges. College Search also allows you to link directly to any college's website, where you can gather more information.

- Consider taking an Advanced Placement (AP) Program course and/or AP Exam. The College Board's Advanced Placement Program provides high school students with the opportunity to study and learn at the college level. AP Exams are administered every year in May.

- If English is not your first language, learn about the English proficiency examination required. Two examples of this type of test are the Test of English as a Foreign Language (TOEFL) and the International English Language Testing System (IELTS). Get the information bulletin and registration materials. See also "Test information" on page 31.

- Be sure you are taking courses that prepare you for college or graduate study at U.S. educational institutions.

- Register for the SAT or SAT Subject Tests if you plan to take the tests in autumn. Information on the SAT is available at sat.org, and on page 31.

### October

- Register for the SAT or SAT Subject Tests if you plan to take the tests in November or December.

- Discuss your plans with an adviser. Ask your adviser or counselor whether U.S. college representatives will be visiting your country. Note the dates and places, and try to attend at least one meeting.

### November

- Register for the SAT or SAT Subject Tests if you plan to take the tests in December.

- Discuss your plans with your teachers, family, people who work in your field of study and, if possible, people who have studied in the United States.

- Contact colleges by visiting their websites, or by airmail or email to request catalogs.

### December

- Register for the SAT or SAT Subject Tests if you plan to take the tests in May or June.

## January

- Review college information you have collected from guidebooks, college catalogs and online sources. Choose three to six colleges to research more fully.

## February

- Develop your financial plan. Consider how you will pay for your education, living expenses and transportation for each year of study in the United States.
- Find out about scholarships and other types of financial aid available in your country. Request the application materials.

## March

- Register for the SAT or SAT Subject Tests if you plan to take the tests in May or June.
- Schedule an appointment to take the TOEFL, or another English proficiency test.

## April

- Register for the SAT or SAT Subject Tests if you plan to take the tests in June.
- Write to the colleges you have selected to request a current catalog and application form, or go to their websites to get that material. Be sure to request financial aid and scholarship application forms if you intend to apply for aid.

## May

- Identify the teachers, counselors and other adults you will ask for letters of recommendation.

## June

- If there is a break in your school schedule, use the time to improve your English skills by reading, writing and speaking in English whenever you can.

## July

- Read college application instructions carefully to find out what information is required and when it must reach each college to which you are applying.

# One year before admission...

## August

- Request information on intensive English language programs in the event you do not meet English proficiency requirements.
- If an essay is required for your applications, begin your first draft.
- If you have not yet taken admission tests, or if you and your adviser think you can improve your scores, register for a test date, preferably no later than November.

## September

- Find out the procedures at your school (and any other secondary school or college you have attended) for sending your academic records (transcripts) to the colleges to which you are applying.
- If colleges have provided forms for recommendations, give them to the teachers and other adults you have contacted.
- Register for the SAT or SAT Subject Tests if you plan to take the tests in October or November.

## October

- Register for the SAT or SAT Subject Tests if you plan to take the tests in November or December.
- Complete the essay for your applications.
- Complete the financial aid application forms.
- Apply early to colleges.

## November

- Be sure you request that your scores on all required tests be sent to all the colleges on your list.

- Check to see that the people from whom you requested recommendations have sent them.

- Be sure that your school or college has sent your academic records to all the colleges on your list.

## December

- Reply promptly and completely to any requests for additional information you may receive from colleges to which you have applied.

## January

- Be sure to keep up the quality of your studies. Your complete academic record can be important in admission decisions.

- If you have not already completed all financial aid application forms, be sure to do so now and mail them as soon as possible.

## February

- Review your financial plan for your education. If you think you may need additional help, investigate any sources of financial aid in your country that you may have overlooked.

## March

- Some colleges with a rolling admission policy require a response and a deposit soon. Note any reply dates that apply to you.

## April

- You will probably hear from colleges this month or next. Review the section in this book on what to do if you are accepted at more than one college.

- Be sure to send your reply and deposit by the acceptance deadline.

- Apply for a passport, if you do not have one already.

## May

- Write to colleges from which you have not heard.

- Review predeparture procedures.

- Confirm housing reservations at the college of your choice.

- Apply for a visa appropriate for your student status. Check with the U.S. embassy or consulate to be sure you meet all requirements for entry into the United States.

## June

- Investigate predeparture orientation programs in your country. Ask the adviser at the EducationUSA advising center in your country (see Part III).

- Make travel arrangements.

## July

- Use this opportunity to continue upgrading your English proficiency.

- If possible, earn money toward your expenses.

## August

- Make sure all your predeparture activities are complete.

- Have a wonderful trip!

# Why study in the United States?

Although travel of any kind is both exciting and informative, studying outside your home country offers unique possibilities. It allows you to completely immerse yourself in a new environment: in the classroom you gain exposure to new learning techniques and perspectives; outside the classroom you have the opportunity to meet people from different cultures. This can be a life-changing experience, giving you a new understanding of international political, social and economic issues. In addition, study abroad develops self-confidence, cross-cultural awareness and open-mindedness to new ideas and values. Employers worldwide consider these important assets.

Of all the possible places international students choose to study, the largest proportion choose the United States. In fact, today about 18 percent of all international students in the world are studying in the United States. There are a number of features that make U.S. education so popular.

**Quality.** The U.S. higher education system has an international reputation for quality. There are distinguished programs available at both the undergraduate and graduate levels in almost every field of study. Many universities attract world-renowned faculty and stand at the forefront of research and technological development. State-of-the-art facilities include libraries, laboratories, computers and other resources.

**Diversity of institutions and programs available.** The range of educational opportunities in the United States is enormous. No matter what college experience you are seeking, you can find it at one of more than 4,500 higher education institutions throughout the country. Here are just a few of the features you can choose among.

- **Size:** Institutions range from fewer than 1,000 to more than 50,000 students.

- **Student body:** Most colleges are coeducational, but there are some colleges for men only, and some for women only (these colleges are listed in the Special characteristics index in the back of this book).

- **Selectivity:** College admission policies range from highly selective to open admission.

- **Setting:** Campuses are located in small and large cities, suburban areas, and rural communities, and in a variety of climates.

- **Field of study:** With more than 1200 major fields of study to select from, you are likely to find a program that suits your interests.

- **Type of institution:** Choices range from liberal arts colleges that emphasize broad preparation in academic disciplines to technical schools that provide focused, career-related training. Some offer vocational programs, and a growing number of colleges offer options in distance learning.

**Flexibility.** One of the hallmarks of U.S. education is flexibility. At the undergraduate level, universities emphasize a broad, well-rounded education. You will be offered a wide range of classes — mathematics, science, the arts, social science, and languages — before finally having to choose a specialization. Even at the graduate level, related courses might be offered outside the department and in interdisciplinary fields. Students are actively involved in designing their course schedules because so many options are available. It is even possible to combine academic classes with work experience that will be recognized as part of the degree program. Most institutions have qualified staff on hand to help you make the best decisions to attain your academic goals. In the classroom, you are encouraged to be an active participant in the learning process. Faculty welcome, and generally expect, student input and encourage you to develop your own ideas and questions, and to express them.

**Campus life.** A successful college experience involves more than academic work. You will find a wide range of social, cultural and sports activities outside the classroom that will match your interests, such as internships and clubs. These give you a chance to make friends and at the same time develop team and leadership skills that will be useful in your future career.

It is important to understand the differences between the U.S. system of education and your own country's system. Please review the next section on U.S. higher education before continuing.

# U.S. higher education

## Organization of the U.S. education system

How education systems are organized varies from country to country. Higher education in the United States may be very different from education in your country.

Preuniversity studies in the United States consist of one or more years of preschool and kindergarten and 12 years of elementary and secondary school (also called "high school"). The chart in this section shows that the structure of preuniversity studies varies in how it is organized, but the body of knowledge to be covered is similar across the 50 states, regardless of how the school system is organized. The United States does not have a mandated course for secondary schools or a national examination. However, educators apply a common set of standards for assessing the basic competencies expected of secondary school graduates. The typical student receives a secondary school diploma at age 17 or 18.

The first level of higher (postsecondary) education is called "undergraduate" study and includes two-year and four-year programs. Two-year programs generally lead to an associate degree. An associate degree may be earned at a two-year community or junior college, or at a four-year college or university. There are two types of associate degree programs. Transfer programs provide the first two years of general education for transfer to a four-year program. Terminal programs (sometimes called vocational or technical) prepare students for a career in a specific trade.

Four-year colleges and universities offer programs that lead to a bachelor's degree (sometimes called the baccalaureate). The first two years usually are spent in courses that give you a broad foundation for future specialization. They may include English composition, world history, natural sciences, mathematics, languages and social sciences, plus some courses determined by your chosen field of study. The second two years are devoted to your major

academic subject. Five years of undergraduate study may be required for some fields. A few specialized institutions offer only the last two years of undergraduate study; these are called upper-division institutions.

"Graduate study" follows the completion of undergraduate education at the bachelor's degree level. It leads to the master's and doctoral degrees in academic disciplines or professional degrees such as law (J.D.), medicine (M.D.) and dentistry (D.D.S.). A master's degree generally requires one or two years of full-time study, but three-year master's degree programs exist. Doctoral and professional degrees require at least three years of full-time study and, with some research projects, will take even longer. Admission to graduate programs can be very competitive, and some first-professional degree programs limit admission to applicants who earned their bachelor's degrees at a U.S. college.

## Types of institutions

Degree programs are offered at many different types of institutions in the United States. Some institutions are public and some private. Although nearly all institutions receive some financial support from federal and state governments, public institutions rely heavily on public funds, while private institutions depend more on tuition, fees and contributions from foundations and private citizens. There are also some postsecondary schools called "proprietary" schools, which are operated on a for-profit basis by their owners.

### Admission Advice

*"One advantage of community colleges is pricing. Students can earn two years of credit at a much lower cost to them and their families than at a public or private university. Community colleges also have smaller classes, and there's a lot of support available to international students for improving their English."*

— Ken Bus, Glendale Community College, Glendale, Ariz.

*"Plain and simple, women's colleges in the United States are devoted to developing the untapped potential and ensuring success of women throughout their education, their careers and their lives."*

— Jennifer Fondiller, Barnard College NY

# Education in the United States

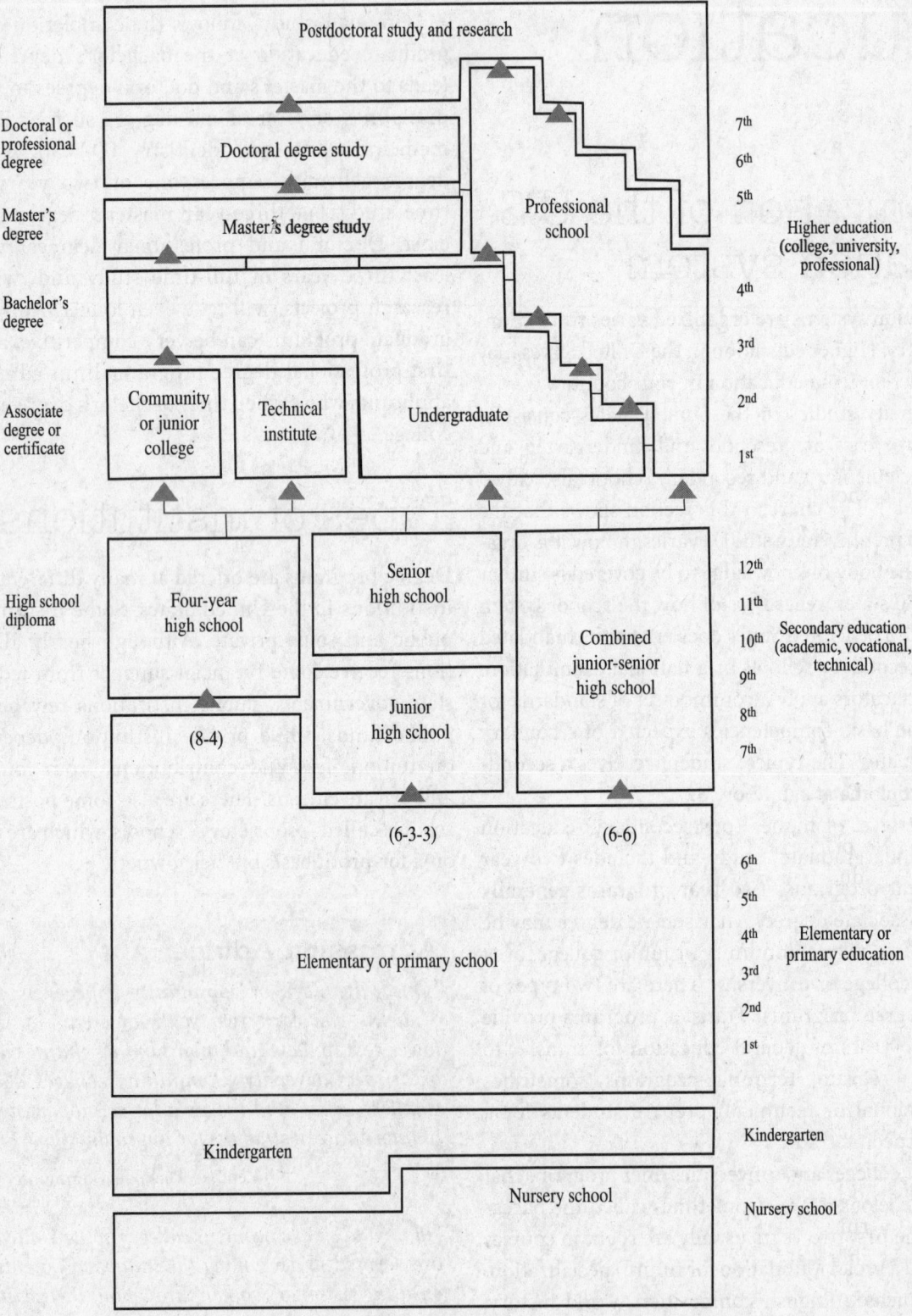

Postdoctoral study and research

Doctoral or professional degree

Doctoral degree study

Master's degree

Master's degree study

Professional school

Bachelor's degree

Associate degree or certificate

Community or junior college

Technical institute

Undergraduate

7th
6th
5th
4th
3rd
2nd
1st

Higher education (college, university, professional)

High school diploma

Four-year high school

(8-4)

Senior high school

Junior high school

(6-3-3)

Combined junior-senior high school

(6-6)

12th
11th
10th
9th
8th
7th

Secondary education (academic, vocational, technical)

6th
5th
4th
3rd
2nd
1st

Elementary or primary school

Elementary or primary education

Kindergarten

Nursery school

Kindergarten

Nursery school

# Degrees offered

## Undergraduate degrees

Associate degree programs are offered at two-year colleges, most of which are public *community colleges*, though some are private institutions called *junior colleges*. Associate degrees are also offered at some four-year colleges and universities. If you plan to earn an associate degree and then go on to a four-year bachelor's degree program, after you have enrolled be sure to consult with a transfer adviser to develop a program of study comparable to the first two years of a bachelor's program.

Bachelor's degrees are earned at four-year public or private *colleges* and *universities*. The terms *college* and *university* are used interchangeably in the United States and imply an institution that offers a bachelor's degree. Some *institutes*, such as the California Institute of Technology or the Massachusetts Institute of Technology, also offer bachelor's degrees. Some colleges and institutes, and all universities, also offer graduate degrees. Whether your bachelor's degree is earned at a college, university or institute, it will have the same value as a credential for applying to graduate school, provided that the institution is accredited. (See the accreditation information later in this section.)

## Graduate degrees

Graduate degree programs also are offered at several types of higher education institutions. Master's degrees can be earned at some four-year colleges as well as at universities and institutions that offer graduate study only. Master's degree programs generally take one or two years of full-time study to complete, but there are some that require three years of study. Doctoral and professional degree programs are offered at universities and graduate-only institutions. Doctoral degrees usually require a minimum of three years beyond the bachelor's degree.

It is possible to take a professional degree program without first earning a bachelor's degree, but those programs are highly selective and often require a very heavy course load. Professional degrees require a total of at least six years of study, including appropriate undergraduate preparation. An example of this type of program is the six-year medical program.

# Academic calendar

The academic year can be divided in a variety of ways. The most common is the semester system, in which the academic year is divided into two 16-week terms in fall and spring, with a long summer vacation and a shorter winter break. In the quarter system, the 12-month academic year is divided into four equal parts; most students take classes for three quarters of the year and take a break in the remaining quarter. There is also a trimester system, which divides the year into three 15-week terms. Under that system, students can attend school year-round and earn the same number of credits in the summer as they do in the fall or spring semesters. Some schools use a modified semester system called 4-1-4; they have a one-month intersession (or "winter term") between the two semesters, during which students take short courses, travel for a short study abroad experience, or do an internship. Regardless of how the calendar is arranged, you will cover approximately the same amount of material in a year of study. If you transfer from a college using the semester system to a university using a quarter system, the university will know how to convert your semester credits to quarter credits, and you will not lose any time.

# Accreditation

Accreditation in the United States is managed entirely by the institutions themselves, in cooperation with regional accrediting bodies. Reviews are conducted by committees of educators and other private citizens rather than by the government. Although institutions are not required to seek accreditation, most do because accreditation indicates that an institution meets standards of quality in its faculty and academic programs.

There are six regional accrediting associations that cover the entire country. A college or university that is regionally accredited has the highest type of institutional accreditation granted in the United States. Some institutions are accredited by national agencies that accredit specific types of schools, such as religious or technical schools.

Accreditation by a recognized agency is important for several reasons:

- Credits are more easily transferred from one accredited institution to another.

- Most scholarship, fellowship and grant programs are available only for study in accredited institutions.

- Degrees and diplomas are more generally recognized among accredited institutions within the United States as well as by governments and universities in other countries.

Specific academic or professional programs at a university, such as the engineering department, may also be accredited. Professional associations, concerned about standards of education, offer accreditation reviews to assure that the course offerings, facilities and program administration (such as faculty qualifications and teaching load) meet agreed-upon standards. Two examples of such professional accrediting agencies are the Association to Advance Collegiate Schools of Business and the Accreditation Board for Engineering and Technology, but there are many others. Each institution you consider will be able to tell you the standing of their academic programs with accrediting bodies.

Accreditation alone is not a guarantee of high standards, but the lack of accreditation may be a warning that the degree or credit earned may not be accepted by other institutions or your country's government. All the colleges and universities listed in Part II of this book are accredited by either regional associations or national agencies recognized by the U.S. Department of Education and the Council for Higher Education Accreditation. (A list of these agencies appears on page 14.)

You can verify a college's accreditation by going to the *U.S. Department of Education Database of Accredited Postsecondary Institutions and Programs* website at ope.ed.gov/accreditation, or on the Council for Higher Education Accreditation's website (chea.org). If a college is not accredited by a regional accrediting association or other nationally recognized agency, you should consult an adviser to find out more about the college before you send any application forms or money.

# Credits, grading and evaluation

The "credit" system in the United States is sometimes confusing. Each course is assigned a value, called a credit or unit. The number of credits usually reflects the number of hours the class will meet with the professor during one week. In a three-credit course, the class typically will meet Monday, Wednesday and Friday for one hour of lecture each day. A four-credit course might meet Tuesday and Thursday for two hours of lecture each day, or meet three days a week for lecture and have one hour of discussion or lab. Each professor will give reading or writing assignments, usually weekly, and students should plan to work two to three hours outside of class for every hour inside class. In other words, a three-credit course may produce nine hours of homework a week.

Classroom examinations are given frequently throughout the years of undergraduate education in the United States. While small weekly written tests are common, testing may be limited to two or three large written examinations each semester, often called midterms. Almost all classes conclude with a final examination or large project. Testing gives the instructor or professor a basis for awarding grades and gives students an indication of their academic progress compared with other students in the class. At the graduate level, grades are more likely to be based on research papers in combination with some written or oral examinations.

Grades are determined by a series of evaluations and may include the cumulative assessment of all of the following: weekly quizzes, midterms, final exams, and papers, as well as class attendance and class participation. Each assignment or examination is usually graded, but your permanent record reflects only the final grade earned by the end of the course. If you do not do well on a midterm examination, there are other opportunities during the balance of the term to show the professor that you have improved. Most professors distribute a syllabus outlining the course requirements and grading system to be used. Although there is great variation in grading practices, particularly at the graduate level, most colleges in the United States use some version of the following grading system.

| Grade | Represents |
|-------|-----------|
| A or 4 | Consistently high performance |
| B or 3 | Above average |
| C or 2 | Average |
| D or 1 | Minimally passing |
| E, F or 0 | Failure |

Grades are recorded in your permanent record at the end of each term by the registrar. Using the points noted above and the credits assigned to each course, a grade point average is determined for each semester and accumulated for the entire time you are in the degree program. Each university has its own grading policies, and that information is usually explained in the university catalog or can be obtained from the office of the registrar.

# Regional Accrediting Associations

**Middle States Commission on Higher Education**
3624 Market Street
Philadelphia, PA 19104-2680
msche.org
> Delaware, District of Columbia, Maryland, New Jersey, New York, Pennsylvania, Puerto Rico, Virgin Islands

**New England Association of Schools and Colleges**
3 Burlington Woods Drive, Suite 100
Burlington, MA 01803-4514
neasc.org
> Connecticut, Maine, Massachusetts, New Hampshire, Rhode Island, Vermont

**North Central Association of Colleges and Schools Higher Learning Commission**
The Higher Learning Commission
230 South LaSalle Street, Suite 7-500
Chicago, IL 60604-1411
ncahlc.org
> Arizona, Arkansas, Colorado, Illinois, Indiana, Iowa, Kansas, Michigan, Minnesota, Missouri, Nebraska, New Mexico, North Dakota, Ohio, Oklahoma, South Dakota, West Virginia, Wisconsin, Wyoming

**Northwest Commission on Colleges and Universities**
8060 165th Avenue N.E., Suite 100
Redmond, WA 98052
nwccu.org
> Alaska, Idaho, Montana, Nevada, Oregon, Utah, Washington

**Southern Association of Colleges and Schools**
1866 Southern Lane
Decatur, GA 30033-4097
sacs.org
> Alabama, Florida, Georgia, Kentucky, Louisiana, Mississippi, North Carolina, South Carolina, Tennessee, Texas, Virginia

**Western Association of Schools and Colleges**
WASC Senior College and University Commission
985 Atlantic Avenue, Suite 100
Alameda, CA 94501
wascsenior.org
Accrediting Commission for Community and Junior Colleges
10 Commercial Boulevard, Suite 204
Novato, CA 94949
accjc.org
> American Samoa, California, Guam, Hawaii, Pacific Basin

# National Accrediting Associations

**ACICS** — **Accrediting Council for Independent Colleges and Schools**
Washington, DC
acics.org

**ACCSC** — **Accrediting Commission of Career Schools and Colleges**
Arlington, VA
accsc.org

**ABHE** — **The Association for Biblical Higher Education**
Orlando, FL
abhe.org

**AARTS** — **Association of Advanced Rabbinical and Talmudic Schools**
11 Broadway, Suite 405
New York, NY 10004

**ATS** — **Association of Theological Schools in the United States and Canada**
Pittsburgh, PA
ats.edu

**DETC** — **Distance Education Accrediting Commission**
Washington, DC
deac.org

**TRACS** — **Transnational Association of Christian Colleges and Schools**
Forest, VA
tracs.org

> For specialized program accreditation, see *Accredited Institutions of Postsecondary Education* available from:
> American Council on Education
> One Dupont Circle NW
> Washington, DC 20036
> acenet.edu

# Community Colleges in the United States

*Judy Irwin*
*Executive Vice President, Global and College Alliances*
*Center for Global Advancement of Community Colleges*

U.S. community colleges are a vital part of the higher education system structure in the United States, attracting nearly 90,000 international students each year. Sometimes called junior or technical colleges, these institutions provide the first two years of a four-year undergraduate degree program, at an affordable cost, leading to an associate degree.

Students with associate degrees can transfer course credits earned at a community college toward a bachelor's degree at a four-year college or university. To ensure a seamless transfer process from one institution to the other, community colleges and universities have developed "2+2" agreements specifying transfer criteria and requirements. The term "2+2" refers to the two years of course work taken at a community college plus two years of course work at a university. See 2plus2.org for more information.

All U.S. higher education institutions (community colleges, four-year colleges and major universities) are accredited by the same regional accrediting agencies throughout the United States. Community college programs must meet the same stringent criteria as four-year colleges and universities to attain accreditation status. This is the reason why universities will accept course credits obtained at community colleges.

There are nearly 1,700 two-year, associate-degree granting institutions in the United States, serving more than 12.4 million students. Forty-four percent of all U.S. undergraduates begin their higher education studies at a community college.

International students are attracted to community colleges because of significantly lower (at least 50 percent) tuition costs; numerous opportunities to transfer to four-year colleges and universities; excellent intensive English programs to advance language ability and skills; small class sizes with a focus on individual student success; a wide range of student support services; cutting-edge technologies; hundreds of programs from which to choose; hands-on access to U.S. culture; and the ability to take one year of optional practical training (OPT) related to one's degree upon completing an associate degree. A second year of OPT can be taken upon completing a bachelor's degree.

Community colleges differ in a variety of ways. Some are large, multi-campus institutions located in an urban/suburban location, while others are small and in rural settings. Over 300 community colleges provide campus living in dormitories, while others recommend nearby apartments to rent or offer home stays with host families.

Alumni from community colleges include U.S. government officials, Nobel and Pulitzer Prize recipients, Gold/Silver Olympic champions, award-winning producers, actors, and musicians. Some well-known alumni include Arnold Schwarzenegger, former governor of California; Eileen Collins, NASA space shuttle commander; Calvin Klein, fashion designer; George Lucas, producer/director of "Star Wars" movie series; Tom Hanks and Clint Eastwood, film actors; Walt Disney, founder of the Disney corporate empire; and Craig Ventnor, genome scientist.

Community colleges are a key component of higher education in the United States. As a stepping stone to 4-year universities, they offer opportunities for academically qualified and motivated international students to obtain a high-quality and affordable education in a supportive learning environment.

# Planning for study in the United States

Applying to college in the United States from another country can be exciting and challenging. The process may be different from the one in your country, but it need not be difficult if you get accurate information and follow the required procedures carefully.

There are over 880,000 students from other countries enrolled in degree programs at over 3,000 two-year and four-year colleges and universities in the United States. This represents 4.2 percent of the U.S. higher education enrollment each year. Many of these institutions have more applicants than they can accept in any year. As a result, college admission can be very competitive, especially for applicants from outside the United States.

The key to successful admission lies in careful planning and timely completion of the required steps. Keep in mind the following advice during your college planning.

## Consider your own characteristics

- What kind of person are you?

- What makes you happy?

- What are your interests?

- Are you sure you know what you want to study?

- Why do you think studying in another country will be good for you?

- What about studying in another country makes you feel anxious?

- Have you been away from your family for long periods of time before?

## Planning Guide

- Begin planning about 24 months before the date you wish to start studying in the United States. Contact universities that interest you at least one year in advance.

- Identify the things that are most important to you when looking for a college in the United States. Make a list of those characteristics to help you compare the colleges that interest you.

- Review and use this book. If you have access to a computer with an Internet browser, link to the College Search on collegeboard.org, where you can find out quickly which colleges have the features you want. College Search also allows you to link directly to college websites, which are a rich source of information about degrees and courses offered, costs, student services and financial aid. Some even provide a virtual campus tour.

- Consult an EducationUSA advising center or the EducationUSA website (http://educationusa.state.gov). Locate the center nearest you in the list at the back of this book.

- Talk with students in your country who have studied in the United States.

- Start planning your college budget. Be realistic about how you will pay for your education.

- If you plan to apply for scholarships, do so before leaving home. Little financial help is available once the school year starts.

- Be sure that your information is current and correct. Don't rely on hearsay or someone else's experience. Contact universities directly to get information and instructions about admission.

- Complete all the steps in the admission and financial aid process as early as possible. If you do not understand why a college asks for particular information or requires a particular process, ask them for more information about it.

The picture you have of yourself — your academic ability, interests, attitudes and personality — is very useful in choosing colleges and in completing the application forms you will be asked to submit. Colleges will ask you about yourself because they are interested in you and believe that personal factors play an important role in academic success.

# Consider your English language skills

One of the main challenges many international students face is their English language proficiency. If your first language is not English and if your previous education was not in English, it is important to take all English language proficiency tests as soon as possible.

You will be expected to read, write, understand and speak English properly and fluently to carry out your studies. Conversational English will not be sufficient. Colleges and universities require proof of English language proficiency when you apply and measure your skills by asking you to take a standardized test of English. Even with excellent academic qualifications, you may not be admitted if your English language proficiency is too low.

International students often underestimate the stress caused by suddenly changing cultures, education and economic systems, friends, methods of teaching and learning, and living environments. Moving suddenly from speaking and thinking in the language of your country to thinking, listening and speaking in English is very stressful. Get an accurate estimate of your ability in English so that you can enroll in a language school if needed to improve your ability before starting studies in the United States. Be sure to ask the admission office if the institution offers an intensive course in English as a second language.

Answer the questions below to help you assess your English.

## Circle one

1.  **I can read textbooks written in English …**
    A.      easily with the help of a dictionary to check new or difficult words.
    B.      with difficulty and the frequent use of a dictionary.
    C.      with great difficulty, constant use of a dictionary and help from others.
    D.      I have never tried reading a textbook in English.

2.  **I can write an essay in English …**
    A.      easily, using a dictionary to check the spelling and meaning of some words.
    B.      with difficulty and the frequent use of a dictionary and grammar book.
    C.      with great difficulty, translating what I have written in my language into English, with constant use of a dictionary and help from others.
    D.      I have never tried writing an essay in English.

3.  **I can understand spoken English about a current news topic…**
    A.      easily except for special words.
    B.      with some difficulty, and only if the information is repeated at least once.
    C.      with difficulty and the use of a dictionary.
    D.      I have not listened to someone speak in English about a current news topic.

4.  **I can speak in English …**
    A.      about any topic, with the occasional use of a dictionary.
    B.      about certain topics with which I am most familiar.
    - if I am asked simple questions.
    - I have not had the opportunity to speak in English.

# College cost and paying for your education

## College cost

The profiles in Part II of this book give academic-year costs broken down by tuition and fees and living expenses. Remember that college costs are rising and are likely to be higher by the time you enter a program of study. Confirm current costs with the school when you apply.

Just as the types of educational institutions in the United States vary widely, so does the cost of education. Cost may be a major factor in deciding which college to attend. You must consider living expenses during holidays and the summer and round-trip transportation from your home country. Actual tuition, fees and estimated living expenses for international students are listed in Part II of this book. The estimates do not include expenses for an automobile, unless specified. The cost of going to college in the United States is something you and your family should think about early in your college planning. Cost differs from one institution to another, so you should estimate a budget for the college you are considering. Your total budget should include the following expenses for each year of study.

## Tuition and fees

Tuition and fees are generally charged on the basis of a nine-month (September-May) academic year. Some colleges also offer course work in the summer period (June-August); if you plan to take courses in the summer, increase your budget to allow for expenses for a 12-month period. Some universities charge a flat rate for tuition and some calculate tuition by the credit hour. Each course is assigned a number of credits, usually reflecting the number of "contact hours" with the professor per week for one term. A typical course in a U.S. institution is worth three credit hours. Thus, to calculate the additional cost of a summer program, multiply the number of courses you intend to take by three to obtain the total number of credit hours, then multiply that by the tuition per credit hour charge.

Tuition and fees for international students listed in this book are for the 2017-18 academic year unless otherwise stated; the costs tend to increase each year. Be sure to confirm current costs with the college when you apply. To estimate future costs, add an increase for each year. Over the past decade, average annual costs have risen 3.2 percent at private four-year institutions.

The items included in fees vary from institution to institution. To compare accurately, ask what is included in the fees. Some typical fees are health insurance, student activity fees, scholarship funds, building funds, lab fees and computer usage fees.

## Room and board

Room and board means basic living expenses for food and housing. No matter where you go to college, you will have to consider these expenses. Many colleges have on-campus housing. Some require students to live in a college dormitory, at least for the first year. Others do not, and students commute from housing near the college. Commuting students in general pay somewhat less for housing than students living in college dormitories, but their cost of transportation is higher. Most colleges have housing offices that can help you find local housing in an apartment or a home that you can share with other students.

The room and board cost for colleges with on-campus housing assumes that you will share a room with one student, and have regular meals in the college cafeteria. Find out if the room charges include bedding (sheets, pillows and blankets) and regular linen service.

If you will be attending college during the summer, add an estimate of the cost for housing and meals for three additional months to your budget.

## Books and supplies

Colleges estimate the cost for books and supplies for the academic year. If you are planning to study in a field that requires special supplies, such as engineering, art or film, your expenses are likely to be greater than the average. If you attend summer school, add a sum to your budget for books for the summer classes.

## Computers

Computers are a common requirement on college campuses today. Most universities have computer labs for student use, but some require students to have their own computers. Ask whether the university you are applying to requires you to have a personal computer. If so, calculate that into your expenses.

## Transportation

The living cost figures in this book do not cover trips between the United States and your home country. Be sure to add expenses to your yearly budget for round-trip travel between your home country and college.

If you plan to live off campus and commute to college, you will incur local travel expenses. Commuter colleges have included an estimate of these expenses.

## Personal expenses

These expenses include the cost of basic goods such as clothing, services such as laundry and activities such as movies and sports events. Health insurance is required. If you have dependents or if you have special medical needs, substantial additional funds will be needed to meet your living expenses. Most institutions have an estimate of the basic cost.

# Sources of funding

Although there are U.S. government-sponsored and institutional financial aid programs, most of those funds are for U.S. citizens or permanent residents. For international students, the cost of higher education in the United States is primarily the student's responsibility. Although many colleges have some financial aid available for students from outside the United States, there is not enough aid to meet the need of all students.

There is usually more financial aid available for graduate students than for undergraduate students. In Part II of this book, which lists detailed information about undergraduate institutions, the far right-hand column indicates whether an institution offers financial aid to international students, the number of awards and the average amount of the awards. These lists will give you a realistic idea of your chances of receiving financial assistance from a specific institution.

You are responsible for planning how you will pay for your educational, living and travel expenses. Answer the questions below to begin your financial plan.

- Have you consulted your family, a prospective sponsor or others about your plans for financing your stay in the United States?

- Have they agreed to support you?

- If you are applying for a scholarship, have you submitted all the required documents?

- When will you be notified of the results?

# Financial aid

Financial aid to students in the United States includes (1) scholarships or grants, (2) loans, which have to be repaid and (3) jobs, which provide money to help pay college costs. Financial aid may cover all college costs or only a very small fraction. Jobs require a commitment of a specified number of hours per week; teaching and research assistantships for graduate students require up to 20 hours per week.

U.S. sources of financial aid include federal and state governments, private foundations, companies and universities. Financial aid programs usually have specific requirements, such as financial need, citizenship or a particular field and level of study. International students may apply for privately sponsored scholarships where the criteria allow, but should be aware that these scholarships have a very early deadline for applications. If you have Internet access, be sure to use the Scholarship Search on the College Board's website bigfuture.collegeboard.org/scholarship-search to find potential sources of funding.

It is a good idea to investigate sources of financial aid in your own country as well as those in the United States. Keep in mind that the application process for scholarships and other financial aid programs may begin as early as 18 months before your planned date of enrollment. Contact an EducationUSA advising center, the U.S. embassy or consulate in your country, your ministry of education, or other organizations about financial aid as soon as possible.

Part-time work outside of the college or university is sometimes a possible source of additional income once a student is in the United States. Keep in mind, however, that people traveling in the United States on a student visa are not allowed to work off campus until one year of academic study has been completed successfully. Then you have to get permission from the college and the Bureau of Citizenship and Immigration Services before you can work off campus part time. International students can usually work on campus. In either case, your earnings from part-time work will not cover much more than personal expenses. You should not count on employment to pay the major cost of your education.

## Understanding your U.S. federal income tax obligations

Many students from other countries studying in the United States are not aware that they may incur U.S. federal income tax obligations. According to the U.S. Internal Revenue Service, the international students most likely to incur U.S. tax obligations are those who receive grants or stipends or who earn income as graduate assistants.

According to IRS officials, a large number of international students actually overpay their taxes because they mistakenly believe that the government will automatically withhold the correct amount of taxes and that they therefore do not have to file a return. Seek advice in the personnel office on your campus about your tax withholding, and familiarize yourself with the U.S. tax regulations. Watch for tax seminars on your campus, or ask your international student adviser for advice.

Be sure to check out the financial aid feature on our BigFuture site (bigfuture.collegeboard.org) which includes explanations of aid packages, comparing costs and grant awards.

# Advice for undergraduate applicants

## Choosing a college

Attending college in another country can be a very exciting and rewarding experience. It is important that you select an institution that best matches your interests and needs and offers the academic program you want to study. To find a college that offers what you need, decide what college characteristics are important to you. When you compare your own needs and interests with the characteristics of the college, you will find a good match.

### Choosing a college

Make a list of what is important to you when choosing a college. Consider this list and then add other characteristics you seek.

- Does the college offer the degree you are seeking in your desired field of study?

- What type of college is it (for example, two-year community college, four-year university, private or public, urban or rural, religious affiliation)?

- How many students are enrolled? How many of them specialize in the field you're interested in? How many of them are from outside the United States?

- Can you describe the campus environment from what you have read about it?

- Is housing available on campus?

- What is the total cost of tuition, fees, room, and board (meals)? Are scholarships or other forms of financial aid available for international students?

- Is there an orientation program specifically for international students? Are there student services to help you outside the classroom, including an international student advising office? If you need help with your English skills, does the college offer an intensive language learning program?

### Admission Advice

*"It's all about finding the right fit, or the best fit, for that student. What you need to do is ask questions about yourself first. What kind of environment do I want to be in? What do I want to study? Do I want a preprofessional education or a liberal arts education? Do I want a big city or a small city? Do I want a religiously affiliated institution? Once you ask those questions, you can start plugging your desires and priorities into the schools that fit best."*

— Joseph DeCrosta, Duquesne University, Pittsburgh, Pa.

*"It's important to decide whether you need an active international student community and how much support you think you will need. If there's an international student organization that you can become a part of, how active is it? If you can, determine whether international students are mainstreamed into the college community or whether they're more of a segregated population. That said, any international student should be sure that the college has an international student adviser."*

— David Dillman, Austin College, Sherman, Texas

## Finding out more about colleges

Learning as much as you can about the colleges you are considering increases your chances of making a good decision on where to apply. One of the best sources is the Internet. Most U.S. colleges have websites that provide you with complete information about academic programs and course offerings, admission requirements and procedures for applying. Their sites may include photos of the campus and its environment or a virtual campus tour. The College Board's website (bigfuture.collegeboard.org) provides detailed resources to plan for, apply to and pay for college. In addition, there are many other sources of information and advising that may be available in your country. The U.S. government, foreign governments and nonprofit organizations support these activities. There is usually no cost to you, although a minimal charge may be requested to cover the expense of printing booklets or the postage if you request information by mail. The U.S. Department of State promotes American higher education through its EducationUSA advising network, located in the following types of centers:

- U.S. embassies, consulates, American centers, American corners and libraries

- Fulbright commissions and foundations

- Binational centers

- Nonprofit exchange organizations, such as the Institute of International Education or AMIDEAST

- University information centers and libraries

- Public libraries

You may also check listings in local telephone books or call or write the U.S. embassy or the ministry of education in your country, stating that (1) you are seeking information and advice about academic study in the United States and (2) you would like to know where to visit or write.

A list of advising centers is provided in Part III of this book. Advice from knowledgeable and experienced advisers can help you make realistic plans and complete the admission process successfully.

Another helpful source of information in your country is people who have studied in the United States. Talk to them, but remember that their experiences will be influenced by how recently they were there and by the location and type of institution they attended. The environment they chose may be different from the one you seek. However, they should be able to give you some ideas about adjusting to college life in the United States. An advising center may offer discussions or workshops with returnees and U.S. college alumni.

## Admission Advice

*"It's very important for prospective international students to communicate with current students, especially from their home country, even perhaps from their own high school, who may be attending an institution. That way, culturally at least, they can ask the types of questions that are most relevant to them. A student from small-town Iowa and a student calling from Thailand — they might not quite relate on the same level. Speaking with someone from your own culture is probably most helpful. Speaking to parents of current students from your home country is also very helpful."*

— Mark G. Reid,
University of Miami, Fla.

# The following sources can provide important facts about U.S. colleges:

**The Internet.** Most colleges have websites, and their addresses are listed in the alphabetical list of colleges in Part III. Search for colleges with the features you want, using a free service such as the College Board's BigFuture website (bigfuture.org).

**Other college guidebooks and software.** The book you're reading provides current information on international student enrollment, tests required, application deadlines, application fees, tuition and fees, room and board, financial aid, and the availability of international student advisers, orientation and intensive English language programs at U.S. colleges. The *College Board College Handbook* provides in-depth, current information on size, location, degrees and majors offered, admission requirements, cost, student profile, activities, athletics, and special programs and services. The *College Board Book of Majors* provides lists of major fields of study at the undergraduate and graduate degree levels and the colleges that offer each major. It also provides descriptions of the most popular majors.

**College catalogs.** Colleges produce catalogs and bulletins that give up-to-date information on their admission requirements, major fields of study, faculty, college costs and other important factors. Most catalogs are available on the Internet and less often in paper form.

**College representatives.** Some institutions send representatives to other countries to talk about their colleges and to meet students who may be interested in applying. Contact the U.S. embassy, an advising center or the ministry of education to find out whether representatives from colleges will be visiting your country or participating in an online college fair.

Once you have investigated the colleges that you are considering and determined where you wish to study, you are ready to send an application. Since the procedures for applying to college in the United States are likely to be different from those in your own country, here are guidelines to help make this a smooth process.

# When to apply

You should begin the application process as soon as you have decided which colleges best meet your needs. This usually should be no later than 12 months before the date you expect to begin study in the United States. Review the planning calendar at the beginning of this book.

Colleges may give a deadline for applications. Usually the deadline is the final date by which they must receive the application. Some colleges will continue to accept applications after the deadline, but they will only process the application if they do not fill their class with applications from students who applied by the deadline. For late applicants, there may be no housing and no financial assistance.

Make a checklist of the admission requirements and deadlines from your college comparison worksheet. Set your own completion dates well ahead of the colleges' stated deadlines, and check off each step as you complete it. Remember to send all required documents and forms as soon as possible. U.S. colleges usually review applications only when *all* the required documents have been received.

# Applying to college in the United States

## Requesting and filing the application

Most colleges will respond to email requests for information. Whether writing by airmail or using electronic mail, when you first contact a college in the United States, supply enough information so that you will receive correct information in return. Include your intended field of study, your educational background, the term in which you wish to start and information about your source of funds for paying for your education.

The use of computers in the application process and in completing other college procedures is very common. If at all possible, use the electronic application provided by the college. This will accelerate the application process for you and make it easier for the college to process your application.

After you have received an application packet from the colleges of your choice, you should:

- Review the programs offered and the academic preparation required for them.

- Note the important dates, such as deadlines.

- Note which parts of the application will require a contribution by another person. For example, does the college ask for teacher recommendations?

- Pay special attention to the information about tuition, fees and living costs to be sure you understand the financial commitment involved.

You are now ready to file your application for admission. Plan to apply to more than one college in order to increase your opportunities for admission.

## Admission Advice

*"Some international students will have limited English skills, especially when they are looking at our intensive English program, and may be shy about asking questions because of this. I encourage students to email us anyway."*

— Ann Gogerty, formerly of Iowa State University, Ames, Iowa

*"What's most important when deciding where to go? It's somehow about getting into the right school, and that the school is somehow going to make something out of you. The truth of the matter is, at any good school, you're going to make something out of the school. That is, it's far more important that you be prepared to go to college and that you fully engage the infinite opportunities that are available at any good college, than to obsess on which one you're going to."*

- Jeff Brenzel, Yale University

*"Don't write chat-room English to college administrators!"*

— Ken Bus, Glendale Community College, Glendale, Ariz.

## Completing the application form

Many colleges use a preliminary application for an initial review of your background. This preliminary decision may save both you and the university some time and money. Whether you complete a preliminary application or the official application, be sure to read all instructions carefully and answer every question. Many colleges offer an electronic application on the Internet. Be sure to look for it and use it if you have access to appropriate technology.

## Application fee

Most colleges charge a nonrefundable application fee. Some colleges waive the fee if you use their electronic application. The fee must be sent in U.S. dollars; follow the instructions provided with the application form.

## Writing the essay

As part of the application for admission, most colleges require one or more essays in which you respond to questions provided by the college, write a biographical statement, or describe your academic goals, your previous accomplishments, and reasons why you wish to attend college. Instructions for specific information requested as part of the essays will be included in the application packet. Give each essay a lot of thought because it is given careful consideration by the admission staff when making a decision about your application. Type the essay or write very clearly.

### Admission Advice

*"We ask for an essay and give students flexibility on what they write about. It's important for us to see that they can communicate well in English, grammatically and logically."*

— David Dillman, Austin College, Sherman, Texas

*"I want the essay to come alive. I want to know that person as well as I can on paper. And that's a hard thing, because we want somebody to self-disclose, and that's not necessarily the model in a lot of non-Western cultures."*

— Peter Briggs, Michigan State University, East Lansing, Mich.

# Your academic records

The colleges to which you apply will require a complete set of records of your academic performance at previous schools attended. Many colleges will accept unofficial copies for their preliminary evaluation but will require original or official documents to confirm their review. If your original records are not in English, submit an official translation with your academic records. Some EducationUSA advising centers can provide "apostille," or internationally certified, copies or translations of your academic records.

## Admission and placement tests

Almost all institutions will require you to take one or more tests as part of the application process. Most colleges and universities require admission tests, such as the SAT and SAT Subject Tests. The tests can be used for admission decisions or for placement — that is, deciding whether you need additional study in some areas or whether you are equal to or ahead of other students being accepted to the college. Tests that are computer-based may be taken any time that is convenient for you. You are advised to register in advance. Where tests are given on a fixed date, you must register well in advance for a space to take the test. See the test registration schedule on page 32.

Each college will list the required tests in its application instructions. Be sure to take all required tests as early as possible because they will be considered when the college makes a decision about your admission to the university. Check the college application for required tests. See the test information section on page 31 for a description of the various tests.

Undergraduates may also be required to take placement tests in specific subject areas such as English, mathematics or the sciences to assess knowledge in a particular subject. Placement tests are usually taken

### Important things to remember when completing your application

- Use the same translation of your name on all documents, preferably the one on your passport. If the name is different on some records, enclose an explanation.

- Note the proper dates for filing the application.

- Read and follow the essay instructions carefully.

- Enclose proper financial documentation.

- Include all fees requested.

- If you have an email address and/or fax number, be sure to include it.

- Type the application form and essay, or write clearly.

- Send complete official academic records or certified copies of your academic records along with your application. Have official translations prepared, where necessary, and attach them to the original/official documents.

- Take all required tests in time for your scores to be considered with your application.

after arrival on campus, and the information is used in course selection so that students neither repeat things they already know nor are placed in a course for which they do not have the sufficient background.

## Letters of recommendation

Some colleges require letters of recommendation from one or more adults who know you well. Letters of recommendation by themselves will not ensure admission, and letters that do not appear to assess the candidate honestly may hinder an applicant's chance. The following guidelines may be useful when requesting letters of recommendation:

- Letters of recommendation should be honest and balanced. A letter that is unrealistically favorable is less useful than one that explains possible areas where you need improvement.

- You should request letters from two or three different people who are familiar with your academic or professional achievement — among them teachers, professors, school counselors and employers. A family member or personal friend is usually not acceptable.

- Letters should focus on your academic abilities more than on your character, but may include information about your community service, volunteer work, employment, service to others and leadership qualities.

- Admission officers reading letters of recommendation find the following information useful:

*Academic record:* discussion of your stronger and weaker academic areas; explanation of any gaps in your schooling, such as time off, school closings and so forth.

*Achievements:* special accomplishments in school, work or family should be mentioned. Awards you have received should be described so that the admission officer will understand their significance.

*Unusual talents:* special skills with languages or in the arts, athletic ability and so on, should be mentioned.

- Give the person writing the letter clear instructions for scanning and emailing the letter or for sending the letter airmail to the address the college provides. Ask them to type or print clearly.

## Auditions and portfolios

Schools of architecture, film and the arts usually require additional information about you in order to assess your qualifications for admission to their programs. This may include portfolios of your work for art, architecture, and design programs, and auditions for music and theater programs. They will often accept audiotaped or videotaped representations of auditions from applicants who are unable to perform in person.

## Interviews

Some colleges require interviews for admission to some or all of their programs. Interviews may be conducted in your home country by alumni, by visiting staff from the colleges, at recruitment fairs or by individuals designated by the college. During the interview, be clear about your education goals and the reasons you want to attend this particular college, and be prepared to ask questions.

## Your English skills

Strong English language skills will be very important to your success while studying in the United States. The level of proficiency expected by each college should be identified in the application for admission. Some colleges offer English as a second language (ESL) programs on the campus or nearby to help you improve your English language skills. Be sure to take the English language test required by your chosen college so the college can assess your readiness to study in English. Please refer to the test information on page 34 to find out more about the Test of English as a Foreign Language (TOEFL).

# Other Requirements

## Health forms and health insurance

Once you are admitted, you may be required to complete forms about your health. If a form is not provided, have a health examination and obtain a certificate written in English.

Most colleges and universities require health insurance while you are enrolled. Refer to the section on health on page 40 for more detailed information.

## Financial documentation

A document certifying the amount and sources of income available to you for study in the United States will be required. Most U.S. institutions will send you instructions and a special form to complete. The documentation must show that you have resources to pay for the first year of your college program and a reasonable financial plan for paying for the balance of your education. Once an admission decision is made, the college will send you the appropriate U.S. government form so you can apply for a student or exchange visitor visa. Refer to the visa information on page 35 for more information regarding financial documentation and procedures for coming to the United States.

## Financial aid forms

Many colleges and universities that offer financial aid to international students require applicants to complete a detailed financial aid application form, which is separate from the college application form. Typically, these forms ask the following kinds of questions:

- What is your parents' total annual income?

- What is your annual income?

- What are your annual living expenses?

- What is the value of any assets you and your parents have, such as a house, a car, savings and investments?

- How many family members are in college?

- What plans do you have for locating financial aid from sources other than the college or university?

- Most colleges will provide information about the financial aid application process on their websites. The forms required may vary by college, and you need to make sure you understand each college's specific financial aid application requirements. Some institutions use their own forms. Others use the CSS/Financial Aid PROFILE®, an online application that allows you to enter information once and electronically submit the data to several institutions.

Complete and submit all the financial aid application materials when you apply for admission. Be sure to answer the questions as completely as possible. Most colleges will ask for documentation of the information you provide on the financial aid application; gather and save those documents as you complete the forms. Be sure to submit any paper financial aid materials by fax or use airmail or courier to the correct address, which may be different from the address you use for the college application.

## What happens next

**Notice of receipt.** Most colleges will send you a notice confirming that they have received your application. If you have not received such a notice within a month to six weeks from the time you submit your application (either by mail or email), you should inquire to be sure it was received and is complete. Be consistent in using the same email address throughout the process.

**Evaluating your application.** The evaluation of all the admission applications a college receives can take several months. Some colleges send notifications to all students at one time; others respond as soon as an individual admission decision is made. You can eliminate delays in your evaluation by following application instructions carefully and responding to requests for additional information immediately.

**Offers of admission.** Accompanying your offer of admission will be a packet of information about the college and its programs — things you need to know to get ready to enter the college. It will usually include information about campus housing and orientation programs, and may have forms for you to complete and return. You may be asked to submit a fee to hold a place at the college once you have been offered admission. (See "After colleges decide" on page 35.)

**Orientation.** Most colleges have orientation programs for new students; many offer special orientation programs for international students. You should try to attend these programs to acquaint yourself with the college environment as well as to obtain program advice.

# Other things you should know

**Transferring from one U.S. college to another.** It is quite common in the United States for students to transfer from one college to another. They may attend a community college for one or two years and then transfer to a four-year college or university; sometimes they transfer from one four-year college to another. If you begin your studies in a community college and want to go on to a four-year college for a bachelor's degree, be sure to plan your studies with an adviser. Without careful course selection, you may extend the time it takes to earn your degree because the college you transfer to may require basic courses other than the ones you have taken.

**Transferring academic credits.** In the United States, colleges allow the transfer of university-level academic credits from one institution to another and will apply those credits toward your degree at the new institution. This is particularly important when transferring from a two-year to a four-year college. Transferring credits is also possible at the graduate level, though usually only a limited number are allowed. The previous course work must be comparable in content to an equivalent course offered at your new university and must be applicable to the degree you are pursuing. Although there is no guarantee that all previous course work will be accepted, universities make every effort to apply courses either as general education credit or as fulfillment of a major subject requirement. Your new

university will provide you with an evaluation of your credentials as well as documentation of your progress toward your degree. This information will enable you to determine the length of time it may take you to complete your degree.

# Comparing colleges and universities

The more information you can gather on colleges and universities, the better your chance of making a good decision about applying to appropriate institutions. Look at the college listings in Part II of this book. If you are interested in undergraduate study, also use the College Search on bigfuture.org to identify colleges that have the features you want, read the descriptions in the *College Board College Handbook*, and consult other sources of information that are available to you.

There is no ideal number of colleges and universities to select for application, but advisers often recommend that students identify at least three to six institutions.

The worksheets on the following pages can help you compare institutions on the basis of the characteristics important in choosing and applying to colleges. For each characteristic, write how each college matches (or does not match) your preference. Some of the characteristics you may be comparing are:

- **Degree level.** For which degree do you plan to study at this college or university?

- **Location.** In what city or town, state and region of the country is the college or university located?

- **Type of institution.** Is this a public or private institution? Is it a two-year community college, four-year liberal arts college, university or graduate institution? Does the college admit men only, women only or is it coeducational?

- **Major/field of study.** What field or fields of study that interest you does the institution offer?

- **Religious affiliation.** Was the college or university founded by or is it administered by a religious organization? Does this affect student lifestyle?

- **Enrollment size.** How many students are enrolled in the undergraduate colleges or graduate divisions in which you would be enrolled?

- **International student enrollment.** Does the college enroll many or few students from outside the United States? Are the students from diverse regions?

- **Campus environment.** Is the institution's campus urban, suburban or rural?

- **Housing.** Is on-campus housing available?

- **Academic background of students.** Do most students successfully complete their first year at the college? Do they return as sophomores?

- **Student activities.** Are there groups or organizations on campus to support the cultural, political, social or other activities that interest you?

- **Athletics.** If athletic competition is important to you, does the college offer the sports programs you want?

- **Test requirements.** Is TOEFL required? What is the minimum acceptable score? Is an admission test (e.g., SAT) required?

- **Cost.** What is the estimated international student cost for tuition, fees, room and board for nine months? For 12 months? (Remember, your miscellaneous personal expenses, health insurance and travel expenses will also be part of your total budget.)

- **Financial aid.** Is financial aid available to international students? How many international students receive aid? What is the average amount available for each student who receives aid?

- **English as a second language program.** Is an intensive ESL program available on campus? Is there a writing center for additional help?

- **Conditional admission based on English proficiency.** Will the institution provisionally accept students for academic study who do not meet English proficiency requirements?

- **Deadlines.** When must applications for admission and financial aid be completed and received by the institution?

# College comparison worksheet (sample)

| Characteristics important to you | College 1 | College 2 | College 3 |
|---|---|---|---|
| | Yoder College | State university | Harrison University |
| Degree level | Bachelor's | Bachelor's | Bachelor's |
| Location | Baltimore, MD (Mid-Atlantic) | Minneapolis, MN (Midwest) | Boston, MA (New England) |
| Type of institution | Private college | Public university | Private university |
| Major | Engineering | Engineering | Engineering |
| Enrollment size | 2,100 | 10,500 (very large) | 6,800 |
| International student enr. | 18 | 113 | 182 |
| Housing | yes | yes | yes |
| Academic background | Top half of class, 90% continue after first year | Top half | Most in top third, 45% continue to graduate studies |
| Test requirements | TOEFL SAT | TOEFL 550 mins. | TOEFL 550 mins. SAT |
| Cost | $8,030 (9 months) $11,100 (12 months) | $13,400 (9 months) $17,850 (12 months) | $11,950 (9 months) $15,180 (12 months) |
| Financial aid | yes 12 applied for financial aid, 50% received aid | no | yes 109 applied for aid, 30% received aid |
| Application deadline | 15 February | 30 January | 1 March |
| Financial aid deadline | 15 March | | 30 December |

# College comparison worksheet

| Characteristics important to you | College 1 | College 2 | College 3 |
|---|---|---|---|
| | | | |
| | | | |
| | | | |
| | | | |
| | | | |
| | | | |
| | | | |
| | | | |
| | | | |
| | | | |
| | | | |
| | | | |
| | | | |
| | | | |
| | | | |
| | | | |
| | | | |

# Test information

The information tables in this book tell you which tests may be required of international students. Verify which tests are required by the colleges that interest you. Also, familiarize yourself with the format of the test you will be taking. When you register to take a test, ask for the available practice materials and work through the sample questions and sample test.

If you have access to the Internet, go to the websites of the various testing organizations to review the test formats, or take a sample test.

It is important to get up-to-date information about tests that are required by colleges to which you may apply. Although these standardized tests are offered at test centers throughout the world, they are not offered in every country on each test date or in each test format. For example, TOEFL, the test used by most colleges to evaluate English language proficiency, is now most widely offered in an Internet-based format, but is also offered as a paper-based test at designated testing centers. Write or call for information well ahead of time; registration slots are often closed out two months before the test date, particularly between October and February.

College Board tests commonly required or recommended by U.S. institutions are described below.

## The SAT®

**Overview:** The SAT is a globally recognized admission test used by colleges and universities, and is administered widely outside the United States (a calendar of testing dates appears on page 32). To learn more about the SAT, visit sat.org.

**Type of test:** Undergraduate admission and placement.

**Purpose:** A student's SAT score combined with his or her academic record is the best indicator of how well that student will do in college. The SAT gives colleges an objective way to evaluate a student's potential for succeeding in college. It also helps equalize the academic experiences of students from diverse education systems.

**Generally required of:** Students seeking admission to the first year of undergraduate study in the U.S.

**Format:** The SAT consists of a multiple-choice Evidence-Based Reading and Writing section, which includes a reading test and a writing and language test, and a multiple-choice mathematics section. Both sections are scored on a scale of 200-800. There is also an optional 50 minute essay section, that is scored on a scale of 2 to 8.

**For more information:** Visit sat.org/international, where you can register online. You can also refer to the *SAT and SAT Subject Tests* or to either *Getting Ready for the SAT* or *Getting Ready for the Redesigned SAT*, which you can usually obtain from your local EducationUSA advising center at no charge. **Free SAT test preparation** programs and resources are available to all students worldwide at sat.org and satpractice.org.

## SAT Subject Tests™

**Overview:** SAT Subject Tests are designed to measure students' knowledge and achievement in particular subject areas. The SAT Subject Tests are the only U.S. admission tests that give students the opportunity to demonstrate mastery of content in specific subjects, such as English, history, mathematics, science, and various foreign languages. **NOTE:** SAT Subject Tests have not been redesigned.

**Type of test:** Undergraduate admission and placement.

**Purpose:** Many colleges use the SAT Subject Tests to make admission decisions, for course placement, and to advise students about course selection. Some colleges specify the SAT Subject Tests they require for admission or placement; others allow applicants to choose which tests to take.

**Generally required of:** Undergraduates applying for admission as first-year students to selective U.S. institutions. One or more Subject Tests may be required. See the list of colleges that require or recommend the Subject Tests in Part III of this book.

**Format:** One-hour multiple-choice tests in the following subjects: English Literature, U.S. History, World History, Mathematics Level 1 and Level 2 (a graphic or scientific calculator is required for some of the questions in the math tests), Biology Ecological/Molecular, Chemistry, Physics, Chinese with Listening, French, French with Listening, German, German with Listening, Modern Hebrew, Italian, Japanese with Listening, Korean with Listening, Latin, Spanish, and Spanish with Listening.

| 2017-18 SAT International Test Calendar | | | | | |
|---|---|---|---|---|---|
| **Test Dates** | Oct. 7 | Nov. 4 | Dec. 2 | May 5 | June 2 |
| **Registration Deadlines** | | | | | |
| *Early** | Aug 31 | Sept 28 | Oct 26 | Mar 29 | Apr 26 |
| *Regular* | Sept 7 | Oct 6 | Nov 2 | Apr 6 | May 3 |
| SAT | ■ | ■ | ■ | ■ | ■ |
| SAT Subject Tests | | | | | |
| Literature | ■ | ■ | ■ | ■ | ■ |
| United States (U.S.) History | ■ | ■ | ■ | ■ | ■ |
| World History | | | ■ | | ■ |
| Math Level 1 | ■ | ■ | ■ | ■ | ■ |
| Math Level 2 | ■ | ■ | ■ | ■ | ■ |
| Biology E/M (Ecological/Molecular) | ■ | ■ | ■ | ■ | ■ |
| Chemistry | ■ | ■ | ■ | ■ | ■ |
| Physics | ■ | ■ | ■ | ■ | ■ |
| Languages: *Reading Only* | | | | | |
| French | ■ | | ■ | ■ | ■ |
| German | | | | | ■ |
| Modern Hebrew | | | | | ■ |
| Italian | | | | | ■ |
| Latin | | | ■ | | ■ |
| Spanish | ■ | | ■ | ■ | ■ |
| Languages: *Reading and Listening* | | | | | |
| Chinese | | ■ | | | |
| French | | ■ | | | |
| German | | ■ | | | |
| Japanese | | ■ | | | |
| Korean | | ■ | | | |
| Spanish | | ■ | | | |

*\* Applies to closer-to-home testing and registration through SAT International Representatives.*
*Note: Registration deadlines are subject to change. Visit sat.org/international for updated listings. Sunday test dates immediately follow each Saturday test date (except in October, when it is usually one week later) for students who cannot test on Saturday because of religious observance. Sunday testing is not offered in India or Pakistan.*

# AP® Exams

**Type of test:** Subject-matter exam. Most colleges and universities in the United States recognize AP when making credit, advancement placement and/or admission decisions.

**Purpose:** To measure students' mastery of content and skills within college-level courses taught in secondary schools throughout the world. Colleges and universities grant advanced placement, credit or both for successful AP Exam scores.

**Format:** Most AP Exams are approximately two to three hours in length and include a multiple-choice section and a free-response section. Exceptions: Computer Science Principles (multiple-choice only), AP Seminar (written exam), AP Research (paper, presentation, and oral defense), and all three Studio Art exams (portfolio assessment). AP Exams in world languages and cultures include a speaking section (recorded), and the AP Music Theory Exam includes a sight-singing section (recorded).

**For more information:** Visit the College Board website (apstudent.collegeboard.org) or contact:

**AP Services for Students**
P.O. Box 6671
Princeton, NJ 08541-6671
USA
+1212-632-1780
email: apstudents@info.collegeboard.org

# 2018 AP Exam Schedule

| Week 1 | Morning Session 8 a.m. | Afternoon Session 12 p.m. | |
|---|---|---|---|
| Monday, May 7 | Chemistry<br>Spanish Literature and Culture | Psychology | |
| Tuesday, May 8 | AP Seminar<br>Spanish Language and Culture | Art History<br>Physics 1: Algebra-Based | |
| Wednesday, May 9 | English Literature and Composition | Japanese Language and Culture<br>Physics 2: Algebra-Based | |
| Thursday, May 10 | United States Government and Politics | Chinese Language and Culture<br>Environmental Science | |
| Friday, May 11* | German Language and Culture<br>United States History | Computer Science Principles | |

| Week 2 | Morning Session 8 a.m. | Afternoon Session<br>12 p.m. | 2 p.m. |
|---|---|---|---|
| Monday, May 14 | Biology<br>Music Theory | Physics C: Mechanics | Physics C: Electricity and Magnetism |
| Tuesday, May 15 | Calculus AB<br>Calculus BC | Computer Science A<br>French Language and Culture | |
| Wednesday, May 16 | English Language and Composition | Italian Language and Culture<br>Macroeconomics | |
| Thursday, May 17 | Comparative Government and Politics<br>World History | Statistics | |
| Friday, May 18 | Human Geography<br>Microeconomics | European History<br>Latin | |

*Studio Art: Last day for coordinators to submit digital portfolios (by 8 p.m. EDT) and gather 2-D Design and Drawing students for physical portfolio assembly.

Up-to-date information on AP credit policies of U.S. universities may be found at collegeboard.org/apcreditpolicy.

Policies of universities outside the United States may be found at international.collegeboard.org.

# CLEP® (College-Level Examination Program®)

**Type of test:** Undergraduate credit-by-examination program.

**Purpose:** To test knowledge of material normally taught in introductory college courses and give students the opportunity to earn undergraduate credit. Knowledge may have been acquired in the classroom or through independent study, academic interests, or on-the-job training. Each college sets its own policy regarding which CLEP exams it will grant credit for and how many credits it will award. There are 33 CLEP exams available in various subject areas, including mathematics, science, social sciences and history, literature, world languages and business. CLEP is administered at over 1,800 test centers and accepted by approximately 2,900 colleges and universities.

**Who takes CLEP:** High school and college students, adults returning to college, military personnel and veterans, and international students who wish to obtain credit from a U.S. university for knowledge acquired at an institution in another country.

**Format:** The exam is administered on computer at 1,800 colleges and universities in the United States and at some international locations.

**For more information:** Consult the CLEP website (clep.collegeboard.org), call +001 212-237-1331, or write to:
CLEP
P.O. Box 6600
Princeton, NJ 08541-6600
USA
email: clep@info.collegeboard.org

# Other Tests

## ACT

The ACT is another admission test. Consult the ACT website for more information.

## TOEFL (Test of English as a Foreign Language)

**Type of test:** English proficiency.

**Purpose:** To measure the ability of nonnative English speakers to communicate in an academic setting.

**Required of:** Undergraduates seeking a first degree and graduate students seeking an advanced degree.

**Format:** There are two versions of the TOEFL test: Internet-based (TOEFL iBT) and paper-based (TOEFL PBT). Results for all versions are valid for two years from the test administration date. It is important to understand where each version will be administered and the differences between them.

**Internet-based test (TOEFL iBT):** Test-takers have up to four hours to complete the TOEFL iBT test, which has four sections: Reading, Listening, Speaking and Writing. The test is offered on selected dates at authorized ETS test centers. The test emphasizes the use of language for communication by combining, or integrating, the language skills needed to succeed in an academic setting. For more information, consult the TOEFL website (ets.org/toefl).

**Paper-based test:** The TOEFL paper-based test (TOEFL PBT) has three sections: Listening Comprehension, Structure and Written Expression, and Reading Comprehension. There is also a 30-minute essay called the Test of Written English (TWE) that is given at every TOEFL PBT administration. The entire administration takes approximately 3 1/2 hours. The paper-based test will be administered on a limited basis in selected locations on specific dates in countries where TOEFL iBT is not available and to supplement the TOEFL iBT test center network.

# After colleges decide

You should receive a reply about two or three months after the college receives all your application documents. If not, write to the admission office and ask about its decision.

**If you are accepted.** You will be asked to let the college know by a specific date whether you will enroll. Many colleges require a deposit to confirm enrollment, usually $50 to $100, which may not be refundable. This is credited to your tuition when you register. In your admission packet, you will receive a document for use in applying for a visa (SEVIS Form I-20A-B or Form DS-2019 for study in the United States). Be sure to confirm housing reservations with the college and submit the required housing deposits, which average about $200.

**If you are accepted by more than one college.** If you already know which college you prefer, notify the other colleges that you will not attend, so that admission can be offered to another student. If you are not sure which college you prefer, review your college comparison worksheet to help you decide.

## Admission Advice

*"International students, given that they can seldom visit campuses, are strongly influenced by family members and others who have been to the institution. Ask around and try to get a feel for each institution. If you're from Malaysia, try to contact a Malaysian student association at the college and ask everything from 'What's it really like there?' to 'Will you pick me up at the airport?'"*

— Peter Briggs, Michigan State University,
East Lansing, Mich.

**If you are not offered the financial aid you need.** Some colleges may not be able to offer financial aid, or you may have to choose between one that offers aid and another that offers none or a lesser amount. If you can't meet the college expense budget without additional help, find out if there are any resources in your country from which you can get financial help. Contact an EducationUSA advising center or the ministry of education to see if there are organizations that have helped other students in your country in recent years. However, keep in mind that deadlines for scholarships and financial aid are often earlier than the college application deadlines. Start your financial planning as soon as possible. Your admitting institution may ask you to submit a special form documenting your financial status or to complete the College Board International Student Certification of Finances and/or International Student Financial Aid Application.

# Looking ahead

Once you have made your decision, there are many responsibilities to take care of.

**Obtaining a passport and visa.** You must have a valid passport to apply for a student visa. Your U.S. college or university will send you the documentation necessary to obtain a nonimmigrant student visa from the U.S. embassy or consulate in the country where you are located. The U.S. Department of State maintains consular offices at U.S. embassies and in many major cities around the world. Information on their location and details about the visa application process can be found at unitedstatesvisas.gov. Apply for a visa early to avoid any possible delays.

An F-1 student visa is granted to most students who have been accepted for admission to an academic institution in the United States. To obtain an F-1 visa, you must have a SEVIS Form I-20A-B, Certificate of Eligibility for Nonimmigrant (F-1) Student Status, from your U.S. college or university, as well as financial documentation proving that you have the funds to complete an academic program at that college. The documentation may consist of a notarized affidavit from a relative or other person who is supporting you financially, a bank statement showing that you have funds to meet at least your first-year expenses at college, and/or a letter from a government or private agency that is providing funds to support you.

Students entering on an international exchange program or with funding other than their personal funds may have to get a J-1 nonimmigrant Exchange Visitor visa rather than an F-1 visa. This includes students who are being supported by funds from the U.S. government, the government of the student's country, international organizations or a U.S. college or university. If your U.S. college requires a J-1 visa, the college will send you a Form DS-2019, Certificate of Eligibility for Exchange Visitor (J-1) Status. You must take the Form DS-2019, with required financial documentation, to the U.S. embassy or consulate in your country to apply for a J-1 visa.

Students applying for either an F-1 or J-1 visa may have to provide additional documentation. For complete information about U.S. visa issuance requirements, contact the U.S. embassy or consulate. Be sure to read the rules governing the visa status on the form you receive from the university, as it provides different privileges for employment, dependents, practical training and length of stay in the United States. With either visa, you are eligible to enroll as a full-time student and pursue the educational objective for which you entered the United States. You are advised not to enter the United States as a tourist (B-2) or without a visa, because you will not be eligible to enroll in college and pursue full-time studies in the United States.

If you wish to bring a spouse and/or children under age 21 with you, you must prove that you have the funds to support them. The college or university you will be attending will determine the amount of money necessary to support dependents.

Be sure to contact your local EducationUSA advising center for information about the visa application process and tips on preparing for your consular interview.

**Upon arrival in the United States.** As a guest in the United States, from the time you enter the United States until the time you complete studies and return home, you will be subject to U.S. laws and regulations. These affect your ability to enter the United States, study, work and travel. Although you don't need to know every detail about U.S. immigration law, you should become familiar with the most important regulations that affect your status as a student.

While in the United States, you alone will be responsible for maintaining your status as a student in the United States. The best place to find accurate information about immigration regulations is the international student office on your campus. Although your friends might be willing to share their own experiences and advice with you, every student's situation is different, and the information given by your friends might not be the right information for you.

When you arrive at the U.S. port of entry, usually an airport, you will encounter various representatives of the U.S. government. One will request the Arrival-Departure Record (Form I-94), which you will have received on the airplane, and your passport. The inspector may ask you some questions about your plans and your source of support while in the United States. Such questions are routine, and if you have the proper documents you will be admitted without delay. The I-94 will be stapled into your passport. This card indicates the period of time you have permission to remain in the United States to study. For nonimmigrant students, the notation is "D/S," or "Duration of Status," to signify that you may remain in the United States for the time necessary to complete your program of study.

The inspector will take either your SEVIS Form I-20A-B or DS-2019. After making appropriate notations on the form, part of it will be returned to you — page 3 of Form I-20A-B if you are an F-1 student or a copy of the Form DS-2019 if you are a J-1 Exchange Visitor. It is very important that you check the immigration notations on your documents immediately for possible errors and retain this copy with your passport; it is a record of your stay in the United States, which includes date of entry, employment authorization and expected school graduation date. Keep these documents in a safe place at all times. Also make copies and file them separately.

**Upon arrival on your campus.** Meet the international student adviser on your campus as soon as possible. Most colleges and universities hold orientation programs for new students, and many have special sessions for new international students. Most of your questions will be answered during these programs, and you will meet other new students before classes begin.

In addition to providing an orientation to your new surroundings and important details about your new community and college, the international adviser can help you with any required modifications to your immigration status, such as getting stay extensions once you are in the United States. Note that your passport must be valid for six months into the future at all times. The international adviser can also give you information on work eligibility and practical training. Students with F-1 or J-1 immigrant status may get permission to work in the United States subject to certain restrictions and the availability of jobs. Be sure not to work without permission, or you will jeopardize your student status.

# Important regulations for F-1 and J-1 students

There are some important regulations that apply to international students while studying in the United States. You are responsible for being aware of, and following, these guidelines.

## Full course of study

International students are expected to register for a full course of study during each semester or term. For undergraduate students, this means a minimum of 12 credit hours or its equivalent each semester. You are not required to carry a full course of study during your annual vacation or during your final semester of study. The full course of study requirements may vary at colleges that are on the quarter or trimester system. Consult your international student adviser about the requirements for you. Failure to carry a full course of study could result in your losing eligibility for employment and other important benefits. Note that there are limits on online enrollments for international students.

## Processing changes in your I-20A-B or DS-2019

If you change your major field of study or your degree objective, transfer from one college to another or need an extension of the expected completion date of the academic program indicated on your I-20A-B or DS-2019, you must process the change officially with a new form or entry in the SEVIS system database. Consult your international student adviser or J-1 sponsor.

## Departing and reentering the United States

You must have your I-20A-B or DS-2019 form endorsed each time you leave and reenter the United States. For an endorsement, F-1 students should consult the international student adviser; J-1 students should contact the sponsor.

Many international students make plans to travel during winter, spring or summer breaks. International student offices can be very busy in the weeks leading up to a break, so you should make an appointment to have your I-20 A-B or DS-2019 form endorsed as soon as you have made your travel plans.

# Employment in the United States

Many international students are anxious to work in the United States. Employment can be a means of learning about American culture, developing professional skills and earning additional income. However, employment of nonimmigrants in the United States is strictly regulated, and failure to follow U.S. employment law can result in loss of your student or exchange visitor status. Therefore, it is important to understand and follow the rules that govern your prospective employment. Refer to the overview provided below for general information, and consult your international student adviser for details.

You are eligible to apply for and accept employment only if you are in good standing with the immigration authorities. This means that you must carry a full course of study and process all the appropriate forms for change of major, degree objective and school transfer for approval. If you do not maintain your approved status, you may face serious consequences.

Most student employment falls into one of these three categories:

- **Part-time employment on campus:** F-1 students are eligible to accept on-campus employment up to 20 hours per week while school is in session, and full-time (more than 20 hours per week) during holidays, school breaks and vacation periods. Provided that a student is properly maintaining F-1 status, no written authorization is required. J-1 students are also eligible for part-time on-campus employment, but J-1 employment must be authorized in writing on the DS-2019 or in a separate letter from the sponsor.

- **Employment for economic necessity:** Some students experience unexpected financial crises after beginning study in the United States. Examples of such crises could include sudden devaluation of home-country currency, loss of scholarship, or the illness or death of a private sponsor. In such cases, if a student is able to show that off-campus part-time employment could provide a solution to the emergency, he or she may request employment authorization. Check with the international student office for the most current regulations and procedures. Off-campus employment must always be authorized in writing before a student begins work.

- **F-1 Practical Training/J-1 Academic Training:** Employment that applies the concepts learned in the student's academic program is considered practical or curricular training, and may be requested regardless of a student's economic need. Such employment is generally authorized only after the student has had a chance to participate in classroom activities and gain some theoretical background, which she or he would then apply in a practical setting. F-1 students are required to maintain their full-time student status for a minimum of one academic year or nine consecutive months before they become eligible to request practical training. J-1 students, similarly, may not request academic training for

# Predeparture checklist

❑ Get or renew your passport.

❑ Obtain a student or exchange visitor visa.

❑ Make airline reservations. Find out about baggage charges or shipping rates. Plan to arrive in time for the orientation program. Try to arrive at the college during regular office hours (8 a.m. to 5 p.m., Monday through Friday).

❑ Make hotel reservations if you will be stopping en route. If you have not received a housing assignment or need to find temporary living accommodations, be sure to have sufficient funds to cover these living expenses.

❑ Get inoculations and have your doctor complete a World Health Organization yellow immunization card. Have a physical examination and send the report to your college if it is requested. If you wear glasses, get and carry with you a prescription from your doctor. If you take special medication, get a reasonable supply and a new prescription, written in English, from your doctor to take with you.

❑ Request information on health insurance and services from your college. Obtain health insurance.

❑ If you want on-campus housing, send in your housing reservation form and deposit.

❑ Write to the international student adviser to notify him or her of the date and approximate time of your arrival. Ask about airport arrival services.

❑ If you would like help on arrival, check with your local EducationUSA adviser, or inquire about the help offered by the YMCA Arrivals Program, c/o International YMCA, 5 West 63rd Street, 2nd floor, New York, NY 10023 USA. Visit its website at internationalymca.org.

❑ Be sure you understand U.S. currency (bills and coins) and the exchange rate between your country and the United States.

❑ Arrange to set up and transfer money to an account at a bank in the United States.

❑ Be sure to have funds (in U.S. currency) to cover expenses while traveling to college and for your first month in the United States. A credit card in your name, such as a Visa or MasterCard, will also be extremely helpful.

❑ If possible, take about $150 in U.S. currency in small denominations ($1, $5, $10, $20) for use on arrival. Do not keep all the cash in one place.

❑ Ask the college or check on its website about the best transportation from the airport to the college. If arriving in a large city, ask how much it should cost to get from the airport to the college. If you take a taxi, be sure to confirm the price of the trip with the driver before leaving the airport. Some colleges offer airport pickup services, particularly if arranged in advance.

❑ Arrange in advance to ship belongings that will be over the baggage limit on airlines, unless you are willing to pay the excess baggage charges.

❑ Prepare items to be carried on your person or in a carry-on bag (not checked). Be sure to set aside your passport, visa documents, U.S. currency, medication and prescriptions, and the college deposit receipt or registration form to carry with you. Your carry-on bag should contain any items you will need in case your regular baggage is temporarily delayed.

❑ Label all of your luggage on the inside and outside with your name and the name and address of the college to which you are going.

a period longer than their length of study in the United States. Both academic training and practical training may be undertaken prior to or following a student's completion of his or her program of studies. The length of authorization for academic or practical training, the type of job, and the employer are all generally regulated for both F-1 and J-1 students. In every case, employment for practical or academic training must be authorized in writing before a student begins work.

## Admission Advice

*"Many international students will get internships or co-ops. What international students need to keep in mind is that they need to adhere to U.S. immigration regulations, as far as working goes. They need to get involved right away with their international student adviser on campus. They should maintain good standing so that they can get the correct visa and work legally."*

— Ann Gogerty, Iowa State University, Ames, Iowa

*"Some students want to gain some practical on-the-job training, and they can do that through immigration's OPT program — that's 'Optional Practical Training' — which allows them to stay in the United States after earning an associate degree for one year and work in the field for which they were trained."*

— Ken Bus, Glendale Community College, Glendale, Ariz.

# Accompanying dependents

Students in F-1 and J-1 status may bring eligible dependents (spouse and children), who enter the United States with F-2 or J-2 visas. Additional funds are required for the support of dependents, and these funds must be documented before the dependents can enter the United States. F-2 dependents are not permitted to work under any circumstances. J-2 dependents may request employment authorization but can earn money only to support themselves and other J-2 dependents. If you wish to bring dependents with you when you first come to the United States, notify your university or your J-1 program sponsor so the required dependent information can be included on your I-20A-B or DS-2019 form. If you want your dependents to follow separately after you are settled, consult your international student adviser or sponsor for advice several months before your dependents plan to travel.

# SEVIS (Student and Exchange Visitor Information System)

Students planning to study in the United States must be aware of the automated tracking system called "SEVIS." This system is designed to track international students through an electronic network among colleges and universities, U.S. immigration services, and U.S. consular posts overseas. While you are a student in the United States, it will be important to maintain contact with the international student adviser at your institution to report any changes to your status. You can learn more about visa procedures by logging on to the website http://travel.state.gov.

## Admission Advice

*"International students help diversify our campuses and teach us about the rest of the world, as much as we're able to educate them in the academic areas. We encourage students to look at the United States and the educational options they have here."*

— Joseph DeCrosta, Duquesne University, Pittsburgh, Pa.

# Consider your health

Your good health is essential for your success as a student. If you have been relatively healthy for most of your life, you may take your good health for granted. But before you leave for the United States, you should take steps to prepare for the big changes ahead.

If you have any unresolved health concerns, take care of them before you leave home. Do you need a new pair of glasses? Have you had a recent dental examination? Have you experienced some unexplained symptoms that need to be checked? Be sure to have these and any similar problems solved before you depart for the United States.

Your U.S. university may request health records from your physician at home, but you should bring copies of your records for yourself. These include your medical history, immunization records, eyeglass prescription, drug prescriptions and a written record of any remedy that you use on a regular basis. These records should be written in English or you should bring translations with you.

Learn as much as you can about health resources on your chosen campus ahead of time so you are prepared when you arrive. These may include a small infirmary or a large hospital, depending on the size of your college. After arriving on campus, find out where you can go for emergency health care if the health center is closed. Do not wait for an emergency to find out where such a facility is located.

Expect changes in your health as you adjust to your new surroundings. Many factors, including your eating habits, sleeping patterns, local climate and level of stress, contribute to your physical health and emotional well-being. When you arrive in a new place and are surrounded by a different culture, these factors change and your health may be affected. Give yourself time to adjust, and if you become uncomfortable or unhappy, consult the international student adviser, student health service or counselors available at your college or university.

## Student health insurance

There is no socialized medicine in the United States. Be sure that you have health insurance. If your sponsor provides health coverage, be sure that it covers treatment in the United States and that it covers catastrophic illnesses. Otherwise, purchase medical insurance for yourself and your dependents through your campus health insurance plan or through a U.S. health insurance agent. Medical insurance is absolutely essential to meet health care costs in the United States. Many U.S. universities require medical insurance for international students who enroll, and all J-1 exchange visitor students are required by law to carry medical insurance. But whether your school requires insurance or not, you should buy it as soon as you arrive. Policies differ in the expenses they will pay; find a policy with a reasonable deductible, affordable copayments and limited exclusions. To learn more about how to shop for a health insurance policy, consult with the student health service or international student adviser on your campus.

# Glossary

**Accelerated program.** A college program of study completed in less time than is usually required, most often by attending classes in summer or by taking extra courses during the regular academic terms. Completion of a bachelor's degree program in three years is an example of acceleration.

**Accreditation.** Recognition by an accrediting organization or agency that a college meets certain acceptable standards in its educational programs, services and facilities. Regional accreditation applies to a college as a whole and not to any particular programs or courses of study. Specialized accreditation of specific types of schools, such as Bible colleges or trade and technical schools, may also be determined by a national organization. Information about the accreditation of specialized programs within a college by organizations, such as the American Chemical Society, American Dietetic Association, etc., is given in *Accredited Institutions of Postsecondary Education*, published for the Commission on Recognition of Postsecondary Accreditation by the American Council on Education.

**ACT.** A college admission test given at test centers on specified dates throughout the year. Please visit the organization's website for further information.

**Advanced placement.** Admission or assignment of a freshman to an advanced course in a certain subject on the basis of evidence that the student has already completed the equivalent of the college's freshman course in that subject.

**Advanced Placement Program® (AP®).** An academic program of the College Board that provides high school students with the opportunity to study and learn at the college level. AP offers courses in 38 subjects, each culminating in a rigorous exam. Most colleges and universities accept qualifying AP Exam scores for credit, advanced placement or both.

**Associate degree.** A degree granted by a college or university after the satisfactory completion of a two-year full-time program of study or its part-time equivalent. In general, the associate of arts (A.A.) or associate of science (A.S.) degree is granted after students complete a program of study similar to the first two years of a four-year college curriculum. The associate in applied science (A.A.S.) is awarded by many colleges upon completion of technological or vocational programs of study.

**Bachelor's, or baccalaureate, degree.** A degree received after the satisfactory completion of a four- or five-year full-time program of study (or its part-time equivalent) at a college or university. The bachelor of arts (B.A.) and bachelor of science (B.S.) are the most common baccalaureates. There is no absolute difference between the degrees, and policies concerning their award vary from college to college.

**Calendar.** The system by which an institution divides its year into shorter periods for instruction and awarding credit. The most common calendars are those based on the semester, trimester, quarter, and 4-1-4.

**Certificate.** An award for completing a particular program or course of study, sometimes given by two-year colleges or vocational or technical schools.

**College-Level Examination Program® (CLEP®).** A program in which students receive college credit by earning a qualifying score in any of 33 examinations in business, composition and literature, world languages, history and social sciences, and science and mathematics. Sponsored by the College Board, exams are administered at over 1,800 test centers. Approximately 2,900 colleges and universities grant credit for passing a CLEP exam.

**College-preparatory subjects.** A term used to describe subjects required for admission to, or recommended as preparation for, college. It is usually understood to mean subjects from the fields of English, history and social studies, foreign languages, mathematics, science, and the arts.

**Combined bachelor's/graduate degree.** A program in which students complete a bachelor's degree and a master's degree or first-professional degree in less than the usual amount of time. In most programs, students apply to undergraduate study, and begin the graduate program in their fourth year of college. Successful completion results in the awarding of both bachelor's and graduate degrees. At some colleges, this option is called a joint-degree program.

**Common Application.** The standard application form distributed by the National Association of Secondary School Principals to private colleges that are subscribers to the Common Application Group.

**Community/junior college.** A college offering a two-year program rather than a four-year program. A junior college usually offers vocational programs as well as the first two years of a four-year program. The student in the vocational program usually goes directly into a vocation after graduation, while the student in the academic program transfers to a four-year institution.

**Comprehensive fee.** If the college combines tuition, fees, room and board expenses, that single figure is called a comprehensive fee.

**Consortium.** When there are several colleges and universities within close geographical proximity, they often join together in a consortium. The advantages of attending a college that is a member of a consortium are that students have the resources of many libraries instead of just one; they have the opportunity to take courses not available at their own college by doing so at a member institution; and they can take advantage of many of the combined cultural and educational opportunities offered when the members of the consortium unite and present panel discussions, special lectures and unusual courses.

**Consumer Price Index (CPI).** A measure of inflation or deflation at the consumer level, updated monthly by the U.S. Bureau of Labor Statistics.

**Cooperative education (co-op).** A program that provides for alternative class attendance and employment in business, industry or government. Students are typically paid for their work. Under a cooperative plan, five years are normally required to complete a bachelor's degree, but graduates have the advantage of about a year's practical work experience in addition to their studies.

**Credit by examination.** Academic credit granted by a college to entering students who have demonstrated proficiency in college-level studies through examinations, such as those administered by the College Board's AP and CLEP programs. This is a means of cutting college costs by reducing the number of courses needed to earn a degree.

**Credit hour.** A unit of measure representing an hour of instruction over a 15-week period in a semester or trimester system, or a 10-week period in a quarter system. It is applied toward the total number of hours needed for completing the requirements of a degree, diploma, certificate or other formal award.

**Credit/no credit grading system.** *See* Pass/fail grading system.

**Cross-registration.** The practice, through agreements between colleges, of permitting students enrolled at one college or university to enroll in courses at another institution without formally applying for admission to the second institution.

**Deferred admission.** The practice of permitting students to postpone enrollment, usually for one year, after acceptance to college.

**Distance learning.** An option for earning course credit off campus via cable television, the Internet, satellite classes, videotapes, correspondence courses, or other means.

**Double major.** Any program in which a student completes the requirements of two majors concurrently.

**Exchange student program.** Any arrangement that permits a student to study for a semester or more at another college in the United States without extending the amount of time required for a degree.

**4-1-4.** A variation of the semester calendar system, the 4-1-4 calendar consists of two terms of about 16 weeks each, separated by a one-month intersession used for intensive short courses, independent study, off-campus work or other types of instruction.

**Gift aid.** Scholarships and grants that do not have to be repaid.

**Grade point average or ratio (GPA).** A system used by many schools for evaluating the overall scholastic performance of students. Grade points are determined by first multiplying the number of hours given for a course by the numerical value of the grade and then dividing the sum of all grade points by the total number of hours carried. The most common system of numerical values for grades is: A = 4, B = 3, C = 2, D = 1, and E or F = 0. Also called a quality point average ratio.

**Graduate study.** A program leading to a master's degree or doctoral degree; advanced study generally following a bachelor's degree.

**High school.** The final three to four years of preuniversity education in the United States. Students usually receive their high school diplomas when they are 17 or 18. Also called "secondary school."

**Honors program.** A plan designed to encourage superior students to engage in more challenging programs in their areas of concentration than are required. Students who succeed in meeting the stringent requirements of an honors program are usually granted "honor" degrees.

**Independent study.** Academic work chosen or designed by the student with the approval of the department concerned, under an instructor's supervision. This work is usually undertaken outside of the regular classroom structure.

**Interdisciplinary.** Refers to programs or courses that use the knowledge from a number of academic disciplines, such as a combination of environmental science and government policy, or of engineering and business.

**International Baccalaureate (IB).** A high school curriculum offered by some schools in the United States and other countries. Some colleges award credit for completion of this curriculum. For further information, visit the organization's website.

**Internships.** Short-term supervised work experiences, usually related to a student's major field, for which the student earns academic credit. The work can be full time or part time, on or off campus, paid or unpaid. Student teaching and apprenticeships are examples.

**Liberal arts.** The study of the humanities (literature, the arts and philosophy), history, foreign languages, social sciences, mathematics and natural sciences. Study of the liberal arts and humanities prepares students to develop general knowledge and reasoning ability rather than specific skills.

**Major.** Short for "major field of concentration," a student's academic field of specialization. In general, most courses in the major are taken at the degree-granting institution during the junior and senior years.

**Master's degree.** A degree awarded after one or more years of graduate work following the bachelor's degree.

**Matriculation.** The process whereby a student is accepted, pays fees and enrolls in classes, officially becoming a student at the college. This term is only applied to freshmen or to a transfer student's first enrollment.

**Open admission.** The college admission policy of admitting high school graduates and other adults generally without regard to conventional academic qualifications, such as high school subjects, high school grades and admission test scores. Virtually all applicants with high school diplomas or their equivalent are accepted.

**Optional Practical Training (OPT).** This program, sponsored by the U.S. Citizenship and Immigration Services, gives students on F-1 visas the opportunity to work for up to a year in a field related to their program of study.

**Pass/fail grading system.** Some colleges permit students to take courses where their performance is simply rated as either passing or failing, rather than graded to indicate various levels of passing work. The college's entire grading system may follow this pattern, or it may be an option for individual students in specific courses. It may also be referred to as a credit/no credit grading option.

**Prerequisite.** A requirement that must be met before a certain course can be taken.

**Private institution.** An institution of higher education not supported by public taxes. It may be independent or related to a church.

**Professional degree.** A degree granted upon completion of academic requirements to become licensed in a recognized profession, such as medicine or the law. The programs of study require at least two years of previous college work for entrance, and at least six years of college work for completion.

**Public college/university.** An institution of higher education supported by public taxes.

**Quarter system.** An academic calendar period of about 12 weeks. Four quarters make up an academic year, but at colleges using the quarter system, students make normal academic progress by attending three quarters each year. In some colleges, students can accelerate their progress by attending all four quarters in one or more years.

**Residency requirements.** Most colleges and universities require that a student spend a minimum number of terms taking courses on campus (as opposed to independent study, transfer credits from other colleges or credit by examination) to be eligible for graduation. Also, residency requirements can refer to the minimum amount of time a student is required to have lived in a state to be eligible for in-state tuition at a public (state-controlled) college or university.

**Rolling admission.** An admission procedure by which the college considers each student's application as soon as all the required credentials, such as school records and test scores, have been received. The college usually notifies an applicant of its decision without delay. At many colleges, rolling admission allows for early notification and works much like nonbinding Early Action programs.

**SAT Question-and-Answer Service.** A service of the College Board that provides students with a copy of their SAT, their answers and the correct answers, scoring instructions, and information about the questions. The service is only available for certain test dates.

**SAT®.** A college admission exam that tests reading, writing and language, and mathematics skills. It is given on specified dates through the year at test centers in the Unites States and other countries. The SAT is used by most colleges and sponsors of financial aid programs in the U.S., and at many universities across the world.

**SAT Subject Tests™.** Admission tests in specific subjects are given at test centers in the United States and other countries on specified dates throughout the year. The tests are used by colleges for help in both evaluating applicants for admission and determining course placement and exemption of enrolled first-year students.

**Secondary school.** *See* High school.

**Semester.** A period of about 16 weeks. Colleges on a semester system offer two semesters of instruction a year; there may also be an additional summer session.

**Student and Exchange Visitor Information System (SEVIS).** An automated system created by the U.S. government to track international students.

**Terminal program.** A program of study in which the student completes his or her studies in a preselected period of time. This type of program is usually directed toward vocational preparation. The amount of time taken to complete the program will vary, but is not usually longer than two years.

**Test of English as a Foreign Language (TOEFL).** A test generally used by international students to demonstrate their English language proficiency at the advanced level required for study at colleges and universities worldwide. Please visit the organization's website for further information.

**Transcript.** A copy of a student's official academic record listing all courses taken and grades required.

**Transfer program.** An educational program in a two-year college (or four-year college that offers associate degrees) primarily for students who plan to continue their studies in a four-year college or university.

**Transfer student.** A student who has attended another college for any period, which may be defined by various colleges as any time from a single term up to three years. A transfer student may receive credit for all or some of the courses successfully completed before the transfer.

**Trimester.** An academic calendar period of about 15 weeks. Three trimesters make up one year. Students normally progress by attending two of the trimesters each year and in some colleges can accelerate their progress by attending all three trimesters in one or more years.

**Undergraduate study.** A program leading to an associate or a bachelor's degree; generally follows high school.

**Upper-division college.** A college offering bachelor's degree programs that begin with the junior year. Entering students must have completed the freshman and sophomore years at other colleges.

**Virtual university.** A degree-granting, accredited institution wherein all courses are delivered by distance learning, with no physical campus.

# **Part II:**
# Information tables on U.S. colleges and universities

# How to use the information tables

The information tables provide detailed information on more than 3,200 undergraduate institutions in the United States. The data were collected directly from the institutions responding to the College Board's Annual Survey of Colleges in the spring of 2017.

## Colleges and Universities

The names of the colleges are listed alphabetically by state. Institutions are listed by their full names, which are not always the ones in popular use. For example, UCLA is listed as University of California: Los Angeles. The mailing address, telephone number, website address and fax number (when available) of each college are given in the *College addresses* in the back of this book.

The columns in this table include the following information.

**Control/degrees.** This column shows whether the institution is private (Pr) or public (Pu), and whether the college offers associate degrees (A), bachelor's degrees (B), or both (AB).

**Undergraduate enrollment.** The first figure is the total number of undergraduate students enrolled in the fall of 2016. The second figure is the number of undergraduate international students enrolled.

**Tests required.** If the college requires one or more of the following standardized admission tests, they are indicated

in this column: SAT, SAT Subject Test, ACT, or TOEFL. A slash (/) between two tests means that either test is required; for example, SAT/TOEFL means that applicants must take either the SAT or the TOEFL. A plus (+) between tests means that both are required; for example, SAT + TOEFL means that applicants must take both the SAT and the TOEFL.

**TOEFL minimum and average.** The minimum score listed is generally acceptable to the college as an indicator of English language proficiency. The average may be significantly higher at some colleges. The scores indicated, which range from 0 to 120, are for the iBT (Internet-based) test. For paper-based test scores, which range from 310 to 667, see the concordance table on the TOEFL website.

**Applications.** The deadline is generally the last date by which the college will accept application forms, test scores, transcripts and other documents required for the admission process. Remember that many colleges fill their classes well in advance of this date, so complete your applications as soon as possible before the deadline. The application fee is required at the time you send your application form; the figure here is in U.S. dollars.

**Student services.** These columns indicate whether the college offers the following services for international students: student adviser, student orientation program or English as a second language (ESL) program on campus.

**Housing.** These two columns indicate whether the college has housing during the academic year (September-May) and/or summer months (June, July and August) for international students.

**Academic year cost.** The figure for tuition/fees represents the tuition and general fees the college charges most first-year, full-time international students for the nine-month academic year. For colleges with on-campus housing, the nine-month living cost includes room and board. For colleges that do not offer on-campus housing, the living cost figure includes an estimated expense for room and board. The cost per credit is indicated along with the maximum number of credits the institution allows a student to take during the summer. The cost does not include travel to and from your home country. Cost is for 2017-18, unless otherwise indicated.

**Financial aid.** The first column indicates whether the institution offers financial aid for undergraduates from other countries. The number of international students who received aid is shown next, followed by the average award (in U.S. dollars). The last column shows the deadline for applying for financial aid. Remember that there is not enough financial aid to meet the needs of all applicants, so complete any financial aid application requirements as soon as possible.

# Lists and indexes

**International undergraduate student enrollment.** Colleges are listed in descending order by enrollment size. If a college did not provide international enrollment information this year, it is not included on the list.

**Total financial aid for international undergraduate students.** Colleges are listed in descending order by the total dollar amount of financial aid awarded to international students.

**Conditional admission based on English language proficiency.** Colleges that will admit applicants whose English skills will not permit them to pursue academic course work during their first term are listed here. These colleges require that the student spend time in the first term increasing their English language skills to the required level. English language proficiency is defined differently by different institutions. If you have questions about your English language skills, be sure to check with the colleges of interest to you.

**SAT Subject Tests required or recommended.** Some colleges require one or more SAT Subject Tests of undergraduate international applicants, and some recommend these tests.

**Credit/placement for International Baccalaureate (IB).** These colleges offer credit or advanced standing for the IB diploma and/or certificates from individual IB exams. They do not necessarily offer credit for every IB exam, and qualifying scores will vary. Check with the colleges to learn more about their policies.

**Credit/placement for Advanced Placement® (AP).** These colleges offer credit or advanced placement to students with qualifying scores on AP Exams. They do not necessarily offer credit for every AP Exam, and qualifying scores will vary. Check with the colleges, or use the AP Credit Policy Info tool at collegeboard.org/apcreditpolicy, to learn more about the colleges' policies.

**ESL programs on campus.** Colleges that offer English as a second language programs on campus are listed in alphabetical order by state.

**Special housing for international students.** Colleges that offer a special on-campus dormitory for international students are listed in alphabetical order by state.

**Housing guaranteed for all freshmen.** These colleges guarantee that incoming freshmen will be offered on-campus accommodations.

**College size (undergraduate enrollment).** Colleges are grouped into categories from very small (fewer than 750 undergraduates) to very large (15,000 or more undergraduates).

**College type.** Colleges are grouped into types that describe the type of courses you'll find at the college, such as liberal arts colleges, business colleges, engineering colleges and military academies. Separate lists show colleges that are affiliated with a religious denomination and colleges that cater to a specific type of student — colleges for women, for example.

# College addresses

This listing gives the full name and mailing address for each institution listed in the undergraduate and graduate tables in this section. It includes the school's telephone number and, when available, the website address, fax number, and email address. The office to contact for further information about the institution and for application procedures and forms is also given.

# Colleges and universities

| Institution | Control/ degrees | Undergraduates | | Tests required (Fall 2017) | TOEFL | | Application | |
|---|---|---|---|---|---|---|---|---|
| | | Total | Internat'l | | minimum | average | Deadline | Fee |
| **Alabama** | | | | | | | | |
| Alabama Agricultural and Mechanical University. . . . . . . . . . . . . . . . . | .Pu/B | 4,616 | | TOEFL | 61 | | 5/15 | 30 |
| Alabama State University . . . . . . . . . . . . . . . | .Pu/B | 4,703 | 75 | TOEFL | | | | 25 |
| Athens State University. . . . . . . . . . . . . . . . . | .Pu/B | 2,889 | | TOEFL | | | | 30 |
| Auburn University. . . . . . . . . . . . . . . . . . . . | .Pu/B | 22,095 | 473 | TOEFL, SAT/ACT | 79 | | | 60 |
| Auburn University at Montgomery . . . . . . . . . . . . | .Pu/B | 4,179 | 172 | TOEFL | 61 | 70 | 7/15 | |
| Birmingham-Southern College . . . . . . . . . . . . . | .Pr/B | 1,290 | | TOEFL | 81 | 93 | 6/1 | 50 |
| Bishop State Community College . . . . . . . . . . . | .Pu/A | 3,029 | | TOEFL | | | | |
| Brown Mackie College: Birmingham . . . . . . . . . | .Pr/AB | | | | | | | |
| Calhoun Community College. . . . . . . . . . . . . . . | .Pu/A | 9,900 | | TOEFL | 61 | | None | |
| Chattahoochee Valley Community College . . . . . . . | .Pu/A | 1,529 | | TOEFL | 61 | | None | |
| Columbia Southern University . . . . . . . . . . . . . . | .Pr/AB | 24,713 | 9 | TOEFL | 61 | | None | |
| Concordia College . . . . . . . . . . . . . . . . . . . . | .Pr/AB | 610 | | TOEFL | | | | 25 |
| Faulkner State Community College . . . . . . . . . . . | .Pu/A | 1,342 | | TOEFL | 61 | | | |
| Faulkner University . . . . . . . . . . . . . . . . . . . . | .Pr/AB | 2,298 | 56 | TOEFL | 61 | | None | 25 |
| Gadsden State Community College . . . . . . . . . . . | .Pu/A | 5,109 | | TOEFL | | | | |
| George C. Wallace Community College at Dothan. . . . . . . . . . . . . . . . . . . . . . . . . . | .Pu/A | 3,904 | | TOEFL | 61 | | 5/15 | |
| Heritage Christian University . . . . . . . . . . . . . . | .Pr/AB | 60 | | | | | | 25 |
| Herzing University: Birmingham. . . . . . . . . . . . . | .Pr/AB | 481 | | | | | | |
| Huntingdon College . . . . . . . . . . . . . . . . . . . . | .Pr/B | 1,140 | 2 | TOEFL, SAT/ACT | 45 | 75 | | |
| Huntsville Bible College . . . . . . . . . . . . . . . . . | .Pr/AB | 119 | | | | | | 35 |
| Jacksonville State University . . . . . . . . . . . . . . | .Pu/B | 6,714 | | TOEFL | 61 | | | 35 |
| Jefferson State Community College. . . . . . . . . . . | .Pu/A | 7,256 | | TOEFL | 61 | | | |
| Judson College . . . . . . . . . . . . . . . . . . . . . . | .Pr/AB | 334 | | TOEFL | 61 | | None | 42 |
| Lawson State Community College. . . . . . . . . . . . | .Pu/A | 3,090 | | TOEFL | | | | 10 |
| Lurleen B. Wallace Community College. . . . . . . . . | .Pu/A | 1,419 | 3 | TOEFL | 61 | | None | |
| Marion Military Institute . . . . . . . . . . . . . . . . . | .Pu/A | 422 | | TOEFL | | | | 30 |
| Miles College . . . . . . . . . . . . . . . . . . . . . . . | .Pr/B | 1,690 | | TOEFL | | | | |
| Oakwood University. . . . . . . . . . . . . . . . . . . . | .Pr/AB | 1,703 | | TOEFL | | | | 30 |
| Remington College: Mobile . . . . . . . . . . . . . . . | .Pr/A | 881 | | | | | | 50 |
| Samford University . . . . . . . . . . . . . . . . . . . . | .Pr/B | 3,324 | 77 | TOEFL, SAT/ACT | 90 | | 5/1 | 40 |
| Selma University. . . . . . . . . . . . . . . . . . . . . . | .Pr/AB | 399 | | | | | | 20 |
| Southern Union State Community College . . . . . . . | .Pu/A | 4,734 | | TOEFL | | | | |
| Spring Hill College . . . . . . . . . . . . . . . . . . . . | .Pr/B | 1,379 | 39 | TOEFL | 80 | | | 35 |
| Stillman College . . . . . . . . . . . . . . . . . . . . . | .Pr/B | 1,000 | | TOEFL, SAT/ACT | | | | 25 |
| Talladega College . . . . . . . . . . . . . . . . . . . . | .Pr/B | 1,016 | | TOEFL | 65 | | | 25 |
| Troy University. . . . . . . . . . . . . . . . . . . . . . . | .Pu/AB | 14,149 | 638 | | 61 | | | 30 |
| Tuskegee University. . . . . . . . . . . . . . . . . . . . | .Pr/B | 2,485 | | TOEFL, SAT/ACT | 69 | 80 | | 35 |
| United States Sports Academy . . . . . . . . . . . . . | .Pr/B | 270 | | TOEFL | 79 | | | 100 |
| University of Alabama . . . . . . . . . . . . . . . . . . | .Pu/B | 31,663 | 607 | | 79 | | 5/1 | 40 |
| University of Alabama at Birmingham. . . . . . . . . . | .Pu/B | 12,092 | 254 | TOEFL | 77 | | 6/1 | 30 |
| University of Alabama in Huntsville . . . . . . . . . . | .Pu/B | 6,338 | 184 | TOEFL, SAT/ACT | 62 | 89 | | 50 |
| University of Mobile. . . . . . . . . . . . . . . . . . . . | .Pr/AB | 1,373 | 59 | TOEFL | 61 | | | 50 |
| University of Montevallo. . . . . . . . . . . . . . . . . | .Pu/B | 2,399 | 31 | TOEFL | 71 | | | 30 |
| University of North Alabama . . . . . . . . . . . . . . . | .Pu/B | 5,869 | 200 | TOEFL | 61 | 72 | 7/1 | 100 |
| University of Phoenix: Birmingham. . . . . . . . . . . | .Pr/B | 198 | | | | | | |
| University of South Alabama . . . . . . . . . . . . . . . | .Pu/B | 11,483 | 1,014 | TOEFL | 61 | | | 45 |
| University of West Alabama . . . . . . . . . . . . . . . | .Pu/AB | 1,974 | 117 | TOEFL, SAT/ACT | 61 | | 6/15 | 40 |
| Virginia College in Birmingham. . . . . . . . . . . . . | .Pr/AB | 2,711 | | | | | | 250 |
| Virginia College in Mobile . . . . . . . . . . . . . . . | .Pr/A | 575 | | | | | | |
| Virginia College in Montgomery. . . . . . . . . . . . . | .Pr/A | 622 | | | | | | |
| Wallace State Community College at Hanceville . . . . . . . . . . . . . . . . . . . . . . . . | .Pu/A | 4,856 | 52 | TOEFL | 61 | | | |
| **Alaska** | | | | | | | | |
| Alaska Pacific University . . . . . . . . . . . . . . . . | .Pr/AB | 266 | | TOEFL | | | | 25 |
| University of Alaska Anchorage . . . . . . . . . . . . . | .Pu/AB | 11,843 | 221 | TOEFL, SAT/ACT | 45 | 70 | | 50 |

| Student services | | | Housing | | Academic year costs | | Maximum credits/ summer | Credit hour charge | International financial aid | | | |
|---|---|---|---|---|---|---|---|---|---|---|---|---|
| Adviser | Orientation | ESL | Academic year | Summer | Tuition/ fees | Living costs | | | Available | Number receiving aid | Average award | Deadline |
| Yes | Yes | | Yes | Yes | 17,964 † | 7,030 | | 542 | Yes | | | 3/1 |
| Yes | Yes | | Yes | Yes | 15,656 † | 5,422 | 9 | 578 | Yes | | | None |
| Yes | | | No | | 12,210 † | | 19 | | Yes | | | None |
| Yes | Yes | Yes | Yes | | 28,840 † | 13,028 | | 1134 | | | | |
| Yes | Yes | Yes | Yes | Yes | 20,710 † | 5,650 | 18 | 665 | Yes | 17 | $2,243 | None |
| Yes | Yes | | Yes | | 34,448 † | 13,020 | 12 | 1383.25 | Yes | | | None |
| Yes | Yes | | No | | 7,890 † | | 15 | 234 | | | | |
| Yes | | | No | | 7,890 † | 4,500 | 19 | 234 | Yes | | | None |
| | | Yes | No | | 7,950 † | | | 234 | | | | |
| | | | No | | 6,335 † | 6,372 | | 210 | | | | |
| Yes | | | Yes | | 10,120 † | 5,700 | | | | | | |
| Yes | | | Yes | | 7,910 † | 5,800 | | 234 | | | | |
| Yes | Yes | Yes | Yes | Yes | 20,130 † | 7,230 | 12 | 620 | Yes | | | 5/1 |
| Yes | Yes | Yes | Yes | Yes | 7,590 † | 3,600 | 14 | 234 | Yes | | | None |
| Yes | | | No | | 7,830 † | 2,983 | 19 | 234 | | | | |
| Yes | Yes | | Yes | Yes | | | 15 | | | | | |
| | Yes | | Yes | | 25,450 † | 9,100 | 14 | 1020 | Yes | 3 | $7,500 | None |
| | | | No | | 5,390 † | | | 175 | Yes | | | 6/30 |
| Yes | | | Yes | Yes | 18,525 ‡ | 7,128 | 18 | 600 | | 108 | $10,982 | |
| Yes | Yes | | No | | 7,950 † | | 19 | 234 | | | | |
| Yes | | | Yes | | 17,376 † | 9,978 | 10 | 550 | Yes | | | None |
| Yes | | | Yes | | 7,910 † | 4,760 | 21 | 234 | | | | |
| | | | No | | 7,890 † | 9,450 | 12 | 234 | | | | |
| Yes | | | Yes | | 15,418 † | 4,950 | | 400 | | | | |
| Yes | | | Yes | | 11,604 † | 7,042 | | 448 | | | | |
| Yes | Yes | | Yes | | 16,720 † | 9,312 | | | | | | |
| | | | No | | | | 16 | | | | | |
| Yes | Yes | | Yes | Yes | 30,490 | 10,280 | 16 | 991 | Yes | 25 | $21,794 | None |
| | | | Yes | | 7,145 † | 6,000 | | | Yes | | | 6/30 |
| Yes | | | Yes | | 7,610 † | 3,200 | | 234 | | | | |
| Yes | | | Yes | Yes | 37,584 | 13,070 | 12 | 1024 | Yes | | | None |
| | | | Yes | | 10,938 † | 7,180 | 12 | 539 | Yes | | | 8/15 |
| Yes | Yes | | Yes | | 13,828 † | 6,704 | | 466.33 | Yes | | | 3/1 |
| Yes | Yes | Yes | Yes | Yes | 20,831 ‡ | 7,853 | 21 | 602 | | | | |
| Yes | | | Yes | | 21,470 † | 9,104 | 9 | | | | | |
| | | | | | 11,850 | | | 395 | | | | |
| Yes | Yes | Yes | Yes | Yes | 26,950 † | 9,550 | 12 | | Yes | 90 | $25,514 | None |
| Yes | Yes | Yes | Yes | Yes | 22,612 † | 9,970 | 18 | 746 | Yes | 251 | $13,979 | None |
| Yes | Yes | Yes | Yes | Yes | 20,612 † | 9,603 | 18 | | Yes | 51 | $11,040 | 7/31 |
| Yes | | | Yes | Yes | 21,400 † | 9,600 | 18 | 720 | Yes | 53 | $20,932 | None |
| Yes | | Yes | Yes | Yes | 24,310 | 7,462 | 14 | 788 | Yes | | | None |
| Yes | Yes | Yes | Yes | Yes | 17,840 † | 6,696 | 12 | 528 | Yes | 57 | $5,841 | None |
| Yes | Yes | Yes | Yes | | 18,120 † | 7,340 | | 604 | | | | |
| Yes | Yes | Yes | Yes | Yes | 16,162 † | 6,640 | | 608 | Yes | 77 | $2,928 | None |
| | | | No | | | | 12 | | | | | |
| Yes | | | Yes | | 7,890 † | 4,600 | 19 | 234 | | | | |
| Yes | | | Yes | | 20,830 | 7,210 | 15 | 848 | Yes | | | None |
| Yes | Yes | Yes | Yes | Yes | 21,744 † | 12,475 | 19 | 681 | | | | |

† Actual for 2016-17.  ‡ Estimated for 2017-18.  * Includes room and board

| Institution | Control/degrees | Undergraduates Total | Undergraduates Internat'l | Tests required (Fall 2017) | TOEFL minimum | TOEFL average | Application Deadline | Application Fee |
|---|---|---|---|---|---|---|---|---|
| University of Alaska Fairbanks............... | Pu/AB | 5,164 | 58 | TOEFL | 79 | 89 | 1/15 | 50 |
| University of Alaska Southeast............... | Pu/AB | 2,695 | | TOEFL | 80 | | | 50 |
| **Arizona** | | | | | | | | |
| Argosy University: Online............... | Pr/AB | 10,703 | | | | | | 50 |
| Argosy University: Phoenix............... | Pr/AB | 219 | | | | | | 50 |
| Arizona Christian University............... | Pr/AB | 684 | 18 | TOEFL | 61 | 80 | | 30 |
| Arizona State University............... | Pu/B | 42,224 | 5,339 | TOEFL | 61 | 79 | 5/1 | 85 |
| Arizona Western College............... | Pu/A | 5,996 | 140 | | | | 10/1 | 25 |
| Art Institute of Phoenix............... | Pr/AB | 1,009 | | TOEFL | 61 | | | 50 |
| Art Institute of Tucson............... | Pr/AB | 348 | | | | | | 35 |
| Brookline College: Phoenix............... | Pr/AB | 1,429 | | | | | | |
| Brookline College: Tempe............... | Pr/A | 418 | | | | | | |
| Brown Mackie College: Phoenix............... | Pr/AB | | | | | | | |
| Bryan University............... | Pr/AB | 928 | | TOEFL | 61 | | | 25 |
| Carrington College: Mesa............... | Pr/A | 718 | | | | | | |
| Carrington College: Phoenix............... | Pr/AB | 617 | | | | | | |
| Carrington College: Phoenix Westside........... | Pr/A | 503 | | | | | | |
| Carrington College: Tucson............... | Pr/A | 424 | | | | | | |
| Central Arizona College............... | Pu/A | 5,585 | | TOEFL | | | | |
| Chamberlain College of Nursing: Phoenix........ | Pr/AB | 674 | | | | | | 95 |
| Chandler-Gilbert Community College........... | Pu/A | 14,630 | | | | | None | |
| Cochise College............... | Pu/A | 3,719 | 41 | | | | None | 75 |
| DeVry University: Phoenix............... | Pr/AB | 730 | | TOEFL | | | | 50 |
| Dine College............... | Pu/AB | 1,490 | | TOEFL | | | | 20 |
| Dunlap-Stone University............... | Pr/AB | 42 | | TOEFL | 85 | 105 | | 50 |
| Eastern Arizona College............... | Pu/A | 5,082 | 67 | TOEFL | | | 8/1 | 25 |
| Embry-Riddle Aeronautical University: Prescott Campus............... | Pr/B | 2,363 | 178 | TOEFL | 79 | | None | 50 |
| Estrella Mountain Community College........... | Pu/A | 9,344 | | TOEFL | | | | |
| GateWay Community College............... | Pu/A | 5,058 | | TOEFL | | | 7/1 | |
| Glendale Community College............... | Pu/A | | | TOEFL | 61 | | | 50 |
| Golf Academy of America: Phoenix............. | Pr/A | 154 | | | | | | |
| Grand Canyon University............... | Pr/B | 39,400 | | TOEFL | 61 | | | |
| International Baptist College............... | Pr/AB | 57 | | TOEFL | | | | |
| Le Cordon Bleu College of Culinary Arts: Scottsdale............... | Pr/AB | 1,567 | | TOEFL | | | | 125 |
| Mesa Community College............... | Pu/A | 16,672 | 553 | TOEFL | 61 | | | |
| Mohave Community College............... | Pu/A | 2,770 | | TOEFL | 70 | | None | |
| National Paralegal College............... | Pr/AB | 938 | | | | | | |
| Northern Arizona University............... | Pu/B | 26,400 | 1,152 | TOEFL | 70 | | | 50 |
| Paradise Valley Community College........... | Pu/A | 9,555 | | TOEFL | | | | |
| Paralegal Institute............... | Pr/A | | | | | | | |
| Penn Foster College............... | Pr/AB | 31,991 | | TOEFL | | | | |
| Phoenix College............... | Pu/A | 11,508 | | TOEFL | | | | |
| Prescott College............... | Pr/B | 350 | 3 | TOEFL | 61 | | None | |
| Refrigeration School............... | Pr/A | 1,185 | | | | | None | |
| Rio Salado College............... | Pu/A | 18,724 | | TOEFL | | | None | |
| Scottsdale Community College............... | Pu/A | 9,410 | | TOEFL | | | None | |
| Sessions College for Professional Design........ | Pr/A | 124 | | TOEFL | 61 | | | 50 |
| South Mountain Community College........... | Pu/A | 4,083 | | | | | | 15 |
| Southwest University of Visual Arts........... | Pr/B | 119 | | TOEFL | 61 | | None | 25 |
| Tohono O'odham Community College........... | Pu/A | 299 | | | | | | |
| Universal Technical Institute............... | Pr/A | 2,000 | | | | | | 50 |
| University of Advancing Technology........... | Pr/AB | 784 | | TOEFL | 79 | | | |
| University of Arizona............... | Pu/B | 33,780 | 2,276 | TOEFL | | 70 | | 75 |
| University of Phoenix: Phoenix-Hohokam......... | Pr/AB | 155,872 | | | | | | |
| University of Phoenix: Southern Arizona......... | Pr/B | 1,620 | | | | | | |
| Yavapai College............... | Pu/A | 8,273 | | TOEFL | 70 | | | 50 |

| Student services | | | Housing | | Academic year costs | | Maximum credits/ summer | Credit hour charge | International financial aid | | | |
|---|---|---|---|---|---|---|---|---|---|---|---|---|
| Adviser | Orien- tation | ESL | Academic year | Summer | Tuition/ fees | Living costs | | | Avail- able | Number receiving aid | Average award | Deadline |
| Yes | Yes | Yes | Yes | Yes | 21,854† | 8,380 | 18 | 681 | Yes | 33 | $19,335 | 7/1 |
| Yes | Yes | | Yes | Yes | 22,080† | 9,200 | 12 | 681 | Yes | | | None |
| Yes | | | Yes | | 24,958 | 10,334 | 6 | | Yes | 17 | $13,554 | None |
| Yes | Yes | Yes | Yes | Yes | 28,270† | 11,386 | 14 | 1074 | Yes | 1022 | $6,358 | None |
| Yes | Yes | Yes | Yes | Yes | 9,450 | 6,595 | 8 | 315 | | | | |
| Yes | Yes | | Yes | | | | 15 | | | | | |
| | | | Yes | | | | 16 | | | | | |
| | | | No | | | 9,000 | | | | | | |
| | | | No | | | 9,000 | | | | | | |
| | | | No | | | | | | | | | |
| Yes | | Yes | Yes | | 10,980† | 6,900 | 6 | 168 | Yes | | | 7/15 |
| | | | | | 19,500† | | | 675 | | | | |
| | | | | | 9,840 | 5,652 | | 327 | | | | |
| Yes | Yes | Yes | Yes | Yes | 7,500† | 10,280 | 8 | 250 | Yes | 12 | $9,479 | 6/15 |
| | | | | | 17,512† | | | 609 | | | | |
| | | | Yes | Yes | 1,410‡ | 4,610 | 12 | | Yes | 2 | $3,462 | None |
| | | | No | | | | | | | | | |
| Yes | | | Yes | | 10,800† | 6,280 | 18 | 360 | Yes | | | None |
| Yes | Yes | Yes | Yes | Yes | 34,662‡ | 10,468 | | 1392 | Yes | 58 | $10,639 | None |
| Yes | | | No | | 9,840† | | 12 | | Yes | | | None |
| Yes | Yes | Yes | No | | 9,840† | 7,272 | | 327 | Yes | | | 4/15 |
| Yes | Yes | Yes | No | | 9,840† | 5,832 | 12 | 327 | Yes | | | None |
| | | | | | 17,250† | | | | | | | |
| Yes | Yes | | Yes | Yes | 17,170† | 15,100 | 15 | 688 | Yes | | | None |
| | | | Yes | | 10,500† | 5,900 | | 350 | | | | |
| Yes | | | | | | 7,876 | | | | | | |
| Yes | Yes | Yes | No | | 9,825† | 5,724 | 9 | 327 | Yes | | | None |
| | | Yes | No | | 8,715† | | 7 | 283.5 | | | | |
| | | | | | 7,995 | 8,072 | | 325 | | | | |
| Yes | Yes | Yes | Yes | Yes | 24,144† | 12,482 | 18 | 964 | Yes | | | None |
| | | | No | | 9,840† | 7,902 | 6 | 327 | | | | |
| | | | No | | | | | 79 | | | | |
| Yes | Yes | Yes | No | | 9,840† | 9,216 | 12 | | | | | |
| | | | Yes | | 28,693† | 7,300 | 16 | | Yes | | | None |
| Yes | | | No | | 9,850† | 3,996 | 18 | 325 | Yes | | | None |
| Yes | Yes | Yes | No | | 9,840† | 5,724 | | 327 | | | | |
| | | | | | 10,000† | | | | | | | |
| | | Yes | No | | 9,840† | | | 325 | | | | |
| Yes | | | No | | 22,944† | | | | Yes | | | None |
| | | | Yes | | 2,075† | 2,400 | | | Yes | | | None |
| Yes | | | No | | | | | | | | | |
| | | | Yes | | 23,150† | 9,700 | 21 | | | | | |
| Yes | Yes | Yes | Yes | Yes | 36,017† | 12,300 | 12 | 1415 | Yes | 209 | $11,610 | None |
| Yes | Yes | | Yes | Yes | 10,980† | 9,212 | 12 | 366 | Yes | | | None |

† Actual for 2016-17.   ‡ Estimated for 2017-18.   * Includes room and board

| Institution | Control/degrees | Undergraduates Total | Internat'l | Tests required (Fall 2017) | TOEFL minimum | average | Application Deadline | Fee |
|---|---|---|---|---|---|---|---|---|
| **Arkansas** | | | | | | | | |
| Arkansas Baptist College | Pr/AB | 990 | | | | | | 75 |
| Arkansas State University | Pu/AB | 9,592 | | TOEFL | 61 | 76 | | 40 |
| | | | | | | | | |
| Arkansas State University Mid-South | Pu/A | 1,836 | | TOEFL | 61 | | 7/1 | 25 |
| Arkansas State University: Beebe | Pu/A | 2,826 | 10 | TOEFL | 63 | | None | |
| Arkansas State University: Mountain Home | Pu/A | 1,384 | | TOEFL | | | | |
| Arkansas Tech University | Pu/AB | 8,463 | 331 | TOEFL, SAT/ACT | 61 | | 6/18 | 50 |
| Bryan University: Rogers | Pr/A | 61 | | | | | | 50 |
| | | | | | | | | |
| College of the Ouachitas | Pu/A | 707 | 1 | TOEFL | | | | 100 |
| Cossatot Community College of the University of Arkansas | Pu/A | 1,519 | | TOEFL, SAT/ACT | | | | 150 |
| East Arkansas Community College | Pu/A | 1,268 | | TOEFL, ACT | | | | 25 |
| Ecclesia College | Pr/AB | 246 | | TOEFL | 80 | | 6/1 | 75 |
| Harding University | Pr/B | 4,411 | | TOEFL, SAT/ACT | 79 | | 6/1 | 100 |
| | | | | | | | | |
| Henderson State University | Pu/AB | 3,048 | 43 | TOEFL, SAT/ACT | 61 | | | 30 |
| Hendrix College | Pr/B | 1,316 | 52 | TOEFL | 79 | 94 | 5/1 | 40 |
| John Brown University | Pr/AB | 1,662 | 94 | TOEFL | 80 | | None | 100 |
| Lyon College | Pr/B | 678 | 19 | TOEFL, SAT/ACT | 79 | | | 50 |
| National Park College | Pu/A | 3,244 | | TOEFL | | | | |
| | | | | | | | | |
| Ouachita Baptist University | Pr/AB | 1,474 | 33 | TOEFL | 80 | | | |
| Philander Smith College | Pr/B | 765 | | TOEFL, SAT/ACT | | | | 75 |
| Pulaski Technical College | Pu/A | 5,776 | 27 | TOEFL, ACT | | | 5/15 | 50 |
| Remington College: Little Rock | Pr/A | 383 | | | | | | 50 |
| South Arkansas Community College | Pu/A | 1,112 | | TOEFL | | | None | |
| | | | | | | | | |
| Southeast Arkansas College | Pu/A | 1,493 | | TOEFL, ACT | 89 | | | 100 |
| Southern Arkansas University | Pu/AB | 3,013 | 95 | TOEFL | 61 | 74 | | 50 |
| Southern Arkansas University Tech | Pu/A | 779 | | TOEFL | | | 5/15 | 50 |
| University of Arkansas | Pu/B | 22,243 | 678 | TOEFL, SAT/ACT | 79 | 83 | 5/31 | 50 |
| University of Arkansas at Fort Smith | Pu/AB | 6,823 | | TOEFL, SAT/ACT | 61 | | | 50 |
| | | | | | | | | |
| University of Arkansas at Little Rock | Pu/AB | 9,374 | | TOEFL, SAT/ACT | 71 | | | 40 |
| University of Arkansas at Monticello | Pu/AB | 3,733 | | TOEFL, SAT/ACT | | | | 30 |
| University of Arkansas at Pine Bluff | Pu/AB | 2,721 | | TOEFL, SAT/ACT | 70 | 71 | | |
| University of Arkansas for Medical Sciences | Pu/AB | 656 | 4 | TOEFL | | | | 50 |
| University of Central Arkansas | Pu/AB | 9,081 | 469 | TOEFL | 61 | | | 50 |
| | | | | | | | | |
| University of the Ozarks | Pr/B | 651 | | TOEFL | | | | |
| University of Phoenix: Little Rock | Pr/B | 551 | | | | | | |
| University of Phoenix: Northwest Arkansas | Pr/B | 530 | | | | | | |
| Williams Baptist College | Pr/AB | 434 | | TOEFL | 61 | | | |
| | | | | | | | | |
| **California** | | | | | | | | |
| Academy of Art University | Pr/AB | 8,182 | 2,340 | | | | None | 50 |
| | | | | | | | | |
| Allan Hancock College | Pu/A | 15,687 | | TOEFL | | | | |
| Alliant International University | Pr/B | 1,424 | | TOEFL | 75 | | | 65 |
| American Academy of Dramatic Arts: West | Pr/A | 303 | | | | | | 50 |
| American Jewish University | Pr/B | 150 | | TOEFL | 75 | | | 35 |
| American River College | Pu/A | 31,280 | | TOEFL | | | 7/1 | 50 |
| | | | | | | | | |
| Antelope Valley College | Pu/A | 14,552 | | TOEFL | 45 | | | |
| Antioch University Los Angeles | Pr/B | 1,437 | | | 79 | | | 60 |
| Antioch University Santa Barbara | Pr/B | 118 | | TOEFL | | | | 60 |
| Argosy University: Inland Empire | Pr/AB | 367 | | | | | | 50 |
| Argosy University: Los Angeles | Pr/B | 298 | | | | | | 50 |
| | | | | | | | | |
| Argosy University: Orange County | Pr/B | 222 | | | | | | 50 |
| Argosy University: San Diego | Pr/B | 234 | | | | | | 50 |
| Argosy University: San Francisco Bay Area | Pr/B | 139 | | | | | | 50 |
| Art Institute of California: Hollywood | Pr/AB | 1,602 | | TOEFL | 61 | | | 50 |
| Art Institute of California: Inland Empire | Pr/AB | 1,092 | | | | | | 50 |
| | | | | | | | | |
| Art Institute of California: Los Angeles | Pr/AB | 1,436 | | TOEFL | | | | 50 |

| Student services | | | Housing | | Academic year costs | | Maximum credits/ summer | Credit hour charge | International financial aid | | | |
|---|---|---|---|---|---|---|---|---|---|---|---|---|
| Adviser | Orien- tation | ESL | Academic year | Summer | Tuition/ fees | Living costs | | | Avail- able | Number receiving aid | Average award | Deadline |
| Yes | Yes | Yes | Yes | Yes | 8,760 † | 8,190 | 6 | | Yes | | | 4/1 |
| | | | Yes | Yes | 15,080 † | 9,630 | 12 | 404 | Yes | | | 7/1 |
| Yes | | | No | | 9,490 † | 9,354 | 6 | 300 | | | | |
| | | | Yes | | 5,520 † | 5,180 | 12 | 169 | Yes | | | None |
| Yes | | | No | | 5,460 † | | 6 | 160 | | | | |
| Yes | Yes | Yes | Yes | Yes | 14,850 † | 7,036 | 12 | 438 | Yes | 44 | $9,625 | None |
| | | | No | | 9,380 | | ·12 | 380 | Yes | | | None |
| Yes | | | No | | 6,345 † | 3,624 | | 180 | Yes | | | None |
| | | | No | | 3,660 † | 4,800 | | 111 | Yes | | | 7/1 |
| Yes | | | Yes | Yes | 15,140 † | 7,510 | 11 | 475 | Yes | | | None |
| Yes | | Yes | Yes | Yes | 19,190 ‡ | 6,894 | 16 | 598 | Yes | 82 | $9,806 | None |
| Yes | Yes | Yes | Yes | Yes | 14,956 † | 6,870 | 14 | 443 | Yes | | | None |
| Yes | Yes | Yes | Yes | | 42,440 † | 11,580 | | 1315 | Yes | | | None |
| Yes | Yes | Yes | Yes | | 25,324 † | 10,340 | | 807 | Yes | 86 | $29,142 | None |
| Yes | Yes | | Yes | | 26,290 † | 8,440 | 10 | 860 | Yes | 9 | $20,881 | None |
| Yes | | | No | | | 6,976 | 12 | | Yes | | | None |
| Yes | Yes | Yes | Yes | Yes | 25,870 | 11,030 | 15 | 700 | Yes | | | 6/1 |
| Yes | Yes | | Yes | Yes | 12,414 † | 8,250 | 12 | 495 | Yes | | | None |
| Yes | | | No | | 6,360 † | 8,967 | 6 | 168 | Yes | | | 5/15 |
| | | | No | | 5,418 ‡ | | 14 | 172 | Yes | | | 7/1 |
| | | | No | | 5,830 † | 2,900 | 12 | 176 | Yes | | | None |
| Yes | Yes | Yes | Yes | Yes | 11,856 † | 5,832 | 12 | 345 | Yes | | | None |
| Yes | Yes | | Yes | Yes | 4,680 † | 2,600 | 18 | | | | | |
| Yes | Yes | Yes | Yes | Yes | 23,168 † | 10,332 | 18 | 718.39 | Yes | | | None |
| Yes | Yes | Yes | Yes | Yes | 15,701 † | 8,242 | 12 | 460 | | | | |
| Yes | Yes | Yes | Yes | | 20,888 † | 8,170 | 12 | 625 | | | | |
| | | | Yes | Yes | 13,060 † | 6,389 | 12 | 350 | Yes | | | None |
| Yes | | | Yes | Yes | 12,706 † | 7,418 | 12 | 358 | | | | |
| Yes | | | Yes | | 19,472 † | | | 597 | | | | |
| Yes | Yes | Yes | Yes | Yes | 14,447 † | 6,248 | 12 | 415 | Yes | | | 7/1 |
| Yes. | Yes | | Yes | | 23,750 † | 7,100 | | | Yes | | | None |
| Yes | | | Yes | Yes | 17,320 ‡ | 8,550 | | 675 | Yes | 22 | $11,281 | None |
| Yes | Yes | Yes | Yes | Yes | 26,490 ‡ | 15,792 | 6 | 873 | Yes | 70 | $15,592 | None |
| | | Yes | No | | 7,358 † | | 8 | 244 | | | | |
| Yes | Yes | Yes | | Yes | 21,340 † | 8,090 | 18 | 700 | Yes | | | |
| Yes | | | No | | 33,190 † | 12,850 | | | Yes | | | None |
| | | | Yes | | 30,184 † | 15,550 | | 1208 | Yes | | | None |
| Yes | Yes | | No | | 8,846 ‡ | 11,494 | 8 | 275 | | | | |
| | | | No | | 7,750 † | 12,492 | 9 | 257 | | | | |
| Yes | | | No | | 20,670 † | | 15 | 679 | | | | |
| Yes | Yes | | No | | 22,575 † | | 15 | 495 | Yes | | | None |
| Yes | Yes | | Yes | Yes | | 11,268 | 15 | | | | | |
| Yes | Yes | | Yes | Yes | | 11,268 | | | Yes | | | None |

† Actual for 2016-17.      ‡ Estimated for 2017-18.      * Includes room and board

| Institution | Control/ degrees | Undergraduates | | Tests required (Fall 2017) | TOEFL | | Application | |
|---|---|---|---|---|---|---|---|---|
| | | Total | Internat'l | | minimum | average | Deadline | Fee |
| Art Institute of California: Orange County . . . . . . . | Pr/AB | 1,417 | | TOEFL | | | | 50 |
| Art Institute of California: Sacramento . . . . . . . . . | Pr/AB | 993 | | | | | | 50 |
| Art Institute of California: San Diego . . . . . . . . . | Pr/AB | 1,634 | | TOEFL | | | | 50 |
| Art Institute of California: San Francisco . . . . . . . | Pr/AB | 1,070 | | TOEFL | | | | 150 |
| Ashford University. . . . . . . . . . . . . . . . . . . | Pr/AB | 35,252 | | TOEFL | 61 | | | |
| Azusa Pacific University. . . . . . . . . . . . . . . . | Pr/B | 5,762 | 153 | TOEFL | | | | 65 |
| Bakersfield College . . . . . . . . . . . . . . . . . . | Pu/A | 23,187 | | TOEFL | 45 | | | 50 |
| Bergin University of Canine Studies . . . . . . . . . | Pr/AB | 40 | | TOEFL | 61 | | | 50 |
| Berkeley City College. . . . . . . . . . . . . . . . . | Pu/A | 6,974 | | TOEFL | 61 | | | 50 |
| Bethesda University of California . . . . . . . . . . . | Pr/B | 256 | | TOEFL | 61 | | | 280 |
| Beverly Hills Design Institute. . . . . . . . . . . . . | Pr/AB | 25 | | | 61 | | | 160 |
| Biola University . . . . . . . . . . . . . . . . . . . | Pr/B | 4,083 | 126 | TOEFL | 100 | | | 55 |
| Bryan College: Sacramento . . . . . . . . . . . . . | Pr/A | 544 | | | | | | 20 |
| Butte College . . . . . . . . . . . . . . . . . . . . | Pu/A | 12,978 | | TOEFL | 45 | | | |
| Cabrillo College . . . . . . . . . . . . . . . . . . . | Pu/A | 12,318 | | TOEFL | | | | |
| California Baptist University . . . . . . . . . . . . . | Pr/AB | 6,904 | 130 | TOEFL | 71 | 84 | 7/1 | 45 |
| California Christian College. . . . . . . . . . . . . . | Pr/AB | 18 | | | | | | 50 |
| California Coast University . . . . . . . . . . . . . . | Pr/AB | 5,447 | | | | | | 75 |
| California College of the Arts . . . . . . . . . . . . | Pr/B | 1,515 | 524 | TOEFL | 80 | 94 | | 70 |
| California College San Diego. . . . . . . . . . . . . | Pr/AB | 768 | | | | | None | |
| California Institute of the Arts . . . . . . . . . . . . | Pr/B | 951 | 143 | TOEFL | 80 | 93 | None | 85 |
| California Institute of Integral Studies . . . . . . . . | Pr/B | 70 | 1 | TOEFL | 80 | 103 | 6/1 | 65 |
| California Institute of Technology. . . . . . . . . . . | Pr/B | 979 | 89 | | | | | 75 |
| California Lutheran University . . . . . . . . . . . . | Pr/B | 2,887 | 97 | TOEFL | 79 | 82 | 1/1 | 25 |
| California Maritime Academy . . . . . . . . . . . . . | Pu/B | 1,107 | 9 | TOEFL, SAT/ACT | | | | 55 |
| California Miramar University . . . . . . . . . . . . . | Pr/AB | 361 | | | | | | 25 |
| California National University for Advanced Studies. . . . . . . . . . . . . . . . . . . . . . . . | Pr/B | 59 | | | | | | 100 |
| California Polytechnic State University: San Luis Obispo . . . . . . . . . . . . . . . . . . . . . | Pu/B | 20,367 | 403 | TOEFL, SAT/ACT | 80 | | | 55 |
| California State Polytechnic University: Pomona. . . . . . . . . . . . . . . . . . . . . . . . . | Pu/B | 23,611 | 1,442 | TOEFL, SAT, SAT Subject Test(s), or ACT | 70 | 88 | 4/1 | 55 |
| California State University: Bakersfield . . . . . . . . | Pu/B | 8,058 | 451 | TOEFL | | | | 55 |
| California State University: Channel Islands . . . . . | Pu/B | 5,653 | | TOEFL | 61 | | | 55 |
| California State University: Chico. . . . . . . . . . . | Pu/B | 16,471 | 591 | TOEFL | 61 | 70 | | 55 |
| California State University: Dominguez Hills . . . . . | Pu/B | 12,613 | 495 | TOEFL | 61 | | 11/30 | 55 |
| California State University: East Bay. . . . . . . . . | Pu/B | 13,289 | 837 | TOEFL | | | 3/30 | 55 |
| California State University: Fresno . . . . . . . . . . | Pu/B | 21,148 | 1,196 | TOEFL | 61 | 70 | 4/1 | 55 |
| California State University: Fullerton. . . . . . . . . | Pu/B | 34,416 | 2,052 | TOEFL | 61 | | 11/30 | 55 |
| California State University: Long Beach. . . . . . . . | Pu/B | 32,246 | 2,139 | TOEFL, SAT/ACT | | | | 55 |
| California State University: Los Angeles . . . . . . . | Pu/B | 24,031 | 1,362 | TOEFL | | | | 55 |
| California State University: Monterey Bay . . . . . . | Pu/B | 6,923 | 348 | TOEFL | 61 | 76 | | 55 |
| California State University: Sacramento . . . . . . . . | Pu/B | 27,810 | 777 | TOEFL | | | | 55 |
| California State University: San Bernardino . . . . . | Pu/B | 18,453 | 1,237 | TOEFL | | | | 55 |
| California State University: San Marcos . . . . . . . . | Pu/B | 12,470 | 593 | TOEFL | | | | 55 |
| California State University: Stanislaus . . . . . . . . | Pu/B | 8,610 | 309 | TOEFL | 61 | | 5/31 | 55 |
| California University of Management and Sciences. . . . . . . . . . . . . . . . . . . . . . . . | Pr/AB | 19 | 14 | TOEFL | 51 | 70 | | 100 |
| Canada College. . . . . . . . . . . . . . . . . . . . | Pu/A | 6,944 | | TOEFL | 56 | | | 50 |
| Carrington College: Citrus Heights . . . . . . . . . . | Pr/A | 517 | | | | | | |
| Carrington College: Pleasant Hill . . . . . . . . . . | Pr/A | 599 | | | | | | |
| Carrington College: Sacramento . . . . . . . . . . . | Pr/A | 1,385 | | | | | | |
| Carrington College: San Jose . . . . . . . . . . . . | Pr/A | 805 | | | | | | |
| Carrington College: Stockton . . . . . . . . . . . . | Pr/A | 549 | | | | | | |
| Cerritos College . . . . . . . . . . . . . . . . . . . | Pu/A | 24,678 | | TOEFL | | | | 40 |
| Cerro Coso Community College . . . . . . . . . . . | Pu/A | 5,233 | | TOEFL | | | | |
| Chabot College. . . . . . . . . . . . . . . . . . . . | Pu/A | 14,076 | | TOEFL | | | | 100 |
| Chaffey College . . . . . . . . . . . . . . . . . . . | Pu/A | 22,962 | | TOEFL | | | | 35 |
| Chapman University. . . . . . . . . . . . . . . . . . | Pr/B | 6,338 | 251 | TOEFL, SAT/ACT | 80 | 99 | 1/15 | 70 |

| Student services | | | Housing | | Academic year costs | | Maximum credits/ summer | Credit hour charge | International financial aid | | | |
|---|---|---|---|---|---|---|---|---|---|---|---|---|
| Adviser | Orien- tation | ESL | Academic year | Summer | Tuition/ fees | Living costs | | | Avail- able | Number receiving aid | Average award | Deadline |
| Yes | | | Yes | Yes | | 11,268 | 18 | | Yes | | | None |
| | | | | | | 11,268 | | | | | | |
| Yes | Yes | | Yes | | | 11,268 | | | | | | |
| Yes | Yes | | Yes | | | 11,268 | 15 | | | | | |
| | | | No | | 11,032† | 7,162 | | 443 | Yes | | | None |
| Yes | Yes | Yes | Yes | Yes | 36,120† | 9,492 | 16 | 1481 | Yes | | | 7/1 |
| Yes | Yes | Yes | No | | 8,378† | 12,492 | | 278 | | | | |
| | | | No | | 10,650† | | | | | | | |
| Yes | Yes | Yes | No | | 8,332† | 12,636 | 6 | 276 | | | | |
| Yes | | Yes | | | 7,930† | 5,800 | 18 | 251 | Yes | | | None |
| Yes | Yes | Yes | | Yes | 35,092‡ | | | 729 | Yes | | | None |
| Yes | Yes | Yes | Yes | Yes | 38,448 | 10,238 | 6 | 1602 | Yes | 144 | $10,499 | None |
| Yes | Yes | | No | | 7,948† | 10,962 | 9 | 261 | Yes | | | None |
| Yes | Yes | Yes | No | | 7,609† | 12,492 | 8 | 250 | | | | |
| Yes | Yes | Yes | Yes | Yes | 32,566 | 11,540 | 6 | 1171 | Yes | 15 | $4,000 | None |
| | | | Yes | | 8,990† | 4,750 | | 350 | | | | |
| Yes | Yes | Yes | Yes | Yes | 47,266 | 9,840 | | | Yes | 234 | $8,490 | None |
| | | | No | | | | | | | | | |
| Yes | Yes | Yes | Yes | | 45,646† | 11,715 | 6 | | Yes | 143 | $6,334 | None |
| Yes | Yes | | No | | 18,978† | 19,236 | | 778 | Yes | | | 4/15 |
| Yes | Yes | | Yes | Yes | 47,577† | 14,100 | | | Yes | 31 | $47,612 | None |
| Yes | Yes | | Yes | | 39,760† | 15,560 | 12 | 1265 | Yes | | | 7/1 |
| Yes | | | Yes | Yes | 17,976† | 11,756 | | 372 | Yes | | | None |
| | | | | | 9,750† | | | 325 | | | | |
| | | | | | | | | 330 | | | | |
| Yes | Yes | | Yes | | 20,235† | 12,507 | | 248 | Yes | 26 | $12,446 | None |
| Yes | Yes | Yes | Yes | Yes | 18,187† | 14,514 | | 248 | | | | |
| Yes | | Yes | Yes | | 18,001† | 13,968 | | 372 | Yes | | | None |
| Yes | | | Yes | | 17,692† | 16,146 | | 372 | | | | |
| Yes | Yes | Yes | Yes | Yes | 19,776† | 12,824 | 12 | 372 | | | | |
| Yes | Yes | Yes | Yes | Yes | 17,578† | 12,790 | 12 | 372 | | | | |
| Yes | Yes | Yes | Yes | Yes | 17,724† | 14,184 | 22 | 248 | | | | |
| Yes | Yes | Yes | Yes | | 17,471† | 9,386 | | 372 | Yes | 63 | $21,304 | |
| Yes | Yes | Yes | Yes | | 17,596† | 15,642 | | 372 | Yes | | | 6/6 |
| Yes | Yes | Yes | Yes | Yes | 17,620† | 12,398 | 12 | 372 | Yes | | | None |
| Yes | Yes | Yes | Yes | Yes | 17,191† | 12,860 | 12 | 372 | Yes | 26 | $13,132 | None |
| Yes | Yes | | Yes | Yes | 17,387† | 11,930 | | 372 | | | | |
| Yes | Yes | Yes | Yes | | 18,060† | 13,916 | 12 | 372 | | | | |
| Yes | Yes | Yes | Yes | Yes | 16,632† | 12,966 | | 248 | | | | |
| Yes | Yes | Yes | Yes | | 18,524† | 13,240 | 12 | 372 | Yes | 206 | $6,439 | None |
| Yes | Yes | Yes | Yes | Yes | 17,888† | 10,074 | | 372 | | | | |
| Yes | Yes | Yes | No | | 9,570† | 12,300 | 24 | | Yes | | | 5/30 |
| Yes | Yes | | No | | 8,130† | 13,293 | 19 | 265 | | | | |
| Yes | | Yes | No | | 9,208† | 11,268 | | 305 | | | | |
| Yes | | Yes | | | 8,342† | 11,268 | 7 | 278 | | | | |
| Yes | Yes | | No | | 8,704† | 11,268 | 18 | 289 | | | | |
| Yes | Yes | Yes | No | | 8,104† | 11,268 | 14 | 269 | | | | |
| Yes | Yes | | Yes | Yes | 50,594 | 14,910 | | 1560 | Yes | 104 | $17,011 | None |

† Actual for 2016-17.          ‡ Estimated for 2017-18.          * Includes room and board

| Institution | Control/ degrees | Undergraduates | | Tests required (Fall 2017) | TOEFL | | Application | |
|---|---|---|---|---|---|---|---|---|
| | | Total | Internat'l | | minimum | average | Deadline | Fee |
| Charles Drew University of Medicine and Science | Pr/AB | 88 | 2 | TOEFL | | | | 35 |
| Citrus College | Pu/A | 13,498 | | | 45 | | | 40 |
| City College of San Francisco | Pu/A | 21,786 | | TOEFL | | | | 50 |
| Claremont McKenna College | Pr/B | 1,344 | 229 | TOEFL, SAT/ACT | 100 | | | 70 |
| Coastline Community College | Pu/A | 14,284 | | TOEFL | | | | 30 |
| Cogswell Polytechnical College | Pr/B | 653 | 3 | TOEFL | 69 | | | |
| Coleman University | Pr/AB | 342 | | TOEFL | | | | 25 |
| College of Alameda | Pu/A | 6,560 | | TOEFL | 61 | | | |
| College of the Canyons | Pu/A | 20,917 | 134 | TOEFL | 45 | | 6/15 | |
| College of the Desert | Pu/A | 12,762 | | TOEFL | 32 | 45 | | 30 |
| College of Marin | Pu/A | 6,830 | | TOEFL | | | | 50 |
| College of the Redwoods | Pu/A | 5,631 | | TOEFL | | | | 100 |
| College of San Mateo | Pu/A | 9,633 | | TOEFL | 56 | | | 50 |
| College of the Sequoias | Pu/A | 12,677 | | TOEFL | | | | 100 |
| College of the Siskiyous | Pu/A | 3,341 | | TOEFL | 55 | | | 35 |
| Columbia College | Pu/A | 2,901 | | | | | | |
| Columbia College Hollywood | Pr/AB | 367 | | TOEFL | 80 | | | 25 |
| Concorde Career College: Garden Grove | Pr/A | 974 | | | | | | 100 |
| Concorde Career College: North Hollywood | Pr/A | 620 | | | | | | |
| Concorde Career College: San Bernardino | Pr/A | 668 | | | | | | |
| Concordia University Irvine | Pr/AB | 1,895 | 85 | TOEFL | 79 | 80 | 6/1 | 125 |
| Contra Costa College | Pu/A | 6,795 | | TOEFL | 54 | | | 50 |
| Copper Mountain College | Pu/A | 1,951 | | | | | | |
| Cosumnes River College | Pu/A | 14,330 | | TOEFL | | | | 50 |
| Crafton Hills College | Pu/A | 6,021 | | TOEFL | | | | 100 |
| Cuesta College | Pu/A | 11,238 | | TOEFL | | | | |
| Cuyamaca College | Pu/A | 9,884 | | TOEFL | | 60 | | |
| Cypress College | Pu/A | 16,242 | | TOEFL | 61 | | | 40 |
| De Anza College | Pu/A | 21,891 | | TOEFL | | | 6/30 | |
| Deep Springs College | Pr/A | 26 | 6 | TOEFL | | | | |
| Design Institute of San Diego | Pr/B | 143 | 12 | TOEFL | 61 | | | 25 |
| DeVry University: Pomona | Pr/AB | 781 | 18 | TOEFL | | | | 50 |
| Diablo Valley College | Pu/A | 19,739 | | TOEFL | 54 | | | 50 |
| Dominican University of California | Pr/B | 1,374 | 20 | TOEFL | 80 | | | 40 |
| East Los Angeles College | Pu/A | 40,121 | | TOEFL | 45 | | | 35 |
| El Camino College | Pu/A | 24,113 | | TOEFL | 45 | 48 | | 50 |
| Epic Bible College | Pr/AB | 170 | | | | | | |
| Evergreen Valley College | Pu/A | 9,150 | | TOEFL | | | | 100 |
| Ex'pression College | Pr/B | 445 | | | | | | 60 |
| Fashion Institute of Design and Merchandising: Los Angeles | Pr/AB | 2,624 | 373 | TOEFL | 65 | 76 | | 525 |
| Fashion Institute of Design and Merchandising: San Diego | Pr/A | 75 | | TOEFL | 65 | 76 | None | 525 |
| Fashion Institute of Design and Merchandising: San Francisco | Pr/AB | 332 | | TOEFL | 65 | 76 | None | 525 |
| Feather River College | Pu/AB | 1,674 | | TOEFL | 65 | | 6/15 | |
| Folsom Lake College | Pu/A | 8,769 | | TOEFL | 45 | | | 50 |
| Foothill College | Pu/AB | 16,671 | | TOEFL | | | | 75 |
| Fremont College | Pr/AB | 387 | | TOEFL | 61 | | | 85 |
| Fresno City College | Pu/A | 24,100 | | TOEFL | | | | |
| Fresno Pacific University | Pr/AB | 2,429 | 20 | TOEFL | 61 | | | 40 |
| Fullerton College | Pu/A | 24,661 | | TOEFL | | | 4/15 | 40 |
| Glendale Community College | Pu/A | 20,061 | | TOEFL | | | | 50 |
| Golden Gate University | Pr/AB | 444 | 17 | | | | | |
| Golden West College | Pu/A | 12,032 | | TOEFL | | | | 30 |
| Golf Academy of America: San Diego | Pr/A | 168 | | | | | | 100 |
| Grossmont College | Pu/A | 18,789 | | TOEFL | 45 | | | |
| Hartnell College | Pu/A | 12,385 | | TOEFL | 48 | | | |

| Student services | | | Housing | | Academic year costs | | Maximum credits/ summer | Credit hour charge | International financial aid | | | |
|---|---|---|---|---|---|---|---|---|---|---|---|---|
| Adviser | Orientation | ESL | Academic year | Summer | Tuition/ fees | Living costs | | | Available | Number receiving aid | Average award | Deadline |
| | | | No | | 16,780† | | | 556 | | | | |
| Yes | Yes | Yes | No | | 8,680† | 12,400 | 6 | 287 | Yes | | | 3/1 |
| Yes | Yes | Yes | No | | 8,074† | 11,268 | 7 | 268 | | | | |
| Yes | Yes | | Yes | | 50,945† | 15,740 | | | Yes | 25 | $39,044 | 1/1 |
| Yes | | Yes | No | | 9,080† | 12,762 | 9 | 302 | Yes | | | None |
| Yes | Yes | | Yes | Yes | 19,096† | 12,415 | 16 | | Yes | | | None |
| Yes | Yes | | No | | 20,725† | 8,190 | 12 | 345 | | | | |
| Yes | | | No | | 8,496† | 11,160 | 10 | 282 | | | | |
| Yes | Yes | Yes | No | | 6,194† | 3,006 | | 267 | Yes | | | 3/2 |
| Yes | Yes | Yes | No | | 8,230† | 12,492 | 9 | 273 | Yes | | | None |
| Yes | | Yes | No | | 9,248† | 13,673 | | 307 | | | | |
| Yes | | | Yes | | 7,778† | 7,809 | 12 | 258 | | | | |
| Yes | Yes | Yes | No | | 8,288† | 11,160 | 8 | 275 | Yes | | | None |
| Yes | | Yes | No | | 7,780† | 9,000 | 8 | 257 | | | | |
| Yes | Yes | | Yes | | 7,790† | 8,000 | 9 | 258 | | | | |
| | | | Yes | | 8,288† | 11,970 | | 275 | Yes | | | 6/1 |
| Yes | Yes | | Yes | Yes | 21,789† | 12,492 | 16 | | | | | |
| Yes | Yes | Yes | Yes | Yes | 34,100‡ | 10,760 | 12 | 995 | Yes | 46 | $6,325 | 3/2 |
| Yes | | Yes | No | | 8,502† | | 6 | 283 | | | | |
| | | | No | | 10,830† | 11,268 | | 361 | | | | |
| Yes | | Yes | No | | 8,286† | 10,863 | 9 | 275 | | | | |
| Yes | | Yes | No | | 8,715† | 11,493 | 6 | 289 | | | | |
| Yes | Yes | Yes | No | | 7,748† | 11,268 | 6 | 257 | | | | |
| Yes | Yes | Yes | No | | 7,848† | 11,100 | | 260 | | | | |
| Yes | Yes | Yes | No | | 8,104† | 11,970 | | 269 | | | | |
| Yes | Yes | | No | | 8,400† | 12,594 | 17 | 156 | | | | |
| | | | Yes | Yes | | | | | Yes | | | None |
| | | | No | | 21,460† | 13,293 | | | | | | |
| Yes | | | | | 17,512† | 7,110 | | 609 | | | | |
| Yes | Yes | | No | | 8,500† | 11,268 | 6 | 283 | Yes | | | 5/1 |
| Yes | Yes | Yes | Yes | | 44,690 | 14,650 | 18 | 1850 | Yes | 13 | $20,015 | None |
| Yes | Yes | Yes | No | | 8,064† | 11,268 | 6 | 268 | | | | |
| Yes | Yes | Yes | No | | 8,679† | 14,098 | 10 | 288 | | | | |
| Yes | | | No | | 7,866† | 11,556 | 6 | 261 | | | | |
| | | | Yes | | | 11,088 | | | | | | |
| Yes | Yes | | Yes | Yes | 32,790† | 14,148 | 45 | 355 | | | | |
| Yes | Yes | | | Yes | 32,790† | 14,148 | 45 | 355 | | | | |
| Yes | Yes | | No | Yes | 32,790† | 14,148 | 45 | 355 | | | | |
| | | | Yes | | 7,821† | 10,873 | 19 | 258 | Yes | | | None |
| Yes | | Yes | No | | 8,304† | 13,293 | | 275 | | | | |
| Yes | Yes | | No | | 8,519† | 11,475 | 12 | 187 | | | | |
| | | | No | | | 8,370 | | | | | | |
| Yes | Yes | Yes | No | | 8,470† | 9,820 | 11 | 281 | | | | |
| Yes | Yes | Yes | Yes | Yes | 29,170† | 8,540 | 18 | 1028 | | | | |
| Yes | Yes | Yes | No | | 8,133† | 11,970 | | 269 | | | | |
| Yes | Yes | Yes | No | | 7,901† | 12,492 | 7 | 261 | | | | |
| | | | No | | 15,584 | 13,200 | | 660 | Yes | | | None |
| Yes | Yes | | No | | 7,752† | 12,492 | 9 | 256 | | | | |
| | | | | | 17,250† | | | | | | | |
| Yes | Yes | Yes | No | | 7,838† | 11,100 | 8 | 260 | | | | |
| Yes | Yes | | No | | 7,670† | 11,970 | | 255 | | | | |

† Actual for 2016-17.  ‡ Estimated for 2017-18.  * Includes room and board

| Institution | Control/ degrees | Undergraduates | | Tests required (Fall 2017) | TOEFL | | Application | |
|---|---|---|---|---|---|---|---|---|
| | | Total | Internat'l | | minimum | average | Deadline | Fee |
| Harvey Mudd College | Pr/B | 829 | 92 | TOEFL, SAT/ACT, SAT Subject Test(s) | 100 | | 1/5 | 70 |
| Holy Names University | Pr/B | 515 | 20 | TOEFL | 57 | | 7/1 | 20 |
| Hope International University | Pr/AB | 828 | 9 | TOEFL | 83 | | None | 50 |
| Horizon University | Pr/AB | 73 | | | | | | 100 |
| Hult International Business School | Pr/B | 1,147 | 1,059 | TOEFL | | | None | 75 |
| Humboldt State University | Pu/B | 7,942 | 108 | TOEFL | 71 | 73 | 4/1 | 55 |
| Humphreys College | Pr/AB | 617 | | TOEFL | | | | 200 |
| Institute of Technology: Clovis | Pr/A | 1,509 | | | | | | 75 |
| Irvine Valley College | Pu/A | 16,126 | | | | | | 39 |
| John F. Kennedy University | Pr/B | 251 | | TOEFL | 80 | 90 | | 65 |
| John Paul the Great Catholic University | Pr/B | 227 | | TOEFL | | | None | 50 |
| Kaplan College: Palm Springs | Pr/A | 379 | | | | | | 10 |
| Kaplan College: Riverside | Pr/A | 167 | | TOEFL | | | | 100 |
| Kaplan College: Sacramento | Pr/A | 429 | | | | | | 20 |
| Kaplan College: Salida | Pr/A | 429 | | | | | | 10 |
| Kaplan College: San Diego | Pr/A | 1,297 | | | | | | 10 |
| Kaplan College: Vista | Pr/A | 812 | | | | | | 10 |
| La Sierra University | Pr/B | 2,103 | | TOEFL | 79 | | | 30 |
| Laguna College of Art and Design | Pr/B | 567 | | TOEFL | 79 | 6 | 6/1 | |
| Lake Tahoe Community College | Pu/A | 2,297 | | TOEFL | 61 | | | 100 |
| Laney College | Pu/A | 11,232 | | TOEFL | 61 | | 6/15 | 50 |
| Las Positas College | Pu/A | 9,223 | | TOEFL | | | | 100 |
| Lassen Community College | Pu/A | 2,237 | | TOEFL | 61 | | None | |
| Le Cordon Bleu College of Culinary Arts: Los Angeles | Pr/A | 1,792 | | TOEFL | 61 | | | 50 |
| Le Cordon Bleu College of Culinary Arts: San Francisco | Pr/A | 442 | | TOEFL | | | | 65 |
| Life Pacific College | Pr/AB | 534 | 5 | TOEFL | | | | 35 |
| Lincoln University | Pr/AB | 122 | | TOEFL | 61 | 71 | | 75 |
| Loma Linda University | Pr/AB | 1,157 | | TOEFL | 80 | 88 | | 60 |
| Long Beach City College | Pu/A | 25,746 | | TOEFL | 61 | 69 | | 40 |
| Los Angeles City College | Pu/A | 20,606 | | | 45 | | | |
| Los Angeles Harbor College | Pu/A | 9,971 | | TOEFL | | | | |
| Los Angeles Mission College | Pu/A | 11,632 | | TOEFL | 45 | | | |
| Los Angeles Pierce College | Pu/A | 22,196 | | | | | | 35 |
| Los Angeles Southwest College | Pu/A | 8,780 | | | | | | |
| Los Angeles Trade and Technical College | Pu/A | 16,200 | | TOEFL | | | | |
| Los Angeles Valley College | Pu/A | 16,200 | | TOEFL | | | | 35 |
| Los Medanos College | Pu/A | 8,918 | | TOEFL | 54 | | | 50 |
| Loyola Marymount University | Pr/B | 6,126 | 594 | TOEFL | 80 | 97 | 1/15 | 60 |
| Marymount California University | Pr/AB | 942 | 171 | | | | | 40 |
| The Master's University | Pr/B | 1,154 | 50 | TOEFL | 80 | | None | 40 |
| Menlo College | Pr/B | 774 | 110 | TOEFL | 61 | 70 | 4/1 | 40 |
| Merritt College | Pu/A | 6,977 | | TOEFL | 61 | | | 50 |
| Mills College | Pr/B | 806 | 6 | TOEFL | 80 | 97 | None | 50 |
| MiraCosta College | Pu/A | 18,685 | 632 | | 46 | | | |
| Mission College | Pu/A | 9,289 | | TOEFL | 61 | | | 100 |
| Modesto Junior College | Pu/A | 18,615 | | TOEFL | | | 5/10 | |
| Monterey Peninsula College | Pu/A | 9,007 | | TOEFL | | | | |
| Moorpark College | Pu/A | 14,141 | | TOEFL | | | | 50 |
| Moreno Valley College | Pu/A | 9,300 | | | | | | |
| Mount Saint Mary's University | Pr/AB | 2,789 | 18 | TOEFL, SAT/ACT | 75 | | 6/1 | 50 |
| Mount San Antonio College | Pu/A | 38,297 | | TOEFL | | | | 50 |
| Mount San Jacinto College | Pu/A | 17,200 | | TOEFL | 45 | | | 90 |
| Mt. Sierra College | Pr/B | 530 | | TOEFL | 65 | | | 50 |
| MTI College | Pr/A | 1,020 | | | | | | 50 |
| Napa Valley College | Pu/A | 6,869 | | TOEFL | | | | 25 |
| National University | Pr/AB | 7,979 | 68 | TOEFL | 70 | | None | 65 |

| Student services | | | Housing | | Academic year costs | | Maximum credits/ summer | Credit hour charge | International financial aid | | | |
|---|---|---|---|---|---|---|---|---|---|---|---|---|
| Adviser | Orien-tation | ESL | Academic year | Summer | Tuition/ fees | Living costs | | | Avail-able | Number receiving aid | Average award | Deadline |
| Yes | Yes | | Yes | | 52,916‡ | 17,051 | | 1637 | Yes | 32 | $24,577 | 2/1 |
| Yes | Yes | | Yes | | 37,074† | 12,434 | | 1254 | Yes | | | None |
| Yes | Yes | Yes | Yes | Yes | 31,800 | 9,930 | | 1395 | Yes | 4 | $11,000 | None |
| | | | No | | 7,700† | | | 250 | | | | None |
| | | | Yes | | 41,550‡ | 14,500 | | | Yes | | | None |
| Yes | Yes | Yes | Yes | | 18,372† | 14,638 | | 372 | | | | |
| Yes | | | Yes | Yes | 14,004† | | 16 | 389 | Yes | | | None |
| | | | No | | | 11,493 | | | | | | |
| Yes | Yes | Yes | No | | 9,698† | 10,872 | 16 | 322 | | | | |
| Yes | | | No | | 17,469† | | | 478 | Yes | | | None |
| | | | Yes | Yes | 24,900† | 8,100 | 18 | 667 | Yes | | | 4/15 |
| | | | No | | | | | | | | | |
| | | | No | | | | | | | | | |
| | | | | | | 8,442 | | | | | | |
| Yes | Yes | Yes | Yes | Yes | 31,590† | 10,100 | 105 | 850 | Yes | | | 8/15 |
| Yes | | | Yes | | 29,800 | 9,700 | | 1242 | Yes | | | None |
| Yes | Yes | | No | | 8,160† | 11,406 | 9 | 181 | Yes | | | 6/30 |
| Yes | Yes | | No | | 8,054† | 12,800 | 12 | 267 | | | | |
| Yes | Yes | Yes | No | | 8,726† | 11,268 | | 289 | | | | |
| Yes | Yes | | Yes | Yes | 7,433† | 7,024 | | 247 | | | | |
| Yes | | | | | | | | | | | | |
| Yes | | | | | | | | | | | | |
| | | | Yes | Yes | 14,884 | 8,990 | | 591 | Yes | | | None |
| Yes | Yes | Yes | No | | 13,110† | 9,300 | 9 | 425 | Yes | | | 8/22 |
| Yes | Yes | | Yes | Yes | 32,520† | 3,960 | 16 | | | | | |
| Yes | Yes | Yes | No | | 9,188† | 11,268 | | 305 | Yes | | | None |
| Yes | | Yes | No | | 8,692† | 11,493 | 7 | 289 | | | | |
| Yes | Yes | Yes | No | | 8,064† | 11,268 | 6 | 268 | | | | |
| Yes | | Yes | No | | 8,694† | 11,970 | 6 | 289 | | | | |
| Yes | Yes | Yes | No | | 8,694† | 11,493 | 5 | 289 | Yes | | | |
| Yes | Yes | Yes | No | | 8,708† | 10,872 | 7 | 289 | | | | None |
| Yes | | Yes | No | | 8,708† | 11,268 | 6 | 289 | | | | |
| Yes | Yes | Yes | No | | 9,444† | 10,872 | 7 | 314 | | | | |
| | | Yes | No | | 8,500† | | 6 | 283 | | | | |
| Yes | Yes | | Yes | | 46,386 | 14,255 | 16 | 1897 | Yes | 199 | $10,352 | |
| Yes | Yes | Yes | Yes | Yes | 35,834† | 14,412 | 9 | 1475 | Yes | 41 | $20,963 | 2/15 |
| Yes | Yes | | Yes | Yes | 33,020 | 13,850 | | 1370 | Yes | 47 | $16,429 | None |
| Yes | Yes | | Yes | Yes | 41,350 | 13,680 | | 1693 | Yes | | | 8/1 |
| Yes | | Yes | No | | 8,500† | 11,160 | 18 | 282 | Yes | | | 6/30 |
| Yes | Yes | | Yes | Yes | 45,620† | 12,702 | 12 | | Yes | 5 | $13,780 | 3/1 |
| Yes | Yes | Yes | No | | 7,758† | 11,970 | 7 | 257 | | | | |
| Yes | | Yes | No | | 7,904† | 11,493 | 6 | 261 | | | | |
| Yes | Yes | Yes | No | | 8,286† | 11,268 | 12 | 275 | | | | |
| Yes | Yes | Yes | No | | 7,780† | 13,788 | | 257 | | | | |
| Yes | | | No | | 8,918† | 11,268 | 7 | 295 | Yes | | | |
| | | | | | 9,456† | 13,558 | | 314 | | | | None |
| | | | Yes | | 37,722† | 11,451 | | 1528 | Yes | 82 | $16,541 | None |
| Yes | | Yes | No | | 8,671† | 12,492 | 12 | 287 | | | | |
| | | | No | | 8,264† | | 8 | 275 | | | | |
| | | | No | | 26,596† | 12,492 | | 395 | Yes | | | None |
| | | | No | | | 1,208 | | | | | | |
| Yes | Yes | | No | | 7,774† | 11,493 | 6 | 258 | | | | |
| Yes | Yes | Yes | No | | 13,092† | 11,104 | 18 | 362 | | | | |

| Institution | Control/ degrees | Undergraduates Total | Undergraduates Internat'l | Tests required (Fall 2017) | TOEFL minimum | TOEFL average | Application Deadline | Application Fee |
|---|---|---|---|---|---|---|---|---|
| NewSchool of Architecture & Design | Pr/B | 408 | | TOEFL | 79 | | | 75 |
| Norco College | Pu/A | 10,323 | | | | | | |
| Northcentral University | Pr/B | 133 | | TOEFL | 79 | | None | |
| Northwestern Polytechnic University | Pr/B | 52 | | TOEFL, SAT | 70 | | | 60 |
| Notre Dame de Namur University | Pr/B | 1,097 | | TOEFL | 61 | | | 50 |
| Occidental College | Pr/B | 2,050 | 133 | TOEFL, SAT/ACT | 100 | 106 | 1/15 | 65 |
| Ohlone College | Pu/A | 9,955 | | TOEFL | 57 | | | 50 |
| Orange Coast College | Pu/A | 21,928 | | TOEFL | 61 | | 7/8 | 55 |
| Otis College of Art and Design | Pr/B | 1,023 | | TOEFL, SAT/ACT | 79 | | | 60 |
| Pacific College of Oriental Medicine: San Diego | Pr/AB | 128 | 2 | TOEFL | | | | 50 |
| Pacific Oaks College | Pr/B | 522 | | TOEFL | | | | 55 |
| Pacific States University | Pr/AB | 32 | | TOEFL | 45 | | 8/1 | 200 |
| Pacific Union College | Pr/AB | 1,550 | | TOEFL, SAT/ACT | 80 | 86 | | 30 |
| Palo Verde College | Pu/A | 4,404 | | TOEFL | | | | |
| Palomar College | Pu/A | 25,998 | | TOEFL | | | | 25 |
| Pasadena City College | Pu/A | 30,961 | | TOEFL | | | | 40 |
| Patten University | Pr/AB | 1,492 | | TOEFL, SAT/ACT | | | | 30 |
| Pepperdine University | Pr/B | 3,528 | | TOEFL, SAT/ACT | 80 | 101 | 1/5 | 65 |
| Pitzer College | Pr/B | 1,062 | 91 | TOEFL | 95 | | | 70 |
| Platt College: Los Angeles | Pr/AB | 661 | | TOEFL | | | | 75 |
| Platt College: Ontario | Pr/AB | 431 | | TOEFL | | | | 75 |
| Platt College: San Diego | Pr/AB | 255 | 1 | | | | | |
| Point Loma Nazarene University | Pr/B | 3,042 | 35 | TOEFL | 80 | | | 55 |
| Pomona College | Pr/B | 1,642 | 180 | TOEFL, SAT/ACT | 100 | | 1/1 | 70 |
| Porterville College | Pu/A | 4,393 | | TOEFL | | | | |
| Professional Golfers Career College | Pr/A | 311 | | TOEFL | 52 | | | 125 |
| Providence Christian College | Pr/B | 147 | | | | | | 200 |
| Reedley College | Pu/A | 10,370 | | TOEFL | 60 | 66 | | |
| Rio Hondo College | Pu/AB | 21,013 | | TOEFL | | | | 20 |
| Riverside City College | Pu/A | 20,472 | | TOEFL | 45 | | | 50 |
| Sacramento City College | Pu/A | 22,593 | | TOEFL | | | | 50 |
| Saddleback College | Pu/A | 27,510 | | TOEFL | 52 | | | 54 |
| St. Mary's College of California | Pr/B | 2,789 | 60 | TOEFL | 79 | 92 | | 60 |
| Samuel Merritt University | Pr/B | 584 | | TOEFL | | | | 50 |
| San Bernardino Valley College | Pu/A | 12,941 | | TOEFL | | | | 25 |
| San Diego Christian College | Pr/AB | 668 | 8 | TOEFL | 61 | | None | 100 |
| San Diego City College | Pu/A | 16,917 | | TOEFL | 61 | 81 | | 100 |
| San Diego Mesa College | Pu/A | 23,630 | | TOEFL | | | | 100 |
| San Diego Miramar College | Pu/A | 14,768 | | TOEFL | 61 | | | 100 |
| San Diego State University | Pu/B | 29,853 | 2,042 | TOEFL | 80 | | 5/1 | 55 |
| San Francisco Art Institute | Pr/B | 332 | 66 | TOEFL | 79 | 91 | | 85 |
| San Francisco Conservatory of Music | Pr/B | 187 | 63 | TOEFL | 71 | 76 | 12/1 | 110 |
| San Francisco State University | Pu/B | 24,882 | 1,553 | TOEFL | 61 | | | 55 |
| San Joaquin Delta College | Pu/A | 19,430 | | TOEFL | 61 | 80 | | 50 |
| San Joaquin Valley College | Pr/A | 1,892 | | | | | | |
| San Jose City College | Pu/A | 8,194 | | TOEFL | | | | 100 |
| San Jose State University | Pu/B | 26,432 | 1,879 | TOEFL | 61 | | | 55 |
| Santa Ana College | Pu/A | 42,024 | | TOEFL | | | | 50 |
| Santa Barbara Business College | Pr/AB | 94 | | | | | | 25 |
| Santa Barbara Business College: Bakersfield | Pr/AB | 405 | | | | | | 25 |
| Santa Barbara Business College: Rancho Mirage | Pr/AB | 256 | | | | | | 25 |
| Santa Barbara Business College: Santa Maria | Pr/AB | 222 | | | | | | 25 |
| Santa Barbara Business College: Ventura | Pr/AB | 106 | | | | | | 25 |
| Santa Barbara City College | Pu/A | 17,807 | | | | | | 50 |
| Santa Clara University | Pr/B | 5,411 | 213 | TOEFL, SAT/ACT | 90 | 97 | 1/7 | 60 |
| Santa Monica College | Pu/A | 34,226 | 2,060 | TOEFL | | | 6/16 | 75 |
| Santa Rosa Junior College | Pu/A | 27,289 | | TOEFL | 53 | 57 | | 50 |

| Student services | | | Housing | | Academic year costs | | Maximum credits/ summer | Credit hour charge | International financial aid | | | |
|---|---|---|---|---|---|---|---|---|---|---|---|---|
| Adviser | Orien- tation | ESL | Academic year | Summer | Tuition/ fees | Living costs | | | Avail- able | Number receiving aid | Average award | Deadline |
| | Yes | | Yes | | 26,463 † | 13,707 | | 751 | | | | |
| | | | | | 9,456 † | 13,558 | | 371 | | | | |
| | | | No | | 10,360 † | | | | | | | |
| Yes | Yes | Yes | Yes | Yes | 10,700 † | 6,900 | 16 | | | | | |
| Yes | Yes | Yes | Yes | Yes | 33,418 † | 13,398 | | 1065 | Yes | | | None |
| Yes | Yes | | Yes | | 51,070 † | 14,460 | 12 | | Yes | 7 | $32,539 | 1/15 |
| Yes | Yes | Yes | No | | 8,378 † | 13,713 | | 278 | Yes | | | |
| Yes | Yes | | No | | 7,738 † | 12,492 | 12 | 256 | Yes | | | None |
| Yes | Yes | | Yes | Yes | 43,270 | 14,690 | 18 | 1412 | Yes | | | None |
| Yes | | | | | | | | | Yes | | | 8/1 |
| Yes | | | No | | 23,430 † | 11,268 | 12 | 781 | | | | |
| Yes | Yes | Yes | Yes | Yes | 16,005 † | | 20 | 345 | Yes | | | None |
| Yes | Yes | | Yes | Yes | 28,329 † | 9,370 | | 810 | Yes | 34 | $9,600 | None |
| Yes | | Yes | No | | 8,340 † | 11,268 | 6 | 278 | Yes | | | None |
| Yes | Yes | Yes | No | | 7,910 † | 12,826 | | 262 | | | | |
| Yes | Yes | | No | | 8,340 † | 9,710 | 8 | 276 | | | | |
| Yes | Yes | | | | 3,432 † | | 12 | | Yes | | | None |
| Yes | Yes | | Yes | Yes | 50,022 † | 14,330 | 18 | 1565 | Yes | 139 | $20,809 | |
| Yes | Yes | Yes | Yes | Yes | 50,430 † | 15,762 | | | Yes | 13 | $56,339 | 2/1 |
| | | | No | | | 9,600 | | | | | | |
| | | | No | | | 15,960 | | | | | | |
| Yes | Yes | | Yes | Yes | 34,600 | 10,150 | 12 | 1417 | Yes | | | None |
| Yes | Yes | | Yes | | 49,352 † | 15,605 | | | Yes | | | 3/1 |
| Yes | | Yes | No | | 8,364 † | 8,500 | 6 | 278 | | | | |
| Yes | Yes | | No | | 15,600 † | | | | | | | |
| | | | Yes | | 28,014 † | 8,408 | | 1132 | Yes | | | 5/1 |
| Yes | | | Yes | | 8,470 † | 6,668 | 18 | 281 | Yes | | | None |
| Yes | | | No | | 7,452 † | 11,970 | 15 | 246 | | | | |
| Yes | Yes | | | | 9,456 † | 13,558 | | 314 | | | | |
| Yes | Yes | Yes | No | | 8,286 † | 11,970 | 7 | 275 | | | | |
| Yes | Yes | Yes | No | | 9,698 † | 12,492 | 19 | 322 | | | | |
| Yes | Yes | Yes | Yes | Yes | 44,360 † | 14,880 | 2 | 1583 | Yes | 47 | $39,555 | None |
| Yes | | Yes | | Yes | 45,491 † | | | 1917 | | | | |
| Yes | | | No | | 8,710 † | | | 289 | | | | |
| Yes | Yes | | Yes | Yes | 29,550 † | 10,974 | 12 | 1210 | Yes | | | 7/15 |
| Yes | Yes | | No | | 7,748 † | 11,970 | 12 | 239 | | | | |
| Yes | Yes | | No | | 7,748 † | 11,493 | 12 | 257 | | | | |
| Yes | Yes | | No | | 7,767 † | 11,268 | 12 | 257 | | | | |
| Yes | Yes | Yes | Yes | Yes | 18,244 † | 14,812 | | 372 | Yes | 71 | $18,309 | 3/2 |
| Yes | Yes | Yes | Yes | | 44,778 | 15,523 | 15 | 1923 | Yes | 65 | $4,743 | None |
| Yes | Yes | | Yes | | 44,810 | 16,060 | | 1924 | Yes | 62 | $22,528 | 3/1 |
| Yes | Yes | Yes | Yes | | 17,644 † | 12,698 | 12 | 372 | | | | |
| Yes | Yes | Yes | No | | 7,950 † | 12,492 | 9 | 257 | | | | |
| | | | No | | | | | | | | | |
| Yes | | Yes | No | | 7,878 † | 13,293 | 7 | 261 | Yes | | | None |
| Yes | Yes | Yes | Yes | | 16,346 ‡ | 13,002 | | 372 | Yes | 440 | $9,091 | None |
| Yes | Yes | Yes | No | | 9,068 † | 11,000 | 6 | 301 | | | | |
| | | | | | 13,619 † | | | 375.54 | | | | |
| | | | | | 13,619 † | | | 375.54 | | | | |
| | | | | | 13,619 † | | | 375.54 | | | | |
| | | | | | 13,619 † | | | 375.54 | | | | |
| | | | No | | 13,619 † | | | 375.54 | | | | |
| Yes | Yes | Yes | | | 7,880 † | 11,494 | 3 | 261 | | | | |
| Yes | Yes | | Yes | Yes | 47,112 † | 13,965 | | 1309 | Yes | 28 | $36,235 | None |
| Yes | Yes | Yes | No | | 10,114 † | 11,809 | 8 | 335 | | | | |
| Yes | Yes | | No | | 7,378 † | 13,812 | | 270 | Yes | | | None |

† Actual for 2016-17.    ‡ Estimated for 2017-18.    * Includes room and board

| Institution | Control/ degrees | Undergraduates Total | Internat'l | Tests required (Fall 2017) | TOEFL minimum | average | Application Deadline | Fee |
|---|---|---|---|---|---|---|---|---|
| Santiago Canyon College | Pu/A | 19,071 | | TOEFL | 45 | 47 | | 50 |
| | | | | | | | | |
| Scripps College | Pr/B | 1,030 | 50 | TOEFL, SAT/ACT | 100 | | 1/1 | 60 |
| Shasta Bible College and Graduate School | Pr/AB | 46 | | TOEFL | | | | 50 |
| Shasta College | Pu/A | 10,334 | | TOEFL | 45 | 61 | | |
| Sierra College | Pu/A | 18,488 | | TOEFL | 45 | | 7/1 | 100 |
| Silicon Valley University | Pr/B | 206 | | TOEFL | 61 | 84 | | 75 |
| | | | | | | | | |
| Simpson University | Pr/AB | 788 | 10 | TOEFL | 79 | | 6/1 | 35 |
| Skyline College | Pu/A | 9,774 | | TOEFL | | | 7/1 | |
| Soka University of America | Pr/B | 419 | 179 | TOEFL, SAT/ACT | | | 1/15 | 45 |
| Solano Community College | Pu/A | 9,994 | | TOEFL | | | | |
| Sonoma State University | Pu/B | 8,615 | | TOEFL | 61 | 87 | | 55 |
| | | | | | | | | |
| South Coast College | Pr/A | 365 | | | | | | 99 |
| Southern California Institute of Architecture | Pr/B | 255 | | TOEFL | 92 | | | 85 |
| Southern California Institute of Technology | Pr/AB | 367 | | TOEFL | 65 | | None | 100 |
| Southern California Seminary | Pr/AB | 62 | | TOEFL | | | | 126 |
| Southwestern College | Pu/A | 20,364 | | | | | | |
| | | | | | | | | |
| Stanbridge University | Pr/AB | 1,073 | | TOEFL | | | | |
| Stanford University | Pr/B | 7,032 | 640 | | | | | 90 |
| SUM Bible College & Theological Seminary | Pr/AB | 446 | | TOEFL | | | | 20 |
| Taft College | Pu/A | 6,088 | | TOEFL | 45 | | | 100 |
| Thomas Aquinas College | Pr/B | 389 | | TOEFL, SAT/ACT | | | None | |
| | | | | | | | | |
| Touro University Worldwide | Pr/AB | 405 | | TOEFL | 57 | | None | |
| Trident University International | Pr/B | 4,760 | | TOEFL | | | | |
| University of Antelope Valley | Pr/AB | 643 | | TOEFL | 61 | | None | 100 |
| University of California: Berkeley | Pu/B | 27,496 | | TOEFL | 80 | | | 80 |
| University of California: Davis | Pu/B | 29,348 | 3,918 | TOEFL | | | | 70 |
| | | | | | | | | |
| University of California: Irvine | Pu/B | 27,331 | 4,440 | TOEFL, SAT/ACT | 80 | 100 | 11/30 | 80 |
| University of California: Los Angeles | Pu/B | 30,856 | 3,645 | TOEFL, SAT/ACT | 83 | | 11/30 | 70 |
| University of California: Merced | Pu/B | 6,815 | 451 | TOEFL, SAT/ACT | 80 | | 11/30 | 80 |
| University of California: Riverside | Pu/B | 19,788 | 493 | TOEFL, SAT/ACT | 80 | | 11/30 | 80 |
| University of California: San Diego | Pu/B | 23,850 | | TOEFL, SAT/ACT | 83 | | | 70 |
| | | | | | | | | |
| University of California: Santa Barbara | Pu/B | 21,574 | 1,810 | TOEFL, SAT/ACT | 80 | | 11/30 | 80 |
| University of California: Santa Cruz | Pu/B | 16,962 | 762 | TOEFL, SAT/ACT | 80 | | | 70 |
| University of La Verne | Pr/AB | 2,802 | 157 | TOEFL | 80 | | | 50 |
| University of the Pacific | Pr/B | 3,474 | 212 | TOEFL | 52 | | | 60 |
| University of Phoenix: Bay Area | Pr/B | 1,659 | | | | | | |
| | | | | | | | | |
| University of Phoenix: Central Valley | Pr/B | 2,375 | | | | | | |
| University of Phoenix: Sacramento Valley | Pr/B | 3,190 | | | | | | |
| University of Phoenix: San Diego | Pr/AB | 5,885 | | | | | | |
| University of Phoenix: Southern California | Pr/B | 19,688 | | | | | | |
| University of Redlands | Pr/B | 2,402 | 57 | TOEFL, SAT/ACT | 81 | | | 30 |
| | | | | | | | | |
| University of San Diego | Pr/B | 5,604 | 476 | TOEFL | 80 | | 12/17 | 55 |
| University of San Francisco | Pr/B | 6,664 | 1,200 | TOEFL | 80 | 87 | None | 65 |
| University of Southern California | Pr/B | 18,557 | | | | | | 80 |
| University of the West | Pr/B | 106 | 39 | TOEFL | 61 | 70 | | 100 |
| Vanguard University of Southern California | Pr/AB | 1,765 | | TOEFL | | | | 45 |
| | | | | | | | | |
| Ventura College | Pu/A | 13,121 | | TOEFL | | | | 50 |
| Victor Valley College | Pu/A | 12,505 | | TOEFL | | | | 50 |
| West Hills College: Coalinga | Pu/A | 3,794 | | | | | | 50 |
| West Hills College: Lemoore | Pu/A | 4,345 | | | | | | 50 |
| West Los Angeles College | Pu/A | 13,032 | | TOEFL | | | | 35 |
| | | | | | | | | |
| West Valley College | Pu/A | 10,587 | | TOEFL | | | | |
| Westmont College | Pr/B | 1,275 | 35 | TOEFL, SAT/ACT | 83 | | | 50 |
| Whittier College | Pr/B | 1,598 | 46 | TOEFL, SAT/ACT | 100 | | | 50 |
| William Jessup University | Pr/AB | 1,158 | 21 | TOEFL | 80 | 523 | 5/15 | 50 |
| Woodbury University | Pr/B | 1,096 | 258 | TOEFL | 61 | 78 | | 50 |
| | | | | | | | | |
| Woodland Community College | Pu/A | 4,095 | | | | | | |
| World Mission University | Pr/B | 142 | | | | | | 50 |

| Student services | | | Housing | | Academic year costs | | Maximum credits/ summer | Credit hour charge | International financial aid | | | |
|---|---|---|---|---|---|---|---|---|---|---|---|---|
| Adviser | Orientation | ESL | Academic year | Summer | Tuition/ fees | Living costs | | | Available | Number receiving aid | Average award | Deadline |
| Yes | Yes | Yes | No | | 9,068 † | 11,268 | 6 | 301 | | | | |
| Yes | Yes | | Yes | | 50,982 † | 15,682 | | 1587 | Yes | 9 | $34,441 | 2/1 |
| | | | Yes | | 11,310 † | 2,800 | | 350 | | | | |
| Yes | | Yes | Yes | | 7,838 † | 11,494 | | 260 | | | | |
| Yes | Yes | Yes | Yes | Yes | 7,998 † | 7,400 | 18 | 265 | | | | |
| Yes | Yes | Yes | | | 9,750 † | | | 325 | | | | |
| Yes | | | Yes | Yes | 25,950 † | 8,100 | | 1095 | Yes | 7 | $13,554 | None |
| Yes | Yes | | No | | 9,432 † | 12,492 | 9 | 269 | | | | |
| Yes | Yes | Yes | Yes | Yes | 30,106 ‡ | 13,166 | | 1255 | Yes | 178 | $37,434 | 3/2 |
| | | Yes | No | | 7,886 † | 10,863 | | 262 | | | | |
| Yes | Yes | Yes | Yes | Yes | 18,548 † | 13,146 | | 372 | | | | |
| Yes | | | No | | 11,594 † | 12,492 | | | Yes | | | 3/2 |
| Yes | Yes | Yes | No | | 42,900 † | 14,520 | 18 | | | | | |
| Yes | | | Yes | Yes | 12,250 † | 9,410 | | | | | | |
| Yes | Yes | Yes | | | 7,758 | | | 257 | | | | |
| | | | | | | | | | Yes | | | 3/2 |
| Yes | Yes | Yes | Yes | | 47,940 † | 14,601 | | | Yes | 169 | $56,082 | None |
| | | | Yes | | 9,125 ‡ | 2,500 | 6 | 277.33 | Yes | | | None |
| | | | Yes | | 7,380 † | 4,707 | | 246 | | | | |
| | | | Yes | | 24,500 ‡ | 7,950 | | 681 | Yes | | | 3/2 |
| | | | | | 9,600 † | | | 400 | Yes | | | None |
| | | | | | | 6,118 | | | | | | |
| | | | Yes | Yes | 16,900 † | 5,800 | 21 | 490 | | | | |
| Yes | Yes | | Yes | | 40,167 † | 15,115 | 10 | | | | | |
| | | | Yes | | 40,728 † | 14,838 | | | Yes | 175 | $8,691 | None |
| Yes | Yes | Yes | Yes | Yes | 41,708 † | 13,661 | | | Yes | 144 | $10,980 | 6/26 |
| Yes | Yes | | Yes | | 40,091 † | 15,069 | 18 | | Yes | 116 | $22,145 | None |
| Yes | Yes | | Yes | Yes | 39,944 † | 15,933 | | | Yes | 8 | $5,000 | 3/2 |
| Yes | Yes | | Yes | Yes | 40,263 † | 16,400 | | | Yes | 12 | $10,166 | 6/15 |
| Yes | Yes | Yes | Yes | | 40,255 † | 10,976 | | | Yes | | | 6/1 |
| Yes | Yes | Yes | Yes | Yes | 40,696 † | 13,605 | | | Yes | 26 | $28,558 | 5/31 |
| Yes | Yes | | Yes | Yes | 40,197 † | 13,874 | 20 | | Yes | | | 3/2 |
| Yes | Yes | | Yes | Yes | 41,450 ‡ | 13,140 | | 1165 | Yes | 71 | $10,617 | None |
| Yes | Yes | Yes | Yes | Yes | 44,588 † | 12,858 | 18 | 1520 | | | | |
| Yes | Yes | | Yes | | 48,072 | 13,862 | | | Yes | 39 | $7,739 | 3/2 |
| Yes | Yes | Yes | Yes | | 46,140 † | 12,302 | 13 | 1570 | Yes | 28 | $8,803 | None |
| Yes | Yes | Yes | Yes | Yes | 44,494 † | 13,990 | 18 | 1565 | Yes | 167 | $44,257 | None |
| Yes | Yes | Yes | Yes | Yes | 52,283 † | 14,348 | | 1733 | Yes | | | None |
| Yes | Yes | Yes | Yes | Yes | 14,040 † | 7,156 | 6 | 438 | Yes | | | None |
| | | | Yes | Yes | 30,980 † | 9,310 | 9 | | Yes | | | 3/2 |
| Yes | | Yes | No | | 8,888 † | 10,962 | 8 | 295 | | | | |
| Yes | | Yes | No | | 9,172 † | 11,268 | 8 | 305 | Yes | | | None |
| Yes | Yes | Yes | Yes | Yes | 8,190 † | 9,177 | | 273 | | | | |
| Yes | Yes | Yes | | Yes | 8,190 † | 11,970 | | 273 | | | | |
| Yes | Yes | Yes | No | | 8,076 † | 11,493 | 18 | 268 | | | | |
| Yes | Yes | Yes | No | | 7,868 † | 11,268 | 6 | 261 | | | | |
| Yes | Yes | | Yes | Yes | 44,044 ‡ | 13,886 | 9 | 2120 | | | | |
| Yes | Yes | | Yes | | 44,774 † | 12,902 | 13 | 1841 | Yes | | | 6/30 |
| Yes | Yes | | Yes | | 29,950 | 10,950 | | | Yes | 8 | $13,038 | None |
| Yes | Yes | Yes | Yes | Yes | 37,882 † | 11,133 | 18 | 1200 | Yes | | | 2/1 |
| Yes | | Yes | | | 8,000 † | | | 266 | | | | |
| | | | | | 7,200 † | 9,738 | | 230 | | | | |

† Actual for 2016-17.   ‡ Estimated for 2017-18.   * Includes room and board

| Institution | Control/ degrees | Undergraduates | | Tests required (Fall 2017) | TOEFL | | Application | |
|---|---|---|---|---|---|---|---|---|
| | | Total | Internat'l | | minimum | average | Deadline | Fee |
| Yuba College . . . . . . . . . . . . . . . . . . . . . . . . . | Pu/A | 6,666 | | TOEFL | | | | 25 |
| **Colorado** | | | | | | | | |
| Adams State University. . . . . . . . . . . . . . . . . . | Pu/AB | 1,974 | 20 | TOEFL, SAT/ACT | 79 | | 6/1 | 30 |
| Aims Community College . . . . . . . . . . . . . . . . | Pu/A | 3,672 | 10 | TOEFL | 57 | | 6/1 | |
| American Sentinel University. . . . . . . . . . . . . | Pr/AB | 1,712 | | TOEFL | | | | |
| Argosy University: Denver . . . . . . . . . . . . . . | Pr/AB | 129 | | | | | | 50 |
| Aspen University. . . . . . . . . . . . . . . . . . . . . . | Pr/AB | 231 | | TOEFL | 61 | | | |
| CollegeAmerica: Fort Collins. . . . . . . . . . . . | Pr/AB | 230 | | | | | | |
| Colorado Christian University . . . . . . . . . . . | Pr/AB | 6,313 | | TOEFL | | | | 30 |
| Colorado College. . . . . . . . . . . . . . . . . . . . . . | Pr/B | 2,084 | 162 | | | | 1/15 | 60 |
| Colorado Mesa University. . . . . . . . . . . . . . . . | Pu/AB | 8,734 | 83 | TOEFL | 70 | | None | 30 |
| Colorado Mountain College . . . . . . . . . . . . . . | Pu/AB | 5,690 | | TOEFL | | | 5/1 | |
| Colorado Northwestern Community College . . . . . . | Pu/A | 957 | 13 | TOEFL | 57 | | 7/1 | |
| Colorado School of Mines . . . . . . . . . . . . . . . | Pu/B | 4,566 | 278 | TOEFL | 79 | 91 | 4/1 | 50 |
| Colorado School of Trades . . . . . . . . . . . . . . | Pr/A | 153 | | | | | | 25 |
| Colorado State University . . . . . . . . . . . . . . . | Pu/B | 23,768 | 951 | | 79 | 86 | | 50 |
| Colorado State University: Pueblo. . . . . . . . . . | Pu/B | 5,192 | | TOEFL | 61 | 75 | | 30 |
| Colorado Technical University . . . . . . . . . . . . | Pr/AB | 1,144 | | TOEFL | | | | 100 |
| Community College of Aurora . . . . . . . . . . . . | Pu/A | 5,831 | 209 | TOEFL | | | None | |
| Community College of Denver. . . . . . . . . . . . . | Pu/A | 10,432 | | TOEFL | | | | |
| Concorde Career College: Aurora . . . . . . . . . . | Pr/A | 761 | | | | | | |
| Denver School of Nursing. . . . . . . . . . . . . . . | Pr/AB | 653 | | | | | | 100 |
| DeVry University: Westminster . . . . . . . . . . . | Pr/AB | 237 | 1 | TOEFL | | | | 50 |
| Ecotech Institute . . . . . . . . . . . . . . . . . . . . . | Pr/A | 375 | | | | | | |
| Fort Lewis College . . . . . . . . . . . . . . . . . . . . | Pu/B | 3,458 | 19 | TOEFL, SAT/ACT | 61 | | 8/1 | 40 |
| Front Range Community College . . . . . . . . . . . | Pu/A | 14,543 | 371 | TOEFL | 53 | | | |
| IBMC College: Fort Collins. . . . . . . . . . . . . . | Pr/A | 1,058 | | | | | | 50 |
| IntelliTec College . . . . . . . . . . . . . . . . . . . . . | Pr/A | 828 | | | | | None | |
| IntelliTec College: Grand Junction . . . . . . . . . | Pr/A | 218 | | | | | | |
| Johnson & Wales University: Denver. . . . . . . . . | Pr/AB | 1,227 | 15 | TOEFL | 80 | 90 | | |
| Lamar Community College . . . . . . . . . . . . . . . | Pu/A | 475 | 16 | TOEFL | 46 | | | |
| Lincoln College of Technology: Denver. . . . . . . . | Pr/A | 900 | | | | | | 150 |
| Metropolitan State University of Denver. . . . . . . | Pu/B | 19,334 | 112 | TOEFL | | | | 40 |
| Morgan Community College . . . . . . . . . . . . . . | Pu/A | 1,475 | | TOEFL | | | | |
| Naropa University . . . . . . . . . . . . . . . . . . . . . | Pr/B | 374 | 12 | TOEFL | 80 | | 1/15 | 50 |
| National American University: Denver. . . . . . . . | Pr/AB | 218 | | TOEFL | | | | 45 |
| Nazarene Bible College. . . . . . . . . . . . . . . . . . | Pr/AB | 716 | | TOEFL | 61 | | None | |
| Northeastern Junior College. . . . . . . . . . . . . . | Pu/A | 1,554 | | TOEFL | 52 | | | |
| Otero Junior College . . . . . . . . . . . . . . . . . . . | Pu/A | 1,466 | | TOEFL | | | | |
| Pikes Peak Community College . . . . . . . . . . . . | Pu/A | 12,525 | 125 | TOEFL | | | None | |
| Pueblo Community College . . . . . . . . . . . . . . . | Pu/AB | 4,544 | | TOEFL | 45 | | None | |
| Red Rocks Community College . . . . . . . . . . . . | Pu/AB | 8,221 | | | | | | |
| Redstone College. . . . . . . . . . . . . . . . . . . . . . | Pr/A | 552 | | TOEFL | | | | 25 |
| Regis University . . . . . . . . . . . . . . . . . . . . . . | Pr/B | 3,972 | 50 | TOEFL | 82 | | | |
| Rocky Mountain College of Art & Design . . . . . . | Pr/B | 1,079 | | TOEFL | 80 | | | 50 |
| Trinidad State Junior College. . . . . . . . . . . . . . | Pu/A | 1,783 | | TOEFL | 53 | | | 10 |
| University of Colorado Boulder . . . . . . . . . . . | Pu/B | 27,418 | 1,959 | TOEFL | 75 | 87 | 1/15 | 70 |
| University of Colorado Colorado Springs . . . . . . | Pu/B | 10,147 | 100 | TOEFL | 80 | 91 | None | 100 |
| University of Colorado Denver. . . . . . . . . . . . . | Pu/B | 10,855 | 864 | TOEFL | 75 | 86 | 5/15 | 75 |
| University of Denver . . . . . . . . . . . . . . . . . . . | Pr/B | 5,738 | 475 | TOEFL | 80 | 81 | 1/15 | 65 |
| University of Northern Colorado. . . . . . . . . . . . | Pu/B | 9,095 | 114 | TOEFL | 70 | | 5/31 | 60 |
| University of Phoenix: Denver . . . . . . . . . . . . | Pr/B | 1,351 | | | | | | |
| University of Phoenix: Southern Colorado . . . . . . | Pr/B | 600 | | | | | | |
| Western State Colorado University . . . . . . . . . . | Pu/B | 1,988 | 8 | TOEFL, SAT/ACT | | | | 40 |
| Westwood College: Denver North. . . . . . . . . . . | Pr/AB | 863 | | TOEFL | 53 | | | |

| Student services | | | Housing | | Academic year costs | | Maximum credits/ summer | Credit hour charge | International financial aid | | | |
|---|---|---|---|---|---|---|---|---|---|---|---|---|
| Adviser | Orien- tation | ESL | Academic year | Summer | Tuition/ fees | Living costs | | | Avail- able | Number receiving aid | Average award | Deadline |
| | | Yes | No | | 7,850 † | 4,968 | 9 | 261 | Yes | | | 3/1 |
| Yes | | | Yes | Yes | 19,785 † | 7,950 | 15 | 682 | | | | |
| | | | No | | 13,018 † | 8,982 | | 425 | | | | |
| | | | No | | 11,640 † | | | 380 | | | | |
| Yes | Yes | | Yes | | 29,360 † | 11,010 | 12 | | Yes | | | None |
| Yes | Yes | Yes | Yes | | 52,818 | 12,076 | 12 | 2201 | Yes | 117 | $46,144 | 1/15 |
| Yes | Yes | | Yes | Yes | 20,353 † | 13,152 | 12 | 651 | Yes | | | None |
| Yes | Yes | | Yes | | 13,170 ‡ | 9,098 | | 429 | Yes | | | None |
| Yes | | | Yes | | 7,472 † | 8,304 | 12 | 234 | | | | |
| Yes | Yes | | Yes | Yes | 36,172 † | 11,477 | | 1134 | Yes | | | |
| | | | | | | 17,500 | | | | | | |
| Yes | Yes | Yes | Yes | Yes | 28,346 † | 14,326 | 18 | 1301 | Yes | 146 | $14,817 | None |
| Yes | Yes | Yes | Yes | Yes | 24,101 † | 10,521 | 18 | 728.37 | Yes | | | 3/1 |
| Yes | Yes | | Yes | Yes | | | 17 | 325 | | | | |
| Yes | | Yes | No | | 17,118 † | 9,694 | 15 | 562 | | | | |
| Yes | | Yes | No | | 17,917 † | 9,072 | | 234 | Yes | | | None |
| Yes | | | | | 17,512 † | | | 609 | | | | |
| Yes | Yes | Yes | Yes | Yes | 17,817 † | 9,130 | 18 | 670 | Yes | 25 | $15,063 | None |
| Yes | Yes | Yes | No | | 17,222 † | 9,603 | 18 | 562 | Yes | | | None |
| | | | No | | | 9,152 | | | | | | |
| | | | No | | | | | | | | | |
| | | | No | | | | | | | | | |
| Yes | Yes | | Yes | Yes | 31,872 † | 11,961 | | | Yes | | | None |
| Yes | | | Yes | | 7,464 † | 6,200 | 18 | 234 | | | | |
| Yes | Yes | Yes | No | | 20,096 † | | 12 | | Yes | | | 7/21 |
| | | | No | | 17,073 † | | | 562 | | | | |
| Yes | Yes | | Yes | | 31,790 | 11,880 | | 995 | Yes | 7 | $19,171 | None |
| Yes | | Yes | No | | 17,100 † | 7,272 | 20 | 360 | | | | |
| | | | No | | 14,620 | 9,450 | 16 | 450 | Yes | | | None |
| Yes | Yes | Yes | Yes | Yes | 7,635 † | 7,874 | 12 | 235 | | | | |
| Yes | Yes | | Yes | | 7,382 † | 6,558 | 10 | 234 | | | | |
| Yes | | Yes | No | | 17,157 † | 9,603 | | 562 | | | | |
| Yes | | Yes | No | | 17,438 † | 9,309 | | 562 | | | | |
| Yes | Yes | Yes | No | | 17,438 † | 4,767 | 18 | 562 | | | | |
| | | | Yes | | | | | | | | | |
| | Yes | | Yes | | 34,450 | 10,420 | 12 | 1066 | Yes | 25 | $12,048 | None |
| Yes | | | Yes | Yes | 15,870 † | 8,640 | 18 | 594 | Yes | | | None |
| | | Yes | Yes | Yes | 7,620 † | 6,414 | 12 | 234 | | | | |
| Yes | Yes | Yes | Yes | Yes | 36,711 † | 13,590 | 16 | | Yes | | | None |
| Yes | Yes | Yes | Yes | Yes | 23,273 † | 9,800 | 12 | | | | | |
| Yes | Yes | Yes | | | 30,361 † | 9,693 | 12 | 934 | Yes | 207 | $2,239 | None |
| Yes | Yes | Yes | Yes | Yes | 48,669 | 12,612 | 18 | 1320 | Yes | 300 | $23,039 | None |
| Yes | Yes | Yes | Yes | Yes | 20,474 † | 10,566 | 15 | 735.5 | Yes | 43 | $5,409 | None |
| Yes | | | Yes | | 21,274 | 11,846 | 8 | 754 | Yes | | | None |
| Yes | | | No | | | | 21 | | Yes | | | None |

| Institution | Control/ degrees | Undergraduates | | Tests required (Fall 2017) | TOEFL | | Application | |
|---|---|---|---|---|---|---|---|---|
| | | Total | Internat'l | | minimum | average | Deadline | Fee |
| **Connecticut** | | | | | | | | |
| Albertus Magnus College . . . . . . . . . . . . . . . | .Pr/AB | 1,218 | 20 | TOEFL | | | 7/1 | 35 |
| Asnuntuck Community College . . . . . . . . . . . . . | .Pu/A | 1,658 | | TOEFL | | | | 20 |
| Capital Community College. . . . . . . . . . . . . . . | .Pu/A | 3,503 | | TOEFL | | | | 20 |
| Central Connecticut State University . . . . . . . . . . | .Pu/B | 9,269 | 141 | TOEFL | 61 | | | 50 |
| Charter Oak State College . . . . . . . . . . . . . . . | .Pu/AB | 1,459 | 15 | TOEFL | | | None | 75 |
| Connecticut College . . . . . . . . . . . . . . . . . . | .Pr/B | 1,822 | 125 | TOEFL | | 104 | | 60 |
| Eastern Connecticut State University . . . . . . . . . . | .Pu/AB | 4,818 | 46 | TOEFL | 79 | | | 50 |
| Fairfield University . . . . . . . . . . . . . . . . . | .Pr/B | 3,955 | 111 | TOEFL | 80 | 93 | 1/15 | 60 |
| Gateway Community College. . . . . . . . . . . . . . . | .Pu/A | 7,217 | | TOEFL | | | | 20 |
| Goodwin College. . . . . . . . . . . . . . . . . . . . | .Pr/AB | 3,440 | | TOEFL | | | | 50 |
| Holy Apostles College and Seminary . . . . . . . . . . | .Pr/AB | 135 | | TOEFL | | | | 50 |
| Housatonic Community College . . . . . . . . . . . . . | .Pu/A | 5,143 | | TOEFL | | | | 20 |
| Lyme Academy College of Fine Arts. . . . . . . . . . | .Pr/B | 78 | | TOEFL, SAT/ACT | | | | 55 |
| Manchester Community College . . . . . . . . . . . . . | .Pu/A | 6,891 | | TOEFL | | | | 20 |
| Middlesex Community College. . . . . . . . . . . . . . | .Pu/A | 2,740 | | TOEFL | | | | 20 |
| Mitchell College . . . . . . . . . . . . . . . . . . . | .Pr/AB | 677 | | TOEFL | 71 | | | 30 |
| Naugatuck Valley Community College. . . . . . . . . . | .Pu/A | 5,976 | 19 | TOEFL | | | | 20 |
| Norwalk Community College. . . . . . . . . . . . . . . | .Pu/A | 4,598 | | | | | | 20 |
| Paier College of Art . . . . . . . . . . . . . . . . . | .Pr/AB | 95 | | TOEFL | | | 7/18 | 25 |
| Post University . . . . . . . . . . . . . . . . . . . . | .Pr/AB | 709 | 8 | | | 46 | 8/1 | |
| Quinnipiac University. . . . . . . . . . . . . . . . . . | .Pr/B | 7,042 | 153 | TOEFL | 80 | 85 | 2/1 | 65 |
| Sacred Heart University . . . . . . . . . . . . . . . . | .Pr/AB | 5,325 | 69 | TOEFL | 80 | | | 50 |
| Southern Connecticut State University . . . . . . . . . | .Pu/B | 7,963 | 48 | TOEFL | 72 | | | 50 |
| Trinity College . . . . . . . . . . . . . . . . . . . . | .Pr/B | 2,289 | | TOEFL, SAT/ACT | | 105 | | 60 |
| Tunxis Community College . . . . . . . . . . . . . . . | .Pu/A | 3,307 | 4 | TOEFL | | | | 20 |
| United States Coast Guard Academy . . . . . . . . . . | .Pu/B | 986 | 24 | TOEFL, SAT/ACT | | | 2/1 | |
| University of Bridgeport . . . . . . . . . . . . . . . . | .Pr/AB | 2,941 | 426 | TOEFL, SAT/ACT | 60 | | None | 50 |
| University of Connecticut . . . . . . . . . . . . . . . | .Pu/AB | 18,826 | | TOEFL, SAT/ACT | 79 | 95 | | 70 |
| University of Hartford . . . . . . . . . . . . . . . . . | .Pr/AB | 4,924 | 295 | TOEFL | 79 | | 8/1 | 35 |
| University of New Haven . . . . . . . . . . . . . . . . | .Pr/AB | 4,850 | 364 | TOEFL | 75 | | 6/1 | 25 |
| University of Saint Joseph. . . . . . . . . . . . . . . | .Pr/B | 843 | 9 | TOEFL | 65 | | None | 50 |
| Wesleyan University . . . . . . . . . . . . . . . . . . | .Pr/B | 2,913 | 293 | TOEFL, SAT, SAT Subject Test(s), or ACT | 100 | 115 | | 55 |
| Western Connecticut State University . . . . . . . . . | .Pu/AB | 5,001 | 11 | TOEFL | 79 | | 3/1 | 50 |
| Yale University. . . . . . . . . . . . . . . . . . . . | .Pr/B | 5,471 | 587 | TOEFL, SAT, SAT Subject Test(s), or ACT | 100 | | | 75 |
| **Delaware** | | | | | | | | |
| Delaware College of Art and Design . . . . . . . . . . | .Pr/A | 169 | 4 | TOEFL | 79 | | | 80 |
| Delaware State University . . . . . . . . . . . . . . . | .Pu/B | 3,692 | | TOEFL | 79 | | | 35 |
| Delaware Technical Community College: Stanton/Wilmington Campus . . . . . . . . . . . . . | .Pu/A | 6,732 | | TOEFL | | | | 10 |
| Goldey-Beacom College . . . . . . . . . . . . . . . . | .Pr/AB | 630 | | TOEFL | 60 | | | |
| University of Delaware. . . . . . . . . . . . . . . . . | .Pu/AB | 17,669 | 743 | TOEFL | 90 | | | 60 |
| Wesley College. . . . . . . . . . . . . . . . . . . . | .Pr/AB | 1,345 | 4 | TOEFL | | | | |
| **District of Columbia** | | | | | | | | |
| American University . . . . . . . . . . . . . . . . . . | .Pr/AB | 7,277 | 522 | TOEFL | 80 | | 1/10 | 70 |
| Catholic University of America . . . . . . . . . . . . | .Pr/AB | 3,217 | 156 | TOEFL | 80 | | 1/15 | 55 |
| Gallaudet University. . . . . . . . . . . . . . . . . . | .Pr/B | 1,112 | 79 | TOEFL, SAT/ACT | | | | 50 |
| George Washington University . . . . . . . . . . . . . | .Pr/AB | 11,244 | 1,216 | TOEFL, SAT/ACT | | | 1/1 | 75 |
| Georgetown University. . . . . . . . . . . . . . . . . | .Pr/B | 7,112 | 830 | TOEFL, SAT/ACT | | | 1/10 | 75 |
| Howard University. . . . . . . . . . . . . . . . . . . | .Pr/B | 6,883 | | TOEFL, SAT/ACT, SAT Subject Test(s) | | 92 | | 45 |
| Strayer University . . . . . . . . . . . . . . . . . . . | .Pr/AB | 1,192 | | TOEFL | 61 | | | 50 |
| Trinity Washington University . . . . . . . . . . . . . | .Pr/AB | 2,129 | | TOEFL | 79 | | | 40 |
| University of the District of Columbia . . . . . . . . . | .Pu/AB | 4,463 | | TOEFL | 79 | | | 50 |

| Student services | | | Housing | | Academic year costs | | Maximum credits/ summer | Credit hour charge | International financial aid | | | |
|---|---|---|---|---|---|---|---|---|---|---|---|---|
| Adviser | Orien- tation | ESL | Academic year | Summer | Tuition/ fees | Living costs | | | Avail- able | Number receiving aid | Average award | Deadline |
| Yes | | | Yes | | 30,526† | 14,016 | | 1252 | Yes | | | None |
| | | | No | | 12,484† | 9,545 | 18 | 465 | | | | |
| Yes | | Yes | No | | 11,642† | | | 465 | | | | |
| Yes | Yes | Yes | Yes | Yes | 22,602† | 11,462 | 12 | 223 | | | | |
| | | | No | | 12,093† | | | 377 | | | | |
| Yes | Yes | | Yes | Yes | 52,850 | 14,590 | | 1562.5 | Yes | | | None |
| Yes | Yes | | Yes | Yes | 22,166† | 12,559 | | 496 | Yes | | | None |
| Yes | Yes | | Yes | Yes | 47,165 | 14,280 | 18 | 725 | Yes | 100 | $38,297 | 1/15 |
| Yes | | Yes | No | | 12,524† | 7,766 | 12 | 465 | | | | |
| | | | No | | 20,400† | 4,701 | | 690 | | | | |
| | | Yes | No | | 9,670† | 8,755 | 9 | 320 | | | | |
| Yes | | Yes | No | | 12,514† | 9,600 | 12 | 465 | | | | |
| | | | | | 32,222† | 9,300 | 3 | 1270 | | | | |
| Yes | | Yes | No | | 12,524† | 5,572 | 12 | 465 | | | | |
| Yes | | Yes | No | | 12,524† | 7,722 | .6 | 465 | | | | |
| Yes | | | Yes | Yes | 32,442‡ | 12,750 | 11 | 500 | Yes | | | None |
| Yes | Yes | Yes | No | | 12,524† | | 6 | 465 | | | | |
| Yes | | Yes | No | | 11,628† | 8,755 | | 465 | | | | |
| Yes | | | | | 15,450† | | | | Yes | | | None |
| Yes | Yes | Yes | Yes | Yes | 29,550† | 10,600 | | 945 | Yes | 70 | $24,268 | None |
| Yes | Yes | | Yes | | 43,940† | 16,170 | 12 | 995 | Yes | 137 | $35,258 | None |
| Yes | Yes | Yes | Yes | | 38,300† | 14,450 | | 600 | Yes | 43 | $27,318 | None |
| Yes | Yes | | Yes | Yes | 21,720† | 11,870 | 12 | 535 | Yes | | | |
| Yes | Yes | | Yes | Yes | 52,760† | 13,680 | | 1678 | Yes | | | 3/1 |
| Yes | | Yes | No | | 12,524† | 6,479 | 15 | 465 | Yes | | | None |
| Yes | Yes | | Yes | Yes | | | | | | | | |
| Yes | Yes | Yes | Yes | Yes | 32,250 | 13,590 | 12 | 1005 | Yes | | | None |
| Yes | Yes | Yes | Yes | Yes | 36,948 | 12,514 | 14 | 1421 | | | | |
| Yes | Yes | Yes | Yes | Yes | 38,910‡ | 15,346 | 15 | 556 | Yes | | | None |
| Yes | Yes | | Yes | | 37,060† | 15,130 | | 1190 | Yes | 59 | $16,025 | |
| Yes | Yes | Yes | | Yes | 36,870† | 11,095 | 6 | 795 | | | | |
| Yes | Yes | | Yes | Yes | 50,912† | 13,950 | | | Yes | 80 | $58,920 | 2/15 |
| Yes | | | Yes | Yes | 22,281† | 12,089 | | 223 | | | | |
| Yes | Yes | Yes | Yes | | 49,480† | 15,170 | | | Yes | | | 3/1 |
| Yes | | | Yes | | 24,830† | 12,000 | 18 | 1005 | Yes | | | 8/1 |
| Yes | | Yes | Yes | Yes | 16,138† | 11,090 | 9 | 638 | | | | |
| Yes | Yes | Yes | No | | 8,698† | | | 350 | | | | |
| Yes | | | Yes | Yes | 23,400† | 5,975 | 12 | 780 | Yes | | | 7/15 |
| Yes | Yes | Yes | Yes | Yes | 32,250† | 12,843 | 14 | 1290 | | | | |
| Yes | | | Yes | Yes | 25,646† | 11,244 | 12 | | Yes | | | None |
| Yes | Yes | Yes | Yes | Yes | 44,853† | 14,526 | 12 | 1467 | Yes | 73 | $24,241 | 1/10 |
| Yes | Yes | Yes | Yes | Yes | 44,060 | 14,316 | | 1715 | Yes | | | 4/10 |
| Yes | Yes | Yes | Yes | Yes | 31,630† | 13,204 | 8 | 1296 | Yes | | | None |
| Yes | Yes | Yes | Yes | Yes | 53,518 | 13,000 | 12 | 1520 | Yes | 341 | $17,742 | 2/1 |
| Yes | Yes | Yes | Yes | Yes | 50,547† | 15,572 | 12 | 2082 | Yes | | | None |
| Yes | Yes | | Yes | Yes | 24,908† | 11,416 | 12 | 980 | Yes | | | 5/1 |
| Yes | | | No | | 42,730† | 10,287 | 18 | | | | | |
| Yes | Yes | | Yes | | 23,690‡ | 12,990 | 9 | 730 | | | | |
| Yes | Yes | Yes | No | | 15,500† | 15,027 | 9 | | Yes | | | None |

† Actual for 2016-17.    ‡ Estimated for 2017-18.    * Includes room and board

| Institution | Control/ degrees | Undergraduates Total | Internat'l | Tests required (Fall 2017) | TOEFL minimum | average | Application Deadline | Fee |
|---|---|---|---|---|---|---|---|---|
| University of Phoenix: Washington DC . . . . . . . . . .Pr/B | | 251 | | | | | | |
| University of the Potomac. . . . . . . . . . . . . . . . . .Pr/AB | | 145 | | TOEFL | 61 | | | |
| **Florida** | | | | | | | | |
| Adventist University of Health Sciences. . . . . . . . .Pr/AB | | 1,529 | 10 | TOEFL | 79 | | 7/1 | 20 |
| Argosy University: Sarasota. . . . . . . . . . . . . . . . .Pr/AB | | 145 | | | | | | 50 |
| Argosy University: Tampa. . . . . . . . . . . . . . . . . .Pr/B | | 132 | | | | | | 50 |
| Art Institute of Fort Lauderdale . . . . . . . . . . . . .Pr/AB | | 1,514 | | TOEFL | | | | 50 |
| Ave Maria University. . . . . . . . . . . . . . . . . . . . .Pr/B | | 1,050 | 26 | TOEFL, SAT/ACT | 85 | | | |
| Baptist College of Florida . . . . . . . . . . . . . . . . .Pr/AB | | 430 | | TOEFL, SAT/ACT | 55 | | 8/1 | 25 |
| Barry University . . . . . . . . . . . . . . . . . . . . . . .Pr/B | | 3,461 | 272 | TOEFL | 61 | | | |
| Beacon College. . . . . . . . . . . . . . . . . . . . . . . .Pr/AB | | 314 | 10 | TOEFL | 80 | | None | 50 |
| Bethune-Cookman University. . . . . . . . . . . . . . .Pr/B | | 3,741 | 79 | TOEFL, SAT/ACT | 80 | | | 25 |
| Broward College . . . . . . . . . . . . . . . . . . . . . . .Pu/AB | | 38,674 | 1,592 | | 61 | | 6/30 | 75 |
| Brown Mackie College: Miami. . . . . . . . . . . . . .Pr/AB | | | | TOEFL | | | | |
| Carlos Albizu University. . . . . . . . . . . . . . . . . .Pr/B | | 305 | | | | | | 25 |
| Chamberlain College of Nursing: Jacksonville . . . . .Pr/B | | 485 | | | | | | 95 |
| Chamberlain College of Nursing: Miramar . . . . . . .Pr/B | | 567 | 1 | | | | | 95 |
| Chipola College. . . . . . . . . . . . . . . . . . . . . . . .Pu/AB | | 1,673 | | TOEFL, SAT/ACT | 70 | 75 | | 100 |
| City College: Altamonte Springs. . . . . . . . . . . . . .Pr/A | | 340 | | | | | | 25 |
| City College: Fort Lauderdale . . . . . . . . . . . . . . .Pr/AB | | 750 | | | | | | 40 |
| City College: Gainesville. . . . . . . . . . . . . . . . . .Pr/AB | | 430 | | | | | | 40 |
| City College: Miami. . . . . . . . . . . . . . . . . . . . .Pr/AB | | 228 | | | | | | 25 |
| College of Business and Technology: Cutler Bay. . . . . . . . . . . . . . . . . . . . . . . . . . . . .Pr/A | | 123 | | TOEFL | 90 | | None | 250 |
| College of Business and Technology: Flagler . . . . .Pr/A | | 301 | 2 | TOEFL | 90 | | None | 250 |
| College of Business and Technology: Hialeah . . . . .Pr/A | | 248 | | TOEFL | 90 | | | 250 |
| College of Business and Technology: Kendall . . . . .Pr/AB | | 10 | | TOEFL | 90 | | | 250 |
| College of Business and Technology: Miami Gardens . . . . . . . . . . . . . . . . . . . . . . . . . .Pr/AB | | 116 | | TOEFL | 90 | | None | 250 |
| College of Central Florida . . . . . . . . . . . . . . . . .Pu/AB | | 6,154 | | | 61 | 65 | | 45 |
| Daytona State College . . . . . . . . . . . . . . . . . . .Pu/AB | | 12,112 | 89 | TOEFL | 61 | | 5/28 | 50 |
| DeVry University: Miramar. . . . . . . . . . . . . . . . .Pr/AB | | 245 | | TOEFL | | | | 50 |
| DeVry University: Orlando . . . . . . . . . . . . . . . . .Pr/AB | | 533 | 13 | TOEFL | | | | 50 |
| Digital Media Arts College . . . . . . . . . . . . . . . .Pr/AB | | 300 | | TOEFL | 80 | | | 50 |
| Eastern Florida State College. . . . . . . . . . . . . . .Pu/AB | | 15,825 | | TOEFL | 61 | | | 60 |
| Eckerd College . . . . . . . . . . . . . . . . . . . . . . . .Pr/B | | 1,831 | 86 | TOEFL, SAT/ACT | 79 | | 4/16 | 40 |
| Edward Waters College. . . . . . . . . . . . . . . . . . .Pr/B | | 933 | | TOEFL | 53 | | | 75 |
| Embry-Riddle Aeronautical University . . . . . . . . .Pr/AB | | 5,407 | 711 | TOEFL | 79 | | None | 50 |
| Embry-Riddle Aeronautical University: Worldwide Campus . . . . . . . . . . . . . . . . . . .Pr/AB | | 10,932 | 446 | TOEFL | 79 | | None | 50 |
| Everest University: Orange Park. . . . . . . . . . . . . .Pr/AB | | 558 | | | | | | |
| Everglades University. . . . . . . . . . . . . . . . . . . . .Pr/B | | 1,359 | | | | | None | 50 |
| Flagler College . . . . . . . . . . . . . . . . . . . . . . . .Pr/B | | 2,611 | 85 | TOEFL | 75 | 80 | 3/1 | 50 |
| Florida Agricultural and Mechanical University . . . .Pu/AB | | 7,365 | 65 | TOEFL, SAT/ACT | 61 | 67 | 5/15 | 30 |
| Florida Atlantic University . . . . . . . . . . . . . . . . .Pu/AB | | 24,221 | 653 | TOEFL, SAT/ACT | 80 | 100 | 4/1 | 30 |
| Florida Career College: Hialeah . . . . . . . . . . . . .Pr/AB | | | | | | | | 100 |
| Florida Career College: Miami. . . . . . . . . . . . . .Pr/AB | | 6,227 | | | | | | 100 |
| Florida Career College: Riverview . . . . . . . . . . .Pr/AB | | | | | | | | 100 |
| Florida Career College: West Palm Beach. . . . . . .Pr/AB | | | | | | | | 100 |
| Florida College of Natural Health: Bradenton . . . . .Pr/A | | 143 | | | | | | 50 |
| Florida College of Natural Health: Maitland . . . . . .Pr/A | | 418 | | | | | | |
| Florida College of Natural Health: Miami. . . . . . .Pr/A | | 202 | | | | | | |
| Florida College of Natural Health: Pompano Beach . . . . . . . . . . . . . . . . . . . . . . . . . . .Pr/AB | | 203 | | | | | | |
| Florida Gateway College. . . . . . . . . . . . . . . . . .Pu/AB | | 3,197 | | TOEFL | 61 | | | |
| Florida Gulf Coast University. . . . . . . . . . . . . . .Pu/AB | | 13,659 | 238 | TOEFL, SAT/ACT | 79 | | | 30 |
| Florida Institute of Technology. . . . . . . . . . . . . .Pr/B | | 3,419 | 1,125 | TOEFL | 79 | | | |
| Florida International University . . . . . . . . . . . . .Pu/AB | | 41,133 | 2,427 | TOEFL, SAT/ACT | | | 11/1 | 30 |

| Student services | | | Housing | | Academic year costs | | Maximum credits/summer | Credit hour charge | International financial aid | | | |
|---|---|---|---|---|---|---|---|---|---|---|---|---|
| Adviser | Orien-tation | ESL | Academic year | Summer | Tuition/fees | Living costs | | | Avail-able | Number receiving aid | Average award | Deadline |
| Yes | | | No | | | 9,360 | | | | | | |
| Yes | Yes | | Yes | Yes | 14,250 | 4,200 | 12 | 455 | Yes | 8 | $2,961 | None |
| Yes | Yes | Yes | Yes | Yes | 22,105 † | 7,077 | 18 | 489 | | | | |
| Yes | Yes | | Yes | Yes | 19,970 | 10,865 | 16 | | Yes | | | None |
| Yes | | | Yes | | 11,100 ‡ | 4,138 | 10 | 340 | Yes | | | 4/15 |
| | | Yes | Yes | | 28,800 † | 10,600 | 12 | 865 | Yes | | | None |
| | | | Yes | | 36,172 † | 12,690 | 6 | 866 | Yes | | | None |
| Yes | Yes | | Yes | Yes | 14,410 † | 8,710 | 9 | | Yes | 91 | $17,617 | None |
| Yes | Yes | Yes | No | | 11,058 † | 13,500 | 18 | 369 | Yes | | | None |
| Yes | | | | | | 5,541 | 12 | | | | | |
| Yes | Yes | Yes | No | | 10,294 † | | 18 | 323 | | | | |
| | | | | | 19,500 † | | | 675 | | | | |
| | | | | | 19,500 † | | | 675 | | | | |
| Yes | | | No | | 8,891 † | | 12 | | | | | |
| | | | | | 14,550 † | | | 320 | | | | |
| Yes | Yes | | No | | 14,550 † | | | 320 | | | | |
| | | | | | 14,550 † | 9,513 | | 320 | | | | |
| | | | | | 14,625 † | | | 320 | | | | |
| Yes | Yes | Yes | No | | | | | 498 | Yes | | | None |
| Yes | Yes | Yes | No | | | | | 498 | Yes | | | None |
| Yes | Yes | Yes | No | | | | | 498 | Yes | | | None |
| Yes | Yes | Yes | No | | | | | 498 | Yes | | | None |
| Yes | Yes | | No | | 15,210 † | | | 498 | Yes | | | None |
| Yes | Yes | Yes | Yes | Yes | 12,656 † | | 18 | 422 | Yes | | | None |
| Yes | Yes | Yes | | | 12,001 † | 6,000 | 18 | 398.65 | | | | |
| Yes | | | | | 17,512 † | | | 609 | | | | |
| Yes | | | | | 17,512 † | | | 609 | | | | |
| Yes | | | | | 17,610 † | 7,888 | 18 | 582 | Yes | | | None |
| Yes | | Yes | No | | 12,183 † | | 18 | 406 | | | | |
| Yes | Yes | Yes | Yes | Yes | 41,538 † | 11,336 | 14 | 1412 | Yes | | | None |
| Yes | | | Yes | | 13,325 † | 7,282 | | 555 | Yes | | | 4/15 |
| Yes | Yes | Yes | Yes | Yes | 33,886 † | 10,826 | | 1358 | Yes | 251 | $5,469 | None |
| Yes | | Yes | No | | 9,076 ‡ | | | 375 | Yes | | | None |
| | | | No | | 16,400 ‡ | 7,872 | | 650 | | | | |
| Yes | Yes | | Yes | | 18,200 ‡ | 10,688 | 9 | 620 | Yes | 53 | $10,055 | None |
| Yes | Yes | | Yes | Yes | 17,730 † | 10,058 | 12 | 586.18 | Yes | | | None |
| Yes | Yes | Yes | Yes | Yes | 21,595 † | 12,006 | 12 | 719.84 | Yes | 75 | $19,344 | 6/30 |
| Yes | | | | | | | | | | | | |
| | | | No | | | | | | | | | |
| | | | No | | 11,747 † | | 12 | 391.57 | | | | |
| Yes | Yes | | Yes | Yes | 25,214 † | 9,120 | 12 | 840.48 | Yes | | | 6/30 |
| Yes | Yes | Yes | Yes | Yes | 40,446 † | 13,670 | 12 | 1148 | Yes | 792 | $17,545 | None |
| Yes | Yes | | Yes | Yes | 18,956 † | 10,846 | | 619 | Yes | 276 | $8,878 | 5/15 |

† Actual for 2016-17.    ‡ Estimated for 2017-18.    * Includes room and board

| Institution | Control/ degrees | Undergraduates | | Tests required (Fall 2017) | TOEFL | | Application | |
|---|---|---|---|---|---|---|---|---|
| | | Total | Internat'l | | minimum | average | Deadline | Fee |
| Florida Keys Community College . . . . . . . . . . . . . | Pu/AB | 1,023 | | TOEFL | 61 | | | 50 |
| Florida Memorial University . . . . . . . . . . . . . . . | Pr/B | 1,399 | | TOEFL, SAT/ACT | | | | 15 |
| Florida National University . . . . . . . . . . . . . . . . | Pr/AB | 3,157 | 361 | | | | | |
| Florida Southern College. . . . . . . . . . . . . . . . . | Pr/B | 2,370 | 100 | TOEFL | 79 | 85 | | 30 |
| Florida SouthWestern State College . . . . . . . . . | Pu/AB | 15,887 | 370 | TOEFL | 79 | | | 60 |
| Florida State College at Jacksonville . . . . . . . . . | Pu/AB | 20,507 | 231 | TOEFL | 61 | | 5/31 | 80 |
| Florida State University . . . . . . . . . . . . . . . . . | Pu/AB | 32,562 | 463 | TOEFL, SAT/ACT | 80 | | 2/7 | 30 |
| Florida Technical College: Deland . . . . . . . . . . . | Pr/A | | | TOEFL | | | | 25 |
| Florida Technical College: Orlando . . . . . . . . . . | Pr/AB | 2,977 | | TOEFL | | | | 25 |
| Fortis College: Orange Park. . . . . . . . . . . . . . . | Pr/A | 312 | | | | | | 67 |
| Fortis College: Winter Park . . . . . . . . . . . . . . . | Pr/A | 14 | | | | | | 50 |
| Full Sail University . . . . . . . . . . . . . . . . . . . . . | Pr/AB | 17,318 | | TOEFL | 79 | | | 75 |
| Golf Academy of America: Orlando . . . . . . . . . . | Pr/A | 192 | | | | | | 50 |
| Gulf Coast State College. . . . . . . . . . . . . . . . . . | Pu/AB | 4,017 | 16 | TOEFL | 79 | | | 40 |
| Herzing University: Winter Park. . . . . . . . . . . . . | Pr/AB | 478 | | TOEFL | | | | |
| Hillsborough Community College . . . . . . . . . . . . | Pu/A | 23,216 | | TOEFL | 61 | | | 50 |
| Hodges University . . . . . . . . . . . . . . . . . . . . . . | Pr/AB | 1,487 | | TOEFL | | | | 20 |
| Indian River State College. . . . . . . . . . . . . . . . . | Pu/AB | 17,665 | | | | | | |
| Jacksonville University . . . . . . . . . . . . . . . . . . . | Pr/B | 2,841 | 172 | TOEFL | 76 | 103 | None | 30 |
| Johnson & Wales University: North Miami. . . . . . | Pr/AB | 1,553 | 144 | TOEFL | 80 | | | |
| Johnson University: Florida . . . . . . . . . . . . . . . | Pr/AB | 179 | 2 | TOEFL, SAT/ACT | 71 | | | 35 |
| Jones College . . . . . . . . . . . . . . . . . . . . . . . . . | Pr/AB | 449 | | TOEFL | 60 | | | |
| Jose Maria Vargas University. . . . . . . . . . . . . . . | Pr/AB | 154 | | TOEFL | 50 | 50 | | 50 |
| Keiser University. . . . . . . . . . . . . . . . . . . . . . . | Pr/AB | 17,361 | | | | | None | 55 |
| Key College . . . . . . . . . . . . . . . . . . . . . . . . . . | Pr/A | 59 | | TOEFL | | | | 35 |
| Lake-Sumter State College . . . . . . . . . . . . . . . . | Pu/AB | 4,500 | | TOEFL | 80 | | | 70 |
| Le Cordon Bleu College of Culinary Arts: Miami . . . . . . . . . . . . . . . . . . . . . . . . . . . . | Pr/A | 789 | | | | | | |
| Le Cordon Bleu College of Culinary Arts: Orlando . . . . . . . . . . . . . . . . . . . . . . . . . . | Pr/A | 972 | | TOEFL | | | | 50 |
| Lincoln College of Technology: West Palm Beach . . . . . . . . . . . . . . . . . . . . . . . . . . . | Pr/AB | 713 | | | | | | 25 |
| Lynn University . . . . . . . . . . . . . . . . . . . . . . . | Pr/B | 2,053 | 440 | TOEFL | 71 | 79 | None | 45 |
| Miami Dade College . . . . . . . . . . . . . . . . . . . . | Pu/AB | 50,604 | 3,244 | | | | 6/26 | 50 |
| Miami International University of Art and Design. . . . . . . . . . . . . . . . . . . . . . . . . . . | Pr/AB | 3,167 | | TOEFL | 61 | | | 50 |
| New College of Florida. . . . . . . . . . . . . . . . . . . | Pu/B | 861 | 17 | TOEFL, SAT/ACT | 83 | 105 | 4/15 | 30 |
| North Florida Community College. . . . . . . . . . . . | Pu/A | 1,455 | | TOEFL | 61 | | None | 20 |
| Northwest Florida State College . . . . . . . . . . . . | Pu/AB | 5,889 | | TOEFL | 61 | | | |
| Nova Southeastern University. . . . . . . . . . . . . . . | Pr/AB | 4,230 | 242 | TOEFL, SAT/ACT | 79 | | | 50 |
| Palm Beach Atlantic University . . . . . . . . . . . . . | Pr/B | 2,474 | 97 | TOEFL | 79 | 84 | None | 50 |
| Palm Beach State College . . . . . . . . . . . . . . . . . | Pu/AB | 26,916 | 518 | TOEFL | | | 8/1 | 75 |
| Pasco-Hernando State College . . . . . . . . . . . . . | Pu/AB | 11,575 | | TOEFL | 69 | | | 25 |
| Pensacola State College . . . . . . . . . . . . . . . . . . | Pu/AB | 7,723 | 29 | TOEFL | 61 | | | 30 |
| Polk State College. . . . . . . . . . . . . . . . . . . . . . | Pu/AB | 8,583 | 109 | TOEFL | 61 | | 5/15 | |
| Professional Golfers Career College: Orlando . . . . . | Pr/A | | | TOEFL | | | | 125 |
| Rasmussen College: Fort Myers . . . . . . . . . . . . . | Pr/AB | 423 | | TOEFL | | | | |
| Rasmussen College: New Port Richey . . . . . . . . . | Pr/AB | 370 | | TOEFL | | | | |
| Rasmussen College: Ocala. . . . . . . . . . . . . . . . . | Pr/AB | 5,042 | | TOEFL | | | | |
| Rasmussen College: Pasco/Land O'Lakes . . . . . . | Pr/AB | 197 | | TOEFL | | | | |
| Rasmussen College: Tampa/Brandon . . . . . . . . . | Pr/AB | 358 | | TOEFL | | | | |
| Remington College of Nursing . . . . . . . . . . . . . | Pr/B | 184 | | | | | | 50 |
| Remington College: Tampa . . . . . . . . . . . . . . . | Pr/AB | 350 | | | | | | 50 |
| Ringling College of Art and Design. . . . . . . . . . | Pr/B | 1,331 | 214 | TOEFL | 61 | | | 70 |
| Rollins College . . . . . . . . . . . . . . . . . . . . . . . . | Pr/B | 1,925 | 188 | TOEFL | 80 | | 2/15 | 50 |
| Saint Leo University . . . . . . . . . . . . . . . . . . . . | Pr/AB | 2,262 | 272 | TOEFL | 78 | | | 40 |
| St. Petersburg College . . . . . . . . . . . . . . . . . . . | Pu/AB | 25,583 | 196 | | | | | 140 |
| Saint Thomas University . . . . . . . . . . . . . . . . . | Pr/B | 838 | | TOEFL | 71 | | None | 40 |
| Santa Fe College . . . . . . . . . . . . . . . . . . . . . . . | Pu/AB | 13,799 | 318 | TOEFL | 32 | | | |

| Adviser | Orien-tation | ESL | Academic year | Summer | Tuition/fees | Living costs | Maximum credits/summer | Credit hour charge | Avail-able | Number receiving aid | Average award | Deadline |
|---|---|---|---|---|---|---|---|---|---|---|---|---|
| | | | *Student services* | | *Academic year costs* | | | | | *International financial aid* | | |
| | | | *Housing* | | | | | | | | | |
| Yes | | | Yes | | 13,162 † | 13,200 | 15 | 438.73 | Yes | | | None |
| Yes | | | Yes | Yes | 15,536 † | 6,734 | 12 | | Yes | | | None |
| Yes | | Yes | Yes | | 13,250 | 7,816 | 15 | 525 | | | | |
| Yes | | | Yes | Yes | 33,100 † | 10,680 | 18 | 936 | Yes | 94 | $25,384 | 7/1 |
| Yes | Yes | | Yes | Yes | 12,979 † | 8,860 | | 325 | Yes | | | 9/16 |
| Yes | Yes | Yes | No | | 12,038 † | | 12 | | Yes | | | None |
| Yes | Yes | Yes | Yes | Yes | 21,673 † | 10,304 | 15 | 721.1 | | | | |
| | | | No | | | | | | Yes | | | None |
| | | | No | | | | | | | | | |
| Yes | Yes | | No | | | | | | | | | |
| Yes | | | No | | 17,250 † | | | | | | | |
| | | | | | 10,791 † | 7,580 | 12 | | | | | |
| Yes | Yes | Yes | Yes | Yes | 11,388 † | 8,784 | | | | | | |
| | | Yes | No | | 17,000 † | | 16 | 550 | Yes | | | None |
| Yes | | Yes | Yes | Yes | 11,715 † | | 12 | | | | | |
| Yes | Yes | Yes | Yes | Yes | 33,930 † | 13,550 | 18 | 1130 | Yes | 155 | $46,335 | None |
| Yes | Yes | Yes | Yes | Yes | 30,746 † | 11,961 | | | Yes | | | None |
| | | | Yes | | 14,270 † | 3,200 | | 440 | Yes | | | 7/15 |
| Yes | | | No | | 9,540 † | | 15 | 315 | Yes | | | None |
| Yes | | Yes | | | | 6,000 | 12 | | | | | |
| | | | No | | 28,768 ‡ | 11,240 | | | Yes | | | None |
| Yes | Yes | | | | | 9,153 | 16 | | Yes | | | None |
| Yes | | | No | | 13,276 † | 6,734 | 18 | 442.54 | Yes | | | None |
| Yes | | | | | | | | | | | | |
| Yes | Yes | | No | Yes | | | 23 | | | | | |
| Yes | Yes | | Yes | Yes | 37,010 ‡ | 14,782 | 18 | | Yes | 238 | $17,313 | None |
| Yes | Yes | Yes | No | | 12,075 † | 16,326 | 12 | 403 | Yes | 802 | $1,411 | 6/30 |
| Yes | Yes | | | | 22,105 † | 5,100 | | 489 | | | | |
| Yes | | | Yes | | 29,944 † | 9,009 | | 832 | Yes | 17 | $17,749 | None |
| | | | No | | 12,095 † | 5,400 | 12 | | | | | |
| Yes | | | No | | 11,941 † | 8,930 | 12 | | Yes | | | None |
| Yes | Yes | | Yes | Yes | 27,660 † | 11,540 | 18 | 897 | Yes | 143 | $6,387 | None |
| Yes | Yes | | Yes | Yes | 29,950 | 9,770 | | 675 | Yes | 93 | $13,155 | None |
| Yes | | Yes | | | 10,890 † | 9,050 | 17 | 363 | Yes | | | None |
| | | | No | | 12,032 † | 2,966 | | | | | | |
| Yes | | | No | | 12,593 † | 7,650 | 15 | 419.76 | | | | |
| Yes | | Yes | No | | 12,272 † | 8,080 | 18 | 409.06 | Yes | | | |
| Yes | | | | | 15,600 † | | | | | | | |
| | | | | | 13,455 † | | | 299 | Yes | | | None |
| | | | | | 13,455 † | | | 299 | Yes | | | None |
| | | | No | | 13,455 † | | | 299 | Yes | | | None |
| | | | | | 13,455 † | | | 299 | | | | |
| | | | | | 13,455 † | | | 299 | Yes | | | None |
| | | | No | | | | 15 | | | | | |
| Yes | Yes | Yes | Yes | | 42,990 † | 14,390 | | 1840 | Yes | 105 | $21,045 | None |
| Yes | Yes | Yes | Yes | | 48,335 | 14,730 | 4 | | Yes | 115 | $24,645 | None |
| Yes | Yes | Yes | Yes | Yes | 22,280 | 14,570 | 12 | | Yes | 238 | $14,021 | None |
| Yes | Yes | Yes | No | | 11,697 † | 9,527 | 12 | | Yes | | | None |
| Yes | Yes | Yes | Yes | Yes | 28,800 † | 8,200 | 18 | 960 | Yes | | | None |
| Yes | | Yes | No | | 11,487 † | | 18 | | | | | |

† Actual for 2016-17.    ‡ Estimated for 2017-18.    * Includes room and board

73

| Institution | Control/ degrees | Undergraduates | | Tests required (Fall 2017) | TOEFL | | Application | |
|---|---|---|---|---|---|---|---|---|
| | | Total | Internat'l | | minimum | average | Deadline | Fee |
| Schiller International University ............. | Pr/AB | 145 | | TOEFL | 61 | | | 65 |
| Seminole State College of Florida ............. | Pu/AB | 17,706 | | | 45 | | | 50 |
| South Florida State College ................. | Pu/AB | 2,063 | 37 | TOEFL | 61 | | | 15 |
| Southeastern College: Greenacres ......... | Pr/A | 1,013 | | | | | | 50 |
| Southeastern College: Miami Lakes ........... | Pr/A | | | | | | | |
| Southeastern University ................... | Pr/AB | 4,155 | 78 | TOEFL, SAT/ACT | | | | 40 |
| Southern Technical College ................. | Pr/AB | 15,389 | | TOEFL | 61 | | | 25 |
| Southwest Florida College: Tampa ........... | Pr/AB | | | | | | | 25 |
| State College of Florida, Manatee-Sarasota ........ | Pu/AB | 8,752 | 51 | TOEFL, SAT/ACT | | | | 75 |
| Stenotype Institute: Jacksonville ............... | Pr/A | 130 | | | | | | 100 |
| Stetson University ...................... | Pr/B | 3,052 | 166 | TOEFL | 79 | 91 | 4/15 | 50 |
| Tallahassee Community College ............. | Pu/A | 11,030 | 171 | TOEFL | 61 | 75 | 7/1 | |
| Talmudic University ..................... | Pr/B | 29 | | | | | | 250 |
| Trinity Baptist College .................. | Pr/AB | 314 | | | | | | 150 |
| Trinity College of Florida ................. | Pr/AB | 199 | 2 | TOEFL, SAT/ACT | 61 | | 7/1 | 35 |
| University of Central Florida .............. | Pu/AB | 55,292 | 736 | | 80 | | 3/1 | 30 |
| University of Florida .................... | Pu/AB | 33,219 | | | 80 | | | 30 |
| University of Miami ..................... | Pr/B | 10,615 | 1,480 | TOEFL | 80 | 100 | 1/1 | 70 |
| University of North Florida ............... | Pu/AB | 13,585 | 195 | TOEFL, SAT/ACT | 61 | | 5/1 | 30 |
| University of Phoenix: Central Florida ........... | Pr/B | 3,059 | | | | | | |
| University of Phoenix: North Florida ........... | Pr/B | 1,100 | | | | | | |
| University of Phoenix: South Florida ........... | Pr/B | 1,400 | | | | | | |
| University of Phoenix: West Florida ........... | Pr/B | 800 | | | | | | |
| University of South Florida ............... | Pu/AB | 30,553 | 1,844 | TOEFL, SAT/ACT | 79 | | 6/1 | 30 |
| University of South Florida: Saint Petersburg ...... | Pu/AB | 4,028 | 31 | | 79 | | | 30 |
| University of South Florida: Sarasota-Manatee...... | Pu/AB | 1,800 | 26 | TOEFL, SAT/ACT | 79 | | 3/1 | 30 |
| University of Tampa ..................... | Pr/B | 7,363 | 795 | TOEFL | 79 | 84 | None | 40 |
| University of West Florida ................. | Pu/AB | 9,652 | 181 | TOEFL | | 78 | | 30 |
| Valencia College ....................... | Pu/AB | 38,044 | | TOEFL | 45 | | 7/18 | 35 |
| Virginia College in Jacksonville .............. | Pr/A | 687 | | | | | | 100 |
| Virginia College in Pensacola ............... | Pr/A | 384 | | | | | | 100 |
| Warner University ...................... | Pr/AB | 1,056 | | TOEFL, SAT/ACT | 61 | 102 | | 20 |
| Webber International University .............. | Pr/AB | 654 | 144 | TOEFL | 61 | 78 | | 75 |
| Yeshiva Gedolah Rabbinical College ........... | Pr/B | 46 | | | | | | |

## Georgia

| Institution | Control/ degrees | Total | Internat'l | Tests required | minimum | average | Deadline | Fee |
|---|---|---|---|---|---|---|---|---|
| Abraham Baldwin Agricultural College ......... | Pu/AB | 3,458 | | TOEFL | 69 | | | 20 |
| Agnes Scott College ..................... | Pr/B | 886 | 83 | TOEFL, SAT/ACT | 80 | | 5/1 | |
| Albany State University .................. | Pu/B | 2,576 | 11 | TOEFL, SAT/ACT | 69 | | 5/1 | 25 |
| Albany Technical College ................. | Pu/A | 3,894 | | TOEFL, SAT/ACT | | | | 15 |
| Andrew College ...................... | Pr/A | 274 | 6 | TOEFL | 61 | | None | 20 |
| Argosy University: Atlanta ................. | Pr/AB | 434 | | | | | | 50 |
| Armstrong State University ............... | Pu/AB | 6,367 | 93 | TOEFL | 70 | | 5/1 | 25 |
| Art Institute of Atlanta .................... | Pr/AB | 2,623 | | TOEFL | 61 | | | 50 |
| Ashworth College ...................... | Pr/AB | 6,126 | | TOEFL | | | | |
| Athens Technical College ................. | Pu/A | 4,564 | | | | | | 20 |
| Atlanta Metropolitan State College ............ | Pu/AB | 3,016 | | TOEFL | 69 | | | 20 |
| Atlanta Technical College ................. | Pu/A | 3,771 | 33 | | | | | 20 |
| Bainbridge State College .................. | Pu/AB | 2,450 | | TOEFL | 77 | | 8/15 | |
| Bauder College ........................ | Pr/AB | 751 | | TOEFL | | | | 100 |
| Berry College .......................... | Pr/B | 2,055 | 11 | TOEFL, SAT/ACT | 80 | | | 50 |
| Beulah Heights University ................. | Pr/AB | 405 | | TOEFL | | | None | 35 |
| Brenau University ...................... | Pr/AB | 1,638 | 49 | TOEFL | 71 | 73 | None | |
| Brewton-Parker College .................. | Pr/AB | 616 | | | | | | 35 |
| Carver College ........................ | Pr/AB | 55 | | TOEFL | | | | 35 |
| Central Georgia Technical College ............ | Pu/A | 7,762 | | | | | None | 25 |
| Chamberlain College of Nursing: Atlanta ........ | Pr/B | 996 | 6 | | | | | 95 |
| Chattahoochee Technical College ............. | Pu/A | 9,997 | | TOEFL | 61 | | 8/4 | 25 |
| Clark Atlanta University ................... | Pr/B | 3,093 | 131 | TOEFL, SAT/ACT | | | 5/1 | 55 |

| Student services | | | Housing | | Academic year costs | | Maximum credits/ summer | Credit hour charge | International financial aid | | | |
|---|---|---|---|---|---|---|---|---|---|---|---|---|
| Adviser | Orien- tation | ESL | Academic year | Summer | Tuition/ fees | Living costs | | | Avail- able | Number receiving aid | Average award | Deadline |
| Yes | Yes | Yes | | Yes | | | 10 | | Yes | | | 4/1 |
| Yes | Yes | Yes | No | | 11,456 † | | 18 | | Yes | | | None |
| Yes | Yes | | Yes | Yes | 11,829 † | 5,920 | 7 | | | | | |
| Yes | | | Yes | Yes | 24,160 † | 9,562 | 12 | 965 | Yes | 69 | $13,233 | None |
| Yes | | | No | | | 7,024 | | | | | | |
| Yes | | | No | | 11,596 † | 16,529 | 12 | | Yes | | | 7/28 |
| | | | | | | 12,660 | | | | | | |
| Yes | Yes | | Yes | Yes | 44,480 | 12,684 | 10 | 1144 | Yes | 160 | $32,186 | None |
| Yes | Yes | | No | | 11,288 † | | 18 | | Yes | | | None |
| | | | Yes | Yes | 13,250 † | 8,000 | 10 | | Yes | | | None |
| | | | Yes | | 11,040 † | 6,270 | | | Yes | | | None |
| Yes | | | Yes | | 15,690 ‡ | 6,450 | | 495 | Yes | | | 9/16 |
| Yes | Yes | Yes | Yes | Yes | 22,467 † | 9,554 | 15 | | Yes | 37 | $1,275 | 6/30 |
| Yes | Yes | Yes | Yes | | 28,658 † | 9,910 | 15 | 856.45 | | | | |
| Yes | Yes | Yes | Yes | Yes | 47,004 † | 13,310 | 12 | 1900 | Yes | 136 | $38,950 | 4/15 |
| Yes | Yes | Yes | Yes | Yes | 20,112 † | 9,602 | 18 | 693.26 | Yes | 114 | $2,634 | 4/1 |
| Yes | Yes | Yes | Yes | Yes | 17,324 † | 9,700 | 12 | 577.48 | Yes | 468 | $8,276 | None |
| | | | Yes | | 16,766 † | 11,284 | | 557.85 | Yes | 6 | $3,084 | |
| Yes | | | No | | 16,502 † | 4,850 | | 550.07 | Yes | 3 | $5,466 | None |
| Yes | Yes | Yes | Yes | Yes | 27,740 † | 10,196 | 16 | 550 | Yes | 474 | $4,080 | None |
| Yes | Yes | Yes | Yes | Yes | 19,241 † | 10,062 | 15 | 641.37 | Yes | | | None |
| Yes | Yes | Yes | No | | 11,729 † | 9,366 | 19 | | | | | |
| | | | Yes | | 20,712 † | 8,104 | 12 | | Yes | | | None |
| Yes | Yes | Yes | Yes | Yes | 25,358 ‡ | 12,230 | 12 | 356 | Yes | 46 | $14,790 | 8/1 |
| | | | | | 8,400 † | 8,500 | | | | | | |
| Yes | | Yes | Yes | | 12,324 † | 8,060 | 18 | 378 | | | | |
| Yes | Yes | | Yes | Yes | 39,960 | 12,970 | | 1655 | Yes | 83 | $25,831 | 5/1 |
| Yes | Yes | | Yes | Yes | 19,280 † | 7,844 | 12 | 590 | | | | |
| | | | No | | 11,202 † | 9,304 | | 356 | | | | |
| | Yes | | Yes | | 15,770 † | 9,650 | 12 | 460 | Yes | | | 8/1 |
| Yes | Yes | | Yes | Yes | 19,152 † | 11,352 | 18 | 590 | Yes | | | 4/20 |
| Yes | Yes | | Yes | Yes | | 11,292 | | | Yes | | | None |
| | | | | | 1,399 † | | | | | | | |
| Yes | Yes | Yes | No | | 11,168 † | 9,600 | 18 | 356 | | | | |
| Yes | Yes | | | | 11,872 † | | 12 | 361 | | | | |
| | | Yes | No | | 11,300 † | 5,000 | 21 | 356 | | | | |
| Yes | | | No | | 11,366 † | 6,000 | 18 | 344 | | | | |
| Yes | | | Yes | | | 8,442 | | | Yes | | | None |
| Yes | Yes | | Yes | Yes | 35,176 | 12,260 | 12 | 1165 | Yes | 12 | $22,737 | None |
| Yes | Yes | Yes | Yes | Yes | 9,390 † | 10,800 | 12 | 303 | Yes | | | 6/30 |
| Yes | Yes | Yes | Yes | Yes | 28,510 | 13,138 | 65 | 937 | Yes | 47 | $19,097 | None |
| Yes | Yes | | Yes | Yes | 17,410 † | 7,440 | 12 | | Yes | | | 7/1 |
| | | | Yes | | 12,200 † | 8,600 | | 390 | Yes | | | None |
| | Yes | | No | | 5,878 ‡ | 2,100 | | 356 | | | | |
| | | | | | 19,500 † | | | 675 | | | | |
| Yes | | | No | | 11,198 † | | | 356 | | | | |
| Yes | Yes | | Yes | Yes | 22,396 † | 9,256 | 9 | 828 | | | | |

† Actual for 2016-17.     ‡ Estimated for 2017-18.     * Includes room and board

| Institution | Control/ degrees | Undergraduates | | Tests required (Fall 2017) | TOEFL | | Application | |
|---|---|---|---|---|---|---|---|---|
| | | Total | Internat'l | | minimum | average | Deadline | Fee |
| Clayton State University | Pu/AB | 5,723 | 74 | TOEFL | | | | 40 |
| Coastal Pines Technical College | Pu/A | 2,783 | | | | | | 24 |
| College of Coastal Georgia | Pu/AB | 3,478 | | TOEFL, SAT/ACT | 69 | | None | 25 |
| Columbus State University | Pu/AB | 6,529 | | TOEFL | 79 | | 6/1 | 40 |
| Columbus Technical College | Pu/A | 3,739 | | TOEFL | | | | 15 |
| Covenant College | Pr/B | 981 | 30 | TOEFL, SAT/ACT | | | | 35 |
| Darton State College | Pu/AB | 6,195 | | TOEFL | 54 | | | 20 |
| DeVry University: Decatur | Pr/AB | 1,684 | | TOEFL | | | | 50 |
| East Georgia State College | Pu/AB | 2,885 | | TOEFL, SAT/ACT | 70 | | | 20 |
| Emory University | Pr/B | 6,717 | 1,093 | TOEFL, SAT/ACT | | 100 | 1/1 | 75 |
| Fort Valley State University | Pu/AB | 3,250 | | TOEFL, SAT/ACT | | | | 20 |
| Georgia College and State University | Pu/B | 5,923 | 37 | TOEFL | 79 | 93 | 4/1 | 40 |
| Georgia Gwinnett College | Pu/B | 11,444 | 237 | TOEFL | 74 | 80 | | 20 |
| Georgia Highlands College | Pu/AB | 6,014 | | TOEFL, SAT/ACT | 80 | | 8/1 | 30 |
| Georgia Institute of Technology | Pu/B | 14,766 | 1,480 | | | | 1/1 | 85 |
| Georgia Military College | Pu/AB | 6,519 | 22 | TOEFL | | | | 35 |
| Georgia Perimeter College | Pu/A | 21,088 | | TOEFL | | | | 20 |
| Georgia Piedmont Technical College | Pu/A | 4,050 | | | | | | 25 |
| Georgia Southern University | Pu/B | 17,349 | 279 | TOEFL | 69 | | 5/1 | 30 |
| Georgia Southwestern State University | Pu/B | 2,413 | 45 | TOEFL | 70 | | 7/1 | 25 |
| Georgia State University | Pu/AB | 24,729 | 553 | TOEFL, SAT/ACT | 79 | 83 | 3/1 | 60 |
| Gordon State College | Pu/AB | 3,890 | | TOEFL | 71 | | | 30 |
| Gupton Jones College of Funeral Service | Pr/A | 215 | | | | | | 50 |
| Gwinnett College | Pr/A | 115 | | | | | None | |
| Gwinnett Technical College | Pu/A | 7,234 | | | | | | 20 |
| Herzing University: Atlanta | Pr/AB | 602 | | TOEFL | | | | |
| Kennesaw State University | Pu/B | 31,613 | 506 | TOEFL, SAT/ACT | 79 | | 6/16 | 40 |
| LaGrange College | Pr/B | 902 | 7 | TOEFL | 61 | | | |
| Le Cordon Bleu College of Culinary Arts: Atlanta | Pr/A | 1,108 | | | | | | 50 |
| Life University | Pr/AB | 718 | 39 | TOEFL, SAT/ACT | 90 | | 8/15 | 50 |
| Mercer University | Pr/B | 3,032 | 95 | TOEFL | 80 | | 6/1 | 50 |
| Middle Georgia State University | Pu/AB | 7,164 | | TOEFL, SAT/ACT | 69 | | | 20 |
| Morehouse College | Pr/B | 2,104 | 35 | TOEFL, SAT/ACT | | 78 | 2/1 | 50 |
| Oglethorpe University | Pr/B | 1,147 | | TOEFL | 79 | | | 50 |
| Oxford College of Emory University | Pr/A | 978 | 160 | TOEFL, SAT/ACT | 100 | | 1/1 | 75 |
| Paine College | Pr/B | 419 | 12 | TOEFL, SAT/ACT | 61 | | 7/1 | 40 |
| Piedmont College | Pr/B | 1,276 | | TOEFL, SAT/ACT | 80 | 100 | | |
| Point University | Pr/B | 1,358 | 30 | TOEFL | 80 | | 7/1 | |
| Reinhardt University | Pr/AB | 1,326 | 2 | TOEFL | | | | 25 |
| Savannah College of Art and Design | Pr/B | 10,483 | 2,165 | TOEFL, SAT/ACT | 85 | | None | 40 |
| Savannah State University | Pu/AB | 4,611 | | TOEFL, SAT/ACT | 70 | | | |
| Savannah Technical College | Pu/A | 4,784 | | | | | | 20 |
| Shorter University | Pr/AB | 1,342 | 45 | TOEFL, SAT/ACT | 61 | | 7/15 | 25 |
| South Georgia State College | Pu/AB | 2,648 | | TOEFL | 70 | | | 20 |
| South University: Savannah | Pr/AB | 777 | | TOEFL | | | | 50 |
| Southeastern Technical College | Pu/A | 1,542 | | TOEFL | 61 | | 3/31 | 25 |
| Southern Crescent Technical College | Pu/A | 4,899 | | | | | | 20 |
| Southern Regional Technical College | Pu/A | 2,337 | | | | | | 20 |
| Spelman College | Pr/B | 2,122 | | TOEFL, SAT/ACT | 120 | | | 35 |
| Thomas University | Pr/AB | 769 | | TOEFL | | | | 125 |
| Toccoa Falls College | Pr/AB | 796 | 10 | TOEFL | | | 8/1 | 25 |
| Truett McConnell University | Pr/B | 740 | 14 | TOEFL, SAT/ACT | | | | 25 |
| University of Georgia | Pu/B | 27,828 | 468 | TOEFL, SAT/ACT | 80 | | | 60 |
| University of North Georgia | Pu/AB | 17,648 | 274 | TOEFL, SAT/ACT | 79 | | | 30 |
| University of Phoenix: Atlanta | Pr/B | 2,523 | | | | | | |
| University of Phoenix: Augusta | Pr/B | 930 | | | | | | |
| University of Phoenix: Columbus | Pr/B | 1,000 | | | | | | |

| Student services | | | Housing | | Academic year costs | | Maximum credits/ summer | Credit hour charge | International financial aid | | | |
|---|---|---|---|---|---|---|---|---|---|---|---|---|
| Adviser | Orien-tation | ESL | Academic year | Summer | Tuition/ fees | Living costs | | | Avail-able | Number receiving aid | Average award | Deadline |
| Yes | Yes | | Yes | | 19,132 † | 9,742 | 12 | 590 | Yes | | | None |
| | | | No | | 11,178 † | | | 356 | | | | |
| Yes | Yes | | Yes | Yes | 12,692 † | 9,688 | | 378 | Yes | | | None |
| Yes | Yes | Yes | Yes | Yes | 20,294 † | 9,124 | 13 | 615 | Yes | 13 | $6,936 | None |
| | | | No | | 11,198 † | 11,000 | | 356 | | | | |
| Yes | | | Yes | Yes | 32,230 † | 9,630 | 3 | 1340 | Yes | 29 | $17,503 | None |
| Yes | Yes | Yes | Yes | Yes | 11,534 † | 10,070 | 15 | | Yes | | | None |
| Yes | | | | | 17,512 † | | | 609 | | | | |
| Yes | Yes | | Yes | | 11,356 † | 8,338 | | 344 | Yes | | | None |
| Yes | Yes | Yes | Yes | Yes | 49,392 | 14,894 | 16 | 2029 | Yes | 48 | $41,876 | 3/1 |
| Yes | Yes | | Yes | Yes | 19,386 † | 8,010 | 18 | 590 | | | | |
| Yes | Yes | | Yes | Yes | 27,550 † | 12,526 | 18 | | | | | |
| Yes | Yes | Yes | Yes | Yes | 16,052 † | 12,222 | | 479 | Yes | | | None |
| Yes | | | No | | 11,384 † | | 17 | 344 | | | | |
| Yes | Yes | Yes | Yes | Yes | 32,404 † | 11,088 | 16 | | | | | |
| | | | | | 6,128 † | | 15 | | | | | |
| Yes | Yes | Yes | No | | 11,400 † | | | 344 | Yes | | | 6/1 |
| Yes | | | No | | 11,194 † | 9,000 | | 356 | | | | |
| Yes | Yes | Yes | Yes | Yes | 20,536 † | 10,070 | 12 | 615 | Yes | 32 | $9,169 | None |
| | | Yes | Yes | Yes | 19,054 † | 7,672 | 18 | 590 | Yes | | | 6/15 |
| Yes | Yes | Yes | Yes | | 28,896 † | 10,972 | 18 | 893 | Yes | 162 | $4,260 | 4/1 |
| | | Yes | Yes | | 12,422 † | 6,370 | 18 | 378 | | | | |
| | | | No | | 11,150 ‡ | | | | | | | |
| | | | | | 9,850 † | 1,017 | | | | | | |
| | | | No | | 11,200 † | | | 356 | Yes | | | 7/8 |
| Yes | | | No | | | 9,594 | 16 | | | | | |
| Yes | Yes | Yes | Yes | Yes | 20,782 † | 10,500 | 12 | 626 | | | | |
| Yes | Yes | | Yes | Yes | 28,460 † | 11,440 | 17 | 1160 | Yes | 4 | $7,215 | None |
| Yes | Yes | Yes | Yes | Yes | 11,220 † | 12,450 | 20 | | Yes | 3 | $2,166 | |
| Yes | Yes | Yes | Yes | Yes | 35,130 † | 11,106 | 12 | 1161 | Yes | 25 | $27,165 | None |
| Yes | | | Yes | Yes | 13,328 † | 8,510 | 18 | 402 | Yes | | | 7/16 |
| Yes | | | Yes | | 27,278 ‡ | 13,557 | 9 | 1013 | Yes | | | 4/1 |
| Yes | Yes | Yes | Yes | Yes | 35,280 † | 12,710 | 16 | 1467 | Yes | | | None |
| Yes | Yes | | Yes | | 43,254 † | 13,006 | 16 | 1775 | Yes | | | 3/1 |
| Yes | | | Yes | | 14,224 † | 6,662 | 12 | 529 | Yes | | | None |
| Yes | | | Yes | Yes | 23,112 † | 11,400 | | 963 | Yes | 8 | $15,951 | None |
| | | | Yes | | 20,600 | 7,900 | | 650 | Yes | | | 12/31 |
| Yes | Yes | | | Yes | 21,644 † | 7,948 | 21 | 692 | Yes | | | None |
| Yes | Yes | Yes | Yes | Yes | 35,190 ‡ | 13,905 | 15 | 782 | Yes | | | None |
| Yes | Yes | | Yes | Yes | 19,436 † | 8,068 | | 590 | Yes | | | 4/1 |
| Yes | Yes | Yes | No | | 11,168 † | | 21 | 356 | Yes | | | None |
| Yes | Yes | | Yes | Yes | 21,910 † | 9,460 | 19 | | Yes | | | None |
| | | | Yes | | 11,350 † | 8,390 | | 344 | | | | |
| Yes | | | Yes | | | | | | Yes | | | None |
| Yes | | | | | 11,328 † | | 21 | 356 | | | | |
| | | | | | 11,208 † | 3,400 | | 356 | | | | |
| | | | | | 5,828 † | 7,440 | | 178 | | | | |
| Yes | Yes | | Yes | | 27,564 ‡ | 12,795 | | | Yes | 12 | $14,020 | None |
| Yes | | | Yes | Yes | 16,715 † | 4,800 | 15 | 630 | Yes | | | None |
| Yes | | | Yes | | 21,314 † | 7,635 | 12 | 863 | Yes | 12 | $13,465 | 8/1 |
| Yes | | | Yes | | 18,510 † | 7,220 | 12 | 595 | Yes | 16 | $17,980 | None |
| Yes | Yes | | Yes | Yes | 29,844 † | 9,600 | 9 | | | | | |
| Yes | Yes | Yes | Yes | Yes | 20,770 † | 7,812 | 20 | 630 | | | | |

† Actual for 2016-17.   ‡ Estimated for 2017-18.   * Includes room and board

| Institution | Control/ degrees | Undergraduates | | Tests required (Fall 2017) | TOEFL | | Application | |
|---|---|---|---|---|---|---|---|---|
| | | Total | Internat'l | | minimum | average | Deadline | Fee |
| University of Phoenix: Savannah | .Pr/B | 490 | | | | | | |
| University of West Georgia | .Pu/B | 11,155 | 125 | TOEFL, SAT/ACT | 69 | | None | 40 |
| Valdosta State University | .Pu/AB | 8,726 | 221 | TOEFL | 69 | | 6/1 | 40 |
| Virginia College in Augusta | .Pr/A | 902 | | | | | | 250 |
| Virginia College in Columbus | .Pr/A | 741 | | | | | | 100 |
| Virginia College in Macon | .Pr/A | 451 | | | | | | 100 |
| Virginia College in Savannah | .Pr/A | 620 | | | | | | 100 |
| Wesleyan College | .Pr/B | 608 | 103 | TOEFL, SAT/ACT | 80 | 92 | | 30 |
| Wiregrass Georgia Technical College | .Pu/A | 826 | | TOEFL | 61 | | None | 25 |
| Young Harris College | .Pr/AB | 1,200 | | TOEFL, SAT/ACT | 79 | 100 | | 30 |
| **Hawaii** | | | | | | | | |
| Argosy University: Hawaii | .Pr/AB | 431 | | | | | | 50 |
| Brigham Young University-Hawaii | .Pr/AB | 2,901 | | TOEFL | | | | 30 |
| Chaminade University of Honolulu | .Pr/AB | 1,167 | 17 | TOEFL, SAT/ACT | 79 | | None | 50 |
| Hawaii Pacific University | .Pr/AB | 3,384 | 372 | TOEFL | 80 | | | 50 |
| Hawaii Tokai International College | .Pr/A | 80 | 69 | | 45 | 55 | 6/1 | 100 |
| Remington College: Honolulu | .Pr/AB | 763 | | TOEFL | | | | 50 |
| University of Hawaii at Hilo | .Pu/B | 3,260 | | | 61 | 73 | | 50 |
| University of Hawaii at Manoa | .Pu/B | 12,767 | 334 | TOEFL, SAT/ACT | 61 | | 1/5 | 70 |
| University of Hawaii: Hawaii Community College | .Pu/A | 2,758 | | TOEFL | 61 | | 4/15 | 25 |
| University of Hawaii: Honolulu Community College | .Pu/A | 4,144 | | TOEFL | | | | 25 |
| University of Hawaii: Kapiolani Community College | .Pu/A | 7,994 | | TOEFL | | | | 50 |
| University of Hawaii: Kauai Community College | .Pu/A | 1,425 | | TOEFL | 45 | | | 25 |
| University of Hawaii: Leeward Community College | .Pu/A | 5,789 | | TOEFL | 61 | | | 25 |
| University of Hawaii: Maui College | .Pu/AB | 2,825 | | TOEFL | 61 | | 11/1 | 25 |
| University of Hawaii: West Oahu | .Pu/B | 2,757 | 12 | TOEFL | 79 | | 6/15 | 50 |
| University of Hawaii: Windward Community College | .Pu/A | 2,610 | | TOEFL | | | | 25 |
| University of Phoenix: Hawaii | .Pr/B | 1,408 | | | | | | |
| **Idaho** | | | | | | | | |
| Boise State University | .Pu/AB | 16,053 | 634 | TOEFL, SAT/ACT | 61 | | 5/15 | 85 |
| Brigham Young University-Idaho | .Pr/AB | 32,042 | 2,813 | TOEFL | 66 | | 2/1 | 35 |
| Broadview University: Boise | .Pr/AB | 142 | | | | | | 50 |
| Brown Mackie College: Boise | .Pr/AB | | | | | | | |
| Carrington College: Boise | .Pr/A | 494 | | | | | | |
| College of Idaho | .Pr/B | 953 | 69 | TOEFL | 79 | | None | |
| College of Southern Idaho | .Pu/A | 4,159 | 40 | TOEFL | 45 | | | |
| College of Western Idaho | .Pu/A | 8,777 | 33 | | | | | 25 |
| Idaho State University | .Pu/AB | 8,314 | 796 | TOEFL | 61 | | None | 50 |
| Lewis-Clark State College | .Pu/AB | 3,038 | 66 | TOEFL | 61 | | | 45 |
| New Saint Andrews College | .Pr/AB | 136 | | TOEFL, SAT/ACT | | | | 50 |
| North Idaho College | .Pu/A | 5,779 | | TOEFL | | | | 25 |
| Northwest Nazarene University | .Pr/AB | 1,481 | | TOEFL, SAT/ACT | | | | 40 |
| Stevens-Henager College: Boise | .Pr/AB | 350 | | TOEFL | | | | 100 |
| University of Idaho | .Pu/B | 7,735 | | TOEFL | 70 | | 5/1 | 70 |
| University of Phoenix: Idaho | .Pr/B | 410 | | | | | | |
| **Illinois** | | | | | | | | |
| American Academy of Art | .Pr/B | 297 | | TOEFL | 61 | | | 25 |
| American InterContinental University | .Pr/AB | 10,876 | | TOEFL | | | | |
| Argosy University: Chicago | .Pr/B | 247 | | TOEFL | 61 | | | 50 |
| Argosy University: Schaumburg | .Pr/B | 90 | | | | | | 50 |
| Augustana College | .Pr/B | 2,522 | 120 | TOEFL, SAT/ACT | 80 | 85 | None | |

| | Student services | | | Housing | | Academic year costs | | Maximum credits/ summer | Credit hour charge | International financial aid | | | |
|---|---|---|---|---|---|---|---|---|---|---|---|---|---|
| Adviser | Orientation | ESL | Academic year | Summer | Tuition/ fees | Living costs | | | | Available | Number receiving aid | Average award | Deadline |
| Yes | | | Yes | Yes | 20,406 † | 10,352 | 18 | 615 | Yes | | | | 7/1 |
| Yes | Yes | Yes | Yes | Yes | 20,560 † | 7,840 | | 615 | | | | | |
| | | | No | | | | 12 | | | | | | |
| Yes | Yes | | Yes | Yes | 21,750 † | 11,290 | 12 | | Yes | 51 | $9,784 | 6/1 |
| Yes | | Yes | No | | 11,288 † | | | 356 | Yes | | | None |
| Yes | | | Yes | | 29,217 † | 11,576 | 6 | | Yes | | | None |
| Yes | Yes | Yes | Yes | Yes | 5,240 † | 6,050 | 9 | | Yes | | | 3/15 |
| Yes | | | Yes | Yes | 23,310 † | 12,690 | 12 | 773 | Yes | 25 | $15,608 | None |
| Yes | Yes | Yes | Yes | | 23,440 † | 13,898 | 21 | 775 | Yes | | | None |
| Yes | Yes | Yes | Yes | Yes | 12,885 | 9,000 | 10 | | Yes | | | None |
| | | | No | | | | | | | | | |
| Yes | Yes | Yes | Yes | Yes | 20,580 † | 8,786 | 12 | 840 | Yes | | | None |
| Yes | Yes | Yes | Yes | Yes | 33,764 † | 13,975 | 16 | 1371 | Yes | | | None |
| Yes | Yes | Yes | Yes | Yes | 10,260 † | | 10 | 340 | | | | |
| | | | No | | 10,230 † | | 6 | 340 | | | | |
| Yes | Yes | | | | 10,260 † | | 6 | 340 | | | | |
| Yes | Yes | | No | | 10,308 † | | 6 | 340 | | | | |
| Yes | Yes | Yes | No | | 10,260 † | | | 340 | Yes | | | None |
| Yes | Yes | Yes | | Yes | 10,326 † | 14,662 | 6 | 340 | Yes | | | 4/1 |
| Yes | | | No | | 20,400 † | | 18 | 840 | | | | |
| | | | No | | 10,240 † | | | 340 | Yes | | | None |
| Yes | Yes | Yes | Yes | Yes | 21,530 † | 7,566 | 12 | 567 | Yes | 37 | $5,731 | None |
| Yes | Yes | | Yes | Yes | 3,920 † | 4,000 | 21 | 163 | Yes | | | None |
| | | | No | | | 5,148 | | | | | | |
| Yes | Yes | Yes | Yes | | 28,755 | 10,834 | 6 | 1165 | Yes | | | None |
| Yes | Yes | Yes | Yes | | 8,400 † | 5,590 | | 280 | Yes | | | None |
| | | | | | 9,180 ‡ | | | | Yes | | | None |
| Yes | Yes | Yes | Yes | Yes | 21,023 † | 6,663 | | 576 | Yes | 53 | $5,377 | None |
| Yes | Yes | Yes | Yes | Yes | 17,620 † | 7,392 | 15 | | Yes | 64 | $4,000 | 4/1 |
| | | | No | | 12,350 | 4,500 | | 475 | Yes | 2 | $5,750 | 3/1 |
| Yes | Yes | Yes | Yes | | 10,200 † | 7,500 | 6 | | Yes | | | None |
| Yes | | | Yes | | 29,000 | 7,000 | 6 | 1200 | Yes | 40 | $19,571 | None |
| | | | No | | | | | | | | | |
| Yes | Yes | Yes | Yes | Yes | 22,040 † | 8,354 | 18 | 1042 | Yes | 113 | $5,400 | None |
| | | | Yes | | 33,100 | | 16 | | | | | |
| Yes | Yes | | | | | | | | | | | |
| Yes | Yes | Yes | Yes | Yes | 39,621 † | 11,037 | 9 | 1700 | Yes | 86 | $24,502 | None |

† Actual for 2016-17.  ‡ Estimated for 2017-18.  * Includes room and board

| Institution | Control/ degrees | Undergraduates | | Tests required (Fall 2017) | TOEFL | | Application | |
|---|---|---|---|---|---|---|---|---|
| | | Total | Internat'l | | minimum | average | Deadline | Fee |
| Aurora University | Pr/B | 3,784 | 9 | TOEFL | 79 | | | |
| Benedictine University | Pr/AB | 3,132 | 21 | TOEFL | 79 | 82 | | 40 |
| Benedictine University at Springfield | Pr/AB | 788 | | TOEFL | | | | 50 |
| Black Hawk College | Pu/A | 3,397 | 6 | | 80 | | 6/1 | 20 |
| Blackburn College | Pr/B | 588 | 7 | TOEFL | | | | |
| Blessing-Rieman College of Nursing & Health Sciences | Pr/AB | 255 | | TOEFL | 80 | | | |
| Bradley University | Pr/B | 4,464 | 66 | TOEFL | 79 | 99 | 6/1 | 50 |
| Carl Sandburg College | Pu/A | 1,927 | | TOEFL | | | | |
| Chamberlain College of Nursing: Addison | Pr/B | 14,255 | 37 | | | | | 95 |
| Chamberlain College of Nursing: Chicago | Pr/B | 939 | 9 | | | | | 95 |
| Chamberlain College Of Nursing: Tinley Park | Pr/B | 664 | | | | | | 95 |
| Chicago State University | Pu/B | 3,462 | | TOEFL | 70 | | | 30 |
| City Colleges of Chicago: Harold Washington College | Pu/A | 7,943 | | TOEFL | | | | |
| City Colleges of Chicago: Kennedy-King College | Pu/A | 2,821 | | TOEFL | | | | |
| City Colleges of Chicago: Malcolm X College | Pu/A | 4,027 | | TOEFL | | | | |
| City Colleges of Chicago: Olive-Harvey College | Pu/A | 2,149 | | | | | | |
| City Colleges of Chicago: Richard J. Daley College | Pu/A | 3,953 | | TOEFL | | | | |
| City Colleges of Chicago: Wilbur Wright College | Pu/A | 7,691 | | TOEFL | | | | |
| College of DuPage | Pu/A | 14,442 | 221 | | 79 | | | 20 |
| College of Lake County | Pu/A | 15,410 | | | | | | |
| College of Office Technology | Pr/A | | | | | | | 50 |
| Columbia College Chicago | Pr/B | 7,739 | 266 | TOEFL | 80 | | 5/1 | 100 |
| Concordia University Chicago | Pr/B | 1,458 | | TOEFL, SAT/ACT | | | | |
| Coyne College | Pr/A | 590 | | | | | | |
| Danville Area Community College | Pu/A | 1,668 | | TOEFL | 61 | | 7/15 | |
| DePaul University | Pr/B | 15,151 | 543 | TOEFL | 80 | | | |
| DeVry University: Chicago | Pr/AB | 584 | 21 | TOEFL | | | | 50 |
| DeVry University: Online | Pr/AB | 11,908 | 101 | | | | | 40 |
| Dominican University | Pr/B | 2,288 | 69 | TOEFL | 79 | | 6/1 | 100 |
| East-West University | Pr/AB | 524 | | TOEFL | | | | 200 |
| Eastern Illinois University | Pu/B | 5,750 | | TOEFL | 61 | 78 | 5/15 | 30 |
| Elgin Community College | Pu/A | 8,057 | 42 | TOEFL | | | | 50 |
| Elmhurst College | Pr/B | 2,763 | | TOEFL | 79 | | 7/15 | |
| Eureka College | Pr/B | 664 | 7 | TOEFL | 79 | | 5/1 | |
| Governors State University | Pu/B | 3,467 | 42 | TOEFL, SAT/ACT | 68 | 75 | 4/1 | 25 |
| Greenville College | Pr/B | 961 | 33 | TOEFL | | | | |
| Harper College | Pu/A | 10,172 | | TOEFL | | | | 25 |
| Heartland Community College | Pu/A | 3,649 | 32 | TOEFL | 79 | | 6/15 | |
| Illinois Central College | Pu/A | 7,211 | | TOEFL | | | None | |
| Illinois College | Pr/B | 952 | 38 | TOEFL | 79 | 96 | | |
| Illinois Eastern Community Colleges: Frontier Community College | Pu/A | 364 | | TOEFL | | | None | 100 |
| Illinois Eastern Community Colleges: Lincoln Trail College | Pu/A | 514 | | TOEFL | | | None | 100 |
| Illinois Eastern Community Colleges: Olney Central College | Pu/A | 735 | | TOEFL | | | None | 100 |
| Illinois Eastern Community Colleges: Wabash Valley College | Pu/A | 636 | | TOEFL | | | | 100 |
| Illinois Institute of Art: Chicago | Pr/AB | 1,807 | | TOEFL | | | | 150 |
| Illinois Institute of Art: Schaumburg | Pr/AB | 902 | | TOEFL | | | | |
| Illinois Institute of Technology | Pr/B | 2,800 | 602 | TOEFL | 80 | | | |
| Illinois State University | Pu/B | 18,571 | 76 | TOEFL, SAT/ACT | 79 | | 4/1 | 50 |
| Illinois Wesleyan University | Pr/B | 1,763 | 159 | TOEFL, SAT/ACT | 80 | 96 | | |

| Student services | | | Housing | | Academic year costs | | Maximum credits/ summer | Credit hour charge | International financial aid | | | |
|---|---|---|---|---|---|---|---|---|---|---|---|---|
| Adviser | Orientation | ESL | Academic year | Summer | Tuition/ fees | Living costs | | | Available | Number receiving aid | Average award | Deadline |
| Yes | | | Yes | Yes | 23,520‡ | 11,470 | 8 | 670 | Yes | 9 | $10,055 | None |
| Yes | Yes | Yes | Yes | Yes | 33,900‡ | 9,200 | 12 | 1030 | Yes | | | None |
| Yes | Yes | | Yes | Yes | 32,170† | 8,930 | 12 | 1030 | | | | |
| Yes | Yes | Yes | No | | 7,650† | 6,676 | 12 | 255 | Yes | 16 | $2,183 | None |
| Yes | | | Yes | | 21,992 | 7,660 | 6 | 720 | Yes | | | None |
| | | | | | 22,900† | | | 763 | | | | |
| Yes | Yes | | Yes | Yes | 32,120† | 10,010 | 15 | 850 | | | | |
| Yes | | Yes | No | | 7,950† | | | 260 | Yes | | | None |
| | | | | | 19,500† | | | 675 | | | | |
| | | | | | 19,500† | | | 675 | | | | |
| | | | | | 18,160‡ | | | 665 | | | | |
| Yes | Yes | | Yes | | 20,716† | 8,724 | 6 | 584 | Yes | | | None |
| | | | No | | 17,906† | | | | | | | |
| | | Yes | | | 17,906† | | | | | | | |
| | | | | | 17,906† | | 6 | | | | | |
| | | | | | 17,906† | | | | | | | |
| | | | | | 17,906† | | | | | | | |
| | | | | | 17,906† | | | | | | | |
| Yes | Yes | Yes | No | | 11,760 | 8,818 | 18 | 392 | Yes | 10 | $1,248 | None |
| Yes | Yes | Yes | No | | 12,390† | 5,180 | 6 | 390 | Yes | | | None |
| Yes | Yes | Yes | Yes | Yes | 25,294† | 13,298 | 12 | | | | | |
| Yes | | | Yes | Yes | 30,640† | 9,172 | 16 | 899 | Yes | | | 6/1 |
| | | | No | | | | | | | | | |
| Yes | | | No | | 7,050† | | 9 | 220 | Yes | | | None |
| Yes | Yes | Yes | Yes | Yes | 37,020† | 14,277 | 16 | 600 | | | | |
| Yes | | Yes | | Yes | 17,512† | | | 609 | | | | |
| | | | | | 17,512† | | | 690 | | | | |
| Yes | Yes | Yes | Yes | Yes | 32,530‡ | 11,542 | 12 | 1072 | Yes | 4 | $13,853 | None |
| Yes | | | No | | 20,820† | 8,811 | 16 | | | | | |
| Yes | Yes | Yes | Yes | | 13,740† | 9,546 | 15 | 361 | | | | |
| Yes | Yes | Yes | No | | 14,952† | | | 498 | | | | |
| Yes | Yes | | Yes | Yes | 36,295‡ | 10,144 | 8 | 1026 | Yes | 9 | $15,528 | None |
| Yes | Yes | | Yes | Yes | 25,390‡ | 9,370 | | 700 | Yes | 6 | $4,033 | None |
| Yes | Yes | Yes | Yes | Yes | 18,676† | 7,058 | 16 | 544 | Yes | 3 | $4,597 | 10/1 |
| | | | Yes | Yes | 26,356 | 8,922 | 12 | | Yes | | | None |
| | | | No | | 14,090† | | | 451.75 | | | | |
| Yes | | Yes | No | | 12,420† | 8,700 | 9 | 405 | | | | |
| Yes | Yes | Yes | Yes | Yes | 10,500† | 7,200 | 10 | 350 | Yes | | | None |
| Yes | Yes | | Yes | Yes | 32,140 | 9,190 | 6 | 970 | Yes | 43 | $22,365 | None |
| Yes | Yes | Yes | No | | 10,678† | 6,121 | 9 | 331 | Yes | | | None |
| Yes | Yes | Yes | No | | 10,678† | 6,121 | 9 | 331 | Yes | | | None |
| Yes | Yes | Yes | No | | 10,678† | 6,121 | 9 | 331 | Yes | | | None |
| Yes | Yes | Yes | No | | 10,678† | 6,121 | 9 | 331 | Yes | | | None |
| Yes | | | | | | | 9 | | Yes | | | None |
| | | | Yes | | | | | | | | | |
| Yes | Yes | Yes | Yes | Yes | 44,884† | 11,612 | 9 | 1359 | Yes | 691 | $20,414 | None |
| Yes | Yes | Yes | Yes | Yes | 25,168† | 9,948 | 9 | 740.5 | Yes | | | None |
| Yes | Yes | | Yes | Yes | 45,856 | 10,574 | | 1427 | Yes | 149 | $20,144 | None |

† Actual for 2016-17.   ‡ Estimated for 2017-18.   * Includes room and board

| Institution | Control/ degrees | Undergraduates | | Tests required (Fall 2017) | TOEFL | | Application | |
|---|---|---|---|---|---|---|---|---|
| | | Total | Internat'l | | minimum | average | Deadline | Fee |
| International Academy of Design and Technology: Chicago | Pr/AB | 229 | | TOEFL | | | | 50 |
| John A. Logan College | Pu/A | 2,600 | | TOEFL | | | | |
| John Wood Community College | Pu/A | 1,968 | | TOEFL | | | | |
| Joliet Junior College | Pu/A | 14,944 | | TOEFL | | | | |
| Judson University | Pr/AB | 1,093 | 43 | TOEFL | 79 | | | 50 |
| Kankakee Community College | Pu/A | 2,457 | 4 | TOEFL | 68 | | | 250 |
| Kaskaskia College | Pu/A | 1,949 | | TOEFL | 79 | | 6/1 | |
| Kendall College | Pr/AB | 1,516 | | TOEFL | 71 | | | 50 |
| Kishwaukee College | Pu/A | 4,900 | | TOEFL | | | | 15 |
| Knox College | Pr/B | 1,334 | 186 | TOEFL | 80 | | None | 50 |
| Lake Forest College | Pr/B | 1,514 | 116 | TOEFL, SAT/ACT | 83 | 98 | | |
| Lake Land College | Pu/A | 5,107 | | TOEFL | 61 | | | |
| Le Cordon Bleu College of Culinary Arts: Chicago | Pr/A | 958 | | TOEFL | 61 | | | 50 |
| Lewis University | Pr/AB | 4,433 | 57 | TOEFL, SAT/ACT | 79 | | None | 40 |
| Lincoln Christian University | Pr/AB | 446 | 19 | TOEFL | 75 | | 3/1 | 25 |
| Lincoln College | Pr/AB | 995 | | TOEFL, SAT/ACT | 55 | 63 | | 25 |
| Lincoln Land Community College | Pu/A | 6,447 | | TOEFL | | | | |
| Loyola University Chicago | Pr/AB | 10,906 | 536 | TOEFL, SAT/ACT | 79 | 92 | | |
| MacCormac College | Pr/A | 216 | | TOEFL | 61 | | | 20 |
| McHenry County College | Pu/A | 4,483 | 2 | TOEFL | 79 | | None | 15 |
| McKendree University | Pr/AB | 2,243 | 61 | TOEFL, SAT/ACT | 70 | 84 | | |
| Methodist College | Pr/B | 672 | | | | | | 50 |
| Midstate College | Pr/AB | 521 | | | | | | 25 |
| Millikin University | Pr/B | 1,917 | 35 | TOEFL | 79 | | 6/1 | |
| Monmouth College | Pr/B | 1,133 | 80 | TOEFL | 79 | 100 | | |
| Moody Bible Institute | Pr/AB | 2,850 | | TOEFL | 79 | | | 50 |
| Moraine Valley Community College | Pu/A | 11,556 | | | | | 7/18 | 25 |
| Morrison Institute of Technology | Pr/A | 86 | | TOEFL | | | | 100 |
| Morton College | Pu/A | 3,371 | | TOEFL | | | | 10 |
| National-Louis University | Pr/B | 1,405 | 10 | TOEFL | 61 | | | 40 |
| North Central College | Pr/B | 2,626 | 48 | TOEFL | 79 | | 4/15 | 25 |
| North Park University | Pr/B | 2,152 | | TOEFL | 80 | | | 40 |
| Northern Illinois University | Pu/B | 14,036 | 259 | TOEFL | | | | 40 |
| Northwestern College | Pr/A | 671 | 1 | TOEFL | 79 | | | 100 |
| Northwestern University | Pr/B | 8,351 | 818 | TOEFL, SAT/ACT | | | 1/1 | 75 |
| Oakton Community College | Pu/A | 9,363 | | TOEFL | 68 | | | 50 |
| Olivet Nazarene University | Pr/AB | 3,348 | 37 | TOEFL, ACT | 61 | | | 25 |
| Parkland College | Pu/A | 6,990 | 25 | | 61 | | | 40 |
| Prairie State College | Pu/A | 4,571 | | TOEFL | | | | 10 |
| Quincy University | Pr/AB | 1,161 | | TOEFL | 61 | 88 | | 25 |
| Rasmussen College: Aurora | Pr/AB | 410 | | | | | | |
| Rasmussen College: Mokena/Tinley Park | Pr/AB | 396 | | TOEFL | | | | |
| Rasmussen College: Rockford | Pr/AB | 429 | | TOEFL | | | | |
| Rasmussen College: Romeoville/Joliet | Pr/AB | 542 | | TOEFL | | | | |
| Resurrection University | Pr/B | 603 | | | | | | 50 |
| Richland Community College | Pu/A | 2,606 | | TOEFL | 61 | | | |
| Robert Morris University: Chicago | Pr/AB | 2,345 | 17 | TOEFL | 80 | 85 | None | 100 |
| Rock Valley College | Pu/A | 6,516 | | | 79 | | | |
| Rockford University | Pr/B | 1,039 | 29 | TOEFL | 79 | | | 50 |
| Roosevelt University | Pr/B | 2,710 | 110 | TOEFL | 80 | | 7/1 | 25 |
| Rush University | Pr/B | 122 | | TOEFL | | | | 40 |
| St. Augustine College | Pr/AB | 1,754 | | | | | | |
| Saint Xavier University | Pr/B | 2,974 | | TOEFL | | | | 25 |
| Sauk Valley Community College | Pu/A | 1,491 | 1 | TOEFL | 66 | | 8/1 | |
| School of the Art Institute of Chicago | Pr/B | 2,842 | 920 | TOEFL | 82 | | | 85 |
| Shimer College | Pr/B | 63 | | TOEFL | | | | 25 |

| Adviser | Orientation | ESL | Housing Academic year | Housing Summer | Tuition/ fees | Living costs | Maximum credits/ summer | Credit hour charge | Available | Number receiving aid | Average award | Deadline |
|---|---|---|---|---|---|---|---|---|---|---|---|---|
| Yes | | | | | | | 16 | | Yes | | | None |
| | | Yes | No | | 12,152† | | | 400.08 | | | | |
| | | Yes | No | | 8,010† | | 10 | 267 | | | | |
| Yes | Yes | | No | | 11,187† | | 9 | 341.9 | Yes | | | 6/12 |
| Yes | Yes | | Yes | Yes | 29,434‡ | 12,840 | | 1145 | Yes | | | 5/1 |
| Yes | Yes | | Yes | No | 20,143† | 6,000 | 9 | 648 | Yes | | | 7/13 |
| Yes | | | No | | 12,330† | | 9 | 395 | Yes | | | None |
| Yes | Yes | | Yes | Yes | 25,278† | 10,500 | | 655 | | | | |
| Yes | Yes | Yes | No | | 11,970† | | 9 | 387 | | | | |
| Yes | Yes | | Yes | Yes | 44,958 | 9,696 | | 5892 | Yes | 183 | $25,484 | None |
| Yes | Yes | | Yes | Yes | 44,116† | 9,810 | 12 | | Yes | | | 5/1 |
| Yes | Yes | Yes | No | | 13,616 | | 10 | | | | | |
| Yes | | | No | | | 6,904 | | | Yes | | | None |
| Yes | Yes | Yes | Yes | Yes | 31,250 | 10,460 | 8 | 913 | Yes | 29 | $23,614 | 5/1 |
| Yes | | | Yes | | 13,020† | 7,564 | 3 | 434 | Yes | | | None |
| Yes | | | Yes | | 17,700† | 10,100 | 9 | | | | | |
| | | Yes | No | | 10,680† | 6,975 | 10 | 345 | | | | |
| Yes | Yes | Yes | Yes | | 43,078 | 14,080 | 12 | 770 | Yes | | | None |
| Yes | | Yes | No | | 12,820† | | 16 | | | | | |
| | | Yes | No | | 14,003‡ | 12,164 | 9 | 458 | | | | |
| Yes | Yes | | Yes | Yes | 28,740† | 11,200 | 12 | 910 | Yes | 62 | $21,264 | None |
| | | | | | 20,650† | 6,290 | | 640 | | | | |
| | | | No | | 16,230† | | | 381.25 | Yes | | | None |
| Yes | Yes | Yes | Yes | Yes | 33,166 | 11,498 | 9 | 465 | Yes | 19 | $12,534 | None |
| Yes | Yes | Yes | Yes | | 36,400 | 11,820 | | | Yes | | | None |
| Yes | Yes | | Yes | Yes | 12,630† | 11,680 | 9 | 320 | Yes | | | None |
| Yes | Yes | Yes | No | | 11,292‡ | 5,000 | 12 | 356 | Yes | | | None |
| | | | Yes | Yes | 15,790† | 5,400 | | | | | | |
| Yes | | Yes | No | | 9,420† | 7,556 | 19 | 280 | | | | |
| Yes | | Yes | No | | 18,000† | | 21 | | | | | |
| Yes | Yes | Yes | Yes | Yes | 36,654† | 10,356 | 9 | 1013 | Yes | 49 | $22,483 | None |
| Yes | Yes | Yes | Yes | Yes | 26,840† | 13,310 | 12 | 850 | Yes | | | 8/1 |
| Yes | Yes | | Yes | | 21,727 | 9,784 | 12 | 697 | Yes | 91 | $15,514 | None |
| Yes | | | No | | | | 20 | | Yes | | | 6/30 |
| Yes | Yes | | Yes | | 50,855† | 15,489 | | | Yes | 93 | $47,878 | None |
| Yes | | | No | | 12,655† | 8,419 | | 415 | Yes | | | None |
| Yes | | | Yes | Yes | 34,940 | 8,800 | 12 | 1415 | Yes | 26 | $31,776 | None |
| Yes | Yes | Yes | No | | 15,870† | 5,500 | | 508.5 | | | | |
| Yes | | | No | | 12,735† | 6,264 | 9 | 399 | | | | |
| Yes | Yes | | Yes | Yes | 27,128† | 10,500 | 12 | 710 | Yes | | | None |
| | | | | | 13,455† | | | 299 | Yes | | | None |
| | | | | | 13,455† | | | 299 | Yes | | | None |
| | | | | | 13,455† | | | 299 | Yes | | | None |
| | | | | | 13,455† | | | 299 | Yes | | | None |
| | | | | | 25,632† | | | 849 | | | | |
| Yes | | Yes | No | | 14,640‡ | 5,400 | 6 | | | | | |
| Yes | | | Yes | Yes | 27,180 | 13,200 | 16 | 742 | Yes | 55 | $13,808 | None |
| Yes | | | No | | 15,584‡ | 7,614 | 9 | 509 | | | | |
| Yes | Yes | Yes | Yes | Yes | 30,050‡ | 9,820 | 9 | 785 | Yes | 17 | $11,739 | None |
| Yes | Yes | Yes | Yes | Yes | 28,119† | 15,427 | 12 | 759 | | | | |
| Yes | | | | | | | 12 | | | | | |
| Yes | | Yes | No | | 16,500† | | | 550 | | | | |
| Yes | Yes | | Yes | Yes | 32,250† | 11,060 | 6 | 680 | Yes | | | None |
| Yes | | Yes | | | 10,194‡ | | 9 | | Yes | | | None |
| Yes | Yes | Yes | Yes | | 45,750† | 13,100 | 9 | | Yes | 674 | $4,805 | None |
| Yes | | | Yes | Yes | 33,790† | 14,516 | | 1130 | Yes | | | None |

† Actual for 2016-17.    ‡ Estimated for 2017-18.    * Includes room and board

| Institution | Control/ degrees | Undergraduates | | Tests required (Fall 2017) | TOEFL | | Application | |
|---|---|---|---|---|---|---|---|---|
| | | Total | Internat'l | | minimum | average | Deadline | Fee |
| Southeastern Illinois College | Pu/A | 964 | 3 | TOEFL | | | None | |
| Southern Illinois University Carbondale | Pu/AB | 12,056 | 450 | TOEFL | 68 | | None | 40 |
| Southern Illinois University Edwardsville | Pu/B | 11,652 | 129 | TOEFL | 79 | | 7/1 | 40 |
| Southwestern Illinois College | Pu/A | 9,943 | | TOEFL | | | | |
| Spoon River College | Pu/A | 1,133 | | TOEFL | | | | |
| Taylor Business Institute | Pr/A | 257 | | | | | | 25 |
| Telshe Yeshiva-Chicago | Pr/B | 67 | | | | | | |
| Trinity Christian College | Pr/B | 1,085 | 17 | TOEFL | 79 | | | 30 |
| Trinity International University | Pr/B | 947 | 19 | TOEFL, SAT/ACT | 71 | | | 35 |
| Triton College | Pu/A | 9,880 | 18 | TOEFL | 61 | | | |
| University of Chicago | Pr/B | 5,930 | 717 | TOEFL, SAT/ACT | 100 | | | 75 |
| University of Illinois at Chicago | Pu/B | 17,804 | 479 | TOEFL, SAT/ACT | 80 | | | 50 |
| University of Illinois at Urbana-Champaign | Pu/B | 32,752 | 5,097 | | 80 | | 12/1 | 75 |
| University of Illinois: Springfield | Pu/B | 2,877 | 133 | TOEFL, SAT/ACT | 61 | | None | 60 |
| University of Phoenix: Chicago | Pr/B | 781 | | | | | | |
| University of St. Francis | Pr/B | 1,343 | 39 | TOEFL | 79 | | 6/15 | |
| VanderCook College of Music | Pr/B | 103 | 2 | TOEFL | 70 | | None | 35 |
| Vatterott College: Quincy | Pr/A | 200 | | | | | | |
| Western Illinois University | Pu/B | 8,543 | 141 | TOEFL | 73 | | 5/1 | 30 |
| Wheaton College | Pr/B | 2,432 | 76 | TOEFL | 95 | | 1/10 | 50 |

### Indiana

| Institution | Control/ degrees | Undergraduates | | Tests required (Fall 2017) | TOEFL | | Application | |
|---|---|---|---|---|---|---|---|---|
| | | Total | Internat'l | | minimum | average | Deadline | Fee |
| American National University: Fort Wayne | Pr/A | 26 | | | | | | 50 |
| American National University: Indianapolis | Pr/AB | 128 | | | | | | 50 |
| American National University: South Bend | Pr/A | 63 | | | | | | 50 |
| Ancilla College | Pr/A | 558 | | TOEFL | 79 | | None | |
| Ball State University | Pu/AB | 16,095 | | TOEFL | 79 | 85 | | 55 |
| Bethel College | Pr/AB | 1,335 | 17 | TOEFL | 76 | | 2/1 | |
| Brown Mackie College: Fort Wayne | Pr/AB | | | | | | | 20 |
| Brown Mackie College: Indianapolis | Pr/AB | | | | | | | |
| Brown Mackie College: Merrillville | Pr/AB | | | | | | | 20 |
| Butler University | Pr/AB | 4,235 | 36 | TOEFL, SAT/ACT | 79 | 98 | 7/1 | 35 |
| Calumet College of St. Joseph | Pr/AB | 744 | | TOEFL | 68 | 75 | | |
| Chamberlain College of Nursing: Indianapolis | Pr/B | 264 | | | | | | 95 |
| College of Court Reporting | Pr/A | 239 | | | | | | 50 |
| Crossroads Bible College | Pr/AB | 249 | | TOEFL | 70 | | | 80 |
| DePauw University | Pr/B | 2,181 | 180 | TOEFL, SAT/ACT | | | 2/1 | 40 |
| Earlham College | Pr/B | 994 | 225 | TOEFL | 80 | 100 | | |
| Fortis College: Indianapolis | Pr/A | 218 | | | | | | 25 |
| Franklin College | Pr/B | 977 | 11 | TOEFL | 79 | | None | 40 |
| Goshen College | Pr/B | 793 | 69 | TOEFL | 79 | | 7/1 | 25 |
| Hanover College | Pr/B | 1,083 | 41 | TOEFL, SAT/ACT | 80 | | | |
| Harrison College: Indianapolis | Pr/AB | 3,498 | | TOEFL | 65 | | | |
| Holy Cross College | Pr/AB | 601 | | TOEFL | 71 | 75 | | |
| Huntington University | Pr/AB | 924 | 47 | TOEFL | 65 | 88 | 8/1 | 25 |
| Indiana Institute of Technology | Pr/AB | 8,685 | | TOEFL | 70 | | | 50 |
| Indiana State University | Pu/B | 10,601 | 632 | TOEFL | 61 | | 6/15 | 65 |
| Indiana University Bloomington | Pu/AB | 32,924 | 3,533 | TOEFL, SAT/ACT | 79 | | None | 65 |
| Indiana University East | Pu/B | 3,082 | 28 | | 79 | | | 65 |
| Indiana University Kokomo | Pu/AB | 2,771 | 17 | TOEFL, SAT/ACT | 61 | | | 60 |
| Indiana University Northwest | Pu/AB | 3,727 | 12 | TOEFL, SAT/ACT | 71 | | 6/1 | 60 |
| Indiana University South Bend | Pu/AB | 4,981 | 151 | TOEFL | 71 | | | 60 |
| Indiana University Southeast | Pu/AB | 4,964 | 24 | TOEFL, SAT/ACT | 75 | | | 60 |
| Indiana University-Purdue University Fort Wayne | Pu/AB | 8,302 | | TOEFL | 79 | 99 | 8/1 | 50 |
| Indiana University-Purdue University Indianapolis | Pu/AB | 21,001 | 849 | TOEFL, SAT/ACT | 60 | | | 65 |
| Indiana Wesleyan University | Pr/AB | 2,679 | 26 | TOEFL, SAT/ACT | 79 | | 5/1 | 25 |
| International Business College | Pr/AB | 406 | | | | | | 50 |

| Student services | | | Housing | | Academic year costs | | Maximum credits/ summer | Credit hour charge | International financial aid | | | |
| Adviser | Orientation | ESL | Academic year | Summer | Tuition/ fees | Living costs | | | Available | Number receiving aid | Average award | Deadline |
|---|---|---|---|---|---|---|---|---|---|---|---|---|
| Yes | | | No | | 5,700† | | 12 | 180 | Yes | | | None |
| Yes | Yes | Yes | Yes | Yes | 25,880† | 10,186 | 12 | 758 | Yes | 86 | $18,865 | None |
| Yes | Yes | Yes | Yes | Yes | 23,536† | 10,491 | 12 | 696 | | | | None |
| Yes | | Yes | No | | 15,750† | | | 520 | Yes | | | 5/31 |
| Yes | | Yes | No | | 10,470† | | 9 | 324 | | | | |
| | | | | | 15,000† | | | | | | | |
| Yes | | Yes | Yes | Yes | 27,675† | 9,580 | | 908 | Yes | | | None |
| Yes | Yes | | Yes | Yes | 30,750† | 9,240 | 6 | 1260 | Yes | 19 | $17,761 | None |
| Yes | | Yes | No | | 11,629† | 6,346 | 12 | 371 | Yes | | | None |
| Yes | | Yes | Yes | | 52,491† | 15,093 | | | Yes | 126 | $62,736 | |
| Yes | Yes | Yes | Yes | | 26,520† | 10,960 | 12 | | Yes | 24 | $5,780 | None |
| Yes | Yes | Yes | Yes | Yes | 32,848‡ | 11,308 | 9 | | Yes | | | None |
| Yes | Yes | Yes | Yes | Yes | 20,938† | 11,600 | 8 | 631 | Yes | 33 | $6,837 | 11/15 |
| Yes | Yes | Yes | Yes | Yes | 30,840† | 9,084 | | 825 | Yes | 17 | $23,980 | None |
| | | | Yes | Yes | 28,344 | 12,074 | | 1115 | Yes | | | None |
| Yes | Yes | Yes | Yes | Yes | 15,515† | 9,580 | 6 | 427 | Yes | 34 | $8,170 | None |
| Yes | Yes | | Yes | | 34,050† | 12,848 | 8 | 1419 | Yes | 41 | $18,084 | None |
| | | | | | 15,411† | | | 317 | | | | |
| | | | | | 15,411† | | | 317 | | | | |
| | | | | | 15,411† | | | 317 | | | | |
| Yes | | | Yes | | 15,830 | 9,200 | 9 | | Yes | | | 3/10 |
| Yes | Yes | Yes | Yes | Yes | 25,428† | 9,936 | 12 | 980 | | | | |
| Yes | Yes | | Yes | Yes | 27,930 | 8,800 | | | Yes | 12 | $22,500 | 3/10 |
| | | | | | | 5,611 | | | | | | |
| | | | | | | 5,611 | | | | | | |
| Yes | | Yes | Yes | Yes | 40,175 | 13,030 | 12 | 1558 | Yes | | | None |
| Yes | | | | | 17,570† | 5,600 | 18 | 550 | Yes | | | None |
| | | | | | 19,500† | | | 675 | | | | |
| | | | No | | 12,400 | | | 395 | Yes | | | 3/10 |
| Yes | Yes | | Yes | | 47,838 | 12,529 | | 1470 | Yes | 176 | $18,769 | 2/1 |
| Yes | Yes | Yes | Yes | Yes | 45,300† | 11,570 | | 1479 | Yes | | | 3/1 |
| | | | | | | 9,153 | | | | | | |
| Yes | Yes | Yes | Yes | Yes | 30,920 | 9,630 | | 1135 | Yes | 7 | $21,247 | 3/10 |
| Yes | Yes | | Yes | Yes | 33,200‡ | 11,850 | 8 | 1380 | Yes | 65 | $23,398 | None |
| Yes | Yes | | Yes | Yes | 36,520 | 12,230 | | 993 | Yes | | | None |
| Yes | | | No | | | | | | Yes | | | None |
| Yes | | | Yes | | 28,760† | 10,500 | | | | | | |
| Yes | Yes | Yes | Yes | | 25,540‡ | 8,456 | 8 | | Yes | 47 | $18,836 | None |
| Yes | Yes | Yes | Yes | Yes | 26,370† | 9,580 | 9 | | Yes | | | None |
| Yes | Yes | Yes | Yes | Yes | 19,076† | 9,785 | 12 | 669 | | | | |
| Yes | Yes | Yes | Yes | Yes | 34,246† | 10,040 | | 1030 | Yes | 1035 | $4,448 | None |
| | | | No | | 18,683† | 7,170 | 18 | 603 | | 6 | $2,385 | |
| Yes | | Yes | No | | 18,683† | 7,170 | | 603 | | 9 | $2,327 | |
| | | | No | | 18,683† | 7,170 | 18 | 603 | | 1 | $17,786 | None |
| Yes | Yes | Yes | Yes | Yes | 18,683† | 7,222 | 12 | 603 | | 39 | $3,670 | |
| Yes | Yes | | Yes | | 18,683† | 6,520 | 12 | 603 | Yes | 6 | $3,656 | None |
| Yes | Yes | Yes | Yes | Yes | 19,727† | 9,340 | 12 | 622.75 | Yes | | | None |
| Yes | Yes | Yes | Yes | Yes | 29,791† | 8,462 | 12 | 958 | | 246 | $7,171 | |
| Yes | Yes | | Yes | Yes | 25,346† | 8,148 | 12 | | Yes | | | 3/10 |
| | | | | | | 5,980 | | | | | | |

† Actual for 2016-17.    ‡ Estimated for 2017-18.    * Includes room and board

| Institution | Control/ degrees | Undergraduates Total | Internat'l | Tests required (Fall 2017) | TOEFL minimum | average | Application Deadline | Fee |
|---|---|---|---|---|---|---|---|---|
| International Business College: Indianapolis | Pr/A | 399 | | | | | | 50 |
| Ivy Tech Community College: Bloomington | Pu/A | 3,940 | | TOEFL | 79 | | | |
| Ivy Tech Community College: Central Indiana | Pu/A | 16,060 | 1 | TOEFL | 79 | | 4/15 | |
| Ivy Tech Community College: Columbus | Pu/A | 2,095 | | TOEFL | 79 | | 4/15 | |
| Ivy Tech Community College: East Central | Pu/A | 4,941 | | TOEFL | 79 | | 4/15 | |
| Ivy Tech Community College: Kokomo | Pu/A | 2,075 | | TOEFL | 79 | | 4/15 | |
| Ivy Tech Community College: Lafayette | Pu/A | 3,804 | | TOEFL | 79 | | 4/15 | |
| Ivy Tech Community College: North Central | Pu/A | 4,555 | 1 | TOEFL | 79 | | | |
| Ivy Tech Community College: Northeast | Pu/A | 6,858 | 1 | TOEFL | 79 | | 4/15 | |
| Ivy Tech Community College: Northwest | Pu/A | 7,222 | | TOEFL | 79 | | 4/15 | |
| Ivy Tech Community College: Richmond | Pu/A | 1,613 | | TOEFL | 79 | | 4/15 | |
| Ivy Tech Community College: South Central | Pu/A | 3,616 | 2 | TOEFL | 79 | | 4/15 | |
| Ivy Tech Community College: Southeast | Pu/A | 1,794 | | TOEFL | 79 | | 4/15 | |
| Ivy Tech Community College: Southwest | Pu/A | 3,428 | | TOEFL | 79 | | | |
| Ivy Tech Community College: Wabash Valley | Pu/A | 3,127 | 1 | TOEFL | 79 | | | |
| Kaplan College: Hammond | Pr/A | 299 | | | | | | 10 |
| Lincoln College of Technology: Indianapolis | Pr/A | 1,199 | | | | | | 100 |
| Manchester University | Pr/AB | 1,254 | 50 | TOEFL | 79 | | 5/1 | 25 |
| Marian University | Pr/AB | 2,019 | 24 | TOEFL | 79 | | 6/1 | 35 |
| Martin University | Pr/B | 286 | | | | | | 25 |
| Mid-America College of Funeral Service | Pr/AB | 60 | | | | | | 50 |
| Oakland City University | Pr/AB | 496 | 21 | TOEFL, SAT/ACT | 70 | | | |
| Purdue University | Pu/AB | 29,866 | 5,129 | TOEFL | | | | 60 |
| Purdue University North Central | Pu/AB | 9,619 | 377 | TOEFL | 79 | | | 30 |
| Purdue University Northwest | Pu/B | 9,619 | 377 | TOEFL | | | | 25 |
| Rose-Hulman Institute of Technology | Pr/B | 2,186 | 281 | TOEFL, SAT/ACT | 80 | | 3/1 | 40 |
| Saint Joseph's College | Pr/AB | 948 | 26 | TOEFL | 80 | | | 35 |
| St. Mary-of-the-Woods College | Pr/AB | 569 | 5 | TOEFL | 62 | | | |
| Saint Mary's College | Pr/B | 1,576 | 24 | TOEFL | 80 | | 2/15 | |
| Taylor University | Pr/AB | 1,845 | 104 | TOEFL, SAT/ACT | 84 | | | 25 |
| Trine University | Pr/AB | 1,780 | | TOEFL | 79 | | 6/1 | |
| University of Evansville | Pr/AB | 2,164 | 329 | TOEFL | 61 | | | |
| University of Indianapolis | Pr/AB | 4,242 | 344 | TOEFL, SAT/ACT | 61 | 84 | | |
| University of Notre Dame | Pr/B | 8,496 | 494 | TOEFL, SAT/ACT | 100 | 111 | 1/1 | 75 |
| University of Phoenix: Indianapolis | Pr/B | 275 | | | | | | |
| University of Saint Francis | Pr/AB | 1,758 | 9 | TOEFL, SAT/ACT | 80 | | None | |
| University of Southern Indiana | Pu/AB | 7,894 | 158 | TOEFL | 71 | 87 | | 40 |
| Valparaiso University | Pr/AB | 3,255 | 173 | TOEFL, SAT/ACT | 80 | | 6/1 | |
| Vincennes University | Pu/AB | 7,563 | 50 | | 70 | | | 50 |
| Wabash College | Pr/B | 843 | 57 | TOEFL, SAT/ACT | | | 2/1 | 50 |

## Iowa

| Institution | Control/ degrees | Undergraduates Total | Internat'l | Tests required (Fall 2017) | TOEFL minimum | average | Application Deadline | Fee |
|---|---|---|---|---|---|---|---|---|
| Allen College | Pr/AB | 358 | | | 92 | | | 50 |
| Briar Cliff University | Pr/AB | 972 | 46 | TOEFL, SAT | 70 | | | 20 |
| Brown Mackie College: Quad Cities | Pr/A | | | | | | | |
| Buena Vista University | Pr/B | 781 | 36 | TOEFL | 59 | | 6/1 | |
| Central College | Pr/B | 1,184 | 2 | TOEFL | 71 | | 5/1 | 25 |
| Clarke University | Pr/AB | 788 | 7 | TOEFL, SAT/ACT | 70 | | None | 25 |
| Clinton Community College | Pu/A | 1,909 | | TOEFL | | | | |
| Coe College | Pr/B | 1,323 | 34 | TOEFL, SAT/ACT | 68 | 89 | 3/1 | 30 |
| Cornell College | Pr/B | 974 | | TOEFL | 79 | | | 30 |
| Des Moines Area Community College | Pu/A | 12,814 | 181 | TOEFL | 45 | | | 100 |
| Divine Word College | Pr/AB | 47 | | TOEFL | | | | 25 |
| Dordt College | Pr/AB | 1,379 | | TOEFL, SAT/ACT | 79 | 90 | | |
| Drake University | Pr/B | 3,196 | 210 | TOEFL, SAT/ACT | | | | 25 |
| Ellsworth Community College | Pu/A | 949 | | TOEFL | | | | |
| Emmaus Bible College | Pr/AB | 251 | 18 | TOEFL, SAT/ACT | | | 5/1 | 25 |

| | Student services | | Housing | | Academic year costs | | Maximum credits/ summer | Credit hour charge | | International financial aid | | |
|---|---|---|---|---|---|---|---|---|---|---|---|---|
| Adviser | Orien- tation | ESL | Academic year | Summer | Tuition/ fees | Living costs | | | Avail- able | Number receiving aid | Average award | Deadline |
| | | | No | | | | | | | | | |
| Yes | | | No | | 8,052† | | 18 | 264 | Yes | | | 3/1 |
| Yes | | | No | | 8,052† | | 18 | 264 | Yes | | | 3/1 |
| Yes | | | No | | 8,052† | | 18 | 264 | Yes | | | 3/1 |
| Yes | | | No | | 8,052† | | 18 | 264 | Yes | | | 3/1 |
| Yes | | | No | | 8,052† | | 18 | 264 | Yes | | | 3/1 |
| Yes | | | No | | 8,052† | | 18 | 264 | Yes | | | 3/1 |
| Yes | | | No | | 8,052† | | 18 | 264 | Yes | | | 3/1 |
| Yes | | | No | | 8,052† | | 18 | 264 | Yes | | | 3/1 |
| Yes | | | No | | 8,052† | | 18 | 264 | Yes | | | 3/1 |
| Yes | | | No | | 8,052† | | 18 | 264 | Yes | | | 3/1 |
| Yes | | | No | | 8,052† | | 18 | 264 | Yes | | | 3/1 |
| Yes | | | No | | 8,052† | | 18 | 264 | Yes | | | 3/1 |
| Yes | | | No | | 8,052† | | 18 | 264 | Yes | | | 3/1 |
| Yes | | | No | | 8,052† | | 18 | 264 | Yes | | | 3/1 |
| Yes | Yes | | Yes | Yes | 31,660 | 12,080 | | 700 | Yes | 48 | $20,873 | None |
| Yes | Yes | | Yes | Yes | 33,000 | 10,206 | 9 | 1450 | Yes | | | 3/10 |
| Yes | Yes | | No | | 15,630† | | 12 | | Yes | | | 6/30 |
| | | | No | | | | | | | | | |
| Yes | Yes | | Yes | | 23,400† | 9,980 | 15 | 780 | Yes | | | None |
| Yes | Yes | | Yes | Yes | 30,804† | 10,030 | 9 | 1018 | Yes | 256 | $2,320 | None |
| Yes | | | Yes | | | | 9 | | Yes | | | 6/30 |
| Yes | Yes | Yes | Yes | Yes | 16,895† | 7,560 | 9 | | Yes | | | 6/30 |
| Yes | Yes | Yes | Yes | Yes | 47,997 | 14,061 | 16 | 1309 | Yes | 262 | $4,852 | None |
| Yes | | | Yes | | 30,080† | 10,080 | 9 | 990 | Yes | 21 | $21,506 | None |
| Yes | Yes | | Yes | | 29,510‡ | 13,059 | | 496 | Yes | | | 3/10 |
| Yes | Yes | Yes | Yes | Yes | 40,800 | 12,600 | 6 | 1580 | Yes | 23 | $19,784 | 3/1 |
| Yes | Yes | Yes | Yes | | 32,885 | 9,245 | 12 | 1150 | Yes | 102 | $22,445 | 3/10 |
| Yes | Yes | Yes | Yes | Yes | 31,540 | 10,570 | 18 | 970 | Yes | 12 | $10,226 | None |
| Yes | Yes | Yes | Yes | Yes | 33,966† | 11,690 | 10 | 920 | Yes | 207 | $24,309 | None |
| Yes | Yes | Yes | Yes | Yes | 27,420† | 9,648 | | 1120 | Yes | 166 | $18,579 | |
| Yes | Yes | Yes | Yes | | 51,505 | 14,890 | | 2125 | Yes | 241 | $43,712 | |
| | | | Yes | | 29,430 | 9,090 | | 900 | Yes | 9 | $14,854 | None |
| Yes | Yes | Yes | Yes | Yes | 17,848‡ | 10,696 | 12 | 578 | | | | None |
| Yes | Yes | Yes | Yes | Yes | 37,450† | 10,920 | 14 | 1615 | Yes | 89 | $17,780 | None |
| Yes | Yes | Yes | Yes | Yes | 13,184† | 10,332 | 12 | 431.18 | Yes | | | None |
| Yes | Yes | | Yes | Yes | 42,250 | 9,850 | | 1733 | Yes | 54 | $32,475 | None |
| | | | Yes | Yes | 20,010† | 7,281 | | 588 | Yes | | | None |
| Yes | Yes | | Yes | Yes | 28,788† | 9,282 | 10 | 910 | Yes | 28 | $16,068 | None |
| Yes | Yes | Yes | Yes | Yes | 32,210† | 9,304 | 12 | 1083 | Yes | 34 | $22,843 | None |
| Yes | Yes | | Yes | Yes | 34,612† | 9,980 | 9 | 1442 | Yes | 2 | $22,306 | None |
| Yes | Yes | | Yes | Yes | 30,900† | 11,200 | 9 | 700 | Yes | 4 | $10,571 | None |
| Yes | | Yes | No | | 6,480† | 7,650 | 12 | 216 | | | | |
| Yes | Yes | Yes | Yes | Yes | 42,430 | 12,950 | 2 | 1315 | Yes | 30 | $17,885 | None |
| Yes | Yes | Yes | Yes | | 39,900‡ | 9,850 | | 1240 | Yes | | | None |
| Yes | Yes | Yes | Yes | | 8,820† | 5,748 | | 294 | | | | |
| | Yes | Yes | Yes | | 12,600† | 3,500 | | 420 | Yes | | | None |
| Yes | Yes | Yes | Yes | Yes | 30,000‡ | 10,640 | | 1190 | Yes | | | None |
| Yes | Yes | Yes | Yes | Yes | 35,206† | 13,660 | 16 | | Yes | 165 | $12,080 | None |
| Yes | | | Yes | Yes | 6,780† | 8,300 | 15 | 200 | Yes | | | 4/1 |
| Yes | | | Yes | | 17,520‡ | 8,100 | | 730 | Yes | | | None |

| Institution | Control/ degrees | Undergraduates | | Tests required (Fall 2017) | TOEFL | | Application | |
|---|---|---|---|---|---|---|---|---|
| | | Total | Internat'l | | minimum | average | Deadline | Fee |
| Faith Baptist Bible College and Theological Seminary | Pr/AB | 249 | | TOEFL | | | None | 45 |
| Graceland University | Pr/B | 1,261 | | TOEFL, SAT/ACT | 79 | | None | |
| Grand View University | Pr/B | 1,876 | 43 | TOEFL | 77 | | 6/15 | |
| Grinnell College | Pr/B | 1,657 | 304 | TOEFL, SAT/ACT | | | 1/15 | |
| Iowa Central Community College | Pu/A | 3,437 | 77 | TOEFL | | | | |
| Iowa Lakes Community College | Pu/A | 1,200 | | TOEFL | | | 6/1 | |
| Iowa State University | Pu/B | 30,224 | 2,063 | TOEFL | 71 | | 2/1 | 50 |
| Iowa Wesleyan College | Pr/B | 599 | | TOEFL | 61 | | | 20 |
| Iowa Western Community College | Pu/A | 4,208 | | TOEFL | | | None | |
| Kaplan University: Cedar Falls | Pr/AB | 306 | | TOEFL | | | | 100 |
| Kaplan University: Cedar Rapids | Pr/AB | 454 | | TOEFL | 71 | | | 25 |
| Kaplan University: Davenport | Pr/AB | 35,040 | 149 | TOEFL | 71 | | | 25 |
| Kaplan University: Des Moines | Pr/AB | 780 | | TOEFL | | | | 100 |
| Kaplan University: Mason City | Pr/AB | 228 | | TOEFL | 71 | | | 20 |
| Loras College | Pr/AB | 1,422 | 18 | TOEFL | 79 | 97 | 8/31 | 25 |
| Luther College | Pr/B | 2,121 | 143 | TOEFL | 80 | 90 | 3/1 | |
| Maharishi University of Management | Pr/B | 320 | 17 | | | | | 30 |
| Marshalltown Community College | Pu/A | 2,101 | | TOEFL | | | | 100 |
| Mercy College of Health Sciences | Pr/AB | 771 | | TOEFL | | | | |
| Morningside College | Pr/B | 1,278 | 62 | TOEFL | 61 | | 8/15 | |
| Mount Mercy University | Pr/B | 1,570 | 68 | TOEFL, SAT/ACT | 79 | | | |
| Muscatine Community College | Pu/A | 1,600 | | TOEFL | | | | |
| North Iowa Area Community College | Pu/A | 1,745 | 54 | TOEFL | 60 | | | 75 |
| Northeast Iowa Community College | Pu/A | 2,262 | 7 | TOEFL | | | | |
| Northwest Iowa Community College | Pu/A | 1,634 | | TOEFL | 61 | 63 | | |
| Northwestern College | Pr/B | 1,076 | 39 | TOEFL | 53 | 77 | None | |
| St. Ambrose University | Pr/B | 2,381 | 82 | TOEFL | 79 | 88 | None | |
| St. Luke's College | Pr/AB | 267 | | | | | | 50 |
| Scott Community College | Pu/A | 4,634 | | TOEFL | | | | |
| Shiloh University | Pr/AB | 13 | | TOEFL | 61 | 66 | 7/3 | |
| Simpson College | Pr/B | 1,525 | | TOEFL | 79 | | | |
| Southeastern Community College | Pu/A | 1,762 | 16 | TOEFL | | | | |
| Southwestern Community College | Pu/A | 1,646 | | TOEFL | 68 | | | 75 |
| University of Dubuque | Pr/B | 1,921 | | TOEFL | 61 | | None | 25 |
| University of Iowa | Pu/B | 22,990 | 2,421 | TOEFL | 80 | | 3/1 | 80 |
| University of Northern Iowa | Pu/B | 9,943 | 365 | TOEFL | 79 | | None | 50 |
| University of Phoenix: Des Moines | Pr/B | 30 | | | | | | |
| Upper Iowa University | Pr/AB | 3,859 | 64 | TOEFL | 61 | | | |
| Vatterott College: Des Moines | Pr/A | 239 | | | | | | |
| Waldorf University | Pr/AB | 1,983 | 61 | TOEFL | 61 | | | |
| Wartburg College | Pr/B | 1,448 | 122 | TOEFL | 55 | | None | |
| Western Iowa Tech Community College | Pu/A | 5,660 | | TOEFL | 45 | | None | |
| William Penn University | Pr/AB | 1,307 | 61 | TOEFL, SAT/ACT | 61 | | 8/15 | 50 |

**Kansas**

| Institution | Control/ degrees | Undergraduates | | Tests required (Fall 2017) | TOEFL | | Application | |
|---|---|---|---|---|---|---|---|---|
| | | Total | Internat'l | | minimum | average | Deadline | Fee |
| Allen County Community College | Pu/A | 2,377 | | TOEFL | | | | 50 |
| Baker University | Pr/B | 858 | 19 | TOEFL, SAT/ACT | 70 | | 7/1 | |
| Barclay College | Pr/AB | 250 | 5 | | | | | 10 |
| Barton County Community College | Pu/A | 8,114 | | TOEFL | | | | 150 |
| Benedictine College | Pr/B | 1,936 | 31 | TOEFL, SAT/ACT | | | None | 50 |
| Bethany College | Pr/B | 650 | 49 | TOEFL | 71 | 83 | None | |
| Bethel College | Pr/B | 460 | | TOEFL | 76 | | | 20 |
| Brown Mackie College: Kansas City | Pr/AB | | | | | | | |
| Bryan University: Topeka | Pr/A | 63 | | | | | | 50 |
| Butler Community College | Pu/A | 9,363 | | TOEFL | | | | |
| Central Christian College of Kansas | Pr/AB | 827 | 8 | TOEFL | 64 | | None | 35 |
| Cloud County Community College | Pu/A | 1,110 | | TOEFL | 61 | | | |

| Student services | | | Housing | | Academic year costs | | Maximum credits/ summer | Credit hour charge | International financial aid | | | |
|---|---|---|---|---|---|---|---|---|---|---|---|---|
| Adviser | Orien-tation | ESL | Academic year | Summer | Tuition/ fees | Living costs | | | Avail-able | Number receiving aid | Average award | Deadline |
| Yes | | | Yes | Yes | 16,766 † | 6,800 | 8 | 595 | Yes | | | None |
| Yes | Yes | | Yes | | 28,110 | 12,112 | 18 | 800 | Yes | 72 | $19,554 | None |
| Yes | Yes | Yes | Yes | Yes | 26,516 | 8,834 | | 642 | Yes | 43 | $21,440 | None |
| Yes | Yes | | Yes | | 48,758 † | 12,380 | | 1510 | Yes | 222 | $36,599 | 1/15 |
| Yes | | Yes | Yes | Yes | 7,395 † | 6,600 | 10 | 232.5 | Yes | | | None |
| Yes | | | Yes | Yes | 5,655 † | 6,030 | 12 | 178 | Yes | | | None |
| Yes | Yes | Yes | Yes | Yes | 22,083 † | 8,356 | 12 | 874 | Yes | 316 | $6,731 | None |
| Yes | | | Yes | Yes | 28,646 † | 10,554 | 14 | 710 | Yes | | | None |
| Yes | Yes | Yes | Yes | Yes | 5,405 † | 8,200 | 12 | 162 | Yes | | | None |
| | | | No | | | | | | Yes | | | None |
| | | | No | | | 8,190 | | | Yes | | | None |
| | | | No | | | | | | | | | |
| | | | No | | | 8,649 | 16 | | | | | |
| | | | No | | | | | | | | | |
| Yes | Yes | | Yes | Yes | 31,525 † | 7,700 | 9 | 610 | Yes | 17 | $12,620 | None |
| Yes | Yes | | Yes | | 41,020 | 8,970 | 8 | 1454 | Yes | 143 | $31,363 | None |
| Yes | Yes | | Yes | Yes | 26,530 † | 8,480 | | | Yes | | | 7/30 |
| Yes | Yes | Yes | Yes | | 6,030 † | | 12 | 175 | | | | |
| | | | | | 17,600 | 5,430 | | 610 | Yes | | | None |
| Yes | Yes | Yes | Yes | Yes | 30,390 | 9,390 | 8 | 910 | Yes | | | None |
| Yes | Yes | | Yes | Yes | 30,582 | 9,166 | 16 | 920 | Yes | | | None |
| Yes | Yes | Yes | Yes | Yes | 6,480 † | | 12 | 216 | | | | |
| | | | Yes | Yes | 7,113 † | 6,718 | | | Yes | 48 | $3,709 | None |
| | | Yes | No | | 5,880 | 7,010 | 9 | 188 | Yes | | | None |
| | | Yes | Yes | Yes | 6,060 † | 4,942 | 18 | 167 | | | | |
| Yes | Yes | Yes | Yes | Yes | 29,500 † | 8,900 | 8 | | Yes | 34 | $21,153 | 6/30 |
| Yes | Yes | Yes | Yes | Yes | 30,016 | 10,164 | 18 | 915 | Yes | | | None |
| | | | No | | 20,460 ‡ | | | 525 | | | | |
| Yes | Yes | Yes | | | 6,480 † | | 12 | 216 | | | | |
| | | | | | 4,510 ‡ | | 12 | 150 | | | | |
| Yes | Yes | | Yes | Yes | 37,663 ‡ | 9,963 | 12 | 415 | Yes | 15 | $29,734 | None |
| Yes | | Yes | Yes | | 5,424 † | 7,400 | 6 | | | | | |
| Yes | | | Yes | Yes | 5,310 † | 6,960 | 12 | 165 | Yes | | | 7/1 |
| Yes | Yes | Yes | Yes | Yes | 28,700 † | 11,950 | 16 | 775 | Yes | | | None |
| Yes | Yes | Yes | Yes | Yes | 28,413 † | 12,048 | 12 | 1124 | Yes | 948 | $4,888 | None |
| Yes | Yes | Yes | Yes | Yes | 18,851 † | 8,629 | 12 | 735 | Yes | 106 | $4,777 | None |
| Yes | Yes | Yes | Yes | Yes | 29,600 | 8,370 | 6 | 1200 | Yes | 96 | $16,861 | None |
| | | | No | | | | | | | | | |
| Yes | Yes | | Yes | Yes | 21,674 | 7,884 | 17 | 558 | Yes | 5 | $12,115 | None |
| Yes | Yes | | Yes | Yes | 38,380 † | 9,460 | 4 | | Yes | | | None |
| Yes | Yes | Yes | Yes | Yes | 5,280 † | 5,855 | | 144 | | | | |
| Yes | Yes | | Yes | Yes | 25,000 | 8,752 | 12 | | Yes | | | None |
| Yes | | | Yes | | 5,160 † | 5,830 | 9 | 147 | | | | |
| Yes | | | Yes | Yes | 28,030 † | 8,270 | 14 | 830 | Yes | | | None |
| Yes | | | Yes | | 15,990 † | 8,400 | 6 | 295 | Yes | | | 7/15 |
| Yes | | Yes | Yes | Yes | 5,490 † | 5,624 | 12 | 155 | | | | |
| Yes | Yes | Yes | Yes | Yes | 27,480 † | 9,670 | | 775 | Yes | 37 | $12,871 | None |
| Yes | Yes | | Yes | Yes | 27,472 | 11,175 | 12 | 545 | Yes | | | None |
| Yes | Yes | | Yes | | 27,720 ‡ | 13,270 | 15 | | Yes | 9 | $13,636 | None |
| Yes | Yes | Yes | Yes | | 6,420 † | 5,800 | 9 | | Yes | | | None |
| Yes | Yes | Yes | Yes | Yes | 25,040 † | 8,451 | 6 | 751 | Yes | | | None |
| | | Yes | Yes | | 3,270 † | 5,800 | 9 | 79 | Yes | | | None |

† Actual for 2016-17.       ‡ Estimated for 2017-18.       * Includes room and board

| Institution | Control/ degrees | Undergraduates | | Tests required (Fall 2017) | TOEFL | | Application | |
|---|---|---|---|---|---|---|---|---|
| | | Total | Internat'l | | minimum | average | Deadline | Fee |
| Coffeyville Community College . . . . . . . . . . . . | Pu/A | 1,703 | | TOEFL | 45 | | None | 100 |
| Colby Community College . . . . . . . . . . . . . . . | Pu/A | 1,311 | | TOEFL | 80 | | | 150 |
| Cowley County Community College . . . . . . . . . . | Pu/A | 4,013 | | TOEFL | 61 | | | |
| Dodge City Community College. . . . . . . . . . . . | Pu/A | 1,804 | | TOEFL | 61 | | None | 100 |
| Donnelly College. . . . . . . . . . . . . . . . . . . | Pr/AB | 318 | 7 | | 69 | | | 250 |
| Emporia State University. . . . . . . . . . . . . . . | Pu/B | 3,578 | 257 | TOEFL | 72 | | | 50 |
| Fort Hays State University. . . . . . . . . . . . . . | Pu/AB | 11,698 | | TOEFL | | | | 35 |
| Friends University . . . . . . . . . . . . . . . . . . | Pr/AB | 1,164 | 2 | TOEFL, SAT/ACT | 63 | | | 50 |
| Garden City Community College . . . . . . . . . . . | Pu/A | 2,034 | | TOEFL | 61 | | | 150 |
| Grantham University . . . . . . . . . . . . . . . . . | Pr/AB | 9,341 | | TOEFL | 61 | | None | |
| Haskell Indian Nations University. . . . . . . . . . . | Pu/AB | 821 | | | | | | 10 |
| Hesston College . . . . . . . . . . . . . . . . . . . | Pr/AB | 398 | 35 | TOEFL | | | 7/1 | |
| Hutchinson Community College . . . . . . . . . . . . | Pu/A | 5,527 | 28 | TOEFL | | | | 100 |
| Independence Community College. . . . . . . . . . . | Pu/A | 669 | 14 | TOEFL | 61 | | | 85 |
| Kansas City Kansas Community College . . . . . . . | Pu/A | 4,790 | 179 | TOEFL | | | | |
| Kansas State University . . . . . . . . . . . . . . . | Pu/AB | 19,151 | 999 | TOEFL | 79 | 80 | | 80 |
| Kansas Wesleyan University . . . . . . . . . . . . . | Pr/AB | 678 | 13 | TOEFL | 61 | 69 | None | 30 |
| Labette Community College. . . . . . . . . . . . . . | Pu/A | 1,574 | | TOEFL | 65 | | | 40 |
| McPherson College . . . . . . . . . . . . . . . . . . | Pr/B | 643 | | TOEFL | 79 | 84 | None | |
| MidAmerica Nazarene University . . . . . . . . . . . | Pr/AB | 1,224 | | TOEFL | 76 | | None | |
| Neosho County Community College . . . . . . . . . | Pu/A | 1,334 | | TOEFL | | | | 75 |
| Newman University . . . . . . . . . . . . . . . . . . | Pr/AB | 1,095 | 85 | TOEFL | 74 | | 7/1 | |
| North Central Kansas Technical College. . . . . . . | Pu/A | 785 | | | | | | 50 |
| Northwest Kansas Technical College . . . . . . . . . | Pu/A | 626 | | TOEFL, SAT/ACT | 61 | | | 25 |
| Ottawa University . . . . . . . . . . . . . . . . . . | Pr/B | 539 | | TOEFL | 80 | | | 25 |
| Pittsburg State University . . . . . . . . . . . . . . | Pu/AB | 5,636 | 181 | TOEFL | 68 | 77 | | 50 |
| Pratt Community College . . . . . . . . . . . . . . . | Pu/A | 1,197 | | TOEFL | 61 | 65 | | |
| Seward County Community College . . . . . . . . . | Pu/A | 1,700 | | TOEFL | 61 | | 7/1 | 100 |
| Southwestern College. . . . . . . . . . . . . . . . . | Pr/AB | 1,157 | 49 | TOEFL | 80 | | 8/1 | 25 |
| Sterling College. . . . . . . . . . . . . . . . . . . . | Pr/B | 587 | 10 | TOEFL | 70 | | 8/15 | 25 |
| Tabor College. . . . . . . . . . . . . . . . . . . . . | Pr/AB | 637 | 24 | TOEFL | 70 | 85 | 8/1 | 50 |
| University of Kansas . . . . . . . . . . . . . . . . . | Pu/B | 18,337 | 1,091 | TOEFL | | | 5/1 | 85 |
| University of Kansas Medical Center. . . . . . . . . | Pu/B | 506 | 9 | TOEFL | | | | 60 |
| University of St. Mary . . . . . . . . . . . . . . . . | Pr/AB | 765 | 11 | TOEFL | | | | 25 |
| Washburn University . . . . . . . . . . . . . . . . . | Pu/AB | 4,967 | 178 | TOEFL | 72 | | | 70 |
| Wichita Area Technical College . . . . . . . . . . . | Pu/A | 3,318 | | TOEFL | 94 | | | |
| Wichita State University . . . . . . . . . . . . . . . | Pu/AB | 11,037 | 777 | TOEFL | 72 | 85 | | 75 |
| **Kentucky** | | | | | | | | |
| Alice Lloyd College. . . . . . . . . . . . . . . . . . | Pr/B | 431 | | TOEFL | | | | |
| Asbury University . . . . . . . . . . . . . . . . . . . | Pr/AB | 1,493 | 44 | TOEFL | 80 | | | |
| Ashland Community and Technical College . . . . . . | Pu/A | 2,228 | | TOEFL, ACT | | | | |
| Bellarmine University. . . . . . . . . . . . . . . . . | Pr/B | 2,571 | 24 | TOEFL | 80 | | 5/1 | 25 |
| Berea College. . . . . . . . . . . . . . . . . . . . . | Pr/B | 1,612 | 122 | TOEFL | | | 1/15 | |
| Big Sandy Community and Technical College . . . . . | Pu/A | 5,057 | | TOEFL | | | | |
| Bluegrass Community and Technical College . . . . . | Pu/A | 10,392 | | TOEFL | 61 | | | |
| Brescia University . . . . . . . . . . . . . . . . . . | Pr/AB | 953 | 23 | TOEFL | 79 | | None | 75 |
| Campbellsville University . . . . . . . . . . . . . . | Pr/AB | 2,215 | 213 | TOEFL, SAT/ACT | 61 | | | 20 |
| Centre College . . . . . . . . . . . . . . . . . . . . | Pr/B | 1,422 | 95 | TOEFL | 90 | 98 | 1/15 | 40 |
| Daymar College: Louisville . . . . . . . . . . . . . | Pr/AB | 68 | | | | | | |
| Daymar College: Owensboro . . . . . . . . . . . . . | Pr/AB | 94 | | | | | | |
| Eastern Kentucky University . . . . . . . . . . . . . | Pu/AB | 14,293 | | TOEFL, SAT/ACT | | | | 30 |
| Elizabethtown Community and Technical College . . . . . . . . . . . . . . . . . . . . . . . | Pu/A | 6,898 | | TOEFL, ACT | 61 | 71 | None | |
| Gateway Community and Technical College . . . . . . | Pu/A | 2,958 | | | | | None | |
| Georgetown College. . . . . . . . . . . . . . . . . . | Pr/B | 982 | 8 | TOEFL | 68 | 75 | | 30 |
| Hazard Community and Technical College . . . . . . | Pu/A | 3,280 | | TOEFL, SAT/ACT | | | | |
| Henderson Community College . . . . . . . . . . . . | Pu/A | 1,332 | | | | | | |

| Student services | | | Housing | | Academic year costs | | Maximum credits/ summer | Credit hour charge | International financial aid | | | |
|---|---|---|---|---|---|---|---|---|---|---|---|---|
| Adviser | Orientation | ESL | Academic year | Summer | Tuition/ fees | Living costs | | | Available | Number receiving aid | Average award | Deadline |
| Yes | | | Yes | Yes | 5,970† | 5,900 | 9 | 162 | | | | |
| Yes | | | Yes | Yes | 5,700† | 7,140 | 14 | 150 | | | | |
| Yes | | Yes | Yes | | 5,790† | 4,900 | 12 | 159 | | | | |
| Yes | | Yes | Yes | Yes | 3,000† | 6,400 | 19 | 60 | Yes | | | None |
| | | Yes | Yes | Yes | 8,400† | 7,650 | 6 | | Yes | 65 | $3,131 | |
| Yes | Yes | | Yes | Yes | 19,392† | 8,391 | 12 | 603.5 | Yes | | | None |
| Yes | Yes | Yes | Yes | Yes | 14,426† | 7,669 | | 444.4 | Yes | | | None |
| Yes | Yes | | Yes | Yes | 27,465‡ | 7,740 | 12 | 905 | Yes | 22 | $12,219 | None |
| | | | Yes | | 4,032† | 5,250 | 12 | | Yes | | | None |
| | | | No | | 6,540‡ | | | 265 | | | | |
| | | | Yes | | 2,010† | 850 | | | | | | |
| Yes | Yes | Yes | Yes | | 26,318 | 8,578 | 9 | | Yes | | | 4/1 |
| Yes | | | Yes | Yes | 4,290 | 7,100 | 9 | 124 | | | | |
| | | | Yes | | 5,730† | 5,014 | | 151 | Yes | | | None |
| Yes | | Yes | Yes | | 7,830† | | | 246 | | | | |
| Yes | Yes | Yes | Yes | Yes | 24,775† | 9,150 | 6 | 797 | | | | |
| Yes | Yes | | Yes | Yes | 28,000† | 8,600 | 6 | 280 | | | | |
| Yes | | | | | 5,280† | 9,040 | 12 | 133 | | | | |
| Yes | | | Yes | | 26,498† | 8,411 | 12 | 716 | Yes | 34 | $20,185 | None |
| Yes | Yes | | Yes | Yes | 29,670 | 8,138 | 15 | 1050 | Yes | | | None |
| Yes | Yes | | Yes | | 5,130† | 9,500 | 12 | 140 | Yes | | | None |
| Yes | Yes | | Yes | Yes | 27,716† | 7,674 | 12 | 881 | Yes | 69 | $12,106 | |
| | | | Yes | | 3,557† | 5,274 | | | Yes | | | None |
| Yes | | Yes | Yes | Yes | 8,300† | 4,425 | | | | | | |
| Yes | Yes | | Yes | Yes | 27,096† | 9,550 | 9 | 1079 | Yes | | | None |
| Yes | Yes | Yes | Yes | Yes | 17,662† | 7,572 | 12 | 538 | | | | |
| Yes | | | Yes | Yes | 3,660† | 5,530 | 8 | | Yes | | | 8/1 |
| Yes | | | Yes | Yes | 3,810† | 6,300 | 9 | 93 | | | | |
| Yes | Yes | Yes | Yes | Yes | 27,250† | 7,250 | | 1129 | Yes | 17 | $9,260 | |
| | | | Yes | | 24,835‡ | 8,280 | | | Yes | 9 | $14,535 | None |
| Yes | | | Yes | | 26,590† | 11,155 | 6 | 535 | Yes | 23 | $16,088 | None |
| Yes | Yes | Yes | Yes | Yes | 28,239† | 10,436 | | 909 | Yes | 99 | $15,771 | None |
| Yes | Yes | Yes | No | | 25,794† | | | 832 | | | | |
| Yes | Yes | | Yes | Yes | 27,720 | 8,140 | 12 | 875 | Yes | | | None |
| Yes | Yes | Yes | Yes | Yes | 18,620† | 10,027 | 9 | 617 | Yes | | | None |
| Yes | | | No | | 3,444† | | | 82.8 | Yes | | | None |
| Yes | Yes | Yes | Yes | Yes | 16,634† | 6,712 | | 504.16 | Yes | 50 | $1,594 | |
| Yes | | | Yes | | 11,550† | 9,740 | | 212 | Yes | 2 | $2,320 | 7/1 |
| Yes | Yes | | Yes | Yes | 29,500 | 6,950 | 12 | 1127 | Yes | | | None |
| | | | No | | 16,620† | 6,976 | 14 | 546 | Yes | | | None |
| Yes | Yes | | Yes | Yes | 40,350 | 11,750 | | 905 | Yes | 17 | $23,205 | None |
| Yes | Yes | Yes | Yes | Yes | 25,760 | 6,534 | 6 | | Yes | 166 | $32,823 | None |
| | | | No | | 16,620† | 6,952 | | 546 | Yes | | | None |
| Yes | Yes | Yes | Yes | Yes | 16,620† | 6,976 | | 546 | Yes | | | None |
| Yes | Yes | | Yes | Yes | 21,850 | 9,150 | 9 | 590 | Yes | | | 8/23 |
| Yes | Yes | Yes | Yes | Yes | 24,596† | 8,496 | 12 | 972 | Yes | 32 | $20,042 | None |
| Yes | Yes | | Yes | Yes | 39,300† | 11,450 | | | Yes | 98 | $17,545 | 1/31 |
| Yes | | | No | | | 9,120 | 12 | | | | | |
| Yes | Yes | Yes | Yes | Yes | 18,180† | 8,666 | 12 | 745 | Yes | | | None |
| | | | No | | 16,620† | | 10 | 546 | | | | |
| | | | | | 16,420† | | | 546 | | | | |
| Yes | Yes | | Yes | Yes | 35,850† | 9,050 | 14 | 1470 | Yes | | | |
| | | | No | | 16,620† | | 6 | 546 | | | | |
| | | | No | | 16,620† | 6,952 | 9 | 546 | | | | |

† Actual for 2016-17.  ‡ Estimated for 2017-18.  * Includes room and board

| Institution | Control/ degrees | Undergraduates | | Tests required (Fall 2017) | TOEFL | | Application | |
|---|---|---|---|---|---|---|---|---|
| | | Total | Internat'l | | minimum | average | Deadline | Fee |
| Jefferson Community and Technical College . . . . . | .Pu/A | 11,969 | | TOEFL, ACT | | | | |
| Kentucky Christian University . . . . . . . . . . . . . | .Pr/B | 602 | | TOEFL | 61 | | | 30 |
| Kentucky Mountain Bible College. . . . . . . . . . . . | .Pr/AB | 79 | 5 | TOEFL | 61 | | | 75 |
| Kentucky State University. . . . . . . . . . . . . . . . | .Pu/AB | 1,287 | 6 | TOEFL, SAT/ACT | 71 | | 7/15 | 100 |
| Kentucky Wesleyan College. . . . . . . . . . . . . . . | .Pr/B | 693 | | TOEFL, SAT/ACT | | | | |
| Lindsey Wilson College . . . . . . . . . . . . . . . . . | .Pr/AB | 2,038 | 1 | TOEFL | 45 | | 7/30 | |
| Maysville Community and Technical College . . . . . | .Pu/A | 3,525 | | | | | | |
| Midway College . . . . . . . . . . . . . . . . . . . . . | .Pr/AB | 1,005 | | TOEFL | | | | 25 |
| Morehead State University. . . . . . . . . . . . . . . . | .Pu/AB | 6,647 | 174 | TOEFL, SAT/ACT | 61 | 73 | | 30 |
| Murray State University . . . . . . . . . . . . . . . . . | .Pu/AB | 7,655 | 320 | TOEFL | 71 | 79 | 6/15 | 50 |
| National College: Danville. . . . . . . . . . . . . . . . | .Pr/A | 81 | | | | | | 125 |
| National College: Florence . . . . . . . . . . . . . . . | .Pr/A | 40 | | | | | | 125 |
| National College: Lexington. . . . . . . . . . . . . . . | .Pr/AB | 98 | | | | | | 125 |
| Northern Kentucky University . . . . . . . . . . . . . | .Pu/AB | 11,042 | 301 | TOEFL | 61 | 84 | None | 40 |
| Owensboro Community and Technical College . . . . | .Pu/A | 2,647 | | TOEFL, SAT/ACT | 61 | | None | |
| St. Catharine College . . . . . . . . . . . . . . . . . . | .Pr/AB | 636 | | TOEFL | | 71 | | |
| Somerset Community College . . . . . . . . . . . . . | .Pu/A | 6,639 | | TOEFL, ACT | | | | |
| Southeast Kentucky Community and Technical College . . . . . . . . . . . . . . . . . . . . . . . | .Pu/A | 3,111 | | TOEFL, ACT | | | | |
| Southern Baptist Theological Seminary . . . . . . . . | .Pr/AB | 799 | | | | | | 35 |
| Spalding University . . . . . . . . . . . . . . . . . . . . | .Pr/AB | 1,141 | 3 | TOEFL, SAT/ACT | 75 | | | 100 |
| Spencerian College . . . . . . . . . . . . . . . . . . . | .Pr/AB | 392 | | TOEFL | 61 | | | 50 |
| Spencerian College: Lexington . . . . . . . . . . . . . | .Pr/A | 73 | | TOEFL | 61 | | | 50 |
| Sullivan College of Technology and Design . . . . . | .Pr/AB | 379 | | | | | | 50 |
| Sullivan University . . . . . . . . . . . . . . . . . . . . | .Pr/AB | 2,386 | 7 | TOEFL | 70 | | 9/18 | 200 |
| Thomas More College . . . . . . . . . . . . . . . . . . | .Pr/AB | 1,401 | 9 | TOEFL | 66 | | None | 25 |
| Transylvania University . . . . . . . . . . . . . . . . . | .Pr/B | 960 | 35 | TOEFL | 80 | | None | |
| Union College. . . . . . . . . . . . . . . . . . . . . . . | .Pr/B | 912 | | TOEFL, SAT/ACT | | | | 20 |
| University of the Cumberlands . . . . . . . . . . . . . | .Pr/AB | 1,938 | 78 | | 79 | 82 | 6/1 | |
| University of Kentucky. . . . . . . . . . . . . . . . . . | .Pu/B | 22,223 | | TOEFL | 71 | | | 60 |
| University of Louisville . . . . . . . . . . . . . . . . . | .Pu/AB | 15,033 | 185 | TOEFL, SAT/ACT | 79 | | 5/1 | 50 |
| University of Phoenix: Louisville . . . . . . . . . . . . | .Pr/B | 184 | | | | | 7/1 | |
| University of Pikeville . . . . . . . . . . . . . . . . . . | .Pr/AB | 1,150 | 26 | TOEFL, SAT/ACT | 80 | | | |
| Western Kentucky University. . . . . . . . . . . . . . . | .Pu/AB | 14,956 | 816 | TOEFL, SAT/ACT | 71 | 84 | | 75 |
| **Louisiana** | | | | | | | | |
| Baton Rouge Community College . . . . . . . . . . . . | .Pu/A | 10,698 | | TOEFL | | | | 52 |
| Baton Rouge School of Computers . . . . . . . . . . . | .Pr/A | 78 | | | | | | 25 |
| Blue Cliff College: Metairie. . . . . . . . . . . . . . . | .Pr/A | 892 | | | | | | 25 |
| Blue Cliff College: Shreveport . . . . . . . . . . . . . | .Pr/A | 253 | | | | | | 25 |
| Bossier Parish Community College . . . . . . . . . . . | .Pu/A | 5,198 | 14 | TOEFL | 61 | | | |
| Centenary College of Louisiana . . . . . . . . . . . . | .Pr/B | 473 | 6 | TOEFL | 79 | | | |
| Delgado Community College . . . . . . . . . . . . . . | .Pu/A | 15,455 | | | | | 7/1 | 50 |
| Delta College of Arts & Technology . . . . . . . . . . | .Pr/A | 316 | | | | | | 100 |
| Delta School of Business & Technology. . . . . . . . | .Pr/A | 208 | | | | | | |
| Dillard University . . . . . . . . . . . . . . . . . . . . . | .Pr/B | 1,200 | | TOEFL, SAT/ACT | 79 | | | 50 |
| Grambling State University . . . . . . . . . . . . . . . | .Pu/AB | 4,153 | | TOEFL, SAT/ACT | 62 | | | 30 |
| Herzing University: Kenner . . . . . . . . . . . . . . . | .Pr/AB | 468 | | TOEFL | | | | |
| ITI Technical College. . . . . . . . . . . . . . . . . . . | .Pr/A | 575 | | TOEFL | | | | |
| Louisiana College . . . . . . . . . . . . . . . . . . . . . | .Pr/AB | 868 | 28 | TOEFL, SAT/ACT | 80 | 90 | 5/1 | 25 |
| Louisiana State University and Agricultural and Mechanical College . . . . . . . . . . . . . . . . | .Pu/B | 26,118 | | TOEFL | 79 | 92 | 4/15 | 40 |
| Louisiana State University at Eunice . . . . . . . . . . | .Pu/A | 2,397 | 10 | TOEFL | | | | 25 |
| Louisiana State University Health Sciences Center . . . . . . . . . . . . . . . . . . . . . . . . . . | .Pu/AB | 873 | 1 | | | | | 50 |
| Louisiana State University in Shreveport . . . . . . . | .Pu/B | 2,233 | 44 | TOEFL, ACT | 61 | | | 20 |
| Louisiana Tech University. . . . . . . . . . . . . . . . . | .Pu/AB | 11,281 | | TOEFL | | | | 30 |
| Loyola University New Orleans . . . . . . . . . . . . . | .Pr/B | 2,399 | 53 | TOEFL, SAT/ACT | 79 | | 4/15 | |
| McNeese State University . . . . . . . . . . . . . . . . | .Pu/AB | 6,155 | 417 | TOEFL | 61 | | 5/15 | 30 |

| Student services | | | Housing | | Academic year costs | | Maximum credits/ summer | Credit hour charge | Available | International financial aid | | |
|---|---|---|---|---|---|---|---|---|---|---|---|---|
| Adviser | Orientation | ESL | Academic year | Summer | Tuition/ fees | Living costs | | | | Number receiving aid | Average award | Deadline |
| Yes | Yes | Yes | No | | 16,620† | 6,976 | 6 | 546 | | | | |
| Yes | | | Yes | | 18,560† | 8,000 | | 605 | Yes | | | None |
| Yes | | | Yes | Yes | 7,610† | 7,850 | | 230 | Yes | | | None |
| Yes | | Yes | Yes | | 18,704† | 6,690 | 9 | 763 | Yes | | | None |
| Yes | | | Yes | Yes | 24,300† | 10,680 | 12 | 670 | Yes | 5 | $10,810 | None |
| Yes | Yes | | Yes | | 24,246 | 9,300 | 12 | 1000 | Yes | | | None |
| | | | No | | 16,620† | | | 546 | Yes | | | None |
| Yes | | | Yes | Yes | 23,250† | 10,200 | 12 | 860 | Yes | | | None |
| Yes | Yes | | Yes | Yes | 21,326† | 8,560 | 12 | 884 | Yes | | | None |
| Yes | Yes | Yes | Yes | Yes | 21,648† | 8,588 | | 902 | Yes | 38 | $27,854 | None |
| | | | No | | 14,460† | 5,202 | | 317 | | | | |
| | | | No | | 14,460† | 5,202 | | 317 | | | | |
| | | | No | | 14,460† | 5,202 | | 317 | | | | |
| Yes | Yes | Yes | Yes | Yes | 18,384† | 8,768 | | 750 | Yes | 55 | $4,913 | None |
| Yes | | | No | | 16,620† | 6,976 | 9 | 546 | Yes | | | None |
| Yes | Yes | | Yes | | 22,100† | 9,500 | 9 | 730 | | | | |
| | | | No | | 16,620† | 6,952 | 10 | 546 | Yes | | | None |
| Yes | | | No | | 16,620† | 6,952 | 10 | 546 | Yes | | | None |
| | | | Yes | | 11,600† | | | | | | | |
| Yes | Yes | | Yes | Yes | 24,000† | 7,600 | | 800 | Yes | | | |
| | | | | | 20,905† | 8,925 | | | Yes | | | None |
| | | | Yes | | 19,260† | 5,940 | 20 | 299 | | | | |
| Yes | Yes | Yes | Yes | Yes | | | 20 | | Yes | | | None |
| Yes | Yes | | Yes | | | | 20 | | | | | |
| Yes | Yes | | Yes | Yes | 29,450† | 7,304 | 12 | 620 | Yes | 8 | $23,077 | 3/15 |
| Yes | | | Yes | Yes | 37,290‡ | 10,160 | | 995 | Yes | 34 | $15,919 | None |
| | | | Yes | Yes | 25,135† | 9,250 | 15 | 345 | Yes | | | None |
| Yes | Yes | | Yes | Yes | 23,000† | 12,500 | 14 | 690 | Yes | | | None |
| Yes | Yes | Yes | Yes | Yes | 26,156† | 9,230 | 15 | 1075 | Yes | | | |
| Yes | Yes | Yes | Yes | Yes | 26,286† | 8,130 | 17 | 1088 | | | | |
| Yes | Yes | Yes | Yes | Yes | 20,350 | 7,500 | 12 | 842 | Yes | | | None |
| Yes | Yes | Yes | Yes | Yes | 25,440† | 7,713 | | 1060 | Yes | 175 | $9,637 | None |
| Yes | Yes | | No | | 8,299† | 7,459 | 9 | | Yes | | | 6/30 |
| Yes | | | No | | 8,816† | 9,073 | 21 | | Yes | | | None |
| Yes | | | Yes | | 35,430† | 12,980 | 12 | | Yes | | | None |
| Yes | Yes | Yes | No | | 8,200† | 8,789 | 9 | | | | | |
| | | | No | | | 8,236 | | | | | | |
| Yes | Yes | | Yes | | 17,004† | 9,874 | 9 | | Yes | | | 3/1 |
| Yes | Yes | | Yes | Yes | 16,394† | 6,594 | 14 | | Yes | | | 6/1 |
| | | | No | | | 10,224 | | | | | | |
| | | | No | | | | | | | | | |
| Yes | Yes | Yes | Yes | Yes | 13,838‡ | 8,724 | 14 | | Yes | | | None |
| Yes | Yes | Yes | Yes | Yes | 27,491† | 11,540 | 12 | | Yes | | | None |
| Yes | | | Yes | Yes | 9,670† | 9,072 | 12 | | Yes | 1 | $2,682 | None |
| Yes | Yes | Yes | Yes | Yes | 13,705† | 5,370 | | | | | | |
| | | | | Yes | 20,418† | 11,789 | 12 | | | | | |
| Yes | | Yes | Yes | | 29,370† | 6,330 | 12 | | Yes | | | None |
| Yes | Yes | Yes | Yes | Yes | 39,242 | 13,214 | 12 | 1073 | Yes | | | None |
| Yes | | Yes | Yes | Yes | 18,399† | 5,810 | 12 | | Yes | | | None |

† Actual for 2016-17.    ‡ Estimated for 2017-18.    * Includes room and board

| Institution | Control/ degrees | Undergraduates | | Tests required (Fall 2017) | TOEFL | | Application | |
|---|---|---|---|---|---|---|---|---|
| | | Total | Internat'l | | minimum | average | Deadline | Fee |
| New Orleans Baptist Theological Seminary | Pr/AB | 1,230 | | TOEFL | | | | 25 |
| Nicholls State University | Pu/AB | 5,280 | 82 | TOEFL, SAT/ACT | 61 | | | 30 |
| Northwestern State University | Pu/AB | 7,401 | 115 | TOEFL, SAT/ACT | 61 | | None | 30 |
| Nunez Community College | Pu/A | 1,454 | 2 | | | | | 20 |
| Remington College: Baton Rouge | Pr/A | 547 | | | | | | 50 |
| Remington College: Lafayette | Pr/A | 585 | | | | | | 50 |
| Remington College: Shreveport | Pr/AB | 582 | | | | | | 50 |
| St. Joseph Seminary College | Pr/B | 140 | | TOEFL, SAT/ACT | | | | |
| South Louisiana Community College | Pu/A | 6,958 | | | | | | 5 |
| Southeastern Louisiana University | Pu/AB | 10,836 | 164 | TOEFL, ACT | 75 | | 5/1 | 30 |
| Southern University and Agricultural and Mechanical College | Pu/B | 5,181 | | TOEFL, SAT/ACT | 61 | | | 30 |
| Southern University at New Orleans | Pu/AB | 1,981 | | TOEFL, SAT/ACT | | | | 15 |
| Southern University at Shreveport | Pu/A | 2,327 | 209 | | | | | 30 |
| Southwest University | Pr/AB | 601 | | TOEFL | 61 | 71 | | 50 |
| Tulane University | Pr/AB | 6,821 | 225 | TOEFL, SAT/ACT | | | 1/15 | |
| University of Holy Cross | Pr/AB | 980 | | TOEFL | | | | 25 |
| University of Louisiana at Lafayette | Pu/B | 15,870 | | TOEFL | 71 | | | 30 |
| University of Louisiana at Monroe | Pu/AB | 7,778 | | TOEFL, SAT/ACT | 61 | | 3/1 | 40 |
| University of New Orleans | Pu/B | 5,987 | 255 | | | | 6/25 | 20 |
| University of Phoenix: Baton Rouge | Pr/B | 865 | | | | | | |
| University of Phoenix: Louisiana | Pr/B | 530 | | | | | | |
| University of Phoenix: Shreveport | Pr/B | 310 | | | | | | |
| Virginia College in Baton Rouge | Pr/A | 589 | | | | | | 100 |
| Virginia College in Shreveport | Pr/AB | 264 | | | | | | |
| Xavier University of Louisiana | Pr/B | 2,293 | 44 | TOEFL, SAT/ACT | | | | 25 |
| **Maine** | | | | | | | | |
| Bates College | Pr/B | 1,780 | 122 | TOEFL | | | 1/1 | 60 |
| Bowdoin College | Pr/B | 1,799 | 85 | TOEFL | 100 | | 1/1 | 65 |
| Central Maine Community College | Pu/A | 2,404 | 14 | TOEFL | | | None | 20 |
| Colby College | Pr/B | 1,879 | 213 | TOEFL | 100 | 111 | 1/1 | |
| College of the Atlantic | Pr/B | 333 | 70 | TOEFL | 100 | | 2/1 | 50 |
| Eastern Maine Community College | Pu/A | 1,964 | | TOEFL | | | | 20 |
| Husson University | Pr/AB | 2,724 | 77 | TOEFL | 75 | 83 | | 40 |
| Kaplan University: South Portland | Pr/AB | 903 | | TOEFL | | | | 100 |
| Kennebec Valley Community College | Pu/A | 1,613 | | TOEFL | | | | 20 |
| Landing School of Boatbuilding and Design | Pr/A | 37 | | | | | None | |
| Maine College of Art | Pr/B | 434 | | TOEFL | 79 | | None | 60 |
| Maine Maritime Academy | Pu/AB | 1,014 | | TOEFL, SAT/ACT | | | 3/1 | 50 |
| Northern Maine Community College | Pu/A | 637 | 15 | TOEFL | | | | 20 |
| Saint Joseph's College of Maine | Pr/AB | 1,016 | | TOEFL | | | | 50 |
| Southern Maine Community College | Pu/A | 5,051 | 31 | TOEFL | 61 | | | 20 |
| Thomas College | Pr/AB | 892 | 24 | TOEFL | 72 | 82 | 7/1 | 40 |
| Unity College | Pr/AB | 729 | | TOEFL | 80 | | None | |
| University of Maine | Pu/B | 8,757 | 184 | TOEFL | 79 | | | 40 |
| University of Maine at Augusta | Pu/AB | 4,416 | | TOEFL | 61 | | | 40 |
| University of Maine at Farmington | Pu/B | 1,753 | 7 | TOEFL | 79 | | 3/1 | |
| University of Maine at Fort Kent | Pu/AB | 1,076 | | TOEFL | | | | 40 |
| University of Maine at Machias | Pu/AB | 560 | 11 | TOEFL | | | | 40 |
| University of Maine at Presque Isle | Pu/AB | 790 | 53 | TOEFL | 71 | | None | 40 |
| University of New England | Pr/B | 2,374 | 12 | TOEFL | 80 | | | 40 |
| University of Southern Maine | Pu/B | 5,233 | 77 | TOEFL | | | | 40 |
| Washington County Community College | Pu/A | 309 | | TOEFL | 61 | | None | |
| York County Community College | Pu/A | 1,277 | 4 | TOEFL | 80 | | None | 20 |
| **Maryland** | | | | | | | | |
| Allegany College of Maryland | Pu/A | 2,926 | | TOEFL | | | None | |

| Student services | | | Housing | | Academic year costs | | Maximum credits/ summer | Credit hour charge | International financial aid | | | |
|---|---|---|---|---|---|---|---|---|---|---|---|---|
| Adviser | Orientation | ESL | Academic year | Summer | Tuition/ fees | Living costs | | | Available | Number receiving aid | Average award | Deadline |
| | | | Yes | | 7,475† | 2,400 | 16 | 230 | | | | |
| Yes | Yes | | Yes | Yes | 18,602† | 7,692 | 12 | | Yes | | | 6/30 |
| Yes | | | Yes | | 17,890† | 8,914 | 12 | | Yes | | | None |
| | | | No | | 7,602† | 7,010 | | | | | | |
| | | | No | | | | | | | | | |
| | | | No | | | | | | | | | |
| | | Yes | Yes | | 16,550† | 14,120 | | 260 | | | | |
| | | | No | | 7,810† | 8,400 | | | Yes | | | None |
| Yes | Yes | Yes | Yes | Yes | 20,521† | 6,460 | 10 | | Yes | 176 | $18,052 | None |
| Yes | Yes | | Yes | Yes | 15,444† | 14,922 | | | | | | |
| Yes | Yes | | No | | 10,839† | 8,780 | 10 | | | | | |
| Yes | | | Yes | | 7,296† | 9,780 | 10 | | | | | |
| | | | No | | 8,554† | | | 275 | | | | |
| Yes | Yes | Yes | Yes | Yes | 51,010† | 13,844 | 18 | 1964 | Yes | 45 | $33,367 | None |
| | | | No | | 14,242† | 8,921 | | 435 | Yes | | | None |
| Yes | Yes | Yes | Yes | Yes | 24,788† | 8,112 | 10 | | Yes | | | None |
| Yes | Yes | Yes | Yes | Yes | 19,758† | 7,400 | 6 | | Yes | | | 6/30 |
| Yes | Yes | Yes | Yes | Yes | 22,511† | 9,730 | | 663 | | 139 | $19,134 | |
| Yes | | | Yes | Yes | 23,606 | 8,784 | 12 | 884 | Yes | 28 | $15,582 | None |
| Yes | Yes | | Yes | | 50,310† | 14,190 | | | Yes | 79 | $54,496 | 1/1 |
| Yes | | | Yes | Yes | 49,900† | 13,600 | | 965 | Yes | 41 | $49,038 | 2/15 |
| | | Yes | Yes | | 6,330† | 8,770 | | 184 | | | | |
| Yes | Yes | | Yes | | 53,120 | 14,860 | | 1960 | Yes | 95 | $54,727 | 2/1 |
| Yes | Yes | | Yes | | 43,542 | 13,397 | | 1433 | Yes | 69 | $43,207 | 2/1 |
| | | | Yes | Yes | 6,436† | 8,130 | 12 | 184 | | | | |
| Yes | Yes | Yes | Yes | Yes | 17,037† | 10,220 | 12 | 535 | Yes | 38 | $6,932 | None |
| | | | | | | | 18 | | Yes | | | None |
| Yes | | | No | | 6,185† | 7,238 | 9 | 138 | Yes | | | None |
| | | | No | | 22,296† | 9,265 | | | Yes | | | None |
| | | | Yes | | 33,522† | 11,086 | | 1340 | Yes | | | None |
| Yes | | | Yes | Yes | 26,158† | 10,030 | 12 | | Yes | | | 4/15 |
| | | | Yes | | 6,218† | 7,818 | | 184 | | | | |
| | | | Yes | | 34,800† | 15,985 | | 1120 | Yes | | | None |
| | | | Yes | Yes | 6,520† | 9,238 | 12 | 184 | | | | |
| Yes | | | Yes | | 25,150† | 11,482 | | | Yes | 21 | $10,630 | None |
| Yes | | | Yes | | 27,570† | 10,100 | | 950 | Yes | 1 | $13,185 | None |
| Yes | Yes | Yes | Yes | Yes | 29,498† | 11,442 | 9 | 908 | Yes | 33 | $5,303 | 4/15 |
| Yes | | | No | | 17,048† | | 12 | 537 | Yes | | | None |
| Yes | Yes | | Yes | Yes | 19,026‡ | 10,834 | 16 | 567 | Yes | 4 | $7,625 | None |
| Yes | | Yes | Yes | Yes | 11,205† | 8,910 | 9 | 341 | Yes | | | None |
| Yes | | | Yes | | 19,300† | 8,486 | | 616 | Yes | 7 | $5,500 | None |
| Yes | | | Yes | Yes | 11,634‡ | 8,264 | 12 | 353 | Yes | 21 | $2,899 | None |
| Yes | Yes | | Yes | Yes | 35,598† | 16,250 | | 1210 | Yes | | | None |
| Yes | Yes | Yes | Yes | Yes | 21,280† | 9,200 | | 665 | Yes | | | None |
| | | | Yes | | 6,200† | 5,490 | | 184 | Yes | | | None |
| | | | No | | 6,300† | 6,740 | | 184 | Yes | 1144 | $266 | None |
| Yes | | Yes | Yes | Yes | 8,345† | | 8 | 270 | Yes | | | None |

† Actual for 2016-17.   ‡ Estimated for 2017-18.   * Includes room and board

| Institution | Control/ degrees | Undergraduates | | Tests required (Fall 2017) | TOEFL | | Application | |
|---|---|---|---|---|---|---|---|---|
| | | Total | Internat'l | | minimum | average | Deadline | Fee |
| Anne Arundel Community College . . . . . . . . . . . . | Pu/A | 11,821 | 173 | TOEFL | 79 | | 6/1 | |
| Baltimore City Community College. . . . . . . . . . . . | Pu/A | 5,269 | | | | | | 10 |
| Bowie State University. . . . . . . . . . . . . . . . . . . . . | Pu/B | 4,711 | 59 | TOEFL | | | | 40 |
| Brightwood College: Baltimore. . . . . . . . . . . . . | Pr/A | 582 | | | | | | 10 |
| Brightwood College: Beltsville. . . . . . . . . . . . . | Pr/A | 388 | | | | | | 10 |
| Brightwood College: Towson. . . . . . . . . . . . . . . | Pr/A | 318 | | | | | | 10 |
| Capitol Technology University . . . . . . . . . . . . . . | Pr/AB | 441 | | TOEFL | | | | 200 |
| Carroll Community College. . . . . . . . . . . . . . . . | Pu/A | 2,942 | 5 | TOEFL | | | 6/16 | |
| Chesapeake College . . . . . . . . . . . . . . . . . . . . . | Pu/A | 1,807 | 24 | TOEFL | | | 7/1 | |
| College of Southern Maryland . . . . . . . . . . . . . . | Pu/A | 8,781 | | TOEFL | 61 | | | |
| Community College of Baltimore County . . . . . . . . | Pu/A | 19,390 | 972 | TOEFL | 45 | | 8/10 | |
| Coppin State University . . . . . . . . . . . . . . . . . . | Pu/B | 2,920 | | TOEFL | | | | 35 |
| Frostburg State University . . . . . . . . . . . . . . . . | Pu/B | 4,779 | 59 | TOEFL, SAT | 79 | | | 30 |
| Garrett College . . . . . . . . . . . . . . . . . . . . . . . . | Pu/A | 506 | 10 | TOEFL | 80 | | 6/1 | |
| Goucher College . . . . . . . . . . . . . . . . . . . . . . . . | Pr/B | 1,461 | 47 | TOEFL | 79 | 98 | 2/1 | 55 |
| Harford Community College . . . . . . . . . . . . . . . . | Pu/A | 5,155 | 59 | TOEFL | 61 | | 6/1 | |
| Hood College . . . . . . . . . . . . . . . . . . . . . . . . . . | Pr/B | 1,151 | 19 | TOEFL | 79 | | | |
| Howard Community College . . . . . . . . . . . . . . . . | Pu/A | 9,114 | 434 | TOEFL | 74 | 84 | 6/1 | 50 |
| Johns Hopkins University . . . . . . . . . . . . . . . . . | Pr/B | 5,691 | 598 | TOEFL, SAT/ACT | 100 | | | 70 |
| Johns Hopkins University: Peabody Conservatory of Music . . . . . . . . . . . . . . . . . . . | Pr/B | 265 | | TOEFL | 79 | | | 100 |
| Kaplan University: Hagerstown . . . . . . . . . . . . . . | Pr/AB | 672 | | | | | | 20 |
| Loyola University Maryland. . . . . . . . . . . . . . . . | Pr/B | 4,067 | 23 | TOEFL | 79 | 96 | 1/15 | 60 |
| Maryland Institute College of Art . . . . . . . . . . . . | Pr/B | 1,673 | 308 | TOEFL | 80 | | 2/1 | 70 |
| McDaniel College . . . . . . . . . . . . . . . . . . . . . . . | Pr/B | 1,528 | | TOEFL | 80 | | 2/1 | 50 |
| Morgan State University . . . . . . . . . . . . . . . . . . | Pu/B | 6,333 | 724 | TOEFL, SAT/ACT | | | | 35 |
| Mount St. Mary's University . . . . . . . . . . . . . . . | Pr/B | 1,717 | 15 | TOEFL | 83 | | 3/1 | 45 |
| Notre Dame of Maryland University . . . . . . . . . . | Pr/B | 869 | 16 | TOEFL | | | | |
| Prince George's Community College . . . . . . . . . . | Pu/A | 13,733 | | TOEFL | | | | 25 |
| St. John's College . . . . . . . . . . . . . . . . . . . . . . | Pr/B | 434 | 78 | TOEFL, SAT/ACT | 100 | 103 | None | |
| St. Mary's College of Maryland . . . . . . . . . . . . . | Pu/B | 1,618 | 8 | TOEFL | 90 | 97 | 2/15 | 50 |
| Salisbury University. . . . . . . . . . . . . . . . . . . . . . | Pu/B | 7,657 | 122 | TOEFL | 79 | | 1/15 | 50 |
| Stevenson University . . . . . . . . . . . . . . . . . . . . | Pr/B | 3,598 | 17 | TOEFL | | | | 40 |
| Towson University. . . . . . . . . . . . . . . . . . . . . . . | Pu/B | 18,968 | 299 | TOEFL | 61 | 82 | 5/15 | 45 |
| United States Naval Academy . . . . . . . . . . . . . . . | Pu/B | 4,526 | 58 | TOEFL, SAT/ACT | | | 12/1 | |
| University of Baltimore. . . . . . . . . . . . . . . . . . . | Pu/B | 3,344 | | TOEFL, SAT/ACT | 79 | | | 30 |
| University of Maryland: Baltimore . . . . . . . . . . . | Pu/B | 904 | 18 | TOEFL | | | 1/15 | 50 |
| University of Maryland: Baltimore County . . . . . . | Pu/B | 11,025 | 428 | TOEFL | 80 | | | 50 |
| University of Maryland: College Park . . . . . . . . . | Pu/B | 27,864 | 1,145 | TOEFL | 100 | | 11/1 | 75 |
| University of Maryland: Eastern Shore. . . . . . . . . | Pu/B | 3,163 | 89 | TOEFL | 67 | | 7/15 | 25 |
| University of Maryland: University College . . . . . . | Pu/AB | 41,068 | 564 | TOEFL | 79 | | None | 50 |
| University of Phoenix: Maryland . . . . . . . . . . . . . | Pr/B | 395 | | | | | | |
| Washington Adventist University . . . . . . . . . . . . . | Pr/AB | 911 | | TOEFL | | | | 25 |
| Washington College. . . . . . . . . . . . . . . . . . . . . . | Pr/B | 1,446 | 153 | TOEFL | 79 | 90 | 2/15 | 50 |
| Yeshiva College of the Nations Capital . . . . . . . . . | Pr/B | 35 | | | | | | |
| **Massachusetts** | | | | | | | | |
| American International College. . . . . . . . . . . . . . | Pr/AB | 1,408 | 50 | TOEFL, SAT/ACT | | | None | 35 |
| Amherst College . . . . . . . . . . . . . . . . . . . . . . . . | Pr/B | 1,849 | 174 | TOEFL, SAT/ACT | 100 | | 1/1 | 60 |
| Anna Maria College. . . . . . . . . . . . . . . . . . . . . . | Pr/B | 1,057 | 4 | TOEFL | 79 | | | 25 |
| Assumption College. . . . . . . . . . . . . . . . . . . . . . | Pr/B | 1,976 | 48 | TOEFL | 80 | | | 50 |
| Babson College. . . . . . . . . . . . . . . . . . . . . . . . . | Pr/B | 2,283 | 608 | TOEFL, SAT/ACT | 100 | | 1/3 | 75 |
| Bard College at Simon's Rock . . . . . . . . . . . . . . | Pr/AB | 362 | 50 | TOEFL | 100 | | | |
| Bay Path University . . . . . . . . . . . . . . . . . . . . . | Pr/AB | 1,886 | 11 | TOEFL | 76 | | 7/1 | 25 |
| Bay State College . . . . . . . . . . . . . . . . . . . . . . . | Pr/AB | 884 | 21 | TOEFL | 65 | | None | 50 |
| Becker College . . . . . . . . . . . . . . . . . . . . . . . . . | Pr/AB | 1,951 | 14 | TOEFL | 79 | | | |
| Benjamin Franklin Institute of Technology . . . . . . . | Pr/AB | 493 | | TOEFL | 61 | | | 50 |
| Bentley University. . . . . . . . . . . . . . . . . . . . . . . | Pr/B | 4,152 | 563 | TOEFL, SAT/ACT | 90 | 97 | 1/18 | 75 |
| Berklee College of Music . . . . . . . . . . . . . . . . . . | Pr/B | 5,972 | 1,779 | TOEFL | | | 1/15 | 150 |

| Student services | | | Housing | | Academic year costs | | Maximum credits/ summer | Credit hour charge | International financial aid | | | |
|---|---|---|---|---|---|---|---|---|---|---|---|---|
| Adviser | Orientation | ESL | Academic year | Summer | Tuition/ fees | Living costs | | | Available | Number receiving aid | Average award | Deadline |
| Yes | Yes | Yes | No | | 11,780† | 10,354 | 7 | 367 | | 12 | $229 | |
| Yes | | Yes | No | | 7,952† | | 12 | 245 | Yes | | | None |
| Yes | Yes | | Yes | Yes | 18,416† | 10,200 | 12 | 667 | Yes | | | 3/1 |
| Yes | | | Yes | Yes | 24,362† | 5,536 | 12 | 772 | | | | |
| | | Yes | No | | 9,744† | 5,500 | | 324 | Yes | | | None |
| | | Yes | No | | 9,050† | 4,100 | | 265 | | | | |
| Yes | | | No | | 10,148† | 9,449 | 6 | 275 | | | | |
| Yes | Yes | Yes | No | | 11,602† | | | 337 | Yes | | | None |
| Yes | Yes | | Yes | | 12,178† | 9,753 | 9 | 563 | | | | |
| Yes | Yes | | Yes | Yes | 21,226† | 9,312 | 12 | 530 | | | | |
| | | | Yes | | 9,170 | 6,009 | 6 | 270 | Yes | | | None |
| Yes | Yes | | Yes | Yes | 43,416† | 12,300 | | | Yes | 38 | $32,422 | 4/1 |
| Yes | Yes | | No | | 9,684† | 9,000 | 6 | 298 | Yes | 18 | $1,207 | None |
| Yes | Yes | | Yes | Yes | 37,960 | 13,580 | 12 | 1090 | Yes | 17 | $30,772 | None |
| Yes | Yes | Yes | No | | 8,533† | 15,133 | 12 | 262 | Yes | 1 | $500 | None |
| Yes | Yes | | Yes | Yes | 50,910† | 14,976 | | 1680 | Yes | | | 3/1 |
| Yes | Yes | | Yes | | 45,632† | 15,122 | | 1258 | Yes | | | 2/1 |
| | | | Yes | | | | | | | | | |
| Yes | Yes | | Yes | Yes | 46,430† | 13,870 | 12 | | | | | |
| Yes | Yes | | Yes | Yes | 46,990 | 15,360 | | 1890 | Yes | | | 2/15 |
| Yes | Yes | | Yes | | 41,800 | 11,110 | 12 | 1306 | Yes | 16 | $31,576 | None |
| Yes | | | Yes | | 17,504† | 9,910 | 6 | 592 | Yes | 137 | $4,984 | None |
| Yes | | | Yes | Yes | 40,550 | 12,830 | 12 | 1275 | Yes | 14 | $38,027 | 3/1 |
| Yes | Yes | Yes | Yes | | 35,019† | 11,446 | 9 | 1126 | Yes | | | None |
| | Yes | | No | | 10,100† | 6,893 | 12 | 290 | | | | |
| Yes | Yes | | Yes | | 51,670 | 12,233 | | | Yes | | | None |
| Yes | Yes | | Yes | | 29,340† | 12,442 | 8 | | Yes | 1 | $6,000 | None |
| Yes | Yes | Yes | Yes | Yes | 17,776† | 11,350 | 9 | 631 | Yes | 11 | $2,607 | None |
| Yes | | | Yes | | 33,168† | 12,702 | | 780 | Yes | | | None |
| Yes | Yes | Yes | Yes | Yes | 21,076† | 11,754 | 15 | 768 | Yes | 62 | $8,364 | None |
| Yes | Yes | | Yes | Yes | | | | | | | | |
| Yes | Yes | | Yes | | 20,242† | 13,100 | 6 | 954 | Yes | | | None |
| Yes | Yes | | Yes | | 34,780† | 19,350 | | 1179 | Yes | | | None |
| Yes | Yes | Yes | Yes | Yes | 24,492† | 11,218 | 12 | 890 | Yes | 67 | $17,142 | None |
| Yes | Yes | Yes | Yes | Yes | 32,045† | 11,758 | 16 | 1258 | | | | |
| Yes | Yes | | Yes | Yes | 17,188† | 10,913 | 6 | 534 | Yes | | | 4/1 |
| Yes | | | No | | 12,426† | | 18 | 499 | | | | |
| Yes | | Yes | Yes | Yes | 23,400† | 8,930 | 6 | | Yes | | | 3/31 |
| Yes | Yes | | Yes | | 44,700 | 11,040 | | | Yes | | | None |
| | | | Yes | | 9,700† | 9,200 | | | | | | |
| Yes | Yes | | Yes | Yes | 33,200† | 13,490 | 12 | 685 | Yes | 36 | $37,792 | None |
| Yes | Yes | | Yes | | 52,476† | 14,510 | | | Yes | 156 | $59,163 | None |
| | | Yes | Yes | | 36,110† | 13,510 | 18 | 1410 | Yes | | | None |
| Yes | | | Yes | Yes | 36,260† | 11,660 | 12 | 1184 | Yes | 28 | $23,308 | 2/15 |
| Yes | Yes | | Yes | Yes | 48,288† | 15,376 | 8 | | Yes | 79 | $31,708 | 2/15 |
| Yes | Yes | | Yes | | 52,385† | 16,560 | | | Yes | | | None |
| Yes | Yes | | Yes | Yes | 32,739† | 15,210 | 6 | | Yes | 5 | $21,049 | None |
| Yes | Yes | | Yes | Yes | 27,750† | 14,500 | | 905 | Yes | | | 6/30 |
| Yes | Yes | | Yes | | 38,250‡ | 16,700 | | 1444 | Yes | 21 | $12,333 | None |
| Yes | | Yes | Yes | Yes | 16,950† | 15,050 | 17 | 707 | Yes | | | None |
| Yes | Yes | | Yes | Yes | 45,760† | 15,130 | 15 | | Yes | 118 | $19,823 | 1/7 |
| Yes | Yes | Yes | Yes | Yes | 42,750 | 18,180 | 16 | 1510 | Yes | 926 | $19,014 | None |

† Actual for 2016-17.    ‡ Estimated for 2017-18.    * Includes room and board

| Institution | Control/ degrees | Undergraduates | | Tests required (Fall 2017) | TOEFL | | Application | |
|---|---|---|---|---|---|---|---|---|
| | | Total | Internat'l | | minimum | average | Deadline | Fee |
| Berkshire Community College | Pu/A | 1,666 | 3 | TOEFL | 61 | | None | |
| Boston Baptist College | Pr/AB | 98 | | | | | | 50 |
| Boston College | Pr/B | 9,309 | 609 | TOEFL, SAT/ACT | 100 | 106 | 1/1 | 75 |
| Boston Conservatory | Pr/B | 565 | | TOEFL | 73 | | | 110 |
| Boston University | Pr/B | 16,511 | 3,614 | TOEFL, SAT/ACT | 90 | 105 | 1/2 | 80 |
| Brandeis University | Pr/B | 3,597 | 742 | TOEFL, SAT/ACT | 100 | 105 | 1/1 | 80 |
| Bridgewater State University | Pu/B | 9,387 | 35 | TOEFL | 61 | | | 50 |
| Bristol Community College | Pu/A | 8,476 | | TOEFL | 61 | | | 35 |
| Bunker Hill Community College | Pu/A | 12,004 | | TOEFL | 38 | | | |
| Cambridge College | Pr/B | 1,209 | | TOEFL | 79 | | | 30 |
| Cape Cod Community College | Pu/A | 2,764 | | TOEFL | 68 | | 6/1 | |
| Clark University | Pr/B | 2,247 | 320 | TOEFL | 80 | 100 | | 60 |
| College of the Holy Cross | Pr/B | 2,910 | 75 | TOEFL | 100 | | 1/15 | 60 |
| Curry College | Pr/B | 2,653 | 50 | TOEFL, SAT/ACT | 68 | 79 | 4/1 | 50 |
| Dean College | Pr/AB | 1,300 | 83 | TOEFL | 60 | 72 | 7/31 | |
| Eastern Nazarene College | Pr/AB | 780 | 19 | TOEFL, SAT/ACT | 63 | | None | |
| Elms College | Pr/AB | 1,155 | 8 | TOEFL | | | None | 30 |
| Emerson College | Pr/B | 3,782 | 318 | TOEFL | 80 | 100 | | 65 |
| Emmanuel College | Pr/B | 1,907 | 37 | TOEFL | | | 2/15 | 60 |
| Endicott College | Pr/AB | 3,081 | 60 | TOEFL | 79 | | 2/15 | 50 |
| Fisher College | Pr/AB | 1,556 | 141 | TOEFL | 61 | | | 50 |
| Fitchburg State University | Pu/B | 3,985 | 19 | TOEFL, SAT/ACT | 79 | 85 | None | 50 |
| Framingham State University | Pu/B | 4,100 | 18 | TOEFL | 79 | | | 50 |
| Franklin W. Olin College of Engineering | Pr/B | 331 | 26 | | | | 1/1 | 100 |
| Gordon College | Pr/B | 1,631 | 150 | TOEFL | 85 | 101 | 2/1 | 50 |
| Greenfield Community College | Pu/A | 1,649 | | TOEFL | 71 | | | 35 |
| Hampshire College | Pr/B | 1,396 | 70 | TOEFL | 91 | 98 | 11/1 | |
| Harvard College | Pr/B | 6,648 | 772 | | | | | 75 |
| Hellenic College/Holy Cross | Pr/B | 119 | | TOEFL | 61 | | | 50 |
| Holyoke Community College | Pu/A | 5,364 | 45 | TOEFL | 61 | | 5/1 | 100 |
| Lasell College | Pr/B | 1,778 | 114 | TOEFL | 71 | 81 | 8/15 | 40 |
| Lesley University | Pr/AB | 1,521 | | TOEFL, SAT/ACT | 80 | 94 | | 50 |
| Massachusetts Bay Community College | Pu/A | 3,850 | 89 | TOEFL | | | | 20 |
| Massachusetts College of Art and Design | Pu/B | 1,722 | 79 | TOEFL | 85 | 87 | 2/1 | 70 |
| Massachusetts College of Liberal Arts | Pu/B | 1,408 | 8 | TOEFL, SAT/ACT | | | | |
| Massachusetts Institute of Technology | Pr/B | 4,489 | 428 | TOEFL, SAT Subject Test(s) | 90 | | 1/1 | 75 |
| Massachusetts Maritime Academy | Pu/B | 1,641 | 10 | TOEFL, SAT/ACT | 75 | | | 50 |
| Massasoit Community College | Pu/A | 7,905 | | TOEFL | 53 | | | |
| MCPHS University | Pr/B | 3,791 | | TOEFL, SAT/ACT | 79 | 98 | | |
| Merrimack College | Pr/B | 3,416 | 112 | TOEFL | 79 | 85 | 2/15 | |
| Middlesex Community College | Pu/A | 7,709 | | TOEFL | 61 | | 7/15 | |
| Montserrat College of Art | Pr/B | 378 | | TOEFL | 68 | | | 50 |
| Mount Holyoke College | Pr/B | 2,179 | 587 | TOEFL | 100 | 106 | 1/15 | 60 |
| Mount Ida College | Pr/AB | 1,317 | | TOEFL | 70 | | | 45 |
| Mount Wachusett Community College | Pu/A | 3,570 | 11 | TOEFL | | | | |
| New England College of Business and Finance | Pr/AB | 690 | | TOEFL | 80 | | | 50 |
| New England Conservatory of Music | Pr/B | 382 | 145 | TOEFL | 61 | | | 115 |
| Newbury College | Pr/AB | 747 | | TOEFL | 71 | 79 | 5/1 | |
| Nichols College | Pr/AB | 1,259 | 18 | TOEFL | 72 | 90 | None | 25 |
| North Shore Community College | Pu/A | 5,893 | 4 | TOEFL | | | | |
| Northeastern University | Pr/B | 17,795 | 3,414 | TOEFL | 92 | 104 | | 75 |
| Northern Essex Community College | Pu/A | 5,530 | 32 | TOEFL | 61 | | | |
| Northpoint Bible College | Pr/AB | 227 | | TOEFL | 61 | | | 75 |
| Pine Manor College | Pr/AB | 287 | | TOEFL | 65 | | None | 25 |
| Quincy College | Pu/A | 4,732 | | TOEFL | 38 | | | 30 |
| Quinsigamond Community College | Pu/A | 6,917 | | TOEFL | 61 | | 7/1 | 50 |
| Regis College | Pr/AB | 1,235 | 22 | TOEFL | 79 | | 6/1 | 50 |

| Student services | | | Housing | | Academic year costs | | Maximum credits/ summer | Credit hour charge | International financial aid | | | |
|---|---|---|---|---|---|---|---|---|---|---|---|---|
| Adviser | Orien- tation | ESL | Academic year | Summer | Tuition/ fees | Living costs | | | Avail- able | Number receiving aid | Average award | Deadline |
| Yes | Yes | Yes | No | | 13,260† | 13,620 | | 260 | Yes | | | None |
| | | | Yes | | 15,040† | 8,102 | | 475 | Yes | | | None |
| Yes | Yes | | Yes | | 51,296† | 15,468 | 12 | | | | | |
| Yes | Yes | Yes | Yes | Yes | 43,860† | 20,174 | 6 | 1670 | Yes | | | None |
| Yes | Yes | Yes | Yes | Yes | 50,240† | 16,487 | 16 | 1537 | Yes | 171 | $34,277 | 2/1 |
| Yes | Yes | Yes | Yes | | 51,548† | 14,380 | | 1549 | Yes | 67 | $46,310 | None |
| Yes | Yes | Yes | Yes | Yes | 15,750† | 12,200 | | 294 | | | | |
| Yes | | Yes | No | | 11,895† | | 15 | 230 | | | | |
| Yes | Yes | Yes | No | | 10,740† | | 12 | 230 | Yes | | | None |
| Yes | Yes | | No | | 13,760† | 8,000 | | 401 | Yes | | | 10/1 |
| | | | No | | 13,116† | 7,000 | 6 | 386 | | | | |
| Yes | Yes | Yes | Yes | Yes | 43,150† | 8,450 | 8 | 1337.5 | Yes | 234 | $28,172 | 2/1 |
| Yes | Yes | | Yes | | 48,940† | 13,225 | | | Yes | 26 | $48,767 | 1/15 |
| Yes | Yes | | Yes | | 38,596 | 15,415 | 12 | 1226 | Yes | 39 | $15,952 | None |
| Yes | Yes | Yes | Yes | Yes | 38,390 | 16,846 | | | Yes | | | None |
| Yes | | | Yes | | 31,780 | 9,334 | | 1260 | Yes | | | 8/1 |
| Yes | Yes | Yes | Yes | | 34,578 | 12,664 | | 668 | Yes | 6 | $13,683 | None |
| Yes | Yes | | Yes | Yes | 42,908† | 16,320 | 16 | 1317 | Yes | | | 3/1 |
| Yes | | | Yes | | 39,144‡ | 14,628 | | 1205.75 | Yes | 30 | $6,363 | None |
| Yes | | | Yes | Yes | 31,312† | 14,500 | | | Yes | 32 | $16,753 | None |
| Yes | Yes | Yes | Yes | Yes | 30,499‡ | 15,768 | 12 | 984 | Yes | | | 3/15 |
| Yes | Yes | | Yes | | 16,249† | 10,170 | 18 | 294 | | | | |
| Yes | | Yes | Yes | | 15,420† | 11,250 | 16 | 294 | | | | |
| Yes | | | Yes | | 49,986† | 15,800 | | 1560 | Yes | 25 | $26,361 | 2/15 |
| Yes | Yes | | Yes | Yes | 36,740 | 13,000 | | 879 | Yes | 157 | $19,984 | None |
| Yes | Yes | | No | | 14,282‡ | 5,840 | 12 | | | | | |
| Yes | Yes | | Yes | | 50,550† | 13,274 | | | Yes | | | 1/15 |
| Yes | Yes | | Yes | | 48,859 | 16,660 | 3 | | Yes | | | 3/1 |
| Yes | | | Yes | Yes | 22,490† | 16,192 | 6 | 950 | Yes | 2 | $19,000 | |
| | | Yes | No | | 11,750† | | | 230 | | | | |
| Yes | Yes | Yes | Yes | | 34,600 | 14,800 | | 1110 | Yes | 2 | $8,000 | None |
| Yes | Yes | | Yes | Yes | 26,250† | 15,300 | 9 | | Yes | | | None |
| Yes | Yes | Yes | No | | 12,090† | 8,606 | | 230 | Yes | | | None |
| Yes | Yes | | Yes | Yes | 32,800† | 13,100 | | | | | | |
| | | | Yes | Yes | 18,820† | 10,078 | | 416 | | | | |
| Yes | Yes | | Yes | | 49,892 | 14,720 | | | Yes | 328 | $46,968 | 2/15 |
| Yes | | | Yes | | 24,600† | 11,978 | | 1013.88 | | | | |
| | | Yes | No | | 12,030† | 9,000 | 12 | 230 | | | | |
| Yes | Yes | Yes | Yes | Yes | 31,670‡ | 15,834 | 12 | 1125 | | | | |
| Yes | Yes | | Yes | Yes | 38,825† | 14,345 | 32 | 1310 | Yes | 75 | $24,388 | None |
| Yes | Yes | | No | | 12,080† | | | 401 | | | | |
| | | | Yes | | 29,550† | 11,100 | | | Yes | | | None |
| Yes | Yes | | Yes | Yes | 45,866† | 13,440 | 8 | 1430 | Yes | 365 | $33,039 | 2/1 |
| Yes | Yes | Yes | Yes | Yes | 35,720‡ | 13,680 | | | Yes | | | None |
| Yes | Yes | Yes | Yes | | 12,700† | 7,400 | 12 | | Yes | 2 | $2,947 | None |
| | | | No | | | | 6 | | | | | |
| Yes | Yes | Yes | Yes | | 44,755† | 13,900 | | 1420 | Yes | | | 12/1 |
| Yes | | | Yes | | 33,685† | 15,700 | 18 | 1020 | Yes | | | 5/1 |
| Yes | | | Yes | | 34,000 | 13,800 | 6 | 350 | Yes | | | 6/1 |
| Yes | Yes | | No | | 13,020† | | 12 | 257 | | | | |
| Yes | Yes | Yes | Yes | Yes | 47,655† | 15,600 | 16 | | Yes | 461 | $19,760 | None |
| Yes | Yes | | No | | 13,540† | | 12 | 266 | | | | |
| Yes | | | Yes | | 11,510† | 8,600 | 8 | 345 | | | | |
| Yes | Yes | Yes | Yes | Yes | 28,620† | 13,280 | 8 | | Yes | | | None |
| Yes | Yes | Yes | No | | 11,298† | | 12 | 220 | | | | |
| Yes | | | No | | 12,720† | 8,854 | 12 | 230 | | | | |
| Yes | Yes | Yes | Yes | Yes | 39,040† | 14,740 | 12 | 1301.33 | Yes | 11 | $23,357 | None |

† Actual for 2016-17.  ‡ Estimated for 2017-18.  * Includes room and board

| Institution | Control/ degrees | Undergraduates | | Tests required (Fall 2017) | TOEFL | | Application | |
|---|---|---|---|---|---|---|---|---|
| | | Total | Internat'l | | minimum | average | Deadline | Fee |
| Roxbury Community College................. | Pu/A | 2,437 | | | | | | 135 |
| Salem State University..................... | Pu/B | 7,346 | | TOEFL, SAT/ACT | 61 | | | 40 |
| School of the Museum of Fine Arts............ | Pr/B | 349 | | TOEFL | 79 | | | 65 |
| Simmons College......................... | Pr/B | 1,772 | 73 | TOEFL, SAT/ACT | 83 | 98 | 2/1 | 55 |
| Smith College........................... | Pr/B | 2,501 | 358 | TOEFL | | 90 | | 60 |
| Springfield College ...................... | Pr/B | 2,182 | | TOEFL, SAT | 69 | | | 50 |
| Springfield Technical Community College ........ | Pu/A | 5,622 | | TOEFL | 80 | | | |
| Stonehill College......................... | Pr/B | 2,472 | 22 | TOEFL | 90 | 93 | 1/15 | 60 |
| Suffolk University........................ | Pr/AB | 5,185 | 1,162 | TOEFL, SAT/ACT | 77 | 84 | | 50 |
| Tufts University ......................... | Pr/B | 5,459 | 563 | TOEFL, SAT, SAT Subject Test(s), or ACT | 100 | 110 | 1/1 | 75 |
| University of Massachusetts Amherst........... | Pu/AB | 22,958 | 1,138 | TOEFL, SAT/ACT | 80 | | 1/15 | 75 |
| University of Massachusetts Boston............ | Pu/B | 12,210 | 1,503 | TOEFL | | | | 100 |
| University of Massachusetts Dartmouth ......... | Pu/B | 6,758 | 112 | TOEFL, SAT/ACT | 79 | 83 | | 60 |
| University of Massachusetts Lowell............ | Pu/AB | 12,914 | 464 | TOEFL, SAT/ACT | 79 | 93 | 7/18 | 60 |
| University of Phoenix: Boston ............... | Pr/B | 179 | | | | | | |
| Wellesley College ....................... | Pr/B | 2,188 | 260 | TOEFL, SAT/ACT | | 110 | 1/15 | 50 |
| Wentworth Institute of Technology ............ | Pr/AB | 3,931 | 343 | TOEFL | 79 | | | 50 |
| Western New England University ............. | Pr/AB | 2,717 | 94 | TOEFL | 79 | | None | 40 |
| Westfield State University.................. | Pu/B | 5,474 | 22 | TOEFL, SAT/ACT | 79 | | 2/1 | 50 |
| Wheaton College......................... | Pr/B | 1,637 | 193 | TOEFL | 90 | 102 | 1/1 | 60 |
| Wheelock College ....................... | Pr/B | 721 | 16 | TOEFL, SAT/ACT | 80 | | | 15 |
| Williams College......................... | Pr/B | 2,042 | 162 | | | | 1/1 | 65 |
| Worcester Polytechnic Institute............... | Pr/B | 4,320 | 483 | TOEFL | 80 | 103 | 2/1 | 65 |
| Worcester State University ................. | Pu/B | 4,891 | 35 | TOEFL, SAT/ACT | 79 | | | 50 |
| **Michigan** | | | | | | | | |
| Adrian College .......................... | Pr/AB | 1,622 | | | | | 3/15 | |
| Albion College .......................... | Pr/B | 1,393 | 31 | TOEFL | 79 | 90 | | |
| Alma College ........................... | Pr/B | 1,414 | 20 | TOEFL | 79 | 84 | None | 25 |
| Andrews University....................... | Pr/AB | 1,467 | 248 | TOEFL | | | | 30 |
| Aquinas College ......................... | Pr/AB | 1,549 | 29 | TOEFL | | | 5/1 | |
| Art Institute of Michigan................... | Pr/AB | 986 | | | | | | 50 |
| Baker College of Allen Park ............... | Pr/AB | 4,000 | | | | | | 20 |
| Baker College of Auburn Hills.............. | Pr/AB | 3,400 | | TOEFL | | | | 20 |
| Baker College of Cadillac.................. | Pr/AB | 1,800 | | TOEFL | | | | 20 |
| Baker College of Jackson .................. | Pr/AB | 2,009 | | TOEFL | | | | 20 |
| Baker College of Muskegon................. | Pr/AB | 4,500 | | TOEFL | 61 | | | 20 |
| Baker College of Owosso .................. | Pr/AB | 3,000 | | TOEFL | | | | 20 |
| Baker College of Port Huron ............... | Pr/AB | 1,200 | | TOEFL | | | | 20 |
| Bay College ............................ | Pu/A | 1,422 | | TOEFL | 61 | | | |
| Calvin College .......................... | Pr/B | 3,722 | 392 | TOEFL | 80 | 96 | 4/1 | 35 |
| Central Michigan University ................ | Pu/B | 19,551 | 400 | | 79 | | 6/1 | 35 |
| Cleary University......................... | Pr/AB | 454 | | TOEFL | 70 | | | 25 |
| College for Creative Studies ............... | Pr/B | 1,377 | 97 | TOEFL | 71 | | 7/1 | |
| Concordia University ..................... | Pr/AB | 592 | | TOEFL, SAT/ACT | 68 | | | 100 |
| Cornerstone University .................... | Pr/AB | 1,856 | 60 | TOEFL | 80 | | | 25 |
| Davenport University ..................... | Pr/AB | 5,398 | 128 | TOEFL | 61 | | | 50 |
| Delta College .......................... | Pu/A | 9,291 | | TOEFL | | | | 20 |
| Eastern Michigan University ............... | Pu/B | 17,256 | | TOEFL | 61 | | | 35 |
| Ferris State University ................... | Pu/AB | 12,006 | 108 | TOEFL | 61 | | None | 30 |
| Finlandia University....................... | Pr/AB | 600 | | TOEFL | | | | |
| Glen Oaks Community College ............. | Pu/A | 1,104 | | TOEFL | | | | |
| Gogebic Community College ............... | Pu/A | 793 | 3 | TOEFL | 61 | | | 100 |
| Grand Rapids Community College ........... | Pu/A | 13,244 | 58 | TOEFL | 71 | | 6/1 | |
| Grand Valley State University .............. | Pu/B | 22,081 | 265 | TOEFL | 80 | | | 30 |
| Henry Ford College....................... | Pu/AB | 10,958 | 209 | | | | | 30 |
| Hillsdale College......................... | Pr/B | 1,482 | | | 83 | | 5/1 | 35 |

| Student services | | | Housing | | Academic year costs | | Maximum credits/ summer | Credit hour charge | International financial aid | | | |
|---|---|---|---|---|---|---|---|---|---|---|---|---|
| Adviser | Orientation | ESL | Academic year | Summer | Tuition/ fees | Living costs | | | Available | Number receiving aid | Average award | Deadline |
| Yes | Yes | Yes | No | | 11,610† | | 9 | 247 | Yes | | | 5/1 |
| Yes | Yes | Yes | Yes | Yes | 15,466† | 13,110 | 18 | 293.75 | | | | |
| Yes | Yes | | Yes | | 52,430† | 16,556 | | | Yes | | | 3/15 |
| Yes | Yes | | Yes | Yes | 38,590† | 14,500 | 16 | | Yes | | | None |
| Yes | Yes | | Yes | Yes | 50,044 | 16,730 | 12 | 1560 | Yes | 155 | $51,569 | 2/15 |
| | | | | | | | | | | | | |
| Yes | Yes | Yes | Yes | Yes | 35,475† | 11,890 | | | | | | |
| Yes | | | No | | 12,246† | | 12 | 242 | Yes | | | None |
| Yes | Yes | | Yes | Yes | 39,900† | 15,130 | | 1330 | Yes | | | 2/1 |
| Yes | Yes | Yes | Yes | Yes | 37,510 | 16,576 | 12 | 1092 | Yes | 650 | $13,701 | 3/1 |
| Yes | Yes | | | Yes | 52,430† | 13,566 | | | Yes | 136 | $57,728 | 2/15 |
| | | | | | | | | | | | | |
| Yes | Yes | Yes | Yes | Yes | 32,389† | 13,341 | 12 | 1255 | Yes | 488 | $7,508 | None |
| Yes | Yes | Yes | No | | 32,023† | | 12 | | | | | |
| Yes | Yes | | Yes | Yes | 27,473† | 12,470 | | 1127.83 | | | | |
| Yes | Yes | | Yes | Yes | 30,875† | 12,073 | 20 | 1286 | Yes | | | None |
| | | | | | | | | | | | | |
| Yes | Yes | | Yes | Yes | 48,802† | 15,114 | | | Yes | 91 | $54,873 | None |
| Yes | Yes | | Yes | | 31,840‡ | 12,570 | | 995 | Yes | 168 | $4,627 | None |
| Yes | Yes | Yes | Yes | | 35,740 | 13,442 | | 628 | Yes | | | None |
| Yes | Yes | | Yes | | 15,355† | 11,865 | | | | | | |
| Yes | Yes | | Yes | Yes | 49,012† | 12,500 | | 1522 | Yes | 161 | $20,350 | 2/1 |
| | | | | | | | | | | | | |
| | | Yes | Yes | | 36,350 | 14,975 | | 1090 | Yes | | | |
| Yes | Yes | | Yes | | 51,790† | 13,690 | | | Yes | 98 | $60,944 | None |
| Yes | Yes | Yes | Yes | Yes | 48,628 | 14,218 | | 1333 | Yes | 436 | $21,341 | None |
| Yes | Yes | Yes | Yes | Yes | 15,282† | 11,775 | 12 | 293.75 | | | | |
| | | | | | | | | | | | | |
| | Yes | Yes | Yes | | 36,010‡ | 10,988 | 12 | 890 | Yes | | | None |
| | | | | | | | | | | | | |
| Yes | Yes | | Yes | | 41,040† | 15,410 | | 1720 | Yes | 29 | $30,495 | None |
| Yes | | | Yes | | 37,310† | 13,238 | | 1150 | Yes | 3 | $28,553 | None |
| Yes | Yes | Yes | Yes | Yes | 27,684† | 8,742 | | 1116 | Yes | 249 | $27,519 | None |
| Yes | Yes | | Yes | Yes | 31,244 | 9,070 | 12 | 498 | Yes | 15 | $17,898 | None |
| | | | | | | | | | | | | |
| Yes | | | No | | 11,250† | | | 250 | | | | |
| Yes | | | No | | 11,250† | 7,200 | 16 | 250 | | | | |
| Yes | | | | | 11,250† | | 16 | 250 | | | | |
| | | | Yes | Yes | 11,250† | | 16 | 250 | | | | |
| | | | | | | | | | | | | |
| Yes | | | Yes | | 11,250† | 7,200 | 16 | 250 | | | | |
| Yes | | | No | | 11,250† | | 16 | 250 | | | | |
| Yes | | | Yes | Yes | 11,928† | 3,000 | 8 | 362 | | | | |
| Yes | Yes | | Yes | Yes | 31,730† | 11,240 | 13 | 760 | Yes | 374 | $19,569 | None |
| Yes | Yes | Yes | Yes | Yes | 23,670† | 10,406 | 12 | 789 | Yes | 53 | $5,979 | None |
| | | | | | | | | | | | | |
| Yes | | | | | 17,500† | 9,600 | 12 | 625 | Yes | | | None |
| Yes | Yes | | Yes | Yes | 42,460 | 8,650 | 6 | 1368 | Yes | | | None |
| | | | Yes | | 27,710† | 9,680 | | | Yes | | | 3/1 |
| Yes | Yes | | Yes | | 27,520 | 10,930 | | 1030 | Yes | 54 | $12,207 | None |
| Yes | Yes | Yes | Yes | Yes | 20,680† | 9,358 | | 664 | Yes | | | None |
| | | | | | | | | | | | | |
| Yes | Yes | | No | | 9,680† | 4,122 | | 320 | | | | None |
| Yes | Yes | Yes | Yes | Yes | 27,712† | 9,344 | | 873 | Yes | 202 | $18,692 | None |
| Yes | Yes | Yes | Yes | Yes | 18,990† | 9,651 | | 633 | Yes | 19 | $6,329 | None |
| Yes | Yes | Yes | Yes | | 22,758† | 8,800 | 12 | | Yes | | | None |
| Yes | | | No | | 7,050† | 6,560 | 18 | 206 | Yes | | | None |
| | | | | | | | | | | | | |
| Yes | | | Yes | Yes | 9,142† | 5,804 | 12 | 260 | | | | |
| Yes | Yes | | No | | 11,049† | 4,064 | | 353 | | | | |
| Yes | Yes | Yes | Yes | Yes | 16,392† | 8,400 | 16 | 683 | Yes | 168 | $8,032 | None |
| Yes | | | No | | 7,592† | 8,649 | | 230 | Yes | | | |
| | | | Yes | | 25,522† | 10,200 | | 985 | Yes | 27 | $25,394 | None |

† Actual for 2016-17.     ‡ Estimated for 2017-18.     * Includes room and board

| Institution | Control/ degrees | Undergraduates Total | Undergraduates Internat'l | Tests required (Fall 2017) | TOEFL minimum | TOEFL average | Application Deadline | Application Fee |
|---|---|---|---|---|---|---|---|---|
| Hope College . . . . . . . . . . . . . . . . . . . . : . . | Pr/B | 2,915 | 64 | TOEFL | 80 | | None | 35 |
| International Academy of Design and Technology: Detroit . . . . . . . . . . . . . . . . . . . . | Pr/AB | 134 | | | | | | 50 |
| Kalamazoo College . . . . . . . . . . . . . . . . . . . | Pr/B | 1,417 | 109 | TOEFL | | | 2/15 | |
| Kalamazoo Valley Community College . . . . . . . . | Pu/A | 7,148 | 77 | TOEFL | | | None | |
| Kellogg Community College . . . . . . . . . . . . . . . | Pu/A | 3,627 | | TOEFL | 61 | 65 | | |
| Kettering University. . . . . . . . . . . . . . . . . . . . | Pr/B | 1,866 | 77 | TOEFL | 79 | 92 | | 35 |
| Kirtland Community College . . . . . . . . . . . . . . . | Pu/A | 1,114 | | TOEFL | 61 | | None | |
| Kuyper College. . . . . . . . . . . . . . . . . . . . . . . | Pr/AB | 201 | | TOEFL | | | None | 25 |
| Lake Michigan College. . . . . . . . . . . . . . . . . . | Pu/AB | 2,820 | | | 63 | | | |
| Lake Superior State University . . . . . . . . . . . . . | Pu/AB | 2,063 | 139 | TOEFL | 61 | | 8/15 | 25 |
| Lansing Community College . . . . . . . . . . . . . . . | Pu/A | 12,673 | 187 | TOEFL | | | | |
| Lawrence Technological University. . . . . . . . . . . | Pr/AB | 2,004 | 330 | TOEFL, SAT/ACT | 79 | 87 | | 30 |
| Macomb Community College. . . . . . . . . . . . . . . | Pu/A | 16,543 | | TOEFL , | 61 | | None | |
| Madonna University. . . . . . . . . . . . . . . . . . . . | Pr/AB | 2,445 | 379 | | 70 | | | 25 |
| Manthano Christian College. . . . . . . . . . . . . . . | Pr/AB | 24 | | | | | | 25 |
| Marygrove College . . . . . . . . . . . . . . . . . . . . | Pr/AB | 492 | | TOEFL | | | 3/15 | |
| Michigan Jewish Institute . . . . . . . . . . . . . . . . | Pr/AB | 2,204 | | | | | | 50 |
| Michigan State University . . . . . . . . . . . . . . . . | Pu/B | 38,851 | 4,846 | TOEFL, SAT/ACT | 79 | | | 50 |
| Michigan Technological University . . . . . . . . . . . | Pu/AB | 5,753 | 186 | TOEFL | | | | |
| Mid Michigan Community College . . . . . . . . . . . | Pu/A | 4,120 | | TOEFL | | | | |
| Montcalm Community College. . . . . . . . . . . . . . | Pu/A | 1,832 | | TOEFL | | | | |
| Mott Community College . . . . . . . . . . . . . . . . . | Pu/A | 6,817 | 20 | TOEFL | 61 | | None | |
| Muskegon Community College. . . . . . . . . . . . . . | Pu/A | 3,441 | 12 | TOEFL | | | | |
| North Central Michigan College . . . . . . . . . . . . | Pu/A | 2,581 | | TOEFL | | | | |
| Northern Michigan University . . . . . . . . . . . . . . | Pu/AB | 8,233 | | TOEFL | 61 | | | 30 |
| Northwestern Michigan College . . . . . . . . . . . . | Pu/AB | 3,724 | 39 | TOEFL | 79 | 85 | | 25 |
| Northwood University: Michigan . . . . . . . . . . . . | Pr/AB | 1,422 | 97 | TOEFL | 61 | | 6/1 | 30 |
| Oakland Community College. . . . . . . . . . . . . . . | Pu/A | 21,260 | | TOEFL | 79 | | | |
| Oakland University . . . . . . . . . . . . . . . . . . . . | Pu/B | 16,233 | 322 | TOEFL, SAT/ACT | 79 | | 7/18 | |
| Olivet College. . . . . . . . . . . . . . . . . . . . . . . | Pr/B | 993 | | TOEFL, SAT/ACT | 80 | | 9/1 | 25 |
| Robert B. Miller College. . . . . . . . . . . . . . . . . | Pr/B | 327 | | | | | | 25 |
| Rochester College . . . . . . . . . . . . . . . . . . . . | Pr/AB | 1,117 | | TOEFL, ACT | | | | 30 |
| Sacred Heart Major Seminary. . . . . . . . . . . . . . | Pr/AB | 260 | | TOEFL | | | | 25 |
| Saginaw Chippewa Tribal College. . . . . . . . . . . | Pu/A | 141 | | | | | | 25 |
| Saginaw Valley State University . . . . . . . . . . . . | Pu/B | 7,913 | 466 | TOEFL | 61 | | 7/15 | 80 |
| St. Clair County Community College. . . . . . . . . . | Pu/A | 3,625 | | TOEFL | 68 | | 6/1 | |
| Schoolcraft College . . . . . . . . . . . . . . . . . . . | Pu/AB | 10,145 | | TOEFL | 52 | | None | |
| Siena Heights University. . . . . . . . . . . . . . . . . | Pr/AB | 2,289 | | TOEFL | | | | |
| Southwestern Michigan College . . . . . . . . . . . . | Pu/A | 1,807 | 1 | | | | | |
| Spring Arbor University . . . . . . . . . . . . . . . . . | Pr/AB | 2,100 | | TOEFL | 79 | | | 30 |
| University of Detroit Mercy. . . . . . . . . . . . . . . | Pr/B | 2,530 | 145 | | | | | |
| University of Michigan. . . . . . . . . . . . . . . . . . | Pu/B | 28,761 | 1,949 | TOEFL, SAT/ACT | 100 | | 2/1 | 75 |
| University of Michigan: Dearborn. . . . . . . . . . . . | Pu/B | 6,886 | 131 | TOEFL, SAT/ACT | 80 | 95 | 7/1 | 75 |
| University of Michigan: Flint. . . . . . . . . . . . . . . | Pu/B | 5,827 | 301 | TOEFL | 61 | 80 | 5/1 | 30 |
| University of Phoenix: Metro Detroit. . . . . . . . . . | Pr/AB | 1,126 | | | | | | |
| University of Phoenix: West Michigan. . . . . . . . . . | Pr/B | 660 | | | | | | |
| Walsh College of Accountancy and Business Administration. . . . . . . . . . . . . . . . . . . . . | Pr/B | 912 | 22 | TOEFL | 79 | | None | 35 |
| Washtenaw Community College . . . . . . . . . . . . . | Pu/A | 12,151 | | TOEFL | | | | |
| Wayne County Community College. . . . . . . . . . . | Pu/A | 11,747 | 114 | TOEFL | 61 | | | |
| Wayne State University. . . . . . . . . . . . . . . . . . | Pu/B | 16,671 | 415 | TOEFL | 79 | | 8/1 | 25 |
| Western Michigan University . . . . . . . . . . . . . . | Pu/B | 17,984 | 709 | TOEFL | 80 | | 4/1 | 100 |
| Yeshiva Beth Yehuda-Yeshiva Gedolah of Greater Detroit . . . . . . . . . . . . . . . . . . . . | Pr/B | 57 | | | | | | |

**Minnesota**

| Institution | Control/ degrees | Undergraduates Total | Undergraduates Internat'l | Tests required (Fall 2017) | TOEFL minimum | TOEFL average | Application Deadline | Application Fee |
|---|---|---|---|---|---|---|---|---|
| Academy College . . . . . . . . . . . . . . . . . . . . | Pr/AB | 105 | | TOEFL | | | None | 40 |
| Alexandria Technical and Community College. . . . . | Pu/A | 2,577 | | TOEFL | 61 | | 5/1 | 20 |

| Adviser | Orientation | ESL | Academic year | Summer | Tuition/ fees | Living costs | Maximum credits/ summer | Credit hour charge | Available | Number receiving aid | Average award | Deadline |
|---|---|---|---|---|---|---|---|---|---|---|---|---|
| Yes | Yes | Yes | Yes | Yes | 31,560† | 9,690 | 12 | | Yes | 62 | $16,412 | None |
| | | | | | | | | | | | | |
| Yes | Yes | Yes | Yes | | 44,857† | 9,174 | | | Yes | 105 | $27,151 | None |
| Yes | | Yes | No | | 8,050† | 4,194 | | 261 | | | | |
| Yes | | | No | | 7,721† | 5,470 | | | | | | |
| | | | | | | | | | | | | |
| Yes | Yes | | Yes | Yes | 42,490 | 8,040 | 20 | 1417 | Yes | 64 | $14,074 | None |
| | | | No | | 8,130 | 4,550 | 9 | 250 | Yes | | | None |
| Yes | Yes | | Yes | Yes | 20,342† | 7,280 | | 945 | Yes | 6 | $19,793 | None |
| Yes | | | Yes | | 7,905† | 7,000 | 18 | 219.5 | Yes | | | None |
| Yes | | | Yes | Yes | 11,089† | 9,442 | | | Yes | | | None |
| | | | | | | | | | | | | |
| Yes | Yes | Yes | No | | 10,790‡ | | | | | | | None |
| Yes | Yes | Yes | Yes | Yes | 32,130 | 9,500 | | 1122 | Yes | | | |
| Yes | | Yes | No | | 7,170† | 6,224 | | 230 | | | | |
| Yes | Yes | Yes | Yes | Yes | 19,640† | 13,068 | 18 | 650 | Yes | | | None |
| | | | | | 7,050† | | | 235 | | | | |
| | | | | | | | | | | | | |
| Yes | Yes | | Yes | | 22,750 | 7,800 | 7 | 740 | | | | |
| Yes | Yes | | No | | 10,600† | | | 350 | | | | |
| Yes | Yes | Yes | Yes | Yes | 37,890† | 11,234 | 6 | 1263 | Yes | 315 | $28,099 | None |
| Yes | Yes | Yes | Yes | Yes | 30,968† | 10,105 | 18 | 1136 | Yes | 134 | $9,618 | None |
| Yes | | | No | | 12,508† | 5,876 | 9 | 412 | Yes | | | None |
| | | | | | | | | | | | | |
| Yes | | | No | | 8,832† | | 8 | 325 | | | | |
| Yes | | | No | | 8,598† | 8,838 | 9 | 261 | | | | |
| Yes | | | No | | 8,920† | 5,694 | | | | | | |
| Yes | | | Yes | | 7,684† | 7,050 | 6 | 232 | Yes | | | None |
| Yes | Yes | Yes | Yes | Yes | 15,508† | 9,604 | 16 | 607 | Yes | | | None |
| | | | | | | | | | | | | |
| Yes | Yes | Yes | Yes | Yes | 9,975† | 8,750 | 18 | 302.25 | Yes | | | None |
| Yes | Yes | Yes | Yes | Yes | 26,080 | 10,170 | 15 | | Yes | | | None |
| Yes | Yes | Yes | No | | 5,230† | | 16 | 171 | Yes | | | None |
| Yes | Yes | Yes | Yes | Yes | 24,540† | 9,620 | | 795.75 | Yes | | | None |
| Yes | | | Yes | | 26,695 | 9,310 | | | Yes | | | None |
| | | | | | | | | | | | | |
| | | | No | | 11,970† | | | | Yes | | | None |
| Yes | | | Yes | Yes | 22,544† | 6,952 | | | Yes | | | None |
| Yes | | Yes | Yes | | 18,706† | 10,062 | | 434 | Yes | | | None |
| | | | No | | 2,550† | | | | | | | |
| Yes | Yes | Yes | Yes | Yes | 21,947† | 10,609 | 12 | | Yes | | | None |
| | | | | | | | | | | | | |
| Yes | | | No | | 9,514† | 5,710 | | 298 | Yes | | | None |
| Yes | Yes | Yes | No | | 7,316† | | 8 | 218 | Yes | | | None |
| Yes | Yes | Yes | Yes | Yes | 24,856† | 10,040 | | | Yes | | | 8/15 |
| | | | Yes | | 7,651† | 6,160 | | 207 | | | | |
| Yes | Yes | Yes | Yes | Yes | 27,750‡ | 9,640 | 8 | 660 | Yes | | | None |
| | | | | | | | | | | | | |
| Yes | Yes | Yes | Yes | Yes | 41,158‡ | 9,220 | | 1049 | Yes | 99 | $21,474 | None |
| Yes | Yes | Yes | Yes | Yes | 45,410† | 10,872 | 18 | 1848 | | | | |
| Yes | Yes | Yes | | | 24,272† | | 18 | 937 | | | | |
| Yes | Yes | Yes | Yes | Yes | 20,802† | 8,178 | | 823 | Yes | 42 | $4,952 | None |
| | | | | | | | | | | | | |
| Yes | Yes | | No | | 13,450† | 14,385 | 12 | 440 | Yes | | | None |
| Yes | | Yes | No | | 7,590† | | 12 | 246 | | | | |
| Yes | Yes | | No | | 4,777† | 4,598 | 9 | 149 | Yes | | | None |
| Yes | Yes | Yes | Yes | Yes | 26,220† | 9,747 | 18 | 825.42 | Yes | 141 | $9,430 | 6/30 |
| | | | | | | | | | | | | |
| Yes | Yes | Yes | Yes | Yes | 26,851† | 9,561 | | 943 | | | | |
| | | | Yes | | 6,800† | 4,200 | | | | | | |
| | | | | | | | | | | | | |
| Yes | | | No | | | | | | | | | |
| Yes | | | No | | 5,358† | 5,200 | | | Yes | | | None |

† Actual for 2016-17.    ‡ Estimated for 2017-18.    * Includes room and board

| Institution | Control/ degrees | Undergraduates | | Tests required (Fall 2017) | TOEFL | | Application | |
|---|---|---|---|---|---|---|---|---|
| | | Total | Internat'l | | minimum | average | Deadline | Fee |
| Argosy University: Twin Cities .............. | Pr/AB | 1,072 | | | | | | 50 |
| Art Institutes International Minnesota. . . . . . . . . . | Pr/AB | 820 | | TOEFL | | | | 50 |
| Augsburg College . . . . . . . . . . . . . . . . . . . . . | Pr/B | 2,530 | 85 | TOEFL | 80 | | | 25 |
| Bemidji State University . . . . . . . . . . . . . . . . . . | Pu/AB | 4,421 | 92 | TOEFL | 61 | | | 20 |
| Bethany Lutheran College . . . . . . . . . . . . . . . . | Pr/B | 513 | 29 | TOEFL | 75 | | 7/1 | |
| Bethel University . . . . . . . . . . . . . . . . . . . . . . | Pr/AB | 2,846 | 9 | TOEFL | 70 | 72 | None | |
| Capella University . . . . . . . . . . . . . . . . . . . . . | Pr/B | 8,750 | | | | | | 100 |
| Carleton College . . . . . . . . . . . . . . . . . . . . . . | Pr/B | 2,045 | 208 | TOEFL, SAT/ACT | | 100 | 1/15 | 30 |
| Central Lakes College. . . . . . . . . . . . . . . . . . . | Pu/A | 3,754 | | TOEFL | | | 8/1 | 20 |
| Century College . . . . . . . . . . . . . . . . . . . . . . . | Pu/A | 7,743 | 172 | TOEFL | 61 | 75 | | 20 |
| College of St. Benedict . . . . . . . . . . . . . . . . . . | Pr/B | 1,958 | 87 | TOEFL | 80 | | 4/1 | |
| College of St. Scholastica . . . . . . . . . . . . . . . . | Pr/B | 2,792 | 79 | TOEFL | 79 | 94 | 6/1 | |
| Concordia College: Moorhead . . . . . . . . . . . . . | Pr/B | 2,035 | 69 | TOEFL | 73 | 87 | | |
| Concordia University St. Paul . . . . . . . . . . . . . . | Pr/AB | 2,356 | 108 | TOEFL | 65 | | 8/1 | 30 |
| Crossroads College . . . . . . . . . . . . . . . . . . . . | Pr/AB | 109 | | TOEFL | 61 | | | 100 |
| Crown College . . . . . . . . . . . . . . . . . . . . . . . . | Pr/AB | 1,090 | | TOEFL, SAT/ACT | 61 | 86 | | 20 |
| Dakota County Technical College . . . . . . . . . . . . | Pu/A | 2,067 | | TOEFL | 61 | | 6/1 | 20 |
| Dunwoody College of Technology . . . . . . . . . . . | Pr/AB | 1,216 | | | | | | 50 |
| Fond du Lac Tribal and Community College. . . . . . | Pu/A | 1,419 | | TOEFL | | | | 20 |
| Globe University: Minneapolis . . . . . . . . . . . . . . | Pr/AB | 164 | | TOEFL | 61 | | | 50 |
| Globe University: Moorhead . . . . . . . . . . . . . . | Pr/AB | 220 | | TOEFL | 61 | | | 50 |
| Globe University: Woodbury . . . . . . . . . . . . . . . | Pr/AB | 717 | | TOEFL | 61 | | | 50 |
| Gustavus Adolphus College . . . . . . . . . . . . . . . | Pr/B | 2,229 | 101 | TOEFL | 80 | 96 | | |
| Hamline University . . . . . . . . . . . . . . . . . . . . . | Pr/B | 2,117 | 21 | TOEFL | 79 | | 6/1 | 40 |
| Hennepin Technical College. . . . . . . . . . . . . . . . | Pu/A | 5,272 | 17 | TOEFL | 61 | | | |
| Herzing University: Minneapolis. . . . . . . . . . . . . | Pr/AB | 310 | | TOEFL | | | | |
| Hibbing Community College . . . . . . . . . . . . . . . | Pu/A | 1,319 | | TOEFL | | | 6/1 | 20 |
| Institute of Production and Recording . . . . . . . . . | Pr/A | 243 | | TOEFL | 61 | | | 50 |
| Inver Hills Community College . . . . . . . . . . . . . . | Pu/A | 3,759 | | TOEFL | 61 | | | 20 |
| Itasca Community College. . . . . . . . . . . . . . . . . | Pu/A | 1,218 | | TOEFL | 61 | | 6/1 | 20 |
| Lake Superior College . . . . . . . . . . . . . . . . . . . | Pu/A | 3,240 | 24 | TOEFL | 61 | | | 20 |
| Le Cordon Bleu College of Culinary Arts: | | | | | | | | |
|   Minneapolis-St. Paul. . . . . . . . . . . . . . . . . . . | Pr/A | 491 | | TOEFL | 61 | | | 50 |
| Macalester College. . . . . . . . . . . . . . . . . . . . . | Pr/B | 2,122 | 307 | TOEFL, SAT/ACT | 100 | | 1/15 | 40 |
| McNally Smith College of Music . . . . . . . . . . . . | Pr/AB | 408 | 29 | TOEFL | | | | 75 |
| Mesabi Range College . . . . . . . . . . . . . . . . . . | Pu/A | 1,373 | | TOEFL | | | | 20 |
| Minneapolis Business College . . . . . . . . . . . . . . | Pr/A | 235 | | | | | | 50 |
| Minneapolis College of Art and Design . . . . . . . . | Pr/B | 690 | 20 | TOEFL | 79 | 100 | | 50 |
| Minneapolis Community and Technical | | | | | | | | |
|   College . . . . . . . . . . . . . . . . . . . . . . . . . | Pu/A | 9,465 | | TOEFL | 61 | | | 20 |
| Minnesota School of Business: Blaine . . . . . . . . . | Pr/AB | 239 | | TOEFL | 61 | | | 50 |
| Minnesota School of Business: Brooklyn | | | | | | | | |
|   Center . . . . . . . . . . . . . . . . . . . . . . . . . . . | Pr/AB | 109 | | TOEFL | 61 | | | 50 |
| Minnesota School of Business: Elk River . . . . . . . | Pr/AB | 236 | | TOEFL | 61 | | | 50 |
| Minnesota School of Business: Lakeville . . . . . . . | Pr/AB | 195 | | TOEFL | 61 | | | 50 |
| Minnesota School of Business: Plymouth . . . . . . . | Pr/AB | 130 | | TOEFL | 61 | | | 50 |
| Minnesota School of Business: Richfield . . . . . . . | Pr/AB | 693 | | TOEFL | 61 | | | 50 |
| Minnesota School of Business: Rochester . . . . . . . | Pr/AB | 183 | | TOEFL | 61 | | | 50 |
| Minnesota School of Business: Shakopee . . . . . . . | Pr/AB | 210 | | TOEFL | 61 | | | 50 |
| Minnesota School of Business: St. Cloud . . . . . . . | Pr/AB | 218 | | TOEFL | 61 | | | 50 |
| Minnesota State College - Southeast Technical . . . . | Pu/A | 1,473 | 7 | TOEFL | 61 | | None | 20 |
| Minnesota State Community and Technical | | | | | | | | |
|   College . . . . . . . . . . . . . . . . . . . . . . . . . | Pu/A | 4,299 | | TOEFL | 80 | | 7/1 | 20 |
| Minnesota State University Mankato . . . . . . . . . . | Pu/AB | 13,335 | | TOEFL | 50 | | | 20 |
| Minnesota State University Moorhead . . . . . . . . . | Pu/AB | 4,966 | 384 | TOEFL | 61 | | | 20 |
| Minnesota West Community and Technical | | | | | | | | |
|   College . . . . . . . . . . . . . . . . . . . . . . . . . | Pu/A | 3,182 | | TOEFL | | | | 20 |
| National American University: Bloomington . . . . . . | Pr/AB | 422 | | TOEFL | | | | 45 |
| National American University: Roseville . . . . . . . . | Pr/AB | 264 | | | | | | 25 |

| Student services | | | Housing | | Academic year costs | | Maximum credits/summer | Credit hour charge | International financial aid | | | |
| Adviser | Orien-tation | ESL | Academic year | Summer | Tuition/fees | Living costs | | | Avail-able | Number receiving aid | Average award | Deadline |
|---|---|---|---|---|---|---|---|---|---|---|---|---|
| Yes | | | Yes | | | | 16 | | Yes | | | None |
| Yes | Yes | Yes | Yes | Yes | 37,615‡ | 9,939 | | 1155 | Yes | 82 | $21,509 | 8/1 |
| Yes | Yes | Yes | Yes | Yes | 8,393† | 7,924 | | 257 | | | | |
| Yes | Yes | | Yes | Yes | 26,020† | 9,960 | | 1080 | Yes | | | None |
| Yes | Yes | | Yes | Yes | 36,210 | 10,340 | 8 | 1510 | Yes | 9 | $23,127 | None |
| Yes | Yes | | No | | | | | | | | | |
| Yes | Yes | | Yes | Yes | 52,782 | 13,632 | | | Yes | 79 | $42,366 | 2/15 |
| Yes | | Yes | No | | 5,348† | | 16 | | Yes | | | None |
| Yes | Yes | Yes | No | | 5,393† | | 18 | | | | | |
| Yes | Yes | Yes | Yes | Yes | 42,271† | 10,535 | | 1719 | Yes | 75 | $23,645 | None |
| Yes | Yes | | Yes | Yes | 35,326† | 11,314 | | 1088 | Yes | | | None |
| Yes | Yes | | Yes | Yes | 36,878† | 9,440 | 12 | 1380 | Yes | 42 | $21,864 | None |
| Yes | Yes | | Yes | Yes | 29,400 | 8,750 | 19 | | Yes | 13 | $11,424 | None |
| | | | Yes | | 16,500† | 7,200 | | | Yes | | | 4/15 |
| Yes | Yes | Yes | Yes | | 24,700† | 8,160 | 12 | | Yes | | | None |
| Yes | Yes | | No | | 5,662† | 7,470 | | | | | | |
| Yes | | | No | | 24,230† | | | | | | | |
| | | | Yes | | 5,210† | 3,598 | 9 | | Yes | | | None |
| Yes | Yes | | No | | | 5,148 | | | | | | |
| Yes | Yes | | No | | | 5,148 | | | | | | |
| Yes | Yes | | No | | | 5,148 | | | | | | |
| Yes | Yes | | Yes | Yes | 42,840† | 9,400 | | | Yes | 106 | $30,635 | 4/15 |
| Yes | Yes | Yes | Yes | Yes | 40,822 | 10,156 | 8 | 1225 | Yes | 22 | $16,736 | None |
| Yes | Yes | Yes | No | | 5,156† | 7,958 | 12 | | | | | |
| Yes | | | Yes | | 6,432† | 3,140 | 6 | 195.05 | | | | |
| Yes | Yes | | No | | | 5,148 | | | | | | |
| Yes | | Yes | No | | 5,285† | 6,084 | | | Yes | | | None |
| | | | Yes | Yes | 6,448† | 7,760 | 12 | 195.05 | | | | |
| Yes | | | No | | 9,483† | 6,440 | 18 | 291.56 | | | | |
| Yes | | | No | | | | | | | | | |
| Yes | Yes | | Yes | Yes | 52,464‡ | 11,672 | | 1632 | Yes | 252 | $43,785 | 3/1 |
| | | | Yes | | 27,940† | 5,100 | | 1040 | Yes | | | 8/1 |
| Yes | | | Yes | Yes | 6,451† | 3,754 | 9 | 195.05 | | | | |
| | | | Yes | | | | | | | | | |
| Yes | Yes | Yes | Yes | Yes | 36,548† | 7,420 | 12 | 1505 | Yes | 20 | $12,457 | 3/1 |
| Yes | | Yes | No | | 5,349† | | | | Yes | | | None |
| Yes | Yes | | No | | | 5,148 | | | | | | |
| Yes | Yes | | No | | | 5,148 | | | | | | |
| Yes | Yes | | No | | | 5,148 | | | | | | |
| Yes | Yes | | No | | | 5,148 | | | | | | |
| Yes | Yes | | No | | | 5,148 | | | | | | |
| Yes | Yes | | No | | | 5,148 | | | | | | |
| Yes | Yes | | No | | | 5,148 | | | | | | |
| Yes | Yes | | No | | | 5,148 | | | | | | |
| Yes | | | Yes | | 5,553† | 6,606 | | | | | | |
| | | Yes | Yes | Yes | 5,313† | 4,800 | 20 | 159.15 | Yes | | | None |
| Yes | Yes | Yes | Yes | Yes | 15,602† | 8,758 | 12 | 584 | Yes | | | None |
| Yes | Yes | | Yes | Yes | 15,251† | 8,076 | 12 | 460.5 | Yes | | | None |
| Yes | | Yes | No | | 5,637† | 2,500 | 20 | 339.67 | | | | |
| | Yes | Yes | No | | 17,685† | | 20 | 373 | | | | |
| | | | | | 17,760† | | | 373 | | | | |

| Institution | Control/degrees | Undergraduates Total | Internat'l | Tests required (Fall 2017) | TOEFL minimum | average | Application Deadline | Fee |
|---|---|---|---|---|---|---|---|---|
| Normandale Community College . . . . . . . . . . . . . | Pu/A | 9,296 | | TOEFL | 61 | | | 20 |
| North Central University . . . . . . . . . . . . . . . . . . . | Pr/AB | 1,301 | | TOEFL, SAT/ACT | | | | 25 |
| North Hennepin Community College . . . . . . . . . . . | Pu/A | 5,494 | | TOEFL | 61 | | | 20 |
| Northland Community & Technical College . . . . . . | Pu/A | 2,386 | | TOEFL | 61 | | None | 20 |
| Northwest Technical College . . . . . . . . . . . . . . . | Pu/A | 1,114 | | TOEFL | | | | 20 |
| Northwestern Health Sciences University . . . . . . . . | Pr/AB | 163 | | TOEFL | 76 | | None | 50 |
| Pine Technical & Community College . . . . . . . . . . | Pu/A | 1,083 | | TOEFL | | | | |
| Rainy River Community College . . . . . . . . . . . . . | Pu/A | 268 | | TOEFL | 61 | | | 20 |
| Rasmussen College: Blaine . . . . . . . . . . . . . . . . . | Pr/AB | 403 | | TOEFL | | | | |
| Rasmussen College: Bloomington . . . . . . . . . . . . . | Pr/AB | 429 | | TOEFL | | | | 60 |
| Rasmussen College: Brooklyn Park . . . . . . . . . . . . | Pr/AB | 529 | | TOEFL | | | | |
| Rasmussen College: Eagan . . . . . . . . . . . . . . . . . | Pr/AB | 499 | | TOEFL | | | | |
| Rasmussen College: Lake Elmo/Woodbury . . . . . . . | Pr/AB | 1,343 | | TOEFL | | | | |
| Rasmussen College: Mankato . . . . . . . . . . . . . . . . | Pr/AB | 381 | | TOEFL | | | | |
| Rasmussen College: Moorhead . . . . . . . . . . . . . . . | Pr/AB | 190 | | TOEFL | | | | |
| Rasmussen College: St. Cloud . . . . . . . . . . . . . . . | Pr/AB | 542 | | TOEFL | | | | |
| Ridgewater College . . . . . . . . . . . . . . . . . . . . . . | Pu/A | 3,580 | | | | | | 20 |
| Riverland Community College . . . . . . . . . . . . . . . | Pu/A | 3,068 | | TOEFL | | | | 20 |
| Rochester Community and Technical College . . . . . | Pu/A | 5,289 | | TOEFL | | | | 20 |
| St. Catherine University . . . . . . . . . . . . . . . . . . | Pr/AB | 3,086 | 25 | TOEFL | 61 | 73 | | 20 |
| Saint Cloud State University . . . . . . . . . . . . . . . . | Pu/AB | 13,630 | | TOEFL | 61 | | | 20 |
| St. Cloud Technical and Community College . . . . . . | Pu/A | 4,420 | | TOEFL | | | | 20 |
| St. John's University . . . . . . . . . . . . . . . . . . . . . | Pr/B | 1,754 | 76 | TOEFL | 80 | | 4/1 | |
| St. Mary's University of Minnesota . . . . . . . . . . . | Pr/B | 1,552 | 51 | TOEFL | 59 | 79 | | 25 |
| St. Olaf College . . . . . . . . . . . . . . . . . . . . . . . . | Pr/B | 2,991 | 248 | TOEFL, SAT/ACT | 90 | 101 | 1/15 | |
| South Central College . . . . . . . . . . . . . . . . . . . . | Pu/A | 2,823 | | TOEFL | | | 3/1 | 20 |
| Southwest Minnesota State University . . . . . . . . . . | Pu/AB | 2,285 | | | 61 | | 6/15 | 20 |
| University of Minnesota: Crookston . . . . . . . . . . . . | Pu/B | 1,821 | 97 | TOEFL | 68 | 74 | None | 30 |
| University of Minnesota: Duluth . . . . . . . . . . . . . | Pu/B | 9,051 | 178 | TOEFL | 80 | | 6/15 | 50 |
| University of Minnesota: Morris . . . . . . . . . . . . . | Pu/B | 1,680 | 191 | TOEFL, SAT/ACT | 79 | | 3/16 | 25 |
| University of Minnesota: Rochester . . . . . . . . . . . . | Pu/B | 424 | 3 | TOEFL | 95 | | 6/1 | 30 |
| University of Minnesota: Twin Cities . . . . . . . . . . | Pu/B | 30,975 | 2,779 | TOEFL | | | None | 55 |
| University of Northwestern - St. Paul . . . . . . . . . . | Pr/AB | 1,958 | | TOEFL, SAT/ACT | 71 | 98 | | 25 |
| University of Phoenix: Minneapolis-St. Paul . . . . . . | Pr/B | 132 | | | | | | |
| University of St. Thomas . . . . . . . . . . . . . . . . . | Pr/B | 6,111 | 165 | TOEFL | 71 | 88 | | |
| Walden University . . . . . . . . . . . . . . . . . . . . . . . | Pr/B | 7,329 | 150 | TOEFL | 79 | 81 | None | |
| White Earth Tribal and Community College . . . . . . | Pr/A | 71 | | | | | | |
| Winona State University . . . . . . . . . . . . . . . . . . . | Pu/AB | 7,486 | 202 | TOEFL | 68 | 80 | 7/1 | 20 |

**Mississippi**

| Institution | Control/degrees | Undergraduates Total | Internat'l | Tests required (Fall 2017) | TOEFL minimum | average | Application Deadline | Fee |
|---|---|---|---|---|---|---|---|---|
| Alcorn State University . . . . . . . . . . . . . . . . . . . . | Pu/AB | 2,812 | 47 | TOEFL, SAT/ACT | 71 | | None | |
| Antonelli College: Jackson . . . . . . . . . . . . . . . . | Pr/A | 352 | | | | | | |
| Belhaven University . . . . . . . . . . . . . . . . . . . . . . | Pr/AB | 2,566 | | TOEFL | 71 | 73 | | 25 |
| Blue Cliff College: Gulfport . . . . . . . . . . . . . . . . | Pr/A | 274 | | | | | | |
| Blue Mountain College . . . . . . . . . . . . . . . . . . . . | Pr/B | 541 | 9 | TOEFL, SAT/ACT | 61 | | | |
| Coahoma Community College . . . . . . . . . . . . . . . . | Pu/A | 1,759 | 6 | TOEFL, SAT/ACT | | | | |
| Delta State University . . . . . . . . . . . . . . . . . . . . . | Pu/B | 2,763 | | TOEFL, SAT/ACT | | | | 25 |
| East Mississippi Community College . . . . . . . . . . . | Pu/A | 3,902 | | TOEFL, ACT | | 61 | None | |
| Hinds Community College . . . . . . . . . . . . . . . . . . | Pu/A | 10,042 | 2 | TOEFL | 61 | | None | |
| Jackson State University . . . . . . . . . . . . . . . . . . . | Pu/B | 7,492 | 162 | TOEFL, SAT/ACT | 69 | | 9/2 | |
| Jones County Junior College . . . . . . . . . . . . . . . . | Pu/A | 4,549 | | | | | | |
| Meridian Community College . . . . . . . . . . . . . . . . | Pu/A | 3,188 | | | 61 | 72 | | |
| Millsaps College . . . . . . . . . . . . . . . . . . . . . . . . | Pr/B | 797 | 31 | TOEFL | 80 | | | |
| Mississippi College . . . . . . . . . . . . . . . . . . . . . . | Pr/B | 2,954 | | TOEFL | | | | 25 |
| Mississippi Gulf Coast Community College . . . . . . | Pu/A | 9,555 | | TOEFL | | | | |
| Mississippi State University . . . . . . . . . . . . . . . . | Pu/B | 17,371 | 219 | TOEFL, SAT/ACT | 71 | | None | 60 |
| Mississippi University for Women . . . . . . . . . . . . | Pu/AB | 2,745 | | TOEFL | | | | 25 |
| Mississippi Valley State University . . . . . . . . . . . . | Pu/B | 1,808 | | TOEFL, SAT/ACT | | | | |
| Northeast Mississippi Community College . . . . . . . | Pu/A | 3,524 | | | | | | |

| Student services | | | Housing | | Academic year costs | | Maximum credits/ summer | Credit hour charge | International financial aid | | | |
|---|---|---|---|---|---|---|---|---|---|---|---|---|
| Adviser | Orien-tation | ESL | Academic year | Summer | Tuition/ fees | Living costs | | | Avail-able | Number receiving aid | Average award | Deadline |
| | | Yes | No | | 5,714 † | 8,004 | 12 | 159.88 | Yes | | | None |
| Yes | Yes | | Yes | Yes | 22,240 † | 6,670 | 15 | | Yes | | | None |
| Yes | Yes | Yes | No | | 5,460 † | 8,004 | | | Yes | | | None |
| Yes | | | Yes | | 5,485 † | 6,000 | | 163.35 | | | | |
| Yes | | | Yes | Yes | 5,428 † | 7,924 | | 171.27 | | | | |
| | | | No | | 12,618 † | 8,500 | | 404 | Yes | | | |
| | Yes | | No | | 9,586 † | 7,206 | 9 | 303.26 | | | | None |
| Yes | | | Yes | Yes | 6,448 † | 3,930 | | 195.05 | Yes | | | None |
| | | | | | 13,455 † | | | 299 | Yes | | | None |
| | | | No | | 13,455 † | 7,011 | | 299 | Yes | | | None |
| | | | No | | 13,455 † | 7,011 | | 299 | Yes | | | None |
| | | | No | | 13,455 † | 7,011 | | 299 | Yes | | | None |
| | | | | | 13,455 † | 7,011 | | 299 | Yes | | | None |
| | | | No | | 13,455 † | 7,011 | | 299 | Yes | | | None |
| | | | | | 13,455 † | | | 299 | Yes | | | None |
| | | | No | | 13,455 † | 7,011 | | 299 | Yes | | | None |
| | | | No | | 5,370 † | | | | | | | |
| Yes | Yes | Yes | | Yes | 5,508 † | 5,800 | 6 | | Yes | | | None |
| Yes | Yes | | No | | 5,579 † | 7,200 | | | | | | |
| Yes | Yes | | Yes | Yes | 38,349 | 12,326 | | 1253 | Yes | | | None |
| Yes | Yes | Yes | Yes | Yes | 15,718 † | 8,230 | | 491 | | | | |
| Yes | Yes | Yes | No | | 5,295 † | 6,260 | | | | | | |
| Yes | Yes | Yes | Yes | Yes | 41,732 † | 9,892 | | 1709 | Yes | 72 | $23,341 | None |
| Yes | Yes | Yes | Yes | | 33,560 | 8,800 | 18 | 1110 | Yes | 37 | $12,613 | None |
| Yes | Yes | | Yes | | 44,180 † | 10,080 | | 1381 | Yes | | | 1/15 |
| Yes | Yes | | No | | 5,369 † | | | | Yes | | | None |
| Yes | Yes | | Yes | Yes | 8,344 † | 8,742 | 20 | | Yes | 19 | $823 | None |
| Yes | Yes | Yes | Yes | Yes | 11,700 † | 8,418 | 10 | 392 | Yes | 2 | $3,250 | None |
| Yes | Yes | Yes | Yes | | 17,485 † | 7,460 | | 625 | Yes | 75 | $8,036 | None |
| Yes | Yes | Yes | Yes | Yes | 14,846 ‡ | 7,981 | 20 | | Yes | 24 | $3,951 | None |
| Yes | | | Yes | Yes | 13,232 † | 9,420 | | 458 | Yes | 3 | $4,079 | None |
| Yes | Yes | Yes | Yes | Yes | 23,806 † | 9,377 | | 854 | Yes | 242 | $3,389 | None |
| Yes | Yes | | Yes | | 29,510 † | 9,060 | 12 | | Yes | | | 8/1 |
| Yes | | | Yes | | 39,594 † | 10,970 | | 1210 | Yes | 22 | $26,582 | None |
| Yes | | | No | | 15,105 † | | | 325 | Yes | | | None |
| | | | | | 3,518 † | 4,500 | | 130 | | | | |
| Yes | Yes | Yes | Yes | Yes | 14,772 † | 8,460 | | 426 | Yes | 200 | $5,616 | None |
| Yes | | | Yes | | 6,546 † | 8,667 | 12 | | Yes | 2 | $4,633 | None |
| | | | No | | | 8,610 | | | | | | |
| Yes | Yes | Yes | Yes | Yes | 23,016 † | 8,000 | 15 | 425 | Yes | | | None |
| | | | No | | | | | | | | | |
| | | | Yes | | 11,212 † | 5,839 | 14 | 317 | Yes | | | 7/31 |
| | | | Yes | | 3,472 | 4,420 | 12 | 235 | | | | |
| Yes | Yes | | Yes | Yes | 6,418 † | 8,801 | 12 | 263 | Yes | | | None |
| | Yes | | Yes | | 5,240 † | 4,600 | | 140 | | | | |
| Yes | | | Yes | Yes | 6,120 | 6,120 | | 240 | Yes | | | None |
| Yes | Yes | Yes | Yes | Yes | 17,614 † | 8,788 | 12 | 729 | Yes | | | None |
| | | | Yes | | | | 14 | | | | | |
| Yes | Yes | Yes | Yes | Yes | 4,030 † | | 12 | 177 | Yes | | | None |
| Yes | Yes | | Yes | Yes | 37,110 † | 14,303 | 12 | 1072 | | 32 | $26,633 | |
| Yes | Yes | Yes | Yes | | 16,740 † | 9,190 | 12 | 495 | Yes | | | None |
| Yes | | | Yes | | 5,660 † | 6,100 | | | | | | |
| Yes | Yes | Yes | Yes | Yes | 20,900 † | 9,570 | | 866 | Yes | 100 | $4,782 | None |
| Yes | | | Yes | Yes | 16,634 † | 6,902 | | 689 | Yes | | | None |
| Yes | | | Yes | Yes | 6,116 † | 7,659 | 12 | | | | | |
| | | | Yes | | 5,180 † | 3,850 | | | | | | |

† Actual for 2016-17.    ‡ Estimated for 2017-18.    * Includes room and board

| Institution | Control/ degrees | Undergraduates | | Tests required (Fall 2017) | TOEFL | | Application | |
| --- | --- | --- | --- | --- | --- | --- | --- | --- |
| | | Total | Internat'l | | minimum | average | Deadline | Fee |
| Rust College | Pr/AB | 1,004 | 17 | TOEFL, SAT/ACT | | | | 10 |
| Southeastern Baptist College | Pr/AB | 52 | | | | | | 25 |
| Tougaloo College | Pr/AB | 839 | | TOEFL | 70 | | 5/18 | 25 |
| University of Mississippi | Pu/B | 18,975 | 270 | TOEFL | 79 | 86 | | 60 |
| University of Phoenix: Jackson | Pr/B | 49 | | | | | | |
| University of Southern Mississippi | Pu/B | 11,689 | 243 | TOEFL, SAT/ACT | 71 | | 6/1 | 35 |
| Virginia College in Biloxi | Pr/A | 470 | | | | | | 100 |
| Virginia College in Jackson | Pr/A | 376 | | | | | | 100 |
| William Carey University | Pr/B | 2,487 | | TOEFL, SAT/ACT | 70 | | | 30 |
| **Missouri** | | | | | | | | |
| Avila University | Pr/B | 1,279 | 118 | TOEFL | 79 | 88 | | 25 |
| Bolivar Technical College | Pr/A | 134 | | | | | | 50 |
| Brown Mackie College: St. Louis | Pr/AB | | | | | | | |
| Calvary Bible College and Theological Seminary | Pr/AB | 194 | | TOEFL, SAT/ACT | 80 | | | |
| Central Methodist University | Pr/AB | 1,090 | 61 | TOEFL, SAT/ACT | | | | 20 |
| College of the Ozarks | Pr/B | 1,512 | 21 | TOEFL | 79 | 80 | 2/15 | |
| Columbia College | Pr/AB | 924 | 82 | TOEFL | 61 | 77 | | 35 |
| Concorde Career College: Kansas City | Pr/A | 783 | | | | | | 100 |
| Cottey College | Pr/AB | 283 | 42 | TOEFL | 68 | 78 | | 20 |
| Cox College | Pr/AB | 735 | | TOEFL | | | | 50 |
| Crowder College | Pu/A | 3,629 | 48 | TOEFL | | | None | 25 |
| Culver-Stockton College | Pr/B | 998 | | TOEFL, SAT/ACT | 79 | | 8/1 | |
| DeVry University: Kansas City | Pr/AB | 230 | | TOEFL | | | | 50 |
| Drury University | Pr/AB | 1,367 | 138 | TOEFL | 72 | 89 | None | |
| East Central College | Pu/A | 2,338 | 1 | TOEFL | 60 | 75 | 7/1 | |
| Evangel University | Pr/AB | 1,619 | 16 | TOEFL | | | | 25 |
| Fontbonne University | Pr/B | 953 | 66 | TOEFL | 61 | | | 25 |
| Global University | Pr/AB | | | | | | | 40 |
| Goldfarb School of Nursing at Barnes-Jewish College | Pr/B | 616 | | TOEFL | | | | 50 |
| Hannibal-LaGrange University | Pr/AB | 1,292 | | TOEFL | 70 | | | 150 |
| Harris-Stowe State University | Pu/B | 1,445 | 4 | TOEFL, SAT/ACT | 61 | | | 20 |
| Jefferson College | Pu/A | 4,496 | | TOEFL | 52 | | None | 25 |
| Kansas City Art Institute | Pr/B | 629 | 5 | TOEFL | 80 | | | 45 |
| L'Ecole Culinaire | Pr/A | 269 | | | | | | |
| Lincoln University | Pu/AB | 2,113 | 49 | TOEFL, SAT/ACT | 61 | | 7/15 | |
| Lindenwood University | Pr/B | 7,331 | 895 | TOEFL | 61 | 80 | 6/18 | 100 |
| Logan University | Pr/B | 93 | 1 | TOEFL | 79 | | None | 25 |
| Maryville University of Saint Louis | Pr/B | 2,892 | 143 | TOEFL | 61 | | 7/1 | |
| Metro Business College: Rolla | Pr/A | 76 | | | | | | 25 |
| Metropolitan Community College - Kansas City | Pu/A | 15,158 | 143 | | | | | 50 |
| Missouri Baptist University | Pr/AB | 1,846 | | TOEFL | 80 | | None | 35 |
| Missouri College | Pr/AB | 553 | | | | | | 35 |
| Missouri Southern State University | Pu/AB | 6,117 | | TOEFL, SAT/ACT | 68 | | | 50 |
| Missouri State University | Pu/B | 17,300 | 762 | TOEFL | 61 | | | 50 |
| Missouri State University: West Plains | Pu/A | 1,993 | | TOEFL | 61 | | | 15 |
| Missouri University of Science and Technology | Pu/B | 6,857 | 300 | TOEFL | 79 | | | 50 |
| Missouri Valley College | Pr/AB | 1,683 | | TOEFL | 61 | | | 75 |
| Missouri Western State University | Pu/AB | 5,120 | | TOEFL | 61 | | | 50 |
| Moberly Area Community College | Pu/A | 5,800 | | TOEFL | | | | |
| National American University: Kansas City | Pr/AB | 646 | | TOEFL | | | | 45 |
| National American University: Lee's Summit | Pr/AB | 360 | | | | | | |
| North Central Missouri College | Pu/A | 1,720 | | TOEFL | 61 | | | 20 |
| Northwest Missouri State University | Pu/AB | 5,240 | 226 | TOEFL | 61 | 71 | | 50 |
| Ozarks Technical Community College | Pu/A | 13,260 | | TOEFL | 61 | | None | 78 |

| Student services | | | Housing | | Academic year costs | | Maximum credits/ summer | Credit hour charge | International financial aid | | | |
|---|---|---|---|---|---|---|---|---|---|---|---|---|
| Adviser | Orientation | ESL | Academic year | Summer | Tuition/ fees | Living costs | | | Available | Number receiving aid | Average award | Deadline |
| Yes | | | Yes | | 9,500 † | 4,100 | 6 | 396 | | | | |
| Yes | | | Yes | | 6,550 † | 2,200 | 12 | 210 | | | | |
| Yes | | | Yes | | 10,607 † | 10,350 | 12 | 423 | Yes | | | None |
| Yes | Yes | Yes | Yes | Yes | 22,022 † | 9,099 | 12 | 913 | Yes | 183 | $16,530 | None |
| Yes | Yes | Yes | Yes | Yes | 16,204 † | 8,610 | 18 | 675 | Yes | 109 | $14,078 | None |
| Yes | Yes | | Yes | Yes | 11,700 † | 5,900 | 12 | 360 | Yes | | | 9/1 |
| Yes | Yes | Yes | Yes | Yes | 28,820 | 6,900 | 12 | 758 | Yes | | | 4/1 |
| | | | No | | 13,301 † | | | | Yes | | | None |
| Yes | | | Yes | Yes | 12,370 † | 5,630 | | 375 | Yes | | | 4/1 |
| | | | Yes | | 23,770 ‡ | 7,730 | 9 | 210 | Yes | 56 | $17,962 | None |
| Yes | Yes | | Yes | Yes | 19,200 | 7,100 | | | Yes | 26 | $18,500 | None |
| Yes | Yes | Yes | Yes | Yes | 20,936 † | 6,440 9,024 | 8 | 450 | Yes | 61 | $18,628 | None |
| Yes | Yes | | Yes | | 20,200 14,010 † | 8,840 | 18 | 125 400 | Yes | 46 | $19,377 | None |
| Yes | Yes | Yes | Yes | | 6,270 | 5,402 | 9 | 186 | Yes | | | None |
| Yes | Yes | | Yes | | 26,040 | 10,810 | 6 | 590 | Yes | 52 | $16,223 | 6/1 |
| Yes | | | | | 17,512 † | | | 609 | | | | |
| Yes | Yes | Yes | Yes | Yes | 27,005 ‡ | 10,536 | 13 | 862 | Yes | 116 | $15,771 | None |
| Yes | | | No | | 6,120 ‡ | | 9 | 181 | Yes | | | None |
| Yes | | | Yes | | 22,081 † | 7,882 | 12 | | Yes | 12 | $7,303 | None |
| Yes | Yes | Yes | Yes | Yes | 24,610 † | 9,107 | 15 | 648 | Yes | | | None |
| | | | No | | 4,560 † | | 6 | 135 | | | | |
| Yes | | | No | | 20,188 | | 22 | 733 | | | | |
| Yes | Yes | Yes | Yes | Yes | 21,710 † | 7,608 | 17 | | Yes | | | None |
| Yes | | | Yes | | 9,853 † | 9,250 | 9 | 392 | Yes | | | 4/1 |
| Yes | Yes | Yes | Yes | Yes | 6,450 | 9,306 | 9 | 210 | Yes | 7 | $9,306 | None |
| Yes | | | Yes | | 37,800 | 10,400 | 6 | 1510 | Yes | | | 4/1 |
| Yes | Yes | | Yes | Yes | 13,432 † | 6,560 | 9 | 418 | Yes | 20 | $17,652 | None |
| Yes | Yes | Yes | Yes | Yes | 16,960 | 8,800 | 16 | 460 | Yes | 873 | $10,867 | None |
| | | | No | | 8,380 † | 8,456 | | 275 | | | | |
| Yes | Yes | | Yes | Yes | 27,958 † | 10,088 | 16 | 766 | Yes | 78 | $15,946 | None |
| Yes | Yes | Yes | No | | 6,910 † | | | 229 | | | | |
| Yes | Yes | | Yes | Yes | 26,020 | 10,380 | 21 | 857 | Yes | | | None |
| | | | No | | | | | | | | | |
| Yes | Yes | Yes | Yes | Yes | 11,283 † | 6,627 | 9 | 357 | Yes | | | None |
| Yes | Yes | Yes | Yes | Yes | 14,746 | 8,084 | 10 | 458 | Yes | 608 | $8,977 | None |
| Yes | | | Yes | Yes | 7,460 † | 5,702 | 10 | 238 | Yes | | | None |
| Yes | Yes | Yes | Yes | Yes | 26,897 † | 9,935 | 9 | 852 | | 175 | $13,517 | |
| Yes | Yes | Yes | Yes | Yes | 19,750 † | 8,400 | 12 | | Yes | | | None |
| Yes | Yes | Yes | Yes | Yes | 13,080 † | 8,565 | | 412 | Yes | | | None |
| Yes | Yes | | Yes | | 6,750 † | 5,200 | 12 | 207 | Yes | | | None |
| | | | | | 16,200 † | | 16 | 360 | Yes | | | None |
| | | | | | 16,200 † | | | 360 | | | | |
| | | | Yes | | 5,340 † | 5,849 | 12 | 148 | Yes | | | |
| Yes | Yes | Yes | Yes | Yes | 15,499 † | 12,312 | 18 | 517 | Yes | 229 | $5,848 | None |
| Yes | Yes | Yes | No | | 6,600 ‡ | | 6 | 198 | | | | |

† Actual for 2016-17.    ‡ Estimated for 2017-18.    * Includes room and board

| Institution | Control/ degrees | Undergraduates | | Tests required (Fall 2017) | TOEFL | | Application | |
|---|---|---|---|---|---|---|---|---|
| | | Total | Internat'l | | minimum | average | Deadline | Fee |
| Park University . . . . . . . . . . . . . . . . . . . . . . . . . | Pr/AB | 9,356 | 262 | TOEFL | | | | 25 |
| Pinnacle Career Institute: Kansas City . . . . . . . . . . | Pr/A | 491 | | | | | | |
| Ranken Technical College . . . . . . . . . . . . . . . . . . | Pr/AB | 1,929 | | | | | | 25 |
| Research College of Nursing . . . . . . . . . . . . . . . | Pr/B | 294 | | TOEFL, SAT/ACT | 79 | | | 50 |
| Rockhurst University . . . . . . . . . . . . . . . . . . . . | Pr/B | 1,495 | 21 | TOEFL, SAT/ACT | 79 | | None | 50 |
| St. Louis Community College at Florissant Valley . . . . . . . . . . . . . . . . . . . . . . . . . . . . | Pu/A | | | TOEFL | | | | |
| Saint Louis University . . . . . . . . . . . . . . . . . . . . | Pr/AB | 7,354 | 400 | TOEFL | 80 | | 6/1 | |
| Southeast Missouri Hospital College of Nursing and Health Sciences . . . . . . . . . . . . . . | Pr/AB | 210 | | | | | | 100 |
| Southeast Missouri State University . . . . . . . . . . . | Pu/AB | 9,028 | 589 | TOEFL | 61 | 75 | | 40 |
| Southwest Baptist University . . . . . . . . . . . . . . . | Pr/AB | 3,691 | | TOEFL, SAT/ACT | | | | 100 |
| State Fair Community College . . . . . . . . . . . . . . | Pu/A | 3,886 | | TOEFL | 61 | | | |
| State Technical College of Missouri . . . . . . . . . . | Pu/A | 1,127 | | TOEFL, ACT | 80 | | None | |
| Stephens College . . . . . . . . . . . . . . . . . . . . . . . | Pr/AB | 724 | 1 | TOEFL, SAT/ACT | 79 | | None | 50 |
| Stevens Institute of Business & Arts . . . . . . . . . . | Pr/AB | 131 | | | | | | 15 |
| Texas County Technical College . . . . . . . . . . . . . | Pr/A | 91 | | | | | | 50 |
| Three Rivers Community College . . . . . . . . . . . . | Pu/A | 3,087 | | TOEFL | | | | |
| Truman State University . . . . . . . . . . . . . . . . . . | Pu/B | 5,302 | 385 | TOEFL | 79 | 88 | None | |
| University of Central Missouri . . . . . . . . . . . . . . | Pu/B | 8,744 | 159 | TOEFL, SAT/ACT | | | None | 50 |
| University of Missouri: Columbia . . . . . . . . . . . . | Pu/B | 25,544 | 949 | TOEFL | 61 | | | 60 |
| University of Missouri: Kansas City . . . . . . . . . . | Pu/B | 7,904 | 356 | TOEFL | 61 | 91 | 7/1 | 50 |
| University of Missouri: St. Louis . . . . . . . . . . . . | Pu/B | 7,737 | 255 | TOEFL | 61 | 78 | 6/1 | 40 |
| University of Phoenix: Kansas City . . . . . . . . . . . | Pr/B | 660 | | | | | | |
| University of Phoenix: St. Louis . . . . . . . . . . . . . | Pr/B | 952 | | | | | | |
| Vatterott College: Berkeley . . . . . . . . . . . . . . . | Pr/AB | 1,344 | | | | | | 25 |
| Vatterott College: Joplin . . . . . . . . . . . . . . . . . | Pr/A | 236 | | | | | | |
| Vatterott College: Kansas City . . . . . . . . . . . . . | Pr/A | 540 | | | | | | |
| Vatterott College: O'Fallon . . . . . . . . . . . . . . . | Pr/A | 305 | | | | | | |
| Vatterott College: Sunset Hills . . . . . . . . . . . . . | Pr/AB | 624 | | | | | | |
| Washington University in St. Louis . . . . . . . . . . . | Pr/AB | 7,116 | 538 | TOEFL, SAT/ACT | | | 1/15 | 75 |
| Webster University . . . . . . . . . . . . . . . . . . . . . | Pr/B | 2,591 | 101 | TOEFL | 80 | | 8/1 | 35 |
| Wentworth Military Junior College . . . . . . . . . . . | Pr/A | 343 | | | | | | 100 |
| Westminster College . . . . . . . . . . . . . . . . . . . . | Pr/B | 863 | 80 | TOEFL | | | 5/1 | 25 |
| William Jewell College . . . . . . . . . . . . . . . . . . . | Pr/B | 992 | 49 | TOEFL | 80 | 96 | None | |
| William Woods University . . . . . . . . . . . . . . . . . | Pr/AB | 943 | 41 | TOEFL, SAT/ACT | 60 | 65 | None | |
| **Montana** | | | | | | | | |
| Carroll College . . . . . . . . . . . . . . . . . . . . . . . . | Pr/AB | 1,342 | 17 | TOEFL | 80 | | | 35 |
| Dawson Community College . . . . . . . . . . . . . . . | Pu/A | 193 | 11 | TOEFL | 61 | | | 30 |
| Flathead Valley Community College . . . . . . . . . . | Pu/A | 2,206 | | TOEFL | 61 | | | 15 |
| Little Big Horn College . . . . . . . . . . . . . . . . . . | Pr/A | 596 | | | | | | |
| Montana Bible College . . . . . . . . . . . . . . . . . . . | Pr/B | 89 | 1 | | | | None | 50 |
| Montana State University . . . . . . . . . . . . . . . . . | Pu/AB | 14,205 | 470 | TOEFL | 71 | 89 | | 30 |
| Montana State University: Billings . . . . . . . . . . . | Pu/AB | 3,570 | 83 | TOEFL | 68 | | | 30 |
| Montana State University: Northern . . . . . . . . . . . | Pu/AB | 1,218 | | TOEFL, SAT/ACT | 53 | | | 30 |
| Montana Tech of the University of Montana . . . . . . | Pu/AB | 2,277 | 243 | TOEFL | 71 | | 8/1 | 30 |
| Rocky Mountain College . . . . . . . . . . . . . . . . . . | Pr/AB | 885 | 33 | TOEFL, SAT/ACT | 72 | | None | 40 |
| Salish Kootenai College . . . . . . . . . . . . . . . . . . | Pr/AB | 859 | | | | | | |
| Stone Child College . . . . . . . . . . . . . . . . . . . . . | Pu/A | 180 | | | | | | 10 |
| University of Great Falls . . . . . . . . . . . . . . . . . . | Pr/AB | 881 | | TOEFL | | | | 35 |
| University of Montana . . . . . . . . . . . . . . . . . . . | Pu/AB | 9,356 | 177 | TOEFL | | | 6/15 | 30 |
| University of Montana: Western . . . . . . . . . . . . . | Pu/AB | 1,467 | | TOEFL | 61 | 71 | 3/1 | 30 |
| **Nebraska** | | | | | | | | |
| Bellevue University . . . . . . . . . . . . . . . . . . . . . | Pr/B | 6,224 | | TOEFL | 61 | | | 75 |
| BryanLGH College of Health Sciences . . . . . . . . . . | Pr/AB | 590 | | | | | | 50 |
| Chadron State College . . . . . . . . . . . . . . . . . . . | Pu/B | 2,046 | 51 | TOEFL | | | | 15 |

| Student services | | | Housing | | Academic year costs | | Maximum credits/ summer | Credit hour charge | International financial aid | | | |
|---|---|---|---|---|---|---|---|---|---|---|---|---|
| Adviser | Orientation | ESL | Academic year | Summer | Tuition/ fees | Living costs | | | Available | Number receiving aid | Average award | Deadline |
| Yes | Yes | Yes | Yes | Yes | 12,130† | 8,340 | 6 | 391 | Yes | | | 8/1 |
| | | | No | | | 7,587 | | | | | | |
| Yes | Yes | | Yes | | 17,790† | 5,900 | | 593 | Yes | | | None |
| | | | Yes | Yes | 35,800† | 9,055 | 12 | | | | | None |
| | | | Yes | Yes | 35,670† | 10,880 | 18 | 1164 | Yes | 26 | $19,780 | None |
| | | | | | 6,540† | | 9 | | | | | |
| Yes | Yes | Yes | Yes | Yes | 40,726† | 10,640 | | 1400 | Yes | 140 | $20,641 | None |
| | | | No | | 12,330† | | | 390 | | | | |
| Yes | Yes | Yes | Yes | Yes | 12,375‡ | 8,508 | 9 | 379 | Yes | 487 | $2,862 | None |
| | Yes | | Yes | Yes | 23,290 | 7,600 | 12 | | Yes | | | None |
| Yes | | Yes | Yes | Yes | 7,500† | 5,000 | 9 | 250 | Yes | | | None |
| Yes | | | Yes | | 10,665† | 5,300 | | 319.5 | Yes | | | None |
| | | | Yes | | 30,344 | 10,424 | 18 | | Yes | 6 | $9,829 | None |
| | Yes | | | | 14,760‡ | 7,479 | 18 | 265 | | | | |
| | | | No | | 15,810† | 3,700 | | 424 | | | | |
| | | | Yes | | 6,330† | 3,440 | 12 | 178 | | | | |
| Yes | Yes | Yes | Yes | Yes | 13,940† | 8,558 | 9 | 568 | Yes | 268 | $5,798 | None |
| Yes | Yes | Yes | Yes | Yes | 13,767† | 8,318 | | 429.7 | Yes | 199 | $2,280 | None |
| Yes | Yes | Yes | Yes | Yes | 25,892† | 10,100 | | 822 | Yes | | | None |
| Yes | Yes | Yes | Yes | | 23,363† | 10,257 | 6 | 732 | | | | |
| Yes | Yes | Yes | Yes | Yes | 26,277† | 12,220 | 15 | 876 | Yes | 84 | $14,946 | None |
| Yes | Yes | Yes | Yes | Yes | 51,533 | 16,006 | 14 | | Yes | 101 | $34,481 | 2/1 |
| Yes | Yes | Yes | Yes | Yes | 26,425† | 11,190 | 9 | 670 | Yes | 44 | $12,270 | None |
| Yes | Yes | Yes | Yes | Yes | 20,900† | 6,800 | | 180 | Yes | | | 4/30 |
| Yes | Yes | Yes | Yes | Yes | 25,940 | 10,745 | 3 | 800 | Yes | | | None |
| Yes | Yes | | Yes | Yes | 33,620 | 9,640 | 8 | 960 | Yes | 44 | $22,824 | None |
| Yes | | | Yes | Yes | 23,260 | 10,900 | 18 | 665 | Yes | 38 | $24,730 | None |
| Yes | Yes | Yes | Yes | Yes | 33,192† | 9,584 | 13 | 1340 | Yes | | | None |
| Yes | | | Yes | | 7,650‡ | 5,775 | 12 | 201 | | | | |
| Yes | | Yes | | | 11,254† | | 12 | | | | | |
| | | | No | | 3,200† | | | | Yes | | | None |
| | | | Yes | Yes | 7,640 | 3,000 | | 220 | | | | |
| Yes | Yes | Yes | Yes | Yes | 23,042† | 8,900 | | 889 | Yes | 53 | $4,176 | None |
| Yes | Yes | Yes | Yes | Yes | 18,093† | 7,690 | 18 | 555 | Yes | 51 | $3,665 | None |
| Yes | | | Yes | Yes | 17,122† | 6,410 | 18 | 523 | Yes | | | None |
| Yes | Yes | | Yes | Yes | 20,046† | 8,932 | | 761 | Yes | 47 | $3,153 | None |
| Yes | Yes | Yes | Yes | Yes | 27,566 | 8,960 | 12 | 1127 | Yes | 33 | $22,756 | None |
| | | | Yes | | 11,463† | | | 285 | Yes | | | None |
| | | | No | | 2,775† | | | | Yes | | | None |
| Yes | Yes | | Yes | Yes | 25,050 | 8,500 | 12 | 789 | Yes | 24 | $18,767 | None |
| Yes | Yes | Yes | Yes | Yes | 23,669† | 8,826 | 18 | 728 | Yes | 157 | $5,881 | None |
| Yes | | | Yes | | 16,206† | 7,482 | 12 | 626 | Yes | | | None |
| Yes | Yes | | Yes | Yes | 11,475† | 6,649 | 15 | 385 | Yes | | | None |
| | | | No | | 16,890† | 10,341 | | 533 | Yes | | | 5/1 |
| Yes | | | Yes | | 6,686† | 6,352 | 18 | 161 | Yes | | | None |

† Actual for 2016-17.          ‡ Estimated for 2017-18.          * Includes room and board

| Institution | Control/ degrees | Undergraduates | | Tests required (Fall 2017) | TOEFL | | Application | |
|---|---|---|---|---|---|---|---|---|
| | | Total | Internat'l | | minimum | average | Deadline | Fee |
| College of Saint Mary . . . . . . . . . . . . . . . . . . . . | .Pr/AB | 744 | 5 | TOEFL | 80 | | | 30 |
| Concordia University . . . . . . . . . . . . . . . . . . . . . | .Pr/B | 1,233 | 28 | TOEFL, SAT/ACT | 78 | | 6/15 | |
| Creighton University . . . . . . . . . . . . . . . . . . . . . | .Pr/AB | 4,149 | 120 | TOEFL | 88 | | 5/1 | 40 |
| Doane University. . . . . . . . . . . . . . . . . . . . . . . . | .Pr/B | 1,041 | 21 | TOEFL, SAT/ACT | | | | 15 |
| Grace University . . . . . . . . . . . . . . . . . . . . . . . . | .Pr/AB | 238 | | TOEFL, SAT/ACT | 81 | | None | 35 |
| Hastings College . . . . . . . . . . . . . . . . . . . . . . . . | .Pr/B | 1,108 | | TOEFL, SAT/ACT | | | | 50 |
| Herzing University: Omaha School of Massage Therapy and Healthcare. . . . . . . . . . . . . . . . . | .Pr/AB | 105 | | | | | | |
| Kaplan University: Lincoln . . . . . . . . . . . . . . . . | .Pr/AB | 449 | | TOEFL | | | | 25 |
| Metropolitan Community College . . . . . . . . . . . . | .Pu/A | 6,899 | | TOEFL | | | | |
| Mid-Plains Community College . . . . . . . . . . . . . | .Pu/A | 1,215 | 27 | TOEFL | 61 | | 2/15 | |
| Midland University . . . . . . . . . . . . . . . . . . . . . . | .Pr/B | 1,213 | 13 | TOEFL, SAT/ACT | | | | 30 |
| Myotherapy Institute . . . . . . . . . . . . . . . . . . . . | .Pr/A | 15 | | | | | | 150 |
| Nebraska College of Technical Agriculture . . . . . . | .Pu/A | 265 | | TOEFL | 70 | | | 45 |
| Nebraska Indian Community College. . . . . . . . . . . | .Pu/A | 135 | | | | | None | 50 |
| Nebraska Wesleyan University . . . . . . . . . . . . . . | .Pr/B | 1,788 | 21 | TOEFL | 71 | | 5/1 | |
| Northeast Community College . . . . . . . . . . . . . . | .Pu/A | 5,061 | | TOEFL | 61 | | 6/1 | |
| Peru State College . . . . . . . . . . . . . . . . . . . . . . | .Pu/B | 1,483 | | TOEFL | 22 | | | |
| Union College. . . . . . . . . . . . . . . . . . . . . . . . . | .Pr/AB | 759 | 66 | TOEFL, ACT | 79 | | None | |
| University of Nebraska - Kearney . . . . . . . . . . . . | .Pu/B | 4,672 | 228 | TOEFL | 61 | | | 45 |
| University of Nebraska - Lincoln . . . . . . . . . . . . | .Pu/B | 20,833 | 1,746 | | 70 | 79 | 5/1 | 45 |
| University of Nebraska - Omaha. . . . . . . . . . . . . | .Pu/B | 12,488 | | TOEFL | 61 | | | 45 |
| Wayne State College . . . . . . . . . . . . . . . . . . . . | .Pu/B | 2,641 | 12 | TOEFL | | | | |
| Western Nebraska Community College . . . . . . . . . | .Pu/A | 1,143 | 88 | TOEFL | 32 | | 6/1 | 150 |
| York College . . . . . . . . . . . . . . . . . . . . . . . . . | .Pr/AB | 417 | | TOEFL, SAT/ACT | | | | 100 |

**Nevada**

| Institution | Control/ degrees | Undergraduates | | Tests required (Fall 2017) | TOEFL | | Application | |
|---|---|---|---|---|---|---|---|---|
| | | Total | Internat'l | | minimum | average | Deadline | Fee |
| Art Institute of Las Vegas . . . . . . . . . . . . . . . . . | .Pr/AB | 952 | | TOEFL | 61 | | | 150 |
| Career College of Northern Nevada. . . . . . . . . . . | .Pr/A | 350 | | TOEFL | | | | 25 |
| Carrington College: Las Vegas . . . . . . . . . . . . . . | .Pr/A | 325 | | | | | | |
| Carrington College: Reno . . . . . . . . . . . . . . . . . | .Pr/A | 343 | | | | | | |
| College of Southern Nevada . . . . . . . . . . . . . . . | .Pu/AB | 33,313 | | TOEFL | | | | 50 |
| Great Basin College. . . . . . . . . . . . . . . . . . . . . | .Pu/AB | 3,397 | | TOEFL | 61 | | | 25 |
| International Academy of Design and Technology: Henderson. . . . . . . . . . . . . . . . . | .Pr/AB | 510 | | TOEFL | 79 | | | 50 |
| Roseman University of Health Sciences . . . . . . . . | .Pr/B | 385 | | TOEFL | 79 | | 6/15 | 40 |
| Sierra Nevada College . . . . . . . . . . . . . . . . . . . | .Pr/B | 478 | 7 | TOEFL | 59 | | 8/26 | |
| Truckee Meadows Community College . . . . . . . . | .Pu/A | 8,538 | 51 | TOEFL | 61 | | | 20 |
| University of Nevada: Las Vegas . . . . . . . . . . . . | .Pu/B | 24,197 | 913 | TOEFL | 61 | | 7/1 | 95 |
| University of Nevada: Reno. . . . . . . . . . . . . . . . | .Pu/B | 17,794 | 133 | TOEFL | 61 | 82 | 2/1 | 95 |
| University of Phoenix: Las Vegas . . . . . . . . . . . . | .Pr/B | 2,000 | | | | | | |
| University of Phoenix: Northern Nevada . . . . . . . | .Pr/B | 300 | | | | | | |
| Western Nevada College. . . . . . . . . . . . . . . . . . | .Pu/AB | 3,005 | 1 | TOEFL | 61 | | | 15 |

**New Hampshire**

| Institution | Control/ degrees | Undergraduates | | Tests required (Fall 2017) | TOEFL | | Application | |
|---|---|---|---|---|---|---|---|---|
| | | Total | Internat'l | | minimum | average | Deadline | Fee |
| Colby-Sawyer College . . . . . . . . . . . . . . . . . . | .Pr/AB | 1,062 | | TOEFL | 61 | | | 45 |
| Dartmouth College. . . . . . . . . . . . . . . . . . . . . | .Pr/B | 4,230 | 358 | TOEFL, SAT/ACT, SAT Subject Test(s) | | | 1/1 | 80 |
| Franklin Pierce University. . . . . . . . . . . . . . . . . | .Pr/AB | 1,743 | | TOEFL | | | None | 40 |
| Granite State College . . . . . . . . . . . . . . . . . . . | .Pu/AB | 1,802 | 1 | TOEFL | 80 | | None | |
| Great Bay Community College. . . . . . . . . . . . . . | .Pu/A | 2,137 | | TOEFL | 61 | | | 10 |
| Keene State College. . . . . . . . . . . . . . . . . . . . . | .Pu/AB | 4,068 | 3 | TOEFL | 79 | 83 | 4/1 | 50 |
| Lakes Region Community College . . . . . . . . . . . | .Pu/A | 845 | | TOEFL | | | | 20 |
| Manchester Community College . . . . . . . . . . . . . | .Pu/A | 3,276 | | TOEFL | 61 | | | 20 |
| Nashua Community College. . . . . . . . . . . . . . . . | .Pu/A | 1,562 | | TOEFL | 61 | | None | 100 |
| New England College. . . . . . . . . . . . . . . . . . . . | .Pr/AB | 1,751 | 71 | TOEFL | 100 | 90 | None | 35 |
| New Hampshire Institute of Art . . . . . . . . . . . . . | .Pr/B | 339 | | TOEFL | 71 | | None | 70 |
| NHTI-Concord's Community College . . . . . . . . . . | .Pu/A | 4,109 | | TOEFL | | | | 20 |

| Student services | | | Housing | | Academic year costs | | Maximum credits/ summer | Credit hour charge | International financial aid | | | |
|---|---|---|---|---|---|---|---|---|---|---|---|---|
| Adviser | Orientation | ESL | Academic year | Summer | Tuition/ fees | Living costs | | | Available | Number receiving aid | Average award | Deadline |
| Yes | Yes | | Yes | Yes | 19,950 | 7,550 | 9 | 985 | Yes | 5 | $27,133 | None |
| Yes | Yes | | Yes | Yes | 31,000 | 8,400 | 12 | 890 | Yes | | | None |
| Yes | Yes | Yes | Yes | Yes | 37,606† | 10,600 | 15 | 1125 | Yes | | | None |
| Yes | Yes | Yes | Yes | Yes | 30,434† | 8,750 | 12 | 990 | Yes | 13 | $18,405 | None |
| | | | Yes | Yes | 21,928† | 7,558 | 6 | | Yes | | | 4/1 |
| Yes | Yes | | Yes | Yes | 28,250† | 8,880 | 9 | | Yes | | | 5/1 |
| | | | No | | | 15,150 | | | Yes | | | None |
| | | | | | | 4,928 | | | | | | |
| Yes | Yes | Yes | Yes | Yes | 4,208 | 6,255 | | 88.5 | | | | None |
| Yes | Yes | | Yes | | 3,720† | 6,100 | 9 | 109 | Yes | 4 | $657 | None |
| Yes | | | Yes | Yes | 30,430† | 9,223 | 12 | | Yes | | | None |
| Yes | Yes | | Yes | | 9,450† | 7,098 | | 256.5 | Yes | | | None |
| | | | No | | 5,150‡ | 10,776 | | | Yes | | | None |
| Yes | Yes | | Yes | Yes | 31,394† | 8,758 | 12 | 1120 | Yes | 9 | $15,844 | None |
| Yes | | Yes | Yes | Yes | 4,365† | 7,800 | | 126 | | | | |
| | | | Yes | Yes | 6,821† | 7,214 | | 161 | Yes | | | None |
| Yes | Yes | Yes | Yes | Yes | 23,070‡ | 6,926 | | 916 | Yes | 58 | $7,653 | None |
| Yes | Yes | Yes | Yes | Yes | 13,381† | 10,094 | 15 | 396.25 | Yes | 193 | $5,298 | None |
| Yes | Yes | Yes | Yes | Yes | 23,058† | 14,794 | 17 | 709.25 | Yes | 768 | $6,924 | None |
| Yes | Yes | Yes | Yes | Yes | 20,939† | 10,018 | 12 | 642.5 | Yes | | | None |
| Yes | | | Yes | Yes | 6,457† | 7,110 | | 161 | Yes | 11 | $1,367 | None |
| Yes | Yes | Yes | Yes | | 3,660† | 7,360 | 12 | 104.5 | Yes | 57 | $6,099 | None |
| Yes | | | Yes | | 17,700† | 9,100 | 9 | 600 | Yes | | | None |
| Yes | | | Yes | Yes | 22,645† | 6,377 | 16 | 481 | Yes | | | None |
| | | | No | | | | | | Yes | | | None |
| Yes | Yes | Yes | No | | 9,688† | | 12 | | | | | |
| Yes | | Yes | Yes | | 9,688† | 3,325 | 6 | | Yes | | | None |
| | | | No | | 36,530† | 21,794 | | 644 | Yes | | | None |
| Yes | | Yes | Yes | Yes | 32,639 | 13,764 | 15 | 1348 | Yes | 30 | $13,091 | 8/17 |
| Yes | Yes | | No | | 9,688† | 9,736 | 12 | | | | | |
| Yes | Yes | Yes | Yes | Yes | 20,973† | 11,024 | 18 | | Yes | 250 | $11,744 | None |
| Yes | Yes | Yes | Yes | Yes | 21,053† | 12,172 | 15 | | Yes | | | None |
| Yes | | | No | | 9,688† | 9,220 | 12 | | Yes | | | None |
| Yes | Yes | Yes | Yes | | 40,386 | 13,650 | | | Yes | | | None |
| Yes | Yes | Yes | Yes | Yes | 51,438† | 15,141 | 4 | | Yes | 271 | $57,326 | 2/1 |
| Yes | Yes | Yes | Yes | Yes | 34,050† | 15,400 | 16 | 1050 | Yes | 28 | $9,102 | None |
| Yes | | | No | | 10,200† | 8,919 | | 335 | | | | |
| Yes | Yes | Yes | No | | 14,310† | 13,160 | 18 | 455 | | | | |
| Yes | Yes | Yes | Yes | Yes | 21,997† | 10,390 | 20 | 806 | | | | 3/1 |
| | | | Yes | | 13,830† | 8,100 | | 455 | | | | |
| Yes | | Yes | No | | 14,130† | 13,160 | | 455 | | | | |
| Yes | | | No | | 14,130† | 13,896 | | 455 | | | | |
| Yes | Yes | Yes | Yes | Yes | 36,954 | 15,374 | 18 | 1715 | Yes | 39 | $20,816 | 9/1 |
| | | | Yes | | 26,880 | 11,160 | | 1095 | Yes | | | None |
| Yes | | Yes | Yes | Yes | 14,310† | 9,056 | | 455 | | | | |

| Institution | Control/ degrees | Undergraduates Total | Undergraduates Internat'l | Tests required (Fall 2017) | TOEFL minimum | TOEFL average | Application Deadline | Application Fee |
|---|---|---|---|---|---|---|---|---|
| Plymouth State University . . . . . . . . . . . . . . . . . . | Pu/B | 4,073 | 65 | TOEFL | 68 | 81 | 5/1 | 50 |
| River Valley Community College . . . . . . . . . . . . | Pu/A | 955 | | TOEFL | 61 | | | 20 |
| Rivier University . . . . . . . . . . . . . . . . . . . . . . . . | Pr/AB | 1,375 | | TOEFL | | | 7/1 | 25 |
| Saint Anselm College . . . . . . . . . . . . . . . . . . . . | Pr/B | 1,916 | 10 | TOEFL | 80 | 90 | None | 50 |
| | | | | | | | | |
| Southern New Hampshire University . . . . . . . . . . . | Pr/AB | 3,002 | 213 | TOEFL | 71 | | None | 40 |
| Thomas More College of Liberal Arts . . . . . . . . . . | Pr/B | 89 | | TOEFL | | | | |
| University of New Hampshire . . . . . . . . . . . . . . . | Pu/AB | 12,653 | 381 | TOEFL, SAT/ACT | 80 | | 2/1 | 65 |
| University of New Hampshire at Manchester . . . . . . | Pu/AB | 712 | | TOEFL | | | 4/1 | 60 |
| | | | | | | | | |
| **New Jersey** | | | | | | | | |
| | | | | | | | | |
| Atlantic Cape Community College . . . . . . . . . . . . | Pu/A | 7,254 | | | 54 | | | 100 |
| | | | | | | | | |
| Berkeley College . . . . . . . . . . . . . . . . . . . . . . . . | Pr/AB | 3,813 | | TOEFL | 61 | | | 50 |
| Bloomfield College . . . . . . . . . . . . . . . . . . . . . . | Pr/B | 1,941 | 83 | TOEFL | 79 | | 8/1 | 40 |
| Brookdale Community College . . . . . . . . . . . . . . . | Pu/A | 14,144 | | TOEFL | 45 | | | 25 |
| Caldwell University . . . . . . . . . . . . . . . . . . . . . . | Pr/B | 1,632 | 125 | TOEFL | 70 | | | 50 |
| Centenary University . . . . . . . . . . . . . . . . . . . . . | Pr/AB | 1,490 | 45 | TOEFL | | | None | 50 |
| | | | | | | | | |
| The College of New Jersey . . . . . . . . . . . . . . . . . | Pu/B | 6,666 | 15 | TOEFL, SAT/ACT | 90 | | 1/15 | 75 |
| College of St. Elizabeth . . . . . . . . . . . . . . . . . . . | Pr/B | 740 | 21 | TOEFL | | | | 35 |
| County College of Morris . . . . . . . . . . . . . . . . . . | Pu/A | 8,067 | | TOEFL | 32 | | 7/1 | 30 |
| Cumberland County College . . . . . . . . . . . . . . . . | Pu/A | 3,080 | | TOEFL | | | None | |
| DeVry University: North Brunswick . . . . . . . . . . . | Pr/AB | 583 | 11 | TOEFL | | | | 50 |
| | | | | | | | | |
| Drew University . . . . . . . . . . . . . . . . . . . . . . . . | Pr/B | 1,407 | 109 | TOEFL | 80 | | 2/1 | 40 |
| Eastern International College . . . . . . . . . . . . . . . . | Pr/AB | 433 | | | | | | 125 |
| Eastwick College . . . . . . . . . . . . . . . . . . . . . . . . | Pr/A | 865 | | | | | | 100 |
| Eastwick College: Hackensack . . . . . . . . . . . . . . . | Pr/A | 375 | | | | | | 25 |
| Essex County College . . . . . . . . . . . . . . . . . . . . . | Pu/A | 10,954 | | | | | | 25 |
| | | | | | | | | |
| Fairleigh Dickinson University: College at Florham . . . . . . . . . . . . . . . . . . . . . . . . . . . . . | Pr/B | 2,483 | 12 | TOEFL | 79 | | | 40 |
| Fairleigh Dickinson University: Metropolitan Campus . . . . . . . . . . . . . . . . . . . . . . . . . . . . | Pr/AB | 3,450 | | TOEFL | 79 | | | 40 |
| Felician University . . . . . . . . . . . . . . . . . . . . . . . | Pr/AB | 1,639 | 34 | TOEFL | 61 | 64 | 6/1 | 30 |
| Georgian Court University . . . . . . . . . . . . . . . . . . | Pr/B | 1,409 | 21 | TOEFL | 79 | | | 40 |
| Hudson County Community College . . . . . . . . . . . | Pu/A | 7,893 | | | | | | 25 |
| | | | | | | | | |
| Kean University . . . . . . . . . . . . . . . . . . . . . . . . . | Pu/B | 11,656 | 284 | TOEFL | 79 | | None | 75 |
| Mercer County Community College . . . . . . . . . . . . | Pu/A | 6,609 | 295 | TOEFL | | | | 50 |
| Middlesex County College . . . . . . . . . . . . . . . . . . | Pu/A | 11,380 | | | | | 6/17 | 25 |
| Monmouth University . . . . . . . . . . . . . . . . . . . . . | Pr/AB | 4,668 | 35 | TOEFL | 79 | 90 | | 50 |
| Montclair State University . . . . . . . . . . . . . . . . . . | Pu/B | 16,653 | 241 | TOEFL | 80 | | 3/1 | 65 |
| | | | | | | | | |
| New Jersey City University . . . . . . . . . . . . . . . . . | Pu/B | 6,465 | 60 | TOEFL, SAT | 61 | 68 | | 35 |
| New Jersey Institute of Technology . . . . . . . . . . . | Pu/B | 7,336 | 345 | TOEFL, SAT/ACT | 79 | | 4/1 | 75 |
| Ocean County College . . . . . . . . . . . . . . . . . . . . | Pu/A | 7,374 | 80 | TOEFL | 61 | | | |
| Passaic County Community College . . . . . . . . . . . | Pu/A | 8,389 | | | | | | |
| Pillar College . . . . . . . . . . . . . . . . . . . . . . . . . . | Pr/AB | 496 | | TOEFL | 80 | | | 2500 |
| | | | | | | | | |
| Princeton University . . . . . . . . . . . . . . . . . . . . . . | Pr/B | 5,236 | 625 | TOEFL, SAT/ACT | | | 1/1 | 65 |
| Rabbi Jacob Joseph School . . . . . . . . . . . . . . . . . | Pr/B | 86 | | | | | | |
| Rabbinical College of America . . . . . . . . . . . . . . . | Pr/B | 249 | | | | | | 150 |
| Ramapo College of New Jersey . . . . . . . . . . . . . . | Pu/B | 5,445 | 90 | TOEFL | 90 | | | 75 |
| Raritan Valley Community College . . . . . . . . . . . . | Pu/A | 7,005 | 153 | TOEFL | 65 | | | 225 |
| | | | | | | | | |
| Rider University . . . . . . . . . . . . . . . . . . . . . . . . | Pr/AB | 3,978 | 123 | TOEFL, SAT/ACT | 80 | 93 | 3/15 | 50 |
| Rowan College at Burlington County . . . . . . . . . . . | Pu/A | 7,939 | | | | | None | 100 |
| Rowan College at Gloucester . . . . . . . . . . . . . . . . | Pu/A | 6,229 | | TOEFL | 61 | | | 20 |
| Rowan University . . . . . . . . . . . . . . . . . . . . . . . | Pu/B | 14,208 | 119 | TOEFL | 79 | | 3/1 | 65 |
| Rutgers, The State University of New Jersey: Camden Campus . . . . . . . . . . . . . . . . . . . . . . . | Pu/B | 4,978 | 59 | TOEFL, SAT/ACT | 79 | | 4/15 | 70 |
| | | | | | | | | |
| Rutgers, The State University of New Jersey: New Brunswick/Piscataway Campus . . . . . . . . . . . | Pu/AB | 35,782 | 2,904 | TOEFL, SAT/ACT | 79 | | 4/15 | 70 |
| Rutgers, The State University of New Jersey: Newark Campus . . . . . . . . . . . . . . . . . . . . . . | Pu/AB | 7,691 | 349 | TOEFL, SAT/ACT | 79 | | 4/15 | 70 |
| Saint Peter's University . . . . . . . . . . . . . . . . . . . . | Pr/AB | 2,589 | 53 | TOEFL | 79 | 82 | 7/1 | |
| Salem Community College . . . . . . . . . . . . . . . . . | Pu/A | 912 | | TOEFL | 68 | | | 27 |

| Student services | | | Housing | | Academic year costs | | Maximum credits/ summer | Credit hour charge | International financial aid | | | |
|---|---|---|---|---|---|---|---|---|---|---|---|---|
| Adviser | Orien- tation | ESL | Academic year | Summer | Tuition/ fees | Living costs | | | Avail- able | Number receiving aid | Average award | Deadline |
| Yes | Yes | | Yes | Yes | 21,732 † | 11,008 | 9 | 803 | Yes | 19 | $1,921 | None |
| | | | No | | 13,800 † | 6,000 | 18 | 455 | | | | |
| Yes | Yes | | Yes | | 29,700 † | 11,610 | 12 | 970 | Yes | | | None |
| Yes | Yes | | Yes | Yes | 38,826 † | 13,734 | 9 | | Yes | 9 | $44,902 | 2/15 |
| Yes | Yes | Yes | Yes | Yes | 31,136 † | 12,812 | 18 | 1282 | Yes | 45 | $20,237 | 6/30 |
| | | | Yes | | 20,400 † | 9,700 | | 850 | Yes | | | None |
| Yes | Yes | Yes | Yes | Yes | 31,424 † | 11,538 | 12 | 1175 | Yes | 62 | $30,580 | 3/1 |
| | | Yes | No | | 28,293 † | | | 1160 | Yes | | | 3/1 |
| Yes | | Yes | No | | 7,753 † | 18,700 | | 230 | Yes | | | None |
| Yes | Yes | | | | | 13,989 | 18 | | Yes | | | None |
| Yes | Yes | | Yes | Yes | 29,300 | 11,700 | 16 | 918 | Yes | | | 4/15 |
| | | | No | | 9,049 † | 9,287 | | 270.5 | | | | |
| Yes | Yes | | Yes | Yes | 33,900 | 11,710 | 12 | 700 | Yes | 122 | $24,002 | None |
| Yes | Yes | Yes | Yes | Yes | 32,580 ‡ | 11,110 | 18 | 600 | Yes | | | 9/1 |
| Yes | Yes | | Yes | | 26,971 † | 12,881 | 12 | 789 | Yes | 5 | $2,100 | 10/1 |
| Yes | Yes | Yes | Yes | Yes | 32,282 † | 14,744 | 9 | 843 | Yes | | | 10/1 |
| Yes | | Yes | No | | 11,790 | 10,800 | 11 | 357 | Yes | | | None |
| | | Yes | No | | 8,580 † | 8,564 | 12 | 256 | | | | |
| Yes | | | No | | 17,512 † | | | 609 | | | | |
| Yes | Yes | Yes | Yes | Yes | 47,752 † | 13,296 | | 1955 | Yes | 84 | $25,347 | 2/1 |
| | | | | | | 4,221 | | | Yes | | | 6/1 |
| Yes | Yes | Yes | No | | 8,370 † | 11,076 | | 239 | Yes | | | None |
| Yes | Yes | Yes | Yes | Yes | 40,887 † | 12,840 | | | Yes | | | None |
| Yes | Yes | Yes | Yes | Yes | 38,641 † | 13,521 | | | | | | |
| Yes | Yes | Yes | Yes | Yes | 32,990 † | 12,380 | 9 | 1015 | Yes | | | None |
| Yes | | Yes | Yes | Yes | 31,618 † | 10,808 | 9 | 690 | Yes | 21 | $32,249 | None |
| | Yes | Yes | No | | 13,093 † | 10,442 | 6 | 387 | | | | |
| Yes | Yes | Yes | Yes | Yes | 18,637 † | 12,780 | 12 | 513 | Yes | 27 | $5,109 | 4/17 |
| Yes | Yes | Yes | No | | 8,835 † | 8,003 | 18 | 254 | Yes | | | 5/1 |
| Yes | Yes | Yes | No | | 9,236 † | | 12 | 216 | | | | |
| Yes | Yes | | Yes | Yes | 35,364 † | 13,038 | 12 | 1003 | Yes | 37 | $28,104 | None |
| Yes | Yes | ESL | Yes | Yes | 20,007 † | 14,094 | 8 | 555.3 | Yes | | | None |
| Yes | Yes | Yes | Yes | Yes | 20,458 ‡ | 12,446 | 12 | 571 | | | | |
| Yes | Yes | Yes | Yes | | 31,034 † | 13,420 | 24 | 1206 | Yes | 86 | $28,343 | None |
| Yes | Yes | Yes | No | | 7,735 † | | 18 | 225 | | | | |
| Yes | | Yes | No | | 7,973 † | | 8 | 228 | | | | |
| Yes | | Yes | No | | 23,100 † | 10,450 | 35 | 785 | | | | |
| Yes | Yes | | Yes | Yes | 47,500 ‡ | 15,495 | | | Yes | 427 | $49,642 | 2/1 |
| | | | | | 11,700 † | 3,300 | | | | | | |
| | | | Yes | | | | | | | | | |
| Yes | Yes | | Yes | Yes | 22,870 † | 12,030 | 12 | 562 | Yes | 58 | $22,462 | None |
| Yes | Yes | Yes | No | | 6,294 † | | 12 | 179 | Yes | | | None |
| Yes | Yes | Yes | Yes | Yes | 39,820 † | 14,230 | | 1140 | Yes | 95 | $25,988 | None |
| Yes | | Yes | No | | 6,495 † | 9,900 | | 181 | Yes | | | None |
| Yes | | | No | | 9,075 | 9,928 | 16 | | Yes | | | None |
| | | Yes | Yes | | 21,378 † | 11,688 | 12 | 682 | Yes | | | None |
| Yes | | | Yes | | 29,381 † | 11,908 | 12 | 862 | Yes | | | None |
| Yes | Yes | Yes | Yes | Yes | 30,023 † | 12,260 | 12 | 878 | Yes | | | None |
| Yes | Yes | Yes | Yes | | 29,480 † | 13,459 | 12 | 878 | Yes | | | None |
| Yes | Yes | | Yes | Yes | 35,192 † | 16,456 | 12 | | Yes | | | None |
| Yes | | | No | | 5,844 † | 5,400 | 12 | 150 | | | | |

† Actual for 2016-17.     ‡ Estimated for 2017-18.     * Includes room and board

| Institution | Control/ degrees | Undergraduates | | Tests required (Fall 2017) | TOEFL | | Application | |
|---|---|---|---|---|---|---|---|---|
| | | Total | Internat'l | | minimum | average | Deadline | Fee |
| Seton Hall University . . . . . . . . . . . . . . . . . . . . . | Pr/B | 6,090 | | TOEFL | 79 | | | 55 |
| | | | | | | | | |
| Stevens Institute of Technology . . . . . . . . . . . . . | Pr/B | 3,109 | 144 | TOEFL | 80 | | | 65 |
| Stockton University . . . . . . . . . . . . . . . . . . . . . | Pu/B | 7,825 | 26 | TOEFL | 80 | | 3/15 | 50 |
| Sussex County Community College. . . . . . . . . . . . | Pu/A | 2,738 | | | | | | 25 |
| Talmudical Academy of New Jersey . . . . . . . . . . . | Pr/B | 45 | | | | | | |
| Thomas Edison State University . . . . . . . . . . . . . | Pu/AB | 16,506 | 197 | TOEFL | 79 | | | 75 |
| | | | | | | | | |
| Union County College . . . . . . . . . . . . . . . . . . | Pu/A | 9,704 | 194 | TOEFL | 30 | | 6/1 | |
| University of Phoenix: Jersey City . . . . . . . . . . . | Pr/B | 371 | | | | | | |
| William Paterson University of New Jersey. . . . . . . | Pu/B | 8,972 | 80 | TOEFL, SAT/ACT | 79 | | 6/1 | 50 |
| | | | | | | | | |
| **New Mexico** | | | | | | | | |
| | | | | | | | | |
| Brookline College: Albuquerque . . . . . . . . . . . . . | Pr/AB | 357 | | | | | | |
| Brown Mackie College: Albuquerque. . . . . . . . . . . | Pr/AB | 767 | | | | | | |
| | | | | | | | | |
| Carrington College: Albuquerque . . . . . . . . . . . . | Pr/A | 586 | | | | | | |
| Dona Ana Community College of New | | | | | | | | |
|   Mexico State University . . . . . . . . . . . . . . . . . | Pu/A | 9,280 | | TOEFL | 61 | | | 15 |
| Eastern New Mexico University . . . . . . . . . . . . . | Pu/AB | 4,574 | | TOEFL, SAT/ACT | | | | |
| Eastern New Mexico University: Roswell. . . . . . . . | Pu/A | 1,724 | | | | | None | |
| Institute of American Indian Arts . . . . . . . . . . . . | Pu/AB | 463 | | TOEFL | | | | 25 |
| | | | | | | | | |
| Luna Community College . . . . . . . . . . . . . . . . . | Pu/A | 699 | | | | | None | |
| Mesalands Community College. . . . . . . . . . . . . . | Pu/A | 869 | | TOEFL | | | | |
| National American University: Albuquerque . . . . . . | Pr/AB | 352 | | TOEFL | | | | 25 |
| Navajo Technical University . . . . . . . . . . . . . . . | Pu/AB | 1,351 | 3 | | | | | |
| New Mexico Highlands University . . . . . . . . . . . . | Pu/AB | 2,123 | 101 | TOEFL | 61 | 76 | | 15 |
| | | | | | | | | |
| New Mexico Institute of Mining and | | | | | | | | |
|   Technology. . . . . . . . . . . . . . . . . . . . . . . . . | Pu/AB | 1,460 | 38 | TOEFL | 76 | | | 50 |
| New Mexico Junior College. . . . . . . . . . . . . . . . | Pu/A | 2,949 | | TOEFL | | | | |
| New Mexico Military Institute . . . . . . . . . . . . . . | Pu/A | 422 | | TOEFL | 61 | | 7/10 | 85 |
| New Mexico State University. . . . . . . . . . . . . . . | Pu/AB | 11,421 | 603 | TOEFL | 79 | | 3/1 | 50 |
| New Mexico State University at Alamogordo . . . . . | Pu/A | 1,914 | | TOEFL | 61 | | | 50 |
| | | | | | | | | |
| New Mexico State University at Carlsbad. . . . . . . . | Pu/A | 1,360 | | TOEFL | 61 | | | |
| New Mexico State University at Grants . . . . . . . . . | Pu/A | 1,160 | | TOEFL | 61 | | | 20 |
| Northern New Mexico College. . . . . . . . . . . . . . | Pu/AB | 1,601 | | TOEFL | | | | |
| St. John's College . . . . . . . . . . . . . . . . . . . . . | Pr/B | 326 | 83 | TOEFL | | 102 | | |
| San Juan College. . . . . . . . . . . . . . . . . . . . . . | Pu/A | 5,581 | 56 | TOEFL | 61 | | | 10 |
| | | | | | | | | |
| Santa Fe Community College. . . . . . . . . . . . . . . | Pu/A | 4,911 | | TOEFL | | | | |
| Santa Fe University of Art and Design. . . . . . . . . | Pr/B | 911 | | TOEFL | 79 | | | 50 |
| University of New Mexico . . . . . . . . . . . . . . . . | Pu/B | 19,648 | | TOEFL | 68 | | | 50 |
| University of Phoenix: New Mexico . . . . . . . . . . . | Pr/B | 1,238 | | | | | | |
| University of the Southwest. . . . . . . . . . . . . . . . | Pr/B | 536 | | TOEFL, SAT/ACT | 79 | | | |
| | | | | | | | | |
| Western New Mexico University . . . . . . . . . . . . . | Pu/AB | 1,798 | | TOEFL | 79 | | 3/1 | 30 |
| | | | | | | | | |
| **New York** | | | | | | | | |
| | | | | | | | | |
| Adelphi University. . . . . . . . . . . . . . . . . . . . . . | Pr/AB | 5,135 | 160 | TOEFL | 80 | 94 | | 50 |
| Adirondack Community College. . . . . . . . . . . . . . | Pu/A | 3,111 | 11 | TOEFL | | | | 35 |
| Albany College of Pharmacy and Health | | | | | | | | |
|   Sciences. . . . . . . . . . . . . . . . . . . . . . . . . . | Pr/B | 901 | 55 | TOEFL, SAT/ACT | 84 | | | 75 |
| Alfred University. . . . . . . . . . . . . . . . . . . . . . . | Pr/B | 1,725 | 30 | TOEFL | 80 | | | 50 |
| | | | | | | | | |
| American Academy of Dramatic Arts . . . . . . . . . . | Pr/A | 288 | | | | | | 50 |
| ASA College . . . . . . . . . . . . . . . . . . . . . . . . . | Pr/A | 4,641 | 930 | | 70 | 75 | None | 25 |
| Bard College . . . . . . . . . . . . . . . . . . . . . . . . . | Pr/AB | 1,926 | 185 | TOEFL | 100 | | | 50 |
| Barnard College . . . . . . . . . . . . . . . . . . . . . . . | Pr/B | 2,572 | 216 | TOEFL, SAT/ACT | 100 | 108 | 1/1 | 75 |
| Beis Medrash Heichal Dovid . . . . . . . . . . . . . . . | Pr/AB | 110 | | | | | | 100 |
| | | | | | | | | |
| Berkeley College. . . . . . . . . . . . . . . . . . . . . . . | Pr/AB | 467 | | TOEFL | 61 | | | 50 |
| Berkeley College of New York City . . . . . . . . . . . | Pr/AB | 3,968 | | TOEFL | 61 | | | 50 |
| Beth Hamedrash Shaarei Yosher Institute . . . . . . . | Pr/B | 49 | | | | | | 100 |
| Beth Hatalmud Rabbinical College . . . . . . . . . . . | Pr/B | 47 | | | | | | |
| Bramson ORT College . . . . . . . . . . . . . . . . . . . | Pr/A | 508 | | | | | | 50 |

| Student services | | | Housing | | Academic year costs | | Maximum credits/ summer | Credit hour charge | International financial aid | | | |
|---|---|---|---|---|---|---|---|---|---|---|---|---|
| Adviser | Orien- tation | ESL | Academic year | Summer | Tuition/ fees | Living costs | | | Avail- able | Number receiving aid | Average award | Deadline |
| Yes | Yes | Yes | Yes | Yes | 39,558 † | 14,732 | | 1130 | Yes | | | None |
| Yes | Yes | Yes | Yes | Yes | 50,554 ‡ | 14,400 | 18 | 1626 | Yes | | | None |
| Yes | Yes | | Yes | Yes | 19,861 † | 11,982 | 24 | | | | | |
| | | Yes | No | | 10,950 † | 5,100 | | | | | | |
| | | | Yes | | 13,000 † | 3,000 | | | | | | |
| Yes | | | No | | 9,352 † | | | 499 | | | | |
| Yes | Yes | Yes | No | | 9,608 | 7,250 | | 382 | Yes | | | None |
| Yes | Yes | | Yes | Yes | 20,466 † | 11,103 | | 579 | Yes | 46 | $5,292 | None |
| | | | No | | | 9,000 | | | | | | |
| Yes | Yes | Yes | Yes | Yes | 5,184 † | | 14 | 216 | | | | |
| | Yes | | Yes | Yes | 11,258 † | 6,760 | 9 | 470.21 | Yes | | | None |
| Yes | | | Yes | | 4,920 † | 8,160 | 12 | | Yes | | | None |
| | | | Yes | | 9,160 † | 8,612 | | 372 | Yes | | | None |
| | | Yes | No | | 2,426 † | 6,538 | | 99 | | | | |
| | | Yes | No | | 3,465 † | 5,542 | | 99 | | | | |
| | | | No | | 16,200 † | 7,272 | 16 | 360 | | | | |
| | | | Yes | | 4,070 † | 6,270 | | | | | | |
| Yes | Yes | | Yes | Yes | 8,500 † | 7,836 | 9 | 293.82 | | | | |
| Yes | Yes | | Yes | Yes | 20,041 † | 9,642 | 6 | 791 | Yes | 4 | $12,862 | None |
| Yes | | | Yes | Yes | 1,896 † | 5,350 | 14 | 62 | Yes | | | None |
| Yes | | | Yes | | 14,027 † | 5,325 | 2 | | Yes | | | None |
| Yes | Yes | Yes | Yes | Yes | 21,234 † | 7,988 | | | Yes | 228 | $18,286 | 6/30 |
| Yes | Yes | | No | | 5,280 † | | 10 | | | | | |
| Yes | | | No | | 3,868 † | 8,320 | 14 | | | | | |
| | | Yes | No | | 3,936 † | 7,526 | 9 | | | | | |
| Yes | | | Yes | | 13,032 † | | 9 | | | | | |
| | Yes | | Yes | Yes | 52,320 ‡ | 14,336 | | 1506 | Yes | 70 | $52,607 | None |
| Yes | | | No | | 10,750 | 8,370 | 12 | 346 | | | | |
| Yes | | Yes | No | | 2,940 † | 11,013 | 7 | | Yes | | | None |
| | | Yes | Yes | Yes | | | | | Yes | | | None |
| Yes | Yes | Yes | Yes | Yes | 21,936 † | 9,472 | 9 | | Yes | | | None |
| Yes | | | Yes | | 16,560 † | 11,535 | 12 | 552 | Yes | | | 6/1 |
| | | Yes | Yes | Yes | 15,261 † | 8,936 | 12 | | Yes | | | None |
| Yes | Yes | Yes | Yes | Yes | 35,740 † | 13,930 | 24 | 1040 | Yes | 109 | $18,723 | None |
| | | | Yes | | 8,787 † | 11,410 | 12 | 348 | | | | |
| Yes | Yes | | Yes | | 31,981 † | 10,700 | | 1040 | Yes | | | 5/1 |
| Yes | Yes | Yes | Yes | | 32,264 | 12,272 | 16 | 998 | Yes | | | 3/15 |
| Yes | Yes | | Yes | | 33,190 † | | | | Yes | | | |
| Yes | | Yes | Yes | | 14,065 ‡ | 9,500 | 18 | 546 | Yes | | | None |
| Yes | | Yes | Yes | Yes | 54,496 | 15,066 | | 1635 | Yes | 68 | $46,527 | 2/15 |
| Yes | Yes | | Yes | | 50,394 † | 15,598 | | | Yes | | | 2/15 |
| | | | | | 9,450 † | 5,500 | | | | | | |
| Yes | Yes | | Yes | Yes | 24,750 † | 9,000 | 18 | 525 | Yes | | | None |
| Yes | Yes | Yes | | | 24,750 † | 14,382 | 18 | 810 | Yes | | | None |
| | | | Yes | | 10,950 † | | | | | | | |
| | | Yes | No | | 11,280 † | 8,432 | 12 | 450 | | | | |

† Actual for 2016-17.      ‡ Estimated for 2017-18.      * Includes room and board

| Institution | Control/ degrees | Undergraduates Total | Internat'l | Tests required (Fall 2017) | TOEFL minimum | average | Application Deadline | Fee |
|---|---|---|---|---|---|---|---|---|
| Briarcliffe College . . . . . . . . . . . . . . . . . . . . . . . | Pr/AB | 1,719 | | TOEFL | 61 | | | 35 |
| Broome Community College . . . . . . . . . . . . | Pu/A | 5,343 | 6 | TOEFL | | | | 50 |
| Bryant & Stratton College: Albany . . . . . . . . . . . . | Pr/AB | 481 | | TOEFL | | | | 35 |
| Bryant & Stratton College: Amherst . . . . . . . . . . | Pr/AB | 340 | | | | | | 35 |
| Bryant & Stratton College: Buffalo . . . . . . . . . . . . | Pr/AB | 671 | | | | | | 35 |
| Bryant & Stratton College: Henrietta . . . . . . . . . . . | Pr/A | 393 | | | | | | 35 |
| Bryant & Stratton College: Rochester . . . . . . . . . . . | Pr/AB | 401 | | | | | | 25 |
| Bryant & Stratton College: Southtowns . . . . . . . . . | Pr/AB | 2,330 | | | | | | 35 |
| Bryant & Stratton College: Syracuse North . . . . . . . | Pr/AB | 466 | | | | | | 35 |
| Canisius College . . . . . . . . . . . . . . . . . . . . . . . . | Pr/AB | 2,488 | 106 | TOEFL | 79 | | 7/15 | 40 |
| Cayuga Community College . . . . . . . . . . . . . . . | Pu/A | 2,285 | 15 | TOEFL | | | | |
| Cazenovia College . . . . . . . . . . . . . . . . . . . . . . | Pr/AB | 991 | 4 | TOEFL | 79 | | | 30 |
| Central Yeshiva Tomchei Tmimim-Lubavitch . . . . . | Pr/B | 648 | | | | | | |
| City University of New York: Baruch College . . . . . | Pu/B | 14,858 | 1,672 | TOEFL | 80 | | | 65 |
| City University of New York: Borough of Manhattan Community College . . . . . . . . . . . . . . | Pu/A | 25,548 | 1,589 | TOEFL | 45 | | | 65 |
| City University of New York: Bronx Community College . . . . . . . . . . . . . . . . . . . . . | Pu/A | 10,919 | | TOEFL | 60 | | | 65 |
| City University of New York: Brooklyn College . . . . . . . . . . . . . . . . . . . . . . . . . . | Pu/B | 13,380 | 452 | TOEFL | | | | 65 |
| City University of New York: City College . . . . . . . | Pu/B | 12,606 | 741 | TOEFL | 61 | | | 65 |
| City University of New York: College of Staten Island . . . . . . . . . . . . . . . . . . . . . . . | Pu/AB | 12,139 | 320 | TOEFL | 45 | | None | 65 |
| City University of New York: Hostos Community College . . . . . . . . . . . . . . . . . . . | Pu/A | 6,983 | | | | | | 65 |
| City University of New York: Hunter College . . . . . . | Pu/B | 15,632 | 910 | TOEFL | | | | 65 |
| City University of New York: John Jay College of Criminal Justice . . . . . . . . . . . . . . . . | Pu/B | 12,175 | | TOEFL, SAT/ACT | 61 | | None | 65 |
| City University of New York: Kingsborough Community College . . . . . . . . . . . . . . . . . . . | Pu/A | 17,033 | | TOEFL | | | | 65 |
| City University of New York: LaGuardia Community College . . . . . . . . . . . . . . . . . . . | Pu/A | 16,141 | 666 | TOEFL | 45 | | | 70 |
| City University of New York: Lehman College . . . . | Pu/B | 10,992 | 312 | TOEFL | | | | 65 |
| City University of New York: Medgar Evers College . . . . . . . . . . . . . . . . . . . . . . . . . | Pu/AB | 6,405 | | TOEFL | | | | 65 |
| City University of New York: New York City College of Technology . . . . . . . . . . . . . . . . . . | Pu/AB | 16,040 | 799 | TOEFL | 61 | | 2/1 | 65 |
| City University of New York: Queens College . . . . . | Pu/B | 15,426 | 822 | TOEFL, SAT/ACT | 62 | 74 | | 65 |
| City University of New York: Queensborough Community College . . . . . . . . . . . . . . . . . . . | Pu/A | 13,596 | 694 | TOEFL | | 53 | | 65 |
| City University of New York: York College . . . . . . | Pu/B | 7,140 | 324 | TOEFL | | | | 65 |
| Clarkson University . . . . . . . . . . . . . . . . . . . . . . | Pr/B | 3,176 | 75 | TOEFL, SAT/ACT | 80 | 91 | 1/17 | 50 |
| Clinton Community College . . . . . . . . . . . . . . . . . | Pu/A | 1,023 | 15 | TOEFL | 62 | | | |
| Colgate University . . . . . . . . . . . . . . . . . . . . . . . | Pr/B | 2,868 | 260 | TOEFL, SAT/ACT | | | | 60 |
| College of Mount St. Vincent . . . . . . . . . . . . . . . . | Pr/AB | 1,683 | 32 | TOEFL, SAT/ACT | | | | 35 |
| College of New Rochelle . . . . . . . . . . . . . . . . . . | Pr/B | 672 | 8 | TOEFL | 100 | | | 35 |
| College of Saint Rose . . . . . . . . . . . . . . . . . . . . | Pr/B | 2,581 | 52 | TOEFL | 80 | 82 | 5/1 | |
| Columbia University . . . . . . . . . . . . . . . . . . . . . | Pr/B | 6,158 | 897 | TOEFL, SAT/ACT | 100 | | 1/1 | 85 |
| Columbia University: School of General Studies . . . . . . . . . . . . . . . . . . . . . . . . . . . . | Pr/B | 2,068 | 424 | TOEFL | 100 | | | 80 |
| Columbia-Greene Community College . . . . . . . . . . | Pu/A | 1,183 | | TOEFL | | | None | |
| Concordia College . . . . . . . . . . . . . . . . . . . . . . . | Pr/AB | 944 | | TOEFL | | | | 100 |
| Cooper Union for the Advancement of Science and Art . . . . . . . . . . . . . . . . . . . . . . . . . . . | Pr/B | 857 | 156 | TOEFL, SAT/ACT | 100 | 110 | 1/9 | 75 |
| Cornell University . . . . . . . . . . . . . . . . . . . . . . . | Pr/B | 14,471 | 1,461 | TOEFL, SAT/ACT | 100 | | 1/2 | 80 |
| Corning Community College . . . . . . . . . . . . . . . . | Pu/A | 2,327 | 2 | TOEFL | | | | |
| Culinary Institute of America . . . . . . . . . . . . . . . . | Pr/AB | 2,774 | | TOEFL | 80 | 88 | None | 50 |
| Daemen College . . . . . . . . . . . . . . . . . . . . . . . . | Pr/B | 1,884 | 24 | TOEFL | 63 | | None | 25 |
| Davis College . . . . . . . . . . . . . . . . . . . . . . . . . | Pr/AB | 390 | | TOEFL, SAT/ACT | 68 | | | 45 |

| Adviser | Orientation | ESL | Academic year | Summer | Tuition/fees | Living costs | Maximum credits/summer | Credit hour charge | Available | Number receiving aid | Average award | Deadline |
|---|---|---|---|---|---|---|---|---|---|---|---|---|
| Yes | Yes | Yes | No | | 9,441† | 11,078 | | 368 | | | | |
| Yes | | | No | | 17,190† | | 18 | 573 | | | | |
| | | | | | 17,190† | | | 573 | | | | |
| | | | No | | 17,190† | | 21 | 573 | | | | |
| | | | No | | 17,190† | | | 573 | | | | |
| | | | | | 17,190† | 4,865 | | 573 | | | | |
| | | | | | 17,190† | 4,820 | | 573 | | | | |
| | | | | | 17,190† | 8,880 | 18 | 573 | Yes | | | 9/17 |
| Yes | Yes | | Yes | Yes | 35,424† | 13,022 | 9 | 970 | Yes | 102 | $26,885 | None |
| Yes | | | No | | 9,568† | | 15 | 374 | | | | |
| | | | Yes | | 32,674† | 13,198 | 7 | | Yes | | | None |
| | | | | | 6,700† | 2,500 | | | | | | |
| Yes | Yes | | Yes | | 17,331† | 16,936 | 12 | 560 | Yes | | | None |
| Yes | Yes | Yes | No | | 9,969† | | 6 | 320 | | | | |
| Yes | | Yes | No | | 10,005† | 10,386 | | 320 | | | | |
| Yes | Yes | Yes | No | | 17,308† | | 6 | 560 | | | | |
| Yes | Yes | Yes | Yes | | 17,210† | 22,068 | 6 | 560 | Yes | | | None |
| Yes | | Yes | Yes | Yes | 17,359† | 17,227 | 8 | 560 | Yes | | | None |
| Yes | Yes | Yes | No | | 10,006† | | 6 | 320 | | | | |
| Yes | | Yes | Yes | | 17,250† | 16,568 | 7 | 560 | Yes | | | None |
| Yes | Yes | Yes | No | | 17,280† | 16,350 | 6 | 560 | Yes | | | None |
| Yes | | Yes | No | | 10,053† | | 8 | 320 | | | | |
| Yes | Yes | Yes | No | | 10,017† | 15,188 | 6 | 320 | Yes | | | 4/15 |
| Yes | Yes | Yes | No | | 17,279† | 13,498 | 8 | 560 | Yes | | | None |
| Yes | | Yes | No | | 17,213† | 10,386 | 9 | 560 | | | | |
| Yes | Yes | Yes | No | | 17,190† | 10,386 | 6 | 560 | | | | |
| Yes | | | Yes | Yes | 17,408† | 14,953 | | 560 | | | | |
| Yes | Yes | Yes | No | | 10,009† | 1,918 | | 320 | | | | |
| Yes | Yes | Yes | No | | 17,217† | 10,386 | 12 | 560 | Yes | | | 5/30 |
| Yes | Yes | Yes | Yes | | 47,950 | 14,488 | 12 | 1556 | Yes | 65 | $17,300 | 3/1 |
| Yes | Yes | | Yes | Yes | 10,347† | 9,310 | 12 | 383 | | | | |
| Yes | Yes | | Yes | Yes | 53,980 | 13,520 | | | Yes | 150 | $43,829 | 1/15 |
| | Yes | | Yes | | 36,540‡ | 9,500 | 9 | 1020 | Yes | | | None |
| Yes | | Yes | Yes | Yes | 36,618 | 14,136 | 6 | 1170 | Yes | | | None |
| Yes | Yes | | Yes | Yes | 30,692† | 12,356 | 12 | 986 | Yes | 44 | $21,867 | 4/1 |
| Yes | Yes | | Yes | Yes | 55,161† | 13,244 | | | Yes | | | |
| Yes | Yes | Yes | Yes | | 53,445† | 13,586 | 15 | 1692 | Yes | | | 6/1 |
| | | | No | | 9,136† | | | 366 | | | | |
| Yes | Yes | Yes | Yes | Yes | 30,550† | 13,575 | | | Yes | | | None |
| Yes | Yes | | Yes | | 47,110 | 18,280 | 6 | 1272 | Yes | 141 | $24,740 | 5/1 |
| Yes | Yes | Yes | Yes | Yes | 50,953† | 13,900 | | | Yes | 196 | $58,139 | 2/15 |
| | | | Yes | | 9,182† | 9,224 | 12 | 360 | | | | |
| Yes | | | Yes | | 31,616 | 10,870 | | 955 | Yes | 174 | $6,284 | None |
| Yes | Yes | | Yes | Yes | 26,940† | 12,925 | 9 | 880 | Yes | | | None |
| | | | Yes | Yes | 16,500† | 7,700 | | 500 | Yes | | | None |

| Institution | Control/ degrees | Undergraduates | | Tests required (Fall 2017) | TOEFL | | Application | |
|---|---|---|---|---|---|---|---|---|
| | | Total | Internat'l | | minimum | average | Deadline | Fee |
| DeVry College of New York: Midtown Campus | Pr/AB | 936 | | TOEFL | | | | 50 |
| Dominican College of Blauvelt | Pr/AB | 1,461 | 20 | TOEFL, SAT/ACT | 80 | | None | 35 |
| Dutchess Community College | Pu/A | 6,503 | | TOEFL | 61 | | 6/15 | |
| D'Youville College | Pr/B | 1,652 | 31 | TOEFL | 61 | 63 | | |
| Eastman School of Music of the University of Rochester | Pr/B | 566 | | TOEFL | 83 | 87 | 12/1 | 125 |
| Elmira College | Pr/AB | 1,067 | 50 | TOEFL | 79 | | 6/1 | |
| Erie Community College | Pu/A | 9,479 | 282 | TOEFL | 48 | 50 | 6/30 | 25 |
| Eugene Lang College The New School for Liberal Arts | Pr/B | 1,658 | 127 | TOEFL | 100 | | 1/15 | 50 |
| Excelsior College | Pr/AB | 35,161 | 252 | TOEFL | 69 | | None | 50 |
| Fashion Institute of Technology | Pu/AB | 8,168 | 1,039 | TOEFL | 80 | | 1/1 | 50 |
| Five Towns College | Pr/AB | 631 | | TOEFL | | 80 | | 35 |
| Fordham University | Pr/B | 9,096 | 692 | TOEFL, SAT/ACT | 90 | 100 | 1/1 | 70 |
| Fulton-Montgomery Community College | Pu/A | 2,634 | | TOEFL | | | | |
| Genesee Community College | Pu/A | 3,374 | | TOEFL | | | | |
| Globe Institute of Technology | Pr/AB | 450 | | | | | | 250 |
| Hamilton College | Pr/B | 1,867 | 122 | TOEFL | | 110 | 1/1 | 50 |
| Hartwick College | Pr/B | 1,396 | 40 | TOEFL | 79 | | | |
| Herkimer County Community College | Pu/A | 1,987 | | | | | | |
| Hilbert College | Pr/AB | 791 | 4 | TOEFL | | | 6/1 | 25 |
| Hobart and William Smith Colleges | Pr/B | 2,241 | 143 | TOEFL | 100 | | 2/1 | 45 |
| Hofstra University | Pr/B | 6,810 | 342 | TOEFL | 80 | | 8/1 | 75 |
| Houghton College | Pr/AB | 1,037 | 125 | TOEFL | 80 | | 3/1 | 40 |
| Hudson Valley Community College | Pu/A | 13,750 | | TOEFL | | | | 30 |
| Iona College | Pr/B | 3,120 | 84 | TOEFL, SAT/ACT | 80 | | 12/1 | 50 |
| Island Drafting and Technical Institute | Pr/A | 106 | | TOEFL | | | | 25 |
| Ithaca College | Pr/B | 6,181 | 116 | TOEFL | 80 | | 2/1 | 60 |
| Jamestown Community College | Pu/A | 2,657 | 17 | TOEFL | 61 | | | |
| Jewish Theological Seminary of America | Pr/B | 157 | | TOEFL, SAT/ACT | | | | 65 |
| Juilliard School | Pr/B | 499 | | TOEFL | | | | 100 |
| Kehilath Yakov Rabbinical Seminary | Pr/B | 155 | | | | | | |
| Keuka College | Pr/B | 1,722 | 42 | TOEFL | 53 | | None | |
| The King's College | Pr/B | 520 | 17 | TOEFL, SAT/ACT | 83 | | None | 30 |
| Le Moyne College | Pr/B | 2,793 | 27 | TOEFL | 79 | | 2/1 | 35 |
| LIM College | Pr/AB | 1,499 | 90 | TOEFL | 80 | 91 | 7/30 | 40 |
| LIU Brooklyn | Pr/AB | 4,177 | 137 | TOEFL | 75 | | 6/1 | 50 |
| LIU Post | Pr/AB | 3,133 | 237 | TOEFL | 75 | | 7/15 | 50 |
| Long Island Business Institute | Pr/A | 1,102 | 79 | | | | None | |
| Machzikei Hadath Rabbinical College | Pr/B | 148 | | | | | | 150 |
| Manhattan College | Pr/B | 3,637 | 110 | TOEFL, SAT/ACT | 80 | | | 60 |
| Manhattan School of Music | Pr/B | 410 | | TOEFL | 79 | | | 100 |
| Manhattanville College | Pr/B | 1,735 | 147 | TOEFL | 80 | 95 | None | 50 |
| Maria College | Pr/AB | 770 | | TOEFL, SAT/ACT | 61 | | None | 35 |
| Marist College | Pr/B | 5,308 | 122 | TOEFL | 80 | 95 | 2/15 | 50 |
| Marymount Manhattan College | Pr/AB | 2,027 | 94 | TOEFL | 80 | | None | 60 |
| Medaille College | Pr/AB | 1,635 | | TOEFL, SAT/ACT | | | | 25 |
| Medaille College: Rochester | Pr/AB | 145 | | | | | | 25 |
| Mercy College | Pr/AB | 6,286 | 95 | TOEFL | 71 | | None | 40 |
| Mesivta Torah Vodaath Seminary | Pr/B | 210 | | | | | | 200 |
| Metropolitan College of New York | Pr/AB | 693 | 18 | TOEFL | 75 | | 8/1 | 30 |
| Mildred Elley: Albany | Pr/A | 748 | | | | | | 50 |
| Mildred Elley: New York City | Pr/A | 590 | | | | | | 50 |
| Mirrer Yeshiva Central Institute | Pr/B | 161 | | | | | | |
| Mohawk Valley Community College | Pu/A | 4,298 | 59 | | 61 | | | |
| Molloy College | Pr/AB | 3,562 | 15 | TOEFL | 79 | | None | 40 |
| Monroe College | Pr/AB | 5,888 | | TOEFL | | | | 35 |
| Monroe Community College | Pu/A | 12,425 | 132 | TOEFL | | | | 20 |

| Student services | | | Housing | | Academic year costs | | Maximum credits/ summer | Credit hour charge | International financial aid | | | |
|---|---|---|---|---|---|---|---|---|---|---|---|---|
| Adviser | Orien-tation | ESL | Academic year | Summer | Tuition/ fees | Living costs | | | Avail-able | Number receiving aid | Average award | Deadline |
| Yes | | | Yes | | 17,512† | | | 609 | | | | |
| Yes | | | Yes | | 28,448 | 12,670 | | 834 | Yes | | | None |
| Yes | | | Yes | Yes | 7,596† | 10,478 | 12 | 294 | Yes | | | None |
| Yes | Yes | | Yes | Yes | 25,210† | 11,570 | | 770 | Yes | | | None |
| | | | | | | | | | | | | |
| Yes | Yes | Yes | Yes | Yes | 51,106† | 16,343 | 6 | 1550 | Yes | 102 | $24,319 | 2/28 |
| | Yes | | Yes | | 41,900 | 15,500 | 9 | 1200 | Yes | 49 | $24,509 | None |
| Yes | Yes | Yes | No | | 10,141† | | | 396 | | | | |
| Yes | Yes | Yes | Yes | Yes | 44,540† | 18,420 | | 1480 | Yes | | | 2/1 |
| Yes | | | No | | | | | 510 | | | | |
| | | | | | | | | | | | | |
| Yes | Yes | Yes | Yes | Yes | 14,515† | 13,386 | 18 | 574 | Yes | 18 | $1,066 | None |
| Yes | | | Yes | | 19,700† | 16,270 | 12 | | Yes | | | None |
| Yes | Yes | Yes | Yes | Yes | 49,073† | 16,845 | 8 | 1595 | Yes | 59 | $31,704 | 2/10 |
| Yes | Yes | Yes | Yes | | 8,920† | 11,350 | 12 | 350 | Yes | | | None |
| Yes | Yes | Yes | Yes | Yes | 5,060† | 8,585 | 12 | | | | | |
| | | | | | | | | | | | | |
| Yes | Yes | Yes | Yes | Yes | | | 19 | | Yes | | | None |
| Yes | Yes | Yes | Yes | Yes | 51,240† | 13,010 | | | Yes | 63 | $55,246 | 2/15 |
| Yes | Yes | | Yes | | 44,534 | 12,093 | | 1390 | Yes | | | None |
| Yes | Yes | Yes | Yes | | 7,780† | 9,620 | 15 | 278 | | | | |
| | | | Yes | | 21,800 | 9,000 | 12 | 545 | Yes | 3 | $7,750 | None |
| | | | | | | | | | | | | |
| Yes | Yes | Yes | Yes | Yes | 51,523† | 13,050 | | | Yes | 104 | $21,867 | 2/1 |
| Yes | Yes | Yes | Yes | Yes | 42,160† | 13,800 | 15 | 1380 | Yes | 167 | $23,827 | None |
| Yes | Yes | | Yes | | 31,540 | 9,018 | | 1267 | Yes | 66 | $16,084 | None |
| Yes | | | No | | 9,562† | 5,850 | 12 | 358 | | | | |
| Yes | | | Yes | Yes | 36,584† | 14,400 | 12 | 1142 | Yes | 73 | $27,048 | None |
| | | | | | | | | | | | | |
| | | | | | 16,200 | 10,395 | | 525 | | | | |
| Yes | Yes | | Yes | Yes | 42,884 | 15,274 | 15 | 1429 | Yes | 100 | $28,806 | None |
| Yes | | | Yes | Yes | 10,130† | 10,750 | 12 | 386 | | | | |
| | | | Yes | Yes | 20,910† | 15,460 | | 1115 | Yes | | | 3/1 |
| Yes | Yes | Yes | Yes | Yes | 41,460† | 15,380 | | | Yes | | | 3/1 |
| | | | | | | | | | | | | |
| Yes | Yes | Yes | Yes | Yes | 9,600† | 2,800 | 15 | 999 | Yes | | | |
| Yes | | | Yes | | 30,946 | 11,452 | | 1460 | Yes | 12 | $19,440 | None |
| | | | Yes | | 35,400 | 16,652 | | | Yes | 22 | $26,401 | None |
| Yes | Yes | | Yes | Yes | 33,030† | 12,970 | 12 | 672 | Yes | 10 | $5,562 | 11/15 |
| Yes | Yes | | Yes | | 26,350‡ | 20,350 | 9 | 830 | Yes | | | |
| | | | | | | | | | | | | |
| Yes | Yes | Yes | Yes | Yes | 36,256† | 13,426 | 12 | 1072 | Yes | 67 | $40,711 | None |
| Yes | Yes | Yes | Yes | Yes | 36,256† | 13,426 | 12 | 1072 | Yes | 74 | $23,421 | 2/15 |
| Yes | | Yes | No | | 14,769‡ | | 18 | | Yes | | | 5/1 |
| | | | Yes | | | | | | | | | |
| Yes | Yes | | Yes | Yes | 40,365† | 15,010 | 12 | | | | | |
| | | | | | | | | | | | | |
| Yes | Yes | Yes | Yes | Yes | 44,700† | 15,073 | | 1800 | Yes | | | 3/1 |
| Yes | Yes | Yes | Yes | Yes | 37,910‡ | 14,520 | | 825 | Yes | 140 | $28,144 | None |
| | | | No | | 14,210† | | 18 | 595 | | | | |
| Yes | Yes | | Yes | Yes | 35,210† | 14,650 | 9 | 650 | Yes | 75 | $20,013 | 5/1 |
| Yes | Yes | | Yes | | 30,290† | 15,990 | 6 | 965 | Yes | 30 | $5,408 | None |
| | | | | | | | | | | | | |
| | | | Yes | | 27,276† | 13,080 | 6 | 971 | Yes | | | None |
| | | | | | 21,000† | | | | | | | |
| Yes | Yes | Yes | Yes | Yes | 18,392† | 13,700 | 12 | 748 | | | | |
| | | | | | 11,330† | 4,500 | | | | | | |
| Yes | | Yes | No | | 19,180 | 9,600 | 15 | 766 | Yes | 12 | $2,293 | None |
| | | | | | | | | | | | | |
| Yes | | | No | | | | | | | | | |
| Yes | | | No | | | | | | | | | |
| | | | | | 6,983† | | | | | | | |
| Yes | Yes | Yes | Yes | Yes | 8,906† | 10,100 | 22 | 330 | | | | |
| Yes | | Yes | Yes | | 29,100† | 14,250 | | 925 | Yes | 5 | $17,734 | 5/1 |
| | | | | | | | | | | | | |
| Yes | Yes | Yes | Yes | Yes | 14,460† | 9,770 | 15 | 565 | Yes | | | 6/30 |
| Yes | | | Yes | | 8,691† | 6,453 | 12 | 342 | | | | |

† Actual for 2016-17.    ‡ Estimated for 2017-18.    * Includes room and board

| Institution | Control/ degrees | Undergraduates | | Tests required (Fall 2017) | TOEFL | | Application | |
|---|---|---|---|---|---|---|---|---|
| | | Total | Internat'l | | minimum | average | Deadline | Fee |
| Mount Saint Mary College . . . . . . . . . . . . . . . . | Pr/B | 2,106 | 10 | TOEFL, SAT/ACT | 79 | | | 45 |
| Nassau Community College. . . . . . . . . . . . . . . . | Pu/A | 18,204 | 180 | | | | 8/1 | 40 |
| Nazareth College. . . . . . . . . . . . . . . . . . . . . . . | Pr/B | 2,125 | 34 | TOEFL | 79 | | 2/1 | 45 |
| The New School College of Performing Arts. . . . . | Pr/B | 564 | 163 | TOEFL | 79 | 93 | | 50 |
| New York Career Institute. . . . . . . . . . . . . . . . . | Pr/A | 439 | | | | | | 60 |
| New York Institute of Technology . . . . . . . . . . . | Pr/AB | 3,577 | 528 | TOEFL | 79 | 82 | 7/1 | 50 |
| New York School of Interior Design . . . . . . . . . . | Pr/AB | 381 | | TOEFL | 79 | | | 100 |
| New York University. . . . . . . . . . . . . . . . . . . . . | Pr/AB | 25,716 | 4,576 | TOEFL, SAT, SAT Subject Test(s), or ACT | 100 | | 1/1 | 70 |
| Niagara County Community College . . . . . . . . . . | Pu/A | 4,372 | | TOEFL | | | 8/1 | |
| Niagara University. . . . . . . . . . . . . . . . . . . . . . | Pr/AB | 3,045 | 375 | TOEFL | 79 | | 8/15 | |
| North Country Community College. . . . . . . . . . . | Pu/A | 2,680 | | TOEFL | | | | |
| Nyack College . . . . . . . . . . . . . . . . . . . . . . . . | Pr/AB | 1,439 | 86 | TOEFL | 83 | | | 25 |
| Ohr Somayach Tanenbaum Education Center . . . . . | Pr/B | 26 | | | | | | 75 |
| Onondaga Community College. . . . . . . . . . . . . . . | Pu/A | 7,818 | | TOEFL | 61 | | | |
| Orange County Community College . . . . . . . . . . . | Pu/A | 5,271 | | TOEFL | 73 | | 6/1 | 30 |
| Pace University. . . . . . . . . . . . . . . . . . . . . . . . | Pr/AB | 5,916 | 808 | TOEFL | 80 | | | 50 |
| Pace University: Pleasantville/Briarcliff . . . . . . . | Pr/AB | 2,468 | 36 | TOEFL | 80 | | | 50 |
| Parsons The New School for Design . . . . . . . . . . | Pr/AB | 4,299 | 1,925 | TOEFL, SAT/ACT | 92 | 97 | 1/15 | 50 |
| Paul Smith's College . . . . . . . . . . . . . . . . . . . . | Pr/AB | 850 | | TOEFL | 79 | | | 30 |
| Phillips School of Nursing at Mount Sinai Beth Israel . . . . . . . . . . . . . . . . . . . . . . . . | Pr/AB | 202 | | | | | 3/1 | 50 |
| Pratt Institute . . . . . . . . . . . . . . . . . . . . . . . . | Pr/AB | 3,271 | 879 | TOEFL | | | | 90 |
| Rabbinical Academy Mesivta Rabbi Chaim Berlin . . . . . . . . . . . . . . . . . . . . . . . . . . . . | Pr/B | 177 | | | | | | |
| Rabbinical College Beth Shraga . . . . . . . . . . . . . | Pr/B | 47 | | | | | | |
| Rabbinical College Bobover Yeshiva B'nei Zion . . . . . . . . . . . . . . . . . . . . . . . . . . . . . | Pr/B | 232 | | | | | | |
| Rabbinical College Ch'san Sofer of New York . . . . | Pr/B | 32 | | | | | | |
| Rabbinical College of Long Island . . . . . . . . . . . | Pr/B | 126 | | | | | | |
| Rabbinical College of Ohr Shimon Yisroel . . . . . . | Pr/B | 152 | | | | | | |
| Rabbinical Seminary of America. . . . . . . . . . . . . | Pr/B | 276 | | | | | | |
| Rensselaer Polytechnic Institute . . . . . . . . . . . . | Pr/B | 6,200 | 705 | TOEFL, SAT/ACT | 88 | 102 | 1/15 | 70 |
| Roberts Wesleyan College. . . . . . . . . . . . . . . . . | Pr/B | 1,266 | 45 | TOEFL | 75 | | | |
| Rochester Institute of Technology. . . . . . . . . . . . | Pr/AB | 12,704 | 784 | TOEFL | 79 | | | 60 |
| Rockland Community College . . . . . . . . . . . . . . | Pu/A | 7,344 | | | | | | 30 |
| The Sage Colleges. . . . . . . . . . . . . . . . . . . . . . | Pr/AB | 1,431 | 3 | TOEFL | 79 | | 7/1 | 30 |
| Saint Bonaventure University. . . . . . . . . . . . . . . | Pr/B | 1,609 | 46 | TOEFL | 79 | | | |
| St. Elizabeth College of Nursing. . . . . . . . . . . . . | Pr/A | 196 | 4 | TOEFL | | | 3/31 | 65 |
| St. Francis College. . . . . . . . . . . . . . . . . . . . . . | Pr/AB | 2,539 | 144 | TOEFL | 75 | | None | 35 |
| St. John Fisher College. . . . . . . . . . . . . . . . . . . | Pr/B | 2,757 | 4 | TOEFL, SAT/ACT | 79 | 88 | 2/15 | |
| St. John's University . . . . . . . . . . . . . . . . . . . . | Pr/AB | 11,768 | 660 | TOEFL | 80 | | None | |
| St. Joseph's College New York: Suffolk Campus. . . . . . . . . . . . . . . . . . . . . . . . . . | Pr/B | 3,031 | | | 79 | 83 | 3/15 | 25 |
| St. Joseph's College, New York . . . . . . . . . . . . . | Pr/B | 953 | | | 79 | 83 | 3/15 | 25 |
| St. Lawrence University . . . . . . . . . . . . . . . . . . | Pr/B | 2,344 | 199 | | 82 | | 2/1 | 60 |
| St. Thomas Aquinas College . . . . . . . . . . . . . . . | Pr/AB | 1,152 | 34 | TOEFL | | | | 30 |
| Sarah Lawrence College . . . . . . . . . . . . . . . . . . | Pr/B | 1,377 | 187 | TOEFL | 100 | 104 | 1/15 | 60 |
| Schenectady County Community College . . . . . . . | Pu/A | 4,102 | | TOEFL | | | | |
| School of Visual Arts. . . . . . . . . . . . . . . . . . . . | Pr/B | 3,602 | 1,466 | TOEFL | 79 | 87 | | 80 |
| Shor Yoshuv Rabbinical College. . . . . . . . . . . . . | Pr/B | 98 | | | | | | 360 |
| Siena College . . . . . . . . . . . . . . . . . . . . . . . . . | Pr/B | 3,141 | 59 | TOEFL, SAT/ACT | 65 | 85 | 4/15 | 50 |
| Skidmore College . . . . . . . . . . . . . . . . . . . . . . | Pr/B | 2,661 | 279 | TOEFL | 96 | | 1/15 | 65 |
| Suffolk County Community College . . . . . . . . . . | Pu/A | 27,066 | | TOEFL | 61 | | | 35 |
| Sullivan County Community College. . . . . . . . . . | Pu/A | 1,074 | 9 | TOEFL | 45 | | None | |
| SUNY College at Brockport . . . . . . . . . . . . . . . | Pu/B | 7,062 | 71 | TOEFL | 76 | | None | 50 |
| SUNY College at Buffalo . . . . . . . . . . . . . . . . . | Pu/B | 8,360 | 118 | TOEFL, SAT, SAT Subject Test(s), or ACT | 61 | | | 50 |
| SUNY College at Cortland . . . . . . . . . . . . . . . . | Pu/B | 6,292 | 41 | TOEFL | | | | 40 |

| Adviser | Orientation | ESL | Academic year | Summer | Tuition/fees | Living costs | Maximum credits/summer | Credit hour charge | Available | Number receiving aid | Average award | Deadline |
|---|---|---|---|---|---|---|---|---|---|---|---|---|
| Yes | | | Yes | | 29,920 | 14,528 | 12 | 963 | Yes | | | 3/1 |
| Yes | Yes | Yes | No | | 10,116† | | 15 | 406 | Yes | | | None |
| Yes | Yes | Yes | Yes | Yes | 32,424† | 13,150 | 12 | 740 | | 31 | $14,079 | |
| Yes | Yes | Yes | Yes | | 44,540† | 18,420 | | 1480 | Yes | | | 3/1 |
| | | | No | | 13,700† | | | | | | | |
| Yes | Yes | | Yes | | 35,160† | 13,570 | | | Yes | 238 | $14,679 | None |
| Yes | Yes | | Yes | Yes | 30,945† | 22,100 | 6 | 915 | Yes | | | None |
| Yes | Yes | Yes | Yes | Yes | 49,062† | 17,578 | 16 | 1373 | Yes | 595 | $21,479 | 2/15 |
| Yes | | | Yes | | 10,638† | | 12 | 425 | | | | |
| Yes | Yes | Yes | Yes | Yes | 31,950 | 12,950 | | 1020 | Yes | 125 | $14,627 | None |
| Yes | | | Yes | | 11,362† | 9,750 | 12 | 441 | | | | |
| Yes | | Yes | Yes | | 25,350 | 9,450 | | 1040 | Yes | | | None |
| Yes | | Yes | Yes | Yes | | | 12 | | Yes | | | None |
| Yes | Yes | Yes | Yes | | 9,724† | 9,100 | 12 | 380 | | | | |
| Yes | | | No | | 9,896† | 6,000 | 12 | 386 | Yes | | | 7/1 |
| Yes | Yes | Yes | Yes | Yes | 42,722† | 18,280 | 12 | 1180 | Yes | | | None |
| Yes | Yes | Yes | Yes | Yes | 42,772† | 15,476 | 12 | 1180 | Yes | 29 | $29,861 | None |
| Yes | Yes | Yes | Yes | Yes | 46,036† | 17,170 | 18 | 1530 | Yes | | | 2/1 |
| Yes | | | Yes | | 27,621‡ | 13,870 | | | Yes | | | None |
| Yes | | | No | | 26,577† | 22,500 | 12 | 575 | Yes | | | 6/30 |
| Yes | Yes | Yes | Yes | Yes | 50,038‡ | 12,110 | | 1548 | Yes | | | 3/1 |
| | | | | | 12,450† | 3,000 | | | | | | |
| | | | | | 12,450† | 5,400 | | | | | | |
| | | | | | 7,750† | 4,500 | | | | | | |
| | | | Yes | | 8,500† | | | | | | | |
| | | | | | 13,700† | 4,900 | | | | | | |
| | | | | | 12,800† | | | | | | | |
| | | | Yes | | 9,800† | 6,000 | | | | | | |
| Yes | Yes | Yes | Yes | Yes | 50,797† | 14,630 | 16 | 2060 | | | | |
| Yes | | Yes | Yes | Yes | 29,740† | 10,212 | 12 | | Yes | 41 | $19,141 | None |
| Yes | Yes | Yes | Yes | Yes | 38,568† | 13,050 | 18 | 1408 | Yes | 620 | $6,050 | None |
| Yes | Yes | Yes | No | | 9,248† | | 15 | 370 | | | | |
| Yes | | | Yes | | 29,764 | 12,408 | | 945 | Yes | 1 | $2,500 | None |
| Yes | Yes | | Yes | Yes | 32,331† | 13,463 | 12 | 934 | Yes | | | None |
| Yes | | | | | 16,300 | | 2 | 440 | Yes | | | None |
| Yes | Yes | | | | 25,300† | 14,000 | 12 | 815 | Yes | | | None |
| Yes | | | Yes | | 33,120 | 12,150 | 14 | 885 | Yes | 6 | $10,634 | None |
| | Yes | Yes | Yes | | 39,460† | 17,580 | 18 | 1288 | Yes | 391 | $20,799 | None |
| Yes | | | No | | 25,124† | 6,500 | 6 | 795 | Yes | 11 | $11,321 | None |
| Yes | | | Yes | | 25,114† | 6,500 | 6 | 795 | Yes | 22 | $15,660 | None |
| Yes | Yes | | Yes | | 51,200† | 13,540 | 12 | | Yes | 195 | $36,225 | 2/1 |
| Yes | Yes | Yes | Yes | Yes | 29,275† | 12,390 | 12 | 930 | Yes | 42 | $20,276 | 6/30 |
| Yes | Yes | | Yes | | 52,550† | 14,440 | | | Yes | 210 | $23,345 | 2/1 |
| Yes | | | Yes | | 8,088† | 8,069 | 6 | 310 | | | | |
| Yes | Yes | Yes | Yes | Yes | 36,500† | 18,300 | 18 | 1270 | Yes | 267 | $9,231 | 3/1 |
| | | | | | 9,000† | 6,000 | | | | | | |
| Yes | Yes | Yes | Yes | Yes | 36,335 | 15,900 | | 675 | Yes | | | 2/15 |
| Yes | Yes | | Yes | Yes | 50,834† | 13,530 | | 1657 | Yes | 82 | $60,975 | 2/1 |
| Yes | Yes | Yes | No | | 10,270† | 5,980 | 12 | 398 | Yes | | | 6/1 |
| Yes | | | Yes | | 10,224† | 10,648 | 10 | 312 | Yes | | | None |
| Yes | Yes | Yes | Yes | | 17,778† | 13,720 | 18 | 680 | Yes | 17 | $4,070 | None |
| Yes | Yes | Yes | Yes | Yes | 17,550† | 14,442 | 16 | | | | | |
| Yes | Yes | | Yes | | 17,956† | 12,200 | 12 | 680 | Yes | | | None |

† Actual for 2016-17.    ‡ Estimated for 2017-18.    * Includes room and board

| Institution | Control/ degrees | Undergraduates | | Tests required (Fall 2017) | TOEFL | | Application | |
|---|---|---|---|---|---|---|---|---|
| | | Total | Internat'l | | minimum | average | Deadline | Fee |
| SUNY College at Fredonia . . . . . . . . . . . . . . . . | .Pu/B | 4,359 | 78 | TOEFL | 61 | | | 50 |
| SUNY College at Geneseo . . . . . . . . . . . . . . . | .Pu/B | 5,405 | 116 | TOEFL | 71 | 91 | | 50 |
| SUNY College at New Paltz . . . . . . . . . . . . . . . | .Pu/B | 6,582 | 150 | TOEFL | 80 | 97 | 4/1 | 50 |
| SUNY College at Old Westbury . . . . . . . . . . . . | .Pu/B | 4,084 | 1 | TOEFL | 65 | | None | 50 |
| SUNY College at Oneonta . . . . . . . . . . . . . . . . | .Pu/B | 5,709 | 54 | TOEFL | 79 | 83 | | 50 |
| SUNY College at Oswego . . . . . . . . . . . . . . . . | .Pu/B | 7,113 | 138 | TOEFL | 72 | | 5/17 | 50 |
| SUNY College at Plattsburgh . . . . . . . . . . . . . . | .Pu/B | 5,170 | 305 | TOEFL | 76 | 93 | | 50 |
| SUNY College at Potsdam . . . . . . . . . . . . . . . | .Pu/B | 3,406 | 23 | TOEFL | 79 | 89 | | 50 |
| SUNY College at Purchase . . . . . . . . . . . . . . . | .Pu/B | 3,944 | 94 | TOEFL, SAT/ACT | 80 | | | 50 |
| SUNY College of Agriculture and Technology at Cobleskill . . . . . . . . . . . . . . . . . . . . . . . . | .Pu/AB | 2,288 | 22 | TOEFL | 61 | 64 | | 50 |
| SUNY College of Agriculture and Technology at Morrisville . . . . . . . . . . . . . . . . . . . . . . | .Pu/AB | 2,765 | 33 | TOEFL | 61 | | 7/1 | 50 |
| SUNY College of Environmental Science and Forestry . . . . . . . . . . . . . . . . . . . . . . . . . . | .Pu/AB | 1,751 | 38 | TOEFL | 79 | | None | 50 |
| SUNY College of Technology at Alfred . . . . . . . . | .Pu/AB | 3,712 | 45 | TOEFL | 61 | 76 | None | 50 |
| SUNY College of Technology at Canton . . . . . . . . | .Pu/AB | 3,094 | 50 | TOEFL | 61 | | 7/1 | 50 |
| SUNY College of Technology at Delhi . . . . . . . . . | .Pu/AB | 3,391 | 13 | TOEFL | 49 | | 7/15 | 50 |
| SUNY Empire State College . . . . . . . . . . . . . . | .Pu/AB | 9,061 | 91 | TOEFL | | | | 50 |
| SUNY Farmingdale State College . . . . . . . . . . . | .Pu/AB | 8,591 | 138 | TOEFL | 79 | | 6/1 | 50 |
| SUNY Maritime College . . . . . . . . . . . . . . . . . | .Pu/AB | 1,626 | 29 | TOEFL | 79 | 87 | 1/31 | 50 |
| SUNY Polytechnic Institute . . . . . . . . . . . . . . . | .Pu/B | 1,896 | 23 | TOEFL | 79 | 84 | 7/1 | 50 |
| SUNY University at Albany . . . . . . . . . . . . . . | .Pu/B | 12,955 | 723 | TOEFL | 79 | | 3/1 | 50 |
| SUNY University at Binghamton . . . . . . . . . . . . | .Pu/B | 13,578 | 1,257 | TOEFL | | | 2/15 | 50 |
| SUNY University at Buffalo . . . . . . . . . . . . . . . | .Pu/B | 20,102 | 3,249 | TOEFL | 79 | 86 | None | 50 |
| SUNY University at Stony Brook . . . . . . . . . . . . | .Pu/B | 16,863 | 2,354 | TOEFL | 80 | 90 | 3/1 | 50 |
| SUNY Upstate Medical University . . . . . . . . . . . | .Pu/B | 219 | | TOEFL | | | | 50 |
| Swedish Institute . . . . . . . . . . . . . . . . . . . . . | .Pr/A | 725 | | TOEFL | | | | 45 |
| Syracuse University . . . . . . . . . . . . . . . . . . . . | .Pr/AB | 14,777 | 1,829 | TOEFL | 85 | 93 | 1/1 | 75 |
| Talmudical Institute of Upstate New York . . . . . . . | .Pr/B | 9 | | | | | | |
| Talmudical Seminary Oholei Torah . . . . . . . . . . . | .Pr/B | 360 | | | | | | |
| Technical Career Institutes . . . . . . . . . . . . . . . . | .Pr/A | 1,400 | 18 | | | | | |
| Tompkins Cortland Community College . . . . . . . . . | .Pu/A | 2,493 | 49 | TOEFL | 55 | | 6/1 | 15 |
| Torah Temimah Talmudical Seminary . . . . . . . . . . | .Pr/B | 178 | | | | | | |
| Touro College . . . . . . . . . . . . . . . . . . . . . . . . | .Pr/AB | 5,818 | 160 | TOEFL | | | | 30 |
| Trocaire College . . . . . . . . . . . . . . . . . . . . . . | .Pr/AB | 1,369 | | TOEFL | | | | 25 |
| U.T.A. Mesivta-Kiryas Joel . . . . . . . . . . . . . . . | .Pr/B | 1,684 | | | | | | |
| Ulster County Community College . . . . . . . . . . . | .Pu/A | 3,419 | | TOEFL | 70 | | | 25 |
| Union College . . . . . . . . . . . . . . . . . . . . . . . . | .Pr/B | 2,119 | 161 | TOEFL, SAT/ACT | 90 | | | |
| United States Merchant Marine Academy . . . . . . . . | .Pu/B | 902 | 6 | TOEFL, SAT/ACT | 83 | 104 | | |
| United Talmudical Seminary . . . . . . . . . . . . . . . | .Pr/B | 1,845 | | | | | | |
| University of Rochester . . . . . . . . . . . . . . . . . . | .Pr/B | 6,223 | 1,293 | TOEFL | 100 | 108 | 1/5 | 50 |
| Utica College . . . . . . . . . . . . . . . . . . . . . . . . | .Pr/B | 3,433 | 46 | TOEFL | 70 | | | 40 |
| Utica School of Commerce . . . . . . . . . . . . . . . . | .Pr/A | 324 | | | | | | 20 |
| Vassar College . . . . . . . . . . . . . . . . . . . . . . . | .Pr/B | 2,401 | 182 | TOEFL, SAT/ACT | 100 | 112 | 1/1 | 70 |
| Vaughn College of Aeronautics and Technology . . . . . . . . . . . . . . . . . . . . . . . . . | .Pr/AB | 1,532 | 87 | TOEFL | 80 | 112 | | 40 |
| Villa Maria College of Buffalo . . . . . . . . . . . . . . | .Pr/AB | 584 | | TOEFL | 61 | | None | |
| Wagner College . . . . . . . . . . . . . . . . . . . . . . . | .Pr/B | 1,785 | 65 | TOEFL | 79 | | | 75 |
| Wells College . . . . . . . . . . . . . . . . . . . . . . . . | .Pr/B | 506 | 17 | | 75 | | 3/1 | |
| Westchester Community College . . . . . . . . . . . . . | .Pu/A | 11,625 | | TOEFL | | | None | 35 |
| Wood Tobe-Coburn School . . . . . . . . . . . . . . . . | .Pr/A | 476 | | | | | | 50 |
| Yeshiva and Kolel Bais Medrash Elyon . . . . . . . . . | .Pr/B | 26 | | | | | | |
| Yeshiva and Kollel Harbotzas Torah . . . . . . . . . . . | .Pr/B | 29 | | | | | | |
| Yeshiva Derech Chaim . . . . . . . . . . . . . . . . . . . | .Pr/B | 103 | | | | | | |
| Yeshiva D'Monsey Rabbinical College . . . . . . . . . | .Pr/B | 49 | | | | | | |
| Yeshiva Gedolah Imrei Yosef D'Spinka . . . . . . . . . | .Pr/B | 130 | | | | | | |
| Yeshiva Gedolah Zichron Moshe . . . . . . . . . . . . | .Pr/B | 164 | | | | | | |
| Yeshiva Karlin Stolin . . . . . . . . . . . . . . . . . . . . | .Pr/B | 115 | | | | | | |

| Student services | | | Housing | | Academic year costs | | Maximum credits/ summer | Credit hour charge | International financial aid | | | |
|---|---|---|---|---|---|---|---|---|---|---|---|---|
| Adviser | Orientation | ESL | Academic year | Summer | Tuition/ fees | Living costs | | | Available | Number receiving aid | Average award | Deadline |
| Yes | Yes | | Yes | Yes | 17,939† | 12,730 | 12 | 680 | Yes | 4 | $3,500 | None |
| Yes | Yes | Yes | Yes | Yes | 18,026† | 12,264 | 12 | 680 | Yes | 104 | $4,012 | 2/15 |
| Yes | Yes | Yes | Yes | Yes | 17,610† | 12,000 | | 680 | | | | |
| Yes | Yes | | Yes | Yes | 17,533† | 11,590 | 16 | 680 | | | | |
| Yes | Yes | Yes | Yes | Yes | 17,812† | 13,486 | 12 | 680 | | | | |
| Yes | Yes | Yes | Yes | Yes | 17,807† | 15,590 | 12 | 680 | Yes | 3 | $500 | None |
| Yes | Yes | Yes | Yes | Yes | 17,756† | 12,150 | 12 | 680 | Yes | 308 | $6,642 | None |
| Yes | Yes | | Yes | Yes | 17,834† | 12,420 | 18 | 680 | Yes | 12 | $3,971 | None |
| Yes | Yes | Yes | Yes | Yes | 18,117† | 12,952 | 8 | 680 | Yes | | | 5/1 |
| | | | | | | | | | | | | None |
| Yes | Yes | Yes | Yes | Yes | 17,781† | 13,180 | 6 | 680 | Yes | | | None |
| Yes | Yes | | Yes | Yes | 12,553† | 15,338 | 12 | 458 | Yes | 12 | $1,495 | None |
| Yes | Yes | Yes | Yes | Yes | 17,953† | 15,750 | | 680 | Yes | 6 | $4,458 | None |
| Yes | Yes | | Yes | Yes | 17,925† | 12,965 | | 406 | Yes | | | None |
| Yes | Yes | | Yes | Yes | 17,731† | 12,650 | 12 | 680 | Yes | 4 | $2,201 | None |
| Yes | Yes | | Yes | | 17,945† | 11,680 | | 452 | | | | |
| Yes | | | No | | 16,835† | | | 680 | | | | |
| Yes | Yes | | Yes | Yes | 17,710† | 16,264 | 12 | 680 | Yes | | | None |
| Yes | Yes | | Yes | | 17,684† | 11,948 | | 680 | Yes | | | 7/15 |
| Yes | Yes | | Yes | Yes | 17,627† | 12,068 | 8 | 680 | Yes | 13 | $4,653 | None |
| Yes | Yes | Yes | Yes | Yes | 24,204† | 13,142 | | 898 | | | | |
| Yes | Yes | Yes | Yes | Yes | 24,351† | 18,602 | 16 | 898 | Yes | 46 | $10,479 | None |
| Yes | Yes | Yes | Yes | Yes | 26,814† | 13,548 | 19 | 988 | Yes | 63 | $11,537 | None |
| Yes | Yes | Yes | Yes | Yes | 26,240† | 12,882 | 16 | 988 | Yes | 49 | $7,713 | None |
| Yes | | | Yes | Yes | 17,194† | | | 680 | | | | |
| | | | No | | | | | | | | | |
| Yes | Yes | Yes | Yes | Yes | 45,022† | 15,217 | 14 | 1891 | Yes | | | 2/1 |
| | | | Yes | | 5,300† | 4,000 | | | | | | |
| | | | Yes | | | | | | | | | |
| Yes | | Yes | No | | 13,800† | | | 548 | Yes | | | |
| Yes | Yes | Yes | Yes | Yes | 10,922† | 10,540 | 21 | 354 | | | | None |
| Yes | | | Yes | | 10,750† | 3,500 | | | | | | |
| | | | | | 16,980† | 11,970 | 6 | 680 | Yes | 148 | $4,670 | 8/15 |
| | | | No | | 16,770† | | 12 | 680 | | | | |
| | | | | | 10,500† | 3,000 | | | | | | |
| | | | No | | 9,440† | 6,000 | 24 | 330 | Yes | | | None |
| Yes | Yes | | Yes | Yes | 51,696† | 12,678 | 1 | | Yes | 81 | $47,301 | 1/15 |
| Yes | | | Yes | | | | | | | | | |
| | | | | | 13,535† | 3,000 | | | | | | |
| Yes | Yes | Yes | Yes | Yes | 51,898‡ | 15,338 | 16 | 1593 | Yes | 626 | $25,744 | 2/15 |
| Yes | Yes | | Yes | Yes | 19,996† | 10,434 | 12 | | Yes | 55 | $7,963 | None |
| | | | No | | 13,500† | 6,500 | 15 | 540 | | | | |
| Yes | Yes | | Yes | | 55,210 | 12,900 | | | Yes | 73 | $55,561 | 2/1 |
| Yes | Yes | | Yes | Yes | 24,837‡ | 14,185 | 15 | 798 | Yes | 20 | $4,503 | None |
| | | | No | | 20,770† | | 12 | 670 | | | | |
| Yes | Yes | | Yes | Yes | 43,980† | 13,260 | 4 | | Yes | | | None |
| Yes | Yes | Yes | Yes | Yes | 39,600‡ | 14,730 | | 1600 | Yes | 2 | $14,500 | None |
| Yes | Yes | Yes | No | | 12,213† | | | 493 | | | | |
| | | | No | | | | | | Yes | | | None |
| | | | | | 11,200† | 2,800 | | | | | | |
| | | | Yes | | 11,800† | | | | | | | |
| | | | | | 5,900† | 2,150 | | | | | | |
| | | | | | 8,000† | | | | | | | |
| | | | | | 11,500† | 4,000 | | | | | | |

† Actual for 2016-17.  ‡ Estimated for 2017-18.  * Includes room and board

| Institution | Control/ degrees | Undergraduates | | Tests required (Fall 2017) | TOEFL | | Application | |
|---|---|---|---|---|---|---|---|---|
| | | Total | Internat'l | | minimum | average | Deadline | Fee |
| Yeshiva of Nitra . . . . . . . . . . . . . . . . . . . . . . | .Pr/B | 217 | | | | | | 50 |
| Yeshiva of the Telshe Alumni . . . . . . . . . . . . | .Pr/B | 115 | | | | | | 100 |
| Yeshiva Shaar Hatorah . . . . . . . . . . . . . . . . . | .Pr/B | 77 | | | | | | 250 |
| Yeshiva Shaarei Torah of Rockland . . . . . . . . . | .Pr/B | 92 | | | | | | 100 |
| Yeshivas Novominsk . . . . . . . . . . . . . . . . . . . | .Pr/B | 130 | | | | | | |
| | | | | | | | | |
| Yeshivat Mikdash Melech . . . . . . . . . . . . . . . | .Pr/B | 17 | | | | | | 400 |
| Yeshivath Viznitz . . . . . . . . . . . . . . . . . . . . . | .Pr/B | 519 | | | | | | |
| | | | | | | | | |
| **North Carolina** | | | | | | | | |
| Alamance Community College . . . . . . . . . . . . | .Pu/A | 4,011 | | TOEFL | 79 | | | |
| Apex School of Theology . . . . . . . . . . . . . . . | .Pr/AB | 745 | | | | | | 25 |
| Appalachian State University . . . . . . . . . . . . . | .Pu/B | 16,442 | 77 | TOEFL | 75 | | | 55 |
| | | | | | | | | |
| Asheville-Buncombe Technical Community | | | | | | | | |
|   College . . . . . . . . . . . . . . . . . . . . . . . . . . . . | .Pr/A | 7,272 | | TOEFL | 60 | | | |
| Barton College . . . . . . . . . . . . . . . . . . . . . . . | .Pr/B | 979 | 39 | TOEFL | | | | 50 |
| Beaufort County Community College . . . . . . . . . | .Pu/A | 1,442 | | TOEFL | 80 | | | |
| Belmont Abbey College . . . . . . . . . . . . . . . . | .Pr/B | 1,523 | | TOEFL | 79 | | | |
| Bennett College for Women . . . . . . . . . . . . . . | .Pr/B | 400 | | TOEFL, SAT/ACT | | | | 35 |
| | | | | | | | | |
| Bladen Community College . . . . . . . . . . . . . . . | .Pu/A | 1,229 | | | | | None | |
| Brevard College . . . . . . . . . . . . . . . . . . . . . . | .Pr/B | 697 | 25 | TOEFL | | | | |
| Cabarrus College of Health Sciences . . . . . . . . | .Pr/AB | 431 | | | | | | 50 |
| Caldwell Community College and Technical | | | | | | | | |
|   Institute . . . . . . . . . . . . . . . . . . . . . . . . . . . | .Pu/A | 3,719 | | TOEFL | | | | |
| Campbell University . . . . . . . . . . . . . . . . . . . . | .Pr/AB | 4,490 | 80 | TOEFL | 61 | 86 | | 35 |
| | | | | | | | | |
| Carteret Community College . . . . . . . . . . . . . . | .Pu/A | 1,437 | | TOEFL | 64 | | | |
| Catawba College . . . . . . . . . . . . . . . . . . . . . . | .Pr/B | 1,276 | 27 | TOEFL | 69 | | None | |
| Central Piedmont Community College . . . . . . . . | .Pu/A | 17,974 | 1,053 | TOEFL | 66 | | None | 40 |
| Charlotte Christian College and Theological | | | | | | | | |
|   Seminary . . . . . . . . . . . . . . . . . . . . . . . . . . | .Pr/AB | 128 | | | | | | 40 |
| Chowan University . . . . . . . . . . . . . . . . . . . . | .Pr/AB | 1,523 | 44 | TOEFL, SAT/ACT | | | 8/1 | 20 |
| | | | | | | | | |
| College of the Albemarle . . . . . . . . . . . . . . . | .Pu/A | 1,604 | | TOEFL | | | | |
| Craven Community College . . . . . . . . . . . . . . . | .Pu/A | 2,665 | 48 | | | | None | |
| Davidson College . . . . . . . . . . . . . . . . . . . . . | .Pr/B | 1,791 | 121 | TOEFL, SAT/ACT | 100 | 102 | 1/2 | 50 |
| Duke University . . . . . . . . . . . . . . . . . . . . . . | .Pr/B | 6,467 | 661 | TOEFL, SAT, SAT Subject Test(s), or ACT | 100 | | | 75 |
| Durham Technical Community College . . . . . . . . | .Pu/A | 5,120 | | | | | | |
| | | | | | | | | |
| East Carolina University . . . . . . . . . . . . . . . . | .Pu/B | 22,386 | 123 | | 80 | | | 70 |
| Elizabeth City State University . . . . . . . . . . . . | .Pu/B | 2,336 | | TOEFL, SAT/ACT | 80 | | | 30 |
| Elon University . . . . . . . . . . . . . . . . . . . . . . | .Pr/B | 6,008 | 129 | TOEFL, SAT/ACT | 79 | | 6/1 | 50 |
| Fayetteville State University . . . . . . . . . . . . . . | .Pu/B | 5,518 | 14 | TOEFL, SAT/ACT | | | 7/1 | 40 |
| Fayetteville Technical Community College . . . . . . | .Pu/A | 9,623 | | | | | None | |
| | | | | | | | | |
| Gardner-Webb University . . . . . . . . . . . . . . . | .Pr/AB | 2,352 | | TOEFL, SAT/ACT | 61 | 78 | | 100 |
| Greensboro College . . . . . . . . . . . . . . . . . . . | .Pr/B | 789 | | TOEFL | 76 | | 7/15 | 35 |
| Guilford College . . . . . . . . . . . . . . . . . . . . . | .Pr/B | 1,682 | 26 | TOEFL | 65 | | 2/1 | 25 |
| Guilford Technical Community College . . . . . . . . | .Pu/A | 10,852 | 194 | TOEFL | | | | |
| Halifax Community College . . . . . . . . . . . . . . . | .Pu/A | 853 | | | 79 | | None | |
| | | | | | | | | |
| High Point University . . . . . . . . . . . . . . . . . . | .Pr/B | 4,510 | 112 | TOEFL | 79 | | | 50 |
| Johnson & Wales University: Charlotte . . . . . . . | .Pr/AB | 2,101 | 21 | TOEFL | 80 | 90 | | |
| Johnson C. Smith University . . . . . . . . . . . . . | .Pr/B | 1,324 | 31 | TOEFL, SAT/ACT | 79 | | | 25 |
| Johnston Community College . . . . . . . . . . . . . | .Pu/A | 2,718 | | TOEFL | | | | |
| Laurel University . . . . . . . . . . . . . . . . . . . . . | .Pr/AB | 125 | | TOEFL | | | | 20 |
| | | | | | | | | |
| Lees-McRae College . . . . . . . . . . . . . . . . . . | .Pr/B | 991 | 23 | TOEFL | | | None | 35 |
| Lenoir-Rhyne University . . . . . . . . . . . . . . . . . | .Pr/B | 1,590 | 37 | TOEFL | 79 | | | 35 |
| Livingstone College . . . . . . . . . . . . . . . . . . . | .Pr/B | 1,204 | | TOEFL | | | | 25 |
| Louisburg College . . . . . . . . . . . . . . . . . . . . | .Pr/A | 685 | 6 | TOEFL | 60 | | None | 25 |
| Mars Hill University . . . . . . . . . . . . . . . . . . . | .Pr/B | 1,332 | | TOEFL | 61 | | | 25 |
| | | | | | | | | |
| Martin Community College . . . . . . . . . . . . . . . | .Pu/A | 341 | | | | | | |
| McDowell Technical Community College . . . . . . . | .Pu/A | 1,323 | | TOEFL | | | | |
| Meredith College . . . . . . . . . . . . . . . . . . . . . | .Pr/B | 1,650 | 87 | TOEFL | 79 | 87 | 2/15 | 40 |

| Student services | | | Housing | | Academic year costs | | Maximum credits/ summer | Credit hour charge | International financial aid | | | |
|---|---|---|---|---|---|---|---|---|---|---|---|---|
| Adviser | Orientation | ESL | Academic year | Summer | Tuition/ fees | Living costs | | | Available | Number receiving aid | Average award | Deadline |
| | | | Yes | | 8,400 † | 4,300 | | | | | | |
| | | | | | 9,300 † | 4,000 | | | | | | |
| | | | | | 14,230 † | | | | | | | |
| | | | | | 11,750 † | 3,250 | | | | | | |
| | | | Yes | Yes | | | | | Yes | | | None |
| Yes | | | No | | 8,070 † | | 12 | 268 | Yes | | | None |
| | | | | | 6,200 † | 15,998 | | 200 | | | | |
| Yes | Yes | | Yes | Yes | 21,652 † | 8,100 | | | | | | |
| | | Yes | No | | 8,114 † | | 18 | 268 | | | | |
| | | | Yes | | 29,998 | 9,856 | 12 | 1163 | Yes | 15 | $24,279 | 8/19 |
| | | Yes | No | | 8,104 † | | | 268 | | | | |
| | Yes | | Yes | | 18,500 † | 12,890 | 6 | 617 | Yes | | | None |
| Yes | | | Yes | Yes | 18,513 † | 10,614 | | 633 | Yes | | | 4/15 |
| | | | No | | 8,081 † | 5,250 | | 268 | | | | |
| | | | Yes | | 27,790 † | 11,200 | | 535 | Yes | 31 | $19,862 | None |
| | | | No | | 12,950 † | 9,600 | | 384 | | | | |
| Yes | | | No | | 8,116 † | | 18 | 268 | | | | |
| Yes | Yes | | Yes | Yes | 30,050 † | 10,600 | 18 | 575 | | | | |
| Yes | | | No | | 8,132 † | | | 268 | Yes | | | None |
| | | | Yes | | 29,920 | 10,488 | 12 | 785 | Yes | 34 | $27,907 | None |
| Yes | | Yes | No | | 8,206 † | 7,840 | 15 | 268 | Yes | | | 6/1 |
| | | | | | 9,680 † | 9,657 | | 440 | | | | |
| Yes | | | Yes | Yes | 24,480 ‡ | 9,950 | 9 | 400 | Yes | 5 | $23,360 | None |
| Yes | Yes | Yes | No | | 8,167 † | 8,325 | 12 | 268 | Yes | | | 6/1 |
| | | | No | | 8,328 † | 11,187 | | 268 | Yes | | | 6/1 |
| Yes | Yes | | Yes | Yes | 49,949 | 13,954 | | | Yes | 65 | $46,706 | 2/15 |
| Yes | Yes | Yes | Yes | Yes | 51,265 † | 14,438 | 16 | 1489 | Yes | | | None |
| Yes | | Yes | No | | 8,132 † | | | 268 | Yes | | | |
| Yes | Yes | Yes | Yes | Yes | 22,874 † | 10,971 | 14 | | Yes | 51 | $26,175 | None |
| Yes | | | Yes | | 17,859 † | 7,682 | 9 | | Yes | | | 6/1 |
| Yes | Yes | | Yes | | 33,104 † | 11,495 | 8 | 1041 | Yes | 29 | $3,103 | None |
| Yes | | | Yes | | 16,668 † | 7,250 | 18 | | Yes | | | None |
| | | Yes | No | | 8,136 † | 5,436 | 12 | 268 | Yes | | | None |
| Yes | Yes | | Yes | Yes | 30,310 | 12,080 | 12 | 482 | Yes | | | 6/30 |
| Yes | Yes | | Yes | Yes | 28,000 † | 10,400 | 16 | | Yes | | | None |
| Yes | Yes | Yes | Yes | Yes | 34,215 | 10,800 | 16 | 1032 | Yes | | | None |
| Yes | Yes | Yes | No | | 8,040 † | 7,461 | 12 | 268 | Yes | | | 7/25 |
| | | | No | | 8,172 † | 5,400 | | 268 | Yes | | | None |
| Yes | Yes | Yes | Yes | Yes | 33,405 † | 16,072 | 12 | 927 | | | | |
| | | | Yes | | 30,396 † | 13,464 | | | Yes | | | None |
| Yes | Yes | | Yes | Yes | 18,236 ‡ | 7,100 | 9 | 418 | Yes | 30 | $22,308 | None |
| | | | No | | 8,137 † | 9,284 | 9 | 268 | | | | |
| | | | Yes | Yes | 13,330 † | 3,000 | 12 | 420 | Yes | | | None |
| Yes | Yes | | Yes | | 24,878 ‡ | 12,428 | 12 | 710 | Yes | 23 | $20,811 | None |
| Yes | Yes | | Yes | Yes | 33,730 † | 11,060 | 16 | 1395 | Yes | | | None |
| Yes | | | Yes | | 17,763 † | 6,596 | | | Yes | | | 6/30 |
| Yes | | | Yes | | 18,007 † | 10,709 | | | Yes | | | None |
| Yes | | Yes | Yes | | 31,804 ‡ | 10,400 | 18 | 1003 | Yes | | | None |
| | | | No | | 8,078 † | 6,300 | | 268 | | | | |
| Yes | | | No | | 8,093 † | | 18 | 268 | Yes | | | None |
| Yes | Yes | | Yes | | 34,907 † | 10,390 | 12 | 864 | Yes | | | None |

† Actual for 2016-17.  ‡ Estimated for 2017-18.  * Includes room and board

| Institution | Control/ degrees | Undergraduates | | Tests required (Fall 2017) | TOEFL | | Application | |
|---|---|---|---|---|---|---|---|---|
| | | Total | Internat'l | | minimum | average | Deadline | Fee |
| Methodist University | Pr/AB | 2,225 | | TOEFL | 60 | | | 25 |
| Mid-Atlantic Christian University | Pr/AB | 184 | 1 | TOEFL | 80 | | None | 50 |
| Miller-Motte College: Cary | Pr/A | 316 | | | | | | 40 |
| Miller-Motte College: Fayetteville | Pr/A | 741 | | | | | | 40 |
| Montreat College | Pr/AB | 808 | | TOEFL | 61 | | | 30 |
| Nash Community College | Pu/A | 1,987 | | TOEFL | | 80 | | |
| North Carolina Central University | Pu/B | 5,902 | 131 | TOEFL, SAT/ACT | | | 5/1 | 30 |
| North Carolina State University | Pu/AB | 22,346 | 1,002 | TOEFL | 85 | | 1/15 | 100 |
| North Carolina Wesleyan College | Pr/B | 2,085 | 87 | TOEFL, SAT/ACT | | | 5/1 | |
| Pamlico Community College | Pu/A | 520 | | | | | | |
| Pfeiffer University | Pr/B | 917 | | TOEFL, SAT/ACT | 61 | | | 50 |
| Piedmont Community College | Pu/A | 1,298 | | TOEFL | | | | |
| Piedmont International University | Pr/AB | 298 | 1 | TOEFL, ACT | | | None | 39 |
| Queens University of Charlotte | Pr/B | 1,504 | 111 | | 79 | | 7/1 | |
| Richmond Community College | Pu/A | 2,321 | | TOEFL | | | | |
| Roanoke-Chowan Community College | Pu/A | 903 | | TOEFL | | | | |
| Robeson Community College | Pu/A | 1,976 | | | | | | |
| Rockingham Community College | Pu/A | 1,860 | | TOEFL | | | | |
| St. Andrews University | Pr/B | 683 | 91 | TOEFL | | | | 30 |
| Saint Augustine's University | Pr/B | 944 | 6 | TOEFL, SAT/ACT | | | None | 25 |
| Salem College | Pr/B | 946 | | TOEFL, SAT/ACT | 79 | | | 30 |
| Sandhills Community College | Pu/A | 3,900 | | TOEFL | | | 4/1 | |
| Shaw University | Pr/B | 1,711 | 37 | TOEFL | | | 7/30 | 40 |
| Southeastern Community College | Pu/A | 968 | | TOEFL | | | | |
| Southwestern Community College | Pu/A | 1,703 | 19 | TOEFL | | | None | |
| University of Mount Olive | Pr/AB | 3,251 | | TOEFL | 65 | | | |
| University of North Carolina at Asheville | Pu/B | 3,466 | 22 | TOEFL | 80 | 92 | 2/15 | 75 |
| University of North Carolina at Chapel Hill | Pu/B | 18,207 | 452 | TOEFL, SAT/ACT | 100 | 109 | 1/10 | 80 |
| University of North Carolina at Charlotte | Pu/B | 23,246 | 564 | TOEFL | 70 | 80 | 6/1 | 60 |
| University of North Carolina at Greensboro | Pu/B | 15,783 | 280 | TOEFL | 79 | | 3/1 | 55 |
| University of North Carolina at Pembroke | Pu/B | 5,375 | 38 | TOEFL | 61 | | | 45 |
| University of North Carolina at Wilmington | Pu/B | 13,609 | 118 | TOEFL | 71 | | | 75 |
| University of North Carolina School of the Arts | Pu/B | 897 | 16 | TOEFL | | | 3/1 | 100 |
| University of Phoenix: Charlotte | Pr/B | 684 | | | | | | |
| University of Phoenix: Raleigh | Pr/B | 402 | | | | | | |
| Vance-Granville Community College | Pu/A | 3,200 | | TOEFL | | | | |
| Virginia College in Greensboro | Pr/A | 468 | | | | | | |
| Wake Forest University | Pr/B | 4,949 | 436 | TOEFL | 100 | | | 50 |
| Wake Technical Community College | Pu/A | 20,043 | | | 88 | | 4/15 | 40 |
| Warren Wilson College | Pr/B | 648 | 13 | TOEFL | | | | |
| Western Carolina University | Pu/B | 9,003 | 84 | TOEFL, SAT/ACT | 79 | 84 | 4/1 | 65 |
| Wilkes Community College | Pu/A | 2,999 | | | | | | |
| Wilson Community College | Pu/A | 1,786 | | TOEFL | | | | |
| Wingate University | Pr/B | 2,076 | 79 | TOEFL | 80 | | None | |
| Winston-Salem State University | Pu/B | 4,686 | 69 | TOEFL | | | | 50 |
| **North Dakota** | | | | | | | | |
| Bismarck State College | Pu/AB | 3,060 | 9 | TOEFL | 70 | | 8/20 | 35 |
| Dakota College at Bottineau | Pu/A | 692 | | TOEFL, SAT/ACT | 70 | | | 35 |
| Dickinson State University | Pu/AB | 1,310 | | TOEFL | 71 | | | 35 |
| Lake Region State College | Pu/A | 712 | | TOEFL | 65 | | | 35 |
| Mayville State University | Pu/AB | 1,091 | | TOEFL | 68 | 70 | | 35 |
| Minot State University | Pu/AB | 2,563 | 304 | TOEFL, ACT | 71 | 82 | | 35 |
| North Dakota State College of Science | Pu/A | 2,129 | 44 | | | | | 35 |
| North Dakota State University | Pu/B | 11,682 | 224 | TOEFL | 71 | | 5/1 | 35 |
| Nueta Hidatsa Sahnish College | Pu/AB | 205 | | | | | | 25 |
| Rasmussen College: Bismarck | Pr/AB | 15 | | TOEFL | | | | |
| Rasmussen College: Fargo | Pr/AB | 345 | | TOEFL | | | | |

| Adviser | Orientation | ESL | Academic year | Summer | Tuition/ fees | Living costs | Maximum credits/ summer | Credit hour charge | Available | Number receiving aid | Average award | Deadline |
|---|---|---|---|---|---|---|---|---|---|---|---|---|
| Yes | Yes | Yes | Yes | Yes | 31,980† | 11,966 | 18 | 1020 | Yes | | | None |
| | | | Yes | | 13,200 | 10,600 | | 440 | Yes | | | None |
| Yes | | | Yes | | 24,940† | 11,637 | | | Yes | | | None |
| | | Yes | No | | 9,080† | | | 268 | | | | |
| Yes | | Yes | Yes | | 18,509† | 8,270 | | | Yes | | | 3/1 |
| Yes | Yes | Yes | Yes | Yes | 26,399† | 10,635 | 15 | | Yes | 184 | $13,472 | None |
| Yes | | | Yes | | 30,150 | 10,050 | 14 | | Yes | | | None |
| | | | No | | 8,083† | 4,800 | | 268 | | | | |
| Yes | Yes | | Yes | | 28,995† | 10,700 | 15 | 640 | Yes | | | None |
| | | | No | | 8154.5† | 5,772 | 12 | 268 | | | | |
| Yes | Yes | | Yes | Yes | 9,650† | 6,410 | 18 | 295 | Yes | 279 | $2,660 | 8/1 |
| Yes | | | Yes | Yes | 33,532‡ | 11,844 | 12 | 464 | Yes | 98 | $25,712 | None |
| Yes | | | No | | 8,104† | | 9 | 268 | Yes | | | 7/25 |
| | | | No | | 8,154† | 6,000 | 9 | 268 | Yes | | | None |
| | | | No | | 8,153† | | | 268 | Yes | | | None |
| Yes | | | No | | 8,136† | 7,600 | | 268 | | | | |
| Yes | Yes | | Yes | | 25,874† | 14,896 | 6 | | Yes | | | None |
| Yes | Yes | | Yes | Yes | 17,890‡ | 7,692 | 12 | 547 | Yes | | | None |
| Yes | Yes | | Yes | | 27,406† | 11,500 | 16 | | Yes | | | None |
| Yes | | Yes | No | | 8,206† | | | 268 | Yes | | | |
| Yes | Yes | | Yes | Yes | 16,480‡ | 8,158 | 9 | 492 | Yes | | | 6/30 |
| Yes | | | No | | 8,197† | 9,450 | | 268 | | | | |
| | | Yes | No | | 8,131† | 6,750 | | 268 | Yes | | | 6/30 |
| Yes | Yes | | Yes | | 19,000† | 7,600 | 12 | 425 | Yes | | | None |
| Yes | Yes | | Yes | Yes | 23,237† | 8,746 | | | | | | |
| Yes | Yes | | Yes | Yes | 33,648† | 11,218 | 12 | 1331.79 | | | | |
| Yes | Yes | Yes | Yes | Yes | 19,934† | 10,470 | 6 | | | | | |
| Yes | Yes | | Yes | Yes | 21,903† | 8,580 | 6 | | Yes | 30 | $17,935 | None |
| Yes | Yes | Yes | Yes | Yes | 16,760† | 8,573 | 17 | | Yes | 13 | $9,603 | None |
| Yes | Yes | Yes | Yes | Yes | 20,920† | 10,060 | 12 | | Yes | | | None |
| Yes | | | Yes | | 25,081‡ | 8,977 | | | Yes | | | None |
| | | | No | | 8,169† | 5,828 | | 268 | Yes | | | None |
| Yes | Yes | | Yes | Yes | 49,308† | 13,404 | | 2020 | Yes | 64 | $13,665 | 1/1 |
| Yes | Yes | Yes | No | | 8,370† | 9,531 | 14 | 268 | Yes | | | None |
| Yes | Yes | Yes | Yes | Yes | 33,970† | 10,250 | | 1386 | Yes | | | None |
| Yes | Yes | | Yes | Yes | 17,420† | 9,516 | 12 | | | | | |
| | | | No | | 8,180† | | | 268 | | | | |
| | | Yes | No | | 8,175† | 9,550 | | 268 | Yes | | | None |
| Yes | Yes | | Yes | Yes | 31,120‡ | 11,380 | 12 | 1035 | Yes | 82 | $26,105 | None |
| | | | Yes | | 15,824† | 8,846 | | | Yes | 20 | $2,581 | None |
| | | | Yes | | 10,474† | 7,400 | 15 | 324 | Yes | 4 | $5,917 | None |
| Yes | | | Yes | Yes | 6,015† | 6,780 | | 217 | Yes | | | None |
| Yes | | Yes | Yes | Yes | 8,917† | 6,749 | 7 | 321 | Yes | | | None |
| Yes | Yes | | Yes | Yes | 9,193† | 6,425 | 12 | 346 | Yes | | | None |
| Yes | Yes | | Yes | Yes | 14,693† | 8,473 | 10 | 562 | Yes | | | None |
| Yes | Yes | | Yes | Yes | 6,568† | 6,249 | 18 | | Yes | 116 | $2,788 | None |
| | | | Yes | Yes | 10,748† | 6,720 | 12 | 336 | Yes | 2 | $12,050 | 4/15 |
| Yes | Yes | Yes | Yes | Yes | 19,771† | 7,918 | 15 | 814 | Yes | 225 | $9,064 | |
| | | | No | | 4,910† | 10,800 | 18 | | | | | |
| | | | No | | 13,455† | 7,011 | | 299 | Yes | | | None |
| | | | No | | 13,455† | 7,011 | | 299 | Yes | | | None |

† Actual for 2016-17.  ‡ Estimated for 2017-18.  * Includes room and board

| Institution | Control/ degrees | Undergraduates | | Tests required (Fall 2017) | TOEFL | | Application | |
|---|---|---|---|---|---|---|---|---|
| | | Total | Internat'l | | minimum | average | Deadline | Fee |
| Turtle Mountain Community College . . . . . . . . . . . | Pr/AB | 550 | | | | | | |
| | | | | | | | | |
| United Tribes Technical College . . . . . . . . . . . . . | Pr/AB | 456 | | TOEFL | | | | |
| University of Jamestown . . . . . . . . . . . . . . . . . . | Pr/B | 934 | 93 | TOEFL | 70 | | | |
| University of Mary . . . . . . . . . . . . . . . . . . . . . | Pr/B | 2,036 | | TOEFL | 71 | | | 25 |
| University of North Dakota . . . . . . . . . . . . . . . | Pu/B | 10,598 | 523 | TOEFL | 76 | | | 35 |
| Valley City State University . . . . . . . . . . . . . . . | Pu/B | 958 | 25 | TOEFL | 68 | | 5/1 | 35 |
| | | | | | | | | |
| Williston State College . . . . . . . . . . . . . . . . . . . | Pu/A | 751 | | TOEFL | 65 | | | 35 |
| **Ohio** | | | | | | | | |
| Allegheny Wesleyan College . . . . . . . . . . . . . . . | Pr/AB | 85 | | | | | | |
| Antonelli College: Cincinnati . . . . . . . . . . . . . . | Pr/A | 173 | | TOEFL | | | | 100 |
| Art Academy of Cincinnati . . . . . . . . . . . . . . . . | Pr/AB | 207 | | TOEFL, SAT/ACT | 80 | | | |
| Art Institute of Cincinnati . . . . . . . . . . . . . . . . | Pr/AB | 22 | | | | | | 100 |
| | | | | | | | | |
| Ashland University . . . . . . . . . . . . . . . . . . . . . | Pr/AB | 3,559 | 80 | TOEFL | 67 | | | 50 |
| ATS Institute of Technology . . . . . . . . . . . . . . . | Pr/A | 459 | | | | | | 30 |
| Baldwin Wallace University . . . . . . . . . . . . . . . . | Pr/B | 3,245 | 25 | TOEFL | 79 | 81 | 3/1 | 25 |
| Belmont College . . . . . . . . . . . . . . . . . . . . . . . | Pu/A | 1,259 | | TOEFL | | | | |
| Bluffton University . . . . . . . . . . . . . . . . . . . . . | Pr/B | 787 | 8 | TOEFL | 64 | 85 | None | |
| | | | | | | | | |
| Bowling Green State University . . . . . . . . . . . . . | Pu/B | 13,901 | 274 | TOEFL | 71 | 84 | 7/1 | 75 |
| Bowling Green State University: Firelands College . . . . . . . . . . . . . . . . . . . . . . . . . . . | Pu/AB | 1,315 | 2 | TOEFL | 61 | | | 75 |
| Brown Mackie College: Akron . . . . . . . . . . . . . | Pr/AB | | | | | | | |
| Bryant & Stratton College: Eastlake . . . . . . . . . | Pr/AB | 471 | | TOEFL | | | | 35 |
| Bryant & Stratton College: Parma . . . . . . . . . . . | Pr/AB | 541 | | TOEFL | | | | 35 |
| | | | | | | | | |
| Capital University . . . . . . . . . . . . . . . . . . . . . . | Pr/B | 2,600 | 50 | TOEFL | 61 | 79 | 4/15 | 25 |
| Case Western Reserve University . . . . . . . . . . . . | Pr/B | 5,048 | 625 | TOEFL, SAT/ACT | 90 | | 1/15 | |
| Cedarville University . . . . . . . . . . . . . . . . . . . . | Pr/B | 3,065 | 53 | TOEFL | 80 | 89 | | 30 |
| Central Ohio Technical College . . . . . . . . . . . . . | Pu/A | 3,601 | | TOEFL | | | | |
| Central State University . . . . . . . . . . . . . . . . . . | Pu/B | 1,701 | 9 | TOEFL, SAT/ACT | | | | 20 |
| | | | | | | | | |
| Chamberlain College of Nursing: Cleveland . . . . . . | Pr/AB | 218 | 1 | | | | | 95 |
| Chamberlain College of Nursing: Columbus . . . . . . | Pr/AB | 500 | | | | | | 95 |
| Cincinnati Christian University . . . . . . . . . . . . . . | Pr/AB | 681 | | TOEFL | | | | 40 |
| Cincinnati State Technical and Community College . . . . . . . . . . . . . . . . . . . . . . . . . . . | Pu/A | 7,229 | | TOEFL | 61 | 65 | | |
| Clark State Community College . . . . . . . . . . . . . | Pu/A | 5,099 | | TOEFL | 60 | | | 15 |
| | | | | | | | | |
| Cleveland Institute of Art . . . . . . . . . . . . . . . . | Pr/B | 614 | 58 | TOEFL | 79 | 83 | | 40 |
| Cleveland Institute of Music . . . . . . . . . . . . . . | Pr/B | 233 | 57 | TOEFL | 79 | | 12/1 | 110 |
| Cleveland State University . . . . . . . . . . . . . . . . . | Pu/B | 11,764 | 595 | TOEFL | 65 | | | 30 |
| College of Wooster . . . . . . . . . . . . . . . . . . . . . | Pr/B | 1,980 | 215 | TOEFL, SAT/ACT | 81 | 97 | | |
| Columbus College of Art and Design . . . . . . . . . | Pr/B | 1,036 | 77 | TOEFL | 61 | 80 | None | 50 |
| | | | | | | | | |
| Columbus State Community College . . . . . . . . . . | Pu/A | 11,561 | 107 | | | 79 | None | |
| Cuyahoga Community College . . . . . . . . . . . . . . | Pu/A | 12,772 | 292 | | | | | |
| Davis College . . . . . . . . . . . . . . . . . . . . . . . . . | Pr/A | 193 | | TOEFL | 51 | | | 30 |
| Defiance College . . . . . . . . . . . . . . . . . . . . . . . | Pr/AB | 582 | | TOEFL | 79 | | | 25 |
| Denison University . . . . . . . . . . . . . . . . . . . . . | Pr/B | 2,261 | 193 | TOEFL | | | | 40 |
| | | | | | | | | |
| DeVry University: Columbus . . . . . . . . . . . . . . . | Pr/AB | 1,676 | | TOEFL | | | | 50 |
| Edison State Community College . . . . . . . . . . . . | Pu/A | 1,707 | 2 | TOEFL | 61 | | | |
| Fortis College: Cuyahoga . . . . . . . . . . . . . . . . . | Pr/A | 526 | | | | | | 55 |
| Fortis College: Ravenna . . . . . . . . . . . . . . . . . . | Pr/A | 269 | | | | | | 100 |
| Franciscan University of Steubenville . . . . . . . . . | Pr/AB | 2,038 | 13 | TOEFL | 80 | | 4/30 | 20 |
| | | | | | | | | |
| Franklin University . . . . . . . . . . . . . . . . . . . . . | Pr/AB | 4,122 | | TOEFL | 45 | | | 40 |
| God's Bible School and College . . . . . . . . . . . . . | Pr/AB | 304 | | TOEFL, SAT | | | | 50 |
| Harrison College: Grove City . . . . . . . . . . . . . . | Pr/AB | 273 | | | | | | |
| Heidelberg University . . . . . . . . . . . . . . . . . . . . | Pr/B | 1,116 | 1 | TOEFL | | | | 25 |
| Herzing University . . . . . . . . . . . . . . . . . . . . . . | Pr/AB | 5,707 | | | | | | |
| | | | | | | | | |
| Herzing University: Toledo . . . . . . . . . . . . . . . . | Pr/AB | 208 | | | | | | |
| Hiram College . . . . . . . . . . . . . . . . . . . . . . . . | Pr/B | 974 | 18 | TOEFL, SAT/ACT | 61 | | None | 25 |
| Hocking College . . . . . . . . . . . . . . . . . . . . . . . | Pu/A | 3,474 | | | | | | 50 |
| Hondros College . . . . . . . . . . . . . . . . . . . . . . . | Pr/AB | 1,924 | | | | | | 25 |

| Student services | | | Housing | | Academic year costs | | Maximum credits/ summer | Credit hour charge | International financial aid | | | |
|---|---|---|---|---|---|---|---|---|---|---|---|---|
| Adviser | Orien-tation | ESL | Academic year | Summer | Tuition/ fees | Living costs | | | Avail-able | Number receiving aid | Average award | Deadline |
| | | | | | 2,220† | | | 74 | | | | |
| Yes | | | Yes | Yes | 4,482† | 3,284 | 7 | | | | | |
| | | Yes | Yes | Yes | 21,158 | 7,556 | 12 | 435 | Yes | 37 | $13,831 | None |
| Yes | Yes | | Yes | | 17,130† | 6,822 | 12 | | Yes | | | None |
| Yes | Yes | Yes | Yes | Yes | 19,291† | 7,630 | 12 | 743 | Yes | | | None |
| | Yes | | Yes | Yes | 16,016† | 6,966 | 9 | 470 | Yes | | | None |
| | | | Yes | Yes | 6,282† | 10,066 | | 153 | Yes | | | None |
| Yes | | | Yes | | 6,000† | 3,600 | | 200 | | | | |
| | | | Yes | | 29,252† | 6,500 | 18 | 1177 | | | | |
| | | | No | | 16,834† | 6,750 | | | Yes | | | None |
| Yes | Yes | Yes | Yes | Yes | 20,392† | 9,602 / 5,220 | 12 | | Yes | 21 | $8,602 | None |
| Yes | Yes | Yes | Yes | Yes | 31,668 | 9,142 | 18 | 984 | Yes | 21 | $14,614 | None |
| | | | No | | 7,488† | | 21 | 208 | | | | |
| Yes | Yes | | Yes | | 31,672 | 10,484 | 17 | 1301 | Yes | 5 | $18,876 | |
| Yes | Yes | Yes | Yes | Yes | 18,593† | 8,690 | 18 | 693 | Yes | 140 | $11,552 | None |
| Yes | Yes | | No | | 12,254† | | 12 | 501 | Yes | | | None |
| | | | | | 17,190† | | 21 | 573 | Yes | | | None |
| | | | | | 17,190† | | | 573 | | | | |
| Yes | Yes | Yes | Yes | Yes | 34,600 | 10,178 | 18 | 1144 | Yes | 44 | $17,226 | None |
| Yes | Yes | Yes | Yes | Yes | 47,500 | 14,784 | 9 | 1962 | Yes | | | 5/15 |
| Yes | Yes | | Yes | | 29,156 | 7,088 | 12 | 1096 | Yes | 45 | $15,250 | None |
| Yes | | | Yes | | 7,056† | 6,512 | | | Yes | | | None |
| Yes | | Yes | Yes | Yes | 8,096† | 9,934 | 18 | 625 | Yes | | | None |
| | | | | | 19,500† | | | 675 | | | | |
| | | | | | 19,500† | | | 675 | | | | |
| Yes | Yes | | Yes | Yes | 16,664† | 7,860 | 9 | 650 | Yes | 4 | $10,796 | None |
| Yes | | Yes | No | | 9,177† | 5,700 | 18 | | | | | |
| Yes | | | No | | 7,820† | 5,000 | 20 | 243 | | | | |
| Yes | Yes | | Yes | | 40,685‡ | 13,640 | | | Yes | 33 | $10,389 | 3/15 |
| Yes | Yes | Yes | Yes | | 49,106† | 14,382 | | 1967 | Yes | | | 3/1 |
| Yes | Yes | Yes | Yes | Yes | 14,558† | 12,500 | 18 | 604 | Yes | | | None |
| Yes | Yes | | Yes | Yes | 46,860† | 11,040 | | 1440 | Yes | 212 | $25,315 | None |
| Yes | Yes | | Yes | | 33,960 | 9,856 | | 1415 | Yes | 79 | $10,805 | 2/15 |
| Yes | Yes | | No | | 10,887† | 6,484 | | 361.24 | Yes | | | None |
| Yes | Yes | Yes | | | 7,468† | 5,000 | 16 | | Yes | | | None |
| | | Yes | | | 16,800† | 9,396 | 18 | 350 | | | | |
| Yes | Yes | | Yes | Yes | 32,190‡ | 9,950 | 12 | | Yes | 644 | $12,744 | None |
| Yes | Yes | | Yes | | 50,440‡ | 12,330 | | | Yes | 230 | $28,290 | None |
| Yes | | | | | 17,512† | | | 609 | | | | |
| Yes | | | No | | 7,828† | 7,986 | 6 | 241 | | | | |
| Yes | Yes | | Yes | Yes | 25,680† | 8,300 | 15 | 840 | Yes | 11 | $2,363 | None |
| Yes | Yes | Yes | No | | 14,845† | | 18 | 494 | Yes | | | None |
| Yes | | | Yes | Yes | 7,040† | 4,250 | | 225 | Yes | | | None |
| | | | No | | | | | | | | | |
| Yes | Yes | | Yes | Yes | 29,200† | 11,000 | 16 | | Yes | | | None |
| | | | No | | | | | | | | | |
| Yes | Yes | | Yes | Yes | 33,040† | 10,190 | 12 | | | | | |
| Yes | Yes | Yes | Yes | Yes | 8,780† | 6,310 | 18 | | Yes | | | None |
| | | | No | | 18,489† | | | | | | | |

† Actual for 2016-17.   ‡ Estimated for 2017-18.   * Includes room and board

| Institution | Control/ degrees | Undergraduates | | Tests required (Fall 2017) | TOEFL | | Application | |
|---|---|---|---|---|---|---|---|---|
| | | Total | Internat'l | | minimum | average | Deadline | Fee |
| International College of Broadcasting........... | Pr/A | 64 | | | | | | 100 |
| | | | | | | | | |
| James A. Rhodes State College .............. | Pu/A | 4,368 | | TOEFL | | | | 25 |
| John Carroll University..................... | Pr/B | 2,952 | 62 | TOEFL | 79 | 85 | 5/1 | |
| Kaplan College: Dayton .................... | Pr/A | 317 | | TOEFL | | | | 10 |
| Kent State University....................... | Pu/B | 22,907 | 1,177 | TOEFL | 71 | | 6/18 | 70 |
| Kenyon College........................... | Pr/B | 1,688 | 78 | TOEFL, SAT/ACT | 100 | 110 | | 50 |
| | | | | | | | | |
| Kettering College.......................... | Pr/AB | 584 | | TOEFL | 90 | | | |
| Lake Erie College ......................... | Pr/B | 750 | 26 | TOEFL | 79 | | None | 30 |
| Lakeland Community College ................ | Pu/A | 7,932 | | TOEFL | 61 | | | 15 |
| Lorain County Community College............. | Pu/A | 8,271 | 81 | TOEFL | | | | |
| Lourdes University......................... | Pr/AB | 1,108 | | TOEFL | 61 | | | 25 |
| | | | | | | | | |
| Malone University......................... | Pr/B | 1,228 | 7 | TOEFL | 79 | | 7/1 | 20 |
| Marietta College .......................... | Pr/AB | 1,077 | 180 | TOEFL | 79 | | | 50 |
| Miami University: Hamilton ................. | Pu/AB | 3,386 | | TOEFL | 76 | | | 35 |
| Miami University: Middletown................ | Pu/AB | 2,034 | | | | | | 35 |
| Miami University: Oxford ................... | Pu/AB | 16,597 | 1,960 | TOEFL | 80 | 86 | | 70 |
| | | | | | | | | |
| Miami-Jacobs Career College: Columbus ........ | Pr/A | 366 | | | | | | 100 |
| Miami-Jacobs Career College: Dayton ......... | Pr/A | 159 | | TOEFL | | | | 140 |
| Miami-Jacobs Career College: Sharonville ....... | Pr/A | 69 | | | | | | 40 |
| Mount St. Joseph University ................. | Pr/AB | 1,207 | 5 | TOEFL, SAT/ACT | 79 | | 6/18 | 25 |
| Mount Vernon Nazarene University............. | Pr/AB | 1,720 | 13 | TOEFL, SAT/ACT | 80 | | 5/1 | 25 |
| | | | | | | | | |
| Muskingum University ..................... | Pr/B | 1,498 | 55 | TOEFL | 79 | | 6/1 | |
| National College: Canton ................... | Pr/A | 46 | | | | | | 50 |
| National College: Cincinnati ................ | Pr/A | 96 | | | | | | 50 |
| National College: Columbus ................ | Pr/A | 52 | | | | | | 50 |
| National College: Kettering ................. | Pr/A | 112 | | | | | | 50 |
| | | | | | | | | |
| National College: Stow...................... | Pr/A | 58 | | | | | | 50 |
| National College: Willoughby Hills............. | Pr/A | 42 | | | | | | 50 |
| National College: Youngstown ............... | Pr/A | 80 | | | | | | 50 |
| North Central State College.................. | Pu/A | 1,902 | | TOEFL | 61 | | | |
| Notre Dame College........................ | Pr/AB | 1,989 | | TOEFL | | | | |
| | | | | | | | | |
| Oberlin College........................... | Pr/B | 2,895 | 264 | TOEFL, SAT/ACT | 100 | 108 | 1/15 | |
| Ohio Business College: Hilliard .............. | Pr/A | 178 | | | | | | 25 |
| Ohio Business College: Sheffield .............. | Pr/A | 420 | | | | | | 25 |
| Ohio College of Massotherapy ............... | Pr/A | 150 | | | | | | 25 |
| Ohio Dominican University .................. | Pr/AB | 1,158 | 22 | TOEFL | 79 | | None | 25 |
| | | | | | | | | |
| Ohio Northern University ................... | Pr/B | 2,259 | | TOEFL | 79 | | | |
| Ohio State University: Columbus Campus......... | Pu/AB | 44,762 | 3,566 | TOEFL, SAT/ACT | 79 | 98 | 2/1 | 70 |
| Ohio Technical College...................... | Pr/A | 455 | 2 | | | | | 50 |
| Ohio University........................... | Pu/AB | 23,542 | 524 | | 71 | | 2/1 | 70 |
| Ohio University: Eastern Campus ............. | Pu/AB | 1,010 | | TOEFL | | | | 20 |
| | | | | | | | | |
| Ohio University: Southern Campus at Ironton ...... | Pu/AB | 2,131 | | TOEFL, SAT/ACT | | | None | 20 |
| Ohio University: Zanesville Campus ............ | Pu/AB | 1,839 | 8 | | | | | 20 |
| Ohio Wesleyan University.................... | Pr/B | 1,629 | 91 | TOEFL | 80 | 101 | | |
| Otterbein University........................ | Pr/B | 2,485 | 23 | TOEFL | | | | 30 |
| Owens Community College .................. | Pu/A | 9,338 | | TOEFL | 61 | | | 20 |
| | | | | | | | | |
| PowerSport Institute....................... | Pr/A | 109 | | | | | | 50 |
| Rabbinical College of Telshe ................. | Pr/B | 52 | | | | | | 100 |
| Remington College: Cleveland ............... | Pr/A | 911 | | | | | | 50 |
| School of Advertising Art .................... | Pr/A | 197 | | TOEFL | | | None | |
| Shawnee State University ................... | Pu/AB | 3,365 | 39 | TOEFL | 60 | | | 50 |
| | | | | | | | | |
| Sinclair Community College .................. | Pu/A | 14,642 | 295 | TOEFL | 61 | | None | |
| Stark State College ........................ | Pu/A | 8,460 | | TOEFL | 61 | | 6/1 | 95 |
| Terra State Community College ............... | Pu/A | 2,901 | | TOEFL | 68 | | | |
| Tiffin University........................... | Pr/AB | 2,176 | 290 | TOEFL | 79 | 87 | | 20 |
| Union Institute & University ................. | Pr/B | 772 | | TOEFL | 79 | | None | |
| | | | | | | | | |
| University of Akron........................ | Pu/AB | 15,626 | 363 | TOEFL | 71 | 80 | 5/1 | 70 |
| University of Akron: Wayne College........... | Pu/AB | 2,461 | | | | | | 50 |

| Student services | | | Housing | | Academic year costs | | Maximum credits/ summer | Credit hour charge | International financial aid | | | |
|---|---|---|---|---|---|---|---|---|---|---|---|---|
| Adviser | Orientation | ESL | Academic year | Summer | Tuition/fees | Living costs | | | Available | Number receiving aid | Average award | Deadline |
| | | | | | 31,950† | | | 424.67 | | | | |
| Yes | | | | | 9,611† | 7,200 | 21 | 320 | | | | |
| Yes | Yes | | Yes | Yes | 39,790 | 12,580 | 21 | 1275 | Yes | 57 | $24,479 | 3/15 |
| | | | No | | | | 12 | | | | | |
| Yes | Yes | Yes | Yes | Yes | 18,376† | 10,720 | 12 | 818 | Yes | | | None |
| Yes | Yes | | Yes | Yes | 51,200† | 12,130 | | | Yes | 51 | $50,436 | 2/15 |
| Yes | | | Yes | Yes | 14,760† | 6,644 | 13 | 492 | Yes | | | None |
| | Yes | | Yes | | 33,062‡ | 9,132 | 6 | 780 | Yes | 26 | $25,256 | None |
| Yes | Yes | | No | | 9,176† | 6,911 | 12 | 294.05 | Yes | | | 3/1 |
| Yes | | Yes | No | | 7,302† | 3,712 | 18 | 280.84 | Yes | 3 | $833 | None |
| Yes | | | Yes | | 21,540 | 9,700 | | 695 | | | | |
| Yes | | | Yes | Yes | 29,900 | 9,300 | 18 | 500 | Yes | 6 | $29,393 | 7/31 |
| Yes | Yes | Yes | Yes | Yes | 35,330† | 11,100 | 11 | 1140 | Yes | | | None |
| Yes | | Yes | | | 14,830† | | | | | | | |
| | | | No | | 14,830† | | | | Yes | | | None |
| Yes | Yes | Yes | Yes | | 31,592† | 12,014 | | | Yes | 354 | $12,680 | None |
| | | | No | | | | | | | | | |
| | | | No | | | 6,750 | 14 | | | | | |
| | | | | | | 7,885 | | | | | | |
| Yes | | | Yes | Yes | 29,100 | 9,266 | 9 | 525 | Yes | | | None |
| Yes | | | Yes | Yes | 28,090 | 8,054 | 8 | 773 | Yes | | | None |
| Yes | Yes | Yes | Yes | | 25,062‡ | 11,540 | 12 | 595 | Yes | | | None |
| | | | | | 14,460† | | | 317 | | | | |
| | | | | | 14,460† | | | 317 | | | | |
| | | | | | 14,460† | | | 317 | | | | |
| | | | | | 14,460† | | | 317 | | | | |
| | | | | | 14,460† | | | 317 | | | | |
| | | | | | 14,460† | | | 317 | | | | |
| | | | | | 14,460† | | | 317 | | | | |
| | | Yes | Yes | Yes | 9,685† | 4,758 | 18 | 251.32 | Yes | | | None |
| Yes | | | Yes | | 29,300 | 9,850 | 12 | 560 | Yes | | | 5/1 |
| Yes | Yes | Yes | Yes | | 53,460 | 15,862 | | 2200 | Yes | 160 | $34,214 | 2/1 |
| | | | No | | | | | | | | | |
| Yes | Yes | Yes | Yes | Yes | 31,080† | 10,946 | | 720 | Yes | | | None |
| Yes | Yes | Yes | Yes | Yes | 29,820† | 11,050 | 16 | 1180 | Yes | 42 | $9,792 | None |
| Yes | Yes | Yes | Yes | Yes | 28,229† | 11,666 | | 1293.2 | Yes | | | None |
| | | | No | | | | | | | | | |
| Yes | Yes | Yes | Yes | Yes | 21,208† | 11,176 | 18 | 1022 | Yes | | | 1/15 |
| | | | | | 6,718† | | 20 | 303 | Yes | | | None |
| Yes | | | No | | 6,718† | | | 305 | Yes | | | 3/15 |
| | | | No | | 9,530† | | 20 | 416 | Yes | | | None |
| Yes | Yes | | Yes | Yes | 44,090† | 14,770 | | | Yes | 110 | $23,921 | None |
| Yes | Yes | Yes | Yes | Yes | 31,874 | 10,828 | 15 | | Yes | | | None |
| Yes | Yes | Yes | No | | 8,698† | 4,440 | 18 | 306 | Yes | | | None |
| | | | Yes | | 27,000† | | | | Yes | | | None |
| | | | Yes | | 10,500† | 3,000 | | | | | | |
| | | | No | | | | | | | | | |
| | | | No | | 32,379‡ | | | | Yes | | | None |
| Yes | Yes | Yes | Yes | Yes | 13,030† | 9,966 | 20 | | Yes | | | None |
| Yes | Yes | Yes | No | | 8,560† | 5,742 | 19 | 282 | Yes | | | None |
| Yes | | | | | 8,478† | | | 282 | Yes | | | None |
| | | | No | | 8,568† | | | | | | | |
| Yes | Yes | Yes | Yes | Yes | 23,850‡ | 11,150 | 9 | 790 | Yes | 95 | $14,758 | None |
| Yes | | | No | | 12,384† | | | 510 | Yes | | | None |
| Yes | Yes | Yes | Yes | Yes | 20,496† | 12,395 | | 175 | Yes | 69 | $16,572 | None |
| | | | No | | 14,501† | 10,504 | 9 | 526 | Yes | | | 3/15 |

† Actual for 2016-17.    ‡ Estimated for 2017-18.    * Includes room and board

| Institution | Control/ degrees | Undergraduates | | Tests required (Fall 2017) | TOEFL | | Application | |
|---|---|---|---|---|---|---|---|---|
| | | Total | Internat'l | | minimum | average | Deadline | Fee |
| University of Cincinnati . . . . . . . . . . . . . . . . . . . . | Pu/AB | 24,890 | 1,089 | TOEFL | 66 | | | 50 |
| University of Cincinnati: Blue Ash College. . . . . . . | Pu/AB | 4,818 | 61 | TOEFL | 79 | | | 35 |
| University of Cincinnati: Clermont College. . . . . . . | Pu/AB | 2,339 | 8 | TOEFL | 66 | | 7/11 | 50 |
| University of Dayton . . . . . . . . . . . . . . . . . . . . . . | Pr/B | 8,261 | 783 | TOEFL | 70 | | | |
| University of Findlay . . . . . . . . . . . . . . . . . . . . . | Pr/AB | 2,723 | 235 | TOEFL | 61 | 65 | 6/15 | |
| University of Mount Union . . . . . . . . . . . . . . . . | Pr/B | 2,110 | 8 | TOEFL | 79 | | None | |
| University of Northwestern Ohio . . . . . . . . . . . . | Pr/AB | 4,100 | | TOEFL | | | None | 20 |
| University of Phoenix: Cleveland . . . . . . . . . . . . | Pr/B | 483 | | | | | | |
| University of Rio Grande . . . . . . . . . . . . . . . . . | Pr/AB | 2,001 | | TOEFL | | | | 25 |
| University of Toledo . . . . . . . . . . . . . . . . . . . . | Pu/AB | 15,166 | 1,009 | TOEFL | 61 | | 5/1 | 40 |
| Urbana University . . . . . . . . . . . . . . . . . . . . . . | Pr/AB | 1,434 | | TOEFL | | | | 135 |
| Ursuline College . . . . . . . . . . . . . . . . . . . . . . . | Pr/B | 632 | 11 | TOEFL | 60 | 92 | | 25 |
| Vatterott College: Cleveland . . . . . . . . . . . . . . | Pr/A | 218 | | | | | | |
| Virginia Marti College of Art and Design. . . . . . . | Pr/AB | 160 | | TOEFL | 61 | | None | |
| Walsh University. . . . . . . . . . . . . . . . . . . . . . . . | Pr/AB | 2,124 | 88 | TOEFL | 61 | | None | |
| Washington State Community College . . . . . . . . . | Pu/A | 971 | | | | | | |
| Wilberforce University . . . . . . . . . . . . . . . . . . . | Pr/B | 653 | | TOEFL, SAT/ACT | | | | 25 |
| Wilmington College . . . . . . . . . . . . . . . . . . . . . | Pr/B | 1,112 | | TOEFL | | | | |
| Wittenberg University. . . . . . . . . . . . . . . . . . . . | Pr/B | 1,903 | | TOEFL | 79 | | 4/15 | 40 |
| Wright State University. . . . . . . . . . . . . . . . . . . | Pu/AB | 11,664 | 463 | TOEFL | 61 | 70 | 5/15 | 30 |
| Wright State University: Lake Campus. . . . . . . . . | Pu/AB | 1,073 | 11 | TOEFL | 61 | 69 | 5/15 | 30 |
| Xavier University . . . . . . . . . . . . . . . . . . . . . . | Pr/AB | 4,503 | 94 | TOEFL | 79 | 91 | None | 35 |
| Youngstown State University . . . . . . . . . . . . . . . | Pu/AB | 10,188 | 190 | TOEFL | 61 | | | 45 |
| **Oklahoma** | | | | | | | | |
| Bacone College. . . . . . . . . . . . . . . . . . . . . . . . | Pr/AB | 968 | | TOEFL, SAT/ACT | | | | 25 |
| Brown Mackie College: Oklahoma City . . . . . . . . | Pr/AB | | | | | | | |
| Brown Mackie College: Tulsa . . . . . . . . . . . . . . | Pr/AB | | | | | | | |
| Cameron University . . . . . . . . . . . . . . . . . . . . . | Pu/AB | 4,117 | 183 | TOEFL | 61 | 82 | 6/1 | 20 |
| Carl Albert State College . . . . . . . . . . . . . . . . . | Pu/A | 2,902 | | TOEFL, ACT | 61 | | 4/15 | 50 |
| College of the Muscogee Nation. . . . . . . . . . . . . | Pu/A | 202 | | | | | | |
| East Central University. . . . . . . . . . . . . . . . . . . | Pu/B | 3,361 | 367 | TOEFL, SAT/ACT | 61 | | 7/15 | 20 |
| Eastern Oklahoma State College . . . . . . . . . . . . . | Pu/A | 1,341 | | TOEFL, ACT | 61 | | | 25 |
| Family of Faith College . . . . . . . . . . . . . . . . . . | Pr/B | 17 | | | | | | 25 |
| Hillsdale Free Will Baptist College . . . . . . . . . . . | Pr/AB | 311 | | TOEFL | | | | 25 |
| Langston University. . . . . . . . . . . . . . . . . . . . . | Pu/AB | 2,040 | | TOEFL, ACT | 48 | | 7/1 | 25 |
| Murray State College . . . . . . . . . . . . . . . . . . . . | Pu/A | 2,305 | | TOEFL, ACT | | | | |
| Northeastern Oklahoma Agricultural and Mechanical College . . . . . . . . . . . . . . . . . . . . | Pu/A | 2,216 | | TOEFL | 61 | 70 | | |
| Northeastern State University. . . . . . . . . . . . . . . | Pu/B | 6,579 | 143 | TOEFL | 61 | 86 | 8/1 | 25 |
| Northern Oklahoma College. . . . . . . . . . . . . . . . | Pu/A | 5,023 | | TOEFL, SAT/ACT | | | | |
| Northwestern Oklahoma State University . . . . . . . | Pu/B | 1,858 | | TOEFL | 61 | | | 15 |
| Oklahoma Baptist University . . . . . . . . . . . . . . . | Pr/AB | 1,861 | 64 | TOEFL | 61 | | 4/15 | |
| Oklahoma Christian University. . . . . . . . . . . . . . | Pr/B | 1,887 | 127 | TOEFL | 61 | | | 25 |
| Oklahoma City Community College . . . . . . . . . . | Pu/A | 14,000 | | TOEFL | 61 | | | 25 |
| Oklahoma City University. . . . . . . . . . . . . . . . . | Pr/B | 1,751 | | TOEFL | 80 | | None | 70 |
| Oklahoma Panhandle State University . . . . . . . . . | Pu/AB | 1,391 | | TOEFL, SAT, SAT Subject Test(s), or ACT | | | | |
| Oklahoma State University . . . . . . . . . . . . . . . . | Pu/B | 20,828 | 738 | TOEFL | 61 | 85 | 6/1 | 75 |
| Oklahoma State University Institute of Technology: Okmulgee . . . . . . . . . . . . . . . . . . | Pu/AB | 2,293 | 38 | TOEFL | 61 | | None | |
| Oklahoma State University: Oklahoma City . . . . . . | Pu/AB | 5,963 | | TOEFL | | | | |
| Oklahoma Wesleyan University . . . . . . . . . . . . . | Pr/AB | 1,208 | 54 | TOEFL, SAT/ACT | 69 | 71 | None | 25 |
| Oral Roberts University . . . . . . . . . . . . . . . . . . | Pr/B | 2,979 | 228 | TOEFL, SAT/ACT | 61 | | | 35 |
| Platt College: Moore . . . . . . . . . . . . . . . . . . . . | Pr/A | 172 | | | | | | 25 |
| Platt College: Oklahoma City Central . . . . . . . . . | Pr/A | 200 | | | | | | 25 |
| Platt College: Tulsa . . . . . . . . . . . . . . . . . . . . . | Pr/AB | 360 | | | | | | 100 |
| Redlands Community College . . . . . . . . . . . . . . | Pu/A | 2,500 | | TOEFL | 61 | | | 25 |
| Rogers State University. . . . . . . . . . . . . . . . . . . | Pu/AB | 3,889 | | TOEFL | 84 | 92 | | 20 |

| Student services | | | Housing | | Academic year costs | | Maximum credits/ summer | Credit hour charge | International financial aid | | | |
|---|---|---|---|---|---|---|---|---|---|---|---|---|
| Adviser | Orien-tation | ESL | Academic year | Summer | Tuition/ fees | Living costs | | | Avail-able | Number receiving aid | Average award | Deadline |
| Yes | Yes | Yes | Yes | Yes | 26,334† | 10,964 | 19 | 1028 | Yes | 375 | $9,234 | None |
| Yes | | | No | | 14,808‡ | 9,240 | | 617 | | | | |
| Yes | | | No | | 12,548† | 2,981 | | 523 | Yes | | | None |
| Yes | Yes | Yes | Yes | Yes | 40,940† | 12,680 | 18 | | Yes | 340 | $11,003 | 5/1 |
| Yes | Yes | Yes | Yes | Yes | 32,402† | 9,538 | 12 | 697 | Yes | | | 9/1 |
| Yes | Yes | Yes | Yes | Yes | 29,890 | 11,100 | 12 | 1260 | Yes | | | None |
| Yes | | | Yes | Yes | | | 19 | | Yes | | | None |
| Yes | Yes | | Yes | Yes | 24,910† | 10,120 | 15 | 1014 | Yes | | | None |
| Yes | Yes | Yes | Yes | Yes | 19,313† | 11,724 | 21 | 725 | Yes | 431 | $11,344 | None |
| | | | Yes | | 22,452† | 9,182 | 18 | 748 | Yes | | | 8/15 |
| | | | Yes | Yes | 30,000† | 9,964 | 12 | 988 | Yes | 12 | $27,582 | None |
| | | | | | | 5,320 | | | | | | |
| | | | No | | 19,350† | 6,624 | 18 | 390 | Yes | | | None |
| Yes | Yes | Yes | Yes | Yes | 28,720† | 12,740 | 12 | 905 | Yes | 61 | $22,016 | None |
| | | | | | 8,580† | 5,850 | | 278 | | | | |
| Yes | | | Yes | | 13,250† | 10,050 | | 501 | Yes | | | 6/30 |
| Yes | | | Yes | Yes | 25,000† | 9,600 | 18 | | Yes | | | 6/1 |
| Yes | Yes | | Yes | Yes | 38,730 | 11,126 | 15 | 1264 | Yes | 18 | $29,026 | None |
| Yes | Yes | Yes | Yes | Yes | 17,350† | 9,436 | 18 | 791 | Yes | | | None |
| Yes | Yes | | Yes | | 14,462† | | 18 | 662 | Yes | 11 | $4,167 | None |
| Yes | Yes | | Yes | Yes | 37,230 | 12,150 | 12 | 694 | Yes | 71 | $16,096 | None |
| Yes | Yes | Yes | Yes | Yes | 14,327† | 8,990 | 20 | 520 | Yes | | | None |
| | Yes | | Yes | Yes | 14,850† | 10,100 | 9 | 550 | Yes | | | None |
| Yes | Yes | | Yes | Yes | 15,210† | 5,102 | 9 | | Yes | 45 | $5,209 | None |
| Yes | | | Yes | | 4,636† | 3,800 | 9 | 202 | | | | |
| | | | | | 6,600† | 9,100 | | | | | | |
| Yes | Yes | Yes | Yes | Yes | 15,399† | 5,350 | 9 | 470 | Yes | | | 3/1 |
| | | | Yes | | 7,841† | 5,697 | 9 | 225.21 | | | | |
| | | | Yes | | 6,200† | 8,400 | | 195 | | | | |
| | | | Yes | | 12,640† | 6,680 | | 420 | | | | |
| Yes | Yes | | Yes | Yes | 12,850† | 9,186 | | | Yes | | | 5/1 |
| | | | Yes | | 10,330† | 6,600 | 6 | 323 | | | | |
| Yes | Yes | | Yes | Yes | 9,173† | 6,168 | 9 | 256 | Yes | | | None |
| Yes | Yes | Yes | Yes | Yes | 13,707† | 6,650 | 12 | 420 | Yes | 93 | $10,296 | None |
| Yes | | | Yes | Yes | 8,409† | 5,770 | 15 | 250 | Yes | | | None |
| Yes | | | Yes | Yes | 13,238† | 4,885 | | 419.5 | Yes | | | None |
| Yes | Yes | Yes | Yes | Yes | 26,840‡ | 8,150 | 12 | | Yes | | | None |
| Yes | Yes | Yes | Yes | Yes | 21,670‡ | 7,590 | 12 | 900 | Yes | | | 8/31 |
| Yes | Yes | Yes | No | | 8,425† | 8,258 | 12 | 255 | Yes | | | None |
| Yes | Yes | Yes | Yes | Yes | 30,726 | 8,624 | 12 | 925 | Yes | 49 | $24,762 | None |
| Yes | | Yes | Yes | Yes | | 7,561 | 9 | | Yes | | | None |
| Yes | Yes | Yes | Yes | Yes | 22,443† | 7,790 | | 635.5 | Yes | 246 | $3,928 | None |
| Yes | | | Yes | Yes | 10,710† | 6,554 | 21 | 317 | Yes | | | None |
| Yes | | | No | | 9,922† | 5,534 | 9 | 305 | Yes | | | None |
| Yes | | | Yes | | 26,090 | 8,644 | 12 | 1030 | Yes | | | None |
| Yes | Yes | Yes | Yes | Yes | 25,678† | 10,348 | 16 | 1031 | | | | |
| | | | No | | | | | | | | | |
| | | | No | | | | | | | | | |
| Yes | | | Yes | Yes | 6,026† | 9,468 | 6 | 201 | | | | |
| Yes | | | Yes | Yes | 14,460† | 7,950 | 9 | 396 | | | | |

† Actual for 2016-17.    ‡ Estimated for 2017-18.    * Includes room and board

| Institution | Control/ degrees | Undergraduates | | Tests required (Fall 2017) | TOEFL | | Application | |
|---|---|---|---|---|---|---|---|---|
| | | Total | Internat'l | | minimum | average | Deadline | Fee |
| Rose State College | Pu/A | 6,143 | 8 | TOEFL | 61 | | | |
| St. Gregory's University | Pr/AB | 601 | 21 | TOEFL | | | None | |
| Seminole State College | Pu/A | 1,288 | 17 | TOEFL | 61 | | | 15 |
| Southeastern Oklahoma State University | Pu/B | 3,130 | | TOEFL | | | | 55 |
| Southern Nazarene University | Pr/AB | 1,647 | | TOEFL | 61 | 65 | | 25 |
| Southwestern Christian University | Pr/AB | 716 | | TOEFL | | | | 200 |
| Southwestern Oklahoma State University | Pu/AB | 4,542 | 248 | TOEFL, SAT/ACT | 61 | | | 15 |
| Spartan College of Aeronautics and Technology | Pr/AB | 849 | | TOEFL | 61 | | | 100 |
| Tulsa Community College | Pu/A | 14,224 | 381 | TOEFL | | | | 20 |
| Tulsa Welding School | Pr/A | 1,902 | | TOEFL | | | None | |
| University of Central Oklahoma | Pu/AB | 15,067 | | TOEFL | 61 | | | 40 |
| University of Oklahoma | Pu/B | 21,909 | 926 | TOEFL | 79 | 84 | 2/1 | 90 |
| University of Phoenix: Oklahoma City | Pr/B | 428 | | | | | | |
| University of Phoenix: Tulsa | Pr/B | 500 | | | | | | |
| University of Science and Arts of Oklahoma | Pu/B | 841 | 77 | TOEFL, SAT | 61 | 76 | | 40 |
| University of Tulsa | Pr/B | 3,362 | 805 | TOEFL | 70 | 73 | None | 50 |
| Vatterott College: Oklahoma City | Pr/A | 280 | | | | | | |
| Vatterott College: Tulsa | Pr/A | 164 | | | | | | |
| Virginia College in Tulsa | Pr/A | 121 | | | | | | 100 |
| Western Oklahoma State College | Pu/A | 1,178 | | TOEFL | 61 | | None | 15 |

**Oregon**

| Institution | Control/ degrees | Undergraduates | | Tests required (Fall 2017) | TOEFL | | Application | |
|---|---|---|---|---|---|---|---|---|
| | | Total | Internat'l | | minimum | average | Deadline | Fee |
| Art Institute of Portland | Pr/AB | 1,111 | | TOEFL | | | None | |
| Chemeketa Community College | Pu/A | 9,030 | 22 | TOEFL | | | | |
| Clackamas Community College | Pu/A | 5,902 | | | | | 8/17 | 50 |
| Clatsop Community College | Pu/A | 857 | | TOEFL | 68 | | | 150 |
| Concordia University | Pr/AB | 1,174 | 30 | TOEFL | 71 | | | 50 |
| Corban University | Pr/AB | 1,062 | | TOEFL, SAT, SAT Subject Test(s), or ACT | 70 | | | 40 |
| Eastern Oregon University | Pu/AB | 2,721 | 40 | TOEFL | 70 | | | |
| George Fox University | Pr/B | 2,682 | 74 | TOEFL | 70 | 84 | | 40 |
| Gutenberg College | Pr/B | 21 | | | | | None | 40 |
| Lane Community College | Pu/A | 9,236 | | TOEFL | | | | |
| Le Cordon Bleu College of Culinary Arts: Portland | Pr/A | 452 | | | | | | 50 |
| Lewis & Clark College | Pr/B | 2,033 | 104 | TOEFL | 91 | | 3/1 | |
| Linfield College | Pr/B | 1,603 | 49 | TOEFL | 80 | | None | |
| Linn-Benton Community College | Pu/A | 5,727 | 160 | TOEFL | 61 | 68 | | 100 |
| Marylhurst University | Pr/B | 398 | 16 | TOEFL | 79 | | | 50 |
| Mount Angel Seminary | Pr/B | 75 | | TOEFL | 47 | 55 | | 27 |
| Mt. Hood Community College | Pu/A | 5,835 | | TOEFL | 61 | | | 50 |
| New Hope Christian College | Pr/AB | 121 | | TOEFL | 72 | 90 | 5/25 | 35 |
| Northwest Christian University | Pr/AB | 559 | | TOEFL | 80 | | 6/1 | |
| Oregon College of Art & Craft | Pr/B | 122 | 1 | TOEFL | 80 | | None | 45 |
| Oregon Health & Science University | Pu/B | 777 | 8 | TOEFL | 83 | 90 | | 60 |
| Oregon Institute of Technology | Pu/AB | 4,373 | | TOEFL, SAT/ACT | 68 | | | 50 |
| Oregon State University | Pu/B | 24,350 | 1,646 | TOEFL | 80 | 89 | 6/1 | 60 |
| Pacific Northwest College of Art | Pr/B | 399 | 8 | TOEFL | 79 | | None | 45 |
| Pacific University | Pr/B | 1,848 | | TOEFL | 79 | | | 40 |
| Portland Community College | Pu/A | 30,946 | | | | | | 50 |
| Portland State University | Pu/B | 19,119 | 1,042 | TOEFL | 71 | | 7/15 | 50 |
| Reed College | Pr/B | 1,376 | 108 | TOEFL, SAT/ACT | 100 | 110 | | |
| Rogue Community College | Pu/A | 4,097 | 4 | TOEFL | 58 | | | |
| Southern Oregon University | Pu/B | 4,064 | | TOEFL | 68 | | | 50 |
| Southwestern Oregon Community College | Pu/A | 2,245 | | TOEFL | | | | 40 |
| Tillamook Bay Community College | Pu/A | 544 | | | | | | |
| Treasure Valley Community College | Pu/A | 2,170 | | TOEFL | 173 | | None | |
| Umpqua Community College | Pu/A | 1,142 | | TOEFL | 61 | | None | |

| Student services | | | Housing | | Academic year costs | | Maximum credits/ summer | Credit hour charge | International financial aid | | | |
|---|---|---|---|---|---|---|---|---|---|---|---|---|
| Adviser | Orientation | ESL | Academic year | Summer | Tuition/ fees | Living costs | | | Available | Number receiving aid | Average award | Deadline |
| Yes | | Yes | Yes | Yes | 10,184 † | 6,000 | 9 | 313.2 | | | | |
| Yes | Yes | | Yes | Yes | 21,300 † | 8,044 | 12 | 710 | | | | |
| Yes | | | Yes | Yes | 9,735 † | 7,070 | 12 | 277 | Yes | | | None |
| | | | Yes | | 15,720 † | 6,535 | 12 | 507 | Yes | 59 | $11,957 | None |
| Yes | | Yes | Yes | | 24,468 † | 8,330 | 9 | 790 | Yes | | | None |
| Yes | | | Yes | | 15,930 † | 6,300 | 6 | 465 | Yes | | | None |
| Yes | | | Yes | Yes | 13,140 † | 5,400 | | 438 | Yes | | | 3/1 |
| Yes | | | Yes | | 16,150 † | | | | | | | |
| Yes | Yes | Yes | No | | 9,903 † | 11,328 | 9 | 297 | | | | |
| | | | | | | | | | Yes | | | None |
| Yes | Yes | Yes | Yes | Yes | 16,459 † | 7,740 | 12 | | Yes | 297 | $3,351 | None |
| Yes | Yes | Yes | Yes | Yes | 25,203 † | 10,280 | 9 | 630 | Yes | 37 | $4,358 | None |
| Yes | Yes | | Yes | Yes | 16,020 † | 5,800 | 20 | 495 | Yes | 75 | $12,971 | None |
| Yes | Yes | Yes | Yes | Yes | 41,459 ‡ | 11,476 | 12 | 1453 | Yes | 502 | $10,877 | None |
| | | | No | | | | | | | | | |
| | | | Yes | | 8,584 ‡ | 4,950 | 12 | 268 | Yes | | | 3/1 |
| Yes | Yes | | Yes | | | | 18 | | Yes | | | None |
| Yes | Yes | Yes | No | | 11,610 † | 8,022 | | 242 | | | | |
| Yes | Yes | Yes | No | | 11,927 † | 7,500 | 18 | 257 | Yes | | | None |
| | | | No | | 16,110 † | 7,449 | | 346 | Yes | | | None |
| Yes | Yes | Yes | Yes | Yes | 29,140 † | 9,220 | 12 | 890 | | | | |
| | | | Yes | Yes | 30,640 † | 9,666 | | 1250 | Yes | | | None |
| Yes | Yes | | Yes | Yes | 18,804 † | 9,642 | | 383 | Yes | 14 | $4,410 | None |
| Yes | Yes | Yes | Yes | | 35,016 | 10,886 | 10 | 1044 | Yes | 61 | $11,059 | None |
| | | | Yes | Yes | 13,650 | | | | | | | |
| Yes | Yes | Yes | Yes | | 10,995 † | | 18 | 233 | Yes | | | 2/15 |
| Yes | Yes | Yes | Yes | Yes | 46,894 † | 11,540 | 20 | 2327 | Yes | 94 | $30,788 | None |
| Yes | Yes | Yes | Yes | Yes | 41,612 | 12,380 | | 1285 | Yes | 46 | $24,197 | None |
| Yes | Yes | Yes | No | | 13,049 † | | | 282.02 | | | | |
| Yes | Yes | Yes | No | | 20,835 † | | 15 | 463 | | | | |
| | | Yes | Yes | | 15,912 † | 11,089 | | 506 | | | | |
| Yes | | Yes | No | | 11,386 † | 7,380 | 16 | 236 | Yes | | | 4/1 |
| Yes | | | Yes | Yes | 17,530 † | 6,100 | 12 | 550 | Yes | | | 8/1 |
| Yes | | | Yes | Yes | 28,680 | 8,800 | | 950 | Yes | 10 | $17,440 | None |
| | | | | | 33,160 ‡ | 9,900 | | 1315 | Yes | 1 | $13,000 | None |
| Yes | Yes | | No | | 31,380 † | 13,104 | | 662 | Yes | | | None |
| Yes | Yes | | Yes | Yes | 25,570 † | 8,704 | 18 | | Yes | | | None |
| Yes | Yes | Yes | Yes | Yes | 28,846 † | 12,153 | 19 | 582 | Yes | 117 | $8,256 | None |
| Yes | Yes | | Yes | Yes | 34,550 † | 12,504 | | 1368 | Yes | | | None |
| Yes | Yes | Yes | Yes | | 41,054 † | 11,822 | 9 | 1672 | Yes | 22 | $22,063 | None |
| Yes | Yes | Yes | No | | 10,542 † | 10,158 | 9 | 226 | Yes | | | None |
| Yes | Yes | Yes | Yes | Yes | 24,852 † | 10,653 | 21 | 523 | Yes | | | None |
| Yes | Yes | | Yes | Yes | 52,150 † | 14,050 | | | Yes | 48 | $52,840 | 2/1 |
| Yes | | Yes | No | | 15,540 † | 8,721 | 15 | 331 | | | | |
| Yes | Yes | Yes | Yes | Yes | 23,170 † | 12,540 | 18 | 477 | Yes | | | None |
| Yes | Yes | Yes | Yes | Yes | 13,770 † | 7,769 | 18 | 267 | Yes | | | 3/1 |
| | | | | | 5,670 † | 3,846 | | 115 | | | | |
| Yes | | Yes | Yes | Yes | 10,530 † | 7,646 | 20 | | Yes | | | None |
| Yes | | | No | | 8,013 † | 8,550 | | 221 | | | | |

† Actual for 2016-17.  ‡ Estimated for 2017-18.  * Includes room and board

| Institution | Control/ degrees | Undergraduates Total | Internat'l | Tests required (Fall 2017) | TOEFL minimum | average | Application Deadline | Fee |
|---|---|---|---|---|---|---|---|---|
| University of Oregon | Pu/B | 19,773 | 2,571 | TOEFL | 61 | 77 | | 65 |
| University of Phoenix: Oregon | Pr/B | 496 | | | | | | |
| University of Portland | Pr/B | 3,762 | 103 | TOEFL | 71 | 88 | 6/1 | 50 |
| Warner Pacific College | Pr/AB | 478 | | TOEFL | | | | 50 |
| Western Oregon University | Pu/AB | 4,776 | | TOEFL | 68 | | | 50 |
| Willamette University | Pr/B | 1,867 | 25 | TOEFL | | | 2/1 | 50 |
| **Pennsylvania** | | | | | | | | |
| Albright College | Pr/B | 2,291 | | TOEFL | 68 | 88 | 6/1 | 25 |
| Allegheny College | Pr/B | 1,884 | 60 | TOEFL | 80 | 89 | 2/15 | |
| Alvernia University | Pr/AB | 2,225 | 10 | TOEFL | 75 | 80 | | 100 |
| Antonelli Institute of Art and Photography | Pr/A | 189 | | TOEFL | | | | 50 |
| Arcadia University | Pr/B | 2,367 | 94 | TOEFL | 90 | 96 | | 30 |
| Art Institute of Philadelphia | Pr/AB | 1,953 | | TOEFL | 61 | | | 50 |
| Art Institute of Pittsburgh | Pr/AB | 900 | | TOEFL | | | None | 50 |
| Berks Technical Institute | Pr/A | 1,140 | | | | | | 50 |
| Bidwell Training Center | Pr/A | 150 | | | | | | |
| Bloomsburg University of Pennsylvania | Pu/B | 8,734 | 29 | TOEFL | 65 | | 3/1 | 60 |
| Bradford School: Pittsburgh | Pr/A | 439 | | | | | | 50 |
| Bryn Athyn College | Pr/AB | 293 | 6 | TOEFL, SAT/ACT | 70 | 75 | | |
| Bryn Mawr College | Pr/B | 1,371 | 316 | TOEFL, SAT, SAT Subject Test(s), or ACT | 100 | | 1/15 | 50 |
| Bucknell University | Pr/B | 3,531 | 217 | TOEFL, SAT/ACT | 100 | 106 | 1/15 | 40 |
| Bucks County Community College | Pu/A | 8,076 | 3 | TOEFL | | | 7/1 | |
| Butler County Community College | Pu/A | 3,686 | | TOEFL | | | | 25 |
| Cabrini University | Pr/B | 1,475 | 5 | TOEFL | 75 | | 2/1 | 20 |
| Cairn University | Pr/B | 729 | 14 | TOEFL | 68 | | None | 25 |
| California University of Pennsylvania | Pu/AB | 5,426 | 42 | TOEFL | | | | 35 |
| Career Training Academy: Monroeville | Pr/A | 115 | | | | | | 30 |
| Carlow University | Pr/B | 1,393 | | TOEFL | 90 | 92 | | |
| Carnegie Mellon University | Pr/B | 6,574 | 1,492 | TOEFL, SAT/ACT | 102 | 111 | 1/1 | 75 |
| Cedar Crest College | Pr/B | 1,397 | 145 | TOEFL | 61 | | | 35 |
| Central Penn College | Pr/AB | 1,334 | | TOEFL | 80 | | None | |
| Chatham University | Pr/B | 786 | 23 | TOEFL | 79 | 84 | None | 35 |
| Chestnut Hill College | Pr/AB | 1,364 | 33 | TOEFL | 79 | 80 | 5/31 | 35 |
| Cheyney University of Pennsylvania | Pu/B | 708 | | TOEFL, SAT | | | | 20 |
| Clarion University of Pennsylvania | Pu/AB | 4,251 | 21 | TOEFL | 61 | | | 35 |
| Clarks Summit University | Pr/AB | 616 | | TOEFL, SAT/ACT | 65 | | | 30 |
| Community College of Allegheny County | Pu/A | 14,710 | | | | | None | |
| Community College of Beaver County | Pu/A | 2,255 | | TOEFL | | | | |
| Community College of Philadelphia | Pu/A | 17,060 | 1,996 | | | | None | 20 |
| Consolidated School of Business: Lancaster | Pr/A | 99 | | | | | | |
| Curtis Institute of Music | Pr/B | | | TOEFL, SAT | 79 | | | 150 |
| Delaware County Community College | Pu/A | 11,742 | | | | | | 25 |
| Delaware Valley University | Pr/AB | 1,885 | 7 | TOEFL | 74 | | 5/1 | 50 |
| DeSales University | Pr/B | 2,333 | 13 | TOEFL | 79 | | | 30 |
| DeVry University: Fort Washington | Pr/AB | 436 | | TOEFL | | | | 50 |
| Dickinson College | Pr/B | 2,370 | 243 | TOEFL | 90 | 105 | 2/1 | 65 |
| Douglas Education Center | Pr/A | 267 | | TOEFL | 97 | | | 50 |
| Drexel University | Pr/B | 15,210 | | | 79 | | 7/15 | 50 |
| DuBois Business College | Pr/A | 90 | | TOEFL | | | | 25 |
| DuBois Business College: Huntingdon | Pr/A | 80 | | | | | | 25 |
| DuBois Business College: Oil City | Pr/A | 29 | | | | | | 25 |
| Duquesne University | Pr/B | 6,018 | 240 | | 90 | | None | 50 |
| East Stroudsburg University of Pennsylvania | Pu/AB | 6,095 | 40 | TOEFL | 78 | 84 | 5/1 | 25 |
| Eastern University | Pr/B | 2,045 | 51 | TOEFL | 79 | | | 35 |
| Edinboro University of Pennsylvania | Pu/AB | 5,247 | | TOEFL | 61 | 93 | | 30 |
| Elizabethtown College | Pr/B | 1,713 | 51 | TOEFL | 61 | 91 | 5/1 | 30 |

| Student services | | | Housing | | Academic year costs | | Maximum credits/ summer | Credit hour charge | International financial aid | | | |
|---|---|---|---|---|---|---|---|---|---|---|---|---|
| Adviser | Orientation | ESL | Academic year | Summer | Tuition/ fees | Living costs | | | Available | Number receiving aid | Average award | Deadline |
| Yes | Yes | Yes | Yes | Yes | 33,442† | 12,210 | | 702 | Yes | 139 | $9,019 | None |
| Yes | Yes | Yes | Yes | Yes | 42,014† | 12,394 | 9 | 1310 | Yes | 78 | $25,692 | None |
| Yes | Yes | | Yes | Yes | 22,710† | 8,900 | | | Yes | 11 | $9,692 | None |
| Yes | Yes | Yes | Yes | Yes | 23,445† | 9,798 | 12 | 483 | Yes | 38 | $5,398 | None |
| Yes | Yes | | Yes | | 48,164‡ | 11,830 | | 1495 | Yes | | | None |
| Yes | Yes | Yes | Yes | Yes | 43,454 | 11,606 | 8 | 1325 | Yes | 29 | $15,081 | 2/1 |
| Yes | Yes | Yes | Yes | Yes | 45,970 | 13,650 | | 1895 | Yes | 59 | $20,269 | None |
| Yes | Yes | Yes | Yes | | 33,640 | 11,690 | 12 | 900 | Yes | 10 | $21,612 | None |
| Yes | | | | Yes | 20,920† | | | | | | | |
| Yes | Yes | | Yes | | 40,920† | 13,500 | 16 | 660 | Yes | 47 | $14,607 | None |
| Yes | Yes | | Yes | Yes | | 5,610 | 18 | | Yes | | | None |
| Yes | Yes | | Yes | Yes | 23,476† | 10,271 | 15 | | Yes | | | |
| | | | No | | | 6,750 | | | | | | |
| | | | No | | | | | | | | | |
| Yes | | Yes | Yes | Yes | 21,013† | 8,912 | 12 | | Yes | 25 | $11,512 | None |
| | | | Yes | | | | | | | | | |
| Yes | Yes | | Yes | | 19,932† | 13,338 | | 765 | Yes | 8 | $9,529 | None |
| Yes | Yes | | Yes | Yes | 50,500 | 15,910 | 8 | | Yes | 138 | $49,229 | 1/15 |
| Yes | Yes | | Yes | Yes | 53,986 | 15,161 | 8 | 1473 | Yes | 104 | $43,516 | 1/15 |
| | | Yes | No | | 13,760† | | | 420 | | | | |
| | | | No | | 10,830† | | | 312 | | | | |
| Yes | Yes | | Yes | Yes | 31,350‡ | 12,740 | 12 | 550 | Yes | | | None |
| Yes | Yes | | Yes | Yes | 26,493 | 9,803 | 6 | 777 | Yes | 14 | $16,230 | None |
| Yes | Yes | | Yes | Yes | 17,215† | 11,038 | 12 | | Yes | 31 | $13,341 | None |
| | | | No | | | | | | | | | |
| Yes | Yes | | Yes | Yes | 27,764† | 10,784 | 12 | 863 | Yes | | | 5/1 |
| Yes | Yes | | Yes | Yes | 53,910‡ | 13,784 | | 732 | | | | |
| Yes | Yes | | Yes | Yes | 38,092 | 11,208 | 12 | 1250 | Yes | 1 | $18,000 | None |
| | | | Yes | Yes | 18,174 | 7,416 | | 466 | Yes | | | None |
| Yes | Yes | Yes | Yes | Yes | 35,475† | 11,042 | 18 | 829 | Yes | | | None |
| Yes | Yes | Yes | Yes | Yes | 34,950‡ | 10,400 | 12 | | Yes | 28 | $24,928 | None |
| Yes | | | Yes | | 14,240† | 11,252 | | | Yes | | | None |
| Yes | | Yes | Yes | Yes | 14,090† | 11,104 | 15 | 452 | Yes | 6 | $1,607 | None |
| Yes | | | Yes | | 23,170 | 6,150 | 6 | 690 | Yes | | | 5/1 |
| Yes | Yes | Yes | No | | 10,662† | | | 323.25 | Yes | | | None |
| | | | No | | 16,470† | | 15 | 459 | | | | |
| Yes | Yes | Yes | No | | 14,280‡ | | 12 | | | | | |
| | | | No | | | | | | | | | |
| Yes | Yes | Yes | Yes | | | 15,059 | | | Yes | | | None |
| | | | | | | | | | Yes | | | None |
| Yes | Yes | Yes | Yes | Yes | 15,255† | | | 339 | | | | |
| Yes | Yes | | Yes | | 36,750† | 13,254 | 16 | 916 | Yes | 5 | $14,700 | None |
| Yes | | | Yes | | 35,900 | 12,800 | 15 | 1440 | Yes | | | 5/1 |
| Yes | | | Yes | | | | | | | | | |
| Yes | Yes | Yes | Yes | | 51,205† | 12,794 | 4 | 1586 | Yes | 186 | $31,743 | 2/1 |
| Yes | | | Yes | | | | | | | | | |
| Yes | Yes | Yes | Yes | Yes | 52,002‡ | 13,890 | | | | | | |
| Yes | Yes | | | | | | 18 | | | | | |
| | | | | | | 7,200 | | | | | | |
| | | | | | | 7,200 | | | | | | |
| Yes | Yes | Yes | Yes | Yes | 36,394 | 16,114 | 12 | 1206 | Yes | 98 | $23,775 | 5/1 |
| Yes | Yes | | Yes | Yes | 21,044† | 10,490 | 15 | | Yes | 4 | $28,681 | 2/16 |
| Yes | Yes | | Yes | Yes | 32,315 | 12,980 | 12 | 695 | Yes | 49 | $11,756 | None |
| Yes | Yes | | Yes | Yes | 15,817† | 9,396 | 12 | | Yes | | | None |
| Yes | Yes | Yes | Yes | Yes | 45,350 | 12,513 | 9 | | Yes | 53 | $25,605 | None |

† Actual for 2016-17.    ‡ Estimated for 2017-18.    * Includes room and board

| Institution | Control/ degrees | Undergraduates | | Tests required (Fall 2017) | TOEFL | | Application | |
|---|---|---|---|---|---|---|---|---|
| | | Total | Internat'l | | minimum | average | Deadline | Fee |
| Erie Institute of Technology............... | Pr/A | 232 | | | | | | 25 |
| Fortis Institute: Erie.................. | Pr/A | 404 | | | | | | 25 |
| Fortis Institute: Forty Fort............. | Pr/A | 186 | | | | | | 25 |
| Franklin & Marshall College.......... | Pr/B | 2,230 | 337 | TOEFL, SAT/ACT | | | | 60 |
| Gannon University................... | Pr/AB | 2,597 | 236 | TOEFL | 79 | | None | 25 |
| Geneva College.................... | Pr/AB | 1,458 | | TOEFL | 79 | | | 40 |
| Gettysburg College.................. | Pr/B | 2,379 | 157 | TOEFL, SAT/ACT | | | 1/15 | 60 |
| Gratz College..................... | Pr/B | 15 | | TOEFL | | | | 50 |
| Grove City College.................. | Pr/B | 2,346 | 23 | TOEFL, SAT/ACT | 79 | 86 | 2/1 | 50 |
| Gwynedd Mercy University............ | Pr/AB | 1,944 | 3 | TOEFL, SAT/ACT | 71 | | | |
| Harcum College.................... | Pr/A | 1,612 | | TOEFL | 61 | | | 25 |
| Harrisburg Area Community College..... | Pu/A | 14,230 | | | 79 | | | 35 |
| Harrisburg University of Science and Technology.................... | Pr/B | 374 | | TOEFL | 80 | 100 | | |
| Haverford College.................. | Pr/B | 1,261 | 115 | TOEFL, SAT, SAT Subject Test(s), or ACT | 100 | | 1/15 | 65 |
| Holy Family University.............. | Pr/AB | 1,766 | 6 | TOEFL, SAT | 79 | | | 25 |
| Immaculata University............... | Pr/AB | 1,459 | 13 | TOEFL, SAT/ACT | 65 | | | 35 |
| Indiana University of Pennsylvania...... | Pu/AB | 10,357 | 388 | TOEFL | 61 | | 7/1 | 25 |
| JNA Institute of Culinary Arts........ | Pr/A | 65 | | TOEFL | | | None | |
| Johnson College.................... | Pr/A | 437 | | TOEFL | | | | 25 |
| Juniata College.................... | Pr/B | 1,454 | 108 | TOEFL | 79 | 87 | | |
| Kaplan Career Institute: Franklin Mills...... | Pr/A | 640 | | | | | | 10 |
| Keystone College................... | Pr/AB | 1,280 | 5 | TOEFL | 80 | | | 30 |
| Keystone Technical Institute.......... | Pr/A | 341 | | | | | | 20 |
| King's College.................... | Pr/B | 1,946 | 122 | TOEFL | 71 | 101 | | 30 |
| Kutztown University of Pennsylvania...... | Pu/B | 7,683 | 54 | TOEFL | 79 | 85 | | 35 |
| La Roche College.................. | Pr/AB | 1,357 | 222 | | | | | 50 |
| La Salle University................. | Pr/AB | 3,543 | 81 | TOEFL | 80 | 90 | 4/15 | 35 |
| Lackawanna College................. | Pr/A | 1,477 | | TOEFL | 55 | | 6/30 | 35 |
| Lafayette College.................. | Pr/B | 2,518 | 264 | TOEFL, SAT/ACT | | | 1/15 | 65 |
| Lancaster Bible College............. | Pr/AB | 1,530 | | TOEFL | 69 | | | 25 |
| Lansdale School of Business.......... | Pr/A | 344 | | | | | | 40 |
| Laurel Business Institute............. | Pr/A | 233 | | | | | | 55 |
| Laurel Technical Institute............ | Pr/A | 171 | | | | | | 50 |
| Lebanon Valley College.............. | Pr/B | 1,649 | 7 | TOEFL | 80 | | 7/1 | |
| Lehigh Carbon Community College...... | Pu/A | 5,485 | | | | | 6/30 | |
| Lehigh University.................. | Pr/B | 5,061 | 427 | TOEFL, SAT/ACT | 90 | | 1/1 | 70 |
| Lincoln Technical Institute: Allentown........ | Pr/A | 540 | | | | | | 150 |
| Lincoln Technical Institute: Northeast Philadelphia.................... | Pr/A | 310 | | | | | | 150 |
| Lincoln Technical Institute: Philadelphia...... | Pr/A | 360 | | | | | | 150 |
| Lincoln University................. | Pu/B | 1,824 | 65 | TOEFL, SAT/ACT | 71 | | | 20 |
| Lock Haven University of Pennsylvania......... | Pu/AB | 3,786 | 22 | TOEFL | 79 | 81 | None | 25 |
| Lycoming College.................. | Pr/B | 1,246 | 62 | TOEFL | 70 | 97 | 5/1 | |
| Manor College.................... | Pr/A | 601 | 1 | TOEFL | 54 | 72 | 8/15 | |
| Mansfield University of Pennsylvania.......... | Pu/AB | 2,052 | 12 | TOEFL | | | | 25 |
| Marywood University................ | Pr/B | 1,822 | 27 | TOEFL | 71 | 75 | None | 35 |
| McCann School of Business and Technology: Dickson City.................... | Pr/A | | | | | | | 40 |
| McCann School of Business and Technology: Hazleton..................... | Pr/A | 315 | | | | | | 40 |
| McCann School of Business and Technology: Pottsville.................... | Pr/A | 275 | | | | | | 40 |
| McCann School of Business and Technology: Sunbury..................... | Pr/A | | | | | | | 40 |
| Mercyhurst University................ | Pr/B | 2,469 | | TOEFL, SAT/ACT | 79 | 80 | | |
| Messiah College.................... | Pr/B | 2,683 | 126 | TOEFL, SAT/ACT | 80 | | None | 50 |
| Millersville University of Pennsylvania......... | Pu/AB | 6,879 | 35 | TOEFL | 70 | | None | 40 |

| | Student services | | | Housing | | Academic year costs | | Maximum credits/ summer | Credit hour charge | International financial aid | | | |
|---|---|---|---|---|---|---|---|---|---|---|---|---|---|
| | Adviser | Orientation | ESL | Academic year | Summer | Tuition/ fees | Living costs | | | Available | Number receiving aid | Average award | Deadline |
| | | | | No | | | | | | | | | |
| | Yes | Yes | | Yes | Yes | 52,490† | 13,120 | 16 | 1631 | Yes | | | 2/15 |
| | Yes | Yes | Yes | Yes | Yes | 30,042† | 11,990 | 12 | 710 | Yes | 87 | $21,868 | None |
| | Yes | Yes | Yes | Yes | Yes | 26,070 | 9,920 | | 880 | Yes | | | None |
| | Yes | Yes | | Yes | Yes | 50,860† | 12,140 | | | Yes | 87 | $32,481 | 1/15 |
| | Yes | | | No | | | 11,700 | 12 | 783 | | | | |
| | Yes | Yes | | Yes | | 17,254 | 9,400 | 6 | 560 | Yes | 16 | $8,247 | 4/15 |
| | | | | Yes | | 34,380† | 12,150 | 12 | 700 | Yes | 1 | $3,750 | 5/1 |
| | Yes | Yes | Yes | Yes | Yes | 23,670‡ | 9,600 | 12 | 745 | Yes | | | 5/1 |
| | Yes | | Yes | No | | 8,970† | | 12 | 256 | | | | |
| | | Yes | | Yes | Yes | 23,900 | 11,650 | 17 | 1000 | | | | |
| | Yes | Yes | | Yes | Yes | 51,024† | 15,466 | | | Yes | 15 | $52,085 | 2/1 |
| | Yes | | | Yes | | 30,346 | 13,576 | 12 | 627 | Yes | 4 | $32,140 | 4/1 |
| | Yes | Yes | | Yes | | 35,210† | 12,500 | | 530 | Yes | | | 4/15 |
| | Yes | Yes | Yes | Yes | Yes | 21,034† | 12,402 | 12 | | Yes | 27 | $1,085 | None |
| | | | | No | | 12,725† | | | | | | | |
| | | | | Yes | | 18,035† | 7,100 | | 510 | | | | |
| | Yes | Yes | Yes | Yes | Yes | 43,875‡ | 12,040 | 15 | 1765 | Yes | 102 | $20,376 | 2/15 |
| | | | | No | | | | | | | | | |
| | Yes | | | Yes | Yes | 25,548† | 10,352 | 12 | 480 | Yes | | | 5/1 |
| | | | | No | | | 15,250 | | | | | | |
| | Yes | Yes | Yes | Yes | Yes | 34,720† | 12,318 | 12 | 565 | Yes | 3 | $12,333 | None |
| | Yes | Yes | Yes | Yes | Yes | 20,476† | 9,438 | 18 | 754 | Yes | 64 | $22,535 | None |
| | Yes | Yes | Yes | Yes | Yes | 27,720 | 11,220 | 15 | 680 | Yes | 79 | $13,607 | None |
| | Yes | Yes | Yes | Yes | Yes | 41,100† | 15,070 | 12 | | Yes | 89 | $25,457 | None |
| | Yes | | | Yes | Yes | 14,680† | 8,800 | 6 | 499 | Yes | 1284 | $896 | None |
| | Yes | Yes | | Yes | Yes | 48,885† | 14,470 | 16 | | Yes | | | 1/15 |
| | Yes | | | Yes | | 21,800† | 8,580 | 6 | | Yes | | | None |
| | | | | No | | | | | | | | | |
| | | | | No | | | 4,304 | 18 | | | | | |
| | | | | No | | | | | | | | | |
| | Yes | Yes | | Yes | Yes | 42,180 | 11,410 | 15 | | Yes | 6 | $23,312 | None |
| | Yes | | Yes | No | | 10,440† | 4,000 | 12 | 318 | | | | |
| | Yes | Yes | Yes | Yes | Yes | 48,320† | 12,690 | 16 | 2000 | Yes | 75 | $42,318 | 2/15 |
| | | | | No | | | | | | | | | |
| | Yes | Yes | | Yes | | 15,582† | 14,268 | 9 | 519 | Yes | 32 | $14,834 | |
| | | | | Yes | | 21,087† | 9,588 | | | Yes | | | 3/15 |
| | Yes | Yes | | Yes | Yes | 37,387† | 13,418 | 12 | 1139 | Yes | 56 | $24,790 | None |
| | Yes | | | Yes | | 16,550† | 7,500 | 18 | 699 | Yes | | | None |
| | Yes | | Yes | Yes | Yes | 21,058† | 12,438 | 12 | | Yes | 8 | $7,107 | 6/30 |
| | Yes | Yes | Yes | Yes | Yes | 33,000† | 13,900 | 12 | 630 | Yes | | | None |
| | | | | No | | | | | | | | | |
| | | | | No | | | | | | | | | |
| | | | | No | | | | | | | | | |
| | Yes | Yes | | Yes | Yes | 34,480† | 13,624 | 6 | 1081 | Yes | | | None |
| | Yes | Yes | Yes | Yes | Yes | 34,160 | 10,220 | | 1390 | Yes | 126 | $21,743 | None |
| | Yes | Yes | | Yes | Yes | 20,620† | 12,228 | 15 | 754 | Yes | 5 | $9,480 | None |

† Actual for 2016-17.  ‡ Estimated for 2017-18.  * Includes room and board

| Institution | Control/ degrees | Undergraduates | | Tests required (Fall 2017) | TOEFL | | Application | |
|---|---|---|---|---|---|---|---|---|
| | | Total | Internat'l | | minimum | average | Deadline | Fee |
| Misericordia University................. | Pr/B | 2,148 | 3 | TOEFL | 75 | | | 35 |
| Montgomery County Community College........ | Pu/A | 9,791 | 176 | | 79 | | 7/1 | |
| Moore College of Art and Design............. | Pr/B | 368 | | TOEFL | 71 | | | 60 |
| Moravian College ........................ | Pr/B | 1,928 | 129 | TOEFL | | | | |
| Mount Aloysius College ................... | Pr/AB | 1,310 | 68 | TOEFL, SAT/ACT | 61 | 70 | | 30 |
| Muhlenberg College....................... | Pr/AB | 2,375 | 77 | TOEFL | 80 | 90 | | 50 |
| Neumann University....................... | Pr/AB | 2,190 | 29 | TOEFL | 70 | | None | 35 |
| Northampton Community College............. | Pu/A | 9,450 | 124 | | | | 7/1 | 25 |
| Orleans Technical Institute ................. | Pr/A | 548 | | | | | | 125 |
| Peirce College........................... | Pr/AB | 1,484 | 4 | | | | | 50 |
| Penn Commercial Business and Technical School......................... | Pr/A | 307 | | | | | | 25 |
| Penn State Abington...................... | Pu/AB | 3,950 | | TOEFL, SAT/ACT | 80 | | 2/1 | 75 |
| Penn State Altoona ...................... | Pu/AB | 3,491 | 176 | TOEFL, SAT/ACT | 80 | | 2/1 | 75 |
| Penn State Beaver ....................... | Pu/AB | 726 | | TOEFL, SAT/ACT | 80 | | 2/1 | 75 |
| Penn State Berks........................ | Pu/AB | 2,888 | 73 | TOEFL, SAT/ACT | 80 | | 2/1 | 75 |
| Penn State Brandywine.................... | Pu/AB | 1,379 | | TOEFL, SAT/ACT | 80 | | 2/1 | 75 |
| Penn State DuBois....................... | Pu/AB | 608 | | TOEFL, SAT/ACT | 80 | | 2/1 | 75 |
| Penn State Erie, The Behrend College ......... | Pu/AB | 4,420 | 389 | TOEFL, SAT/ACT | 80 | | 2/1 | 75 |
| Penn State Fayette, The Eberly Campus ........ | Pu/AB | 643 | 9 | TOEFL, SAT/ACT | 80 | | 2/1 | 75 |
| Penn State Greater Allegheny................ | Pu/AB | 550 | 17 | TOEFL, SAT/ACT | 80 | | 2/1 | 75 |
| Penn State Harrisburg..................... | Pu/AB | 4,200 | 606 | TOEFL, SAT/ACT | 80 | | 2/1 | 75 |
| Penn State Hazleton...................... | Pu/AB | 863 | | TOEFL, SAT/ACT | 80 | | 2/1 | 75 |
| Penn State Lehigh Valley .................. | Pu/AB | 868 | | TOEFL, SAT/ACT | 80 | | 2/1 | 75 |
| Penn State Mont Alto..................... | Pu/AB | 902 | | TOEFL, SAT/ACT | 80 | | 2/1 | 75 |
| Penn State New Kensington................. | Pu/AB | 686 | | TOEFL, SAT/ACT | 80 | | 2/1 | 75 |
| Penn State Schuylkill .:................... | Pu/AB | 759 | | TOEFL, SAT/ACT | 80 | | 2/1 | 75 |
| Penn State Shenango ..................... | Pu/AB | 462 | | TOEFL, SAT/ACT | 80 | | 2/1 | 75 |
| Penn State University Park ................. | Pu/AB | 41,359 | 4,706 | TOEFL, SAT/ACT | 80 | | 2/1 | 75 |
| Penn State Wilkes-Barre.................... | Pu/AB | 477 | | TOEFL, SAT/ACT | 80 | | 2/1 | 75 |
| Penn State Worthington Scranton ............. | Pu/AB | 1,019 | 6 | TOEFL, SAT/ACT | 80 | | 2/1 | 75 |
| Penn State York ......................... | Pu/AB | 1,060 | | TOEFL, SAT/ACT | 80 | | 2/1 | 75 |
| Pennco Tech............................ | Pr/A | 500 | | | | | | 100 |
| Pennsylvania Academy of the Fine Arts......... | Pr/B | 195 | | TOEFL | 80 | | | 60 |
| Pennsylvania College of Art and Design......... | Pr/B | 231 | | TOEFL | 80 | | | 110 |
| Pennsylvania College of Health Sciences ........ | Pr/AB | 1,395 | | | | | | 35 |
| Pennsylvania College of Technology ........... | Pu/AB | 5,395 | 51 | TOEFL | 68 | | 5/1 | 50 |
| Pennsylvania Highlands Community College...... | Pu/A | 2,656 | | TOEFL | | | | |
| Pennsylvania Institute of Health and Technology........................ | Pr/A | 104 | | | | | | 25 |
| Philadelphia University.................... | Pr/AB | 2,733 | | TOEFL, SAT/ACT | | | | 40 |
| Pittsburgh Institute of Aeronautics............. | Pr/A | 152 | | TOEFL | 61 | | None | 150 |
| Pittsburgh Institute of Mortuary Science.......... | Pr/A | 317 | | TOEFL | | | | 50 |
| Point Park University..................... | Pr/AB | 3,207 | 156 | TOEFL | 61 | 72 | | 40 |
| Reading Area Community College ............ | Pu/A | 4,198 | | TOEFL | 45 | | | |
| Restaurant School at Walnut Hill College........ | Pr/AB | 396 | | TOEFL | | | | 200 |
| Robert Morris University.................... | Pr/B | 4,370 | 542 | TOEFL | 61 | | | 30 |
| Rosedale Technical College.................. | Pr/A | 343 | | | | | | 20 |
| Rosemont College ....................... | Pr/B | 614 | 24 | TOEFL | 61 | | | |
| St. Francis University..................... | Pr/AB | 1,652 | | TOEFL | 70 | 80 | | 30 |
| Saint Joseph's University ................. | Pr/AB | 5,238 | 103 | TOEFL | 79 | 92 | | 60 |
| St. Vincent College ...................... | Pr/B | 1,609 | 9 | TOEFL, SAT/ACT | | | 5/1 | 25 |
| Seton Hill University ..................... | Pr/B | 1,554 | | TOEFL | 79 | | | 35 |
| Shippensburg University of Pennsylvania ........ | Pu/B | 5,853 | 33 | TOEFL | 66 | | None | 45 |
| Slippery Rock University of Pennsylvania......... | Pu/B | 7,569 | 79 | TOEFL | 61 | 85 | 5/1 | 30 |
| Susquehanna University ................... | Pr/B | 2,136 | 37 | TOEFL | 80 | 90 | 3/1 | |
| Swarthmore College....................... | Pr/B | 1,617 | 188 | | | | 1/1 | 60 |
| Temple University........................ | Pu/AB | 28,709 | 1,858 | TOEFL | 79 | 93 | | 55 |
| Thiel College ........................... | Pr/AB | 876 | | TOEFL | 62 | | None | 50 |

| Student services | | | Housing | | Academic year costs | | Maximum credits/ summer | Credit hour charge | International financial aid | | | |
|---|---|---|---|---|---|---|---|---|---|---|---|---|
| Adviser | Orientation | ESL | Academic year | Summer | Tuition/ fees | Living costs | | | Available | Number receiving aid | Average award | Deadline |
| Yes | | | Yes | Yes | 31,660 | 13,550 | 12 | 595 | Yes | | | 5/1 |
| Yes | Yes | Yes | No | | 14,850† | | 12 | 432 | | | | |
| Yes | | | Yes | | 38,480† | 14,390 | 18 | | Yes | | | 5/1 |
| Yes | Yes | | Yes | Yes | 42,024 | 12,694 | 16 | 1119.5 | Yes | 120 | $4,851 | None |
| Yes | | | Yes | Yes | 22,430 | 10,338 | 12 | 800 | Yes | 38 | $12,672 | None |
| Yes | Yes | | Yes | | 48,310† | 11,090 | 8 | 1406.25 | Yes | 36 | $28,937 | 2/15 |
| Yes | | | Yes | Yes | 28,580† | 12,158 | 6 | 625 | Yes | 19 | $15,824 | None |
| Yes | Yes | Yes | Yes | Yes | 13,290† | 8,452 | 12 | 291 | | | | |
| Yes | Yes | | No | | | 6,102 | | | | | | |
| | | | No | | 17,940† | | | 578 | Yes | 4 | $3,375 | None |
| | | | No | | | | 18 | | | | | |
| Yes | Yes | Yes | No | | 21,742† | | | 866 | | | | |
| Yes | Yes | Yes | Yes | | 22,834† | 11,860 | | 911 | | | | |
| Yes | | | Yes | | 20,558† | 11,860 | | 817 | | | | |
| Yes | Yes | Yes | Yes | | 22,834† | 12,940 | | 911 | | | | |
| Yes | Yes | Yes | No | | 21,568† | | | 859 | | | | |
| Yes | Yes | | No | | 20,496† | | | 817 | | | | |
| Yes | Yes | | Yes | Yes | 22,834† | 11,860 | | 911 | | | | |
| Yes | | | No | | 20,496† | | | 817 | | | | |
| Yes | | Yes | | Yes | 20,546† | 11,860 | | 817 | | | | |
| Yes | Yes | | Yes | Yes | 22,834† | 13,460 | | 911 | | | | |
| Yes | Yes | Yes | Yes | | 21,506† | 11,860 | | 859 | | | | |
| | | | No | | 21,568† | | | 859 | | | | |
| Yes | Yes | | Yes | | 20,558† | 11,860 | | 817 | | | | |
| Yes | Yes | | No | | 20,496† | | | 817 | | | | |
| Yes | Yes | Yes | Yes | Yes | 21,506† | 8,240 | | 859 | | | | |
| | | | No | | 20,042† | | | 801 | | | | |
| Yes | Yes | Yes | Yes | Yes | 32,382† | 11,860 | | 1310 | | | | |
| Yes | Yes | | No | | 20,420† | | | 817 | | | | |
| Yes | Yes | | Yes | | 21,506† | | | 859 | | | | |
| Yes | Yes | Yes | No | | 21,568† | | | 859 | | | | |
| | | | | | | 11,550 | | | Yes | | | None |
| Yes | | | | | 36,058† | 15,315 | | 1154 | Yes | | | 3/1 |
| Yes | | | Yes | | 23,800† | | | 929 | Yes | | | None |
| | | | No | | | 8,908 | | | | | | |
| Yes | Yes | Yes | Yes | Yes | 22,890† | 11,244 | | | | | | |
| | | | No | | 11,310 | 2,250 | 12 | 315 | Yes | | | 4/1 |
| Yes | Yes | Yes | Yes | Yes | 37,800† | 12,570 | 12 | 605 | Yes | 41 | $13,011 | None |
| Yes | | | No | | 15,990 | | | | | | | |
| | | | No | | 14,125† | 12,324 | 20 | 290 | | | | |
| Yes | Yes | | Yes | Yes | 29,030† | 10,840 | 12 | 788 | Yes | 92 | $13,208 | 12/1 |
| Yes | Yes | Yes | No | | 11,100† | 10,800 | 15 | | | | | |
| Yes | | | Yes | | | 15,192 | | | Yes | | | None |
| Yes | Yes | | Yes | Yes | 29,420 | 11,180 | 15 | 905 | Yes | 129 | $23,067 | None |
| Yes | Yes | | Yes | Yes | 19,480 | 11,960 | 12 | 700 | Yes | | | None |
| Yes | Yes | Yes | Yes | | 34,956‡ | 13,928 | 16 | 1057 | Yes | | | None |
| Yes | Yes | Yes | Yes | | 43,020† | 14,524 | 12 | | Yes | | | None |
| Yes | Yes | Yes | Yes | Yes | 33,814† | 11,105 | 12 | 1018 | Yes | 7 | $17,258 | None |
| Yes | Yes | | Yes | Yes | 35,010‡ | 12,500 | 12 | 910 | Yes | 38 | $30,347 | None |
| Yes | Yes | | Yes | Yes | 19,308† | 11,756 | 15 | 679 | Yes | 24 | $11,494 | None |
| Yes | Yes | Yes | Yes | Yes | 13,482† | 10,110 | 18 | 452 | Yes | 46 | $3,816 | None |
| Yes | Yes | Yes | Yes | Yes | 43,720† | 11,620 | 8 | 1375 | Yes | 18 | $15,705 | 5/1 |
| Yes | Yes | | Yes | Yes | 49,104† | 14,446 | | | Yes | 65 | $56,833 | 2/15 |
| Yes | Yes | | Yes | Yes | 25,994† | 11,146 | 12 | 899 | Yes | 435 | $8,440 | 3/1 |
| Yes | Yes | Yes | Yes | Yes | 29,740† | 13,200 | 16 | 880 | Yes | | | None |

† Actual for 2016-17.  ‡ Estimated for 2017-18.  * Includes room and board

| Institution | Control/ degrees | Undergraduates Total | Undergraduates Internat'l | Tests required (Fall 2017) | TOEFL minimum | TOEFL average | Application Deadline | Fee |
|---|---|---|---|---|---|---|---|---|
| Thomas Jefferson University ................ | Pr/AB | 842 | | TOEFL | | | | 25 |
| Triangle Tech: Bethlehem ................... | Pr/A | 120 | | | | | | |
| Triangle Tech: Greensburg .................. | Pr/A | 163 | | | | | | |
| University of the Arts...................... | Pr/B | 1,693 | 80 | TOEFL | 80 | | None | 60 |
| University of Pennsylvania ................. | Pr/AB | 10,019 | 1,176 | TOEFL, SAT/ACT | | 112 | | 75 |
| University of Phoenix: Harrisburg............. | Pr/B | 130 | | | | | | |
| University of Phoenix: Philadelphia............ | Pr/B | 639 | | | | | | |
| University of Phoenix: Pittsburgh ............. | Pr/B | 110 | | | | | | |
| University of Pittsburgh ................... | Pu/B | 18,920 | 706 | TOEFL, SAT/ACT | 100 | | 4/1 | 45 |
| University of Pittsburgh at Bradford ........... | Pu/AB | 1,449 | 48 | TOEFL | 80 | 81 | 4/14 | 45 |
| University of Pittsburgh at Greensburg.......... | Pu/B | 1,520 | 14 | TOEFL, SAT/ACT | 80 | 88 | 5/1 | 45 |
| University of Pittsburgh at Johnstown .......... | Pu/AB | 2,816 | | TOEFL | 80 | | | 45 |
| University of Pittsburgh at Titusville ........... | Pu/A | 330 | | TOEFL | | | | 45 |
| University of the Sciences................... | Pr/B | 2,090 | | TOEFL, SAT/ACT | 75 | | | |
| University of Scranton .................... | Pr/AB | 3,757 | 37 | TOEFL | 80 | | 3/1 | |
| University of Valley Forge ................. | Pr/AB | 742 | 2 | TOEFL | 61 | | 3/1 | 25 |
| Ursinus College......................... | Pr/B | 1,540 | 32 | TOEFL | 80 | | | 100 |
| Valley Forge Military College ............. | Pr/A | 204 | | TOEFL | | | | 25 |
| Vet Tech Institute ...................... | Pr/A | 385 | | | | | | 50 |
| Villanova University .................... | Pr/AB | 6,862 | 104 | TOEFL, SAT/ACT | 85 | | | 80 |
| Washington & Jefferson College.............. | Pr/B | 1,371 | 48 | TOEFL | 85 | 93 | 3/1 | 25 |
| Waynesburg University..................... | Pr/B | 1,390 | 2 | TOEFL | 80 | | | 20 |
| West Chester University of Pennsylvania ......... | Pu/B | 14,123 | 59 | TOEFL | 80 | 90 | 5/1 | 45 |
| Westminster College ..................... | Pr/B | 1,158 | 6 | TOEFL | 79 | | 4/1 | 35 |
| Westmoreland County Community College........ | Pu/A | 4,316 | | TOEFL | | | None | |
| Widener University ...................... | Pr/AB | 3,331 | 136 | TOEFL | | | | |
| Wilson College......................... | Pr/AB | 748 | | TOEFL | 61 | 84 | 5/1 | |
| The Workforce Institute's City College .......... | Pr/A | 38 | | | | | | 50 |
| Yeshivath Beth Moshe .................... | Pr/B | 52 | | | | | | |
| York College of Pennsylvania ............... | Pr/AB | 4,154 | 21 | TOEFL | 72 | | | |
| YTI Career Institute: Altoona................ | Pr/A | 334 | | | | | | 50 |
| **Puerto Rico** | | | | | | | | |
| American University of Puerto Rico ........... | Pr/AB | 1,343 | | | | | None | 25 |
| Atlantic University College ................. | Pr/AB | 1,429 | | | | | | 30 |
| Bayamon Central University ............... | Pr/AB | 315 | | | | | None | 25 |
| Caribbean University .................... | Pr/AB | 2,920 | | | | | | 30 |
| Carlos Albizu University: San Juan............ | Pr/B | 189 | | | | | | 75 |
| Centro de Estudios Multidisciplinarios .......... | Pr/AB | 987 | | | | | | 30 |
| Colegio de Cinematografia Artes y Television...... | Pr/A | 761 | | | | | | 25 |
| Columbia Central University: Caguas........... | Pr/AB | 1,383 | | | | | | 50 |
| Conservatory of Music of Puerto Rico .......... | Pu/B | 409 | | | | | 12/1 | 125 |
| EDIC College........................... | Pr/AB | 2,919 | | | | | | 25 |
| EDP University of Puerto Rico: Hato Rey ........ | Pr/AB | 1,560 | | | | | | 15 |
| EDP University of Puerto Rico: San Sebastian...... | Pr/AB | 1,018 | | | | | | 125 |
| Escuela de Artes Plasticas de Puerto Rico......... | Pu/B | 555 | | | | | 5/4 | 25 |
| Humacao Community College ................ | Pr/AB | 465 | | | | | | 15 |
| ICPR Junior College ..................... | Pr/A | 2,554 | | | | | | |
| Inter American University of Puerto Rico: Aguadilla Campus ...................... | Pr/AB | 3,912 | | | | | None | |
| Inter American University of Puerto Rico: Arecibo Campus ....................... | Pr/AB | 4,303 | | | | | | |
| Inter American University of Puerto Rico: Barranquitas Campus ................... | Pr/AB | 1,892 | | | | | | |
| Inter American University of Puerto Rico: Bayamon Campus ..................... | Pr/AB | 4,313 | | | | | | |
| Inter American University of Puerto Rico: Fajardo Campus....................... | Pr/AB | 1,984 | | | | | | |

| Student services | | | Housing | | Academic year costs | | Maximum credits/ summer | Credit hour charge | International financial aid | | | |
| Adviser | Orien-tation | ESL | Academic year | Summer | Tuition/ fees | Living costs | | | Avail-able | Number receiving aid | Average award | Deadline |
|---|---|---|---|---|---|---|---|---|---|---|---|---|
| Yes | | | Yes | | | | | | | | | |
| | | | No | | 16,779† | | | | Yes | | | None |
| | | | | | | | | | Yes | | | None |
| Yes | Yes | Yes | Yes | | 41,464† | 15,120 | | 1728 | Yes | | | None |
| Yes | Yes | Yes | Yes | Yes | 53,534 | 15,066 | 12 | | Yes | | | None |
| Yes | Yes | Yes | Yes | Yes | 29,758† | 10,950 | | 1201 | | | | |
| Yes | Yes | | Yes | Yes | 24,630† | 16,794 | 18 | 987 | Yes | 4 | $8,000 | None |
| | | | Yes | Yes | 24,640† | 9,990 | 15 | 987 | Yes | | | None |
| | | | Yes | | 24,646† | 9,390 | | 987 | Yes | | | None |
| | | | Yes | | 21,552† | 10,472 | 15 | 862 | | | | |
| Yes | | Yes | Yes | | 38,850† | 15,188 | 12 | 1540 | Yes | | | |
| Yes | Yes | | Yes | | 42,162† | 14,264 | 12 | 1072 | Yes | | | None |
| Yes | | | Yes | | 21,271 | 8,611 | | | Yes | | | None |
| Yes | Yes | Yes | Yes | | 49,370† | 12,320 | | 1543 | Yes | 31 | $12,805 | 2/1 |
| Yes | Yes | Yes | Yes | Yes | 29,975† | 15,400 | | | Yes | | | |
| Yes | Yes | Yes | Yes | Yes | 49,430† | 13,093 | 12 | 2701 | Yes | 61 | $43,037 | 1/15 |
| Yes | Yes | Yes | Yes | Yes | 44,900† | 11,854 | 12 | 1113 | Yes | 46 | $19,544 | None |
| Yes | Yes | | Yes | | 24,010 | 9,820 | 12 | 960 | Yes | | | None |
| Yes | Yes | Yes | Yes | | 20,578† | 12,860 | 12 | | Yes | 14 | $13,496 | None |
| Yes | | | Yes | | 36,230 | 11,020 | 7 | 1125 | Yes | 2 | $18,750 | None |
| | | | No | | 12,390† | 5,500 | 18 | 366 | Yes | | | None |
| Yes | Yes | Yes | Yes | Yes | 44,166 | 14,024 | 12 | 1442 | Yes | | | None |
| Yes | Yes | | Yes | | 24,430† | 11,190 | 4 | | Yes | | | None |
| | | | | | 12,147† | 7,385 | | | | | | |
| Yes | Yes | | Yes | Yes | 18,780† | 10,460 | 15 | 525 | Yes | | | None |
| | | | No | | 6,824 | 4,700 | | | | | | |
| | | | | | 6,870† | 2,500 | | 140 | | | | |
| Yes | Yes | Yes | No | | 5,270† | | 12 | 185 | | | | |
| | | | No | | 6,280† | 5,947 | | 183 | Yes | | | None |
| | | | | | 5,656† | | | 167 | | | | |
| | | | | | | 1,200 | | | | | | |
| Yes | Yes | | No | | 4,175‡ | | | | | | | |
| | | | | | 6,745 | | | 280 | | | | |
| Yes | Yes | | No | | | | 15 | | | | | |
| Yes | Yes | | | | 5,940‡ | 8,040 | 12 | | | | | |
| | | | No | | 6,702 | 8,144 | | 180 | Yes | | | 5/18 |
| | | | No | | 5,382† | | | | | | | |
| | | | No | | | 1,600 | | | | | | |
| | | | No | | 6,142† | 3,100 | | 183 | | | | |
| | | Yes | No | | 6,180† | | 12 | 183 | Yes | | | 5/15 |
| | | | No | | 6,142† | | 6 | 183 | Yes | | | 6/30 |
| | | | Yes | | 6,180† | 6,114 | 18 | 183 | Yes | | | None |
| | Yes | | No | | 6,180† | 7,314 | 6 | 183 | | | | |

| Institution | Control/ degrees | Undergraduates Total | Undergraduates Internat'l | Tests required (Fall 2017) | TOEFL minimum | TOEFL average | Application Deadline | Application Fee |
|---|---|---|---|---|---|---|---|---|
| Inter American University of Puerto Rico: Guayama Campus . . . . . . . . . . . . . . . . . . . . . . | Pr/AB | 1,709 | | | | | | |
| Inter American University of Puerto Rico: Metropolitan Campus . . . . . . . . . . . . . . . . . . | Pr/AB | 6,113 | | | | | 4/15 | |
| Inter American University of Puerto Rico: Ponce Campus. . . . . . . . . . . . . . . . . . . . . . . | Pr/AB | 4,750 | | | | | | |
| Inter American University of Puerto Rico: San German Campus . . . . . . . . . . . . . . . . . . . . | Pr/AB | 3,972 | | | | | None | |
| National University College: Arecibo. . . . . . . . . . | Pr/AB | 1,450 | | | | | | 25 |
| National University College: Bayamon. . . . . . . . . | Pr/AB | 3,314 | | | | | | 25 |
| National University College: Ponce . . . . . . . . . . . . | Pr/AB | 1,230 | | | | | | 25 |
| Ponce Paramedical College . . . . . . . . . . . . . . . . | Pr/A | 2,607 | | | | | | 25 |
| Pontifical Catholic University of Puerto Rico . . . . . | Pr/AB | 7,133 | 14 | | | | | 15 |
| Theological University of the Caribbean. . . . . . . . . | Pr/B | 262 | | | | | | 25 |
| Turabo University . . . . . . . . . . . . . . . . . . . . . . | Pr/AB | 14,170 | | | | | None | 15 |
| Universal Technology College of Puerto Rico . . . . . | Pr/AB | 1,260 | | | | | | 20 |
| Universidad Adventista de las Antillas . . . . . . . . . | Pr/AB | 1,235 | | | | | | 20 |
| Universidad Central del Caribe. . . . . . . . . . . . . . | Pr/AB | 144 | | | | | | 25 |
| Universidad del Este . . . . . . . . . . . . . . . . . . . . | Pr/AB | 11,000 | | | | | | 15 |
| Universidad Metropolitana. . . . . . . . . . . . . . . . . | Pr/AB | 11,231 | | | | | | 15 |
| Universidad Pentecostal Mizpa . . . . . . . . . . . . . . | Pr/AB | 347 | | | | | | 45 |
| Universidad Politecnica de Puerto Rico . . . . . . . . | Pr/AB | 3,334 | | | | | | 50 |
| University College of San Juan. . . . . . . . . . . . . . | Pu/AB | 1,528 | | | | | | 15 |
| University of Phoenix: Puerto Rico . . . . . . . . . . . | Pr/B | 313 | | | | | | |
| University of Puerto Rico: Aguadilla . . . . . . . . . . | Pu/AB | 3,170 | | | | | 12/15 | 20 |
| University of Puerto Rico: Arecibo . . . . . . . . . . . | Pu/AB | 4,062 | | | | | 1/31 | 30 |
| University of Puerto Rico: Bayamon University College . . . . . . . . . . . . . . . . . . . . . . | Pu/AB | 5,000 | | | | | | 15 |
| University of Puerto Rico: Carolina Regional College . . . . . . . . . . . . . . . . . . . . . . . . . . | Pu/AB | 3,819 | | | | | 1/31 | |
| University of Puerto Rico: Cayey University College . . . . . . . . . . . . . . . . . . . . . . . . . . | Pu/B | 3,741 | | | | | | 20 |
| University of Puerto Rico: Humacao . . . . . . . . . . | Pu/AB | 4,037 | | | | | | 20 |
| University of Puerto Rico: Mayaguez. . . . . . . . . . | Pu/B | 11,989 | | | | | | 20 |
| University of Puerto Rico: Medical Sciences . . . . . . | Pu/AB | 388 | | | | | | 30 |
| University of Puerto Rico: Ponce . . . . . . . . . . . . | Pu/AB | 3,630 | | | | | | |
| University of Puerto Rico: Rio Piedras. . . . . . . . . . | Pu/B | 13,264 | | | | | 12/15 | |
| University of Puerto Rico: Utuado . . . . . . . . . . . . | Pu/AB | 1,429 | | | | | | 20 |

**Rhode Island**

| Institution | Control/ degrees | Undergraduates Total | Undergraduates Internat'l | Tests required (Fall 2017) | TOEFL minimum | TOEFL average | Application Deadline | Application Fee |
|---|---|---|---|---|---|---|---|---|
| Brown University . . . . . . . . . . . . . . . . . . . . . . | Pr/B | 6,580 | 744 | | 100 | | 1/1 | 75 |
| Bryant University . . . . . . . . . . . . . . . . . . . . . . | Pr/B | 3,443 | 249 | TOEFL | 80 | 94 | | 50 |
| Community College of Rhode Island . . . . . . . . . . . | Pu/A | 14,348 | 11 | TOEFL | | | | 20 |
| Johnson & Wales University: Providence . . . . . . . . | Pr/AB | 8,116 | 610 | TOEFL | | | | |
| New England Institute of Technology . . . . . . . . . . | Pr/AB | 2,853 | | TOEFL | | | None | 25 |
| Providence College . . . . . . . . . . . . . . . . . . . . . | Pr/AB | 4,173 | 83 | TOEFL | 90 | | | 65 |
| Rhode Island College . . . . . . . . . . . . . . . . . . . . | Pu/B | 7,224 | 13 | TOEFL | 79 | | | 50 |
| Rhode Island School of Design. . . . . . . . . . . . . . | Pr/B | 2,000 | 548 | TOEFL, SAT/ACT | 93 | 104 | 2/1 | 60 |
| Roger Williams University . . . . . . . . . . . . . . . . . | Pr/AB | 4,586 | 169 | | 85 | 89 | None | 50 |
| Salve Regina University . . . . . . . . . . . . . . . . . . | Pr/AB | 2,090 | 29 | TOEFL | 80 | 92 | None | 50 |
| University of Rhode Island . . . . . . . . . . . . . . . . | Pu/B | 13,777 | 189 | TOEFL | 79 | 86 | 2/1 | 65 |

**South Carolina**

| Institution | Control/ degrees | Undergraduates Total | Undergraduates Internat'l | Tests required (Fall 2017) | TOEFL minimum | TOEFL average | Application Deadline | Application Fee |
|---|---|---|---|---|---|---|---|---|
| Aiken Technical College. . . . . . . . . . . . . . . . . . . | Pu/A | 2,357 | | TOEFL | 61 | | | |
| Allen University . . . . . . . . . . . . . . . . . . . . . . . | Pr/B | 670 | | | | | | |
| Anderson University. . . . . . . . . . . . . . . . . . . . . | Pr/B | 2,749 | | TOEFL | | | 7/1 | 25 |
| Benedict College . . . . . . . . . . . . . . . . . . . . . . . | Pr/B | 2,464 | | TOEFL | | | | 60 |
| Bob Jones University . . . . . . . . . . . . . . . . . . . . | Pr/AB | 2,361 | 148 | TOEFL, ACT | 61 | 70 | | |
| Brown Mackie College: Greenville . . . . . . . . . . . | Pr/AB | | | | | | | |
| Central Carolina Technical College . . . . . . . . . . . | Pu/A | 4,300 | | | | | | |

| Student services | | | Housing | | Academic year costs | | Maximum credits/summer | Credit hour charge | International financial aid | | | |
| --- | --- | --- | --- | --- | --- | --- | --- | --- | --- | --- | --- | --- |
| Adviser | Orientation | ESL | Academic year | Summer | Tuition/fees | Living costs | | | Available | Number receiving aid | Average award | Deadline |
| Yes | | | | | 6,482 | | 6 | 187 | | | | |
| Yes | | | No | | 7,302 † | | 12 | 183 | Yes | | | 4/30 |
| | | | | | 6,180 † | | | 183 | | | | |
| Yes | | Yes | Yes | Yes | 6,180 † | 7,401 | 6 | 183 | | | | |
| | | | No | | | 6,358 | | | | | | |
| | | | No | | | 6,358 | | | | | | |
| | | | No | | | 6,358 | | | | | | |
| Yes | Yes | | Yes | Yes | | | 12 | | Yes | | | 5/15 |
| | | | Yes | | 4,448 † | 2,400 | | 130 | | | | |
| Yes | Yes | | No | | 5,820 † | 8,000 | | 205 | Yes | | | None |
| | | | No | | | 3,333 | | | Yes | | | 6/30 |
| Yes | | Yes | Yes | Yes | 6,350 † | 7,400 | 12 | 175 | | | | |
| | | | | | | 7,200 | | | | | | |
| Yes | | | No | | 5,820 † | 8,000 | 21 | 205 | | | | |
| Yes | | | Yes | | 5,820 † | 4,600 | 12 | 205 | | | | |
| | | | Yes | | 5,150 ‡ | 3,760 | 12 | 155 | | | | |
| | | | No | | 8,328 | 11,857 | 12 | 208 | Yes | | | 6/30 |
| | | | | | 2,370 † | 7,350 | 9 | | | | | |
| Yes | | | No | | 5,297 † | 8,280 | 6 | | Yes | | | 5/6 |
| | | | No | | 4,600 † | | 6 | 4456 | | | | |
| | | Yes | No | | 4,513 † | | 6 | 55 | | | | |
| | | | No | | 5,404 † | 11,161 | | | | | | |
| | | | No | | | | 7 | | Yes | | | 6/30 |
| | | Yes | No | | 4,513 † | 8,751 | 7 | 55 | Yes | | | 6/30 |
| Yes | | | No | | | | 6 | | | | | |
| | | | No | | 4,585 † | | | 120 | | | | |
| | | | No | | 4,069 † | 8,751 | 6 | | | | | |
| Yes | Yes | | Yes | Yes | 4,630 † | 8,751 | 10 | 87 | Yes | | | 4/1 |
| | | | | | 4,041 † | 8,751 | 9 | 114 | | | | |
| Yes | Yes | | Yes | | 51,366 † | 13,200 | | | Yes | 188 | $52,276 | 2/1 |
| Yes | Yes | Yes | Yes | Yes | 42,109 | 15,394 | | 1033 | Yes | | | 2/15 |
| Yes | | | No | | 11,496 † | 9,382 | 12 | 534 | | | | |
| Yes | Yes | Yes | Yes | Yes | 30,396 † | 12,672 | 18 | | Yes | | | None |
| Yes | Yes | Yes | No | | 28,740 | 7,065 | | 480 | Yes | | | None |
| | | | Yes | | 46,970 † | 13,790 | | 1645 | Yes | 83 | $50,261 | 2/1 |
| Yes | | | Yes | | 19,867 † | 11,133 | 14 | 690 | | | | |
| Yes | Yes | | Yes | | 47,110 † | 12,850 | | | | | | |
| | Yes | Yes | Yes | Yes | 31,850 † | 17,687 | 12 | 1249 | Yes | 58 | $12,506 | 2/1 |
| Yes | Yes | | Yes | | 37,820 † | 14,650 | 12 | 1242 | Yes | | | None |
| Yes | Yes | Yes | Yes | Yes | 28,874 † | 12,022 | 14 | 1130 | | | | |
| Yes | | | No | | 8,192 † | 3,600 | 18 | 259 | | | | |
| Yes | | | Yes | | 12,740 † | 6,560 | | 450 | Yes | | | 7/20 |
| Yes | Yes | | Yes | Yes | 26,920 | 9,680 | | 605 | Yes | 46 | $13,456 | 6/30 |
| Yes | | | Yes | | 19,566 † | 8,672 | | 586 | | | | |
| Yes | | Yes | Yes | | 15,550 † | 6,470 | 14 | 355 | Yes | | | 7/1 |
| | | | No | | 8,700 † | 9,830 | | 290 | | | | |

† Actual for 2016-17.    ‡ Estimated for 2017-18.    * Includes room and board

| Institution | Control/ degrees | Undergraduates Total | Internat'l | Tests required (Fall 2017) | TOEFL minimum | average | Application Deadline | Fee |
|---|---|---|---|---|---|---|---|---|
| Charleston Southern University . . . . . . . . . . . . . . | Pr/B | 3,205 | | TOEFL, SAT/ACT | | | | 40 |
| The Citadel . . . . . . . . . . . . . . . | Pu/B | 2,693 | 24 | TOEFL, SAT/ACT | 79 | | 6/1 | 40 |
| Claflin University . . . . . . . . . . . . . . | Pr/B | 1,904 | 47 | | | | 5/1 | 75 |
| Clemson University . . . . . . . . . . . . . . | Pu/B | 18,395 | 127 | TOEFL, SAT/ACT | 80 | | | 70 |
| Clinton College . . . . . . . . . . . . . . | Pr/AB | 194 | | | | | | 25 |
| Coastal Carolina University . . . . . . . . . . . . . . | Pu/B | 9,460 | 140 | TOEFL | 71 | 82 | | 45 |
| Coker College . . . . . . . . . . . . . . | Pr/B | 1,203 | | TOEFL, SAT/ACT | 61 | | | 25 |
| College of Charleston . . . . . . . . . . . . . . | Pu/B | 10,033 | 73 | TOEFL | 80 | | None | 50 |
| Columbia College . . . . . . . . . . . . . . | Pr/B | 1,465 | | TOEFL, SAT/ACT | | | | 25 |
| Columbia International University . . . . . . . . . . . . . . | Pr/AB | 488 | 23 | TOEFL | 70 | 87 | | 45 |
| Converse College . . . . . . . . . . . . . . | Pr/B | 864 | | TOEFL | 79 | | | |
| Denmark Technical College . . . . . . . . . . . . . . | Pu/A | 579 | | | | | None | 10 |
| Erskine College . . . . . . . . . . . . . . | Pr/B | 622 | | TOEFL, SAT/ACT | | | | 25 |
| Florence-Darlington Technical College . . . . . . . . . . . . . . | Pu/A | 6,214 | | TOEFL | | | | 15 |
| Forrest Junior College . . . . . . . . . . . . . . | Pr/A | 116 | | | | | | 25 |
| Francis Marion University . . . . . . . . . . . . . . | Pu/B | 3,221 | 48 | TOEFL, SAT/ACT | 61 | 68 | 8/15 | 39 |
| Furman University . . . . . . . . . . . . . . | Pr/B | 2,780 | 128 | TOEFL | | | 1/15 | 50 |
| Golf Academy of America: Myrtle Beach . . . . . . . . | Pr/A | 251 | | | | | | 50 |
| Greenville Technical College . . . . . . . . . . . . . . | Pu/A | 10,353 | | | 61 | 70 | None | |
| Horry-Georgetown Technical College . . . . . . . . . . | Pu/A | 7,018 | | TOEFL | 61 | | | 30 |
| Lander University . . . . . . . . . . . . . . | Pu/B | 2,717 | | TOEFL, SAT/ACT | 80 | | | 35 |
| Limestone College . . . . . . . . . . . . . . | Pr/AB | 1,195 | 99 | TOEFL, SAT/ACT | 76 | | 9/2 | 25 |
| Midlands Technical College . . . . . . . . . . . . . . | Pu/A | 10,946 | | TOEFL | | 65 | | 35 |
| Miller-Motte Technical College . . . . . . . . | Pr/A | 460 | | | | | | 40 |
| Miller-Motte Technical College: Conway . . . . . . . . | Pr/A | 622 | | | | | | 40 |
| Morris College . . . . . . . . . . . . . . | Pr/B | 754 | | TOEFL | | | | 20 |
| Newberry College . . . . . . . . . . . . . . | Pr/B | 1,063 | 45 | TOEFL, SAT/ACT | 71 | | None | 30 |
| North Greenville University . . . . . . . . . . . . . . | Pr/B | 2,174 | 6 | TOEFL, SAT/ACT | | | | 35 |
| Orangeburg-Calhoun Technical College . . . . . . . . | Pu/A | 2,718 | | TOEFL | | | | 50 |
| Piedmont Technical College . . . . . . . . . . . . . . | Pu/A | 4,081 | | TOEFL, SAT | 61 | | None | |
| Presbyterian College . . . . . . . . . . . . . . | Pr/B | 950 | 32 | TOEFL | 80 | | 7/1 | |
| Remington College: Columbia . . . . . . . . . . . . . . | Pr/A | | | | | | | |
| South Carolina State University . . . . . . . . . . . . . . | Pu/B | 2,499 | 5 | TOEFL, SAT/ACT | 61 | 75 | | 25 |
| Southern Wesleyan University . . . . . . . . . . . . . . | Pr/AB | 1,400 | | TOEFL, SAT/ACT | 61 | | | 25 |
| Spartanburg Community College . . . . . . . . . . . . . . | Pu/A | 3,900 | | TOEFL | 63 | | None | 25 |
| Spartanburg Methodist College . . . . . . . . . . . . . . | Pr/A | 736 | 5 | TOEFL, SAT/ACT | | | | 25 |
| Tri-County Technical College . . . . . . . . . . . . . . | Pu/A | 6,094 | | TOEFL | 61 | | | 30 |
| Trident Technical College . . . . . . . . . . . . . . | Pu/A | 11,393 | | TOEFL | | | 8/6 | 30 |
| University of Phoenix: Columbia . . . . . . . . . . . . . . | Pr/B | 487 | | | | | | |
| University of South Carolina: Aiken . . . . . . . . | Pu/B | 3,131 | 130 | TOEFL, SAT/ACT | 80 | | 6/1 | 100 |
| University of South Carolina: Beaufort . . . . . . . . | Pu/AB | 1,986 | | TOEFL, SAT/ACT | 77 | | | 40 |
| University of South Carolina: Columbia . . . . . . . . | Pu/AB | 25,108 | | TOEFL | 77 | | | 100 |
| University of South Carolina: Lancaster . . . . . . . . | Pu/A | 1,845 | | TOEFL, SAT/ACT | | | 4/1 | 40 |
| University of South Carolina: Sumter . . . . . . . . . . | Pu/A | 901 | | TOEFL | | | | 40 |
| University of South Carolina: Union . . . . . . . . | Pu/A | 850 | | TOEFL, SAT/ACT | | | | 40 |
| University of South Carolina: Upstate . . . . . . . . . | Pu/B | 5,495 | 141 | TOEFL, SAT/ACT | 61 | | | 40 |
| Virginia College in Charleston . . . . . . . . . . . . . . | Pr/AB | 414 | | | | | | 100 |
| Virginia College in Columbia . . . . . . . . . . . . . . | Pr/A | 589 | | | | | | 100 |
| Virginia College in Florence . . . . . . . . . . . . . . | Pr/A | 414 | | | | | | |
| Virginia College in Greenville . . . . . . . . . . . . . . | Pr/A | 453 | | | | | | 100 |
| Virginia College in Spartanburg . . . . . . . . . . . . . . | Pr/A | 413 | | | | | | 100 |
| Voorhees College . . . . . . . . . . . . . . | Pr/B | 415 | | TOEFL, SAT, SAT Subject Test(s) | | | 5/1 | 25 |
| W.L. Bonner Bible College . . . . . . . . . . . . . . | Pr/AB | 35 | | | | | | 30 |
| Winthrop University . . . . . . . . . . . . . . | Pu/B | 4,790 | 75 | TOEFL | 68 | | | 60 |
| Wofford College . . . . . . . . . . . . . . | Pr/B | 1,606 | 27 | TOEFL | 80 | 92 | 2/1 | 35 |

**South Dakota**

| | | | | | | | | |
|---|---|---|---|---|---|---|---|---|
| Augustana University . . . . . . . . . . . . . . | Pr/B | 1,617 | | TOEFL, SAT/ACT | | | 8/1 | |

| Student services | | | Housing | | Academic year costs | | Maximum credits/ summer | Credit hour charge | International financial aid | | | |
|---|---|---|---|---|---|---|---|---|---|---|---|---|
| Adviser | Orientation | ESL | Academic year | Summer | Tuition/ fees | Living costs | | | Available | Number receiving aid | Average award | Deadline |
| Yes | | | Yes | | 24,100 † | 9,600 | 12 | 470 | Yes | | | None |
| Yes | | Yes | Yes | | 34,518 ‡ | 7,924 | 12 | | Yes | 5 | $35,720 | None |
| Yes | | | Yes | | 15,982 † | 8,932 | 9 | | Yes | | | 4/15 |
| Yes | Yes | | Yes | Yes | 33,300 † | 9,080 | | | | | | |
| Yes | | | | | 6,994 † | 9,551 | | | | | | |
| Yes | Yes | Yes | Yes | Yes | 25,872 | 9,140 | 16 | 1075 | Yes | 52 | $26,020 | None |
| Yes | Yes | Yes | Yes | | 27,624 † | 9,618 | | | Yes | | | 6/1 |
| Yes | Yes | Yes | Yes | Yes | 29,864 † | 13,908 | 15 | 1231 | | | | |
| Yes | Yes | | Yes | | 28,900 † | 8,650 | 16 | 760 | Yes | | | None |
| Yes | Yes | | Yes | | 21,490 † | 7,760 | | 870 | Yes | 18 | $12,176 | None |
| | | Yes | Yes | | 18,030 | 10,610 | 15 | 875 | Yes | 10 | $1,504 | None |
| Yes | | | Yes | Yes | 6,996 † | 3,938 | 9 | | Yes | | | None |
| Yes | | | Yes | | 34,560 † | 10,900 | 14 | 1250 | Yes | | | None |
| Yes | | | No | | 10,405 † | | 25 | 341 | Yes | | | None |
| | | | No | | 9,195 ‡ | 9,657 | | 245 | Yes | | | None |
| Yes | Yes | | Yes | Yes | 20,308 † | 7,716 | 15 | 988 | | | | |
| Yes | Yes | | Yes | Yes | 48,348 | 15,408 | 12 | 1499 | Yes | 126 | $33,505 | 1/15 |
| | | | | | 17,250 † | | | | | | | |
| Yes | | | Yes | Yes | 10,350 † | | 12 | | | | | |
| Yes | | | No | | 9,868 † | 8,590 | | 320 | | | | |
| Yes | Yes | Yes | Yes | | 20,300 † | 11,683 | 17 | | Yes | | | 8/1 |
| Yes | Yes | | Yes | | 24,900 ‡ | 9,582 | 14 | | Yes | 93 | $16,979 | None |
| Yes | Yes | Yes | No | | 14,624 † | 6,201 | 18 | | | | | |
| Yes | | | Yes | | 13,458 | 5,737 | 9 | 504 | | | | |
| Yes | Yes | | Yes | Yes | 25,600 † | 9,790 | 17 | 735 | Yes | 43 | $26,445 | None |
| | | | Yes | | 17,594 † | 9,892 | 12 | | Yes | | | 6/30 |
| Yes | | | No | | 8,690 † | 2,737 | 18 | 280 | | | | |
| Yes | | | No | | 6,188 † | 12,123 | | 250 | | | | |
| Yes | Yes | Yes | Yes | | 37,842 ‡ | 10,298 | 12 | | Yes | | | 6/30 |
| Yes | | | Yes | | 20,500 † | 9,890 | | 854 | Yes | | | 5/1 |
| Yes | | | Yes | | 24,110 † | 8,020 | | | Yes | | | 6/30 |
| Yes | | | No | | 8,592 † | 6,099 | 18 | 358 | Yes | | | 5/1 |
| | | Yes | Yes | | 16,860 † | 8,910 | 7 | 425 | Yes | | | 8/22 |
| Yes | | | No | | 11,303 † | 15,017 | 18 | | Yes | | | 7/30 |
| | | Yes | No | | 7,838 † | 8,793 | | 325.25 | Yes | | | None |
| Yes | | | Yes | Yes | 20,102 † | 7,466 | 6 | 825 | Yes | 64 | $13,391 | None |
| | | | Yes | | 20,805 † | 7,800 | 6 | 844 | Yes | | | None |
| Yes | Yes | Yes | Yes | Yes | 31,282 † | 9,700 | 12 | 1286.75 | Yes | 101 | $7,983 | None |
| | Yes | | No | | 17,184 † | 6,279 | 12 | 679.25 | Yes | | | None |
| | | | No | | 17,184 † | | 12 | 697.25 | | | | |
| | | | No | | 17,134 † | 6,279 | 6 | 697.25 | | | | |
| Yes | Yes | Yes | Yes | | 22,063 † | 8,142 | 12 | 904.5 | Yes | 46 | $7,589 | 7/15 |
| Yes | | | Yes | | 12,630 † | 10,346 | 10 | 484 | Yes | | | None |
| | | | | | 8,868 † | 2,576 | | 286 | | | | |
| Yes | Yes | | Yes | Yes | 28,390 † | 8,572 | | 1170 | Yes | | | None |
| Yes | | | Yes | | 41,955 | 12,140 | 12 | 1605 | Yes | 17 | $25,007 | None |
| Yes | Yes | | Yes | Yes | 31,960 | 9,508 | | 475 | Yes | | | None |

† Actual for 2016-17.    ‡ Estimated for 2017-18.    * Includes room and board

| Institution | Control/ degrees | Undergraduates | | Tests required (Fall 2017) | TOEFL | | Application | |
|---|---|---|---|---|---|---|---|---|
| | | Total | Internat'l | | minimum | average | Deadline | Fee |
| Black Hills State University................ | Pu/AB | 3,139 | | TOEFL | 69 | 72 | 7/1 | 20 |
| Dakota State University ...................... | Pu/AB | 1,936 | 25 | TOEFL | 79 | 81 | 7/15 | 20 |
| Dakota Wesleyan University ................ | Pr/AB | 782 | 15 | TOEFL | 71 | | | |
| Globe University: Sioux Falls............. | Pr/AB | 138 | | TOEFL | 61 | | | 50 |
| Lake Area Technical Institute.............. | Pu/A | 1,802 | | TOEFL | | | 5/1 | 250 |
| Mitchell Technical Institute ............... | Pu/A | 1,093 | 2 | TOEFL | | | | |
| Mount Marty College....................... | Pr/AB | 572 | | TOEFL | | | | 35 |
| National American University: Rapid City ....... | Pr/AB | 1,479 | | TOEFL | | | | 45 |
| Northern State University .................. | Pu/AB | 1,537 | 102 | TOEFL | 61 | | | 20 |
| Oglala Lakota College ..................... | Pu/AB | 1,215 | | | | | | 40 |
| Presentation College....................... | Pr/AB | 750 | | TOEFL, ACT | | | | 25 |
| Sinte Gleska University..................... | Pu/AB | 690 | | TOEFL | | | | 74 |
| Sisseton Wahpeton College ................ | Pu/A | 131 | | | | | | |
| South Dakota School of Mines and Technology........ | Pu/AB | 2,359 | 56 | TOEFL | 83 | 88 | | 20 |
| South Dakota State University .............. | Pu/AB | 9,778 | 422 | TOEFL | 61 | | 6/15 | 20 |
| University of Sioux Falls................... | Pr/AB | 1,207 | 12 | TOEFL | 75 | | | 25 |
| University of South Dakota ................ | Pu/AB | 7,541 | | TOEFL | 79 | | | 20 |
| Western Dakota Technical Institute ........... | Pu/A | 824 | | | | | | |

**Tennessee**

| Institution | Control/ degrees | Total | Internat'l | Tests required (Fall 2017) | minimum | average | Deadline | Fee |
|---|---|---|---|---|---|---|---|---|
| American Baptist College ................... | Pr/AB | 160 | | TOEFL | | | | 40 |
| Aquinas College .......................... | Pr/AB | 299 | 11 | TOEFL | 80 | | | |
| Argosy University: Nashville ............... | Pr/AB | 217 | | | | | | 50 |
| Austin Peay State University ................ | Pu/AB | 9,116 | 25 | TOEFL | 61 | | 8/9 | 25 |
| Belmont University ........................ | Pr/B | 6,232 | 56 | TOEFL, SAT/ACT | | | | 50 |
| Bethel University.......................... | Pr/AB | 4,068 | 61 | TOEFL | 65 | | None | 30 |
| Bryan College: Dayton .................... | Pr/AB | 987 | | TOEFL, SAT/ACT | 75 | | | 35 |
| Carson-Newman University ................ | Pr/AB | 1,748 | 54 | TOEFL, SAT/ACT | 79 | | | 100 |
| Chattanooga College ...................... | Pr/A | 340 | | | | | | 25 |
| Christian Brothers University .............. | Pr/AB | 1,440 | 71 | TOEFL, SAT/ACT | 68 | | None | 100 |
| Cleveland State Community College ........... | Pu/A | 3,054 | 1 | TOEFL, SAT/ACT | 61 | | 7/15 | |
| Cumberland University..................... | Pr/AB | 1,142 | | TOEFL, SAT/ACT | | | | 50 |
| Daymar Institute: Clarksville .............. | Pr/AB | 513 | | | | | | 20 |
| Daymar Institute: Murfreesboro ............ | Pr/AB | 131 | | | | | | |
| Daymar Institute: Nashville ................ | Pr/AB | 410 | | | | | | 75 |
| Dyersburg State Community College........... | Pu/A | 1,855 | | TOEFL, ACT | 45 | | | |
| East Tennessee State University ............. | Pu/B | 10,709 | 412 | TOEFL, SAT/ACT | 61 | 65 | | 35 |
| Fisk University ........................... | Pr/B | 723 | | TOEFL, SAT/ACT | | 91 | | 50 |
| Freed-Hardeman University ................. | Pr/B | 1,362 | | TOEFL | | | | |
| Hiwassee College ......................... | Pr/AB | 286 | | TOEFL | | | | 25 |
| Huntington College of Health Sciences ......... | Pr/AB | 135 | | TOEFL | | | | 75 |
| Jackson State Community College............. | Pu/A | 4,924 | | TOEFL, SAT/ACT | 61 | | | |
| Johnson University........................ | Pr/AB | 842 | | TOEFL | 71 | | | 35 |
| King University........................... | Pr/AB | 2,249 | 70 | TOEFL | 84 | 90 | | 50 |
| Lane College ............................. | Pr/AB | 1,427 | | TOEFL | | | | |
| Lee University ............................ | Pr/B | 4,261 | 161 | TOEFL | 45 | | None | 25 |
| LeMoyne-Owen College ................... | Pr/AB | 959 | 12 | TOEFL | | | None | 25 |
| Lincoln Memorial University ............... | Pr/AB | 1,680 | | TOEFL, SAT/ACT | | | 9/1 | 25 |
| Lipscomb University ...................... | Pr/AB | 2,969 | 79 | TOEFL | | | | 25 |
| Martin Methodist College ................. | Pr/AB | 1,144 | | TOEFL, SAT/ACT | | | | 30 |
| Maryville College ........................ | Pr/B | 1,174 | 36 | | 74 | | None | 50 |
| Memphis College of Art ................... | Pr/B | 337 | 1 | TOEFL, SAT/ACT | 61 | | 8/1 | |
| Middle Tennessee State University ........... | Pu/B | 18,998 | 644 | TOEFL, SAT/ACT | | | | 30 |
| Miller-Motte Technical College: Chattanooga ...... | Pr/A | 348 | | | | | | 40 |
| Miller-Motte Technical College: Clarksville ...... | Pr/A | 404 | | TOEFL | | | | 40 |
| Milligan College .......................... | Pr/B | 820 | | TOEFL | 79 | | | 30 |
| Motlow State Community College........... | Pu/A | 4,803 | | TOEFL, SAT/ACT | | | | |

| Student services | | | Housing | | Academic year costs | | Maximum credits/ summer | Credit hour charge | International financial aid | | | |
|---|---|---|---|---|---|---|---|---|---|---|---|---|
| Adviser | Orientation | ESL | Academic year | Summer | Tuition/ fees | Living costs | | | Available | Number receiving aid | Average award | Deadline |
| Yes | | Yes | Yes | | 10,920 † | 6,695 | 12 | 330 | Yes | | | 2/15 |
| Yes | Yes | | Yes | Yes | 11,843 † | 7,911 | 12 | 330 | Yes | 9 | $2,268 | None |
| Yes | Yes | | Yes | Yes | 26,050 † | 10,200 | 12 | | Yes | 1 | $12,540 | None |
| Yes | Yes | | No | | | 5,148 | | | | | | |
| Yes | | Yes | No | | 6,107 † | 6,700 | | | | | | |
| | | | No | | 6,030 † | 6,000 | | | | | | |
| Yes | | | Yes | Yes | 26,310 | 7,846 | 18 | | Yes | | | None |
| | | | No | | 17,175 † | | | 360 | Yes | | | None |
| Yes | Yes | Yes | Yes | Yes | 10,803 † | 6,984 | 14 | 330 | Yes | 46 | $3,262 | None |
| | | | Yes | | 3,140 † | 7,200 | | | | | | |
| | | | Yes | Yes | 18,710 † | 8,690 | 12 | | Yes | | | None |
| | | | No | | 3,700 † | | | | | | | |
| | | | No | | 3,984 † | 3,000 | | | Yes | | | None |
| Yes | Yes | Yes | Yes | Yes | 13,734 † | 6,734 | | 383 | Yes | | | None |
| Yes | Yes | Yes | Yes | | 11,403 † | 7,743 | | 346.2 | Yes | | | None |
| Yes | Yes | | Yes | Yes | 27,980 | 11,350 | | | Yes | 18 | $15,717 | None |
| Yes | Yes | Yes | Yes | Yes | 11,688 † | 7,646 | 12 | 346 | | | | |
| | | | No | | 6,150 † | 7,934 | | | | | | |
| | | | Yes | Yes | 11,894 † | 6,440 | 6 | | | | | |
| | | | Yes | | 22,850 | 9,500 | | 830 | Yes | | | None |
| Yes | Yes | Yes | Yes | Yes | 25,464 † | 9,711 | 14 | | | | | |
| Yes | Yes | | Yes | Yes | 31,390 † | 11,330 | 12 | 1140 | Yes | | | None |
| Yes | | | Yes | Yes | 16,552 ‡ | 9,198 | | 462 | Yes | | | 6/30 |
| Yes | | | Yes | Yes | 24,450 † | 6,990 | | | Yes | 1 | $12,000 | None |
| Yes | Yes | Yes | Yes | Yes | 26,360 † | 8,430 | 14 | 1050 | Yes | 44 | $8,941 | None |
| Yes | Yes | | Yes | Yes | 30,860 † | 7,000 | 14 | 1070 | Yes | | | None |
| Yes | | | No | | 16,289 † | 2,141 | | 642 | | | | |
| Yes | Yes | | Yes | Yes | 21,210 † | 8,400 | 18 | 840 | Yes | | | None |
| | | | No | | | | | | | | | |
| Yes | | | No | | 16,475 † | 8,828 | 14 | 642 | Yes | | | None |
| Yes | Yes | Yes | Yes | Yes | 26,767 † | 7,952 | 17 | 996 | | | | |
| Yes | Yes | | Yes | Yes | 21,480 † | 10,790 | 12 | 817 | Yes | | | 7/1 |
| Yes | | | Yes | Yes | 21,500 † | 7,950 | 17 | 700 | Yes | | | None |
| Yes | | Yes | Yes | Yes | 15,543 † | 6,784 | | | | | | |
| | | | No | | 16,746 † | 11,144 | 18 | 486 | | | | |
| Yes | | | Yes | Yes | 13,950 † | 5,820 | 6 | | Yes | | | 3/1 |
| Yes | Yes | | Yes | | 27,276 † | 8,180 | 6 | | Yes | 60 | $20,229 | None |
| Yes | | | Yes | | 10,280 † | 8,770 | 8 | 375 | Yes | | | None |
| Yes | Yes | Yes | Yes | Yes | 15,770 † | 7,000 | 18 | 632 | Yes | 106 | $8,966 | None |
| Yes | | | Yes | Yes | 10,880 † | 5,910 | | 436 | Yes | | | None |
| Yes | Yes | Yes | Yes | Yes | 21,050 † | 7,550 | | 855 | Yes | | | None |
| Yes | Yes | | Yes | Yes | 29,756 † | 12,540 | 12 | 1150 | Yes | 96 | $8,201 | None |
| Yes | Yes | Yes | Yes | Yes | | 6,425 | 14 | | Yes | | | None |
| Yes | Yes | Yes | Yes | Yes | 34,196 | 15,144 | 14 | 859 | Yes | | | None |
| Yes | Yes | | Yes | Yes | 31,700 † | 9,750 | 12 | | Yes | | | None |
| Yes | Yes | | Yes | Yes | 26,610 † | 8,850 | | 989 | Yes | 173 | $18,023 | None |
| | | | | | | 6,300 | 12 | | | | | |
| | Yes | | Yes | | 31,450 † | 6,700 | 12 | | Yes | 31 | $22,643 | None |
| | | | | | 11,971 † | | 12 | | | | | |

† Actual for 2016-17.    ‡ Estimated for 2017-18.    * Includes room and board

| Institution | Control/ degrees | Undergraduates | | Tests required (Fall 2017) | TOEFL | | Application | |
|---|---|---|---|---|---|---|---|---|
| | | Total | Internat'l | | minimum | average | Deadline | Fee |
| Nashville State Community College | Pu/A | 7,296 | 51 | | 61 | | | 20 |
| National College: Bartlett | Pr/A | 120 | | | | | | 50 |
| National College: Knoxville | Pr/A | 64 | | | | | | 50 |
| National College: Madison | Pr/A | 94 | | | | | | 50 |
| National College: Memphis | Pr/A | 195 | | | | | | 50 |
| Nossi College of Art | Pr/AB | 256 | | | | | None | 100 |
| O'More College of Design | Pr/B | 159 | | TOEFL | | | | 50 |
| Pellissippi State Community College | Pu/A | 10,325 | | TOEFL | 45 | 55 | | 10 |
| Remington College: Memphis | Pr/AB | 1,361 | | | | | | 50 |
| Remington College: Nashville | Pr/A | 597 | | | | | | 50 |
| Rhodes College | Pr/B | 1,980 | 60 | TOEFL, SAT/ACT | 80 | 96 | | |
| Roane State Community College | Pu/A | 5,832 | | TOEFL | | | | 20 |
| Sewanee: The University of the South | Pr/B | 1,714 | 50 | TOEFL | 90 | 102 | 2/1 | |
| South College | Pr/AB | 1,139 | | TOEFL | | | | 50 |
| Southern Adventist University | Pr/AB | 5,799 | | | 80 | | | 25 |
| Southwest Tennessee Community College | Pu/A | 8,327 | | TOEFL, SAT/ACT | | | None | 30 |
| Tennessee State University | Pu/AB | 6,871 | 747 | TOEFL, SAT/ACT | | | 6/1 | 25 |
| Tennessee Technological University | Pu/B | 9,801 | | TOEFL, SAT/ACT | 57 | | | 30 |
| Tennessee Wesleyan College | Pr/B | 999 | | TOEFL | | | 7/1 | |
| Trevecca Nazarene University | Pr/AB | 1,990 | 48 | TOEFL, SAT/ACT | 61 | | 8/1 | 25 |
| Tusculum College | Pr/AB | 1,585 | 58 | TOEFL, SAT/ACT | 76 | | None | 50 |
| Union University | Pr/AB | 2,106 | 28 | TOEFL, SAT/ACT | | | | 50 |
| University of Memphis | Pu/B | 15,955 | 167 | TOEFL, SAT/ACT | 61 | | | 50 |
| University of Phoenix: Knoxville | Pr/B | 170 | | | | | | |
| University of Phoenix: Memphis | Pr/B | 1,280 | | | | | | |
| University of Phoenix: Nashville | Pr/B | 2,252 | | | | | | |
| University of Tennessee: Chattanooga | Pu/B | 10,058 | 86 | TOEFL | 61 | | | 30 |
| University of Tennessee: Knoxville | Pu/B | 21,984 | 340 | TOEFL | 70 | 77 | 5/15 | 50 |
| University of Tennessee: Martin | Pu/B | 5,576 | 172 | TOEFL | 61 | | | 130 |
| Vanderbilt University | Pr/B | 6,844 | 487 | TOEFL, SAT/ACT | 100 | | 1/1 | 50 |
| Vatterott College: Memphis | Pr/A | 1,020 | | | | | | |
| Virginia College School of Business and Health in Chattanooga | Pr/A | 345 | | | | | | 100 |
| Virginia College School of Business and Health in Knoxville | Pr/AB | 330 | | | | | | |
| Visible Music College | Pr/B | 111 | | TOEFL, SAT/ACT | | | | 40 |
| Volunteer State Community College | Pu/A | 6,973 | 33 | TOEFL, SAT/ACT | 60 | | | |
| Walters State Community College | Pu/A | 5,947 | | TOEFL, SAT/ACT | 61 | 65 | | |
| Watkins College of Art, Design & Film | Pr/B | 238 | | TOEFL, SAT/ACT | 80 | | | 50 |
| Welch College | Pr/AB | 238 | | TOEFL, SAT/ACT | | | | 35 |
| West Tennessee Business College | Pr/A | 211 | | | | | | 50 |
| Williamson College | Pr/AB | 69 | | TOEFL, SAT/ACT | | | | 25 |

**Texas**

| Institution | Control/ degrees | Undergraduates | | Tests required (Fall 2017) | TOEFL | | Application | |
|---|---|---|---|---|---|---|---|---|
| | | Total | Internat'l | | minimum | average | Deadline | Fee |
| Abilene Christian University | Pr/AB | 3,719 | 137 | TOEFL, SAT/ACT | 80 | 85 | 2/15 | 50 |
| Amarillo College | Pu/A | 8,179 | | TOEFL | | | | |
| Angelo State University | Pu/B | 5,781 | 239 | TOEFL | 79 | | | 50 |
| Argosy University: Dallas | Pr/AB | 271 | | | | | | 50 |
| Arlington Baptist College | Pr/B | 185 | | TOEFL | | | | 25 |
| Art Institute of Dallas | Pr/AB | 1,155 | | TOEFL | | | | 50 |
| Art Institute of Houston | Pr/AB | 1,304 | | TOEFL | 61 | | None | |
| Austin College | Pr/B | 1,274 | 37 | TOEFL, SAT/ACT | 80 | 94 | | |
| Austin Community College | Pu/A | 41,543 | | TOEFL | 79 | 79 | | 100 |
| Baptist University of the Americas | Pr/AB | 223 | | | | | | 25 |
| Baylor University | Pr/B | 14,309 | 497 | TOEFL, SAT/ACT | 76 | | 2/1 | |
| Blinn College | Pu/A | 16,851 | 135 | TOEFL | 61 | | | 200 |
| Brazosport College | Pu/AB | 4,173 | | TOEFL | | | | |
| Brookhaven College | Pu/A | 10,226 | | TOEFL | 71 | | | |
| Brown Mackie College: Dallas/Ft Worth | Pr/AB | | | | | | | |

| Adviser | Orientation | ESL | Academic year | Summer | Tuition/fees | Living costs | Maximum credits/summer | Credit hour charge | Available | Number receiving aid | Average award | Deadline |
|---|---|---|---|---|---|---|---|---|---|---|---|---|
| Yes | | Yes | No | | 19,485† | | 12 | | Yes | | | 7/1 |
| | | | | | 14,460† | | | 317 | | | | |
| | | | | | 14,460† | | | 317 | | | | |
| | | | | | 14,460† | | | 317 | | | | |
| | | | | | 14,460† | | | 317 | | | | |
| Yes | Yes | | No | | 17,700‡ | | 12 | | Yes | | | 4/7 |
| Yes | Yes | Yes | | | 28,176† | 7,200 | | 1174 | | | | |
| | | | | | 16,516† | 6,300 | 12 | | | | | |
| Yes | Yes | | Yes | Yes | 44,942† | 11,068 | 12 | 1865 | Yes | | | 3/1 |
| Yes | | | No | | 16,101† | 5,175 | 21 | | Yes | | | None |
| Yes | Yes | | Yes | Yes | 45,120 | 14,880 | 8 | 1425 | Yes | 36 | $36,087 | 12/1 |
| Yes | | | No | | 21,075† | 11,562 | 18 | | Yes | | | |
| Yes | | Yes | Yes | Yes | 21,150† | 6,450 | | 850 | Yes | | | None |
| Yes | Yes | Yes | No | | 16,038† | | | 642 | Yes | | | |
| Yes | Yes | | Yes | Yes | 20,924† | 7,544 | 12 | 789 | | | | |
| Yes | Yes | Yes | Yes | Yes | 25,586† | 8,956 | 16 | 954 | | | | |
| Yes | | | Yes | | 23,800‡ | 7,750 | 18 | 580 | Yes | 990 | $9,707 | None |
| Yes | | | Yes | | 25,100 | 8,808 | | | Yes | 25 | $18,759 | None |
| Yes | | | Yes | | 23,125† | 8,500 | 12 | 718 | Yes | 55 | $20,422 | 2/15 |
| Yes | Yes | | Yes | Yes | 30,330† | 10,200 | 14 | 975 | Yes | 28 | $24,934 | None |
| Yes | Yes | Yes | Yes | Yes | 21,209† | 9,153 | 16 | | Yes | | | 5/1 |
| Yes | Yes | Yes | Yes | Yes | 26,438† | 8,960 | 16 | | Yes | 9 | $5,544 | None |
| Yes | Yes | Yes | Yes | Yes | 30,914† | 10,238 | 12 | 1121 | Yes | 49 | $8,901 | None |
| Yes | Yes | Yes | Yes | Yes | 23,032† | 5,788 | 18 | 875 | Yes | 21 | $26,805 | None |
| Yes | Yes | Yes | Yes | Yes | 46,110† | 14,962 | | 1854 | Yes | 120 | $51,680 | None |
| | | Yes | No | | 19,500† | 5,000 | | 650 | | | | |
| | | | | | 15,701† | 11,755 | 18 | | Yes | 1 | $125 | None |
| Yes | | Yes | No | | 16,464† | 3,600 | 21 | | Yes | | | None |
| | | | Yes | Yes | 23,700† | 6,500 | 9 | 725 | | | | |
| Yes | | | Yes | | 17,920† | 7,260 | 6 | | Yes | | | None |
| | | | No | | | | | | | | | |
| Yes | | Yes | No | | 12,975† | 9,000 | 12 | 425 | Yes | | | None |
| Yes | Yes | Yes | Yes | Yes | 32,070† | 9,730 | 14 | 1334 | Yes | 128 | $10,451 | None |
| | | Yes | Yes | | 5,723† | | | | | | | |
| Yes | Yes | Yes | Yes | Yes | 20,278† | 8,166 | 12 | 573.2 | Yes | 8 | $3,928 | None |
| Yes | | | Yes | Yes | 12,000† | 5,800 | 12 | 335 | Yes | | | None |
| | | | Yes | | 21,960† | | | 488 | Yes | | | None |
| Yes | | | Yes | | 24,024† | 7,320 | | 488 | | | | |
| Yes | Yes | | Yes | | 37,340† | 12,082 | | | Yes | 32 | $19,947 | None |
| Yes | Yes | Yes | No | | 13,080† | 9,280 | 12 | 418 | Yes | | | |
| | | | | | 7,800† | 2,500 | | 230 | | | | |
| Yes | Yes | | Yes | | 43,970‡ | 12,163 | 18 | 1650 | Yes | 400 | $14,568 | None |
| Yes | Yes | Yes | Yes | Yes | 9,330† | 6,250 | 14 | 260 | Yes | | | None |
| Yes | | | No | | 5,145† | | 14 | 150 | Yes | | | None |
| Yes | Yes | Yes | No | | 5,220† | 3,708 | 14 | 200 | | | | |

† Actual for 2016-17.    ‡ Estimated for 2017-18.    * Includes room and board

| Institution | Control/ degrees | Undergraduates | | Tests required (Fall 2017) | TOEFL | | Application | |
|---|---|---|---|---|---|---|---|---|
| | | Total | Internat'l | | minimum | average | Deadline | Fee |
| Brown Mackie College: San Antonio............. | Pr/AB | | | | | | | |
| Cedar Valley College...................... | Pu/A | 7,195 | | | | | | |
| Central Texas College..................... | Pu/A | 10,711 | 37 | TOEFL | 68 | | 7/1 | 500 |
| Chamberlain College of Nursing: Houston ....... | Pr/B | 439 | 4 | | | | | 95 |
| Cisco College............................ | Pu/A | 3,244 | | TOEFL | | | 7/18 | 100 |
| | | | | | | | | |
| Clarendon College........................ | Pu/A | 1,482 | | TOEFL | | | | 200 |
| Coastal Bend College...................... | Pu/A | 5,041 | | TOEFL | 68 | | None | |
| Collin County Community College District........ | Pu/A | 24,894 | 1,125 | TOEFL | 71 | | None | |
| Commonwealth Institute of Funeral Service ...... | Pr/A | 226 | | | | | | 50 |
| Concordia University Texas.................. | Pr/AB | 1,567 | | | 80 | | | 50 |
| | | | | | | | | |
| Criswell College ......................... | Pr/AB | 222 | 2 | TOEFL | | | | 35 |
| Culinary Institute LeNotre.................. | Pr/A | 255 | | | 79 | | None | 50 |
| Dallas Baptist University................... | Pr/AB | 3,109 | 202 | TOEFL | 71 | | None | 25 |
| Del Mar College .......................... | Pu/A | 7,713 | | | | | None | |
| DeVry University: Irving................... | Pr/AB | 403 | 3 | TOEFL | | | | 50 |
| | | | | | | | | |
| East Texas Baptist University................ | Pr/B | 1,218 | 11 | TOEFL | 61 | | 8/29 | 50 |
| Eastfield College......................... | Pu/A | 11,369 | | TOEFL | | | 7/15 | |
| El Centro College ........................ | Pu/A | 10,428 | | TOEFL | | | | |
| Frank Phillips College .................... | Pu/A | 1,350 | | TOEFL | | | | |
| Galveston College........................ | Pu/A | 1,729 | 20 | TOEFL | | | | 30 |
| | | | | | | | | |
| Golf Academy of America: Dallas ............ | Pr/A | 80 | | | | | | |
| Grayson College ......................... | Pu/A | 4,400 | | TOEFL | | | | |
| Hardin-Simmons University................. | Pr/B | 1,621 | 20 | TOEFL | 79 | 107 | | |
| Hill College ............................ | Pu/A | 4,098 | | TOEFL | | | | 50 |
| Houston Baptist University ................. | Pr/B | 2,313 | 80 | TOEFL | 80 | | 6/1 | 25 |
| | | | | | | | | |
| Houston Community College System........... | Pu/A | 56,846 | 6,474 | | | | 7/1 | 75 |
| Howard Payne University .................. | Pr/AB | 1,099 | | TOEFL | 79 | | 6/1 | |
| Huston-Tillotson University................. | Pr/AB | | | TOEFL | 61 | | | 75 |
| International Academy of Design and | | | | | | | | |
| Technology: San Antonio ................. | Pr/AB | 450 | | | | | | 50 |
| Jacksonville College....................... | Pr/A | 304 | | TOEFL | 40 | | 6/1 | 100 |
| | | | | | | | | |
| Jarvis Christian College ................... | Pr/B | 863 | | | | | | 50 |
| Kilgore College........................... | Pu/A | 5,666 | | | | | | |
| The King's University ..................... | Pr/AB | 473 | | TOEFL | | | | 75 |
| Lamar Institute of Technology ............... | Pu/A | 2,739 | | TOEFL | 61 | | 7/1 | |
| Lamar State College at Orange............... | Pu/A | 2,338 | | TOEFL | | | | |
| | | | | | | | | |
| Lamar State College at Port Arthur ........... | Pu/A | 2,051 | | TOEFL | | | None | |
| Lamar University.......................... | Pu/B | 9,079 | 120 | TOEFL, SAT/ACT | 79 | | | 75 |
| Laredo Community College.................. | Pu/A | 8,307 | | TOEFL | | | | |
| Le Cordon Bleu College of Culinary Arts: | | | | | | | | |
| Austin ............................... | Pr/A | 643 | | | | | | 50 |
| Lee College ............................. | Pu/A | 6,817 | | TOEFL | | | | 50 |
| | | | | | | | | |
| LeTourneau University..................... | Pr/AB | 1,823 | 63 | TOEFL | 80 | | None | |
| Lincoln College of Technology: Grand Prairie...... | Pr/A | 947 | | | | | | 100 |
| Lone Star College System................... | Pu/A | 85,661 | | | | | | |
| Lubbock Christian University................ | Pr/AB | 1,471 | 23 | TOEFL, SAT/ACT | 71 | | | 25 |
| McLennan Community College .............. | Pu/A | 8,609 | | TOEFL | | | None | 50 |
| | | | | | | | | |
| McMurry University....................... | Pr/B | 1,016 | 70 | TOEFL, SAT/ACT | 79 | | 3/1 | 50 |
| Midland College .......................... | Pu/AB | 5,644 | | TOEFL | 70 | | | 20 |
| Midwestern State University ................ | Pu/AB | 5,307 | 454 | TOEFL, SAT/ACT | 79 | | | 50 |
| Mountain View College .................... | Pu/A | 9,889 | | TOEFL | | | 7/31 | |
| National American University: Austin .......... | Pr/AB | 207 | | | | | | |
| | | | | | | | | |
| Navarro College ......................... | Pu/A | 9,230 | | TOEFL | 61 | | | 60 |
| North Central Texas College ................ | Pu/A | 9,618 | | TOEFL | | | | |
| North Lake College ....................... | Pu/A | 8,694 | | TOEFL | | | | |
| Northeast Texas Community College........... | Pu/A | 3,037 | | TOEFL | | | | |
| Northwest Vista College ................... | Pu/A | 13,221 | | | | | | |
| | | | | | | | | |
| Northwood University: Texas................. | Pr/B | 209 | | TOEFL | | | | 25 |

| Student services | | | Housing | | Academic year costs | | Maximum credits/ summer | Credit hour charge | International financial aid | | | |
|---|---|---|---|---|---|---|---|---|---|---|---|---|
| Adviser | Orien- tation | ESL | Academic year | Summer | Tuition/ fees | Living costs | | | Avail- able | Number receiving aid | Average award | Deadline |
| Yes | | | No | | 5,220† | 7,154 | 15 | 200 | | | | |
| Yes | Yes | Yes | Yes | Yes | 6,420† | 4,800 | 12 | 214 | | | | |
| | | | | | 19,500† | | | 675 | | | | |
| Yes | | | Yes | | 4,920† | 4,236 | | 164 | | | | |
| | | Yes | Yes | | 4,650† | 4,176 | 12 | | Yes | | | None |
| Yes | | | Yes | | 4,956† | 5,200 | 16 | 147 | | | | |
| Yes | Yes | Yes | No | | 4,284 | 9,683 | 14 | 142 | | | | |
| | | | No | | 15,620† | | 20 | | | | | |
| Yes | | | Yes | | 30,600 | 10,406 | 18 | 970 | Yes | 14 | $15,086 | None |
| Yes | | | Yes | | 12,138 | | 9 | 380 | Yes | | | 4/15 |
| Yes | | | No | | 15,828† | | | 11988 | | | | |
| Yes | Yes | Yes | Yes | Yes | 27,480 | 7,740 | 18 | 886 | Yes | 123 | $6,267 | None |
| | | Yes | No | | 5,700 | | 18 | 148 | | | | |
| Yes | | | | | 17,512† | | | 609 | | | | |
| Yes | Yes | Yes | Yes | Yes | 25,470 | 8,915 | 21 | 814 | Yes | 11 | $9,761 | None |
| Yes | | | No | | 5,220† | 7,154 | 14 | 200 | Yes | | | None |
| Yes | Yes | Yes | No | | 5,220† | 7,408 | 14 | 200 | Yes | | | None |
| Yes | | | Yes | | 3,850† | 5,040 | | | | | | |
| Yes | | | No | | 4,270† | 5,754 | 16 | | | | | |
| | | | | | 17,250† | | | | | | | |
| Yes | Yes | Yes | Yes | | 4,830† | 5,560 | | 133 | Yes | | | None |
| Yes | | | Yes | Yes | 27,440 | 8,420 | 12 | | Yes | 35 | $8,854 | None |
| Yes | | | Yes | | 3,520† | 3,850 | 12 | | Yes | | | 7/31 |
| Yes | Yes | | Yes | Yes | 30,800† | 7,858 | 12 | 1200 | Yes | 68 | $20,689 | None |
| Yes | Yes | Yes | No | | 4,686† | 5,800 | | | Yes | | | None |
| | | | Yes | | 27,690‡ | 8,304 | 14 | 820 | Yes | | | None |
| Yes | | | | | 14,346† | 7,568 | 9 | 410 | Yes | | | None |
| Yes | | | Yes | | 7,900† | 6,400 | 15 | 210 | | | | |
| Yes | | | Yes | | 11,720† | 12,225 | 3 | 435 | Yes | | | None |
| Yes | Yes | Yes | Yes | Yes | 5,700† | 4,710 | 14 | 160 | Yes | | | 7/1 |
| | | | No | | 13,350† | 11,717 | 15 | 415 | Yes | | | None |
| Yes | Yes | Yes | Yes | | 17,680† | | | 540 | | | | |
| | | | No | | 17,255† | 3,500 | 18 | 538 | | | | |
| Yes | | | | | 17,938† | 8,370 | | 540 | | | | |
| Yes | Yes | Yes | Yes | Yes | 22,141† | 10,256 | 12 | 644 | Yes | | | None |
| Yes | | Yes | Yes | | 7,140† | | 14 | 200 | | | | |
| Yes | | | No | | 4,368† | 7,328 | | 127 | Yes | | | None |
| Yes | Yes | Yes | Yes | | 28,480† | 9,770 | | | Yes | 53 | $10,752 | None |
| Yes | Yes | Yes | No | | 4,506‡ | | 12 | | Yes | | | None |
| Yes | | | Yes | | 21,166† | 6,250 | 12 | 685 | Yes | 23 | $13,184 | None |
| Yes | Yes | | Yes | | 5,700† | 7,065 | 14 | 181 | | | | |
| | | | Yes | Yes | 26,100† | 9,744 | 14 | 815 | Yes | 4 | $15,867 | None |
| Yes | | Yes | Yes | | 5,280† | 4,800 | 14 | 456 | Yes | | | 6/1 |
| Yes | Yes | Yes | Yes | Yes | 20,534† | 7,440 | 18 | 581.85 | Yes | | | None |
| Yes | | Yes | No | | 5,220† | | | 200 | Yes | | | None |
| | | | | | 17,685† | | | 373 | | | | |
| Yes | Yes | | Yes | Yes | 5,400 | 5,618 | 14 | | | | | |
| Yes | | | Yes | Yes | 6,000† | 3,928 | 12 | 174 | | | | |
| Yes | Yes | Yes | No | | 5,220† | 7,154 | 14 | 200 | Yes | | | 5/1 |
| | | | Yes | | 5,980† | 6,100. | 14 | 148 | | | | |
| | | | No | | 11,274† | | | | Yes | | | None |
| Yes | Yes | | | Yes | 25,130† | 9,880 | 18 | 918 | Yes | | | None |

† Actual for 2016-17.  ‡ Estimated for 2017-18.  * Includes room and board

| Institution | Control/ degrees | Undergraduates | | Tests required (Fall 2017) | TOEFL | | Application | |
|---|---|---|---|---|---|---|---|---|
| | | Total | Internat'l | | minimum | average | Deadline | Fee |
| Odessa College . . . . . . . . . . . . . . . . . . . .Pu/A | | 6,186 | 45 | TOEFL | 70 | | 6/1 | 50 |
| Our Lady of the Lake University of San Antonio . . . . . . . . . . . . . . . . . . . . . . . . .Pr/B | | 1,326 | 13 | TOEFL | 71 | 80 | | 50 |
| Panola College . . . . . . . . . . . . . . . . . . . .Pu/A | | 2,667 | 65 | TOEFL | 71 | | 6/1 | 50 |
| Paris Junior College . . . . . . . . . . . . . . . . .Pu/A | | 4,806 | | TOEFL | | | 8/1 | |
| Paul Quinn College . . . . . . . . . . . . . . . . .Pr/B | | 424 | | TOEFL, SAT/ACT | | | | |
| Prairie View A&M University . . . . . . . . . . . . . . .Pu/B | | 7,417 | 116 | TOEFL, SAT/ACT | 79 | | 5/1 | 50 |
| Ranger College . . . . . . . . . . . . . . . . . . . . . . . .Pu/A | | 2,047 | 60 | TOEFL | 34 | | | 100 |
| Remington College: Dallas . . . . . . . . . . .Pr/AB | | 1,561 | | | | | | 50 |
| Remington College: Fort Worth . . . . . . . . . . . . . .Pr/AB | | 746 | | | | | | 50 |
| Remington College: Greenspoint Campus . . . . . . . . .Pr/AB | | 868 | | | | | | 50 |
| Remington College: Webster Campus . . . . . . . . . . .Pr/A | | 509 | | | | | | 50 |
| Remington College: Westchase Campus . . . . . . . . . .Pr/A | | 609 | | | | | | 50 |
| Rice University . . . . . . . . . . . . . . . . . . . . . .Pr/B | | 3,879 | 471 | TOEFL, SAT, SAT Subject Test(s), or ACT | 100 | | 1/1 | 75 |
| Richland College . . . . . . . . . . . . . . . . . . . . . . .Pu/A | | 14,546 | | TOEFL | | | | |
| St. Edward's University . . . . . . . . . . . . . . . . . . .Pr/B | | 4,050 | 320 | TOEFL | 61 | | 5/1 | 50 |
| St. Mary's University . . . . . . . . . . . . . . . . . . . . .Pr/B | | 2,268 | 198 | TOEFL | 80 | | None | |
| St. Philip's College . . . . . . . . . . . . . . . . . . .Pu/A | | 11,604 | | TOEFL | 61 | | | 100 |
| Sam Houston State University . . . . . . . . . . . . . . . .Pu/B | | 17,902 | 210 | TOEFL | 79 | | | 75 |
| San Antonio College . . . . . . . . . . . . . . . . . . . . .Pu/A | | 20,420 | | | | | | 15 |
| San Jacinto College . . . . . . . . . . . . . . . . . . . . . .Pu/A | | 24,153 | 485 | TOEFL | 45 | 78 | None | |
| Schreiner University . . . . . . . . . . . . . . . . . . . . . .Pr/AB | | 1,181 | 11 | TOEFL, SAT/ACT | 79 | | 8/1 | 25 |
| South Plains College . . . . . . . . . . . . . . . . . . . . .Pu/A | | 7,639 | 76 | TOEFL | 79 | 82 | 5/18 | 100 |
| South Texas College . . . . . . . . . . . . . . . . . . . . .Pu/AB | | 33,923 | 3 | TOEFL | 61 | 80 | | |
| Southern Methodist University . . . . . . . . . . . . . . . .Pr/B | | 6,487 | 532 | TOEFL | 80 | | None | 60 |
| Southwest Texas Junior College . . . . . . . . . . . . . .Pu/A | | 6,439 | | | | | | |
| Southwestern Adventist University . . . . . . . . . . . . .Pr/AB | | 716 | 47 | TOEFL | 75 | 80 | 5/1 | 25 |
| Southwestern Assemblies of God University . . . . . . . .Pr/AB | | 1,656 | | TOEFL | | | | 35 |
| Southwestern Baptist Theological Seminary . . . . . .Pr/B | | 589 | | TOEFL | 79 | | | 35 |
| Southwestern Christian College . . . . . . . . . . . . . .Pr/AB | | 143 | | | | | | 20 |
| Southwestern University . . . . . . . . . . . . . . . . . . .Pr/B | | 1,477 | 26 | TOEFL | 88 | | | |
| Stephen F. Austin State University . . . . . . . . . . . .Pu/B | | 10,765 | | TOEFL | 79 | | 6/1 | 50 |
| Sul Ross State University . . . . . . . . . . . . . . . . . .Pu/B | | 1,359 | | TOEFL, SAT/ACT | | | | 50 |
| Tarleton State University . . . . . . . . . . . . . . . . . . .Pu/AB | | 11,282 | 30 | TOEFL, SAT/ACT | 69 | | 5/31 | 130 |
| Tarrant County College . . . . . . . . . . . . . . . . . . . .Pu/A | | 52,521 | | | 71 | | 7/15 | |
| Texas A&M International University . . . . . . . . . . .Pu/B | | 6,566 | 103 | TOEFL, SAT/ACT | 69 | | 6/1 | |
| Texas A&M University . . . . . . . . . . . . . . . . . . . .Pu/B | | 50,392 | 630 | TOEFL | 100 | | 12/1 | 90 |
| Texas A&M University-Commerce . . . . . . . . . . . .Pu/B | | 6,797 | 128 | TOEFL, SAT/ACT | 79 | | | |
| Texas A&M University-Corpus Christi . . . . . . . . . .Pu/B | | 10,205 | 247 | TOEFL, SAT/ACT | 80 | | 6/1 | 75 |
| Texas A&M University-Kingsville . . . . . . . . . . . . .Pu/B | | 5,845 | 192 | | 61 | | | 50 |
| Texas A&M University-Texarkana . . . . . . . . . . . .Pu/B | | 1,561 | 58 | TOEFL, SAT/ACT | 79 | | None | 50 |
| Texas Christian University . . . . . . . . . . . . . . . . . .Pr/B | | 8,852 | 403 | TOEFL | 80 | | 2/15 | 50 |
| Texas College . . . . . . . . . . . . . . . . . . . . . . . . . .Pr/AB | | 813 | | TOEFL | | | | 20 |
| Texas Lutheran University . . . . . . . . . . . . . . . . . . .Pr/B | | 1,252 | 6 | TOEFL | | 89 | | 300 |
| Texas Southern University . . . . . . . . . . . . . . . . . .Pu/B | | 6,562 | 641 | TOEFL, SAT/ACT | 61 | | 4/30 | 78 |
| Texas State Technical College . . . . . . . . . . . . . . .Pu/A | | 9,184 | | TOEFL | | | | |
| Texas State University . . . . . . . . . . . . . . . . . . . . .Pu/B | | 34,244 | 187 | TOEFL | 78 | | 3/1 | 150 |
| Texas Tech University . . . . . . . . . . . . . . . . . . . . .Pu/B | | 29,587 | 1,477 | TOEFL, SAT/ACT | 79 | | 5/1 | 60 |
| Texas Tech University Health Sciences Center . . . . .Pu/B | | 1,221 | | | | | | 40 |
| Texas Wesleyan University . . . . . . . . . . . . . . . . .Pr/B | | 1,685 | 272 | TOEFL | 68 | | | |
| Texas Woman's University . . . . . . . . . . . . . . . . .Pu/B | | 9,513 | 59 | TOEFL | 79 | | | 75 |
| Trinity University . . . . . . . . . . . . . . . . . . . . . . . .Pr/B | | 2,317 | 157 | TOEFL, SAT/ACT | 100 | | 2/1 | |
| Trinity Valley Community College . . . . . . . . . . . . .Pu/A | | 6,508 | 56 | TOEFL | | | | 80 |
| University of Dallas . . . . . . . . . . . . . . . . . . . . . . .Pr/B | | 1,393 | 42 | TOEFL | 79 | 96 | 7/1 | 50 |
| University of Houston . . . . . . . . . . . . . . . . . . . . . .Pu/B | | 34,688 | 1,522 | TOEFL | 79 | 96 | | 90 |
| University of Houston-Clear Lake . . . . . . . . . . . . .Pu/B | | 5,557 | 92 | TOEFL, SAT/ACT | 79 | | | 75 |
| University of Houston-Downtown . . . . . . . . . . . . .Pu/B | | 12,758 | 648 | TOEFL | 80 | | | 60 |
| University of Houston-Victoria . . . . . . . . . . . . . . .Pu/B | | 3,012 | | TOEFL | 79 | | | |

| Student services | | | Housing | | Academic year costs | | Maximum credits/ summer | Credit hour charge | International financial aid | | | |
|---|---|---|---|---|---|---|---|---|---|---|---|---|
| Adviser | Orientation | ESL | Academic year | Summer | Tuition/ fees | Living costs | | | Available | Number receiving aid | Average award | Deadline |
| Yes | | Yes | Yes | Yes | 5,440‡ | 6,927 | 16 | | Yes | | | None |
| Yes | Yes | | Yes | Yes | 27,140† | 7,872 | | 843 | Yes | 16 | $18,950 | None |
| Yes | | | Yes | | 4,770 | 4,888 | | 200 | Yes | | | None |
| Yes | Yes | | Yes | Yes | 5,100† | 5,550 | | 150 | | | | |
| | | | Yes | Yes | 8,275† | 6,000 | 9 | 240.63 | Yes | | | None |
| Yes | Yes | | Yes | | 23,378† | 8,626 | 12 | 684.45 | Yes | | | 3/15 |
| Yes | | | Yes | | 4,860† | 6,800 | 12 | 130 | Yes | | | None |
| | | | No | | | | | | | | | |
| Yes | Yes | Yes | Yes | | 43,918† | 13,750 | 12 | 1801 | Yes | 94 | $28,606 | 3/1 |
| Yes | Yes | Yes | No | | 5,220† | 7,154 | 15 | 200 | Yes | | | None |
| Yes | Yes | | Yes | | 40,828† | 12,172 | 15 | 1348 | Yes | 122 | $18,937 | None |
| Yes | Yes | Yes | Yes | Yes | 28,200† | 9,300 | 12 | 855 | Yes | 25 | $26,330 | None |
| Yes | | | No | | 13,670‡ | 8,190 | 14 | | | | | |
| Yes | | | Yes | | 21,756† | 8,986 | | 623.5 | Yes | 75 | $12,401 | None |
| Yes | Yes | Yes | No | | 11,274† | | 18 | | Yes | | | 5/1 |
| Yes | Yes | Yes | No | | 5,100† | | 14 | 160 | Yes | | | None |
| Yes | | | Yes | Yes | 26,750 | 10,152 | 6 | 1069 | Yes | | | None |
| Yes | | | Yes | Yes | 4,562† | 3,900 | 14 | | | | | |
| Yes | | | No | | 7,230† | 3,750 | | | Yes | | | None |
| Yes | Yes | Yes | Yes | Yes | 50,358† | 16,125 | 18 | 1867 | Yes | 201 | $27,784 | None |
| Yes | | | Yes | | 5,678† | 4,660 | | 155 | Yes | | | None |
| Yes | Yes | Yes | Yes | Yes | 20,276† | 7,500 | 12 | 819 | Yes | | | None |
| Yes | | | Yes | Yes | 20,410‡ | 7,060 | 12 | 695 | Yes | | | None |
| Yes | Yes | | Yes | Yes | 11,700 | 1,890 | | 370 | | | | |
| Yes | | | Yes | | 8,074 | 5,600 | | 310 | Yes | | | 6/1 |
| Yes | Yes | | Yes | | 40,560 | 11,170 | | 1690 | Yes | | | 3/1 |
| Yes | | Yes | Yes | Yes | 21,777† | 8,868 | 12 | 650 | Yes | 129 | $1,249 | None |
| | | | Yes | Yes | 20,056† | 9,488 | 14 | | Yes | | | None |
| Yes | Yes | | Yes | | 20,886 | 10,050 | 12 | 561.97 | | | | |
| Yes | Yes | | No | | 7,650† | 8,910 | 14 | 255 | Yes | | | None |
| Yes | Yes | Yes | Yes | Yes | 20,879† | 12,727 | 12 | 567.1 | Yes | | | None |
| Yes | Yes | Yes | Yes | Yes | 30,208‡ | 10,998 | 12 | 895 | Yes | 230 | $22,063 | None |
| Yes | Yes | Yes | Yes | Yes | 20,138† | 8,326 | 14 | 550 | Yes | 100 | $11,157 | None |
| Yes | | | Yes | Yes | 21,193† | 9,874 | 12 | 578.24 | Yes | 207 | $3,026 | |
| | Yes | Yes | Yes | Yes | 21,356† | 8,530 | 12 | | Yes | 89 | $6,584 | None |
| | | Yes | Yes | Yes | 20,616† | 8,105 | 12 | | | | | |
| Yes | Yes | Yes | Yes | Yes | 44,760 | 12,360 | 15 | | Yes | 256 | $34,237 | 5/1 |
| Yes | | | Yes | | 10,008† | 8,000 | 6 | | Yes | | | None |
| Yes | Yes | | Yes | Yes | 29,960 | 12,090 | 14 | 980 | Yes | | | None |
| Yes | Yes | Yes | Yes | Yes | 21,241† | 10,566 | 12 | | Yes | | | None |
| | | | Yes | Yes | 10,080† | 6,420 | | | | | | |
| Yes | Yes | Yes | Yes | Yes | 22,458† | 9,132 | 12 | 666 | Yes | 81 | $12,861 | None |
| Yes | Yes | | Yes | Yes | 21,481† | 8,505 | 16 | 625 | Yes | | | None |
| | | | No | | 21,286† | 9,964 | | | Yes | | | None |
| Yes | Yes | | Yes | | 26,049† | 9,084 | 12 | 780 | | | | |
| Yes | Yes | | Yes | Yes | 21,010† | 8,282 | 16 | 614.26 | Yes | | | None |
| Yes | Yes | | Yes | | 39,560† | 12,754 | | 1624 | Yes | 139 | $22,472 | None |
| Yes | Yes | Yes | Yes | Yes | 4,920‡ | 5,650 | 12 | 118 | Yes | | | 7/1 |
| Yes | Yes | Yes | Yes | | 38,716 | 11,960 | | | Yes | 37 | $11,889 | 8/1 |
| Yes | Yes | | Yes | | 26,126† | | 9 | 819 | Yes | 238 | $3,289 | None |
| Yes | Yes | | Yes | Yes | 22,055† | 9,588 | | 710 | Yes | 49 | $4,675 | None |
| Yes | Yes | Yes | No | | 19,421† | 8,532 | 12 | 609 | Yes | 34 | $2,441 | None |
| Yes | | | Yes | | 19,610† | 7,664 | | 599 | Yes | | | None |

† Actual for 2016-17.      ‡ Estimated for 2017-18.      * Includes room and board

| Institution | Control/ degrees | Undergraduates | | Tests required (Fall 2017) | TOEFL | | Application | |
|---|---|---|---|---|---|---|---|---|
| | | Total | Internat'l | | minimum | average | Deadline | Fee |
| University of the Incarnate Word . . . . . . . . . . . . . | Pr/AB | 6,239 | 344 | TOEFL | 79 | | None | 20 |
| University of Mary Hardin-Baylor. . . . . . . . . . . . . | Pr/B | 3,217 | 40 | TOEFL | 86 | | | 135 |
| University of North Texas. . . . . . . . . . . . . . . . . . | Pu/B | 31,209 | 1,002 | TOEFL | 79 | 89 | | 85 |
| University of North Texas at Dallas. . . . . . . . . . . . | | 1,927 | | | | | | 40 |
| University of Phoenix: Austin . . . . . . . . . . . . . . . | Pr/B | 660 | | | | | | |
| University of Phoenix: Dallas Fort Worth . . . . . . . . | Pr/B | 1,240 | | | | | | |
| University of Phoenix: Houston Westside . . . . . . . . | Pr/B | 4,486 | | | | | | |
| University of Phoenix: San Antonio. . . . . . . . . . . | Pr/B | 930 | | | | | | |
| University of St. Thomas . . . . . . . . . . . . . . . . . . | Pr/B | 1,750 | 157 | TOEFL | 79 | 93 | None | |
| University of Texas at Arlington. . . . . . . . . . . . . . | Pu/B | 30,633 | | TOEFL, SAT/ACT | 79 | | | 60 |
| University of Texas at Austin. . . . . . . . . . . . . . . . | Pu/B | 39,676 | 2,042 | TOEFL, SAT/ACT | 79 | | | 90 |
| University of Texas at Dallas. . . . . . . . . . . . . . . . | Pu/B | 17,059 | 624 | TOEFL, SAT/ACT | 80 | 97 | 5/1 | 100 |
| University of Texas at El Paso . . . . . . . . . . . . . . . | Pu/B | 20,376 | 1,067 | TOEFL | 61 | | | 65 |
| University of Texas at San Antonio. . . . . . . . . . . . | Pu/B | 24,036 | 599 | TOEFL | 79 | | | 60 |
| University of Texas at Tyler . . . . . . . . . . . . . . . . | Pu/B | 6,318 | | TOEFL, SAT/ACT | | | | 75 |
| University of Texas Health Science Center at Houston. . . . . . . . . . . . . . . . . . . . . . . . . . . . . | Pu/B | 677 | | TOEFL | | | | 10 |
| University of Texas Medical Branch at Galveston. . . . . . . . . . . . . . . . . . . . . . . . . . . . . | Pu/B | 738 | 18 | TOEFL | | | | 50 |
| University of Texas of the Permian Basin. . . . . . . . | Pu/B | 3,642 | 97 | TOEFL, SAT/ACT | 79 | | 7/15 | 40 |
| University Of Texas Rio Grande Valley . . . . . . . . . | Pu/B | 24,140 | | TOEFL, SAT/ACT | 61 | | 2/1 | 50 |
| Vet Tech Institute of Houston . . . . . . . . . . . . . . . | Pr/A | 260 | | | | | | 50 |
| Victoria College . . . . . . . . . . . . . . . . . . . . . . . | Pu/A | 3,264 | | TOEFL | 61 | 70 | None | |
| Virginia College in Austin. . . . . . . . . . . . . . . . . . | Pr/A | 569 | | | | | | 100 |
| Wade College. . . . . . . . . . . . . . . . . . . . . . . . . . | Pr/AB | 250 | | TOEFL | | | | 25 |
| Wayland Baptist University . . . . . . . . . . . . . . . . | Pr/AB | 3,567 | 54 | TOEFL, SAT/ACT | 61 | | 8/1 | 35 |
| Weatherford College. . . . . . . . . . . . . . . . . . . . . | Pu/A | 5,637 | | TOEFL | | | | 50 |
| West Texas A&M University . . . . . . . . . . . . . . . . | Pu/B | 7,384 | 135 | TOEFL, SAT/ACT | 71 | | 5/1 | 75 |
| Western Technical College . . . . . . . . . . . . . . . . . | Pr/A | 862 | | | | | | 100 |
| Western Technical College: Diana Drive . . . . . . . . | Pr/A | 456 | | | | | | 100 |
| Western Texas College . . . . . . . . . . . . . . . . . . . | Pu/A | 998 | | TOEFL | 71 | | | 25 |
| Wharton County Junior College . . . . . . . . . . . . . | Pu/A | 7,072 | 1 | TOEFL | 75 | | 7/15 | |
| Wiley College. . . . . . . . . . . . . . . . . . . . . . . . . . | Pr/AB | 1,172 | | TOEFL, SAT/ACT | 61 | | | 83 |
| **Utah** | | | | | | | | |
| Argosy University: Salt Lake City. . . . . . . . . . . . . | Pr/AB | 97 | | | | | | 50 |
| Brigham Young University . . . . . . . . . . . . . . . . . | Pr/B | 30,979 | | TOEFL, SAT/ACT | 80 | 96 | | 35 |
| Broadview Entertainment Arts University . . . . . . . . | Pr/AB | 151 | | | | | | 50 |
| Broadview University: Layton . . . . . . . . . . . . . . . | Pr/AB | 163 | | | | | | 50 |
| Broadview University: Orem . . . . . . . . . . . . . . . . | Pr/AB | 124 | | | | | | 50 |
| Careers Unlimited . . . . . . . . . . . . . . . . . . . . . . | Pr/B | 118 | | | | | | 50 |
| Dixie State University. . . . . . . . . . . . . . . . . . . . . | Pu/AB | 7,432 | 152 | TOEFL | 61 | | | 75 |
| Eagle Gate College: Layton . . . . . . . . . . . . . . . . | Pr/AB | 241 | | | | | | |
| Eagle Gate College: Murray. . . . . . . . . . . . . . . . . | Pr/AB | 290 | | | | | | |
| Independence University . . . . . . . . . . . . . . . . . . | Pr/AB | 1,280 | | TOEFL | | | | |
| Neumont University . . . . . . . . . . . . . . . . . . . . . | Pr/B | 441 | | TOEFL | 79 | | | 125 |
| Provo College. . . . . . . . . . . . . . . . . . . . . . . . . . | Pr/A | 372 | | | | | | |
| Salt Lake Community College . . . . . . . . . . . . . . . | Pu/A | 21,830 | | TOEFL | | | | 75 |
| Snow College . . . . . . . . . . . . . . . . . . . . . . . . . | Pu/AB | 5,350 | 110 | TOEFL | | | | 50 |
| Southern Utah University . . . . . . . . . . . . . . . . . . | Pu/AB | 6,353 | 278 | TOEFL | 71 | | 7/1 | 55 |
| Stevens-Henager College: Logan. . . . . . . . . . . . . | Pr/AB | 140 | | | | | | |
| Stevens-Henager College: Murray . . . . . . . . . . . . | Pr/AB | 2,541 | | | | | | |
| Stevens-Henager College: Ogden . . . . . . . . . . . . | Pr/AB | 320 | | | | | | |
| Stevens-Henager College: Orem . . . . . . . . . . . . . | Pr/AB | 136 | | TOEFL, SAT/ACT | | | | 50 |
| University of Phoenix: Utah. . . . . . . . . . . . . . . . . | Pr/B | 919 | | TOEFL | | | | |
| University of Utah. . . . . . . . . . . . . . . . . . . . . . . | Pu/B | 22,748 | 1,027 | TOEFL | 80 | | 4/1 | 55 |
| Utah State University . . . . . . . . . . . . . . . . . . . . . | Pu/AB | 21,833 | 278 | TOEFL | 71 | | 6/1 | 50 |
| Utah Valley University . . . . . . . . . . . . . . . . . . . . | Pu/AB | 26,571 | 641 | TOEFL, SAT/ACT | 61 | | | 100 |
| Vista College: Online . . . . . . . . . . . . . . . . . . . . . | Pr/A | 207 | | | | | | 100 |

| Student services | | | Housing | | Academic year costs | | Maximum credits/ summer | Credit hour charge | International financial aid | | | |
|---|---|---|---|---|---|---|---|---|---|---|---|---|
| Adviser | Orientation | ESL | Academic year | Summer | Tuition/ fees | Living costs | | | Available | Number receiving aid | Average award | Deadline |
| Yes | Yes | Yes | Yes | Yes | 29,990‡ | 12,436 | | | Yes | 374 | $6,102 | None |
| Yes | Yes | Yes | Yes | Yes | 27,700 | 8,592 | 12 | 845 | Yes | 22 | $1,762 | None |
| Yes | Yes | Yes | Yes | Yes | 23,355 | 9,406 | | 695 | | | | |
| | | | | | 20,088 | | | 696 | | | | |
| Yes | Yes | Yes | Yes | Yes | 32,100† | 8,500 | 12 | 1038 | Yes | 98 | $13,873 | None |
| Yes | Yes | Yes | Yes | Yes | 23,046† | 8,410 | 14 | | Yes | | | None |
| Yes | Yes | Yes | Yes | Yes | 35,906† | 11,456 | | | Yes | 498 | $7,903 | None |
| Yes | Yes | Yes | Yes | | 33,654† | 10,668 | 12 | 1122 | Yes | 176 | $10,534 | 4/12 |
| Yes | Yes | Yes | Yes | Yes | 20,329† | 4,815 | 9 | 625 | Yes | | | None |
| Yes | Yes | Yes | Yes | Yes | 22,290† | 8,074 | 15 | 652 | Yes | 223 | $4,780 | None |
| Yes | Yes | | Yes | Yes | 20,032† | 9,970 | 15 | 458 | Yes | | | None |
| Yes | Yes | | Yes | | 25,986† | | | | Yes | | | None |
| Yes | | | Yes | Yes | 20,735† | | | 677 | | | | |
| Yes | | Yes | Yes | Yes | 19,540† | 14,600 | 18 | 602.6 | Yes | 79 | $4,437 | None |
| Yes | Yes | | Yes | | 19,688† | 7,950 | | 769 | Yes | | | None |
| Yes | | | No | | 4,650† | 8,236 | 16 | 200 | | | | |
| Yes | | | No | | 16,175† | | | 535 | | | | |
| Yes | | | Yes | Yes | 19,110† | 8,896 | 12 | 595 | Yes | 47 | $15,496 | None |
| Yes | Yes | | Yes | Yes | 5,280† | 7,430 | 12 | | | | | |
| Yes | Yes | Yes | Yes | Yes | 21,173† | 7,196 | 12 | 603.82 | Yes | | | None |
| | | | | | | 5,479 | | | Yes | | | None |
| | | | | | | 5,479 | | | | | | |
| Yes | | Yes | Yes | Yes | 5,820† | 8,600 | 10 | | Yes | | | None |
| Yes | | | Yes | | 5,880† | 4,100 | 14 | | | | | |
| Yes | | Yes | Yes | | 12,064† | 7,194 | 9 | 324 | Yes | | | 4/15 |
| Yes | Yes | Yes | Yes | | 5,300† | 7,448 | | 276 | Yes | 466 | $6,044 | None |
| | | | No | | 14,625† | 9,531 | | | | | | |
| | | | No | | 14,625† | 9,531 | | | | | | |
| | | | No | | 14,625† | 9,531 | | | | | | |
| | | | No | | | | | | | | | |
| Yes | Yes | Yes | Yes | Yes | 13,855† | 6,098 | 12 | 547 | | | | |
| Yes | | | No | | | | | | | | | |
| Yes | | | Yes | Yes | 24,450† | 5,670 | | 495 | | | | |
| | | | | | | 5,700 | | | | | | |
| Yes | Yes | Yes | No | | 11,728† | | 18 | | | | | |
| Yes | Yes | Yes | Yes | Yes | 12,071† | 3,670 | 18 | | Yes | | | 6/1 |
| Yes | | Yes | Yes | | 20,770† | 7,067 | | 667 | Yes | | | None |
| Yes | | | No | | | | | | | | | |
| | | | | Yes | | | | | | | | |
| Yes | Yes | | | Yes | | 7,688 | | | Yes | | | None |
| Yes | Yes | Yes | Yes | Yes | 27,039† | 9,406 | | 715.48 | Yes | | | None |
| Yes | Yes | Yes | Yes | Yes | 19,772† | 5,870 | 18 | | | | | |
| Yes | Yes | Yes | No | | 15,690† | 5,960 | | | Yes | 135 | $6,329 | None |

† Actual for 2016-17.     ‡ Estimated for 2017-18.     * Includes room and board

| Institution | Control/ degrees | Undergraduates | | Tests required (Fall 2017) | TOEFL | | Application | |
|---|---|---|---|---|---|---|---|---|
| | | Total | Internat'l | | minimum | average | Deadline | Fee |
| Weber State University . . . . . . . . . . . . . . . . . . . . | Pu/AB | 25,335 | | | | | | 65 |
| Westminster College . . . . . . . . . . . . . . . . . . . . . | Pr/B | 2,095 | 96 | TOEFL, SAT/ACT | 100 | | | 50 |
| **Vermont** | | | | | | | | |
| Bennington College . . . . . . . . . . . . . . . . . . . . . | Pr/B | 701 | 102 | TOEFL | 92 | | 1/3 | |
| Castleton University . . . . . . . . . . . . . . . . . . . . . | Pu/AB | 1,985 | | TOEFL | | | | 40 |
| Champlain College . . . . . . . . . . . . . . . . . . . . . . | Pr/AB | 3,735 | 17 | TOEFL | 79 | | | |
| College of St. Joseph in Vermont . . . . . . . . . . . | Pr/AB | 223 | | TOEFL | 79 | | | |
| Community College of Vermont . . . . . . . . . . . . . | Pu/A | 6,385 | | TOEFL | 80 | | | |
| Goddard College . . . . . . . . . . . . . . . . . . . . . . . | Pr/B | 188 | | | | | | 65 |
| Green Mountain College . . . . . . . . . . . . . . . . . . | Pr/B | 492 | 12 | TOEFL | | | None | |
| Johnson State College . . . . . . . . . . . . . . . . . . . . | Pu/AB | 1,339 | 6 | TOEFL | 65 | | | 40 |
| Landmark College . . . . . . . . . . . . . . . . . . . . . . | Pr/AB | 452 | | TOEFL | 79 | | | 75 |
| Lyndon State College . . . . . . . . . . . . . . . . . . . . | Pu/AB | 1,179 | | TOEFL | 80 | | | 46 |
| Marlboro College . . . . . . . . . . . . . . . . . . . . . . . | Pr/B | 190 | 4 | TOEFL | 80 | | None | 50 |
| Middlebury College . . . . . . . . . . . . . . . . . . . . . | Pr/B | 2,513 | 236 | TOEFL, SAT, SAT  Subject Test(s), or ACT | | | 1/1 | 65 |
| New England Culinary Institute . . . . . . . . . . . . . | Pr/AB | 300 | | TOEFL | | | | 35 |
| Norwich University . . . . . . . . . . . . . . . . . . . . . | Pr/B | 3,085 | | | | | | 35 |
| Saint Michael's College . . . . . . . . . . . . . . . . . . | Pr/B | 1,863 | 67 | TOEFL | 80 | | 5/1 | 50 |
| Southern Vermont College . . . . . . . . . . . . . . . . . | Pr/AB | 358 | 2 | TOEFL | 70 | | 5/1 | 30 |
| Sterling College . . . . . . . . . . . . . . . . . . . . . . . . | Pr/B | 119 | | TOEFL | 61 | | | 35 |
| University of Vermont . . . . . . . . . . . . . . . . . . . . | Pu/B | 10,267 | 528 | TOEFL, SAT/ACT | 90 | | 1/15 | 55 |
| **Virginia** | | | | | | | | |
| American National University: Harrisonburg . . . . . . | Pr/AB | 112 | | | | | | 125 |
| American National University: Salem . . . . . . . . . . | Pr/AB | 160 | | | | | | 125 |
| Argosy University: Washington D.C. . . . . . . . . . . . | Pr/B | 121 | | | | | | 50 |
| Art Institute of Washington . . . . . . . . . . . . . . . . | Pr/AB | 662 | | TOEFL | | | | 50 |
| Averett University . . . . . . . . . . . . . . . . . . . . . . | Pr/AB | 849 | 44 | TOEFL | 61 | | | |
| Blue Ridge Community College . . . . . . . . . . . . . . | Pu/A | 4,388 | | TOEFL | | | | |
| Bluefield College . . . . . . . . . . . . . . . . . . . . . . . | Pr/AB | 886 | 38 | TOEFL | 61 | | 8/15 | 30 |
| Bridgewater College . . . . . . . . . . . . . . . . . . . . . | Pr/B | 1,871 | 22 | TOEFL, SAT/ACT | 79 | | 3/15 | |
| Bryant & Stratton College: Virginia Beach . . . . . . . | Pr/AB | 585 | | TOEFL | | | | 35 |
| Chamberlain College of Nursing: Arlington . . . . . . . | Pr/B | 544 | | | | | | 95 |
| Christendom College . . . . . . . . . . . . . . . . . . . . . | Pr/AB | 477 | | TOEFL | | | | 25 |
| Christopher Newport University . . . . . . . . . . . . . . | Pu/B | 4,921 | 19 | TOEFL | 71 | 90 | 2/1 | 65 |
| College of William and Mary . . . . . . . . . . . . . . . | Pu/B | 6,245 | 375 | TOEFL, SAT/ACT | 100 | | 1/1 | 70 |
| Danville Community College . . . . . . . . . . . . . . . . | Pu/A | 1,739 | 3 | TOEFL | | | | |
| DeVry University: Arlington . . . . . . . . . . . . . . . . | Pr/AB | 251 | 5 | TOEFL | | | | 50 |
| Eastern Mennonite University . . . . . . . . . . . . . . . . | Pr/AB | 1,240 | 44 | TOEFL | 79 | | 6/1 | 25 |
| ECPI University . . . . . . . . . . . . . . . . . . . . . . . . | Pr/AB | 10,840 | | TOEFL | 61 | | | 45 |
| Emory & Henry College . . . . . . . . . . . . . . . . . . | Pr/B | 1,004 | 8 | TOEFL, SAT/ACT | | | | |
| Ferrum College . . . . . . . . . . . . . . . . . . . . . . . . | Pr/B | 1,451 | | TOEFL | | | | 25 |
| George Mason University . . . . . . . . . . . . . . . . . . | Pu/B | 23,174 | 1,127 | TOEFL | 80 | 93 | 1/15 | 80 |
| Germanna Community College . . . . . . . . . . . . . . . | Pu/A | 7,379 | | TOEFL | 80 | | | |
| Hampden-Sydney College . . . . . . . . . . . . . . . . . . | Pr/B | 1,027 | 6 | TOEFL, SAT/ACT | 100 | | 3/1 | 30 |
| Hampton University . . . . . . . . . . . . . . . . . . . . . | Pr/AB | 3,836 | 29 | TOEFL | | | 3/1 | 35 |
| Hollins University . . . . . . . . . . . . . . . . . . . . . . | Pr/B | 647 | 31 | TOEFL | 80 | 95 | | |
| J. Sargeant Reynolds Community College . . . . . . . . | Pu/A | 8,505 | | TOEFL | 80 | | | |
| James Madison University . . . . . . . . . . . . . . . . . . | Pu/B | 19,262 | 411 | TOEFL | 80 | 84 | | 60 |
| Jefferson College of Health Sciences . . . . . . . . . . . | Pr/AB | 800 | | TOEFL | 80 | | | 250 |
| Liberty University . . . . . . . . . . . . . . . . . . . . . . | Pr/AB | 13,587 | 651 | TOEFL | 61 | | None | 40 |
| Longwood University . . . . . . . . . . . . . . . . . . . . . | Pu/B | 4,194 | 62 | TOEFL | 79 | 95 | 3/1 | 50 |
| Lynchburg College . . . . . . . . . . . . . . . . . . . . . . | Pr/B | 1,999 | 52 | TOEFL | 78 | 83 | None | 30 |
| Mary Baldwin University . . . . . . . . . . . . . . . . . . | Pr/B | 1,312 | | TOEFL | | | | 35 |
| Marymount University . . . . . . . . . . . . . . . . . . . . | Pr/B | 2,304 | 329 | TOEFL | 79 | 87 | 7/1 | 40 |
| Norfolk State University . . . . . . . . . . . . . . . . . . . | Pu/AB | 5,356 | | TOEFL | | | | 25 |

| Student services | | | Housing | | Academic year costs | | Maximum credits/ summer | Credit hour charge | International financial aid | | | |
|---|---|---|---|---|---|---|---|---|---|---|---|---|
| Adviser | Orientation | ESL | Academic year | Summer | Tuition/ fees | Living costs | | | Available | Number receiving aid | Average award | Deadline |
| Yes | Yes | Yes | Yes | Yes | 14,749† | 5,907 | | | Yes | | | None |
| Yes | Yes | | Yes | Yes | 32,104† | 8,974 | | 1316 | Yes | 87 | $17,012 | None |
| Yes | Yes | Yes | Yes | Yes | 52,420 | 15,040 | | 2135 | Yes | 83 | $48,895 | 1/3 |
| | Yes | | Yes | | 16,474† | 9,988 | 18 | 642 | Yes | | | None |
| Yes | Yes | | Yes | Yes | 39,818 | 15,906 | 12 | | Yes | 18 | $11,566 | None |
| | | | Yes | | 22,650† | 11,250 | 15 | 285 | | | | None |
| | | | No | | 15,330† | | 15 | 506 | Yes | | | None |
| | | | Yes | | 16,260 | 4,648 | | | Yes | | | None |
| Yes | Yes | | Yes | | 37,002‡ | 12,722 | | 1185 | Yes | 12 | $26,572 | None |
| Yes | | Yes | Yes | | 24,690‡ | 10,290 | | 983 | Yes | | | None |
| Yes | | | Yes | | 52,650† | 10,970 | 12 | | Yes | | | None |
| Yes | | Yes | Yes | Yes | 23,898 | 10,290 | 9 | 950 | | | | |
| Yes | | | Yes | | 40,425‡ | 14,430 | | 1316 | Yes | 3 | $17,028 | 3/1 |
| Yes | Yes | | Yes | Yes | 50,063† | 14,269 | | | Yes | 133 | $54,621 | 2/1 |
| Yes | | | Yes | Yes | 22,910 | 10,466 | | | Yes | | | None |
| Yes | Yes | | Yes | Yes | 38,662 | 13,372 | 20 | 1072 | Yes | 45 | $30,469 | None |
| Yes | Yes | Yes | Yes | Yes | 43,640 | 11,750 | 12 | 1390 | Yes | 61 | $14,275 | None |
| | | | Yes | | 23,975† | 10,800 | 16 | | Yes | 3 | $10,000 | None |
| | | | Yes | | 36,577† | 10,060 | | | Yes | | | None |
| | Yes | | Yes | Yes | 40,364† | 11,578 | | | Yes | 208 | $17,621 | None |
| Yes | Yes | | No | | 18,735‡ | 5,463 | | 412 | | | | |
| Yes | Yes | | Yes | Yes | 14,460† | | | 317 | | | | |
| Yes | Yes | | Yes | Yes | 21,970† | 10,398 | 16 | 486 | | | | |
| | Yes | | Yes | | 31,980† | 8,990 | 18 | 1335 | Yes | 45 | $16,172 | None |
| | | | No | | 10,429† | | | 314 | | | | |
| | | | Yes | Yes | 24,890‡ | 10,687 | 21 | 970 | Yes | | | None |
| Yes | Yes | | Yes | Yes | 33,820 | 12,440 | 11 | 1150 | Yes | 22 | $25,950 | None |
| | | | No | | 17,190† | 4,820 | | 573 | Yes | | | 9/17 |
| | | | | | 19,500† | | | 675 | | | | |
| | | | Yes | | 25,580 | 9,976 | 18 | | Yes | 2 | $11,387 | 6/1 |
| | Yes | | Yes | Yes | 24,680† | 10,914 | 12 | 794 | | | | |
| Yes | Yes | | Yes | | 41,718† | 11,382 | 16 | 1150 | | | | |
| | | | No | | 9,760† | | | 314 | | | | |
| Yes | | | | | 17,512† | | | 609 | | | | |
| Yes | Yes | Yes | Yes | Yes | 34,200† | 10,660 | 7 | 1350 | Yes | | | None |
| Yes | | | | | 15,811† | 8,670 | 24 | | | | | |
| Yes | | | Yes | | 33,700† | 11,200 | 12 | | Yes | 7 | $15,508 | None |
| Yes | | | Yes | | 31,915† | 11,090 | | 635 | Yes | | | None |
| Yes | Yes | Yes | Yes | | 32,582† | 10,730 | | 1229 | | | | |
| | | | No | | 10,577† | 8,004 | | 315 | | | | |
| Yes | | | Yes | | 42,962† | 13,286 | 6 | | Yes | | | 5/1 |
| Yes | Yes | Yes | Yes | Yes | 23,992† | 10,684 | 12 | 548 | Yes | 6 | $31,218 | 4/15 |
| Yes | Yes | | Yes | | 36,835† | 12,800 | 12 | 1132 | Yes | 30 | $33,659 | None |
| Yes | | Yes | No | | 10,663† | | 18 | 315 | | | | |
| Yes | Yes | Yes | Yes | Yes | 26,116† | 9,334 | 15 | 703 | Yes | | | |
| | | | Yes | Yes | 25,150† | 5,870 | 15 | 715 | Yes | | | None |
| Yes | Yes | Yes | Yes | Yes | 23,020† | 9,306 | 12 | 917 | Yes | 604 | $9,699 | 3/1 |
| Yes | Yes | Yes | Yes | | 26,670† | 14,685 | 20 | 706 | Yes | | | None |
| Yes | Yes | Yes | Yes | Yes | 37,690 | 10,680 | 12 | 510 | Yes | 20 | $4,829 | None |
| Yes | Yes | Yes | Yes | | 30,635† | 9,230 | | 455 | Yes | | | None |
| Yes | Yes | | Yes | Yes | 30,426 | 12,805 | | 975 | Yes | | | None |
| Yes | Yes | | Yes | | 21,100† | 9,490 | 9 | 796 | Yes | | | None |

† Actual for 2016-17.     ‡ Estimated for 2017-18.     * Includes room and board

| Institution | Control/degrees | Undergraduates Total | Internat'l | Tests required (Fall 2017) | TOEFL minimum | average | Application Deadline | Fee |
|---|---|---|---|---|---|---|---|---|
| Northern Virginia Community College | Pu/A | 52,078 | | TOEFL | | | | |
| Old Dominion University | Pu/B | 19,606 | 285 | TOEFL | 79 | | 4/15 | 50 |
| Patrick Henry College | Pr/B | 263 | | | | | | 20 |
| Patrick Henry Community College | Pu/A | 3,322 | | TOEFL | 50 | | 7/15 | |
| | | | | | | | | |
| Paul D. Camp Community College | Pu/A | 1,479 | | TOEFL | | | None | |
| Piedmont Virginia Community College | Pu/A | 5,438 | | TOEFL | 61 | | | |
| Radford University | Pu/B | 8,426 | 67 | TOEFL | 68 | | | |
| Randolph College | Pr/B | 649 | 36 | TOEFL | 79 | 86 | | |
| Randolph-Macon College | Pr/B | 1,429 | 23 | TOEFL | 80 | 92 | | 30 |
| | | | | | | | | |
| Rappahannock Community College | Pu/A | 3,464 | | TOEFL | 80 | | | |
| Regent University | Pr/AB | 3,657 | 33 | TOEFL | 90 | 97 | 2/15 | 50 |
| Richard Bland College | Pu/A | 1,089 | 12 | TOEFL | 61 | | 7/1 | 50 |
| Roanoke College | Pr/B | 1,946 | 50 | TOEFL, SAT/ACT | 80 | | 4/15 | 30 |
| Shenandoah University | Pr/B | 2,087 | 84 | TOEFL, SAT/ACT | 79 | 100 | None | 30 |
| | | | | | | | | |
| Southern Virginia University | Pr/B | 705 | | TOEFL, SAT/ACT | 79 | | | 290 |
| Southwest Virginia Community College | Pu/A | 1,758 | | TOEFL | | | | |
| Stratford University: Falls Church | Pr/AB | 640 | | TOEFL | 79 | | None | 50 |
| Stratford University: Woodbridge | Pr/AB | 378 | | TOEFL | 79 | | | 50 |
| Sweet Briar College | Pr/B | 320 | 6 | TOEFL | | | | |
| | | | | | | | | |
| Thomas Nelson Community College | Pu/A | 8,897 | | | | | | |
| Tidewater Community College | Pu/A | 23,946 | | TOEFL | 61 | | | |
| University of Management and Technology | Pr/AB | 943 | | TOEFL | 61 | | None | 30 |
| University of Mary Washington | Pu/B | 4,318 | 40 | TOEFL | 80 | 93 | 2/1 | 50 |
| University of Phoenix: Northern Virginia | Pr/B | 790 | | | | | | |
| | | | | | | | | |
| University of Phoenix: Richmond | Pr/B | 1,115 | | | | | | |
| University of the Potomac | Pr/AB | 23 | | TOEFL | 61 | | None | |
| University of Richmond | Pr/B | 2,950 | 271 | TOEFL, SAT/ACT | 80 | 106 | 1/15 | 50 |
| University of Virginia | Pu/B | 15,844 | 721 | TOEFL, SAT/ACT | | | 1/1 | 60 |
| University of Virginia's College at Wise | Pu/B | 1,376 | | TOEFL, SAT/ACT | 80 | | 4/1 | 25 |
| | | | | | | | | |
| Virginia College in Richmond | Pr/A | 446 | | | | | | 100 |
| Virginia Commonwealth University | Pu/B | 22,758 | 787 | TOEFL | | | | 65 |
| Virginia Military Institute | Pu/B | 1,713 | | TOEFL | | | | 40 |
| Virginia Polytechnic Institute and State University | Pu/AB | 25,725 | 1,499 | TOEFL | 80 | | 1/15 | 70 |
| Virginia State University | Pu/AB | 4,155 | 10 | TOEFL | | | | 25 |
| | | | | | | | | |
| Virginia Union University | Pr/B | 1,337 | 3 | TOEFL, SAT, SAT Subject Test(s) | | | | 25 |
| Virginia University of Lynchburg | Pr/AB | 470 | | | | | | 25 |
| Virginia Wesleyan College | Pr/B | 1,342 | 10 | TOEFL | 80 | | | |
| Virginia Western Community College | Pu/A | 8,632 | | TOEFL | 61 | | | |
| Washington and Lee University | Pr/B | 1,820 | 71 | TOEFL, SAT/ACT | | 100 | 1/1 | 60 |
| | | | | | | | | |
| **Washington** | | | | | | | | |
| | | | | | | | | |
| Argosy University: Seattle | Pr/AB | 153 | | | | | | 50 |
| Art Institute of Seattle | Pr/AB | 1,703 | | TOEFL | 61 | | | 50 |
| Bastyr University | Pr/B | 227 | 3 | TOEFL | 79 | | | 75 |
| Bates Technical College | Pu/A | 3,546 | | TOEFL | | | | 50 |
| Bellevue College | Pu/AB | 13,469 | | TOEFL | 61 | 62 | | 50 |
| | | | | | | | | |
| Bellingham Technical College | Pu/AB | 3,111 | | TOEFL | | | None | |
| Big Bend Community College | Pu/A | 1,676 | 11 | TOEFL | 48 | | None | 30 |
| Carrington College: Spokane | Pr/A | 511 | | | | | | |
| Cascadia College | Pu/AB | 2,310 | 137 | | | | | 50 |
| Central Washington University | Pu/B | 10,492 | 312 | TOEFL | 71 | | None | 50 |
| | | | | | | | | |
| Centralia College | Pu/AB | 2,340 | | | | | | 35 |
| City University of Seattle | Pr/AB | 1,120 | | TOEFL | 76 | | | 50 |
| Clark College | Pu/AB | 8,339 | 71 | | 32 | | | 35 |
| Clover Park Technical College | Pu/A | 4,509 | | | | | | 50 |
| Columbia Basin College | Pu/AB | 2,760 | | TOEFL | 61 | | | 29 |
| | | | | | | | | |
| Cornish College of the Arts | Pr/B | 649 | | TOEFL | | | | 40 |

| Student services | | | Housing | | Academic year costs | | Maximum credits/ summer | Credit hour charge | International financial aid | | | |
| Adviser | Orientation | ESL | Academic year | Summer | Tuition/ fees | Living costs | | | Available | Number receiving aid | Average award | Deadline |
|---|---|---|---|---|---|---|---|---|---|---|---|---|
| Yes | | Yes | No | | 10,965† | 5,810 | | 342 | | | | |
| Yes | Yes | Yes | Yes | Yes | 27,026† | 10,864 | | 891 | Yes | 24 | $7,916 | 3/15 |
| | | | Yes | | 27,922 | 10,728 | | 1163 | | | | |
| Yes | | | No | | 10,371† | | 24 | 314.35 | Yes | | | None |
| Yes | | | No | | 10,286† | 9,136 | | 314 | | | | |
| Yes | | | No | | 9,855† | 6,920 | 12 | 315 | | | | |
| Yes | Yes | | Yes | Yes | 21,716† | 8,946 | | 776 | Yes | | | None |
| Yes | Yes | | Yes | | 38,155 | 13,070 | | 1565 | Yes | | | None |
| Yes | Yes | | Yes | Yes | 40,100 | 12,480 | 8 | | Yes | 22 | $29,212 | 3/1 |
| | | | No | | 9,885† | | 18 | 314 | Yes | | | None |
| Yes | Yes | | Yes | Yes | 17,450‡ | 8,480 | | 555 | Yes | 19 | $6,299 | None |
| Yes | | | Yes | | 21,720 | 11,480 | 12 | 724 | | | | |
| Yes | Yes | Yes | Yes | Yes | 42,694 | 14,358 | 16 | 491 | Yes | 36 | $31,843 | None |
| Yes | Yes | Yes | Yes | Yes | 31,322† | 9,990 | 12 | 877 | Yes | 25 | $6,243 | None |
| | | | Yes | Yes | 15,300† | 8,450 | | 685 | Yes | | | None |
| Yes | | | No | | 10,361† | | 15 | 314.35 | Yes | | | None |
| Yes | | Yes | No | | 16,750† | 6,664 | | 370 | | | | |
| Yes | Yes | Yes | No | | 16,750† | 6,664 | 18 | 370 | | | | |
| Yes | Yes | | Yes | | 36,425† | 12,635 | 18 | 1050 | Yes | | | None |
| | | Yes | No | | 10,076† | 7,874 | | 316 | | | | |
| Yes | | Yes | No | | 10,596† | 6,800 | 18 | 316 | | | | |
| | | | No | | 9,420† | 6,435 | | 390 | | | | |
| Yes | Yes | | Yes | Yes | 26,160† | 11,118 | 12 | 1018 | Yes | 6 | $2,666 | 7/1 |
| Yes | | | No | | | 9,300 | 9 | | | | | |
| Yes | Yes | | Yes | Yes | 49,420† | 11,460 | 9 | 2471 | Yes | 138 | $41,396 | 2/1 |
| Yes | Yes | Yes | Yes | | 46,634‡ | 11,220 | 12 | 1440 | | | | |
| Yes | | | Yes | | 25,617† | 10,346 | 14 | 900 | Yes | | | 2/15 |
| Yes | Yes | Yes | Yes | Yes | 31,608† | 9,919 | | 1013 | Yes | 39 | $8,625 | None |
| | | | | | 43,902 | 10,736 | | | | | | |
| Yes | Yes | Yes | Yes | Yes | 29,975† | 8,424 | 14 | 1137.75 | | | | |
| Yes | | | Yes | Yes | 18,292† | 10,562 | 10 | | Yes | 25 | $4,000 | 5/1 |
| Yes | | | Yes | | 16,734† | 8,412 | 6 | 470 | Yes | | | None |
| | | | Yes | Yes | 7,880† | 8,520 | | | | | | |
| Yes | | | Yes | Yes | 36,660‡ | 8,943 | | 1500 | Yes | 13 | $22,596 | None |
| Yes | | Yes | No | | 10,990† | 6,936 | 12 | 316 | Yes | | | None |
| Yes | Yes | | Yes | | 48,267† | 11,380 | | 1689 | Yes | 65 | $54,012 | 2/15 |
| Yes | Yes | | Yes | Yes | | 9,750 | 18 | | | | | |
| | Yes | | Yes | | 27,834† | 15,555 | | | Yes | | | None |
| Yes | | Yes | No | | 10,011† | | | 201 | Yes | | | None |
| Yes | Yes | Yes | No | | 9,492† | | 18 | 206 | Yes | | | None |
| Yes | | | No | | 9,295† | 9,780 | | 201 | Yes | | | None |
| Yes | Yes | | Yes | Yes | 9,486† | 3,330 | | 206 | | | | |
| Yes | Yes | Yes | No | | 9,361† | | | 203 | | | | |
| Yes | Yes | Yes | Yes | Yes | 21,501† | 10,175 | 12 | | Yes | 128 | $6,120 | 5/1 |
| Yes | Yes | Yes | Yes | Yes | 9,597† | 10,052 | 12 | 206 | Yes | | | 9/1 |
| Yes | Yes | Yes | Yes | | | 9,492 | 15 | | Yes | | | None |
| Yes | Yes | Yes | No | | 9,394† | 9,780 | 18 | 203 | | | | |
| Yes | Yes | Yes | No | | 9,335† | | | 203 | Yes | | | 4/12 |
| Yes | Yes | Yes | No | | 9,828† | 9,492 | 18 | | | | | |
| Yes | | | Yes | | 38,370† | 10,950 | 16 | 1580 | Yes | | | |

† Actual for 2016-17.    ‡ Estimated for 2017-18.    * Includes room and board

| Institution | Control/ degrees | Undergraduates | | Tests required (Fall 2017) | TOEFL | | Application | |
|---|---|---|---|---|---|---|---|---|
| | | Total | Internat'l | | minimum | average | Deadline | Fee |
| DigiPen Institute of Technology . . . . . . . . . . . . . | .Pr/B | 976 | | TOEFL | 80 | | | 35 |
| Eastern Washington University . . . . . . . . . . . . . . | .Pu/B | 10,546 | 477 | TOEFL | 71 | 74 | | 50 |
| Edmonds Community College . . . . . . . . . . . . . . | .Pu/A | 9,540 | | | | | | 50 |
| Everett Community College . . . . . . . . . . . . . . . . | .Pu/A | 6,990 | | | | | | 40 |
| Evergreen State College . . . . . . . . . . . . . . . . | .Pu/B | 3,732 | 26 | TOEFL | 79 | 84 | 2/1 | 50 |
| Fiath International University . . . . . . . . . . . . . . . | .Pr/B | 180 | | TOEFL | 79 | | | 40 |
| Gonzaga University . . . . . . . . . . . . . . . . . . . . | .Pr/B | 5,084 | 74 | TOEFL | 80 | 91 | 2/1 | 50 |
| Grays Harbor College. . . . . . . . . . . . . . . . . . . | .Pu/A | 2,302 | | TOEFL | | | | |
| Green River College . . . . . . . . . . . . . . . . . . . | .Pu/AB | 10,456 | | | | | 8/15 | 50 |
| Heritage University . . . . . . . . . . . . . . . . . . . . | .Pr/AB | 795 | 15 | TOEFL | | | None | 25 |
| Highline College . . . . . . . . . . . . . . . . . . . . . | .Pu/A | 6,489 | | TOEFL | | | | 50 |
| International Academy of Design and Technology: Seattle . . . . . . . . . . . . | .Pr/AB | 340 | | TOEFL | 61 | | | 50 |
| Lake Washington Institute of Technology . . . . . . . | .Pu/AB | 1,770 | | | | | None | 80 |
| Lower Columbia College. . . . . . . . . . . . . . . . . | .Pu/A | 1,263 | | | | | | |
| North Seattle College . . . . . . . . . . . . . . . . . . | .Pu/AB | 5,890 | | | | | | 35 |
| Northwest College of Art & Design. . . . . . . . . . | .Pr/B | 80 | | TOEFL | | | | 100 |
| Northwest School of Wooden Boatbuilding. . . . . . | .Pr/A | 40 | | | | | | 100 |
| Northwest University . . . . . . . . . . . . . . . . . . . | .Pr/AB | 1,712 | | TOEFL | 70 | | 6/1 | 30 |
| Olympic College . . . . . . . . . . . . . . . . . . . . . | .Pu/AB | 7,253 | | | | | | 50 |
| Pacific Lutheran University . . . . . . . . . . . . . . | .Pr/B | 2,743 | 80 | TOEFL | 79 | | | 40 |
| Peninsula College . . . . . . . . . . . . . . . . . . . . | .Pu/AB | 1,994 | | TOEFL | | | | 35 |
| Pierce College. . . . . . . . . . . . . . . . . . . . . . . | .Pu/A | 9,615 | | TOEFL | 61 | | | 30 |
| Renton Technical College . . . . . . . . . . . . . . . . | .Pu/AB | 3,359 | | TOEFL | 39 | | | 30 |
| Saint Martin's University . . . . . . . . . . . . . . . . | .Pr/B | 1,178 | 45 | TOEFL | 71 | | 7/31 | 50 |
| Seattle Central College . . . . . . . . . . . . . . . . . | .Pu/AB | 8,783 | | TOEFL | | | | 50 |
| Seattle Pacific University . . . . . . . . . . . . . . . . | .Pr/B | 3,079 | | TOEFL | | | | 50 |
| Seattle University . . . . . . . . . . . . . . . . . . . . | .Pr/B | 4,748 | 519 | TOEFL | 68 | | 6/1 | 55 |
| Shoreline Community College . . . . . . . . . . . . . | .Pu/A | 6,475 | | | | | | 50 |
| Skagit Valley College. . . . . . . . . . . . . . . . . . . | .Pu/A | 5,977 | | | | | | 25 |
| South Puget Sound Community College . . . . . . . . | .Pu/A | 4,861 | | | 61 | | | 40 |
| South Seattle College. . . . . . . . . . . . . . . . . . . | .Pu/AB | 7,726 | | | 72 | | | 50 |
| Spokane Community College . . . . . . . . . . . . . . | .Pu/A | 6,960 | | TOEFL | | | | 40 |
| Spokane Falls Community College . . . . . . . . . . . | .Pu/A | 8,530 | | TOEFL | | | | 40 |
| Tacoma Community College . . . . . . . . . . . . . . | .Pu/A | 7,384 | | | | | | |
| University of Phoenix: Western Washington . . . . . . | .Pr/B | 607 | | TOEFL, SAT/ACT | 80 | | | 50 |
| University of Puget Sound. . . . . . . . . . . . . . . . | .Pr/B | 2,506 | 12 | TOEFL | 76 | | 12/1 | 80 |
| University of Washington . . . . . . . . . . . . . . . . | .Pu/B | 29,990 | 4,391 | TOEFL | 76 | | 1/15 | 75 |
| University of Washington Bothell . . . . . . . . . . . . | .Pu/B | 5,078 | 498 | TOEFL | 76 | | | 75 |
| University of Washington Tacoma . . . . . . . . . . . | .Pu/B | 4,252 | 208 | TOEFL | 83 | | | 75 |
| Walla Walla Community College . . . . . . . . . . . . | .Pu/A | 6,572 | | TOEFL | 61 | | | |
| Walla Walla University. . . . . . . . . . . . . . . . . . . | .Pr/AB | 1,650 | | TOEFL | | | | 30 |
| Washington State University . . . . . . . . . . . . . . | .Pu/B | 24,362 | 1,130 | TOEFL | 79 | | None | 50 |
| Western Washington University . . . . . . . . . . . . | .Pu/B | 14,483 | 162 | TOEFL | 80 | | 3/1 | 55 |
| Whatcom Community College . . . . . . . . . . . . . | .Pu/A | 4,823 | | | | | | 50 |
| Whitman College. . . . . . . . . . . . . . . . . . . . . | .Pr/B | 1,463 | 84 | TOEFL | 85 | | 1/15 | 50 |
| Whitworth University . . . . . . . . . . . . . . . . . . . | .Pr/B | 2,280 | 69 | TOEFL | 79 | 95 | None | |
| Yakima Valley Community College. . . . . . . . . . . | .Pu/A | 4,105 | | TOEFL | 57 | | | 25 |
| **West Virginia** | | | | | | | | |
| Alderson-Broaddus University . . . . . . . . . . . . . | .Pr/AB | 972 | 45 | TOEFL, ACT | | | 8/1 | |
| American National University: Parkersburg. . . . . . . | .Pr/AB | 52 | | | | | | 50 |
| American Public University System. . . . . . . . . . . | .Pr/AB | 37,826 | 230 | TOEFL | | | None | |
| Appalachian Bible College . . . . . . . . . . . . . . . | .Pr/AB | 160 | | TOEFL | 60 | 65 | None | 20 |
| Bethany College . . . . . . . . . . . . . . . . . . . . . | .Pr/B | 622 | 13 | TOEFL | 90 | | | |
| Bluefield State College. . . . . . . . . . . . . . . . . . | .Pu/AB | 1,362 | 28 | TOEFL | | | | |
| BridgeValley Community and Technical College . . . . . . . . . . . . . . . . . . . . . . . . . | .Pu/A | 1,000 | | TOEFL, SAT/ACT | 61 | | | 50 |
| Catholic Distance University . . . . . . . . . . . . . . | .Pr/AB | 103 | | TOEFL | 61 | | | 25 |

| Student services | | | Housing | | Academic year costs | | Maximum credits/ summer | Credit hour charge | International financial aid | | | |
|---|---|---|---|---|---|---|---|---|---|---|---|---|
| Adviser | Orien-tation | ESL | Academic year | Summer | Tuition/ fees | Living costs | | | Avail-able | Number receiving aid | Average award | Deadline |
| Yes | Yes | Yes | Yes | | 32,180 | 11,350 | 21 | 1066 | Yes | 7 | $1,318 | None |
| Yes | Yes | Yes | Yes | Yes | 23,342 † | 10,945 | 18 | 750 | | | | |
| Yes | Yes | Yes | | Yes | 9,656 † | 8,400 | | 206 | | | | |
| Yes | Yes | Yes | No | | 9,516 † | 13,274 | 18 | 206 | | | | |
| Yes | Yes | | Yes | Yes | 23,887 † | 9,360 | 20 | 767 | Yes | | | None |
| | | | | | 7,890 † | 9,081 | | 165 | | | | |
| Yes | Yes | Yes | Yes | Yes | 41,330 | 11,550 | 14 | 1110 | Yes | 78 | $23,568 | 6/30 |
| Yes | | Yes | No | | 9,677 † | 9,492 | 10 | 206 | Yes | | | 5/1 |
| Yes | Yes | Yes | Yes | Yes | 9,756 † | | 22 | 197 | | | | |
| Yes | Yes | | No | | 18,084 | 9,492 | 9 | 743 | Yes | | | None |
| Yes | Yes | Yes | No | | 9,336 † | 9,630 | 18 | 206 | | | | |
| | | | | | 10,063 † | 10,272 | | 206 | | | | |
| Yes | Yes | Yes | No | Yes | 9,637 † | 11,154 | | 206 | | | | |
| Yes | Yes | Yes | No | | 9,449 † | 9,240 | 18 | 204 | Yes | | | 6/30 |
| | | | | | | 9,630 | 15 | | Yes | | | 6/1 |
| | | | No | | 19,500 | 12,840 | | 225 | Yes | | | None |
| Yes | Yes | Yes | Yes | Yes | 30,320 | 8,400 | 10 | | Yes | | | 8/1 |
| Yes | Yes | Yes | Yes | Yes | 9,366 † | 4,950 | 15 | 206 | Yes | | | None |
| Yes | Yes | Yes | Yes | Yes | 39,450 † | 10,330 | 12 | 1221.25 | Yes | 56 | $16,861 | None |
| Yes | Yes | Yes | | | 9,759 † | 8,495 | | 206 | Yes | | | 4/1 |
| Yes | Yes | Yes | | | 9,602 † | | 18 | 206 | | | | |
| Yes | | Yes | No | | 9,576 † | | | 206 | | | | |
| Yes | Yes | Yes | Yes | Yes | 35,656 | 12,148 | 18 | 1190 | Yes | 6 | $5,000 | None |
| Yes | Yes | Yes | No | | 9,514 † | | 18 | 205 | Yes | | | 7/27 |
| Yes | Yes | Yes | Yes | Yes | 40,893 | 11,232 | 20 | 1124 | Yes | | | None |
| Yes | Yes | Yes | Yes | Yes | 41,265 † | 11,499 | 18 | 900 | Yes | 200 | $17,696 | None |
| Yes | Yes | Yes | No | | 9,561 † | | 15 | 204 | | | | |
| Yes | Yes | Yes | Yes | Yes | 9,874 † | | 18 | 205 | | | | |
| Yes | Yes | Yes | | Yes | 9,513 † | 9,632 | 20 | 206 | | | | |
| Yes | Yes | Yes | No | | 9,666 † | 9,630 | 20 | 206 | | | | |
| Yes | Yes | Yes | No | | 9,627 † | | 15 | 206 | | | | |
| Yes | Yes | Yes | No | | 10,016 † | | 15 | 206 | | | | |
| Yes | Yes | Yes | No | | 9,748 † | | | 282.37 | | | | |
| Yes | Yes | | Yes | | 46,552 † | 11,800 | 16 | 1461 | Yes | 12 | $15,804 | None |
| Yes | Yes | ESL | Yes | Yes | 34,791 † | 11,691 | | 1124 | | | | |
| Yes | Yes | | Yes | Yes | 34,728 † | 10,833 | | 1124 | | | | |
| Yes | Yes | | Yes | Yes | 34,869 † | 10,230 | | 1124 | | | | |
| Yes | | | | | 9,768 † | | 15 | 206 | | | | |
| Yes | Yes | | Yes | Yes | 27,495 ‡ | 10,485 | 12 | 738 | Yes | 5 | $12,700 | None |
| Yes | Yes | Yes | Yes | Yes | 24,516 † | 11,356 | | 1226 | Yes | 330 | $11,182 | 1/31 |
| Yes | Yes | Yes | Yes | Yes | 21,596 † | 10,350 | 18 | | Yes | 58 | $3,132 | None |
| Yes | Yes | Yes | No | | 9,715 † | 8,064 | 20 | 206 | | | | |
| Yes | Yes | | Yes | Yes | 49,780 | 12,524 | | 2058 | Yes | 48 | $40,916 | 2/1 |
| Yes | Yes | | Yes | Yes | 40,562 † | 11,170 | 12 | 1650 | Yes | 69 | $29,243 | None |
| | | Yes | Yes | Yes | 9,734 † | 9,492 | 18 | 206 | | | | |
| Yes | Yes | | Yes | Yes | 26,610 | 8,390 | -6 | 838 | Yes | 48 | $18,581 | None |
| | | | | | 14,460 † | | | 317 | | | | |
| Yes | | | No | | 8,150 † | | | 270 | Yes | 13 | $629 | None |
| Yes | | | Yes | | 14,000 † | 7,570 | | 375 | Yes | | | 9/15 |
| Yes | Yes | | Yes | | 27,438 † | 9,924 | 4 | 1104 | Yes | | | None |
| Yes | Yes | | No | | 12,876 † | 9,800 | 12 | | Yes | 22 | $7,807 | None |
| Yes | | | Yes | Yes | | 5,542 | 12 | | | | | |
| | | | | | 9,150 † | | | 305 | | | | |

† Actual for 2016-17.    ‡ Estimated for 2017-18.    * Includes room and board

| Institution | Control/degrees | Undergraduates Total | Internat'l | Tests required (Fall 2017) | TOEFL minimum | average | Application Deadline | Fee |
|---|---|---|---|---|---|---|---|---|
| Concord University | Pu/AB | 1,996 | 87 | TOEFL, SAT/ACT | | | | 25 |
| Davis and Elkins College | Pr/AB | 874 | | TOEFL | 50 | | | |
| Fairmont State University | Pu/AB | 3,687 | 94 | TOEFL, SAT/ACT | | | | 25 |
| Glenville State College | Pu/AB | 1,347 | 5 | TOEFL, SAT/ACT | | | | 100 |
| Kanawha Valley Community and Technical College | Pu/A | | | TOEFL, SAT/ACT | | | | |
| Marshall University | Pu/AB | 8,699 | 124 | TOEFL, SAT/ACT | 80 | | | 100 |
| Mountain State College | Pr/A | 189 | | | | | | 115 |
| Ohio Valley University | Pr/AB | 157 | | TOEFL, SAT/ACT | 61 | 98 | | 20 |
| Pierpont Community and Technical College | Pu/A | 2,700 | | | | | | |
| Potomac State College of West Virginia University | Pu/AB | 1,204 | 6 | TOEFL | 61 | | | |
| Salem International University | Pr/AB | 402 | | | | | | 20 |
| Shepherd University | Pu/B | 3,094 | 11 | TOEFL | 79 | 83 | None | 45 |
| University of Charleston | Pr/AB | 1,733 | | TOEFL | 61 | | | 25 |
| West Liberty University | Pu/AB | 1,919 | 38 | TOEFL | | | | |
| West Virginia Junior College: Bridgeport | Pr/A | 188 | | | | | | 25 |
| West Virginia Northern Community College | Pu/A | 2,013 | | TOEFL | | | | |
| West Virginia State University | Pu/B | 2,011 | 23 | TOEFL, SAT/ACT | | | | 20 |
| West Virginia University | Pu/B | 21,428 | 1,386 | TOEFL | 61 | | 5/1 | 60 |
| West Virginia University at Parkersburg | Pu/AB | 3,800 | | TOEFL | | | | |
| West Virginia University Institute of Technology | Pu/B | 1,109 | | TOEFL, SAT/ACT | 61 | | 8/1 | 100 |
| West Virginia Wesleyan College | Pr/B | 1,382 | 82 | TOEFL, SAT/ACT | | | | 50 |
| Wheeling Jesuit University | Pr/B | 1,187 | | TOEFL | 80 | 83 | | 25 |

**Wisconsin**

| Institution | Control/degrees | Undergraduates Total | Internat'l | Tests required (Fall 2017) | TOEFL minimum | average | Application Deadline | Fee |
|---|---|---|---|---|---|---|---|---|
| Alverno College | Pr/AB | 1,380 | 4 | TOEFL | 68 | | 5/15 | |
| Beloit College | Pr/B | 1,315 | 177 | TOEFL | 80 | | 1/15 | |
| Blackhawk Technical College | Pu/A | 2,034 | | TOEFL | | | 7/1 | 30 |
| Bryant & Stratton College: Milwaukee | Pr/AB | 2,075 | | TOEFL | | | | 25 |
| Cardinal Stritch University | Pr/AB | 1,503 | 159 | TOEFL | 79 | 82 | None | |
| Carroll University | Pr/B | 2,911 | 88 | TOEFL | 79 | | None | |
| Carthage College | Pr/B | 2,818 | 27 | TOEFL | | | | 40 |
| Chippewa Valley Technical College | Pu/A | 3,283 | | TOEFL | | | None | 30 |
| Concordia University Wisconsin | Pr/AB | 3,551 | 78 | TOEFL | | | | 125 |
| Edgewood College | Pr/B | 1,615 | 62 | TOEFL | 71 | | 5/1 | 30 |
| Fox Valley Technical College | Pu/A | 5,972 | 3 | TOEFL | 70 | 75 | None | 80 |
| Gateway Technical College | Pu/A | 6,180 | | TOEFL | 64 | | | 30 |
| Globe University: Appleton | Pr/AB | 203 | | TOEFL | 61 | | | 50 |
| Globe University: Eau Claire | Pr/AB | 153 | | TOEFL | 61 | | | 50 |
| Globe University: Green Bay | Pr/AB | 185 | | TOEFL | 61 | | | 50 |
| Globe University: La Crosse | Pr/AB | 178 | | TOEFL | 61 | | | 50 |
| Globe University: Madison East | Pr/AB | 217 | | TOEFL | 61 | | | 50 |
| Globe University: Middleton | Pr/AB | 182 | | TOEFL | 61 | | | 50 |
| Globe University: Wausau | Pr/AB | 122 | | TOEFL | 61 | | | 50 |
| Herzing University: Brookfield | Pr/AB | 307 | | | | | | |
| Herzing University: Kenosha | Pr/AB | 316 | | | | | | |
| Herzing University: Madison | Pr/AB | 1,955 | | TOEFL | 61 | | | |
| Lakeland University | Pr/AB | 2,537 | | TOEFL | 61 | | | 20 |
| Lakeshore Technical College | Pu/A | 2,837 | | TOEFL | | | None | 30 |
| Lawrence University | Pr/B | 1,507 | 170 | TOEFL | 90 | 100 | 1/15 | |
| Madison Area Technical College | Pu/A | 16,467 | | TOEFL | | | | 35 |
| Madison Media Institute | Pr/AB | 372 | | | | | | 30 |
| Maranatha Baptist University | Pr/AB | 764 | 8 | TOEFL, SAT/ACT | | | None | 50 |
| Marian University | Pr/B | 1,475 | 27 | TOEFL | 70 | | | 25 |
| Marquette University | Pr/B | 8,053 | 311 | | 78 | 88 | | 40 |
| Mid-State Technical College | Pu/A | 3,100 | | TOEFL | | | | 30 |
| Milwaukee Area Technical College | Pu/A | 13,403 | | TOEFL | | | 7/31 | 30 |

| Student services | | | Housing | | Academic year costs | | Maximum credits/ summer | Credit hour charge | International financial aid | | | |
|---|---|---|---|---|---|---|---|---|---|---|---|---|
| Adviser | Orientation | ESL | Academic year | Summer | Tuition/ fees | Living costs | | | Available | Number receiving aid | Average award | Deadline |
| Yes | Yes | Yes | Yes | | 15,564 † | 8,400 | | 648 | Yes | 64 | $6,975 | None |
| Yes | Yes | | Yes | | 28,842 † | 9,250 | 12 | | Yes | | | 8/1 |
| Yes | Yes | Yes | Yes | Yes | 14,666 † | 9,100 | 12 | 603 | Yes | 21 | $9,582 | |
| | | Yes | Yes | | 16,600 † | 7,964 | 9 | 692 | Yes | | | None |
| Yes | | | | | | 8,556 | | | | | | |
| Yes | Yes | Yes | Yes | Yes | 16,382 † | 10,126 | 24 | 636 | Yes | 45 | $18,470 | None |
| | | | No | | 8,215 † | 5,850 | | | Yes | | | None |
| Yes | | Yes | Yes | Yes | 21,100 ‡ | 7,700 | 12 | 700 | Yes | 17 | $11,172 | None |
| | | | | | 11,124 † | 8,776 | | | | | | |
| | | | Yes | | 10,416 † | 8,752 | 14 | | | | | |
| Yes | Yes | Yes | Yes | Yes | 12,920 † | 7,480 | 20 | 530 | Yes | | | None |
| Yes | Yes | Yes | Yes | Yes | 17,482 † | 10,054 | 12 | 687 | Yes | 6 | $11,395 | None |
| Yes | Yes | Yes | Yes | Yes | 30,400 | 10,100 | 12 | 380 | Yes | | | 8/15 |
| Yes | | | Yes | | | | 18 | | Yes | | | None |
| | | | No | | | 7,350 | | | | | | |
| Yes | | | No | | 10,355 † | | 12 | | | | | |
| Yes | | Yes | Yes | Yes | 15,572 † | 11,388 | 9 | 644 | Yes | | | None |
| Yes | Yes | Yes | Yes | | 22,488 † | 10,218 | | 937 | Yes | | | |
| Yes | | | No | | 7,920 † | 5,000 | 12 | | Yes | | | None |
| Yes | Yes | | Yes | | 16,728 † | 9,814 | 12 | 697 | Yes | | | |
| Yes | | Yes | Yes | Yes | 29,952 † | 8,248 | 12 | | Yes | | | None |
| Yes | Yes | Yes | Yes | Yes | 28,110 † | 7,796 | 12 | | Yes | | | 8/1 |
| Yes | Yes | Yes | Yes | Yes | 26,932 † | 7,884 | 18 | 1093 | Yes | 5 | $3,904 | None |
| Yes | Yes | Yes | Yes | Yes | 47,060 † | 8,146 | | 1394 | Yes | | | 3/1 |
| | | Yes | No | | 6,059 † | 5,795 | 6 | 196 | | | | |
| Yes | | | No | | 17,190 † | | 18 | 573 | | | | |
| Yes | Yes | | Yes | Yes | 28,212 † | 7,940 | | 880 | Yes | 153 | $22,794 | None |
| Yes | Yes | Yes | Yes | Yes | 31,144 | 9,494 | 20 | 390 | Yes | | | None |
| Yes | Yes | | Yes | Yes | 41,950 ‡ | 11,600 | 16 | 575 | Yes | | | None |
| Yes | | Yes | No | | 6,127 † | | 9 | 196 | | | | |
| Yes | | Yes | Yes | Yes | 27,910 † | 10,280 | 10 | 1152 | Yes | | | 4/15 |
| Yes | Yes | | Yes | Yes | 28,500 | 10,494 | 6 | 896 | Yes | 19 | $10,742 | None |
| Yes | Yes | Yes | Yes | Yes | 5,866 † | 7,154 | 12 | 196 | | | | |
| Yes | | Yes | No | | 5,983 ‡ | 7,154 | 18 | | | | | |
| Yes | Yes | | No | | | 5,148 | | | | | | |
| Yes | Yes | | No | | | 5,148 | | | | | | |
| Yes | Yes | | No | | | 5,148 | | | | | | |
| Yes | Yes | | No | | | 5,148 | | | | | | |
| Yes | Yes | | No | | | 5,148 | | | | | | |
| Yes | Yes | | No | | | 5,148 | | | | | | |
| Yes | Yes | | No | | | 5,148 | | | | | | |
| Yes | | | No | | | | | | Yes | | | None |
| Yes | Yes | Yes | Yes | Yes | 26,560 † | 8,620 | 12 | | Yes | | | None |
| Yes | | | No | | 5,866 † | 3,150 | | 196 | | | | |
| Yes | Yes | Yes | Yes | Yes | 44,844 † | 11,154 | | | Yes | 166 | $26,604 | None |
| | | Yes | No | | 6,236 † | | 6 | 196 | | | | |
| Yes | | | Yes | | 14,260 † | 6,720 | 6 | 546 | | | | |
| Yes | Yes | | Yes | Yes | 28,380 † | 8,530 | 12 | 450 | Yes | 34 | $10,084 | None |
| Yes | Yes | | Yes | Yes | 38,470 † | 11,440 | 16 | 995 | Yes | 259 | $14,305 | None |
| | | Yes | No | | 5,866 † | | 6 | 196 | | | | |
| Yes | Yes | Yes | No | | 6,373 † | 7,500 | 6 | 196 | Yes | | | None |

† Actual for 2016-17.   ‡ Estimated for 2017-18.   * Includes room and board

| Institution | Control/ degrees | Undergraduates | | Tests required (Fall 2017) | TOEFL | | Application | |
|---|---|---|---|---|---|---|---|---|
| | | Total | Internat'l | | minimum | average | Deadline | Fee |
| Milwaukee Institute of Art & Design . . . . . . . . . . . | Pr/B | 628 | 8 | TOEFL | 79 | 90 | | 25 |
| Milwaukee School of Engineering . . . . . . . . . . . . . | Pr/B | 2,675 | 289 | TOEFL | 79 | 93 | 8/1 | |
| Moraine Park Technical College . . . . . . . . . . . . . . | Pu/A | 6,041 | | TOEFL | | | | 30 |
| Mount Mary University . . . . . . . . . . . . . . . . . . . | Pr/B | 789 | 16 | TOEFL | 76 | | | 100 |
| Northcentral Technical College . . . . . . . . . . . . . . | Pu/A | 3,449 | | TOEFL | | | None | 30 |
| Northeast Wisconsin Technical College . . . . . . . . . | Pu/A | 8,526 | | TOEFL | | | | 30 |
| Northland College . . . . . . . . . . . . . . . . . . . . . . | Pr/B | 562 | 19 | TOEFL, SAT/ACT | 69 | | 7/1 | |
| Rasmussen College: Appleton . . . . . . . . . . . . . . | Pr/AB | 149 | | | | | | |
| Rasmussen College: Green Bay . . . . . . . . . . . . . . | Pr/AB | 447 | | TOEFL | | | | |
| Rasmussen College: Wausau . . . . . . . . . . . . . . . | Pr/AB | 252 | | TOEFL | | | | |
| St. Norbert College . . . . . . . . . . . . . . . . . . . . . | Pr/B | 2,064 | 54 | TOEFL | | | | 150 |
| Silver Lake College of the Holy Family . . . . . . . . | Pr/B | 354 | 15 | TOEFL, SAT/ACT | | | 6/1 | 50 |
| Southwest Wisconsin Technical College . . . . . . . . | Pu/A | 1,430 | | | | | None | 30 |
| University of Phoenix: Milwaukee . . . . . . . . . . . . | Pr/B | 284 | | | | | | |
| University of Wisconsin-Baraboo/Sauk County . . . . . | Pu/A | 600 | | TOEFL | | | | 35 |
| University of Wisconsin-Barron County . . . . . . . . . | Pu/A | 540 | | TOEFL | | | | 35 |
| University of Wisconsin-Eau Claire . . . . . . . . . . . . | Pu/AB | 9,798 | | TOEFL | 79 | | | 50 |
| University of Wisconsin-Fox Valley . . . . . . . . . . . | Pu/A | 1,393 | | TOEFL | | | | 44 |
| University of Wisconsin-Green Bay . . . . . . . . . . . . | Pu/AB | 5,502 | 75 | TOEFL | | 75 | | 50 |
| University of Wisconsin-La Crosse . . . . . . . . . . . . | Pu/AB | 9,486 | 95 | TOEFL | 73 | | | 50 |
| University of Wisconsin-Madison . . . . . . . . . . . . . | Pu/B | 29,536 | 2,460 | TOEFL, SAT/ACT | 80 | | 2/1 | 60 |
| University of Wisconsin-Marathon County . . . . . . . | Pu/A | 1,138 | | TOEFL, SAT/ACT | | | | 35 |
| University of Wisconsin-Marinette . . . . . . . . . . . . | Pu/A | 350 | | TOEFL, SAT/ACT | 61 | | | 44 |
| University of Wisconsin-Marshfield/Wood County . . . . . . . . . . . . . . . . . . . . . . . . . . . . . | Pu/A | 650 | | TOEFL | | | | 45 |
| University of Wisconsin-Milwaukee . . . . . . . . . . . | Pu/B | 20,000 | 739 | TOEFL | 68 | 85 | | 84 |
| University of Wisconsin-Oshkosh . . . . . . . . . . . . . | Pu/AB | 9,502 | 59 | TOEFL | | | | 44 |
| University of Wisconsin-Parkside . . . . . . . . . . . . . | Pu/AB | 4,154 | 59 | TOEFL | | | | 60 |
| University of Wisconsin-Platteville . . . . . . . . . . . . | Pu/AB | 7,676 | 87 | TOEFL | 64 | | | 50 |
| University of Wisconsin-Richland . . . . . . . . . . . . . | Pu/A | 556 | | TOEFL | | 61 | | 44 |
| University of Wisconsin-River Falls . . . . . . . . . . . | Pu/B | 5,346 | 135 | TOEFL | 65 | 70 | 2/1 | 44 |
| University of Wisconsin-Rock County . . . . . . . . . . | Pu/A | 1,220 | | TOEFL | | | | 35 |
| University of Wisconsin-Sheboygan . . . . . . . . . . . . | Pu/A | 769 | | TOEFL | | | | 44 |
| University of Wisconsin-Stevens Point . . . . . . . . . . | Pu/AB | 8,169 | 134 | TOEFL | 70 | 75 | | 100 |
| University of Wisconsin-Stout . . . . . . . . . . . . . . . | Pu/B | 8,178 | 183 | TOEFL, SAT/ACT | 61 | | None | 50 |
| University of Wisconsin-Superior . . . . . . . . . . . . . | Pu/AB | 2,257 | 211 | TOEFL | 61 | 84 | 7/1 | 44 |
| University of Wisconsin-Washington County . . . . . . | Pu/A | 810 | | TOEFL | | | | 44 |
| University of Wisconsin-Waukesha . . . . . . . . . . . . | Pu/A | 2,239 | | TOEFL | 61 | | | 44 |
| University of Wisconsin-Whitewater . . . . . . . . . . . | Pu/AB | 10,775 | 97 | TOEFL | 61 | 70 | 5/30 | 50 |
| Viterbo University . . . . . . . . . . . . . . . . . . . . . . | Pr/AB | 1,861 | | TOEFL | | | | 25 |
| Western Technical College . . . . . . . . . . . . . . . . . | Pu/A | 4,423 | | TOEFL | | | | 30 |
| Wisconsin Indianhead Technical College . . . . . . . . | Pu/A | 2,667 | | TOEFL | 60 | | None | 30 |
| Wisconsin Lutheran College . . . . . . . . . . . . . . . . | Pr/B | 1,074 | | TOEFL | 79 | | | 20 |

**Wyoming**

| Institution | Control/ degrees | Undergraduates | | Tests required (Fall 2017) | TOEFL | | Application | |
|---|---|---|---|---|---|---|---|---|
| | | Total | Internat'l | | minimum | average | Deadline | Fee |
| Casper College . . . . . . . . . . . . . . . . . . . . . . . . | Pu/A | 2,536 | 23 | TOEFL, SAT/ACT | 61 | | None | |
| Central Wyoming College . . . . . . . . . . . . . . . . . . | Pu/A | 1,058 | 1 | TOEFL | 60 | | None | |
| Eastern Wyoming College . . . . . . . . . . . . . . . . . . | Pu/A | 1,715 | | TOEFL | 61 | | | |
| Laramie County Community College . . . . . . . . . . . | Pu/A | 3,008 | | TOEFL | | | None | |
| Northwest College . . . . . . . . . . . . . . . . . . . . . . | Pu/A | 1,337 | 74 | | | | 8/1 | 50 |
| Sheridan College . . . . . . . . . . . . . . . . . . . . . . . | Pu/A | 2,002 | 16 | TOEFL | 61 | | | 100 |
| University of Wyoming . . . . . . . . . . . . . . . . . . . | Pu/B | 9,622 | 393 | TOEFL | 71 | 76 | | 40 |
| Western Wyoming Community College . . . . . . . . . | Pu/A | 2,553 | 47 | TOEFL | | | 6/15 | 100 |

| Student services | | | Housing | | Academic year costs | | Maximum credits/ summer | Credit hour charge | International financial aid | | | Deadline |
|---|---|---|---|---|---|---|---|---|---|---|---|---|
| Adviser | Orientation | ESL | Academic year | Summer | Tuition/ fees | Living costs | | | Available | Number receiving aid | Average award | |
| Yes |  |  | Yes |  | 36,230 | 9,180 |  | 1160 | Yes | 10 | $13,100 | None |
| Yes | Yes | Yes | Yes | Yes | 39,429 | 9,102 | 19 | 655 | Yes | 131 | $10,327 | None |
| Yes |  | Yes | No |  | 5,866† | 6,523 | 9 | 196 | Yes |  |  | None |
| Yes | Yes |  | Yes | Yes | 29,510 | 8,530 | 12 | 860 | Yes |  |  | None |
| Yes | Yes | Yes | Yes | Yes | 5,866† |  | 12 | 196 |  |  |  |  |
| Yes | Yes | Yes | No |  | 5,866† |  | 6 | 196 |  |  |  |  |
| Yes |  |  | Yes | Yes | 35,157 | 8,886 |  | 650 | Yes | 19 | $24,409 | None |
|  |  |  |  |  | 13,455† |  |  | 299 | Yes |  |  | None |
|  |  |  |  |  | 13,455† | 7,011 |  | 299 | Yes |  |  | None |
|  |  |  |  |  | 13,455† |  |  | 299 | Yes |  |  | None |
| Yes | Yes | Yes | Yes | Yes | 36,593 | 9,467 | 12 | 1121 | Yes | 40 | $21,071 | None |
| Yes |  | Yes | Yes | Yes | 14,650† | 13,760 | 18 |  | Yes | 7 | $22,135 | None |
|  |  | Yes | Yes | Yes | 5,866† | 7,000 | 6 | 196 | Yes |  |  | None |
| Yes |  |  | No |  | 12,266† |  | 12 | 488.92 |  |  |  |  |
| Yes |  | Yes | No |  | 12,248† |  | 9 | 488.92 |  |  |  |  |
| Yes | Yes | Yes | Yes | Yes | 16,386† | 6,984 | 11 | 622 | Yes | 84 | $5,363 | None |
| Yes |  |  | Yes |  | 12,118† | 2,150 | 6 |  | Yes |  |  | None |
| Yes | Yes | Yes | Yes | Yes | 15,451† | 7,186 |  | 578 | Yes |  |  | None |
| Yes | Yes | Yes | Yes | Yes | 17,438† | 6,025 |  | 671.1 | Yes |  |  | None |
| Yes | Yes | Yes | Yes | Yes | 33,738† | 10,446 |  | 1355 |  |  |  |  |
| Yes |  |  | Yes | Yes | 12,196† |  | 6 | 488.92 |  |  |  |  |
| Yes |  | Yes | No |  | 12,139† |  | 12 | 488.92 |  |  |  |  |
|  |  |  | Yes |  | 12,191† |  | 9 | 488.92 | Yes |  |  | 4/15 |
| Yes | Yes | Yes | Yes | Yes | 19,901† | 10,350 |  |  | Yes | 33 | $4,019 | None |
| Yes | Yes |  | Yes | Yes | 15,167† |  | 9 | 583.13 |  |  |  |  |
| Yes | Yes |  | Yes | Yes | 15,496† | 8,474 |  | 595 | Yes |  |  | None |
| Yes | Yes | Yes | Yes | Yes | 15,454† | 7,160 | 8 |  | Yes |  |  | None |
| Yes | Yes |  | Yes |  | 12,352† | 6,330 | 9 | 488.92 |  |  |  |  |
| Yes | Yes | Yes | Yes | Yes | 15,554† | 6,545 | 8 |  |  |  |  |  |
|  |  |  |  |  | 12,171† |  | 9 | 488.92 |  |  |  |  |
| Yes |  |  | No |  | 12,170† |  | 9 | 488.92 | Yes |  |  | None |
| Yes | Yes | Yes | Yes | Yes | 16,297† | 6,714 | 6 | 623.53 | Yes | 74 | $6,434 | 5/1 |
| Yes | Yes | Yes | Yes | Yes | 17,140† | 6,624 | 10 | 492 | Yes | 37 | $5,730 | None |
| Yes | Yes | Yes | Yes | Yes | 15,660† | 6,720 |  | 588 | Yes | 262 | $6,175 | None |
| Yes |  |  | No |  | 12,134† | 5,180 | 9 | 488.92 |  |  |  |  |
| Yes |  |  | No |  | 12,179† |  | 6 | 488.92 | Yes |  |  | None |
| Yes | Yes | Yes | Yes | Yes | 16,223† | 6,376 | 12 | 629 | Yes | 82 | $384 | None |
| Yes | Yes |  | Yes | Yes | 26,150† | 11,430 | 12 |  | Yes |  |  | None |
| Yes |  | Yes | Yes | Yes | 5,866† | 6,250 | 12 | 196 |  |  |  |  |
| Yes |  |  | Yes |  | 5,866† |  |  | 196 | Yes |  |  | None |
| Yes | Yes |  | Yes |  | 27,984† | 11,620 |  | 720 | Yes |  |  | None |
| Yes | Yes |  | Yes |  | 7,104† | 7,392 | 10 | 267 | Yes |  |  | None |
| Yes | Yes |  | Yes | Yes | 7,308† | 5,374 |  | 267 | Yes | 17 | $2,566 | None |
| Yes |  | Yes | Yes |  | 7,248† | 6,136 |  | 267 | Yes |  |  | None |
| Yes |  | Yes | Yes |  | 7,578† | 7,988 |  | 267 | Yes |  |  | None |
| Yes | Yes | Yes | Yes | Yes | 7,463† | 5,512 |  | 267 | Yes |  |  | None |
| Yes |  | Yes | Yes | Yes | 7,428† | 6,907 | 8 | 267 | Yes |  |  | None |
| Yes | Yes |  | Yes | Yes | 16,295† | 12,820 | 12 | 496 | Yes | 214 | $10,660 | None |
| Yes | Yes | Yes | Yes | Yes | 6,628† | 6,065 | 12 | 267 | Yes |  |  | None |

† Actual for 2016-17.   ‡ Estimated for 2017-18.   * Includes room and board

# International undergraduate student enrollment

Houston Community
College System (TX) ............... 6,474
Arizona State
University (AZ) ..................... 5,339
Purdue University (IN) ................. 5,129
University of Illinois at
Urbana-Champaign (IL) ........... 5,097
Michigan State
University (MI) ..................... 4,846
Penn State University
Park (PA) ............................ 4,706
New York University (NY) .......... 4,576
University of California:
Irvine (CA) .......................... 4,440
University of
Washington (WA) ................... 4,391
University of California:
Davis (CA) ........................... 3,918
University of California:
Los Angeles (CA) .................... 3,645
Boston University (MA) ............... 3,614
Ohio State University:
Columbus Campus (OH) .......... 3,566
Indiana University
Bloomington (IN) .................... 3,533
Northeastern
University (MA) ..................... 3,414
SUNY University at
Buffalo (NY) ......................... 3,249
Miami Dade College (FL) ............. 3,244
Rutgers, The State
University of New
Jersey: New Brunswick/
Piscataway Campus (NJ) ......... 2,904
Brigham Young University-
Idaho (ID) ............................ 2,813
University of Minnesota:
Twin Cities (MN) ................... 2,779
University of Oregon (OR) ............ 2,571
University of Wisconsin-
Madison (WI) ........................ 2,460
Florida International
University (FL) ...................... 2,427
University of Iowa (IA) ................ 2,421
SUNY University at Stony
Brook (NY) ........................... 2,354
Academy of Art
University (CA) ...................... 2,340
University of Arizona (AZ) ......... 2,276
Savannah College of Art
and Design (GA) ..................... 2,165
California State University:
Long Beach (CA) .................... 2,139
Iowa State University (IA) ............ 2,063
Santa Monica College (CA) ........ 2,060
California State University:
Fullerton (CA) ....................... 2,052
San Diego State
University (CA) ...................... 2,042
University of Texas at
Austin (TX) .......................... 2,042
Community College of
Philadelphia (PA) .................... 1,996
Miami University:
Oxford (OH) ......................... 1,960
University of Colorado
Boulder (CO) ......................... 1,959

University of
Michigan (MI) ....................... 1,949
Parsons The New School
for Design (NY) ..................... 1,925
San Jose State
University (CA) ...................... 1,879
Temple University (PA) ............... 1,858
University of South
Florida (FL) .......................... 1,844
Syracuse University (NY) ............ 1,829
University of California:
Santa Barbara (CA) ................. 1,810
Berklee College of
Music (MA) ........................... 1,779
University of Nebraska -
Lincoln (NE) ......................... 1,746
City University of New
York: Baruch
College (NY) .......................... 1,672
Oregon State
University (OR) ...................... 1,646
Broward College (FL) ................. 1,592
City University of New
York: Borough of
Manhattan Community
College (NY) .......................... 1,589
San Francisco State
University (CA) ...................... 1,553
University of Houston (TX) ......... 1,522
University of Massachusetts
Boston (MA) .......................... 1,503
Virginia Polytechnic
Institute and State
University (VA) ...................... 1,499
Carnegie Mellon
University (PA) ...................... 1,492
Georgia Institute of
Technology (GA) .................... 1,480
University of Miami (FL) ............ 1,480
Texas Tech
University (TX) ...................... 1,477
School of Visual Arts (NY) ........ 1,466
Cornell University (NY) .............. 1,461
California State Polytechnic
University: Pomona (CA) ......... 1,442
West Virginia
University (WV) ..................... 1,386
California State University:
Los Angeles (CA) .................... 1,362
University of
Rochester (NY) ...................... 1,293
SUNY University at
Binghamton (NY) ................... 1,257
California State University:
San Bernardino (CA) ............... 1,237
George Washington
University (DC) ...................... 1,216
University of San
Francisco (CA) ....................... 1,200
California State University:
Fresno (CA) .......................... 1,196
Kent State University (OH) ......... 1,177
University of
Pennsylvania (PA) .................. 1,176
Suffolk University (MA) .............. 1,162
Northern Arizona
University (AZ) ...................... 1,152

University of Maryland:
College Park (MD) ................... 1,145
University of Massachusetts
Amherst (MA) ........................ 1,138
Washington State
University (WA) ..................... 1,130
George Mason
University (VA) ...................... 1,127
Collin County Community
College District (TX) ............... 1,125
Florida Institute of
Technology (FL) ..................... 1,125
Emory University (GA) ............... 1,093
University of Kansas (KS) .......... 1,091
University of
Cincinnati (OH) ..................... 1,089
University of Texas at El
Paso (TX) ............................. 1,067
Hult International Business
School (CA) .......................... 1,059
Central Piedmont
Community
College (NC) ......................... 1,053
Portland State
University (OR) ...................... 1,042
Fashion Institute of
Technology (NY) ..................... 1,039
University of Utah (UT) ............... 1,027
University of South
Alabama (AL) ......................... 1,014
University of Toledo (OH) ........... 1,009
North Carolina State
University (NC) ...................... 1,002
University of North
Texas (TX) ............................ 1,002
Kansas State
University (KS) ....................... 999
Community College of
Baltimore County (MD) ............. 972
Colorado State
University (CO) ....................... 951
University of Missouri:
Columbia (MO) ....................... 949
ASA College (NY) ...................... 930
University of
Oklahoma (OK) ....................... 926
School of the Art Institute
of Chicago (IL) ........................ 920
University of Nevada: Las
Vegas (NV) ............................. 913
City University of New
York: Hunter
College (NY) ........................... 910
Columbia University (NY) ............ 897
Lindenwood
University (MO) ...................... 895
Pratt Institute (NY) ..................... 879
University of Colorado
Denver (CO) ........................... 864
Indiana University-Purdue
University
Indianapolis (IN) ..................... 849
California State University:
East Bay (CA) ......................... 837
Georgetown
University (DC) ....................... 830
City University of New
York: Queens
College (NY) ........................... 822
Northwestern
University (IL) ........................ 818
Western Kentucky
University (KY) ....................... 816
Pace University (NY) ................... 808
University of Tulsa (OK) .............. 805
City University of New
York: New York City
College of
Technology (NY) ...................... 799
Idaho State University (ID) ............ 796
University of Tampa (FL) .............. 795
Virginia Commonwealth
University (VA) ....................... 787
Rochester Institute of
Technology (NY) ...................... 784

University of Dayton (OH) ............. 783
California State University:
Sacramento (CA) ..................... 777
Wichita State
University (KS) ....................... 777
Harvard College (MA) ................. 772
Missouri State
University (MO) ...................... 762
University of California:
Santa Cruz (CA) ..................... 762
Tennessee State
University (TN) ....................... 747
Brown University (RI) .................. 744
University of
Delaware (DE) ........................ 743
Brandeis University (MA) .............. 742
City University of New
York: City College (NY) ............ 741
University of Wisconsin-
Milwaukee (WI) ...................... 739
Oklahoma State
University (OK) ....................... 738
University of Central
Florida (FL) ........................... 736
Morgan State
University (MD) ...................... 724
SUNY University at
Albany (NY) .......................... 723
University of Virginia (VA) ........... 721
University of Chicago (IL) ............. 717
Embry-Riddle Aeronautical
University (FL) ....................... 711
Western Michigan
University (MI) ....................... 709
University of
Pittsburgh (PA) ...................... 706
Rensselaer Polytechnic
Institute (NY) ........................ 705
City University of New
York: Queensborough
Community
College (NY) ........................... 694
Fordham University (NY) .............. 692
University of
Arkansas (AR) ........................ 678
City University of New
York: LaGuardia
Community
College (NY) ........................... 666
Duke University (NC) ................... 661
St. John's University (NY) .............. 660
Florida Atlantic
University (FL) ....................... 653
Liberty University (VA) ................ 651
University of Houston-
Downtown (TX) ....................... 648
Middle Tennessee State
University (TN) ....................... 644
Texas Southern
University (TX) ....................... 641
Utah Valley
University (UT) ....................... 641
Stanford University (CA) ............... 640
Troy University (AL) .................... 638
Boise State University (ID) ............ 634
Indiana State
University (IN) ....................... 632
MiraCosta College (CA) ................ 632
Texas A&M
University (TX) ....................... 630
Case Western Reserve
University (OH) ....................... 625
Princeton University (NJ) .............. 625
University of Texas at
Dallas (TX) ........................... 624
Johnson & Wales
University:
Providence (RI) ...................... 610
Boston College (MA) ................... 609
Babson College (MA) .................. 608
University of
Alabama (AL) ......................... 607
Penn State Harrisburg (PA) ............ 606
New Mexico State
University (NM) ...................... 603

International undergraduate student enrollment

International undergraduate student enrollment

International undergraduate student enrollment

University of Puget
Sound (WA)...................... 12
University of Sioux
Falls (SD)....................... 12
Wayne State College (NE)............... 12
Adirondack Community
College (NY) ..................... 11
Albany State
University (GA)...................... 11
Aquinas College (TN) ..................... 11
Bay Path University (MA)............ 11
Berry College (GA)........................ 11
Big Bend Community
College (WA)..................... 11
Community College of
Rhode Island (RI) ..................... 11
Dawson Community
College (MT).................... 11
DeVry University: North
Brunswick (NJ) ..................... 11
East Texas Baptist
University (TX)..................... 11
Franklin College (IN)...................... 11
Mount Wachusett
Community
College (MA)..................... 11
Schreiner University (TX)................. 11
Shepherd University (WV)............... 11
University of Maine at
Machias (ME).................... 11
University of St. Mary (KS) ............. 11
Ursuline College (OH) ..................... 11
Western Connecticut State
University (CT)..................... 11
Wright State University:
Lake Campus (OH) ..................... 11
Adventist University of
Health Sciences (FL)..................... 10
Aims Community
College (CO)..................... 10
Alvernia University (PA) ................. 10
Arkansas State University:
Beebe (AR)..................... 10
Beacon College (FL) ........................ 10
Garrett College (MD) ..................... 10
Louisiana State University
at Eunice (LA)..................... 10
Massachusetts Maritime
Academy (MA)..................... 10
Mount Saint Mary
College (NY) ..................... 10
National-Louis
University (IL)..................... 10
Saint Anselm College (NH) ............. 10
Simpson University (CA).................. 10
Sterling College (KS) ..................... 10
Toccoa Falls College (GA) ............. 10
Virginia State
University (VA)..................... 10
Virginia Wesleyan
College (VA) ..................... 10
Aurora University (IL) ..................... 9
Bethel University (MN)..................... 9
Bismarck State
College (ND) ..................... 9
Blue Mountain
College (MS) ..................... 9
California Maritime
Academy (CA)..................... 9
Central State
University (OH) ..................... 9
Chamberlain College of
Nursing: Chicago (IL) ..................... 9
Columbia Southern
University (AL) ..................... 9
Hope International
University (CA)..................... 9
Penn State Fayette, The
Eberly Campus (PA) ..................... 9
St. Vincent College (PA)..................... 9
Sullivan County
Community
College (NY) ..................... 9
Thomas More
College (KY) ..................... 9

University of Kansas
Medical Center (KS) ..................... 9
University of Saint
Francis (IN) ..................... 9
University of Saint
Joseph (CT)..................... 9
Bluffton University (OH) ..................... 8
Central Christian College of
Kansas (KS) ..................... 8
College of New
Rochelle (NY)..................... 8
Elms College (MA) ..................... 8
Emory & Henry
College (VA) ..................... 8
Georgetown College (KY) ..................... 8
Maranatha Baptist
University (WI)..................... 8
Massachusetts College of
Liberal Arts (MA) ..................... 8
Milwaukee Institute of
Art & Design (WI)..................... 8
Ohio University: Zanesville
Campus (OH)..................... 8
Oregon Health & Science
University (OR)..................... 8
Pacific Northwest College
of Art (OR) ..................... 8
Post University (CT) ..................... 8
Rose State College (OK)..................... 8
St. Mary's College of
Maryland (MD)..................... 8
San Diego Christian
College (CA)..................... 8
University of Cincinnati:
Clermont College (OH)..................... 8
University of Mount
Union (OH)..................... 8
Western State Colorado
University (CO) ..................... 8
Blackburn College (IL) ..................... 7
Clarke University (IA)..................... 7
Delaware Valley
University (PA)..................... 7
Donnelly College (KS) ..................... 7
Eureka College (IL)..................... 7
LaGrange College (GA) ..................... 7
Lebanon Valley
College (PA)..................... 7
Malone University (OH) ..................... 7
Minnesota State College -
Southeast
Technical (MN) ..................... 7
Northeast Iowa Community
College (IA) ..................... 7
Sierra Nevada
College (NV) ..................... 7
Sullivan University (KY) ..................... 7
University of Maine at
Farmington (ME)..................... 7
Andrew College (GA) ..................... 6
Black Hawk College (IL)..................... 6
Broome Community
College (NY) ..................... 6
Bryn Athyn College (PA) ..................... 6
Centenary College of
Louisiana (LA)..................... 6
Chamberlain College of
Nursing: Atlanta (GA)..................... 6
Coahoma Community
College (MS) ..................... 6
Deep Springs College (CA) ..................... 6
Hampden-Sydney
College (VA) ..................... 6
Holy Family
University (PA)..................... 6
Johnson State College (VT) ..................... 6
Kentucky State
University (KY) ..................... 6
Louisburg College (NC) ..................... 6
Mills College (CA)..................... 6
North Greenville
University (SC)..................... 6
Penn State Worthington
Scranton (PA) ..................... 6

Potomac State College of
West Virginia
University (WV) ..................... 6
Saint Augustine's
University (NC) ..................... 6
Sweet Briar College (VA)..................... 6
Texas Lutheran
University (TX) ..................... 6
United States Merchant
Marine Academy (NY) ..................... 6
Westminster College (PA)..................... 6
Barclay College (KS) ..................... 5
Cabrini University (PA) ..................... 5
Carroll Community
College (MD) ..................... 5
College of Saint Mary (NE) ..................... 5
DeVry University:
Arlington (VA) ..................... 5
Glenville State
College (WV)..................... 5
Kansas City Art
Institute (MO) ..................... 5
Kentucky Mountain Bible
College (KY) ..................... 5
Keystone College (PA)..................... 5
Life Pacific College (CA) ..................... 5
Mount St. Joseph
University (OH) ..................... 5
St. Mary-of-the-Woods
College (IN)..................... 5
South Carolina State
University (SC)..................... 5
Spartanburg Methodist
College (SC) ..................... 5
Alverno College (WI)..................... 4
Anna Maria College (MA)..................... 4
Cazenovia College (NY) ..................... 4
Chamberlain College of
Nursing: Houston (TX) ..................... 4
Delaware College of Art
and Design (DE)..................... 4
Harris-Stowe State
University (MO) ..................... 4
Hilbert College (NY) ..................... 4
Kankakee Community
College (IL) ..................... 4
Marlboro College (VT) ..................... 4
North Shore Community
College (MA)..................... 4
Peirce College (PA)..................... 4
Rogue Community
College (OR)..................... 4
St. Elizabeth College of
Nursing (NY)..................... 4
St. John Fisher
College (NY) ..................... 4
Tunxis Community
College (CT) ..................... 4
University of Arkansas for
Medical Sciences (AR)..................... 4
Wesley College (DE) ..................... 4
York County Community
College (ME) ..................... 4
Bastyr University (WA) ..................... 3
Berkshire Community
College (MA)..................... 3
Bucks County Community
College (PA)..................... 3
Cogswell Polytechnical
College (CA)..................... 3
Danville Community
College (VA) ..................... 3
DeVry University:
Irving (TX)..................... 3
Fox Valley Technical
College (WI) ..................... 3
Gogebic Community
College (MI) ..................... 3
Gwynedd Mercy
University (PA)..................... 3
Keene State College (NH)..................... 3
Lurleen B. Wallace
Community College (AL) ..................... 3
Misericordia
University (PA)..................... 3

Navajo Technical
University (NM) ..................... 3
Prescott College (AZ)..................... 3
The Sage Colleges (NY) ..................... 3
South Texas College (TX) ..................... 3
Southeastern Illinois
College (IL)..................... 3
Spalding University (KY) ..................... 3
University of Minnesota:
Rochester (MN) ..................... 3
Virginia Union
University (VA) ..................... 3
Bowling Green State
University: Firelands
College (OH) ..................... 2
Central College (IA) ..................... 2
Charles Drew University of
Medicine and
Science (CA)..................... 2
College of Business and
Technology: Flagler (FL) ..................... 2
Corning Community
College (NY) ..................... 2
Criswell College (TX) ..................... 2
Edison State Community
College (OH) ..................... 2
Friends University (KS) ..................... 2
Hinds Community
College (MS) ..................... 2
Huntingdon College (AL) ..................... 2
Ivy Tech Community
College: South
Central (IN) ..................... 2
Johnson University:
Florida (FL) ..................... 2
McHenry County
College (IL) ..................... 2
Mitchell Technical
Institute (SD) ..................... 2
Nunez Community
College (LA) ..................... 2
Ohio Technical
College (OH) ..................... 2
Pacific College of Oriental
Medicine: San
Diego (CA) ..................... 2
Reinhardt University (GA)..................... 2
Southern Vermont
College (VT) ..................... 2
Trinity College of
Florida (FL) ..................... 2
University of Valley
Forge (PA) ..................... 2
VanderCook College of
Music (IL)..................... 2
Waynesburg
University (PA)..................... 2
California Institute of
Integral Studies (CA)..................... 1
Central Wyoming
College (WY)..................... 1
Chamberlain College of
Nursing: Cleveland (OH) ..................... 1
Chamberlain College of
Nursing: Miramar (FL)..................... 1
Cleveland State Community
College (TN)..................... 1
College of the
Ouachitas (AR)..................... 1
DeVry University:
Westminster (CO) ..................... 1
East Central College (MO) ..................... 1
Granite State College (NH)..................... 1
Heidelberg University (OH)..................... 1
Ivy Tech Community
College: Central
Indiana (IN) ..................... 1
Ivy Tech Community
College: North
Central (IN)..................... 1
Ivy Tech Community
College: Northeast (IN) ..................... 1
Ivy Tech Community
College: Wabash
Valley (IN)..................... 1

# Total financial aid for international undergraduate students

Princeton University (NJ).... 21,197,495
Berklee College of
  Music (MA) .................... 17,607,106
University of
  Rochester (NY)............... 16,115,852
Dartmouth College (NH)..... 15,535,530
Massachusetts Institute of
  Technology (MA)............ 15,405,747
Illinois Institute of
  Technology (IL)............... 14,106,074
Florida Institute of
  Technology (FL)............... 13,896,231
New York University (NY). 12,780,487
Mount Holyoke
  College (MA).................. 12,059,426
Cornell University (NY)...... 11,395,314
Macalester College (MN)..... 11,033,957
University of Notre
  Dame (IN)...................... 10,534,603
Brown University (RI)........... 9,828,035
Tennessee Wesleyan
  College (TN)..................... 9,610,154
Lindenwood
  University (MO)................. 9,487,600
Stanford University (CA)....... 9,477,988
Worcester Polytechnic
  Institute (MA)................... 9,304,915
Amherst College (MA).......... 9,229,581
Northeastern
  University (MA) ............... 9,109,529
Suffolk University (MA)....... 8,906,296
Michigan State
  University (MI).................. 8,851,195
Texas Christian
  University (TX) ................ 8,764,807
Defiance College (OH)......... 8,207,704
St. John's University (NY)..... 8,132,691
Grinnell College (IA)........... 8,125,178
Faulkner University (AL)....... 8,054,725
Smith College (MA)............. 7,993,329
University of Chicago (IL)..... 7,904,835
Tufts University (MA)........... 7,851,100
University of San
  Francisco (CA).................. 7,390,919
Calvin College (MI) ............ 7,319,000
Middlebury College (VT)...... 7,264,632
Jacksonville
  University (FL).................. 7,181,955
St. Lawrence
  University (NY) ................ 7,063,912
University of Denver (CO) .. 6,911,714
Andrews University (MI)...... 6,852,231
Bryn Mawr College (PA)...... 6,793,624
Soka University of
  America (CA)................... 6,663,281
Clark University (MA) ......... 6,592,450
Colgate University (NY)....... 6,574,360
Denison University (OH)...... 6,506,835
Arizona State
  University (AZ) ................ 6,498,129
Vanderbilt University (TN)... 6,201,687
George Washington
  University (DC)................. 6,050,029
Williams College (MA)........ 5,972,530
Dickinson College (PA) ....... 5,904,199
Boston University (MA)........ 5,861,421
Liberty University (VA)........ 5,858,503

Baylor University (TX) ......... 5,827,467
University of
  Richmond (VA) ................ 5,712,744
Southern Methodist
  University (TX) ................ 5,584,593
Oberlin College (OH)........... 5,474,317
University of Tulsa (OK)...... 5,460,448
Missouri State
  University (MO) ............... 5,458,016
Berea College (KY).............. 5,448,618
Colorado College (CO) ........ 5,398,931
College of Wooster (OH)...... 5,366,850
University of Nebraska -
  Lincoln (NE)..................... 5,318,287
University of Miami (FL) ..... 5,297,272
Colby College (ME) ............ 5,199,081
Stetson University (FL)......... 5,149,865
Texas A&M
  University (TX) ................ 5,074,581
University of
  Evansville (IN)................... 5,031,975
Skidmore College (NY)......... 5,000,000
Wellesley College (MA) ....... 4,993,477
Sarah Lawrence
  College (NY) .................... 4,902,649
University of Toledo (OH).... 4,889,532
Quinnipiac University (CT)... 4,830,398
Wesleyan University (CT)..... 4,713,639
Knox College (IL) ............... 4,663,594
University of Iowa (IA)......... 4,633,873
Indiana University
  Bloomington (IN).............. 4,604,591
Bucknell University (PA)...... 4,525,665
Miami University:
  Oxford (OH) .................... 4,488,829
Luther College (IA)............. 4,485,027
Northwestern
  University (IL).................. 4,452,744
Lawrence University (WI).... 4,416,397
Bates College (ME)............. 4,305,219
Furman University (SC) ....... 4,221,678
Providence College (RI)....... 4,171,699
New Mexico State
  University (NM) ............... 4,169,233
Lynn University (FL) ........... 4,120,709
Bennington College (VT)...... 4,058,298
Vassar College (NY) ........... 4,055,995
San Jose State
  University (CA) ................ 4,000,416
Hofstra University (NY)....... 3,979,259
Hult International Business
  School (CA)...................... 3,960,014
Manhattanville
  College (NY) .................... 3,940,182
University of Texas at
  Austin (TX)...................... 3,936,112
University of South
  Florida (FL)...................... 3,873,228
Union College (NY)............. 3,831,459
Fairfield University (CT)....... 3,829,744
Eastern Michigan
  University (MI).................. 3,775,960
Rochester Institute of
  Technology (NY)............... 3,751,398
University of Dayton (OH) ... 3,741,173
Marquette University (WI).... 3,705,060
Swarthmore College (PA)..... 3,694,165

Washington State
  University (WA) ............... 3,690,352
St. John's College (NM) ....... 3,682,551
Temple University (PA)........ 3,671,482
University of
  Vermont (VT) ................... 3,665,168
University of Massachusetts
  Amherst (MA) .................. 3,663,999
Seattle University (WA)....... 3,539,374
Washington and Lee
  University (VA)................. 3,510,803
University of Alabama at
  Birmingham (AL)............... 3,508,854
New York Institute of
  Technology (NY)............... 3,493,797
Cooper Union for the
  Advancement of Science
  and Art (NY) .................... 3,488,400
Cardinal Stritch
  University (WI).................. 3,487,626
Washington University in
  St. Louis (MO).................. 3,482,679
Hamilton College (NY)........ 3,480,501
University of
  Cincinnati (OH) ................ 3,463,014
Carleton College (MN)......... 3,346,977
Saint Leo University (FL)..... 3,337,226
DePauw University (IN)........ 3,303,408
Wheaton College (MA)......... 3,276,354
Gustavus Adolphus
  College (MN).................... 3,247,372
School of the Art Institute
  of Chicago (IL).................. 3,238,770
Southeastern Louisiana
  University (LA).................. 3,177,220
Lehigh University (PA)......... 3,173,870
Bard College (NY) .............. 3,163,869
Gordon College (MA) .......... 3,137,567
Trinity University (TX)......... 3,123,693
Middle Tennessee State
  University (TN) ................ 3,118,089
Brandeis University (MA)..... 3,102,796
University of
  Indianapolis (IN)............... 3,084,232
Davidson College (NC) ........ 3,035,933
University of
  Mississippi (MS)................ 3,025,011
Illinois Wesleyan
  University (IL) .................. 3,001,570
College of the
  Atlantic (ME)................... 2,981,327
Robert Morris
  University (PA) ................ 2,975,724
University of Nevada: Las
  Vegas (NV)...................... 2,936,180
Caldwell University (NJ)....... 2,928,248
Lewis & Clark
  College (OR).................... 2,894,091
Pepperdine University (CA).. 2,892,519
Saint Louis
  University (MO) ............... 2,889,797
Ithaca College (NY) ............ 2,880,617
Kalamazoo College (MI)....... 2,850,908
Rollins College (FL)............. 2,834,280
Gettysburg College (PA)....... 2,825,892
Brigham Young
  University (UT).................. 2,816,719
Canisius College (NY) ......... 2,742,295
Messiah College (PA) .......... 2,739,632
LIU Brooklyn (NY)............... 2,727,663
Rice University (TX)............. 2,688,978
University of New
  Orleans (LA)..................... 2,659,729
Ohio Wesleyan
  University (OH)................. 2,631,405
Villanova University (PA)..... 2,625,277
Kenyon College (OH) .......... 2,572,248
University of California:
  Los Angeles (CA).............. 2,568,847
Reed College (OR) .............. 2,536,325
Queens University of
  Charlotte (NC) .................. 2,519,781
John Brown
  University (AR) ................ 2,506,275
Babson College (MA) .......... 2,504,975

Eastman School of Music
  of the University of
  Rochester (NY).................. 2,480,608
North Carolina State
  University (NC) ................ 2,478,939
Rider University (NJ)........... 2,468,882
School of Visual Arts (NY) .. 2,464,804
Florida International
  University (FL) ................. 2,450,526
New Jersey Institute of
  Technology (NJ)................. 2,437,569
University of Arizona (AZ).. 2,426,580
Florida Southern
  College (FL)...................... 2,386,102
Missouri University of
  Science and
  Technology (MO).............. 2,365,647
Bentley University (MA)....... 2,339,218
Duquesne University (PA)..... 2,329,952
St. Edward's
  University (TX) ................ 2,310,364
University of
  Alabama (AL).................... 2,296,300
Taylor University (IN).......... 2,289,489
University of the Incarnate
  Word (TX) ....................... 2,282,459
University of
  Wyoming (WY)................. 2,281,447
Hobart and William Smith
  Colleges (NY)................... 2,274,255
La Salle University (PA)....... 2,265,710
Ringling College of Art and
  Design (FL)....................... 2,209,775
Colorado State
  University (CO) ................ 2,163,399
Agnes Scott College (GA) .... 2,144,009
Wingate University (NC)....... 2,140,684
Drew University (NJ) ........... 2,129,168
Iowa State University (IA)..... 2,127,097
University of Detroit
  Mercy (MI) ...................... 2,125,996
Augustana College (IL)......... 2,107,215
Juniata College (PA) ............ 2,078,361
Loyola Marymount
  University (CA).................. 2,060,125
SUNY College at
  Plattsburgh (NY)............... 2,045,991
Adelphi University (NY)....... 2,040,814
North Dakota State
  University (ND) ................ 2,039,588
Whitworth University (WA) . 2,017,831
Bowdoin College (ME) ......... 2,010,562
Emory University (GA)......... 2,010,077
University of Portland (OR).. 2,003,986
Drake University (IA) ........... 1,993,286
California College of the
  Arts (CA) ......................... 1,986,710
Iona College (NY) ............... 1,974,548
Whitman College (WA) ........ 1,963,990
University of Tampa (FL)..... 1,934,000
Gannon University (PA)........ 1,902,537
University of New
  Hampshire (NH) ............... 1,896,005
Fordham University (NY)..... 1,870,558
St. Mary's College of
  California (CA).................. 1,859,129
University of Texas at
  Dallas (TX)....................... 1,854,053
Gonzaga University (WA)..... 1,838,304
Drury University (MO) ......... 1,829,498
Merrimack College (MA)...... 1,829,106
Niagara University (NY)....... 1,828,461
College of St.
  Benedict (MN)................... 1,773,412
American University (DC).... 1,769,611
Chapman University (CA)..... 1,769,171
Indiana University-Purdue
  University
  Indianapolis (IN)............... 1,764,168
Augsburg College (MN)........ 1,763,815
Wabash College (IN)............ 1,753,650
LIU Post (NY)...................... 1,733,167
Centre College (KY) ............ 1,719,410
Post University (CT) ............ 1,698,799

Western Kentucky
   University (KY) .............. 1,686,634
St. John's University (MN) ... 1,680,604
Southern Illinois University
   Carbondale (IL) .............. 1,622,400
Upper Iowa University (IA).. 1,618,730
University of Wisconsin-
   Superior (WI)................... 1,617,983
Bowling Green State
   University (OH) ............... 1,617,362
Bethune-Cookman
   University (FL) ................. 1,603,197
Valparaiso University (IN).... 1,582,443
University of California:
   Irvine (CA) ..................... 1,581,156
Limestone College (SC) ........ 1,579,135
University of Kansas (KS) .... 1,561,412
Truman State
   University (MO) ............... 1,553,864
University of Southern
   Mississippi (MS)............... 1,534,502
University of California:
   Davis (CA) ..................... 1,521,019
Goshen College (IN) ............ 1,520,880
Biola University (CA) ........... 1,511,922
Tulane University (LA) ........ 1,501,540
Marist College (NY)............. 1,500,994
Westminster College (UT) .... 1,480,062
California Institute of
   Technology (CA) ............... 1,475,982
West Virginia
   University (WV) ............... 1,475,000
Florida Atlantic
   University (FL) ................. 1,450,825
Kutztown University of
   Pennsylvania (PA) ............. 1,442,289
Northern Illinois
   University (IL) .................. 1,411,777
Graceland University (IA)..... 1,407,889
Houston Baptist
   University (TX) ................ 1,406,891
Tiffin University (OH) .......... 1,402,090
San Francisco Conservatory
   of Music (CA) ................... 1,396,790
John Carroll
   University (OH) ................ 1,395,330
Southeast Missouri State
   University (MO) ............... 1,393,794
Lycoming College (PA) ........ 1,388,240
Embry-Riddle Aeronautical
   University (FL) ................. 1,372,837
Norwich University (VT) ...... 1,371,115
American International
   College (MA)..................... 1,360,516
University of St.
   Thomas (TX) .................. 1,359,583
Elizabethtown College (PA).. 1,357,080
Mount Saint Mary's
   University (CA) ................ 1,356,443
Coastal Carolina
   University (SC) ................. 1,353,044
Milwaukee School of
   Engineering (WI)............... 1,352,957
Grand Valley State
   University (MI) ................. 1,349,480
Walsh University (OH) ........ 1,343,015
California State University:
   Fresno (CA) ..................... 1,342,200
Northwest Missouri State
   University (MO) ................ 1,339,192
Abilene Christian
   University (TX) ................ 1,337,850
East Carolina
   University (NC) ................ 1,334,957
Wayne State
   University (MI) ................. 1,329,735
California Lutheran
   University (CA) ................ 1,329,552
California State University:
   San Marcos (CA)............. 1,326,532
McKendree University (IL)... 1,318,377
Ramapo College of New
   Jersey (NJ) ...................... 1,302,834
San Diego State
   University (CA) ................ 1,300,000

Sewanee: The University of
   the South (TN) ................ 1,299,162
Michigan Technological
   University (MI)................. 1,288,939
Rose-Hulman Institute of
   Technology (IN) ............... 1,271,259
College of the Holy
   Cross (MA) ...................... 1,267,965
University of Missouri: St.
   Louis (MO) ...................... 1,255,522
University of Oregon (OR) ... 1,253,665
Maryville University of
   Saint Louis (MO)............. 1,243,793
Goucher College (MD)......... 1,232,073
Palm Beach Atlantic
   University (FL) ................. 1,223,487
Point Park University (PA) ... 1,215,181
King University (TN) ........... 1,213,759
Oklahoma City
   University (OK) ............... 1,213,338
Elmira College (NY) ............ 1,200,975
Allegheny College (PA) ........ 1,195,910
Jacksonville State
   University (AL) ................ 1,186,064
Sacred Heart
   University (CT) ................ 1,174,712
Seton Hill University (PA)... 1,153,212
Lackawanna College (PA).... 1,150,885
University of Maryland:
   Baltimore County (MD).... 1,148,579
Roanoke College (VA)......... 1,146,374
University of Akron (OH) .... 1,143,473
Xavier University (OH)........ 1,142,873
Newberry College (SC) ........ 1,137,172
Columbia College (MO)....... 1,136,308
Miami Dade College (FL).... 1,131,900
Clarkson University (NY) .... 1,124,560
Winona State
   University (MN) ............... 1,123,225
Tusculum College (TN)........ 1,123,224
Texas A&M University-
   Commerce (TX)................ 1,115,728
Linfield College (OR) .......... 1,113,064
University of Mobile (AL).... 1,109,433
North Central College (IL)... 1,101,713
Culinary Institute of
   America (NY) ................... 1,093,462
Academy of Art
   University (CA) ................ 1,091,471
La Roche College (PA)......... 1,075,000
University of Texas at San
   Antonio (TX) ................... 1,066,097
Houghton College (NY) ....... 1,061,577
Murray State
   University (KY) ................ 1,058,479
Texas State
   University (TX) ................ 1,041,809
Muhlenberg College (PA) ..... 1,041,738
Monmouth University (NJ) ... 1,039,875
University of Nebraska -
   Kearney (NE)................... 1,022,674
Hope College (MI) ............... 1,017,582
Santa Clara
   University (CA) ................ 1,014,580
Hollins University (VA)........ 1,009,783
Central Methodist
   University (MO) ............... 1,005,872
William Jewell
   College (MO)..................... 1,004,267
Manchester University (IN)... 1,001,947
University of Central
   Oklahoma (OK) ................ 995,486
Claremont McKenna
   College (CA)...................... 976,115
University of Science and
   Arts of Oklahoma (OK) ....... 972,826
Oklahoma State
   University (OK) ................ 966,391
Oregon State
   University (OR) ................ 965,963
College of Saint Rose (NY)..... 962,182
Illinois College (IL)................. 961,695
Northeastern State
   University (OK) ................ 957,598
Lee University (TN) ................ 950,486

Catawba College (NC) ............ 948,838
University of New
   Haven (CT) ...................... 945,518
Pacific Lutheran
   University (WA) ................ 944,246
William Woods
   University (MO) ............... 939,740
Sam Houston State
   University (TX) ................ 930,075
University of
   Montana (MT) ................. 923,326
Grand View
   University (IA)................... 921,934
Concordia College:
   Moorhead (MN) ............... 918,316
Nova Southeastern
   University (FL) ................. 913,457
Southeastern
   University (FL) ................. 913,097
Southern New Hampshire
   University (NH) ................ 910,704
California Institute of the
   Arts (CA) ........................ 905,762
Kettering University (MI) ........ 900,793
Washington & Jefferson
   College (PA) .................... 899,055
Brenau University (GA) ........ 897,593
Alderson-Broaddus
   University (WV) ............... 891,934
Cottey College (MO)............. 891,375
Huntington University (IN).... 885,313
Albion College (MI) ............. 884,360
Wake Forest
   University (NC) ................ 874,566
Saint Michael's
   College (VT) .................... 870,775
Pace University:
   Pleasantville/
   Briarcliff (NY) ................. 865,980
Marymount California
   University (CA) ................ 859,483
University of South
   Carolina: Aiken (SC)............ 857,058
Utah Valley
   University (UT) ................ 854,506
Columbus College of Art
   and Design (OH) ................ 853,625
Millsaps College (MS) ............ 852,267
St. Thomas Aquinas
   College (NY) ................... 851,610
Culver-Stockton
   College (MO)..................... 843,617
St. Norbert College (WI)........ 842,870
Newman University (KS)........ 835,323
Marshall University (WV)....... 831,179
Olivet Nazarene
   University (IL) .................. 826,176
University of Minnesota:
   Twin Cities (MN) ............. 820,258
New England College (NH)..... 811,852
University of South
   Carolina: Columbia (SC).... 806,336
Harding University (AR)......... 804,147
Lipscomb University (TN)....... 787,344
Harvey Mudd College (CA)..... 786,475
Roberts Wesleyan
   College (NY) ................... 784,792
Central Washington
   University (WA) ................ 783,382
Northwest Nazarene
   University (ID).................. 782,875
University of Houston (TX)..... 782,850
Haverford College (PA) .......... 781,278
Wentworth Institute of
   Technology (MA)............... 777,350
Buena Vista
   University (IA)................... 776,681
The Master's
   University (CA) ................ 772,192
Dallas Baptist
   University (TX) ................ 770,899
Robert Morris University:
   Chicago (IL) .................... 759,494
Capital University (OH) .......... 757,969

University of La
   Verne (CA) ...................... 753,807
Rocky Mountain
   College (MT) ................... 750,948
University of California:
   Santa Barbara (CA) ........... 742,523
Piedmont International
   University (NC) ................ 742,272
Wheaton College (IL)............. 741,444
Pitzer College (CA) ................ 732,418
Wayland Baptist
   University (TX) ................ 728,333
Averett University (VA).......... 727,750
SUNY University at
   Buffalo (NY)..................... 726,831
Roger Williams
   University (RI).................. 725,400
Northwestern College (IA)....... 719,202
Southeastern Oklahoma
   State University (OK) ........... 705,513
Milligan College (TN) ............. 701,962
Union University (TN) ............ 698,159
Chestnut Hill College (PA) ...... 698,007
Touro College (NY) ................ 691,229
Georgia State
   University (GA) ................ 690,138
Arcadia University (PA) .......... 686,529
McPherson College (KS).......... 686,310
Cedarville University (OH) ...... 686,264
Hillsdale College (MI)............. 685,651
Lewis University (IL)............... 684,834
Morgan State
   University (MD) ............... 682,880
Webber International
   University (FL) ................. 680,345
Mercer University (GA) .......... 679,130
Georgian Court
   University (NJ) ................. 677,243
George Fox
   University (OR) ................ 674,600
Johnson C. Smith
   University (NC) ................ 669,240
Cornerstone
   University (MI) ................. 659,231
Franklin W. Olin College
   of Engineering (MA) ............ 659,049
St. Mary's University (TX)...... 658,263
Lake Erie College (OH) ........... 656,662
Assumption College (MA)....... 652,636
Randolph-Macon
   College (VA) .................... 642,666
Campbellsville
   University (KY) ................ 641,344
Austin College (TX)................ 638,315
University of Alaska
   Fairbanks (AK) ................ 638,063
Texas A&M University-
   Corpus Christi (TX).......... 626,499
Curry College (MA) ................ 622,133
Anderson University (SC)........ 618,979
Embry-Riddle Aeronautical
   University: Prescott
   Campus (AZ) ................... 617,101
Brevard College (NC) ............. 615,744
University of Idaho (ID) .......... 610,275
University of Minnesota:
   Duluth (MN) .................... 602,708
Purdue University (IN)............. 594,073
Texas A&M University-
   Kingsville (TX)................. 585,976
University of St.
   Thomas (MN) .................. 584,810
Moravian College (PA) ............ 582,154
Le Moyne College (NY) .......... 580,836
Eastern University (PA) ........... 576,065
Bridgewater College (VA) ....... 570,900
LeTourneau
   University (TX) ................ 569,884
University of Alabama in
   Huntsville (AL)................. 563,046
University of Tennessee:
   Martin (TN) ..................... 562,911
Southern Arkansas
   University (AR) ................ 545,698
Samford University (AL) ......... 544,850

Total financial aid for international undergraduate students

Transylvania University (KY) .................... 541,250
Webster University (MO) ......... 539,923
University of North Carolina at Greensboro (NC) ................. 538,064
Coe College (IA) ................. 536,558
Endicott College (MA) ............. 536,111
Philadelphia University (PA) .................... 533,480
Flagler College (FL) ................ 532,940
Mount St. Mary's University (MD) .................... 532,378
Hood College (MD) ................ 523,137
Wittenberg University (OH) ...... 522,480
Towson University (MD) ........... 518,619
Rockhurst University (MO) ...... 514,294
University of Jamestown (ND) .................... 511,758
Covenant College (GA) ............ 507,591
University of Northern Iowa (IA) ...................... 506,403
McDaniel College (MD) ......... 505,220
Wesleyan College (GA) ............ 499,024
Pacific University (OR) ........... 485,407
SUNY University at Binghamton (NY) ................ 482,047
Mount Aloysius College (PA) ..................... 481,540
College of the Ozarks (MO) ........................ 481,000
Lees-McRae College (NC) ....... 478,670
Mississippi State University (MS) .................... 478,210
Benedictine College (KS) ......... 476,250
University of Wisconsin-Stevens Point (WI) ........... 476,182
Lincoln University (PA) ........... 474,698
Trevecca Nazarene University (TN) .................... 468,989
St. Mary's University of Minnesota (MN) .................. 466,700
Northland College (WI) ............ 463,781
University of Colorado Denver (CO) ........................ 463,549
Eastern Nazarene College (MA) ...................... 460,565
Saint Mary's College (IN) ..... 455,040
University of Central Missouri (MO) ................... 453,720
Saint Joseph's College (IN) ..... 451,635
University of Wisconsin-Eau Claire (WI) ................... 450,510
University of Great Falls (MT) ........................ 450,423
Briar Cliff University (IA) ....... 449,905
Concord University (WV) ........ 446,421
Simpson College (IA) ............. 446,021
Union College (NE) ................. 443,925
University of Dallas (TX) ........ 439,893
Utica College (NY) ................ 437,990
Albright College (PA) .............. 437,370
Nazareth College (NY) ............ 436,452
Xavier University of Louisiana (LA) .................... 436,314
University of Tennessee: Knoxville (TN) .................. 436,170
Wofford College (SC) .............. 425,133
Arkansas Tech University (AR) ................... 423,525
SUNY College at Geneseo (NY) ...................... 417,250
California University of Pennsylvania (PA) ............... 413,595
Ohio Northern University (OH) ................... 411,295
University of St. Francis (IL) ..................... 407,660
Saint Anselm College (NH) ..... 404,123
Ursinus College (PA) .............. 396,977
Bellarmine University (KY) ..... 394,490
Carson-Newman University (TN) ................... 393,435
Sierra Nevada College (NV) ...................... 392,759

Chaminade University of Honolulu (HI) .................... 390,221
SUNY University at Stony Brook (NY) ..................... 377,946
Fort Lewis College (CO) ......... 376,588
Tabor College (KS) ................ 370,040
Hamline University (MN) ......... 368,192
Barton College (NC) ............... 364,186
Lincoln University (MO) ......... 353,046
University of Texas of the Permian Basin (TX) ............. 350,533
University of South Carolina: Upstate (SC) ......... 349,123
Mount Vernon Nazarene University (OH) .................... 347,803
Western Nebraska Community College (NE) .... 347,657
St. Joseph's College, New York (NY) ....................... 344,540
Marian University (WI) ............ 342,882
Cleveland Institute of Art (OH) ......................... 342,863
California State University: Los Angeles (CA) ................. 341,434
Trinity International University (IL) ..................... 337,470
Virginia Commonwealth University (VA) .................... 336,412
University of North Alabama (AL) ...................... 332,965
Ursuline College (OH) ............. 330,994
Pacific Union College (CA) ...... 326,430
California Polytechnic State University: San Luis Obispo (CA) ..................... 323,600
Minot State University (ND) ................... 323,421
Green Mountain College (VT) ..................... 318,864
Central Michigan University (MI) ................... 316,912
Scripps College (CA) .............. 309,970
Hardin-Simmons University (TX) ................... 309,899
San Francisco Art Institute (CA) ...................... 308,313
Baldwin Wallace University (OH) ................... 306,900
York County Community College (ME) .................... 304,488
Lubbock Christian University (TX) ................... 303,251
Our Lady of the Lake University of San Antonio (TX) ..................... 303,209
University of Redlands (CA) ....................... 301,821
New College of Florida (FL) .................... 301,738
Regis University (CO) ............. 301,213
Neumann University (PA) ......... 300,668
University of North Florida (FL) .................... 300,343
Virginia Wesleyan College (VA) ..................... 293,752
Georgia Southern University (GA) ................... 293,408
Concordia University Irvine (CA) ....................... 290,974
Bloomsburg University of Pennsylvania (PA) ............... 287,818
Truett McConnell University (GA) ................... 287,683
Idaho State University (ID) ...... 284,987
University of Sioux Falls (SD) ...................... 282,910
Susquehanna University (PA) .................... 282,700
Western Illinois University (IL) .................... 277,802
Shippensburg University of Pennsylvania (PA) ............... 275,866
Berry College (GA) ................ 272,849
Northern Kentucky University (KY) .................. 270,218

Bethel College (IN) ................ 270,000
Friends University (KS) .......... 268,828
Aquinas College (MI) .............. 268,478
Husson University (ME) .......... 263,425
Dominican University of California (CA) .................... 260,195
Becker College (MA) .............. 259,000
Regis College (MA) ............... 256,930
Lewis-Clark State College (ID) ..................... 256,000
Franklin Pierce University (NH) .................... 254,875
Minneapolis College of Art and Design (MN) ............. 249,146
Williams Baptist College (AR) ..................... 248,185
University of San Diego (CA) ........................ 246,500
William Paterson University of New Jersey (NJ) ..................... 243,450
Doane University (NE) ............ 239,265
Millikin University (IL) ............ 238,164
Cameron University (OK) ......... 234,438
The King's College (NY) ........ 233,280
University of Northern Colorado (CO) .................... 232,623
Arizona Christian University (AZ) .................... 230,425
University of Houston-Clear Lake (TX) ................. 229,109
Occidental College (CA) ......... 227,773
Cairn University (PA) ............. 227,220
University of Illinois: Springfield (IL) ................. 225,627
University of West Alabama (AL) ................... 225,495
Thomas College (ME) .............. 223,250
Montana State University (MT) ................... 221,355
Columbia International University (SC) .................. 219,182
Alvernia University (PA) ......... 216,120
Loras College (IA) ................ 214,553
Boise State University (ID) ...... 212,067
University of Wisconsin-Stout (WI) ........................ 212,040
Concordia University Texas (TX) ....................... 211,205
Champlain College (VT) ......... 208,194
Bethel University (MN) ........... 208,144
University of Michigan: Flint (MI) ........................ 208,018
Western Oregon University (OR) ................. 205,129
Edgewood College (WI) ........... 204,112
Donnelly College (KS) ............ 203,569
Fairmont State University (WV) ................. 201,222
Rockford University (IL) .......... 199,572
Emmanuel College (MA) ......... 190,890
Old Dominion University (VA) ................... 190,000
Ohio Valley University (WV) ................. 189,936
University of Puget Sound (WA) ...................... 189,650
West Chester University of Pennsylvania (PA) ............... 188,945
Lyon College (AR) ................ 187,930
Hampton University (VA) ........ 187,312
Montana State University: Billings (MT) .................. 186,954
Thomas More College (KY) ..................... 184,620
Western Washington University (WA) ................. 181,689
Ashland University (OH) ......... 180,650
The Citadel (SC) ................... 178,604
North Iowa Area Community College (IA) ...... 178,032
Malone University (OH) ......... 176,358
Slippery Rock University of Pennsylvania (PA) ............... 175,542
University of Maine (ME) ........ 175,010

Northwest Christian University (OR) ................. 174,400
Bluefield State College (WV) ..................... 171,754
Spelman College (GA) ............ 168,244
Marymount Manhattan College (NY) ..................... 162,267
Toccoa Falls College (GA) ...... 161,580
University of Oklahoma (OK) .................... 161,265
Stephen F. Austin State University (TX) ................... 161,238
Southwestern College (KS) ..... 157,422
Shenandoah University (VA) .................... 156,097
Silver Lake College of the Holy Family (WI) ............... 154,951
Northern State University (SD) ................... 150,052
Franklin College (IN) ............. 148,733
Concordia University St. Paul (MN) .................... 148,520
Montana Tech of the University of Montana (MT) ..................... 148,217
Indiana University South Bend (IN) ...................... 143,168
Nebraska Wesleyan University (NE) .................... 142,600
Lebanon Valley College (PA) ..................... 139,877
Elmhurst College (IL) ............. 139,752
University of Illinois at Chicago (IL) .................... 138,731
Kean University (NJ) ............. 137,951
College of Saint Mary (NE) ..... 135,665
Naropa University (CO) .......... 134,198
University of Saint Francis (IN) .................... 133,690
University of Wisconsin-Milwaukee (WI) ................. 132,628
Grove City College (PA) .......... 131,960
Milwaukee Institute of Art & Design (WI) ............... 131,000
Sterling College (KS) ............. 130,817
Holy Family University (PA) .................... 128,560
Piedmont College (GA) ............ 127,612
University of North Carolina at Pembroke (NC) .................... 124,839
St. Joseph's College New York: Suffolk Campus (NY) ...................... 124,535
Bethel College (KS) ............... 122,728
Trine University (IN) ............. 122,712
University of California: Riverside (CA) ................... 122,000
St. Vincent College (PA) ......... 120,810
Ferris State University (MI) ...... 120,260
Regent University (VA) ........... 119,692
Kuyper College (MI) .............. 118,760
Chowan University (NC) .......... 116,800
East Stroudsburg University of Pennsylvania (PA) ............. 114,725
Cochise College (AZ) ............. 113,759
Emory & Henry College (VA) ..................... 108,560
East Texas Baptist University (TX) ................... 107,381
Warner Pacific College (OR) ..................... 106,620
Bay Path University (MA) ....... 105,245
William Jessup University (CA) ................... 104,309
Virginia State University (VA) ................... 100,000
Lynchburg College (VA) ............ 96,590
Simpson University (CA) ............ 94,881
University of Minnesota: Morris (MN) ......................... 94,835
Bluffton University (OH) ............ 94,381
Aurora University (IL) ............. 90,500
Columbus State University (GA) ................... 90,179

Vaughn College of
Aeronautics and
Technology (NY).................. 90,077
Elon University (NC) ................ 89,987
Molloy College (NY) ................ 88,670
Evangel University (MO)........... 87,643
Alma College (MI) .................. 85,660
University of Houston-
Downtown (TX)..................... 83,024
Elms College (MA) .................. 82,100
Wichita State
University (KS)................... 79,730
Bryn Athyn College (PA) .......... 76,236
Delaware Valley
University (PA)..................... 73,500
SUNY College at
Brockport (NY)..................... 69,190
Mills College (CA).................. 68,900
Shepherd University (WV)......... 68,373
Jefferson College (MO)............. 65,144
St. John Fisher
College (NY) ......................... 63,804
Walla Walla
University (WA) .................. 63,500
McMurry University (TX)......... 63,470
Eastern Oregon
University (OR) ..................... 61,740
University of Maine at
Presque Isle (ME)............... 60,895
Waldorf University (IA)............ 60,575
SUNY Polytechnic
Institute (NY)....................... 60,500
California Baptist
University (CA) ..................... 60,000
Stephens College (MO) ............. 58,976
Mansfield University of
Pennsylvania (PA)............... 56,856
LIM College (NY).................... 55,624
Dominican University (IL)......... 55,412
Kentucky State
University (KY)..................... 54,054
Winston-Salem State
University (NC) ..................... 51,634
New Mexico Institute of
Mining and
Technology (NM).................. 51,450
Marlboro College (VT) ............. 51,086
University of Tennessee:
Chattanooga (TN).................. 49,898
SUNY College at
Potsdam (NY)......................... 47,653
Millersville University of
Pennsylvania (PA)................. 47,401
University of Central
Florida (FL) .......................... 47,175
Wright State University:
Lake Campus (OH) ............... 45,837
Central College (IA)................. 44,613
Hope International
University (CA) ..................... 44,000
Central Wyoming
College (WY)......................... 43,629
Cincinnati Christian
University (OH)..................... 43,184
Clarke University (IA)............... 42,285
University of California:
Merced (CA).......................... 40,000
University of Mary Hardin-
Baylor (TX) ........................ 38,764
University of Maine at
Machias (ME) ...................... 38,500
Auburn University at
Montgomery (AL) ................. 38,147
Hellenic College/Holy
Cross (MA) ........................... 38,000
Westminster College (PA).......... 37,500
King's College (PA).................. 37,000
Plymouth State
University (NH)..................... 36,500
Black Hawk College (IL)........... 34,928
University of Pittsburgh at
Bradford (PA) ....................... 32,000
University of Wisconsin-
Whitewater (WI)..................... 31,500

Angelo State
University (TX) ..................... 31,430
University of Maine at
Farmington (ME)................... 30,500
Saint Martin's
University (WA) ................... 30,000
Southern Vermont
College (VT)......................... 30,000
Indiana University of
Pennsylvania (PA) ................. 29,301
Wells College (NY) .................. 29,000
LaGrange College (GA) ............ 28,860
Salisbury University (MD)......... 28,678
Metropolitan College of
New York (NY)..................... 27,525
SUNY College of
Environmental Science
and Forestry (NY) ................. 26,750
Franciscan University of
Steubenville (OH) ................. 26,000
Eureka College (IL)................... 24,200
North Dakota State College
of Science (ND)..................... 24,100
Adventist University of
Health Sciences (FL)............. 23,690
Bismarck State
College (ND) ......................... 23,669
Hilbert College (NY)................. 23,250
Christendom College (VA) ........ 22,775
Huntingdon College (AL) .......... 22,500
Indiana University
Southeast (IN)........................ 21,938
Harford Community
College (MD)......................... 21,739
Indiana University
Kokomo (IN) ......................... 20,946
Dakota State
University (SD)...................... 20,413
Alverno College (WI)................ 19,520
Fashion Institute of
Technology (NY)................... 19,200
University of South Florida:
Saint Petersburg (FL) ............. 18,508
Cedar Crest College (PA) .......... 18,000
SUNY College of
Agriculture and
Technology at
Morrisville (NY).................... 17,950
Indiana University
Northwest (IN)....................... 17,786
University of South Florida:
Sarasota-Manatee (FL) ........... 16,398
Lasell College (MA).................. 16,000
University of Mary
Washington (VA)................... 16,000
Southwest Minnesota State
University (MN) .................... 15,650
Converse College (SC).............. 15,045
Wayne State College (NE)......... 15,037
Indiana University
East (IN)................................ 14,313
SUNY College at
Fredonia (NY)....................... 14,000
Governors State
University (IL)....................... 13,792
Peirce College (PA)................... 13,500
Unity College (ME)................... 13,185
Oregon College of Art &
Craft (OR)............................. 13,000
Dakota Wesleyan
University (SD)...................... 12,540
College of DuPage (IL)............. 12,480
University of Minnesota:
Rochester (MN) ..................... 12,238
Bryan College:
Dayton (TN)........................... 12,000
New Saint Andrews
College (ID)........................... 11,500
The College of New
Jersey (NJ) ............................ 10,500
Clarion University of
Pennsylvania (PA) .................. 9,647
Alcorn State
University (MS)........................ 9,267

DigiPen Institute of
Technology (WA)..................... 9,229
SUNY College of
Technology at
Canton (NY) ............................ 8,805
American Public University
System (WV) ........................... 8,186
Dine College (AZ)..................... 6,924
Life University (GA)................... 6,500
University of Minnesota:
Crookston (MN)....................... 6,500
St. Mary's College of
Maryland (MD)....................... 6,000
Mount Wachusett
Community
College (MA)........................... 5,895
Alice Lloyd College (KY)........... 4,640
Gwynedd Mercy
University (PA)....................... 3,750
Anne Arundel Community
College (MD).......................... 2,750
Louisiana State University
at Eunice (LA) ........................ 2,682
Mid-Plains Community
College (NE) .......................... 2,629
Lorain County Community
College (OH) .......................... 2,500
The Sage Colleges (NY) ............. 2,500
SUNY College at
Oswego (NY)........................... 1,500
Howard Community
College (MD)............................ 500
Volunteer State Community
College (TN)............................. 125

# Conditional admission based on English-language proficiency

## Alabama

Alabama Agricultural and Mechanical University
Auburn University
Bishop State Community College
Chattahoochee Valley Community College
Faulkner State Community College
Faulkner University
Gadsden State Community College
Jacksonville State University
Miles College
Samford University
Spring Hill College
United States Sports Academy
University of Alabama
University of Alabama at Birmingham
University of Mobile
University of North Alabama
University of South Alabama
Wallace State Community College at Hanceville

## Alaska

Alaska Pacific University
University of Alaska Anchorage

## Arizona

Arizona State University
Arizona Western College
Bryan University
Cochise College
Dine College
Dunlap-Stone University
Embry-Riddle Aeronautical University: Prescott Campus
Glendale Community College
Northern Arizona University
Prescott College
Rio Salado College
Scottsdale Community College
Southwest University of Visual Arts
University of Advancing Technology
University of Arizona

## Arkansas

Arkansas State University
Arkansas Tech University
Cossatot Community College of the University of Arkansas
Ecclesia College
Harding University
John Brown University
National Park College
Ouachita Baptist University
University of Arkansas
University of Arkansas at Little Rock
University of Central Arkansas

## California

Academy of Art University
Allan Hancock College
Art Institute of California: San Diego
Art Institute of California: San Francisco
Ashford University
Azusa Pacific University
Bethesda University of California
Beverly Hills Design Institute
Biola University
California Baptist University
California College San Diego
California Institute of the Arts
California Lutheran University
California State University: Chico
California State University: Fresno
California State University: Long Beach
California State University: Los Angeles
California State University: Monterey Bay
California State University: Stanislaus
California University of Management and Sciences
Canada College
Chaffey College
Charles Drew University of Medicine and Science
Citrus College
City College of San Francisco
Coastline Community College
Coleman University
College of the Desert
College of the Sequoias
Contra Costa College
East Los Angeles College
El Camino College
Fashion Institute of Design and Merchandising: San Francisco
Feather River College
Foothill College
Fremont College
Fresno Pacific University
Glendale Community College
Holy Names University
Hope International University
Hult International Business School
Humboldt State University
Humphreys College
Kaplan College: Riverside
La Sierra University
Laguna College of Art and Design
Las Positas College
Long Beach City College
Los Angeles City College
Los Angeles Pierce College
Marymount California University
Menlo College
Merritt College
Mills College
MiraCosta College
Mission College
Monterey Peninsula College
Mt. Sierra College
Napa Valley College
National University
NewSchool of Architecture & Design
Northwestern Polytechnic University
Notre Dame de Namur University
Ohlone College
Otis College of Art and Design
Pacific College of Oriental Medicine: San Diego
Palomar College
Patten University
Pepperdine University
Pitzer College
Platt College: San Diego
Point Loma Nazarene University
Providence Christian College
Sacramento City College
Saddleback College
St. Mary's College of California
San Diego Christian College
San Diego Mesa College
San Diego State University
San Francisco Art Institute
San Francisco Conservatory of Music
San Joaquin Delta College
San Jose City College
Santa Ana College
Santa Barbara City College
Santa Monica College
Santiago Canyon College
Scripps College
Shasta College
Sierra College
Silicon Valley University
Soka University of America
Solano Community College
Southern California Institute of Architecture
Southern California Institute of Technology
Southern California Seminary
SUM Bible College & Theological Seminary
Trident University International
University of California: Santa Barbara
University of La Verne
University of San Diego
University of San Francisco
University of Southern California
University of the West
Ventura College
West Hills College: Coalinga
West Los Angeles College
Whittier College
World Mission University
Yuba College

## Colorado

Aims Community College
Colorado Christian University
Colorado Mesa University
Colorado Mountain College
Colorado Northwestern Community College
Colorado State University
Colorado State University: Pueblo
IntelliTec College
Johnson & Wales University: Denver
Northeastern Junior College
Rocky Mountain College of Art & Design
Trinidad State Junior College
University of Colorado Boulder
University of Colorado Colorado Springs
University of Denver
University of Northern Colorado
Westwood College: Denver North

## Connecticut

Asnuntuck Community College
Central Connecticut State University
Gateway Community College
Holy Apostles College and Seminary
Housatonic Community College
Naugatuck Valley Community College
Post University
Quinnipiac University
Sacred Heart University
Tunxis Community College
University of Bridgeport
University of Connecticut
University of Hartford
University of New Haven
University of Saint Joseph

## Delaware

Delaware College of Art and Design
Delaware Technical Community College: Stanton/Wilmington Campus
University of Delaware
Wesley College

## District of Columbia

American University
Catholic University of America
Gallaudet University
George Washington University
Georgetown University
Howard University
Strayer University
Trinity Washington University
University of the District of Columbia
University of the Potomac

## Florida

Ave Maria University
Barry University
Carlos Albizu University
Chipola College
City College: Fort Lauderdale
Eckerd College
Embry-Riddle Aeronautical University
Florida Atlantic University
Florida Institute of Technology
Florida Memorial University
Florida National University
Florida Southern College
Florida State College at Jacksonville
Fortis College: Winter Park
Full Sail University
Johnson & Wales University: North Miami
Jose Maria Vargas University
Key College
Lincoln College of Technology: West Palm Beach
Palm Beach State College
Polk State College
Remington College: Tampa
Ringling College of Art and Design
Saint Leo University
Saint Thomas University
Schiller International University
Seminole State College of Florida
Southern Technical College
Stetson University
Talmudic University
University of Miami

University of South Florida
University of Tampa
Valencia College
Warner University
Webber International University

## Georgia

Abraham Baldwin Agricultural College
Andrew College
Art Institute of Atlanta
Atlanta Technical College
Bauder College
Beulah Heights University
Columbus State University
Darton State College
Fort Valley State University
Georgia Gwinnett College
Georgia Piedmont Technical College
Georgia Southern University
Georgia Southwestern State University
Georgia State University
Life University
Mercer University
Savannah College of Art and Design
Savannah Technical College
Thomas University
University of Georgia
University of North Georgia
Wiregrass Georgia Technical College

## Hawaii

Brigham Young University-Hawaii
Chaminade University of Honolulu
Hawaii Pacific University
Hawaii Tokai International College
University of Hawaii at Manoa
University of Hawaii: Hawaii
    Community College
University of Hawaii: Honolulu
    Community College
University of Hawaii: Kapiolani
    Community College
University of Hawaii: Leeward
    Community College
University of Hawaii: Windward
    Community College

## Idaho

Boise State University
College of Idaho
Idaho State University
Lewis-Clark State College
North Idaho College
Stevens-Henager College: Boise
University of Idaho

## Illinois

American InterContinental University
Augustana College
Benedictine University
Black Hawk College
Carl Sandburg College
College of DuPage
College of Lake County
Columbia College Chicago
Concordia University Chicago
Danville Area Community College
DePaul University
Dominican University
East-West University
Eastern Illinois University
Elgin Community College
Governors State University
Harper College

Heartland Community College
Illinois Central College
Illinois Eastern Community Colleges:
    Frontier Community College
Illinois Eastern Community Colleges:
    Lincoln Trail College
Illinois Eastern Community Colleges:
    Olney Central College
Illinois Eastern Community Colleges:
    Wabash Valley College
Illinois State University
Kishwaukee College
Lake Land College
Lewis University
Lincoln College
Loyola University Chicago
MacCormac College
Millikin University
Monmouth College
Moraine Valley Community College
Morrison Institute of Technology
National-Louis University
North Central College
North Park University
Parkland College
Richland Community College
Rockford University
Roosevelt University
Sauk Valley Community College
School of the Art Institute of Chicago
Southern Illinois University Carbondale
Southern Illinois University
    Edwardsville
Southwestern Illinois College
Trinity Christian College
Triton College
University of St. Francis
Western Illinois University

## Indiana

Ancilla College
Ball State University
Franklin College
Huntington University
Indiana Institute of Technology
Indiana State University
Indiana University Bloomington
Indiana University East
Indiana University Kokomo
Indiana University South Bend
Indiana University Southeast
Indiana University-Purdue University
    Fort Wayne
Indiana University-Purdue University
    Indianapolis
Ivy Tech Community College:
    Bloomington
Ivy Tech Community College: Central
    Indiana
Ivy Tech Community College:
    Columbus
Ivy Tech Community College: East
    Central
Ivy Tech Community College:
    Kokomo
Ivy Tech Community College:
    Lafayette
Ivy Tech Community College: North
    Central
Ivy Tech Community College:
    Northeast
Ivy Tech Community College:
    Northwest
Ivy Tech Community College:
    Richmond
Ivy Tech Community College: South
    Central
Ivy Tech Community College:
    Southeast
Ivy Tech Community College:
    Southwest

Ivy Tech Community College: Wabash
    Valley
Marian University
Oakland City University
Saint Mary's College
Taylor University
Trine University
University of Evansville
University of Indianapolis
University of Southern Indiana
Vincennes University

## Iowa

Buena Vista University
Clarke University
Coe College
Des Moines Area Community College
Drake University
Ellsworth Community College
Iowa State University
Iowa Wesleyan College
Kaplan University: Des Moines
Maharishi University of Management
Marshalltown Community College
Northeast Iowa Community College
Northwestern College
St. Ambrose University
Scott Community College
University of Dubuque
University of Iowa
University of Northern Iowa
Upper Iowa University
Waldorf University
Wartburg College
Western Iowa Tech Community
    College
William Penn University

## Kansas

Barclay College
Barton County Community College
Benedictine College
Cloud County Community College
Colby Community College
Dodge City Community College
Donnelly College
Emporia State University
Fort Hays State University
Hesston College
Independence Community College
Kansas City Kansas Community
    College
Kansas State University
McPherson College
MidAmerica Nazarene University
Neosho County Community College
Northwest Kansas Technical College
Ottawa University
Pittsburg State University
Pratt Community College
Southwestern College
University of Kansas
University of Kansas Medical Center
University of St. Mary
Washburn University
Wichita State University

## Kentucky

Bluegrass Community and Technical
    College
Brescia University
Campbellsville University
Daymar College: Owensboro
Henderson Community College
Jefferson Community and Technical
    College
Kentucky Mountain Bible College

Lindsey Wilson College
Morehead State University
Murray State University
Northern Kentucky University
St. Catharine College
Somerset Community College
Southeast Kentucky Community and
    Technical College
Sullivan College of Technology and
    Design
Thomas More College
Transylvania University
University of Kentucky
University of Louisville
Western Kentucky University

## Louisiana

Bossier Parish Community College
Delgado Community College
Herzing University: Kenner
ITI Technical College
Louisiana State University at Eunice
Louisiana Tech University
Loyola University New Orleans
McNeese State University
Nunez Community College
St. Joseph Seminary College
Southern University and Agricultural
    and Mechanical College
Tulane University
University of Louisiana at Lafayette
University of Louisiana at Monroe
University of New Orleans

## Maine

Central Maine Community College
Colby College
Husson University
Landing School of Boatbuilding and
    Design
Maine Maritime Academy
Thomas College
Unity College
University of Maine
University of Maine at Fort Kent
University of Maine at Presque Isle
University of New England
University of Southern Maine
Washington County Community
    College

## Maryland

Anne Arundel Community College
Baltimore City Community College
Brightwood College: Towson
Capitol Technology University
Carroll Community College
Chesapeake College
Community College of Baltimore
    County
Harford Community College
Hood College
Johns Hopkins University: Peabody
    Conservatory of Music
Maryland Institute College of Art
Notre Dame of Maryland University
Prince George's Community College
Salisbury University
Stevenson University
Towson University
University of Maryland: Baltimore
    County
University of Maryland: College Park
University of Maryland: Eastern Shore
University of Maryland: University
    College
Washington Adventist University

Conditional admission based on English-language proficiency

## Massachusetts

Bard College at Simon's Rock
Bay Path University
Bay State College
Benjamin Franklin Institute of
　Technology
Berklee College of Music
Berkshire Community College
Boston Conservatory
Boston University
Bridgewater State University
Bristol Community College
Bunker Hill Community College
Clark University
Eastern Nazarene College
Elms College
Fisher College
Gordon College
Greenfield Community College
Hellenic College/Holy Cross
Holyoke Community College
Lasell College
Massachusetts Bay Community College
MCPHS University
Merrimack College
Middlesex Community College
Montserrat College of Art
Mount Ida College
Mount Wachusett Community College
New England Conservatory of Music
Nichols College
Northeastern University
Northern Essex Community College
Pine Manor College
Quincy College
Regis College
Springfield College
Suffolk University
University of Massachusetts Boston
University of Massachusetts Lowell
Wentworth Institute of Technology
Western New England University
Wheaton College
Worcester Polytechnic Institute

## Michigan

Alma College
Andrews University
Baker College of Auburn Hills
Baker College of Cadillac
Baker College of Jackson
Baker College of Muskegon
Baker College of Port Huron
Calvin College
Central Michigan University
Cornerstone University
Davenport University
Eastern Michigan University
Finlandia University
Hope College
Kettering University
Kuyper College
Lawrence Technological University
Macomb Community College
Madonna University
Michigan Jewish Institute
Michigan State University
Michigan Technological University
Mid Michigan Community College
Muskegon Community College
Northern Michigan University
Northwood University: Michigan
Oakland Community College
Oakland University
Rochester College
Saginaw Valley State University
St. Clair County Community College
Schoolcraft College
Siena Heights University
Spring Arbor University
University of Detroit Mercy

University of Michigan: Dearborn
University of Michigan: Flint
Wayne State University
Western Michigan University

## Minnesota

Art Institutes International Minnesota
Augsburg College
Bemidji State University
Bethel University
College of St. Benedict
College of St. Scholastica
Concordia University St. Paul
Crown College
Hamline University
Hibbing Community College
Lake Superior College
Le Cordon Bleu College of Culinary
　Arts: Minneapolis-St. Paul
Minneapolis College of Art and Design
Minnesota State Community and
　Technical College
Minnesota West Community and
　Technical College
North Central University
North Hennepin Community College
Northwest Technical College
Pine Technical & Community College
Rainy River Community College
Rochester Community and Technical
　College
St. Catherine University
Saint Cloud State University
St. Cloud Technical and Community
　College
St. John's University
St. Mary's University of Minnesota
University of Minnesota: Crookston
University of Minnesota: Duluth
University of St. Thomas
Winona State University

## Mississippi

Belhaven University
Hinds Community College
Jackson State University
Meridian Community College
Mississippi College
Mississippi State University
Southeastern Baptist College
University of Mississippi
University of Southern Mississippi
William Carey University

## Missouri

Avila University
Crowder College
Culver-Stockton College
Drury University
Fontbonne University
Jefferson College
Kansas City Art Institute
Lindenwood University
Maryville University of Saint Louis
Metropolitan Community College -
　Kansas City
Missouri Baptist University
Missouri Southern State University
Missouri State University
Missouri University of Science and
　Technology
Missouri Valley College
National American University: Kansas
　City
Northwest Missouri State University
Ranken Technical College
Rockhurst University

Southeast Missouri State University
Southwest Baptist University
State Fair Community College
Stephens College
Truman State University
University of Central Missouri
University of Missouri: Columbia
University of Missouri: Kansas City
University of Missouri: St. Louis
Washington University in St. Louis
Webster University
Westminster College

## Montana

Carroll College
Montana State University
Montana State University: Billings
Montana Tech of the University of
　Montana
University of Great Falls
University of Montana

## Nebraska

College of Saint Mary
Creighton University
Doane University
Hastings College
Metropolitan Community College
Nebraska Wesleyan University
Northeast Community College
Union College
University of Nebraska - Kearney
University of Nebraska - Lincoln
University of Nebraska - Omaha
York College

## Nevada

Career College of Northern Nevada
College of Southern Nevada
Great Basin College
Sierra Nevada College
University of Nevada: Las Vegas
University of Nevada: Reno
Western Nevada College

## New Hampshire

Colby-Sawyer College
Franklin Pierce University
Keene State College
Manchester Community College
New England College
NHTI-Concord's Community College
Rivier University
Saint Anselm College
Southern New Hampshire University

## New Jersey

Atlantic Cape Community College
Brookdale Community College
Caldwell University
Centenary University
The College of New Jersey
College of St. Elizabeth
County College of Morris
Fairleigh Dickinson University:
　College at Florham
Fairleigh Dickinson University:
　Metropolitan Campus
Felician University
Hudson County Community College
Mercer County Community College

Middlesex County College
Monmouth University
Montclair State University
New Jersey City University
New Jersey Institute of Technology
Ocean County College
Rowan College at Burlington County
Seton Hall University
Stevens Institute of Technology
Stockton University
Sussex County Community College

## New Mexico

Eastern New Mexico University
Institute of American Indian Arts
Mesalands Community College
National American University:
　Albuquerque
New Mexico Institute of Mining and
　Technology
New Mexico Military Institute
New Mexico State University
New Mexico State University at
　Alamogordo
Santa Fe Community College
Santa Fe University of Art and Design
University of New Mexico

## New York

Adelphi University
ASA College
Bard College
Bramson ORT College
Briarcliffe College
Broome Community College
Bryant & Stratton College: Albany
Bryant & Stratton College: Rochester
Bryant & Stratton College: Syracuse
　North
Canisius College
City University of New York: Baruch
　College
City University of New York: Borough
　of Manhattan Community College
City University of New York: Bronx
　Community College
City University of New York:
　Brooklyn College
City University of New York: City
　College
City University of New York: College
　of Staten Island
City University of New York:
　LaGuardia Community College
City University of New York: New
　York City College of Technology
City University of New York: York
　College
College of Mount St. Vincent
College of Saint Rose
Columbia University: School of
　General Studies
Concordia College
Cooper Union for the Advancement of
　Science and Art
Culinary Institute of America
Daemen College
Dutchess Community College
Eastman School of Music of the
　University of Rochester
Elmira College
Eugene Lang College The New School
　for Liberal Arts
Excelsior College
Five Towns College
Fordham University
Fulton-Montgomery Community
　College
Globe Institute of Technology
Herkimer County Community College

Hofstra University
Iona College
Ithaca College
LIU Brooklyn
LIU Post
Manhattan School of Music
Manhattanville College
Medaille College
Mercy College
Mildred Elley: Albany
Molloy College
Nazareth College
The New School College of
    Performing Arts
New York Institute of Technology
New York University
Niagara County Community College
Niagara University
North Country Community College
Nyack College
Ohr Somayach Tanenbaum Education
    Center
Onondaga Community College
Pace University
Pace University: Pleasantville/Briarcliff
Parsons The New School for Design
Pratt Institute
Rensselaer Polytechnic Institute
Roberts Wesleyan College
Rochester Institute of Technology
Rockland Community College
The Sage Colleges
Saint Bonaventure University
St. Francis College
St. John's University
St. Thomas Aquinas College
School of Visual Arts
Siena College
Suffolk County Community College
SUNY College at Brockport
SUNY College at Geneseo
SUNY College at New Paltz
SUNY College at Oswego
SUNY College at Plattsburgh
SUNY College at Potsdam
SUNY College of Agriculture and
    Technology at Morrisville
SUNY College of Technology at
    Canton
SUNY Polytechnic Institute
SUNY University at Albany
SUNY University at Buffalo
SUNY University at Stony Brook
Syracuse University
Tompkins Cortland Community
    College
Touro College
University of Rochester
Utica College
Vaughn College of Aeronautics and
    Technology
Wagner College
Wells College
Yeshivat Mikdash Melech

## North Carolina

Alamance Community College
Appalachian State University
Beaufort County Community College
Brevard College
Central Piedmont Community College
Chowan University
College of the Albemarle
Elizabeth City State University
Elon University
Guilford College
High Point University
Laurel University
McDowell Technical Community
    College
Methodist University
North Carolina State University

Piedmont Community College
Piedmont International University
Richmond Community College
Southeastern Community College
University of Mount Olive
University of North Carolina at
    Charlotte
University of North Carolina at
    Greensboro
University of North Carolina at
    Pembroke
University of North Carolina at
    Wilmington
University of North Carolina School of
    the Arts
Vance-Granville Community College
Wilson Community College
Wingate University

## North Dakota

Bismarck State College
Dickinson State University
Lake Region State College
North Dakota State College of Science
North Dakota State University
United Tribes Technical College
University of Mary

## Ohio

Antonelli College: Cincinnati
Ashland University
Baldwin Wallace University
Bowling Green State University
Bowling Green State University:
    Firelands College
Capital University
Central Ohio Technical College
Central State University
Cincinnati State Technical and
    Community College
Cleveland Institute of Art
Cleveland Institute of Music
Cleveland State University
Cuyahoga Community College
Defiance College
Edison State Community College
Franklin University
Heidelberg University
Hiram College
Hocking College
John Carroll University
Kent State University
Lake Erie College
Lorain County Community College
Miami University: Middletown
Miami University: Oxford
Muskingum University
North Central State College
Ohio Dominican University
Ohio Northern University
Ohio Technical College
Ohio University
Otterbein University
Shawnee State University
Sinclair Community College
Terra State Community College
Tiffin University
Union Institute & University
University of Akron
University of Dayton
University of Findlay
University of Mount Union
University of Northwestern Ohio
University of Rio Grande
University of Toledo
Urbana University
Virginia Marti College of Art and
    Design
Walsh University
Wilmington College

Wittenberg University
Wright State University
Wright State University: Lake Campus
Xavier University
Youngstown State University

## Oklahoma

Bacone College
Eastern Oklahoma State College
Northeastern Oklahoma Agricultural
    and Mechanical College
Northeastern State University
Oklahoma Baptist University
Oklahoma Christian University
Oklahoma City Community College
Oklahoma City University
Oklahoma State University: Oklahoma
    City
Oklahoma Wesleyan University
Oral Roberts University
St. Gregory's University
Seminole State College
Southern Nazarene University
Southwestern Christian University
Southwestern Oklahoma State
    University
University of Central Oklahoma
University of Oklahoma
University of Tulsa

## Oregon

Chemeketa Community College
Clackamas Community College
Concordia University
George Fox University
Lewis & Clark College
Linfield College
Marylhurst University
Mount Angel Seminary
Mt. Hood Community College
Oregon Institute of Technology
Oregon State University
Pacific University
Portland Community College
Portland State University
Southwestern Oregon Community
    College
University of Oregon
University of Portland
Western Oregon University

## Pennsylvania

Albright College
Arcadia University
Art Institute of Pittsburgh
Bloomsburg University of
    Pennsylvania
Cabrini University
Chatham University
Clarion University of Pennsylvania
Clarks Summit University
Curtis Institute of Music
Douglas Education Center
Drexel University
DuBois Business College
Duquesne University
Gannon University
Geneva College
Gratz College
Harcum College
Harrisburg Area Community College
Immaculata University
Juniata College
Keystone College
Keystone Technical Institute
King's College
Kutztown University of Pennsylvania

La Roche College
La Salle University
Laurel Business Institute
Laurel Technical Institute
Lehigh Carbon Community College
Lehigh University
Lock Haven University of
    Pennsylvania
Lycoming College
Manor College
Mansfield University of Pennsylvania
Marywood University
Mercyhurst University
Millersville University of Pennsylvania
Misericordia University
Montgomery County Community
    College
Moore College of Art and Design
Pennsylvania College of Technology
Pittsburgh Institute of Aeronautics
Pittsburgh Institute of Mortuary
    Science
Point Park University
Robert Morris University
Rosemont College
St. Francis University
Saint Joseph's University
St. Vincent College
Seton Hill University
Slippery Rock University of
    Pennsylvania
Susquehanna University
Temple University
Thiel College
Thomas Jefferson University
University of the Arts
University of Pittsburgh at Greensburg
University of Scranton
Valley Forge Military College
Villanova University
Washington & Jefferson College
West Chester University of
    Pennsylvania
Widener University

## Puerto Rico

ICPR Junior College
Inter American University of Puerto
    Rico: San German Campus
University of Puerto Rico: Mayaguez

## Rhode Island

Bryant University
Johnson & Wales University:
    Providence
New England Institute of Technology
Roger Williams University
University of Rhode Island

## South Carolina

Anderson University
Bob Jones University
Charleston Southern University
The Citadel
Coastal Carolina University
Coker College
College of Charleston
Forrest Junior College
Greenville Technical College
Horry-Georgetown Technical College
Morris College
North Greenville University
Southern Wesleyan University
Spartanburg Community College
Spartanburg Methodist College
Tri-County Technical College
University of South Carolina: Aiken

Conditional admission based on English-language proficiency

University of South Carolina: Beaufort
University of South Carolina:
  Columbia
University of South Carolina: Sumter
University of South Carolina: Upstate
Winthrop University

## South Dakota

Dakota State University
Lake Area Technical Institute
National American University: Rapid
  City
Presentation College
South Dakota School of Mines and
  Technology
South Dakota State University
University of South Dakota

## Tennessee

American Baptist College
Bethel University
Carson-Newman University
East Tennessee State University
Huntington College of Health Sciences
King University
Lane College
Lincoln Memorial University
Lipscomb University
Martin Methodist College
Maryville College
Nossi College of Art
O'More College of Design
Pellissippi State Community College
Southern Adventist University
Tennessee Wesleyan College
University of Memphis
University of Tennessee: Knoxville
University of Tennessee: Martin
Volunteer State Community College
Williamson College

## Texas

Abilene Christian University
Arlington Baptist College
Blinn College
Cedar Valley College
Central Texas College
Cisco College
Dallas Baptist University
East Texas Baptist University
El Centro College
Frank Phillips College
Galveston College
Grayson College
Houston Community College System
Huston-Tillotson University
Jarvis Christian College
Kilgore College
The King's University
Lamar State College at Port Arthur
Lamar University
LeTourneau University
Midland College
Midwestern State University
Mountain View College
Northwood University: Texas
Our Lady of the Lake University of
  San Antonio
Ranger College
Richland College
St. Mary's University
Schreiner University
South Plains College
Southern Methodist University
Southwestern Adventist University
Texas A&M University
Texas Christian University

Texas College
Texas Southern University
Texas State University
Texas Tech University
Texas Woman's University
Trinity Valley Community College
University of the Incarnate Word
University of Mary Hardin-Baylor
University of North Texas
University of Texas at Arlington
University of Texas at El Paso
University of Texas at San Antonio
Wade College
Wayland Baptist University
Weatherford College
West Texas A&M University
Western Technical College
Western Technical College: Diana
  Drive
Wiley College

## Utah

Brigham Young University
Dixie State University
Independence University
Neumont University
Salt Lake Community College
Snow College
Southern Utah University
Stevens-Henager College: Ogden
Utah State University
Utah Valley University
Weber State University
Westminster College

## Vermont

Community College of Vermont
Green Mountain College
Johnson State College
Lyndon State College
Saint Michael's College

## Virginia

Bryant & Stratton College: Virginia
  Beach
Christendom College
Eastern Mennonite University
George Mason University
J. Sargeant Reynolds Community
  College
James Madison University
Jefferson College of Health Sciences
Liberty University
Marymount University
Old Dominion University
Patrick Henry Community College
Paul D. Camp Community College
Roanoke College
Shenandoah University
Stratford University: Falls Church
Stratford University: Woodbridge
Thomas Nelson Community College
Tidewater Community College
University of Mary Washington
University of the Potomac
University of Richmond
University of Virginia's College at
  Wise
Virginia Polytechnic Institute and State
  University
Virginia Union University
Virginia Wesleyan College
Virginia Western Community College

## Washington

Art Institute of Seattle
Bates Technical College
Bellevue College
Cascadia College
Central Washington University
Centralia College
City University of Seattle
Clark College
Clover Park Technical College
DigiPen Institute of Technology
Eastern Washington University
Edmonds Community College
Everett Community College
Fiath International University
Gonzaga University
Grays Harbor College
Heritage University
Highline College
Lake Washington Institute of
  Technology
Lower Columbia College
North Seattle College
Northwest University
Olympic College
Pacific Lutheran University
Peninsula College
Pierce College
Saint Martin's University
Seattle Central College
Seattle Pacific University
Seattle University
Skagit Valley College
South Puget Sound Community
  College
South Seattle College
Spokane Community College
Spokane Falls Community College
Walla Walla Community College
Walla Walla University
Washington State University
Western Washington University
Whatcom Community College
Yakima Valley Community College

## West Virginia

Alderson-Broaddus University
Appalachian Bible College
Bluefield State College
BridgeValley Community and
  Technical College
Concord University
Davis and Elkins College
Glenville State College
Ohio Valley University
Salem International University
University of Charleston
West Virginia Junior College:
  Bridgeport
West Virginia Northern Community
  College
West Virginia University
West Virginia University Institute of
  Technology
West Virginia Wesleyan College
Wheeling Jesuit University

## Wisconsin

Beloit College
Carroll University
Concordia University Wisconsin
Edgewood College
Fox Valley Technical College
Gateway Technical College
Lakeland University
Lakeshore Technical College
Lawrence University
Marquette University

Milwaukee Area Technical College
Milwaukee School of Engineering
Northcentral Technical College
Northland College
St. Norbert College
Silver Lake College of the Holy
  Family
Southwest Wisconsin Technical
  College
University of Wisconsin-Baraboo/Sauk
  County
University of Wisconsin-Eau Claire
University of Wisconsin-La Crosse
University of Wisconsin-Marshfield/
  Wood County
University of Wisconsin-Milwaukee
University of Wisconsin-Platteville
University of Wisconsin-Richland
University of Wisconsin-Rock County
University of Wisconsin-Sheboygan
University of Wisconsin-Stevens Point
University of Wisconsin-Stout
University of Wisconsin-Superior
University of Wisconsin-Waukesha
University of Wisconsin-Whitewater
Viterbo University
Western Technical College

## Wyoming

Central Wyoming College
Western Wyoming Community College

# SAT Subject Tests required or recommended

## Alabama

University of Mobile*

## Arizona

Bryan University*

## Arkansas

John Brown University*

## California

California Institute of Technology
Harvey Mudd College
Stanford University*
University of California: Irvine*
University of California: Merced*
University of California: Santa Barbara*
University of the Pacific*
University of Southern California*

## District of Columbia

Georgetown University*
Howard University

## Georgia

Emory University*
Morehouse College*

## Illinois

Northwestern University*

## Massachusetts

Harvard College
Massachusetts Institute of Technology
Smith College*

## Minnesota

Carleton College*

## Montana

University of Great Falls*

## New Hampshire

Dartmouth College

## New Jersey

Princeton University*
Stevens Institute of Technology*

## New York

Mercy College*
University of Rochester*

## Ohio

Ohio Wesleyan University*

## Pennsylvania

Susquehanna University*
University of Pennsylvania*

## Puerto Rico

EDP University of Puerto Rico: Hato Rey*
Inter American University of Puerto Rico: Barranquitas Campus*
National University College: Arecibo
University of Puerto Rico: Aguadilla
University of Puerto Rico: Arecibo
University of Puerto Rico: Carolina Regional College
University of Puerto Rico: Cayey University College
University of Puerto Rico: Humacao
University of Puerto Rico: Mayaguez
University of Puerto Rico: Utuado

## South Carolina

Voorhees College

## Tennessee

Cumberland University*

## Vermont

Bennington College*
Green Mountain College*

## Virginia

Hampden-Sydney College*
University of Virginia*
Virginia Union University

## Washington

Heritage University*

Colleges that recommend SAT Subject Tests are noted with an asterisk

# Credit/placement for International Baccalaureate (IB)

## Alabama

Auburn University at Montgomery
Birmingham-Southern College
Calhoun Community College
Faulkner University
Huntingdon College
Jefferson State Community College
Judson College
Samford University
Spring Hill College
Tuskegee University
University of Alabama
University of Alabama at Birmingham
University of Alabama in Huntsville
University of Mobile
University of Montevallo
University of North Alabama
University of South Alabama
University of West Alabama

## Alaska

Alaska Pacific University
University of Alaska Anchorage
University of Alaska Fairbanks

## Arizona

Arizona State University
Arizona Western College
Art Institute of Phoenix
Chandler-Gilbert Community College
Cochise College
Dunlap-Stone University
Eastern Arizona College
Embry-Riddle Aeronautical University: Prescott Campus
Estrella Mountain Community College
GateWay Community College
Glendale Community College
Grand Canyon University
Mesa Community College
Mohave Community College
Northern Arizona University
Phoenix College
Prescott College
South Mountain Community College
Southwest University of Visual Arts
University of Arizona
Yavapai College

## Arkansas

Arkansas Tech University
Harding University
Hendrix College
John Brown University
Lyon College
Ouachita Baptist University
Philander Smith College
South Arkansas Community College
University of Arkansas
University of Arkansas at Little Rock
University of Arkansas at Monticello
University of Arkansas at Pine Bluff
University of Central Arkansas
Williams Baptist College

## California

Academy of Art University
Alliant International University
American Jewish University
American River College
Antioch University Los Angeles
Antioch University Santa Barbara
Art Institute of California: Hollywood
Art Institute of California: Orange County
Art Institute of California: San Francisco
Azusa Pacific University
Bethesda University of California
Beverly Hills Design Institute
Biola University
California Baptist University
California Coast University
California College of the Arts
California Lutheran University
California Maritime Academy
California Polytechnic State University: San Luis Obispo
California State Polytechnic University: Pomona
California State University: Chico
California State University: Dominguez Hills
California State University: East Bay
California State University: Fresno
California State University: Fullerton
California State University: Long Beach
California State University: Monterey Bay
California State University: Sacramento
California State University: San Bernardino
California State University: San Marcos
California State University: Stanislaus
Canada College
Chapman University
Charles Drew University of Medicine and Science
Citrus College
Claremont McKenna College
Cogswell Polytechnical College
College of San Mateo
Columbia College
Columbia College Hollywood
Concordia University Irvine
Cypress College
Design Institute of San Diego
Dominican University of California
El Camino College

Fashion Institute of Design and Merchandising: Los Angeles
Fashion Institute of Design and Merchandising: San Diego
Fashion Institute of Design and Merchandising: San Francisco
Fremont College
Fresno Pacific University
Fullerton College
Golden Gate University
Holy Names University
Hope International University
Humboldt State University
Humphreys College
La Sierra University
Lake Tahoe Community College
Long Beach City College
Los Angeles Harbor College
Los Angeles Mission College
Los Angeles Valley College
Loyola Marymount University
Marymount California University
The Master's University
Menlo College
Mills College
MiraCosta College
Mount Saint Mary's University
Mt. Sierra College
National University
Northwestern Polytechnic University
Notre Dame de Namur University
Occidental College
Ohlone College
Otis College of Art and Design
Pacific States University
Pacific Union College
Palomar College
Pepperdine University
Pitzer College
Point Loma Nazarene University
Pomona College
Saddleback College
St. Mary's College of California
San Diego Christian College
San Diego State University
San Francisco Art Institute
San Francisco State University
San Joaquin Delta College
San Jose City College
Santa Barbara City College
Santa Clara University
Santa Rosa Junior College
Scripps College
Southern California Institute of Architecture
Southwestern College
Stanford University
University of Antelope Valley
University of California: Irvine
University of California: Merced
University of California: Riverside
University of California: San Diego
University of California: Santa Barbara
University of California: Santa Cruz
University of the Pacific
University of Redlands
University of San Diego
University of San Francisco
University of Southern California
University of the West
Vanguard University of Southern California
Westmont College
Whittier College
William Jessup University
Woodbury University
World Mission University

## Colorado

Adams State University
Aims Community College
Colorado Christian University
Colorado College
Colorado Mesa University
Colorado Mountain College
Colorado Northwestern Community College
Colorado School of Mines
Colorado State University
Colorado State University: Pueblo
Community College of Aurora
Fort Lewis College
Metropolitan State University of Denver
Naropa University
Nazarene Bible College
Northeastern Junior College
Pikes Peak Community College
Pueblo Community College
Red Rocks Community College
Regis University
Rocky Mountain College of Art & Design
University of Colorado Boulder
University of Colorado Colorado Springs
University of Colorado Denver
University of Denver
University of Northern Colorado
Western State Colorado University

## Connecticut

Central Connecticut State University
Connecticut College
Fairfield University
Holy Apostles College and Seminary
Norwalk Community College
Paier College of Art
Post University
Quinnipiac University
Sacred Heart University
Trinity College
University of Bridgeport
University of Connecticut
University of New Haven
Wesleyan University
Western Connecticut State University
Yale University

## Delaware

Delaware State University
University of Delaware

## District of Columbia

American University
Catholic University of America
George Washington University
Georgetown University
Howard University
Strayer University
Trinity Washington University
University of the District of Columbia

## Florida

Adventist University of Health Sciences
Art Institute of Fort Lauderdale
Ave Maria University
Baptist College of Florida
Barry University
Bethune-Cookman University
Broward College
Carlos Albizu University
Chipola College
City College: Fort Lauderdale
College of Central Florida

Daytona State College
Digital Media Arts College
Eastern Florida State College
Eckerd College
Embry-Riddle Aeronautical University
Flagler College
Florida Agricultural and Mechanical
University
Florida Atlantic University
Florida Gateway College
Florida Gulf Coast University
Florida Institute of Technology
Florida International University
Florida Keys Community College
Florida Southern College
Florida SouthWestern State College
Florida State University
Florida Technical College: Deland
Gulf Coast State College
Herzing University: Winter Park
Hillsborough Community College
Hodges University
Indian River State College
Jacksonville University
Johnson University: Florida
Jose Maria Vargas University
Lake-Sumter State College
Lynn University
Miami Dade College
Miami International University of Art
and Design
North Florida Community College
Nova Southeastern University
Palm Beach Atlantic University
Palm Beach State College
Pasco-Hernando State College
Pensacola State College
Polk State College
Rasmussen College: New Port Richey
Rasmussen College: Ocala
Ringling College of Art and Design
Rollins College
Saint Leo University
St. Petersburg College
Saint Thomas University
Santa Fe College
Schiller International University
Seminole State College of Florida
South Florida State College
Southeastern University
Stetson University
Tallahassee Community College
University of Central Florida
University of Florida
University of Miami
University of North Florida
University of South Florida
University of South Florida: Sarasota-
Manatee
University of Tampa
University of West Florida
Valencia College
Warner University
Webber International University

### Georgia

Agnes Scott College
Albany State University
Armstrong State University
Art Institute of Atlanta
Atlanta Technical College
Bainbridge State College
Berry College
Beulah Heights University
Brenau University
Chattahoochee Technical College
Clark Atlanta University
Clayton State University
College of Coastal Georgia
Columbus State University
Covenant College
Darton State College

East Georgia State College
Emory University
Georgia College and State University
Georgia Gwinnett College
Georgia Highlands College
Georgia Institute of Technology
Georgia Military College
Georgia Perimeter College
Georgia Southern University
Georgia Southwestern State University
Georgia State University
Gordon State College
Herzing University: Atlanta
Kennesaw State University
LaGrange College
Mercer University
Middle Georgia State University
Morehouse College
Oglethorpe University
Oxford College of Emory University
Point University
Savannah College of Art and Design
Shorter University
South Georgia State College
South University: Savannah
Spelman College
University of Georgia
University of West Georgia
Valdosta State University
Wesleyan College
Wiregrass Georgia Technical College
Young Harris College

### Hawaii

Brigham Young University-Hawaii
Chaminade University of Honolulu
Hawaii Pacific University
Hawaii Tokai International College
University of Hawaii at Hilo
University of Hawaii at Manoa
University of Hawaii: Leeward
Community College
University of Hawaii: West Oahu

### Idaho

Brigham Young University-Idaho
College of Idaho
Idaho State University
Lewis-Clark State College
Northwest Nazarene University
University of Idaho

### Illinois

American InterContinental University
Augustana College
Bradley University
City Colleges of Chicago: Wilbur
Wright College
Columbia College Chicago
Concordia University Chicago
Danville Area Community College
DePaul University
Dominican University
Eastern Illinois University
Elmhurst College
Eureka College
Governors State University
Greenville College
Illinois College
Illinois Institute of Technology
Illinois State University
Illinois Wesleyan University
International Academy of Design and
Technology: Chicago
Judson University
Kendall College
Knox College

Lake Forest College
Lewis University
Loyola University Chicago
MacCormac College
McKendree University
Midstate College
Millikin University
Monmouth College
Moody Bible Institute
Morrison Institute of Technology
Morton College
North Central College
North Park University
Northwestern University
Olivet Nazarene University
Quincy University
St. Augustine College
School of the Art Institute of Chicago
Southern Illinois University Carbondale
Southern Illinois University
Edwardsville
Spoon River College
Trinity Christian College
Trinity International University
University of Chicago
University of Illinois at Chicago
University of Illinois at Urbana-
Champaign
University of Illinois: Springfield
University of St. Francis
VanderCook College of Music
Western Illinois University
Wheaton College

### Indiana

Ball State University
Bethel College
Butler University
DePauw University
Earlham College
Franklin College
Goshen College
Hanover College
Holy Cross College
Indiana Institute of Technology
Indiana University Bloomington
Indiana University East
Indiana University Kokomo
Indiana University Northwest
Indiana University South Bend
Indiana University Southeast
Indiana University-Purdue University
Fort Wayne
Indiana University-Purdue University
Indianapolis
Manchester University
Marian University
Oakland City University
Purdue University
Rose-Hulman Institute of Technology
Saint Joseph's College
St. Mary-of-the-Woods College
Saint Mary's College
Taylor University
Trine University
University of Evansville
University of Indianapolis
University of Notre Dame
University of Saint Francis
Valparaiso University
Vincennes University
Wabash College

### Iowa

Allen College
Briar Cliff University
Buena Vista University
Central College
Clarke University
Coe College

Cornell College
Dordt College
Drake University
Emmaus Bible College
Faith Baptist Bible College and
Theological Seminary
Graceland University
Grinnell College
Iowa State University
Iowa Wesleyan College
Loras College
Luther College
Maharishi University of Management
Morningside College
Mount Mercy University
Northwestern College
St. Ambrose University
Shiloh University
Simpson College
University of Dubuque
University of Iowa
University of Northern Iowa
Upper Iowa University
William Penn University

### Kansas

Baker University
Barclay College
Barton County Community College
Benedictine College
Bethany College
Bethel College
Central Christian College of Kansas
Donnelly College
Emporia State University
Friends University
Grantham University
Hesston College
Hutchinson Community College
Kansas City Kansas Community
College
Kansas State University
Kansas Wesleyan University
McPherson College
MidAmerica Nazarene University
Newman University
Ottawa University
Pittsburg State University
Pratt Community College
Sterling College
Tabor College
University of Kansas
University of St. Mary
Wichita State University

### Kentucky

Alice Lloyd College
Asbury University
Bellarmine University
Brescia University
Centre College
Georgetown College
Jefferson Community and Technical
College
Kentucky State University
Kentucky Wesleyan College
Midway College
Morehead State University
Murray State University
Northern Kentucky University
St. Catharine College
Spencerian College: Lexington
Thomas More College
Transylvania University
University of the Cumberlands
University of Kentucky
University of Louisville
Western Kentucky University

Credit/placement for International Baccalaureate (IB)

## Louisiana

Centenary College of Louisiana
Dillard University
Herzing University: Kenner
Louisiana State University and
   Agricultural and Mechanical College
Loyola University New Orleans
Northwestern State University
St. Joseph Seminary College
South Louisiana Community College
Tulane University
University of New Orleans

## Maine

Bates College
Bowdoin College
Central Maine Community College
Colby College
College of the Atlantic
Husson University
Maine College of Art
Unity College
University of Maine
University of Maine at Farmington
University of Maine at Fort Kent
University of Maine at Presque Isle
University of New England
University of Southern Maine
Washington County Community
   College

## Maryland

Anne Arundel Community College
Baltimore City Community College
Coppin State University
Frostburg State University
Harford Community College
Hood College
Howard Community College
Johns Hopkins University
Johns Hopkins University: Peabody
   Conservatory of Music
Loyola University Maryland
Maryland Institute College of Art
McDaniel College
Mount St. Mary's University
Notre Dame of Maryland University
St. Mary's College of Maryland
Salisbury University
Stevenson University
Towson University
United States Naval Academy
University of Baltimore
University of Maryland: Baltimore
   County
University of Maryland: College Park
University of Maryland: Eastern Shore
University of Maryland: University
   College
Washington College

## Massachusetts

American International College
Amherst College
Assumption College
Babson College
Bay Path University
Bay State College
Becker College
Benjamin Franklin Institute of
   Technology
Bentley University
Berkshire Community College
Boston Baptist College
Boston College

Boston University
Brandeis University
Bridgewater State University
Clark University
College of the Holy Cross
Curry College
Dean College
Eastern Nazarene College
Elms College
Emerson College
Emmanuel College
Endicott College
Fisher College
Fitchburg State University
Framingham State University
Gordon College
Harvard College
Hellenic College/Holy Cross
Lasell College
Lesley University
Massachusetts Bay Community College
Massachusetts College of Art and
   Design
Massachusetts College of Liberal Arts
Massachusetts Institute of Technology
Massachusetts Maritime Academy
MCPHS University
Merrimack College
Montserrat College of Art
Mount Holyoke College
Mount Ida College
Mount Wachusett Community College
New England College of Business and
   Finance
New England Conservatory of Music
Newbury College
Nichols College
Northeastern University
Pine Manor College
Quinsigamond Community College
Regis College
Simmons College
Smith College
Springfield College
Stonehill College
Suffolk University
Tufts University
University of Massachusetts Amherst
University of Massachusetts Dartmouth
University of Massachusetts Lowell
Wellesley College
Wentworth Institute of Technology
Western New England University
Wheaton College
Williams College
Worcester Polytechnic Institute
Worcester State University

## Michigan

Adrian College
Albion College
Alma College
Andrews University
Baker College of Auburn Hills
Baker College of Cadillac
Baker College of Jackson
Baker College of Muskegon
Baker College of Owosso
Baker College of Port Huron
Calvin College
Central Michigan University
College for Creative Studies
Concordia University
Cornerstone University
Davenport University
Delta College
Eastern Michigan University
Finlandia University
Grand Valley State University
Hillsdale College
Hope College
Kalamazoo College

Kellogg Community College
Kettering University
Kuyper College
Lake Superior State University
Lansing Community College
Lawrence Technological University
Madonna University
Michigan Jewish Institute
Michigan State University
Michigan Technological University
North Central Michigan College
Northern Michigan University
Northwood University: Michigan
Oakland University
Olivet College
Rochester College
Saginaw Valley State University
Siena Heights University
Spring Arbor University
University of Detroit Mercy
University of Michigan
University of Michigan: Dearborn
Walsh College of Accountancy and
   Business Administration
Wayne State University
Western Michigan University

## Minnesota

Academy College
Alexandria Technical and Community
   College
Augsburg College
Bemidji State University
Bethany Lutheran College
Bethel University
Capella University
Carleton College
Central Lakes College
Century College
College of St. Benedict
College of St. Scholastica
Concordia College: Moorhead
Concordia University St. Paul
Crown College
Dakota County Technical College
Dunwoody College of Technology
Fond du Lac Tribal and Community
   College
Gustavus Adolphus College
Hamline University
Hennepin Technical College
Inver Hills Community College
Itasca Community College
Macalester College
Minneapolis College of Art and Design
Minneapolis Community and Technical
   College
Minnesota State College - Southeast
   Technical
Minnesota State Community and
   Technical College
Minnesota State University Mankato
Minnesota State University Moorhead
Minnesota West Community and
   Technical College
National American University:
   Bloomington
Normandale Community College
North Hennepin Community College
Northland Community & Technical
   College
Northwest Technical College
Rainy River Community College
Rasmussen College: Mankato
Riverland Community College
St. Catherine University
Saint Cloud State University
St. John's University
St. Mary's University of Minnesota
St. Olaf College
South Central College
Southwest Minnesota State University

University of Minnesota: Crookston
University of Minnesota: Duluth
University of Minnesota: Morris
University of Minnesota: Rochester
University of Minnesota: Twin Cities
University of Northwestern - St. Paul
University of St. Thomas
Walden University
Winona State University

## Mississippi

Belhaven University
Blue Mountain College
Hinds Community College
Jackson State University
Millsaps College
Mississippi College
Mississippi State University
Tougaloo College
University of Mississippi
University of Southern Mississippi
William Carey University

## Missouri

Avila University
Calvary Bible College and Theological
   Seminary
Central Methodist University
College of the Ozarks
Columbia College
Cottey College
Culver-Stockton College
Drury University
Evangel University
Fontbonne University
Goldfarb School of Nursing at Barnes-
   Jewish College
Jefferson College
Kansas City Art Institute
Lincoln University
Lindenwood University
Maryville University of Saint Louis
Metropolitan Community College -
   Kansas City
Missouri Baptist University
Missouri Southern State University
Missouri State University
Missouri State University: West Plains
Missouri University of Science and
   Technology
Missouri Western State University
Moberly Area Community College
Northwest Missouri State University
Ozarks Technical Community College
Ranken Technical College
Research College of Nursing
Rockhurst University
Saint Louis University
Southeast Missouri State University
Southwest Baptist University
Stephens College
Truman State University
University of Central Missouri
University of Missouri: Columbia
University of Missouri: Kansas City
University of Missouri: St. Louis
Washington University in St. Louis
Webster University
Westminster College
William Jewell College
William Woods University

## Montana

Carroll College
Dawson Community College
Flathead Valley Community College
Montana State University

Montana State University: Northern
Montana Tech of the University of
  Montana
Rocky Mountain College
University of Great Falls
University of Montana
University of Montana: Western

### Nebraska

Bellevue University
College of Saint Mary
Concordia University
Creighton University
Doane University
Hastings College
Nebraska Wesleyan University
Peru State College
University of Nebraska - Lincoln
Western Nebraska Community College
York College

### Nevada

Art Institute of Las Vegas
Roseman University of Health Sciences
Sierra Nevada College
Truckee Meadows Community College
University of Nevada: Las Vegas
University of Nevada: Reno

### New Hampshire

Colby-Sawyer College
Dartmouth College
Franklin Pierce University
Keene State College
Lakes Region Community College
New England College
New Hampshire Institute of Art
NHTI-Concord's Community College
Plymouth State University
Rivier University
Saint Anselm College
Southern New Hampshire University
University of New Hampshire
University of New Hampshire at
  Manchester

### New Jersey

Caldwell University
Centenary University
The College of New Jersey
College of St. Elizabeth
Cumberland County College
Drew University
Felician University
Hudson County Community College
Kean University
Monmouth University
Montclair State University
New Jersey City University
Pillar College
Princeton University
Ramapo College of New Jersey
Rider University
Rowan University
Rutgers, The State University of New
  Jersey: Camden Campus
Rutgers, The State University of New
  Jersey: New Brunswick/Piscataway
  Campus
Rutgers, The State University of New
  Jersey: Newark Campus
Saint Peter's University
Seton Hall University
Stevens Institute of Technology

Stockton University
Sussex County Community College

### New Mexico

Eastern New Mexico University:
  Roswell
Institute of American Indian Arts
Navajo Technical University
Northern New Mexico College
Santa Fe University of Art and Design
University of New Mexico
University of the Southwest
Western New Mexico University

### New York

Adelphi University
Adirondack Community College
Albany College of Pharmacy and
  Health Sciences
Alfred University
Bard College
Barnard College
Briarcliffe College
Canisius College
Cazenovia College
City University of New York: Baruch
  College
City University of New York: Bronx
  Community College
City University of New York:
  Brooklyn College
City University of New York: City
  College
City University of New York: College
  of Staten Island
City University of New York: Hunter
  College
City University of New York: John Jay
  College of Criminal Justice
City University of New York: Lehman
  College
City University of New York: Medgar
  Evers College
City University of New York: New
  York City College of Technology
City University of New York: Queens
  College
City University of New York: York
  College
Clarkson University
Clinton Community College
Colgate University
College of Mount St. Vincent
College of New Rochelle
College of Saint Rose
Columbia University
Concordia College
Cooper Union for the Advancement of
  Science and Art
Cornell University
Culinary Institute of America
Daemen College
Davis College
Dominican College of Blauvelt
D'Youville College
Elmira College
Eugene Lang College The New School
  for Liberal Arts
Excelsior College
Fashion Institute of Technology
Five Towns College
Fordham University
Genesee Community College
Hamilton College
Hartwick College
Hilbert College
Hobart and William Smith Colleges
Hofstra University
Houghton College
Iona College

Ithaca College
Jewish Theological Seminary of
  America
The King's College
Le Moyne College
LIU Brooklyn
LIU Post
Manhattan College
Manhattanville College
Maria College
Marist College
Marymount Manhattan College
Medaille College
Metropolitan College of New York
Molloy College
Monroe College
Mount Saint Mary College
Nassau Community College
Nazareth College
New York Institute of Technology
New York School of Interior Design
New York University
Niagara County Community College
Niagara University
Pace University
Pace University: Pleasantville/Briarcliff
Parsons The New School for Design
Paul Smith's College
Rensselaer Polytechnic Institute
Roberts Wesleyan College
Rochester Institute of Technology
Rockland Community College
The Sage Colleges
Saint Bonaventure University
St. Francis College
St. John Fisher College
St. John's University
St. Joseph's College New York:
  Suffolk Campus
St. Joseph's College, New York
St. Lawrence University
St. Thomas Aquinas College
Sarah Lawrence College
School of Visual Arts
Siena College
Skidmore College
Suffolk County Community College
SUNY College at Brockport
SUNY College at Buffalo
SUNY College at Cortland
SUNY College at Fredonia
SUNY College at Geneseo
SUNY College at New Paltz
SUNY College at Old Westbury
SUNY College at Oswego
SUNY College at Plattsburgh
SUNY College at Potsdam
SUNY College of Agriculture and
  Technology at Morrisville
SUNY College of Environmental
  Science and Forestry
SUNY College of Technology at
  Alfred
SUNY College of Technology at
  Canton
SUNY College of Technology at Delhi
SUNY Empire State College
SUNY Farmingdale State College
SUNY Maritime College
SUNY Polytechnic Institute
SUNY University at Albany
SUNY University at Binghamton
SUNY University at Buffalo
SUNY University at Stony Brook
Syracuse University
Tompkins Cortland Community
  College
Union College
United States Merchant Marine
  Academy
University of Rochester
Utica College
Vassar College
Vaughn College of Aeronautics and
  Technology

Wagner College
Wells College
Westchester Community College

### North Carolina

Alamance Community College
Appalachian State University
Barton College
Belmont Abbey College
Bennett College for Women
Brevard College
Campbell University
Catawba College
Chowan University
Davidson College
Duke University
East Carolina University
Elizabeth City State University
Elon University
Fayetteville Technical Community
  College
Gardner-Webb University
Greensboro College
Guilford College
Guilford Technical Community College
High Point University
Johnson C. Smith University
Johnston Community College
Laurel University
Lees-McRae College
Lenoir-Rhyne University
Mars Hill University
Meredith College
Methodist University
Montreat College
Nash Community College
North Carolina State University
Pfeiffer University
Queens University of Charlotte
Robeson Community College
St. Andrews University
Saint Augustine's University
Salem College
Shaw University
University of North Carolina at
  Asheville
University of North Carolina at Chapel
  Hill
University of North Carolina at
  Charlotte
University of North Carolina at
  Greensboro
University of North Carolina at
  Wilmington
Wake Forest University
Wake Technical Community College
Warren Wilson College
Western Carolina University
Wilkes Community College
Wingate University
Winston-Salem State University

### North Dakota

Mayville State University
North Dakota State University
Rasmussen College: Fargo
University of Jamestown
University of Mary
University of North Dakota
Williston State College

### Ohio

Ashland University
Baldwin Wallace University
Bowling Green State University
Bryant & Stratton College: Parma
Capital University

Case Western Reserve University
Cedarville University
Central Ohio Technical College
Cincinnati Christian University
Cincinnati State Technical and
  Community College
Cleveland Institute of Art
Cleveland Institute of Music
Cleveland State University
College of Wooster
Columbus College of Art and Design
Columbus State Community College
Defiance College
Denison University
Edison State Community College
Franciscan University of Steubenville
Franklin University
Heidelberg University
Hiram College
John Carroll University
Kent State University
Kenyon College
Lake Erie College
Lourdes University
Marietta College
Miami University: Hamilton
Miami University: Middletown
Miami University: Oxford
Mount Vernon Nazarene University
Muskingum University
North Central State College
Oberlin College
Ohio Dominican University
Ohio Northern University
Ohio State University: Columbus
  Campus
Ohio University
Ohio Wesleyan University
Otterbein University
Tiffin University
Union Institute & University
University of Akron
University of Cincinnati
University of Cincinnati: Blue Ash
  College
University of Cincinnati: Clermont
  College
University of Dayton
University of Findlay
University of Mount Union
University of Rio Grande
University of Toledo
Walsh University
Wilmington College
Wittenberg University
Wright State University: Lake Campus
Xavier University
Youngstown State University

## Oklahoma

Cameron University
Northeastern State University
Oklahoma Baptist University
Oklahoma Christian University
Oklahoma City Community College
Oklahoma City University
Oklahoma State University
Oklahoma State University Institute of
  Technology: Okmulgee
Rogers State University
Rose State College
St. Gregory's University
Southeastern Oklahoma State
  University
Southern Nazarene University
Southwestern Oklahoma State
  University
Tulsa Community College
University of Oklahoma
University of Tulsa
Western Oklahoma State College

## Oregon

Art Institute of Portland
Chemeketa Community College
Clackamas Community College
Clatsop Community College
Corban University
Eastern Oregon University
George Fox University
Lane Community College
Lewis & Clark College
Linfield College
Linn-Benton Community College
Marylhurst University
Mt. Hood Community College
Northwest Christian University
Oregon College of Art & Craft
Oregon State University
Pacific University
Reed College
Southern Oregon University
University of Oregon
University of Portland
Western Oregon University
Willamette University

## Pennsylvania

Albright College
Allegheny College
Alvernia University
Arcadia University
Art Institute of Philadelphia
Art Institute of Pittsburgh
Bryn Athyn College
Bryn Mawr College
Bucknell University
Cabrini University
Cairn University
California University of Pennsylvania
Carlow University
Carnegie Mellon University
Cedar Crest College
Central Penn College
Chatham University
Chestnut Hill College
Clarion University of Pennsylvania
Clarks Summit University
Dickinson College
Drexel University
Duquesne University
East Stroudsburg University of
  Pennsylvania
Eastern University
Elizabethtown College
Franklin & Marshall College
Gannon University
Geneva College
Gettysburg College
Grove City College
Harrisburg Area Community College
Harrisburg University of Science and
  Technology
Haverford College
Holy Family University
Immaculata University
Indiana University of Pennsylvania
Juniata College
Keystone College
King's College
Kutztown University of Pennsylvania
La Roche College
Lafayette College
Lebanon Valley College
Lincoln University
Lock Haven University of
  Pennsylvania
Lycoming College
Mansfield University of Pennsylvania
Marywood University
Mercyhurst University
Messiah College
Millersville University of Pennsylvania

Misericordia University
Moore College of Art and Design
Moravian College
Muhlenberg College
Penn State Abington
Penn State Altoona
Penn State Beaver
Penn State Berks
Penn State Brandywine
Penn State DuBois
Penn State Erie, The Behrend College
Penn State Fayette, The Eberly
  Campus
Penn State Greater Allegheny
Penn State Harrisburg
Penn State Hazleton
Penn State Lehigh Valley
Penn State Mont Alto
Penn State New Kensington
Penn State Schuylkill
Penn State Shenango
Penn State University Park
Penn State Wilkes-Barre
Penn State Worthington Scranton
Penn State York
Pennsylvania Academy of the Fine
  Arts
Point Park University
Rosemont College
St. Francis University
Saint Joseph's University
St. Vincent College
Seton Hill University
Shippensburg University of
  Pennsylvania
Slippery Rock University of
  Pennsylvania
Susquehanna University
Swarthmore College
Temple University
Thiel College
University of the Arts
University of Pennsylvania
University of Pittsburgh
University of Pittsburgh at Bradford
University of Pittsburgh at Johnstown
University of the Sciences
University of Scranton
University of Valley Forge
Ursinus College
Villanova University
Washington & Jefferson College
West Chester University of
  Pennsylvania
Westminster College
Widener University
Wilson College
York College of Pennsylvania

## Puerto Rico

Bayamon Central University
Conservatory of Music of Puerto Rico
University of Puerto Rico: Arecibo

## Rhode Island

Brown University
Bryant University
Providence College
Rhode Island School of Design
Roger Williams University
Salve Regina University
University of Rhode Island

## South Carolina

Anderson University
Central Carolina Technical College
Charleston Southern University

The Citadel
Clemson University
Coastal Carolina University
Coker College
College of Charleston
Columbia College
Columbia International University
Converse College
Erskine College
Florence-Darlington Technical College
Francis Marion University
Furman University
Greenville Technical College
Horry-Georgetown Technical College
Lander University
Newberry College
North Greenville University
Piedmont Technical College
Presbyterian College
Southern Wesleyan University
Spartanburg Community College
Tri-County Technical College
Trident Technical College
University of South Carolina: Aiken
University of South Carolina: Beaufort
University of South Carolina:
  Columbia
University of South Carolina:
  Lancaster
University of South Carolina: Upstate
Voorhees College
Winthrop University
Wofford College

## South Dakota

Augustana University
Dakota State University
Dakota Wesleyan University
Mount Marty College
National American University: Rapid
  City
Northern State University
South Dakota School of Mines and
  Technology
South Dakota State University
University of Sioux Falls

## Tennessee

Aquinas College
Austin Peay State University
Belmont University
Bryan College: Dayton
Christian Brothers University
East Tennessee State University
Fisk University
Freed-Hardeman University
Hiwassee College
Lee University
LeMoyne-Owen College
Lincoln Memorial University
Lipscomb University
Martin Methodist College
Maryville College
Memphis College of Art
Middle Tennessee State University
Milligan College
O'More College of Design
Pellissippi State Community College
Rhodes College
Roane State Community College
Sewanee: The University of the South
Tennessee Technological University
Tennessee Wesleyan College
Trevecca Nazarene University
Union University
University of Memphis
University of Tennessee: Chattanooga
University of Tennessee: Knoxville
Vanderbilt University

Watkins College of Art, Design & Film
Welch College

## Texas

Abilene Christian University
Austin College
Austin Community College
Baylor University
Blinn College
Brookhaven College
Central Texas College
Cisco College
Collin County Community College District
Concordia University Texas
Dallas Baptist University
Del Mar College
East Texas Baptist University
Eastfield College
El Centro College
Frank Phillips College
Houston Baptist University
Houston Community College System
Howard Payne University
Jarvis Christian College
The King's University
Lamar Institute of Technology
Lamar University
LeTourneau University
Lone Star College System
Lubbock Christian University
McMurry University
Midland College
Midwestern State University
Mountain View College
Northwood University: Texas
Our Lady of the Lake University of San Antonio
Ranger College
Rice University
St. Edward's University
Sam Houston State University
San Antonio College
San Jacinto College
Schreiner University
South Texas College
Southern Methodist University
Southwestern Adventist University
Southwestern University
Stephen F. Austin State University
Texas A&M International University
Texas A&M University
Texas A&M University-Commerce
Texas A&M University-Corpus Christi
Texas A&M University-Kingsville
Texas A&M University-Texarkana
Texas Christian University
Texas Lutheran University
Texas Southern University
Texas State Technical College
Texas State University
Texas Tech University
Texas Wesleyan University
Texas Woman's University
Trinity University
University of Dallas
University of Houston
University of Houston-Clear Lake
University of Houston-Downtown
University of the Incarnate Word
University of Mary Hardin-Baylor
University of North Texas
University of St. Thomas
University of Texas at Arlington
University of Texas at Austin
University of Texas at Dallas
University of Texas at El Paso
University of Texas at San Antonio
University of Texas at Tyler
University of Texas Medical Branch at Galveston

University of Texas of the Permian Basin
Victoria College
Wade College
Wayland Baptist University
West Texas A&M University

## Utah

Brigham Young University
Neumont University
Salt Lake Community College
Stevens-Henager College: Orem
University of Utah
Utah State University
Utah Valley University
Weber State University
Westminster College

## Vermont

Bennington College
Champlain College
College of St. Joseph in Vermont
Community College of Vermont
Goddard College
Green Mountain College
Johnson State College
Lyndon State College
Marlboro College
Middlebury College
Norwich University
Saint Michael's College
Sterling College
University of Vermont

## Virginia

Art Institute of Washington
Averett University
Blue Ridge Community College
Bluefield College
Bridgewater College
Christopher Newport University
College of William and Mary
Eastern Mennonite University
Emory & Henry College
Ferrum College
George Mason University
Hampden-Sydney College
Hampton University
Hollins University
J. Sargeant Reynolds Community College
James Madison University
Jefferson College of Health Sciences
Liberty University
Longwood University
Lynchburg College
Mary Baldwin University
Marymount University
Northern Virginia Community College
Old Dominion University
Patrick Henry College
Radford University
Randolph College
Randolph-Macon College
Regent University
Roanoke College
Shenandoah University
Southern Virginia University
Sweet Briar College
University of Mary Washington
University of Richmond
University of Virginia
University of Virginia's College at Wise
Virginia Commonwealth University
Virginia Military Institute

Virginia Polytechnic Institute and State University
Virginia Union University
Virginia University of Lynchburg
Virginia Wesleyan College
Virginia Western Community College
Washington and Lee University

## Washington

Art Institute of Seattle
Bates Technical College
Bellingham Technical College
Cascadia College
Central Washington University
Centralia College
City University of Seattle
Clark College
Columbia Basin College
Cornish College of the Arts
Eastern Washington University
Everett Community College
Evergreen State College
Gonzaga University
Lake Washington Institute of Technology
North Seattle College
Northwest School of Wooden Boatbuilding
Northwest University
Olympic College
Pacific Lutheran University
Saint Martin's University
Seattle Central College
Seattle Pacific University
Seattle University
Shoreline Community College
Skagit Valley College
South Puget Sound Community College
South Seattle College
Tacoma Community College
University of Puget Sound
University of Washington
University of Washington Bothell
University of Washington Tacoma
Walla Walla Community College
Walla Walla University
Washington State University
Western Washington University
Whatcom Community College
Whitman College
Whitworth University
Yakima Valley Community College

## West Virginia

American Public University System
Bethany College
Bluefield State College
Davis and Elkins College
Fairmont State University
Marshall University
Ohio Valley University
Potomac State College of West Virginia University
Salem International University
Shepherd University
University of Charleston
West Virginia State University
West Virginia University
West Virginia University at Parkersburg
West Virginia Wesleyan College
Wheeling Jesuit University

## Wisconsin

Alverno College
Beloit College

Cardinal Stritch University
Carroll University
Carthage College
Concordia University Wisconsin
Edgewood College
Lakeland University
Lawrence University
Marian University
Marquette University
Milwaukee Area Technical College
Milwaukee School of Engineering
Mount Mary University
Northcentral Technical College
Northland College
St. Norbert College
Silver Lake College of the Holy Family
University of Wisconsin-Baraboo/Sauk County
University of Wisconsin-Eau Claire
University of Wisconsin-Green Bay
University of Wisconsin-La Crosse
University of Wisconsin-Madison
University of Wisconsin-Marathon County
University of Wisconsin-Milwaukee
University of Wisconsin-Oshkosh
University of Wisconsin-Parkside
University of Wisconsin-River Falls
University of Wisconsin-Sheboygan
University of Wisconsin-Stevens Point
University of Wisconsin-Stout
University of Wisconsin-Superior
University of Wisconsin-Washington County
University of Wisconsin-Waukesha
University of Wisconsin-Whitewater
Viterbo University
Wisconsin Lutheran College

## Wyoming

Casper College
Eastern Wyoming College
Laramie County Community College
University of Wyoming
Western Wyoming Community College

# Credit/placement for Advanced Placement (AP)

## Alabama

Alabama Agricultural and Mechanical University
Alabama State University
Athens State University
Auburn University
Auburn University at Montgomery
Birmingham-Southern College
Calhoun Community College
Chattahoochee Valley Community College
Faulkner University
Gadsden State Community College
George C. Wallace Community College at Dothan
Heritage Christian University
Huntingdon College
Jacksonville State University
Jefferson State Community College
Judson College
Lawson State Community College
Lurleen B. Wallace Community College
Marion Military Institute
Oakwood University
Samford University
Spring Hill College
Talladega College
Troy University
Tuskegee University
University of Alabama
University of Alabama at Birmingham
University of Alabama in Huntsville
University of Mobile
University of Montevallo
University of North Alabama
University of South Alabama
University of West Alabama
Wallace State Community College at Hanceville

## Alaska

Alaska Pacific University
University of Alaska Anchorage
University of Alaska Fairbanks
University of Alaska Southeast

## Arizona

Arizona Christian University
Arizona State University
Arizona Western College
Art Institute of Phoenix
Art Institute of Tucson
Central Arizona College
Chandler-Gilbert Community College
Cochise College
DeVry University: Phoenix
Dunlap-Stone University
Embry-Riddle Aeronautical University: Prescott Campus
GateWay Community College
Glendale Community College
Grand Canyon University
Northern Arizona University
Paradise Valley Community College
Phoenix College
Prescott College
Rio Salado College
Scottsdale Community College
Sessions College for Professional Design
University of Advancing Technology
University of Arizona
Yavapai College

## Arkansas

Arkansas State University
Arkansas State University Mid-South
Arkansas State University: Beebe
Arkansas State University: Mountain Home
Arkansas Tech University
College of the Ouachitas
Cossatot Community College of the University of Arkansas
East Arkansas Community College
Ecclesia College
Harding University
Henderson State University
Hendrix College
John Brown University
Lyon College
National Park College
Ouachita Baptist University
Philander Smith College
Pulaski Technical College
Remington College: Little Rock
South Arkansas Community College
Southeast Arkansas College
Southern Arkansas University
Southern Arkansas University Tech
University of Arkansas
University of Arkansas at Fort Smith
University of Arkansas at Little Rock
University of Arkansas at Monticello
University of Central Arkansas
University of the Ozarks
Williams Baptist College

## California

Academy of Art University
Allan Hancock College
Alliant International University
American Academy of Dramatic Arts: West
American Jewish University
American River College
Antelope Valley College
Antioch University Los Angeles
Antioch University Santa Barbara
Art Institute of California: Hollywood
Art Institute of California: Inland Empire
Art Institute of California: Los Angeles
Art Institute of California: Orange County
Art Institute of California: Sacramento
Art Institute of California: San Diego
Art Institute of California: San Francisco
Ashford University
Azusa Pacific University
Bakersfield College
Bergin University of Canine Studies
Berkeley City College
Beverly Hills Design Institute
Biola University
Butte College
Cabrillo College
California Baptist University
California Christian College
California College of the Arts
California Institute of the Arts
California Institute of Integral Studies
California Institute of Technology
California Lutheran University
California Maritime Academy
California Polytechnic State University: San Luis Obispo
California State Polytechnic University: Pomona
California State University: Bakersfield
California State University: Channel Islands
California State University: Chico
California State University: Dominguez Hills
California State University: East Bay
California State University: Fresno
California State University: Fullerton
California State University: Long Beach
California State University: Los Angeles
California State University: Monterey Bay
California State University: Sacramento
California State University: San Bernardino
California State University: San Marcos
California State University: Stanislaus
California University of Management and Sciences
Canada College
Cerritos College
Cerro Coso Community College
Chabot College
Chapman University
Charles Drew University of Medicine and Science
Citrus College
City College of San Francisco
Claremont McKenna College
Coastline Community College
Cogswell Polytechnical College
College of the Canyons
College of the Desert
College of San Mateo
College of the Sequoias
College of the Siskiyous
Columbia College
Columbia College Hollywood
Concordia University Irvine
Contra Costa College
Copper Mountain College
Cosumnes River College
Crafton Hills College
Cuesta College
Cuyamaca College
Cypress College
De Anza College
Design Institute of San Diego
DeVry University: Pomona
Diablo Valley College
Dominican University of California
East Los Angeles College
El Camino College
Evergreen Valley College
Fashion Institute of Design and Merchandising: Los Angeles
Fashion Institute of Design and Merchandising: San Diego
Fashion Institute of Design and Merchandising: San Francisco
Feather River College
Folsom Lake College
Foothill College
Fresno Pacific University
Fullerton College
Glendale Community College
Golden Gate University
Golden West College
Grossmont College
Hartnell College
Holy Names University
Hope International University
Humboldt State University
Humphreys College
Irvine Valley College
John F. Kennedy University
John Paul the Great Catholic University
Kaplan College: Riverside
Kaplan College: San Diego
La Sierra University
Laguna College of Art and Design
Lake Tahoe Community College
Las Positas College
Lassen Community College
Le Cordon Bleu College of Culinary Arts: Los Angeles
Life Pacific College
Loma Linda University
Long Beach City College
Los Angeles Harbor College
Los Angeles Mission College
Los Angeles Trade and Technical College
Los Angeles Valley College
Loyola Marymount University
Marymount California University
The Master's University
Menlo College
Mills College
MiraCosta College
Modesto Junior College
Moorpark College
Mount Saint Mary's University
Mount San Antonio College
Mount San Jacinto College
Mt. Sierra College
National University
NewSchool of Architecture & Design
Norco College
Northwestern Polytechnic University
Notre Dame de Namur University
Occidental College
Ohlone College
Orange Coast College
Otis College of Art and Design
Pacific Oaks College
Pacific Union College
Palo Verde College
Palomar College
Patten University
Pepperdine University
Pitzer College
Platt College: San Diego
Point Loma Nazarene University
Pomona College
Providence Christian College
Reedley College
Rio Hondo College
Riverside City College
Sacramento City College
Saddleback College
St. Mary's College of California
San Bernardino Valley College
San Diego Christian College
San Diego City College
San Diego Mesa College
San Diego Miramar College
San Diego State University
San Francisco Art Institute
San Francisco Conservatory of Music
San Francisco State University
San Joaquin Delta College
San Jose City College
San Jose State University

Santa Ana College
Santa Barbara City College
Santa Clara University
Santa Monica College
Santa Rosa Junior College
Santiago Canyon College
Scripps College
Shasta Bible College and Graduate
  School
Shasta College
Sierra College
Simpson University
Skyline College
Solano Community College
Sonoma State University
Southern California Institute of
  Architecture
Southwestern College
Stanford University
SUM Bible College & Theological
  Seminary
Taft College
Trident University International
University of Antelope Valley
University of California: Berkeley
University of California: Davis
University of California: Irvine
University of California: Los Angeles
University of California: Merced
University of California: Riverside
University of California: San Diego
University of California: Santa Barbara
University of California: Santa Cruz
University of La Verne
University of the Pacific
University of Redlands
University of San Diego
University of San Francisco
University of Southern California
University of the West
Vanguard University of Southern
  California
Ventura College
Victor Valley College
West Hills College: Coalinga
West Hills College: Lemoore
West Valley College
Westmont College
Whittier College
William Jessup University
Woodbury University
Yuba College

## Colorado

Adams State University
Aims Community College
American Sentinel University
Colorado Christian University
Colorado College
Colorado Mesa University
Colorado Mountain College
Colorado Northwestern Community
  College
Colorado School of Mines
Colorado State University
Colorado State University: Pueblo
Community College of Aurora
Community College of Denver
DeVry University: Westminster
Fort Lewis College
Front Range Community College
IBMC College: Fort Collins
IntelliTec College
Johnson & Wales University: Denver
Metropolitan State University of
  Denver
Morgan Community College
Naropa University
National American University: Denver
Nazarene Bible College
Northeastern Junior College
Otero Junior College

Pikes Peak Community College
Pueblo Community College
Red Rocks Community College
Regis University
Rocky Mountain College of Art &
  Design
Trinidad State Junior College
University of Colorado Boulder
University of Colorado Colorado
  Springs
University of Colorado Denver
University of Denver
University of Northern Colorado
Western State Colorado University

## Connecticut

Albertus Magnus College
Capital Community College
Central Connecticut State University
Charter Oak State College
Connecticut College
Eastern Connecticut State University
Fairfield University
Gateway Community College
Goodwin College
Holy Apostles College and Seminary
Lyme Academy College of Fine Arts
Manchester Community College
Middlesex Community College
Mitchell College
Naugatuck Valley Community College
Norwalk Community College
Paier College of Art
Post University
Quinnipiac University
Sacred Heart University
Southern Connecticut State University
Trinity College
Tunxis Community College
United States Coast Guard Academy
University of Bridgeport
University of Connecticut
University of Hartford
University of New Haven
University of Saint Joseph
Wesleyan University
Western Connecticut State University
Yale University

## Delaware

Delaware College of Art and Design
Delaware State University
Delaware Technical Community
  College: Stanton/Wilmington
  Campus
Goldey-Beacom College
University of Delaware
Wesley College

## District of Columbia

American University
Catholic University of America
Gallaudet University
George Washington University
Georgetown University
Howard University
Strayer University
Trinity Washington University
University of the District of Columbia

## Florida

Adventist University of Health
  Sciences
Art Institute of Fort Lauderdale

Ave Maria University
Baptist College of Florida
Barry University
Beacon College
Bethune-Cookman University
Broward College
Chipola College
College of Central Florida
Daytona State College
DeVry University: Miramar
DeVry University: Orlando
Digital Media Arts College
Eastern Florida State College
Eckerd College
Edward Waters College
Embry-Riddle Aeronautical University
Embry-Riddle Aeronautical University:
  Worldwide Campus
Everglades University
Flagler College
Florida Agricultural and Mechanical
  University
Florida Atlantic University
Florida Gateway College
Florida Gulf Coast University
Florida Institute of Technology
Florida International University
Florida Keys Community College
Florida Memorial University
Florida National University
Florida Southern College
Florida SouthWestern State College
Florida State College at Jacksonville
Florida State University
Full Sail University
Gulf Coast State College
Herzing University: Winter Park
Hillsborough Community College
Hodges University
Indian River State College
Jacksonville University
Johnson & Wales University: North
  Miami
Johnson University: Florida
Jones College
Jose Maria Vargas University
Key College
Lake-Sumter State College
Lincoln College of Technology: West
  Palm Beach
Lynn University
Miami Dade College
Miami International University of Art
  and Design
New College of Florida
North Florida Community College
Northwest Florida State College
Nova Southeastern University
Palm Beach Atlantic University
Palm Beach State College
Pasco-Hernando State College
Pensacola State College
Polk State College
Rasmussen College: New Port Richey
Rasmussen College: Ocala
Ringling College of Art and Design
Rollins College
Saint Leo University
St. Petersburg College
Saint Thomas University
Santa Fe College
Schiller International University
Seminole State College of Florida
South Florida State College
Southeastern University
Southern Technical College
State College of Florida, Manatee-
  Sarasota
Stetson University
Tallahassee Community College
Trinity Baptist College
Trinity College of Florida
University of Central Florida
University of Florida
University of Miami

University of North Florida
University of South Florida
University of South Florida: Sarasota-
  Manatee
University of Tampa
University of West Florida
Valencia College
Warner University
Webber International University

## Georgia

Abraham Baldwin Agricultural College
Agnes Scott College
Albany State University
Andrew College
Armstrong State University
Art Institute of Atlanta
Ashworth College
Atlanta Metropolitan State College
Bainbridge State College
Bauder College
Berry College
Brenau University
Brewton-Parker College
Central Georgia Technical College
Chattahoochee Technical College
Clark Atlanta University
Clayton State University
College of Coastal Georgia
Columbus State University
Columbus Technical College
Covenant College
Darton State College
DeVry University: Decatur
East Georgia State College
Emory University
Fort Valley State University
Georgia College and State University
Georgia Gwinnett College
Georgia Highlands College
Georgia Institute of Technology
Georgia Military College
Georgia Perimeter College
Georgia Piedmont Technical College
Georgia Southern University
Georgia Southwestern State University
Georgia State University
Gordon State College
Kennesaw State University
LaGrange College
Le Cordon Bleu College of Culinary
  Arts: Atlanta
Life University
Mercer University
Middle Georgia State University
Morehouse College
Oglethorpe University
Oxford College of Emory University
Paine College
Piedmont College
Point University
Reinhardt University
Savannah College of Art and Design
Savannah State University
Savannah Technical College
Shorter University
South Georgia State College
Southern Regional Technical College
Spelman College
Thomas University
Toccoa Falls College
Truett McConnell University
University of Georgia
University of North Georgia
University of West Georgia
Valdosta State University
Wesleyan College
Wiregrass Georgia Technical College
Young Harris College

Credit/placement for Advanced Placement (AP)

## Hawaii

Brigham Young University-Hawaii
Chaminade University of Honolulu
Hawaii Pacific University
Hawaii Tokai International College
University of Hawaii at Manoa
University of Hawaii: Hawaii
  Community College
University of Hawaii: Honolulu
  Community College
University of Hawaii: Kauai
  Community College
University of Hawaii: West Oahu

## Idaho

Boise State University
Brigham Young University-Idaho
College of Idaho
College of Southern Idaho
College of Western Idaho
Idaho State University
Lewis-Clark State College
Northwest Nazarene University
Stevens-Henager College: Boise
University of Idaho

## Illinois

American Academy of Art
American InterContinental University
Augustana College
Aurora University
Benedictine University
Benedictine University at Springfield
Black Hawk College
Blackburn College
Blessing-Rieman College of Nursing &
  Health Sciences
Bradley University
Carl Sandburg College
Chicago State University
City Colleges of Chicago: Harold
  Washington College
City Colleges of Chicago: Kennedy-
  King College
City Colleges of Chicago: Olive-
  Harvey College
City Colleges of Chicago: Wilbur
  Wright College
College of DuPage
College of Lake County
Columbia College Chicago
Concordia University Chicago
Danville Area Community College
DePaul University
DeVry University: Chicago
DeVry University: Online
Dominican University
Eastern Illinois University
Elgin Community College
Elmhurst College
Eureka College
Governors State University
Greenville College
Harper College
Heartland Community College
Illinois Central College
Illinois College
Illinois Eastern Community Colleges:
  Frontier Community College
Illinois Eastern Community Colleges:
  Lincoln Trail College
Illinois Eastern Community Colleges:
  Olney Central College
Illinois Eastern Community Colleges:
  Wabash Valley College
Illinois Institute of Art: Chicago
Illinois Institute of Technology
Illinois State University

Illinois Wesleyan University
International Academy of Design and
  Technology: Chicago
John Wood Community College
Joliet Junior College
Judson University
Kankakee Community College
Kendall College
Kishwaukee College
Knox College
Lake Forest College
Lake Land College
Le Cordon Bleu College of Culinary
  Arts: Chicago
Lewis University
Lincoln Christian University
Lincoln College
Lincoln Land Community College
Loyola University Chicago
McHenry County College
McKendree University
Millikin University
Monmouth College
Moody Bible Institute
Moraine Valley Community College
Morrison Institute of Technology
Morton College
National-Louis University
North Central College
North Park University
Northern Illinois University
Northwestern College
Northwestern University
Oakton Community College
Olivet Nazarene University
Parkland College
Quincy University
Resurrection University
Richland Community College
Robert Morris University: Chicago
Rock Valley College
Rockford University
Roosevelt University
Saint Xavier University
Sauk Valley Community College
School of the Art Institute of Chicago
Southeastern Illinois College
Southern Illinois University Carbondale
Southern Illinois University
  Edwardsville
Southwestern Illinois College
Spoon River College
Trinity Christian College
Trinity International University
Triton College
University of Chicago
University of Illinois at Chicago
University of Illinois at Urbana-
  Champaign
University of Illinois: Springfield
University of St. Francis
VanderCook College of Music
Western Illinois University
Wheaton College

## Indiana

Ancilla College
Ball State University
Bethel College
Butler University
Calumet College of St. Joseph
Crossroads Bible College
DePauw University
Earlham College
Franklin College
Goshen College
Hanover College
Holy Cross College
Huntington University
Indiana Institute of Technology
Indiana State University
Indiana University Bloomington

Indiana University East
Indiana University Kokomo
Indiana University Northwest
Indiana University South Bend
Indiana University Southeast
Indiana University-Purdue University
  Fort Wayne
Indiana University-Purdue University
  Indianapolis
Indiana Wesleyan University
Ivy Tech Community College:
  Bloomington
Ivy Tech Community College: Central
  Indiana
Ivy Tech Community College:
  Columbus
Ivy Tech Community College: East
  Central
Ivy Tech Community College:
  Kokomo
Ivy Tech Community College:
  Lafayette
Ivy Tech Community College: North
  Central
Ivy Tech Community College:
  Northeast
Ivy Tech Community College:
  Northwest
Ivy Tech Community College:
  Richmond
Ivy Tech Community College: South
  Central
Ivy Tech Community College:
  Southeast
Ivy Tech Community College:
  Southwest
Ivy Tech Community College: Wabash
  Valley
Lincoln College of Technology:
  Indianapolis
Manchester University
Marian University
Oakland City University
Purdue University
Purdue University North Central
Purdue University Northwest
Rose-Hulman Institute of Technology
Saint Joseph's College
St. Mary-of-the-Woods College
Saint Mary's College
Taylor University
Trine University
University of Evansville
University of Indianapolis
University of Notre Dame
University of Saint Francis
University of Southern Indiana
Valparaiso University
Vincennes University
Wabash College

## Iowa

Allen College
Briar Cliff University
Buena Vista University
Central College
Clarke University
Clinton Community College
Coe College
Cornell College
Des Moines Area Community College
Divine Word College
Dordt College
Drake University
Ellsworth Community College
Emmaus Bible College
Faith Baptist Bible College and
  Theological Seminary
Graceland University
Grand View University
Grinnell College
Iowa Central Community College

Iowa State University
Iowa Wesleyan College
Iowa Western Community College
Kaplan University: Cedar Falls
Kaplan University: Cedar Rapids
Kaplan University: Des Moines
Loras College
Luther College
Marshalltown Community College
Mercy College of Health Sciences
Morningside College
Mount Mercy University
Muscatine Community College
North Iowa Area Community College
Northeast Iowa Community College
Northwest Iowa Community College
Northwestern College
St. Ambrose University
St. Luke's College
Scott Community College
Shiloh University
Simpson College
Southeastern Community College
Southwestern Community College
University of Dubuque
University of Iowa
University of Northern Iowa
Upper Iowa University
Waldorf University
Wartburg College
Western Iowa Tech Community
  College
William Penn University

## Kansas

Allen County Community College
Baker University
Barclay College
Barton County Community College
Benedictine College
Bethany College
Bethel College
Butler Community College
Central Christian College of Kansas
Cloud County Community College
Coffeyville Community College
Colby Community College
Cowley County Community College
Dodge City Community College
Donnelly College
Emporia State University
Fort Hays State University
Friends University
Garden City Community College
Grantham University
Hesston College
Hutchinson Community College
Independence Community College
Kansas City Kansas Community
  College
Kansas State University
Kansas Wesleyan University
Labette Community College
McPherson College
MidAmerica Nazarene University
Newman University
Pittsburg State University
Seward County Community College
Southwestern College
Sterling College
Tabor College
University of Kansas
University of St. Mary
Washburn University
Wichita State University

## Kentucky

Alice Lloyd College
Asbury University

Ashland Community and Technical
  College
Bellarmine University
Berea College
Big Sandy Community and Technical
  College
Bluegrass Community and Technical
  College
Brescia University
Campbellsville University
Centre College
Daymar College: Louisville
Daymar College: Owensboro
Eastern Kentucky University
Elizabethtown Community and
  Technical College
Georgetown College
Henderson Community College
Jefferson Community and Technical
  College
Kentucky Christian University
Kentucky Mountain Bible College
Kentucky State University
Kentucky Wesleyan College
Lindsey Wilson College
Maysville Community and Technical
  College
Midway College
Morehead State University
Murray State University
Northern Kentucky University
Owensboro Community and Technical
  College
St. Catharine College
Somerset Community College
Southeast Kentucky Community and
  Technical College
Spalding University
Sullivan College of Technology and
  Design
Thomas More College
Transylvania University
Union College
University of the Cumberlands
University of Kentucky
University of Louisville
University of Pikeville
Western Kentucky University

## Louisiana

Bossier Parish Community College
Centenary College of Louisiana
Delgado Community College
Dillard University
Grambling State University
Louisiana College
Louisiana State University and
  Agricultural and Mechanical College
Louisiana State University at Eunice
Louisiana State University Health
  Sciences Center
Louisiana State University in
  Shreveport
Louisiana Tech University
Loyola University New Orleans
McNeese State University
Nicholls State University
Northwestern State University
Nunez Community College
St. Joseph Seminary College
Southeastern Louisiana University
Southern University and Agricultural
  and Mechanical College
Southern University at New Orleans
Tulane University
University of Holy Cross
University of Louisiana at Lafayette
University of Louisiana at Monroe
University of New Orleans
Xavier University of Louisiana

## Maine

Bates College
Bowdoin College
Central Maine Community College
Colby College
College of the Atlantic
Eastern Maine Community College
Husson University
Kennebec Valley Community College
Maine College of Art
Maine Maritime Academy
Saint Joseph's College of Maine
Southern Maine Community College
Thomas College
Unity College
University of Maine
University of Maine at Augusta
University of Maine at Farmington
University of Maine at Fort Kent
University of Maine at Machias
University of Maine at Presque Isle
University of New England
University of Southern Maine
Washington County Community
  College
York County Community College

## Maryland

Allegany College of Maryland
Anne Arundel Community College
Bowie State University
Brightwood College: Baltimore
Capitol Technology University
Carroll Community College
Chesapeake College
College of Southern Maryland
Community College of Baltimore
  County
Coppin State University
Frostburg State University
Garrett College
Goucher College
Harford Community College
Hood College
Howard Community College
Johns Hopkins University
Johns Hopkins University: Peabody
  Conservatory of Music
Kaplan University: Hagerstown
Loyola University Maryland
Maryland Institute College of Art
McDaniel College
Morgan State University
Mount St. Mary's University
Notre Dame of Maryland University
Prince George's Community College
St. Mary's College of Maryland
Salisbury University
Stevenson University
Towson University
United States Naval Academy
University of Baltimore
University of Maryland: Baltimore
  County
University of Maryland: College Park
University of Maryland: Eastern Shore
University of Maryland: University
  College
Washington College

## Massachusetts

American International College
Amherst College
Anna Maria College
Assumption College
Babson College
Bard College at Simon's Rock
Bay Path University

Bay State College
Becker College
Bentley University
Berklee College of Music
Berkshire Community College
Boston Baptist College
Boston College
Boston Conservatory
Boston University
Brandeis University
Bridgewater State University
Bristol Community College
Bunker Hill Community College
Cape Cod Community College
Clark University
College of the Holy Cross
Curry College
Dean College
Eastern Nazarene College
Elms College
Emerson College
Emmanuel College
Endicott College
Fitchburg State University
Framingham State University
Gordon College
Greenfield Community College
Hampshire College
Harvard College
Hellenic College/Holy Cross
Holyoke Community College
Lasell College
Lesley University
Massachusetts Bay Community College
Massachusetts College of Art and
  Design
Massachusetts College of Liberal Arts
Massachusetts Institute of Technology
Massachusetts Maritime Academy
Massasoit Community College
MCPHS University
Merrimack College
Middlesex Community College
Montserrat College of Art
Mount Holyoke College
Mount Ida College
Mount Wachusett Community College
New England Conservatory of Music
Newbury College
Nichols College
North Shore Community College
Northeastern University
Northern Essex Community College
Northpoint Bible College
Pine Manor College
Quincy College
Quinsigamond Community College
Regis College
Salem State University
School of the Museum of Fine Arts
Simmons College
Smith College
Springfield College
Springfield Technical Community
  College
Stonehill College
Suffolk University
Tufts University
University of Massachusetts Amherst
University of Massachusetts Boston
University of Massachusetts Dartmouth
University of Massachusetts Lowell
Wellesley College
Wentworth Institute of Technology
Western New England University
Westfield State University
Wheaton College
Wheelock College
Williams College
Worcester Polytechnic Institute
Worcester State University

## Michigan

Adrian College
Albion College

Alma College
Andrews University
Aquinas College
Baker College of Auburn Hills
Baker College of Cadillac
Baker College of Jackson
Baker College of Muskegon
Baker College of Owosso
Baker College of Port Huron
Bay College
Calvin College
Central Michigan University
College for Creative Studies
Concordia University
Cornerstone University
Davenport University
Delta College
Eastern Michigan University
Ferris State University
Finlandia University
Glen Oaks Community College
Gogebic Community College
Grand Rapids Community College
Grand Valley State University
Henry Ford College
Hillsdale College
Hope College
Kalamazoo College
Kellogg Community College
Kettering University
Kirtland Community College
Kuyper College
Lake Michigan College
Lake Superior State University
Lansing Community College
Lawrence Technological University
Macomb Community College
Madonna University
Marygrove College
Michigan Jewish Institute
Michigan State University
Michigan Technological University
Mid Michigan Community College
Montcalm Community College
Mott Community College
Muskegon Community College
North Central Michigan College
Northern Michigan University
Northwestern Michigan College
Northwood University: Michigan
Oakland Community College
Oakland University
Olivet College
Rochester College
Sacred Heart Major Seminary
Saginaw Valley State University
St. Clair County Community College
Schoolcraft College
Siena Heights University
Southwestern Michigan College
Spring Arbor University
University of Detroit Mercy
University of Michigan
University of Michigan: Dearborn
University of Michigan: Flint
Washtenaw Community College
Wayne State University
Western Michigan University

## Minnesota

Academy College
Alexandria Technical and Community
  College
Art Institutes International Minnesota
Augsburg College
Bemidji State University
Bethany Lutheran College
Bethel University
Carleton College
Central Lakes College
Century College
College of St. Benedict

College of St. Scholastica
Concordia College: Moorhead
Concordia University St. Paul
Crossroads College
Crown College
Dakota County Technical College
Dunwoody College of Technology
Gustavus Adolphus College
Hamline University
Hennepin Technical College
Inver Hills Community College
Itasca Community College
Lake Superior College
Macalester College
Minneapolis College of Art and Design
Minneapolis Community and Technical
  College
Minnesota State College - Southeast
  Technical
Minnesota State Community and
  Technical College
Minnesota State University Mankato
Minnesota State University Moorhead
Minnesota West Community and
  Technical College
National American University:
  Bloomington
Normandale Community College
North Central University
North Hennepin Community College
Northland Community & Technical
  College
Northwest Technical College
Pine Technical & Community College
Rainy River Community College
Rasmussen College: Bloomington
Rasmussen College: Brooklyn Park
Rasmussen College: Eagan
Rasmussen College: Mankato
Rasmussen College: St. Cloud
Ridgewater College
Riverland Community College
Rochester Community and Technical
  College
St. Catherine University
Saint Cloud State University
St. Cloud Technical and Community
  College
St. John's University
St. Mary's University of Minnesota
St. Olaf College
South Central College
Southwest Minnesota State University
University of Minnesota: Crookston
University of Minnesota: Duluth
University of Minnesota: Morris
University of Minnesota: Rochester
University of Minnesota: Twin Cities
University of Northwestern - St. Paul
University of St. Thomas
Walden University
Winona State University

## Mississippi

Alcorn State University
Belhaven University
Blue Mountain College
Delta State University
East Mississippi Community College
Hinds Community College
Jackson State University
Jones County Junior College
Meridian Community College
Millsaps College
Mississippi College
Mississippi Gulf Coast Community
  College
Mississippi State University
Mississippi University for Women
Mississippi Valley State University
Northeast Mississippi Community
  College

Rust College
Tougaloo College
University of Mississippi
University of Southern Mississippi
William Carey University

## Missouri

Avila University
Calvary Bible College and Theological
  Seminary
Central Methodist University
College of the Ozarks
Columbia College
Cottey College
Crowder College
Culver-Stockton College
DeVry University: Kansas City
Drury University
East Central College
Evangel University
Fontbonne University
Goldfarb School of Nursing at Barnes-
  Jewish College
Hannibal-LaGrange University
Harris-Stowe State University
Jefferson College
Kansas City Art Institute
Lincoln University
Lindenwood University
Logan University
Maryville University of Saint Louis
Metropolitan Community College -
  Kansas City
Missouri Baptist University
Missouri Southern State University
Missouri State University
Missouri State University: West Plains
Missouri University of Science and
  Technology
Missouri Valley College
Missouri Western State University
Moberly Area Community College
North Central Missouri College
Northwest Missouri State University
Park University
Ranken Technical College
Research College of Nursing
Rockhurst University
Saint Louis University
Southeast Missouri Hospital College of
  Nursing and Health Sciences
Southeast Missouri State University
Southwest Baptist University
Stephens College
Stevens Institute of Business & Arts
Three Rivers Community College
Truman State University
University of Central Missouri
University of Missouri: Columbia
University of Missouri: Kansas City
University of Missouri: St. Louis
Washington University in St. Louis
Webster University
Westminster College
William Jewell College
William Woods University

## Montana

Carroll College
Dawson Community College
Flathead Valley Community College
Montana Bible College
Montana State University
Montana State University: Billings
Montana State University: Northern
Montana Tech of the University of
  Montana
Rocky Mountain College
University of Great Falls
University of Montana: Western

## Nebraska

Bellevue University
BryanLGH College of Health Sciences
Chadron State College
College of Saint Mary
Concordia University
Creighton University
Doane University
Grace University
Hastings College
Metropolitan Community College
Mid-Plains Community College
Midland University
Nebraska College of Technical
  Agriculture
Nebraska Wesleyan University
Northeast Community College
Peru State College
Union College
University of Nebraska - Kearney
University of Nebraska - Lincoln
University of Nebraska - Omaha
Wayne State College
Western Nebraska Community College
York College

## Nevada

College of Southern Nevada
Great Basin College
International Academy of Design and
  Technology: Henderson
Roseman University of Health Sciences
Sierra Nevada College
Truckee Meadows Community College
University of Nevada: Las Vegas
University of Nevada: Reno
Western Nevada College

## New Hampshire

Colby-Sawyer College
Dartmouth College
Franklin Pierce University
Granite State College
Keene State College
Lakes Region Community College
Nashua Community College
New England College
New Hampshire Institute of Art
NHTI-Concord's Community College
Plymouth State University
Rivier University
Saint Anselm College
Southern New Hampshire University
University of New Hampshire
University of New Hampshire at
  Manchester

## New Jersey

Atlantic Cape Community College
Berkeley College
Bloomfield College
Brookdale Community College
Caldwell University
Centenary University
The College of New Jersey
College of St. Elizabeth
County College of Morris
Cumberland County College
DeVry University: North Brunswick
Drew University
Essex County College
Fairleigh Dickinson University:
  College at Florham
Fairleigh Dickinson University:
  Metropolitan Campus

Felician University
Georgian Court University
Hudson County Community College
Kean University
Mercer County Community College
Middlesex County College
Monmouth University
Montclair State University
New Jersey City University
New Jersey Institute of Technology
Ocean County College
Passaic County Community College
Pillar College
Princeton University
Ramapo College of New Jersey
Raritan Valley Community College
Rider University
Rowan College at Burlington County
Rowan University
Rutgers, The State University of New
  Jersey: Camden Campus
Rutgers, The State University of New
  Jersey: New Brunswick/Piscataway
  Campus
Rutgers, The State University of New
  Jersey: Newark Campus
Saint Peter's University
Salem Community College
Seton Hall University
Stevens Institute of Technology
Stockton University
Thomas Edison State University
Union County College
William Paterson University of New
  Jersey

## New Mexico

Eastern New Mexico University
Eastern New Mexico University:
  Roswell
Mesalands Community College
National American University:
  Albuquerque
New Mexico Highlands University
New Mexico Institute of Mining and
  Technology
New Mexico Junior College
New Mexico State University
New Mexico State University at
  Alamogordo
New Mexico State University at
  Carlsbad
Northern New Mexico College
San Juan College
Santa Fe Community College
Santa Fe University of Art and Design
University of New Mexico
University of the Southwest
Western New Mexico University

## New York

Adelphi University
Adirondack Community College
Albany College of Pharmacy and
  Health Sciences
Alfred University
ASA College
Bard College
Barnard College
Berkeley College
Berkeley College of New York City
Briarcliffe College
Broome Community College
Bryant & Stratton College: Amherst
Bryant & Stratton College: Buffalo
Bryant & Stratton College: Syracuse
  North
Canisius College
Cayuga Community College
Cazenovia College

City University of New York: Baruch College
City University of New York: Borough of Manhattan Community College
City University of New York: Bronx Community College
City University of New York: Brooklyn College
City University of New York: City College
City University of New York: College of Staten Island
City University of New York: Hostos Community College
City University of New York: Hunter College
City University of New York: John Jay College of Criminal Justice
City University of New York: Kingsborough Community College
City University of New York: LaGuardia Community College
City University of New York: Lehman College
City University of New York: Medgar Evers College
City University of New York: New York City College of Technology
City University of New York: Queens College
City University of New York: Queensborough Community College
City University of New York: York College
Clarkson University
Clinton Community College
Colgate University
College of Mount St. Vincent
College of New Rochelle
College of Saint Rose
Columbia University
Columbia University: School of General Studies
Columbia-Greene Community College
Concordia College
Cooper Union for the Advancement of Science and Art
Cornell University
Corning Community College
Daemen College
Davis College
DeVry College of New York: Midtown Campus
Dominican College of Blauvelt
Dutchess Community College
D'Youville College
Eastman School of Music of the University of Rochester
Elmira College
Erie Community College
Eugene Lang College The New School for Liberal Arts
Excelsior College
Fashion Institute of Technology
Five Towns College
Fordham University
Fulton-Montgomery Community College
Genesee Community College
Globe Institute of Technology
Hamilton College
Hartwick College
Herkimer County Community College
Hilbert College
Hobart and William Smith Colleges
Hofstra University
Houghton College
Hudson Valley Community College
Iona College
Ithaca College
Jamestown Community College
Jewish Theological Seminary of America
Juilliard School
Keuka College

The King's College
Le Moyne College
LIM College
LIU Brooklyn
LIU Post
Manhattan College
Manhattanville College
Maria College
Marist College
Marymount Manhattan College
Medaille College
Medaille College: Rochester
Mercy College
Mildred Elley: Albany
Mildred Elley: New York City
Mohawk Valley Community College
Molloy College
Monroe College
Monroe Community College
Mount Saint Mary College
Nassau Community College
Nazareth College
New York Career Institute
New York Institute of Technology
New York School of Interior Design
New York University
Niagara County Community College
Niagara University
North Country Community College
Nyack College
Onondaga Community College
Orange County Community College
Pace University
Pace University: Pleasantville/Briarcliff
Parsons The New School for Design
Paul Smith's College
Phillips School of Nursing at Mount Sinai Beth Israel
Pratt Institute
Rensselaer Polytechnic Institute
Roberts Wesleyan College
Rochester Institute of Technology
Rockland Community College
The Sage Colleges
Saint Bonaventure University
St. Elizabeth College of Nursing
St. Francis College
St. John Fisher College
St. John's University
St. Joseph's College New York: Suffolk Campus
St. Joseph's College, New York
St. Lawrence University
St. Thomas Aquinas College
Sarah Lawrence College
Schenectady County Community College
School of Visual Arts
Siena College
Skidmore College
Suffolk County Community College
Sullivan County Community College
SUNY College at Brockport
SUNY College at Buffalo
SUNY College at Cortland
SUNY College at Fredonia
SUNY College at Geneseo
SUNY College at New Paltz
SUNY College at Old Westbury
SUNY College at Oneonta
SUNY College at Oswego
SUNY College at Plattsburgh
SUNY College at Potsdam
SUNY College at Purchase
SUNY College of Agriculture and Technology at Cobleskill
SUNY College of Agriculture and Technology at Morrisville
SUNY College of Environmental Science and Forestry
SUNY College of Technology at Alfred
SUNY College of Technology at Canton
SUNY College of Technology at Delhi

SUNY Empire State College
SUNY Farmingdale State College
SUNY Maritime College
SUNY Polytechnic Institute
SUNY University at Albany
SUNY University at Binghamton
SUNY University at Buffalo
SUNY University at Stony Brook
SUNY Upstate Medical University
Syracuse University
Technical Career Institutes
Tompkins Cortland Community College
Touro College
Union College
United States Merchant Marine Academy
University of Rochester
Utica College
Vassar College
Vaughn College of Aeronautics and Technology
Villa Maria College of Buffalo
Wagner College
Wells College
Westchester Community College

## North Carolina

Alamance Community College
Appalachian State University
Barton College
Beaufort County Community College
Belmont Abbey College
Bennett College for Women
Brevard College
Cabarrus College of Health Sciences
Caldwell Community College and Technical Institute
Campbell University
Carteret Community College
Catawba College
Central Piedmont Community College
Chowan University
College of the Albemarle
Craven Community College
Davidson College
Duke University
Durham Technical Community College
East Carolina University
Elizabeth City State University
Elon University
Fayetteville State University
Fayetteville Technical Community College
Gardner-Webb University
Greensboro College
Guilford College
Guilford Technical Community College
High Point University
Johnson C. Smith University
Johnston Community College
Laurel University
Lees-McRae College
Lenoir-Rhyne University
Louisburg College
Mars Hill University
Martin Community College
Meredith College
Methodist University
Mid-Atlantic Christian University
Montreat College
Nash Community College
North Carolina Central University
North Carolina State University
North Carolina Wesleyan College
Pfeiffer University
Piedmont International University
Queens University of Charlotte
Richmond Community College
Roanoke-Chowan Community College
Robeson Community College
St. Andrews University

Saint Augustine's University
Salem College
Sandhills Community College
Southeastern Community College
Southwestern Community College
University of Mount Olive
University of North Carolina at Asheville
University of North Carolina at Chapel Hill
University of North Carolina at Charlotte
University of North Carolina at Greensboro
University of North Carolina at Pembroke
University of North Carolina at Wilmington
University of North Carolina School of the Arts
Wake Forest University
Wake Technical Community College
Warren Wilson College
Western Carolina University
Wilkes Community College
Wilson Community College
Wingate University
Winston-Salem State University

## North Dakota

Bismarck State College
Dakota College at Bottineau
Dickinson State University
Lake Region State College
Mayville State University
Minot State University
North Dakota State University
Rasmussen College: Bismarck
Rasmussen College: Fargo
University of Jamestown
University of Mary
University of North Dakota
Valley City State University
Williston State College

## Ohio

Allegheny Wesleyan College
Art Academy of Cincinnati
Art Institute of Cincinnati
Ashland University
Baldwin Wallace University
Belmont College
Bluffton University
Bowling Green State University
Bowling Green State University: Firelands College
Bryant & Stratton College: Eastlake
Bryant & Stratton College: Parma
Capital University
Case Western Reserve University
Cedarville University
Central Ohio Technical College
Central State University
Cincinnati Christian University
Cincinnati State Technical and Community College
Clark State Community College
Cleveland Institute of Art
Cleveland Institute of Music
Cleveland State University
College of Wooster
Columbus College of Art and Design
Columbus State Community College
Cuyahoga Community College
Defiance College
Denison University
DeVry University: Columbus
Edison State Community College
Franciscan University of Steubenville
Franklin University

Credit/placement for Advanced Placement (AP)

Heidelberg University
Hiram College
Hocking College
James A. Rhodes State College
John Carroll University
Kaplan College: Dayton
Kent State University
Kenyon College
Kettering College
Lake Erie College
Lakeland Community College
Lorain County Community College
Lourdes University
Malone University
Marietta College
Miami University: Hamilton
Miami University: Middletown
Miami University: Oxford
Miami-Jacobs Career College: Dayton
Mount St. Joseph University
Mount Vernon Nazarene University
Muskingum University
North Central State College
Notre Dame College
Oberlin College
Ohio Dominican University
Ohio Northern University
Ohio State University: Columbus
   Campus
Ohio University
Ohio University: Eastern Campus
Ohio University: Southern Campus at
   Ironton
Ohio University: Zanesville Campus
Ohio Wesleyan University
Otterbein University
Owens Community College
Shawnee State University
Sinclair Community College
Terra State Community College
Tiffin University
Union Institute & University
University of Akron
University of Akron: Wayne College
University of Cincinnati
University of Cincinnati: Blue Ash
   College
University of Cincinnati: Clermont
   College
University of Dayton
University of Findlay
University of Mount Union
University of Northwestern Ohio
University of Rio Grande
University of Toledo
Urbana University
Ursuline College
Walsh University
Washington State Community College
Wilberforce University
Wilmington College
Wittenberg University
Wright State University
Wright State University: Lake Campus
Xavier University
Youngstown State University

## Oklahoma

Bacone College
Cameron University
Carl Albert State College
East Central University
Eastern Oklahoma State College
Hillsdale Free Will Baptist College
Langston University
Murray State College
Northeastern Oklahoma Agricultural
   and Mechanical College
Northeastern State University
Northern Oklahoma College
Northwestern Oklahoma State
   University

Oklahoma Baptist University
Oklahoma Christian University
Oklahoma City Community College
Oklahoma City University
Oklahoma Panhandle State University
Oklahoma State University
Oklahoma State University Institute of
   Technology: Okmulgee
Oklahoma State University: Oklahoma
   City
Oklahoma Wesleyan University
Oral Roberts University
Redlands Community College
Rogers State University
Rose State College
St. Gregory's University
Seminole State College
Southeastern Oklahoma State
   University
Southern Nazarene University
Southwestern Christian University
Southwestern Oklahoma State
   University
Tulsa Community College
University of Central Oklahoma
University of Oklahoma
University of Science and Arts of
   Oklahoma
University of Tulsa
Western Oklahoma State College

## Oregon

Art Institute of Portland
Chemeketa Community College
Clackamas Community College
Clatsop Community College
Concordia University
Corban University
Eastern Oregon University
George Fox University
Lane Community College
Lewis & Clark College
Linfield College
Linn-Benton Community College
Marylhurst University
Mt. Hood Community College
New Hope Christian College
Northwest Christian University
Oregon College of Art & Craft
Oregon Health & Science University
Oregon Institute of Technology
Oregon State University
Pacific Northwest College of Art
Pacific University
Portland Community College
Portland State University
Reed College
Rogue Community College
Southern Oregon University
Southwestern Oregon Community
   College
Treasure Valley Community College
Umpqua Community College
University of Oregon
University of Portland
Warner Pacific College
Western Oregon University
Willamette University

## Pennsylvania

Albright College
Allegheny College
Alvernia University
Arcadia University
Art Institute of Philadelphia
Art Institute of Pittsburgh
Bloomsburg University of
   Pennsylvania
Bryn Athyn College
Bryn Mawr College

Bucknell University
Bucks County Community College
Butler County Community College
Cabrini University
Cairn University
California University of Pennsylvania
Carlow University
Carnegie Mellon University
Cedar Crest College
Central Penn College
Chatham University
Chestnut Hill College
Cheyney University of Pennsylvania
Clarion University of Pennsylvania
Clarks Summit University
Community College of Allegheny
   County
Community College of Beaver County
Community College of Philadelphia
Curtis Institute of Music
Delaware County Community College
Delaware Valley University
DeSales University
DeVry University: Fort Washington
Dickinson College
Drexel University
DuBois Business College
Duquesne University
East Stroudsburg University of
   Pennsylvania
Eastern University
Edinboro University of Pennsylvania
Elizabethtown College
Fortis Institute: Erie
Franklin & Marshall College
Gannon University
Geneva College
Gettysburg College
Grove City College
Gwynedd Mercy University
Harcum College
Harrisburg Area Community College
Harrisburg University of Science and
   Technology
Haverford College
Holy Family University
Immaculata University
Indiana University of Pennsylvania
Johnson College
Juniata College
Keystone College
King's College
Kutztown University of Pennsylvania
La Roche College
La Salle University
Lafayette College
Lancaster Bible College
Laurel Business Institute
Laurel Technical Institute
Lebanon Valley College
Lehigh University
Lincoln Technical Institute: Allentown
Lincoln University
Lock Haven University of
   Pennsylvania
Lycoming College
Manor College
Mansfield University of Pennsylvania
Marywood University
Mercyhurst University
Messiah College
Millersville University of Pennsylvania
Misericordia University
Montgomery County Community
   College
Moore College of Art and Design
Moravian College
Mount Aloysius College
Muhlenberg College
Neumann University
Northampton Community College
Penn Commercial Business and
   Technical School
Penn State Abington
Penn State Altoona

Penn State Beaver
Penn State Berks
Penn State Brandywine
Penn State DuBois
Penn State Erie, The Behrend College
Penn State Fayette, The Eberly
   Campus
Penn State Greater Allegheny
Penn State Harrisburg
Penn State Hazleton
Penn State Lehigh Valley
Penn State Mont Alto
Penn State New Kensington
Penn State Schuylkill
Penn State Shenango
Penn State University Park
Penn State Wilkes-Barre
Penn State Worthington Scranton
Penn State York
Pennsylvania Academy of the Fine
   Arts
Pennsylvania College of Art and
   Design
Pennsylvania College of Health
   Sciences
Pennsylvania College of Technology
Philadelphia University
Pittsburgh Institute of Aeronautics
Point Park University
Reading Area Community College
Robert Morris University
Rosemont College
St. Francis University
Saint Joseph's University
St. Vincent College
Seton Hill University
Shippensburg University of
   Pennsylvania
Slippery Rock University of
   Pennsylvania
Susquehanna University
Swarthmore College
Temple University
Thiel College
Thomas Jefferson University
University of the Arts
University of Pennsylvania
University of Pittsburgh
University of Pittsburgh at Bradford
University of Pittsburgh at Greensburg
University of Pittsburgh at Johnstown
University of Pittsburgh at Titusville
University of the Sciences
University of Scranton
University of Valley Forge
Ursinus College
Valley Forge Military College
Vet Tech Institute
Villanova University
Washington & Jefferson College
Waynesburg University
West Chester University of
   Pennsylvania
Westminster College
Westmoreland County Community
   College
Widener University
Wilson College
York College of Pennsylvania

## Puerto Rico

American University of Puerto Rico
Bayamon Central University
Conservatory of Music of Puerto Rico
EDP University of Puerto Rico: Hato
   Rey
Humacao Community College
Inter American University of Puerto
   Rico: Aguadilla Campus
Inter American University of Puerto
   Rico: Arecibo Campus

Inter American University of Puerto Rico: Barranquitas Campus
Inter American University of Puerto Rico: Bayamon Campus
Inter American University of Puerto Rico: Ponce Campus
Inter American University of Puerto Rico: San German Campus
National University College: Arecibo
National University College: Bayamon
National University College: Ponce
Pontifical Catholic University of Puerto Rico
Universidad Adventista de las Antillas
Universidad del Este
Universidad Politecnica de Puerto Rico
University College of San Juan
University of Puerto Rico: Arecibo
University of Puerto Rico: Bayamon University College
University of Puerto Rico: Carolina Regional College
University of Puerto Rico: Cayey University College
University of Puerto Rico: Humacao
University of Puerto Rico: Mayaguez
University of Puerto Rico: Rio Piedras
University of Puerto Rico: Utuado

## Rhode Island

Brown University
Bryant University
Community College of Rhode Island
Johnson & Wales University: Providence
New England Institute of Technology
Providence College
Rhode Island College
Rhode Island School of Design
Roger Williams University
Salve Regina University
University of Rhode Island

## South Carolina

Aiken Technical College
Anderson University
Benedict College
Bob Jones University
Central Carolina Technical College
Charleston Southern University
The Citadel
Claflin University
Clemson University
Coastal Carolina University
Coker College
College of Charleston
Columbia College
Columbia International University
Converse College
Denmark Technical College
Erskine College
Florence-Darlington Technical College
Francis Marion University
Furman University
Greenville Technical College
Lander University
Limestone College
Midlands Technical College
Morris College
Newberry College
North Greenville University
Orangeburg-Calhoun Technical College
Presbyterian College
South Carolina State University
Southern Wesleyan University
Spartanburg Community College
Tri-County Technical College
Trident Technical College
University of South Carolina: Aiken
University of South Carolina: Beaufort

University of South Carolina: Columbia
University of South Carolina: Lancaster
University of South Carolina: Sumter
University of South Carolina: Union
University of South Carolina: Upstate
Voorhees College
Winthrop University
Wofford College

## South Dakota

Augustana University
Black Hills State University
Dakota State University
Dakota Wesleyan University
Lake Area Technical Institute
Mitchell Technical Institute
Mount Marty College
National American University: Rapid City
Northern State University
South Dakota School of Mines and Technology
South Dakota State University
University of Sioux Falls
University of South Dakota

## Tennessee

Aquinas College
Austin Peay State University
Belmont University
Bethel University
Bryan College: Dayton
Carson-Newman University
Christian Brothers University
Cleveland State Community College
Cumberland University
Dyersburg State Community College
East Tennessee State University
Fisk University
Freed-Hardeman University
Hiwassee College
Jackson State Community College
Johnson University
King University
Lee University
LeMoyne-Owen College
Lincoln Memorial University
Lipscomb University
Martin Methodist College
Maryville College
Memphis College of Art
Middle Tennessee State University
Milligan College
Motlow State Community College
Nashville State Community College
Nossi College of Art
O'More College of Design
Pellissippi State Community College
Rhodes College
Roane State Community College
Sewanee: The University of the South
Southern Adventist University
Southwest Tennessee Community College
Tennessee State University
Tennessee Technological University
Tennessee Wesleyan College
Trevecca Nazarene University
Tusculum College
Union University
University of Memphis
University of Tennessee: Chattanooga
University of Tennessee: Knoxville
University of Tennessee: Martin
Vanderbilt University
Volunteer State Community College
Walters State Community College

Watkins College of Art, Design & Film
Welch College
Williamson College

## Texas

Abilene Christian University
Angelo State University
Arlington Baptist College
Art Institute of Houston
Austin College
Austin Community College
Baylor University
Blinn College
Brookhaven College
Central Texas College
Cisco College
Clarendon College
Collin County Community College District
Concordia University Texas
Dallas Baptist University
Del Mar College
DeVry University: Irving
East Texas Baptist University
Eastfield College
El Centro College
Frank Phillips College
Grayson College
Hardin-Simmons University
Hill College
Houston Baptist University
Houston Community College System
Howard Payne University
Huston-Tillotson University
Jacksonville College
Jarvis Christian College
Kilgore College
The King's University
Lamar University
Laredo Community College
Lee College
LeTourneau University
Lone Star College System
Lubbock Christian University
McLennan Community College
McMurry University
Midland College
Midwestern State University
Mountain View College
North Central Texas College
North Lake College
Northeast Texas Community College
Northwest Vista College
Northwood University: Texas
Odessa College
Our Lady of the Lake University of San Antonio
Panola College
Paris Junior College
Paul Quinn College
Prairie View A&M University
Ranger College
Rice University
Richland College
St. Edward's University
St. Mary's University
St. Philip's College
Sam Houston State University
San Antonio College
San Jacinto College
Schreiner University
South Plains College
South Texas College
Southern Methodist University
Southwestern Adventist University
Southwestern Assemblies of God University
Southwestern Christian College
Southwestern University
Stephen F. Austin State University
Sul Ross State University

Tarleton State University
Tarrant County College
Texas A&M International University
Texas A&M University
Texas A&M University-Commerce
Texas A&M University-Corpus Christi
Texas A&M University-Kingsville
Texas A&M University-Texarkana
Texas Christian University
Texas College
Texas Lutheran University
Texas Southern University
Texas State Technical College
Texas State University
Texas Tech University
Texas Wesleyan University
Texas Woman's University
Trinity University
Trinity Valley Community College
University of Dallas
University of Houston
University of Houston-Clear Lake
University of Houston-Downtown
University of Houston-Victoria
University of the Incarnate Word
University of Mary Hardin-Baylor
University of North Texas
University of North Texas at Dallas
University of St. Thomas
University of Texas at Arlington
University of Texas at Austin
University of Texas at Dallas
University of Texas at El Paso
University of Texas at San Antonio
University of Texas at Tyler
University of Texas of the Permian Basin
University Of Texas Rio Grande Valley
Victoria College
Wade College
Wayland Baptist University
Weatherford College
West Texas A&M University
Western Texas College
Wharton County Junior College
Wiley College

## Utah

Brigham Young University
Dixie State University
Neumont University
Salt Lake Community College
Snow College
Southern Utah University
Stevens-Henager College: Ogden
Stevens-Henager College: Orem
University of Utah
Utah State University
Utah Valley University
Weber State University
Westminster College

## Vermont

Bennington College
Castleton University
Champlain College
College of St. Joseph in Vermont
Community College of Vermont
Goddard College
Green Mountain College
Johnson State College
Landmark College
Lyndon State College
Marlboro College
Middlebury College
New England Culinary Institute
Norwich University
Saint Michael's College
Southern Vermont College

Sterling College
University of Vermont

## Virginia

Art Institute of Washington
Averett University
Blue Ridge Community College
Bluefield College
Bridgewater College
Bryant & Stratton College: Virginia Beach
Christendom College
Christopher Newport University
College of William and Mary
Danville Community College
DeVry University: Arlington
Eastern Mennonite University
ECPI University
Emory & Henry College
Ferrum College
George Mason University
Germanna Community College
Hampden-Sydney College
Hampton University
Hollins University
J. Sargeant Reynolds Community College
James Madison University
Jefferson College of Health Sciences
Liberty University
Longwood University
Lynchburg College
Mary Baldwin University
Marymount University
Norfolk State University
Northern Virginia Community College
Old Dominion University
Patrick Henry College
Patrick Henry Community College
Paul D. Camp Community College
Piedmont Virginia Community College
Radford University
Randolph College
Randolph-Macon College
Rappahannock Community College
Regent University
Richard Bland College
Roanoke College
Shenandoah University
Southern Virginia University
Southwest Virginia Community College
Stratford University: Falls Church
Stratford University: Woodbridge
Sweet Briar College
Thomas Nelson Community College
University of Mary Washington
University of Richmond
University of Virginia
University of Virginia's College at Wise
Virginia Commonwealth University
Virginia Military Institute
Virginia Polytechnic Institute and State University
Virginia State University
Virginia Union University
Virginia University of Lynchburg
Virginia Wesleyan College
Virginia Western Community College
Washington and Lee University

## Washington

Art Institute of Seattle
Bastyr University
Bellevue College
Big Bend Community College
Cascadia College
Central Washington University
Centralia College
Clark College
Clover Park Technical College
Columbia Basin College
Cornish College of the Arts
DigiPen Institute of Technology
Eastern Washington University
Edmonds Community College
Everett Community College
Evergreen State College
Gonzaga University
Grays Harbor College
Green River College
Heritage University
Lake Washington Institute of Technology
Lower Columbia College
North Seattle College
Northwest College of Art & Design
Northwest School of Wooden Boatbuilding
Northwest University
Olympic College
Pacific Lutheran University
Peninsula College
Pierce College
Saint Martin's University
Seattle Central College
Seattle Pacific University
Seattle University
Shoreline Community College
Skagit Valley College
South Puget Sound Community College
South Seattle College
Spokane Community College
Spokane Falls Community College
Tacoma Community College
University of Puget Sound
University of Washington
University of Washington Bothell
University of Washington Tacoma
Walla Walla Community College
Walla Walla University
Washington State University
Western Washington University
Whatcom Community College
Whitman College
Whitworth University
Yakima Valley Community College

## West Virginia

Alderson-Broaddus University
American Public University System
Appalachian Bible College
Bethany College
Bluefield State College
BridgeValley Community and Technical College
Concord University
Davis and Elkins College
Fairmont State University
Glenville State College
Kanawha Valley Community and Technical College
Marshall University
Ohio Valley University
Potomac State College of West Virginia University
Salem International University
Shepherd University
University of Charleston
West Liberty University
West Virginia Northern Community College
West Virginia State University
West Virginia University
West Virginia University at Parkersburg
West Virginia University Institute of Technology
West Virginia Wesleyan College
Wheeling Jesuit University

## Wisconsin

Alverno College
Beloit College
Bryant & Stratton College: Milwaukee
Cardinal Stritch University
Carroll University
Carthage College
Chippewa Valley Technical College
Concordia University Wisconsin
Edgewood College
Fox Valley Technical College
Gateway Technical College
Herzing University: Madison
Lakeland University
Lakeshore Technical College
Lawrence University
Madison Area Technical College
Maranatha Baptist University
Marian University
Marquette University
Mid-State Technical College
Milwaukee Area Technical College
Milwaukee Institute of Art & Design
Milwaukee School of Engineering
Moraine Park Technical College
Mount Mary University
Northcentral Technical College
Northeast Wisconsin Technical College
Northland College
St. Norbert College
Silver Lake College of the Holy Family
Southwest Wisconsin Technical College
University of Wisconsin-Baraboo/Sauk County
University of Wisconsin-Barron County
University of Wisconsin-Eau Claire
University of Wisconsin-Fox Valley
University of Wisconsin-Green Bay
University of Wisconsin-La Crosse
University of Wisconsin-Madison
University of Wisconsin-Marathon County
University of Wisconsin-Marinette
University of Wisconsin-Marshfield/Wood County
University of Wisconsin-Milwaukee
University of Wisconsin-Oshkosh
University of Wisconsin-Parkside
University of Wisconsin-Platteville
University of Wisconsin-Richland
University of Wisconsin-River Falls
University of Wisconsin-Rock County
University of Wisconsin-Sheboygan
University of Wisconsin-Stevens Point
University of Wisconsin-Stout
University of Wisconsin-Superior
University of Wisconsin-Washington County
University of Wisconsin-Waukesha
University of Wisconsin-Whitewater
Viterbo University
Western Technical College
Wisconsin Indianhead Technical College
Wisconsin Lutheran College

## Wyoming

Casper College
Central Wyoming College
Eastern Wyoming College
Laramie County Community College
Northwest College
Sheridan College
University of Wyoming
Western Wyoming Community College

# ESL programs on campus

## Alabama

Auburn University
Auburn University at Montgomery
Chattahoochee Valley Community
  College
Faulkner University
Gadsden State Community College
Troy University
University of Alabama
University of Alabama at Birmingham
University of Alabama in Huntsville
University of Montevallo
University of North Alabama
University of South Alabama
University of West Alabama

## Alaska

University of Alaska Anchorage
University of Alaska Fairbanks

## Arizona

Arizona State University
Arizona Western College
Central Arizona College
Cochise College
Embry-Riddle Aeronautical University:
  Prescott Campus
GateWay Community College
Glendale Community College
Mesa Community College
Mohave Community College
Northern Arizona University
Phoenix College
Scottsdale Community College
South Mountain Community College
University of Arizona

## Arkansas

Arkansas State University
Arkansas Tech University
Harding University
Henderson State University
Hendrix College
John Brown University
Ouachita Baptist University
Southern Arkansas University
University of Arkansas
University of Arkansas at Fort Smith
University of Arkansas at Little Rock
University of Central Arkansas

## California

Academy of Art University
Allan Hancock College
Alliant International University
Azusa Pacific University
Bakersfield College
Berkeley City College

Bethesda University of California
Beverly Hills Design Institute
Biola University
Cabrillo College
California Baptist University
California College of the Arts
California Institute of the Arts
California State Polytechnic University:
  Pomona
California State University: Bakersfield
California State University: Chico
California State University: Dominguez
  Hills
California State University: East Bay
California State University: Fresno
California State University: Fullerton
California State University: Long
  Beach
California State University: Los
  Angeles
California State University: Sacramento
California State University: San
  Bernardino
California State University: San
  Marcos
California State University: Stanislaus
California University of Management
  and Sciences
Cerritos College
Cerro Coso Community College
Chaffey College
Citrus College
City College of San Francisco
Coastline Community College
College of the Canyons
College of the Desert
College of Marin
College of San Mateo
College of the Sequoias
Concordia University Irvine
Contra Costa College
Cosumnes River College
Crafton Hills College
Cuesta College
Cuyamaca College
Cypress College
Dominican University of California
East Los Angeles College
El Camino College
Folsom Lake College
Fresno City College
Fresno Pacific University
Fullerton College
Glendale Community College
Grossmont College
Hope International University
Humboldt State University
Irvine Valley College
La Sierra University
Las Positas College
Lincoln University
Long Beach City College
Los Angeles City College
Los Angeles Harbor College
Los Angeles Mission College
Los Angeles Pierce College
Los Angeles Southwest College
Los Angeles Trade and Technical
  College
Los Angeles Valley College
Los Medanos College
Marymount California University

Menlo College
Merritt College
MiraCosta College
Mission College
Modesto Junior College
Monterey Peninsula College
Mount San Antonio College
National University
Northwestern Polytechnic University
Notre Dame de Namur University
Ohlone College
Pacific States University
Palo Verde College
Palomar College
Pitzer College
Porterville College
Sacramento City College
Saddleback College
St. Mary's College of California
Samuel Merritt University
San Diego State University
San Francisco Art Institute
San Francisco State University
San Joaquin Delta College
San Jose City College
San Jose State University
Santa Ana College
Santa Barbara City College
Santa Monica College
Santiago Canyon College
Shasta College
Sierra College
Silicon Valley University
Soka University of America
Solano Community College
Sonoma State University
Southern California Institute of
  Technology
Southwestern College
Stanford University
University of California: Irvine
University of California: San Diego
University of California: Santa Barbara
University of the Pacific
University of San Diego
University of San Francisco
University of Southern California
University of the West
Ventura College
Victor Valley College
West Hills College: Coalinga
West Hills College: Lemoore
West Los Angeles College
West Valley College
Woodbury University
World Mission University
Yuba College

## Colorado

Colorado College
Colorado State University
Colorado State University: Pueblo
Community College of Aurora
Community College of Denver
Front Range Community College
Metropolitan State University of
  Denver
National American University: Denver
Northeastern Junior College
Pikes Peak Community College
Pueblo Community College
Red Rocks Community College
Trinidad State Junior College
University of Colorado Boulder
University of Colorado Colorado
  Springs
University of Colorado Denver
University of Denver
University of Northern Colorado

## Connecticut

Capital Community College
Central Connecticut State University
Gateway Community College
Holy Apostles College and Seminary
Housatonic Community College
Manchester Community College
Middlesex Community College
Naugatuck Valley Community College
Norwalk Community College
Post University
Sacred Heart University
Tunxis Community College
University of Bridgeport
University of Connecticut
University of Hartford
University of Saint Joseph
Yale University

## Delaware

Delaware State University
Delaware Technical Community
  College: Stanton/Wilmington
  Campus
University of Delaware

## District of Columbia

American University
Catholic University of America
Gallaudet University
George Washington University
Georgetown University
University of the District of Columbia

## Florida

Art Institute of Fort Lauderdale
Barry University
Broward College
Carlos Albizu University
College of Business and Technology:
  Cutler Bay
College of Business and Technology:
  Flagler
College of Business and Technology:
  Hialeah
College of Business and Technology:
  Kendall
College of Central Florida
Daytona State College
Eastern Florida State College
Eckerd College
Embry-Riddle Aeronautical University
Embry-Riddle Aeronautical University:
  Worldwide Campus
Florida Atlantic University
Florida Institute of Technology
Florida National University
Florida State College at Jacksonville
Florida State University
Hillsborough Community College
Hodges University
Indian River State College
Jacksonville University
Johnson & Wales University: North
  Miami
Jose Maria Vargas University
Miami Dade College
Palm Beach State College
Polk State College
Ringling College of Art and Design
Saint Leo University
St. Petersburg College
Saint Thomas University
Santa Fe College
Schiller International University

Seminole State College of Florida
University of Central Florida
University of Florida
University of Miami
University of North Florida
University of South Florida
University of Tampa
University of West Florida
Valencia College
Webber International University

## Georgia

Abraham Baldwin Agricultural College
Athens Technical College
Atlanta Technical College
Beulah Heights University
Brenau University
Central Georgia Technical College
Columbus State University
Darton State College
Emory University
Georgia Gwinnett College
Georgia Institute of Technology
Georgia Perimeter College
Georgia Southern University
Georgia Southwestern State University
Georgia State University
Gordon State College
Kennesaw State University
Life University
Mercer University
Oglethorpe University
Savannah College of Art and Design
Savannah Technical College
University of North Georgia
Valdosta State University
Wiregrass Georgia Technical College

## Hawaii

Brigham Young University-Hawaii
Hawaii Pacific University
Hawaii Tokai International College
University of Hawaii at Hilo
University of Hawaii at Manoa
University of Hawaii: Hawaii
  Community College
University of Hawaii: Leeward
  Community College
University of Hawaii: Maui College

## Idaho

Boise State University
College of Idaho
College of Southern Idaho
Idaho State University
Lewis-Clark State College
North Idaho College
University of Idaho

## Illinois

Augustana College
Benedictine University
Black Hawk College
Carl Sandburg College
City Colleges of Chicago: Kennedy-
  King College
College of DuPage
College of Lake County
Columbia College Chicago
DePaul University
DeVry University: Chicago
Dominican University
Eastern Illinois University
Elgin Community College

Governors State University
Heartland Community College
Illinois Central College
Illinois Eastern Community Colleges:
  Frontier Community College
Illinois Eastern Community Colleges:
  Lincoln Trail College
Illinois Eastern Community Colleges:
  Olney Central College
Illinois Eastern Community Colleges:
  Wabash Valley College
Illinois Institute of Technology
Illinois State University
John Wood Community College
Joliet Junior College
Kishwaukee College
Lake Land College
Lewis University
Lincoln Land Community College
Loyola University Chicago
MacCormac College
McHenry County College
Millikin University
Monmouth College
Moraine Valley Community College
Morton College
National-Louis University
North Central College
North Park University
Parkland College
Richland Community College
Rockford University
Roosevelt University
St. Augustine College
Sauk Valley Community College
School of the Art Institute of Chicago
Southern Illinois University Carbondale
Southern Illinois University
  Edwardsville
Southwestern Illinois College
Spoon River College
Trinity Christian College
Triton College
University of Chicago
University of Illinois at Chicago
University of Illinois at Urbana-
  Champaign
University of Illinois: Springfield
University of St. Francis
Western Illinois University

## Indiana

Ball State University
Butler University
Earlham College
Franklin College
Huntington University
Indiana Institute of Technology
Indiana State University
Indiana University Bloomington
Indiana University Kokomo
Indiana University South Bend
Indiana University-Purdue University
  Fort Wayne
Indiana University-Purdue University
  Indianapolis
Purdue University Northwest
Rose-Hulman Institute of Technology
Saint Mary's College
Taylor University
Trine University
University of Evansville
University of Indianapolis
University of Notre Dame
University of Southern Indiana
Valparaiso University
Vincennes University

## Iowa

Buena Vista University
Clinton Community College

Coe College
Cornell College
Des Moines Area Community College
Divine Word College
Dordt College
Drake University
Grand View University
Iowa Central Community College
Iowa State University
Iowa Western Community College
Marshalltown Community College
Morningside College
Muscatine Community College
Northeast Iowa Community College
Northwest Iowa Community College
Northwestern College
St. Ambrose University
Scott Community College
Southeastern Community College
University of Dubuque
University of Iowa
University of Northern Iowa
Upper Iowa University
Western Iowa Tech Community
  College

## Kansas

Barton County Community College
Benedictine College
Butler Community College
Central Christian College of Kansas
Cloud County Community College
Cowley County Community College
Dodge City Community College
Donnelly College
Fort Hays State University
Hesston College
Kansas City Kansas Community
  College
Kansas State University
Northwest Kansas Technical College
Pittsburg State University
Southwestern College
University of Kansas
University of Kansas Medical Center
Washburn University
Wichita State University

## Kentucky

Berea College
Bluegrass Community and Technical
  College
Campbellsville University
Eastern Kentucky University
Jefferson Community and Technical
  College
Kentucky State University
Murray State University
Northern Kentucky University
Sullivan University
University of Kentucky
University of Louisville
University of Pikeville
Western Kentucky University

## Louisiana

Delgado Community College
Louisiana College
Louisiana State University and
  Agricultural and Mechanical College
Louisiana State University Health
  Sciences Center
Louisiana Tech University
Loyola University New Orleans
McNeese State University
St. Joseph Seminary College
Southeastern Louisiana University

Tulane University
University of Louisiana at Lafayette
University of Louisiana at Monroe
University of New Orleans

## Maine

Central Maine Community College
Husson University
University of Maine
University of Maine at Fort Kent
University of Southern Maine

## Maryland

Allegany College of Maryland
Anne Arundel Community College
Baltimore City Community College
Capitol Technology University
Carroll Community College
Chesapeake College
Community College of Baltimore
  County
Howard Community College
Notre Dame of Maryland University
Prince George's Community College
Salisbury University
Towson University
University of Maryland: Baltimore
  County
University of Maryland: College Park
Washington Adventist University

## Massachusetts

Benjamin Franklin Institute of
  Technology
Berklee College of Music
Berkshire Community College
Boston Conservatory
Boston University
Brandeis University
Bridgewater State University
Bristol Community College
Bunker Hill Community College
Clark University
Dean College
Elms College
Fisher College
Framingham State University
Holyoke Community College
Lasell College
Massachusetts Bay Community College
Massasoit Community College
MCPHS University
Mount Ida College
Mount Wachusett Community College
New England Conservatory of Music
Northeastern University
Pine Manor College
Quincy College
Regis College
Roxbury Community College
Salem State University
Springfield College
Suffolk University
University of Massachusetts Amherst
University of Massachusetts Boston
Western New England University
Wheelock College
Worcester Polytechnic Institute
Worcester State University

## Michigan

Adrian College
Andrews University
Central Michigan University

Davenport University
Eastern Michigan University
Ferris State University
Finlandia University
Grand Valley State University
Hope College
Kalamazoo College
Kalamazoo Valley Community College
Lansing Community College
Lawrence Technological University
Macomb Community College
Madonna University
Michigan State University
Michigan Technological University
Northern Michigan University
Northwestern Michigan College
Northwood University: Michigan
Oakland Community College
Oakland University
Sacred Heart Major Seminary
Saginaw Valley State University
Schoolcraft College
Siena Heights University
Spring Arbor University
University of Detroit Mercy
University of Michigan
University of Michigan: Dearborn
University of Michigan: Flint
Washtenaw Community College
Wayne State University
Western Michigan University

## Minnesota

Augsburg College
Bemidji State University
Central Lakes College
Century College
College of St. Benedict
Crown College
Hamline University
Hennepin Technical College
Inver Hills Community College
Minneapolis College of Art and Design
Minneapolis Community and Technical
  College
Minnesota State Community and
  Technical College
Minnesota State University Mankato
Minnesota West Community and
  Technical College
National American University:
  Bloomington
Normandale Community College
North Hennepin Community College
Riverland Community College
Saint Cloud State University
St. Cloud Technical and Community
  College
St. John's University
St. Mary's University of Minnesota
University of Minnesota: Crookston
University of Minnesota: Duluth
University of Minnesota: Morris
University of Minnesota: Twin Cities
Winona State University

## Mississippi

Belhaven University
Jackson State University
Meridian Community College
Mississippi College
Mississippi State University
University of Mississippi
University of Southern Mississippi

## Missouri

Avila University
Columbia College

Crowder College
Drury University
Fontbonne University
Hannibal-LaGrange University
Jefferson College
Lindenwood University
Metropolitan Community College -
  Kansas City
Missouri Southern State University
Missouri State University
Missouri University of Science and
  Technology
Missouri Valley College
Missouri Western State University
Northwest Missouri State University
Ozarks Technical Community College
Park University
Saint Louis University
Southeast Missouri State University
State Fair Community College
Truman State University
University of Central Missouri
University of Missouri: Columbia
University of Missouri: Kansas City
University of Missouri: St. Louis
Washington University in St. Louis
Webster University
Wentworth Military Junior College
Westminster College

## Montana

Carroll College
Flathead Valley Community College
Montana State University
Montana State University: Billings
Rocky Mountain College
University of Montana

## Nebraska

Creighton University
Doane University
Metropolitan Community College
Northeast Community College
Union College
University of Nebraska - Kearney
University of Nebraska - Lincoln
University of Nebraska - Omaha
Western Nebraska Community College

## Nevada

College of Southern Nevada
Great Basin College
Sierra Nevada College
University of Nevada: Las Vegas
University of Nevada: Reno

## New Hampshire

Colby-Sawyer College
Dartmouth College
Franklin Pierce University
Great Bay Community College
Keene State College
Manchester Community College
New England College
NHTI-Concord's Community College
Southern New Hampshire University
University of New Hampshire
University of New Hampshire at
  Manchester

## New Jersey

Atlantic Cape Community College
Centenary University
College of St. Elizabeth
County College of Morris
Cumberland County College
Drew University
Essex County College
Fairleigh Dickinson University:
  College at Florham
Fairleigh Dickinson University:
  Metropolitan Campus
Felician University
Georgian Court University
Hudson County Community College
Kean University
Mercer County Community College
Middlesex County College
Montclair State University
New Jersey City University
New Jersey Institute of Technology
Ocean County College
Passaic County Community College
Pillar College
Raritan Valley Community College
Rider University
Rowan College at Burlington County
Rowan University
Rutgers, The State University of New
  Jersey: New Brunswick/Piscataway
  Campus
Rutgers, The State University of New
  Jersey: Newark Campus
Seton Hall University
Stevens Institute of Technology
Sussex County Community College
Union County College

## New Mexico

Dona Ana Community College of New
  Mexico State University
Luna Community College
Mesalands Community College
New Mexico State University
New Mexico State University at Grants
Santa Fe Community College
Santa Fe University of Art and Design
University of New Mexico
Western New Mexico University

## New York

Adelphi University
Alfred University
ASA College
Bard College
Berkeley College of New York City
Bramson ORT College
Broome Community College
City University of New York: Borough
  of Manhattan Community College
City University of New York: Bronx
  Community College
City University of New York:
  Brooklyn College
City University of New York: City
  College
City University of New York: College
  of Staten Island
City University of New York: Hostos
  Community College
City University of New York: Hunter
  College
City University of New York: John Jay
  College of Criminal Justice
City University of New York:
  Kingsborough Community College
City University of New York:
  LaGuardia Community College

City University of New York: Lehman
  College
City University of New York: Medgar
  Evers College
City University of New York: New
  York City College of Technology
City University of New York:
  Queensborough Community College
City University of New York: York
  College
Clarkson University
College of New Rochelle
Columbia University: School of
  General Studies
Concordia College
Cornell University
Eastman School of Music of the
  University of Rochester
Erie Community College
Eugene Lang College The New School
  for Liberal Arts
Fashion Institute of Technology
Fordham University
Fulton-Montgomery Community
  College
Genesee Community College
Globe Institute of Technology
Hamilton College
Herkimer County Community College
Hobart and William Smith Colleges
Hofstra University
Juilliard School
Keuka College
LIU Brooklyn
LIU Post
Long Island Business Institute
Manhattan School of Music
Manhattanville College
Mercy College
Metropolitan College of New York
Mohawk Valley Community College
Molloy College
Monroe College
Nassau Community College
Nazareth College
The New School College of
  Performing Arts
New York Institute of Technology
New York University
Niagara University
Nyack College
Ohr Somayach Tanenbaum Education
  Center
Onondaga Community College
Pace University
Pace University: Pleasantville/Briarcliff
Parsons The New School for Design
Pratt Institute
Rensselaer Polytechnic Institute
Roberts Wesleyan College
Rochester Institute of Technology
Rockland Community College
St. John's University
St. Thomas Aquinas College
School of Visual Arts
Siena College
Suffolk County Community College
SUNY College at Brockport
SUNY College at Buffalo
SUNY College at Geneseo
SUNY College at New Paltz
SUNY College at Oneonta
SUNY College at Oswego
SUNY College at Plattsburgh
SUNY College at Purchase
SUNY College of Agriculture and
  Technology at Cobleskill
SUNY College of Environmental
  Science and Forestry
SUNY University at Albany
SUNY University at Binghamton
SUNY University at Buffalo
SUNY University at Stony Brook
Syracuse University
Technical Career Institutes

ESL programs on campus

Tompkins Cortland Community
College
University of Rochester
Wells College
Westchester Community College

## North Carolina

Asheville-Buncombe Technical
Community College
Beaufort County Community College
Central Piedmont Community College
College of the Albemarle
Duke University
Durham Technical Community College
East Carolina University
Fayetteville Technical Community
College
Guilford College
Guilford Technical Community College
High Point University
Mars Hill University
Methodist University
Nash Community College
North Carolina Central University
North Carolina State University
Sandhills Community College
Southwestern Community College
University of North Carolina at
Charlotte
University of North Carolina at
Pembroke
University of North Carolina at
Wilmington
Wake Technical Community College
Warren Wilson College
Wilson Community College

## North Dakota

Dickinson State University
North Dakota State University
University of Jamestown
University of North Dakota

## Ohio

Ashland University
Baldwin Wallace University
Bowling Green State University
Capital University
Case Western Reserve University
Central State University
Cincinnati State Technical and
Community College
Cleveland Institute of Music
Cleveland State University
Cuyahoga Community College
Davis College
Franklin University
Hocking College
Kent State University
Lorain County Community College
Marietta College
Miami University: Hamilton
Miami University: Oxford
Muskingum University
North Central State College
Oberlin College
Ohio Dominican University
Ohio Northern University
Ohio State University: Columbus
Campus
Ohio University
Otterbein University
Owens Community College
Shawnee State University
Sinclair Community College
Tiffin University
University of Akron

University of Cincinnati
University of Dayton
University of Findlay
University of Mount Union
University of Toledo
Walsh University
Wright State University
Xavier University
Youngstown State University

## Oklahoma

East Central University
Northeastern State University
Oklahoma Baptist University
Oklahoma Christian University
Oklahoma City Community College
Oklahoma City University
Oklahoma Panhandle State University
Oklahoma State University
Oral Roberts University
Rose State College
Southern Nazarene University
Tulsa Community College
University of Central Oklahoma
University of Oklahoma
University of Tulsa

## Oregon

Chemeketa Community College
Clackamas Community College
Concordia University
George Fox University
Lane Community College
Lewis & Clark College
Linfield College
Linn-Benton Community College
Marylhurst University
Mount Angel Seminary
Mt. Hood Community College
Oregon State University
Pacific University
Portland Community College
Portland State University
Rogue Community College
Southern Oregon University
Southwestern Oregon Community
College
Treasure Valley Community College
University of Oregon
University of Portland
Western Oregon University

## Pennsylvania

Albright College
Allegheny College
Alvernia University
Bloomsburg University of
Pennsylvania
Bucks County Community College
Chatham University
Chestnut Hill College
Clarion University of Pennsylvania
Community College of Allegheny
County
Community College of Philadelphia
Curtis Institute of Music
Delaware County Community College
Dickinson College
Drexel University
Duquesne University
Elizabethtown College
Gannon University
Geneva College
Harcum College
Harrisburg Area Community College
Indiana University of Pennsylvania
Juniata College

King's College
Kutztown University of Pennsylvania
La Roche College
La Salle University
Lehigh Carbon Community College
Lehigh University
Mansfield University of Pennsylvania
Marywood University
Messiah College
Montgomery County Community
College
Northampton Community College
Penn State Abington
Penn State Altoona
Penn State Berks
Penn State Brandywine
Penn State Greater Allegheny
Penn State Hazleton
Penn State Schuylkill
Penn State University Park
Penn State York
Pennsylvania College of Technology
Philadelphia University
Reading Area Community College
St. Francis University
Saint Joseph's University
St. Vincent College
Seton Hill University
Slippery Rock University of
Pennsylvania
Susquehanna University
Temple University
Thiel College
University of the Arts
University of Pennsylvania
University of Pittsburgh
University of the Sciences
Ursinus College
Valley Forge Military College
Villanova University
Washington & Jefferson College
West Chester University of
Pennsylvania
Widener University

## Puerto Rico

Bayamon Central University
Inter American University of Puerto
Rico: Arecibo Campus
Inter American University of Puerto
Rico: San German Campus
Universidad Adventista de las Antillas
University of Puerto Rico: Bayamon
University College
University of Puerto Rico: Mayaguez

## Rhode Island

Bryant University
Johnson & Wales University:
Providence
New England Institute of Technology
Roger Williams University
University of Rhode Island

## South Carolina

Bob Jones University
The Citadel
Coastal Carolina University
Coker College
College of Charleston
Converse College
Lander University
Midlands Technical College
Presbyterian College
Spartanburg Methodist College
Trident Technical College

University of South Carolina:
Columbia
University of South Carolina: Upstate

## South Dakota

Black Hills State University
Lake Area Technical Institute
Northern State University
South Dakota School of Mines and
Technology
South Dakota State University
University of South Dakota

## Tennessee

Austin Peay State University
Carson-Newman University
East Tennessee State University
Hiwassee College
Lee University
Lincoln Memorial University
Martin Methodist College
Maryville College
Nashville State Community College
Pellissippi State Community College
Southern Adventist University
Southwest Tennessee Community
College
Tennessee Technological University
University of Memphis
University of Tennessee: Chattanooga
University of Tennessee: Knoxville
University of Tennessee: Martin
Vanderbilt University
Volunteer State Community College
Walters State Community College
Williamson College

## Texas

Abilene Christian University
Amarillo College
Angelo State University
Austin Community College
Blinn College
Brookhaven College
Central Texas College
Clarendon College
Collin County Community College
District
Dallas Baptist University
Del Mar College
East Texas Baptist University
El Centro College
Grayson College
Houston Community College System
Kilgore College
Lamar Institute of Technology
Lamar University
Laredo Community College
LeTourneau University
Lone Star College System
Midland College
Midwestern State University
Mountain View College
North Lake College
Odessa College
Rice University
Richland College
St. Mary's University
Sam Houston State University
San Antonio College
San Jacinto College
Southern Methodist University
Southwest Texas Junior College
Southwestern Adventist University
Stephen F. Austin State University
Texas A&M International University
Texas A&M University

Texas A&M University-Commerce
Texas A&M University-Kingsville
Texas A&M University-Texarkana
Texas Christian University
Texas Southern University
Texas State University
Trinity Valley Community College
University of Dallas
University of Houston-Downtown
University of the Incarnate Word
University of Mary Hardin-Baylor
University of North Texas
University of St. Thomas
University of Texas at Arlington
University of Texas at Austin
University of Texas at El Paso
University of Texas at San Antonio
University of Texas of the Permian
  Basin
West Texas A&M University
Western Texas College
Wiley College

## Utah

Brigham Young University
Dixie State University
Salt Lake Community College
Snow College
Southern Utah University
University of Utah
Utah State University
Utah Valley University
Weber State University

## Vermont

Bennington College
Johnson State College
Lyndon State College
Saint Michael's College

## Virginia

Eastern Mennonite University
George Mason University
Hampton University
J. Sargeant Reynolds Community
  College
James Madison University
Liberty University
Longwood University
Lynchburg College
Mary Baldwin University
Northern Virginia Community College
Old Dominion University
Roanoke College
Shenandoah University
Stratford University: Falls Church
Stratford University: Woodbridge
Thomas Nelson Community College
Tidewater Community College
University of Virginia
Virginia Commonwealth University
Virginia Polytechnic Institute and State
  University
Virginia Western Community College

## Washington

Bates Technical College
Bellevue College
Cascadia College
Central Washington University
Centralia College
City University of Seattle
Clark College
Clover Park Technical College

Columbia Basin College
DigiPen Institute of Technology
Eastern Washington University
Edmonds Community College
Everett Community College
Gonzaga University
Grays Harbor College
Green River College
Highline College
Lower Columbia College
North Seattle College
Northwest University
Olympic College
Pacific Lutheran University
Peninsula College
Pierce College
Renton Technical College
Saint Martin's University
Seattle Central College
Seattle Pacific University
Seattle University
Shoreline Community College
Skagit Valley College
South Puget Sound Community
  College
South Seattle College
Spokane Community College
Spokane Falls Community College
Tacoma Community College
University of Washington
Washington State University
Western Washington University
Whatcom Community College
Yakima Valley Community College

## West Virginia

Concord University
Fairmont State University
Glenville State College
Marshall University
Ohio Valley University
Salem International University
Shepherd University
University of Charleston
West Virginia State University
West Virginia University
West Virginia Wesleyan College
Wheeling Jesuit University

## Wisconsin

Alverno College
Beloit College
Blackhawk Technical College
Carroll University
Chippewa Valley Technical College
Concordia University Wisconsin
Fox Valley Technical College
Gateway Technical College
Lakeland University
Lawrence University
Madison Area Technical College
Mid-State Technical College
Milwaukee Area Technical College
Milwaukee School of Engineering
Moraine Park Technical College
Northcentral Technical College
Northeast Wisconsin Technical College
St. Norbert College
Silver Lake College of the Holy
  Family
Southwest Wisconsin Technical
  College
University of Wisconsin-Barron
  County
University of Wisconsin-Eau Claire
University of Wisconsin-Green Bay
University of Wisconsin-La Crosse
University of Wisconsin-Madison
University of Wisconsin-Marinette
University of Wisconsin-Milwaukee

University of Wisconsin-Platteville
University of Wisconsin-River Falls
University of Wisconsin-Stevens Point
University of Wisconsin-Stout
University of Wisconsin-Superior
University of Wisconsin-Whitewater
Western Technical College

## Wyoming

Eastern Wyoming College
Laramie County Community College
Northwest College
Sheridan College
Western Wyoming Community College

# Special housing for international students

## Alabama

Alabama State University
Auburn University at Montgomery
Jacksonville State University
Troy University
University of Alabama
University of Alabama at Birmingham
University of North Alabama

## Alaska

University of Alaska Anchorage

## Arizona

Northern Arizona University
University of Arizona

## Arkansas

Henderson State University
University of Arkansas
University of Central Arkansas

## California

California Polytechnic State University:
    San Luis Obispo
California State University: Channel
    Islands
California State University: Chico
California State University: Long
    Beach
California State University: Monterey
    Bay
California State University: San
    Bernardino
Columbia College Hollywood
Concordia University Irvine
Humboldt State University
Loyola Marymount University
San Diego State University
San Francisco State University
San Jose State University
Simpson University
Soka University of America
Sonoma State University
University of California: Berkeley
University of California: Irvine
University of California: Riverside
University of California: San Diego
University of California: Santa Barbara
University of California: Santa Cruz
University of La Verne
University of the Pacific
University of San Francisco
University of Southern California

## Connecticut

University of Connecticut

## Florida

Jacksonville University
New College of Florida
University of Florida
University of South Florida

## Georgia

Carver College
Columbus State University
Georgia College and State University
Georgia Southern University
Georgia Southwestern State University
Georgia State University
Mercer University
Morehouse College
Toccoa Falls College
University of Georgia
University of West Georgia
Valdosta State University

## Idaho

Lewis-Clark State College
University of Idaho

## Illinois

Illinois State University
Illinois Wesleyan University
Loyola University Chicago
Monmouth College
Quincy University
Rockford University
Southern Illinois University Carbondale
University of Chicago
University of Illinois at Urbana-
    Champaign
University of Illinois: Springfield
Western Illinois University

## Indiana

Ball State University
DePauw University
Earlham College
Indiana University Bloomington
Indiana University South Bend
Indiana University-Purdue University
    Indianapolis
University of Southern Indiana

## Iowa

Allen College
Iowa State University
William Penn University

## Kansas

Emporia State University
Kansas State University

## Kentucky

Bellarmine University
Eastern Kentucky University
Morehead State University
Northern Kentucky University
Sullivan University
University of Kentucky
Western Kentucky University

## Louisiana

McNeese State University

## Maine

University of Maine
University of Southern Maine

## Maryland

Frostburg State University
Maryland Institute College of Art
St. Mary's College of Maryland
Salisbury University
Towson University
University of Maryland: Baltimore
    County
University of Maryland: College Park

## Massachusetts

Endicott College
Framingham State University
MCPHS University
Tufts University
University of Massachusetts Amherst
Westfield State University
Wheaton College

## Michigan

Alma College
Central Michigan University
Eastern Michigan University
Ferris State University
Michigan State University
Michigan Technological University
Oakland University
Olivet College
Siena Heights University
Spring Arbor University

## Minnesota

Bemidji State University
College of St. Scholastica
Gustavus Adolphus College
Northwest Technical College
Saint Cloud State University
University of Minnesota: Rochester
University of Minnesota: Twin Cities
University of St. Thomas

## Missouri

Fontbonne University
Missouri State University
Missouri Western State University
Saint Louis University
University of Missouri: St. Louis
Webster University

## Montana

Montana State University
University of Montana

## Nebraska

University of Nebraska - Lincoln

## Nevada

University of Nevada: Las Vegas

## New Hampshire

Dartmouth College
Plymouth State University
Southern New Hampshire University
University of New Hampshire

## New Jersey

The College of New Jersey
Drew University
Kean University
Montclair State University
Rowan University

## New Mexico

Dona Ana Community College of New
    Mexico State University
New Mexico State University

## New York

Alfred University
Canisius College
Clarkson University
Columbia University: School of
    General Studies
Cornell University
Genesee Community College
Globe Institute of Technology
Herkimer County Community College
Hobart and William Smith Colleges
Iona College
LIM College
LIU Post
Manhattan College
Mohawk Valley Community College
Rochester Institute of Technology
Saint Bonaventure University
St. Lawrence University
Siena College
SUNY College at Buffalo
SUNY College at Cortland
SUNY College at Geneseo
SUNY College at New Paltz
SUNY College at Oneonta
SUNY College at Purchase

SUNY College of Agriculture and Technology at Cobleskill
SUNY College of Agriculture and Technology at Morrisville
SUNY College of Technology at Alfred
SUNY Polytechnic Institute
SUNY University at Albany
SUNY University at Buffalo
Tompkins Cortland Community College
University of Rochester
Vassar College

## North Carolina

Elon University
Livingstone College
Methodist University
North Carolina State University
University of North Carolina at Asheville
University of North Carolina at Chapel Hill
University of North Carolina at Charlotte
University of North Carolina at Greensboro

## North Dakota

Minot State University
North Dakota State University

## Ohio

Baldwin Wallace University
Columbus College of Art and Design
Heidelberg University
Kent State University
Kenyon College
Miami University: Oxford
Ohio Northern University
Ohio University
Ohio Wesleyan University
University of Dayton
University of Mount Union
Walsh University
Wittenberg University

## Oklahoma

Northeastern Oklahoma Agricultural and Mechanical College
Oklahoma City University
University of Oklahoma

## Oregon

Eastern Oregon University
Oregon State University
Portland State University
Southern Oregon University
Western Oregon University

## Pennsylvania

Albright College
Bucknell University
Chatham University
Delaware County Community College
Drexel University
East Stroudsburg University of Pennsylvania

Franklin & Marshall College
Indiana University of Pennsylvania
Juniata College
Lehigh University
Lycoming College
Messiah College
Millersville University of Pennsylvania
Moravian College
Muhlenberg College
St. Francis University
Saint Joseph's University
Susquehanna University
Ursinus College
Washington & Jefferson College
West Chester University of Pennsylvania

## Puerto Rico

Theological University of the Caribbean
Universidad Politecnica de Puerto Rico

## Rhode Island

University of Rhode Island

## South Carolina

Coastal Carolina University
Furman University
Presbyterian College
University of South Carolina: Columbia

## South Dakota

Northern State University

## Tennessee

Belmont University
Tennessee Technological University
University of Tennessee: Chattanooga

## Texas

Baylor University
Dallas Baptist University
Kilgore College
LeTourneau University
McLennan Community College
Texas A&M University
Texas A&M University-Commerce
University of the Incarnate Word
University of North Texas
University of Texas at Austin
Western Texas College

## Utah

Southern Utah University
Utah State University

## Vermont

Champlain College
Saint Michael's College

## Virginia

College of William and Mary
Emory & Henry College
Ferrum College
George Mason University
Hampden-Sydney College
Hampton University
Lynchburg College
Mary Baldwin University
Old Dominion University
Radford University
Randolph-Macon College
Roanoke College
Sweet Briar College
University of Mary Washington
University of Virginia
Virginia Commonwealth University
Virginia Polytechnic Institute and State University
Washington and Lee University

## Washington

Central Washington University
Centralia College
DigiPen Institute of Technology
Evergreen State College
Gonzaga University
Green River College
Washington State University
Western Washington University

## West Virginia

West Virginia University
Wheeling Jesuit University

## Wisconsin

Marquette University
University of Wisconsin-La Crosse
University of Wisconsin-Madison
University of Wisconsin-Parkside
University of Wisconsin-Stevens Point
University of Wisconsin-Superior
University of Wisconsin-Whitewater

# Housing guaranteed for all freshmen

## Alabama

Alabama Agricultural and Mechanical
    University
Alabama State University
Birmingham-Southern College
Faulkner University
Heritage Christian University
Huntingdon College
Judson College
Marion Military Institute
Samford University
Spring Hill College
Stillman College
Talladega College
Tuskegee University
University of Alabama
University of Alabama in Huntsville
University of Mobile
University of Montevallo
University of West Alabama

## Alaska

Alaska Pacific University

## Arizona

Arizona Christian University
Arizona State University
Embry-Riddle Aeronautical University:
    Prescott Campus
Grand Canyon University
Prescott College
University of Advancing Technology

## Arkansas

Arkansas Tech University
Harding University
Henderson State University
Hendrix College
John Brown University
Lyon College
Ouachita Baptist University
Southern Arkansas University
University of Arkansas
University of Arkansas at Monticello
University of Central Arkansas
University of the Ozarks
Williams Baptist College

## California

Academy of Art University
American Jewish University
Art Institute of California: Los Angeles
Biola University
California Baptist University
California Institute of Technology
California Maritime Academy
California State University: Bakersfield
California State University: Monterey
    Bay
Chapman University
Claremont McKenna College
College of the Siskiyous
Concordia University Irvine
Deep Springs College
Harvey Mudd College
Holy Names University
Hope International University
Hult International Business School
John Paul the Great Catholic
    University
La Sierra University
Life Pacific College
Loma Linda University
Loyola Marymount University
Menlo College
Mills College
Mount Saint Mary's University
Notre Dame de Namur University
Occidental College
Pacific States University
Pacific Union College
Pepperdine University
Pitzer College
Point Loma Nazarene University
Pomona College
Providence Christian College
St. Mary's College of California
San Diego Christian College
San Francisco Conservatory of Music
Scripps College
Simpson University
Soka University of America
Sonoma State University
Stanford University
SUM Bible College & Theological
    Seminary
Thomas Aquinas College
University of California: Berkeley
University of California: Davis
University of California: Irvine
University of California: Los Angeles
University of California: Merced
University of California: Riverside
University of California: San Diego
University of California: Santa Barbara
University of California: Santa Cruz
University of the Pacific
University of Redlands
University of San Diego
University of San Francisco
University of Southern California
University of the West
Vanguard University of Southern
    California
Westmont College
Whittier College
William Jessup University

## Colorado

Adams State University
Colorado Christian University
Colorado College
Colorado Mesa University
Colorado Mountain College
Colorado Northwestern Community
    College
Colorado School of Mines
Colorado State University
Colorado State University: Pueblo
Fort Lewis College
Lamar Community College
Naropa University
Northeastern Junior College
Regis University
Trinidad State Junior College
University of Colorado Boulder
University of Denver
University of Northern Colorado
Western State Colorado University

## Connecticut

Connecticut College
Fairfield University
Mitchell College
Post University
Quinnipiac University
Sacred Heart University
Trinity College
United States Coast Guard Academy
University of Bridgeport
University of Hartford
University of New Haven
Wesleyan University
Yale University

## Delaware

Delaware College of Art and Design
Delaware State University
University of Delaware

## District of Columbia

American University
Catholic University of America
Gallaudet University
George Washington University
Georgetown University
Howard University

## Florida

Art Institute of Fort Lauderdale
Ave Maria University
Beacon College
Bethune-Cookman University
Eckerd College
Edward Waters College
Embry-Riddle Aeronautical University
Flagler College
Florida Agricultural and Mechanical
    University
Florida Atlantic University
Florida Institute of Technology
Florida Memorial University
Florida Southern College
Jacksonville University
Johnson & Wales University: North
    Miami
Lynn University
New College of Florida
Nova Southeastern University
Palm Beach Atlantic University
Rollins College
Saint Leo University
Southeastern University
Stetson University
Talmudic University
Trinity College of Florida
University of Miami
University of North Florida

Warner University
Webber International University

## Georgia

Agnes Scott College
Andrew College
Art Institute of Atlanta
Berry College
Brenau University
Brewton-Parker College
Clark Atlanta University
College of Coastal Georgia
Covenant College
Emory University
Georgia College and State University
Georgia Gwinnett College
Georgia Southern University
LaGrange College
Mercer University
Middle Georgia State University
Morehouse College
Oglethorpe University
Oxford College of Emory University
Piedmont College
Point University
Reinhardt University
Shorter University
Spelman College
Thomas University
Toccoa Falls College
University of Georgia
University of West Georgia
Wesleyan College
Young Harris College

## Hawaii

Brigham Young University-Hawaii
Chaminade University of Honolulu
Hawaii Tokai International College
University of Hawaii at Manoa

## Idaho

College of Idaho
Northwest Nazarene University
University of Idaho

## Illinois

Augustana College
Blackburn College
Bradley University
Concordia University Chicago
Dominican University
Eastern Illinois University
Eureka College
Governors State University
Greenville College
Illinois College
Illinois Institute of Technology
Illinois State University
Illinois Wesleyan University
Judson University
Knox College
Lake Forest College
Lincoln Christian University
Lincoln College
Loyola University Chicago
McKendree University
Millikin University
Monmouth College
Moody Bible Institute
Morrison Institute of Technology
North Central College
North Park University
Northern Illinois University

Northwestern University
Olivet Nazarene University
Quincy University
Roosevelt University
Saint Xavier University
Shimer College
Southern Illinois University Carbondale
Trinity Christian College
Trinity International University
University of Chicago
University of Illinois at Urbana-Champaign
University of Illinois: Springfield
University of St. Francis
VanderCook College of Music
Western Illinois University
Wheaton College

## Indiana

Ball State University
Bethel College
Butler University
DePauw University
Earlham College
Franklin College
Goshen College
Hanover College
Huntington University
Indiana Institute of Technology
Indiana State University
Indiana University Bloomington
Indiana Wesleyan University
Manchester University
Marian University
Oakland City University
Rose-Hulman Institute of Technology
Saint Joseph's College
St. Mary-of-the-Woods College
Saint Mary's College
Taylor University
University of Evansville
University of Notre Dame
University of Saint Francis
Valparaiso University
Wabash College

## Iowa

Briar Cliff University
Buena Vista University
Central College
Clarke University
Coe College
Cornell College
Dordt College
Drake University
Ellsworth Community College
Emmaus Bible College
Faith Baptist Bible College and
    Theological Seminary
Graceland University
Grinnell College
Iowa State University
Iowa Wesleyan College
Loras College
Luther College
Maharishi University of Management
Morningside College
Mount Mercy University
Northwestern College
St. Ambrose University
Simpson College
University of Dubuque
University of Northern Iowa
Upper Iowa University
Waldorf University
Wartburg College
William Penn University

## Kansas

Baker University
Barclay College
Barton County Community College
Benedictine College
Bethany College
Bethel College
Central Christian College of Kansas
Dodge City Community College
Emporia State University
Fort Hays State University
Hesston College
Kansas Wesleyan University
McPherson College
MidAmerica Nazarene University
Neosho County Community College
Newman University
Northwest Kansas Technical College
Ottawa University
Pittsburg State University
Southwestern College
Sterling College
Tabor College
University of St. Mary
Wichita State University

## Kentucky

Alice Lloyd College
Asbury University
Bellarmine University
Berea College
Brescia University
Campbellsville University
Centre College
Eastern Kentucky University
Georgetown College
Kentucky Christian University
Kentucky Mountain Bible College
Kentucky Wesleyan College
Midway College
Murray State University
Spencerian College: Lexington
Sullivan College of Technology and
    Design
Transylvania University
Union College
University of the Cumberlands
University of Louisville

## Louisiana

Centenary College of Louisiana
Dillard University
Louisiana College
Louisiana Tech University
Loyola University New Orleans
Nicholls State University
St. Joseph Seminary College
Southern University and Agricultural
    and Mechanical College
Tulane University

## Maine

Bates College
Bowdoin College
Colby College
College of the Atlantic
Husson University
Maine Maritime Academy
Saint Joseph's College of Maine
Unity College
University of Maine
University of Maine at Farmington
University of Maine at Machias
University of Maine at Presque Isle
University of New England

Washington County Community
College

## Maryland

Goucher College
Hood College
Johns Hopkins University
Johns Hopkins University: Peabody
    Conservatory of Music
Loyola University Maryland
Maryland Institute College of Art
McDaniel College
Mount St. Mary's University
Notre Dame of Maryland University
St. John's College
St. Mary's College of Maryland
Salisbury University
Towson University
United States Naval Academy
University of Baltimore
University of Maryland: Baltimore
    County
University of Maryland: College Park
University of Maryland: Eastern Shore
Washington Adventist University
Washington College

## Massachusetts

American International College
Amherst College
Anna Maria College
Assumption College
Babson College
Bard College at Simon's Rock
Bay Path University
Becker College
Bentley University
Boston College
Boston Conservatory
Boston University
Brandeis University
Clark University
College of the Holy Cross
Dean College
Eastern Nazarene College
Elms College
Emmanuel College
Endicott College
Franklin W. Olin College of
    Engineering
Gordon College
Hampshire College
Harvard College
Hellenic College/Holy Cross
Lasell College
Massachusetts College of Art and
    Design
Massachusetts College of Liberal Arts
Massachusetts Institute of Technology
Massachusetts Maritime Academy
MCPHS University
Merrimack College
Mount Holyoke College
Mount Ida College
New England Conservatory of Music
Newbury College
Nichols College
Northeastern University
Northpoint Bible College
Pine Manor College
Regis College
School of the Museum of Fine Arts
Simmons College
Smith College
Springfield College
Tufts University
University of Massachusetts Amherst
Wellesley College
Western New England University
Wheaton College

Wheelock College
Williams College
Worcester Polytechnic Institute

## Michigan

Adrian College
Albion College
Alma College
Andrews University
Aquinas College
Baker College of Owosso
Calvin College
Central Michigan University
Cleary University
Concordia University
Cornerstone University
Ferris State University
Finlandia University
Grand Valley State University
Hillsdale College
Hope College
Kalamazoo College
Kettering University
Kuyper College
Lake Superior State University
Michigan State University
Michigan Technological University
Northern Michigan University
Northwood University: Michigan
Oakland University
Olivet College
Rochester College
Spring Arbor University
University of Detroit Mercy
University of Michigan
Western Michigan University
Yeshiva Beth Yehuda-Yeshiva Gedolah
    of Greater Detroit

## Minnesota

Augsburg College
Bethany Lutheran College
Bethel University
Carleton College
College of St. Benedict
College of St. Scholastica
Concordia College: Moorhead
Concordia University St. Paul
Crossroads College
Crown College
Gustavus Adolphus College
Hamline University
Macalester College
Minneapolis College of Art and Design
Minnesota State University Moorhead
St. Catherine University
St. John's University
St. Mary's University of Minnesota
St. Olaf College
Southwest Minnesota State University
University of Minnesota: Morris
University of Minnesota: Rochester
University of Minnesota: Twin Cities
University of Northwestern - St. Paul
Winona State University

## Mississippi

Alcorn State University
Belhaven University
Delta State University
Millsaps College
Mississippi State University
Mississippi University for Women
Rust College
Southeastern Baptist College
University of Mississippi
William Carey University

Housing guaranteed for all freshmen

## Missouri

Avila University
Calvary Bible College and Theological
 Seminary
Central Methodist University
College of the Ozarks
Cottey College
Crowder College
Culver-Stockton College
Drury University
Evangel University
Hannibal-LaGrange University
Harris-Stowe State University
Kansas City Art Institute
Maryville University of Saint Louis
Missouri State University
Missouri University of Science and
 Technology
Missouri Valley College
Northwest Missouri State University
Park University
Ranken Technical College
Research College of Nursing
Rockhurst University
Saint Louis University
Southwest Baptist University
Stephens College
Truman State University
University of Central Missouri
University of Missouri: Columbia
University of Missouri: St. Louis
Washington University in St. Louis
Westminster College
William Jewell College
William Woods University

## Montana

Carroll College
Montana Bible College
Montana State University
Montana State University: Northern
Montana Tech of the University of
 Montana
Rocky Mountain College
University of Great Falls
University of Montana
University of Montana: Western

## Nebraska

Chadron State College
College of Saint Mary
Concordia University
Creighton University
Doane University
Grace University
Hastings College
Midland University
Nebraska College of Technical
 Agriculture
Nebraska Wesleyan University
Peru State College
Union College
University of Nebraska - Kearney
University of Nebraska - Lincoln
Wayne State College
York College

## Nevada

Sierra Nevada College
University of Nevada: Las Vegas

## New Hampshire

Colby-Sawyer College
Dartmouth College
Franklin Pierce University
Keene State College
New England College
New Hampshire Institute of Art
Plymouth State University
Rivier University
Saint Anselm College
Thomas More College of Liberal Arts
University of New Hampshire

## New Jersey

Caldwell University
The College of New Jersey
College of St. Elizabeth
Drew University
Fairleigh Dickinson University:
 College at Florham
Felician University
Georgian Court University
Monmouth University
Montclair State University
New Jersey Institute of Technology
Princeton University
Rabbinical College of America
Ramapo College of New Jersey
Rider University
Rowan University
Rutgers, The State University of New
 Jersey: New Brunswick/Piscataway
 Campus
Saint Peter's University
Stevens Institute of Technology
Stockton University
William Paterson University of New
 Jersey

## New Mexico

Eastern New Mexico University
Institute of American Indian Arts
Navajo Technical University
New Mexico Highlands University
New Mexico Military Institute
New Mexico State University
St. John's College
Santa Fe University of Art and Design
University of the Southwest
Western New Mexico University

## New York

Albany College of Pharmacy and
 Health Sciences
Alfred University
American Academy of Dramatic Arts
ASA College
Bard College
Barnard College
Cazenovia College
Clarkson University
Clinton Community College
Colgate University
College of Mount St. Vincent
College of New Rochelle
College of Saint Rose
Columbia University
Concordia College
Corning Community College
Culinary Institute of America
Daemen College
Davis College
Dominican College of Blauvelt
D'Youville College

Eastman School of Music of the
 University of Rochester
Elmira College
Eugene Lang College The New School
 for Liberal Arts
Hamilton College
Hartwick College
Hobart and William Smith Colleges
Hofstra University
Houghton College
Iona College
Ithaca College
Juilliard School
Keuka College
The King's College
Le Moyne College
LIU Brooklyn
LIU Post
Manhattan College
Manhattan School of Music
Manhattanville College
Marist College
Mount Saint Mary College
Nazareth College
The New School College of
 Performing Arts
New York Institute of Technology
New York University
Niagara County Community College
Niagara University
Nyack College
Parsons The New School for Design
Paul Smith's College
Pratt Institute
Rensselaer Polytechnic Institute
Roberts Wesleyan College
Rochester Institute of Technology
The Sage Colleges
Saint Bonaventure University
St. John Fisher College
St. Lawrence University
St. Thomas Aquinas College
Sarah Lawrence College
Siena College
Skidmore College
Sullivan County Community College
SUNY College at Brockport
SUNY College at Cortland
SUNY College at Fredonia
SUNY College at Geneseo
SUNY College at New Paltz
SUNY College at Old Westbury
SUNY College at Oswego
SUNY College at Plattsburgh
SUNY College at Potsdam
SUNY College of Agriculture and
 Technology at Cobleskill
SUNY College of Agriculture and
 Technology at Morrisville
SUNY College of Environmental
 Science and Forestry
SUNY College of Technology at
 Alfred
SUNY College of Technology at
 Canton
SUNY College of Technology at Delhi
SUNY Polytechnic Institute
SUNY University at Albany
SUNY University at Binghamton
SUNY University at Buffalo
Syracuse University
Talmudical Institute of Upstate New
 York
Union College
United States Merchant Marine
 Academy
University of Rochester
Utica College
Vassar College
Vaughn College of Aeronautics and
 Technology
Wagner College
Wells College
Yeshivat Mikdash Melech

## North Carolina

Appalachian State University
Barton College
Belmont Abbey College
Bennett College for Women
Brevard College
Campbell University
Catawba College
Chowan University
Davidson College
Duke University
East Carolina University
Elizabeth City State University
Elon University
Gardner-Webb University
Greensboro College
Guilford College
High Point University
Johnson C. Smith University
Lees-McRae College
Lenoir-Rhyne University
Louisburg College
Mars Hill University
Meredith College
Methodist University
Mid-Atlantic Christian University
Montreat College
North Carolina State University
North Carolina Wesleyan College
Pfeiffer University
Piedmont International University
Queens University of Charlotte
St. Andrews University
Saint Augustine's University
Salem College
University of Mount Olive
University of North Carolina at
 Asheville
University of North Carolina at Chapel
 Hill
University of North Carolina School of
 the Arts
Wake Forest University
Warren Wilson College
Western Carolina University
Wingate University

## North Dakota

Dakota College at Bottineau
Dickinson State University
Mayville State University
Minot State University
North Dakota State College of Science
North Dakota State University
University of Jamestown
University of Mary
Valley City State University

## Ohio

Ashland University
Baldwin Wallace University
Bluffton University
Bowling Green State University
Capital University
Case Western Reserve University
Cedarville University
Central State University
Cincinnati Christian University
Cleveland Institute of Music
College of Wooster
Columbus College of Art and Design
Defiance College
Denison University
Franciscan University of Steubenville
God's Bible School and College
Heidelberg University
Hiram College
John Carroll University

Kenyon College
Lake Erie College
Lourdes University
Marietta College
Miami University: Oxford
Mount St. Joseph University
Mount Vernon Nazarene University
Muskingum University
Oberlin College
Ohio Dominican University
Ohio Northern University
Ohio State University: Columbus Campus
Ohio University
Ohio Wesleyan University
Otterbein University
Tiffin University
University of Cincinnati
University of Dayton
University of Findlay
University of Mount Union
University of Northwestern Ohio
University of Rio Grande
University of Toledo
Urbana University
Walsh University
Wilberforce University
Wilmington College
Wittenberg University
Xavier University
Youngstown State University

## Oklahoma

Langston University
Murray State College
Northeastern Oklahoma Agricultural and Mechanical College
Northeastern State University
Northwestern Oklahoma State University
Oklahoma Baptist University
Oklahoma Christian University
Oklahoma City University
Oklahoma Panhandle State University
Oklahoma State University
Oklahoma Wesleyan University
Oral Roberts University
St. Gregory's University
Southern Nazarene University
University of Oklahoma
University of Science and Arts of Oklahoma
University of Tulsa

## Oregon

Concordia University
Corban University
Eastern Oregon University
Lewis & Clark College
Linfield College
Mount Angel Seminary
New Hope Christian College
Northwest Christian University
Oregon State University
Pacific Northwest College of Art
Pacific University
Reed College
Southern Oregon University
Southwestern Oregon Community College
University of Portland
Warner Pacific College
Western Oregon University
Willamette University

## Pennsylvania

Albright College
Allegheny College

Alvernia University
Arcadia University
Art Institute of Philadelphia
Bloomsburg University of Pennsylvania
Bryn Athyn College
Bryn Mawr College
Bucknell University
Cabrini University
Cairn University
Carnegie Mellon University
Cedar Crest College
Central Penn College
Chatham University
Cheyney University of Pennsylvania
Clarion University of Pennsylvania
Clarks Summit University
Curtis Institute of Music
Delaware Valley University
DeSales University
Dickinson College
Drexel University
East Stroudsburg University of Pennsylvania
Edinboro University of Pennsylvania
Elizabethtown College
Franklin & Marshall College
Gannon University
Geneva College
Gettysburg College
Grove City College
Harcum College
Harrisburg University of Science and Technology
Haverford College
Holy Family University
Indiana University of Pennsylvania
Juniata College
Keystone College
King's College
Kutztown University of Pennsylvania
La Salle University
Lackawanna College
Lafayette College
Lancaster Bible College
Lebanon Valley College
Lehigh University
Lincoln University
Lycoming College
Mansfield University of Pennsylvania
Marywood University
Mercyhurst University
Messiah College
Millersville University of Pennsylvania
Moore College of Art and Design
Moravian College
Mount Aloysius College
Muhlenberg College
Penn State Beaver
Penn State Erie, The Behrend College
Penn State Schuylkill
Penn State University Park
Philadelphia University
Point Park University
Restaurant School at Walnut Hill College
Rosemont College
St. Francis University
Saint Joseph's University
St. Vincent College
Seton Hill University
Shippensburg University of Pennsylvania
Slippery Rock University of Pennsylvania
Susquehanna University
Swarthmore College
Thiel College
Thomas Jefferson University
University of Pennsylvania
University of Pittsburgh
University of Pittsburgh at Bradford
University of Pittsburgh at Johnstown
University of Pittsburgh at Titusville

University of the Sciences
University of Scranton
University of Valley Forge
Ursinus College
Valley Forge Military College
Villanova University
Washington & Jefferson College
Waynesburg University
Westminster College
Widener University
Wilson College
York College of Pennsylvania

## Puerto Rico

Inter American University of Puerto Rico: San German Campus
Universidad Adventista de las Antillas

## Rhode Island

Brown University
Bryant University
Johnson & Wales University: Providence
Providence College
Rhode Island School of Design
Roger Williams University
Salve Regina University
University of Rhode Island

## South Carolina

Allen University
Anderson University
Benedict College
Charleston Southern University
The Citadel
Claflin University
Clemson University
Coker College
Columbia College
Columbia International University
Converse College
Erskine College
Furman University
Limestone College
Newberry College
North Greenville University
Presbyterian College
South Carolina State University
Southern Wesleyan University
Spartanburg Methodist College
University of South Carolina: Columbia
Voorhees College
Winthrop University
Wofford College

## South Dakota

Augustana University
Black Hills State University
Dakota State University
Dakota Wesleyan University
Mount Marty College
South Dakota School of Mines and Technology
South Dakota State University
University of Sioux Falls
University of South Dakota

## Tennessee

American Baptist College
Aquinas College

Belmont University
Bethel University
Bryan College: Dayton
Carson-Newman University
Christian Brothers University
Fisk University
Freed-Hardeman University
Johnson University
King University
Lee University
Lincoln Memorial University
Martin Methodist College
Maryville College
Milligan College
Rhodes College
Sewanee: The University of the South
Southern Adventist University
Tennessee Technological University
Tennessee Wesleyan College
Tusculum College
Union University
University of Tennessee: Chattanooga
University of Tennessee: Knoxville
University of Tennessee: Martin
Vanderbilt University
Watkins College of Art, Design & Film
Welch College

## Texas

Abilene Christian University
Arlington Baptist College
Austin College
Baylor University
Clarendon College
Concordia University Texas
East Texas Baptist University
Hardin-Simmons University
Houston Baptist University
Howard Payne University
Huston-Tillotson University
Jacksonville College
Jarvis Christian College
Lamar University
LeTourneau University
Lubbock Christian University
McMurry University
Midwestern State University
Our Lady of the Lake University of San Antonio
Paul Quinn College
Prairie View A&M University
Rice University
St. Edward's University
St. Mary's University
Sam Houston State University
Schreiner University
Southern Methodist University
Southwestern Adventist University
Southwestern Assemblies of God University
Southwestern Christian College
Southwestern University
Stephen F. Austin State University
Sul Ross State University
Tarleton State University
Texas A&M University-Commerce
Texas A&M University-Corpus Christi
Texas A&M University-Kingsville
Texas A&M University-Texarkana
Texas Christian University
Texas College
Texas Lutheran University
Texas Southern University
Texas State University
Texas Tech University
Texas Wesleyan University
Texas Woman's University
Trinity University
University of Dallas
University of Mary Hardin-Baylor
University of North Texas

Housing guaranteed for all freshmen

Wayland Baptist University
West Texas A&M University
Western Texas College

## Utah

Neumont University
Westminster College

## Vermont

Bennington College
Castleton University
Champlain College
College of St. Joseph in Vermont
Green Mountain College
Johnson State College
Landmark College
Lyndon State College
Marlboro College
Middlebury College
New England Culinary Institute
Norwich University
Saint Michael's College
Southern Vermont College
Sterling College
University of Vermont

## Virginia

Averett University
Christendom College
Christopher Newport University
College of William and Mary
Eastern Mennonite University
Emory & Henry College
Ferrum College
George Mason University
Hampden-Sydney College
Hampton University
Hollins University
James Madison University
Liberty University
Longwood University
Lynchburg College
Mary Baldwin University
Marymount University
Old Dominion University
Patrick Henry College
Radford University
Randolph College
Randolph-Macon College
Regent University
Roanoke College
Shenandoah University
Southern Virginia University
Sweet Briar College
University of Mary Washington
University of Richmond
University of Virginia
Virginia Commonwealth University
Virginia Military Institute
Virginia Polytechnic Institute and State
   University
Virginia State University
Virginia Wesleyan College
Washington and Lee University

## Washington

Art Institute of Seattle
Central Washington University
City University of Seattle
Cornish College of the Arts
Eastern Washington University
Evergreen State College
Gonzaga University
Northwest University

Pacific Lutheran University
Saint Martin's University
Seattle University
University of Puget Sound
Walla Walla University
Washington State University
Whitman College
Whitworth University

## West Virginia

Bethany College
Concord University
Davis and Elkins College
Fairmont State University
Glenville State College
Marshall University
Ohio Valley University
Potomac State College of West
   Virginia University
Salem International University
Shepherd University
University of Charleston
West Liberty University
West Virginia State University
West Virginia University
West Virginia University Institute of
   Technology
West Virginia Wesleyan College
Wheeling Jesuit University

## Wisconsin

Beloit College
Carroll University
Carthage College
Edgewood College
Lakeland University
Lawrence University
Maranatha Baptist University
Marian University
Marquette University
Milwaukee School of Engineering
Mount Mary University
Northland College
St. Norbert College
Silver Lake College of the Holy
   Family
University of Wisconsin-Eau Claire
University of Wisconsin-Oshkosh
University of Wisconsin-Platteville
University of Wisconsin-River Falls
University of Wisconsin-Stout
University of Wisconsin-Superior
University of Wisconsin-Whitewater
Viterbo University
Wisconsin Lutheran College

## Wyoming

Northwest College
University of Wyoming

# College size (undergraduate enrollment)

## Very small (fewer than 750)

### Four-year

**Alabama**
Concordia College
Heritage Christian University
Herzing University
    Birmingham
Huntsville Bible College
Judson College
Selma University
United States Sports Academy
University of Phoenix
    Birmingham

**Alaska**
Alaska Pacific University

**Arizona**
Arizona Christian University
Art Institute of Tucson
Chamberlain College of Nursing
    Phoenix
DeVry University
    Phoenix
Dunlap-Stone University
International Baptist College
Prescott College
Southwest University of Visual Arts

**Arkansas**
Ecclesia College
Lyon College
University of Arkansas
    for Medical Sciences
University of Phoenix
    Little Rock
    Northwest Arkansas
University of the Ozarks
Williams Baptist College

**California**
American Jewish University
Antioch University
    Santa Barbara
Argosy University
    Inland Empire
    Los Angeles
    Orange County
    San Diego
    San Francisco Bay Area
Bergin University of Canine Studies
Bethesda University of California
Beverly Hills Design Institute
California Christian College
California Institute of Integral Studies
California Miramar University
California National University for
    Advanced Studies
California University of Management
    and Sciences
Charles Drew University of Medicine
    and Science
Cogswell Polytechnical College
Coleman University
Columbia College
    Hollywood
Design Institute of San Diego
Ex'pression College
Golden Gate University
Holy Names University
Horizon University
Humphreys College
John F. Kennedy University
John Paul the Great Catholic
    University
Laguna College of Art and Design
Life Pacific College
Lincoln University
Mt. Sierra College
NewSchool of Architecture & Design
Northcentral University
Northwestern Polytechnic University
Pacific Oaks College
Pacific States University
Platt College
    Ontario
    San Diego
Providence Christian College
Samuel Merritt University
San Diego Christian College
San Francisco Art Institute
San Francisco Conservatory of Music
Shasta Bible College and Graduate
    School
Silicon Valley University
Soka University of America
Southern California Institute of
    Architecture
Southern California Institute of
    Technology
Southern California Seminary
SUM Bible College & Theological
    Seminary
Thomas Aquinas College
Touro University Worldwide
University of Antelope Valley
University of the West
World Mission University

**Colorado**
Argosy University
    Denver
Aspen University
CollegeAmerica
    Fort Collins
DeVry University
    Westminster
Naropa University
National American University
    Denver
Nazarene Bible College
University of Phoenix
    Southern Colorado

**Connecticut**
Holy Apostles College and Seminary
Lyme Academy College of Fine Arts
Mitchell College
Paier College of Art
Post University

**Delaware**
Goldey-Beacom College

**District of Columbia**
University of Phoenix
    Washington DC
University of the Potomac

**Florida**
Argosy University
    Sarasota
    Tampa
Baptist College of Florida
Beacon College
Carlos Albizu University
Chamberlain College of Nursing
    Jacksonville
    Miramar
DeVry University
    Miramar
    Orlando
Digital Media Arts College
Everest University
    Orange Park
Johnson University: Florida
Jones College
Jose Maria Vargas University
Rasmussen College
    Fort Myers
    New Port Richey
    Tampa/Brandon
Remington College
    Tampa
    of Nursing
Talmudic University
Trinity Baptist College
Trinity College of Florida
Webber International University
Yeshiva Gedolah Rabbinical College

**Georgia**
Beulah Heights University
Brewton-Parker College
Carver College
Herzing University
    Atlanta
Life University
Paine College
Truett McConnell University
Wesleyan College

**Hawaii**
Argosy University
    Hawaii

**Idaho**
New Saint Andrews College
University of Phoenix
    Idaho

**Illinois**
American Academy of Art
Argosy University
    Chicago
    Schaumburg
Blackburn College
Blessing-Rieman College of Nursing &
    Health Sciences
Chamberlain College Of Nursing
    Tinley Park
DeVry University
    Chicago
East-West University
Eureka College
International Academy of Design and
    Technology
    Chicago
Lincoln Christian University
Methodist College
Midstate College
Rasmussen College
    Mokena/Tinley Park
Resurrection University
Rush University
Shimer College
Telshe Yeshiva-Chicago
VanderCook College of Music

**Indiana**
Calumet College of St. Joseph
Chamberlain College of Nursing
    Indianapolis
Crossroads Bible College
Holy Cross College
International Business College
Martin University
Oakland City University
St. Mary-of-the-Woods College
University of Phoenix
    Indianapolis

**Iowa**
Allen College
Divine Word College
Emmaus Bible College
Faith Baptist Bible College and
    Theological Seminary
Iowa Wesleyan College
Kaplan University
    Cedar Falls
    Mason City
Maharishi University of Management
Shiloh University
University of Phoenix
    Des Moines

**Kansas**
Barclay College
Bethany College
Bethel College
Kansas Wesleyan University
McPherson College
Ottawa University
Sterling College
Tabor College
University of Kansas Medical Center

**Kentucky**
Alice Lloyd College
Kentucky Christian University
Kentucky Mountain Bible College
Kentucky Wesleyan College
St. Catharine College
University of Phoenix
    Louisville

**Louisiana**
Centenary College of Louisiana
Herzing University
    Kenner
St. Joseph Seminary College
University of Phoenix
    Louisiana
    Shreveport

**Maine**
College of the Atlantic
Maine College of Art
Unity College
University of Maine
    Machias

**Maryland**
Capitol Technology University
Johns Hopkins University: Peabody
    Conservatory of Music
St. John's College
University of Phoenix
    Maryland
Yeshiva College of the Nations Capital

**Massachusetts**
Bard College at Simon's Rock
Boston Baptist College
Boston Conservatory
Franklin W. Olin College of
    Engineering
Hellenic College/Holy Cross
Montserrat College of Art
New England Conservatory of Music
Northpoint Bible College
Pine Manor College
School of the Museum of Fine Arts
University of Phoenix
    Boston
Wheelock College

Very small (fewer than 750)

**Michigan**
Cleary University
Concordia University
Finlandia University
International Academy of Design and
Technology
Detroit
Kuyper College
Marygrove College
Robert B Miller College
Robert B. Miller College
Sacred Heart Major Seminary
University of Phoenix
West Michigan
Yeshiva Beth Yehuda-Yeshiva Gedolah
of Greater Detroit

**Minnesota**
Bethany Lutheran College
Crossroads College
Globe University
Minneapolis
Moorhead
Woodbury
McNally Smith College of Music
Minneapolis College of Art and Design
Minnesota School of Business
Blaine
Elk River
Lakeville
Plymouth
Richfield
Rochester
St. Cloud
Shakopee
National American University
Bloomington
Roseville
Northwestern Health Sciences
University
Rasmussen College
Blaine
Moorhead
University of Minnesota
Rochester
University of Phoenix
Minneapolis-St. Paul

**Mississippi**
Blue Mountain College
Southeastern Baptist College
University of Phoenix
Jackson

**Missouri**
Calvary Bible College and Theological
Seminary
Cottey College
Cox College
DeVry University
Kansas City
Goldfarb School of Nursing at Barnes-
Jewish College
Kansas City Art Institute
Logan University
National American University
Kansas City
Lee's Summit
Research College of Nursing
Stephens College

**Montana**
Montana Bible College

**Nebraska**
College of Saint Mary
Grace University
Herzing University
Omaha School of Massage
Therapy and Healthcare
York College

**Nevada**
International Academy of Design and
Technology
Henderson
Roseman University of Health Sciences

Sierra Nevada College
University of Phoenix
Northern Nevada

**New Hampshire**
New Hampshire Institute of Art
Thomas More College of Liberal Arts
University of New Hampshire at
Manchester

**New Jersey**
College of St. Elizabeth
DeVry University
North Brunswick
Pillar College
Rabbi Jacob Joseph School
Rabbinical College of America
Talmudical Academy of New Jersey
University of Phoenix
Jersey City

**New Mexico**
Institute of American Indian Arts
National American University
Albuquerque
St. John's College
University of the Southwest

**New York**
Beis Medrash Heichal Dovid
Berkeley College
Beth Hamedrash Shaarei Yosher
Institute
Beth Hatalmud Rabbinical College
Central Yeshiva Tomchei Tmimim-
Lubavitch
College of New Rochelle
Davis College
Eastman School of Music of the
University of Rochester
Five Towns College
Globe Institute of Technology
Jewish Theological Seminary of
America
Juilliard School
Kehilath Yakov Rabbinical Seminary
The King's College
Machzikei Hadath Rabbinical College
Manhattan School of Music
Medaille College: Rochester
Mesivta Torah Vodaath Seminary
Metropolitan College of New York
Mirrer Yeshiva Central Institute
The New School College of
Performing Arts
New York School of Interior Design
Rabbinical Academy Mesivta Rabbi
Chaim Berlin
Rabbinical College Beth Shraga
Rabbinical College Bobover Yeshiva
B'nei Zion
Rabbinical College Ch'san Sofer of
New York
Rabbinical College of Long Island
Rabbinical College of Ohr Shimon
Yisroel
Rabbinical Seminary of America
Shor Yoshuv Rabbinical College
SUNY
Upstate Medical University
Talmudical Institute of Upstate New
York
Talmudical Seminary Oholei Torah
Torah Temimah Talmudical Seminary
Wells College
Yeshiva and Kolel Bais Medrash Elyon
Yeshiva and Kollel Harbotzas Torah
Yeshiva D'Monsey Rabbinical College
Yeshiva Derech Chaim
Yeshiva Gedolah Imrei Yosef
D'Spinka
Yeshiva Gedolah Zichron Moshe
Yeshiva Karlin Stolin
Yeshiva of Nitra
Yeshiva of the Telshe Alumni
Yeshiva Shaar Hatorah
Yeshiva Shaarei Torah of Rockland

Yeshivas Novominsk
Yeshivat Mikdash Melech
Yeshivath Viznitz

**North Carolina**
Apex School of Theology
Bennett College for Women
Brevard College
Cabarrus College of Health Sciences
Laurel University
Mid-Atlantic Christian University
Piedmont International University
St. Andrews University
University of Phoenix
Charlotte
Raleigh
Warren Wilson College

**North Dakota**
Rasmussen College
Fargo

**Ohio**
Allegheny Wesleyan College
Art Academy of Cincinnati
Bryant & Stratton College
Eastlake
Parma
Chamberlain College of Nursing
Columbus
Chamberlain College Of Nursing
Chamberlain College of Nursing:
Cleveland
Cincinnati Christian University
Cleveland Institute of Art
Cleveland Institute of Music
Defiance College
God's Bible School and College
Herzing University
Toledo
Kettering College
Rabbinical College of Telshe
University of Phoenix
Cleveland
Ursuline College
Wilberforce University

**Oklahoma**
Family of Faith College
Hillsdale Free Will Baptist College
St. Gregory's University
Southwestern Christian University
University of Phoenix
Oklahoma City
Tulsa

**Oregon**
Gutenberg College
Marylhurst University
Mount Angel Seminary
New Hope Christian College
Northwest Christian University
Oregon College of Art & Craft
Pacific Northwest College of Art
University of Phoenix
Oregon
Warner Pacific College

**Pennsylvania**
Bryn Athyn College
Cairn University
Cheyney University of Pennsylvania
Clarks Summit University
DeVry University
Fort Washington
Gratz College
Harrisburg University of Science and
Technology
Moore College of Art and Design
Penn State
Beaver
DuBois
Fayette, The Eberly Campus
Greater Allegheny
New Kensington
Shenango
Wilkes-Barre

Pennsylvania Academy of the Fine
Arts
Pennsylvania Colleg of Art and Design
Pennsylvania College of Art and
Design
Restaurant School at Walnut Hill
College
Rosemont College
University of Phoenix
Harrisburg
Philadelphia
Pittsburgh
University of Valley Forge
Wilson College
Yeshivath Beth Moshe

**Puerto Rico**
Bayamon Central University
Carlos Albizu University: San Juan
Conservatory of Music of Puerto Rico
Escuela de Artes Plasticas de Puerto
Rico
Theological University of the
Caribbean
Universidad Central del Caribe
Universidad Pentecostal Mizpa
University of Phoenix
Puerto Rico
University of Puerto Rico
Medical Sciences

**South Carolina**
Allen University
Columbia International University
Erskine College
University of Phoenix
Columbia
Voorhees College
W.L. Bonner Bible College

**South Dakota**
Mount Marty College
Sinte Gleska University

**Tennessee**
Aquinas College
Argosy University
Nashville
Fisk University
Memphis College of Art
O'More College of Design
University of Phoenix
Knoxville
Virginia College
School of Business and Health in
Knoxville
Visible Music College
Watkins College of Art, Design &
Film
Welch College
Williamson College

**Texas**
Argosy University
Dallas
Arlington Baptist College
Baptist University of the Americas
Chamberlain College of Nursing
Houston
Criswell College
DeVry University
Irving
The King's University
National American University
Austin
Northwood University
Texas
Paul Quinn College
Southwestern Adventist University
Southwestern Baptist Theological
Seminary
Southwestern Christian College
University of Phoenix
Austin
University of Texas
Health Science Center at Houston
Medical Branch at Galveston

## Utah

Argosy University
  Salt Lake City
Broadview University
  Orem
Stevens-Henager College
  Logan
  Ogden
  Orem

## Vermont

Bennington College
College of St. Joseph in Vermont
Goddard College
Green Mountain College
Marlboro College
Southern Vermont College
Sterling College

## Virginia

Argosy University
  Washington D.C.
Art Institute of Washington
Chamberlain College of Nursing
  Arlington
Christendom College
DeVry University
  Arlington
Hollins University
Patrick Henry College
Randolph College
Southern Virginia University
Stratford University: Falls Church
Stratford University: Woodbridge
Sweet Briar College
University of the Potomac
Virginia University of Lynchburg

## Washington

Argosy University
  Seattle
Bastyr University
Cornish College of the Arts
Faith International University
  Fiath International University
International Academy of Design and
  Technology
  Seattle
Northwest College of Art & Design
University of Phoenix
  Western Washington

## West Virginia

Appalachian Bible College
Bethany College
Catholic Distance University
Ohio Valley University
Salem International University

## Wisconsin

Globe University
  Green Bay
Herzing University
  Brookfield
  Kenosha
Milwaukee Institute of Art & Design
Northland College
Rasmussen College
  Appleton
Silver Lake College of the Holy
  Family
University of Phoenix
  Milwaukee

## *Two-year*

## Alabama

Marion Military Institute
Virginia College
  Mobile
  Montgomery

## Arizona

Brookline College
  Tempe
Carrington College
  Mesa
  Phoenix

Phoenix Westside
  Tucson
Golf Academy of America
  Phoenix
Sessions College for Professional
  Design
Tohono O'odham Community College

## Arkansas

Bryan University
  Rogers
College of the Ouachitas
Remington College
  Little Rock

## California

American Academy of Dramatic Arts:
  West
Bryan College: Sacramento
Carrington College
  Citrus Heights
  Pleasant Hill
  Stockton
Concorde Career College
  North Hollywood
  San Bernardino
Deep Springs College
Epic Bible College
Fashion Institute of Design and
  Merchandising
  San Diego
  San Francisco
Fremont College
Golf Academy of America
  San Diego
Kaplan College
  Palm Springs
  Riverside
  Sacramento
  Salida
Le Cordon Bleu College of Culinary
  Arts
  San Francisco
Pacific College of Oriental Medicine:
  San Diego
Platt College
  Los Angeles
Professional Golfers Career College
Santa Barbara Business College
  Bakersfield
  Rancho Mirage
  Santa Maria
  Ventura
South Coast College

## Colorado

Ecotech Institute
IntelliTec College: Grand Junction
Lamar Community College
Redstone College

## Delaware

Delaware College of Art and Design

## Florida

City College
  Altamonte Springs
  Gainesville
  Miami
College of Business and Technology
  Cutler Bay
  Flagler
  Hialeah
  Kendall
  Miami Gardens
Florida College of Natural Health
  Bradenton
  Maitland
  Miami
  Pompano Beach
Fortis College
  Orange Park
  Winter Park
Golf Academy of America
  Orlando
Herzing University
  Winter Park

Key College
Lincoln College of Technology
  West Palm Beach
Rasmussen College
  Pasco/Land O'Lakes
Stenotype Institute: Jacksonville
Virginia College
  Jacksonville
  Pensacola

## Georgia

Andrew College
Gupton Jones College of Funeral
  Service
Virginia College
  Columbus
  Macon
  Savannah

## Hawaii

Hawaii Tokai International College

## Idaho

Broadview University
  Boise
Carrington College
  Boise
Stevens-Henager College
  Boise

## Illinois

Coyne College
Illinois Eastern Community Colleges
  Frontier Community College
  Lincoln Trail College
  Olney Central College
  Wabash Valley College
MacCormac College
Morrison Institute of Technology
Northwestern College
Rasmussen College
  Aurora
  Rockford
  Romeoville/Joliet
Taylor Business Institute
Vatterott College
  Quincy

## Indiana

Ancilla College
College of Court Reporting
Fortis College
  Indianapolis
International Business College:
  Indianapolis
Kaplan College
  Hammond
Mid-America College of Funeral
  Service

## Iowa

Kaplan University
  Cedar Rapids
St. Luke's College
Vatterott College
  Des Moines

## Kansas

Bryan University
  Topeka
Donnelly College
Hesston College
Independence Community College
Northwest Kansas Technical College

## Kentucky

Daymar College
  Louisville
  Owensboro
Spencerian College
Spencerian College: Lexington
Sullivan College of Technology and
  Design

## Louisiana

Baton Rouge School of Computers
Blue Cliff College
  Shreveport
Delta College of Arts & Technology

Delta School of Business &
  Technology
ITI Technical College
Remington College
  Baton Rouge
  Lafayette
  Shreveport
Virginia College
  Baton Rouge
  Shreveport

## Maine

Landing School of Boatbuilding and
  Design
Northern Maine Community College
Washington County Community
  College

## Maryland

Brightwood College
  Beltsville
  Towson
Garrett College
Kaplan University
  Hagerstown
TESST College of Technology
  Brightwood College: Baltimore

## Massachusetts

Benjamin Franklin Institute of
  Technology
New England College of Business and
  Finance

## Michigan

Saginaw Chippewa Tribal College

## Minnesota

Academy College
Herzing University
  Minneapolis
Institute of Production and Recording
Le Cordon Bleu College of Culinary
  Arts
  Minneapolis-St. Paul
Minneapolis Business College
Minnesota School of Business
  Brooklyn Center
Rainy River Community College
Rasmussen College
  Bloomington
  Brooklyn Park
  Eagan
  Mankato
  St. Cloud
White Earth Tribal and Community
  College

## Mississippi

Antonelli College
  Jackson
Blue Cliff College
  Gulfport
Virginia College
  Biloxi
  Jackson

## Missouri

Bolivar Technical College
L'Ecole Culinaire
Metro Business College
  Rolla
Missouri College
Pinnacle Career Institute: Kansas City
Stevens Institute of Business & Arts
Texas County Technical College
Vatterott College
  Joplin
  Kansas City
  O'Fallon
  Sunset Hills

## Montana

Dawson Community College
Little Big Horn College
Stone Child College

Very small (fewer than 750)

**Nebraska**
Kaplan University
  Lincoln
Myotherapy Institute
Nebraska College of Technical
  Agriculture
Nebraska Indian Community College

**Nevada**
Career College of Northern Nevada
Carrington College
  Las Vegas
  Reno

**New Jersey**
Eastern International College
Eastwick College
  Hackensack

**New Mexico**
Brookline College
  Albuquerque
Carrington College
  Albuquerque
Luna Community College
New Mexico Military Institute

**New York**
American Academy of Dramatic Arts
Bramson ORT College
Island Drafting and Technical Institute
Mildred Elley
  Albany
  New York City
New York Career Institute
Phillips School of Nursing at Mount
  Sinai Beth Israel
    Phillips School of Nursing at
      Mount Sinai Beth Israel
St. Elizabeth College of Nursing
Swedish Institute
Utica School of Commerce
Villa Maria College of Buffalo
Wood Tobe-Coburn School

**North Carolina**
Louisburg College
Martin Community College
Miller-Motte College
  Cary
  Fayetteville
Pamlico Community College
Virginia College in Greensboro

**North Dakota**
Dakota College at Bottineau
Lake Region State College
Nueta Hidatsa Sahnish College
Turtle Mountain Community College
United Tribes Technical College

**Ohio**
Antonelli College
  Cincinnati
Art Institute of Cincinnati
ATS Institute of Technology
Davis College
Fortis College
  Cuyahoga
  Ravenna
Harrison College
  Grove City
International College of Broadcasting
Kaplan College
  Dayton
Miami-Jacobs Career College
  Columbus
  Dayton
  Sharonville
Ohio Business College
  Hilliard
  Sheffield
Ohio College of Massotherapy
Ohio Technical College
PowerSport Institute
School of Advertising Art
Vatterott College
  Cleveland

Virginia Marti College of Art and
  Design

**Oklahoma**
College of the Muscogee Nation
Platt College
  Moore
  Oklahoma City Central
  Tulsa
Vatterott College
  Oklahoma City
  Tulsa
Virginia College
  Tulsa

**Oregon**
Le Cordon Bleu College of Culinary
  Arts
    Portland
Tillamook Bay Community College

**Pennsylvania**
Antonelli Institute of Art and
  Photography
Bidwell Training Center
Bradford School: Pittsburgh
Career Training Academy: Monroeville
Consolidated School of Business
  Lancaster
Douglas Education Center
DuBois Business College
  Huntingdon
  Oil City
Erie Institute of Technology
Fortis Institute
  Erie
  Forty Fort
JNA Institute of Culinary Arts
Johnson College
Kaplan Career Institute
  Franklin Mills
Keystone Technical Institute
Lansdale School of Business
Laurel Business Institute
Laurel Technical Institute
Lincoln Technical Institute
  Allentown
  Northeast Philadelphia
  Philadelphia
Manor College
McCann School of Business and
  Technology
    Hazleton
    Pottsville
Orleans Technical Institute
Penn Commercial Business and
  Technical School
Pennco Tech
Pennsylvania Institute of Health and
  Technology
Pittsburgh Institute of Aeronautics
Pittsburgh Institute of Mortuary
  Science
Rosedale Technical College
Triangle Tech
  Bethlehem
  Greensburg
University of Pittsburgh
  Titusville
Valley Forge Military College
Vet Tech Institute
The Workforce Institute's City College
YTI Career Institute
  Altoona

**Puerto Rico**
Humacao Community College

**South Carolina**
Clinton College
Denmark Technical College
Forrest Junior College
Golf Academy of America
  Myrtle Beach
Miller-Motte Technical College
  Conway
Spartanburg Methodist College

Virginia College
  Charleston
  Columbia
  Florence
  Greenville
  Spartanburg

**South Dakota**
Globe University
  Sioux Falls
Sisseton Wahpeton College

**Tennessee**
Chattanooga College
Daymar Institute
  Clarksville
  Murfreesboro
  Nashville
Hiwassee College
Huntington College of Health Sciences
Miller-Motte Technical College
  Chattanooga
  Clarksville
Nossi College of Art
Remington College
  Nashville
Virginia College
  School of Business and Health in
    Chattanooga
West Tennessee Business College

**Texas**
Commonwealth Institute of Funeral
  Service
Culinary Institute LeNotre
Golf Academy of America
  Dallas
International Academy of Design and
  Technology
    San Antonio
Jacksonville College
Le Cordon Bleu College of Culinary
  Arts
    Austin
Remington College
  Fort Worth
  Webster Campus
  Westchase Campus
Virginia College
  Austin
Wade College
Western Technical College: Diana
  Drive

**Utah**
Broadview University
  Broadview Entertainment Arts
    University
  Layton
Careers Unlimited
Eagle Gate College: Layton
Eagle Gate College: Murray
Provo College
Vista College: Online

**Vermont**
Landmark College
New England Culinary Institute

**Virginia**
Virginia College
  Richmond

**Washington**
Carrington College
  Spokane
Northwest School of Wooden
  Boatbuilding

**West Virginia**
West Virginia Junior College
  Bridgeport

**Wisconsin**
Globe University
  Appleton
  Eau Claire
  La Crosse
  Madison East

  Middleton
  Wausau
Madison Media Institute
Rasmussen College
  Green Bay
  Wausau
University of Wisconsin
  Barron County
  Marshfield/Wood County
  Richland

Small (750-1,999)

*Four-year*

**Alabama**
Birmingham-Southern College
Huntingdon College
Miles College
Oakwood University
Spring Hill College
Stillman College
Talladega College
University of Mobile
University of West Alabama

**Arizona**
Art Institute of Phoenix
National Paralegal College
University of Advancing Technology

**Arkansas**
Arkansas Baptist College
Hendrix College
John Brown University
Ouachita Baptist University
Philander Smith College

**California**
Alliant International University
Antioch University
  Los Angeles
Art Institute of California
  Hollywood
  Inland Empire
  Orange County
  Sacramento
  San Diego
  San Francisco
California College of the Arts
California College San Diego
California Institute of Technology
California Institute of the Arts
California Maritime Academy
Claremont McKenna College
Concordia University Irvine
DeVry University
  Pomona
Dominican University of California
Harvey Mudd College
Hope International University
Hult International Business School
Loma Linda University
Marymount California University
The Master's University
Menlo College
Mills College
Notre Dame de Namur University
Otis College of Art and Design
Pacific Union College
Patten University
Pitzer College
Pomona College
Scripps College
Simpson University
Stanbridge University
University of Phoenix
  Bay Area
Vanguard University of Southern
  California
Westmont College
Whittier College
William Jessup University
Woodbury University

## Colorado

Adams State University
American Sentinel University
Colorado Technical University
Johnson & Wales University
  Denver
Rocky Mountain College of Art &
  Design
University of Phoenix
  Denver
Western State Colorado University
Westwood College
  Denver North

## Connecticut

Albertus Magnus College
Charter Oak State College
Connecticut College
United States Coast Guard Academy
University of Saint Joseph

## Delaware

Wesley College

## District of Columbia

Gallaudet University
Strayer University

## Florida

Adventist University of Health
  Sciences
Art Institute of Fort Lauderdale
Ave Maria University
City College
  Fort Lauderdale
Eckerd College
Edward Waters College
Everglades University
Florida Memorial University
Hodges University
Johnson & Wales University
  North Miami
New College of Florida
Ringling College of Art and Design
Rollins College
Saint Thomas University
University of Phoenix
  North Florida
  South Florida
  West Florida
University of South Florida
  Sarasota-Manatee
Warner University

## Georgia

Agnes Scott College
Bauder College
Brenau University
Chamberlain College of Nursing
  Atlanta
Covenant College
DeVry University
  Decatur
LaGrange College
Oglethorpe University
Piedmont College
Point University
Reinhardt University
Shorter University
South University
  Savannah
Thomas University
Toccoa Falls College
University of Phoenix
  Augusta
Young Harris College

## Hawaii

Chaminade University of Honolulu
University of Phoenix
  Hawaii

## Idaho

College of Idaho
Northwest Nazarene University

## Illinois

Chamberlain College of Nursing
  Chicago
Concordia University Chicago
Greenville College
Illinois College
Illinois Institute of Art
  Chicago
  Schaumburg
Illinois Wesleyan University
Judson University
Kendall College
Knox College
Lake Forest College
Millikin University
Monmouth College
National-Louis University
Quincy University
Rockford University
Trinity Christian College
Trinity International University
University of Phoenix
  Chicago
University of St. Francis

## Indiana

Bethel College
Earlham College
Franklin College
Goshen College
Hanover College
Huntington University
Manchester University
Saint Joseph's College
Saint Mary's College
Taylor University
Trine University
University of Saint Francis
Wabash College

## Iowa

Briar Cliff University
Buena Vista University
Central College
Clarke University
Coe College
Cornell College
Dordt College
Graceland University
Grand View University
Grinnell College
Kaplan University
  Des Moines
Loras College
Mercy College of Health Sciences
Morningside College
Mount Mercy University
Northwestern College
Simpson College
University of Dubuque
Waldorf University
Wartburg College
William Penn University

## Kansas

Baker University
Benedictine College
Central Christian College of Kansas
Friends University
Haskell Indian Nations University
MidAmerica Nazarene University
Newman University
Southwestern College
University of St. Mary

## Kentucky

Asbury University
Berea College
Brescia University
Centre College
Georgetown College
Kentucky State University
Midway College
Southern Baptist Theological Seminary
Spalding University
Thomas More College
Transylvania University

Union College
University of Pikeville
University of the Cumberlands

## Louisiana

Dillard University
Louisiana College
Louisiana State University
  Health Sciences Center
Southern University
  New Orleans
University of Holy Cross
University of Phoenix
  Baton Rouge

## Maine

Bates College
Bowdoin College
Colby College
Maine Maritime Academy
Saint Joseph's College of Maine
Thomas College
University of Maine
  Farmington
  Fort Kent
  Presque Isle

## Maryland

Goucher College
Hood College
Maryland Institute College of Art
McDaniel College
Mount St. Mary's University
Notre Dame of Maryland University
St. Mary's College of Maryland
University of Maryland
  Baltimore
Washington Adventist University
Washington College

## Massachusetts

American International College
Amherst College
Anna Maria College
Assumption College
Bay Path University
Becker College
Cambridge College
Eastern Nazarene College
Elms College
Emmanuel College
Fisher College
Gordon College
Hampshire College
Lasell College
Lesley University
Massachusetts College of Art and
  Design
Massachusetts College of Liberal Arts
Massachusetts Maritime Academy
Mount Ida College
Nichols College
Regis College
Simmons College
Wheaton College

## Michigan

Adrian College
Albion College
Alma College
Andrews University
Aquinas College
Art Institute of Michigan
Baker College
  of Cadillac
  of Port Huron
College for Creative Studies
Cornerstone University
Hillsdale College
Kalamazoo College
Kettering University
Northwood University
  Michigan
Olivet College
Rochester College
University of Phoenix
  Metro Detroit

Walsh College of Accountancy and
  Business Administration

## Minnesota

Argosy University
  Twin Cities
Art Institute International Minnesota
  Art Institutes International
  Minnesota
College of St. Benedict
Crown College
North Central University
Rasmussen College
  Lake Elmo/Woodbury
St. John's University
St. Mary's University of Minnesota
University of Minnesota
  Crookston
  Morris
University of Northwestern - St. Paul

## Mississippi

Millsaps College
Mississippi Valley State University
Rust College
Tougaloo College

## Missouri

Avila University
Central Methodist University
College of the Ozarks
Columbia College
Culver-Stockton College
Drury University
Evangel University
Fontbonne University
Hannibal-LaGrange University
Harris-Stowe State University
Missouri Baptist University
Missouri Valley College
Rockhurst University
University of Phoenix
  St. Louis
Westminster College
William Jewell College
William Woods University

## Montana

Carroll College
Montana State University
  Northern
Rocky Mountain College
Salish Kootenai College
University of Great Falls
University of Montana: Western

## Nebraska

Concordia University
Doane University
Hastings College
Midland University
Nebraska Wesleyan University
Peru State College
Union College

## Nevada

Art Institute of Las Vegas

## New Hampshire

Colby-Sawyer College
Franklin Pierce University
Granite State College
New England College
Rivier University
Saint Anselm College

## New Jersey

Bloomfield College
Caldwell University
Centenary University
Drew University
Felician University
Georgian Court University

## New Mexico

New Mexico Institute of Mining and
  Technology
Northern New Mexico College
Santa Fe University of Art and Design

# Small (750-1,999)

University of Phoenix
New Mexico
Western New Mexico University

## New York

Albany College of Pharmacy and
Health Sciences
Alfred University
Bard College
Briarcliffe College
Cazenovia College
College of Mount St. Vincent
Concordia College
Cooper Union for the Advancement of
Science and Art
D'Youville College
Daemen College
DeVry College of New York
Midtown Campus
Dominican College of Blauvelt
Elmira College
Eugene Lang College The New School
for Liberal Arts
Hamilton College
Hartwick College
Hilbert College
Houghton College
Keuka College
LIM College
Manhattanville College
Medaille College
Nyack College
Paul Smith's College
Roberts Wesleyan College
The Sage Colleges
Saint Bonaventure University
St. Joseph's College, New York
St. Thomas Aquinas College
Sarah Lawrence College
SUNY
College of Environmental Science
and Forestry
Maritime College
SUNY Polytechnic Institute
U.T.A. Mesivta-Kiryas Joel
United States Merchant Marine
Academy
United Talmudical Seminary
Vaughn College of Aeronautics and
Technology
Wagner College

## North Carolina

Barton College
Belmont Abbey College
Catawba College
Chowan University
Davidson College
Greensboro College
Guilford College
Johnson C. Smith University
Lees-McRae College
Lenoir-Rhyne University
Livingstone College
Mars Hill University
Meredith College
Montreat College
Pfeiffer University
Queens University of Charlotte
Saint Augustine's University
Salem College
Shaw University
University of North Carolina
School of the Arts

## North Dakota

Dickinson State University
Mayville State University
University of Jamestown
Valley City State University

## Ohio

Bluffton University
Central State University
College of Wooster
Columbus College of Art and Design

DeVry University
Columbus
Heidelberg University
Hiram College
Kenyon College
Lake Erie College
Lourdes University
Malone University
Marietta College
Mount St. Joseph University
Mount Vernon Nazarene University
Muskingum University
Notre Dame College
Ohio Dominican University
Ohio University
Zanesville Campus
Ohio Wesleyan University
Union Institute & University
Urbana University
Wilmington College
Wittenberg University

## Oklahoma

Bacone College
Northwestern Oklahoma State
University
Oklahoma Baptist University
Oklahoma Christian University
Oklahoma City University
Oklahoma Panhandle State University
Oklahoma Wesleyan University
Southern Nazarene University
Spartan College of Aeronautics and
Technology
University of Science and Arts of
Oklahoma

## Oregon

Art Institute of Portland
Concordia University
Corban University
Linfield College
Oregon Health & Science University
Pacific University
Reed College
Willamette University

## Pennsylvania

Allegheny College
Art Institute of Philadelphia
Art Institute of Pittsburgh
Bryn Mawr College
Cabrini University
Carlow University
Cedar Crest College
Central Penn College
Chatham University
Chestnut Hill College
Delaware Valley University
Elizabethtown College
Geneva College
Gwynedd Mercy University
Haverford College
Holy Family University
Immaculata University
Juniata College
Keystone College
King's College
La Roche College
Lancaster Bible College
Lebanon Valley College
Lincoln University
Lycoming College
Marywood University
Moravian College
Mount Aloysius College
Peirce College
Penn State
Brandywine
Hazleton
Lehigh Valley
Mont Alto
Schuylkill
Worthington Scranton
York

Pennsylvania College of Health
Sciences
St. Francis University
St. Vincent College
Seton Hill University
Swarthmore College
Thiel College
Thomas Jefferson University
University of Pittsburgh
Bradford
Greensburg
University of the Arts
Ursinus College
Washington & Jefferson College
Waynesburg University
Westminster College

## Puerto Rico

American University of Puerto Rico
Atlantic University College
Columbia Central University
Caguas
EDP University of Puerto Rico: Hato
Rey
EDP University of Puerto Rico: San
Sebastian
Inter American University of Puerto
Rico
Barranquitas Campus
Fajardo Campus
Guayama Campus
National University College
Arecibo
Ponce
Universidad Adventista de las Antillas
University College of San Juan
University of Puerto Rico
Utuado

## South Carolina

Claflin University
Coker College
Columbia College
Converse College
Limestone College
Morris College
Newberry College
Presbyterian College
Southern Wesleyan University
University of South Carolina
Beaufort
Wofford College

## South Dakota

Augusta University
Augustana University
Dakota State University
Dakota Wesleyan University
National American University
Rapid City
Northern State University
Oglala Lakota College
Presentation College
University of Sioux Falls

## Tennessee

Bryan College
Dayton
Carson-Newman University
Christian Brothers University
Freed-Hardeman University
Johnson University
Lane College
LeMoyne-Owen College
Lincoln Memorial University
Martin Methodist College
Maryville College
Milligan College
Rhodes College
Sewanee: The University of the South
South College
Tennessee Wesleyan College
Trevecca Nazarene University
Tusculum College
University of Phoenix
Memphis

## Texas

Art Institute of Dallas
Art Institute of Houston
Austin College
Concordia University Texas
East Texas Baptist University
Hardin-Simmons University
Howard Payne University
Jarvis Christian College
LeTourneau University
Lubbock Christian University
McMurry University
Our Lady of the Lake University of
San Antonio
Schreiner University
Southwestern Assemblies of God
University
Southwestern University
Sul Ross State University
Texas A&M University
Texarkana
Texas College
Texas Lutheran University
Texas Tech University Health Sciences
Center
Texas Wesleyan University
University of Dallas
University of Phoenix
Dallas Fort Worth
San Antonio
University of St. Thomas
Wiley College

## Utah

Independence University
University of Phoenix
Utah

## Vermont

Castleton University
Johnson State College
Lyndon State College
Saint Michael's College

## Virginia

Averett University
Bluefield College
Bridgewater College
Eastern Mennonite University
Emory & Henry College
Ferrum College
Hampden-Sydney College
Jefferson College of Health Sciences
Lynchburg College
Mary Baldwin University
Randolph-Macon College
Roanoke College
University of Management and
Technology
University of Phoenix
Northern Virginia
Richmond
University of Virginia's College at
Wise
Virginia Military Institute
Virginia Union University
Virginia Wesleyan College
Washington and Lee University

## Washington

Art Institute of Seattle
City University of Seattle
DigiPen Institute of Technology
Heritage University
Northwest University
Saint Martin's University
Walla Walla University
Whitman College

## West Virginia

Alderson-Broaddus University
Bluefield State College
Concord University
Davis and Elkins College
Glenville State College
University of Charleston
West Liberty University

West Virginia University Institute of
    Technology
West Virginia Wesleyan College
Wheeling Jesuit University

### Wisconsin

Alverno College
Beloit College
Cardinal Stritch University
Edgewood College
Herzing University
    Madison
Lawrence University
Maranathan Baptist University
    Maranatha Baptist University
Marian University
Mount Mary University
Viterbo University
Wisconsin Lutheran College

## Two-year

### Alabama

Chattahoochee Valley Community
    College
Faulkner State Community College
Lurleen B. Wallace Community
    College
Remington College
    Mobile

### Arizona

Brookline College
    Phoenix
Bryan University
Dine College
Le Cordon Bleu College of Culinary
    Arts
    Scottsdale
Refrigeration School

### Arkansas

Arkansas State University
    Mid-South
    Mountain Home
Cossatot Community College
    of the University of Arkansas
East Arkansas Community College
South Arkansas Community College
Southeast Arkansas College
Southern Arkansas University Tech

### California

Art Institute of California
    Los Angeles
Carrington College
    Sacramento
    San Jose
Concorde Career College
    Garden Grove
Copper Mountain College
Feather River College
Institute of Technology: Clovis
Kaplan College
    San Diego
    Vista
Le Cordon Bleu College of Culinary
    Arts
    Los Angeles
MTI College
San Joaquin Valley College

### Colorado

Colorado Northwestern Community
    College
Concorde Career College
    Aurora
IBMC College
    Fort Collins
IntelliTec College
Lincoln College of Technology
    Denver
Morgan Community College
Northeastern Junior College
Otero Junior College
Trinidad State Junior College

### Connecticut

Asnuntuck Community College

### Florida

Chipola College
Florida Keys Community College
Le Cordon Bleu College of Culinary
    Arts
    Miami
    Orlando
North Florida Community College
Southeastern College
    Greenacres

### Georgia

Le Cordon Bleu College of Culinary
    Arts
    Atlanta
Oxford College of Emory University
Southeastern Technical College
Virginia College
    Augusta
Wiregrass Georgia Technical College

### Hawaii

Remington College
    Honolulu
University of Hawaii
    Kauai Community College

### Illinois

Benedictine University at Springfield
Carl Sandburg College
Danville Area Community College
John Wood Community College
Kaskaskia College
Le Cordon Bleu College of Culinary
    Arts
    Chicago
Lincoln College
Sauk Valley Community College
Southeastern Illinois College
Spoon River College

### Indiana

Ivy Tech Community College
    Richmond
    Southeast
Lincoln College of Technology
    Indianapolis

### Iowa

Clinton Community College
Ellsworth Community College
Iowa Lakes Community College
Muscatine Community College
North Iowa Area Community College
Northwest Iowa Community College
Southeastern Community College
Southwestern Community College

### Kansas

Cloud County Community College
Coffeyville Community College
Colby Community College
Dodge City Community College
Labette Community College
Neosho County Community College
Pratt Community College
Seward County Community College

### Kentucky

Henderson Community College

### Louisiana

Blue Cliff College
    Metairie
Nunez Community College

### Maine

Eastern Maine Community College
Kaplan University
    South Portland
Kennebec Valley Community College
York County Community College

### Maryland

Chesapeake College

### Massachusetts

Bay State College
Berkshire Community College
Dean College
Greenfield Community College

### Michigan

Bay College
Glen Oaks Community College
Gogebic Community College
Kirtland Community College
Montcalm Community College
Southwestern Michigan College

### Minnesota

Dunwoody College of Technology
Fond du Lac Tribal and Community
    College
Hibbing Community College
Itasca Community College
Mesabi Range College
Minnesota State College - Southeast
    Technical
Northwest Technical College
Pine Technical & Community College

### Mississippi

Coahoma Community College

### Missouri

Concorde Career College
    Kansas City
Missouri State University
    West Plains
North Central Missouri College
Ranken Technical College
State Technical College of Missouri
Vatterott College
    Berkeley

### Nebraska

Mid-Plains Community College
Western Nebraska Community College

### New Hampshire

Lakes Region Community College
Nashua Community College
River Valley Community College

### New Jersey

Eastwick College
Salem Community College

### New Mexico

Brown Mackie College
    Albuquerque
Eastern New Mexico University:
    Roswell
Mesalands Community College
Navajo Technical University
New Mexico State University
    Alamogordo
    Grants

### New York

Clinton Community College
Columbia-Greene Community College
Herkimer County Community College
Long Island Business Institute
Maria College
Sullivan County Community College
Technical Career Institutes
Trocaire College

### North Carolina

Beaufort County Community College
Bladen Community College
Carteret Community College
College of the Albemarle
Halifax Community College
McDowell Technical Community
    College
Nash Community College
Piedmont Community College
Roanoke-Chowan Community College
Robeson Community College
Rockingham Community College
Southeastern Community College

Southwestern Community College
Wilson Community College

### North Dakota

Williston State College

### Ohio

Belmont College
Bowling Green State University:
    Firelands College
Edison State Community College
Hondros College
North Central State College
Remington College
    Cleveland
Washington State Community College
Wright State University: Lake Campus

### Oklahoma

Eastern Oklahoma State College
Seminole State College
Tulsa Welding School

### Oregon

Clatsop Community College
Umpqua Community College

### Pennsylvania

Berks Technical Institute
Harcum College
Lackawanna College

### Puerto Rico

Centro de Estudios Multidisciplinarios
Colegio de Cinematografia Artes y
    Television
Universal Technology College of
    Puerto Rico

### South Carolina

University of South Carolina
    Lancaster
    Sumter
    Union

### South Dakota

Lake Area Technical Institute
Mitchell Technical Institute
Western Dakota Technical Institute

### Tennessee

Dyersburg State Community College
Remington College
    Memphis
Vatterott College
    Memphis

### Texas

Clarendon College
Frank Phillips College
Galveston College
Lincoln College of Technology
    Grand Prairie
Remington College
    Dallas
    Greenspoint Campus
Western Technical College
Western Texas College

### Virginia

Danville Community College
Paul D. Camp Community College
Richard Bland College
Southwest Virginia Community
    College

### Washington

Big Bend Community College
Lake Washington Institute of
    Technology
Lower Columbia College
Peninsula College

### West Virginia

BridgeValley Community and
    Technical College
Potomac State College of West
    Virginia University

Small (750-1,999)

**Wisconsin**
Southwest Wisconsin Technical
College
University of Wisconsin
Fox Valley
Rock County
Sheboygan
Washington County

**Wyoming**
Central Wyoming College
Eastern Wyoming College
Northwest College

## Medium to large (2,000-7,499)

### Four-year

**Alabama**
Alabama Agricultural and Mechanical
University
Alabama State University
Athens State University
Auburn University at Montgomery
Faulkner University
Jacksonville State University
Samford University
Tuskegee University
University of Alabama
Huntsville
University of Montevallo
University of North Alabama
Virginia College
Birmingham

**Alaska**
University of Alaska
Fairbanks
Southeast

**Arizona**
Embry-Riddle Aeronautical University
Prescott Campus

**Arkansas**
Harding University
Henderson State University
Southern Arkansas University
University of Arkansas
Fort Smith
Monticello
Pine Bluff

**California**
Azusa Pacific University
Biola University
California Baptist University
California Coast University
California Lutheran University
California State University
Channel Islands
Monterey Bay
Chapman University
Fashion Institute of Design and
Merchandising
Los Angeles
Fresno Pacific University
La Sierra University
Loyola Marymount University
Mount Saint Mary's University
Occidental College
Pepperdine University
Point Loma Nazarene University
St. Mary's College of California
Santa Clara University
Stanford University
Trident University International
University of California
Merced
University of La Verne
University of Phoenix
Central Valley
Sacramento Valley
San Diego

University of Redlands
University of San Diego
University of San Francisco
University of the Pacific

**Colorado**
Colorado Christian University
Colorado College
Colorado School of Mines
Colorado State University
Pueblo
Fort Lewis College
Regis University
University of Denver

**Connecticut**
Eastern Connecticut State University
Fairfield University
Quinnipiac University
Sacred Heart University
Trinity College
University of Bridgeport
University of Hartford
University of New Haven
Wesleyan University
Western Connecticut State University
Yale University

**Delaware**
Delaware State University

**District of Columbia**
American University
Catholic University of America
Georgetown University
Howard University
Trinity Washington University
University of the District of Columbia

**Florida**
Barry University
Bethune-Cookman University
Embry-Riddle Aeronautical University
Flagler College
Florida Agricultural and Mechanical
University
Florida Institute of Technology
Florida Southern College
Jacksonville University
Lynn University
Miami International University of Art
and Design
Nova Southeastern University
Palm Beach Atlantic University
Rasmussen College
Ocala
Saint Leo University
Southeastern University
Stetson University
University of Phoenix
Central Florida
University of South Florida
Saint Petersburg
University of Tampa

**Georgia**
Albany State University
Armstrong State University
Art Institute of Atlanta
Berry College
Clark Atlanta University
Clayton State University
College of Coastal Georgia
Columbus State University
Emory University
Fort Valley State University
Georgia College and State University
Georgia Southwestern State University
Mercer University
Morehouse College
Savannah State University
South Georgia State College
Spelman College
University of Phoenix
Atlanta

**Hawaii**
Brigham Young University-Hawaii
Hawaii Pacific University
University of Hawaii
Hilo
West Oahu

**Idaho**
Lewis-Clark State College

**Illinois**
Augustana College
Aurora University
Benedictine University
Bradley University
Chicago State University
Dominican University
Eastern Illinois University
Elmhurst College
Governors State University
Illinois Institute of Technology
Lewis University
McKendree University
Moody Bible Institute
North Central College
North Park University
Olivet Nazarene University
Robert Morris College
Robert Morris University: Chicago
Roosevelt University
Saint Xavier University
School of the Art Institute of Chicago
University of Chicago
University of Illinois
Springfield
Wheaton College

**Indiana**
Butler University
DePauw University
Indiana University
East
Kokomo
Northwest
South Bend
Southeast
Indiana Wesleyan University
Marian University
Rose-Hulman Institute of Technology
University of Evansville
University of Indianapolis
Valparaiso University

**Iowa**
Drake University
Luther College
St. Ambrose University
Upper Iowa University

**Kansas**
Emporia State University
Pittsburg State University
Washburn University

**Kentucky**
Bellarmine University
Campbellsville University
Lindsey Wilson College
Morehead State University
Sullivan University

**Louisiana**
Grambling State University
Louisiana State University
Shreveport
Loyola University New Orleans
McNeese State University
Nicholls State University
Northwestern State University
Southern University and Agricultural
and Mechanical College
Tulane University
University of New Orleans
Xavier University of Louisiana

**Maine**
Husson University
University of Maine
Augusta
University of New England
University of Southern Maine

**Maryland**
Bowie State University
Coppin State University
Frostburg State University
Johns Hopkins University
Loyola University Maryland
Morgan State University
Stevenson University
United States Naval Academy
University of Baltimore
University of Maryland
Eastern Shore

**Massachusetts**
Babson College
Bentley University
Berklee College of Music
Brandeis University
Clark University
College of the Holy Cross
Curry College
Emerson College
Endicott College
Fitchburg State University
Framingham State University
Harvard College
Massachusetts Institute of Technology
MCPHS University
Merrimack College
Mount Holyoke College
Salem State University
Smith College
Springfield College
Stonehill College
Suffolk University
Tufts University
University of Massachusetts
Dartmouth
Wellesley College
Wentworth Institute of Technology
Western New England University
Westfield State University
Williams College
Worcester Polytechnic Institute
Worcester State University

**Michigan**
Baker College
of Allen Park
of Auburn Hills
of Jackson
of Muskegon
of Owosso
Calvin College
Davenport University
Hope College
Lake Superior State University
Lawrence Technological University
Madonna University
Michigan Jewish Institute
Michigan Technological University
Siena Heights University
Spring Arbor University
University of Detroit Mercy
University of Michigan
Dearborn
Flint

**Minnesota**
Augsburg College
Bemidji State University
Bethel University
Carleton College
College of St. Scholastica
Concordia College: Moorhead
Concordia University St. Paul
Gustavus Adolphus College
Hamline University
Macalester College

Minnesota State University
Moorhead
St. Catherine University
St. Olaf College
Southwest Minnesota State University
University of St. Thomas
Walden University
Winona State University

**Mississippi**
Alcorn State University
Belhaven University
Delta State University
Jackson State University
Mississippi College
Mississippi University for Women
William Carey University

**Missouri**
Lincoln University
Lindenwood University
Maryville University of Saint Louis
Missouri Southern State University
Missouri University of Science and
Technology
Missouri Western State University
Northwest Missouri State University
Saint Louis University
Southwest Baptist University
Truman State University
Washington University in St. Louis
Webster University

**Montana**
Montana State University
Billings
Montana Tech of the University of
Montana

**Nebraska**
Bellevue University
Chadron State College
Creighton University
University of Nebraska
Kearney
Wayne State College

**Nevada**
Great Basin College

**New Hampshire**
Dartmouth College
Keene State College
Plymouth State University
Southern New Hampshire University

**New Jersey**
Berkeley College
The College of New Jersey
Fairleigh Dickinson University
College at Florham
Metropolitan Campus
Monmouth University
New Jersey City University
New Jersey Institute of Technology
Princeton University
Ramapo College of New Jersey
Rider University
Rutgers, The State University of New
Jersey
Camden Campus
Saint Peter's University
Seton Hall University
Stevens Institute of Technology

**New Mexico**
Eastern New Mexico University
New Mexico Highlands University

**New York**
Adelphi University
Barnard College
Berkeley College of New York City
Canisius College
City University of New York
Medgar Evers College
York College
Clarkson University
Colgate University

College of Saint Rose
Columbia University
School of General Studies
Culinary Institute of America
Hobart and William Smith Colleges
Hofstra University
Iona College
Ithaca College
Le Moyne College
Long Island University
LIU Brooklyn
LIU Post
Manhattan College
Marist College
Marymount Manhattan College
Mercy College
Molloy College
Monroe College
Mount Saint Mary College
Nazareth College
New York Institute of Technology
Niagara University
Pace University
Pace University: Pleasantville/Briarcliff
Parsons the New School for Design
Parsons The New School for
Design
Pratt Institute
Rensselaer Polytechnic Institute
St. Francis College
St. John Fisher College
St. Joseph's College New York:
Suffolk Campus
St. Lawrence University
School of Visual Arts
Siena College
Skidmore College
SUNY
College at Brockport
College at Cortland
College at Fredonia
College at Geneseo
College at New Paltz
College at Old Westbury
College at Oneonta
College at Oswego
College at Plattsburgh
College at Potsdam
College at Purchase
College of Agriculture and
Technology at Morrisville
Touro College
Union College
University of Rochester
Utica College
Vassar College

**North Carolina**
Campbell University
Duke University
Elizabeth City State University
Elon University
Fayetteville State University
Gardner-Webb University
High Point University
Johnson & Wales University
Charlotte
Methodist University
North Carolina Central University
North Carolina Wesleyan College
University of Mount Olive
University of North Carolina
Asheville
Pembroke
Wake Forest University
Wingate University
Winston-Salem State University

**North Dakota**
Minot State University
University of Mary

**Ohio**
Ashland University
Baldwin Wallace University
Capital University

Case Western Reserve University
Cedarville University
Denison University
Franciscan University of Steubenville
Franklin University
John Carroll University
Oberlin College
Ohio Northern University
Ohio University
Southern Campus at Ironton
Otterbein University
Shawnee State University
Tiffin University
University of Findlay
University of Mount Union
University of Rio Grande
Walsh University
Xavier University

**Oklahoma**
Cameron University
East Central University
Langston University
Northeastern State University
Oral Roberts University
Rogers State University
Southeastern Oklahoma State
University
Southwestern Oklahoma State
University
University of Tulsa

**Oregon**
Eastern Oregon University
George Fox University
Lewis & Clark College
Oregon Institute of Technology
Southern Oregon University
University of Portland
Western Oregon University

**Pennsylvania**
Albright College
Alvernia University
Arcadia University
Bucknell University
California University of Pennsylvania
Carnegie Mellon University
Clarion University of Pennsylvania
DeSales University
Dickinson College
Duquesne University
East Stroudsburg University of
Pennsylvania
Eastern University
Edinboro University
of Pennsylvania
Franklin & Marshall College
Gannon University
Gettysburg College
Grove City College
La Salle University
Lafayette College
Lehigh University
Lock Haven University of
Pennsylvania
Mansfield University of Pennsylvania
Mercyhurst University
Messiah College
Millersville University of Pennsylvania
Misericordia University
Muhlenberg College
Neumann University
Penn State
Abington
Altoona
Berks
Erie, The Behrend College
Harrisburg
Pennsylvania College of Technology
Philadelphia University
Point Park University
Robert Morris University
Saint Joseph's University
Shippensburg University of
Pennsylvania

Susquehanna University
University of Pittsburgh
Johnstown
University of Scranton
University of the Sciences
Villanova University
Widener University
York College of Pennsylvania

**Puerto Rico**
Caribbean University
Inter American University of Puerto
Rico
Aguadilla Campus
Arecibo Campus
Bayamon Campus
Metropolitan Campus
Ponce Campus
San German Campus
National University College
Bayamon
Pontifical Catholic University of Puerto
Rico
Universidad Politecnica de Puerto Rico
University of Puerto Rico
Aguadilla
Arecibo
Bayamon University College
Carolina Regional College
Cayey University College
Humacao
Ponce

**Rhode Island**
Brown University
Bryant University
New England Institute of Technology
Providence College
Rhode Island College
Rhode Island School of Design
Roger Williams University
Salve Regina University

**South Carolina**
Anderson University
Benedict College
Bob Jones University
Charleston Southern University
The Citadel
Francis Marion University
Furman University
Lander University
North Greenville University
South Carolina State University
University of South Carolina
Aiken
Upstate
Winthrop University

**South Dakota**
Black Hills State University
South Dakota School of Mines and
Technology

**Tennessee**
Belmont University
Bethel University
King University
Lee University
Lipscomb University
Southern Adventist University
Tennessee State University
Union University
University of Phoenix
Nashville
University of Tennessee
Martin
Vanderbilt University

**Texas**
Abilene Christian University
Angelo State University
Dallas Baptist University
Houston Baptist University
Midwestern State University
Prairie View A&M University
Rice University
St. Edward's University

223

Medium to large (2,000-7,499)

St. Mary's University
Southern Methodist University
Texas A&M International University
Texas A&M University
    Commerce
    Kingsville
Texas Southern University
Trinity University
University of Houston
    Clear Lake
    Victoria
University of Mary Hardin-Baylor
University of Phoenix
    Houston Westside
University of Texas
    Tyler
    of the Permian Basin
University of the Incarnate Word
Wayland Baptist University
West Texas A&M University

**Utah**

Dixie State University
Southern Utah University
Stevens-Henager College
    Murray
Westminster College

**Vermont**

Champlain College
Middlebury College
Norwich University

**Virginia**

Christopher Newport University
College of William and Mary
Hampton University
Longwood University
Marymount University
Norfolk State University
Regent University
Shenandoah University
University of Mary Washington
University of Richmond
Virginia State University

**Washington**

Evergreen State College
Gonzaga University
Pacific Lutheran University
Seattle Pacific University
Seattle University
University of Puget Sound
University of Washington Bothell
University of Washington Tacoma
Whitworth University

**West Virginia**

Fairmont State University
Shepherd University
West Virginia State University

**Wisconsin**

Carroll University
Carthage College
Concordia University Wisconsin
Lakeland University
Milwaukee School of Engineering
St. Norbert College
University of Wisconsin
    Green Bay
    Parkside
    River Falls
    Superior

*Two-year*

**Alabama**

Bishop State Community College
Gadsden State Community College
George C. Wallace Community
    College at Dothan
Jefferson State Community College
Lawson State Community College
Southern Union State Community
    College
Wallace State Community College at
    Hanceville

**Arizona**

Arizona Western College
Central Arizona College
Cochise College
Eastern Arizona College
GateWay Community College
Mohave Community College
South Mountain Community College
Universal Technical Institute

**Arkansas**

Arkansas State University
    Beebe
National Park College
Pulaski Technical College

**California**

Berkeley City College
Canada College
Cerro Coso Community College
College of Alameda
College of Marin
College of the Redwoods
College of the Siskiyous
Columbia College
Contra Costa College
Crafton Hills College
Lake Tahoe Community College
Lassen Community College
Merritt College
Napa Valley College
Palo Verde College
Porterville College
Taft College
West Hills College: Coalinga
West Hills College: Lemoore
Woodland Community College
Yuba College

**Colorado**

Aims Community College
Colorado Mountain College
Community College of Aurora
Pueblo Community College

**Connecticut**

Capital Community College
Gateway Community College
Goodwin College
Housatonic Community College
Manchester Community College
Middlesex Community College
Naugatuck Valley Community College
Norwalk Community College
Tunxis Community College

**Delaware**

Delaware Technical Community
    College
        Stanton/Wilmington Campus

**Florida**

College of Central Florida
Florida Career College
    Miami
Florida Gateway College
Florida National University
Florida Technical College
    Orlando
Gulf Coast State College
Lake-Sumter State College
Northwest Florida State College
South Florida State College

**Georgia**

Abraham Baldwin Agricultural College
Ashworth College
Athens Technical College
Atlanta Metropolitan State College
Atlanta Technical College
Bainbridge State College
Coastal Pines Technical College
Darton State College
East Georgia State College
Georgia Highlands College
Georgia Military College
Georgia Piedmont Technical College
Gordon State College

Savannah Technical College
Southern Crescent Technical College
Southern Regional Technical College

**Hawaii**

University of Hawaii
    Hawaii Community College
    Honolulu Community College
    Maui College
    Windward Community College

**Idaho**

College of Southern Idaho
North Idaho College

**Illinois**

Black Hawk College
Heartland Community College
Illinois Central College
Kankakee Community College
Kishwaukee College
Lake Land College
Lincoln Land Community College
McHenry County College
Morton College
Parkland College
Prairie State College
Richland Community College
Rock Valley College

**Indiana**

Harrison College
    Indianapolis
Ivy Tech Community College
    Bloomington
    Columbus
    East Central
    Kokomo
    Lafayette
    North Central
    Northeast
    Northwest
    South Central
    Southwest
    Wabash Valley

**Iowa**

Iowa Central Community College
Iowa Western Community College
Marshalltown Community College
Northeast Iowa Community College
Scott Community College
Western Iowa Tech Community
    College

**Kansas**

Allen County Community College
Cowley County Community College
Garden City Community College
Hutchinson Community College
Kansas City Kansas Community
    College
Wichita Area Technical College

**Kentucky**

Ashland Community and Technical
    College
Big Sandy Community and Technical
    College
Elizabethtown Community and
    Technical College
Gateway Community and Technical
    College
Hazard Community and Technical
    College
Maysville Community and Technical
    College
Owensboro Community and Technical
    College
Somerset Community College
Southeast Kentucky Community and
    Technical College

**Louisiana**

Bossier Parish Community College
Louisiana State University
    Eunice
South Louisiana Community College

Southern University
    Shreveport

**Maine**

Central Maine Community College
Southern Maine Community College

**Maryland**

Allegany College of Maryland
Baltimore City Community College
Carroll Community College
Harford Community College

**Massachusetts**

Cape Cod Community College
Holyoke Community College
Massachusetts Bay Community College
Mount Wachusett Community College
North Shore Community College
Northern Essex Community College
Quincy College
Quinsigamond Community College
Roxbury Community College
Springfield Technical Community
    College

**Michigan**

Kalamazoo Valley Community College
Kellogg Community College
Lake Michigan College
Mid Michigan Community College
Mott Community College
Muskegon Community College
North Central Michigan College
Northwestern Michigan College
St. Clair County Community College

**Minnesota**

Alexandria Technical and Community
    College
Central Lakes College
Dakota County Technical College
Hennepin Technical College
Inver Hills Community College
Lake Superior College
Minnesota State Community and
    Technical College
Minnesota West Community and
    Technical College
North Hennepin Community College
Northland Community & Technical
    College
Ridgewater College
Riverland Community College
Rochester Community and Technical
    College
St. Cloud Technical and Community
    College
South Central College

**Mississippi**

East Mississippi Community College
Jones County Junior College
Meridian Community College
Northeast Mississippi Community
    College

**Missouri**

Crowder College
East Central College
Jefferson College
Moberly Area Community College
State Fair Community College

**Montana**

Flathead Valley Community College

**Nebraska**

Metropolitan Community College
Northeast Community College

**Nevada**

Western Nevada College

**New Hampshire**

Great Bay Community College
Manchester Community College
NHTI-Concord's Community College

**New Jersey**
Atlantic Cape Community College
Cumberland County College
Mercer County Community College
Ocean County College
Raritan Valley Community College
Rowan College at Gloucester
Sussex County Community College

**New Mexico**
New Mexico Junior College
San Juan College
Santa Fe Community College

**New York**
Adirondack Community College
ASA College
Broome Community College
Cayuga Community College
City University of New York
    Hostos Community College
Corning Community College
Dutchess Community College
Fulton-Montgomery Community
    College
Genesee Community College
Jamestown Community College
Mohawk Valley Community College
Niagara County Community College
North Country Community College
Orange County Community College
Rockland Community College
Schenectady County Community
    College
SUNY
    College of Agriculture and
        Technology at Cobleskill
    College of Technology at Alfred
    College of Technology at Canton
    College of Technology at Delhi
Tompkins Cortland Community
    College
Ulster County Community College

**North Carolina**
Alamance Community College
Asheville-Buncombe Technical
    Community College
Craven Community College
Johnston Community College
Richmond Community College
Sandhills Community College
Vance-Granville Community College
Wilkes Community College

**North Dakota**
Bismarck State College
North Dakota State College of Science

**Ohio**
Central Ohio Technical College
Cincinnati State Technical and
    Community College
Clark State Community College
Herzing University
Hocking College
James A. Rhodes State College
Miami University
    Hamilton
    Middletown
Terra State Community College
University of Akron: Wayne College
University of Cincinnati
    Blue Ash College
    Clermont College
University of Northwestern Ohio

**Oklahoma**
Carl Albert State College
Murray State College
Northeastern Oklahoma Agricultural
    and Mechanical College
Oklahoma State University
    Institute of Technology:
        Okmulgee
        Oklahoma City

Redlands Community College
Rose State College

**Oregon**
Clackamas Community College
Linn-Benton Community College
Mt. Hood Community College
Rogue Community College
Southwestern Oregon Community
    College
Treasure Valley Community College

**Pennsylvania**
Butler County Community College
Community College of Beaver County
Lehigh Carbon Community College
Pennsylvania Highlands Community
    College
Reading Area Community College
Westmoreland County Community
    College

**Puerto Rico**
EDIC College
ICPR Junior College
Ponce Paramedical College

**South Carolina**
Aïken Technical College
Florence-Darlington Technical College
Horry-Georgetown Technical College
Orangeburg-Calhoun Technical College
Piedmont Technical College
Spartanburg Community College
Tri-County Technical College

**Tennessee**
Cleveland State Community College
Jackson State Community College
Motlow State Community College
Nashville State Community College
Roane State Community College
Volunteer State Community College
Walters State Community College

**Texas**
Brazosport College
Cedar Valley College
Cisco College
Coastal Bend College
Grayson College
Hill College
Kilgore College
Lamar Institute of Technology
Lamar State College at Orange
Lamar State College at Port Arthur
Midland College
Northeast Texas Community College
Odessa College
Panola College
Paris Junior College
Ranger College
Southwest Texas Junior College
Trinity Valley Community College
Victoria College
Weatherford College
Wharton County Junior College

**Utah**
Snow College

**Vermont**
Community College of Vermont

**Virginia**
Blue Ridge Community College
Germanna Community College
Patrick Henry Community College
Piedmont Virginia Community College
Rappahannock Community College

**Washington**
Bates Technical College
Bellingham Technical College
Cascadia College
Centralia College
Clover Park Technical College
Columbia Basin College
Everett Community College

Grays Harbor College
Highline College
North Seattle College
Olympic College
Renton Technical College
Shoreline Community College
Skagit Valley College
South Puget Sound Community
    College
Spokane Community College
Tacoma Community College
Walla Walla Community College
Whatcom Community College
Yakima Valley Community College

**West Virginia**
Pierpont Community and Technical
    College
West Virginia Northern Community
    College
West Virginia University at
    Parkersburg

**Wisconsin**
Blackhawk Technical College
Bryant & Stratton College
    Milwaukee
Chippewa Valley Technical College
Fox Valley Technical College
Gateway Technical College
Lakeshore Technical College
Moraine Park Technical College
Northcentral Technical College
University of Wisconsin
    Waukesha
Western Technical College
Wisconsin Indianhead Technical
    College

**Wyoming**
Casper College
Laramie County Community College
Sheridan College
Western Wyoming Community College

---

### Large (7,500-14,499)

*Four-year*

**Alabama**
Troy University
University of Alabama
    Birmingham
University of South Alabama

**Alaska**
University of Alaska
    Anchorage

**Arizona**
Argosy University
    Online

**Arkansas**
Arkansas State University
Arkansas Tech University
University of Arkansas
    Little Rock
University of Central Arkansas

**California**
Academy of Art University
California State University
    Bakersfield
    Dominguez Hills
    East Bay
    San Marcos
    Stanislaus
Humboldt State University
National University
Sonoma State University

**Colorado**
Colorado Mesa University
University of Colorado
    Colorado Springs

    Denver
University of Northern Colorado

**Connecticut**
Central Connecticut State University
Southern Connecticut State University

**District of Columbia**
George Washington University

**Florida**
Embry-Riddle Aeronautical University
    Worldwide Campus
Florida Gulf Coast University
University of Miami
University of North Florida
University of West Florida

**Georgia**
Georgia Gwinnett College
Georgia Institute of Technology
Savannah College of Art and Design
University of West Georgia
Valdosta State University

**Hawaii**
University of Hawaii
    Manoa

**Idaho**
Idaho State University
University of Idaho

**Illinois**
Chamberlain College of Nursing
    Addison
Columbia College Chicago
DeVry University
    Online
Loyola University Chicago
Northern Illinois University
Northwestern University
Southern Illinois University Carbondale
Southern Illinois University
    Edwardsville
Western Illinois University

**Indiana**
Indiana Institute of Technology
Indiana State University
Indiana University
    Purdue University Fort Wayne
Purdue University
    North Central
    Northwest
University of Notre Dame
University of Southern Indiana

**Iowa**
University of Northern Iowa

**Kansas**
Fort Hays State University
Grantham University
Wichita State University

**Kentucky**
Eastern Kentucky University
Murray State University
Northern Kentucky University
Western Kentucky University

**Louisiana**
Louisiana Tech University
Southeastern Louisiana University
University of Louisiana
    Monroe

**Maine**
University of Maine

**Maryland**
Salisbury University
University of Maryland
    Baltimore County

**Massachusetts**
Boston College
Bridgewater State University

225

Large (7,500-14,499)

University of Massachusetts
   Boston
   Lowell

**Michigan**
Ferris State University
Northern Michigan University
Saginaw Valley State University

**Minnesota**
Capella University
Minnesota State University
   Mankato
Saint Cloud State University
University of Minnesota
   Duluth

**Mississippi**
University of Mississippi
   University of Southern Mississippi

**Missouri**
Park University
Southeast Missouri State University
University of Central Missouri
University of Missouri
   Kansas City
   St. Louis

**Montana**
Montana State University
University of Montana

**Nebraska**
University of Nebraska
   Omaha

**New Hampshire**
University of New Hampshire

**New Jersey**
Kean University
Rowan University
Rutgers, The State University of New
   Jersey
     Newark Campus
Stockton University
William Paterson University of New
   Jersey

**New Mexico**
New Mexico State University

**New York**
City University of New York
   Baruch College
   Brooklyn College
   City College
   College of Staten Island
   John Jay College of Criminal
     Justice
   Lehman College
Cornell University
Fashion Institute of Technology
Fordham University
Rochester Institute of Technology
St. John's University
SUNY
   College at Buffalo
   Empire State College
   Farmingdale State College
   University at Albany
   University at Binghamton
Syracuse University

**North Carolina**
University of North Carolina
   Wilmington
Western Carolina University

**North Dakota**
North Dakota State University
University of North Dakota

**Ohio**
Bowling Green State University
Cleveland State University
University of Dayton
Wright State University
Youngstown State University

**Pennsylvania**
Bloomsburg University of
   Pennsylvania
Indiana University of Pennsylvania
Kutztown University of Pennsylvania
Slippery Rock University of
   Pennsylvania
University of Pennsylvania
West Chester University of
   Pennsylvania

**Puerto Rico**
Turabo University
Universidad del Este
Universidad Metropolitana
University of Puerto Rico
   Mayaguez
   Rio Piedras

**Rhode Island**
Johnson & Wales University
   Providence
University of Rhode Island

**South Carolina**
Coastal Carolina University
College of Charleston

**South Dakota**
South Dakota State University
University of South Dakota

**Tennessee**
Austin Peay State University
East Tennessee State University
Tennessee Technological University
University of Tennessee
   Chattanooga

**Texas**
Baylor University
Lamar University
Stephen F. Austin State University
Tarleton State University
Texas A&M University
   Corpus Christi
Texas Christian University
Texas Woman's University
University of Houston
   Downtown

**Vermont**
University of Vermont

**Virginia**
ECPI University
Liberty University
Radford University

**Washington**
Central Washington University
Eastern Washington University
Green River College
Western Washington University

**West Virginia**
Marshall University

**Wisconsin**
Marquette University
University of Wisconsin
   Eau Claire
   La Crosse
   Oshkosh
   Platteville
   Stevens Point
   Stout
   Whitewater

**Wyoming**
University of Wyoming

***Two-year***

**Alabama**
Calhoun Community College

**Arizona**
Chandler-Gilbert Community College
Estrella Mountain Community College

Paradise Valley Community College
Phoenix College
Scottsdale Community College
Yavapai College

**California**
Antelope Valley College
Butte College
Cabrillo College
Chabot College
Citrus College
Coastline Community College
College of San Mateo
College of the Desert
College of the Sequoias
Cosumnes River College
Cuesta College
Cuyamaca College
Evergreen Valley College
Folsom Lake College
Golden West College
Hartnell College
Laney College
Las Positas College
Los Angeles Harbor College
Los Angeles Mission College
Los Angeles Southwest College
Los Medanos College
Mission College
Monterey Peninsula College
Moorpark College
Moreno Valley College
Norco College
Ohlone College
Reedley College
San Bernardino Valley College
San Deigo Miramar College
   San Diego Miramar College
San Jose City College
Shasta College
Skyline College
Solano Community College
Ventura College
Victor Valley College
West Los Angeles College
West Valley College

**Colorado**
Community College of Denver
Front Range Community College
Pikes Peak Community College
Red Rocks Community College

**Florida**
Daytona State College
Pasco-Hernando State College
Pensacola State College
Polk State College
Santa Fe College
State College of Florida, Manatee-
   Sarasota
Tallahassee Community College

**Georgia**
Central Georgia Technical College
Chattahoochee Technical College

**Hawaii**
University of Hawaii
   Kapiolani Community College

**Idaho**
College of Western Idaho

**Illinois**
College of DuPage
Elgin Community College
Harper College
Joliet Junior College
Moraine Valley Community College
Oakton Community College
Southwestern Illinois College
Triton College

**Indiana**
Vincennes University

**Iowa**
Des Moines Area Community College

**Kansas**
Barton County Community College
Butler Community College

**Kentucky**
Bluegrass Community and Technical
   College
Jefferson Community and Technical
   College

**Louisiana**
Baton Rouge Community College

**Maryland**
Anne Arundel Community College
College of Southern Maryland
Howard Community College
Prince George's Community College

**Massachusetts**
Bristol Community College
Bunker Hill Community College
Massasoit Community College
Middlesex Community College

**Michigan**
Delta College
Grand Rapids Community College
Henry Ford College
Lansing Community College
Schoolcraft College
Washtenaw Community College
Wayne County Community College

**Minnesota**
Century College
Minneapolis Community and Technical
   College
Normandale Community College

**Mississippi**
Hinds Community College
Mississippi Gulf Coast Community
   College

**Missouri**
Ozarks Technical Community College

**Nevada**
Truckee Meadows Community College

**New Jersey**
Brookdale Community College
County College of Morris
Essex County College
Hudson County Community College
Middlesex County College
Passaic County Community College
Rowan College at Burlington County
Union County College

**New Mexico**
Dona Ana Community College of New
   Mexico State University

**New York**
City University of New York
   Bronx Community College
   Queensborough Community
     College
Erie Community College
Hudson Valley Community College
Monroe Community College
Onondaga Community College
Westchester Community College

**North Carolina**
Fayetteville Technical Community
   College
Guilford Technical Community College

**Ohio**
Columbus State Community College
Cuyahoga Community College
Lakeland Community College
Lorain County Community College
Owens Community College
Sinclair Community College
Stark State College

**Oklahoma**
Oklahoma City Community College
Tulsa Community College

**Oregon**
Chemeketa Community College
Lane Community College

**Pennsylvania**
Bucks County Community College
Community College of Allegheny
County
Delaware County Community College
Harrisburg Area Community College
Montgomery County Community
College
Northampton Community College

**Rhode Island**
Community College of Rhode Island

**South Carolina**
Greenville Technical College
Midlands Technical College
Trident Technical College

**Tennessee**
Pellissippi State Community College
Southwest Tennessee Community
College

**Texas**
Amarillo College
Brookhaven College
Central Texas College
Del Mar College
Eastfield College
El Centro College
Laredo Community College
McLennan Community College
Mountain View College
Navarro College
North Central Texas College
North Lake College
Northwest Vista College
Richland College
St. Philip's College
South Plains College
Texas State Technical College

**Virginia**
J. Sargeant Reynolds Community
College
Thomas Nelson Community College
Virginia Western Community College

**Washington**
Bellevue College
Clark College
Edmonds Community College
Pierce College
Seattle Central College
South Seattle College
Spokane Falls Community College

**Wisconsin**
Milwaukee Area Technical College

---

**Very large (15,000 or more)**

*Four-year*

**Alabama**
Auburn University
Columbia Southern University
University of Alabama

**Arizona**
Arizona State University
Grand Canyon University
Northern Arizona University
University of Arizona
University of Phoenix
Phoenix-Hohokam

**Arkansas**
University of Arkansas

**California**
Ashford University
California Polytechnic State University:
San Luis Obispo
California State Polytechnic University:
Pomona
California State University
Chico
Fresno
Fullerton
Long Beach
Los Angeles
Sacramento
San Bernardino
San Diego State University
San Francisco State University
San Jose State University
University of California
Berkeley
Davis
Irvine
Los Angeles
Riverside
San Diego
Santa Barbara
Santa Cruz
University of Phoenix
Southern California
University of Southern California

**Colorado**
Colorado State University
Metropolitan State University of
Denver
University of Colorado
Boulder

**Connecticut**
University of Connecticut

**Delaware**
University of Delaware

**Florida**
Florida Atlantic University
Florida International University
Florida State University
Full Sail University
Keiser University
University of Central Florida
University of Florida
University of South Florida

**Georgia**
Georgia Southern University
Georgia State University
Kennesaw State University
University of Georgia
University of North Georgia

**Idaho**
Boise State University
Brigham Young University-Idaho

**Illinois**
DePaul University
Illinois State University
University of Illinois
Chicago
Urbana-Champaign

**Indiana**
Ball State University
Indiana University
Bloomington
Purdue University Indianapolis
Purdue University

**Iowa**
Iowa State University
Kaplan University
Davenport
University of Iowa

**Kansas**
Kansas State University
University of Kansas

**Kentucky**
University of Kentucky
University of Louisville

**Louisiana**
Louisiana State University and
Agricultural and Mechanical College
University of Louisiana at Lafayette

**Maryland**
Towson University
University of Maryland
College Park
University College

**Massachusetts**
Boston University
Northeastern University
University of Massachusetts
Amherst

**Michigan**
Central Michigan University
Eastern Michigan University
Grand Valley State University
Michigan State University
Oakland University
University of Michigan
Wayne State University
Western Michigan University

**Minnesota**
University of Minnesota
Twin Cities

**Mississippi**
Mississippi State University
University of Mississippi

**Missouri**
Missouri State University
University of Missouri
Columbia

**Nebraska**
University of Nebraska
Lincoln

**Nevada**
University of Nevada
Las Vegas
Reno

**New Jersey**
Montclair State University
Rutgers, The State University of New
Jersey
New Brunswick/Piscataway
Campus
Thomas Edison State University

**New Mexico**
University of New Mexico

**New York**
City University of New York
Hunter College
New York City College of
Technology
Queens College
Excelsior College
New York University
SUNY
University at Buffalo
University at Stony Brook

**North Carolina**
Appalachian State University
East Carolina University
North Carolina State University
University of North Carolina
Chapel Hill
Charlotte
Greensboro

**Ohio**
Kent State University
Miami University
Oxford

Ohio State University
Columbus Campus
Ohio University
University of Akron
University of Cincinnati
University of Toledo

**Oklahoma**
Oklahoma State University
University of Central Oklahoma
University of Oklahoma

**Oregon**
Oregon State University
Portland State University
University of Oregon

**Pennsylvania**
Drexel University
Penn State
University Park
Temple University
University of Pittsburgh

**South Carolina**
Clemson University
University of South Carolina
Columbia

**Tennessee**
Middle Tennessee State University
University of Memphis
University of Tennessee
Knoxville

**Texas**
Sam Houston State University
Texas A&M University
Texas State University
Texas Tech University
University of Houston
University of North Texas
University of Texas
Arlington
Austin
Dallas
El Paso
San Antonio
University Of Texas Rio Grande
Valley

**Utah**
Brigham Young University
University of Utah
Utah State University
Utah Valley University
Weber State University

**Virginia**
George Mason University
James Madison University
Old Dominion University
University of Virginia
Virginia Commonwealth University
Virginia Polytechnic Institute and State
University

**Washington**
University of Washington
Washington State University

**West Virginia**
American Public University System
West Virginia University

**Wisconsin**
University of Wisconsin
Madison
Milwaukee

*Two-year*

**Arizona**
Mesa Community College
Penn Foster College
Rio Salado College

**California**
Allan Hancock College
American River College

Very large (15,000 or more)

Bakersfield College
Cerritos College
Chaffey College
City College of San Francisco
College of the Canyons
Cypress College
De Anza College
Diablo Valley College
East Los Angeles College
El Camino College
Foothill College
Fresno City College
Fullerton College
Glendale Community College
Grossmont College
Irvine Valley College
Long Beach City College
Los Angeles City College
Los Angeles Pierce College
Los Angeles Trade and Technical
    College
Los Angeles Valley College
MiraCosta College
Modesto Junior College
Mount San Antonio College
Mount San Jacinto College
Orange Coast College
Palomar College
Pasadena City College
Rio Hondo College
Riverside City College
Sacramento City College
Saddleback College
San Diego City College
San Diego Mesa College
San Joaquin Delta College
Santa Ana College
Santa Barbara City College
Santa Monica College
Santa Rosa Junior College
Santiago Canyon College
Sierra College
Southwestern College

**Florida**
Broward College
Eastern Florida State College
Florida SouthWestern State College
Florida State College at Jacksonville
Hillsborough Community College
Indian River State College
Miami Dade College
Palm Beach State College
St. Petersburg College
Seminole State College of Florida
Southern Technical College
Valencia College

**Georgia**
Georgia Perimeter College

**Illinois**
College of Lake County

**Indiana**
Ivy Tech Community College
    Central Indiana

**Louisiana**
Delgado Community College

**Maryland**
Community College of Baltimore
    County

**Michigan**
Macomb Community College
Oakland Community College

**Missouri**
Metropolitan Community College -
    Kansas City

**Nevada**
College of Southern Nevada

**New York**
City University of New York
    Borough of Manhattan
        Community College
    Kingsborough Community College
    LaGuardia Community College
Nassau Community College
Suffolk County Community College

**North Carolina**
Central Piedmont Community College
Wake Technical Community College

**Oregon**
Portland Community College

**Pennsylvania**
Community College of Philadelphia

**Texas**
Austin Community College
Blinn College
Collin County Community College
    District
Houston Community College System
Lone Star College System
San Antonio College
San Jacinto College
South Texas College
Tarrant County College

**Utah**
Salt Lake Community College

**Virginia**
Northern Virginia Community College
Tidewater Community College

**Wisconsin**
Madison Area Technical College

# College type

## Four-year

### Alabama
Athens State University
Birmingham-Southern College
Concordia College
Faulkner University
Huntingdon College
Judson College
Miles College
Oakwood University
Spring Hill College
Stillman College
Talladega College
University of Mobile
University of Montevallo

### Alaska
Alaska Pacific University
University of Alaska
    Southeast

### Arizona
Arizona Christian University
Prescott College

### Arkansas
Arkansas Baptist College
Arkansas Tech University
Ecclesia College
Henderson State University
Hendrix College
John Brown University
Lyon College
Ouachita Baptist University
Philander Smith College
University of the Ozarks
Williams Baptist College

### California
American Jewish University
Antioch University
    Los Angeles
    Santa Barbara
California Lutheran University
California State University
    Bakersfield
    Chico
    Monterey Bay
    San Bernardino
    Stanislaus
Chapman University
Claremont McKenna College
Concordia University Irvine
Fresno Pacific University
Harvey Mudd College
Hope International University
Horizon University
Humboldt State University
Humphreys College
La Sierra University
Marymount California University
The Master's University
Menlo College
Mills College
Mount Saint Mary's University
NewSchool of Architecture & Design
Notre Dame de Namur University
Occidental College
Pacific Union College
Patten University
Pepperdine University
Pitzer College
Point Loma Nazarene University
Pomona College

Providence Christian College
St. Mary's College of California
San Diego Christian College
San Jose State University
Scripps College
Soka University of America
Sonoma State University
Southern California Institute of
    Architecture
Stanford University
Thomas Aquinas College
University of Redlands
University of the West
Vanguard University of Southern
    California
Westmont College
Whittier College
William Jessup University

### Colorado
Adams State University
Colorado Christian University
Colorado College
Colorado Mesa University
Fort Lewis College
Metropolitan State University of
    Denver
Naropa University
Regis University
Western State Colorado University

### Connecticut
Albertus Magnus College
Charter Oak State College
Connecticut College
Eastern Connecticut State University
Holy Apostles College and Seminary
Mitchell College
Trinity College
University of Saint Joseph
Wesleyan University

### Delaware
Wesley College

### District of Columbia
Gallaudet University
Trinity Washington University
University of the District of Columbia

### Florida
Ave Maria University
Beacon College
Bethune-Cookman University
Eckerd College
Edward Waters College
Flagler College
Florida Memorial University
Florida Southern College
Jacksonville University
New College of Florida
Palm Beach Atlantic University
Rollins College
Southeastern University
University of Tampa
Warner University

### Georgia
Agnes Scott College
Berry College
Brenau University
Brewton-Parker College
Carver College
College of Coastal Georgia
Columbus State University
Covenant College
Fort Valley State University
Georgia College and State University
Georgia Gwinnett College

LaGrange College
Middle Georgia State University
Morehouse College
Oglethorpe University
Paine College
Point University
Reinhardt University
Shorter University
South Georgia State College
Spelman College
Thomas University
Toccoa Falls College
Truett McConnell University
University of North Georgia
Wesleyan College
Young Harris College

### Hawaii
Brigham Young University-Hawaii
Hawaii Pacific University
University of Hawaii
    Hilo
    West Oahu

### Idaho
College of Idaho
Lewis-Clark State College
New Saint Andrews College

### Illinois
Augustana College
Benedictine University
Blackburn College
Concordia University Chicago
Dominican University
Elmhurst College
Eureka College
Greenville College
Illinois College
Illinois Wesleyan University
Judson University
Knox College
Lake Forest College
McKendree University
Monmouth College
North Central College
North Park University
Olivet Nazarene University
Quincy University
Rockford University
St. Augustine College
Shimer College
Trinity Christian College
Trinity International University
University of Chicago
University of Illinois
    Springfield
University of St. Francis
Wheaton College

### Indiana
Bethel College
Calumet College of St. Joseph
DePauw University
Earlham College
Franklin College
Goshen College
Hanover College
Holy Cross College
Huntington University
Indiana Wesleyan University
Manchester University
Marian University
Martin University
Oakland City University
Saint Joseph's College
Saint Mary's College
St. Mary-of-the-Woods College
Taylor University
University of Evansville
University of Indianapolis
University of Southern Indiana
Wabash College

### Iowa
Briar Cliff University
Buena Vista University

Central College
Clarke University
Coe College
Cornell College
Divine Word College
Dordt College
Graceland University
Grand View University
Grinnell College
Iowa Wesleyan College
Loras College
Luther College
Maharishi University of Management
Morningside College
Mount Mercy University
Northwestern College
Simpson College
Upper Iowa University
Waldorf University
Wartburg College
William Penn University

### Kansas
Baker University
Benedictine College
Bethany College
Bethel College
Central Christian College of Kansas
Friends University
Kansas Wesleyan University
McPherson College
MidAmerica Nazarene University
Newman University
Ottawa University
Southwestern College
Sterling College
Tabor College

### Kentucky
Alice Lloyd College
Asbury University
Bellarmine University
Berea College
Brescia University
Centre College
Georgetown College
Kentucky State University
Kentucky Wesleyan College
Lindsey Wilson College
Midway College
St. Catharine College
Thomas More College
Transylvania University
Union College
University of Pikeville
University of the Cumberlands

### Louisiana
Centenary College of Louisiana
Dillard University
Louisiana College
Loyola University New Orleans
St. Joseph Seminary College
University of Holy Cross

### Maine
Bates College
Bowdoin College
Colby College
College of the Atlantic
Saint Joseph's College of Maine
Thomas College
Unity College
University of Maine
    Farmington
    Machias

### Maryland
Coppin State University
Goucher College
Hood College
McDaniel College
Mount St. Mary's University
Notre Dame of Maryland University
St. John's College
St. Mary's College of Maryland
Salisbury University

Liberal arts colleges

University of Baltimore
Washington Adventist University
Washington College

**Massachusetts**

American International College
Amherst College
Anna Maria College
Assumption College
Bard College at Simon's Rock
Bay Path University
Becker College
Cambridge College
Clark University
College of the Holy Cross
Curry College
Eastern Nazarene College
Elms College
Emmanuel College
Endicott College
Fisher College
Fitchburg State University
Gordon College
Hampshire College
Harvard College
Hellenic College/Holy Cross
Lasell College
Lesley University
Massachusetts College of Liberal Arts
Mount Holyoke College
Mount Ida College
Newbury College
Nichols College
Pine Manor College
Regis College
Simmons College
Smith College
Springfield College
Stonehill College
Wellesley College
Wheaton College
Wheelock College
Williams College
Worcester State University

**Michigan**

Adrian College
Albion College
Alma College
Aquinas College
Calvin College
Concordia University
Cornerstone University
Finlandia University
Hillsdale College
Hope College
Kalamazoo College
Kuyper College
Madonna University
Marygrove College
Michigan Jewish Institute
Olivet College
Robert B Miller College
    Robert B. Miller College
Rochester College
Siena Heights University
Spring Arbor University

**Minnesota**

Augsburg College
Bethany Lutheran College
Bethel University
Carleton College
College of St. Benedict
College of St. Scholastica
Concordia College: Moorhead
Crown College
Gustavus Adolphus College
Hamline University
Macalester College
St. Catherine University
St. John's University
St. Olaf College
Southwest Minnesota State University
University of Minnesota
    Morris

University of Northwestern - St. Paul
University of St. Thomas

**Mississippi**

Belhaven University
Blue Mountain College
Millsaps College
Mississippi University for Women
Mississippi Valley State University
Rust College
Tougaloo College
William Carey University

**Missouri**

Avila University
Central Methodist University
College of the Ozarks
Columbia College
Cottey College
Culver-Stockton College
Drury University
Evangel University
Fontbonne University
Hannibal-LaGrange University
Lincoln University
Lindenwood University
Missouri Baptist University
Missouri Southern State University
Missouri Valley College
Missouri Western State University
Rockhurst University
Stephens College
Truman State University
Westminster College
William Jewell College

**Montana**

Carroll College
Rocky Mountain College
Salish Kootenai College
University of Great Falls
University of Montana
University of Montana: Western

**Nebraska**

Chadron State College
College of Saint Mary
Doane University
Hastings College
Midland University
Nebraska Wesleyan University
Peru State College
Union College
Wayne State College
York College

**Nevada**

Sierra Nevada College

**New Hampshire**

Colby-Sawyer College
Dartmouth College
Franklin Pierce University
Granite State College
Keene State College
New England College
Saint Anselm College
Thomas More College of Liberal Arts
University of New Hampshire at
    Manchester

**New Jersey**

Bloomfield College
Caldwell University
Centenary University
The College of New Jersey
College of St. Elizabeth
Drew University
Felician University
Georgian Court University
Kean University
Pillar College
Ramapo College of New Jersey
Stockton University
William Paterson University of New
    Jersey

**New Mexico**

Institute of American Indian Arts
New Mexico Institute of Mining and
    Technology
St. John's College
Santa Fe University of Art and Design
University of the Southwest

**New York**

Bard College
Barnard College
Canisius College
Cazenovia College
City University of New York
    Baruch College
    Brooklyn College
    City College
    College of Staten Island
    Hunter College
    John Jay College of Criminal
        Justice
    Lehman College
    Medgar Evers College
    Queens College
    York College
Colgate University
College of Mount St. Vincent
College of New Rochelle
College of Saint Rose
Columbia University
    School of General Studies
Concordia College
D'Youville College
Daemen College
Dominican College of Blauvelt
Elmira College
Eugene Lang College The New School
    for Liberal Arts
Excelsior College
Hamilton College
Hartwick College
Hilbert College
Hobart and William Smith Colleges
Houghton College
Iona College
Ithaca College
Jewish Theological Seminary of
    America
Keuka College
The King's College
Le Moyne College
Long Island University
    LIU Brooklyn
    LIU Post
Manhattan College
Manhattanville College
Marist College
Marymount Manhattan College
Medaille College
Medaille College: Rochester
Mercy College
Metropolitan College of New York
Molloy College
Mount Saint Mary College
Nazareth College
Nyack College
Paul Smith's College
Roberts Wesleyan College
St. Francis College
St. John Fisher College
St. Joseph's College New York:
    Suffolk Campus
St. Joseph's College, New York
St. Lawrence University
St. Thomas Aquinas College
Sarah Lawrence College
Siena College
Skidmore College
SUNY
    College at Brockport
    College at Buffalo
    College at Cortland
    College at Fredonia
    College at Geneseo
    College at New Paltz
    College at Old Westbury

College at Oneonta
College at Plattsburgh
College at Potsdam
College at Purchase
College of Environmental Science
    and Forestry
Empire State College
Touro College
Union College
Utica College
Vassar College
Wagner College
Wells College

**North Carolina**

Barton College
Belmont Abbey College
Bennett College for Women
Brevard College
Campbell University
Catawba College
Chowan University
Davidson College
Elizabeth City State University
Elon University
Gardner-Webb University
Greensboro College
Guilford College
High Point University
Johnson C. Smith University
Lees-McRae College
Lenoir-Rhyne University
Livingstone College
Mars Hill University
Meredith College
Methodist University
Montreat College
North Carolina Wesleyan College
Pfeiffer University
St. Andrews University
Saint Augustine's University
Salem College
Shaw University
University of North Carolina
    Asheville
    Pembroke
Warren Wilson College

**North Dakota**

Minot State University
University of Jamestown
Valley City State University

**Ohio**

Ashland University
Bluffton University
Cedarville University
Central State University
College of Wooster
Defiance College
Denison University
Heidelberg University
Hiram College
Kenyon College
Lake Erie College
Marietta College
Mount St. Joseph University
Muskingum University
Notre Dame College
Oberlin College
Ohio Dominican University
Ohio Wesleyan University
Otterbein University
Tiffin University
University of Rio Grande
Ursuline College
Walsh University
Wilberforce University
Wilmington College
Wittenberg University

**Oklahoma**

Bacone College
Hillsdale Free Will Baptist College
Langston University
Oklahoma Baptist University
Oklahoma City University

Oklahoma Panhandle State University
Oklahoma Wesleyan University
Oral Roberts University
St. Gregory's University
Southeastern Oklahoma State
  University
Southern Nazarene University
Southwestern Christian University
University of Science and Arts of
  Oklahoma

## Oregon
Art Institute of Portland
Concordia University
Corban University
Eastern Oregon University
Gutenberg College
Lewis & Clark College
Linfield College
Marylhurst University
Reed College
Southern Oregon University
Warner Pacific College
Western Oregon University
Willamette University

## Pennsylvania
Albright College
Allegheny College
Alvernia University
Bryn Athyn College
Bryn Mawr College
Cabrini University
Cedar Crest College
Chatham University
Chestnut Hill College
Dickinson College
Elizabethtown College
Franklin & Marshall College
Geneva College
Gettysburg College
Gratz College
Grove City College
Gwynedd Mercy University
Haverford College
Immaculata University
Juniata College
Keystone College
King's College
La Roche College
La Salle University
Lafayette College
Lebanon Valley College
Lincoln University
Lock Haven University of
  Pennsylvania
Lycoming College
Mercyhurst University
Messiah College
Millersville University of Pennsylvania
Misericordia University
Moravian College
Mount Aloysius College
Muhlenberg College
Rosemont College
St. Francis University
St. Vincent College
Seton Hill University
Susquehanna University
Swarthmore College
Thiel College
University of Pittsburgh
  Greensburg
  Johnstown
University of Scranton
University of Valley Forge
Ursinus College
Washington & Jefferson College
Waynesburg University
Westminster College
Wilson College
York College of Pennsylvania

## Puerto Rico
Atlantic University College
Bayamon Central University

Inter American University of Puerto
  Rico
  Aguadilla Campus
  Arecibo Campus
Universidad Adventista de las Antillas
Universidad Metropolitana
University of Puerto Rico
  Aguadilla
  Arecibo
  Cayey University College
  Humacao

## Rhode Island
Brown University
Bryant University
Providence College
Rhode Island College
Salve Regina University

## South Carolina
Allen University
Benedict College
Bob Jones University
Charleston Southern University
Claflin University
Coker College
College of Charleston
Columbia College
Converse College
Erskine College
Francis Marion University
Furman University
Lander University
Limestone College
Morris College
Newberry College
North Greenville University
Presbyterian College
Southern Wesleyan University
University of South Carolina
  Aiken
  Beaufort
Voorhees College
Wofford College

## South Dakota
Dakota Wesleyan University
Mount Marty College
Northern State University
Sinte Gleska University
University of Sioux Falls

## Tennessee
American Baptist College
Aquinas College
Austin Peay State University
Bethel University
Bryan College
  Dayton
Carson-Newman University
Cumberland University
Fisk University
Freed-Hardeman University
King University
Lane College
Lee University
LeMoyne-Owen College
Lincoln Memorial University
Lipscomb University
Martin Methodist College
Maryville College
Milligan College
Rhodes College
Sewanee: The University of the South
Southern Adventist University
Tennessee Wesleyan College
Trevecca Nazarene University
Tusculum College
Union University
Williamson College

## Texas
Austin College
Concordia University Texas
East Texas Baptist University
Houston Baptist University
Howard Payne University

Huston-Tillotson University
Jarvis Christian College
Lubbock Christian University
McMurry University
Midwestern State University
Paul Quinn College
St. Mary's University
Schreiner University
Southwestern Adventist University
Southwestern Christian College
Southwestern University
Texas College
Texas Lutheran University
University of Dallas
University of St. Thomas
Wayland Baptist University
Wiley College

## Utah
Stevens-Henager College
  Ogden
Westminster College

## Vermont
Bennington College
Castleton University
Champlain College
College of St. Joseph in Vermont
Goddard College
Green Mountain College
Johnson State College
Lyndon State College
Marlboro College
Middlebury College
Saint Michael's College
Southern Vermont College
Sterling College

## Virginia
Averett University
Bluefield College
Bridgewater College
Christendom College
Christopher Newport University
Eastern Mennonite University
Emory & Henry College
Ferrum College
Hampden-Sydney College
Hollins University
Lynchburg College
Mary Baldwin University
Patrick Henry College
Randolph College
Randolph-Macon College
Roanoke College
Southern Virginia University
Sweet Briar College
University of Richmond
University of Virginia's College at
  Wise
Virginia Military Institute
Virginia Union University
Virginia University of Lynchburg
Virginia Wesleyan College
Washington and Lee University

## Washington
Evergreen State College
Gonzaga University
Heritage University
Northwest University
University of Puget Sound
Walla Walla University
Whitman College
Whitworth University

## West Virginia
Alderson-Broaddus University
Bethany College
Bluefield State College
Concord University
Davis and Elkins College
Glenville State College
Ohio Valley University
Salem International University
West Virginia State University

West Virginia University Institute of
  Technology
West Virginia Wesleyan College
Wheeling Jesuit University

## Wisconsin
Alverno College
Beloit College
Carroll University
Carthage College
Concordia University Wisconsin
Edgewood College
Lakeland University
Lawrence University
Maranathan Baptist University
  Maranatha Baptist University
Marian University
Mount Mary University
Northland College
St. Norbert College
Silver Lake College of the Holy
  Family
University of Wisconsin
  Green Bay
  River Falls
  Superior
Wisconsin Lutheran College

## *Two-year*

## Arkansas
National Park College

## California
Antelope Valley College
Deep Springs College
Feather River College
Fresno City College

## Colorado
Colorado Mountain College

## Florida
Florida SouthWestern State College

## Georgia
Andrew College
Georgia Highlands College
Georgia Perimeter College
Gordon State College
Oxford College of Emory University

## Hawaii
Hawaii Tokai International College

## Illinois
Lincoln College

## Indiana
Ancilla College

## Iowa
Kaplan University
  Cedar Rapids

## Kansas
Donnelly College
Hesston College

## Massachusetts
Dean College

## Michigan
Montcalm Community College

## Missouri
Crowder College
Missouri State University
  West Plains
Stevens Institute of Business & Arts

## New Jersey
Rowan College at Gloucester

## New Mexico
Luna Community College

## New York
Maria College
SUNY
  College of Technology at Alfred

Liberal arts colleges

College of Technology at Delhi
Villa Maria College of Buffalo

**Pennsylvania**
University of Pittsburgh
  Titusville

**Puerto Rico**
Colegio de Cinematografia Artes y
  Television

**South Carolina**
Clinton College
Spartanburg Methodist College
University of South Carolina
  Union

**Tennessee**
Hiwassee College

**Texas**
Eastfield College
Jacksonville College
Lamar State College at Orange
North Lake College

**Vermont**
Community College of Vermont
Landmark College

**Virginia**
Richard Bland College

**Washington**
Olympic College

**Wisconsin**
University of Wisconsin
  Baraboo/Sauk County
  Fox Valley
  Marathon County
  Marinette
  Richland
  Rock County
  Sheboygan
  Washington County

## Upper-division colleges

**Alabama**
Athens State University
United States Sports Academy

**California**
Antioch University
  Los Angeles
  Santa Barbara
California Institute of Integral Studies
John F. Kennedy University
Northcentral University
Pacific Oaks College
Samuel Merritt University

**Illinois**
Resurrection University
Rush University

**Kansas**
University of Kansas Medical Center

**Louisiana**
Louisiana State University
  Health Sciences Center

**Maryland**
University of Maryland
  Baltimore

**Michigan**
Walsh College of Accountancy and
  Business Administration

**Minnesota**
Northwestern Health Sciences
  University

**Missouri**
Goldfarb School of Nursing at Barnes-
  Jewish College

**Nevada**
Roseman University of Health Sciences

**New York**
SUNY
  Upstate Medical University

**Puerto Rico**
Carlos Albizu University: San Juan

**Texas**
Texas A&M University
  Texarkana
Texas Tech University Health Sciences
  Center
University of Texas
  Health Science Center at Houston
  Medical Branch at Galveston

**Washington**
Bastyr University

**West Virginia**
Catholic Distance University

## Agricultural and technical colleges

### Four-year

Alabama Agricultural and Mechanical
  University, AL
Alcorn State University, MS
Art Institute of Fort Lauderdale, FL
Baker College
  of Auburn Hills, MI
  of Muskegon, MI
  of Owosso, MI
  of Port Huron, MI
Bluefield State College, WV
Central Penn College, PA
City College
  Fort Lauderdale, FL
City University of New York
  New York City College of
  Technology, NY
Coleman University, CA
CollegeAmerica
  Fort Collins, CO
Colorado Technical University, CO
DeVry College of New York
  Midtown Campus, NY
Ex'pression College, CA
Florida Career College
  Riverview, FL
Herzing University
  Atlanta, GA
  Birmingham, AL
  Brookfield, WI
  Kenner, LA
  Kenosha, WI
  Toledo, OH
International Academy of Design and
  Technology
  Chicago, IL
  Detroit, MI
  Henderson, NV
Lewis-Clark State College, ID
Louisiana State University and
  Agricultural and Mechanical
  College, LA
Mississippi State University, MS
Montana State University
  Billings, MT
Montana Tech of the University of
  Montana, MT
National American University
  Rapid City, SD
Neumont University, UT
New England Institute of Technology,
  RI
Peirce College, PA
Pennsylvania College of Technology,
  PA

Platt College
  Ontario, CA
  San Diego, CA
Remington College
  Tampa, FL
Spartan College of Aeronautics and
  Technology, OK
Stanbridge University, CA
Stevens-Henager College
  Logan, UT
SUNY
  College of Agriculture and
    Technology at Morrisville, NY
  Farmingdale State College, NY
  Maritime College, NY
University of Arkansas
  Monticello, AR
University of Puerto Rico
  Aguadilla, PR
  Bayamon University College, PR
  Mayaguez, PR
  Utuado, PR
Utah Valley University, UT
Wentworth Institute of Technology,
  MA
Wilmington College, OH

### Two-year

Abraham Baldwin Agricultural
  College, GA
Academy College, MN
Aiken Technical College, SC
Albany Technical College, GA
Alexandria Technical and Community
  College, MN
Antelope Valley College, CA
Antonelli College
  Cincinnati, OH
  Jackson, MS
Arkansas State University
  Mid-South, AR
  Mountain Home, AR
ASA College, NY
Asheville-Buncombe Technical
  Community College, NC
Asnuntuck Community College, CT
Athens Technical College, GA
Atlanta Technical College, GA
ATS Institute of Technology, OH
Bainbridge State College, GA
Bates Technical College, WA
Baton Rouge School of Computers, LA
Bellingham Technical College, WA
Belmont College, OH
Benjamin Franklin Institute of
  Technology, MA
Berks Technical Institute, PA
Big Sandy Community and Technical
  College, KY
Bismarck State College, ND
Blackhawk Technical College, WI
Blue Cliff College
  Metairie, LA
  Shreveport, LA
Bluegrass Community and Technical
  College, KY
Bolivar Technical College, MO
Bramson ORT College, NY
BridgeValley Community and
  Technical College, WV
Brightwood College
  Beltsville, MD
  Towson, MD
Bryan University
  Topeka, KS
Caldwell Community College and
  Technical Institute, NC
Capital Community College, CT
Carrington College
  Citrus Heights, CA
  Pleasant Hill, CA
  Sacramento, CA
  San Jose, CA
  Stockton, CA
Carteret Community College, NC

Central Carolina Technical College, SC
Central Georgia Technical College, GA
Central Lakes College, MN
Central Maine Community College,
  ME
Central Ohio Technical College, OH
Century College, MN
Chattahoochee Technical College, GA
Chattanooga College, TN
Chippewa Valley Technical College,
  WI
Cincinnati State Technical and
  Community College, OH
Clover Park Technical College, WA
Coastal Pines Technical College, GA
Coffeyville Community College, KS
Colegio de Cinematografia Artes y
  Television, PR
College of Business and Technology
  Cutler Bay, FL
  Flagler, FL
  Hialeah, FL
  Kendall, FL
  Miami Gardens, FL
College of Court Reporting, IN
College of the Ouachitas, AR
College of Western Idaho, ID
Colorado School of Trades, CO
Columbus State Community College,
  OH
Columbus Technical College, GA
Concorde Career College
  Garden Grove, CA
  San Bernardino, CA
Cowley County Community College,
  KS
Coyne College, IL
Culinary Institute LeNotre, TX
Dakota County Technical College, MN
Daytona State College, FL
Delaware Technical Community
  College
  Stanton/Wilmington Campus, DE
Delta College of Arts & Technology,
  LA
Delta School of Business &
  Technology, LA
Denmark Technical College, SC
Dodge City Community College, KS
DuBois Business College, PA
Dunwoody College of Technology,
  MN
Durham Technical Community
  College, NC
Eagle Gate College: Murray, UT
Eastern Maine Community College,
  ME
EDIC College, PR
Elizabethtown Community and
  Technical College, KY
Erie Institute of Technology, PA
Fayetteville Technical Community
  College, NC
Florence-Darlington Technical College,
  SC
Florida Career College
  Hialeah, FL
  Miami, FL
  West Palm Beach, FL
Florida Technical College
  Deland, FL
  Orlando, FL
Fortis College
  Cuyahoga, OH
  Winter Park, FL
Fortis Institute
  Forty Fort, PA
Fox Valley Technical College, WI
Fullerton College, CA
Gadsden State Community College, AL
Gateway Community and Technical
  College, KY
GateWay Community College, AZ
Gateway Technical College, WI

Georgia Piedmont Technical College, GA
Grayson College, TX
Great Bay Community College, NH
Greenville Technical College, SC
Guilford Technical Community College, NC
Gupton Jones College of Funeral Service, GA
Gwinnett Technical College, GA
Hazard Community and Technical College, KY
Hennepin Technical College, MN
Herzing University
    Minneapolis, MN
Hibbing Community College, MN
Hocking College, OH
Horry-Georgetown Technical College, SC
IBMC College
    Fort Collins, CO
IntelliTec College, CO
IntelliTec College: Grand Junction, CO
International Academy of Design and Technology
    San Antonio, TX
International College of Broadcasting, OH
Iowa Western Community College, IA
Island Drafting and Technical Institute, NY
ITI Technical College, LA
James A. Rhodes State College, OH
Jefferson College, MO
Jefferson Community and Technical College, KY
JNA Institute of Culinary Arts, PA
Johnson College, PA
Johnston Community College, NC
Kanawha Valley Community and Technical College, WV
Kaplan Career Institute
    Franklin Mills, PA
Kaplan College
    Dayton, OH
    Hammond, IN
    Palm Springs, CA
    Riverside, CA
    Sacramento, CA
    Salida, CA
    Vista, CA
Kennebec Valley Community College, ME
Key College, FL
Keystone Technical Institute, PA
Lake Area Technical Institute, SD
Lake Region State College, ND
Lake Superior College, MN
Lake Washington Institute of Technology, WA
Lakeland Community College, OH
Lakes Region Community College, NH
Lakeshore Technical College, WI
Lamar Institute of Technology, TX
Lamar State College at Port Arthur, TX
Landing School of Boatbuilding and Design, ME
Laurel Business Institute, PA
Laurel Technical Institute, PA
Le Cordon Bleu College of Culinary Arts
    Atlanta, GA
    Scottsdale, AZ
Lincoln College of Technology
    Denver, CO
    Grand Prairie, TX
    Indianapolis, IN
    West Palm Beach, FL
Lincoln Technical Institute
    Allentown, PA
    Northeast Philadelphia, PA
    Philadelphia, PA
Los Angeles Trade and Technical College, CA

Madison Area Technical College, WI
Manchester Community College, NH
Martin Community College, NC
Maysville Community and Technical College, KY
McCann School of Business and Technology
    Dickson City, PA
    Hazleton, PA
    Pottsville, PA
    Sunbury, PA
McDowell Technical Community College, NC
Mesabi Range College, MN
Mesalands Community College, NM
Metropolitan Community College, NE
Mid-Plains Community College, NE
Mid-State Technical College, WI
Midlands Technical College, SC
Miller-Motte College
    Cary, NC
    Fayetteville, NC
Miller-Motte Technical College, SC
    Chattanooga, TN
Milwaukee Area Technical College, WI
Minneapolis Business College, MN
Minneapolis Community and Technical College, MN
Minnesota State College - Southeast Technical, MN
Minnesota State Community and Technical College, MN
Minnesota West Community and Technical College, MN
Missouri College, MO
Mitchell Technical Institute, SD
Moraine Park Technical College, WI
Morrison Institute of Technology, IL
MTI College, CA
Nash Community College, NC
Nashua Community College, NH
Nashville State Community College, TN
National College
    Kettering, OH
    Knoxville, TN
National Park College, AR
Naugatuck Valley Community College, CT
Nebraska College of Technical Agriculture, NE
New Mexico Junior College, NM
NHTI-Concord's Community College, NH
North Central Kansas Technical College, KS
North Central State College, OH
North Dakota State College of Science, ND
Northcentral Technical College, WI
Northeast Iowa Community College, IA
Northeast Wisconsin Technical College, WI
Northern Maine Community College, ME
Northland Community & Technical College, MN
Northwest Florida State College, FL
Northwest Kansas Technical College, KS
Northwest School of Wooden Boatbuilding, WA
Northwest Technical College, MN
Northwestern College, IL
Nossi College of Art, TN
Nunez Community College, LA
Ohio Technical College, OH
Oklahoma City Community College, OK
Oklahoma State University Institute of Technology:
    Okmulgee, OK
    Oklahoma City, OK

Orangeburg-Calhoun Technical College, SC
Orleans Technical Institute, PA
Owensboro Community and Technical College, KY
Ozarks Technical Community College, MO
Pellissippi State Community College, TN
Penn Commercial Business and Technical School, PA
Pennco Tech, PA
Piedmont Technical College, SC
Pierpont Community and Technical College, WV
Pine Technical & Community College, MN
Pinnacle Career Institute: Kansas City, MO
Pittsburgh Institute of Aeronautics, PA
Pittsburgh Institute of Mortuary Science, PA
Platt College
    Los Angeles, CA
PowerSport Institute, OH
Pratt Community College, KS
Pulaski Technical College, AR
Rainy River Community College, MN
Ranken Technical College, MO
Redstone College, CO
Refrigeration School, AZ
Remington College
    Baton Rouge, LA
    Cleveland, OH
    Columbia, SC
    Dallas, TX
    Fort Worth, TX
    Greenspoint Campus, TX
    Little Rock, AR
    Memphis, TN
    Nashville, TN
    Shreveport, LA
    Westchase Campus, TX
Renton Technical College, WA
Ridgewater College, MN
Riverland Community College, MN
Rochester Community and Technical College, MN
Rosedale Technical College, PA
St. Cloud Technical and Community College, MN
Salt Lake Community College, UT
San Jacinto College, TX
San Juan College, NM
Santa Barbara Business College, CA
    Bakersfield, CA
    Rancho Mirage, CA
    Santa Maria, CA
    Ventura, CA
Savannah Technical College, GA
Seattle Central College, WA
Seward County Community College, KS
Sisseton Wahpeton College, SD
Somerset Community College, KY
South Central College, MN
South Florida State College, FL
South Texas College, TX
Southeast Kentucky Community and Technical College, KY
Southeastern Technical College, GA
Southern Arkansas University Tech, AR
Southern Crescent Technical College, GA
Southern Maine Community College, ME
Southern Regional Technical College, GA
Southern Union State Community College, AL
Southwest Wisconsin Technical College, WI
Spartanburg Community College, SC

Springfield Technical Community College, MA
State Technical College of Missouri, MO
Stevens-Henager College
    Boise, ID
Sullivan College of Technology and Design, KY
SUNY
    College of Agriculture and Technology at Cobleskill, NY
    College of Technology at Alfred, NY
    College of Technology at Canton, NY
    College of Technology at Delhi, NY
Technical Career Institutes, NY
Terra State Community College, OH
TESST College of Technology
    Brightwood College: Baltimore, MD
Texas County Technical College, MO
Texas State Technical College, TX
Tri-County Technical College, SC
Triangle Tech
    Bethlehem, PA
    Greensburg, PA
Trident Technical College, SC
Truckee Meadows Community College, NV
Tulsa Welding School, OK
United Tribes Technical College, ND
Universal Technical Institute, AZ
University of Hawaii
    Honolulu Community College, HI
University of Northwestern Ohio, OH
Vatterott College
    Berkeley, MO
    Cleveland, OH
    Des Moines, IA
    Joplin, MO
    Kansas City, MO
    Memphis, TN
    O'Fallon, MO
    Oklahoma City, OK
    Quincy, IL
    Sunset Hills, MO
    Tulsa, OK
Vet Tech Institute, PA
Vet Tech Institute of Houston, TX
Virginia College
    Jacksonville, FL
    Mobile, AL
    Spartanburg, SC
Wake Technical Community College, NC
Walla Walla Community College, WA
Washington County Community College, ME
West Virginia Northern Community College, WV
Western Dakota Technical Institute, SD
Western Technical College, TX
Western Technical College, WI
Western Technical College: Diana Drive, TX
Wichita Area Technical College, KS
Wiregrass Georgia Technical College, GA
Wisconsin Indianhead Technical College, WI
The Workforce Institute's City College, PA
York County Community College, ME
YTI Career Institute
    Altoona, PA

## Arts/music colleges

### Four-year

Academy of Art University, CA
American Academy of Art, IL

Art Academy of Cincinnati, OH
Art Institute International Minnesota
    Art Institutes International
      Minnesota, MN
Art Institute of Atlanta, GA
Art Institute of California
    Hollywood, CA
    Inland Empire, CA
    Orange County, CA
    Sacramento, CA
    San Diego, CA
    San Francisco, CA
Art Institute of Dallas, TX
Art Institute of Fort Lauderdale, FL
Art Institute of Houston, TX
Art Institute of Las Vegas, NV
Art Institute of Michigan, MI
Art Institute of Philadelphia, PA
Art Institute of Phoenix, AZ
Art Institute of Pittsburgh, PA
Art Institute of Portland, OR
Art Institute of Seattle, WA
Art Institute of Tucson, AZ
Art Institute of Washington, VA
Berklee College of Music, MA
Boston Conservatory, MA
California College of the Arts, CA
California Institute of the Arts, CA
Cleveland Institute of Art, OH
Cleveland Institute of Music, OH
Cogswell Polytechnical College, CA
College for Creative Studies, MI
Columbia College
    Hollywood, CA
Columbia College Chicago, IL
Columbus College of Art and Design, OH
Conservatory of Music of Puerto Rico, PR
Cooper Union for the Advancement of Science and Art, NY
Cornish College of the Arts, WA
Curtis Institute of Music, PA
DePauw University, IN
DigiPen Institute of Technology, WA
Digital Media Arts College, FL
Eastman School of Music of the University of Rochester, NY
Escuela de Artes Plasticas de Puerto Rico, PR
Ex'pression College, CA
Fashion Institute of Design and Merchandising
    Los Angeles, CA
Fashion Institute of Technology, NY
Five Towns College, NY
Full Sail University, FL
Illinois Institute of Art
    Chicago, IL
    Schaumburg, IL
Institute of American Indian Arts, NM
International Academy of Design and Technology
    Chicago, IL
    Detroit, MI
    Henderson, NV
Johns Hopkins University: Peabody Conservatory of Music, MD
Juilliard School, NY
Kansas City Art Institute, MO
Laguna College of Art and Design, CA
Lawrence University, WI
Lyme Academy College of Fine Arts, CT
Lyndon State College, VT
Maine College of Art, ME
Manhattan School of Music, NY
Maryland Institute College of Art, MD
Marymount Manhattan College, NY
Massachusetts College of Art and Design, MA
McNally Smith College of Music, MN
Memphis College of Art, TN
Miami International University of Art and Design, FL

Milwaukee Institute of Art & Design, WI
Minneapolis College of Art and Design, MN
Montserrat College of Art, MA
Moore College of Art and Design, PA
Mt. Sierra College, CA
New England Conservatory of Music, MA
New Hampshire Institute of Art, NH
The New School College of Performing Arts, NY
New York School of Interior Design, NY
NewSchool of Architecture & Design, CA
Northwest College of Art & Design, WA
O'More College of Design, TN
Oberlin College, OH
Oregon College of Art & Craft, OR
Otis College of Art and Design, CA
Pacific Northwest College of Art, OR
Paier College of Art, CT
Parsons the New School for Design
    Parsons The New School for Design, NY
Pennsylvania Academy of the Fine Arts, PA
Pennsylvania Colleg of Art and Design
    Pennsylvania College of Art and Design, PA
Platt College
    San Diego, CA
Pratt Institute, NY
Rhode Island School of Design, RI
Ringling College of Art and Design, FL
Rocky Mountain College of Art & Design, CO
San Francisco Art Institute, CA
San Francisco Conservatory of Music, CA
Santa Fe University of Art and Design, NM
Savannah College of Art and Design, GA
School of the Art Institute of Chicago, IL
School of the Museum of Fine Arts, MA
School of Visual Arts, NY
Southern California Institute of Architecture, CA
Southwest University of Visual Arts, AZ
Southwestern University, TX
University of North Carolina School of the Arts, NC
University of the Arts, PA
VanderCook College of Music, IL
Visible Music College, TN
Watkins College of Art, Design & Film, TN

### Two-year

American Academy of Dramatic Arts, NY
American Academy of Dramatic Arts: West, CA
Antonelli College
    Cincinnati, OH
Antonelli Institute of Art and Photography, PA
Art Institute of California
    Los Angeles, CA
Art Institute of Cincinnati, OH
Broadview University
    Broadview Entertainment Arts University, UT
Dean College, MA
Delaware College of Art and Design, DE
Delta College of Arts & Technology, LA

Douglas Education Center, PA
Fashion Institute of Design and Merchandising
    San Diego, CA
    San Francisco, CA
Madison Media Institute, WI
Nossi College of Art, TN
Platt College
    Los Angeles, CA
School of Advertising Art, OH
Sessions College for Professional Design, AZ
Villa Maria College of Buffalo, NY
Virginia Marti College of Art and Design, OH

### Bible colleges

#### Four-year

Allegheny Wesleyan College, OH
American Baptist College, TN
Apex School of Theology, NC
Appalachian Bible College, WV
Arizona Christian University, AZ
Arlington Baptist College, TX
Baptist College of Florida, FL
Baptist University of the Americas, TX
Barclay College, KS
Beulah Heights University, GA
Biola University, CA
Boston Baptist College, MA
California Christian College, CA
Calvary Bible College and Theological Seminary, MO
Carver College, GA
Clarks Summit University, PA
Columbia International University, SC
Criswell College, TX
Crossroads Bible College, IN
Crossroads College, MN
Davis College, NY
Ecclesia College, AR
Emmaus Bible College, IA
Faith Baptist Bible College and Theological Seminary, IA
Family of Faith College, OK
Global University, MO
God's Bible School and College, OH
Grace University, NE
Heritage Christian University, AL
Horizon University, CA
Huntsville Bible College, AL
International Baptist College, AZ
Johnson University, TN
Kentucky Christian University, KY
Kentucky Mountain Bible College, KY
The King's University, TX
Kuyper College, MI
La Sierra University, CA
Lancaster Bible College, PA
Laurel University, NC
Life Pacific College, CA
Lincoln Christian University, IL
Maranathan Baptist University
    Maranatha Baptist University, WI
Mid-Atlantic Christian University, NC
Montana Bible College, MT
Moody Bible Institute, IL
Nazarene Bible College, CO
New Hope Christian College, OR
New Orleans Baptist Theological Seminary, LA
Northpoint Bible College, MA
Pillar College, NJ
Point University, GA
Shasta Bible College and Graduate School, CA
Southeastern Baptist College, MS
Southern Baptist Theological Seminary, KY
Southern California Seminary, CA
Southwestern Assemblies of God University, TX

Southwestern Baptist Theological Seminary, TX
Southwestern Christian College, TX
SUM Bible College & Theological Seminary, CA
Theological University of the Caribbean, PR
Toccoa Falls College, GA
Trinity Baptist College, FL
Trinity College of Florida, FL
Universidad Pentecostal Mizpa, PR
W.L. Bonner Bible College, SC
Welch College, TN
William Jessup University, CA
World Mission University, CA

#### Two-year

Epic Bible College, CA

### Business colleges

#### Four-year

American National University
    Salem, VA
American University of Puerto Rico, PR
Babson College, MA
Baker College
    of Allen Park, MI
    of Auburn Hills, MI
    of Cadillac, MI
    of Muskegon, MI
    of Owosso, MI
    of Port Huron, MI
Bellevue University, NE
Bentley University, MA
Berkeley College, NY
Berkeley College, NJ
Berkeley College of New York City, NY
Briarcliffe College, NY
Bryant & Stratton College
    Eastlake, OH
Bryant University, RI
California College San Diego, CA
California Miramar University, CA
California State University
    Stanislaus, CA
California University of Management and Sciences, CA
Capitol Technology University, MD
Central Penn College, PA
Chadron State College, NE
City College
    Fort Lauderdale, FL
City University of New York
    Baruch College, NY
Clarion University of Pennsylvania, PA
Cleary University, MI
DeVry College of New York
    Midtown Campus, NY
Everest University
    Orange Park, FL
Fashion Institute of Design and Merchandising
    Los Angeles, CA
Fashion Institute of Technology, NY
Fisher College, MA
Five Towns College, NY
Fort Lewis College, CO
Franklin University, OH
Globe Institute of Technology, NY
Goldey-Beacom College, DE
Harris-Stowe State University, MO
Herzing University
    Atlanta, GA
    Birmingham, AL
    Brookfield, WI
    Kenosha, WI
    Madison, WI
    Toledo, OH
Hult International Business School, CA

Husson University, ME
Huston-Tillotson University, TX
Independence University, UT
Indiana Institute of Technology, IN
International Business College, IN
Iona College, NY
Jones College, FL
Keystone College, PA
King's College, PA
Lasell College, MA
LIM College, NY
Lincoln University, CA
Mayville State University, ND
Menlo College, CA
Metropolitan College of New York, NY
Midstate College, IL
Millsaps College, MS
Monroe College, NY
Mount Ida College, MA
Mt. Sierra College, CA
National American University
    Albuquerque, NM
    Bloomington, MN
    Rapid City, SD
Newbury College, MA
Nichols College, MA
Northern New Mexico College, NM
Northwestern Polytechnic University, CA
Northwood University
    Michigan, MI
    Texas, TX
Peirce College, PA
Post University, CT
Presentation College, SD
Restaurant School at Walnut Hill College, PA
Rockhurst University, MO
Silicon Valley University, CA
Southeastern Baptist College, MS
Southern California Institute of Technology, CA
Stevens-Henager College
    Murray, UT
Stonehill College, MA
SUNY
    College at Old Westbury, NY
SUNY Polytechnic Institute, NY
Touro University Worldwide, CA
University of the Potomac, VA
University of the Potomac, DC
University of the West, CA
Walsh College of Accountancy and Business Administration, MI
Webber International University, FL

### Two-year

American National University
    Harrisonburg, VA
Bay State College, MA
Berks Technical Institute, PA
Bidwell Training Center, PA
Brown Mackie College
    Akron, OH
    Fort Wayne, IN
    Merrillville, IN
    Miami, FL
Bryant & Stratton College
    Albany, NY
    Amherst, NY
    Buffalo, NY
    Henrietta, NY
    Milwaukee, WI
    Rochester, NY
    Southtowns, NY
    Virginia Beach, VA
City College
    Gainesville, FL
College of Court Reporting, IN
Concorde Career College
    Kansas City, MO
Daymar College
    Louisville, KY
    Owensboro, KY

Daymar Institute
    Clarksville, TN
Delta School of Business & Technology, LA
Douglas Education Center, PA
DuBois Business College, PA
    Huntingdon, PA
    Oil City, PA
Eagle Gate College: Murray, UT
Fashion Institute of Design and Merchandising
    San Diego, CA
    San Francisco, CA
Florida Career College
    Miami, FL
Fortis College
    Orange Park, FL
    Ravenna, OH
Harrison College
    Grove City, OH
    Indianapolis, IN
Herzing University
    Winter Park, FL
Humacao Community College, PR
International Business College:
    Indianapolis, IN
Kaplan College
    Hammond, IN
    San Diego, CA
Kaplan University
    Hagerstown, MD
    South Portland, ME
Key College, FL
Long Island Business Institute, NY
McCann School of Business and Technology
    Dickson City, PA
    Hazleton, PA
Metro Business College
    Rolla, MO
Miami-Jacobs Career College
    Sharonville, OH
Miller-Motte Technical College
    Clarksville, TN
Minneapolis Business College, MN
MTI College, CA
National College
    Danville, KY
    Florence, KY
    Kettering, OH
    Knoxville, TN
    Lexington, KY
New England College of Business and Finance, MA
Ohio Business College
    Hilliard, OH
    Sheffield, OH
Penn Commercial Business and Technical School, PA
Pennsylvania Institute of Health and Technology, PA
Remington College
    Memphis, TN
South Coast College, CA
Southeastern College
    Greenacres, FL
    Miami Lakes, FL
Stenotype Institute: Jacksonville, FL
Stevens Institute of Business & Arts, MO
Taylor Business Institute, IL
University of Northwestern Ohio, OH
Utica School of Commerce, NY
Virginia College
    Austin, TX
    Biloxi, MS
    Greenville, SC
    Pensacola, FL
    School of Business and Health in Chattanooga, TN
Virginia Marti College of Art and Design, OH
Wade College, TX

## Culinary schools

### Four-year

Art Institute International Minnesota
    Art Institutes International Minnesota, MN
Art Institute of Atlanta, GA
Art Institute of California
    Hollywood, CA
    Inland Empire, CA
    Orange County, CA
    Sacramento, CA
    San Francisco, CA
Art Institute of Houston, TX
Art Institute of Las Vegas, NV
Art Institute of Phoenix, AZ
Art Institute of Pittsburgh, PA
Art Institute of Seattle, WA
Art Institute of Tucson, AZ
Art Institute of Washington, VA
Culinary Institute of America, NY
Kendall College, IL
Paul Smith's College, NY
Restaurant School at Walnut Hill College, PA
Southern New Hampshire University, NH

### Two-year

Atlantic Cape Community College, NJ
Culinary Institute LeNotre, TX
Institute of Technology: Clovis, CA
Keystone Technical Institute, PA
L'Ecole Culinaire, MO
Le Cordon Bleu College of Culinary Arts
    Austin, TX
    Chicago, IL
    Los Angeles, CA
    Miami, FL
    Minneapolis-St. Paul, MN
    Orlando, FL
    Portland, OR
    San Francisco, CA
    Scottsdale, AZ
New England Culinary Institute, VT
Platt College
    Moore, OK
    Tulsa, OK
Schoolcraft College, MI
Southwestern Oregon Community College, OR
Virginia College
    Richmond, VA
    Savannah, GA
Walters State Community College, TN

## Engineering colleges

### Four-year

Capitol Technology University, MD
Clemson University, SC
Cogswell Polytechnical College, CA
Colorado School of Mines, CO
Cooper Union for the Advancement of Science and Art, NY
DigiPen Institute of Technology, WA
Franklin W. Olin College of Engineering, MA
Harvey Mudd College, CA
Illinois Institute of Technology, IL
Indiana Institute of Technology, IN
Inter American University of Puerto Rico
    Bayamon Campus, PR
Kettering University, MI
Lafayette College, PA
Lake Superior State University, MI
Manhattan College, NY
Massachusetts Maritime Academy, MA

Montana Tech of the University of Montana, MT
Neumont University, UT
New Mexico Institute of Mining and Technology, NM
New York Institute of Technology, NY
Northwestern Polytechnic University, CA
Rose-Hulman Institute of Technology, IN
Silicon Valley University, CA
Southern California Institute of Technology, CA
Stevens Institute of Technology, NJ
SUNY Polytechnic Institute, NY
Trine University, IN
Turabo University, PR
Union College, NY
United States Coast Guard Academy, CT
Universidad Politecnica de Puerto Rico, PR
University of Pittsburgh
    Johnstown, PA
University of Puerto Rico
    Mayaguez, PR
Vaughn College of Aeronautics and Technology, NY
Wentworth Institute of Technology, MA
West Virginia University Institute of Technology, WV

## Maritime colleges

### Four-year

California Maritime Academy, CA
Maine Maritime Academy, ME
Massachusetts Maritime Academy, MA
SUNY
    Maritime College, NY
United States Merchant Marine Academy, NY

### Two-year

Clatsop Community College, OR
Northwest School of Wooden Boatbuilding, WA
Northwestern Michigan College, MI

## Military colleges

### Four-year

The Citadel, SC
Norwich University, VT
United States Coast Guard Academy, CT
United States Merchant Marine Academy, NY
United States Naval Academy, MD
Virginia Military Institute, VA

### Two-year

Georgia Military College, GA
Marion Military Institute, AL
New Mexico Military Institute, NM
Valley Forge Military College, PA
Wentworth Military Junior College, MO

## Nursing and health science colleges

### Four-year

Albany College of Pharmacy and Health Sciences, NY

235

Allen College, IA
American International College, MA
Baker College
    of Allen Park, MI
    of Cadillac, MI
Bastyr University, WA
Blessing-Rieman College of Nursing & Health Sciences, IL
Bloomfield College, NJ
BryanLGH College of Health Sciences, NE
Bryant & Stratton College
    Parma, OH
Cabarrus College of Health Sciences, NC
California College San Diego, CA
Chamberlain College Of Nursing
    Chamberlain College of Nursing: Cleveland, OH
Chamberlain College of Nursing
    Addison, IL
    Arlington, VA
    Atlanta, GA
    Chicago, IL
    Columbus, OH
    Houston, TX
    Indianapolis, IN
    Jacksonville, FL
    Miramar, FL
    Phoenix, AZ
Charles Drew University of Medicine and Science, CA
Coe College, IA
College of New Rochelle, NY
CollegeAmerica
    Fort Collins, CO
Cox College, MO
D'Youville College, NY
Denver School of Nursing, CO
Dominican College of Blauvelt, NY
ECPI University, VA
Felician University, NJ
Globe University
    Woodbury, MN
Goldfarb School of Nursing at Barnes-Jewish College, MO
Gwynedd Mercy University, PA
Herzing University
    Omaha School of Massage Therapy and Healthcare, NE
Husson University, ME
Independence University, UT
Ithaca College, NY
Jefferson College of Health Sciences, VA
Keiser University, FL
Kettering College, OH
King University, TN
Linfield College, OR
Loma Linda University, CA
Louisiana State University
    Health Sciences Center, LA
MCPHS University, MA
Mercy College of Health Sciences, IA
Methodist College, IL
Misericordia University, PA
Monroe College, NY
National American University
    Bloomington, MN
New England Institute of Technology, RI
New York Institute of Technology, NY
Northern New Mexico College, NM
Northwestern Health Sciences University, MN
Notre Dame College, OH
Oregon Health & Science University, OR
Pennsylvania College of Health Sciences, PA
Piedmont College, GA
Presentation College, SD
Regis College, MA
Remington College
    of Nursing, FL

Research College of Nursing, MO
Resurrection University, IL
Rivier University, NH
Rush University, IL
Saint Anselm College, NH
St. Catharine College, KY
St. Catherine University, MN
Samuel Merritt University, CA
Simmons College, MA
Springfield College, MA
Stanbridge University, CA
Stevens-Henager College
    Logan, UT
    Murray, UT
    Orem, UT
SUNY
    Upstate Medical University, NY
Thomas Jefferson University, PA
University of Arkansas
    for Medical Sciences, AR
University of Findlay, OH
University of Kansas Medical Center, KS
University of Maryland
    Baltimore, MD
University of Minnesota
    Rochester, MN
University of Montana, MT
University of Phoenix
    Central Florida, FL
University of Texas
    Health Science Center at Houston, TX
    Medical Branch at Galveston, TX
University of the Sciences, PA
Utica College, NY
Virginia College
    Birmingham, AL
Wesleyan College, GA
Winston-Salem State University, NC

### Two-year

Abraham Baldwin Agricultural College, GA
ATS Institute of Technology, OH
Bay State College, MA
Bidwell Training Center, PA
Brookline College
    Phoenix, AZ
Careers Unlimited, UT
Carrington College
    Citrus Heights, CA
    Pleasant Hill, CA
    Reno, NV
    Sacramento, CA
Centro de Estudios Multidisciplinarios, PR
City College
    Gainesville, FL
Concorde Career College
    Aurora, CO
    Garden Grove, CA
    Kansas City, MO
    North Hollywood, CA
Dakota College at Bottineau, ND
Eastern International College, NJ
Eastwick College, NJ
EDIC College, PR
Florida College of Natural Health
    Bradenton, FL
    Maitland, FL
Fortis College
    Cuyahoga, OH
    Orange Park, FL
Fortis Institute
    Erie, PA
Goodwin College, CT
Grossmont College, CA
Gwinnett College, GA
Harrison College
    Grove City, OH
    Indianapolis, IN
Herzing University
    Winter Park, FL
Hondros College, OH

Huntington College of Health Sciences, TN
Kaplan College
    Palm Springs, CA
    Salida, CA
    San Diego, CA
Louisiana State University
    Eunice, LA
Maria College, NY
Miller-Motte Technical College
    Clarksville, TN
    Conway, SC
Myotherapy Institute, NE
Ohio Business College
    Hilliard, OH
Ohio College of Massotherapy, OH
Pacific College of Oriental Medicine:
    San Diego, CA
Philliips School of Nursing at Mount Sinai Beth Israel
    Phillips School of Nursing at Mount Sinai Beth Israel, NY
Platt College
    Moore, OK
    Tulsa, OK
Ponce Paramedical College, PR
Remington College
    Greenspoint Campus, TX
St. Elizabeth College of Nursing, NY
St. Luke's College, IA
Southeast Missouri Hospital College of Nursing and Health Sciences, MO
Southeastern College
    Greenacres, FL
    Miami Lakes, FL
State College of Florida, Manatee-Sarasota, FL
Swedish Institute, NY
Texas County Technical College, MO
Trocaire College, NY
Universal Technology College of Puerto Rico, PR
Vatterott College
    Des Moines, IA
Vet Tech Institute, PA
Virginia College
    Augusta, GA
    Austin, TX
    Baton Rouge, LA
    Biloxi, MS
    Charleston, SC
    Columbia, SC
    Columbus, GA
    Macon, GA
    Montgomery, AL
    Pensacola, FL
    Tulsa, OK
Wallace State Community College at Hanceville, AL
West Virginia Junior College
    Bridgeport, WV

### Schools of mortuary science

### Two-year

Commonwealth Institute of Funeral Service, TX
Eastwick College
    Hackensack, NJ
Mid-America College of Funeral Service, IN

### Seminary/rabbinical colleges

### Four-year

Beis Medrash Heichal Dovid, NY
Beth Hamedrash Shaarei Yosher Institute, NY

Beth Hatalmud Rabbinical College, NY
Beulah Heights University, GA
Calvary Bible College and Theological Seminary, MO
Central Yeshiva Tomchei Tmimim-Lubavitch, NY
Charlotte Christian College and Theological Seminary, NC
Criswell College, TX
Divine Word College, IA
Earlham College, IN
Erskine College, SC
Faith Baptist Bible College and Theological Seminary, IA
Faith International University
    Fiath International University, WA
George Fox University, OR
Global University, MO
Hellenic College/Holy Cross, MA
Holy Apostles College and Seminary, CT
International Baptist College, AZ
Kehilath Yakov Rabbinical Seminary, NY
The King's University, TX
Machzikei Hadath Rabbinical College, NY
Manthano Christian College, MI
The Master's University, CA
Mesivta Torah Vodaath Seminary, NY
Mirrer Yeshiva Central Institute, NY
Moody Bible Institute, IL
Moravian College, PA
Mount Angel Seminary, OR
New Orleans Baptist Theological Seminary, LA
Nyack College, NY
Ohr Somayach Tanenbaum Education Center, NY
Piedmont International University, NC
Rabbi Jacob Joseph School, NJ
Rabbinical Academy Mesivta Rabbi Chaim Berlin, NY
Rabbinical College Beth Shraga, NY
Rabbinical College Bobover Yeshiva B'nei Zion, NY
Rabbinical College Ch'san Sofer of New York, NY
Rabbinical College of America, NJ
Rabbinical College of Long Island, NY
Rabbinical College of Ohr Shimon Yisroel, NY
Rabbinical College of Telshe, OH
Rabbinical Seminary of America, NY
Sacred Heart Major Seminary, MI
St. Joseph Seminary College, LA
Shasta Bible College and Graduate School, CA
Shiloh University, IA
Shor Yoshuv Rabbinical College, NY
Southern Baptist Theological Seminary, KY
Southern California Seminary, CA
Southwestern Baptist Theological Seminary, TX
SUM Bible College & Theological Seminary, CA
Talmudic University, FL
Talmudical Academy of New Jersey, NJ
Talmudical Institute of Upstate New York, NY
Talmudical Seminary Oholei Torah, NY
Telshe Yeshiva-Chicago, IL
Theological University of the Caribbean, PR
Torah Temimah Talmudical Seminary, NY
U.T.A. Mesivta-Kiryas Joel, NY
United Talmudical Seminary, NY
University of Dubuque, IA
Virginia University of Lynchburg, VA
World Mission University, CA

Yeshiva and Kolel Bais Medrash
Elyon, NY
Yeshiva and Kollel Harbotzas Torah,
NY
Yeshiva Beth Yehuda-Yeshiva Gedolah
of Greater Detroit, MI
Yeshiva College of the Nations
Capital, MD
Yeshiva D'Monsey Rabbinical College,
NY
Yeshiva Derech Chaim, NY
Yeshiva Gedolah Imrei Yosef
D'Spinka, NY
Yeshiva Gedolah Rabbinical College,
FL
Yeshiva Gedolah Zichron Moshe, NY
Yeshiva Karlin Stolin, NY
Yeshiva of Nitra, NY
Yeshiva of the Telshe Alumni, NY
Yeshiva Shaar Hatorah, NY
Yeshiva Shaarei Torah of Rockland,
NY
Yeshivas Novominsk, NY
Yeshivat Mikdash Melech, NY
Yeshivath Beth Moshe, PA
Yeshivath Viznitz, NY

College at Plattsburgh, NY
College at Potsdam, NY
Tennessee Wesleyan College, TN
Thomas College, ME
Trinity Baptist College, FL
Union College, KY
University of Hawaii
West Oahu, HI
University of Maine
Farmington, ME
University of Montana: Western, MT
University of the Southwest, NM
Valley City State University, ND
VanderCook College of Music, IL
Wayne State College, NE
Welch College, TN
West Virginia State University, WV
Western Oregon University, OR
Wheelock College, MA
William Woods University, MO
Worcester State University, MA
York College, NE

## Teacher's colleges

### Four-year

Arlington Baptist College, TX
Athens State University, AL
Austin College, TX
Baker University, KS
Baptist College of Florida, FL
Bluefield College, VA
California State University
Monterey Bay, CA
Cambridge College, MA
Canisius College, NY
Clarion University of Pennsylvania, PA
College of St. Joseph in Vermont, VT
Concordia University, OR
Concordia University, MI
Elmira College, NY
Fitchburg State University, MA
Fort Valley State University, GA
Frostburg State University, MD
Glenville State College, WV
Great Basin College, NV
Harris-Stowe State University, MO
Heritage University, WA
Humphreys College, CA
Kendall College, IL
Lander University, SC
Lesley University, MA
Louisiana State University
Shreveport, LA
Manhattanville College, NY
Mayville State University, ND
National-Louis University, IL
New England College, NH
Northwestern Oklahoma State
University, OK
Pacific Oaks College, CA
Peru State College, NE
Piedmont College, GA
Plymouth State University, NH
Rabbinical College of Long Island, NY
Rabbinical College of Telshe, OH
Reinhardt University, GA
Rhode Island College, RI
Rust College, MS
St. Joseph's College New York:
Suffolk Campus, NY
St. Joseph's College, New York, NY
Southeastern Oklahoma State
University, OK
Southeastern University, FL
SUNY
College at Buffalo, NY
College at Cortland, NY
College at Geneseo, NY

# Special characteristics

## Colleges for men

### Four-year

Beis Medrash Heichal Dovid, NY
Beth Hamedrash Shaarei Yosher
    Institute, NY
Beth Hatalmud Rabbinical College, NY
Central Yeshiva Tomchei Tmimim-
    Lubavitch, NY
Hampden-Sydney College, VA
Kehilath Yakov Rabbinical Seminary,
    NY
Machzikei Hadath Rabbinical College,
    NY
Mesivta Torah Vodaath Seminary, NY
Mirrer Yeshiva Central Institute, NY
Morehouse College, GA
Mount Angel Seminary, OR
Ohr Somayach Tanenbaum Education
    Center, NY
Rabbinical Academy Mesivta Rabbi
    Chaim Berlin, NY
Rabbinical College Beth Shraga, NY
Rabbinical College Bobover Yeshiva
    B'nei Zion, NY
Rabbinical College Ch'san Sofer of
    New York, NY
Rabbinical College of America, NJ
Rabbinical College of Long Island, NY
Rabbinical College of Ohr Shimon
    Yisroel, NY
Rabbinical College of Telshe, OH
Rabbinical Seminary of America, NY
St. Joseph Seminary College, LA
Shor Yoshuv Rabbinical College, NY
Talmudic University, FL
Talmudical Academy of New Jersey,
    NJ
Talmudical Institute of Upstate New
    York, NY
Talmudical Seminary Oholei Torah,
    NY
Telshe Yeshiva-Chicago, IL
Torah Temimah Talmudical Seminary,
    NY
U.T.A. Mesivta-Kiryas Joel, NY
United Talmudical Seminary, NY
Wabash College, IN
Yeshiva and Kolel Bais Medrash
    Elyon, NY
Yeshiva and Kollel Harbotzas Torah,
    NY
Yeshiva Beth Yehuda-Yeshiva Gedolah
    of Greater Detroit, MI
Yeshiva College of the Nations
    Capital, MD
Yeshiva D'Monsey Rabbinical College,
    NY
Yeshiva Derech Chaim, NY
Yeshiva Gedolah Imrei Yosef
    D'Spinka, NY
Yeshiva Gedolah Rabbinical College,
    FL
Yeshiva Gedolah Zichron Moshe, NY
Yeshiva Karlin Stolin, NY
Yeshiva of Nitra, NY
Yeshiva of the Telshe Alumni, NY
Yeshiva Shaar Hatorah, NY
Yeshiva Shaarei Torah of Rockland,
    NY
Yeshivas Novominsk, NY
Yeshivat Mikdash Melech, NY
Yeshivath Beth Moshe, PA
Yeshivath Viznitz, NY

### Two-year

Deep Springs College, CA

## Colleges for women

### Four-year

Agnes Scott College, GA
Alverno College, WI
Barnard College, NY
Bay Path University, MA
Bennett College for Women, NC
Bryn Mawr College, PA
Cedar Crest College, PA
College of Saint Mary, NE
Columbia College, SC
Converse College, SC
Cottey College, MO
Hollins University, VA
Judson College, AL
Mary Baldwin University, VA
Meredith College, NC
Mills College, CA
Moore College of Art and Design, PA
Mount Holyoke College, MA
Mount Mary University, WI
Mount Saint Mary's University, CA
Notre Dame of Maryland University,
    MD
St. Catherine University, MN
Saint Mary's College, IN
Salem College, NC
Scripps College, CA
Simmons College, MA
Smith College, MA
Spelman College, GA
Stephens College, MO
Sweet Briar College, VA
University of Saint Joseph, CT
Wellesley College, MA
Wesleyan College, GA

## Affiliated with a religion

### African Methodist Episcopal Church

#### Four-year

Allen University, SC
Edward Waters College, FL
Paul Quinn College, TX
Wilberforce University, OH

### African Methodist Episcopal Zion Church

#### Four-year

Livingstone College, NC

### American Baptist Churches in the USA

#### Four-year

Alderson-Broaddus University, WV
Arkansas Baptist College, AR
Bacone College, OK
Benedict College, SC
Eastern University, PA
Florida Memorial University, FL
Franklin College, IN
Judson University, IL
Keuka College, NY
Linfield College, OR

Ottawa University, KS
University of Sioux Falls, SD

### Assemblies of God

#### Four-year

Evangel University, MO
Global University, MO
North Central University, MN
Northpoint Bible College, MA
Northwest University, WA
Southeastern University, FL
Southwestern Assemblies of God
    University, TX
SUM Bible College & Theological
    Seminary, CA
University of Valley Forge, PA
Vanguard University of Southern
    California, CA

### Baptist faith

#### Four-year

American Baptist College, TN
Arlington Baptist College, TX
Averett University, VA
Baptist University of the Americas, TX
Baylor University, TX
Bluefield College, VA
Boston Baptist College, MA
Campbell University, NC
Campbellsville University, KY
Cedarville University, OH
Clarks Summit University, PA
Corban University, OR
Dallas Baptist University, TX
East Texas Baptist University, TX
Georgetown College, KY
Hardin-Simmons University, TX
Houston Baptist University, TX
Howard Payne University, TX
International Baptist College, AZ
Judson College, AL
LeMoyne-Owen College, TN
Maranathan Baptist University
    Maranatha Baptist University, WI
Mars Hill University, NC
Missouri Baptist University, MO
Morris College, SC
Ouachita Baptist University, AR
Piedmont International University, NC
Samford University, AL
Selma University, AL
Shasta Bible College and Graduate
    School, CA
Shaw University, NC
Southeastern Baptist College, MS
University of Mary Hardin-Baylor, TX
University of Mobile, AL
University of the Cumberlands, KY
Virginia Union University, VA
William Carey University, MS

#### Two-year

Jacksonville College, TX

### Brethren Church

#### Four-year

Ashland University, OH
Elizabethtown College, PA
Emmaus Bible College, IA

### Christian and Missionary Alliance

#### Four-year

Crown College, MN
Nyack College, NY
Simpson University, CA
Toccoa Falls College, GA

### Christian Church

#### Four-year

Belmont University, TN
Bethesda University of California, CA
Bryn Athyn College, PA

Cairn University, PA
Cincinnati Christian University, OH
Crossroads College, MN
Hillsdale College, MI
Hope International University, CA
Johnson University, TN
Johnson University: Florida, FL
Kentucky Mountain Bible College, KY
Liberty University, VA
Life Pacific College, CA
Malone University, OH
Milligan College, TN
New Saint Andrews College, ID
Piedmont College, GA
Pillar College, NJ
Point University, GA
Shiloh University, IA
Southwestern Baptist Theological
    Seminary, TX
Visible Music College, TN

### Christian Church (Disciples of Christ)

#### Four-year

Barton College, NC
Bethany College, WV
Chapman University, CA
Columbia College, MO
Culver-Stockton College, MO
Eureka College, IL
Hiram College, OH
Jarvis Christian College, TX
Lynchburg College, VA
Midway College, KY
Northwest Christian University, OR
Texas Christian University, TX
Transylvania University, KY
William Woods University, MO

### Christian Methodist Episcopal Church

#### Four-year

Lane College, TN
Miles College, AL
Paine College, GA
Texas College, TX

### Christian Reformed Church

#### Four-year

Calvin College, MI
Dordt College, IA
Kuyper College, MI

### Church of Christ

#### Four-year

Abilene Christian University, TX
Faulkner University, AL
Freed-Hardeman University, TN
Graceland University, IA
Harding University, AR
Heritage Christian University, AL
Lincoln Christian University, IL
Lipscomb University, TN
Lubbock Christian University, TX
Mid-Atlantic Christian University, NC
Ohio Valley University, WV
Oklahoma Christian University, OK
Pepperdine University, CA
Rochester College, MI
Southwestern Christian College, TX
York College, NE

### Church of God

#### Four-year

Lee University, TN
Theological University of the
    Caribbean, PR
University of Findlay, OH
Warner Pacific College, OR
Warner University, FL

## Church of Jesus Christ of Latter-day Saints

**Four-year**

Brigham Young University, UT
Brigham Young University-Hawaii, HI
Brigham Young University-Idaho, ID
Southern Virginia University, VA

## Church of the Brethren

**Four-year**

Bridgewater College, VA
Manchester University, IN
McPherson College, KS

## Church of the Nazarene

**Four-year**

Eastern Nazarene College, MA
MidAmerica Nazarene University, KS
Mount Vernon Nazarene University, OH
Nazarene Bible College, CO
Northwest Nazarene University, ID
Olivet Nazarene University, IL
Point Loma Nazarene University, CA
Southern Nazarene University, OK
Trevecca Nazarene University, TN

## Converge Worldwide

**Four-year**

Bethel University, MN
Oakland City University, IN

## Cumberland Presbyterian Church

**Four-year**

Bethel University, TN

## Episcopal Church

**Four-year**

Bard College, NY
St. Augustine College, IL
Saint Augustine's University, NC
Sewanee: The University of the South, TN
Voorhees College, SC

## Evangelical Covenant Church of America

**Four-year**

North Park University, IL

## Evangelical Free Church of America

**Four-year**

Trinity International University, IL

## Evangelical Lutheran Church in America

**Four-year**

Augsburg College, MN
Augusta University
    Augustana University, SD
Augustana College, IL
Bethany College, KS
California Lutheran University, CA
Capital University, OH
Carthage College, WI
Concordia College: Moorhead, MN
Finlandia University, MI
Gettysburg College, PA
Grand View University, IA
Gustavus Adolphus College, MN
Lenoir-Rhyne University, NC
Luther College, IA
Midland University, NE
Muhlenberg College, PA
Newberry College, SC
Pacific Lutheran University, WA
Roanoke College, VA
St. Olaf College, MN

Susquehanna University, PA
Texas Lutheran University, TX
Thiel College, PA
Waldorf University, IA
Wartburg College, IA
Wittenberg University, OH

## Evangelical Lutheran Synod

**Four-year**

Bethany Lutheran College, MN

## Free Methodist Church of North America

**Four-year**

Central Christian College of Kansas, KS
Greenville College, IL
Roberts Wesleyan College, NY
Seattle Pacific University, WA
Spring Arbor University, MI

## Free Will Baptists

**Four-year**

California Christian College, CA
University of Mount Olive, NC
Welch College, TN

## General Association of Regular Baptist Churches

**Four-year**

Faith Baptist Bible College and Theological Seminary, IA

## interdenominational tradition

**Four-year**

Asbury University, KY
Azusa Pacific University, CA
Biola University, CA
Bryan College
    Dayton, TN
College of the Ozarks, MO
Columbia International University, SC
Cornerstone University, MI
Ecclesia College, AR
Faith International University
    Fiath International University, WA
God's Bible School and College, OH
Grace University, NE
Heritage University, WA
John Brown University, AR
Laurel University, NC
Messiah College, PA
Moody Bible Institute, IL
Nazareth College, NY
Palm Beach Atlantic University, FL
Patten University, CA
Regent University, VA
Taylor University, IN
Trinity College of Florida, FL
Williamson College, TN

## Jewish faith

**Four-year**

American Jewish University, CA
Beis Medrash Heichal Dovid, NY
Beth Hamedrash Shaarei Yosher Institute, NY
Beth Hatalmud Rabbinical College, NY
Central Yeshiva Tomchei Tmimim-Lubavitch, NY
Gratz College, PA
Jewish Theological Seminary of America, NY
Kehilath Yakov Rabbinical Seminary, NY
Machzikei Hadath Rabbinical College, NY
Mesivta Torah Vodaath Seminary, NY
Michigan Jewish Institute, MI
Mirrer Yeshiva Central Institute, NY
Ohr Somayach Tanenbaum Education Center, NY

Rabbinical Academy Mesivta Rabbi Chaim Berlin, NY
Rabbinical College Beth Shraga, NY
Rabbinical College Bobover Yeshiva B'nei Zion, NY
Rabbinical College Ch'san Sofer of New York, NY
Rabbinical College of America, NJ
Rabbinical College of Long Island, NY
Rabbinical College of Telshe, OH
Rabbinical Seminary of America, NY
Shor Yoshuv Rabbinical College, NY
Talmudic University, FL
Talmudical Academy of New Jersey, NJ
Talmudical Institute of Upstate New York, NY
Talmudical Seminary Oholei Torah, NY
Telshe Yeshiva-Chicago, IL
Torah Temimah Talmudical Seminary, NY
U.T.A. Mesivta-Kiryas Joel, NY
United Talmudical Seminary, NY
Yeshiva and Kolel Bais Medrash Elyon, NY
Yeshiva and Kollel Harbotzas Torah, NY
Yeshiva Beth Yehuda-Yeshiva Gedolah of Greater Detroit, MI
Yeshiva College of the Nations Capital, MD
Yeshiva D'Monsey Rabbinical College, NY
Yeshiva Derech Chaim, NY
Yeshiva Gedolah Imrei Yosef D'Spinka, NY
Yeshiva Gedolah Rabbinical College, FL
Yeshiva Gedolah Zichron Moshe, NY
Yeshiva Karlin Stolin, NY
Yeshiva of Nitra, NY
Yeshiva of the Telshe Alumni, NY
Yeshiva Shaar Hatorah, NY
Yeshiva Shaarei Torah of Rockland, NY
Yeshivas Novominsk, NY
Yeshivat Mikdash Melech, NY
Yeshivath Beth Moshe, PA

**Two-year**

Bramson ORT College, NY

## Lutheran Church

**Four-year**

Valparaiso University, IN

## Lutheran Church - Missouri Synod

**Four-year**

Concordia College, NY
Concordia College, AL
Concordia University, OR
Concordia University, MI
Concordia University, NE
Concordia University Chicago, IL
Concordia University Irvine, CA
Concordia University St. Paul, MN
Concordia University Texas, TX
Concordia University Wisconsin, WI

## Lutheran Church in America

**Four-year**

Wagner College, NY

## Mennonite Brethren Church

**Four-year**

Fresno Pacific University, CA
Tabor College, KS

## Mennonite Church

**Four-year**

Bethel College, KS
Bluffton University, OH
Eastern Mennonite University, VA
Goshen College, IN

**Two-year**

Hesston College, KS

## Missionary Church

**Four-year**

Bethel College, IN

## Moravian Church in America

**Four-year**

Moravian College, PA
Salem College, NC

## nondenominational tradition

**Four-year**

Appalachian Bible College, WV
Arizona Christian University, AZ
Beulah Heights University, GA
Bob Jones University, SC
Calvary Bible College and Theological Seminary, MO
Colorado Christian University, CO
Davis College, NY
Friends University, KS
Gordon College, MA
Horizon University, CA
Kenyon College, OH
The King's College, NY
The King's University, TX
Lancaster Bible College, PA
LeTourneau University, TX
Limestone College, SC
The Master's University, CA
New Hope Christian College, OR
Occidental College, CA
Oral Roberts University, OK
Patrick Henry College, VA
Providence Christian College, CA
San Diego Christian College, CA
University of Northwestern - St. Paul, MN
University of the Southwest, NM
Westmont College, CA
Wheaton College, IL
William Jessup University, CA
World Mission University, CA

## Pentecostal Holiness Church

**Four-year**

Southwestern Christian University, OK
Universidad Pentecostal Mizpa, PR

## Presbyterian Church (USA)

**Four-year**

Agnes Scott College, GA
Alma College, MI
Arcadia University, PA
Austin College, TX
Belhaven University, MS
Blackburn College, IL
Bloomfield College, NJ
Buena Vista University, IA
Carroll University, WI
Centre College, KY
Coe College, IA
Covenant College, GA
Davidson College, NC
Davis and Elkins College, WV
Eckerd College, FL
Grove City College, PA
Hampden-Sydney College, VA
Hanover College, IN
Hastings College, NE
Illinois College, IL
King University, TN
Lees-McRae College, NC

## Affiliated with a religion

Lindenwood University, MO
Lyon College, AR
Macalester College, MN
Mary Baldwin University, VA
Maryville College, TN
Millikin University, IL
Missouri Valley College, MO
Monmouth College, IL
Muskingum University, OH
Presbyterian College, SC
Queens University of Charlotte, NC
Rhodes College, TN
Rocky Mountain College, MT
St. Andrews University, NC
Schreiner University, TX
Sterling College, KS
Stillman College, AL
Trinity University, TX
Tusculum College, TN
University of Dubuque, IA
University of Jamestown, ND
University of Pikeville, KY
University of the Ozarks, AR
University of Tulsa, OK
Waynesburg University, PA
Westminster College, MO
Westminster College, PA
Whitworth University, WA
Wilson College, PA

### Reformed Church in America

**Four-year**
Central College, IA
Hope College, MI
Northwestern College, IA

### Reformed Presbyterian Church of North America

**Four-year**
Erskine College, SC
Geneva College, PA
Montreat College, NC

### Roman Catholic Church

**Four-year**
Albertus Magnus College, CT
Alvernia University, PA
Alverno College, WI
Anna Maria College, MA
Aquinas College, MI
Aquinas College, TN
Assumption College, MA
Ave Maria University, FL
Avila University, MO
Barry University, FL
Bayamon Central University, PR
Bellarmine University, KY
Belmont Abbey College, NC
Benedictine College, KS
Benedictine University, IL
Boston College, MA
Brescia University, KY
Briar Cliff University, IA
Cabrini University, PA
Caldwell University, NJ
Calumet College of St. Joseph, IN
Canisius College, NY
Cardinal Stritch University, WI
Carlow University, PA
Carroll College, MT
Catholic Distance University, WV
Catholic University of America, DC
Chaminade University of Honolulu, HI
Chestnut Hill College, PA
Christendom College, VA
Christian Brothers University, TN
Clarke University, IA
College of Mount St. Vincent, NY
College of New Rochelle, NY
College of St. Benedict, MN
College of St. Elizabeth, NJ
College of St. Joseph in Vermont, VT
College of Saint Mary, NE

College of St. Scholastica, MN
College of the Holy Cross, MA
Creighton University, NE
DePaul University, IL
DeSales University, PA
Divine Word College, IA
Dominican University, IL
Duquesne University, PA
Edgewood College, WI
Elms College, MA
Emmanuel College, MA
Fairfield University, CT
Felician University, NJ
Fontbonne University, MO
Fordham University, NY
Franciscan University of Steubenville, OH
Gannon University, PA
Georgetown University, DC
Georgian Court University, NJ
Gonzaga University, WA
Gwynedd Mercy University, PA
Hilbert College, NY
Holy Apostles College and Seminary, CT
Holy Cross College, IN
Holy Family University, PA
Holy Names University, CA
Immaculata University, PA
Iona College, NY
John Carroll University, OH
John Paul the Great Catholic University, CA
King's College, PA
La Roche College, PA
La Salle University, PA
Le Moyne College, NY
Lewis University, IL
Loras College, IA
Lourdes University, OH
Loyola Marymount University, CA
Loyola University Chicago, IL
Loyola University Maryland, MD
Loyola University New Orleans, LA
Madonna University, MI
Manhattan College, NY
Marian University, IN
Marian University, WI
Marquette University, WI
Marygrove College, MI
Marylhurst University, OR
Marymount California University, CA
Marymount University, VA
Marywood University, PA
Mercy College of Health Sciences, IA
Mercyhurst University, PA
Merrimack College, MA
Misericordia University, PA
Molloy College, NY
Mount Aloysius College, PA
Mount Angel Seminary, OR
Mount Marty College, SD
Mount Mary University, WI
Mount Mercy University, IA
Mount St. Joseph University, OH
Mount Saint Mary College, NY
Mount Saint Mary's University, CA
Mount St. Mary's University, MD
Neumann University, PA
Newman University, KS
Niagara University, NY
Notre Dame College, OH
Notre Dame de Namur University, CA
Notre Dame of Maryland University, MD
Ohio Dominican University, OH
Our Lady of the Lake University of San Antonio, TX
Pontifical Catholic University of Puerto Rico, PR
Presentation College, SD
Providence College, RI
Quincy University, IL
Regis College, MA
Regis University, CO

Resurrection University, IL
Rivier University, NH
Rockhurst University, MO
Rosemont College, PA
Sacred Heart Major Seminary, MI
Sacred Heart University, CT
St. Ambrose University, IA
Saint Anselm College, NH
Saint Bonaventure University, NY
St. Catharine College, KY
St. Catherine University, MN
St. Edward's University, TX
St. Francis College, NY
St. Francis University, PA
St. Gregory's University, OK
St. John Fisher College, NY
St. John's University, NY
St. John's University, MN
St. Joseph Seminary College, LA
Saint Joseph's College, IN
Saint Joseph's College of Maine, ME
Saint Joseph's University, PA
Saint Leo University, FL
Saint Louis University, MO
Saint Martin's University, WA
Saint Mary's College, IN
St. Mary's College of California, CA
St. Mary's University, TX
St. Mary's University of Minnesota, MN
St. Mary-of-the-Woods College, IN
Saint Michael's College, VT
St. Norbert College, WI
Saint Peter's University, NJ
Saint Thomas University, FL
St. Vincent College, PA
Saint Xavier University, IL
Salve Regina University, RI
Santa Clara University, CA
Seattle University, WA
Seton Hall University, NJ
Seton Hill University, PA
Siena College, NY
Siena Heights University, MI
Silver Lake College of the Holy Family, WI
Spalding University, KY
Spring Hill College, AL
Stonehill College, MA
Thomas Aquinas College, CA
Thomas More College, KY
Thomas More College of Liberal Arts, NH
Trinity Washington University, DC
University of Dallas, TX
University of Dayton, OH
University of Detroit Mercy, MI
University of Great Falls, MT
University of Holy Cross, LA
University of Mary, ND
University of Notre Dame, IN
University of Portland, OR
University of Saint Francis, IN
University of St. Francis, IL
University of Saint Joseph, CT
University of St. Mary, KS
University of St. Thomas, TX
University of St. Thomas, MN
University of San Diego, CA
University of San Francisco, CA
University of Scranton, PA
University of the Incarnate Word, TX
Ursuline College, OH
Villanova University, PA
Viterbo University, WI
Walsh University, OH
Wheeling Jesuit University, WV
Xavier University, OH
Xavier University of Louisiana, LA

**Two-year**
Ancilla College, IN
Benedictine University at Springfield, IL
Donnelly College, KS
St. Elizabeth College of Nursing, NY

Trocaire College, NY
Villa Maria College of Buffalo, NY

### Seventh-day Adventists

**Four-year**
Adventist University of Health Sciences, FL
Andrews University, MI
Kettering College, OH
La Sierra University, CA
Loma Linda University, CA
Oakwood University, AL
Pacific Union College, CA
Southern Adventist University, TN
Southwestern Adventist University, TX
Union College, NE
Universidad Adventista de las Antillas, PR
Walla Walla University, WA
Washington Adventist University, MD

### Society of Friends (Quaker)

**Four-year**
Barclay College, KS
Earlham College, IN
George Fox University, OR
Guilford College, NC
William Penn University, IA
Wilmington College, OH

### Southern Baptist Convention

**Four-year**
Anderson University, SC
Baptist College of Florida, FL
Blue Mountain College, MS
Brewton-Parker College, GA
California Baptist University, CA
Carson-Newman University, TN
Charleston Southern University, SC
Chowan University, NC
Criswell College, TX
Gardner-Webb University, NC
Hannibal-LaGrange University, MO
Louisiana College, LA
Mississippi College, MS
New Orleans Baptist Theological Seminary, LA
North Greenville University, SC
Oklahoma Baptist University, OK
Shorter University, GA
Southern Baptist Theological Seminary, KY
Southwest Baptist University, MO
Truett McConnell University, GA
Union University, TN
Wayland Baptist University, TX
Williams Baptist College, AR

### Ukrainian Catholic Church

**Two-year**
Manor College, PA

### United Brethren in Christ

**Four-year**
Huntington University, IN

### United Church of Christ

**Four-year**
Catawba College, NC
Defiance College, OH
Dillard University, LA
Doane University, NE
Drury University, MO
Elmhurst College, IL
Heidelberg University, OH
Hood College, MD
Lakeland University, WI
Northland College, WI
Olivet College, MI
Pacific University, OR
Talladega College, AL
Tougaloo College, MS

### United Methodist Church

**Four-year**

Adrian College, MI
Alaska Pacific University, AK
Albion College, MI
Albright College, PA
Allegheny College, PA
Allegheny Wesleyan College, OH
American University, DC
Baker University, KS
Baldwin Wallace University, OH
Bennett College for Women, NC
Bethune-Cookman University, FL
Birmingham-Southern College, AL
Brevard College, NC
BryanLGH College of Health Sciences, NE
Centenary College of Louisiana, LA
Centenary University, NJ
Central Methodist University, MO
Claflin University, SC
Clark Atlanta University, GA
Columbia College, SC
Cornell College, IA
Dakota Wesleyan University, SD
DePauw University, IN
Drew University, NJ
Emory & Henry College, VA
Emory University, GA
Ferrum College, VA
Florida Southern College, FL
Green Mountain College, VT
Greensboro College, NC
Hamline University, MN
Hendrix College, AR
High Point University, NC
Huntingdon College, AL
Huston-Tillotson University, TX
Iowa Wesleyan College, IA
Kansas Wesleyan University, KS
Kentucky Wesleyan College, KY
LaGrange College, GA
Lebanon Valley College, PA
Lindsey Wilson College, KY
Lycoming College, PA
Martin Methodist College, TN
McKendree University, IL
McMurry University, TX
Methodist University, NC
Millsaps College, MS
Morningside College, IA
Nebraska Wesleyan University, NE
North Carolina Wesleyan College, NC
North Central College, IL
Ohio Northern University, OH
Ohio Wesleyan University, OH
Oklahoma City University, OK
Otterbein University, OH
Pfeiffer University, NC
Philander Smith College, AR
Randolph College, VA
Randolph-Macon College, VA
Reinhardt University, GA
Rust College, MS
Shenandoah University, VA
Simpson College, IA
Southern Methodist University, TX
Southwestern College, KS
Southwestern University, TX
Tennessee Wesleyan College, TN
Texas Wesleyan University, TX
Union College, KY
University of Evansville, IN
University of Indianapolis, IN
University of Mount Union, OH
Virginia Wesleyan College, VA
Wesley College, DE
Wesleyan College, GA
West Virginia Wesleyan College, WV
Wiley College, TX
Willamette University, OR
Wofford College, SC
Young Harris College, GA

**Two-year**

Andrew College, GA
Hiwassee College, TN
Louisburg College, NC
Oxford College of Emory University, GA
Spartanburg Methodist College, SC

### Wesleyan Church

**Four-year**

Houghton College, NY
Indiana Wesleyan University, IN
Oklahoma Wesleyan University, OK
Southern Wesleyan University, SC

### Wisconsin Evangelical Lutheran Synod

**Four-year**

Wisconsin Lutheran College, WI

## Historically Black colleges

### Four-year

Alabama Agricultural and Mechanical University, AL
Alabama State University, AL
Albany State University, GA
Alcorn State University, MS
Allen University, SC
Arkansas Baptist College, AR
Benedict College, SC
Bennett College for Women, NC
Bethune-Cookman University, FL
Bluefield State College, WV
Bowie State University, MD
Central State University, OH
Cheyney University of Pennsylvania, PA
Claflin University, SC
Clark Atlanta University, GA
Concordia College, AL
Coppin State University, MD
Delaware State University, DE
Dillard University, LA
Edward Waters College, FL
Elizabeth City State University, NC
Fayetteville State University, NC
Fisk University, TN
Florida Agricultural and Mechanical University, FL
Florida Memorial University, FL
Fort Valley State University, GA
Grambling State University, LA
Hampton University, VA
Harris-Stowe State University, MO
Howard University, DC
Huston-Tillotson University, TX
Jackson State University, MS
Jarvis Christian College, TX
Johnson C. Smith University, NC
Kentucky State University, KY
Lane College, TN
Langston University, OK
LeMoyne-Owen College, TN
Lincoln University, MO
Lincoln University, PA
Livingstone College, NC
Miles College, AL
Mississippi Valley State University, MS
Morehouse College, GA
Morgan State University, MD
Morris College, SC
Norfolk State University, VA
North Carolina Central University, NC
Oakwood University, AL
Paine College, GA
Paul Quinn College, TX
Philander Smith College, AR
Prairie View A&M University, TX
Rust College, MS

Saint Augustine's University, NC
Savannah State University, GA
Selma University, AL
Shaw University, NC
South Carolina State University, SC
Southern University
New Orleans, LA
Southern University and Agricultural and Mechanical College, LA
Southwestern Christian College, TX
Spelman College, GA
Stillman College, AL
Talladega College, AL
Tennessee State University, TN
Texas College, TX
Texas Southern University, TX
Tougaloo College, MS
Tuskegee University, AL
University of Arkansas
Pine Bluff, AR
University of Maryland
Eastern Shore, MD
University of the District of Columbia, DC
Virginia State University, VA
Virginia Union University, VA
Virginia University of Lynchburg, VA
Voorhees College, SC
West Virginia State University, WV
Wilberforce University, OH
Wiley College, TX
Winston-Salem State University, NC
Xavier University of Louisiana, LA

### Two-year

Bishop State Community College, AL
Clinton College, SC
Coahoma Community College, MS
Denmark Technical College, SC
Gadsden State Community College, AL
Hinds Community College, MS
Lawson State Community College, AL
St. Philip's College, TX
Southern University
Shreveport, LA

## Hispanic serving colleges

### Four-year

Adams State University, CO
American University of Puerto Rico, PR
Angelo State University, TX
Antioch University
Santa Barbara, CA
Atlantic University College, PR
Baptist University of the Americas, TX
Bayamon Central University, PR
California Christian College, CA
California State Polytechnic University:
Pomona, CA
California State University
Bakersfield, CA
Dominguez Hills, CA
Fresno, CA
Fullerton, CA
Long Beach, CA
Los Angeles, CA
Monterey Bay, CA
San Bernardino, CA
San Marcos, CA
Stanislaus, CA
Calumet College of St. Joseph, IN
Caribbean University, PR
Carlos Albizu University, FL
Carlos Albizu University: San Juan, PR
City University of New York
City College, NY
John Jay College of Criminal Justice, NY
Lehman College, NY

New York City College of Technology, NY
Conservatory of Music of Puerto Rico, PR
Dominican University, IL
Eastern New Mexico University, NM
EDP University of Puerto Rico: Hato Rey, PR
EDP University of Puerto Rico: San Sebastian, PR
Escuela de Artes Plasticas de Puerto Rico, PR
Florida International University, FL
Fresno Pacific University, CA
Heritage University, WA
Hodges University, FL
Houston Baptist University, TX
Humphreys College, CA
Inter American University of Puerto Rico
Aguadilla Campus, PR
Arecibo Campus, PR
Barranquitas Campus, PR
Bayamon Campus, PR
Fajardo Campus, PR
Guayama Campus, PR
Metropolitan Campus, PR
Ponce Campus, PR
San German Campus, PR
La Sierra University, CA
Mercy College, NY
Mount Angel Seminary, OR
Mount Saint Mary's University, CA
New Jersey City University, NJ
New Mexico Highlands University, NM
New Mexico Institute of Mining and Technology, NM
New Mexico State University, NM
Northern New Mexico College, NM
Northwood University
Texas, TX
Notre Dame de Namur University, CA
Nova Southeastern University, FL
Our Lady of the Lake University of San Antonio, TX
Pacific Oaks College, CA
Pontifical Catholic University of Puerto Rico, PR
St. Augustine College, IL
St. Edward's University, TX
St. Mary's University, TX
Saint Peter's University, NJ
Saint Thomas University, FL
San Diego State University, CA
Sul Ross State University, TX
Texas A&M International University, TX
Texas A&M University
Corpus Christi, TX
Kingsville, TX
Texas State University, TX
Turabo University, PR
Universidad Adventista de las Antillas, PR
Universidad Central del Caribe, PR
Universidad del Este, PR
Universidad Metropolitana, PR
Universidad Pentecostal Mizpa, PR
Universidad Politecnica de Puerto Rico, PR
University College of San Juan, PR
University of California
Merced, CA
Riverside, CA
University of Houston, TX
Clear Lake, TX
Downtown, TX
Victoria, TX
University of La Verne, CA
University of New Mexico, NM
University of Puerto Rico
Aguadilla, PR
Arecibo, PR
Bayamon University College, PR

Carolina Regional College, PR
Cayey University College, PR
Mayaguez, PR
Medical Sciences, PR
Ponce, PR
Rio Piedras, PR
Utuado, PR
University of St. Thomas, TX
University of Texas
El Paso, TX
San Antonio, TX
of the Permian Basin, TX
University of the Incarnate Word, TX
University of the Southwest, NM
Vaughn College of Aeronautics and
Technology, NY
Western New Mexico University, NM
Whittier College, CA
Woodbury University, CA

## Two-year

Allan Hancock College, CA
Amarillo College, TX
Antelope Valley College, CA
Arizona Western College, AZ
Bakersfield College, CA
Big Bend Community College, WA
Brazosport College, TX
Brookhaven College, TX
Broward College, FL
Cabrillo College, CA
Canada College, CA
Capital Community College, CT
Central Arizona College, AZ
Centro de Estudios Multidisciplinarios,
PR
Cerritos College, CA
Chabot College, CA
Chaffey College, CA
Citrus College, CA
City College
Altamonte Springs, FL
Miami, FL
City Colleges of Chicago
Harold Washington College, IL
Malcolm X College, IL
Richard J. Daley College, IL
Wilbur Wright College, IL
City University of New York
Borough of Manhattan
Community College, NY
Bronx Community College, NY
Hostos Community College, NY
LaGuardia Community College,
NY
Queensborough Community
College, NY
Clarendon College, TX
Coastal Bend College, TX
Cochise College, AZ
College of the Canyons, CA
College of the Desert, CA
College of the Sequoias, CA
Contra Costa College, CA
Crafton Hills College, CA
Cuyamaca College, CA
Cypress College, CA
Del Mar College, TX
Dodge City Community College, KS
Dona Ana Community College of New
Mexico State University, NM
Donnelly College, KS
East Los Angeles College, CA
Eastern New Mexico University:
Roswell, NM
Eastfield College, TX
El Camino College, CA
El Centro College, TX
Elgin Community College, IL
Estrella Mountain Community College,
AZ
Evergreen Valley College, CA
Fresno City College, CA
Fullerton College, CA
Galveston College, TX

Garden City Community College, KS
GateWay Community College, AZ
Glendale Community College, AZ
Hartnell College, CA
Houston Community College System,
TX
Hudson County Community College,
NJ
Humacao Community College, PR
Laredo Community College, TX
Lee College, TX
Lone Star College System, TX
Long Beach City College, CA
Los Angeles City College, CA
Los Angeles Harbor College, CA
Los Angeles Mission College, CA
Los Angeles Pierce College, CA
Los Angeles Trade and Technical
College, CA
Los Angeles Valley College, CA
Los Medanos College, CA
Luna Community College, NM
Mesalands Community College, NM
Miami Dade College, FL
Midland College, TX
Modesto Junior College, CA
Monterey Peninsula College, CA
Morton College, IL
Mount San Antonio College, CA
Mount San Jacinto College, CA
Mountain View College, TX
Napa Valley College, CA
New Mexico Junior College, NM
New Mexico State University
Alamogordo, NM
Carlsbad, NM
Grants, NM
North Lake College, TX
Northern Essex Community College,
MA
Northwest Vista College, TX
Norwalk Community College, CT
Odessa College, TX
Otero Junior College, CO
Palo Verde College, CA
Palomar College, CA
Pasadena City College, CA
Passaic County Community College,
NJ
Phoenix College, AZ
Porterville College, CA
Pueblo Community College, CO
Reedley College, CA
Rio Hondo College, CA
Riverside City College, CA
St. Philip's College, TX
San Antonio College, TX
San Bernardino Valley College, CA
San Diego City College, CA
San Diego Mesa College, CA
San Jacinto College, TX
San Joaquin Delta College, CA
San Jose City College, CA
Santa Ana College, CA
Santa Barbara City College, CA
Santa Fe Community College, NM
Santa Monica College, CA
Santiago Canyon College, CA
Seward County Community College,
KS
South Mountain Community College,
AZ
South Plains College, TX
South Texas College, TX
Southwest Texas Junior College, TX
Southwestern College, CA
Taft College, CA
Trinidad State Junior College, CO
Triton College, IL
Union County College, NJ
Universal Technology College of
Puerto Rico, PR
Valencia College, FL
Ventura College, CA
Victor Valley College, CA

Victoria College, TX
West Hills College: Coalinga, CA
West Hills College: Lemoore, CA
West Los Angeles College, CA
Western Texas College, TX
Wharton County Junior College, TX
Woodland Community College, CA
Yakima Valley Community College,
WA

# College addresses

**Abilene Christian University**
www.acu.edu
Office of Admissions
ACU Box 29000
Abilene, TX 79699
Fax: (325) 674-2130
E-mail: jdg99t@acu.edu
Phone: (325) 674-2710

**Abraham Baldwin Agricultural College**
www.abac.edu
Admissions
ABAC 4, 2802 Moore Highway
Tifton, GA 31793-2601
Fax: (229) 391-5002
E-mail: admissions@abac.edu
Phone: (229) 391-5004

**Academy College**
www.academycollege.edu
Admissions Coordinator
1600 West 82nd Street
Suite 100
Bloomington, MN 55431
Fax: (952) 851-0094
E-mail: admissions@academycollege.edu
Phone: (952) 851-0066

**Academy of Art University**
www.academyart.edu
International Admissions Office
79 New Montgomery Street
San Francisco, CA 94105-3410
Fax: (415) 618-6278
E-mail: intladmissions@academyart.edu
Phone: (415) 274-2208

**Adams State University**
www.adams.edu
Assistant Vice President of Enrollment
Management
208 Edgemont Boulevard
Suite 2190
Alamosa, CO 81101
Fax: (719) 587-7522
E-mail: admissions@adams.edu
Phone: (719) 587-7712

**Adelphi University**
www.adelphi.edu
Office of International Admissions
One South Avenue, Nexus Building, Rm. 111
PO Box 701
Garden City, NY 11530-0701
Fax: (516) 877-3039
E-mail: intladmissions@adelphi.edu
Phone: (516) 877-3049

**Adirondack Community College**
www.sunyacc.edu
Director of Admissions
640 Bay Road
Queensbury, NY 12804
Fax: (518) 743-2317
E-mail: linehans@sunyacc.edu
Phone: (518) 743-2264

**Adrian College**
www.adrian.edu
Admissions
110 South Madison Street
Adrian, MI 49221-2575
Fax: (517) 264-3878
E-mail: admissions@adrian.edu
Phone: (800) 877-2246

**Adventist University of Health Sciences**
www.adu.edu
Enrollment Services
671 Winyah Drive
Orlando, FL 32803
Fax: (407) 303-9408
E-mail: erin.merritt@adu.edu
Phone: (407) 303-9498

**Agnes Scott College**
www.agnesscott.edu
Office of Admission
141 East College Avenue
Decatur, GA 30030-3797
Fax: (404) 471-6414
E-mail: admission@agnesscott.edu
Phone: (404) 471-6285

**Aiken Technical College**
www.atc.edu
Director of Admissions and Records
PO Drawer 696
Aiken, SC 29802
Fax: (803) 593-6526
E-mail: moonj@atc.edu
Phone: (803) 593-9954 ext. 1400

**Aims Community College**
www.aims.edu
Admissions & Records
4911 West 20th Street
Greeley, CO 80634
E-mail: kristie.hererra@aims.edu
Phone: (970) 339-6401

**Alabama Agricultural and Mechanical University**
www.aamu.edu
Admissions Office
Box 908
Normal, AL 35762
Fax: (256) 372-5249
E-mail: venita.king@aamu.edu
Phone: (256) 372-5245

**Alabama State University**
www.alasu.edu
International Programs
PO Box 271
Montgomery, AL 36101-0271
Fax: (334) 229-4984
E-mail: cmwilliams@alasu.edu
Phone: (334) 229-4695

**Alamance Community College**
www.alamancecc.edu
Student Success
Box 8000
Graham, NC 27253
Fax: (336) 506-4264
E-mail: elizabeth.brehler@alamance.cc.nc.us
Phone: (336) 506-4120

**Alaska Pacific University**
www.alaskapacific.edu
Admissions
4101 University Drive
Anchorage, AK 99508-3051
Fax: (907) 564-8317
E-mail: ccaywood@alaskapacific.edu
Phone: (907) 563-8338

**Albany College of Pharmacy and Health Sciences**
www.acphs.edu
Admissions
106 New Scotland Avenue
Albany, NY 12208-3492
Fax: (518) 694-7322
E-mail: admissions@acphs.edu
Phone: (518) 694-7183

**Albany State University**
www.asurams.edu
Office of Admissions
504 College Drive
Albany, GA 31705-2717
Fax: (229) 317-6614
E-mail: SueAnn.Balch@asurams.edu
Phone: (229) 317-6924

**Albany Technical College**
www.albanytech.edu
Admissions Office
1704 South Slappy Boulevard
Albany, GA 31701-3514
Fax: (229) 430-6180
Phone: (229) 430-3520

**Albertus Magnus College**
www.albertus.edu
Office of Admission
700 Prospect Street
New Haven, CT 06511-1189
Fax: (203) 773-5248
E-mail: arreich@albertus.edu
Phone: (203) 787-8635

**Albion College**
www.albion.edu
Admission
611 East Porter Street
Albion, MI 49224-1831
Fax: (517) 629-0569
E-mail: emorley@albion.edu
Phone: (517) 630-1424

**Albright College**
www.albright.edu
Admission Office
North 13th and Bern Streets
PO Box 15234
Reading, PA 19612-5234
Fax: (610) 921-7729
E-mail: nchristie@albright.edu
Phone: (610) 921-7700

**Alcorn State University**
www.alcorn.edu
Admissions
1000 ASU Drive #300
Lorman, MS 39096-7500
Fax: (601) 877-6347
E-mail: ksampson@alcorn.edu
Phone: (601) 877-6147

**Alderson-Broaddus University**
www.ab.edu
Admissions
101 College Hill Drive
Campus Box 2003
Philippi, WV 26416
Fax: (304) 457-6239
E-mail: dionnemi@ab.edu
Phone: (304) 457-6326

**Alexandria Technical and Community College**
www.alextech.edu
Registrar's Office
1601 Jefferson Street
Alexandria, MN 56308-3799
Fax: (320) 762-4430
E-mail: international@alextech.edu
Phone: (320) 762-4482

**Alfred University**
www.alfred.edu
Office of Admissions
Alumni Hall
One Saxon Drive
Alfred, NY 14802-1205
Fax: (607) 871-2198
E-mail: unis@alfred.edu
Phone: (607) 871-2115

**Alice Lloyd College**
www.alc.edu
Admissions
100 Purpose Road
Pippa Passes, KY 41844
Fax: (606) 368-6215
E-mail: admissions@alc.edu
Phone: (606) 368-6036

**Allan Hancock College**
www.hancockcollege.edu
Admissions and Records
800 South College Drive
Santa Maria, CA 93454-6399
Fax: (805) 922-3477
E-mail: pwood@hancockcollege.edu
Phone: (805) 922-6366 ext. 3281

**Allegany College of Maryland**
www.allegany.edu
Admissions Office
12401 Willowbrook Road, SE
Cumberland, MD 21502
Fax: (301) 784-5027
E-mail: ckauffman@allegany.edu
Phone: (301) 784-5199

**Allegheny College**
www.allegheny.edu
Admissions
Box 5, 520 North Main Street
Meadville, PA 16335
Fax: (814) 337-0431
E-mail: globalgators@allegheny.edu
Phone: (814) 332-4351

**Allegheny Wesleyan College**
www.awc.edu
2161 Woodside Road
Salem, OH 44460-9598
Fax: (330) 337-6255
E-mail: college@awc.edu
Phone: (330) 337-6403

**Allen College**
www.allencollege.edu
Student Services
1825 Logan Avenue
Waterloo, IA 50703
Fax: (319) 226-2010
E-mail: Joanna.Ramsden-
Meier@AllenCollege.edu
Phone: (319) 226-2014

**Allen County Community College**
www.allencc.edu
Academic Advisor
1801 North Cottonwood
Iola, KS 66749
Fax: (620) 365-3284
E-mail: npeters@allencc.edu
Phone: (620) 365-5116 ext. 255

**Allen University**
www.allenuniversity.edu
Director of Financial Aid
1530 Harden Street
Columbia, SC 29204
Fax: (803) 376-5731
E-mail: swarren@allenuniversity.edu
Phone: (803) 376-5930

**Alliant International University**
www.alliant.edu
10455 Pomerado Road
San Diego, CA 92131-1799
Fax: (858) 635-4739
E-mail: admissions@alliant.edu
Phone: (866) 825-5426

**Alma College**
www.alma.edu
Admissions
614 West Superior Street
Alma, MI 48801-1599
Fax: (989) 463-7057
E-mail: admissions@alma.edu
Phone: (989) 463-7368

**Alvernia University**
www.alvernia.edu
Office of Admissions
400 St. Bernardine Street
Reading, PA 19607-1799
Fax: (610) 790-2873
E-mail: admissions@alvernia.edu
Phone: (610) 796-8269

**Alverno College**
www.alverno.edu
International and Intercultural Center
3400 South 43rd Street
PO Box 343922
Milwaukee, WI 53234-3922
Fax: (414) 382-6160
E-mail: rachel.haos@alverno.edu
Phone: (414) 382-6066

**Amarillo College**
www.actx.edu
Office of Admissions
Box 447
Amarillo, TX 79178
Fax: (806) 371-5066
E-mail: AskAC@actx.edu
Phone: (806) 371-5030

**American Academy of Art**
www.aaart.edu
Office of the Registrar
332 South Michigan Avenue, Suite 300
Chicago, IL 60604-4302
Fax: (312) 294-9570
E-mail: info@aaart.edu
Phone: (312) 461-0600 ext. 134

**American Academy of Dramatic Arts**
www.aada.edu
120 Madison Avenue
New York, NY 10016
Fax: (212) 686-1284
E-mail: admissions-ny@aada.edu
Phone: (212) 686-0620

**American Academy of Dramatic Arts: West**
www.aada.edu
1336 North La Brea Avenue
Los Angeles, CA 90028
Fax: (323) 464-1250
E-mail: jcanales@aada.edu
Phone: (323) 464-2777 ext. 108

**American Baptist College**
www.abcnash.edu
1800 Baptist World Center Drive
Nashville, TN 37207
Fax: (615) 226-7855
E-mail: admissions@abcnash.edu
Phone: (615) 687-6907

**American InterContinental University**
www.aiuniv.edu
Admissions
231 North Martingale Road 6th Floor
Schaumburg, IL 60173
Phone: (855) 377-1888

**American International College**
www.aic.edu
Admissions
1000 State Street
Springfield, MA 01109
Fax: (413) 205-3051
E-mail: jonathan.scully@aic.edu
Phone: (800) 242-3142

**American Jewish University**
www.college.aju.edu
Director of Admissions
Office of Undergraduate Admissions
Familian Campus, 15600 Mulholland Drive
Bel-Air, CA 90077
Fax: (310) 471-3657
E-mail: achernichovski@aju.edu
Phone: (310) 440-1250

**American National University: Fort Wayne**
www.national-college.edu
6131 North Clinton Street
Fort Wayne, IN 46825
Phone: (260) 483-1605

**American National University:
Harrisonburg**
www.an.edu
1515 Country Club Road
Harrisonburg, VA 22802
Fax: (540) 432-1133
E-mail: market@national-college.edu
Phone: (800) 664-1886

**American National University: Indianapolis**
https://www.an.edu
6060 Castleway Drive West
Indianapolis, IN 46250
Phone: (317) 578-7353

**American National University: Parkersburg**
www.an.edu
110 Park Center Drive
Parkersburg, WV 26101
Phone: (304) 699-3005

**American National University: Salem**
www.an.edu
1813 East Main Street
Salem, VA 24153
Fax: (540) 444-4198
Phone: (540) 986-1800

**American National University: South Bend**
www.national-college.edu
1030 East Jefferson Boulevard
South Bend, IN 46617
Phone: (574) 307-7100

**American Public University System**
www.apus.edu
Admissions
111 West Congress Street
Charles Town, WV 25414
Fax: (304) 724-3764
E-mail: ydeal@apus.edu

**American River College**
www.arc.losrios.edu
Admission
4700 College Oak Drive
Sacramento, CA 95841
Fax: (916) 484-8864
E-mail: recadmis@arc.losrios.edu
Phone: (916) 484-8011

**American Sentinel University**
www.americansentinel.edu
Birmingham Office
2260 South Xanadu Way, Suite 310
Aurora, CO 80014
Fax: (866) 505-2450
E-mail: natalie.nixon@americansentinel.edu
Phone: (866) 922-5690

**American University**
www.american.edu
International Undergraduate Admissions
4400 Massachusetts Avenue NW
Washington, DC 20016-8001
Fax: (202) 885-6014
E-mail: intadm@american.edu
Phone: (202) 885-6000

**American University of Puerto Rico**
www.aupr.edu
PO Box 2037
Bayamon, PR 00960-2037
Fax: (787) 785-7377
E-mail: oficinaadmisiones@aupr.edu
Phone: (787) 620-2040 ext. 2020

**Amherst College**
www.amherst.edu
Admission Office
PO Box 5000
Amherst, MA 01002-5000
Fax: (413) 542-2040
E-mail: admission@amherst.edu
Phone: (413) 542-2328

**Ancilla College**
www.ancilla.edu
Admissions
9601 Union Road
PO Box 1
Donaldson, IN 46513
Fax: (574) 935-1773
E-mail: Justin.Crew@ancilla.edu
Phone: (574) 936-8898 ext. 397

**Anderson University**
www.andersonuniversity.edu
Coordinator of International and Multicultural
Recruitment
316 Boulevard
Anderson, SC 29621-4002
Fax: (864) 231-2033
E-mail: ljohnson@andersonuniversity.edu
Phone: (800) 542-3594

**Andrew College**
www.andrewcollege.edu
Office of Admission
501 College Street
Cuthbert, GA 39840-1395
Fax: (229) 732-2176
E-mail: aaronfeyes@andrewcollege.edu
Phone: (229) 732-2171 ext. 5938

**Andrews University**
www.andrews.edu
100 US Highway 31
Berrien Springs, MI 49104
Fax: (269) 471-3228
E-mail: enroll@andrews.edu

**Angelo State University**
www.angelo.edu
Center for International Studies
ASU Station #11014
San Angelo, TX 76909-1014
Fax: (325) 942-2084
E-mail: meghan.pace@angelo.edu
Phone: (325) 942-2083

**Anna Maria College**
www.annamaria.edu
Dean of Admissions and Financial Aid
50 Sunset Lane, Box O
Paxton, MA 01612-1198
Fax: (508) 849-3362
E-mail: pmiller@annamaria.edu
Phone: (508) 849-3586

**Anne Arundel Community College**
www.aacc.edu
Admissions and Enrollment Development
101 College Parkway
Arnold, MD 21012-1895
Fax: (410) 777-4246
E-mail: admissions@aacc.edu
Phone: (410) 777-2152

**Antelope Valley College**
www.avc.edu
Enrollment Services
3041 West Avenue K
Lancaster, CA 93536-5426
Fax: (661) 722-6531
E-mail: earndt@avc.edu
Phone: (661) 722-6300 ext. 6342

**Antioch University Los Angeles**
www.antiochla.edu
Director of Admissions Recruitment
400 Corporate Pointe
Ste 2000
Culver City, CA 90230-7615
Fax: (310) 821-6032
E-mail: MHall@antioch.edu
Phone: (800) 726-8462

**Antioch University Santa Barbara**
www.antiochsb.edu
Admissions
602 Anacapa Street
Santa Barbara, CA 93101
Fax: (805) 962-4786
E-mail: sestomo@antioch.edu
Phone: (805) 962-8179 ext. 5113

**Antonelli College: Cincinnati**
www.antonellicollege.edu
124 East Seventh Street
Cincinnati, OH 45202
Fax: (513) 241-9396
Phone: (513) 241-4338

**Antonelli College: Jackson**
www.antonellicollege.edu
2323 Lakeland Drive
Jackson, MS 39232
E-mail:
jackson.admissions@antonellicollege.edu
Phone: (601) 362-9991

**Antonelli Institute of Art and Photography**
www.antonelli.edu
300 Montgomery Avenue
Erdenheim, PA 19038-8242
Fax: (215) 836-2794
E-mail: admissions@antonelli.edu
Phone: (215) 836-2222

## Apex School of Theology
www.apexsot.edu
1701 TW Alexander Drive
Durham, NC 27703
E-mail: smanning@apexsot.edu
Phone: (919) 572-1625 ext. 7025

## Appalachian Bible College
https://abc.edu
Admissions
Director of Admissions
161 College Drive
Mount Hope, WV 25880
Fax: (304) 877-5082
E-mail: benjamin.cale@abc.edu
Phone: (304) 877-6428

## Appalachian State University
www.appstate.edu
Admissions
ASU Box 32004
Boone, NC 28608
Fax: (828) 262-4037
E-mail: mcdevittkb@appstate.edu
Phone: (828) 262-2120

## Aquinas College
www.aquinas.edu
Admissions Representative
1700 Fulton Street E
Grand Rapids, MI 49506-1801
Fax: (616) 732-4469
E-mail: kmd015@aquinas.edu
Phone: (616) 632-1123

## Aquinas College
www.aquinascollege.edu
Admissions
4210 Harding Pike
Nashville, TN 37205-2086
Fax: (615) 279-3893
E-mail: hansomc@aquinascollege.edu
Phone: (615) 297-7545 ext. 411

## Arcadia University
www.arcadia.edu
Enrollment Management
450 South Easton Road
Glenside, PA 19038-3295
Fax: (215) 572-4049
E-mail: international@arcadia.edu
Phone: (215) 572-2910

## Argosy University: Atlanta
www.argosy.edu/atlanta
980 Hammond Drive, Suite 100
Atlanta, GA 30328
E-mail: auaadmissions@argosy.edu
Phone: (770) 671-1200

## Argosy University: Chicago
www.argosy.edu/chicago
Student Services
225 North Michigan Avenue, Suite 1300
Chicago, IL 60601
E-mail: jlanderson@argosy.edu
Phone: (312) 777-7622

## Argosy University: Dallas
www.argosy.edu/dallas
5001 Lyndon B. Johnson Freeway, Heritage
Square
Farmers Branch, TX 75244
E-mail: audadmis@argosy.edu
Phone: (214) 459-2237

## Argosy University: Denver
www.argosy.edu/locations/denver
7600 East Eastman Avenue
Denver, CO 80231
Phone: (303) 923-4110

## Argosy University: Hawaii
www.argosy.edu/hawaii
400 ASB Tower, 1001 Bishop Street
Honolulu, HI 96813
E-mail: auhonadmissions@argosy.edu
Phone: (808) 791-5214

## Argosy University: Inland Empire
www.argosy.edu/inlandempire
3401 Centre Lake Drive, Suite 200
Ontario, CA 91761
Phone: (909) 915-3800

## Argosy University: Los Angeles
www.argosy.edu/locations/los-angeles
5230 Pacific Concourse, Suite 200
Los Angeles, CA 90045
E-mail: ausmadms@argosy.edu

## Argosy University: Nashville
www.argosy.edu/nashville
100 Centerview Drive, Suite 225
Nashville, TN 37214
Phone: (615) 525-2800

## Argosy University: Online
www.online.argosy.edu
2233 West Dunlap Avenue
Phoenix, AZ 85021
Phone: (866) 427-4679

## Argosy University: Orange County
www.argosy.edu/orangecounty
601 South Lewis Street
Orange, CA 92868
Phone: (714) 620-3715

## Argosy University: Phoenix
www.argosy.edu/phoenix
2233 West Dunlap Avenue
Phoenix, AZ 85021
Phone: (602) 216-2600

## Argosy University: Salt Lake City
www.argosy.edu
121 Election Road, Suite 300
Draper, UT 84020
Phone: (601) 601-5000

## Argosy University: San Diego
www.argosy.edu/locations/san-diego
1615 Murray Canyon Road
San Diego, CA 92108
E-mail: ausdadmissions@argosy.edu

## Argosy University: San Francisco Bay Area
www.argosy.edu/sanfrancisco
1005 Atlantic Avenue
Alameda, CA 94501
E-mail: ausfadmissions@argosy.edu
Phone: (510) 217-4777

## Argosy University: Sarasota
www.argosy.edu/locations/sarasota
5250 17th Street
Sarasota, FL 34235
E-mail: ausradmissions@argosy.edu
Phone: (877) 331-4480

## Argosy University: Schaumburg
www.argosy.edu/schaumburg
999 North Plaza Drive, Suite 111
Schaumburg, IL 60173-5403
Phone: (847) 969-4910

## Argosy University: Seattle
www.argosy.edu/seattle
2601-A Elliott Avenue
Seattle, WA 98121
E-mail: ausadmissions@argosy.edu
Phone: (206) 393-3516

## Argosy University: Tampa
www.argosy.edu/tampa
1403 North Howard Avenue
Tampa, FL 33607
E-mail: autaadmis@argosy.edu
Phone: (866) 357-4426

## Argosy University: Twin Cities
www.argosy.edu/twincities
1515 Central Parkway
Eagan, MN 55121
E-mail: autcadmissions@argosy.edu
Phone: (651) 846-3300

## Argosy University: Washington D.C.
www.argosy.edu/washingtondc
1550 Wilson Boulevard, Suite 600
Arlington, VA 22209
E-mail: auwadmissions@argosy.edu
Phone: (703) 526-5800

## Arizona Christian University
www.arizonachristian.edu
Office of Admissions
2625 East Cactus Road
Phoenix, AZ 85032-7042
Fax: (602) 404-2159
E-mail: admissions@arizonachristian.edu
Phone: (602) 386-4100

## Arizona State University
www.asu.edu
Undergraduate International Admissions
PO Box 870112
Tempe, AZ 85287-0112
Fax: (480) 727-6453
E-mail: asuinternational@asu.edu
Phone: (480) 965-2437

**Arizona Western College**
www.azwestern.edu
International Students Office
PO Box 929
Yuma, AZ 85366-0929
Fax: (928) 317-5888
E-mail: kenneth.kuntzelman@azwestern.edu
Phone: (928) 344-7699

**Arkansas Baptist College**
www.arkansasbaptist.edu
Admissions and Recruitment
1621 Dr. Martin Luther King Drive
Little Rock, AR 72202
Fax: (501) 374-6136
E-mail: admissions@arkansasbaptist.edu
Phone: (501) 244-5104

**Arkansas State University**
www.astate.edu
Admissions, Records, & Registration
PO Box 1570
State University, AR 72467-1570
Fax: (870) 972-3917
E-mail: swess@astate.edu
Phone: (870) 972-2623

**Arkansas State University Mid-South**
www.asumidsouth.edu
Registrar's Office
2000 West Broadway
West Memphis, AR 72301
Fax: (870) 733-6719
E-mail: landerson@asumidsouth.edu
Phone: (870) 733-6732

**Arkansas State University: Beebe**
www.asub.edu
Admissions
PO Box 1000
Beebe, AR 72012-1000
Fax: (501) 882-8895
E-mail: pkcarson@asub.edu
Phone: (501) 882-4426

**Arkansas State University: Mountain Home**
www.asumh.edu
Assistant Vice Chancellor for Enrollment
1600 South College Street
Attention: Admissions
Mountain Home, AR 72653
Fax: (870) 508-6287
E-mail: rblagg@asumh.edu
Phone: (870) 508-6104

**Arkansas Tech University**
www.atu.edu
International and Multicultural Student Services
105 West O Street, Suite 104
Russellville, AR 72801-2222
Fax: (479) 880-2039
E-mail: yonodera@atu.edu
Phone: (479) 964-0832

**Arlington Baptist College**
www.arlingtonbaptistcollege.edu
Admission Office
3001 West Division Street
Arlington, TX 76012
Fax: (817) 274-1138
E-mail: kmarvin@arlingtonbaptistcollege.edu
Phone: (817) 987-1769

**Armstrong State University**
www.armstrong.edu
Admissions Office
11935 Abercorn Street
Savannah, GA 31419-1997
Fax: (912) 344-3417
E-mail: Melanie.Chaffin-Poeling@armstrong.edu
Phone: (912) 344-3503

**Art Academy of Cincinnati**
www.artacademy.edu
Admissions
1212 Jackson Street
Cincinnati, OH 45202
Fax: (513) 562-8778
E-mail: admissions@artacademy.edu
Phone: (513) 562-8740

**Art Institute of Atlanta**
www.artinstitutes.edu/atlanta
Admissions
6600 Peachtree Dunwoody Road, NE
100 Embassy Row
Atlanta, GA 30328
Fax: (770) 394-0008
E-mail: darrieta@aii.edu
Phone: (770) 689-4755

**Art Institute of California: Hollywood**
www.artinstitutes.edu/hollywood
International Student Advisor
5250 Lankershim Boulevard
North Hollywood, CA 91601
Fax: (818) 299-5151
E-mail: thale@aii.edu
Phone: (818) 299-5231

**Art Institute of California: Inland Empire**
www.artinstitutes.edu/inland-empire
674 East Brier Drive
San Bernardino, CA 92408-2800

**Art Institute of California: Los Angeles**
www.artinstitutes.edu/losangeles
Admissions
2900 31st Street
Santa Monica, CA 90405-3035
Fax: (310) 752-4708
E-mail: wilkinso@aii.edu
Phone: (310) 752-4700

**Art Institute of California: Orange County**
www.artinstitutes.edu/orangecounty
Admissions
3601 West Sunflower Avenue
Santa Ana, CA 92704-7931
Fax: (714) 556-1923
E-mail: tkotler@aii.edu
Phone: (714) 830-0200

**Art Institute of California: Sacramento**
www.artinstitutes.edu/sacramento
2850 Gateway Oaks Drive, Suite 100
Sacramento, CA 95833
Phone: (800) 477-1957

**Art Institute of California: San Diego**
www.artinstitutes.edu/sandiego
7650 Mission Valley Road
San Diego, CA 92108-4423
E-mail: aicaadmin@aii.edu

**Art Institute of California: San Francisco**
www.artinstitutes.edu/sanfrancisco
1170 Market Street
San Francisco, CA 94102
Fax: (415) 863-6344
E-mail: aisfadm@aii.edu
Phone: (415) 865-0198

**Art Institute of Cincinnati**
www.aic-arts.edu
Admissions/Marketing
1171 East Kemper Road
Cincinnati, OH 45246
Fax: (513) 751-1209
E-mail: admissions@aic-arts.edu
Phone: (513) 751-1206

**Art Institute of Dallas**
www.aid.edu
Two North Park, 8080 Park Lane
Suite 100
Dallas, TX 75231
E-mail: cwilliams@aii.edu
Phone: (214) 692-8080

**Art Institute of Fort Lauderdale**
www.aifl.edu
Admissions
1799 SE 17th Street
Fort Lauderdale, FL 33316
Fax: (954) 728-8637
E-mail: byusty@aii.edu
Phone: (800) 275-7603 ext. 2159

**Art Institute of Houston**
www.artinstitutes.edu/houston
4140 Southwest Freeway
Houston, TX 77027
Fax: (713) 966-2797
E-mail: aihadm@aii.edu
Phone: (713) 623-2040

**Art Institute of Las Vegas**
www.artinstitutes.edu/lasvegas
Admissions
2350 Corporate Circle
Henderson, NV 89074-7737
Fax: (702) 992-8458
Phone: (800) 833-2678 ext. 8408

**Art Institute of Michigan**
www.artinstitutes.edu/detroit
28175 Cabot Drive
Novi, MI 48377
Fax: (248) 675-3830
Phone: (248) 675-3800

**Art Institute of Philadelphia**
www.artinstitutes.edu/Philadelphia
Admissions
1622 Chestnut Street
Philadelphia, PA 19103-5198
Fax: (215) 405-6399
E-mail: panua@aii.edu
Phone: (215) 405-6363

**Art Institute of Phoenix**
www.artinstitutes.edu/phoenix
Student Affairs
2233 West Dunlap Avenue
Phoenix, AZ 85021-2859
Fax: (602) 331-5301
E-mail: twashington@aii.edu
Phone: (602) 331-7500

**Art Institute of Pittsburgh**
www.artinstitutes.edu/pittsburgh
Assistant Director of Admissions
420 Boulevard of the Allies
Pittsburgh, PA 15219-1328
Fax: (412) 263-3715
E-mail: aipadm@aii.edu
Phone: (412) 291-6224

**Art Institute of Portland**
https://www.artinstitutes.edu/portland
Admissions
1122 Northwest Davis Street
Portland, OR 97209-2911
Fax: (503) 227-1945
E-mail: bkline@aii.edu
Phone: (503) 228-6528

**Art Institute of Seattle**
www.ais.edu
Admissions
2323 Elliott Avenue
Seattle, WA 98121-1622
Fax: (206) 269-0275
E-mail: aisadm@edmc.edu
Phone: (206) 448-6600

**Art Institute of Tucson**
www.artinstitutes.edu/tucson
5099 East Grant Road, #100
Tucson, AZ 85712
Fax: (520) 881-4234
Phone: (520) 881-2900

**Art Institute of Washington**
www.aiw.artinstitutes.edu
Office of Admissions
1820 North Fort Myer Drive
Arlington, VA 22209-1802
Fax: (703) 358-9759
E-mail: aiwadm@aii.edu
Phone: (703) 358-9550

**Art Institutes International Minnesota**
www.artinstitutes.edu/minneapolis
Dean of Student Affairs
15 South Ninth Street
Minneapolis, MN 55402
Fax: (612) 332-3934
E-mail: pboersig@aii.edu
Phone: (612) 332-3361 ext. 6865

**ASA College**
www.asa.edu
International Student Services
81 Willoughby Street
Brooklyn, NY 11201
Fax: (718) 532-1432
E-mail: okuian@asa.edu
Phone: (718) 522-9073 ext. 1243

**Asbury University**
www.asbury.edu
Admissions
One Macklem Drive
Wilmore, KY 40390-1198
Fax: (859) 858-3921
E-mail: international.admissions@asbury.edu
Phone: (859) 858-3511 ext. 2142

**Asheville-Buncombe Technical Community College**
www.abtech.edu
Academic Advisor, College Transfer Advisor, Student Services
340 Victoria Road
Asheville, NC 28801-4897
Fax: (828) 251-6718
E-mail: rhowell@abtech.edu
Phone: (828) 254-1921 ext. 441

**Ashford University**
www.ashford.edu
8620 Spectrum Center Boulevard
San Diego, CA 92123
E-mail: katie.scheie@ashford.edu
Phone: (800) 798-0584 ext. 20406

**Ashland Community and Technical College**
www.ashland.kctcs.edu
Student Affairs/Admissions
1400 College Drive
Ashland, KY 41101-3683
Fax: (606) 326-2912
E-mail: steve.woodburn@kctcs.net
Phone: (606) 326-2193

**Ashland University**
www.ashland.edu
International Admissions
401 College Avenue
Ashland, OH 44805-9981
Fax: (419) 289-5999
E-mail: international-admissions@ashland.edu
Phone: (419) 289-5052

**Ashworth College**
www.ashworthcollege.edu
6625 The Corners Parkway
Norcross, GA 30092-3406
Fax: (770) 729-9389
E-mail: info@ashworthcollege.edu
Phone: (770) 729-8400

**Asnuntuck Community College**
www.asnuntuck.edu
Admissions Office
170 Elm Street
Enfield, CT 06082
Fax: (860) 253-3014
E-mail: Janilowski@asnuntuck.edu
Phone: (860) 253-3000 ext. 3087

**Aspen University**
www.aspen.edu
720 South Colorado Boulevard, Suite 1150N
Denver, CO 80246
Fax: (303) 336-1144
E-mail: admissions@aspen.edu
Phone: (303) 333-4224

**Assumption College**
www.assumption.edu
Office of Undergraduate Admissions
500 Salisbury Street
Worcester, MA 01609-1296
Fax: (508) 799-4412
E-mail: silva@assumption.edu
Phone: (508) 767-7285

**Athens State University**
www.athens.edu
300 North Beaty Street
Athens, AL 35611
Fax: (256) 233-8128
E-mail: laura.allen@athens.edu
Phone: (256) 233-8142

**Athens Technical College**
www.athenstech.edu
Admissions
800 US Highway 29 North
Athens, GA 30601-1500
Fax: (706) 369-5756
E-mail: epew@athenstech.edu
Phone: (706) 355-5045

**Atlanta Metropolitan State College**
www.atlm.edu
Admissions
1630 Metropolitan Parkway, SW
Atlanta, GA 30310-4498
Fax: (404) 756-4407
E-mail: areid@atlm.edu
Phone: (404) 756-4004

**Atlanta Technical College**
www.atlantatech.edu
Student Affairs
1560 Metropolitan Parkway, SW
Atlanta, GA 30310-4446
E-mail: admissions@atlantatech.edu
Phone: (404) 225-4400

**Atlantic Cape Community College**
www.atlantic.edu
Admissions
5100 Black Horse Pike
Mays Landing, NJ 08330-2699
Fax: (609) 343-4921
E-mail: kfletche@atlantic.edu
Phone: (609) 343-4916

**Atlantic University College**
www.atlanticu.edu
Admissions Office
PO Box 3918
Guaynabo, PR 00970
Fax: (787) 720-1092
E-mail: atlancol@coqui.net
Phone: (787) 720-1022 ext. 1104

**ATS Institute of Technology**
www.atsinstitute.com
325 Alpha Park
Highland Heights, OH 44143
Fax: (440) 442-9876
E-mail: info@atsinstitute.com
Phone: (440) 449-1700

**Auburn University**
www.auburn.edu
Office of University Recruitment-International
Admissions
Quad Center
Auburn, AL 36849-5111
Fax: (334) 844-6436
E-mail: mayokat@auburn.edu
Phone: (334) 844-6425

**Auburn University at Montgomery**
www.aum.edu
Office of Global Initiatives
PO Box 244023
7400 East Drive, Room 139 Taylor Center
Montgomery, AL 36124-4023
Fax: (334) 244-3581
E-mail: global@aum.edu
Phone: (334) 244-3375

**Augsburg College**
www.augsburg.edu
2211 Riverside Avenue
Minneapolis, MN 55454
Fax: (612) 330-1590
E-mail: admissions@augsburg.edu
Phone: (612) 330-1001

**Augustana College**
www.augustana.edu
Admissions
639 38th Street
Rock Island, IL 61201-2296
Fax: (309) 794-7422
E-mail: admissions@augustana.edu
Phone: (309) 794-7540

**Augustana University**
www.augie.edu
Office of International Programs
2001 South Summit Avenue
Sioux Falls, SD 57197-9990
Fax: (605) 274-5518
E-mail: donn.grinager@augie.edu
Phone: (605) 274-5050

**Aurora University**
www.aurora.edu
Office of Admission
347 South Gladstone Avenue
Aurora, IL 60506-4892
Fax: (630) 844-6191
E-mail: admission@aurora.edu
Phone: (630) 844-5533

**Austin College**
www.austincollege.edu
Executive Director of Admission
900 North Grand Avenue, Suite 6N
Sherman, TX 75090-4400
Fax: (903) 813-3198
E-mail: admission@austincollege.edu
Phone: (903) 813-2393

**Austin Community College**
www.austincc.edu
International Student Office
PO Box 15306
Austin, TX 78761-5306
Fax: (512) 223-6239
E-mail: international@austincc.edu
Phone: (512) 223-6241

**Austin Peay State University**
www.apsu.edu
Office of Admissions
PO Box 4548
Clarksville, TN 37044-4548
Fax: (931) 221-6168
E-mail: admissions@apsu.edu
Phone: (800) 844-2778

**Ave Maria University**
www.avemaria.edu
Director of Admissions
5050 Ave Maria Boulevard
Ave Maria, FL 34142-9505
Fax: (239) 280-2559
E-mail: Karen.Full@avemaria.edu
Phone: (239) 304-7371

**Averett University**
www.averett.edu
Office of Admissions
420 West Main Street
Danville, VA 24541
Fax: (434) 797-2784
E-mail: joel.nester@averett.edu
Phone: (434) 791-5663

**Avila University**
www.avila.edu
Intensive Language & Culture Program
11901 Wornall Road
Kansas City, MO 64145-1007
Fax: (816) 501-2461
E-mail: bruce.inwards@avila.edu
Phone: (816) 501-3772

**Azusa Pacific University**
www.apu.edu
International Admissions
901 East Alosta Avenue
Box 7000
Azusa, CA 91702-7000
Fax: (626) 815-3801
E-mail: mgrams@apu.edu
Phone: (626) 815-6000 ext. 3055

**Babson College**
www.babson.edu
Undergraduate Admission Office
231 Forest Street
Babson Park, MA 02457-0310
Fax: (781) 239-4006
E-mail: aramsey@babson.edu
Phone: (781) 239-5522

**Bacone College**
www.bacone.edu
Admissions
2299 Old Bacone Road
Muskogee, OK 74403
Fax: (918) 781-7416
E-mail: admissions@bacone.edu
Phone: (918) 683-4581

**Bainbridge State College**
www.bainbridge.edu
Registrars Office
2500 East Shotwell Street
PO Box 990
Bainbridge, GA 39818-0990
Fax: (229) 248-2623
E-mail: robert.thompson@bainbridge.edu
Phone: (229) 243-3016

**Baker College of Allen Park**
www.baker.edu
Admissions
4500 Enterprise Drive
Allen Park, MI 48101
Fax: (313) 425-3776
Phone: (313) 425-3700

**Baker College of Auburn Hills**
www.baker.edu
Academic Office
1500 University Drive
Auburn Hills, MI 48326
Fax: (248) 340-0608
Phone: (248) 276-8229

**Baker College of Cadillac**
www.baker.edu
Admissions
9600 East 13th Street
Cadillac, MI 49601
Fax: (231) 775-8505
E-mail: mike.tisdal@baker.edu
Phone: (231) 876-3100

**Baker College of Jackson**
www.baker.edu
2800 Springport Road
Jackson, MI 49202
Fax: (517) 789-7331
E-mail: adm-jk@baker.edu
Phone: (517) 788-7800

**Baker College of Muskegon**
www.baker.edu
Admissions
1903 Marquette Avenue
Muskegon, MI 49442
Fax: (231) 777-5201
E-mail: kathy.jacobson@baker.edu
Phone: (231) 777-5200

**Baker College of Owosso**
www.baker.edu
Admissions
1020 South Washington Street
Owosso, MI 48867
Fax: (989) 729-3359
E-mail: michael.konopacke@baker.edu
Phone: (989) 729-3350

**Baker College of Port Huron**
www.baker.edu
Admissions Office
3403 Lapeer Road
Port Huron, MI 48060-2597
Fax: (810) 985-7066
E-mail: daniel.kenny@baker.edu
Phone: (810) 985-7000

**Baker University**
www.bakeru.edu
Office of Admissions
618 Eighth Street
PO Box 65
Baldwin City, KS 66006-0065
Fax: (785) 594-8353
E-mail: cheryl.mccrary@bakeru.edu
Phone: (785) 594-8307

**Bakersfield College**
www.bakersfieldcollege.edu
Admissions and Records Office
1801 Panorama Drive
Bakersfield, CA 93305
Fax: (661) 395-4500
Phone: (661) 395-4315

**Baldwin Wallace University**
www.bw.edu
Office of Undergraduate Admission
275 Eastland Road
Berea, OH 44017-2005
Fax: (440) 826-3830
E-mail: admission@bw.edu
Phone: (440) 826-2222

**Ball State University**
www.bsu.edu
Rinker Center for International Programs
Office of Admissions, Ball State University
2000 West University Avenue
Muncie, IN 47306-0855
Fax: (765) 285-1632
E-mail: ivdawson@bsu.edu
Phone: (765) 285-5422

**Baltimore City Community College**
www.bccc.edu
International Student Services
2901 Liberty Heights Avenue
Baltimore, MD 21215-7893
Fax: (410) 462-8345
E-mail: ddangerfield@bccc.edu
Phone: (410) 462-8311

**Baptist College of Florida**
www.baptistcollege.edu
Admissions
5400 College Drive
Graceville, FL 32440
Fax: (850) 263-9026
E-mail: admissions@baptistcollege.edu
Phone: (800) 328-2660 ext. 460

**Baptist University of the Americas**
www.bua.edu
8019 South Pan Am Expressway
San Antonio, TX 78224
E-mail: mary.ranjel@bua.edu
Phone: (210) 924-4338

**Barclay College**
www.barclaycollege.edu
Director of Admissions
607 North Kingman
Haviland, KS 67059
Fax: (620) 862-5403
E-mail: admissions@barclaycollege.edu
Phone: (620) 862-5252 ext. 43

**Bard College**
www.bard.edu
Admissions
30 Campus Road
PO Box 5000
Annandale-on-Hudson, NY 12504-5000
Fax: (845) 758-5208
E-mail: admission@bard.edu
Phone: (845) 758-7472

**Bard College at Simon's Rock**
www.simons-rock.edu
Admissions
Office of Admission
84 Alford Road
Great Barrington, MA 01230-1990
Fax: (413) 541-0081
E-mail: admit@simons-rock.edu
Phone: (413) 528-7312

**Barnard College**
www.barnard.edu
Admissions
3009 Broadway
New York, NY 10027-6598
Fax: (212) 280-8797
E-mail: jmartinez@barnard.edu
Phone: (212) 854-2014

**Barry University**
www.barry.edu
Recruitment and Admissions
11300 NE Second Avenue
Miami Shores, FL 33161-6695
Fax: (305) 899-2971
E-mail: ascott@barry.edu
Phone: (305) 899-3666

**Barton College**
www.barton.edu
Box 5000
Wilson, NC 27893-7000
Fax: (252) 399-6572
E-mail: enroll@barton.edu
Phone: (252) 399-6317

**Barton County Community College**
www.bartonccc.edu
Admissions
245 NE 30 Road
Great Bend, KS 67530-9283
Fax: (620) 786-1160
E-mail: coopert@bartonccc.edu
Phone: (620) 792-9241

**Bastyr University**
www.bastyr.edu
Admissions
14500 Juanita Drive, NE
Kenmore, WA 98028
Fax: (425) 602-3090
E-mail: cmasters@bastyr.edu
Phone: (425) 602-3330

**Bates College**
www.bates.edu
Office of Admission
23 Campus Avenue, Lindholm House
Lewiston, ME 04240
Fax: (207) 786-6025
E-mail: admission@bates.edu
Phone: (207) 786-6000

**Bates Technical College**
www.bates.ctc.edu
Career Specialist
1101 South Yakima Avenue
Tacoma, WA 98405
E-mail: larnold@bates.ctc.edu
Phone: (253) 680-7007

**Baton Rouge Community College**
www.mybrcc.edu
Enrollment Services
201 Community College Drive
Baton Rouge, LA 70806
Fax: (225) 216-8010
E-mail: howardj@mybrcc.edu
Phone: (225) 216-8871

**Baton Rouge School of Computers**
www.brsc.edu
9352 Interline Avenue
Baton Rouge, LA 70809-4095
Fax: (225) 923-2979
E-mail: admissions@brsc.edu
Phone: (225) 923-2524

**Bauder College**
www.bauder.edu
Admissions (International)
384 Northyards Boulevard NW, Ste 190
Atlanta, GA 30313
Fax: (404) 237-1619
E-mail: llanier@bauder.edu
Phone: (404) 237-7573 ext. 1795

**Bay College**
www.baycollege.edu
Dean Enrollment Management
2001 North Lincoln Road
Escanaba, MI 49829-2511
Fax: (906) 217-1649
E-mail: admissions@baycollege.edu
Phone: (906) 217-4068

**Bay Path University**
www.baypath.edu
Director of International Admissions and
Student Services
588 Longmeadow Street
Longmeadow, MA 01106
Fax: (413) 565-1105
E-mail: jbodnar@baypath.edu
Phone: (413) 565-1364

**Bay State College**
www.baystate.edu
Admissions
122 Commonwealth Avenue
Boston, MA 02116
Fax: (617) 249-0400
E-mail: admissions@baystate.edu
Phone: (617) 217-9000

**Bayamon Central University**
www.ucb.edu.pr
Admissions
PO Box 1725
Bayamon, PR 00960-1725
Fax: (787) 740-2200
E-mail: waponte@ucb.edu.pr
Phone: (787) 786-3030 ext. 2100

**Baylor University**
www.baylor.edu
International Programs
One Bear Place #97056
Waco, TX 76798-7056
Fax: (254) 710-1468
E-mail: alexine_burke@baylor.edu
Phone: (254) 710-1461

**Beacon College**
www.beaconcollege.edu
Vice President of Admissions & Enrollment
105 East Main Street
Leesburg, FL 34748
Fax: (352) 787-0796
E-mail: dherold@beaconcollege.edu
Phone: (352) 638-9778

**Beaufort County Community College**
www.beaufortccc.edu
Admissions
Box 1069
Washington, NC 27889
Fax: (252) 940-6393
E-mail: michele.mayo@beaufortccc.edu
Phone: (252) 940-6233

**Becker College**
www.becker.edu
Dean of Admissions
Office of Admissions
61 Sever Street
Worcester, MA 01609
Fax: (508) 890-1500
E-mail: admissions@becker.edu
Phone: (508) 373-9400

**Beis Medrash Heichal Dovid**
257 Beach 17th Street
Far Rockaway, NY 11691
Fax: (718) 406-8359
Phone: (718) 868-2300 ext. 360

**Belhaven University**
www.belhaven.edu
Institutional Advancement
1500 Peachtree Street
Box 153
Jackson, MS 39202
Fax: (601) 968-8946
E-mail: admission@belhaven.edu
Phone: (800) 960-5940

**Bellarmine University**
www.bellarmine.edu
Admission
2001 Newburg Road
Louisville, KY 40205
Fax: (502) 272-8002
E-mail: dkline@bellarmine.edu
Phone: (502) 272-8131

**Bellevue College**
www.bellevuecollege.edu
International Student Programs
3000 Landerholm Circle SE
Bellevue, WA 98007-6484
Fax: (425) 641-0246
E-mail: kazumi.hada@bellevuecollege.edu
Phone: (425) 564-2973

**Bellevue University**
www.bellevue.edu
International Programs
1000 Galvin Road South
Bellevue, NE 68005-3098
Fax: (402) 557-7230
E-mail: sjiang@bellevue.edu
Phone: (402) 557-5235

**Bellingham Technical College**
www.btc.edu
Admissions & Student Resource Center
3028 Lindbergh Avenue
Bellingham, WA 98225-1599
Fax: (360) 676-2798
E-mail: admissions@btc.edu
Phone: (360) 752-8345

**Belmont Abbey College**
www.belmontabbeycollege.edu
Admissions Office
100 Belmont - Mt. Holly Road
Belmont, NC 28012-2795
Fax: (704) 825-6220
E-mail: nicolefocareto@bac.edu
Phone: (888) 222-0110

**Belmont College**
www.belmontcollege.edu
120 Fox Shannon Place
St. Clairsville, OH 43950
Fax: (740) 699-3049
E-mail: thouston@btc.edu
Phone: (740) 695-9500 ext. 1563

**Belmont University**
www.belmont.edu
International Education
1900 Belmont Boulevard
Nashville, TN 37212-3757
Fax: (615) 460-5539
E-mail: kathy.skinner@belmont.edu
Phone: (615) 460-5500

**Beloit College**
www.beloit.edu
Coordinator of International Admission
700 College Street
Beloit, WI 53511-5595
Fax: (608) 363-2075
E-mail: intadmis@beloit.edu
Phone: (608) 363-2500

**Bemidji State University**
www.bemidjistate.edu
International Program Center
102 Deputy Hall #13
1500 Birchmont Drive NE, #13
Bemidji, MN 56601-2699
Fax: (218) 755-2074
E-mail: international@bemidjistate.edu
Phone: (218) 755-4096

**Benedict College**
www.benedict.edu
Student Records
1600 Harden Street
Columbia, SC 29204
Fax: (803) 253-5085
E-mail: scottkinney@benedict.edu
Phone: (803) 705-4680

**Benedictine College**
www.benedictine.edu
Director of International Education
1020 North Second Street
Atchison, KS 66002-1499
Fax: (913) 360-7970
E-mail: dmusso@benedictine.edu
Phone: (800) 367-5340

**Benedictine University**
www.ben.edu
International Programs
5700 College Road
Lisle, IL 60532
Fax: (630) 829-6301
E-mail: admissions@ben.edu
Phone: (630) 829-6304

**Benedictine University at Springfield**
www.ben.edu/springfield
International Student Services
1500 North Fifth Street
Springfield, IL 62702-2694
Fax: (217) 525-1497
E-mail: cschone@ben.edu
Phone: (217) 525-1420

**Benjamin Franklin Institute of Technology**
www.bfit.edu
Admissions Office
41 Berkeley Street
Boston, MA 02116
Fax: (617) 482-3706
E-mail: mchen@bfit.edu
Phone: (617) 423-4630 ext. 121

**Bennett College for Women**
www.bennett.edu
Admissions
900 East Washington Street
Greensboro, NC 27401-3239
Fax: (336) 517-2166
E-mail: admiss@bennett.edu
Phone: (336) 517-1818

**Bennington College**
www.bennington.edu
Office of Admissions
One College Drive
Bennington, VT 05201-6003
Fax: (802) 440-4320
E-mail: jwerkmeister@bennington.edu
Phone: (802) 440-4343

**Bentley University**
www.bentley.edu
Undergraduate Admissions
175 Forest Street
Waltham, MA 02452
Fax: (781) 891-3414
E-mail: ugadmission@bentley.edu
Phone: (781) 891-2244

**Berea College**
www.berea.edu
Admissions
CPO 2220
Berea, KY 40404
Fax: (859) 985-3512
E-mail: askadmissions@berea.edu
Phone: (800) 326-5948

**Bergin University of Canine Studies**
www.berginu.edu
Admissions
5860 Labath Avenue
Rohnert Park, CA 94928
Fax: (707) 545-0800
E-mail: admissions@berginu.edu
Phone: (707) 545-3647 ext. 21

**Berkeley City College**
www.berkeleycitycollege.edu
International Specialist, International
Affairs & Distance Education
2050 Center Street
Berkeley, CA 94704
Fax: (510) 465-3257
E-mail: dgephart@Peralta.edu
Phone: (510) 587-7834

**Berkeley College**
www.berkeleycollege.edu
International Division
44 Rifle Camp Road
Woodland Park, NJ 07424-0440
Fax: (212) 986-7827
E-mail: international@berkeleycollege.edu
Phone: (212) 687-3730

**Berkeley College**
www.berkeleycollege.edu
International Division
99 Church Street
White Plains, NY 10601
Fax: (212) 986-7827
E-mail: international@berkeleycollege.edu
Phone: (212) 687-3730

**Berkeley College of New York City**
www.berkeleycollege.edu
Berkeley College, International Division
3 East 43rd Street
New York, NY 10017
Fax: (212) 986-7827
E-mail: international@berkeleycollege.edu
Phone: (212) 687-3730

**Berklee College of Music**
www.berklee.edu
Office of Admissions
1140 Boylston Street
Boston, MA 02215
Fax: (617) 747-2047
E-mail: admissions@berklee.edu
Phone: (617) 747-2222

**Berks Technical Institute**
www.berks.edu
Office of Admissions
2205 Ridgewood Road
Wyomissing, PA 19610
Fax: (610) 376-4684
E-mail: jeanv@berkstech.com
Phone: (610) 372-1722

**Berkshire Community College**
www.berkshirecc.edu
Multicultural Admissions Counselor
1350 West Street
Pittsfield, MA 01201-5786
Fax: (413) 496-9511
E-mail: evelez@berkshirecc.edu
Phone: (413) 236-1636

**Berry College**
www.berry.edu
Assistant Vice President of Admissions
PO Box 490159
2277 Martha Berry Highway NW
Mount Berry, GA 30149-0159
Fax: (706) 290-2178
E-mail: admissions@berry.edu
Phone: (706) 236-2215

**Beth Hamedrash Shaarei Yosher Institute**
4102 16th Avenue
Brooklyn, NY 11204
Phone: (718) 854-2290

**Beth Hatalmud Rabbinical College**
2127 82nd Street
Brooklyn, NY 11214
Phone: (718) 259-2525

**Bethany College**
https://www.bethanylb.edu/
Admissions
335 East Swensson
Lindsborg, KS 67456-1897
Fax: (785) 227-8993
E-mail: cornettv@bethanylb.edu
Phone: (800) 826-2281 ext. 8388

**Bethany College**
www.bethanywv.edu
Office of Enrollment
Bethany, WV 26032-0428
Fax: (304) 829-7142
E-mail: admission@bethanywv.edu
Phone: (304) 829-7611

**Bethany Lutheran College**
www.blc.edu
700 Luther Drive
Mankato, MN 56001-4490
Fax: (507) 344-7376
E-mail: nick.cook@blc.edu
Phone: (507) 344-7752

**Bethel College**
www.bethelcollege.edu
Admission Office
1001 Bethel Circle
Mishawaka, IN 46545-5591
Fax: (574) 807-7650
E-mail: admissions@BethelCollege.edu
Phone: (574) 807-7600

**Bethel College**
www.bethelks.edu
Admissions
300 East 27th Street
North Newton, KS 67117-8061
Fax: (316) 284-5870
E-mail: admissions@bethelks.edu
Phone: (800) 522-1887 ext. 230

**Bethel University**
www.bethel.edu
Office of Admissions
3900 Bethel Drive
St. Paul, MN 55112-6999
Fax: (651) 635-1490
E-mail: undergrad-admissions@bethel.edu
Phone: (800) 255-8706 ext. 6242

**Bethel University**
www.bethelu.edu
International Enrollment Counselor
325 Cherry Avenue
Attention: Admissions
McKenzie, TN 38201
Fax: (731) 352-4241
E-mail: pruitte@bethelu.edu
Phone: (731) 352-4249

**Bethesda University of California**
www.buc.edu
Admissions
730 North Euclid Street
Anaheim, CA 92801
Fax: (714) 517-1948
E-mail: admission@buc.edu
Phone: (714) 517-1945

**Bethune-Cookman University**
www.cookman.edu
Associate Director
640 Dr. Mary McLeod Bethune Boulevard
Daytona Beach, FL 32114-3099
Fax: (386) 481-2601
E-mail: admissions@cookman.edu
Phone: (386) 481-2607

**Beulah Heights University**
www.beulah.edu
Admissions
892 Berne Street SE
PO Box 18145
Atlanta, GA 30316
Fax: (404) 627-0702
E-mail: arthur.breland@beulah.org
Phone: (404) 627-2681 ext. 117

**Beverly Hills Design Institute**
www.bhdit.edu
Director of Admissions
8484 Wilshire Boulevard Suite 730
Beverly Hills, CA 90211
Fax: (310) 857-6974
E-mail: jennifer@academyofcoutureart.edu
Phone: (310) 360-8888

**Bidwell Training Center**
www.bidwell-training.org
1815 Metropolitan Street
Pittsburgh, PA 15233
Fax: (412) 321-2120
E-mail: dfarah@mcg-btc.org
Phone: (412) 323-4000 ext. 156

**Big Bend Community College**
www.bigbend.edu
Admissions/Registration
7662 Chanute Street NE
Moses Lake, WA 98837-3299
Fax: (509) 762-6243
E-mail: ruthc@bigbend.edu
Phone: (509) 793-2065

**Big Sandy Community and Technical College**
www.bigsandy.kctcs.edu
One Bert T. Combs Drive
Prestonsburg, KY 41653
Fax: (606) 886-6943
E-mail: jimmy.wright@kctcs.edu
Phone: (606) 886-3863 ext. 67366

**Biola University**
www.biola.edu
Admissions
13800 Biola Avenue
La Mirada, CA 90639-0001
Fax: (562) 903-4709
E-mail: fitsum.mulat@biola.edu
Phone: (562) 903-4752

**Birmingham-Southern College**
www.bsc.edu
Director of Admission
900 Arkadelphia Road
Box 549008
Birmingham, AL 35254
Fax: (205) 226-3074
E-mail: admiss@bsc.edu
Phone: (205) 226-4696

**Bishop State Community College**
www.bishop.edu
Student Development Services
351 North Broad Street
Mobile, AL 36603-5898
Fax: (251) 690-6998
E-mail: mvodom@bishop.edu
Phone: (251) 405-7065

**Bismarck State College**
https://bismarckstate.edu
Admissions
PO Box 5587
Bismarck, ND 58506-5587
Fax: (701) 224-5643
E-mail: karen.erickson@bismarckstate.edu
Phone: (701) 224-5424

**Black Hawk College**
www.bhc.edu
International Student Office/ESL
6600-34th Avenue
Moline, IL 61265-5899
Fax: (309) 796-5209
E-mail: franciscoj@bhc.edu
Phone: (309) 796-5183

**Black Hills State University**
www.bhsu.edu
International Student Office
1200 University Street
Spearfish, SD 57799
Fax: (605) 642-6022
E-mail: Katherine.Wildman@bhsu.edu
Phone: (605) 642-6343

**Blackburn College**
www.blackburn.edu
Admissions Office
700 College Avenue
Carlinville, IL 62626
Fax: (217) 854-3713
E-mail: alisha.kapp@blackburn.edu
Phone: (217) 854-5110

**Blackhawk Technical College**
www.blackhawk.edu
Student Services
PO Box 5009
Janesville, WI 53547-5009
Fax: (608) 743-4407
E-mail: erobinson@blackhawk.edu
Phone: (608) 757-7713

**Bladen Community College**
www.bladencc.edu
Post Office Box 266
Dublin, NC 28332-0266
Fax: (910) 879-5564
E-mail: lmclean@bladencc.edu
Phone: (910) 879-5593

**Blessing-Rieman College of Nursing & Health Sciences**
www.brcn.edu
PO Box 7005
Quincy, IL 62305-7005
Fax: (217) 223-4661
E-mail: admissions@brcn.edu
Phone: (217) 228-5520 ext. 6949

**Blinn College**
www.blinn.edu
Student Services
902 College Avenue
Brenham, TX 77833
Fax: (979) 830-4110
E-mail: dennis.crowson@blinn.edu
Phone: (979) 830-4150

**Bloomfield College**
www.bloomfield.edu
Office of Enrollment Management and Admission
One Park Place
Bloomfield, NJ 07003
Fax: (973) 748-0916
E-mail: admission@bloomfield.edu
Phone: (800) 848-4555 ext. 1127

**Bloomsburg University of Pennsylvania**
www.bloomu.edu
Office of Admissions
104 Student Service Center
400 East Second Street
Bloomsburg, PA 17815
Fax: (570) 389-4741
E-mail: buadmiss@bloomu.edu
Phone: (570) 389-4316

**Blue Cliff College: Gulfport**
www.bluecliffcollege.edu
12251 Bernard Parkway
Gulfport, MS 39503
Fax: (228) 896-8659
E-mail: AlbertF@BlueCliffCollege.com
Phone: (288) 896-9727

**Blue Cliff College: Metairie**
www.bluecliffcollege.com
3200 Cleary Avenue
Metairie, LA 70002
Fax: (504) 456-7849
E-mail: pattyr@bluecliffcollege.com
Phone: (504) 456-3141

**Blue Cliff College: Shreveport**
www.bluecliffcollege.com
8731 Park Plaza Drive
Shreveport, LA 71105-5682
Phone: (318) 425-7941

**Blue Mountain College**
www.bmc.edu
Office of Admissions
PO Box 160
201 W Main Street
Blue Mountain, MS 38610-0160
Fax: (662) 685-4776
E-mail: lgibson@bmc.edu
Phone: (662) 685-4771 ext. 176

**Blue Ridge Community College**
www.brcc.edu
Admissions and Records
Box 80
Weyers Cave, VA 24486-9989
Fax: (540) 453-2437
E-mail: mathiasc@brcc.edu
Phone: (540) 453-2360

**Bluefield College**
www.bluefield.edu
Office of Enrollment Management
3000 College Avenue
Bluefield, VA 24605
Fax: (276) 326-4395
E-mail: admissions@bluefield.edu
Phone: (800) 872-0175

**Bluefield State College**
www.bluefieldstate.edu
Enrollment Management
219 Rock Street
Bluefield, WV 24701
Fax: (304) 325-7747
E-mail: bscadmit@bluefield.wvnet.edu
Phone: (304) 327-4567

**Bluegrass Community and Technical College**
www.bluegrass.kctcs.edu
Admissions
200 Oswald Building, Cooper Drive
Lexington, KY 40506-0235
Fax: (859) 246-4666
E-mail: nathan.congleton@kctcs.edu
Phone: (859) 246-4647

**Bluffton University**
www.bluffton.edu
Admissions
1 University Drive
Bluffton, OH 45817-2104
Fax: (419) 358-3081
E-mail: birkeyp@bluffton.edu
Phone: (419) 358-3257

**Bob Jones University**
www.bju.edu
Office of Admission
1700 Wade Hampton Boulevard
Greenville, SC 29614
Fax: (864) 770-1323
E-mail: bboudrea@bju.edu
Phone: (864) 242-5100 ext. 2092

**Boise State University**
www.boisestate.edu
International Admissions Office
1910 University Drive
Boise, ID 83725-1320
Fax: (208) 426-3765
E-mail: internationalinfo@boisestate.edu
Phone: (208) 426-3720

**Bolivar Technical College**
www.bolivarcollege.org
Admissions
PO Box 592
1135 North Oakland Avenue
Bolivar, MO 65613
Fax: (417) 777-8908
E-mail: info@bolivarcollege.org
Phone: (417) 777-5062

**Bossier Parish Community College**
www.bpcc.edu/index.html
Registrar's Office
6220 East Texas Street
Bossier City, LA 71111-6922
Fax: (318) 678-6390
E-mail: rcockerham@bpcc.edu
Phone: (318) 678-6093

**Boston Baptist College**
www.boston.edu
950 Metropolitan Avenue
Boston, MA 02136
E-mail: admissions@boston.edu
Phone: (617) 364-3510 ext. 230

**Boston College**
www.bc.edu
Office of Undergraduate Admissions
140 Commonwealth Avenue, Devlin Hall 208
Chestnut Hill, MA 02467-3809
Fax: (617) 552-0798
Phone: (617) 552-3100

**Boston Conservatory**
www.bostonconservatory.edu
Admissions
8 The Fenway
Boston, MA 02215
Fax: (617) 536-3176
E-mail: admissions@bostonconservatory.edu
Phone: (617) 912-9153

**Boston University**
www.bu.edu
Office of International Admissions
233 Bay State Road
Boston, MA 02215
Fax: (617) 353-5334
E-mail: intadmis@bu.edu
Phone: (617) 353-4492

**Bowdoin College**
www.bowdoin.edu
Admissions Office
5000 College Station
Brunswick, ME 04011-8441
Fax: (207) 725-3101
E-mail: rricciar@bowdoin.edu
Phone: (207) 798-4218

**Bowie State University**
www.bowiestate.edu
Career Co-Op and International Services
14000 Jericho Park Road
Attn: Admissions Office
Bowie, MD 20715
Fax: (301) 860-3824
E-mail: rbatton@bowiestate.edu
Phone: (301) 860-3830

**Bowling Green State University**
www.bgsu.edu
International Programs and Partnerships
110 McFall Center
Bowling Green State University
Bowling Green, OH 43403-0085
Fax: (419) 372-2429
E-mail: international@bgsu.edu
Phone: (419) 372-8185

**Bowling Green State University: Firelands College**
www.firelands.bgsu.edu
Center for International Programs
One University Drive
Huron, OH 44839-9719
Fax: (419) 372-0604
E-mail: avoogd@bgsu.edu
Phone: (419) 372-4761

**Bradford School: Pittsburgh**
www.bradfordpittsburgh.edu
125 West Station Square Drive
Pittsburgh, PA 15219
Fax: (412) 471-6714
Phone: (412) 391-6710

**Bradley University**
www.bradley.edu
Undergraduate Admissions
1501 West Bradley Avenue
Peoria, IL 61625
Fax: (309) 677-2799
E-mail: admissions@bradley.edu
Phone: (309) 677-1000

**Bramson ORT College**
www.bramsonort.edu
6930 Austin Street
Forest Hills, NY 11375
Fax: (718) 575-5118
Phone: (718) 261-5800

**Brandeis University**
www.brandeis.edu
Associate Director of International Admissions
415 South Street, MS003
Waltham, MA 02453
Fax: (781) 736-3536
E-mail: delgado@brandeis.edu
Phone: (781) 736-3500

**Brazosport College**
www.brazosport.edu
Admissions
500 College Drive
Lake Jackson, TX 77566
Fax: (979) 230-3376
E-mail: Carrie.Streeter@brazosport.edu
Phone: (979) 230-3221

**Brenau University**
www.brenau.edu
Office of Admission
500 Washington Street SE
Gainesville, GA 30501
Fax: (770) 531-3118
E-mail: ajohnston5@brenau.edu
Phone: (770) 564-6100

**Brescia University**
www.brescia.edu
717 Frederica Street
Owensboro, KY 42301-3023
Fax: (270) 686-4314
E-mail: admissions@brescia.edu
Phone: (270) 686-4241

**Brevard College**
www.brevard.edu
Admissions
One Brevard College Drive
Brevard, NC 28712
Fax: (828) 884-3790
E-mail: david.volrath@brevard.edu
Phone: (828) 884-8367

**Brewton-Parker College**
www.bpc.edu
Admissions Director
Brewton-Parker College # 2011
201 David-Eliza Fountain Circle
Mount Vernon, GA 30445
Fax: (912) 583-3598
E-mail: kbell@bpc.edu
Phone: (912) 583-3245

**Briar Cliff University**
www.briarcliff.edu
Admissions
3303 Rebecca Street
Sioux City, IA 51104-2324
Fax: (712) 279-1632
E-mail: admissions@briarcliff.edu
Phone: (712) 279-5200

**Briarcliffe College**
www.briarcliffe.edu
1055 Stewart Avenue
Bethpage, NY 11714
Fax: (516) 470-6020
E-mail: gostroske@bcl.edu
Phone: (516) 918-3600

**BridgeValley Community and Technical College**
www.bridgevalley.edu
Office of Admissions
619 Second Avenue
Montgomery, WV 25136
Fax: (304) 734-6698
E-mail: admissions@bridgemont.edu
Phone: (304) 734-6603

**Bridgewater College**
www.bridgewater.edu
Admissions Office
402 East College Street
Bridgewater, VA 22812-1599
Fax: (540) 828-5481
E-mail: admissions@bridgewater.edu
Phone: (540) 828-5375

**Bridgewater State University**
www.bridgew.edu
University Admissions
Office of Admission-Welcome Center
45 Plymouth Street
Bridgewater, MA 02325
Fax: (508) 531-1746
E-mail: admissions@bridgew.edu
Phone: (508) 531-1237

**Brigham Young University**
www.byu.edu
International Admissions
A-153 ASB
Provo, UT 84602
Fax: (801) 422-0973
E-mail: intladm@byu.edu
Phone: (801) 422-2500

**Brigham Young University-Hawaii**
www.byuh.edu
Admissions
55-220 Kulanui Street, #1973
Laie, HI 96762-1294
Fax: (808) 675-3741
E-mail: sudlowm@byuh.edu
Phone: (808) 675-3535

**Brigham Young University-Idaho**
www.byui.edu
Admissions
120 Kimball Building
Rexburg, ID 83460-1615
Fax: (208) 496-1303
E-mail: admissions@byui.edu
Phone: (208) 496-1300

**Brightwood College: Baltimore**
www.tesst.com/tesstPortal
1520 South Caton Avenue
Baltimore, MD 21227-1063
Fax: (410) 644-6481
Phone: (410) 644-6400

**Brightwood College: Beltsville**
www.tesst.com
4600 Powder Mill Road
Beltsville, MD 20705
E-mail: dedmonds@tesst.com
Phone: (301) 937-8448

**Brightwood College: Towson**
www.tesst.com
803 Glen Eagles Court
Towson, MD 21286
Fax: (410) 296-5356
Phone: (410) 296-5350

**Bristol Community College**
www.bristolcc.edu
Office of Admissions
777 Elsbree Street
Fall River, MA 02720-7395
Fax: (508) 730-3265
E-mail: shilo.henriques@bristolcc.edu
Phone: (508) 678-2811 ext. 2947

**Broadview Entertainment Arts University**
www.broadviewuniversity.edu
240 East Morris Avenue
Salt Lake City, UT 84115
Phone: (801) 300-4300

**Broadview University: Boise**
www.broadviewuniversity.edu
2750 East Gala Court
Meridian, ID 83642
Phone: (208) 577-2900

**Broadview University: Layton**
www.broadviewuniversity.edu
869 West Hill Field Road
Layton, UT 84041
Phone: (801) 660-6000

**Broadview University: Orem**
www.broadviewuniversity.edu
898 North 1200 West
Orem, UT 84057
Phone: (801) 822-5800

**Brookdale Community College**
www.brookdalecc.edu
Director/International Education Center
765 Newman Springs Road
Lincroft, NJ 07738
Fax: (732) 224-2271
E-mail: jthomas@brookdalecc.edu
Phone: (732) 224-2375

**Brookhaven College**
www.brookhavencollege.edu
Multi-Cultural Center
3939 Valley View Lane
Farmers Branch, TX 75244-4997
Fax: (972) 860-4886
E-mail: bhcmulticulturalcenter@dcccd.edu
Phone: (972) 860-4613

**Brookline College: Albuquerque**
www.brooklinecollege.edu
4201 Central Avenue NW, Suite J
Albuquerque, NM 87105-1649
Fax: (505) 352-0199
E-mail: awebb@brooklinecollege.edu
Phone: (505) 880-2877

**Brookline College: Phoenix**
www.brooklinecollege.edu
2445 West Dunlap Avenue, Suite 100
Phoenix, AZ 85021-5820
Fax: (602) 973-2572
E-mail: phnx-admissions@brooklinecollege.edu
Phone: (602) 242-6265

**Brookline College: Tempe**
www.brooklinecollege.edu
1140-1150 South Priest Drive
Tempe, AZ 85281-5240
Fax: (480) 926-1371
E-mail: ckindred@brooklinecollege.edu
Phone: (480) 545-8755

**Broome Community College**
www.sunybroome.edu
Admissions Office
Box 1017
Binghamton, NY 13902
Fax: (607) 778-5310
E-mail: carrams@sunybroome.edu
Phone: (607) 778-5001

**Broward College**
www.broward.edu
Office of International Education
225 East Las Olas Boulevard
Fort Lauderdale, FL 33301
Fax: (954) 201-7708
E-mail: rcarvalh@broward.edu
Phone: (954) 201-7705

**Brown Mackie College: Akron**
www.brownmackie.edu
755 White Pond Drive, Suite 101
Akron, OH 44320
Fax: (330) 733-5853
Phone: (330) 733-8766

**Brown Mackie College: Albuquerque**
www.brownmackie.edu/albuquerque

**Brown Mackie College: Birmingham**
www.brownmackie.edu/birmingham.aspx

**Brown Mackie College: Boise**
www.brownmackie.edu/boise.aspx

**Brown Mackie College: Dallas/Ft Worth**
www.brownmackie.edu/dallas.aspx

**Brown Mackie College: Fort Wayne**
www.brownmackie.edu
3000 Coliseum Boulevard, Suite 100
Fort Wayne, IN 46805
Fax: (260) 484-2678
E-mail: ktaboh@brownmackie.edu
Phone: (260) 484-4400

**Brown Mackie College: Greenville**
www.brownmackie.edu/greenville.aspx

**Brown Mackie College: Indianapolis**
www.brownmackie.edu/indianapolis.aspx

**Brown Mackie College: Kansas City**
www.brownmackie.edu/kansas-city.aspx

**Brown Mackie College: Merrillville**
www.brownmackie.edu
1000 East 80th Place, Suite 101N
Merrillville, IN 46410
E-mail: bmcmeadm@brownmackie.edu
Phone: (219) 769-3321

**Brown Mackie College: Miami**
www.brownmackie.edu
Academic Affairs
One Herald Plaza
Miami, FL 33132
Fax: (305) 373-8814
E-mail: psitton@brownmackie.edu
Phone: (305) 341-6619

**Brown Mackie College: Oklahoma City**
www.brownmackie.edu/oklahoma-city.aspx

**Brown Mackie College: Phoenix**
www.brownmackie.edu/phoenix.aspx

**Brown Mackie College: Quad Cities**
www.brownmackie.edu/quad-cities.aspx

**Brown Mackie College: San Antonio**
www.brownmackie.edu/san-antonio.aspx

**Brown Mackie College: St. Louis**
www.brownmackie.edu
#2 Soccer Park Road
Fenton, MO 63026

**Brown Mackie College: Tulsa**
www.brownmackie.eud/tulsa.aspx

**Brown University**
www.brown.edu
International Admission
Box 1876
Providence, RI 02912
Fax: (401) 863-9300
E-mail: Panetha_Ott@brown.edu
Phone: (401) 863-2378

**Bryan College: Dayton**
www.bryan.edu
Admissions Office Manager
721 Bryan Drive
Dayton, TN 37321-7000
Fax: (423) 775-7199
E-mail: admissions@bryan.edu
Phone: (423) 775-7158

**Bryan College: Sacramento**
www.bryancollege.edu
2317 Gold Meadow Way
Gold River, CA 95670
Fax: (916) 641-8649
E-mail: admissions@bryancollege.com
Phone: (916) 649-2400

**Bryan University**
www.bryanuniversity.edu
Admissions
350 West Washington Street #100
Tempe, AZ 85281
Fax: (602) 759-8743
E-mail: info@bryancollege.edu
Phone: (602) 384-2555

**Bryan University: Rogers**
www.bryanu.edu
3704 West Walnut Street
Rogers, AR 72756
Fax: (479) 899-6535
Phone: (479) 899-6644

**Bryan University: Topeka**
www.bryancolleges.edu
1527 SW Fairlawn Road
Topeka, KS 66604
E-mail: csollars@bryancc.edu
Phone: (785) 272-0889

**BryanLGH College of Health Sciences**
www.bryanhealthcollege.edu
5035 Everett Street
Lincoln, NE 68506
Fax: (402) 481-8621
E-mail: briana.genetti@bryanhealth.org
Phone: (402) 481-8697

**Bryant & Stratton College: Albany**
www.bryantstratton.edu
Admissions
1259 Central Avenue
Albany, NY 12205
Fax: (518) 437-1049
E-mail: rpferrell@bryantstratton.edu
Phone: (518) 437-1802 ext. 205

**Bryant & Stratton College: Amherst**
www.bryantstratton.edu
3650 Millersport Highway
Getzville, NY 14068
Fax: (716) 689-6078
Phone: (716) 625-6300

**Bryant & Stratton College: Buffalo**
www.bryantstratton.edu
465 Main Street, Suite 400
Buffalo, NY 14203
Fax: (716) 884-0091
E-mail: mbrobinson@bryantstratton.edu
Phone: (716) 884-9120

**Bryant & Stratton College: Eastlake**
www.bryantstratton.edu
Admissions
35350 Curtis Boulevard
Eastlake, OH 44095
Fax: (440) 306-2015
E-mail: mejohnson@bryantstratton.edu
Phone: (440) 510-1112

**Bryant & Stratton College: Henrietta**
www.bryantstratton.edu
1225 Jefferson Road
Rochester, NY 14623
Phone: (585) 292-5627

**Bryant & Stratton College: Milwaukee**
www.bryantstratton.edu
Admissions
310 West Wisconsin Avenue, Suite 500
Milwaukee, WI 53203
Fax: (414) 276-3930
E-mail: jrpalmer@byrantstratton.edu
Phone: (414) 276-5200

**Bryant & Stratton College: Parma**
www.bryantstratton.edu
Admissions Department
12955 Snow Road
Parma, OH 44130-1013
Fax: (216) 265-0325
E-mail: atinman@bryantstratton.edu
Phone: (216) 265-3151 ext. 229

**Bryant & Stratton College: Rochester**
www.bryantstratton.edu
1225 Jefferson Road
Rochester, NY 14623
Phone: (585) 292-5627

**Bryant & Stratton College: Southtowns**
www.bryantstratton.edu
200 Redtail
Orchard Park, NY 14127
Fax: (716) 677-9599
E-mail: prkehr@bryantstratton.edu
Phone: (716) 677-9500

**Bryant & Stratton College: Syracuse North**
www.bryantstratton.edu
8687 Carling Road
Liverpool, NY 13090
Phone: (315) 652-6500

**Bryant & Stratton College: Virginia Beach**
www.bryantstratton.edu
Admissions
301 Centre Pointe Drive
Virginia Beach, VA 23462-4417
Fax: (757) 499-9977
E-mail: dmsoutherland@bryantstratton.edu
Phone: (757) 499-7900

**Bryant University**
www.bryant.edu
Office of Admission
1150 Douglas Pike
Smithfield, RI 02917-1291
Fax: (401) 232-6741
E-mail: admission@bryant.edu
Phone: (401) 232-6107

**Bryn Athyn College**
www.brynathyn.edu
Admissions
PO Box 462
2965 College Drive
Bryn Athyn, PA 19009-0462
Fax: (267) 502-2593
E-mail: admissions@brynathyn.edu
Phone: (267) 502-6000

**Bryn Mawr College**
www.brynmawr.edu
Office of Admissions
101 North Merion Avenue
Bryn Mawr, PA 19010-2899
Fax: (610) 526-7471
E-mail: jrussell@brynmawr.edu
Phone: (610) 526-7473

**Bucknell University**
www.bucknell.edu
Office of Admissions, Bucknell University
1 Dent Drive
Lewisburg, PA 17837-9988
Fax: (570) 577-3538
E-mail: admissions@bucknell.edu
Phone: (570) 577-3000

**Bucks County Community College**
www.bucks.edu
Adult and Multicultural Student Services
275 Swamp Road
Office of Admissions
Newtown, PA 18940
Fax: (215) 968-8110
E-mail: Marlene.Barlow@bucks.edu
Phone: (215) 968-8137

**Buena Vista University**
www.bvu.edu
Director of Admissions
610 West Fourth Street
Storm Lake, IA 50588
Fax: (712) 749-2035
E-mail: FoxM@bvu.edu
Phone: (712) 749-2078

**Bunker Hill Community College**
www.bhcc.edu
International Center
250 New Rutherford Avenue
Boston, MA 02129-2925
Fax: (617) 228-2442
E-mail: international@bhcc.mass.edu
Phone: (617) 228-2460

**Butler Community College**
www.butlercc.edu
International Specialist
901 South Haverhill Road
El Dorado, KS 67042-3280
Fax: (316) 322-6852
E-mail: mdugger@butlercc.edu
Phone: (316) 322-3255

**Butler County Community College**
www.bc3.edu
Admissions
PO Box 1203
Butler, PA 16003-1203
Fax: (724) 287-3460
E-mail: pattie.bajuszik@bc3.edu
Phone: (724) 287-8711 ext. 8212

**Butler University**
www.butler.edu
International Admissions
4600 Sunset Avenue
Indianapolis, IN 46208
Fax: (317) 940-8150
E-mail: intadmission@butler.edu
Phone: (888) 940-8100

**Butte College**
www.butte.edu
International Admissions
3536 Butte Campus Drive
Oroville, CA 95965
Fax: (530) 879-4313
E-mail: International@butte.edu
Phone: (530) 895-2991

**Cabarrus College of Health Sciences**
www.cabarruscollege.edu
401 Medical Park Drive
Concord, NC 28025-2405
Fax: (704) 403-2077
E-mail: admissions@cabarruscollege.edu
Phone: (704) 403-1556

**Cabrillo College**
www.cabrillo.edu
International Student Advisor/Counselor
6500 Soquel Drive
Aptos, CA 95003
Fax: (831) 479-5769
E-mail: anna.zagorska@cabrillo.edu
Phone: (831) 477-3375

**Cabrini University**
www.cabrini.edu
Admissions Office
610 King of Prussia Road
Radnor, PA 19087-3698
Fax: (610) 902-8508
E-mail: charles.spencer@cabrini.edu
Phone: (610) 902-8556

**Cairn University**
www.cairn.edu
Admissions
200 Manor Avenue
Langhorne, PA 19047-2990
Fax: (215) 702-4248
E-mail: intl-office@cairn.edu
Phone: (215) 702-4244

**Caldwell Community College and Technical Institute**
www.cccti.edu
2855 Hickory Boulevard
Hudson, NC 28638-2672
Fax: (828) 726-2709
E-mail: esetzer@caldwell.cc.nc.us
Phone: (828) 726-2719

**Caldwell University**
www.caldwell.edu
Director of International Student Services
120 Bloomfield Avenue
Caldwell, NJ 07006-6195
Fax: (973) 618-3600
E-mail: mjoshi@caldwell.edu
Phone: (973) 618-3519

**Calhoun Community College**
www.calhoun.edu
Admissions and Records
PO Box 2216
Decatur, AL 35609-2216
Fax: (256) 306-2941
E-mail: ronald.mccall@calhoun.edu
Phone: (256) 306-2500

**California Baptist University**
www.calbaptist.edu
Director of International Students
8432 Magnolia Avenue
Riverside, CA 92504-3297
Fax: (951) 343-4728
E-mail: bdavis@calbaptist.edu
Phone: (951) 343-4721

**California Christian College**
www.calchristiancollege.edu
Director of Admissions
5364 East Belmont
Fresno, CA 93727
Fax: (559) 385-2329
E-mail: admissions@calchristiancollege.edu
Phone: (559) 251-4215 ext. 1002

**California Coast University**
www.calcoast.edu
925 North Spurgeon Street
Santa Ana, CA 92701
E-mail: admissions@calcoast.edu
Phone: (714) 547-9625

**California College of the Arts**
www.cca.edu
Enrollment Services
1111 Eighth Street
San Francisco, CA 94107-2247
Fax: (415) 703-9539
E-mail: schavan@cca.edu
Phone: (415) 703-9520

**California College San Diego**
www.cc-sd.edu
Admissions
6602 Convoy Court, Suite 100
San Diego, CA 92111
Fax: (619) 295-5867
E-mail: baris.yucelt@cc-sd.edu
Phone: (619) 680-4430 ext. 1502

**California Institute of the Arts**
www.calarts.edu
Admissions
24700 McBean Parkway
Valencia, CA 91355
Fax: (661) 253-7710
E-mail: mryan@calarts.edu
Phone: (661) 255-1050

**California Institute of Integral Studies**
www.ciis.edu
Student Affairs Office
1453 Mission Street
San Francisco, CA 94103
Fax: (415) 575-6158
E-mail: joconnor@ciis.edu
Phone: (415) 575-6157

**California Institute of Technology**
www.caltech.edu
Office of Admissions
383 South Hill Avenue, Mail Code 10-90
Pasadena, CA 91125
Fax: (626) 683-3026
E-mail: ugadmissions@caltech.edu
Phone: (626) 395-6341

**California Lutheran University**
www.callutheran.edu
Admission
60 West Olsen Road #1350
Thousand Oaks, CA 91360-2787
Fax: (805) 493-3114
E-mail: admissions@callutheran.edu
Phone: (805) 493-3601

**California Maritime Academy**
www.csum.edu
Director of Admission
200 Maritime Academy Drive
Vallejo, CA 94590
Fax: (707) 654-1336
E-mail: mmcgee@csum.edu
Phone: (707) 654-1330

**California Miramar University**
www.calmu.edu
9750 Miramar Road, Suite 180
San Diego, CA 92126
E-mail: admissions@calmu.edu
Phone: (858) 653-3000

**California National University for Advanced Studies**
www.cnuas.edu
18520 Hawthorne Boulevard
Torrance, CA 90504
Fax: (310) 371-7072
E-mail: cnuadms@mail.cnuas.edu
Phone: (818) 830-2411

**California Polytechnic State University: San Luis Obispo**
www.calpoly.edu
Admissions Office, Cal Poly
San Luis Obispo, CA 93407-0031
Fax: (805) 756-5400
E-mail: tharris@calpoly.edu
Phone: (805) 756-2311

**California State Polytechnic University: Pomona**
www.cpp.edu
Coordinator of International Admissions
3801 W Temple Avenue
Bldg 98-T2
Pomona, CA 91768-4019
Fax: (909) 869-5858
E-mail: kevinmartin@cpp.edu
Phone: (909) 869-2107

**California State University: Bakersfield**
www.csub.edu
Admission Office
9001 Stockdale Highway
Bakersfield, CA 93311-1099
Fax: (661) 654-3389
E-mail: jmimms@csub.edu
Phone: (661) 654-3036

**California State University: Channel Islands**
www.csuci.edu
Center for International Affairs
One University Drive
Camarillo, CA 93012
E-mail: international@csuci.edu
Phone: (805) 437-3107

**California State University: Chico**
www.csuchico.edu
International Undergraduate Admissions
400 West First Street
Chico, CA 95929-0722
Fax: (530) 898-4895
E-mail: cjmckay@csuchico.edu
Phone: (530) 898-5408

**California State University: Dominguez Hills**
www.csudh.edu
Admissions Office
1000 East Victoria Street
Carson, CA 90747
Fax: (310) 516-4573
E-mail: mtaylor@csudh.edu
Phone: (310) 243-3645

**California State University: East Bay**
www.csueastbay.edu
Director, International Admissions
25800 Carlos Bee Boulevard
Hayward, CA 94542-3095
Fax: (510) 885-3816
E-mail: admissions@csueastbay.edu
Phone: (510) 885-4038

**California State University: Fresno**
www.csufresno.edu
International Student Services and Programs
5150 North Maple Avenue, M/S JA 57
Fresno, CA 93740-8026
Fax: (559) 278-4812
E-mail: sarahl@csufresno.edu
Phone: (559) 278-2782

**California State University: Fullerton**
www.fullerton.edu
Admissions and Records
PO Box 6900
Fullerton, CA 92834-6900
Fax: (657) 278-2356
E-mail: admissions@fullerton.edu
Phone: (657) 278-2371

**California State University: Long Beach**
www.csulb.edu
Center for International Education
1250 Bellflower Boulevard
Long Beach, CA 90840-0106
Fax: (562) 985-4973
E-mail: lynn.christopher@csulb.edu
Phone: (562) 985-5476

**California State University: Los Angeles**
www.calstatela.edu
International Programs and Services
5151 State University Drive SA101
Los Angeles, CA 90032
Fax: (323) 343-6478
E-mail: admission@calstatela.edu
Phone: (323) 343-3170

**California State University: Monterey Bay**
www.csumb.edu
Admissions
100 Campus Center, Student Services Building
Building 47
Seaside, CA 93955-8001
Fax: (831) 582-3783
E-mail: pcarter@csumb.edu
Phone: (831) 582-3738

**California State University: Sacramento**
www.csus.edu
Coordinator of International Admissions
6000 J Street
Lassen Hall, Lobby
Sacramento, CA 95819-6048
Fax: (916) 278-7471
E-mail: mlima.wells@csus.edu
Phone: (916) 278-7772

**California State University: San Bernardino**
www.csusb.edu
Admissions (Foreign Evaluations)
5500 University Parkway
San Bernardino, CA 92407-2397
Fax: (909) 537-7020
E-mail: pamaya@csusb.edu
Phone: (909) 537-5193

**California State University: San Marcos**
www.csusm.edu
Office of Global Education
333 South Twin Oaks Valley Road
San Marcos, CA 92096-0001
Fax: (760) 750-3284
E-mail: apply@csusm.edu
Phone: (760) 750-4090

**California State University: Stanislaus**
www.csustan.edu
Office of International Education
One University Circle
Turlock, CA 95382-0256
Fax: (209) 667-3791
E-mail: jhelzer@csustan.edu
Phone: (209) 667-3329

**California University of Management and Sciences**
www.calums.edu
Admissions
721 North Euclid Streeet
Anaheim, CA 92801-4116
Fax: (714) 533-7778
E-mail: lisa@calums.edu
Phone: (714) 533-3946

**California University of Pennsylvania**
www.calu.edu
250 University Avenue
California, PA 15419-1394
Fax: (724) 938-4564
E-mail: sheetz@calu.edu
Phone: (724) 938-4404

**Calumet College of St. Joseph**
www.ccsj.edu
Admissions
2400 New York Avenue
Whiting, IN 46394-2195
Fax: (219) 473-4259
E-mail: rleevey@ccsj.edu
Phone: (877) 700-9100 ext. 215

**Calvary Bible College and Theological Seminary**
www.calvary.edu
Admissions
15800 Calvary Road
Kansas City, MO 64147-1341
Fax: (816) 331-4474
E-mail: admissions@calvary.edu
Phone: (816) 322-0110 ext. 1321

**Calvin College**
www.calvin.edu
Admissions
3201 Burton Street Southeast
Grand Rapids, MI 49546
Fax: (616) 526-6777
E-mail: intladm@calvin.edu
Phone: (616) 526-6106

**Cambridge College**
www.cambridgecollege.edu
International Students Office
1000 Massachusetts Avenue
Cambridge, MA 02138-5304
Fax: (617) 868-2675
E-mail: Molly.Young@cambridgecollege.edu
Phone: (617) 873-0169

**Cameron University**
www.cameron.edu
International Admissions
2800 West Gore Boulevard
Lawton, OK 73505-6377
Fax: (580) 581-5416
E-mail: international@cameron.edu
Phone: (580) 581-2838

**Campbell University**
www.campbell.edu
International Admissions
PO Box 546
Buies Creek, NC 27506
Fax: (910) 893-1288
E-mail: intl@email.campbell.edu
Phone: (800) 334-4111 ext. 1417

**Campbellsville University**
www.campbellsville.edu
International Admissions Counselor
1 University Drive
Campbellsville, KY 42718-2799
Fax: (270) 789-5071
E-mail: admissions@campbellsville.edu
Phone: (800) 264-6014 ext. 5312

**Canada College**
www.canadacollege.edu
International Student Center
4200 Farm Hill Boulevard
Redwood City, CA 94061
Fax: (650) 306-3518
E-mail: caninternational@smccd.edu
Phone: (650) 381-3544

**Canisius College**
www.canisius.edu
Admissions Office
2001 Main Street
Buffalo, NY 14208-1098
Fax: (716) 888-3116
E-mail: ballarom@canisius.edu
Phone: (716) 888-3272

**Cape Cod Community College**
www.capecod.edu
Admissions
2240 Iyannough Road
West Barnstable, MA 02668-1599
Fax: (508) 375-4089
E-mail: mcormier@capecod.edu
Phone: (508) 362-2131 ext. 4466

**Capella University**
www.capella.edu
Enrollment Services
225 South Sixth Street
Minneapolis, MN 55402
Fax: (612) 977-5060
E-mail: info@capella.edu
Phone: (888) 227-2736

**Capital Community College**
www.ccc.commnet.edu
Admissions
950 Main Street
Hartford, CT 06103-1207
E-mail: mball-davis@ccc.commnet.edu
Phone: (860) 906-5127

**Capital University**
www.capital.edu
Office of International Education
1 College and Main
Columbus, OH 43209-2394
Fax: (614) 236-6171
E-mail: international@capital.edu
Phone: (614) 236-7102

**Capitol Technology University**
www.capitol-college.edu
11301 Springfield Road
Laurel, MD 20708
Fax: (301) 953-1442
E-mail: agmiller@capitol-college.edu
Phone: (301) 369-2800

**Cardinal Stritch University**
www.stritch.edu
International Education Office
6801 North Yates Road, Box 516
Milwaukee, WI 53217-7516
Fax: (414) 410-4092
E-mail: srsweenry@stritch.edu
Phone: (414) 410-4187

**Career College of Northern Nevada**
www.ccnn.edu
1421 Pullman Drive
Sparks, NV 89434
E-mail: mclark@ccnn4u.com
Phone: (775) 856-2266

**Career Training Academy: Monroeville**
www.careerta.edu
4314 Old William Penn Highway #103
Monroeville, PA 15146
E-mail: admissions2@careerta.edu
Phone: (412) 372-3900

**Careers Unlimited**
www.ucdh.edu
1176 South 1480 West
Orem, UT 84058
Fax: (801) 224-5437
E-mail: admissions@ucdh.edu
Phone: (801) 426-8234

**Caribbean University**
www.caribbean.edu
PO Box 493
Bayamon, PR 00960-0493
Fax: (787) 269-4890
E-mail: lmatos@caribbean.edu
Phone: (787) 780-0070 ext. 1515

**Carl Albert State College**
www.carlalbert.edu
Admissions
1507 South McKenna
Poteau, OK 74953-5208
Fax: (918) 647-1306
E-mail: asutter@carlalbert.edu
Phone: (918) 647-1303

**Carl Sandburg College**
www.sandburg.edu
2400 Tom L. Wilson Boulevard
Galesburg, IL 61401
Fax: (309) 344-3291
E-mail: ckreider@csc.cc.il.us
Phone: (309) 344-2518

**Carleton College**
www.carleton.edu
Admissions
100 South College Street
Northfield, MN 55057
Fax: (507) 222-4526
E-mail: admissions@carleton.edu
Phone: (507) 222-4190

**Carlos Albizu University**
www.albizu.edu
Student Affairs
2173 NW 99th Avenue
Miami, FL 33172
Fax: (305) 593-1854
E-mail: prubio@albizu.edu
Phone: (305) 593-1223 ext. 208

**Carlos Albizu University: San Juan**
www.albizu.edu
151 Tanca Street
San Juan, PR 00902-3711
Fax: (787) 721-7187
Phone: (787) 725-6500 ext. 21

**Carlow University**
www.carlow.edu
Center for Global Learning
3333 Fifth Avenue
Pittsburgh, PA 15213-3165
Fax: (412) 578-6321
E-mail: bjpilcher@carlow.edu
Phone: (412) 578-6557

**Carnegie Mellon University**
www.cmu.edu
Admissions Office
5000 Forbes Avenue
Warner Hall
Pittsburgh, PA 15213-3890
Fax: (412) 268-7838
E-mail: undergraduate-
admissions@andrew.cmu.edu
Phone: (412) 268-2082

**Carrington College: Albuquerque**
www.carrington.edu
1001 Menaul Boulevard, N.E.
Albuquerque, NM 87107-1642
Phone: (888) 720-5014

**Carrington College: Boise**
www.carrington.edu
1122 North Liberty Street
Boise, ID 83704-8742
Phone: (888) 720-5014

**Carrington College: Citrus Heights**
www.carrington.edu
7301 Greenback Lane, Suite A
Citrus Heights, CA 95621

**Carrington College: Las Vegas**
www.carrington.edu
5740 South Eastern Avenue
#140
Las Vegas, NV 89119-1642
Phone: (888) 720-5014

**Carrington College: Mesa**
www.carrington.edu
1001 Southern Avenue, Suite 130
Mesa, AZ 85210
Phone: (888) 720-5014

**Carrington College: Phoenix**
www.carrington.edu
8503 North 27th Avenue
Phoenix, AZ 85051-4063
Phone: (888) 720-5014

**Carrington College: Phoenix Westside**
www.carrington.edu
2701 West Bethany Home Road
Phoenix, AZ 85017-5885
Phone: (602) 433-1333

**Carrington College: Pleasant Hill**
www.carrington.edu
380 Civic Drive, Suite 300
Pleasant Hill, CA 94523
Fax: (925) 609-6666
Phone: (925) 609-6650

**Carrington College: Reno**
www.carrington.edu
5580 Kietzke Lane
Reno, NV 89511
E-mail: brossini@carrington.edu
Phone: (888) 720-5014

**Carrington College: Sacramento**
www.carrington.edu
8909 Folsom Boulevard
Sacramento, CA 95826

**Carrington College: San Jose**
www.carrington.edu
6201 San Ignacio Avenue
San Jose, CA 95119
Fax: (408) 360-0848
Phone: (408) 960-0161

**Carrington College: Spokane**
www.carrington.edu
10102 East Knox Avenue
Suite 200
Spokane, WA 99206-4187
Phone: (888) 720-5014

**Carrington College: Stockton**
www.carrington.edu
1313 West Robinhood Drive, Suite B
Stockton, CA 95207

**Carrington College: Tucson**
www.carrington.edu
201 North Bonita Avenue
Tucson, AZ 85745
Phone: (888) 720-5014

**Carroll College**
www.carroll.edu
International Programs
1601 North Benton Avenue
Helena, MT 59625
Fax: (406) 447-5461
E-mail: intl@carroll.edu
Phone: (406) 447-5406

**Carroll Community College**
www.carrollcc.edu
Office of Admissions
1601 Washington Road
Westminster, MD 21157
Fax: (410) 386-8446
E-mail: cedwards@carrollcc.edu
Phone: (410) 386-8430

**Carroll University**
www.carrollu.edu
Office of International Education
100 North East Avenue
Waukesha, WI 53186-9988
Fax: (262) 524-7139
E-mail: international@carrollu.edu
Phone: (262) 650-4948

**Carson-Newman University**
www.cn.edu
International Admissions Coordinator
1646 Russell Avenue
Jefferson City, TN 37760
Fax: (865) 471-3502
E-mail: scunningham@cn.edu
Phone: (865) 471-3431

**Carteret Community College**
www.carteret.edu
Admissions Office
3505 Arendell Street
Morehead City, NC 28557-2989
Fax: (252) 222-6265
E-mail: admissions@email.carteret.edu
Phone: (252) 222-6155

**Carthage College**
www.carthage.edu
Admissions
2001 Alford Park Drive
Kenosha, WI 53140-1994
Fax: (262) 551-5762
E-mail: admissions@carthage.edu
Phone: (262) 551-6000

**Carver College**
www.carver.edu
Admissions
3870 Cascade Road, SW
Atlanta, GA 30331
Fax: (404) 527-4524
E-mail: bmack@carver.edu
Phone: (404) 527-4520 ext. 209

**Cascadia College**
www.cascadia.edu
International Programs
18345 Campus Way, NE
Bothell, WA 98011
Fax: (425) 352-8304
E-mail: International@cascadia.edu
Phone: (425) 352-8218

**Case Western Reserve University**
www.case.edu
Undergraduate Admission
Wolstein Hall
11318 Bellflower Road
Cleveland, OH 44106-7055
Fax: (216) 368-5111
E-mail: drew.crawford@case.edu
Phone: (216) 368-4450

**Casper College**
www.caspercollege.edu
Office of Enrollment Services
125 College Drive
Casper, WY 82601
Fax: (307) 268-2611
E-mail: lnichols@caspercollege.edu
Phone: (307) 268-2220

**Castleton University**
www.castleton.edu
Admissions Office
Seminary Street
Castleton, VT 05735
Fax: (802) 468-1476
E-mail: erica.terault@castleton.edu
Phone: (802) 468-1213

**Catawba College**
www.catawba.edu
Assistant Director of Admissions and
International Student Counselor
2300 West Innes Street
Salisbury, NC 28144-2488
Fax: (704) 637-4222
E-mail: abarkova@catawba.edu
Phone: (704) 645-4581

**Catholic Distance University**
www.cdu.edu
Admissions
115 West Congress Street
Charles Town, WV 25414
Fax: (304) 724-5017
E-mail: admissions@cdu.edu
Phone: (888) 254-4238 ext. 700

**Catholic University of America**
www.cua.edu
VP, Enrollment Management & Marketing
102 Father O'Connell Hall
620 Michigan Avenue, NE
Washington, DC 20064
Fax: (202) 319-6533
E-mail: lydon@cua.edu
Phone: (202) 319-5305

**Cayuga Community College**
www.cayuga-cc.edu
Admissions Office
197 Franklin Street
Auburn, NY 13021-3099
Fax: (315) 255-2117
E-mail: blodgett@cayuga-cc.edu
Phone: (315) 255-1743

**Cazenovia College**
www.cazenovia.edu
Admissions
3 Sullivan Street
Cazenovia, NY 13035
Fax: (315) 655-4860
E-mail: bmcarguello@cazenovia.edu
Phone: (315) 655-7150

**Cedar Crest College**
www.cedarcrest.edu
Office of Admissions
100 College Drive
Allentown, PA 18104-6196
Fax: (610) 606-4647
E-mail: admissions@cedarcrest.edu
Phone: (610) 740-3780

**Cedar Valley College**
www.cedarvalleycollege.edu
Admissions
3030 North Dallas Avenue
Lancaster, TX 75134
Fax: (972) 860-8001
E-mail: ljohnson@dccd.edu
Phone: (972) 860-8016

**Cedarville University**
www.cedarville.edu
International Student Services
251 North Main Street
Cedarville, OH 45314-0601
Fax: (937) 766-4129
E-mail: breid@cedarville.edu
Phone: (937) 766-7982

**Centenary College of Louisiana**
www.centenary.edu
Admission Office
Office of Admission
2911 Centenary Boulevard
Shreveport, LA 71104
Fax: (318) 869-5005
E-mail: abrown5@centenary.edu
Phone: (318) 869-5131

**Centenary University**
www.centenaryuniversity.edu
School of International Programs
400 Jefferson Street
Hackettstown, NJ 07840-9989
Fax: (908) 852-3454
E-mail: mahaffeyp@centenaryuniversity.edu
Phone: (908) 852-1400 ext. 2217

**Central Arizona College**
www.centralaz.edu
Registrars Office
Admissions Office
8470 North Overfield Road
Coolidge, AZ 85128-9030
Fax: (520) 494-5083
E-mail: veronica.duran@centralaz.edu
Phone: (520) 494-5260

**Central Carolina Technical College**
www.cctech.edu
506 North Guignard Drive
Sumter, SC 29150-2499
Fax: (803) 778-6696
E-mail: admissions@cctech.edu
Phone: (803) 778-6605

**Central Christian College of Kansas**
www.centralchristian.edu
Admissions
1200 South Main
PO Box 1403
McPherson, KS 67460-5740
Fax: (620) 241-6032
E-mail: admissions@centralchristian.edu
Phone: (620) 241-0723 ext. 380

**Central College**
www.central.edu
Admission Office, Central College
812 University Street
Pella, IA 50219-1999
Fax: (641) 628-7637
E-mail: freiburgerc@central.edu
Phone: (877) 462-3687

**Central Connecticut State University**
www.ccsu.edu
Recruitment and Admissions
1615 Stanley Street
New Britain, CT 06050
Fax: (860) 832-2295
E-mail: admissions@ccsu.edu
Phone: (860) 832-2278

**Central Georgia Technical College**
www.centralgatech.edu
Office of International Students
80 Cohen Walker Drive
Warner Robins, GA 31088
Fax: (478) 988-6947
E-mail: bmitchem@centralgatech.edu
Phone: (478) 445-2313

**Central Lakes College**
www.clcmn.edu
Admissions
501 West College Drive
Brainerd, MN 56401
Fax: (218) 855-8230
E-mail: jbrose@clcmn.edu
Phone: (218) 855-8035

**Central Maine Community College**
www.cmcc.edu
Admissions
1250 Turner Street
Auburn, ME 04210-6498
Fax: (207) 755-5493
E-mail: enroll@cmcc.edu
Phone: (207) 755-5273

**Central Methodist University**
www.centralmethodist.edu
Admissions
411 Central Methodist Square
Fayette, MO 65248-1198
Fax: (660) 248-1872
E-mail: admissions@centralmethodist.edu
Phone: (660) 248-6374

**Central Michigan University**
www.cmich.edu
Office of International Affairs
Admissions Office
Warriner Hall
Mount Pleasant, MI 48859
Fax: (989) 774-3690
E-mail: intlapp@cmich.edu
Phone: (989) 774-4308

**Central Ohio Technical College**
www.cotc.edu
Academic Advisor
1179 University Drive
Newark, OH 43055
Fax: (740) 366-9160
E-mail: jabraham@cotc.edu
Phone: (740) 755-7325

**Central Penn College**
www.centralpenn.edu
Admissions
600 Valley Road
Summerdale, PA 17093-0309
Fax: (717) 732-5254
E-mail: staceyobi@centralpenn.edu
Phone: (800) 759-2727 ext. 2248

**Central Piedmont Community College**
www.cpcc.edu
International Student Adviser
PO Box 35009
Charlotte, NC 28235-5009
Fax: (704) 330-6130
E-mail: margarita.walkup@cpcc.edu
Phone: (704) 330-6456

**Central State University**
www.centralstate.edu
Admissions
PO Box 1004
Wilberforce, OH 45384-1004
Fax: (937) 376-6530
E-mail: admissions@centralstate.edu
Phone: (937) 376-6121

**Central Texas College**
www.ctcd.edu
International Student Services
Central Texas College
PO Box 1800
Killeen, TX 76540-1800
Fax: (254) 526-1481
E-mail: ctc.international@ctcd.edu
Phone: (254) 526-1107

**Central Washington University**
www.cwu.edu
Office of Admissions
400 East University Way
Ellensburg, WA 98926-7463
Fax: (509) 963-3022
E-mail: admissions@cwu.edu
Phone: (509) 963-1211

**Central Wyoming College**
www.cwc.edu
Admissions
2660 Peck Avenue
Riverton, WY 82501
Fax: (307) 855-2065
E-mail: jharris@cwc.edu
Phone: (307) 855-2270

**Central Yeshiva Tomchei Tmimim-Lubavitch**
841-853 Ocean Parkway
Brooklyn, NY 11230
E-mail: uofiop@juno.com
Phone: (718) 859-7600

**Centralia College**
www.centralia.edu
International Programs
600 Centralia College Boulevard
Centralia, WA 98531
Fax: (360) 330-7503
E-mail: intl@centralia.edu
Phone: (360) 736-9391 ext. 492

**Centre College**
www.centre.edu
Admission Office
600 West Walnut Street
Danville, KY 40422-1394
Fax: (859) 238-5373
E-mail: s.miller@centre.edu
Phone: (859) 238-5350

**Centro de Estudios Multidisciplinarios**
www.cempr.edu
PO Box 191317
San Juan, PR 00919-1317
Fax: (787) 765-4277
E-mail: jmrestotorres@yahoo.com
Phone: (787) 765-4210

**Century College**
www.century.edu
Multicultural Center
3300 Century Avenue North
White Bear Lake, MN 55110
Fax: (651) 747-4057
E-mail: katie.vadnais@century.edu
Phone: (651) 779-3274

**Cerritos College**
www.cerritos.edu
11110 Alondra Boulevard
Norwalk, CA 90650
Fax: (562) 467-5068
Phone: (562) 860-2451 ext. 2211

**Cerro Coso Community College**
www.cerrocoso.edu
Vice President
3000 College Heights Boulevard
Ridgecrest, CA 93555-7777
Fax: (760) 384-6377
E-mail: jboard@cerrocoso.edu
Phone: (760) 384-6354

**Chabot College**
www.chabotcollege.edu
Office of Special Admissions, Room 168,
Chabot College
25555 Hesperian Boulevard
Hayward, CA 94545
Fax: (510) 723-7510
E-mail: dbalangitao@chabotcollege.edu
Phone: (510) 723-6715

**Chadron State College**
www.csc.edu
1000 Main Street
Chadron, NE 69337
Fax: (308) 432-6229
E-mail: ccousin@csc.edu
Phone: (308) 432-6496

**Chaffey College**
www.chaffey.edu
International Student Admissions
5885 Haven Avenue
Rancho Cucamonga, CA 91737-3002
Fax: (909) 652-6006
E-mail: donna.colondres@chaffey.edu
Phone: (909) 652-6226

**Chamberlain College of Nursing: Addison**
www.chamberlain.edu
1221 North Swift Road
Addison, IL 60101-6106

**Chamberlain College of Nursing: Arlington**
www.chamberlain.edu
2450 Crystal Drive
Arlington, VA 22202

**Chamberlain College of Nursing: Atlanta**
www.chamberlain.edu
5775 Peachtree Dunwoody Road Northeast
Atlanta, GA 30342
Phone: (404) 250-8500

**Chamberlain College of Nursing: Chicago**
www.chamberlain.edu/nursing-schools/
campuses/Chicago-Illinois
3300 North Campbell Avenue
Chicago, IL 60618

**Chamberlain College of Nursing: Cleveland**
www.chamberlain.edu
6700 Euclid Avenue, Suite 201
Cleveland, OH 44103

**Chamberlain College of Nursing: Columbus**
www.chamberlain.edu
1350 Alum Creek Drive
Columbus, OH 43209

**Chamberlain College of Nursing: Houston**
www.chamberlain.edu
11025 Equity Drive
Houston, TX 77041
Phone: (713) 277-9800

**Chamberlain College of Nursing: Indianapolis**
www.chamberlain.edu
9100 Keystone Crossing, Suite 600
Indianapolis, IN 46240

**Chamberlain College of Nursing: Jacksonville**
www.chamberlain.edu
5200 Belfort Road
Jacksonville, FL 32256

**Chamberlain College of Nursing: Miramar**
www.chamberlain.edu
2300 Southwest 145th Avenue
Miramar, FL 33027

**Chamberlain College of Nursing: Phoenix**
www.chamberlain.edu
2149 West Dunlap Avenue
Phoenix
Phoenix, AZ 85021

**Chamberlain College Of Nursing: Tinley Park**
www.chamberlain.edu
Phone: (708) 560-2000

**Chaminade University of Honolulu**
www.chaminade.edu
Admissions Office
3140 Waialae Avenue
Honolulu, HI 96816
Fax: (808) 739-4647
E-mail: admissions@chaminade.edu
Phone: (808) 735-4735

**Champlain College**
www.champlain.edu
Director of Admissions
PO Box 670
Burlington, VT 05402-0670
Fax: (802) 860-2767
E-mail: cperlongo@champlain.edu
Phone: (802) 865-5740

**Chandler-Gilbert Community College**
www.cgc.maricopa.edu
International Education Programs
2626 East Pecos Road
Chandler, AZ 85225-2499
Fax: (866) 579-8242
E-mail: iss@cgc.edu
Phone: (480) 732-7391

**Chapman University**
www.chapman.edu
Associate Director of Admission/International
Admission Officer
Admission Office
One University Drive
Orange, CA 92866
Fax: (714) 997-6713
E-mail: intladmit@chapman.edu
Phone: (714) 997-6711

**Charles Drew University of Medicine and Science**
www.cdrewu.edu
Office of Enrollment Management
1731 East 120th Street
Los Angeles, CA 90059
Fax: (323) 563-4837
E-mail: admissionsinfo@cdrewu.edu
Phone: (323) 563-4839

**Charleston Southern University**
www.csuniv.edu
Assistant Director of Admissions
9200 University Boulevard
Box 118087
Charleston, SC 29406
Fax: (843) 863-7070
E-mail: psmith@csuniv.edu
Phone: (843) 863-7050

**Charlotte Christian College and Theological Seminary**
www.nlts.edu
PO Box 790106
Charlotte, NC 28206
E-mail: chemphill@nlts.edu
Phone: (704) 334-6882 ext. 115

**Charter Oak State College**
www.charteroak.edu
Admission
55 Paul Manafort Drive
New Britain, CT 06053
E-mail: admissions@charteroak.edu
Phone: (860) 515-3858

**Chatham University**
www.chatham.edu
VP for Enrollment Management
Woodland Road
Office of Admissions
Pittsburgh, PA 15232
Fax: (412) 365-1295
E-mail: abecher@chatham.edu
Phone: (412) 365-1139

**Chattahoochee Technical College**
www.chattahoocheetech.edu
International
980 South Cobb Drive, SE
Marietta, GA 30060-3300
Fax: (770) 528-5818
E-mail: gmoor@chattahoocheetech.edu
Phone: (770) 528-4528

**Chattahoochee Valley Community College**
www.cv.edu
Admissions
2602 College Drive
Phenix City, AL 36869
Fax: (334) 291-4994
E-mail: admissions@cv.edu
Phone: (334) 291-4996

**Chattanooga College**
www.chattanoogacollege.edu
3805 Brainerd Road
Chattanooga, TN 37411
E-mail: tonym@ecpconline.com
Phone: (423) 624-0077

**Chemeketa Community College**
www.chemeketa.edu
International Student Admissions
Admissions Office
PO Box 14007
Salem, OR 97309-7070
Fax: (503) 365-4768
E-mail: teter.kapan@chemeketa.edu
Phone: (503) 399-5141

**Chesapeake College**
www.chesapeake.edu
Registrar
Box 8
1000 College Circle
Wye Mills, MD 21679-0008
Fax: (410) 827-9466
E-mail: jdavidson@chesapeake.edu
Phone: (410) 822-5400 ext. 5846

**Chestnut Hill College**
www.chc.edu
Global Education Office
9601 Germantown Avenue
Philadelphia, PA 19118-2693
Fax: (215) 248-7155
E-mail: brown2@chc.edu
Phone: (215) 242-7989

**Cheyney University of Pennsylvania**
www.cheyney.edu
Admissions Office
1837 University Circle
PO Box 200
Cheyney, PA 19319-0019
Fax: (610) 399-2099
E-mail: abrown@cheyney.edu
Phone: (610) 399-2275

**Chicago State University**
www.csu.edu
Office of International Programs
9501 South King Drive
Chicago, IL 60628
Fax: (773) 995-2840
E-mail: OIP@csu.edu
Phone: (773) 995-2582

**Chipola College**
www.chipola.edu
Vice President Student Affairs
3094 Indian Circle
Marianna, FL 32446
Fax: (850) 718-2255
E-mail: robertsj@chipola.edu
Phone: (850) 718-2209

**Chippewa Valley Technical College**
www.cvtc.edu
620 West Clairemont Avenue
Eau Claire, WI 54701-6162
Fax: (715) 833-6470
E-mail: jmoldenhauer@cvtc.edu
Phone: (715) 833-6247

**Chowan University**
https://www.chowan.edu
Office of Admissions
One University Place
Murfreesboro, NC 27855-9901
Fax: (252) 398-1190
E-mail: parkes@chowan.edu
Phone: (252) 398-6314

**Christendom College**
www.christendom.edu
134 Christendom Drive
Front Royal, VA 22630
Fax: (540) 636-1655
E-mail: admissions@christendom.edu
Phone: (800) 877-5456 ext. 1290

**Christian Brothers University**
www.cbu.edu
Admissions
650 East Parkway South
Memphis, TN 38104-5519
Fax: (901) 321-3202
E-mail: rosie.britton@cbu.edu
Phone: (901) 321-3222

**Christopher Newport University**
www.cnu.edu
Dean of Admission
1 Avenue of the Arts
Newport News, VA 23606-3072
Fax: (757) 594-7333
E-mail: admit@cnu.edu
Phone: (757) 594-8070

**Cincinnati Christian University**
www.ccuniversity.edu
Director Undergraduate Admissions
2700 Glenway Avenue
Cincinnati, OH 45204-3200
Fax: (513) 244-8453
E-mail: cbcadmission@ccuniversity.edu
Phone: (513) 244-8170

**Cincinnati State Technical and Community College**
www.cincinnatistate.edu
3520 Central Parkway
Cincinnati, OH 45223-2690
Fax: (513) 569-4248
E-mail: bryan.wright@cincinnatistate.edu
Phone: (513) 569-4769

**Cisco College**
www.cisco.edu
International Admissions
101 College Heights
Cisco, TX 76437
Fax: (254) 442-1449
E-mail: international.admissions@cisco.edu
Phone: (254) 442-5131

**The Citadel**
www.citadel.edu
Associate Director of Admissions
171 Moultrie Street
Charleston, SC 29409
Fax: (843) 953-7036
E-mail: admissions@citadel.edu
Phone: (843) 953-5230

**Citrus College**
www.citruscollege.edu
International Student Office
1000 West Foothill Boulevard
Glendora, CA 91741-1899
Fax: (626) 963-4854
E-mail: clamoureux@citruscollege.edu
Phone: (626) 914-8549

**City College of San Francisco**
www.ccsf.edu
Director of Foreign Student Admissions
Office of Admissions and Records E-107
50 Phelan Avenue
San Francisco, CA 94112
Fax: (415) 239-3936
E-mail: jlow@ccsf.edu
Phone: (415) 239-3837

**City College: Altamonte Springs**
www.citycollege.edu
853 Semoran Boulevard 436
Casselberry, FL 32707-5353
Fax: (407) 831-1147
Phone: (407) 831-8466

**City College: Fort Lauderdale**
www.citycollege.edu
Admissions
2000 West Commercial Boulevard
Fort Lauderdale, FL 33309
Fax: (954) 491-1965
E-mail: jhernandez@citycollege.edu
Phone: (954) 492-5353

**City College: Gainesville**
www.citycollege.edu
7001 NW 4th Boulevard
Gainesville, FL 32607
Fax: (352) 335-4303
E-mail: kbowden@citycollege.edu
Phone: (352) 335-4000 ext. 410

**City College: Miami**
www.citycollege.edu
9300 South Dadeland Boulevard
2nd Floor
Miami, FL 33156
Fax: (305) 666-9243
E-mail: dsinawi@citycollege.edu
Phone: (305) 666-9242

**City Colleges of Chicago: Harold Washington College**
www.ccc.edu
Admissions Office
30 East Lake Street
Chicago, IL 60601
Fax: (312) 553-6084
Phone: (312) 553-6004

**City Colleges of Chicago: Kennedy-King College**
www.ccc.edu
6301 South Halsted Street
Chicago, IL 60621
Fax: (773) 602-5247
Phone: (773) 602-5273

**City Colleges of Chicago: Malcolm X College**
www.ccc.edu
1900 West Van Buren Street
Chicago, IL 60612
Fax: (312) 850-7092
Phone: (312) 850-7126

**City Colleges of Chicago: Olive-Harvey College**
www.ccc.edu
10001 South Woodlawn Avenue
Chicago, IL 60628
Fax: (773) 291-6185
Phone: (773) 291-6384

**City Colleges of Chicago: Richard J. Daley College**
www.ccc.edu
7500 South Pulaski Road
Chicago, IL 60652
Fax: (773) 838-7605
Phone: (773) 838-7606

**City Colleges of Chicago: Wilbur Wright College**
www.ccc.edu
4300 North Narragansett Avenue
Chicago, IL 60634-4276
Fax: (773) 481-8053
Phone: (773) 481-8259

**City University of New York: Baruch College**
www.baruch.cuny.edu
Office of Undergraduate Admissions
One Bernard Baruch Way
New York, NY 10010
Fax: (646) 312-1279
E-mail: admissions@baruch.cuny.edu
Phone: (646) 312-1383

**City University of New York: Borough of Manhattan Community College**
www.bmcc.cuny.edu
Office of Admissions
199 Chambers Street
Room S-300
New York, NY 10007
Fax: (212) 220-2366
E-mail: lyielkin@bmcc.cuny.edu
Phone: (212) 220-1270

**City University of New York: Bronx Community College**
www.bcc.cuny.edu
2155 University Avenue
Bronx, NY 10453
Fax: (718) 289-6352
E-mail: patricia.ramos@bcc.cuny.edu
Phone: (718) 289-5888

**City University of New York: Brooklyn College**
www.brooklyn.cuny.edu
CUNY Office of Admissions Services
2900 Bedford Avenue
Brooklyn, NY 11210
Fax: (718) 951-4506
E-mail: keishasimon@brooklyn.cuny.edu
Phone: (718) 951-5000 ext. 3833

**City University of New York: City College**
www.ccny.cuny.edu
Admissions
160 Convent Avenue, A100
New York, NY 10031
Fax: (212) 650-6417
E-mail: asabal@ccny.cuny.edu
Phone: (212) 650-6444

**City University of New York: College of Staten Island**
www.csi.cuny.edu
Recruitment & Admissions
2800 Victory Boulevard 2A-103
Staten Island, NY 10314
Fax: (718) 982-2500
E-mail: monika.wojciechowski@csi.cuny.edu
Phone: (718) 982-2246

**City University of New York: Hostos Community College**
www.hostos.cuny.edu
Office of Admissions
500 Grand Concourse
Bronx, NY 10451
Fax: (718) 518-4256
E-mail: rvelez@hostos.cuny.edu
Phone: (718) 518-4406

**City University of New York: Hunter College**
www.hunter.cuny.edu/main/
International Student Office
695 Park Avenue
New York, NY 10065
E-mail:
internationalstudent.ser@hunter.cuny.edu
Phone: (212) 772-4864

**City University of New York: John Jay College of Criminal Justice**
www.jjay.cuny.edu
Admissions
524 West 59th Street
New York, NY 10019
Fax: (212) 237-8777
E-mail: ecohen@jjay.cuny.edu
Phone: (212) 393-6337

**City University of New York: Kingsborough Community College**
www.kbcc.cuny.edu
Office of International Student Affairs
2001 Oriental Boulevard
Brooklyn, NY 11235
Fax: (718) 368-4535
E-mail: isa@kbcc.cuny.edu
Phone: (718) 368-6800

**City University of New York: LaGuardia Community College**
www.lagcc.cuny.edu
International Student Office
31-10 Thomson Avenue
Long Island City, NY 11101
Fax: (718) 482-2033
E-mail: pnicolov@lagcc.cuny.edu
Phone: (718) 482-5143

**City University of New York: Lehman College**
www.lehman.edu
Office for International Students
250 Bedford Park Boulevard West
Bronx, NY 10468
Fax: (718) 960-8712
E-mail: enroll@lehman.cuny.edu
Phone: (718) 960-7274

**City University of New York: Medgar Evers College**
www.mec.cuny.edu
Admissions
1665 Bedford Avenue
Brooklyn, NY 11225-2201
Fax: (718) 270-6411
E-mail: jaugustin@mec.cuny.edu
Phone: (718) 270-6021

**City University of New York: New York City College of Technology**
www.citytech.cuny.edu
300 Jay Street Namm G17
Brooklyn, NY 11201
Fax: (718) 260-5504
E-mail: vvillanueva@citytech.cuny.edu
Phone: (718) 260-5509

**City University of New York: Queens College**
www.qc.cuny.edu
Admissions
6530 Kissena Boulevard, Jefferson 117
Flushing, NY 11367-1597
Fax: (718) 997-5617
E-mail: admissions@qc.cuny.edu
Phone: (718) 997-5600

**City University of New York: Queensborough Community College**
www.qcc.cuny.edu
Admissions Services CUNY
222-05 56th Avenue
Room A-210
Bayside, NY 11364-1497
E-mail: Gmuchita@qcc.cuny.edu
Phone: (718) 631-6211

**City University of New York: York College**
www.york.cuny.edu
Admission Services
94-20 Guy R. Brewer Boulevard., Room 1B07
Jamaica, NY 11451
Fax: (718) 262-2178
E-mail: gprescod@york.cuny.edu
Phone: (718) 262-2165

**City University of Seattle**
www.cityu.edu
International Student Admissions
521 Wall Street
Seattle, WA 98121
Fax: (425) 709-5319
E-mail: intladmissions@cityu.edu
Phone: (206) 239-4721

**Clackamas Community College**
www.clackamas.edu
Registrar/Enroll Srv Oper Mg
19600 Molalla Avenue
Oregon City, OR 97045
Fax: (503) 722-5864
E-mail: chris.sweet@clackamas.edu
Phone: (503) 594-3370

**Claflin University**
www.claflin.edu
Admissions
400 Magnolia Street
Orangeburg, SC 29115
Fax: (803) 535-5382
E-mail: admissions@claflin.edu
Phone: (803) 535-5340

**Claremont McKenna College**
www.cmc.edu
Office of Admission
888 Columbia Avenue
Claremont, CA 91711
Fax: (909) 621-8516
E-mail: admission@cmc.edu
Phone: (909) 621-8088

**Clarendon College**
www.clarendoncollege.edu
Office of Admissions
PO Box 968
Clarendon, TX 79226
Fax: (806) 874-5080
E-mail: martha.smith@clarendoncollege.edu
Phone: (806) 874-3571 ext. 106

**Clarion University of Pennsylvania**
www.clarion.edu
Office of International Programs
840 Wood Street
Clarion, PA 16214
Fax: (814) 393-2341
E-mail: mschlueter@clarion.edu
Phone: (814) 393-2340

**Clark Atlanta University**
www.cau.edu
Admissions
223 James P. Brawley Drive, SW
101 Trevor Arnett Hall
Atlanta, GA 30314-4391
Fax: (404) 880-6174
E-mail: lrice@cau.edu
Phone: (404) 880-8043

**Clark College**
www.clark.edu
International Education
Welcome Center, MS PUB002
1933 Fort Vancouver Way
Vancouver, WA 98663
Fax: (360) 992-2868
E-mail: sktaylor@clark.edu
Phone: (360) 992-2495

**Clark State Community College**
www.clarkstate.edu
Director Retention Services & Student Life
Box 570
Springfield, OH 45501-0570
Fax: (937) 328-6097
E-mail: wileyn@clarkstate.edu
Phone: (937) 328-7936

**Clark University**
www.clarku.edu
950 Main Street
Worcester, MA 01610-1477
Fax: (508) 793-8821
E-mail: intadmissions@clarku.edu
Phone: (508) 793-7431

**Clarke University**
www.clarke.edu
Assistant Director of Admissions
1550 Clarke Drive
Dubuque, IA 52001-3198
Fax: (563) 588-6789
E-mail: alicia.schmitt@clarke.edu
Phone: (563) 588-6373

**Clarks Summit University**
https://www.clarkssummitu.edu/
Admissions
538 Venard Road
South Abington Twp, PA 18411
Fax: (570) 585-9299
E-mail: admissions@bbc.edu
Phone: (570) 585-9370

**Clarkson University**
www.clarkson.edu
Senior Assistant Dean of International &
Preparatory Admission
Holcroft House
8 Clarkson Ave, Box 5605
Potsdam, NY 13699
Fax: (315) 268-7647
E-mail: pdangrem@clarkson.edu
Phone: (315) 268-3711

**Clatsop Community College**
www.clatsopcc.edu
Admissions Office
1651 Lexington Avenue
Astoria, OR 97103
Fax: (503) 325-5738
E-mail: admissions@clatsop.cc.or.us
Phone: (503) 338-2411

**Clayton State University**
www.clayton.edu
International Student Services Office
2000 Clayton State Boulevard
Morrow, GA 30260-0285
Fax: (678) 466-5469
E-mail: RyanPackard@clayton.edu
Phone: (678) 466-5499

**Cleary University**
www.cleary.edu
Admissions
3750 Cleary Drive
Howell, MI 48843
Fax: (517) 338-3336
E-mail: admissions@cleary.edu
Phone: (517) 338-3330

**Clemson University**
www.clemson.edu
Office of Admissions
105 Sikes Hall
Box 345124
Clemson, SC 29634-5124
Fax: (864) 656-2464
E-mail: wolk@clemson.edu
Phone: (864) 656-4584

**Cleveland Institute of Art**
www.cia.edu
Admissions
11610 Euclid Avenue
Cleveland, OH 44106-1710
Fax: (216) 754-3634
E-mail: admissions@cia.edu
Phone: (216) 421-7491

**Cleveland Institute of Music**
www.cim.edu
Admissions
11021 East Boulevard
Cleveland, OH 44106
E-mail: admission@cim.edu
Phone: (216) 795-3107

**Cleveland State Community College**
www.clevelandstatecc.edu
Enrollment Service Center
3535 Adkisson Drive
PO Box 3570
Cleveland, TN 37320-3570
Fax: (423) 614-8711
E-mail: jsewell@clevelandstatecc.edu
Phone: (423) 472-7141 ext. 744

**Cleveland State University**
www.csuohio.edu
Associate Director, International Admissions
2121 Euclid Avenue
EC 100
Cleveland, OH 44115-2214
E-mail: b.turner@csuohio.edu
Phone: (216) 687-4823

**Clinton College**
www.clintoncollege.edu/
Admissions Office
1029 Crawford Road
Rock Hill, SC 29730
E-mail: rcopeland@clintonjuniorcollege.edu
Phone: (803) 327-7402 ext. 242

**Clinton Community College**
www.eicc.edu
Director of Enrollment Management
1000 Lincoln Boulevard
Clinton, IA 52732
Fax: (563) 244-7107
E-mail: esnyder@eicc.edu
Phone: (563) 336-3310

**Clinton Community College**
www.clinton.edu
Admissions
136 Clinton Point Drive
Plattsburgh, NY 12901
Fax: (518) 562-4373
E-mail: internationaladmissions@clinton.edu
Phone: (518) 562-4188

**Cloud County Community College**
www.cloud.edu
Office of Admissions
2221 Campus Drive
Box 1002
Concordia, KS 66901-1002
Fax: (785) 243-9380
E-mail: solson@cloud.edu
Phone: (800) 729-5101 ext. 213

**Clover Park Technical College**
www.cptc.edu
International Programs
4500 Steilacoom Boulevard, SW
Lakewood, WA 98499-4098
Fax: (253) 589-6054
E-mail: international@cptc.edu
Phone: (253) 589-6089

**Coahoma Community College**
www.coahomacc.edu
Admissions and Records
3240 Friars Point Road
Clarksdale, MS 38614-9799
Fax: (662) 621-4297
E-mail: mhouston@coahomacc.edu
Phone: (662) 621-4205

**Coastal Bend College**
www.coastalbend.edu
3800 Charco Road
Beeville, TX 78102
Fax: (361) 354-2254
E-mail: admissions@coastalbend.edu
Phone: (361) 354-2245

**Coastal Carolina University**
www.coastal.edu
Senior Associate Director, International
Recruitment and Admissions
PO Box 261954
Conway, SC 29528-6054
Fax: (843) 349-6436
E-mail: internationaladmissions@coastal.edu
Phone: (843) 349-2521

**Coastal Pines Technical College**
www.coastalpines.edu
1777 West Cherry Street
Jesup, GA 31545
Fax: (912) 427-1901
Phone: (912) 427-1958

**Coastline Community College**
www.coastline.edu
11460 Warner Avenue
Fountain Valley, CA 92708
Fax: (714) 241-6288
E-mail: jmcdonald@cccd.edu
Phone: (714) 241-6165

**Cochise College**
www.cochise.edu
Division Assistant Student Services
901 North Colombo Avenue
Sierra Vista, AZ 85635-2317
Fax: (520) 515-3647
E-mail: skinnerm@cochise.edu
Phone: (520) 417-4050

**Coe College**
www.coe.edu
Admission Office
1220 First Avenue NE
Cedar Rapids, IA 52402
Fax: (319) 399-8816
E-mail: cpaasch@coe.edu
Phone: (319) 399-8101

**Coffeyville Community College**
www.coffeyville.edu
International
400 West 11th Street
Coffeyville, KS 67337-5064
Fax: (620) 252-7098
E-mail: bryant.lachelle@coffeyville.edu
Phone: (620) 252-7700 ext. 2092

**Cogswell Polytechnical College**
www.cogswell.edu
Admissions
191 Baypointe Parkway
San Jose, CA 95134
Fax: (408) 877-7373
E-mail: rhenson@cogswell.edu
Phone: (408) 498-5103

**Coker College**
www.coker.edu
Admissions
300 East College Avenue
Hartsville, SC 29550
Fax: (843) 383-8056
E-mail: admissions@coker.edu
Phone: (800) 950-1908

**Colby College**
www.colby.edu
Admissions
4800 Mayflower Hill
Waterville, ME 04901-8848
Fax: (207) 859-4828
E-mail: admissions@colby.edu
Phone: (207) 859-4825

**Colby Community College**
www.colbycc.edu
Admissions
1255 South Range Avenue
Colby, KS 67701
Fax: (785) 460-4691
E-mail: doug.johnson@colbycc.edu
Phone: (785) 460-5498

**Colby-Sawyer College**
www.colby-sawyer.edu
Office of Admissions
541 Main Street
New London, NH 03257-7835
Fax: (603) 526-3452
E-mail: international@colby-sawyer.edu
Phone: (603) 526-3491

**Colegio de Cinematografia Artes y Television**
www.ccat.edu
PO Box 10774
San Juan, PR 00922
Fax: (787) 995-2525
E-mail: admissions@ccat.edu
Phone: (787) 779-2500

**Coleman University**
www.coleman.edu
Director of Admissions
8888 Balboa Avenue
San Diego, CA 92123
Fax: (858) 499-0233
E-mail: blandrum@coleman.edu
Phone: (858) 223-8449 ext. 12517

**Colgate University**
www.colgate.edu
13 Oak Drive
Hamilton, NY 13346-1383
Fax: (315) 228-7544
E-mail: lwittchen@colgate.edu
Phone: (315) 228-7401

**College for Creative Studies**
www.collegeforcreativestudies.edu
International Student Services
201 East Kirby
Detroit, MI 48202-4034
Fax: (313) 872-2739
E-mail: flopez@collegeforcreativestudies.edu
Phone: (313) 664-7428

**College of Alameda**
www.alameda.peralta.edu
International Specialist, International
Affairs & Distance Education
555 Ralph Appezzato Memorial Parkway
Alameda, CA 94501
Fax: (510) 748-5227
E-mail: dgephart@Peralta.edu
Phone: (510) 587-7834

**College of the Albemarle**
www.albemarle.edu
Admissions
1208 North Road Street
PO Box 2327
Elizabeth City, NC 27909
Fax: (252) 473-5497
E-mail: katie_cross@albemarle.edu
Phone: (252) 473-2264 ext. 7011

**College of the Atlantic**
www.coa.edu
Admission
105 Eden Street
Bar Harbor, ME 04609
Fax: (207) 288-4126
E-mail: nemlen@coa.edu
Phone: (207) 801-5643

**College of Business and Technology: Cutler Bay**
www.cbt.edu
Miami Gardens
19151 South Dixie Highway, #203
Cutler Bay, FL 33157
Fax: (305) 238-2302
E-mail: daniel.ituria@cbt.edu
Phone: (305) 273-4499 ext. 6600

**College of Business and Technology: Flagler**
www.cbt.edu
Miami Gardens
8230 West Flagler Street
Miami, FL 33144
Fax: (305) 485-4411
E-mail: daniel.ituria@cbt.edu
Phone: (305) 273-4499 ext. 6611

**College of Business and Technology: Hialeah**
www.cbt.edu
Miami Gardens
935 West 49th Street Suite 203
Hialeah, FL 33012-3436
Fax: (305) 827-9955
E-mail: daniel.ituria@cbt.edu
Phone: (305) 273-4499 ext. 6611

**College of Business and Technology: Kendall**
www.cbt.edu
Miami Gardens
8700 W Flagler Street
Suite 420
Miami, FL 33174
Fax: (305) 270-0779
E-mail: daniel.iturria@cbt.edu
Phone: (305) 273-4499 ext. 6600

**College of Business and Technology: Miami Gardens**
www.cbt.edu
Miami Gardens
5190 NW 167th Street
Miami Gardens, FL 33014-6338
E-mail: daniel.ituria@cbt.edu
Phone: (305) 273-4499 ext. 611

**College of the Canyons**
www.canyons.edu
International Students Programs
26455 Rockwell Canyon Road
Santa Clarita, CA 91355
Fax: (661) 362-5539
E-mail: isp@canyons.edu
Phone: (661) 362-3580

**College of Central Florida**
www.cf.edu
International Education Specialist
3001 SW College Road
Ocala, FL 34474-4415
Fax: (352) 873-5882
E-mail: bellamyr@cf.edu
Phone: (352) 854-2322 ext. 1543

**College of Charleston**
www.cofc.edu
International Student Admissions
Admissions
66 George Street
Charleston, SC 29424-0001
Fax: (843) 953-6322
E-mail: international@cofc.edu
Phone: (843) 953-7506

**College of Coastal Georgia**
www.ccga.edu
International Initiatives
One College Drive
Brunswick, GA 31520
Fax: (912) 279-5721
E-mail: jlynch@ccga.edu
Phone: (912) 279-5713

**College of Court Reporting**
www.ccr.edu
111 West 10th Street, Suite 111
Hobart, IN 46342
Fax: (219) 942-1631
E-mail: information@ccr.edu
Phone: (219) 942-1459

**College of the Desert**
www.collegeofthedesert.edu
International Education Program
43500 Monterey Avenue
Palm Desert, CA 92260
Fax: (760) 862-1361
E-mail: cdelgado@collegeofthedesert.edu
Phone: (760) 776-7205

**College of DuPage**
www.cod.edu
Coordinator International Student Services
425 Fawell Boulevard
Glen Ellyn, IL 60137-6599
Fax: (630) 942-2323
E-mail: smid@cod.edu
Phone: (630) 942-3328

**College of the Holy Cross**
www.holycross.edu
Admissions
One College Street
Fenwick 105
Worcester, MA 01610-2395
Fax: (508) 793-3888
E-mail: admissions@holycross.edu
Phone: (508) 793-2443

**College of Idaho**
www.collegeofidaho.edu
Vice President for Enrollment Management
2112 Cleveland Boulevard
Caldwell, ID 83605-4432
Fax: (208) 459-5757
E-mail: LHunter@collegeofidaho.edu
Phone: (800) 224-3246

**College of Lake County**
www.clcillinois.edu
International Education
19351 West Washington Street
Grayslake, IL 60030-1198
Fax: (847) 543-3733
E-mail: ssmith2@clcillinois.edu
Phone: (847) 543-2733

**College of Marin**
www.marin.edu
835 College Avenue
Kentfield, CA 94904
Phone: (415) 457-8811 ext. 7719

**College of Mount St. Vincent**
www.mountsaintvincent.edu
Office of Admission
6301 Riverdale Avenue
Riverdale, NY 10471-1093
Fax: (718) 549-7945
E-mail: thomas.rainey@mountsaintvincent.edu
Phone: (718) 405-3268

**College of the Muscogee Nation**
www.mvsktc.org
2170 Raven Circle
Okmulgee, OK 74447
E-mail: emccormack@mcn-nsn.gov
Phone: (918) 549-2808

**The College of New Jersey**
www.tcnj.edu
Admissions
Office of Undergraduate Admissions PO Box 7718
Paul Loser Hall 228
Ewing, NJ 08628-0718
Fax: (609) 637-5174
E-mail: fay2@tcnj.edu
Phone: (609) 771-2131

**College of New Rochelle**
www.cnr.edu
Admissions
29 Castle Place
New Rochelle, NY 10805-2339
Fax: (914) 654-5464
E-mail: international@cnr.edu
Phone: (914) 654-5452

**College of Office Technology**
www.cot.edu
1520 West Division Street
Chicago, IL 60622-3312
Fax: (773) 278-0143
E-mail: info@cotedu.com
Phone: (773) 278-0042

**College of the Ouachitas**
www.coto.edu
Registrar
One College Circle
Malvern, AR 72104
Fax: (501) 337-9382
E-mail: kjohnson@coto.edu
Phone: (501) 337-5000 ext. 1118

**College of the Ozarks**
www.cofo.edu
Admissions
PO Box 17
Point Lookout, MO 65726-0017
Fax: (417) 690-2635
E-mail: admiss4@cofo.edu
Phone: (417) 690-2636

**College of the Redwoods**
www.redwoods.edu
Enrollment Services
7351 Tompkins Hill Road
Eureka, CA 95501-9300
Fax: (707) 476-4406
E-mail: admissions@redwoods.edu
Phone: (707) 476-4200

**College of Saint Mary**
www.csm.edu
International Student Specialist
7000 Mercy Road
Omaha, NE 68106
Fax: (402) 399-2412
E-mail: jgandha@csm.edu
Phone: (402) 399-2421

**College of Saint Rose**
www.strose.edu
International Admissions Office
432 Western Avenue
Albany, NY 12203
Fax: (518) 454-5479
E-mail: International@strose.edu
Phone: (518) 454-5144

**College of San Mateo**
www.collegeofsanmateo.edu
International Student Center
1700 West Hillsdale Boulevard
San Mateo, CA 94402-3784
Fax: (650) 574-6166
E-mail: csminternational@smccd.edu
Phone: (650) 574-6525

**College of the Sequoias**
www.cos.edu
Dean of Student Services
915 South Mooney Boulevard
Visalia, CA 93277
Fax: (559) 737-4883
Phone: (559) 737-5441

**College of the Siskiyous**
www.siskiyous.edu
Student Life
800 College Avenue
Weed, CA 96094-2899
Fax: (530) 938-5367
E-mail: info@siskiyous.edu
Phone: (530) 938-5374

**College of Southern Idaho**
www.csi.edu
International Student Services
Box 1238
Twin Falls, ID 83303-1238
Fax: (208) 736-3014
E-mail: kquataro@csi.edu
Phone: (208) 732-6283

**College of Southern Maryland**
www.csmd.edu
Enrollment Department
College of Southern Maryland-AOD
8730 Mitchell Road, POB 910
La Plata, MD 20646-0910
Fax: (301) 934-7698
E-mail: askme@csmd.edu
Phone: (301) 934-7765

**College of Southern Nevada**
www.csn.edu
International Student Center
6375 West Charleston Boulevard
Las Vegas, NV 89146-1164
Fax: (702) 651-5821
E-mail: mary.sasso@csn.edu
Phone: (702) 651-5820

**College of St. Benedict**
www.csbsju.edu
Admissions
College of Saint Benedict/Saint John's
University
PO Box 7155
Collegeville, MN 56321-7155
Fax: (320) 363-3206
E-mail: aschleper@csbsju.edu
Phone: (320) 363-2263

**College of St. Elizabeth**
www.cse.edu
Director International and Multicultural
Affairs
2 Convent Road
Morristown, NJ 07960-6989
Fax: (973) 290-4710
E-mail: apply@cse.edu
Phone: (973) 290-4227

**College of St. Joseph in Vermont**
www.csj.edu
Director of Admissions
71 Clement Road
Rutland, VT 05701-3899
Fax: (802) 776-5310
E-mail: ken.labate@csj.edu
Phone: (802) 776-5268

**College of St. Scholastica**
www.css.edu
Office of Admissions
1200 Kenwood Avenue
Duluth, MN 55811-4199
Fax: (218) 723-6394
E-mail: omeyer@css.edu
Phone: (218) 723-6045

**College of Western Idaho**
www.cwidaho.cc
One Stop Student Services
MS 3000
PO Box 3010
Nampa, ID 83653
Fax: (888) 562-3216
E-mail: laurawoodall@cwidaho.cc
Phone: (208) 562-3000

**College of William and Mary**
www.wm.edu
Associate Dean of Admission
PO Box 8795
Williamsburg, VA 23187-8795
Fax: (757) 221-1242
E-mail: dlbask@wm.edu
Phone: (757) 221-1837

**College of Wooster**
www.wooster.edu
Admissions
Gault Admissions Center
847 College Avenue
Wooster, OH 44691-2363
Fax: (330) 263-2621
E-mail: admissions@wooster.edu
Phone: (330) 263-2322

**CollegeAmerica: Fort Collins**
www.collegeamerica.edu
4601 South Mason Street
Fort Collins, CO 80525
Phone: (970) 223-6060

**Collin County Community College District**
www.collin.edu
Admissions & Records Office
2800 East Spring Creek Parkway
Plano, TX 75074
Fax: (972) 881-5175
E-mail: tfields@collin.edu
Phone: (972) 881-5710

**Colorado Christian University**
www.ccu.edu
Undergraduate Admission Office
8787 West Alameda Avenue
Lakewood, CO 80226
Fax: (303) 963-3201
E-mail: admission@ccu.edu
Phone: (303) 963-3000

**Colorado College**
www.coloradocollege.edu
Admission Office
14 East Cache La Poudre Street
Colorado Springs, CO 80903-9854
Fax: (719) 389-6816
E-mail: mbonser@coloradocollege.edu
Phone: (719) 389-6344

**Colorado Mesa University**
www.coloradomesa.edu
Associate Director of International
Programs & Services
1100 North Avenue
Grand Junction, CO 81501-3122
Fax: (970) 248-1973
E-mail: agingeri@coloradomesa.edu
Phone: (970) 248-1802

**Colorado Mountain College**
www.coloradomtn.edu
Enrollment Services
802 Grand Avenue
Glenwood Springs, CO 81601
Fax: (970) 947-8328
E-mail: slarson@coloradomtn.edu
Phone: (800) 621-8559 ext. 8328

**Colorado Northwestern Community College**
www.cncc.edu
500 Kennedy Drive
Rangely, CO 81648
Fax: (970) 675-3343
E-mail: kelly.scott@cncc.edu
Phone: (970) 675-3273

**Colorado School of Mines**
www.mines.edu
Office for International Student & Scholar
Services
Undergraduate Admissions Office
1812 Illinois Street
Golden, CO 80401-6114
Fax: (303) 273-3509
E-mail: admissions@mines.edu
Phone: (303) 273-3210

**Colorado School of Trades**
www.schooloftrades.edu
1575 Hoyt Street
Lakewood, CO 80215-2945
Fax: (303) 233-4723
E-mail: info@schooloftrades.edu
Phone: (800) 234-4594 ext. 45

**Colorado State University**
www.colostate.edu
Admissions
Office of Admissions/Colorado State
University
1062 Campus Delivery
Fort Collins, CO 80523-1062
Fax: (970) 491-7799
E-mail:
international.admissions@colostate.edu
Phone: (970) 491-1573

**Colorado State University: Pueblo**
www.csupueblo.edu
International Programs
2200 Bonforte Boulevard
Pueblo, CO 81001-4901
Fax: (719) 549-2221
E-mail: intprog@colostate-pueblo.edu
Phone: (719) 549-2329

**Colorado Technical University**
www.coloradotech.edu
Admissions
4435 North Chestnut Street
Colorado Springs, CO 80907
Fax: (719) 598-3740
E-mail: cosadmissions@coloradotech.edu
Phone: (719) 598-0200

**Columbia Basin College**
www.columbiabasin.edu
Admissions
2600 North 20th Avenue
Pasco, WA 99301
Fax: (509) 546-0401
E-mail: NRoe@columbiabasin.edu
Phone: (509) 542-4400

**Columbia Central University: Caguas**
www.columbiacentral.edu
PO Box 8517
Caguas, PR 00726-8517
Fax: (787) 744-7031
E-mail: info@columbiacentral.edu
Phone: (787) 743-4041 ext. 240

**Columbia College**
www.gocolumbia.edu
11600 Columbia College Drive
Sonora, CA 95370
Fax: (209) 588-5337
Phone: (209) 588-5231

**Columbia College**
www.ccis.edu
International Center
1001 Rogers Street
Columbia, MO 65216
Fax: (573) 875-7456
E-mail: international@ccis.edu
Phone: (573) 875-7736

**Columbia College**
www.columbiasc.edu
Admission
1301 Columbia College Drive
Columbia, SC 29203
Fax: (803) 786-3674
E-mail: admissions@columbiasc.edu
Phone: (803) 786-3871

**Columbia College Chicago**
www.colum.edu
International Student Admissions
600 South Michigan Avenue
Room 301
Chicago, IL 60605-1996
Fax: (312) 369-8024
E-mail: sstrow@colum.edu
Phone: (312) 369-7318

**Columbia College Hollywood**
www.columbiacollege.edu
Admissions Office
18618 Oxnard Street
Tarzana, CA 91356
Fax: (818) 345-9053
E-mail: cmunoz@columbiacollege.edu
Phone: (818) 345-8414

**Columbia International University**
www.ciu.edu
Admissions Office
PO Box 3122
Columbia, SC 29230-3122
Fax: (803) 786-4209
E-mail: yesciu@ciu.edu
Phone: (800) 777-2227 ext. 5024

**Columbia Southern University**
www.columbiasouthern.edu
Admissions
21982 University Lane
PO Box 3110
Orange Beach, AL 36561
Fax: (251) 981-3815
E-mail: admissions@columbiasouthern.edu
Phone: (251) 981-3771 ext. 521

**Columbia University**
www.columbia.edu
Undergraduate Admissions
1130 Amsterdam Avenue
212 Hamilton Hall, MC 2807
New York, NY 10027
Fax: (212) 854-1209
E-mail: ugrad-ask@columbia.edu
Phone: (212) 854-2522

**Columbia University: School of General Studies**
www.gs.columbia.edu
Admissions
408 Lewisohn Hall, Mail Code 4101
2970 Broadway
New York, NY 10027
Fax: (212) 854-6316
E-mail: gsdegree@columbia.edu
Phone: (212) 854-2772

**Columbia-Greene Community College**
www.sunycgcc.edu
Admissions Office
4400 Route 23
Hudson, NY 12534
Fax: (518) 822-2015
E-mail: rachel.kappel@sunycgcc.edu
Phone: (518) 828-4181 ext. 3388

**Columbus College of Art and Design**
www.ccad.edu
Admissions Office
60 Cleveland Avenue
Columbus, OH 43215-3875
Fax: (614) 232-8344
E-mail: jneeley@ccad.edu
Phone: (614) 224-9101 ext. 3265

**Columbus State Community College**
www.cscc.edu
International Student Services
550 East Spring Street
Box 1609
Columbus, OH 43216-1609
Fax: (614) 287-6019
E-mail: istudent@cscc.edu
Phone: (614) 287-2074

**Columbus State University**
www.columbusstate.edu
Admissions Office
4225 University Avenue
Columbus, GA 31907-5645
Fax: (706) 568-5091
E-mail: williams_kristin@columbusstate.edu
Phone: (706) 507-8848

**Columbus Technical College**
www.columbustech.edu
Student Services
928 Manchester Expressway
Columbus, GA 31904-6572
Fax: (404) 649-1885
E-mail: admissions@columbustech.edu
Phone: (706) 649-1800

**Commonwealth Institute of Funeral Service**
www.commonwealthinst.org
415 Barren Springs Drive
Houston, TX 77090-5913
Fax: (281) 873-5232
Phone: (281) 873-0262

**Community College of Allegheny County**
www.ccac.edu
International Student Services Office
808 Ridge Avenue
Pittsburgh, PA 15212
Fax: (412) 237-4581
E-mail: admissions@ccac.edu
Phone: (412) 237-2629

**Community College of Aurora**
www.ccaurora.edu
Advising
16000 East CentreTech Parkway
Aurora, CO 80011-9036
Fax: (303) 361-7432
E-mail: robin.blish@ccaurora.edu
Phone: (303) 340-7508

**Community College of Baltimore County**
www.ccbcmd.edu
International Student Services
800 South Rolling Road
Baltimore, MD 21228-5317
Fax: (443) 840-4433
E-mail: npharrmaletta@ccbcmd.edu
Phone: (443) 840-4094

**Community College of Beaver County**
www.ccbc.edu
Registrar
One Campus Drive
Monaca, PA 15061-2588
Fax: (724) 728-7599
E-mail: dan.slater@ccbc.edu
Phone: (724) 775-8561 ext. 254

**Community College of Denver**
www.ccd.edu
Dean of Students
Campus Box 201, PO Box 173363
Denver, CO 80217-3363
Fax: (303) 556-2431
E-mail: enrollment_services@ccd.edu
Phone: (303) 556-2430

**Community College of Philadelphia**
www.ccp.edu
1700 Spring Garden Street
Philadelphia, PA 19130-3991
Fax: (215) 972-6324
E-mail: internationaladmissions@ccp.edu
Phone: (215) 751-8835

**Community College of Rhode Island**
www.ccri.edu
Enrollment Services
400 East Avenue
Warwick, RI 02886-1807
Fax: (401) 825-2394
E-mail: tkless@ccri.edu
Phone: (401) 825-2278

**Community College of Vermont**
www.ccv.edu
CCV Winooski
PO Box 489
Montpelier, VT 05601
Fax: (802) 654-0561
E-mail: jck07240@ccv.vsc.edu
Phone: (802) 654-0557

**Concord University**
www.concord.edu
Admissions Office
PO Box 1000
Athens, WV 24712-1000
Fax: (304) 384-9044
E-mail: dmckee@concord.edu
Phone: (304) 384-5248

**Concorde Career College: Aurora**
www.concorde.edu
111 North Havana Street
Aurora, CO 80010
Phone: (303) 861-1151

**Concorde Career College: Garden Grove**
www.concorde.edu
12951 Euclid Street, #101
Garden Grove, CA 92840
E-mail: agueco@concorde.edu
Phone: (714) 703-1900

**Concorde Career College: Kansas City**
www.concorde.edu/kansas
3239 Broadway
Kansas City, MO 64111
Fax: (816) 756-3231
E-mail: dcrow@concorde.edu
Phone: (816) 531-5223

**Concorde Career College: North Hollywood**
www.concorde.edu
12412 Victory Boulevard
North Hollywood, CA 91606
Fax: (818) 766-1587
Phone: (818) 766-8151

**Concorde Career College: San Bernardino**
www.concorde.edu
201 East Airport Drive
San Bernardino, CA 92408

**Concordia College**
www.ccal.edu
1712 Broad Street
Selma, AL 36701
Fax: (314) 874-5755
E-mail: admissions@ccal.edu
Phone: (334) 874-7143

**Concordia College**
www.concordia-ny.edu
Admission
171 White Plains Road
Bronxville, NY 10708-1923
Fax: (914) 395-4636
E-mail: jenifer.jules@concordia-ny.edu
Phone: (914) 337-9300 ext. 2152

**Concordia College: Moorhead**
www.concordiacollege.edu
Admissions Office
901 Eighth Street South
Moorhead, MN 56562
Fax: (218) 299-4720
E-mail: beatty@cord.edu
Phone: (218) 299-3004

**Concordia University**
www.cuaa.edu
Office of Admissions
4090 Geddes Road
Ann Arbor, MI 48105
Fax: (734) 995-4610
E-mail: harrica@cuaa.edu
Phone: (734) 995-7322

**Concordia University**
www.cune.edu
Office of Admission
800 North Columbia Avenue
Seward, NE 68434-1556
Fax: (402) 643-4073
E-mail: admiss@cune.edu
Phone: (800) 535-5494 ext. 7233

**Concordia University**
www.cu-portland.edu
Assistant Director of International Admission
2811 Northeast Holman Street
Portland, OR 97211-6099
Fax: (503) 280-8531
E-mail: LNiemeyer@cu-portland.edu
Phone: (503) 493-6548

**Concordia University Chicago**
www.cuchicago.edu
Undergraduate Admission
7400 Augusta Street
River Forest, IL 60305-1499
Fax: (708) 209-3473
E-mail: admission@cuchicago.edu
Phone: (708) 209-3100

**Concordia University Irvine**
www.cui.edu
Global Programs
1530 Concordia West
Irvine, CA 92612-3203
Fax: (949) 214-3520
E-mail: internationaladmissions@cui.edu
Phone: (949) 214-3062

**Concordia University St. Paul**
www.csp.edu
International Student Services
1282 Concordia Avenue
Saint Paul, MN 55104-5494
Fax: (651) 603-6320
E-mail: jabri@csp.edu
Phone: (651) 641-8835

**Concordia University Texas**
www.concordia.edu
Office of Admissions
11400 Concordia University Drive
Austin, TX 78726
Fax: (512) 313-4269
E-mail: admissions@concordia.edu
Phone: (512) 313-3000

**Concordia University Wisconsin**
www.cuw.edu
Admissions
12800 North Lake Shore Drive
Mequon, WI 53097
Fax: (262) 243-4545
E-mail: ken.gaschk@cuw.edu
Phone: (262) 243-4305

**Connecticut College**
www.conncoll.edu
270 Mohegan Avenue
New London, CT 06320
Fax: (860) 439-4301
E-mail: bridget.moore@conncoll.edu
Phone: (860) 439-2200

**Conservatory of Music of Puerto Rico**
www.cmpr.edu
Admissions Coordinator
951 Ponce de Leon Ave
San Juan, PR 00907-3373
Fax: (787) 764-3581
E-mail: aarraiza2@cmpr.pr.gov
Phone: (787) 751-0160 ext. 275

**Consolidated School of Business: Lancaster**
www.csb.edu
2124 Ambassador Circle
Lancaster, PA 17603
Fax: (717) 394-6213
E-mail: admissions@csb.edu
Phone: (717) 394-6211

**Contra Costa College**
www.contracosta.edu
International Education Director
2600 Mission Bell Drive
San Pablo, CA 94806
E-mail: Allich@4cd.edu
Phone: (925) 685-1230

**Converse College**
www.converse.edu
Admissions
580 East Main Street
Spartanburg, SC 29302-0006
Fax: (864) 596-9225
E-mail: admissions@converse.edu
Phone: (864) 596-9040

**Cooper Union for the Advancement of Science and Art**
www.cooper.edu
Admissions and Records
30 Cooper Square, Suite 300
New York, NY 10003-7183
Fax: (212) 353-4342
E-mail: falls@cooper.edu
Phone: (212) 353-4120

**Copper Mountain College**
www.cmccd.edu
6162 Rotary Way
PO Box 1398
Joshua Tree, CA 92252
Fax: (760) 366-5257
E-mail: lburns@cmccd.edu
Phone: (760) 366-3791 ext. 4232

**Coppin State University**
www.coppin.edu
Office of Admissions
2500 West North Avenue
Baltimore, MD 21216
Fax: (410) 523-7351
E-mail: mgross@coppin.edu
Phone: (410) 951-3600

**Corban University**
www.corban.edu
Admissions
5000 Deer Park Drive SE
Salem, OR 97317-9392
Fax: (503) 585-4316
E-mail: admissions@corban.edu
Phone: (800) 845-3005

**Cornell College**
www.cornellcollege.edu
Admissions
600 First Street SW
Mount Vernon, IA 52314-1098
Fax: (319) 895-4451
E-mail: international@cornellcollege.edu
Phone: (319) 895-4215

**Cornell University**
www.cornell.edu
Undergraduate Admissions
410 Thurston Avenue
Ithaca, NY 14850
Fax: (607) 255-0659
E-mail: admissions@cornell.edu
Phone: (607) 255-5241

**Cornerstone University**
www.cornerstone.edu
Director of Admissions
1001 East Beltline NE
Grand Rapids, MI 49525-5897
Fax: (616) 222-1418
E-mail: david.emerson@cornerstone.edu
Phone: (616) 222-1426

**Corning Community College**
www.corning-cc.edu
Admissions
One Academic Drive
Corning, NY 14830
Fax: (607) 962-9582
E-mail: tbush4@corning-cc.edu
Phone: (607) 962-9540

**Cornish College of the Arts**
www.cornish.edu
Admission
1000 Lenora Street
Seattle, WA 98121
Fax: (206) 720-1011
E-mail: admission@cornish.edu
Phone: (206) 726-5016

**Cossatot Community College of the University of Arkansas**
www.cccua.edu
Student Serivces
183 College Drive
PO Box 960
De Queen, AR 71832
Fax: (870) 642-5088
E-mail: girvin@cccua.edu
Phone: (870) 584-4471 ext. 1967

**Cosumnes River College**
www.crc.losrios.edu
8401 Center Parkway
Sacramento, CA 95823
Fax: (916) 691-7467
E-mail: kimuraj@exi.crc.losrios.cc.ca.us
Phone: (916) 691-7469

**Cottey College**
www.cottey.edu
Office of Enrollment Management
1000 West Austin Boulevard
Nevada, MO 64772
Fax: (417) 448-1025
E-mail: amoore@cottey.edu
Phone: (417) 667-8181 ext. 2139

**County College of Morris**
www.ccm.edu
Admissions
214 Center Grove Road
Randolph, NJ 07869-2086
Fax: (973) 328-5199
E-mail: julmer@ccm.edu
Phone: (973) 328-5097

**Covenant College**
www.covenant.edu
Admissions
14049 Scenic Highway
Lookout Mountain, GA 30750
Fax: (706) 820-0893
E-mail: amy.smith@covenant.edu
Phone: (706) 419-1657

**Cowley County Community College**
www.cowley.edu
Associate Director of Enrollment Management
PO Box 1147
Arkansas City, KS 67005-1147
Fax: (620) 441-5350
E-mail: international@cowley.edu
Phone: (620) 442-0430

**Cox College**
www.coxcollege.edu
1423 North Jefferson Avenue
Springfield, MO 65802
Fax: (417) 269-3581
E-mail: admissions@coxcollege.edu
Phone: (417) 269-3068

**Coyne College**
www.coynecollege.edu
330 North Green Street
Chicago, IL 60607
Fax: (312) 226-3818
E-mail: ppauletti@coynecollege.edu
Phone: (773) 577-8102

**Crafton Hills College**
www.craftonhills.edu
Counseling
11711 Sand Canyon Road
Yucaipa, CA 92399-1799
Fax: (909) 794-3863
E-mail: gmolino@craftonhills.edu
Phone: (909) 389-3366

**Craven Community College**
www.cravencc.edu
International Student Enrollment Services
800 College Court
New Bern, NC 28562
Fax: (252) 637-6112
E-mail: internationalstudents@cravencc.edu
Phone: (252) 638-1315

**Creighton University**
www.creighton.edu
International Admissions Counselor
2500 California Plaza
Creighton University, Office of Undergraduate Admissions
Omaha, NE 68178-0001
Fax: (402) 280-2685
E-mail: MeganMankerian@creighton.edu
Phone: (269) 358-9191

**Criswell College**
www.criswell.edu
4010 Gaston Avenue
Dallas, TX 75246-1537
Fax: (214) 821-5433
E-mail: rmarriott@criswell.edu
Phone: (214) 818-1337

**Crossroads Bible College**
www.crossroads.edu
Admissions
601 North Shortridge Road
Indianapolis, IN 46219
Fax: (317) 789-8253
E-mail: Acoleman16@crossroads.edu
Phone: (317) 789-8271

**Crossroads College**
www.crossroadscollege.edu
Admissions
920 Mayowood Road SW
Rochester, MN 55902
Fax: (507) 288-9046
E-mail: admissions@crossroadscollege.edu
Phone: (507) 288-4563

**Crowder College**
www.crowder.edu
Coordinator of International Studies
601 Laclede Avenue
Neosho, MO 64850
Fax: (417) 455-5731
E-mail: sarahhorine@crowder.edu
Phone: (417) 455-5550

**Crown College**
www.crown.edu
Admissions
8700 College View Drive
Saint Bonifacius, MN 55375-9001
Fax: (952) 446-4149
E-mail: international@crown.edu
Phone: (952) 446-4142

**Cuesta College**
www.cuesta.org
Box 8106
San Luis Obispo, CA 93403
Fax: (805) 546-3975
E-mail: admit@bass.cuesta.cc.ca.us
Phone: (805) 546-3140

**Culinary Institute LeNotre**
www.culinaryinstitute.edu
Admissions
7070 Allensby Street
Houston, TX 77022
Fax: (713) 692-7399
E-mail: ehogaboom@ciaml.com
Phone: (713) 692-0077

**Culinary Institute of America**
www.ciachef.edu
1946 Campus Drive
Hyde Park, NY 12538-1499
Fax: (845) 451-1068
E-mail: d_walsh@culinary.edu
Phone: (845) 451-1531

**Culver-Stockton College**
www.culver.edu
Admissions
One College Hill
Canton, MO 63435-1299
Fax: (573) 288-6618
E-mail: admission@culver.edu
Phone: (573) 288-6331

**Cumberland County College**
www.cccnj.edu
Enrollment Services
PO Box 1500
3322 College Drive
Vineland, NJ 08362
Fax: (856) 691-6157
E-mail: tbonsall@cccnj.edu
Phone: (856) 691-8600 ext. 1221

**Cumberland University**
www.cumberland.edu
Admissions
1 Cumberland Square
Lebanon, TN 37087
Fax: (615) 444-2569
E-mail: ppope@cumberland.edu
Phone: (615) 444-2562

**Curry College**
www.curry.edu
Admission
1071 Blue Hill Avenue
Milton, MA 02186-9984
Fax: (617) 333-2114
E-mail: adm@curry.edu
Phone: (617) 333-2210

**Curtis Institute of Music**
www.curtis.edu
1726 Locust Street
Philadelphia, PA 19103-6187
Fax: (215) 893-9065
E-mail: admissions@curtis.edu
Phone: (215) 717-3117

**Cuyahoga Community College**
www.tri-c.edu
Admissions
2900 Community College Avenue
Cleveland, OH 44115-2878
Fax: (216) 696-2567
E-mail: george.koussa@tri-c.edu
Phone: (216) 987-4167

**Cuyamaca College**
www.cuyamaca.edu
Admissions and Records
900 Rancho San Diego Parkway
El Cajon, CA 92019-4304
Fax: (619) 660-4575
E-mail: vanessa.saenz@gcccd.edu
Phone: (619) 660-4565

**Cypress College**
www.cypresscollege.edu
International Students
9200 Valley View Street
Cypress, CA 90630
Fax: (714) 484-7446
E-mail: yhan@cypresscollege.edu
Phone: (714) 484-7050

**Daemen College**
www.daemen.edu
Admissions
4380 Main Street
Amherst, NY 14226-3592
Fax: (716) 839-8229
E-mail: admissions@daemen.edu
Phone: (716) 839-8225

**Dakota College at Bottineau**
www.dakotacollege.edu
Student Services
105 Simrall Boulevard
Bottineau, ND 58318-1198
Fax: (701) 228-5499
E-mail: danny.davis@dakotacollege.edu
Phone: (800) 542-6866

**Dakota County Technical College**
www.dctc.edu
Academic Advisor
1300 145th Street East
Rosemount, MN 55068
Fax: (651) 423-8775
E-mail: natalie.shrestha@dctc.edu
Phone: (651) 423-8537

**Dakota State University**
www.dsu.edu
International Program Office
820 North Washington Avenue
Admissions Office
Madison, SD 57042
Fax: (605) 256-5095
E-mail: international@dsu.edu
Phone: (605) 256-5267

**Dakota Wesleyan University**
www.dwu.edu
Admissions
1200 West University Avenue
Mitchell, SD 57301-4398
Fax: (605) 995-2699
E-mail: delien@dwu.edu
Phone: (605) 995-2644

**Dallas Baptist University**
www.dbu.edu
International and Immigration Office
3000 Mountain Creek Parkway
Dallas, TX 75211-9299
Fax: (214) 333-5409
E-mail: globalinfo@dbu.edu
Phone: (214) 333-6905

**Danville Area Community College**
www.dacc.edu
Admissions and Records
2000 East Main Street
Danville, IL 61832
Fax: (217) 443-8337
E-mail: dnasser@dacc.edu
Phone: (217) 443-8755

**Danville Community College**
www.dcc.vccs.edu
Admissions
1008 South Main Street
Danville, VA 24541
Fax: (434) 797-8451
E-mail: hgraves@dcc.vccs.edu
Phone: (434) 797-8420

**Dartmouth College**
www.dartmouth.edu
International Admissions
6016 McNutt Hall
Hanover, NH 03755
Fax: (603) 646-1216
E-mail: Rebecca.J.Sabky@Dartmouth.edu
Phone: (603) 646-3368

**Darton State College**
www.darton.edu
Student Affairs
2400 Gillionville Road
Albany, GA 31707-3098
Fax: (229) 317-6614
E-mail: karly.boyd@darton.edu
Phone: (229) 317-6775

**Davenport University**
www.davenport.edu
Senior Advisor for Study Abroad and
International Students
6191 Kraft Avenue SE
Grand Rapids, MI 49512-9396
Fax: (616) 555-5214
E-mail: cassie.patton@davenport.edu
Phone: (616) 554-5290

**Davidson College**
www.davidson.edu
Admissions Office
Box 7156
Davidson, NC 28035-7156
Fax: (704) 894-2016
E-mail: admission@davidson.edu
Phone: (704) 894-2230

**Davis and Elkins College**
www.dewv.edu
Admissions
100 Campus Drive
Elkins, WV 26241-3996
Fax: (304) 637-1800
E-mail: kotaa@dewv.edu
Phone: (304) 637-1328

**Davis College**
www.davisny.edu
Enrollment Management
400 Riverside Drive
Johnson City, NY 13790
Fax: (607) 770-6886
E-mail: hhempstead@davisny.edu
Phone: (607) 729-1581 ext. 341

**Davis College**
www.daviscollege.edu
Admissions
4747 Monroe Street
Toledo, OH 43623
Fax: (419) 473-2472
E-mail: dbrunner@daviscollege.edu
Phone: (419) 473-2700

**Dawson Community College**
www.dawson.edu
Registrar
300 College Drive
Box 421
Glendive, MT 59330
Fax: (406) 377-8132
E-mail: vboysun@dawson.edu
Phone: (406) 377-9404

**Daymar College: Louisville**
www.daymarcollege.edu
4112 Fern Valley Road
Louisville, KY 40219-1973
Phone: (502) 495-1040

**Daymar College: Owensboro**
www.daymarcollege.edu
Admissions
3361 Buckland Square
Owensboro, KY 42301
Fax: (304) 685-4090
E-mail: vmcdougal@daymarcollege.edu
Phone: (270) 926-4040

**Daymar Institute: Clarksville**
www.daymarinstitute.edu
1860 Wilma Rudolph Boulevard
Clarksville, TN 37040
E-mail: chays@draughons.edu
Phone: (931) 552-7600

**Daymar Institute: Murfreesboro**
www.daymarinstitute.edu
415 Golden Bear Court
Murfreesboro, TN 37128
E-mail: jviola@daymarinstitute.edu
Phone: (615) 217-9347

**Daymar Institute: Nashville**
www.daymarinstitute.edu
Admissions
340 & 283 Plus Park at Pavilion Boulevard
Nashville, TN 37217
Fax: (615) 367-2736
E-mail: admissions@daymarinstitute.edu
Phone: (615) 361-7555

**Daytona State College**
www.daytonastate.edu
Admissions Office
Admissions Office Daytona State College
1200 West International Speedway Boulevard
Daytona Beach, FL 32114
Fax: (386) 506-3940
E-mail: admissions@daytonastate.edu
Phone: (386) 506-3071

**De Anza College**
www.deanza.edu
International Student Office
21250 Stevens Creek Boulevard
Cupertino, CA 95014
Fax: (408) 864-5638
E-mail: ngjoseph@fhda.edu
Phone: (408) 864-8826

**Dean College**
www.dean.edu
Admissions
99 Main Street
Franklin, MA 02038-1994
Fax: (508) 541-8726
E-mail: mtraylor@dean.edu
Phone: (508) 541-1512

**Deep Springs College**
www.deepsprings.edu
Applications Committee
Applications Committee
HC 72 Box 45001
Dyer, NV 89010-9803
Fax: (760) 874-7077
E-mail: apcom@deepsprings.edu
Phone: (760) 872-2000

**Defiance College**
www.defiance.edu
Admissions
701 North Clinton Street
Defiance, OH 43512-1695
Fax: (419) 783-2468
E-mail: bharsha@defiance.edu
Phone: (419) 783-2365

**Del Mar College**
www.delmar.edu
Admissions and Registrar's Office
101 Baldwin Boulevard
Corpus Christi, TX 78404-3897
Fax: (361) 698-1595
E-mail: bthomps@delmar.edu
Phone: (361) 698-1255

**Delaware College of Art and Design**
www.dcad.edu
Admissions Office
600 North Market Street
Wilmington, DE 19801
Fax: (302) 622-8870
E-mail: jcampbell@dcad.edu
Phone: (302) 622-8867 ext. 123

**Delaware County Community College**
www.dccc.edu
Admissions
901 South Media Line Road
Media, PA 19063
Fax: (610) 359-7322
E-mail: admiss@dccc.edu
Phone: (610) 359-5050

**Delaware State University**
www.desu.edu
1200 North DuPont Highway
Dover, DE 19901
Fax: (302) 857-6352
E-mail: admissions@desu.edu
Phone: (302) 857-6351

**Delaware Technical Community College: Stanton/Wilmington Campus**
https://www.dtcc.edu/our-campuses/stanton
400 Stanton-Christiana Road
Newark, DE 19713
Fax: (302) 453-3084
E-mail: s-admissions@dtcc.edu
Phone: (302) 571-5343

**Delaware Valley University**
www.delval.edu
Admissions
700 East Butler Avenue
Doylestown, PA 18901-2697
Fax: (215) 230-2968
E-mail: maria.cabrera@delval.edu
Phone: (215) 489-2499

**Delgado Community College**
www.dcc.edu
Office of Admissions and Enrollment Services
615 City Park Avenue
New Orleans, LA 70119
Fax: (504) 483-1895
E-mail: gboutt@dcc.edu
Phone: (504) 671-5099

**Delta College**
www.delta.edu
Admissions
1961 Delta Road D101
University Center, MI 48710
Fax: (989) 667-2202
E-mail: danielsegura@delta.edu
Phone: (989) 686-9507

**Delta College of Arts & Technology**
www.deltacollege.com
7380 Exchange Place
Baton Rouge, LA 70806
Fax: (225) 927-9096
E-mail: admissions@deltacollege.com
Phone: (225) 928-7770

**Delta School of Business & Technology**
www.deltatech.edu
517 Broad Street
Lake Charles, LA 70601
Fax: (337) 436-5151
E-mail: barbara@deltatech.edu
Phone: (337) 439-5765

**Delta State University**
www.deltastate.edu
International Students Office
117 Kent Wyatt Hall
Cleveland, MS 38733
Fax: (662) 846-4684
E-mail: emallette@deltastate.edu
Phone: (662) 846-4574

**Denison University**
www.denison.edu
Coordinator of International Admissions
100 West College
Granville, OH 43023
Fax: (740) 587-6306
E-mail: bentonb@denison.edu
Phone: (740) 587-6789

**Denmark Technical College**
www.denmarktech.edu
Admissions
1126 Solomon Blatt Boulevard
PO Box 327
Denmark, SC 29042
Fax: (803) 793-5290
E-mail: braileyc@denmarktech.edu
Phone: (803) 793-5124

**Denver School of Nursing**
www.denverschoolofnursing.edu
1401 19th Street
Denver, CO 80202
E-mail: jjohnson@denverschoolofnursing.edu
Phone: (303) 292-0015

**DePaul University**
www.depaul.edu
Director of International Admission
1 East Jackson Boulevard Suite 9000
DePaul Center, Suite 9000
Chicago, IL 60604-2287
Fax: (312) 362-8521
E-mail: dpruccol@depaul.edu
Phone: (312) 362-5620

**DePauw University**
www.depauw.edu
Admission
204 East Seminary Street
Greencastle, IN 46135-1611
Fax: (765) 658-4007
E-mail: loutfijirari@depauw.edu
Phone: (765) 658-4547

**Des Moines Area Community College**
www.dmacc.edu
International Student Advisor
2006 South Ankeny Boulevard
Ankeny, IA 50023-3993
Fax: (515) 964-6391
E-mail: khuang@dmacc.edu
Phone: (515) 964-6471

**DeSales University**
www.desales.edu
Enrollment Services
2755 Station Avenue
Center Valley, PA 18034-9568
Fax: (610) 282-0131
E-mail: brian.macdonald@desales.edu
Phone: (610) 282-4443

**Design Institute of San Diego**
www.disd.edu
Director of Admissions
8555 Commerce Avenue
San Diego, CA 92121
Fax: (858) 566-2711
E-mail: admissions@disd.edu
Phone: (858) 566-1200 ext. 1018

**DeVry College of New York: Midtown Campus**
www.devry.edu
180 Madison Avenue, Suite 900
New York, NY 10016
Fax: (630) 571-0317
Phone: (630) 571-7700 ext. 3150

**DeVry University: Arlington**
www.devry.edu
2450 Crystal Drive
Arlington, VA 22202
Fax: (630) 571-0317
E-mail: admissions@crys.devry.edu
Phone: (630) 571-7700 ext. 4006

**DeVry University: Chicago**
www.devry.edu
International Student Coordinator
3300 North Campbell Avenue
Chicago, IL 60618-5994
Fax: (630) 571-0317
E-mail: admissions2@devry.edu
Phone: (630) 571-7700 ext. 3150

**DeVry University: Columbus**
www.devry.edu
International Student Coordinator
1350 Alum Creek Drive
Columbus, OH 43209-2705
Fax: (630) 571-0317
E-mail: admissions@devry.edu
Phone: (630) 571-7700 ext. 3150

**DeVry University: Decatur**
www.devry.edu
International Student Coordinator
One West Court Square, Suite 100
Decatur, GA 30030-2556
Fax: (630) 571-0317
E-mail: bsilva@admin.atl.devry.edu
Phone: (630) 571-7700 ext. 3150

**DeVry University: Fort Washington**
www.devry.edu
International Student Coordinator
1140 Virginia Drive
Fort Washington, PA 19034-3204
Fax: (630) 571-0317
E-mail: admissions@phi.devry.edu
Phone: (630) 571-7700 ext. 3150

**DeVry University: Irving**
www.devry.edu
International Student Coordinator
4800 Regent Boulevard, Suite 200
Dallas, TX 75063-2439
Fax: (630) 571-0317
Phone: (630) 571-7700 ext. 3150

**DeVry University: Kansas City**
www.devry.edu
International Student Coordinator
11224 Holmes Street
Kansas City, MO 64131
Fax: (630) 571-0317
E-mail: ssmeed@kc.devry.edu
Phone: (630) 571-7700 ext. 3150

**DeVry University: Miramar**
www.devry.edu
International Student Coordinator
2300 SW 145th Avenue
Miramar, FL 33027
Fax: (630) 571-0317
E-mail: openhouse@mir.devry.edu
Phone: (630) 571-7700 ext. 3150

**DeVry University: North Brunswick**
www.devry.edu
International Student Coordinator
630 US Highway One
North Brunswick, NJ 08902-3362
Fax: (630) 571-0317
E-mail: admissions@devry.edu
Phone: (630) 571-7700 ext. 3150

**DeVry University: Online**
www.devry.edu
One Tower Lane
Oakbrook Terrace, IL 60181

**DeVry University: Orlando**
www.devry.edu
4000 Millennia Boulevard
Orlando, FL 32839-2426
Fax: (630) 571-0317
Phone: (630) 571-7700 ext. 3150

**DeVry University: Phoenix**
www.devry.edu
International Student Coordinator
2149 West Dunlap Avenue
Phoenix, AZ 85021-2995
Fax: (630) 571-0317
E-mail: admissions@phx.devry.edu
Phone: (630) 571-7700 ext. 3150

**DeVry University: Pomona**
www.devry.edu
901 Corporate Center Drive
Pomona, CA 91768-2642
Fax: (630) 517-0317
Phone: (630) 571-7700 ext. 3150

**DeVry University: Westminster**
www.devry.edu
1870 West 122nd Avenue
Westminster, CO 80234-2010
Fax: (630) 571-0317
E-mail: denver-admissions@den.devry.edu
Phone: (630) 571-7700 ext. 3150

**Diablo Valley College**
www.dvc.edu
International Student Admissions and Services
321 Golf Club Road
Pleasant Hill, CA 94523-1529
Fax: (925) 609-8085
E-mail: GZarabozo@dvc.edu
Phone: (925) 685-1230 ext. 2075

**Dickinson College**
www.dickinson.edu
PO Box 1773
Carlisle, PA 17013-2896
Fax: (717) 245-1442
E-mail: studyusa@dickinson.edu
Phone: (800) 644-1773

**Dickinson State University**
www.dickinsonstate.edu
Office of International Programs
291 Campus Drive
Campus Box 169
Dickinson, ND 58601-4896
Fax: (701) 483-9720
E-mail: nicholas.mahan@dickinsonstate.edu
Phone: (701) 483-2322

**DigiPen Institute of Technology**
www.digipen.edu
Admissions Office
9931 Willows Road NE
Redmond, WA 98052
Fax: (425) 558-0378
E-mail: admissions@digipen.edu
Phone: (425) 558-0299

**Digital Media Arts College**
www.dmac.edu
International Coordinator
5400 Broken Sound Boulevard
Boca Raton, FL 33487
Fax: (561) 998-3403
E-mail: lpingatore@dmac.edu
Phone: (561) 391-1148 ext. 3803

**Dillard University**
www.dillard.edu
Admissions
2601 Gentilly Boulevard
New Orleans, LA 70122-3097
Fax: (504) 816-4951
E-mail: tsteffen@dillard.edu
Phone: (800) 216-6637

**Dine College**
www.dinecollege.edu
Registrar
PO Box C 04
Tsaile, AZ 86556
Fax: (928) 724-3349
E-mail: louise@dinecollege.edu
Phone: (928) 724-6631

**Divine Word College**
www.dwci.edu
102 Jacoby Drive SW
PO Box 380
Epworth, IA 52045
Fax: (563) 876-5515
E-mail: svdvocations@dwci.edu
Phone: (563) 876-3332

**Dixie State University**
www.dixie.edu
International Student Admissions Office
225 South 700 East
St. George, UT 84770-3876
Fax: (435) 656-4070
E-mail: mpthompson@dixie.edu
Phone: (435) 652-7689

**Doane University**
www.doane.edu
Admission Office
1014 Boswell Avenue
Crete, NE 68333
Fax: (402) 826-8592
E-mail: admissions@doane.edu
Phone: (402) 826-2161

**Dodge City Community College**
www.dc3.edu
2501 North 14th Avenue
Dodge City, KS 67801-2399
Fax: (620) 227-9350
E-mail: jkumm@dc3.edu
Phone: (620) 227-9217

**Dominican College of Blauvelt**
www.dc.edu
Admissions
470 Western Highway
Orangeburg, NY 10962-1210
Fax: (845) 365-3150
E-mail: admissions@dc.edu
Phone: (845) 848-7901

**Dominican University**
www.dom.edu
Undergraduate Office of Admissions
7900 West Division Street
River Forest, IL 60305-1099
Fax: (708) 524-6864
E-mail: domadmis@dom.edu
Phone: (708) 524-6965

**Dominican University of California**
www.dominican.edu
Admissions Office
50 Acacia Avenue
San Rafael, CA 94901-2298
Fax: (415) 485-3214
E-mail: nichelle.passanisi@dominican.edu
Phone: (415) 485-3206

**Dona Ana Community College of New
Mexico State University**
www.dacc.nmsu.edu
International Programs, New Mexico State
University
MSC-3DA
PO Box 30001
Las Cruces, NM 88003-8001
Fax: (575) 646-1517
E-mail: marjaspe@ad.nmsu.edu
Phone: (575) 646-2017

**Donnelly College**
www.donnelly.edu
Director of Admissions
608 North 18th Street
Kansas City, KS 66102-4210
Fax: (913) 621-8719
E-mail: kstevenson@donnelly.edu
Phone: (913) 621-8762

**Dordt College**
www.dordt.edu
Office of Global Education
498 Fourth Avenue, NE
Sioux Center, IA 51250
Fax: (712) 722-6035
E-mail: admissions@dordt.edu
Phone: (712) 722-6358

**Douglas Education Center**
www.dec.edu
Director of Admissions
130 Seventh Street
Monessen, PA 15062
E-mail: tbaez@dec.edu
Phone: (724) 653-2183

**Drake University**
www.drake.edu
Office of Admission
2507 University Avenue
Des Moines, IA 50311-4505
Fax: (515) 271-2831
E-mail: international@drake.edu
Phone: (515) 271-3181 ext. 2086

**Drew University**
www.drew.edu
Office of Admissions
36 Madison Avenue
Madison, NJ 07940-4063
E-mail: rcoufal@drew.edu
Phone: (973) 937-7677

**Drexel University**
www.drexel.edu
International Admissions
3141 Chestnut Street
Philadelphia, PA 19104-2876
Fax: (215) 895-1285
E-mail: enroll@drexel.edu
Phone: (215) 895-2400

**Drury University**
www.drury.edu
International and IEP Admission
900 North Benton Avenue
Springfield, MO 65802-3712
Fax: (417) 866-3873
E-mail: iadmissions@drury.edu
Phone: (417) 873-7506

**DuBois Business College**
www.dbcollege.edu
One Beaver Drive
DuBois, PA 15801
Fax: (814) 371-3974
E-mail: admissions@dbcollege.edu
Phone: (814) 371-6920

**DuBois Business College: Huntingdon**
www.dbcollege.edu
1001 Moore Street
Huntingdon, PA 16652
Fax: (814) 641-0205
E-mail: hcc@dbcollege.edu
Phone: (814) 641-0440

**DuBois Business College: Oil City**
www.dbcollege.edu
701 East Third Street
Oil City, PA 16301
Fax: (814) 677-8237
E-mail: occ@dbcollege.edu
Phone: (814) 677-1322

**Duke University**
www.duke.edu
2138 Campus Drive
Box 90586
Durham, NC 27708
Fax: (919) 684-8128
E-mail: jennifer.dewar@duke.edu
Phone: (919) 684-0166

**Dunlap-Stone University**
www.dunlap-stone.edu
Registrar
11225 North 28th Drive Suite B201
Phoenix, AZ 85029
Fax: (602) 648-5755
E-mail: registrar@dunlap-stone.edu
Phone: (602) 648-5750

**Dunwoody College of Technology**
www.dunwoody.edu
Director of Admissions
818 Dunwoody Boulevard
attn: Admissions
Minneapolis, MN 55403-1192
Fax: (612) 374-4128
E-mail: kobrien@dunwoody.edu
Phone: (612) 381-3302

**Duquesne University**
www.duq.edu
Office of International Programs
600 Forbes Avenue, Administration Building
Pittsburgh, PA 15282-0201
Fax: (412) 396-5178
E-mail: intladmissions@duq.edu
Phone: (412) 396-6113

**Durham Technical Community College**
www.durhamtech.edu
International Student Adviser
1637 Lawson Street
Durham, NC 27703
Fax: (919) 686-3669
E-mail: whiteh@durhamtech.edu
Phone: (919) 536-7200 ext. 4052

**Dutchess Community College**
www.sunydutchess.edu
VP of Student of Academic Affairs
53 Pendell Road
Poughkeepsie, NY 12601-1595
Fax: (845) 431-8997
E-mail: egambino@sunydutchess.edu
Phone: (845) 431-8974

**Dyersburg State Community College**
www.dscc.edu
Office of Admissions
1510 Lake Road
Dyersburg, TN 38024
Fax: (731) 286-3325
E-mail: enroll@dscc.edu
Phone: (731) 286-3330

**D'Youville College**
www.dyc.edu
International Admissions
320 Porter Avenue
Buffalo, NY 14201-1084
Fax: (716) 829-7788
E-mail: dannecrh@dyc.edu
Phone: (716) 829-8119

**Eagle Gate College: Layton**
www.eaglegatecollege.edu
915 North 400 West Layton
Layton, UT 84041
Fax: (801) 593-6654
E-mail: admissions@eaglegatecollege.edu
Phone: (801) 546-7500 ext. 7512

**Eagle Gate College: Murray**
www.eaglegatecollege.edu
5588 South Green Street
Murray, UT 84123
Phone: (801) 281-7700

**Earlham College**
www.earlham.edu
International Student Admissions
801 National Road West
Richmond, IN 47374-4095
Fax: (765) 983-1560
E-mail: admissions@earlham.edu
Phone: (765) 983-1600

**East Arkansas Community College**
www.eacc.edu
Admissions and Records
1700 Newcastle Road
Forrest City, AR 72335-2204
Fax: (870) 633-3840
E-mail: scollier@eacc.edu
Phone: (870) 633-4480 ext. 219

**East Carolina University**
www.ecu.edu
Assistant Director of Admissions
Office of Undergraduate Admissions
106 Whichard Building
Greenville, NC 27858-4353
Fax: (252) 328-4813
E-mail: robertsje@ecu.edu
Phone: (252) 328-6769

**East Central College**
www.eastcentral.edu
Office of Admissions
1964 Prairie Dell Road
Union, MO 63084-0529
Fax: (636) 584-7347
E-mail: intladmissions@eastcentral.edu
Phone: (636) 584-6588

**East Central University**
www.ecok.edu
International Student Programs and Services
1100 East 14th Street, PMB R-8
Ada, OK 74820
Fax: (580) 559-5167
E-mail: intlstu@ecok.edu
Phone: (580) 559-5669

**East Georgia State College**
www.ega.edu
Admissions
131 College Circle
Swainsboro, GA 30401-2699
Fax: (478) 289-2353
E-mail: gedmond@ega.edu
Phone: (478) 289-2112

**East Los Angeles College**
www.elac.edu
International Student Program
1301 Avenida Cesar Chavez
Monterey Park, CA 91754-6099
Fax: (323) 260-8192
E-mail: elac_iso@elac.edu
Phone: (323) 265-8796

**East Mississippi Community College**
www.eastms.edu
Admissions Office
PO Box 158
Scooba, MS 39358
Fax: (662) 476-5038
E-mail: pmiller@eastms.edu
Phone: (662) 243-1902

**East Stroudsburg University of Pennsylvania**
www.esu.edu
Office of International Programs
200 Prospect Street
East Stroudsburg, PA 18301-2999
Fax: (570) 422-3579
E-mail: sives@esu.edu
Phone: (570) 422-3527

**East Tennessee State University**
www.etsu.edu
Admissions Office
ETSU Box 70731
Johnson City, TN 37614
Fax: (423) 439-4630
E-mail: go2etsu@etsu.edu
Phone: (423) 439-4213

**East Texas Baptist University**
www.etbu.edu
Director of Global Education
One Tiger Drive
Marshall, TX 75670-1498
Fax: (903) 923-2001
E-mail: intstud@etbu.edu
Phone: (903) 927-4448

**East-West University**
www.eastwest.edu
Admission
816 South Michigan Avenue
Chicago, IL 60605-2185
Fax: (312) 939-0083
E-mail: agniezka@eastwest.edu
Phone: (312) 939-0111 ext. 1825

**Eastern Arizona College**
www.eac.edu
Records and Registration
615 North Stadium Avenue
Thatcher, AZ 85552-0769
Fax: (928) 428-2446
E-mail: admissions@eac.edu
Phone: (928) 428-8904

**Eastern Connecticut State University**
www.easternct.edu
Admissions
83 Windham Street
Willimantic, CT 06226-2295
Fax: (860) 465-5544
E-mail: satsukd@easternct.edu
Phone: (860) 465-5286

**Eastern Florida State College**
www.easternflorida.edu
International Admissions
1519 Clearlake Road
Cocoa, FL 32922-9987
Fax: (321) 433-7102
E-mail: eastmanp@easternflorida.edu
Phone: (321) 433-7341

**Eastern Illinois University**
www.eiu.edu
Admissions Counselor
600 Lincoln Avenue
Charleston, IL 61920
Fax: (217) 581-7207
E-mail: kpthomas@eiu.edu
Phone: (217) 581-2321

**Eastern International College**
www.eicollege.edu
684 Newark Avenue
Jersey City, NJ 07306
Fax: (201) 216-9225
E-mail: admissions@eicollege.edu
Phone: (201) 216-9901

**Eastern Kentucky University**
www.eku.edu
Admissions Director
SSB CPO 54, 521 Lancaster Avenue
Richmond, KY 40475-3102
Fax: (859) 622-1552
E-mail: stephen.byrn@eku.edu
Phone: (859) 622-1478

**Eastern Maine Community College**
www.emcc.edu
354 Hogan Road
Bangor, ME 04401
Fax: (207) 974-4683
E-mail: lrussell@emcc.edu
Phone: (207) 974-4680

**Eastern Mennonite University**
www.emu.edu
Admissions Office
1200 Park Road
Harrisonburg, VA 22802-2462
Fax: (540) 432-4444
E-mail: micah.shristi@emu.edu
Phone: (540) 432-4118

**Eastern Michigan University**
www.emich.edu
Admissions
400 Pierce Hall
Ypsilanti, MI 48197
Fax: (734) 487-6559
E-mail: international.admissions@emich.edu
Phone: (734) 487-3060

**Eastern Nazarene College**
www.enc.edu
Office of Admissions
23 East Elm Avenue
Quincy, MA 02170
Fax: (617) 745-3992
E-mail: admissions@enc.edu
Phone: (617) 745-3861

**Eastern New Mexico University**
www.enmu.edu
International Student Advising
1500 South Avenue K
Station 7
Portales, NM 88130
Fax: (575) 562-2118
E-mail: christy.czerwein@enmu.edu
Phone: (575) 562-4698

**Eastern New Mexico University: Roswell**
www.roswell.enmu.edu
Admissions
PO Box 6000
Roswell, NM 88202-6000
Fax: (575) 624-7144
E-mail: griselda.aubert@roswell.enmu.edu
Phone: (575) 624-7149

**Eastern Oklahoma State College**
www.eosc.edu
Registrar
1301 West Main Street
Wilburton, OK 74578-4999
Fax: (918) 465-4435
E-mail: jlabor@eosc.edu
Phone: (918) 465-1828

**Eastern Oregon University**
www.eou.edu
Admissions
One University Boulevard
Office of Admissions
La Grande, OR 97850
Fax: (541) 962-3418
E-mail: admissions@eou.edu
Phone: (541) 962-3406

**Eastern University**
www.eastern.edu
Admissions
1300 Eagle Road
St. Davids, PA 19087-3696
Fax: (610) 341-1723
E-mail: mdziedzi@eastern.edu
Phone: (610) 341-1376

**Eastern Washington University**
www.ewu.edu
EWU Admissions
304 Sutton Hall
Cheney, WA 99004
Fax: (509) 359-6692
E-mail: international@ewu.edu
Phone: (509) 359-2397

**Eastern Wyoming College**
www.ewc.wy.edu
Admissions
3200 West C Street
Torrington, WY 82240
Fax: (307) 532-8222
E-mail: rex.cogdill@ewc.wy.edu
Phone: (800) 658-3195

**Eastfield College**
www.efc.dcccd.edu
Admissions Office
3737 Motley Drive
Mesquite, TX 75150
Fax: (972) 860-8306
E-mail: molivares-urueta@dcccd.edu
Phone: (972) 860-8354

**Eastman School of Music of the University
of Rochester**
www.esm.rochester.edu
Director of Admissions
26 Gibbs Street
Rochester, NY 14604-2599
Fax: (585) 232-8601
E-mail: mardizzone@esm.rochester.edu
Phone: (585) 274-1060

**Eastwick College**
www.eastwick.edu
10 South Franklin Turnpike
Ramsey, NJ 07446
E-mail: admissions2@eastwick.edu
Phone: (201) 327-8877

**Eastwick College: Hackensack**
www.eastwickcollege.edu
250 Moore Street
Hackensack, NJ 07601
E-mail: rzayas@eastwick.edu
Phone: (201) 488-9400

**Ecclesia College**
www.ecollege.edu
International Student Office
9653 Nations Drive
Springdale, AR 72762
Fax: (479) 248-1455
E-mail: hqualls@ecollege.edu
Phone: (479) 248-7236

**Eckerd College**
www.eckerd.edu
Associate Director of Admissions & Intl
Admission Coordinator
4200 54th Avenue South
St. Petersburg, FL 33711
Fax: (727) 866-2304
E-mail: aksud@eckerd.edu
Phone: (727) 864-8032

**Ecotech Institute**
www.ecotechinstitute.com
1400 South Abilene Street
Aurora, CO 80012

**ECPI University**
www.ecpi.edu
Academic Support Services
5555 Greenwich Road, Suite 300
Virginia Beach, VA 23462-6542
Fax: (757) 671-8661
E-mail: rmckain@ecpi.edu
Phone: (757) 490-9090

**Edgewood College**
www.edgewood.edu
International Admissions
1000 Edgewood College Drive
Madison, WI 53711-1997
Fax: (608) 663-2214
E-mail: admissions@edgewood.edu
Phone: (608) 663-2294

**EDIC College**
www.ediccollege.com
Box 9120
Caguas, PR 00726-9120
Fax: (787) 258-6300
E-mail: admisiones@ediccollege.edu
Phone: (787) 745-7010

**Edinboro University of Pennsylvania**
www.edinboro.edu
International Student Services
200 East Normal Street
Academy Hall
Edinboro, PA 16444
Fax: (814) 732-2443
E-mail: international@edinboro.edu
Phone: (814) 732-2770

**Edison State Community College**
www.edisonohio.edu
Director of Student Success
1973 Edison Drive
Piqua, OH 45356-9253
Fax: (937) 778-1920
E-mail: pgibellino@edisonohio.edu
Phone: (937) 778-7856

**Edmonds Community College**
www.edcc.edu
International Student Services Office
20000 68th Avenue West
Lynnwood, WA 98036-5912
Fax: (425) 774-0455
E-mail: Saerom.han@edcc.edu
Phone: (425) 640-1078

**EDP University of Puerto Rico: Hato Rey**
www.edpuniversity.edu
PO Box 192303
Hato Rey, PR 00919-2303
Fax: (787) 777-0025
E-mail: sandraarroyo@edpuniversity.edu
Phone: (787) 765-3560 ext. 1380

**EDP University of Puerto Rico: San Sebastian**
www.edpuniverstiy.edu
Distance Modality Education
PO Box 1674
49 Betances Street
San Sebastian, PR 00685
Fax: (787) 896-5960
E-mail: cquintana@edpuniversity.edu
Phone: (787) 896-2252 ext. 1412

**Edward Waters College**
www.ewc.edu
Admissions Office
1658 Kings Road
Jacksonville, FL 32209
Fax: (904) 470-8048
E-mail: Elin.Iselin@ewc.edu
Phone: (904) 470-8201

**El Camino College**
www.elcamino.edu
International Student Program Office
16007 Crenshaw Boulevard
Torrance, CA 90506
Fax: (310) 660-3818
E-mail: lrachman@elcamino.edu
Phone: (310) 660-3431

**El Centro College**
www.elcentrocollege.edu
International Office Director
801 Main Street
Dallas, TX 75202
Fax: (214) 860-2022
E-mail: rreyes@dcccd.edu
Phone: (214) 860-2664

**Elgin Community College**
www.elgin.edu
International Education and Programs
1700 Spartan Drive
Elgin, IL 60123-7193
Fax: (847) 214-7484
E-mail: LNehlsen@elgin.edu
Phone: (847) 214-7809

**Elizabeth City State University**
www.ecsu.edu
Director of Admissions
1704 Weeksville Road, Campus Box 901
Elizabeth City, NC 27909
Fax: (252) 335-3537
E-mail: btewers@mail.ecsu.edu
Phone: (252) 335-3630

**Elizabethtown College**
www.etown.edu
Admissions
One Alpha Drive
Elizabethtown, PA 17022-2298
Fax: (717) 361-1365
E-mail: admissions@etown.edu
Phone: (717) 361-1400

**Elizabethtown Community and Technical College**
www.elizabethtown.kctcs.edu
Coordinator of Admissions
600 College Street Road
Elizabethtown, KY 42701
Fax: (270) 769-1618
E-mail: bryan.smith@kctcs.edu
Phone: (270) 769-2371 ext. 68616

**Ellsworth Community College**
www.iavalley.cc.ia.us/ecc
Counseling Office
1100 College Avenue
Iowa Falls, IA 50126
Fax: (641) 648-3128
E-mail: nwalters@iavalley.cc.ia.us
Phone: (641) 648-4611 ext. 424

**Elmhurst College**
www.elmhurst.edu
Admission
190 South Prospect Avenue
Elmhurst, IL 60126-3296
Fax: (630) 617-5501
E-mail: admit@elmhurst.edu
Phone: (630) 617-3400

**Elmira College**
www.elmira.edu
Office of Admissions
One Park Place
Elmira, NY 14901
Fax: (607) 735-1718
E-mail: admissions@elmira.edu
Phone: (607) 735-1724

**Elms College**
www.elms.edu
Director of International Programs
291 Springfield Street
Chicopee, MA 01013-2839
Fax: (413) 594-2781
E-mail: garciam@elms.edu
Phone: (413) 594-3951

**Elon University**
www.elon.edu
Associate Dean & Director or International Admissions
2700 Campus Box
100 Campus Drive
Elon, NC 27244-2010
Fax: (336) 278-7699
E-mail: admissions@elon.edu
Phone: (800) 334-8448

**Embry-Riddle Aeronautical University**
www.embryriddle.edu
Office of International Admissions
600 South Clyde Morris Boulevard
Daytona Beach, FL 32114-3900
Fax: (386) 226-7070
E-mail: international.admissions@erau.edu
Phone: (386) 226-6115

**Embry-Riddle Aeronautical University: Prescott Campus**
https://prescott.erau.edu/
International Admissions
3700 Willow Creek Road
Prescott, AZ 86301-3720
Fax: (928) 777-6606
E-mail: Prescott@erau.edu
Phone: (928) 777-6600

**Embry-Riddle Aeronautical University: Worldwide Campus**
https://worldwide.erau.edu/
Admissions
Attn: Worldwide Imaging
600 South Clyde Morris Boulevard
Daytona Beach, FL 32114-3900
Fax: (386) 226-6984
E-mail: worldwide@erau.edu
Phone: (800) 522-6787

**Emerson College**
www.emerson.edu
Office of Undergraduate Admission
120 Boylston Street
Boston, MA 02116-4624
Fax: (617) 824-8609
E-mail: admission@emerson.edu
Phone: (617) 824-8600

**Emmanuel College**
www.emmanuel.edu
Admissions
400 The Fenway
Boston, MA 02115
Fax: (617) 735-9801
E-mail: enroll@emmanuel.edu
Phone: (617) 735-9715

**Emmaus Bible College**
www.emmaus.edu
2570 Asbury Road
Dubuque, IA 52001
Fax: (563) 588-1216
E-mail: lrasmussen@emmaus.edu
Phone: (563) 588-8000 ext. 1310

**Emory & Henry College**
www.ehc.edu
Admissions Office
PO Box 10
Emory, VA 24327
Fax: (276) 944-6935
E-mail: ehadmiss@ehc.edu
Phone: (276) 944-6133

**Emory University**
www.emory.edu
Office of Admissions
1390 Oxford Road NE, 3rd Floor
Atlanta, GA 30322
Fax: (404) 727-4303
E-mail: admiss@emory.edu
Phone: (404) 727-6036

**Emporia State University**
www.emporia.edu
Office of International Education
One Kellogg Circle, Campus Box 4034
Emporia, KS 66801-5415
Fax: (620) 341-5918
E-mail: gswift@emporia.edu
Phone: (620) 341-5374

**Endicott College**
www.endicott.edu
Admission
376 Hale Street
Beverly, MA 01915-9985
Fax: (978) 232-2520
E-mail: tredman@endicott.edu
Phone: (978) 921-1000

**Epic Bible College**
https://epic.edu/
4330 Auburn Boulevard
Sacramento, CA 95841
Phone: (916) 348-4689

**Erie Community College**
www.ecc.edu
Foreign Student Adviser
6205 Main Street
Williamsville, NY 14221-7095
Fax: (716) 851-1429
E-mail: danna@ecc.edu
Phone: (716) 851-1359

**Erie Institute of Technology**
www.erieit.edu
940 Millcreek Mall
Erie, PA 16565
Fax: (814) 868-9977
Phone: (814) 868-9900

**Erskine College**
www.erskine.edu
Admissions
PO Box 338
Due West, SC 29639-0338
Fax: (864) 379-2167
E-mail: frierson@erskine.edu
Phone: (864) 379-8721

**Escuela de Artes Plasticas de Puerto Rico**
www.eap.edu
Officer of Admissions
PO Box 9021112
San Juan, PR 00902-1112
Fax: (787) 721-3798
E-mail: nmelendez@eap.edu
Phone: (787) 725-8120 ext. 333

**Essex County College**
www.essex.edu
Admissions
303 University Avenue
Newark, NJ 07102
E-mail: dizdarev@essex.edu
Phone: (973) 877-3154

**Estrella Mountain Community College**
www.estrellamountain.edu
Admission and Records
3000 North Dysart Road
Avondale, AZ 85392
Fax: (623) 935-8848
E-mail: elaine.trask@emcmail.maricopa.edu
Phone: (623) 935-8881

**Eugene Lang College The New School for Liberal Arts**
www.newschool.edu
Admissions
79 Fifth Avenue
5th Floor
New York, NY 10003
Fax: (212) 229-5355
E-mail: lang@newschool.edu
Phone: (212) 229-5665 ext. 2300

**Eureka College**
www.eureka.edu
Admissions
300 East College Avenue
Box 280
Eureka, IL 61530-1500
Fax: (309) 467-6576
E-mail: admissions@eureka.edu
Phone: (309) 467-6530

**Evangel University**
www.evangel.edu
Admissions
1111 North Glenstone
Springfield, MO 65802
Fax: (417) 865-9599
E-mail: Pochinga@evangel.edu
Phone: (417) 865-2811 ext. 7450

**Everest University: Orange Park**
www.everest.edu
805 Wells Road
Orange Park, FL 32073
Phone: (904) 264-9122

**Everett Community College**
www.everettcc.edu
International Education
2000 Tower Street
Everett, WA 98201-1352
Fax: (425) 388-9173
E-mail: jfitzpatrick@everettcc.edu
Phone: (425) 388-9220

**Everglades University**
www.evergladesuniversity.edu
Admissions Office
5002 T-REX Avenue, Suite 100
Boca Raton, FL 33431
Fax: (561) 912-1191
E-mail:
admissionsEUB@evergladesuniversity.edu
Phone: (561) 912-1211

**Evergreen State College**
www.evergreen.edu
Admissions
2700 Evergreen Parkway NW
Olympia, WA 98505
Fax: (360) 867-5114
E-mail: admissions@evergreen.edu
Phone: (360) 867-6168

**Evergreen Valley College**
www.evc.edu
International Student Coordinator
3095 Yerba Buena Road
San José, CA 95135
Fax: (408) 223-9351
E-mail: beverly.lynch@evc.edu
Phone: (408) 274-7900 ext. 6638

**Excelsior College**
www.excelsior.edu
Admissions
7 Columbia Circle
Albany, NY 12203
Fax: (518) 464-8833
E-mail: admissions@excelsior.edu
Phone: (518) 464-8500 ext. 2

**Ex'pression College**
www.expression.edu
6601 Shellmound Street
Emeryville, CA 94608
E-mail: admissions@expression.edu
Phone: (510) 654-2934

**Fairfield University**
www.fairfield.edu
Undergrad Admissions
1073 North Benson Road
Fairfield, CT 06824
Fax: (203) 254-4199
E-mail: toconnor@fairfield.edu
Phone: (203) 254-4000 ext. 2168

**Fairleigh Dickinson University: College at Florham**
www.fdu.edu
Office of International and Graduate Student Admissions
285 Madison Avenue, M-RI0-01
Madison, NJ 07940
Fax: (201) 692-2560
E-mail: global@fdu.edu
Phone: (201) 692-2205

**Fairleigh Dickinson University: Metropolitan Campus**
www.fdu.edu
Office of International and Graduate Student Admissions
1000 River Road, H-DH3-10
Teaneck, NJ 07666-1996
Fax: (201) 692-2560
E-mail: global@fdu.edu
Phone: (201) 692-2205

**Fairmont State University**
www.fairmontstate.edu
International Student Adviser
Office of Admissions
1201 Locust Avenue
Fairmont, WV 26554-2470
Fax: (304) 367-4995
E-mail: ghines@fairmontstate.edu
Phone: (304) 367-4490

**Faith Baptist Bible College and Theological Seminary**
www.faith.edu
Admissions
1900 NW Fourth Street
Ankeny, IA 50023
Fax: (515) 964-1638
E-mail: admissions@faith.edu
Phone: (515) 964-0601

**Family of Faith College**
www.familyoffaithcollege.edu
PO Box 1805
Shawnee, OK 74802-1805
Fax: (405) 273-8535
E-mail: info@familyoffaithcollege.edu
Phone: (405) 273-5331

**Fashion Institute of Design and Merchandising: Los Angeles**
www.fidm.edu
Admissions
919 South Grand Avenue
Los Angeles, CA 90015-1421
Fax: (213) 624-4799
E-mail: saronson@fidm.edu
Phone: (213) 624-1201 ext. 5400

**Fashion Institute of Design and Merchandising: San Diego**
www.fidm.edu
Admissions
350 Tenth Avenue, Third Floor
San Diego, CA 92101-7496
Fax: (213) 624-1200
E-mail: saronson@fidm.edu
Phone: (213) 624-1201 ext. 5400

**Fashion Institute of Design and Merchandising: San Francisco**
www.fidm.edu
Admissions
55 Stockton Street
San Francisco, CA 94108-5805
Fax: (213) 624-1200
E-mail: saronson@fidm.edu
Phone: (213) 624-1201 ext. 5400

**Fashion Institute of Technology**
www.fitnyc.edu
Admissions
227 West 27th Street
Marvin Feldman Center Room C139
New York, NY 10001-5992
Fax: (212) 217-3761
E-mail: fitinfo@fitnyc.edu
Phone: (212) 217-3760

**Faulkner State Community College**
www.faulknerstate.edu
Admissions
1900 Highway 31 South
Bay Minette, AL 36507
Fax: (251) 580-2136
E-mail: joe.beaty@faulknerstate.edu
Phone: (251) 580-2243

**Faulkner University**
www.faulkner.edu
VP for Enrollment
5345 Atlanta Highway
Montgomery, AL 36109-3398
Fax: (334) 386-7137
E-mail: kmock@faulkner.edu
Phone: (334) 386-7875

**Fayetteville State University**
www.uncfsu.edu
Admissions
1200 Murchison Road
Fayetteville, NC 28301-4298
Fax: (910) 672-1414
E-mail: ubowles@uncfsu.edu
Phone: (910) 672-1371

**Fayetteville Technical Community College**
www.faytechcc.edu
Assistant Registrar, Corporate and Continuing Education
2201 Hull Road
PO Box 35236
Fayetteville, NC 28303-0236
Fax: (910) 678-0085
E-mail: haywoodl@faytechcc.edu
Phone: (910) 678-8306

**Feather River College**
www.frc.edu
Admissions
570 Golden Eagle Avenue
Quincy, CA 95971
Fax: (530) 283-9961
E-mail: Lmikesell@frc.edu
Phone: (530) 283-0202 ext. 285

**Felician University**
www.felician.edu
Assistant Director of International Services
262 South Main Street
Lodi, NJ 07644-2198
Fax: (201) 355-1443
E-mail: greenL@felician.edu
Phone: (201) 355-3516

**Ferris State University**
www.ferris.edu
Admissions Coordinator
1201 South State Street, CSS 201
Big Rapids, MI 49307-2714
Fax: (231) 591-2423
E-mail: valeriecampbell@ferris.edu
Phone: (231) 591-2451

**Ferrum College**
www.ferrum.edu
Spilman-Daniel House, 40 Stratton Lane
PO Box 1000
Ferrum, VA 24088
Fax: (540) 365-4266
E-mail: admissions@ferrum.edu
Phone: (540) 365-4290

**Fiath International University**
www.faithseminary.edu
Faith Evangelical College & Seminary
3504 North Pearl Street
Tacoma, WA 98407
Fax: (253) 759-1790
E-mail: admissions@faithseminary.edu
Phone: (253) 752-2020 ext. 121

**Finlandia University**
www.finlandia.edu
International Enrollment Officer
601 Quincy Street
Hancock, MI 49930-1882
Fax: (906) 487-7383
E-mail: international@finlandia.edu
Phone: (906) 487-7208

**Fisher College**
www.fisher.edu
Senior Assistant Director of International Recruitment
Office of Admissions
118 Beacon Street
Boston, MA 02116
E-mail: aschumacher@fisher.edu
Phone: (617) 236-8819

**Fisk University**
www.fisk.edu
Office of Recruitment and Admission
1000 Seventeenth Avenue North
Nashville, TN 37208-3051
Fax: (615) 329-8774
E-mail: ajones@fisk.edu
Phone: (615) 329-8737

**Fitchburg State University**
www.fitchburgstate.edu
Director, Admissions
160 Pearl Street
Fitchburg, MA 01420-2697
Fax: (978) 665-4540
E-mail: admissions@fitchburgstate.edu
Phone: (978) 665-3144

**Five Towns College**
www.ftc.edu
Admissions Office
305 North Service Road
Dix Hills, NY 11746-6055
Fax: (631) 656-2172
E-mail: cynthia.catalano@ftc.edu
Phone: (631) 656-2109

**Flagler College**
www.flagler.edu
Admissions Office
74 King Street
St. Augustine, FL 32084
Fax: (904) 819-6466
E-mail: SAlbano@flagler.edu
Phone: (800) 304-4208

**Flathead Valley Community College**
www.fvcc.edu
777 Grandview Drive
Kalispell, MT 59901
Fax: (406) 756-3965
E-mail: mstoltz@fvcc.edu
Phone: (406) 756-3846

**Florence-Darlington Technical College**
www.fdtc.edu
Admissions
PO Box 100548
Florence, SC 29501-0548
Fax: (843) 661-8041
E-mail: delores.dingel@fdtc.edu
Phone: (843) 661-8324

**Florida Agricultural and Mechanical University**
www.famu.edu
Office of Admissions
444 Gamble Street Lucy Moten, Room 204
1700 Lee Hall Drive
Tallahassee, FL 32307-3200
Fax: (850) 599-3069
E-mail: barbara.cox@famu.edu
Phone: (850) 599-3796

**Florida Atlantic University**
www.fau.edu
Admissions Office
777 Glades Road
Boca Raton, FL 33431
Fax: (561) 297-2758
E-mail: avandam1@fau.edu
Phone: (561) 297-2627

**Florida Career College: Hialeah**
www.careercollege.edu
3750 West 18th Avenue
Hialeah, FL 33012
Fax: (305) 825-3436
E-mail: pbrum@careercollege.edu
Phone: (954) 547-6989

**Florida Career College: Miami**
www.careercollege.edu
1321 SW 107th Avenue, Suite 201B
Miami, FL 33174-2521
Phone: (305) 553-6065

**Florida Career College: Riverview**
www.careercollege.edu
2662 South Falkenburg Road
Riverview, FL 33578

**Florida Career College: West Palm Beach**
www.careercollege.edu
6058 Okeechobee Boulevard
West Palm Beach, FL 33417
Fax: (561) 689-0739
Phone: (561) 689-0550

**Florida College of Natural Health: Bradenton**
www.fcnh.com
Admissions
616 67th Street Circle East
Bradenton, FL 34208
Fax: (941) 744-1242
E-mail: sarasota@fcnh.com
Phone: (941) 744-1244

**Florida College of Natural Health: Maitland**
www.fcnh.com
2600 Lake Lucien Drive; Suite 240
Maitland, FL 32751
Fax: (407) 261-0342
E-mail: orlando@fcnh.com
Phone: (407) 261-0319

**Florida College of Natural Health: Miami**
www.fcnh.com
7925 Northwest 12th Street, Suite 201
Miami, FL 33126
Fax: (305) 597-9110
E-mail: miami@fcnh.com
Phone: (305) 597-9599

**Florida College of Natural Health: Pompano Beach**
www.fcnh.com
2001 West Sample Road, Suite 100
Pompano Beach, FL 33064
Fax: (954) 975-9633
E-mail: ftlauderdale@fcnh.com
Phone: (954) 975-6400

**Florida Gateway College**
www.fgc.edu
Admissions
149 SE College Place
Lake City, FL 32025-2007
Fax: (386) 754-4736
E-mail: admissions@fgc.edu
Phone: (386) 754-4236

**Florida Gulf Coast University**
www.fgcu.edu
International Admissions Coordinator
10501 FGCU Boulevard South
Fort Myers, FL 33965-6565
Fax: (239) 590-7894
E-mail: sbannwor@fgcu.edu
Phone: (239) 590-7882

**Florida Institute of Technology**
www.fit.edu
International Admissions
150 West University Boulevard
Melbourne, FL 32901-6975
Fax: (321) 674-8004
E-mail: admission@fit.edu
Phone: (321) 674-8030

**Florida International University**
www.fiu.edu
Undergraduate Admissions
Modesto Maidique Campus, PC 140
Miami, FL 33199
Fax: (305) 348-3648
E-mail: admiss@fiu.edu
Phone: (305) 348-2363

**Florida Keys Community College**
www.fkcc.edu
Office of Enrollment Services
5901 College Road
Key West, FL 33040
Fax: (305) 292-5163
E-mail: internationalstudents@fkcc.edu
Phone: (305) 809-3278

**Florida Memorial University**
www.fmuniv.edu
15800 NW 42nd Avenue
Miami Gardens, FL 33054
Fax: (305) 623-1462
E-mail: admit@fmuniv.edu
Phone: (305) 626-3750

**Florida National University**
www.fnu.edu
Office of International Students
4425 West Jose Regueiro (20th) Avenue
Hialeah, FL 33012
Fax: (305) 362-0595
E-mail: jsanchez@fnu.edu
Phone: (305) 821-333 ext. 1059

**Florida Southern College**
www.flsouthern.edu
Admissions Advisor
111 Lake Hollingsworth Drive
Lakeland, FL 33801-5698
Fax: (863) 680-4120
E-mail: phogan@flsouthern.edu
Phone: (863) 680-3910

**Florida SouthWestern State College**
www.fsw.edu
8099 College Parkway
Fort Myers, FL 33919
Fax: (239) 489-9094
E-mail: admissions@fsw.edu
Phone: (239) 489-9054

**Florida State College at Jacksonville**
www.fscj.edu
Director International Studies
501 West State Street
Jacksonville, FL 32202
Fax: (904) 632-5105
E-mail: asiegel@fscj.edu
Phone: (904) 632-3248

**Florida State University**
www.fsu.edu
Admissions
PO Box 3062400
282 Champions Way
Tallahassee, FL 32306-2400
Fax: (850) 644-0197
E-mail: jmrichardson2@fsu.edu
Phone: (850) 644-6200

**Florida Technical College: Deland**
www.ftccollege.edu
1199 South Woodland Boulevard
Deland, FL 32720
Fax: (386) 734-5150
Phone: (386) 734-3303

**Florida Technical College: Orlando**
www.ftccollege.edu
Admissions
12900 Challenger Parkway
Orlando, FL 32826-2707
Fax: (407) 447-7301
E-mail: dboothe@flatech.edu
Phone: (407) 447-7300

**Folsom Lake College**
www.flc.losrios.edu
Admissions & Records
10 College Parkway
Folsom, CA 95630
Fax: (916) 608-6569
E-mail: callawr@flc.losrios.edu
Phone: (916) 608-5000

**Fond du Lac Tribal and Community College**
www.fdltcc.edu
Admissions
2101 14th Street
Cloquet, MN 55720
Fax: (218) 879-0814
E-mail: sbumann@fdltcc.edu
Phone: (218) 879-0808

**Fontbonne University**
www.fontbonne.edu
Office of International Students
6800 Wydown Boulevard
Saint Louis, MO 63105-3098
Fax: (314) 889-1451
E-mail: RBahan@Fontbonne.edu
Phone: (314) 889-4509

**Foothill College**
www.foothill.edu
12345 El Monte Road
Los Altos Hills, CA 94022
E-mail: foothillinternational@fhda.edu
Phone: (650) 949-7293

**Fordham University**
www.fordham.edu
Office of Undergraduate Admission
Office of Undergraduate Admission, Fordham
University
441 East Fordham Road
Bronx, NY 10458-9993
Fax: (718) 367-9404
E-mail: enroll@fordham.edu
Phone: (718) 817-4000

**Forrest Junior College**
www.forrestcollege.edu
Admissions
601 East River Street
Anderson, SC 29624
Fax: (864) 261-7471
E-mail: janieturmon@forrestcollege.edu
Phone: (864) 225-7653 ext. 2210

**Fort Hays State University**
www.fhsu.edu
International Student Advisor
600 Park Street
Hays, KS 67601
Fax: (785) 628-4085
E-mail: csolko@fhsu.edu
Phone: (785) 628-4222

**Fort Lewis College**
www.fortlewis.edu
Admissions
1000 Rim Drive
Durango, CO 81301-3999
Fax: (970) 247-7179
E-mail: burns_a@fortlewis.edu
Phone: (877) 352-2656

**Fort Valley State University**
www.fvsu.edu
1005 State University Drive
Fort Valley, GA 31030-4313
Fax: (478) 825-6169
E-mail: admissap@fvsu.edu
Phone: (478) 825-6307

**Fortis College: Cuyahoga**
www.fortis.edu
2545 Bailey Road
Cuyahoga Falls, OH 44221
Fax: (330) 923-0886
E-mail: LNelly@edaff.com
Phone: (330) 923-9959 ext. 4660

**Fortis College: Indianapolis**
www.fortis.edu
9001 North Wesleyan Road, Suite 101
Indianapolis, IN 46268
Phone: (317) 808-4800

**Fortis College: Orange Park**
www.fortis.edu
560 Wells Road
Orange Park, FL 32073
Phone: (904) 269-7086

**Fortis College: Ravenna**
www.fortis.edu
653 Enterprise Parkway
Ravenna, OH 44266
Fax: (330) 296-2159
E-mail: sonyah@marcogrp.com
Phone: (330) 297-7319

**Fortis College: Winter Park**
www.fortis.edu
Admissions
1573 West Fairbanks Avenue, Suite 100
Winter Park, FL 32789
Fax: (407) 843-9828
E-mail: admissions@centralfloridacollege.edu
Phone: (407) 843-3984

**Fortis Institute: Erie**
www.fortis.edu
5757 West Twenty-Sixth Street
Erie, PA 16506
Fax: (814) 838-8642
E-mail: bborgeson@fortisinstitute.edu
Phone: (814) 838-7673

**Fortis Institute: Forty Fort**
www.fortis.edu
166 Slocum Street
Forty Fort, PA 18704-2936
Phone: (570) 288-8400

**Fox Valley Technical College**
www.fvtc.edu
Global Education and Services
1825 North Bluemound Drive
PO Box 2277
Appleton, WI 54912-2277
Fax: (920) 735-2538
E-mail: martinm@fvtc.edu
Phone: (920) 735-5677

**Framingham State University**
www.framingham.edu
Undergraduate Admissions
PO Box 9101
Framingham, MA 01701-9101
Fax: (508) 626-4017
E-mail: admissions@framingham.edu
Phone: (508) 626-4500

**Francis Marion University**
www.fmarion.edu
Admissions Office
PO Box 100547
Florence, SC 29502-0547
Fax: (843) 661-4635
E-mail: pwilson@fmarion.edu
Phone: (843) 661-1231

**Franciscan University of Steubenville**
www.franciscan.edu
International Student
1235 University Boulevard
Steubenville, OH 43952-1763
Fax: (740) 284-7225
E-mail: jdaugherty@franciscan.edu
Phone: (740) 284-5867

**Frank Phillips College**
www.fpctx.edu
Educational Services
Box 5118
Borger, TX 79008-5118
Fax: (806) 457-4225
E-mail: mcooper@fpctx.edu
Phone: (806) 457-4200 ext. 751

**Franklin & Marshall College**
www.fandm.edu
Admissions
PO Box 3003
Lancaster, PA 17604-3003
Fax: (717) 358-4389
E-mail: carly.mankus@fandm.edu
Phone: (717) 358-4760

**Franklin College**
www.franklincollege.edu
Admissions
101 Branigin Boulevard
Franklin, IN 46131-2623
Fax: (317) 738-8274
E-mail: kmccain@franklincollege.edu
Phone: (317) 738-8061

**Franklin Pierce University**
www.franklinpierce.edu
Admissions
40 University Drive
Rindge, NH 03461-0060
Fax: (603) 899-4394
E-mail: vorfeldp@franklinpierce.edu
Phone: (603) 899-4057

**Franklin University**
www.franklin.edu
International Services and Program
201 South Grant Avenue
Columbus, OH 43215-5399
Fax: (614) 224-8027
E-mail: bridget.banaszak@franklin.edu
Phone: (614) 947-6794

**Franklin W. Olin College of Engineering**
www.olin.edu
Office of Admission
1000 Olin Way
Needham, MA 02492
Fax: (781) 292-2210
E-mail: info@olin.edu
Phone: (781) 292-2202

**Freed-Hardeman University**
www.fhu.edu
International Admissions
158 East Main Street
Henderson, TN 38340
Fax: (731) 989-6047
E-mail: wscott@fhu.edu
Phone: (731) 989-6790

**Fremont College**
www.fremont.edu
Admissions
18000 Studebaker Road
Suite 900 A
Cerritos, CA 90703
Fax: (562) 809-7100
E-mail: mark.dubois@fremont.edu
Phone: (213) 355-8000

**Fresno City College**
www.fresnocitycollege.edu
International Students
1101 East University Avenue
Fresno, CA 93741
Fax: (559) 237-4232
E-mail: fccintad@fresnocitycollege.edu
Phone: (559) 442-8224

**Fresno Pacific University**
www.fresno.edu
Director of International Programs and
Services
1717 South Chestnut Avenue
Fresno, CA 93702-4709
Fax: (559) 453-7147
E-mail: apprieb@fresno.edu
Phone: (559) 453-2128

**Friends University**
www.friends.edu
Admissions
2100 West University Avenue
Wichita, KS 67213
Fax: (316) 295-5101
E-mail: admissions@friends.edu
Phone: (800) 794-6945

**Front Range Community College**
www.frontrange.edu
Office of Admissions and Records
3645 West 112th Avenue
Westminster, CO 80031
Fax: (303) 404-5150
E-mail: mary.james@frontrange.edu
Phone: (303) 678-3633

**Frostburg State University**
www.frostburg.edu
Center for International Education
101 Braddock Road
Frostburg, MD 21532-1099
Fax: (301) 687-1069
E-mail: vmgearhart@frostburg.edu
Phone: (301) 687-4714

**Full Sail University**
www.fullsail.edu
International Liaison
3300 University Boulevard
Winter Park, FL 32792-7429
E-mail: admissions@fullsail.com
Phone: (407) 679-0100

**Fullerton College**
www.fullcoll.edu
International Student Center
321 East Chapman Avenue
Fullerton, CA 92832-2095
Fax: (714) 992-9927
E-mail: pellis@fullcoll.edu
Phone: (714) 992-7078

**Fulton-Montgomery Community College**
www.fmcc.edu
Director, International Students and ESL
Programs
2805 State Highway 67
Johnstown, NY 12095
Fax: (518) 736-6518
E-mail: intl@fmcc.suny.edu
Phone: (518) 736-3622 ext. 8150

**Furman University**
www.furman.edu
Admissions
3300 Poinsett Highway
Greenville, SC 29613
Fax: (864) 294-2018
E-mail: admissions@furman.edu
Phone: (864) 294-2034

**Gadsden State Community College**
www.gadsdenstate.edu
International Student Office
1001 George Wallace Drive
PO Box 227
Gadsden, AL 35902-0227
Fax: (256) 549-8344
E-mail: bduckett@gadsdenstate.edu
Phone: (256) 549-8324

**Gallaudet University**
www.gallaudet.edu
Undergraduate Admissions
800 Florida Avenue, NE
Washington, DC 20002
Fax: (202) 651-5744
E-mail: international@gallaudet.edu
Phone: (202) 651-5750

**Galveston College**
www.gc.edu
Admissions Office
4015 Avenue Q
Galveston, TX 77550-7447
Fax: (409) 944-1501
E-mail: rroark@gc.edu
Phone: (409) 944-1227

**Gannon University**
www.gannon.edu
Global Admissions and Outreach
109 University Square
Erie, PA 16541-0001
Fax: (814) 871-5803
E-mail: cabanill001@gannon.edu
Phone: (814) 871-7254

**Garden City Community College**
www.gcccks.edu
Office of Admissions
801 Campus Drive
Garden City, KS 67846-6333
Fax: (620) 276-9650
E-mail: tammy.tabor@gcccks.edu
Phone: (620) 276-9508

**Gardner-Webb University**
www.gardner-webb.edu
Senior Associate Director of Undergraduate
Admissions
PO Box 817
Boiling Springs, NC 28017
Fax: (704) 406-4488
E-mail: asundell@gardner-webb.edu
Phone: (704) 406-4495

**Garrett College**
www.garrettcollege.edu
Director of Enrollment Management
687 Mosser Road
McHenry, MD 21541
Fax: (301) 387-3038
E-mail: admissions@garrettcollege.edu
Phone: (301) 387-3010

**Gateway Community and Technical College**
www.gateway.kctcs.edu
790 Thomas More Parkway
Edgewood, KY 41017
Fax: (859) 442-1107
Phone: (859) 442-1134

**GateWay Community College**
www.gatewaycc.edu
International Education
108 North 40th Street
Phoenix, AZ 85034
Fax: (602) 286-8072
E-mail: silva@gatewaycc.edu
Phone: (602) 286-8230

**Gateway Community College**
www.gatewayct.edu
Admissions
20 Church Street
Rm. 207
New Haven, CT 06510
Fax: (203) 285-2018
E-mail: csurface@gatewayct.edu
Phone: (203) 285-2028

**Gateway Technical College**
www.gtc.edu
International Education
400 County Road H
Elkhorn, WI 53121
Fax: (262) 741-8115
E-mail: oiss@gtc.edu
Phone: (262) 619-6546

**Genesee Community College**
www.genesee.edu
Admissions
One College Road
Batavia, NY 14020-9704
Fax: (585) 345-6842
E-mail: tmlanemartin@genesee.edu
Phone: (585) 345-6800

**Geneva College**
www.geneva.edu
Admissions Office
3200 College Avenue
Beaver Falls, PA 15010
Fax: (724) 847-6776
E-mail: jgmoomaw@geneva.edu
Phone: (724) 847-6674

**George C. Wallace Community College at Dothan**
www.wallace.edu
Admissions and Records
1141 Wallace Drive
Dothan, AL 36303-0943
Fax: (334) 983-6066
E-mail: dmccallister@wallace.edu
Phone: (334) 556-2470

**George Fox University**
www.georgefox.edu
Office of International Admissions
414 North Meridian Street #6089
Newberg, OR 97132-2697
Fax: (503) 554-3894
E-mail: tpeng@georgefox.edu
Phone: (503) 554-2614

**George Mason University**
www2.gmu.edu
Director, International Admissions
4400 University Drive, MSN 3A4
Fairfax, VA 22030-4444
Fax: (703) 993-2392
E-mail: jtkacz@gmu.edu
Phone: (703) 993-4587

**George Washington University**
www.gwu.edu/explore
2121 I Street NW, Suite 201
Washington, DC 20052
Fax: (202) 994-7266
E-mail: siskmn@gwunix2.gwu.edu
Phone: (202) 994-4940

**Georgetown College**
www.georgetowncollege.edu
Admissions
400 East College Street
Georgetown, KY 40324-1696
Fax: (502) 868-7733
E-mail: international@georgetowncollege.edu
Phone: (502) 863-8390

**Georgetown University**
www.georgetown.edu
Undergraduate Admissions
Room 103 White Gravenor Hall
37th and O Streets, NW
Washington, DC 20057
Fax: (202) 687-5084
E-mail: guadmiss@georgetown.edu
Phone: (202) 687-3600

**Georgia College and State University**
www.gcsu.edu
International Education
Campus Box 23
Milledgeville, GA 31061-0490
Fax: (478) 445-2623
E-mail: intladm@gcsu.edu
Phone: (478) 445-4789

**Georgia Gwinnett College**
www.ggc.edu
Office of Internationalization
1000 University Center Lane
Lawrenceville, GA 30043
Fax: (678) 407-5192
E-mail: cspark@ggc.edu
Phone: (678) 407-5018

**Georgia Highlands College**
www.highlands.edu
Admissions
3175 Cedartown Highway
Rome, GA 30161
Fax: (706) 295-6341
E-mail: cgraham@highlands.edu
Phone: (706) 295-6339

**Georgia Institute of Technology**
www.gatech.edu
Office of Undergraduate Admissions
Atlanta, GA 30332-0320
Fax: (404) 894-9682
E-mail: info@oie.gatech.edu
Phone: (404) 894-7475

**Georgia Military College**
www.gmc.edu
Enrollment Office
201 East Greene Street
Milledgeville, GA 31061
Fax: (478) 445-2705
E-mail: admission@gmc.cc.ga.us
Phone: (478) 387-4392

**Georgia Perimeter College**
www.gpc.edu
International Student Admissions and Advising
555 North Indian Creek Drive
Clarkston, GA 30021-2361
Fax: (678) 891-3280
E-mail: veronique.barnes@gpc.edu
Phone: (678) 891-3235

**Georgia Piedmont Technical College**
www.gptc.edu
Director, Admissions & Records
495 North Indian Creek Drive
Clarkston, GA 30021-2397
E-mail: parkerc@gptc.edu
Phone: (404) 297-9522 ext. 1152

**Georgia Southern University**
www.georgiasouthern.edu
Admissions
PO Box 8024
Statesboro, GA 30458
Fax: (912) 478-7240
E-mail: intladmissions@georgiasouthern.edu
Phone: (912) 478-5391

**Georgia Southwestern State University**
www.gsw.edu
Admissions Office
800 Georgia Southwestern State University Drive
Americus, GA 31709-9957
Fax: (229) 931-9283
E-mail: admissions@gsw.edu
Phone: (229) 928-1273

**Georgia State University**
www.gsu.edu
Admissions
Box 4009
Atlanta, GA 30302-4009
Fax: (404) 413-2002
E-mail: admissions@gsu.edu
Phone: (404) 413-2500

**Georgian Court University**
www.georgian.edu
Admissions
900 Lakewood Avenue
Lakewood, NJ 08701-2697
Fax: (732) 987-2000
E-mail: admissions@georgian.edu
Phone: (732) 987-2700

**Germanna Community College**
www.germanna.edu
Admissions and Records
2130 Germanna Highway
Locust Grove, VA 22508-2102
Fax: (540) 423-9158
Phone: (540) 834-1980

**Gettysburg College**
www.gettysburg.edu
Admissions Office
300 North Washington Street
Gettysburg, PA 17325-1400
Fax: (717) 337-6145
E-mail: intladmiss@gettysburg.edu
Phone: (717) 337-6100

**Glen Oaks Community College**
www.glenoaks.edu
Counseling Office-International Student Adviser
62249 Shimmel Road
Centreville, MI 49032-9719
Fax: (269) 467-9068
E-mail: chayden@glenoaks.edu
Phone: (269) 294-4242

Golf Academy of America: Dallas  **College addresses**

**Glendale Community College**
www.gccaz.edu
International Student Center
6000 West Olive Avenue
Glendale, AZ 85302
Fax: (623) 845-3060
E-mail: ken.bus@gccaz.edu
Phone: (623) 845-3136

**Glendale Community College**
www.glendale.edu
International Students Admission
1500 North Verdugo Road
Glendale, CA 91208-2809
Fax: (818) 549-9436
E-mail: pkamarak@glendale.edu
Phone: (818) 240-1000 ext. 5440

**Glenville State College**
www.glenville.edu
Office of Enrollment Services
200 High Street
Glenville, WV 26351-1292
Fax: (304) 462-8619
E-mail: Jeremy.Long@glenville.edu
Phone: (304) 462-4128 ext. 6137

**Global University**
www.globaluniversity.edu
International Student Services Director
1211 South Glenstone Avenue
Springfield, MO 65804
Fax: (417) 862-0863
E-mail: info@globaluniversity.edu
Phone: (417) 862-9533

**Globe Institute of Technology**
www.globe.edu
Admissions
500 Seventh Avenue, 2nd Floor
New York, NY 10018
Fax: (212) 302-9242
E-mail: admissions@globe.edu
Phone: (212) 349-4330 ext. 1697

**Globe University: Appleton**
www.globeuniversity.edu
Director of Admissions
5045 West Grande Market Drive
Grand Chute, WI 54913
E-mail: ghavlovick@globeuniversity.edu
Phone: (877) 440-1110

**Globe University: Eau Claire**
www.globeuniversity.edu
Admissions
4955 Bullis Farm Road
Eau Claire, WI 54701
E-mail: wescondo@globeuniversity.edu
Phone: (877) 530-8080

**Globe University: Green Bay**
www.globeuniversity.edu
Admissions
2620 Development Drive
Green Bay, WI 54311
E-mail: josieyoung@globeuniversity.edu
Phone: (920) 264-1600

**Globe University: La Crosse**
www.globeuniversity.edu
Admissions
2651 Midwest Drive
Onalaska, WI 54650
E-mail: rkrueger@globeuniversity.edu
Phone: (877) 540-8777

**Globe University: Madison East**
www.globeuniversity.edu
Admissions
4901 Eastpark Boulevard
Madison, WI 53718
E-mail: kgross@globeuniversity.edu
Phone: (608) 216-9400

**Globe University: Middleton**
www.globeuniversity.edu
Admissions
1345 Deming Way
Middleton, WI 53562
E-mail: lcaamal@globeuniversity.edu
Phone: (877) 830-6999

**Globe University: Minneapolis**
www.globeuniversity.edu
Admissions
80 South Eighth Street
Suite 51, IDS Center
Minneapolis, MN 55402
Fax: (612) 455-3001
E-mail: mward@globeuniversity.edu
Phone: (877) 455-3697

**Globe University: Moorhead**
www.globeuniversity.edu
Admissions
2777 34th Street South
Moorhead, MN 56560
E-mail: mrustad@globeuniversity.edu
Phone: (877) 373-7855

**Globe University: Sioux Falls**
www.globeuniversity.edu
Admissions
5101 South Broadband Lane
Sioux Falls, SD 57108
E-mail: cbuehler@globeuniversity.edu
Phone: (866) 437-0705

**Globe University: Wausau**
www.globeuniversity.edu
Admissions
1480 Country Road XX
Rothschild, WI 54474
E-mail: apalas@globeuniversity.edu
Phone: (877) 323-1313

**Globe University: Woodbury**
www.globeuniversity.edu
Admissions
8089 Globe Drive
Woodbury, MN 55125
Fax: (877) 455-3697
E-mail: mward@globeuniversity.edu
Phone: (612) 455-3000

**Goddard College**
www.goddard.edu
Admissions Office
123 Pitkin Road
Plainfield, VT 05667
Fax: (802) 454-1029
E-mail: chip.cummings@goddard.edu
Phone: (802) 454-8311 ext. 221

**God's Bible School and College**
www.gbs.edu
Office of the Registrar
1810 Young Street
Cincinnati, OH 45202-6838
Fax: (513) 721-1357
E-mail: clambeth@gbs.edu
Phone: (513) 721-7944 ext. 210

**Gogebic Community College**
www.gogebic.edu
Dean of Students
E4946 Jackson Road
Ironwood, MI 49938
Fax: (906) 307-1298
E-mail: jeanneg@gogebic.edu
Phone: (906) 932-4231 ext. 211

**Golden Gate University**
www.ggu.edu
536 Mission Street
San Francisco, CA 94105-2968
Fax: (415) 442-7807
E-mail: info@ggu.edu
Phone: (415) 442-7800

**Golden West College**
www.goldenwestcollege.edu
International Students Office
15744 Golden West Street, Box 2748
Huntington Beach, CA 92647-2748
Fax: (714) 895-8960
E-mail: mlyon@gwc.cccd.edu
Phone: (714) 895-8146

**Goldey-Beacom College**
www.gbc.edu
Director of Admissions
4701 Limestone Road
Wilmington, DE 19808
Fax: (302) 996-5408
E-mail: ebylw@gbc.edu
Phone: (302) 225-6289

**Goldfarb School of Nursing at Barnes-Jewish College**
www.barnesjewishcollege.edu
Office of Student Services
4483 Duncan Avenue
St. Louis, MO 63110-1091
Fax: (314) 362-9250
E-mail: MJaime@bjc.org
Phone: (314) 454-8686

**Golf Academy of America: Dallas**
www.golfacademy.edu/dallas
1861 Valley View Lane, Suite 100
Farmers Branch, TX 75234
E-mail: dallas.info@golfacademy.edu

**Golf Academy of America: Myrtle Beach**
www.golfacademy.edu
7373 North Scottsdale Road, Suite B-100
Scottsdale, AZ 82253
Fax: (480) 905-8705
E-mail: myrtlebeach.info@golfacademy.edu
Phone: (480) 236-0481

**Golf Academy of America: Orlando**
www.golfacademy.edu
7373 North Scottsdale Road, Suite B-100
Scottsdale, AZ 85253
E-mail: orlando.info@golfacademy.edu
Phone: (407) 699-1990

**Golf Academy of America: Phoenix**
www.golfacademy.edu
2031 North Arizona Avenue, Suite 2
Chandler, AZ 85225
Fax: (480) 905-8705
E-mail: phoenix.info@golfacademy.edu
Phone: (480) 857-1574

**Golf Academy of America: San Diego**
www.golfacademy.edu
1950 Camino Vida Roble, Suite 125
Carlsbad, CA 92008
E-mail: henry.salgado@golfacademy.edu
Phone: (760) 734-1208

**Gonzaga University**
www.gonzaga.edu
International Student Programs
502 East Boone Avenue
Spokane, WA 99258-0001
Fax: (509) 313-5814
E-mail: isp@gonzaga.edu
Phone: (509) 313-6563

**Goodwin College**
www.goodwin.edu
Enrollment Management
One Riverside Drive
East Hartford, CT 06118-9980
Fax: (860) 291-9550
E-mail: dnoonan@goodwin.edu
Phone: (860) 528-4111

**Gordon College**
www.gordon.edu
Admissions Office
255 Grapevine Road
Wenham, MA 01984-1899
Fax: (978) 867-4682
E-mail: admissions@gordon.edu
Phone: (866) 464-6736

**Gordon State College**
www.gordonstate.edu
Admissions
419 College Drive
Barnesville, GA 30204
Fax: (678) 359-5080
E-mail: nathanb@gordonstate.edu
Phone: (678) 359-5021

**Goshen College**
www.goshen.edu
Admissions
1700 South Main Street
Goshen College
Goshen, IN 46526-4724
Fax: (574) 535-7609
E-mail: admission@goshen.edu
Phone: (574) 535-7535

**Goucher College**
www.goucher.edu
Admissions
1021 Dulaney Valley Road
Baltimore, MD 21204-2753
Fax: (410) 337-6354
E-mail: csurbeck@goucher.edu
Phone: (410) 337-6100

**Governors State University**
www.govst.edu
Office of International Services
One University Parkway
University Park, IL 60484
Fax: (708) 235-7372
E-mail: ois@govst.edu
Phone: (708) 235-7611 ext. 7611

**Grace University**
www.graceuniversity.edu
Admissions Office
1311 South Ninth Street
Omaha, NE 68108-3629
Fax: (402) 449-2999
E-mail: admissions@graceuniversity.edu
Phone: (402) 449-2831

**Graceland University**
www.graceland.edu
Admissions
1 University Place
Lamoni, IA 50140
Fax: (641) 784-5480
E-mail: brown@graceland.edu
Phone: (641) 784-5149

**Grambling State University**
www.gram.edu
Center for International Affairs & Programs
403 Main Street, GSU Box 4200
100 Founder Street- Grambling Hall, Suite 51
Grambling, LA 71245
Fax: (318) 274-6172
E-mail: arnoldg@gram.edu
Phone: (318) 274-6432

**Grand Canyon University**
www.gcu.edu
3300 West Camelback Road
Phoenix, AZ 85017-8562
Fax: (602) 589-2017
E-mail: admissionsonline@gcu.edu
Phone: (800) 800-9776

**Grand Rapids Community College**
www.grcc.edu
Office of Admissions
143 Bostwick Avenue NE
Grand Rapids, MI 49503-3295
Fax: (616) 234-4107
E-mail: internationalstudents@grcc.edu
Phone: (616) 234-3567

**Grand Valley State University**
www.gvsu.edu
Office of Admssions
1 Campus Drive
Allendale, MI 49401-9403
Fax: (616) 331-2000
E-mail: go2gvsu@gvsu.edu
Phone: (800) 748-0246

**Grand View University**
www.admissions.grandview.edu
Admissions
1200 Grandview Avenue
Des Moines, IA 50316-1599
Fax: (515) 263-2974
E-mail: apiedras@grandview.edu
Phone: (515) 263-2801

**Granite State College**
www.granite.edu
Registrar's Office
25 Hall Street
Concord, NH 03301-7317
Fax: (603) 513-1356
E-mail: gsc.admissions@granite.edu
Phone: (603) 228-3000 ext. 339

**Grantham University**
www.grantham.edu
Vice President of Student Enrollment
16025 W 113th Street
Lenexa, KS 66219
Fax: (816) 595-5757
E-mail: admissions@grantham.edu
Phone: (913) 309-4430

**Gratz College**
www.gratz.edu
Admissions
7605 Old York Road
Melrose Park, PA 19027
Fax: (215) 635-7399
E-mail: admissions@gratz.edu
Phone: (215) 635-7300 ext. 150

**Grays Harbor College**
www.ghc.edu
Coordinator for Student Programs
1620 Edward P Smith Drive
Aberdeen, WA 98520
Fax: (360) 538-4293
E-mail: csvoboda@ghc.edu
Phone: (360) 538-4078

**Grayson College**
www.grayson.edu
International Office
6101 Grayson Drive
Denison, TX 75020
Fax: (903) 463-8758
E-mail: mcclennyb@grayson.edu
Phone: (903) 463-8749

**Great Basin College**
www.gbcnv.edu
Admissions and Records
1500 College Parkway
Elko, NV 89801
Fax: (755) 753-2311
E-mail: admissions@gbcnv.edu
Phone: (755) 753-2361

**Great Bay Community College**
www.greatbay.edu
Admissions
320 Corporate Drive
Portsmouth, NH 03801
Fax: (603) 772-1198
E-mail: lshennett@ccsnh.edu
Phone: (603) 775-2306

**Green Mountain College**
www.greenmtn.edu
Admissions
One Brennan Circle
Poultney, VT 05764
Fax: (802) 287-8099
E-mail: charles.harcourt@greenmtn.edu
Phone: (802) 287-8000

**Green River College**
www.greenriver.edu
International Programs
12401 SE 320th Street
Auburn, WA 98092
Fax: (253) 333-4950
E-mail: wstewart@greenriver.edu
Phone: (253) 288-3300

**Greenfield Community College**
www.gcc.mass.edu
Office of Admission
One College Drive
Greenfield, MA 01301
Fax: (413) 775-1827
E-mail: hudgikm@gcc.mass.edu
Phone: (413) 775-1810

**Greensboro College**
www.greensboro.edu
Director of Admissions
815 West Market Street
Greensboro, NC 27401-1875
Fax: (336) 378-0154
E-mail: julies@greensboro.edu
Phone: (336) 272-7102 ext. 389

**Greenville College**
www.greenville.edu
Admissions
315 East College Avenue
Greenville, IL 62246
Fax: (618) 664-9841
E-mail: admissions@greenville.edu
Phone: (618) 664-7100

**Greenville Technical College**
www.gvltec.edu
Admissions Office
PO Box 5616
Greenville, SC 29606-5616
Fax: (864) 250-8534
E-mail: greenvilletech@gvltec.edu
Phone: (864) 250-8000

**Grinnell College**
www.grinnell.edu
Admission
1103 Park Street, 2nd Floor
Grinnell, IA 50112-1690
Fax: (641) 269-4800
E-mail: admission@grinnell.edu
Phone: (641) 269-3600

**Grossmont College**
www.grossmont.edu
Admissions Office
8800 Grossmont College Drive
El Cajon, CA 92020
Fax: (619) 644-7083
E-mail: mika.miller@gcccd.edu
Phone: (619) 644-7182

**Grove City College**
www.gcc.edu
Admissions Office
100 Campus Drive
Grove City, PA 16127-2104
Fax: (724) 458-3395
E-mail: admissions@gcc.edu
Phone: (724) 458-2100

**Guilford College**
www.guilford.edu
Admissions/Enrollment
Admissions, New Garden Hall
5800 West Friendly Avenue
Greensboro, NC 27410-4108
Fax: (336) 316-2954
E-mail: kellyem@guilford.edu
Phone: (336) 316-2124

**Guilford Technical Community College**
www.gtcc.edu
Foreign Student Adviser/Counselor
PO Box 309
Jamestown, NC 27282
Fax: (336) 819-2022
E-mail: admackeywhitworth@gtcc.edu
Phone: (336) 334-4822 ext. 55081

**Gulf Coast State College**
www.gulfcoast.edu
Graduation Specialist
5230 West US Highway 98
Panama City, FL 32401-1041
Fax: (850) 913-3308
E-mail: mdubois@gulfcoast.edu
Phone: (850) 769-1551 ext. 4862

**Gupton Jones College of Funeral Service**
www.gupton-jones.edu
5141 Snapfinger Woods Drive
Decatur, GA 30035
Fax: (770) 593-1891
E-mail: jahinz@yahoo.com
Phone: (770) 593-2257

**Gustavus Adolphus College**
www.gustavus.edu
Center for International and Cultural
Education
800 West College Avenue
St. Peter, MN 56082
Fax: (507) 933-7900
E-mail: jeffa@gustavus.edu
Phone: (507) 933-7493

**Gutenberg College**
www.gutenberg.edu
1883 University Street
Eugene, OR 97403
E-mail: office@gutenberg.edu
Phone: (541) 683-514

**Gwinnett College**
www.gwinnettcollege.edu
Campus Director
4230 Highway 29
Suite 11
Lilburn, GA 30047
Fax: (770) 381-0454
E-mail: admissions@gwinnettcollege.com
Phone: (770) 381-7200

**Gwinnett Technical College**
www.gwinnetttech.edu
5150 Sugarloaf Parkway
Lawrenceville, GA 30043-5702
E-mail: admissions@gwinnetttech.edu
Phone: (678) 762-7580 ext. 434

**Gwynedd Mercy University**
www.gmercyu.edu
Admissions Office
1325 Sumneytown Pike
PO Box 901
Gwynedd Valley, PA 19437-0901
Fax: (215) 542-4610
E-mail: admissions@gmercyu.edu
Phone: (800) 342-5462

**Halifax Community College**
www.halifaxcc.edu
Director of Admissions
100 College Drive, Drawer 809
Weldon, NC 27890
Fax: (252) 538-4311
E-mail: charrell821@halifaxcc.edu
Phone: (252) 536-7220

**Hamilton College**
www.hamilton.edu
Admissions Office
198 College Hill Road
Office of Admission
Clinton, NY 13323-1293
Fax: (315) 859-4457
E-mail: cflores@hamilton.edu
Phone: (315) 859-4011

**Hamline University**
www.hamline.edu
Undergraduate Admission
1536 Hewitt Avenue
MS-C1930
St. Paul, MN 55104-1284
Fax: (651) 523-2458
E-mail: admission@hamline.edu
Phone: (651) 523-2207

**Hampden-Sydney College**
www.hsc.edu
Admissions
PO Box 667
Hampden-Sydney, VA 23943
Fax: (434) 223-6346
E-mail: jferguson@hsc.edu
Phone: (434) 223-6120

**Hampshire College**
www.hampshire.edu
Admissions
893 West Street
Amherst, MA 01002-3359
E-mail: crAD@hampshire.edu
Phone: (413) 559-6697

**Hampton University**
www.hamptonu.edu
Admissions
Office of Admission
Hampton University
Hampton, VA 23668
Fax: (757) 727-5095
E-mail: admissions@hamptonu.edu
Phone: (757) 727-5328

**Hannibal-LaGrange University**
www.hlg.edu
International Student Office
2800 Palmyra Road
Hannibal, MO 63401
Fax: (573) 221-6594
E-mail: Virginia.Gray@hlg.edu
Phone: (573) 629-3031

**Hanover College**
www.hanover.edu
Admission
517 Ball Drive
Hanover, IN 47243-0108
Fax: (812) 866-7031
E-mail: hidalgo@hanover.edu
Phone: (800) 213-2178

**Harcum College**
www.harcum.edu
Center for International Programs or
Admissions
750 Montgomery Avenue
Bryn Mawr, PA 19010-3476
Fax: (610) 526-6191
E-mail: elaharcum@harcum.edu
Phone: (610) 526-6116

**Hardin-Simmons University**
www.hsutx.edu
PO Box 16050
Abilene, TX 79698-0001
Fax: (325) 671-2115
E-mail: jjones@hsutx.edu
Phone: (325) 670-1207

**Harding University**
www.harding.edu
International Student Advisor
915 East Market Avenue
HU 12255
Searcy, AR 72149-2255
Fax: (501) 279-4122
E-mail: nboyd@harding.edu
Phone: (501) 279-4023

**Harford Community College**
www.harford.edu
Admissions
401 Thomas Run Road
Bel Air, MD 21015
Fax: (443) 412-2169
E-mail: jlares@harford.edu
Phone: (443) 412-2562

**Harper College**
www.harpercollege.edu
International Students Office
1200 West Algonquin Road
Palatine, IL 60067-7398
Fax: (847) 925-6048
E-mail: jizumika@harpercollege.edu
Phone: (847) 925-6756

**Harris-Stowe State University**
www.hssu.edu
Office of Admissions
3026 Laclede Avenue
St. Louis, MO 63103-2199
Fax: (314) 340-3555
E-mail: admissions@hssu.edu
Phone: (314) 340-3300

**Harrisburg Area Community College**
www.hacc.edu
International Admissions
One HACC Drive
Harrisburg, PA 17110-2999
Fax: (717) 231-7674
E-mail: jlmatoly@hacc.edu
Phone: (717) 780-2403

**Harrisburg University of Science and Technology**
www.harrisburgu.edu
Admissions
326 Market Street
Harrisburg, PA 17101-2208
Fax: (717) 901-3150
E-mail: Admissions@HarrisburgU.edu
Phone: (717) 901-5150

**Harrison College: Grove City**
www.harrison.edu
3880 Jackpot Road
Grove City, OH 43123
E-mail: admissions@harrison.edu

**Harrison College: Indianapolis**
www.harrison.edu
International Student Admissions
550 East Washington Street
Indianapolis, IN 46204
Fax: (317) 264-5650
E-mail: Admissions@harrison.edu
Phone: (888) 544-4422

**Hartnell College**
www.hartnell.edu
International Student Services
411 Central Avenue
Salinas, CA 93901
Fax: (831) 755-6759
E-mail: ihaneta@hartnell.edu
Phone: (831) 755-6711

**Hartwick College**
www.hartwick.edu
Senior Assistant Director of Admissions
1 Hartwick Drive
Oneonta, NY 13820-4022
Fax: (607) 431-4102
E-mail: admissions@hartiwck.edu
Phone: (607) 431-4150

**Harvard College**
www.college.harvard.edu
Undergraduate Admissions Office
86 Brattle Street
Cambridge, MA 02138
Fax: (617) 495-8328
E-mail: intladm@fas.harvard.edu
Phone: (617) 495-1551

**Harvey Mudd College**
https://www.hmc.edu/
Admission
301 Platt Boulevard
Claremont, CA 91711-5901
Fax: (909) 607-7046
E-mail: posgood@hmc.edu
Phone: (909) 621-8011

**Haskell Indian Nations University**
www.haskell.edu
155 Indian Avenue, Box #5031
Lawrence, KS 66046-4800
Fax: (785) 749-8429
E-mail: admissions@haskell.edu
Phone: (785) 749-8454

**Hastings College**
www.hastings.edu
Admissions Office
710 North Turner Avenue
Hastings, NE 68901-7621
Fax: (402) 461-7490
E-mail: smeeske@hastings.edu
Phone: (402) 461-7398

**Haverford College**
www.haverford.edu
Admission
370 Lancaster Avenue
Haverford, PA 19041-1392
Fax: (610) 896-1338
E-mail: mmaier@haverford.edu
Phone: (610) 896-1350

**Hawaii Pacific University**
www.hpu.edu
Admissions
1 Aloha Tower Drive
Honolulu, HI 96813
Fax: (808) 544-1136
E-mail: international@hpu.edu
Phone: (808) 687-7020

**Hawaii Tokai International College**
www.hawaiitokai.edu
Office of Admissions
91-971 Farrington Highway
Kapolei, HI 96707-2657
Fax: (808) 983-4173
E-mail: admissions@tokai.edu
Phone: (808) 983-4202

**Hazard Community and Technical College**
www.hazard.kctcs.edu
Office of Diversity
One Community College Drive
Hazard, KY 41701
Fax: (606) 487-3614
E-mail: Elbert.Hagans@kctcs.edu
Phone: (800) 246-7521 ext. 73178

**Heartland Community College**
www.heartland.edu
Student Services
1500 West Raab Road
Normal, IL 61761
Fax: (309) 268-7992
E-mail: ben.stone@heartland.edu
Phone: (309) 268-8010

**Heidelberg University**
www.heidelberg.edu
Office of Admission
310 East Market Street
Tiffin, OH 44883-2462
Fax: (419) 448-2334
E-mail: adminfo@heidelberg.edu
Phone: (419) 448-2330

**Hellenic College/Holy Cross**
www.hchc.edu
Admissions
50 Goddard Avenue
Brookline, MA 02445
Fax: (617) 850-1460
E-mail: admissions@hchc.edu
Phone: (617) 850-1260

**Henderson Community College**
www.henderson.kctcs.edu
Admissions & Records
2660 South Green Street
Henderson, KY 42420
Fax: (270) 831-9612
E-mail: cary.conley@kctcs.edu
Phone: (270) 831-9610

**Henderson State University**
www.hsu.edu
Director of International Student Program
1100 Henderson Street
Box 7560
Arkadelphia, AR 71999-0001
Fax: (870) 230-5419
E-mail: smithc@hsu.edu
Phone: (870) 230-5265

**Hendrix College**
www.hendrix.edu
Office of Admission
1600 Washington Avenue
Conway, AR 72032-3080
Fax: (501) 450-3843
E-mail: lucio@hendrix.edu
Phone: (501) 450-1362

**Hennepin Technical College**
www.hennepintech.edu
Assistant Director of Admissions
9000 Brooklyn Boulevard
Brooklyn Park, MN 55445
Fax: (952) 952-1391
E-mail:
yolanda.matinezpineda@hennepintech.edu
Phone: (763) 488-2550

**Henry Ford College**
www.hfcc.edu
5101 Evergreen Road
Dearborn, MI 48128
Fax: (313) 845-9891
E-mail: pdwebb1@hfcc.edu
Phone: (313) 317-6519

**Heritage Christian University**
www.hcu.edu
Office of Admissions
3625 Helton Drive
PO Box HCU
Florence, AL 35630
Fax: (256) 766-9289
E-mail: hcu@hcu.edu
Phone: (256) 766-6610

**Heritage University**
www.heritage.edu
Student Services Office
3240 Fort Road
Toppenish, WA 98948-9599
Fax: (509) 865-8659
E-mail: collins_j@heritage.edu
Phone: (509) 865-8500 ext. 2020

**Herkimer County Community College**
www.herkimer.edu
International Programs
100 Reservoir Road
Herkimer, NY 13350-1598
Fax: (315) 866-0062
E-mail: gambierjm@herkimer.edu
Phone: (315) 866-0300 ext. 8318

**Herzing University**
www.herzing.edu
1600 South Arlington Street, Suite 100
Akron, OH 44306
Fax: (330) 724-9688
E-mail: info@akr.herzing.edu
Phone: (330) 724-1600

**Herzing University: Atlanta**
www.herzing.edu
Admissions
3393 Peachtree Road NE, Suite 1003
Atlanta, GA 30326
Fax: (404) 816-5576
E-mail: rhinton@atl.herzing.edu
Phone: (404) 816-4533

**Herzing University: Birmingham**
www.herzing.edu
280 West Valley Avenue
Birmingham, AL 35209
Fax: (205) 916-2807
E-mail: admiss@bhm.herzing.edu
Phone: (205) 916-2800

**Herzing University: Brookfield**
www.herzing.edu
555 South Executive Drive
Brookfield, WI 53005
E-mail: info@brk.herzing.edu

**Herzing University: Kenner**
www.herzing.edu
2500 Williams Boulevard
Kenner, LA 70062
Fax: (504) 733-0020
E-mail: info@nor.herzing.edu
Phone: (504) 733-0074

**Herzing University: Kenosha**
www.herzing.edu
4006 Washington Road
Kenosha, WI 53144
E-mail: info@ken.herzing.edu

**Herzing University: Madison**
www.herzing.edu/madison
Admissions Advisor
5218 East Terrace Drive
Madison, WI 53718
Fax: (608) 249-8593
E-mail: info@msn.herzing.edu
Phone: (608) 249-6611

**Herzing University: Minneapolis**
www.herzing.edu
5700 West Broadway
Minneapolis, MN 55428
E-mail: info@mpls.herzing.edu
Phone: (763) 535-3000

**Herzing University: Omaha School of Massage Therapy and Healthcare**
www.osmhc.com
9748 Park Drive
Omaha, NE 68127
E-mail: info@osmhc.com

**Herzing University: Toledo**
www.herzing.edu
5212 Hill Avenue
Toledo, OH 43615
E-mail: info@tol.herzing.edu

**Herzing University: Winter Park**
www.herzing.edu
1595 South Semoran Boulevard
Winter Park, FL 32792
Fax: (401) 418-0501
E-mail: info@orl.herzing.edu
Phone: (407) 478-0500

**Hesston College**
www.hesston.edu
Director of International Admissions
Box 3000
Hesston, KS 67062-2093
Fax: (620) 327-8300
E-mail: daveo@hesston.edu
Phone: (620) 327-8133

**Hibbing Community College**
www.hibbing.edu
Student Services
1515 East 25th Street
Hibbing, MN 55746
Fax: (218) 263-2992
E-mail: karidoucette@hibbing.edu
Phone: (218) 262-6735

**High Point University**
www.highpoint.edu
Admissions
One University Parkway
Box 3188
High Point, NC 27268-3598
Fax: (336) 888-6382
E-mail: jsmith9@highpoint.edu
Phone: (336) 841-9144

**Highline College**
www.highline.edu
International Student Programs
2400 South 240th Street
PO Box 98000
Des Moines, WA 98198-9800
Fax: (206) 870-3782
E-mail: mkuwasaki@highline.edu
Phone: (206) 878-3710 ext. 3725

**Hilbert College**
www.hilbert.edu
Admissions
5200 South Park Avenue
Hamburg, NY 14075-1597
Fax: (716) 926-8886
E-mail: jyale@hilbert.edu
Phone: (800) 649-8003

**Hill College**
www.hillcollege.edu
Admissions
112 Lamar Drive
Hillsboro, TX 76645
Fax: (254) 582-7591
E-mail: cclay@hillcollege.edu
Phone: (254) 659-7606

**Hillsborough Community College**
www.hccfl.edu
International Education
Box 31127
Tampa, FL 33631-3127
Fax: (813) 253-7070
E-mail: acarlson6@hccfl.edu
Phone: (813) 253-7397

**Hillsdale College**
www.hillsdale.edu
Admissions
33 East College Street
Hillsdale, MI 49242
Fax: (517) 607-2223
E-mail: admissions@hillsdale.edu
Phone: (517) 607-2327

**Hillsdale Free Will Baptist College**
www.hc.edu
PO Box 7208
Moore, OK 73153
Fax: (405) 912-9050
E-mail: tmorris@hc.edu
Phone: (405) 912-9000 ext. 29111

**Hinds Community College**
www.hindscc.edu
Foreign Student Counseling Office
HCC Office of Admissions and Records
PO Box 1100
Raymond, MS 39154-1100
E-mail: records@hindscc.edu
Phone: (601) 857-3219

**Hiram College**
www.hiram.edu
PO Box 96
Hiram, OH 44234
Fax: (330) 569-5944
E-mail: interal@hiram.edu
Phone: (330) 569-6103

**Hiwassee College**
www.hiwassee.edu
225 Hiwassee College Drive
Office of Admission
Madisonville, TN 37354-6099
Fax: (423) 545-9575
E-mail: enroll@hiwassee.edu
Phone: (423) 420-1892

**Hobart and William Smith Colleges**
www.hws.edu
Admissions
629 South Main Street
Geneva, NY 14456
Fax: (315) 781-3914
E-mail: admissions@hws.edu
Phone: (315) 781-3622

**Hocking College**
www.hocking.edu
3301 Hocking Parkway
Nelsonville, OH 45764-9704
Fax: (740) 753-7065
E-mail: admissions@hocking.edu
Phone: (740) 753-7049

**Hodges University**
www.hodges.edu
Admissions
2655 Northbrooke Drive
Naples, FL 34119
Fax: (239) 513-9071
E-mail: bpassey@hodges.edu
Phone: (239) 513-1122

**Hofstra University**
www.hofstra.edu
Office of Admission
Admissions Center, 100 Hofstra University
Hempstead, NY 11549
Fax: (516) 463-5100
E-mail: Steven.C.Richman@hofstra.edu
Phone: (516) 463-6292

**Hollins University**
www.hollins.edu
Admission Office
PO Box 9707
8060 Quadrangle Lane
Roanoke, VA 24020-1707
Fax: (540) 362-6218
E-mail: huadm@hollins.edu
Phone: (800) 456-9595

**Holy Apostles College and Seminary**
www.holyapostles.edu
Admissions
33 Prospect Hill Road
Cromwell, CT 06416-2005
Fax: (860) 632-3030
E-mail: admissions@holyapostles.edu
Phone: (860) 632-3012

**Holy Cross College**
www.hcc-nd.edu
Admissions
54515 State Road 933 North
PO Box 308
Notre Dame, IN 46556-0308
Fax: (574) 239-8323
E-mail: cstaubin@hcc-nd.edu
Phone: (574) 239-8397

**Holy Family University**
www.holyfamily.edu
Admissions
9801 Frankford Avenue
Philadelphia, PA 19114-2009
Fax: (215) 281-1022
E-mail: admissions@holyfamily.edu
Phone: (215) 637-3050

**Holy Names University**
www.hnu.edu
Undergraduate Admission
3500 Mountain Boulevard
Oakland, CA 94619-1699
Fax: (510) 436-1325
E-mail: admission@hnu.edu
Phone: (800) 430-1321

**Holyoke Community College**
www.hcc.edu
Office of Admissions
303 Homestead Avenue
Holyoke, MA 01040
Fax; (413) 552-2192
E-mail: admissions@hcc.edu
Phone: (413) 552-2321

**Hondros College**
www.nursing.hondros.edu
4140 Executive Parkway
Westerville, OH 43081-3855
Fax: (614) 508-7280
E-mail: admissions@hondros.edu

**Hood College**
www.hood.edu
Office of Admission
401 Rosemont Avenue
Frederick, MD 21701-8575
Fax: (301) 696-3819
E-mail: international@hood.edu
Phone: (301) 696-3400

**Hope College**
www.hope.edu
Admissions
69 East 10th Street
PO Box 9000
Holland, MI 49422-9000
Fax: (616) 395-7130
E-mail: admissions@hope.edu
Phone: (616) 395-7850

**Hope International University**
www.hiu.edu
International Student Programs
2500 East Nutwood Avenue
Fullerton, CA 92831-3199
Fax: (714) 681-7423
E-mail: isp@hiu.edu
Phone: (714) 879-3901 ext. 2234

**Horizon University**
www.horizonuniversity.edu
5331 Mount Alifan Drive
San Diego, CA 92111
Fax: (858) 695-9527
E-mail: info@horizoncollege.org
Phone: (858) 695-8587

**Horry-Georgetown Technical College**
www.hgtc.edu
Admissions
PO Box 261966
2050 Highway 501 East
Conway, SC 29528-6066
Fax: (843) 349-7501
E-mail: admissions@hgtc.edu
Phone: (843) 349-5277

**Houghton College**
www.houghton.edu
Office of Admission
1 Willard Avenue/PO Box 128
Houghton, NY 14744-0128
Fax: (585) 567-9522
E-mail: admission@houghton.edu
Phone: (585) 567-9353

**Housatonic Community College**
www.hcc.commnet.edu
Admissions
900 Lafayette Boulevard
Bridgeport, CT 06604-4704
Fax: (203) 332-5123
E-mail: egraham@hcc.commnet.edu
Phone: (203) 332-5290

**Houston Baptist University**
www.hbu.edu
International Student Coordinator
7502 Fondren Road
Houston, TX 77074-3298
Fax: (281) 649-3217
E-mail: sbedo@hbu.edu
Phone: (281) 649-3000 ext. 3292

**Houston Community College System**
www.hccs.edu
Office of International Student Services and
Study Abroad
PO Box 667517, MC 1136
Houston, TX 77266-7517
Fax: (713) 718-2112
E-mail: oiss.international@hccs.edu
Phone: (713) 718-8521

**Howard Community College**
www.howardcc.edu
Admissions and Advising
10901 Little Patuxent Parkway
Columbia, MD 21044-3197
Fax: (443) 518-4589
E-mail: intlstudent@howardcc.edu
Phone: (443) 518-4420

**Howard Payne University**
www.hputx.edu
Admission Office
1000 Fisk Street
Brownwood, TX 76801-2794
Fax: (325) 649-8901
E-mail: cmangrum@hputx.edu
Phone: (325) 649-8027

**Howard University**
www.howard.edu
Visa and Administrative Coordinator
2400 Sixth Street NW
Suite 111
Washington, DC 20059
Fax: (202) 238-8521
E-mail: pugbong@howard.edu
Phone: (202) 806-2777

**Hudson County Community College**
www.hccc.edu
Enrollment Services
70 Sip Avenue, 1st Floor
Jersey City, NJ 07306
Fax: (201) 714-2136
E-mail: internationalstudents@hccc.edu
Phone: (201) 360-4136

**Hudson Valley Community College**
www.hvcc.edu
International Student Office
80 Vandenburgh Avenue
Troy, NY 12180
Fax: (518) 629-4576
E-mail: j.deitchman@hvcc.edu
Phone: (518) 629-7567

**Hult International Business School**
www.hult.edu/en/undergraduate/bachelor-of-
business-administration/
E-mail: jessica.szubart@hult.edu

**Humacao Community College**
www.hccpr.edu
Admissions
PO Box 9139
Georgetti St. #69
Humacao, PR 00792-9139
Fax: (787) 850-1577
E-mail: adela.aponte@hccpr.edu
Phone: (787) 852-1430 ext. 225

**Humboldt State University**
www.humboldt.edu
Center for International Programs
One Harpst Street
Arcata, CA 95521-8299
Fax: (707) 826-3939
E-mail: mefford@humbodlt.edu
Phone: (707) 826-4142

**Humphreys College**
www.humphreys.edu
Enrollment Management
6650 Inglewood Avenue
Stockton, CA 95207-3896
Fax: (209) 478-8721
E-mail: salopez@humphreys.edu
Phone: (209) 478-0800 ext. 202

**Huntingdon College**
www.huntingdon.edu
Office of Admission
1500 East Fairview Avenue
Montgomery, AL 36106-2148
Fax: (334) 833-4347
E-mail: admiss@huntingdon.edu
Phone: (334) 833-4497

**Huntington College of Health Sciences**
www.hchs.edu
117 Legacy View Way
Knoxville, TN 37918
Fax: (865) 524-8339
E-mail: kgalyon@hchs.edu
Phone: (865) 524-8079

**Huntington University**
www.huntington.edu
Admissions
2303 College Avenue
Huntington, IN 46750-1237
Fax: (260) 358-3699
E-mail: admissions@huntington.edu
Phone: (260) 359-4000

**Huntsville Bible College**
www.hbc1.edu
906 Oakwood Avenue
Huntsville, AL 35811-1632
E-mail: huntsvillebiblecollege@gmail.com
Phone: (256) 469-7536

**Husson University**
www.husson.edu
International Initiatives
1 College Circle
Bangor, ME 04401-2999
Fax: (207) 941-7935
E-mail: groverc@husson.edu
Phone: (207) ext. 7621

**Huston-Tillotson University**
www.htu.edu
Enrollment Management
900 Chicon Street
Austin, TX 78702-2795
Fax: (512) 505-3190
E-mail: slstinson@htu.edu
Phone: (512) 505-3027

**Hutchinson Community College**
www.hutchcc.edu
Student Success Center
1300 North Plum
Hutchinson, KS 67501
Fax: (620) 728-8155
E-mail: ellise@hutchcc.edu
Phone: (620) 665-3439

**IBMC College: Fort Collins**
www.ibmc.edu
3842 South Mason Street
Fort Collins, CO 80525
Fax: (970) 223-2796
E-mail: info@ibmc.edu
Phone: (970) 223-2669

**ICPR Junior College**
www.icprjc.edu
Marketing Manager
PO Box 190304
San Juan, PR 00919-0304
Fax: (787) 622-3416
E-mail: vasencio@icprjc.edu
Phone: (787) 753-6335 ext. 4101

**Idaho State University**
www.isu.edu
International Programs Office
921 South Eighth Stop 8270
Pocatello, ID 83209-8270
Fax: (208) 282-2924
E-mail: ipomail@isu.edu
Phone: (208) 282-4320

**Illinois Central College**
www.icc.edu
International Education Program Director
1 College Drive
East Peoria, IL 61635-0001
Fax: (309) 694-8461
E-mail: Barbara.Burton@icc.edu
Phone: (309) 694-8817

**Illinois College**
www.ic.edu
Admission
1101 West College Avenue
Jacksonville, IL 62650
Fax: (217) 245-3034
E-mail: rlbystry@ic.edu
Phone: (217) 245-3030

**Illinois Eastern Community Colleges:
Frontier Community College**
www.iecc.edu/fcc
Program Director of International Students
Two Frontier Drive
Fairfield, IL 62837-9801
Fax: (618) 392-3293
E-mail: swansonp@iecc.edu
Phone: (618) 395-7777

**Illinois Eastern Community Colleges:
Lincoln Trail College**
www.iecc.edu/ltc
Program Director of International Students
11220 State Highway 1
Robinson, IL 62454-5707
Fax: (618) 392-3293
E-mail: swansonp@iecc.edu
Phone: (618) 395-7777

**Illinois Eastern Community Colleges: Olney
Central College**
www.iecc.edu/occ
Program Director of International Students
305 North West Street
Olney, IL 62450
Fax: (618) 392-3293
E-mail: swansonp@iecc.edu
Phone: (618) 395-7777

**Illinois Eastern Community Colleges:
Wabash Valley College**
www.iecc.edu/wvc
Program Director of International Students
2200 College Drive
Mount Carmel, IL 62863-2657
Fax: (618) 392-3293
E-mail: swansonp@iecc.edu
Phone: (618) 395-7777

**Illinois Institute of Art: Chicago**
www.ilic.artinstitutes.edu
350 North Orleans Street
Chicago, IL 60654
E-mail: antonj@aii.edu
Phone: (312) 280-3500

**Illinois Institute of Art: Schaumburg**
www.artinstitutes.edu/schaumburg
1000 North Plaza Drive
Suite 100
Schaumburg, IL 60173
Fax: (847) 619-3064
E-mail: ILISadmissions@aii.edu
Phone: (847) 619-3450

**Illinois Institute of Technology**
www.iit.edu
Office of Undergraduate Admission
10 West 33rd Street
Perlstein Hall 101
Chicago, IL 60616-3793
Fax: (312) 567-6939
E-mail: amarti18@iit.edu
Phone: (312) 567-6935

**Illinois State University**
www.ilstu.edu
Office of Admissions
Campus Box 2200
Normal, IL 61790-2200
Fax: (309) 438-3932
E-mail: admissions@IllinoisState.edu
Phone: (309) 438-2181

**Illinois Wesleyan University**
www.iwu.edu
Admissions Office
PO Box 2900
Bloomington, IL 61702-2900
Fax: (309) 556-3820
E-mail: bgeraty@iwu.edu
Phone: (309) 556-3031

**Immaculata University**
www.immaculata.edu
Admissions
1145 King Road
Lillian P. Lettiere Center #118
Immaculata, PA 19345
Fax: (610) 640-0836
E-mail: admiss@immaculata.edu
Phone: (610) 647-4400 ext. 3046

**Independence Community College**
www.indycc.edu
Admissions
1057 West College Avenue
Independence, KS 67301
Fax: (620) 331-0946
E-mail: bthornton@indycc.edu
Phone: (620) 332-5495

**Independence University**
www.independence.edu
Admissions
4021 South 700 East, Suite 400
Murray, UT 84107
Fax: (619) 477-4360
E-mail: gfairley@cchs.edu
Phone: (619) 477-4800 ext. 355

**Indian River State College**
www.irsc.edu
3209 Virginia Avenue
Fort Pierce, FL 34981-5596
Fax: (772) 462-4699
E-mail: tspivey@ircc.edu
Phone: (772) 462-4327

**Indiana Institute of Technology**
www.indianatech.edu
Assistant Director of International Students
Admission and Orientation
1600 East Washington Boulevard
Fort Wayne, IN 46803
Fax: (260) 422-7696
E-mail: srrodriguez@indianatech.edu
Phone: (260) 422-5561 ext. 2251

**Indiana State University**
www.indstate.edu
Center for Global Engagement
Office of Admissions, John W. Moore
Welcome Center
318 North 6th Street
Terre Haute, IN 47809-9989
Fax: (812) 237-8023
E-mail: isu-ips@mail.indstate.edu
Phone: (812) 237-2440

**Indiana University Bloomington**
www.iub.edu
International Admissions
300 North Jordan Avenue
Bloomington, IN 47405-1106
Fax: (812) 855-4418
E-mail: ois@iu.edu
Phone: (812) 855-9086

**Indiana University East**
www.iue.edu
Admissions
2325 Chester Boulevard
Whitewater Hall 151
Richmond, IN 47374-1289
Fax: (765) 973-8209
E-mail: applynow@iue.edu
Phone: (765) 973-8300

**Indiana University Kokomo**
www.iuk.edu
International Student Services
Kelley Student Center, Room 230
2300 South Washington Street
Kokomo, IN 46902-9003
Fax: (765) 455-9537
E-mail: broekerc@iuk.edu
Phone: (765) 455-9535

**Indiana University Northwest**
www.iun.edu
3400 Broadway
Hawthorn Hall, Room 100
Gary, IN 46408-1197
Fax: (219) 981-4219
E-mail: kmspicer@iun.edu
Phone: (219) 980-6848

**Indiana University of Pennsylvania**
www.iup.edu
Office of International Education
120 Sutton Hall, 1011 South Drive
Indiana, PA 15705-1088
Fax: (724) 357-2514
E-mail: intl-education@iup.edu
Phone: (724) 357-2295

**Indiana University South Bend**
www.iusb.edu
Office of International Student Services
1700 Mishawaka Avenue
PO Box 7111
South Bend, IN 46634-7111
Fax: (574) 520-5031
E-mail: copmille@iusb.edu
Phone: (574) 520-4419

**Indiana University Southeast**
www.ius.edu
Admissions
4201 Grant Line Road
University Center South, Room 102
New Albany, IN 47150-6405
Fax: (812) 941-2595
E-mail: seintadm@ius.edu
Phone: (812) 941-2212

**Indiana University-Purdue University Fort Wayne**
www.ipfw.edu
International Student Services
2101 East Coliseum Boulevard
Fort Wayne, IN 46805-1499
Fax: (260) 481-6674
E-mail: iss@ipfw.edu
Phone: (260) 481-6034

**Indiana University-Purdue University Indianapolis**
www.iupui.edu
Office of International Admissions
420 University Boulevard, CE 255
Indianapolis, IN 46202-5143
Fax: (317) 278-2213
E-mail: oia@iupui.edu
Phone: (317) 274-7000

**Indiana Wesleyan University**
www.indwes.edu
Admissions
4201 South Washington Street
Marion, IN 46953-4999
Fax: (765) 677-2140
E-mail: tony.stevens@indwes.edu
Phone: (765) 677-2254

**Institute of American Indian Arts**
www.iaia.edu
Admissions
83 Avan Nu Po Road
Santa Fe, NM 87508-1300
Fax: (505) 424-4500
E-mail: mary.curley@iaia.edu
Phone: (505) 424-2307

**Institute of Production and Recording**
www.ipr.edu
Admissions
300 North First Avenue, Suite 500
Minneapolis, MN 55401
E-mail: sferkingstad@ipr.edu
Phone: (866) 477-4840

**Institute of Technology: Clovis**
www.it-colleges.edu
564 West Herndon Avenue
Clovis, CA 93612
E-mail: rgardner@it-email.com
Phone: (559) 297-4500

**IntelliTec College**
http://intelliteccollege.com
Financial Aid
2315 East Pikes Peak Avenue
Colorado Springs, CO 80909
Fax: (719) 632-7451
E-mail: twright@intelliteccollege.com
Phone: (719) 632-7626

**IntelliTec College: Grand Junction**
http://intelliteccollege.com
772 Horizon Drive
Grand Junction, CO 81506
Fax: (970) 243-8074
E-mail: frontdeskGJ@intellitec.edu
Phone: (970) 245-8101

**Inter American University of Puerto Rico: Aguadilla Campus**
www.aguadilla.inter.edu
Box 20000
Aguadilla, PR 00605
Fax: (787) 882-3020
Phone: (787) 891-0925 ext. 2101

**Inter American University of Puerto Rico: Arecibo Campus**
www.arecibo.inter.edu
Admission Office
PO Box 4050
Arecibo, PR 00614-4050
Fax: (787) 880-1624
E-mail: pmontalvo@arecibo.inter.edu
Phone: (787) 878-5475 ext. 2268

**Inter American University of Puerto Rico: Barranquitas Campus**
www.br.uipr.edu
Admission Office
PO Box 517
Barranquitas, PR 00794
Fax: (787) 857-2244
E-mail: ecintron@br.inter.edu
Phone: (787) 857-3600 ext. 2011

**Inter American University of Puerto Rico: Bayamon Campus**
www.bayamon.inter.edu
Admissions
500 Dr. John Will Harris Road
Bayamon, PR 00957
Fax: (787) 279-2205
E-mail: abaez@bayamon.inter.edu
Phone: (787) 279-1912 ext. 2017

**Inter American University of Puerto Rico: Fajardo Campus**
www.fajardo.inter.edu
Admissions Office
Call Box 70003
Fajardo, PR 00738-7003
Fax: (787) 863-3470
E-mail: ada.caraballo@fajardo.inter.edu
Phone: (787) 863-2390 ext. 2210

**Inter American University of Puerto Rico: Guayama Campus**
www.guayama.inter.edu
Director of Admissions
PO Box 10004
Guayama, PR 00785
Fax: (787) 864-8232
E-mail: laura.ferrer@guayama.inter.edu
Phone: (787) 864-7059

**Inter American University of Puerto Rico: Metropolitan Campus**
www.metro.inter.edu/index.asp
International Relations Office
Box 191293
San Juan, PR 00919-1293
Fax: (787) 763-1464
E-mail: rayala@metro.inter.edu
Phone: (787) 250-1912 ext. 2305

**Inter American University of Puerto Rico: Ponce Campus**
ponce.inter.edu
Admissio Director
104 Turpo Industrial Park
Mercedita, PR 00715-1602
Fax: (787) 841-0103
E-mail: fldiaz@ponce.inter.edu
Phone: (787) 284-1912 ext. 2024

**Inter American University of Puerto Rico: San German Campus**
www.sg.inter.edu
Director Campus Learning Center
Box 5100
San German, PR 00683-9801
Fax: (787) 892-6154
E-mail: smorales@intersg.edu
Phone: (787) 264-1912 ext. 7261

**International Academy of Design and Technology: Chicago**
www.iadtchicago.edu
Registrar's Office
One North State Street, Suite 500
Chicago, IL 60602
Fax: (312) 980-4829
E-mail: ttimmons@iadtchicago.com
Phone: (312) 980-9200

**International Academy of Design and Technology: Detroit**
www.iadt.edu
1850 Research Drive
Troy, MI 48083
Phone: (248) 457-2700

**International Academy of Design and Technology: Henderson**
www.iadtvegas.com
2495 Village View Drive
Henderson, NV 89074
Fax: (702) 990-0161
E-mail: vegas_web@iadtvegas.com
Phone: (702) 990-0150

**International Academy of Design and Technology: San Antonio**
www.iadt.edu
4511 Horizon Hill Boulevard
San Antonio, TX 78229
E-mail: ngarcia@iadtsanantonio.com
Phone: (210) 530-9449

**International Academy of Design and Technology: Seattle**
www.iadt.edu/seattle
645 Andover Park West
Seattle, WA 98188
Fax: (206) 575-1724
Phone: (206) 575-1865

**International Baptist College**
www.ibcs.edu
Admissions
2211 West Germann Road
Chandler, AZ 85286
Fax: (480) 245-7909
E-mail: info@ibcs.edu
Phone: (800) 422-4858

**International Business College**
www.ibcfortwayne.edu
5699 Coventry Lane
Fort Wayne, IN 46804
Fax: (260) 436-1896
E-mail: admission@ibcfortwayne.edu
Phone: (260) 459-4500

**International Business College: Indianapolis**
www.ibcindianapolis.edu
7205 Shadeland Station
Indianapolis, IN 46256
Phone: (317) 841-6400

**International College of Broadcasting**
www.icb.edu
Director of Admission
6 South Smithville Road
Dayton, OH 45431
Fax: (937) 258-8714
E-mail: Admissions@icbcollege.com
Phone: (937) 258-8251

**Inver Hills Community College**
www.inverhills.edu
Admissions Office
2500 80th Street East
Inver Grove Heights, MN 55076-3224
Fax: (651) 450-3883
E-mail: admissions@inverhills.edu
Phone: (651) 450-3902

**Iona College**
www.iona.edu
Admissions
715 North Avenue
New Rochelle, NY 10801-1890
Fax: (914) 633-2182
E-mail: jcavallo@iona.edu
Phone: (800) 231-4662

**Iowa Central Community College**
www.iowacentral.edu
One Triton Circle
Fort Dodge, IA 50501
Fax: (515) 576-7724
E-mail: scharf_s@iowacentral.edu
Phone: (515) 574-1175

**Iowa Lakes Community College**
www.iowalakes.edu
Admissions
300 South 18th Street
Estherville, IA 51334-2725
Fax: (712) 792-3
E-mail: bgrandstaff@iowalakes.edu
Phone: (800) 346-6018

**Iowa State University**
www.iastate.edu
Admissions
100 Enrollment Services Center
Ames, IA 50011-2011
Fax: (515) 294-2592
E-mail: admissions@iastate.edu
Phone: (515) 294-7095

**Iowa Wesleyan College**
www.iwc.edu
Admissions Office
601 North Main Street
Mount Pleasant, IA 52641-1398
Fax: (319) 385-6240
E-mail: admit@iwc.edu
Phone: (319) 385-6468

**Iowa Western Community College**
www.iwcc.edu
Admissions Advisor and International
Specialist
2700 College Road
Box 4-C
Council Bluffs, IA 51502-3004
Fax: (712) 388-6803
E-mail: jcata@iwcc.edu
Phone: (712) 325-3419

**Irvine Valley College**
www.ivc.edu
International Student Office
5500 Irvine Center Drive
Irvine, CA 92618-4399
Fax: (949) 451-5466
E-mail: gvendley@ivc.edu
Phone: (949) 451-5624

**Island Drafting and Technical Institute**
www.idti.edu
Admissions
128 Broadway
Amityville, NY 11701-2704
Fax: (631) 691-8738
E-mail: info@idti.edu
Phone: (631) 691-8733 ext. 117

**Itasca Community College**
www.itascacc.edu
Enrollment Management Office
1851 Highway 169 East
Grand Rapids, MN 55744
Fax: (218) 322-2332
E-mail: william.marshall@itascacc.edu
Phone: (218) 322-2340

**Ithaca College**
www.ithaca.edu
Admission
953 Danby Road
Ithaca, NY 14850-7002
Fax: (607) 274-1900
E-mail: neversley@ithaca.edu
Phone: (800) 429-4274

**ITI Technical College**
www.iticollege.edu
Director of Admissions
13944 Airline Highway
Baton Rouge, LA 70817
Fax: (225) 756-0903
E-mail: mstevens@iticollege.edu
Phone: (225) 752-4233 ext. 261

**Ivy Tech Community College: Bloomington**
www.ivytech.edu
Registrar
200 Daniels Way
Bloomington, IN 47404-1511
Fax: (812) 332-8147
E-mail: askeens@ivytech.edu
Phone: (812) 330-6016

**Ivy Tech Community College: Central Indiana**
www.ivytech.edu
Assistant Director of International Student
Relations
50 West Fall Creek Parkway North Drive
Indianapolis, IN 46208-5752
Fax: (317) 917-5919
E-mail: tywebb@ivytech.edu
Phone: (317) 921-4613

**Ivy Tech Community College: Columbus**
www.ivytech.edu
Assistant Director of Admissions
4475 Central Avenue
Columbus, IN 47203-1868
Fax: (812) 372-0311
E-mail: kbaker17@ivytech.edu
Phone: (812) 374-5255

**Ivy Tech Community College: East Central**
www.ivytech.edu/eastcentral
Dean of Student Affairs
4301 South Cowan Road
Box 3100
Muncie, IN 47302-9448
Fax: (765) 289-2292 ext. 502
E-mail: mlewelle@ivytech.edu
Phone: (765) 289-2291 ext. 1391

**Ivy Tech Community College: Kokomo**
www.ivytech.edu
1815 East Morgan Street
Kokomo, IN 46903-1373
Fax: (765) 454-5111
E-mail: mfedersp@ivytech.edu
Phone: (765) 459-0561 ext. 318

**Ivy Tech Community College: Lafayette**
www.ivytech.edu
Director of Admissions
3101 South Creasy Lane
Lafayette, IN 47905-6299
Fax: (765) 722-9293
E-mail: ihernand@ivytech.edu
Phone: (765) 269-5253

**Ivy Tech Community College: North Central**
www.ivytech.edu
Assistant Director of Admissions
220 Dean Johnson Boulevard
South Bend, IN 46601-3415
Fax: (574) 236-7177
E-mail: tteat@ivytech.edu
Phone: (574) 289-7001 ext. 5399

**Ivy Tech Community College: Northeast**
www.ivytech.edu
Assistant Director of Diversity Affairs
3800 North Anthony Boulevard
Fort Wayne, IN 46805-1489
Fax: (260) 480-2053
E-mail: djackson@ivytech.edu
Phone: (260) 480-4115

**Ivy Tech Community College: Northwest**
www.ivytech.edu
1440 East 35th Avenue
Gary, IN 46409-1499
Fax: (219) 981-4415
E-mail: kwhite112@ivytech.edu
Phone: (219) 392-3600 ext. 3216

**Ivy Tech Community College: Richmond**
www.ivytech.edu
Assistant Director of Admissions
2357 Chester Boulevard
Richmond, IN 47374-1298
Fax: (765) 962-8174
E-mail: lprzybys@ivytech.edu
Phone: (765) 966-2656 ext. 1214

**Ivy Tech Community College: South Central**
www.ivytech.edu
Assistant Director of Admissions
8204 Highway 311
Sellersburg, IN 47172-1897
Fax: (812) 246-9905
E-mail: jgoodman17@ivytech.edu
Phone: (812) 246-3301 ext. 4315

**Ivy Tech Community College: Southeast**
www.ivytech.edu
Dir Express Enrollment
590 Ivy Tech Drive
Madison, IN 47250-1881
Fax: (812) 265-4028
E-mail: sgrubbs5@ivytech.edu
Phone: (812) 537-4010

**Ivy Tech Community College: Southwest**
www.ivytech.edu
Director of Admissions
3501 First Avenue
Evansville, IN 47710-3398
Fax: (812) 429-9878
E-mail: ajohnson@ivytech.edu
Phone: (812) 429-1430

**Ivy Tech Community College: Wabash Valley**
www.ivytech.edu
International Student Coordinator
8000 South Education Drive
Terre Haute, IN 47802-4898
Fax: (812) 299-5723
E-mail: bcandler@ivytech.edu
Phone: (812) 298-2286

**J. Sargeant Reynolds Community College**
www.reynolds.edu
Admissions and Records
PO Box 85622
Richmond, VA 23285-5622
Fax: (804) 371-3650
E-mail: kcossey@reynolds.edu
Phone: (804) 523-5028

**Jackson State Community College**
www.jscc.edu
Office of High School Initiatives and Recruiting
2046 North Parkway
Jackson, TN 38301-3797
Fax: (731) 425-9559
E-mail: awinchester@jscc.edu
Phone: (731) 425-8844 ext. 50484

**Jackson State University**
www.jsums.edu
JSU Global
1400 John R. Lynch Street
Box 17330
Jackson, MS 39217
Fax: (601) 973-9227
E-mail: priscilla.d.slade@jsums.edu
Phone: (601) 979-1611

**Jacksonville College**
www.jacksonville-college.edu
International Student Adviser
105 B.J. Albritton Drive
Jacksonville, TX 75766-4759
Fax: (903) 541-4091
E-mail: admissions@jacksonville-college.edu
Phone: (903) 586-2518 ext. 7107

**Jacksonville State University**
www.jsu.edu
Director of Admission
700 Pelham Road North
Jacksonville, AL 36265-1602
Fax: (256) 782-5291
E-mail: green@jsu.edu
Phone: (256) 782-5400

**Jacksonville University**
www.ju.edu
Chief International Affairs Officer
2800 University Boulevard North
Jacksonville, FL 32211-3394
Fax: (904) 256-8941
E-mail: ckwai@ju.edu
Phone: (904) 256-7775

**James A. Rhodes State College**
www.rhodesstate.edu
Student Affairs Division
4240 Campus Drive, PS 148
Lima, OH 45804-3597
Fax: (419) 995-8098
E-mail: admissions@rhodesstate.edu
Phone: (419) 995-8304

**James Madison University**
www.jmu.edu
Office of Admissions
Sonner Hall, MSC 0101
Harrisonburg, VA 22807
Fax: (540) 568-3332
E-mail: mooneyms@jmu.edu
Phone: (540) 568-3453

**Jamestown Community College**
www.sunyjcc.edu
Admissions
525 Falconer Street
PO Box 20
Jamestown, NY 14702-0020
Fax: (716) 338-1450
E-mail: wendypresent@mail.sunyjcc.edu
Phone: (716) 338-1070

**Jarvis Christian College**
www.jarvis.edu
Admissions and Enrollment Management
PO Box 1470
Hawkins, TX 75765-1470
Fax: (903) 769-1282
E-mail: sfriar@jarvis.edu
Phone: (903) 730-4890 ext. 2601

**Jefferson College**
www.jeffco.edu
Admissions and Student Records
1000 Viking Drive
Hillsboro, MO 63050-2441
Fax: (636) 789-5103
E-mail: mconway@jeffco.edu
Phone: (636) 481-3209

**Jefferson College of Health Sciences**
www.jchs.edu
Office of Admissions
101 Elm Avenue, SE
Roanoke, VA 24013-2222
Fax: (540) 224-6703
E-mail: jomckeon@jchs.edu
Phone: (540) 985-9773

**Jefferson Community and Technical College**
www.jefferson.kctcs.edu
International Student Services
109 East Broadway
Louisville, KY 40202
E-mail: susanj.panfil@kctcs.edu
Phone: (502) 213-2496

**Jefferson State Community College**
www.jeffersonstate.edu
International Student Office
2601 Carson Road
Birmingham, AL 35215
Fax: (205) 856-6070
E-mail: sthompson@jeffersonstate.edu
Phone: (205) 856-7920

**Jewish Theological Seminary of America**
www.jtsa.edu/list
Office of Admissions
3080 Broadway
New York, NY 10025
Fax: (212) 280-6022
E-mail: lcadmissions@jtsa.edu
Phone: (212) 678-8832

**JNA Institute of Culinary Arts**
www.culinaryarts.edu
Admissions
1212 South Broad Street
Philadelphia, PA 19146
Fax: (215) 468-8838
E-mail: admissions@culinaryarts.edu
Phone: (215) 468-8800

**John A. Logan College**
www.jalc.edu
Admissions
700 Logan College Road
Carterville, IL 62918
Fax: (618) 985-4433
E-mail: terry.crain@jal.cc.il.us
Phone: (618) 985-3741

**John Brown University**
www.jbu.edu
Admissions
2000 West University Street
Siloam Springs, AR 72761-2121
Fax: (479) 524-4196
E-mail: jbuinfo@jbu.edu
Phone: (479) 524-7262

**John Carroll University**
www.jcu.edu
Undergraduate Admission
Office of Admission
1 John Carroll Boulevard
University Heights, OH 44118-4581
Fax: (216) 397-4981
E-mail: international@jcu.edu
Phone: (216) 397-4294

**John F. Kennedy University**
www.jfku.edu
International Student Advisor
100 Ellinwood Way
Pleasant Hill, CA 94523-4817
Fax: (925) 969-3331
E-mail: ssermeno@jfku.edu
Phone: (925) 969-3339

**John Paul the Great Catholic University**
https://jpcatholic.edu/
Admissions Office
220 West Grand Avenue
Escondido, CA 92025
E-mail: mharold@jpcatholic.com
Phone: (858) 653-6740 ext. 1101

**John Wood Community College**
www.jwcc.edu
Admissions
1301 South 48th Street
Quincy, IL 62305-8736
Fax: (217) 224-4208
E-mail: admissions@jwcc.edu
Phone: (217) 641-4314

**Johns Hopkins University**
www.jhu.edu
Office of Undergraduate Admissions
3400 North Charles Street, Mason Hall
Baltimore, MD 21218-2683
Fax: (410) 516-6025
E-mail: gotojhu@jhu.edu
Phone: (410) 516-6484

**Johns Hopkins University: Peabody
Conservatory of Music**
www.peabody.jhu.edu
One East Mount Vernon Place
Baltimore, MD 21202
Fax: (410) 659-8102
E-mail: admissions@peabody.jhu.edu
Phone: (410) 659-8100 ext. 3075

**Johnson & Wales University: Charlotte**
https://www1.jwu.edu/admissions/
Admissions Office
801 West Trade Street
Charlotte, NC 28202
Fax: (980) 598-1111
E-mail: erika.ulanday@jwu.edu
Phone: (980) 598-1100

**Johnson & Wales University: Denver**
www.jwu.edu
Academic Services Associate
7150 Montview Boulevard
Denver, CO 80220
Fax: (303) 256-9389
E-mail: cabrahamson@jwu.edu
Phone: (303) 256-9557

**Johnson & Wales University: North Miami**
www.jwu.edu
International Admissions
1701 Northeast 127th Street
North Miami, FL 33181
Fax: (305) 892-7020
E-mail: mia@admissions.jwu.edu
Phone: (305) 892-7005

**Johnson & Wales University: Providence**
http://admissions.jwu.edu/
International Admissions
8 Abbott Park Place
Providence, RI 02903
Fax: (401) 598-4773
E-mail: admissons.pvd@jwu.edu
Phone: (401) 598-1074

**Johnson C. Smith University**
www.jcsu.edu
Admissions
100 Beatties Ford Road
Charlotte, NC 28216-5398
Fax: (704) 378-1242
E-mail: admissions@jcsu.edu
Phone: (704) 378-1010

**Johnson College**
www.johnson.edu
Admissions
3427 North Main Avenue
Scranton, PA 18508
Fax: (570) 348-2181
E-mail: admit@johnson.edu
Phone: (570) 702-8900

**Johnson State College**
www.jsc.edu
Admissions
337 College Hill
Johnson, VT 05656
Fax: (802) 635-1230
E-mail: jscadmissions@jsc.edu
Phone: (802) 635-1219

**Johnson University**
www.johnsonu.edu
Admissions
7900 Johnson Drive
Knoxville, TN 37998-0001
Fax: (865) 251-2336
E-mail: jschultz@johnsonu.edu
Phone: (865) 251-2233

**Johnson University: Florida**
www.johnsonu.edu/florida
Registrar's Office
1011 Bill Beck Boulevard
Kissimmee, FL 34744-4402
Fax: (321) 206-2007
E-mail: dadams@johnsonu.edu
Phone: (407) 569-1341

**Johnston Community College**
www.johnstoncc.edu
Director of Admissions and Counseling
PO Box 2350
Smithfield, NC 27577
Fax: (919) 989-7862
E-mail: jsmclendon@johnstoncc.edu
Phone: (919) 209-2079

**Joliet Junior College**
www.jjc.edu
Admissions and Records
1215 Houbolt Road
Joliet, IL 60431-8938
Fax: (815) 744-5507
E-mail: awalsh@jjc.edu
Phone: (815) 729-9020 ext. 2247

**Jones College**
www.jones.edu
Director International Student Support
5353 Arlington Expressway
Jacksonville, FL 32211
Fax: (904) 743-4446
E-mail: mbarber@jones.edu
Phone: (904) 743-1122 ext. 274

**Jones County Junior College**
www.jcjc.edu
900 South Court Street
Ellisville, MS 39437
Fax: (601) 477-4017
E-mail: admissions@jcjc.edu
Phone: (601) 477-4025

**Jose Maria Vargas University**
www.jmvu.edu
Admissions Department
10131 Pines Boulevard
Pembroke Pines, FL 33026
Fax: (954) 322-4131
E-mail: admissions@jmvu.edu
Phone: (954) 322-4460

**Judson College**
www.judson.edu
Admissions Office
302 Bibb Street
Marion, AL 36756
Fax: (334) 683-5282
E-mail: tolkie@judson.edu
Phone: (334) 683-5110

**Judson University**
www.judsonu.edu
Student Development
1151 North State Street
Elgin, IL 60123-1404
Fax: (847) 628-2526
E-mail: rafael.heck@judsonu.edu
Phone: (847) 628-1546

**Juilliard School**
www.juilliard.edu
Admissions Office
60 Lincoln Center Plaza
New York, NY 10023-6588
Fax: (212) 724-0263
E-mail: admissions@juilliard.edu
Phone: (212) 799-5000 ext. 223

**Juniata College**
www.juniata.edu
Enrollment Office
1700 Moore Street
Huntingdon, PA 16652-2196
Fax: (814) 641-3100
E-mail: tur@juniata.edu
Phone: (814) 641-3427

**Kalamazoo College**
www.kzoo.edu
1200 Academy Street
Kalamazoo, MI 49006
Fax: (269) 337-7390
E-mail: roderick.malcolm@kzoo.edu
Phone: (269) 337-7173

**Kalamazoo Valley Community College**
www.kvcc.edu
6767 West O Avenue
PO Box 4070
Kalamazoo, MI 49003-4070
Fax: (269) 488-4161
E-mail: shubbell@kvcc.edu
Phone: (269) 488-4207

**Kanawha Valley Community and Technical College**
www.kvctc.edu
Division of Student Services
2001 Union Carbide Drive
South Charleston, WV 25303
Fax: (304) 414-4441
E-mail: admissions@kvctc.edu
Phone: (304) 205-6600

**Kankakee Community College**
www.kcc.edu
Admissions
100 College Drive
Kankakee, IL 60901-6505
Fax: (815) 802-8521
E-mail: mdriscoll@kcc.edu
Phone: (815) 802-8524

**Kansas City Art Institute**
www.kcai.edu
Admissions
4415 Warwick Boulevard
Kansas City, MO 64111
Fax: (816) 802-3309
E-mail: admiss@kcai.edu
Phone: (800) 522-5224

**Kansas City Kansas Community College**
www.kckcc.edu
Admissions
7250 State Avenue
Kansas City, KS 66112
Fax: (913) 288-7648
E-mail: tchurch@kckcc.edu
Phone: (913) 288-7201

**Kansas State University**
www.k-state.edu
International Admissions and Recruiting
119 Anderson Hall
Manhattan, KS 66506
Fax: (785) 532-6550
E-mail: intladmit@k-state.edu
Phone: (785) 532-7277

**Kansas Wesleyan University**
www.kwu.edu
Assistant Director of Admissions
100 East Claflin Avenue
Salina, KS 67401-6196
Fax: (785) 404-1485
E-mail: jessica.fuller@kwu.edu
Phone: (785) 833-4308

**Kaplan Career Institute: Franklin Mills**
www.kaplancareerinstitute.com
177 Franklin Mills Boulevard
Philadelphia, PA 19154
Fax: (215) 612-6695
Phone: (215) 612-6600

**Kaplan College: Dayton**
www.dayton.kaplancollege.com
Admissions Office
2800 East River Road
Dayton, OH 45439
Fax: (937) 294-2259
E-mail: ckirby@kaplan.edu
Phone: (937) 294-6155

**Kaplan College: Hammond**
www.kaplan.com
7833 Indianapolis Boulevard
Hammond, IN 46324
Fax: (219) 844-0105
Phone: (219) 844-0100

**Kaplan College: Palm Springs**
www.kc-palmsprings.com
2475 East Tahquitz Canyon Way
Palm Springs, CA 92262
Phone: (760) 327-4562

**Kaplan College: Riverside**
www.riverside.kaplancollege.com
Admissions
4040 Vine Street
Riverside, CA 92507
Fax: (818) 672-8919
E-mail: enalvarez@kaplan.edu
Phone: (818) 672-3000 ext. 3005

**Kaplan College: Sacramento**
https://www.kaplancollege.com/sacramento-ca
4330 Watt Avenue, Suite 400
Sacramento, CA 95821
Fax: (916) 649-8344
Phone: (916) 649-8168

**Kaplan College: Salida**
www.modesto.kaplancollege.com
5172 Kiernan Court
Salida, CA 95368
Fax: (888) 280-9565
Phone: (209) 543-7000

**Kaplan College: San Diego**
www.kaplancollege.com
9055 Balboa Avenue
San Diego, CA 92123
Fax: (858) 279-4885
Phone: (858) 279-4500

**Kaplan College: Vista**
www.mariccollege.edu
2022 University Drive
Vista, CA 92083
Fax: (760) 630-1656
Phone: (760) 630-1555

**Kaplan University: Cedar Falls**
www.kaplanuniversity.edu/cedar-falls-iowa.aspx
7009 Nordic Drive
Cedar Falls, IA 50613
Fax: (319) 243-2961
Phone: (319) 277-0220

**Kaplan University: Cedar Rapids**
www.kaplanuniversity.edu/cedar-rapids-iowa.aspx
Admissions
3165 Edgewood Parkway, SW
Cedar Rapids, IA 52404
Fax: (319) 363-3812
E-mail: druddy@kaplan.edu
Phone: (319) 363-0481

**Kaplan University: Davenport**
www.kaplanuniversity.edu/davenport-iowa.aspx
Director of Admissions
1801 East Kimberly Road, Suite 1
Davenport, IA 52807-2095
Fax: (563) 355-1320
E-mail: rhoffmann@kucampus.edu
Phone: (563) 441-2496

**Kaplan University: Des Moines**
www.kaplanuniversity.edu/des-moines-iowa.aspx
Admissions Office
4655 121st Street
Urbandale, IA 50323
Fax: (515) 727-2115
E-mail: erogan_dm@hamiltonia.edu
Phone: (515) 727-2100

**Kaplan University: Hagerstown**
www.hagerstown.kaplanuniversity.edu
18618 Crestwood Drive
Hagerstown, MD 21742
Fax: (301) 791-7661
E-mail: info@ku-hagerstown.edu
Phone: (301) 739-2670

**Kaplan University: Lincoln**
www.lincoln.kaplanuniversity.edu
Admissions
1821 K Street
Lincoln, NE 68508
Fax: (402) 474-5302
E-mail: kfrette@kaplan.edu
Phone: (402) 474-5315

**Kaplan University: Mason City**
www.kaplanuniversity.edu/mason-city-iowa.aspx
Plaza West 2570 Fourth Street, SW
Mason City, IA 50401
Fax: (641) 423-7512
E-mail: mklacik@kaplan.edu
Phone: (641) 423-2530

**Kaplan University: South Portland**
www.kaplanuniversity.edu
265 Western Avenue
South Portland, ME 04106
Fax: (207) 774-1715
E-mail: enroll@andovercollege.edu
Phone: (207) 774-6126 ext. 8701

**Kaskaskia College**
www.kaskaskia.edu
Enrollment Center
27210 College Road
Centralia, IL 62801
Fax: (618) 545-3393
E-mail: cboehne@kaskaskia.edu
Phone: (618) 545-3184

**Kean University**
www.kean.edu
Admissions Office
Office of Admissions - Kean Hall
1000 Morris Avenue
Union, NJ 07083-0411
Fax: (908) 737-7105
E-mail: ksneerin@kean.edu
Phone: (908) 737-7100

**Keene State College**
www.keene.edu
Admissions
229 Main Street
Keene, NH 03435-2604
Fax: (603) 358-2767
E-mail: bpoirier@keene.edu
Phone: (603) 358-2276

**Kehilath Yakov Rabbinical Seminary**
www.kehilathyakov.com
340 Ilington Road
Ossining, NY 10562
Phone: (718) 963-1212

**Keiser University**
www.keiseruniversity.edu
2600 North Military Trail
West Palm Beach, FL 33409
Fax: (561) 640-3328
E-mail:
ResidentialAdmissions@keiseruniversity.edu
Phone: (954) 776-4456

**Kellogg Community College**
www.kellogg.edu
Admissions
450 North Avenue
Battle Creek, MI 49017-3397
Fax: (269) 565-2085
E-mail: admissions@kellogg.edu
Phone: (269) 965-4153

**Kendall College**
www.kendall.edu
International Enrollment
900 N. North Branch Street
Chicago, IL 60642-4278
Fax: (312) 752-2021
E-mail: patricia.corcoran@kendall.edu
Phone: (312) 752-2288

**Kennebec Valley Community College**
www.kvcc.me.edu
Assistant Dean of Enrollment
92 Western Avenue
Fairfield, ME 04937-1367
Fax: (207) 453-5011
E-mail: cmckenna@kvcc.me.edu
Phone: (207) 453-5155

**Kennesaw State University**
www.kennesaw.edu
Division of Global Admissions
3391 Town Point Drive
Mail Drop #9111
Kennesaw, GA 30144
Fax: (470) 578-9169
E-mail: KSUAdmit@kennesaw.edu
Phone: (470) 578-2368

**Kent State University**
www.kent.edu
Office of Global Education
161 Schwartz Center
PO Box 5190
Kent, OH 44242-0001
Fax: (330) 672-4025
E-mail: intladm@kent.edu
Phone: (330) 672-7980

**Kentucky Christian University**
www.kcu.edu
Athletic Director/ISIS Coordinator
100 Academic Parkway
Box 2021
Grayson, KY 41143-2205
Fax: (606) 474-3189
E-mail: bdixon@kcu.edu
Phone: (606) 474-3215

**Kentucky Mountain Bible College**
www.kmbc.edu
Office of Recruiting
855 Highway 541
Jackson, KY 41339
Fax: (888) 742-1124
E-mail: kmbc@kmbc.edu
Phone: (606) 693-5000 ext. 138

**Kentucky State University**
www.kysu.edu
Office of Admissions
400 East Main Street, ASB 312
Frankfort, KY 40601
Fax: (502) 597-5814
E-mail: admissionis@kysu.edu
Phone: (502) 597-6813

**Kentucky Wesleyan College**
www.kwc.edu
Admissions Office
3000 Frederica Street
Owensboro, KY 42301
Fax: (270) 926-3196
E-mail: cwalker@kwc.edu
Phone: (270) 852-3120

**Kenyon College**
www.kenyon.edu
Admissions
Kenyon College Admissions Office, Ransom
Hall
106 College Park Street
Gambier, OH 43022-9623
Fax: (740) 427-5770
E-mail: morse@kenyon.edu
Phone: (800) 848-2468

**Kettering College**
www.kc.edu
3737 Southern Boulevard
Kettering, OH 45429-1299
Fax: (937) 395-8338
E-mail: studentadmissions@kc.edu
Phone: (800) 422-5262

**Kettering University**
www.kettering.edu
Admissions
1700 University Avenue
Flint, MI 48504-6214
Fax: (810) 762-9837
E-mail:
InternationalAdmissions@kettering.edu
Phone: (810) 762-9568

**Keuka College**
www.keuka.edu
Admissions
141 Central Avenue
Keuka Park, NY 14478-0098
Fax: (315) 536-5386
E-mail: admissions@keuka.edu
Phone: (800) 335-3852

**Key College**
www.keycollege.edu
Financial Services
225 East Dania Beach Boulevard
Dania Beach, FL 33004-3046
Fax: (954) 923-9226
E-mail: financialaid@keycollege.edu
Phone: (954) 923-4440

**Keystone College**
www.keystone.edu
Office of Admissions
One College Green
PO Box 50
La Plume, PA 18440-0200
Fax: (570) 945-7916
E-mail: lauren.risboskin@keystone.edu
Phone: (570) 945-8115

**Keystone Technical Institute**
www.kti.edu
2301 Academy Drive
Harrisburg, PA 17112-1012
Fax: (717) 901-9090
E-mail: info@kti.edu
Phone: (717) 545-4747

**Kilgore College**
www.kilgore.edu
1100 Broadway
Kilgore, TX 75662-3299
Fax: (903) 983-8607
E-mail: cgore@kilgore.edu
Phone: (903) 983-7446

**King University**
www.king.edu
Admission Office
1350 King College Road
Bristol, TN 37620-2699
Fax: (423) 652-4861
E-mail: eabrowne@king.edu
Phone: (423) 652-4769

**The King's College**
www.tkc.edu
Office of Admissions
56 Broadway
New York, NY 10004
Fax: (212) 659-3611
E-mail: ktamm@tkc.edu
Phone: (212) 659-7291

**King's College**
www.kings.edu
Office of International Student Recruitment
133 North River Street
Wilkes-Barre, PA 18711
Fax: (570) 208-5971
E-mail: internationaladmissions@kings.edu
Phone: (570) 208-8401

**The King's University**
www.tku.edu
Office of Admission
2121 E Southlake Blvd
Southlake, TX 76092
Fax: (818) 779-8429
E-mail: admissions@kingsuniversity.edu
Phone: (818) 779-8040

**Kirtland Community College**
www.kirtland.edu
Student Services
10775 North Saint Helen Road
Roscommon, MI 48653
Fax: (989) 275-6727
E-mail: ryan.madis@kirtland.edu
Phone: (989) 275-5000 ext. 248

**Kishwaukee College**
www.kishwaukeecollege.edu
Vice President of Student Services
21193 Malta Road
Malta, IL 60150-9699
Fax: (815) 825-2306
E-mail: apperson@kishwaukeecollege.edu
Phone: (815) 825-2086 ext. 249

**Knox College**
www.knox.edu
Office of Admission
2 East South Street
Campus Box 148
Galesburg, IL 61401
Fax: (309) 341-7070
E-mail: admission@knox.edu
Phone: (309) 341-7100

**Kutztown University of Pennsylvania**
www.kutztown.edu
Admissions
Admissions Office
PO Box 730
Kutztown, PA 19530-0730
Fax: (610) 683-1356
E-mail: nbecker@kutztown.edu
Phone: (484) 646-4257

**Kuyper College**
www.kuyper.edu
Admissions Office
3333 East Beltline Avenue NE
Grand Rapids, MI 49525-9781
Fax: (616) 988-3608
E-mail: everrett@kuyper.edu
Phone: (616) 222-3000

**La Roche College**
www.laroche.edu
Admissions
9000 Babcock Boulevard
Pittsburgh, PA 15237
Fax: (412) 536-1048
E-mail: michael.bauer@laroche.edu
Phone: (412) 536-1010

**La Salle University**
www.lasalle.edu
Office of Undergraduate Admission
1900 West Olney Avenue
Philadelphia, PA 19141-1199
Fax: (215) 951-1656
E-mail: admiss@lasalle.edu
Phone: (215) 951-1500

**La Sierra University**
www.lasierra.edu
Admissions and Records
4500 Riverwalk Parkway
Riverside, CA 92515-8247
Fax: (951) 785-2447
E-mail: admissions@lasierra.edu
Phone: (951) 785-2176

**Labette Community College**
www.labette.edu
Admissions
200 South 14th Street
Parsons, KS 67357
Fax: (620) 421-2309
E-mail: tammyf@labette.edu
Phone: (620) 421-6700 ext. 1228

**Lackawanna College**
www.lackawanna.edu
Admissions Office
501 Vine Street
Scranton, PA 18509
Fax: (570) 961-7843
E-mail: kettenm@lackawanna.edu
Phone: (570) 504-8094

**Lafayette College**
www.lafayette.edu
Admissions
118 Markle Hall
730 High Street
Easton, PA 18042
Fax: (610) 330-5355
E-mail: internatl@lafayette.edu
Phone: (610) 330-5100

**LaGrange College**
www.lagrange.edu
Office of Admission
601 Broad Street
LaGrange, GA 30240-2999
Fax: (706) 880-8010
E-mail: jcmiller@lagrange.edu
Phone: (706) 880-8217

**Laguna College of Art and Design**
www.lcad.edu
Admissions
2222 Laguna Canyon Road
Laguna Beach, CA 92651-1136
Fax: (949) 715-8084
E-mail: cbrown@lcad.edu
Phone: (949) 376-6000 ext. 223

**Lake Area Technical Institute**
www.lakeareatech.edu
Registrar
PO Box 730
Watertown, SD 57201
Fax: (605) 882-6299
E-mail: Eric.Schultz@lakeareatech.edu
Phone: (605) 882-5284 ext. 228

**Lake Erie College**
www.lec.edu
Senior Assistant Director of Admission,
International Recruitment
391 West Washington Street
Painesville, OH 44077-3389
Fax: (440) 375-7005
E-mail: mgaudio@lec.edu
Phone: (440) 375-7060

**Lake Forest College**
www.lakeforest.edu
Admission Office
555 North Sheridan Road
Lake Forest, IL 60045-2338
Fax: (847) 735-6271
E-mail: international@lakeforest.edu
Phone: (847) 735-5000

**Lake Land College**
www.lakelandcollege.edu
Admissions
5001 Lake Land Boulevard
Mattoon, IL 61938-9366
Fax: (217) 234-5390
E-mail: admissions@lakeland.cc.il.us
Phone: (217) 234-5382

**Lake Michigan College**
www.lakemichigancollege.edu
International and Veteran Affairs Office
2755 East Napier Avenue
Benton Harbor, MI 49022-1899
Fax: (269) 927-6718
E-mail: pliml@lakemichigancollege.edu
Phone: (269) 927-6181

**Lake Region State College**
www.lrsc.edu
Student Services
1801 College Drive North
Devils Lake, ND 58301-1598
Fax: (701) 662-1581
E-mail: kristi.hernandez@lrsc.edu
Phone: (701) 662-1692

**Lake Superior College**
www.lsc.edu
Intercultural Services Coordinator
2101 Trinity Road
Duluth, MN 55811
Fax: (218) 733-5945
E-mail: c.crawford@lsc.edu
Phone: (218) 733-7678

**Lake Superior State University**
www.lssu.edu
Admissions
650 West Easterday Avenue
Sault Sainte Marie, MI 49783-1699
Fax: (906) 635-6696
E-mail: ahackbarthonson@lssu.edu
Phone: (906) 635-2231

**Lake Tahoe Community College**
www.ltcc.edu
Admissions & Records
One College Drive
South Lake Tahoe, CA 96150-4524
Fax: (530) 542-1781
E-mail: admissions@ltcc.edu
Phone: (530) 541-4660 ext. 211

**Lake Washington Institute of Technology**
www.lwtech.edu
International Programs
West Building, W201
11605 132nd Avenue, NE
Kirkland, WA 98034
E-mail: international.student@lwtech.edu
Phone: (425) 739-8145

**Lake-Sumter State College**
www.lssc.edu
Senior Program Specialist
9501 US Highway 441
Leesburg, FL 34788-8751
Fax: (352) 365-3553
E-mail: murphyd@lssc.edu
Phone: (352) 323-3686

**Lakeland Community College**
www.lakelandcc.edu
Admissions
7700 Clocktower Drive
Kirtland, OH 44094-5198
Fax: (440) 525-7651
E-mail: tcooper@lakelandcc.edu
Phone: (440) 525-7230

**Lakeland University**
www.lakeland.edu
International Student Advisor
Box 359
Sheboygan, WI 53082-0359
Fax: (920) 565-1556
E-mail: international@lakeland.edu
Phone: (920) 565-1337

**Lakes Region Community College**
www.lrcc.edu
Admission
379 Belmont Road
Laconia, NH 03246-9204
Fax: (603) 524-8084
E-mail: wfraser@ccsnh.edu
Phone: (603) 524-3207

**Lakeshore Technical College**
www.gotoltc.edu
1290 North Avenue
Cleveland, WI 53015-9761
Fax: (920) 693-3561
E-mail: doug.gossen@gotoltc.edu
Phone: (920) 693-1378

**Lamar Community College**
www.lamarcc.edu
Admissions
2401 South Main Street
Lamar, CO 81052-3999
Fax: (719) 336-2400
E-mail: jenna.davis@lamarcc.edu
Phone: (719) 336-1589

**Lamar Institute of Technology**
www.lit.edu
International Admissions Office
PO Box 10043
Beaumont, TX 77705
Fax: (409) 880-8414
E-mail: mingming.zhang@lamar.edu
Phone: (409) 880-7466

**Lamar State College at Orange**
www.lsco.edu
410 Front Street
Orange, TX 77630
Fax: (409) 882-3374
Phone: (409) 883-7750

**Lamar State College at Port Arthur**
www.lamarpa.edu
Dean for Student Services
Box 310
Port Arthur, TX 77641-0310
Fax: (409) 984-6025
E-mail: hebertda@lamarpa.edu
Phone: (409) 984-6156

**Lamar University**
www.lamar.edu
Office of Admissions
Box 10009
Beaumont, TX 77710
Fax: (409) 880-8463
E-mail: international@lamar.edu
Phone: (409) 880-8356

**Lancaster Bible College**
www.lbc.edu
Admissions
901 Eden Road
Lancaster, PA 17601-5036
Fax: (717) 560-8213
E-mail: admissions@lbc.edu
Phone: (717) 560-8200 ext. 5328

**Lander University**
www.lander.edu
Office of Admissions
Stanley Avenue
Box 6007
Greenwood, SC 29649-2099
Fax: (864) 388-8125
E-mail: jmathis@lander.edu
Phone: (864) 388-8307

**Landing School of Boatbuilding and Design**
www.landingschool.edu
Admissions
286 River Road
Arundel, ME 04046
Fax: (207) 985-7942
E-mail: matthewbarry@landingschool.edu
Phone: (207) 985-7976

**Landmark College**
www.landmark.edu
Admissions
19 River Road South
Putney, VT 05346
Fax: (802) 387-6868
E-mail: admissions@landmark.edu
Phone: (802) 387-6718

**Lane College**
www.lanecollege.edu
Admissions
545 Lane Avenue
Jackson, TN 38301-4598
Fax: (731) 426-7559
E-mail: mclayborne@lanecollege.edu
Phone: (731) 426-7533

**Lane Community College**
www.lanecc.edu
International/Multi-Cultural Services
4000 East 30th Avenue
Eugene, OR 97405
Fax: (541) 463-3991
E-mail: Sheldonc@lanecc.edu
Phone: (541) 463-5165

**Laney College**
www.laney.edu
International Services Manager, Office of
International Education
900 Fallon Street
Oakland, CA 94607
Fax: (510) 663-0937
E-mail: dgephart@peralta.edu
Phone: (510) 466-7834

**Langston University**
www.langston.edu
Admissions
Box 728
Langston, OK 73050
Fax: (405) 466-3391
E-mail: mavaugh@langston.edu
Phone: (405) 466-3428

**Lansdale School of Business**
www.lsb.edu
290 Wissahickon Avenue
North Wales, PA 19454-4114
Fax: (215) 699-8770
E-mail: mjohnson@lsb.edu
Phone: (215) 699-5700

**Lansing Community College**
www.lcc.edu
Admissions
1121 Enrollment Services
PO BOX 40010
Lansing, MI 48901-7210
Fax: (517) 483-9668
E-mail: admissions@lcc.edu
Phone: (517) 483-1200

**Laramie County Community College**
www.lccc.wy.edu
1400 East College Drive
Cheyenne, WY 82007-3299
Fax: (307) 778-1350
E-mail: hallison@lccc.wy.edu
Phone: (307) 778-1117

**Laredo Community College**
www.laredo.edu
International Student and Veteran Office
West End Washington Street
Laredo, TX 78040-4395
Fax: (956) 721-5493
E-mail: vghernandez@laredo.edu
Phone: (956) 764-5768

**Las Positas College**
www.laspositascollege.edu
Admissions and Records
3033 Collier Canyon Road
Livermore, CA 94551
Fax: (925) 606-6437
E-mail: sdupree@clpccd.cc.ca.us
Phone: (925) 373-5815

**Lasell College**
www.lasell.edu
Undergraduate Admission
1844 Commonwealth Avenue
Newton, MA 02466-2709
Fax: (617) 243-2380
E-mail: internationaladmiss@lasell.edu
Phone: (617) 243-2225

**Lassen Community College**
www.lassencollege.edu
Admission & Records
PO Box 3000
Susanville, CA 96130
Fax: (530) 251-8802
E-mail: kclain@lassencollege.edu
Phone: (530) 251-8808

**Laurel Business Institute**
www.laurel.edu
11 East Penn Street
PO Box 877
Uniontown, PA 15401
Fax: (724) 439-3607
E-mail: ddecker@laurel.edu
Phone: (724) 439-4900

**Laurel Technical Institute**
www.laurel.edu
200 Sterling Avenue
Sharon, PA 16146
Fax: (724) 983-8355
E-mail: lti.admission@laurel.edu
Phone: (724) 983-0700

**Laurel University**
www.laureluniversity.edu
Admissions
1215 Eastchester Drive
High Point, NC 27265-3115
Fax: (336) 889-2261
E-mail: admissions@laureluniversity.edu
Phone: (336) 887-3000 ext. 127

**Lawrence Technological University**
www.ltu.edu
Director of Admissions
21000 West Ten Mile Road
Southfield, MI 48075-1058
Fax: (248) 204-2228
E-mail: international@ltu.edu
Phone: (248) 204-3160

**Lawrence University**
www.lawrence.edu
Admissions
711 East Boldt Way SPC 29
Appleton, WI 54911-5699
Fax: (920) 832-6782
E-mail: international.admissions@lawrence.edu
Phone: (920) 832-6889

**Lawson State Community College**
www.lawsonstate.edu
Admissions and Records
3060 Wilson Road SW
Birmingham, AL 35221-1717
Fax: (205) 923-7106
E-mail: jshelley@lawsonstate.edu
Phone: (205) 929-6361

**Le Cordon Bleu College of Culinary Arts: Atlanta**
www.chefs.edu/Atlanta
1927 Lakeside Parkway
Tucker, GA 30084
Fax: (773) 938-4571
Phone: (770) 938-4711

**Le Cordon Bleu College of Culinary Arts: Austin**
www.chefs.edu/austin
Admissions
3110 Esperanza Crossing, Suite 100
Austin, TX 78758-3641
E-mail: info@austin.chefs.edu
Phone: (888) 553-2433

**Le Cordon Bleu College of Culinary Arts: Chicago**
www.chefs.edu/Chicago
Admissions
361 West Chestnut
Chicago, IL 60610-3050
Fax: (312) 798-2922
E-mail: mcalafiore@chicnet.org
Phone: (312) 873-2018

**Le Cordon Bleu College of Culinary Arts: Los Angeles**
www.chefs.edu/los-angeles
530 East Colorado Boulevard
Pasadena, CA 91101
Fax: (626) 585-0486
E-mail: admissionsinfo@csca.edu
Phone: (626) 229-1300

**Le Cordon Bleu College of Culinary Arts: Miami**
www.chefs.edu/Miami
3221 Enterprise Way
Miramar, FL 33025
Phone: (954) 438-8882

**Le Cordon Bleu College of Culinary Arts: Minneapolis-St. Paul**
www.chefs.edu/Minneapolis-St-Paul
Admissions
1315 Mendota Heights Road
Mendota Heights, MN 55120-1129
Fax: (651) 452-5282
E-mail: dpeterson@msp.chefs.edu
Phone: (651) 675-4787

**Le Cordon Bleu College of Culinary Arts: Orlando**
www.chefs.edu/Orlando
Registrar
8511 Commodity Circle, Suite 100
Orlando, FL 32819
Fax: (407) 996-1544
E-mail: mwhite@orlandoculinary.com
Phone: (407) 313-8780

**Le Cordon Bleu College of Culinary Arts: Portland**
www.chefs.edu/portland
600 SW 10th Avenue, Suite #500
Portland, OR 97205
Phone: (888) 848-3202

**Le Cordon Bleu College of Culinary Arts: San Francisco**
www.chefs.edu/San-Francisco
Admissions Office
350 Rhode Island Street
San Francisco, CA 94103
Fax: (415) 771-2194
E-mail: admissions@baychef.com
Phone: (415) 771-3500

**Le Cordon Bleu College of Culinary Arts: Scottsdale**
www.chefs.edu/Scottsdale
8100 East Camelback Road, Suite 1001
Scottsdale, AZ 85251
Fax: (480) 990-0351
E-mail: sciadmissions@scichefs.com
Phone: (480) 990-3773

**Le Moyne College**
www.lemoyne.edu
Admission Office
1419 Salt Springs Road
Syracuse, NY 13214-1301
Fax: (315) 445-4711
E-mail: admission@lemoyne.edu
Phone: (315) 445-4300

**Lebanon Valley College**
www.lvc.edu
Admission Office
101 North College Avenue
Annville, PA 17003-1400
Fax: (717) 867-6026
E-mail: mcauley@lvc.edu
Phone: (717) 867-6129

**L'Ecole Culinaire**
www.lecoleculinaire.com
9811 South Outer Forty Drive
St. Louis, MO 63124
Phone: (314) 587-2433

**Lee College**
www.lee.edu
Registrar
Box 818
Baytown, TX 77522-0818
Fax: (281) 425-6831
E-mail: emorris@lee.edu
Phone: (281) 425-6396

**Lee University**
www.leeuniversity.edu
Office of Admissions
1120 North Ocoee Street
PO Box 3450
Cleveland, TN 37320-3450
Fax: (423) 614-8533
E-mail: admissions@leeuniversity.edu
Phone: (423) 614-8500

**Lees-McRae College**
www.lmc.edu
Admissions
Box 128
Banner Elk, NC 28604
Fax: (828) 898-8707
E-mail: shirahk@lmc.edu
Phone: (828) 898-2519

**Lehigh Carbon Community College**
www.lccc.edu
Student Services
4525 Education Park Drive
Schnecksville, PA 18078-2502
Fax: (610) 799-1527
E-mail: corban@lccc.edu
Phone: (610) 799-1137

**Lehigh University**
www.lehigh.edu
Admissions
27 Memorial Drive West
Bethlehem, PA 18015
Fax: (610) 758-4361
E-mail: mbv2@lehigh.edu
Phone: (610) 758-6602

**LeMoyne-Owen College**
www.loc.edu
Admissions
807 Walker Avenue
Memphis, TN 38126
Fax: (901) 435-1524
E-mail: june_chinn-jointer@loc.edu
Phone: (901) 435-1507

**Lenoir-Rhyne University**
www.lr.edu
Office of Enrollment Management
LR Box 7227
Hickory, NC 28603
Fax: (828) 328-7378
E-mail: admission@lr.edu
Phone: (800) 277-5721

**Lesley University**
www.lesley.edu
Director of Admissions
29 Everett Street
Cambridge, MA 02140-2790
Fax: (617) 349-8810
E-mail: dkocar@lesley.edu
Phone: (617) 349-8800

**LeTourneau University**
www.letu.edu
Office of International Studies
PO Box 7001
Longview, TX 75607-7001
Fax: (903) 233-4301
E-mail: alanclipperton@letu.edu
Phone: (903) 233-3170

**Lewis & Clark College**
www.lclark.edu
Associate Dean/Director, International
Students and Scholars
0615 SW Palatine Hill Road
MSC 32
Portland, OR 97219-7899
Fax: (503) 768-7055
E-mail: bdwhite@lclark.edu
Phone: (503) 768-7307

**Lewis University**
www.lewisu.edu
Admission Office
Unit #297
One University Parkway
Romeoville, IL 60446-2200
Fax: (815) 836-5002
E-mail: kingty@lewisu.edu
Phone: (815) 836-7211

**Lewis-Clark State College**
www.lcsc.edu
International Admissions
500 Eighth Avenue
Lewiston, ID 83501-2698
Fax: (208) 792-2876
E-mail: camartin@lcsc.edu
Phone: (208) 792-2877

**Liberty University**
www.liberty.edu
Office of International Admissions
1971 University Boulevard
Lynchburg, VA 24515
Fax: (434) 582-2424
E-mail: international@liberty.edu
Phone: (434) 592-4118

**Life Pacific College**
www.lifepacific.edu
Admissions
Attn: Admissions
1100 West Covina Boulevard
San Dimas, CA 91773
Fax: (909) 599-6690
E-mail: admissions@lifepacific.edu
Phone: (909) 599-5433

**Life University**
www.life.edu
New Student Development - International
1269 Barclay Circle
Marietta, GA 30060
Fax: (770) 426-2895
E-mail: matthew.davidson@life.edu
Phone: (678) 331-4330

**LIM College**
www.limcollege.edu
Admissions Office
12 East 53rd Street
New York, NY 10022
Fax: (212) 750-3432
E-mail: jacqueline.bonsignore@limcollege.edu
Phone: (212) 310-0610

**Limestone College**
www.limestone.edu
Admissions
1115 College Drive
Gaffney, SC 29340-3799
Fax: (864) 487-8706
E-mail: cphenicie@limestone.edu
Phone: (800) 795-7151 ext. 4554

**Lincoln Christian University**
www.lincolnchristian.edu
Admissions Office Manager
100 Campus View Drive
Lincoln, IL 62656-2111
Fax: (217) 732-4199
E-mail: admissions@lincolnchristian.edu
Phone: (217) 732-3168 ext. 2251

**Lincoln College**
www.lincolncollege.edu
Admissions
300 Keokuk Street
Lincoln, IL 62656
Fax: (217) 732-7715
E-mail: gbree@lincolncollege.edu
Phone: (800) 569-0556

**Lincoln College of Technology: Denver**
www.lincolnedu.com
11194 East 45th Ave
Denver, CO 80239
Phone: (303) 722-5724

**Lincoln College of Technology: Grand Prairie**
www.lincolntech.com
2915 Alouette Drive
Grand Prairie, TX 75052

**Lincoln College of Technology: Indianapolis**
www.lincolntech.com
7225 Winton Drive, Building 128
Indianapolis, IN 46268
Fax: (317) 634-1089
Phone: (317) 632-5553

**Lincoln College of Technology: West Palm Beach**
www.lincolnedu.com
Admissions
2410 Metrocentre Boulevard
West Palm Beach, FL 33407
Fax: (561) 842-9503
E-mail: tguibert@newenglandtech.com
Phone: (561) 712-5095

**Lincoln Land Community College**
www.llcc.edu
Special Admissions
5250 Shepherd Road
Box 19256
Springfield, IL 62794-9256
Fax: (217) 786-2492
E-mail: ron.gregoire@llcc.cc.il.us
Phone: (217) 786-2296

**Lincoln Memorial University**
www.lmunet.edu
6965 Cumberland Gap Parkway
Harrogate, TN 37752-1901
Fax: (423) 869-6444
E-mail: admissions@lmunet.edu
Phone: (423) 869-6280

**Lincoln Technical Institute: Allentown**
www.lincolntech.com
5151 Tilghman Street
Allentown, PA 18104
Fax: (610) 395-2706
Phone: (610) 398-5300

**Lincoln Technical Institute: Northeast Philadelphia**
www.lincolntech.com
2180 Hornig Road
Philadelphia, PA 19116
Fax: (215) 969-3457
Phone: (215) 969-0869

**Lincoln Technical Institute: Philadelphia**
www.lincolntech.com
9191 Torresdale Avenue
Philadelphia, PA 19136
Fax: (215) 335-1443
E-mail: dcunningham@lincolntech.com
Phone: (215) 335-0800

**Lincoln University**
www.lincolnuca.edu
Admissions
401 15th Street
Oakland, CA 94612
Fax: (510) 628-8012
E-mail: peggyau@lincolnuca.edu
Phone: (510) 628-8010

**Lincoln University**
www.lincolnu.edu
International Student Affairs
820 Chestnut Street, B7 Young Hall
Jefferson City, MO 65101
Fax: (573) 681-5596
E-mail: clarkd@lincolnu.edu
Phone: (573) 681-5477

**Lincoln University**
www.lincoln.edu
International Programs and Services
1570 Baltimore Pike
Lincoln University, PA 19352-0999
Fax: (484) 365-7822
E-mail: clundy@lincoln.edu
Phone: (484) 365-7785

**Lindenwood University**
www.lindenwood.edu
Director, International Students and Scholars
209 South Kingshighway
St. Charles, MO 63301
Fax: (636) 949-4108
E-mail: international@lindenwood.edu
Phone: (636) 949-4982

**Lindsey Wilson College**
www.lindsey.edu
Office Manager/Admissions Counselor
210 Lindsey Wilson Street
Columbia, KY 42728
Fax: (270) 384-8060
E-mail: talleyd@lindsey.edu
Phone: (270) 384-8236

**Linfield College**
www.linfield.edu
Admission Office
900 Southeast Baker Street
McMinnville, OR 97128-6894
Fax: (503) 883-2472
E-mail: admission@linfield.edu
Phone: (503) 883-2213

**Linn-Benton Community College**
www.linnbenton.edu
Admissions
6500 Pacific Blvd SW
Albany, OR 97321
Fax: (541) 917-4868
E-mail: bakerce@linnbenton.edu
Phone: (541) 917-4813

**Lipscomb University**
www.lipscomb.edu
Office of Transfer and International Students
One University Park Drive
Nashville, TN 37204-3951
Fax: (615) 966-1804
E-mail: sylvia.braden@lipscomb.edu
Phone: (615) 966-6151

**Little Big Horn College**
www.lbhc.edu
Box 370
Crow Agency, MT 59022
Fax: (406) 638-3169
E-mail: mccormickm@lbhc.edu
Phone: (406) 638-3116

**LIU Brooklyn**
http://liu.edu/brooklyn
International Admissions
1 University Plaza
Office of Admissions
Brooklyn, NY 11201-8423
Fax: (718) 780-6110
E-mail: bkln-admissions@liu.edu
Phone: (718) 488-1389

**LIU Post**
www.liu.edu/post
International Admissions
720 Northern Boulevard
Brookville, NY 11548-1300
Fax: (516) 299-2137
E-mail: post-enroll@liu.edu
Phone: (516) 299-2900

**Livingstone College**
www.livingstone.edu
Admissions
701 West Monroe Street
Salisbury, NC 28144-5213
Fax: (704) 216-6215
E-mail: admissions@livingstone.edu
Phone: (704) 216-6001

**Lock Haven University of Pennsylvania**
www.lhup.edu
LHU Office of Admissions
Lock Haven, PA 17745
Fax: (570) 484-2201
E-mail: admissions@lhup.edu
Phone: (570) 484-2027

**Logan University**
www.logan.edu
Admissions
1851 Schoettler Road
Chesterfield, MO 63017
E-mail: Admissions@logan.edu
Phone: (800) 533-9210

**Loma Linda University**
www.llu.edu
Director, International Student and Scholar Services
Admissions Processing
Loma Linda University
Loma Linda, CA 92350
Fax: (909) 558-7949
E-mail: maguirre@llu.edu
Phone: (909) 558-4560

**Lone Star College System**
www.lonestar.edu
F-1 International Student Advising
5000 Research Forest Drive
The Woodlands, TX 77381-4356
E-mail: nithy@lonestar.edu
Phone: (832) 813-6813

**Long Beach City College**
www.lbcc.edu
International Student Program
4901 East Carson Street
Mail Code R6
Long Beach, CA 90808
Fax: (562) 938-4747
E-mail: international_staff@lbcc.edu
Phone: (562) 938-4745

**Long Island Business Institute**
www.libi.edu
Financial Aid
136-18 39th Avenue, 5th Floor
Flushing, NY 11354
Fax: (718) 939-9235
E-mail: lzhu@libi.edu
Phone: (718) 939-5100

**Longwood University**
www.longwood.edu
International Admissions Office
201 High Street
Farmville, VA 23909-1898
Fax: (434) 395-2332
E-mail: internationalaffairs@longwood.edu
Phone: (434) 395-2172

**Lorain County Community College**
www.lorainccc.edu
International Education
1005 Abbe Road North
Elyria, OH 44035-1691
Fax: (440) 366-4167
E-mail: aremmert@lorainccc.edu
Phone: (440) 366-7042

**Loras College**
www.loras.edu
Admissions Office
1450 Alta Vista Street
Dubuque, IA 52001-0178
Fax: (563) 588-7119
E-mail: rebecca.ohnesorge@loras.edu
Phone: (563) 588-7234

**Los Angeles City College**
www.lacitycollege.edu
International Student Center
855 North Vermont Avenue
Los Angeles, CA 90029-3589
Fax: (323) 953-4013
E-mail: bradyr@lacitycollege.edu
Phone: (323) 953-4000 ext. 2470

**Los Angeles Harbor College**
www.lahc.edu
International Student Office
1111 Figueroa Place
Wilmington, CA 90744-2397
Fax: (310) 233-4223
E-mail: gradyp@lahc.edu
Phone: (310) 233-4112

**Los Angeles Mission College**
www.lamission.edu
Counseling Office
13356 Eldridge Avenue
Sylmar, CA 91342-3245
Fax: (818) 365-3623
Phone: (818) 364-7600

**Los Angeles Pierce College**
www.piercecollege.edu
Evaluation Tech/DSO, International
Admissions
6201 Winnetka Avenue
Woodland Hills, CA 91371
Fax: (818) 347-8704
E-mail: intlstu@piercecollege.edu
Phone: (818) 710-2511

**Los Angeles Southwest College**
www.lasc.edu
1600 West Imperial Highway
Los Angeles, CA 90047-4899
Phone: (323) 241-5321

**Los Angeles Trade and Technical College**
www.lattc.edu
International Students Program Coordinator/
DSO
400 West Washington Boulevard
Los Angeles, CA 90015-4181
Fax: (213) 286-5386
E-mail: cruzj@lattc.edu
Phone: (213) 763-5327

**Los Angeles Valley College**
www.lavc.edu
International Students Coordinator
5800 Fulton Avenue
Valley Glen, CA 91401-4096
Fax: (818) 778-5519
E-mail: dunnae@lavc.edu
Phone: (818) 778-5518

**Los Medanos College**
www.losmedanos.edu
International Students Admissions
2700 East Leland Road
Pittsburg, CA 94565
E-mail: ailich@4cd.edu
Phone: (925) 685-1230 ext. 2563

**Louisburg College**
www.louisburg.edu
Admissions
501 North Main Street
Louisburg, NC 27549
Fax: (919) 496-1788
E-mail: stolbert@louisburg.edu
Phone: (919) 497-3233

**Louisiana College**
www.lacollege.edu
Admissions
LC Box 566
Pineville, LA 71359
Fax: (318) 487-7550
E-mail: admissions@lacollege.edu
Phone: (318) 487-7259

**Louisiana State University and Agricultural and Mechanical College**
www.lsu.edu
Undergraduate Admissions
1146 Pleasant Hall
Baton Rouge, LA 70803-2750
Fax: (225) 578-4433
E-mail: intrntladm@lsu.edu
Phone: (225) 578-1175

**Louisiana State University at Eunice**
www.lsue.edu
Admissions
PO Box 1129
Eunice, LA 70535
Fax: (337) 550-1306
E-mail: admissions@lsue.edu
Phone: (337) 550-1329

**Louisiana State University Health Sciences Center**
www.lsuhsc.edu
433 Bolivar Street
New Orleans, LA 70112-7021
Phone: (504) 568-4808

**Louisiana State University in Shreveport**
www.lsus.edu
Registrar
One University Place
Shreveport, LA 71115-2399
Fax: (318) 797-5286
E-mail: darlena.atkins@lsus.edu
Phone: (318) 797-5063

**Louisiana Tech University**
www.latech.edu
Office of Admissions
Box 3178
Ruston, LA 71272
Fax: (318) 257-2499
E-mail: usjba@vm.cc.latech.edu
Phone: (318) 257-3036

**Lourdes University**
www.lourdes.edu
Associate Director of Admissions
6832 Convent Boulevard
Sylvania, OH 43560-2898
Fax: (419) 824-3916
E-mail: AdmissionsLCAdmits@lourdes.edu
Phone: (419) 885-5291

**Lower Columbia College**
www.lowercolumbia.edu
International Programs
1600 Maple Street
Box 3010
Longview, WA 98632-0310
Fax: (360) 442-2379
E-mail: mboisvert@lowercolumbia.edu
Phone: (360) 442-2313

**Loyola Marymount University**
www.lmu.edu
Office of Admissions
1 LMU Drive
Los Angeles, CA 90045-2659
Fax: (310) 338-2797
E-mail: admissions@lmu.edu
Phone: (310) 338-2750

**Loyola University Chicago**
www.luc.edu
Office of Undergraduate Admission
1032 West Sheridan Road.
Chicago, IL 60660
Fax: (773) 508-8926
E-mail: lnieto@luc.edu
Phone: (773) 508-3080

**Loyola University Maryland**
www.loyola.edu
Undergraduate Admission
4501 North Charles Street
Baltimore, MD 21210-2699
Fax: (410) 617-5012
E-mail: admission@loyola.edu
Phone: (800) 221-9107

**Loyola University New Orleans**
www.loyno.edu
Director, Undergraduate Admissions
6363 St. Charles Avenue
Campus Box 18
New Orleans, LA 70118-6195
Fax: (504) 865-3383
E-mail: admit@loyno.edu
Phone: (504) 865-3240

**Lubbock Christian University**
www.lcu.edu
Admissions Office
5601 19th Street
Lubbock, TX 79407-2099
Fax: (806) 720-7162
E-mail: shelley.parnell@lcu.edu
Phone: (806) 720-7160

**Luna Community College**
www.luna.edu
Admissions
366 Luna Drive
Las Vegas, NM 87701
Fax: (505) 454-5338
E-mail: mmarquez@luna.edu
Phone: (505) 454-5312

**Lurleen B. Wallace Community College**
www.lbwcc.edu
Office of Admissions and Records
Box 1418
Andalusia, AL 36420
Fax: (334) 881-2201
E-mail: jriley@lbwcc.edu
Phone: (334) 881-2281

**Luther College**
www.luther.edu
Center for Global Learning
700 College Drive
Decorah, IA 52101-1042
Fax: (563) 387-1060
E-mail: global@luther.edu
Phone: (563) 387-1062

**Lycoming College**
www.lycoming.edu
Admissions Office
700 College Place
Williamsport, PA 17701
Fax: (570) 321-4317
E-mail: zhang@lycoming.edu
Phone: (570) 321-4319

**Lyme Academy College of Fine Arts**
www.lymeacademy.edu
84 Lyme Street
Old Lyme, CT 06371
Fax: (860) 434-8725
E-mail: admissions@lymeacademy.edu
Phone: (860) 434-3571

**Lynchburg College**
www.lynchburg.edu
Admissions
1501 Lakeside Drive
Lynchburg, VA 24501-3199
Fax: (434) 544-8653
E-mail: admissions@lynchburg.edu
Phone: (800) 426-8101 ext. 8300

**Lyndon State College**
www.lyndonstate.edu
Office of Admissions
1001 College Road
PO Box 919
Lyndonville, VT 05851
Fax: (802) 626-6335
E-mail: trevor.barski@lyndonstate.edu
Phone: (800) 225-1998

**Lynn University**
www.lynn.edu
Office of Admission
3601 North Military Trail
Boca Raton, FL 33431-5598
Fax: (561) 237-7100
E-mail: admission@lynn.edu
Phone: (561) 237-7900

**Lyon College**
www.lyon.edu
Enrollment Services
PO Box 2317
Batesville, AR 72501-2317
Fax: (870) 307-7250
E-mail: admissions@lyon.edu
Phone: (800) 423-2542

**Macalester College**
www.macalester.edu
Admissions
1600 Grand Avenue
St. Paul, MN 55105-1899
Fax: (651) 696-6724
E-mail:
internationaladmissions@macalester.edu
Phone: (651) 696-6349

**MacCormac College**
www.maccormac.edu
Registrar's Office
29 East Madison Street
Chicago, IL 60602
Fax: (312) 922-4286
E-mail: msilva@maccormac.edu
Phone: (312) 922-1884 ext. 203

**Machzikei Hadath Rabbinical College**
5407 16th Avenue
Brooklyn, NY 11204
Fax: (718) 851-1265
Phone: (718) 854-8777 ext. 23

**Macomb Community College**
www.macomb.edu
Center Campus - G110
14500 East Twelve Mile Road
Warren, MI 48088-3896
Fax: (586) 286-2187
E-mail: jeffersc@macomb.cc.mi.us
Phone: (586) 286-4787

**Madison Area Technical College**
www.madisoncollege.edu
International Education
1701 Wright Street
Madison, WI 53704-2599
Fax: (608) 258-2329
E-mail: GBradshaw@madisoncollege.edu
Phone: (608) 246-6165

**Madison Media Institute**
www.mediainstitute.edu
2702 Agriculture Drive
Madison, WI 53718
E-mail: mmi@madisonmedia.com

**Madonna University**
www.madonna.edu
International Students Office
36600 Schoolcraft Road
Livonia, MI 48150-1176
Fax: (734) 432-5393
E-mail: gphilson@madonna.edu
Phone: (734) 432-5791

**Maharishi University of Management**
www.mum.edu
Office for International Student Admissions
Office of Admissions
1000 North Fourth Street
Fairfield, IA 52557
Fax: (641) 472-1179
E-mail: intadmiss@mum.edu
Phone: (641) 472-1110

**Maine College of Art**
www.meca.edu
Admissions
522 Congress Street
Portland, ME 04101
Fax: (207) 699-5080
E-mail: jrudnicki@meca.edu
Phone: (207) 699-5021

**Maine Maritime Academy**
www.mainemaritime.edu
Admissions Office
Pleasant Street
Castine, ME 04420
Fax: (207) 326-2515
E-mail: admissions@mma.edu
Phone: (207) 326-2207

**Malone University**
www.malone.edu
Admissions
2600 Cleveland Avenue NW
Canton, OH 44709-3308
Fax: (330) 471-8149
E-mail: lhoffman@malone.edu
Phone: (330) 471-8139

**Manchester Community College**
www.mcc.commnet.edu
PO Box 1046, MS#12
Manchester, CT 06045-1046
Fax: (860) 512-3221
E-mail: jmesquita@mcc.commnet.edu
Phone: (860) 512-3205

**Manchester Community College**
www.mccnh.edu
Admissions Department
1066 Front Street
Manchester, NH 03102-8518
Fax: (603) 668-5354
E-mail: lbaia@ccsnh.edu
Phone: (603) 206-8101

**Manchester University**
www.manchester.edu
Admissions
604 East College Avenue
North Manchester, IN 46962-0365
Fax: (260) 982-5239
E-mail: KLGrubbs@manchester.edu
Phone: (260) 982-5022

**Manhattan College**
www.manhattan.edu
International Admissions Counselor
4513 Manhattan College Parkway
Riverdale, NY 10471
Fax: (718) 862-8019
E-mail: admit_
internationalstudents@manhattan.edu
Phone: (718) 862-7200

**Manhattan School of Music**
www.msmnyc.edu
Admission and Financial Aid
120 Claremont Avenue
New York, NY 10027-4698
Fax: (212) 749-3025
E-mail: admission@msmnyc.edu
Phone: (212) 749-2802 ext. 4501

**Manhattanville College**
www.mville.edu
Admissions
2900 Purchase Street
Purchase, NY 10577
Fax: (914) 694-1732
E-mail: admissions@mville.edu
Phone: (914) 323-5464

**Manor College**
www.manor.edu
Full-Time Admissions
700 Fox Chase Road
Jenkintown, PA 19046-3319
Fax: (215) 576-6564
E-mail: enroll@manor.edu
Phone: (215) 884-2216 ext. 205

**Mansfield University of Pennsylvania**
www.mansfield.edu
Center for International Cooperation and
Exchange
71 Academy Street
Mansfield, PA 16933
Fax: (570) 662-4121
E-mail: mdomenec@mansfield.edu
Phone: (570) 662-4810

**Manthano Christian College**
www.manthanochristian.org
6420 North Newburgh
Westland, MI 48185
Phone: (734) 895-3280 ext. 30


**Maranatha Baptist University**
www.mbu.edu
Admissions Office
745 West Main Street
Watertown, WI 53094
Fax: (920) 261-9109
E-mail: admissions@mbbc.edu
Phone: (920) 261-9300


**Maria College**
www.mariacollege.edu
Admissions Office
700 New Scotland Avenue
Albany, NY 12208
Fax: (518) 453-1366
E-mail: admissions@mariacollege.edu
Phone: (518) 861-2517


**Marian University**
www.marian.edu
Office of Admission
3200 Cold Spring Road
Indianapolis, IN 46222-1997
Fax: (317) 955-6401
E-mail: jjohnson2@marian.edu
Phone: (317) 955-6390


**Marian University**
www.marianuniversity.edu
Admissions
45 South National Avenue
Fond du Lac, WI 54935-4699
Fax: (920) 923-8755
E-mail: jhartzell@marianuniversity.edu
Phone: (920) 923-8117


**Marietta College**
www.marietta.edu
Office of Admission
215 Fifth Street
Marietta, OH 45750-4005
Fax: (740) 376-8888
E-mail: nkh001@marietta.edu
Phone: (800) 331-7896


**Marion Military Institute**
www.marionmilitary.edu
Admissions
1101 Washington Street
Marion, AL 36756-0420
Fax: (334) 683-2382
E-mail: bcrawford@marionmilitary.edu
Phone: (800) 664-1842 ext. 382


**Marist College**
www.marist.edu
Undergraduate Admission
3399 North Road
Poughkeepsie, NY 12601-1387
Fax: (845) 575-3215
E-mail: admission@marist.edu
Phone: (845) 575-3226


**Marlboro College**
www.marlboro.edu
Admissions Office
PO Box A
2582 South Road
Marlboro, VT 05344-0300
Fax: (802) 451-7555
E-mail: admissions@marlboro.edu
Phone: (800) 343-0049


**Marquette University**
www.marquette.edu
Office of International Education
PO Box 1881
Milwaukee, WI 53201-1881
Fax: (414) 288-3701
E-mail: ellen.blauw@marquette.edu
Phone: (414) 288-7289


**Mars Hill University**
www.mhu.edu
Admissions
Mars Hill University Admissions Office
PO Box 370
Mars Hill, NC 28754
Fax: (828) 689-1473
E-mail: kvance@mhu.edu
Phone: (828) 689-1353


**Marshall University**
www.marshall.edu
Graduate/International Admissions
One John Marshall Drive
Huntington, WV 25755
Fax: (304) 696-3135
E-mail: international@marshall.edu
Phone: (304) 696-4304


**Marshalltown Community College**
www.iavalley.edu/mcc/
Carole Permar
3700 South Center Street
Marshalltown, IA 50158
Fax: (641) 752-8149
Phone: (641) 752-7106


**Martin Community College**
www.martincc.edu
1161 Kehukee Park Road
Williamston, NC 27892-9988
Fax: (252) 792-0826
E-mail: admissions@martincc.edu
Phone: (252) 798-0268


**Martin Methodist College**
www.martinmethodist.edu
Admissions
433 West Madison
Pulaski, TN 38478-2799
Fax: (931) 363-9800
E-mail: rhood@martinmethodist.edu
Phone: (931) 363-9805


**Martin University**
www.martin.edu
2171 Avondale Place
Box 18567
Indianapolis, IN 46218
Fax: (317) 543-3257
E-mail: hglinsey@martin.edu
Phone: (317) 543-3671


**Mary Baldwin University**
http://www.marybaldwin.edu/
Spencer Center Civic & Global Engagement
Office of Admissions
Box 1500
Staunton, VA 24401
Fax: (540) 887-7185
E-mail: rvance-cheng@mbc.edu
Phone: (540) 887-7113


**Marygrove College**
www.marygrove.edu
Admissions
8425 West McNichols Road
Detroit, MI 48221-2599
Fax: (313) 927-1399
E-mail: info@marygrove.edu
Phone: (313) 927-1240


**Maryland Institute College of Art**
www.mica.edu
Undergraduate Admission
1300 Mount Royal Avenue
Baltimore, MD 21217-4134
Fax: (410) 225-2337
E-mail: kyee@mica.edu
Phone: (410) 225-2222


**Marylhurst University**
www.marylhurst.edu
Admissions Office
PO Box 261
Marylhurst, OR 97036-0261
Fax: (503) 699-6268
E-mail: admissions@marylhurst.edu
Phone: (800) 634-9982 ext. 6268


**Marymount California University**
www.marymountcalifornia.edu
Office of Admission
30800 Palos Verdes Drive East
Rancho Palos Verdes, CA 90275-6299
Fax: (310) 265-0962
E-mail: admissions@marymountcalifornia.edu
Phone: (310) 377-5501 ext. 211


**Marymount Manhattan College**
www.mmm.edu
Office of International Admissions
221 East 71st Street
New York, NY 10021-4597
Fax: (212) 517-0448
E-mail: aberry@mmm.edu
Phone: (212) 517-0418


**Marymount University**
www.marymount.edu
Office of Admissions
2807 North Glebe Road
Arlington, VA 22207-4224
Fax: (703) 522-0349
E-mail:
international.admissions@marymount.edu
Phone: (703) 284-1500


**Maryville College**
www.maryvillecollege.edu
Center for International Education
502 East Lamar Alexander Parkway
Maryville, TN 37804-5907
Fax: (865) 981-8010
E-mail: kirsten.sheppard@maryvillecollege.edu
Phone: (865) 273-8991

**Maryville University of Saint Louis**
www.maryville.edu
Office of Admissions
650 Maryville University Drive
St. Louis, MO 63141-7299
Fax: (314) 529-9927
E-mail: mmace@maryville.edu
Phone: (314) 529-9350 ext. 6857

**Marywood University**
www.marywood.edu
Office of University Admissions
2300 Adams Avenue
Scranton, PA 18509-1598
Fax: (570) 961-4763
E-mail: digregorio@marywood.edu
Phone: (570) 348-6234 ext. 2434

**Massachusetts Bay Community College**
www.massbay.edu
International Education & Study Abroad
Programs
50 Oakland Street
Wellesley Hills, MA 02481
Fax: (781) 239-2707
E-mail: internationaled@massbay.edu
Phone: (781) 239-2642

**Massachusetts College of Art and Design**
www.massart.edu
Admissions
621 Huntington Avenue
Boston, MA 02115-5882
Fax: (617) 879-7250
E-mail: admissions@massart.edu
Phone: (617) 879-7222

**Massachusetts College of Liberal Arts**
www.mcla.edu
Office of Admission
375 Church Street
North Adams, MA 01247
Fax: (413) 662-5179
E-mail: admissions@mcla.edu
Phone: (413) 662-5410

**Massachusetts Institute of Technology**
web.mit.edu
Undergraduate Admissions
77 Massachusetts Avenue, Room 3-108
Cambridge, MA 02139-4307
Fax: (617) 258-8304
E-mail: mitintl@mit.edu
Phone: (617) 253-3400

**Massachusetts Maritime Academy**
www.maritime.edu
Admissions
101 Academy Drive
Flanagan Hall
Buzzards Bay, MA 02532
E-mail: cavila@maritime.edu
Phone: (508) 830-6686

**Massasoit Community College**
www.massasoit.mass.edu
One Massasoit Boulevard
Brockton, MA 02302-3996
Fax: (508) 427-1257
E-mail: mhughes@massasoit.mass.edu
Phone: (508) 588-9100 ext. 1412

**The Master's University**
www.masters.edu
International Student Office
Office of Admissions
21726 Placerita Canyon Road
Santa Clarita, CA 91321-1200
Fax: (661) 362-2695
E-mail: abryerton@masters.edu
Phone: (661) 362-2249

**Maysville Community and Technical College**
www.maysville.kctcs.edu
1755 US HIghway 68
Maysville, KY 41056
Fax: (606) 759-5818
E-mail: jessica.kern@kctcs.edu
Phone: (606) 759-7141 ext. 66186

**Mayville State University**
www.mayvillestate.edu
Admissions and Extended Learning
330 Third Street, NE
Mayville, ND 58257-1299
Fax: (701) 788-4748
E-mail: misti.wuori@mayvillestate.edu
Phone: (701) 788-4631

**McCann School of Business and Technology: Dickson City**
www.mccann.edu
2227 Scranton Carbondale Highway
Dickson City, PA 18519
Phone: (570) 307-2000

**McCann School of Business and Technology: Hazleton**
www.mccann.edu
370 Maplewood Drive
Hazle Township, PA 18202
Fax: (570) 454-6286
E-mail: info@mccann.edu
Phone: (570) 454-6172

**McCann School of Business and Technology: Pottsville**
www.mccann.edu
2650 Woodglen Road
Pottsville, PA 17901
Fax: (570) 622-7770
E-mail: info@mccann.edu
Phone: (570) 622-7622

**McCann School of Business and Technology: Sunbury**
www.mccann.edu
1147 North Fourth Street
Sunbury, PA 17801
E-mail: info@mccann.edu
Phone: (570) 286-3058

**McDaniel College**
www.mcdaniel.edu
Office of Admissions
2 College Hill
Westminster, MD 21157-4390
Fax: (410) 857-2757
E-mail: bbeveridge@mcdaniel.edu
Phone: (410) 857-2230

**McDowell Technical Community College**
www.mcdowelltech.edu
Admissions
54 College Drive
Marion, NC 28752
Fax: (828) 652-1014
E-mail: wingatecain@mcdowelltech.edu
Phone: (828) 652-0632

**McHenry County College**
www.mchenry.edu
Recruitment and Admissions Office
8900 US Highway 14
Crystal Lake, IL 60012-2738
Fax: (815) 455-3766
E-mail: aweaver@mchenry.edu
Phone: (815) 479-7782

**McKendree University**
www.mckendree.edu
Admission
701 College Road
Lebanon, IL 62254-1299
Fax: (618) 537-6496
E-mail: jlblasdel@mckendree.edu
Phone: (618) 537-6836

**McLennan Community College**
www.mclennan.edu
Admissions
1400 College Drive
Waco, TX 76708
Fax: (254) 299-8622
E-mail: astraten@mclennan.edu
Phone: (254) 299-8657

**McMurry University**
ww2.mcm.edu
Admission
South 14th and Sayles Boulevard
1 McMurry University, #278
Abilene, TX 79697-0001
Fax: (325) 793-4701
E-mail: admissions@mcm.edu
Phone: (325) 793-4700

**McNally Smith College of Music**
www.mcnallysmith.edu
19 Exchange Street East
St. Paul, MN 55101
E-mail: admissions@mcnallysmith.edu
Phone: (651) 361-3460

**McNeese State University**
www.mcneese.edu
International Programs
MSU Box 91740
Lake Charles, LA 70609-1740
Fax: (337) 562-4238
E-mail: internationaloffice@mcneese.edu
Phone: (337) 475-5962

**McPherson College**
www.mcpherson.edu
Admissions
1600 East Euclid Street
Box 1402
McPherson, KS 67460-1402
Fax: (620) 241-8443
E-mail: admiss@mcpherson.edu
Phone: (620) 242-0400

**MCPHS University**
www.mcphs.edu
Director of Undergraduate and International
Recruitment
179 Longwood Avenue
Boston, MA 02115-5896
Fax: (617) 732-2118
E-mail: Rene.cabrera@mcphs.edu
Phone: (617) 879-5974

**Medaille College**
www.medaille.edu
Admissions
18 Agassiz Circle
Buffalo, NY 14214
Fax: (716) 880-2007
E-mail: admissionsug@medaille.edu
Phone: (716) 880-2200

**Medaille College: Rochester**
www.medaille.edu
1880 South Winton Road
Rochester, NY 14618
E-mail: sageadmissions@medaille.edu
Phone: (585) 272-0030

**Memphis College of Art**
www.mca.edu
Admissions
1930 Poplar Avenue
Overton Park
Memphis, TN 38104-2764
Fax: (901) 272-5158
E-mail: info@mca.edu
Phone: (901) 272-5151

**Menlo College**
www.menlo.edu
Admissions & Enrollment Management
1000 El Camino Real
Atherton, CA 94027
Fax: (650) 543-4496
E-mail: manasi.mane@menlo.edu
Phone: (650) 543-3831

**Mercer County Community College**
www.mccc.edu
International Students Coordinator
PO Box B
Trenton, NJ 08690-1099
Fax: (609) 570-3861
E-mail: bambhrol@mccc.edu
Phone: (609) 570-3438

**Mercer University**
www.mercer.edu
Admissions
1501 Mercer University Drive
Macon, GA 31207-0001
Fax: (478) 301-2828
E-mail: admissions@mercer.edu
Phone: (478) 301-5123

**Mercy College**
www.mercy.edu
Office of Admissions
555 Broadway
Dobbs Ferry, NY 10522
Fax: (914) 674-7382
E-mail: admissions@mercy.edu
Phone: (877) 637-2946

**Mercy College of Health Sciences**
www.mchs.edu
921 6th Avenue
Des Moines, IA 50309-1200
Fax: (515) 643-6702
E-mail: hgaumer@mercydesmoines.org
Phone: (515) 643-6604

**Mercyhurst University**
www.mercyhurst.edu
International House
501 East 38th Street
Erie, PA 16546-0001
Fax: (814) 824-2071
E-mail: eevans@mercyhurst.edu
Phone: (814) 824-2478

**Meredith College**
www.meredith.edu
Office of Admissions
3800 Hillsborough Street
Raleigh, NC 27607-5298
Fax: (919) 760-2348
E-mail: admissions@meredith.edu
Phone: (919) 760-8581

**Meridian Community College**
www.meridiancc.edu
Admissions
910 Highway 19 North
Meridian, MS 39307-5890
Fax: (601) 484-8838
E-mail: apayne@meridiancc.edu
Phone: (601) 481-1357

**Merrimack College**
www.merrimack.edu
Admissions
510 Turnpike Street, Suite 201
North Andover, MA 01845
Fax: (978) 837-5133
E-mail: admission@merrimack.edu
Phone: (978) 837-5000 ext. 5100

**Merritt College**
www.merritt.edu
International Specialist, International
Affairs & Distance Education
12500 Campus Drive
Oakland, CA 94619
Fax: (510) 436-2512
E-mail: dgephart@Peralta.edu
Phone: (510) 587-7834

**Mesa Community College**
www.mesacc.edu
International Education
1833 West Southern Avenue
Mesa, AZ 85202
Fax: (480) 461-7805
E-mail: supaluck.senaluang@mesacc.edu
Phone: (480) 461-7658

**Mesabi Range College**
www.mesabirange.edu
Enrollment Services
1001 Chestnut Street West
Virginia, MN 55792-3448
Fax: (218) 749-0318
E-mail: s.twaddle@mr.mnscu.edu
Phone: (218) 749-0313

**Mesalands Community College**
www.mesalands.edu
911 South Tenth Street
Tucumcari, NM 88401
Phone: (575) 461-4413

**Mesivta Torah Vodaath Seminary**
independentrabbinicalcolleges.org/index.html
425 East Ninth Street
Brooklyn, NY 11218
Phone: (718) 621-3651

**Messiah College**
www.messiah.edu
Admissions
One College Avenue, Suite 3005
Mechanicsburg, PA 17055
Fax: (717) 691-2307
E-mail: Intladmiss@messiah.edu
Phone: (717) 691-6000

**Methodist College**
www.methodistcol.edu
7600 North Academic Drive
Peoria, IL 61615
E-mail: admissions@methodistcol.edu
Phone: (309) 671-5143

**Methodist University**
www.methodist.edu
Director of International Programs
5400 Ramsey Street
Fayetteville, NC 28311-1420
Fax: (910) 630-7672
E-mail: bvamasiri@methodist.edu
Phone: (910) 630-7225

**Metro Business College: Rolla**
www.metrobusinesscollege.edu
1202 East Highway 72
Rolla, MO 65401
Fax: (573) 364-8077
E-mail: dana@metrobusinesscollege.edu
Phone: (573) 364-8464

**Metropolitan College of New York**
www.metropolitan.edu
Office of Admissions
60 West Street
New York, NY 10006-1735
Fax: (212) 343-8470
E-mail: admissions@mcny.edu
Phone: (212) 343-1234 ext. 5001

**Metropolitan Community College**
www.mccneb.edu
Associate Vice President for Student Affairs
Box 3777
Omaha, NE 68103-0777
Fax: (402) 457-2238
E-mail: plewisrodriguez@mccneb.edu
Phone: (402) 457-2430

**Metropolitan Community College - Kansas
City**
www.mcckc.edu
Office of Student Services
3200 Broadway
Kansas City, MO 64111
Fax: (816) 759-4589
E-mail: Bobbie.Gustin@mcckc.edu
Phone: (816) 604-4683

**Metropolitan State University of Denver**
www.msudenver.edu
Admission
Campus Box 16
Box 173362
Denver, CO 80217
Fax: (303) 556-6345
E-mail: gomezr@mscd.edu
Phone: (303) 556-5714

**Miami Dade College**
www.mdc.edu/
International Student Services
11011 SW 104th Street
Miami, FL 33176-3393
Fax: (305) 237-7596
E-mail: cflorez1@mdc.edu
Phone: (305) 237-7993

**Miami International University of Art and Design**
www.mymiu.edu
Senior Director of Admissions
1501 Biscayne Boulevard, Suite 100
Miami, FL 33132-1418
Fax: (305) 374-5933
E-mail: kryan@aii.edu
Phone: (305) 428-5700 ext. 5600

**Miami University: Hamilton**
www.ham.muohio.edu
Office of Admission
1601 University Boulevard
Hamilton, OH 45011-3399
Fax: (513) 785-1807
E-mail: leeje1@muohio.edu
Phone: (513) 785-3111

**Miami University: Middletown**
www.mid.muohio.edu
4200 East University Boulevard
Middletown, OH 45042
Fax: (513) 727-3223
E-mail: mlflynn@muohio.edu
Phone: (513) 727-3216

**Miami University: Oxford**
www.MiamiOH.edu
Assistant Director of Admission for
International Recruitment
301 South Campus Avenue
Oxford, OH 45056
Fax: (513) 529-1550
E-mail: ann.rahmat@miamioh.edu
Phone: (513) 529-2288

**Miami-Jacobs Career College: Columbus**
www.miamijacobs.edu
150 East Gay Street, 15th Floor
Columbus, OH 43215
Fax: (614) 221-8429
Phone: (614) 221-7770

**Miami-Jacobs Career College: Dayton**
www.miamijacobs.edu
Admissions
110 North Patterson Boulevard
Dayton, OH 45402
Fax: (937) 461-3384
E-mail: susan.cooper@miamijacobs.edu
Phone: (937) 222-7337

**Miami-Jacobs Career College: Sharonville**
www.miamijacobs.edu
Two Crowne Point Court, Suite 100
Sharonville, OH 45241
Phone: (513) 723-0520

**Michigan Jewish Institute**
www.mji.edu
Admissions
6888 West Maple Road
West Bloomfield, MI 48322
Fax: (248) 414-6907
E-mail: yepstein@mji.edu
Phone: (248) 414-6900

**Michigan State University**
www.msu.edu
International Students and Scholars
250 Administration Building
East Lansing, MI 48824
Fax: (517) 355-4657
E-mail: pbriggs@msu.edu
Phone: (517) 353-1720

**Michigan Technological University**
www.mtu.edu
International Programs and Services
1400 Townsend Drive
Houghton, MI 49931-1295
Fax: (906) 487-1891
E-mail: dslade@mtu.edu
Phone: (906) 487-2160

**Mid Michigan Community College**
www.midmich.edu
Admissions Office
1375 South Clare Avenue
Harrison, MI 48625-9442
Fax: (989) 772-2386
E-mail: jkridler@midmich.edu
Phone: (989) 773-6622 ext. 258

**Mid-America College of Funeral Service**
www.mid-america.edu
3111 Hamburg Pike
Jeffersonville, IN 47130
Fax: (812) 288-5942
E-mail: macfs@mindspring.com
Phone: (812) 288-8878

**Mid-Atlantic Christian University**
www.macuniversity.edu
Registrar
715 North Poindexter Street
Elizabeth City, NC 27909
Fax: (252) 334-2071
E-mail: yolanda.teske@macuniversity.edu
Phone: (252) 334-2029

**Mid-Plains Community College**
www.mpcc.edu
Student Advising
1101 Halligan Drive
North Platte, NE 69101
Fax: (308) 535-3710
E-mail: pucketh@mpcc.edu
Phone: (800) 658-4308 ext. 3710

**Mid-State Technical College**
www.mstc.edu
Enrollment Advisor
500 32nd Street North
Wisconsin Rapids, WI 54494
Fax: (715) 422-5561
E-mail: laurie.inda@mstc.edu
Phone: (715) 422-5430

**MidAmerica Nazarene University**
www.mnu.edu
Admissions Office
2030 East College Way
Olathe, KS 66062-1899
Fax: (913) 971-3410
E-mail: mmiller2@mnu.edu
Phone: (913) 971-3779

**Middle Georgia State University**
www.mga.edu
Admissions
100 College Station Drive
Macon, GA 31206
Fax: (478) 934-3403
E-mail: sbrantley@mgc.edu
Phone: (478) 934-3136

**Middle Tennessee State University**
www.mtsu.edu
International Programs and Services Office
1301 East Main Street
Cope Administration Building 208
Murfreesboro, TN 37132
Fax: (615) 898-5178
E-mail: twubneh@mtsu.edu
Phone: (615) 898-2238

**Middlebury College**
www.middlebury.edu
The Emma Willard House
Middlebury, VT 05753-6002
Fax: (802) 443-2056
E-mail: admissions@middlebury.edu
Phone: (802) 443-3000

**Middlesex Community College**
www.mxcc.edu
Admissions
100 Training Hill Road
Middletown, CT 06457-4889
Fax: (860) 344-7488
E-mail: dreome@mxcc.edu
Phone: (860) 343-5897

**Middlesex Community College**
www.middlesex.mass.edu
International Student Office
33 Kearney Square
Lowell, MA 01852-1987
Fax: (978) 656-3322
E-mail: international@middlesex.mass.edu
Phone: (978) 656-3207

**Middlesex County College**
www.middlesexcc.edu
Admissions
2600 Woodbridge Avenue
Box 3050
Edison, NJ 08818-3050
Fax: (732) 956-7728
E-mail: studentvisa@middlesexcc.edu
Phone: (732) 548-6000

**Midland College**
www.midland.edu
Director of Counseling
3600 North Garfield
Midland, TX 79705
Fax: (432) 685-4623
E-mail: sgrinnan@midland.edu
Phone: (432) 685-4505

**Midland University**
www.midlandu.edu
Admissions Office
900 North Clarkson Street
Fremont, NE 68025
Fax: (402) 941-6513
E-mail: watson@midlandu.edu
Phone: (402) 941-6503

**Midlands Technical College**
www.midlandstech.edu
International Admissions
PO Box 2408
Columbia, SC 29202
Fax: (803) 790-7584
E-mail: grossmanr@midlandstech.edu
Phone: (803) 738-7811

**Midstate College**
www.midstate.edu
411 West Northmoor Road
Peoria, IL 61614-3558
Fax: (309) 692-3893
E-mail: admissions@midstate.edu
Phone: (309) 692-4092

**Midway College**
www.midway.edu
Director of Admissions
512 East Stephens Street
Midway, KY 40347-1120
Fax: (859) 846-5787
E-mail: admissions@midway.edu
Phone: (859) 846-5347

**Midwestern State University**
www.mwsu.edu
Office of International Services
3410 Taft Boulevard
Wichita Falls, TX 76308-2099
Fax: (940) 397-4087
E-mail: kerrie.cale@mwsu.edu
Phone: (940) 397-4344

**Mildred Elley: Albany**
www.mildred-elley.edu
Admissions
855 Central Avenue
Albany, NY 12206-1513
Fax: (518) 786-0011
E-mail: admissions@mildred-elley.edu
Phone: (518) 786-3171

**Mildred Elley: New York City**
www.mildred-elley.edu
Admissions
25 Broadway, 16th Floor
New York, NY 10004
Fax: (518) 786-0011
E-mail: admissions@mildred-elley.edu
Phone: (518) 786-0855 ext. 1362

**Miles College**
www.miles.edu
Office of the Dean of Students
5500 Myron Massey Boulevard
Fairfield, AL 35064
Fax: (205) 923-9292
E-mail: carolyn@miles.edu
Phone: (205) 929-1655

**Miller-Motte College: Cary**
www.miller-motte.edu
2205 Walnut Street
Cary, NC 27518

**Miller-Motte College: Fayetteville**
www.miller-motte.edu
3725 Ramsey Street, Suite 103A
Fayetteville, NC 28311

**Miller-Motte Technical College**
www.miller-motte.edu
8085 Rivers Avenue, Suite E
North Charleston, SC 29406
Fax: (843) 329-4992
Phone: (843) 574-0101

**Miller-Motte Technical College: Chattanooga**
www.miller-motte.edu
6020 Shallowford Road, Suite 100
Chattanooga, TN 37421
Fax: (423) 510-1985
E-mail: gwheelous@miller-motte.com
Phone: (423) 510-9675

**Miller-Motte Technical College: Clarksville**
www.miller-motte.edu
Admissions
1820 Business Park Drive
Clarksville, TN 37040
Fax: (931) 552-2916
E-mail: rgmmb@usit.net
Phone: (931) 553-0071

**Miller-Motte Technical College: Conway**
www.miller-motte.edu
2451 Highway 501 East
Conway, SC 29526
E-mail: jill.miskelly@miller-motte.edu
Phone: (843) 591-1102

**Millersville University of Pennsylvania**
www.millersville.edu
Admissions Office
PO Box 1002
Lyle Hall
Millersville, PA 17551-0302
Fax: (717) 871-2147
E-mail: smita.prabhu@millersville.edu
Phone: (717) 871-4625

**Milligan College**
www.milligan.edu
Admissions
Box 210
Milligan College, TN 37682
Fax: (423) 461-8982
E-mail: kjwright@milligan.edu
Phone: (423) 461-8700

**Millikin University**
www.millikin.edu
International Recruitment
1184 West Main Street
Decatur, IL 62522-2084
Fax: (217) 425-4669
E-mail: international@millikin.edu
Phone: (217) 424-6202

**Mills College**
www.mills.edu
Admission Office
5000 MacArthur Boulevard
Oakland, CA 94613
Fax: (510) 430-3298
E-mail: admission@mills.edu
Phone: (510) 430-2135

**Millsaps College**
www.millsaps.edu
Office of Admissions
1701 North State Street
Jackson, MS 39210-0001
Fax: (601) 974-1059
E-mail: admissions@millsaps.edu
Phone: (601) 974-1063

**Milwaukee Area Technical College**
www.matc.edu
MATC International Student Admissions
Office
700 West State Street
Milwaukee, WI 53233-1443
Fax: (414) 297-8143
E-mail: adamss4@matc.edu
Phone: (414) 297-8177

**Milwaukee Institute of Art & Design**
www.miad.edu
Admissions
273 East Erie Street
Milwaukee, WI 53202
Fax: (414) 291-8077
E-mail: davidsigman@miad.edu
Phone: (414) 847-3267

**Milwaukee School of Engineering**
www.msoe.edu
International Admission Counselor
1025 North Broadway
Milwaukee, WI 53202-3109
Fax: (414) 277-7475
E-mail: andersonm@msoe.edu
Phone: (414) 277-4544

**Minneapolis Business College**
www.minneapolisbusinesscollege.edu
1711 West County Road B
Roseville, MN 55113
Fax: (651) 636-8185
Phone: (651) 636-7406

**Minneapolis College of Art and Design**
www.mcad.edu
Admissions
2501 Stevens Avenue
Minneapolis, MN 55404
Fax: (612) 874-3701
E-mail: admissions@mcad.edu
Phone: (612) 874-3760

**Minneapolis Community and Technical College**
www.minneapolis.edu
International Admissions Advisor
1501 Hennepin Avenue
Minneapolis, MN 55403-1710
Fax: (612) 659-6210
E-mail: sherry.brewer@minneapolis.edu
Phone: (612) 659-6201

**Minnesota School of Business: Blaine**
www.msbcollege.edu
Admissions
3680 Pheasant Ridge Dr. NE
Blaine, MN 55449
E-mail: jokoye@msbcollege.edu
Phone: (877) 225-8201

**Minnesota School of Business: Brooklyn Center**
www.msbcollege.edu
Admissions
5910 Shingle Creek Parkway
Brooklyn Center, MN 55430
E-mail: kellyobrien@msbcollege.edu
Phone: (800) 231-9154

**Minnesota School of Business: Elk River**
www.msbcollege.edu
Admissions
11500 193rd Avenue NW
Elk River, MN 55330
E-mail: telliott@msbcollege.edu
Phone: (877) 333-9757

**Minnesota School of Business: Lakeville**
www.msbcollege.edu
Admissions
17685 Juniper Path
Lakeville, MN 55044
E-mail: jpullin@msbcollege.edu
Phone: (877) 560-8777

**Minnesota School of Business: Plymouth**
www.msbcollege.edu
Admissions
1455 County Road 101 North
Plymouth, MN 55447
Fax: (736) 476-1000
E-mail: candria@msbcollege.edu
Phone: (763) 476-2000

**Minnesota School of Business: Richfield**
www.msbcollege.edu
Admissions
1401 West 76 Street, Suite 500
Richfield, MN 55423
Fax: (612) 861-5548
E-mail: ssultan@globeuniversity.edu
Phone: (800) 752-4223

**Minnesota School of Business: Rochester**
www.msbcollege.edu
Admissions
2521 Pennington Drive NW
Rochester, MN 55901
E-mail: ahelm@msbcollege.edu
Phone: (888) 662-8772

**Minnesota School of Business: Shakopee**
www.msbcollege.edu
Admissions
1200 Shakopee Town Square
Shakopee, MN 55379
E-mail: rkilpatrick@msbcollege.edu
Phone: (866) 776-1200

**Minnesota School of Business: St. Cloud**
www.msbcollege.edu
Admissions
1201 Second Street South
Waite Park, MN 56387
E-mail: info@msbcollege.edu
Phone: (866) 403-3333

**Minnesota State College - Southeast Technical**
www.southeastmn.edu
Admissions
1250 Homer Road
PO Box 409
Winona, MN 55987-0409
Fax: (507) 453-2715
E-mail: glanning@southeastmn.edu
Phone: (877) 853-8324

**Minnesota State Community and Technical College**
www.minnesota.edu
Solution Center
405 Colfax Avenue SW
Wadena, MN 56482-1447
Fax: (218) 736-1510
E-mail: kyle.Johnston@minnesota.edu
Phone: (877) 450-3322

**Minnesota State University Mankato**
www.mnsu.edu
Admissions Office
122 Taylor Center
Mankato, MN 56001
Fax: (507) 389-1511
E-mail: diane.berge@mnsu.edu
Phone: (507) 389-1822

**Minnesota State University Moorhead**
www.mnstate.edu
International Student Services
MSUM Office of Admissions, Box 67
1104 Seventh Avenue South
Moorhead, MN 56563
Fax: (218) 299-5928
E-mail: intladms@mnstate.edu
Phone: (218) 477-2956

**Minnesota West Community and Technical College**
www.mnwest.edu
Student Services
1314 North Hiawatha Avenue
Pipestone, MN 56164
Fax: (501) 372-5803
E-mail: beth.bents@mnwest.edu
Phone: (507) 372-3418

**Minot State University**
www.minotstateu.edu
Admissions Counselor
500 University Avenue West
Minot, ND 58707-5002
Fax: (701) 858-3386
E-mail: meghan.stewart@minotstateu.edu
Phone: (701) 858-3348

**MiraCosta College**
www.miracosta.edu
Institute for International Perspectives
One Barnard Drive
Oceanside, CA 92056-3899
Fax: (760) 757-8209
E-mail: iip@miracosta.edu
Phone: (760) 795-6897

**Mirrer Yeshiva Central Institute**
1795 Ocean Parkway
Brooklyn, NY 11223-2010
Phone: (718) 645-0536

**Misericordia University**
www.misericordia.edu
Admissions
301 Lake Street
Dallas, PA 18612-1098
Fax: (570) 675-2441
E-mail: gbozinsk@misericordia.edu
Phone: (570) 674-6434

**Mission College**
www.missioncollege.edu
International Students
3000 Mission College Boulevard
Santa Clara, CA 95054-1897
Fax: (408) 980-8980
E-mail: chigusa.katoku@missioncollege.edu
Phone: (408) 855-5025

**Mississippi College**
www.mc.edu
Global Education Center
Box 4026
200 South Capitol Street
Clinton, MS 39058-0001
Fax: (601) 925-7704
E-mail: mcpiletz@mc.edu
Phone: (601) 925-7635

**Mississippi Gulf Coast Community College**
www.mgccc.edu
College Registrar
PO Box 548
Perkinston, MS 39573
Fax: (601) 928-6345
E-mail: michelle.sekul@mgccc.edu
Phone: (601) 928-6760

**Mississippi State University**
www.msstate.edu
Mississippi State University International Insititute
Box 6334
Mississippi State, MS 39762
Fax: (662) 325-1678
E-mail: international@msstate.edu
Phone: (662) 325-2835

**Mississippi University for Women**
www.muw.edu
Admissions
1100 College St. MUW-1613
Columbus, MS 39701
Fax: (662) 241-7481
E-mail: smcnees@admissions.muw.edu
Phone: (662) 329-7106

**Mississippi Valley State University**
www.mvsu.edu
Director of Admissions
14000 Highway 82 West
Box 7222
Itta Bena, MS 38941-1400
Fax: (662) 254-3759
E-mail: jawill@mvsu.edu
Phone: (662) 254-3347

**Missouri Baptist University**
www.mobap.edu
Admissions Office
One College Park Drive
St. Louis, MO 63141-8660
Fax: (314) 392-2232
E-mail: Fitzgerald@mobap.edu
Phone: (314) 744-5301

**Missouri College**
www.missouricollege.com
1405 South Hanley Road
Brentwood, MO 63144
E-mail: kjefferson@missouricollege.com
Phone: (314) 821-7700

**Missouri Southern State University**
www.mssu.edu
International Student Exchange Program
3950 East Newman Road
Joplin, MO 64801-1595
Fax: (417) 659-4429
E-mail: zaidarhzauva-1@mssu.edu
Phone: (417) 625-3126

**Missouri State University**
www.missouristate.edu
Office of International Student Services
901 South National Avenue
Springfield, MO 65897
Fax: (417) 836-7656
E-mail:
internationalstudentservices@missouristate.edu
Phone: (417) 836-6618

**Missouri State University: West Plains**
www.wp.missouristate.edu
Office of Admissions
128 Garfield Avenue
West Plains, MO 65775-2715
Fax: (417) 255-7959
E-mail: wpadmissions@missouristate.edu
Phone: (417) 255-7955

**Missouri University of Science and Technology**
www.mst.edu
Admissions
106 Parker Hall
300 West 13th Street
Rolla, MO 65409-1060
Fax: (573) 341-4082
E-mail: admissions@mst.edu
Phone: (573) 341-4164

**Missouri Valley College**
www.moval.edu
Admissions
500 East College Street
Marshall, MO 65340
Fax: (660) 831-4233
E-mail: johnsoni@moval.edu
Phone: (660) 831-4125

**Missouri Western State University**
www.missouriwestern.edu
Admissions
4525 Downs Drive
Saint Joseph, MO 64507
Fax: (816) 271-5833
E-mail: cwashburn@missouriwestern.edu
Phone: (816) 271-4182

**Mitchell College**
www.mitchell.edu
Admissions
437 Pequot Avenue
New London, CT 06320-4498
Fax: (860) 444-1209
E-mail: martin_b@mitchell.edu
Phone: (800) 443-2811

**Mitchell Technical Institute**
www.mitchelltech.edu
1800 E Spruce Street
Mitchell, SD 57301
Fax: (605) 995-3083
E-mail: questions@mitchelltech.edu
Phone: (605) 995-3025

**Moberly Area Community College**
www.macc.edu
Student Services Office
101 College Avenue
Moberly, MO 65270-1304
Fax: (660) 263-2406
E-mail: jamesg@macc.edu
Phone: (660) 263-4110 ext. 235

**Modesto Junior College**
www.mjc.edu
Counseling Office
435 College Avenue
Modesto, CA 95350-5800
Fax: (209) 575-6859
E-mail: sturbainb@yosemite.cc.ca.us
Phone: (209) 575-6013

**Mohave Community College**
www.mohave.edu
Registrar
1971 Jagerson Avenue
Kingman, AZ 86409
Fax: (928) 757-0808
E-mail: mbrehmeyer@mohave.edu
Phone: (928) 757-0809

**Mohawk Valley Community College**
www.mvcc.edu
International Admissions Counselor
1101 Sherman Drive
Utica, NY 13501-5394
Fax: (315) 792-5527
E-mail: international.admissions@mvcc.edu
Phone: (315) 792-5351

**Molloy College**
www.molloy.edu
Admissions
PO Box 5002
Rockville Centre, NY 11571
E-mail: mlane@molloy.edu
Phone: (516) 323-4000

**Monmouth College**
www.monmouthcollege.edu
Admission
700 East Broadway
Monmouth College Admissions Office
Monmouth, IL 61462-1998
Fax: (309) 457-2141
E-mail: international@monmouthcollege.edu
Phone: (309) 457-2134

**Monmouth University**
www.monmouth.edu
Undergraduate Admission
400 Cedar Avenue
West Long Branch, NJ 07764-1898
Fax: (732) 263-5166
E-mail: ortiz-torres@monmouth.edu
Phone: (732) 571-3456

**Monroe College**
www.monroecollege.edu
International Admissions
2501 Jerome Avenue
Bronx, NY 10468
Fax: (718) 364-3552
E-mail: glopez@monroecollege.edu
Phone: (914) 632-5400

**Monroe Community College**
www.monroecc.edu
Admission Office
Office of Admissions-Monroe Community
College
Box 92808
Rochester, NY 14692-8908
Fax: (585) 292-3860
Phone: (585) 292-2200

**Montana Bible College**
www.montanabiblecollege.edu
3625 South 19th Avenue
Bozeman, MT 59718
Phone: (406) 586-3585

**Montana State University**
www.montana.edu
International Programs
PO Box 172190, 201 Strand Union Building
Bozeman, MT 59717-2190
Fax: (406) 994-1619
E-mail: international@montana.edu
Phone: (406) 994-4031

**Montana State University: Billings**
www.msubillings.edu
International Studies
1500 University Drive
Billings, MT 59101-0298
Fax: (406) 896-5907
E-mail: paul.foster4@msubillings.edu
Phone: (406) 657-1705

**Montana State University: Northern**
www.msun.edu
Admissions Office
Box 7751
Havre, MT 59501-7751
Fax: (406) 265-3792
E-mail: kshuttle@msun.edu
Phone: (800) 662-6132 ext. 3704

**Montana Tech of the University of Montana**
www.mtech.edu
Office of Enrollment Services
1300 West Park Street
Butte, MT 59701-8997
Fax: (406) 496-4710
E-mail: enrollment@mtech.edu
Phone: (406) 496-4256

**Montcalm Community College**
www.montcalm.edu
Associate Dean of Student Services
2800 College Drive
Sidney, MI 48885
Fax: (989) 328-2950
E-mail: debraj@montcalm.edu
Phone: (989) 328-1276

**Montclair State University**
www.montclair.edu
Undergraduate Admissions Office
One Normal Avenue
Montclair, NJ 07043
Fax: (973) 655-7700
Phone: (973) 655-6862

**Monterey Peninsula College**
www.mpc.edu
International Student Programs
980 Fremont Street
Monterey, CA 93940-4799
Fax: (831) 645-1390
E-mail: international_center@mpc.cc.ca.us
Phone: (831) 645-1357

**Montgomery County Community College**
www.mc3.edu
Office of Admissions
340 DeKalb Pike
PO Box 400
Blue Bell, PA 19422
Fax: (215) 619-7188
E-mail: international@mc3.edu
Phone: (215) 641-6676

**Montreat College**
www.montreat.edu
Admissions
P.O. Box 1267
Montreat, NC 28757
Fax: (828) 669-0120
E-mail: sgardner@montreat.edu
Phone: (828) 669-8012 ext. 3783

**Montserrat College of Art**
www.montserrat.edu
Admissions
23 Essex Street
Beverly, MA 01915
Fax: (978) 921-4241
E-mail: jeffrey.newell@montserrat.edu
Phone: (978) 921-4242 ext. 1152

**Moody Bible Institute**
www.moody.edu
Dean of Admissions
820 N LaSalle Boulevard
Chicago, IL 60610
Fax: (312) 329-8987
E-mail: charles.dresser@moody.edu
Phone: (312) 329-4267

**Moore College of Art and Design**
www.moore.edu
Admissions Office
The Parkway at 20th Street
Philadelphia, PA 19103-1179
Fax: (215) 568-3547
E-mail: admiss@moore.edu
Phone: (215) 965-4014

**Moorpark College**
www.moorparkcollege.edu
International Student
7075 Campus Road
Moorpark, CA 93021
Fax: (805) 378-1499
E-mail: mrauchfuss@vcccd.edu
Phone: (805) 378-1414

**Moraine Park Technical College**
www.morainepark.edu
Student Services
235 North National Avenue
Box 1940
Fond du Lac, WI 54935-1940
Fax: (920) 924-3421
E-mail: lholte@morainepark.edu
Phone: (920) 924-6378

**Moraine Valley Community College**
www.morainevalley.edu
Office of International Student Affairs
9000 West College Parkway
Palos Hills, IL 60465-2478
Fax: (708) 974-0561
E-mail: viverito@morainevalley.edu
Phone: (708) 974-5334

**Moravian College**
www.moravian.edu
Admissions
1200 Main Street
Bethlehem, PA 18018
Fax: (610) 861-1445
E-mail: apgarr@moravian.edu
Phone: (610) 861-1320

**Morehead State University**
www.moreheadstate.edu
Senior ES (Enrollment Services) Counselor
for International Recruitment
121 E Second Street
Morehead, KY 40351
Fax: (606) 783-5038
E-mail: w.sun@moreheadstate.edu
Phone: (606) 783-2000

**Morehouse College**
www.morehouse.edu
Office of Admissions
830 Westview Drive SW
Atlanta, GA 30314
Fax: (404) 572-3668
E-mail: admissions@morehouse.edu
Phone: (844) 512-6672

**Moreno Valley College**
www.rcc.edu/morenovalley
16130 Lasselle Street
Moreno Valley, CA 92551
Phone: (951) 571-6101

**Morgan Community College**
www.morgancc.edu
Student Services
920 Barlow Road
Fort Morgan, CO 80701
Fax: (970) 867-6608
Phone: (970) 867-3081

**Morgan State University**
www.morgan.edu
Admission/ Recruiting
1700 East Cold Spring Lane
Baltimore, MD 21251
Fax: (443) 885-8200
E-mail: admissions@morgan.edu
Phone: (443) 885-3000

**Morningside College**
www.morningside.edu
Admissions
1501 Morningside Avenue
Sioux City, IA 51106
Fax: (712) 274-5101
E-mail: curryte@morningside.edu
Phone: (712) 274-5511

**Morris College**
www.morris.edu
Admissions and Records
100 West College Street
Sumter, SC 29150-3502
Fax: (803) 773-8241
E-mail: dcalhoun@morris.edu
Phone: (803) 934-3225

**Morrison Institute of Technology**
www.morrisontech.edu
Admissions
701 Portland Avenue
Morrison, IL 61270-2959
Fax: (815) 772-7584
E-mail: admissions@morrisontech.edu
Phone: (815) 772-7218 ext. 207

**Morton College**
www.morton.edu
Director of Student Development
3801 South Central Avenue
Cicero, IL 60804-4398
Fax: (708) 656-9592
E-mail: M.Avalos-Thompson@morton.edu
Phone: (708) 656-8000 ext. 2245

**Motlow State Community College**
www.mscc.edu
Admissions and Records
Box 8500
Lynchburg, TN 37352-8500
Fax: (931) 393-1971
E-mail: sgilbreath@mscc.edu
Phone: (931) 393-1529 ext. 1597

**Mott Community College**
www.mcc.edu
Executive Director, Admissions & Recruitment
1401 East Court Street
Flint, MI 48503-2089
Fax: (810) 232-9503
E-mail: jennifer.mcdonald@mcc.edu
Phone: (810) 232-8225

**Mount Aloysius College**
www.mtaloy.edu
Admissions
7373 Admiral Peary Highway
Cresson, PA 16630
Fax: (814) 886-6441
E-mail: admissions@mtaloy.edu
Phone: (814) 886-6383

**Mount Angel Seminary**
www.mountangelabbey.org
Director of Immigration Services
One Abbey Drive
St. Benedict, OR 97373
Fax: (503) 845-3128
E-mail: tamara.swanson@mtangel.edu
Phone: (503) 845-3951 ext. 3549

**Mount Holyoke College**
www.mtholyoke.edu
Office of Admission
Newhall Center
50 College Street
South Hadley, MA 01075-1488
Fax: (413) 538-2409
E-mail: admission@mtholyoke.edu
Phone: (413) 538-2775

**Mount Ida College**
www.mountida.edu
Admissions Office
777 Dedham Street
Newton, MA 02459
Fax: (617) 928-4507
E-mail: admissions@mountida.edu
Phone: (617) 928-4553

**Mount Marty College**
www.mtmc.edu
Admissions
1105 West Eighth Street
Yankton, SD 57078
Fax: (605) 668-1508
E-mail: mmcadmit@mtmc.edu
Phone: (800) 658-4552

**Mount Mary University**
www.mtmary.edu
Admissions
2900 North Menomonee River Parkway
Milwaukee, WI 53222-4597
Fax: (414) 930-3708
E-mail: mmu-admiss@mtmary.edu
Phone: (414) 930-3620

**Mount Mercy University**
www.mtmercy.edu
Admissions
1330 Elmhurst Drive NE
Cedar Rapids, IA 52402-4797
Fax: (319) 363-5270
E-mail: acasella@mtmercy.edu
Phone: (319) 368-6460

**Mount Saint Mary College**
www.msmc.edu
International Programs
330 Powell Avenue
Newburgh, NY 12550
Fax: (845) 562-3520
E-mail: internationaladmissions@msmc.edu
Phone: (845) 569-3798

**Mount Saint Mary's University**
www.msmu.edu
Admissions
12001 Chalon Road
Los Angeles, CA 90049
Fax: (213) 477-2569
E-mail: vsharma1@msmu.edu
Phone: (800) 999-9893

**Mount San Antonio College**
www.mtsac.edu
1100 North Grand Avenue
Walnut, CA 91789
Phone: (909) 274-4415

**Mount San Jacinto College**
www.msjc.edu
Student Services
1499 North State Street
San Jacinto, CA 92583
Fax: (951) 654-6738
E-mail: jpadilla@msjc.edu
Phone: (951) 487-3211

**Mount St. Joseph University**
www.msj.edu
Office of Admission
ATTN: Office of Admission 5701 Delhi Road
Cincinnati, OH 45233-1670
Fax: (513) 244-4629
E-mail: international.admission@msj.edu
Phone: (513) 244-4814

**Mount St. Mary's University**
www.msmary.edu
Admissions Office
16300 Old Emmitsburg Road
Emmitsburg, MD 21727
Fax: (301) 447-5860
E-mail: mcintyre@msmary.edu
Phone: (800) 447-4347

**Mount Vernon Nazarene University**
www.mvnu.edu
Admissions
800 Martinsburg Road
Mount Vernon, OH 43050
Fax: (740) 393-0511
E-mail: admissions@mvnu.edu
Phone: (866) 462-6868 ext. 4510

**Mount Wachusett Community College**
www.mwcc.edu
Admissions
444 Green Street
Gardner, MA 01440-1000
Fax: (978) 630-9554
E-mail: rforsythe@mwcc.mass.edu
Phone: (978) 630-9290

**Mountain State College**
www.msc.edu
1508 Spring Street
Parkersburg, WV 26101-3993
Fax: (304) 485-3524
E-mail: adm@msc.edu
Phone: (304) 485-5487

**Mountain View College**
www.mvc.dcccd.edu
Office of Enrollment Management
Attn: Admissions
4849 West Illinois Avenue
Dallas, TX 75211-6599
Fax: (214) 860-3074
E-mail: ghall@dcccd.edu
Phone: (214) 860-8600

**Mt. Hood Community College**
www.mhcc.edu
Admissions
26000 SE Stark Street
Gresham, OR 97030
Fax: (503) 491-7388
E-mail: john.hamblin@mhcc.edu
Phone: (503) 491-7384

**Mt. Sierra College**
www.mtsierra.edu
Admissions
101 East Huntington Drive
Monrovia, CA 91016
Fax: (626) 359-1378
E-mail: snavarro@mtsierra.edu
Phone: (626) 873-2100

**MTI College**
www.mticollege.edu
Admissions
5221 Madison Avenue
Sacramento, CA 95841
Fax: (916) 339-0305
E-mail: epatterson@mticollege.edu
Phone: (916) 339-1500

**Muhlenberg College**
www.muhlenberg.edu
Office of Admissions
2400 Chew Street
Allentown, PA 18104
Fax: (484) 334-3032
E-mail: knguyen@muhlenberg.edu
Phone: (484) 664-3212

**Murray State College**
www.mscok.edu
Registrar
One Murray Campus
Tishomingo, OK 73460
Fax: (580) 387-7239
E-mail: pward@mscok.edu
Phone: (580) 387-7232

**Murray State University**
www.murraystate.edu
International Admissions
102 Curris Center
Murray State University
Murray, KY 42071
Fax: (270) 809-3211
E-mail: msu.intl@murraystate.edu
Phone: (270) 809-4223

**Muscatine Community College**
www.eicc.edu
Admissions
152 Colorado Street
Muscatine, IA 52761-5396
Fax: (563) 288-6104
E-mail: bhuntington@eicc.edu
Phone: (563) 288-6007

**Muskegon Community College**
www.muskegoncc.edu
Special Services / Enrollment Services
221 South Quarterline Road
Muskegon, MI 49442
Fax: (231) 777-0443
E-mail: donella.cooper@muskegoncc.edu
Phone: (231) 777-0404

**Muskingum University**
www.muskingum.edu
Director of International Admission and
Immigration Services Operations
163 Stormont Street
New Concord, OH 43762-1199
Fax: (740) 826-8100
E-mail: mccollum@muskingum.edu
Phone: (740) 826-8127

**Myotherapy Institute**
www.myotherapy.edu
4001 Pioneer Woods Drive
Lincoln, NE 68516
E-mail: info@myotherapy.edu
Phone: (402) 421-7410

**Napa Valley College**
www.napavalley.edu
2277 Napa-Vallejo Highway
Napa, CA 94558
Fax: (707) 253-3064
E-mail: dwhite@napavalley.edu
Phone: (707) 256-7200

**Naropa University**
www.naropa.edu
Admissions
2130 Arapahoe Avenue
Boulder, CO 80302-6697
Fax: (303) 546-3536
E-mail: admissions@naropa.edu
Phone: (303) 546-6572

**Nash Community College**
www.nashcc.edu
Admissions
Box 7488
Rocky Mount, NC 27804-0488
Fax: (252) 451-8401
E-mail: sgeanes@nashcc.edu
Phone: (252) 451-8308

**Nashua Community College**
www.nashuacc.edu
Admissions
505 Amherst Street
Nashua, NH 03063-1026
Fax: (603) 882-8690
E-mail: jcurtis@ccsnh.edu
Phone: (603) 578-8900 ext. 1547

**Nashville State Community College**
www.nscc.edu
Adriane Gordon
120 White Bridge Road
Nashville, TN 37209-4515
Fax: (615) 353-3243
E-mail: adriane.gordon@nscc.edu
Phone: (615) 353-3219

**Nassau Community College**
www.ncc.edu
Admissions
One Education Drive
Garden City, NY 11530
Fax: (516) 572-9743
E-mail: Rosemary.Ortlieb@ncc.edu
Phone: (516) 572-7053

**National American University:
Albuquerque**
www.national.edu
4775 Indian School Road NE, Suite 200
Albuquerque, NM 87110
Fax: (505) 348-3755
E-mail: albadmissions@national.edu
Phone: (505) 348-3750

**National American University: Austin**
www.national.edu
13801 Burnet Road, Suite 300
Austin, TX 78727
E-mail: sljones@national.edu
Phone: (512) 651-4700

**National American University: Bloomington**
www.national.edu
Director of Admissions
7801 Metro Parkway Suite 200
Bloomington, MN 55425
Fax: (952) 356-3605
E-mail: speterson2@national.edu
Phone: (651) 855-6315

**National American University: Denver**
www.national.edu
Admissions
1325 South Colorado Boulevard, Suite 100
Denver, CO 80222-3308
Fax: (303) 876-7105
E-mail: sthompson@national.edu
Phone: (303) 876-7100

**National American University: Kansas City**
www.national.edu
Admissions
3620 Arrowhead Avenue
Independence, MO 64057
Fax: (816) 412-7705
Phone: (816) 412-7702

**National American University: Lee's
Summit**
www.national.edu
401 NW Murray Road
Lee's Summit, MO 64081
E-mail: lsadmissions@national.edu
Phone: (816) 600-3900

**National American University: Rapid City**
www.national.edu
International Admissions
5301 South Highway 16
Rapid City, SD 57701
Fax: (605) 394-4900
E-mail: patfox@national.edu
Phone: (605) 394-4800

**National American University: Roseville**
www.national.edu
Regional Vice President Enrollment
Management
1550 West Highway 36
Roseville, MN 55113
E-mail: mmottl@national.edu
Phone: (651) 855-6315

**National College: Bartlett**
www.ncbt.edu
5760 Stage Road
Bartlett, TN 38134
Phone: (901) 213-1681

**National College: Canton**
www.national-college.edu
4736 Dressler Road NW
Canton, OH 44718
Phone: (330) 492-5300

**National College: Cincinnati**
www.national-college.edu
6871 Steger Drive
Cincinnati, OH 45237
Phone: (513) 761-1291

**National College: Columbus**
www.ncbt.edu
5665 Forest Hills Boulevard
Columbus, OH 43231
Phone: (614) 282-2800

**National College: Danville**
www.national-college.edu
115 East Lexington Avenue
Danville, KY 40422
Fax: (859) 236-1063
E-mail: market@educorp.edu
Phone: (859) 236-6991

**National College: Florence**
www.national-college.edu
8095 Connector Drive
Florence, KY 41042
Fax: (606) 525-8961
E-mail: market@educorp.edu
Phone: (606) 525-6510

**National College: Kettering**
www.national-college.edu
1837 Woodman Center Drive
Kettering, OH 45420
Phone: (937) 299-9450

**National College: Knoxville**
www.ncbt.edu
8415 Kingston Pike
Knoxville, TN 37919
Phone: (865) 539-2011

**National College: Lexington**
www.national-college.edu
2376 Sir Barton Way
Lexington, KY 40509
Fax: (859) 233-3054
E-mail: market@educorp.edu
Phone: (859) 253-0621

**National College: Madison**
www.national-college.edu
900 Madison Square
Madison, TN 37115
Phone: (615) 612-3015

**National College: Memphis**
www.ncbt.edu
3545 Lamar Avenue, Suite 1
Memphis, TN 38118
Phone: (901) 363-9046

**National College: Stow**
www.national-college.edu
3855 Fishercreek Road
Stow, OH 44224
Phone: (330) 676-1351

**National College: Willoughby Hills**
www.national-college.edu
27557 Chardon Road
Willoughby Hills, OH 44092
Phone: (440) 944-0825

**National College: Youngstown**
www.national-college.edu
3487 Belmont Avenue
Youngstown, OH 44505
Phone: (330) 759-0205

**National Paralegal College**
https://nationalparalegal.edu
717 East Maryland Avenue
Phoenix, AZ 85014-1561
Fax: (866) 347-2744
E-mail: info@nationalparalegal.edu
Phone: (800) 371-6105 ext. 0

**National Park College**
www.np.edu
Vice President of Student Affairs
101 College Drive
Hot Springs, AR 71913
Fax: (501) 760-4100
E-mail: mpicking@gccc.edu
Phone: (501) 760-4222

**National University**
www.nu.edu
International Programs Office
11255 North Torrey Pines Road
La Jolla, CA 92037-1011
Fax: (858) 541-7995
E-mail: ipo@nu.edu
Phone: (858) 541-7967

**National University College: Arecibo**
www.nuc.edu
High School Coordinator
PO Box 4035, MSC 452
Arecibo, PR 00614
Fax: (787) 879-5047
E-mail: jecandelaria@nuc.edu
Phone: (787) 879-5044 ext. 5211

**National University College: Bayamon**
www.nuc.edu
Special Assistant to the President
PO Box 2036
Bayamon, PR 00960
Fax: (787) 779-4909
E-mail: aaviles@nuc.edu
Phone: (787) 780-5134 ext. 4133

**National University College: Ponce**
www.nuc.edu
Admissions and Marketing Director
PO Box 801243
Coto Laurel, PR 00780-1243
Fax: (787) 841-1360
E-mail: mbermudez@nuc.edu
Phone: (787) 840-4474 ext. 7005

**National-Louis University**
www.nl.edu
Student Affairs
122 South Michigan Avenue
Chicago, IL 60603
Fax: (847) 465-5730
E-mail: brouzan@nl.edu
Phone: (312) 261-3461

**Naugatuck Valley Community College**
www.nv.edu
Admissions
750 Chase Parkway
Waterbury, CT 06708-3089
Fax: (203) 596-8766
E-mail: lstango@nvcc.commnet.edu
Phone: (203) 575-8054

**Navajo Technical University**
www.navajotech.edu
PO Box 849
Crownpoint, NM 87313
Fax: (505) 786-5644
E-mail: tbegay@navajotech.edu
Phone: (505) 786-4326

**Navarro College**
www.navarrocollege.edu
3200 West Seventh Avenue
Corsicana, TX 75110
Fax: (903) 875-7353
E-mail: elizabeth.wilson@navarrocollege.edu
Phone: (903) 875-7370

**Nazarene Bible College**
www.nbc.edu
Admissions Office
1111 Academy Park Loop
Colorado Springs, CO 80910-3704
Fax: (719) 884-5199
E-mail: admissions@nbc.edu
Phone: (719) 884-5062

**Nazareth College**
www.naz.edu
Undergraduate Admissions
4245 East Avenue
Rochester, NY 14618-3790
Fax: (585) 389-2826
E-mail: imortim4@naz.edu
Phone: (585) 389-2860

**Nebraska College of Technical Agriculture**
www.ncta.unl.edu
Office of Admissions
404 East 7th Street
Curtis, NE 69025-0069
Fax: (308) 367-5212
E-mail: tsmith24@unl.edu
Phone: (308) 367-5267

**Nebraska Indian Community College**
www.thenicc.edu
PO Box 428
Macy, NE 68039-0428
Fax: (402) 837-4183
E-mail: tmunhofen@thenicc.edu
Phone: (402) 494-2311

**Nebraska Wesleyan University**
www.nebrwesleyan.edu
Admissions Office
5000 St. Paul Avenue
Lincoln, NE 68504
Fax: (402) 465-2177
E-mail: marmstro@nebrwesleyan.edu
Phone: (402) 465-2100

**Neosho County Community College**
www.neosho.edu
Coordinator for International Services
800 West 14th Street
Chanute, KS 66720
Fax: (620) 431-0082
E-mail: scadwallader@neosho.edu
Phone: (620) 431-2820 ext. 240

**Neumann University**
www.neumann.edu
Admissions
Office of Admissions
One Neumann Drive
Aston, PA 19014-1298
Fax: (610) 361-2548
E-mail: neumann@neumann.edu
Phone: (610) 558-5616

**Neumont University**
www.neumont.edu
Office of Admissions
143 South Main Street
Salt Lake City, UT 84111
Fax: (801) 302-2880
E-mail: admissions@neumont.edu
Phone: (801) 302-2879

**New College of Florida**
www.ncf.edu
Office of Admissions
5800 Bay Shore Road
Sarasota, FL 34243-2109
Fax: (941) 487-5010
E-mail: admissions@ncf.edu
Phone: (941) 487-5001

**New England College**
www.nec.edu
Admissions
15 Main Street
Henniker, NH 03242
Fax: (603) 428-7230
E-mail: bpoznanski@nec.edu
Phone: (603) 428-2223

**New England College of Business and Finance**
www.necb.edu
Admissions
10 High Street, Suite 204
Boston, MA 02110
Fax: (617) 951-2533
E-mail: pamela.dellaporta@necb.edu
Phone: (617) 603-6914

**New England Conservatory of Music**
www.necmusic.edu
Admissions
290 Huntington Avenue
Boston, MA 02115-5018
Fax: (617) 585-1115
E-mail: ADMstaff@necmusic.edu
Phone: (617) 585-1101

**New England Culinary Institute**
www.neci.edu
Admissions
7 School Street
Montpelier, VT 05602
Fax: (802) 225-3280
E-mail: admissions@neci.edu
Phone: (877) 225-3210

**New England Institute of Technology**
www.neit.edu
Admissions Office
One New England Tech Boulevard
East Greenwich, RI 02818
Fax: (401) 886-0868
E-mail: rgroleau@neit.edu
Phone: (401) 467-7744 ext. 3746

**New Hampshire Institute of Art**
www.nhia.edu
Admissions
148 Concord Street
Manchester, NH 03104
E-mail: laurastevenson@nhia.edu
Phone: (603) 836-25148

**New Hope Christian College**
www.newhope.edu
Admissions
2155 Bailey Hill Road
Eugene, OR 97405
Fax: (541) 343-5801
E-mail: markkelley@newhope.edu
Phone: (541) 485-1780

**New Jersey City University**
www.njcu.edu
2039 Kennedy Boulevard
Jersey City, NJ 07305-1597
E-mail: admissions@njcu.edu
Phone: (201) 200-3022

**New Jersey Institute of Technology**
www.njit.edu
Office of International Students and Faculty
University Heights
Newark, NJ 07102
Fax: (973) 596-5450
E-mail: grundy@njit.edu
Phone: (973) 596-2451

**New Mexico Highlands University**
www.nmhu.edu
International Education Center
Box 9000
Las Vegas, NM 87701
Fax: (505) 454-3511
E-mail: eclayton@nmhu.edu
Phone: (505) 454-3058

**New Mexico Institute of Mining and Technology**
www.nmt.edu
International & Exchange Programs
801 Leroy Place
Socorro, NM 87801
Fax: (575) 835-5959
E-mail: michael.voegerl@nmt.edu
Phone: (575) 835-5060

**New Mexico Junior College**
www.nmjc.edu
Office of Admission
5317 Lovington Highway
Hobbs, NM 88240
Fax: (575) 392-0322
E-mail: jmcdonald@nmjc.edu
Phone: (575) 392-5112

**New Mexico Military Institute**
www.nmmi.edu
Office of Admissions
101 West College Boulevard
Roswell, NM 88201-5173
Fax: (575) 624-8058
E-mail: admissions@nmmi.edu
Phone: (800) 421-5376

**New Mexico State University**
www.nmsu.edu
International Programs, MSC 3567
Box 30001, MSC 3A
Las Cruces, NM 88003-8001
Fax: (575) 646-2558
E-mail: ibp@nmsu.edu
Phone: (575) 646-2834

**New Mexico State University at Alamogordo**
www.nmsua.edu
International Student Services
2400 North Scenic Drive
Alamogordo, NM 88310
E-mail: admissnmsua@nmsu.edu
Phone: (575) 439-3700

**New Mexico State University at Carlsbad**
www.cavern.nmsu.edu
International Student Services Office
1500 University Drive
Carlsbad, NM 88220
Fax: (575) 646-2558
E-mail: marjaspe@ad.nmsu.edu
Phone: (575) 646-2017

**New Mexico State University at Grants**
www.grants.nmsu.edu
Graduate and International Student Services
1500 North Third Street
Grants, NM 87020
Fax: (575) 646-2558
E-mail: marjaspe@ad.nmsu.edu
Phone: (575) 646-2017

**New Orleans Baptist Theological Seminary**
www.nobts.edu
3939 Gentilly Boulevard
New Orleans, LA 70126-4858
E-mail: leavelladmission@nobts.edu
Phone: (504) 282-4455

**New Saint Andrews College**
www.nsa.edu
PO Box 9025
Moscow, ID 83843
Fax: (208) 882-4293
E-mail: admissions@nsa.edu
Phone: (208) 882-1566 ext. 113

**The New School College of Performing Arts**
www.newschool.edu
Admissions
79 Fifth Avenue, Floor 5
New York, NY 10003
Fax: (212) 580-1738
E-mail: mannesadmissions@newschool.edu
Phone: (212) 580-0210 ext. 4862

**New York Career Institute**
www.nyci.edu
11 Park Place
New York, NY 10007
Fax: (212) 385-7574
E-mail: lstieglitz@nyci.edu
Phone: (212) 962-0002

**New York Institute of Technology**
www.nyit.edu
Admissions
Box 8000
Northern Boulevard
Old Westbury, NY 11568-8000
Fax: (516) 686-7613
E-mail: nparis@nyit.edu
Phone: (516) 686-1486

**New York School of Interior Design**
www.nysid.edu
Dean of Students
170 East 70th Street
New York, NY 10021-5110
Fax: (212) 472-1867
E-mail: khigginbotham@nysid.edu
Phone: (212) 472-1500 ext. 202

**New York University**
www.nyu.edu
Undergraduate Admissions
665 Broadway, 11th floor
New York, NY 10012-2339
Fax: (212) 995-4902
E-mail: admissions@nyu.edu
Phone: (212) 998-4500

**Newberry College**
www.newberry.edu
Admission
2100 College Street
Newberry, SC 29108
Fax: (803) 321-5138
E-mail: admission@newberry.edu
Phone: (803) 321-5127

**Newbury College**
www.newbury.edu
Office of Admission
129 Fisher Avenue
Office of Admission
Brookline, MA 02445
Fax: (617) 731-9618
E-mail: Shannon.mccarthy@newbury.edu
Phone: (617) 730-7104

**Newman University**
www.newmanu.edu
Admissions
3100 McCormick
Wichita, KS 67213-2097
Fax: (316) 942-4483
E-mail: jonesn@newmanu.edu
Phone: (316) 942-4291 ext. 2233

**NewSchool of Architecture & Design**
www.newschoolarch.edu
International Enrollment
1249 F Street
San Diego, CA 92101
E-mail:
newschooladmissions@newschoolarch.edu
Phone: (619) 684-8887

**NHTI-Concord's Community College**
www.nhti.edu
Admissions
31 College Drive
Concord, NH 03301
Fax: (603) 230-9302
E-mail: nhtiadm@nhctc.edu
Phone: (603) 271-6484 ext. 4178

**Niagara County Community College**
www.niagaracc.suny.edu
Admissions Office
3111 Saunders Settlement Road
Sanborn, NY 14132-9460
Fax: (716) 614-6820
E-mail: drilling@niagaracc.suny.edu
Phone: (716) 614-6282

**Niagara University**
www.niagara.edu
International Relations
Gacioch Center
PO Box 2011
Niagara University, NY 14109
Fax: (716) 286-8303
E-mail: bmb@niagara.edu
Phone: (716) 286-8331

**Nicholls State University**
www.nicholls.edu
Office of Admissions
PO Box 2004-NSU
Thibodaux, LA 70310
Fax: (985) 448-4929
E-mail: marilyn.gonzales@nicholls.edu
Phone: (985) 449-7038

**Nichols College**
www.nichols.edu
Admissions
PO Box 5000
Dudley, MA 01571-5000
Fax: (508) 943-9885
E-mail: emily.reardon@nichols.edu
Phone: (508) 213-2275

**Norco College**
www.norcocollege.edu
2001 Third Street
Norco, CA 92860
Phone: (951) 372-7003

**Norfolk State University**
www.nsu.edu
Admissions
700 Park Avenue
Norfolk, VA 23504
Fax: (757) 823-2078
E-mail: internationaladmissions@nsu.edu
Phone: (757) 823-8396

**Normandale Community College**
www.normandale.edu
Admissions
9700 France Avenue South
Bloomington, MN 55431
Fax: (952) 358-8230
E-mail: antoinette.bowling-
harris@normandale.edu
Phone: (952) 358-8207

**North Carolina Central University**
www.nccu.edu
Student Affairs
PO Box 19717
Durham, NC 27707
Fax: (919) 530-7645
E-mail: emosby@nccu.edu
Phone: (919) 530-7492

**North Carolina State University**
www.ncsu.edu
Director of International Admissions
Campus Box 7103
203 Peele Hall, 10 Watauga Club Drive
Raleigh, NC 27695-7103
Fax: (919) 515-5039
E-mail: jeong_powell@ncsu.edu
Phone: (919) 515-2434

**North Carolina Wesleyan College**
www.ncwc.edu
Office of Admissions
3400 North Wesleyan Boulevard
Rocky Mount, NC 27804
Fax: (252) 985-5319
E-mail: dpatterson@ncwc.edu
Phone: (800) 488-6292

**North Central College**
www.northcentralcollege.edu
Office of Admissions
30 North Brainard Street
Naperville, IL 60566-7063
Fax: (630) 637-5819
E-mail: msotermat@noctrl.edu
Phone: (630) 637-5800

**North Central Kansas Technical College**
www.ncktc.edu
Registrar
PO Box 507
3033 US Highway 24
Beloit, KS 67420
Fax: (785) 738-2903
E-mail: jheidrick@ncktc.edu
Phone: (785) 738-9058

**North Central Michigan College**
www.ncmich.edu
Student Services
1515 Howard Street
Petoskey, MI 49770
Fax: (231) 348-6672
E-mail: pwelmers@ncmich.edu
Phone: (888) 298-6605

**North Central Missouri College**
www.ncmissouri.edu
Admissions Office
1301 Main Street
Trenton, MO 64683
Fax: (660) 359-2211
E-mail: kcross@mail.ncmissouri.edu
Phone: (660) 359-3948 ext. 1401

**North Central State College**
www.ncstatecollege.edu
Registrar
2441 Kenwood Circle, PO Box 698
Mansfield, OH 44901-0698
Fax: (419) 755-4757
E-mail: mmonnes@ncstatecollege.edu
Phone: (419) 755-4824

**North Central Texas College**
www.nctc.edu
1525 West California Street
Gainesville, TX 76240
Fax: (940) 668-6049
E-mail: admissions@nctc.edu
Phone: (940) 668-4404

**North Central University**
www.northcentral.edu
Admissions
910 Elliot Avenue
Minneapolis, MN 55404
Fax: (612) 343-4146
E-mail: camonten@northcentral.edu
Phone: (612) 343-4465

**North Country Community College**
www.nccc.edu
Enrollment Management
23 Santanoni Avenue
PO Box 89
Saranac Lake, NY 12983
Fax: (518) 891-0898
E-mail: admissions@nccc.edu
Phone: (888) 879-6222 ext. 233

**North Dakota State College of Science**
www.ndscs.edu
Admissions Office
800 North 6th Street
Wahpeton, ND 58076-0001
Fax: (701) 671-2201
E-mail: ndscs.admissions@ndscs.edu
Phone: (800) 342-4325 ext. 32202

**North Dakota State University**
www.ndsu.edu
Office of Admission
Dept. 2832, PO Box 6050
Fargo, ND 58108-6050
Fax: (701) 231-8643
E-mail: ndsu.admission@ndsu.edu
Phone: (701) 231-863

**North Florida Community College**
www.nfcc.edu
Admissions
325 NW Turner Davis Drive
Madison, FL 32340
Fax: (850) 973-1697
E-mail: bethead@nfcc.edu
Phone: (850) 973-1622

**North Greenville University**
www.ngu.edu
Admissions
PO Box 1892
7801 North Tigerville Road
Tigerville, SC 29688-1892
Fax: (864) 977-7177
E-mail: Katie.Marshall@ngc.edu
Phone: (864) 977-7001

**North Hennepin Community College**
www.nhcc.edu
Associate Director of Admissions & Outreach
7411 85th Avenue North
Brooklyn Park, MN 55445
Fax: (763) 493-0563
E-mail: solson2@nhcc.edu
Phone: (763) 488-0491

**North Idaho College**
www.nic.edu
Office of Admissions
1000 West Garden Avenue
Coeur d'Alene, ID 83814-2199
Fax: (208) 769-3399
E-mail: cahanhi@nic.edu
Phone: (208) 769-3311

**North Iowa Area Community College**
www.niacc.edu
Student Development
500 College Drive
Mason City, IA 50401
Fax: (641) 422-4150
E-mail: Sandy.Harrington@niacc.edu
Phone: (641) 422-4208

**North Lake College**
www.northlakecollege.edu
International Center
5001 North MacArthur Boulevard
Irving, TX 75038-3899
Fax: (972) 273-3138
E-mail: nlcintl@dcccd.edu
Phone: (972) 273-3155

**North Park University**
www.northpark.edu
Admission
3225 West Foster Avenue Box 19
Chicago, IL 60625-4895
Fax: (773) 279-7952
E-mail: internationals@northpark.edu
Phone: (773) 244-5510

**North Seattle College**
www.northseattle.edu
International Student Programs
9600 College Way North
Seattle, WA 98103-3599
Fax: (206) 934-3794
E-mail: international@sccd.ctc.edu
Phone: (206) 934-3672

**North Shore Community College**
www.northshore.edu
Enrollment Services
One Ferncroft Road
Box 3340
Danvers, MA 01923-0840
Fax: (781) 477-2143
E-mail: lbarrett@northshore.edu
Phone: (978) 762-4000 ext. 4333

**Northampton Community College**
www.northampton.edu
Admissions
3835 Green Pond Road
Bethlehem, PA 18020-7599
Fax: (610) 861-4560
E-mail: pboulous@northampton.edu
Phone: (610) 861-5500

**Northcentral Technical College**
www.ntc.edu
International Education
1000 West Campus Drive
Wausau, WI 54401
E-mail: knight@ntc.edu
Phone: (715) 803-1038

**Northcentral University**
www.ncu.edu
Senior Director of Admissions
8667 East Hartford Drive
Scottsdale, AZ 85255
Fax: (928) 541-7817
E-mail: kboutelle@ncu.edu
Phone: (480) 253-3535

**Northeast Community College**
www.northeast.edu
Admissions
801 East Benjamin Avenue
Box 469
Norfolk, NE 68702-0469
Fax: (402) 844-7413
E-mail: admission@northeast.edu
Phone: (402) 844-7262

**Northeast Iowa Community College**
www.nicc.edu
Admissions
PO Box 400
Calmar, IA 52132
Fax: (563) 562-4369
E-mail: vamstadh@nicc.edu
Phone: (800) 728-2256

**Northeast Mississippi Community College**
www.nemcc.edu
101 Cunningham Boulevard
Booneville, MS 38829
Fax: (662) 728-1165
E-mail: admitme@nemcc.edu
Phone: (662) 720-7290

**Northeast Texas Community College**
www.ntcc.edu
Admissions
2886 FM 1735
PO Box 1307
Mount Pleasant, TX 75455
Fax: (903) 572-6712
E-mail: twhite@ntcc.edu
Phone: (903) 434-8122

**Northeast Wisconsin Technical College**
www.nwtc.edu
2740 West Mason Street
Box 19042
Green Bay, WI 54307-9042
Fax: (920) 498-6882
E-mail: mark.franks@nwtc.edu
Phone: (920) 498-6269

**Northeastern Junior College**
www.njc.edu
Admissions
100 College Avenue
Sterling, CO 80751-2399
Fax: (970) 521-6715
E-mail: sarah.stone-robinson@njc.edu
Phone: (970) 521-6854

**Northeastern Oklahoma Agricultural and Mechanical College**
www.neo.edu
International Student Office
200 I Street Northeast
Box 3843
Miami, OK 74354-6497
Fax: (918) 542-7065
E-mail: scbrown@neo.edu
Phone: (918) 540-6393

**Northeastern State University**
www.nsuok.edu
International Programs
600 N Grand Ave
Tahlequah, OK 74464-2399
Fax: (918) 458-2056
E-mail: international@nsuok.edu
Phone: (918) 444-2050

**Northeastern University**
www.northeastern.edu
International Admissions
200 Kerr Hall
360 Huntington Avenue
Boston, MA 02115
Fax: (617) 373-8780
E-mail: internationaladmissions@neu.edu
Phone: (617) 373-2200

**Northern Arizona University**
www.nau.edu
Center for International Education
PO Box 4084
Flagstaff, AZ 86011-4084
Fax: (928) 523-9489
E-mail: Jacob.Eavis@nau.edu
Phone: (928) 523-8009

**Northern Essex Community College**
www.necc.mass.edu
Admissions and Recruitment
100 Elliott Street
Haverhill, MA 01830-2399
E-mail: iiem@necc.mass.edu
Phone: (978) 556-3726

**Northern Illinois University**
www.niu.edu
International Student Office
1425 West Lincoln Highway
DeKalb, IL 60115-2854
Fax: (815) 753-1488
E-mail: isfo@niu.edu
Phone: (815) 753-8276

**Northern Kentucky University**
www.nku.edu
International Students and Scholars
Administrative Center 400, Northern
Kentucky University
Nunn Drive
Highland Heights, KY 41099
Fax: (859) 572-6178
E-mail: isss@nku.edu
Phone: (859) 572-6517

**Northern Maine Community College**
www.nmcc.edu
Admissions
33 Edgemont Drive
Presque Isle, ME 04769
Fax: (207) 768-2848
E-mail: admission@nmcc.edu
Phone: (207) 768-2785

**Northern Michigan University**
www.nmu.edu
International Studies
1401 Presque Isle Avenue
Marquette, MI 49855
Fax: (906) 227-2533
E-mail: ipo@nmu.edu
Phone: (906) 227-2510

**Northern New Mexico College**
www.nnmc.edu
Director of Recruitment & Admissions
921 Paseo de Onate
Espanola, NM 87532
Fax: (505) 747-2191
E-mail: forona@nnmc.edu
Phone: (505) 747-2161

**Northern Oklahoma College**
www.noc.edu
Registrar's Office
Box 310
1220 East Grand
Tonkawa, OK 74653-0310
Fax: (580) 628-6371
E-mail: rick.edgington@north-ok.edu
Phone: (580) 628-6220

**Northern State University**
www.northern.edu
Admissions
1200 South Jay Street
Aberdeen, SD 57401-7198
Fax: (605) 626-2531
E-mail: admission2@northern.edu
Phone: (800) 678-5330

**Northern Virginia Community College**
www.nvcc.edu
8333 Little River Turnpike
Annandale, VA 22003-3796
Phone: (703) 323-3000

**Northland College**
www.northland.edu
Admission Office
1411 Ellis Avenue
Ashland, WI 54806-3999
Fax: (715) 682-1258
E-mail: admit@northland.edu
Phone: (715) 682-1224

**Northland Community & Technical College**
www.northlandcollege.edu
Student Affairs
2022 Central Avenue NE
East Grand Forks, MN 56721
Fax: (218) 793-2852
E-mail: mary.fontes@northlandcollege.edu
Phone: (218) 793-2460

**Northpoint Bible College**
www.northpoint.edu
Admissions Office
320 South Main Street
Haverhill, MA 01835
Fax: (978) 478-3406
E-mail: admissions@northpoint.edu
Phone: (978) 478-3400 ext. 3432

**Northwest Christian University**
www.nwcu.edu
Admissions
828 East 11th Avenue
Eugene, OR 97401-3745
Fax: (541) 684-7317
E-mail: admissions@nwcu.edu
Phone: (541) 684-7334

**Northwest College**
www.nwc.edu
Intercultural Program Office
Orendorff Bldg
231 West Sixth Street
Powell, WY 82435-1898
Fax: (307) 754-6249
E-mail: amanda.enriquez@nwc.edu
Phone: (307) 754-6424

**Northwest College of Art & Design**
www.ncad.edu
Admissions
16301 Creative Drive NE
Poulsbo, WA 98370-8651
Fax: (360) 779-9933
E-mail: admissions@ncad.edu
Phone: (360) 779-9993

**Northwest Florida State College**
www.nwfsc.edu
Advising
100 College Boulevard
Niceville, FL 32578-1347
Fax: (850) 729-5206
E-mail: dibattin@nwfsc.edu
Phone: (850) 729-5319

**Northwest Iowa Community College**
www.nwicc.edu
Enrollment
603 West Park Street
Sheldon, IA 51201
Fax: (712) 324-4136
E-mail: lstory@nwicc.edu
Phone: (712) 324-5061 ext. 115

**Northwest Kansas Technical College**
www.nwktc.edu
Student Services
1209 Harrison
PO Box 668
Goodland, KS 67735
Fax: (785) 899-5711
E-mail: reina.branum@nwktc.edu
Phone: (785) 890-1516

**Northwest Missouri State University**
www.nwmissouri.edu
Admissions
800 University Drive
248 Administration Building
Maryville, MO 64468-6001
Fax: (660) 562-1821
E-mail: intladm@nwmissouri.edu
Phone: (660) 562-1149

**Northwest Nazarene University**
www.nnu.edu
Student Development
623 South University Boulevard
Nampa, ID 83686-5897
Fax: (208) 467-8468
E-mail: plrogers@nnu.edu
Phone: (208) 467-8768

**Northwest School of Wooden Boatbuilding**
www.nwswb.edu
Director of Education
42 North Water Street
Port Hadlock, WA 98339
Fax: (360) 385-5089
E-mail: info@nwswb.edu
Phone: (360) 385-4948 ext. 307

**Northwest Technical College**
www.ntcmn.edu
Admissions Office
905 Grant Avenue Southeast
Bemidji, MN 56601-4907
Fax: (218) 333-6697
E-mail: sue.ludwig@ntcmn.edu
Phone: (218) 333-6647

**Northwest University**
www.northwestu.edu
International Student Services Office
5520 108th Avenue, NE
Kirkland, WA 98083-0579
Fax: (425) 889-5224
E-mail: international@northwestu.edu
Phone: (425) 889-5764

**Northwest Vista College**
www.alamo.edu/nvc
3535 North Ellison Drive
San Antonio, TX 78251-4217
Fax: (210) 486-9091
E-mail: dgarcia620@alamo.edu
Phone: (210) 486-4157

**Northwestern College**
www.nc.edu
Office of the Registrar
4811 N. Milwaukee Avenue, STE 203
Chicago, IL 60630
Fax: (773) 777-2861
E-mail: bwilliams@nc.edu
Phone: (773) 777-4220

**Northwestern College**
www.nwciowa.edu
Director of International and Multicultural
Affairs
101 Seventh Street SW
Orange City, IA 51041
Fax: (712) 707-7164
E-mail: kmcmahan@nwciowa.edu
Phone: (712) 707-7016

**Northwestern Health Sciences University**
www.nwhealth.edu
2501 West 84th Street
Bloomington, MN 55431
E-mail: admit@nwhealth.edu
Phone: (952) 888-4777 ext. 409

**Northwestern Michigan College**
www.nmc.edu
Admissions Office
1701 East Front Street
Traverse City, MI 49686
Fax: (231) 995-1339
E-mail: ldickinson@nmc.edu
Phone: (231) 995-1082

**Northwestern Oklahoma State University**
www.nwosu.edu
International Student Advisor
709 Oklahoma Boulevard
Alva, OK 73717-2799
Fax: (580) 327-8413
E-mail: rlcook@nwosu.edu
Phone: (580) 327-8435

**Northwestern Polytechnic University**
www.npu.edu
Director of Admissions
47671 Westinghouse Drive
Fremont, CA 94539
Fax: (510) 657-8975
E-mail: judyweng@npu.edu
Phone: (510) 592-9688 ext. 21

**Northwestern State University**
www.nsula.edu
Admissions Office
175 Sam Sibley Drive, Student Services
Center, Suite 235
Northwestern State University
Natchitoches, LA 71497
Fax: (318) 357-4660
E-mail: admissions@nsula.edu
Phone: (318) 357-4078

**Northwestern University**
www.northwestern.edu
Office of Undergraduate Admission
1801 Hinman Avenue
PO Box 3060
Evanston, IL 60208-3060
Fax: (847) 467-2331
E-mail: fss@northwestern.edu
Phone: (847) 491-7271

**Northwood University: Michigan**
www.northwood.edu
International Programs
4000 Whiting Drive
Midland, MI 48640
E-mail: milamb@northwood.edu
Phone: (989) 837-4205

**Northwood University: Texas**
www.northwood.edu
Admissions
1114 West FM 1382
Cedar Hill, TX 75104-1204
Fax: (972) 291-3824
E-mail: txadmit@northwood.edu
Phone: (800) 927-9663

**Norwalk Community College**
http://norwalk.edu/default.asp
International Student Office
188 Richards Avenue
Norwalk, CT 06854-1655
Fax: (203) 857-6948
E-mail: dbogusky@ncc.commnet.edu
Phone: (203) 857-7289

**Norwich University**
www.norwich.edu
158 Harmon Drive
Northfield, VT 05663
Fax: (802) 485-2032
E-mail: tyang@norwich.edu
Phone: (802) 485-2716

**Nossi College of Art**
www.nossi.edu
Admissions
590 Cheron Road
Nashville, TN 37115
Fax: (615) 514-2788
E-mail: admissions@nossi.com
Phone: (615) 514-2787

**Notre Dame College**
www.notredamecollege.edu
Admissions
4545 College Road
Cleveland, OH 44121-4293
Fax: (216) 381-3802
E-mail: cnolan@ndc.edu
Phone: (216) 381-1680 ext. 5355

**Notre Dame de Namur University**
www.ndnu.edu
Admission Office
1500 Ralston Avenue
Belmont, CA 94002-1908
Fax: (650) 508-3426
E-mail: admiss@ndnu.edu
Phone: (650) 508-3600

**Notre Dame of Maryland University**
www.ndm.edu
Admissions Office
4701 North Charles Street
Baltimore, MD 21210
Fax: (410) 532-6287
E-mail: admiss@ndm.edu
Phone: (410) 532-5390

**Nova Southeastern University**
www.nova.edu
Individual Program Offices
3301 College Avenue
Fort Lauderdale, FL 33314
Fax: (954) 262-3811
E-mail: intl@nsu.nova.edu
Phone: (954) 262-8126

**Nueta Hidatsa Sahnish College**
https://nhsc.edu/
Box 490
220 Eighth Avenue North
New Town, ND 58763
Fax: (701) 627-4790
E-mail: taulau@fbcc.bia.edu
Phone: (701) 627-4738 ext. 286

**Nunez Community College**
www.nunez.edu
Admissions Office
3710 Paris Road
Chalmette, LA 70043
Fax: (504) 278-6487
E-mail: bmaillet@nunez.edu
Phone: (504) 278-6467

**Nyack College**
www.nyack.edu
Admissions
1 South Boulevard
Nyack, NY 10960-3698
Fax: (845) 358-3047
E-mail: admissions@nyack.edu
Phone: (845) 675-4401

**Oakland City University**
www.oak.edu
Admissions
138 North Lucretia Street
Oakland City, IN 47660
Fax: (812) 749-1433
E-mail: ocuadmit@oak.edu
Phone: (800) 737-5125 ext. 219

**Oakland Community College**
www.oaklandcc.edu
International Student Advisor
2480 Opdyke Road
Bloomfield Hills, MI 48304-2266
Fax: (248) 232-4441
E-mail: ddschack@oaklandcc.edu
Phone: (248) 232-4440

**Oakland University**
www.oakland.edu
Senior Recruitment Advisor
318 Meadow Brook Road
Oakland University
Rochester, MI 48309-4454
Fax: (248) 370-4462
E-mail: adpanche@oakland.edu
Phone: (248) 370-3310

**Oakton Community College**
www.oakton.edu
Enrollment Services
Enrollment Center
1600 East Golf Road
Des Plaines, IL 60016
Fax: (847) 635-1706
E-mail: lynn@oakton.edu
Phone: (847) 635-1713

**Oakwood University**
www.oakwood.edu
Enrollment Management
7000 Adventist Boulevard, NW
Huntsville, AL 35896
Fax: (256) 726-7154
E-mail: jbartholomew@oakwood.edu
Phone: (256) 726-7423

**Oberlin College**
www.oberlin.edu
Associate Diretor of Admissions
Carnegie Building, 101 North Professor Street
Oberlin, OH 44074-1075
Fax: (440) 775-6905
E-mail: leslie.braat@oberlin.edu
Phone: (440) 775-8411

**Occidental College**
www.oxy.edu
Admission Office
1600 Campus Road
Los Angeles, CA 90041
Fax: (323) 341-4875
E-mail: admission@oxy.edu
Phone: (323) 259-2700

**Ocean County College**
www.ocean.edu
Admissions
College Drive
PO Box 2001
Toms River, NJ 08754-2001
Fax: (732) 255-0444
E-mail: lkasper@ocean.edu
Phone: (732) 255-0400 ext. 2949

**Odessa College**
www.odessa.edu
201 West University
Odessa, TX 79764-7127
Fax: (432) 335-6636
E-mail: admissions@odessa.edu
Phone: (432) 335-6432

**Oglala Lakota College**
www.olc.edu
Box 490
Kyle, SD 57752-0490
Fax: (605) 455-2787
Phone: (605) 455-6000

**Oglethorpe University**
www.oglethorpe.edu
Office of Admission
4484 Peachtree Road NE
Atlanta, GA 30319-2797
Fax: (404) 364-8491
E-mail: admission@oglethorpe.edu
Phone: (404) 364-8455

**Ohio Business College: Hilliard**
www.ohiobusinesscollege.edu
4525 Trueman Boulevard
Hilliard, OH 43026
Phone: (614) 891-5030

**Ohio Business College: Sheffield**
www.ohiobusinesscollege.edu
5095 Waterford Drive
Sheffield Village, OH 44055
Fax: (440) 277-7989
E-mail: lorain@ohiobusinesscollege.edu
Phone: (440) 277-0021

**Ohio College of Massotherapy**
www.ocm.edu
225 Heritage Woods Drive
Akron, OH 44321
Fax: (330) 665-5021
E-mail: admissions@ocm.edu
Phone: (330) 665-1084

**Ohio Dominican University**
www.ohiodominican.edu
International Office
1216 Sunbury Road
Columbus, OH 43219
Fax: (614) 251-4639
E-mail: shined@ohiodominican.edu
Phone: (614) 251-4645

**Ohio Northern University**
www.onu.edu
Director of International Admissions
525 South Main Street
Ada, OH 45810
Fax: (419) 772-2484
E-mail: r-edmond@onu.edu
Phone: (419) 772-2483

**Ohio State University: Columbus Campus**
www.osu.edu
Office of Undergraduate Admission
Student Academic Services Building, 281
West Lane Avenue
Columbus, OH 43210
Fax: (614) 292-4818
E-mail: askabuckeye@osu.edu
Phone: (614) 292-3980

**Ohio Technical College**
www.ohiotech.edu
Admissions
1374 East 51st Street
Cleveland, OH 44103-1269
Fax: (216) 881-9145
E-mail: gkozarik@ohiotech.edu
Phone: (800) 233-7000

**Ohio University**
www.ohio.edu
Office of Undergraduate Admissions
120 Chubb Hall
Athens, OH 45701-2979
Fax: (740) 593-0560
E-mail: admissions.international@ohio.edu
Phone: (740) 593-4100

**Ohio University: Eastern Campus**
www.eastern.ohiou.edu
45425 National Road West
St. Clairsville, OH 43950-9724
Fax: (740) 695-7077
E-mail: admissions@ohio.edu
Phone: (740) 695-1720

**Ohio University: Southern Campus at Ironton**
www.ohio.edu/southern
Student Services
1804 Liberty Avenue
Ironton, OH 45638
Fax: (740) 533-4632
E-mail: queenn@ohio.edu
Phone: (740) 533-4600

**Ohio University: Zanesville Campus**
www.ohio.edu/zanesville
Student Services
1425 Newark Road
Zanesville, OH 43701
Fax: (740) 588-1444
E-mail: ouzservices@ohio.edu
Phone: (740) 588-1439

**Ohio Valley University**
www.ovu.edu
Admissions Office
One Campus View Drive
Vienna, WV 26105
Fax: (304) 865-6175
E-mail: gerald.cole@ovu.edu
Phone: (304) 865-6205

**Ohio Wesleyan University**
www.owu.edu
International Recruitment
61 South Sandusky Street
Delaware, OH 43015-2398
Fax: (740) 368-3314
E-mail: owuintl@owu.edu
Phone: (740) 368-3020

**Ohlone College**
www.ohlone.edu
International Programs and Services
43600 Mission Boulevard
Fremont, CA 94539-0390
Fax: (510) 659-6500
E-mail: international@ohlone.edu
Phone: (510) 659-6439

**Ohr Somayach Tanenbaum Education Center**
www.os.edu
244 Route 306
Box 334
Monsey, NY 10952
Fax: (845) 425-8865
E-mail: ohr@os.edu
Phone: (845) 425-1370

**Oklahoma Baptist University**
www.okbu.edu
Office of Admissions
500 West University
OBU Box 61174
Shawnee, OK 74804
Fax: (405) 585-2068
E-mail: matthew.regier@okbu.edu
Phone: (405) 585-5011

**Oklahoma Christian University**
www.oc.edu
Office of International Programs
Box 11000
Oklahoma City, OK 73136-1100
Fax: (405) 425-5477
E-mail: greg.gillham@oc.edu
Phone: (405) 425-5478

**Oklahoma City Community College**
www.occc.edu
Coordinator of International Admissions
7777 South May Avenue
Oklahoma City, OK 73159
Fax: (405) 682-7817
E-mail: international@occc.edu
Phone: (405) 682-1611 ext. 7884

**Oklahoma City University**
www.okcu.edu
International Admission Office
2501 North Blackwelder Avenue
Oklahoma City, OK 73106-1493
Fax: (405) 208-5279
E-mail: jkenyon@okcu.edu
Phone: (405) 208-5006

**Oklahoma Panhandle State University**
www.opsu.edu
International Students Office
OPSU Admissions
Box 430
Goodwell, OK 73939-0430
Fax: (580) 349-2302
E-mail: international@opsu.edu
Phone: (580) 349-1314

**Oklahoma State University**
go.okstate.edu
International Students and Scholars
219 Student Union
Stillwater, OK 74078
Fax: (405) 744-8120
E-mail: admissions-iss@okstate.edu
Phone: (405) 744-5459

**Oklahoma State University Institute of Technology: Okmulgee**
www.osuit.edu
Director, International Students
1801 East Fourth Street
Okmulgee, OK 74447-3901
Fax: (918) 293-4643
E-mail: kkern@okstate.edu
Phone: (918) 293-4998

**Oklahoma State University: Oklahoma City**
www.osuokc.edu/home
Director of Recruitment and Admissions
900 North Portland Avenue
Oklahoma City, OK 73107-6195
Fax: (405) 945-3277
E-mail: jason.rockwell@osuokc.edu
Phone: (405) 945-3315

**Oklahoma Wesleyan University**
www.okwu.edu
Admissions Office
2201 Silver Lake Road
Bartlesville, OK 74006
Fax: (918) 335-6229
E-mail: admissions@okwu.edu
Phone: (918) 335-6219

**Old Dominion University**
www.odu.edu
Office of International Admissions
108 Rollins Hall
Norfolk, VA 23529
Fax: (757) 683-3651
E-mail: intladm@odu.edu
Phone: (757) 683-3701

**Olivet College**
www.olivetcollege.edu
Admissions
320 South Main Street
Olivet, MI 49076
Fax: (269) 749-6617
E-mail: mlang@olivetcollege.edu
Phone: (269) 749-7635

**Olivet Nazarene University**
www.olivet.edu
Director of International Programs
One University Avenue
Bourbonnais, IL 60914
Fax: (815) 939-5069
E-mail: mcmountain@olivet.edu
Phone: (815) 928-5794

**Olympic College**
www.olympic.edu
International Student Programs
1600 Chester Avenue
Bremerton, WA 98337-1699
Fax: (360) 473-2856
E-mail: international@olympic.edu
Phone: (360) 475-7412

**O'More College of Design**
www.omorecollege.edu
Admissions Office
423 South Margin Street
Franklin, TN 37064-0908
Fax: (615) 790-1662
E-mail: lsmith@omorecollege.edu
Phone: (615) 794-4254 ext. 229

**Onondaga Community College**
www.sunyocc.edu
Office of Recruitment & Admission
4585 West Seneca Turnpike
Syracuse, NY 13215-4585
Fax: (315) 498-7260
E-mail: m.b.peryea@sunyocc.edu
Phone: (315) 498-7217

**Oral Roberts University**
www.oru.edu
International Admissions
7777 South Lewis Avenue
Tulsa, OK 74171
Fax: (918) 495-6788
E-mail: thannon@oru.edu
Phone: (918) 495-6488

**Orange Coast College**
www.orangecoastcollege.edu
Global Engagement Center
2701 Fairview Road
Box 5005
Costa Mesa, CA 92628-5005
Fax: (714) 432-5191
E-mail: njensen@occ.cccd.edu
Phone: (714) 432-5940

**Orange County Community College**
www.sunyorange.edu
Admissions
115 South Street
Middletown, NY 10940-0115
Fax: (845) 342-8662
E-mail: laura.morcone@sunyorange.edu
Phone: (845) 341-4040

**Orangeburg-Calhoun Technical College**
www.octech.edu
Student Services - Admissions
3250 St. Matthews Road
Orangeburg, SC 29118-8222
Fax: (803) 535-1388
E-mail: felderb@octech.edu
Phone: (803) 536-0311

**Oregon College of Art & Craft**
www.ocac.edu
Admissions Office Coordinator and Counselor
8245 SW Barnes Road
Portland, OR 97225-6349
Fax: (503) 297-9651
E-mail: alund@ocac.edu
Phone: (971) 255-4229

**Oregon Health & Science University**
www.ohsu.edu
Office of Admissions
3181 SW Sam Jackson Park Road
Mail Code L109
Portland, OR 97239-3098
Fax: (503) 494-4629
E-mail: proginfo@ohsu.edu
Phone: (503) 494-7725

**Oregon Institute of Technology**
www.oit.edu
Admissions Director
3201 Campus Drive
Klamath Falls, OR 97601
Fax: (541) 885-1115
E-mail: oit@oit.edu
Phone: (541) 885-1150

**Oregon State University**
www.oregonstate.edu
International Admissions
104 Kerr Administration Building
Corvallis, OR 97331-2130
Fax: (541) 737-4220
E-mail: intladmit@oregonstate.edu
Phone: (541) 737-5719

**Orleans Technical Institute**
www.orleanstech.edu
2770 Red Lion Road
Philadelphia, PA 19114
Fax: (215) 745-1689
E-mail: gettingstarted@jevs.org
Phone: (215) 728-4426

**Otero Junior College**
https://www.ojc.edu
1802 Colorado Avenue
La Junta, CO 81050
Fax: (719) 384-6933
E-mail: Rochelle.Wallace@ojc.edu
Phone: (719) 384-6805

**Otis College of Art and Design**
www.otis.edu
Office of Admissions
9045 Lincoln Boulevard
Los Angeles, CA 90045-9785
Fax: (310) 665-6821
E-mail: admissions@otis.edu
Phone: (310) 665-6820

**Ottawa University**
www.ottawa.edu
Foreign Student Advisor
1001 South Cedar Street, #17
Ottawa, KS 66067-3399
Fax: (785) 229-1007
E-mail: murle.mordy@ottawa.edu
Phone: (785) 229-1072

**Otterbein University**
www.otterbein.edu
Office of International Admission
One Otterbein College
Westerville, OH 43081
Fax: (614) 823-3099
E-mail: alibby@otterbein.edu
Phone: (614) 823-1644

**Ouachita Baptist University**
www.obu.edu
International Programs
OBU Box 3776
Arkadelphia, AR 71998-0001
Fax: (870) 245-5312
E-mail: gattisa@obu.edu
Phone: (870) 245-5224

**Our Lady of the Lake University of San Antonio**
www.ollusa.edu
Office of International Admissions
411 Southwest 24th Street
San Antonio, TX 78207-4689
Fax: (210) 431-4036
E-mail: international@ollusa.edu
Phone: (210) 431-3961

**Owens Community College**
www.owens.edu
International Student Services
30335 Oregon Road
PO Box 10000
Toledo, OH 43699-1947
Fax: (567) 661-2046
E-mail: annette_swanson@owens.edu
Phone: (567) 661-7510

**Owensboro Community and Technical College**
www.owensboro.kctcs.edu
Office of Diversity and International Student Services
4800 New Hartford Road
Owensboro, KY 42303-1899
Fax: (270) 686-4648
E-mail: lewatis.mcneal@kctcs.edu
Phone: (270) 852-8607

**Oxford College of Emory University**
www.oxford.emory.edu
Enrollment Services
122 Few Circle
Oxford, GA 30054-1418
Fax: (770) 784-8359
E-mail: maura.klein@emory.edu
Phone: (800) 723-8328

**Ozarks Technical Community College**
www.otc.edu
1001 East Chestnut Expressway
Springfield, MO 65802
Fax: (417) 447-6906
E-mail: lundstrl@otc.edu
Phone: (417) 447-8197

**Pace University**
www.pace.edu
International Programs & Services
1 Pace Plaza
New York, NY 10038-1598
Fax: (212) 346-1116
E-mail: acordon@pace.edu
Phone: (212) 346-1654

**Pace University: Pleasantville/Briarcliff**
www.pace.edu
International Programs & Services
861 Bedford Road
Pleasantville, NY 10570
Fax: (212) 346-1116
E-mail: acordon@pace.edu
Phone: (212) 346-1654

**Pacific College of Oriental Medicine: San Diego**
www.pacificcollege.edu
7445 Mission Valley Road, Suite 105
San Diego, CA 92108
E-mail: admissions-sd@pacificcollege.edu
Phone: (619) 574-6909

**Pacific Lutheran University**
www.plu.edu
Office of International Admission
12180 Park Ave South
Tacoma, WA 98447-0003
Fax: (235) 536-5136
E-mail: intl@plu.edu
Phone: (800) 274-6758

**Pacific Northwest College of Art**
www.pnca.edu
Admissions
511 NW Broadway
Portland, OR 97209
Fax: (503) 821-8978
E-mail: lhux@pnca.edu
Phone: (503) 821-8972

**Pacific Oaks College**
www.pacificoaks.edu
Admissions Office
55 Eureka Street
Pasadena, CA 91103
Fax: (626) 529-8075
E-mail: mpatton@pacificoaks.edu
Phone: (877) 314-2380

**Pacific States University**
www.psuca.edu
Admission office
3424 Wilshire Boulevard 12th floor
Los Angeles, CA 90010
Fax: (323) 731-7276
E-mail: admissions@psuca.edu
Phone: (323) 731-2383 ext. 202

**Pacific Union College**
www.puc.edu
Enrollment Services
One Angwin Avenue
Angwin, CA 94508-9707
Fax: (707) 965-6671
E-mail: admissions@puc.edu
Phone: (707) 965-6336

**Pacific University**
www.pacificu.edu
Office of International Admissions
2043 College Way
Forest Grove, OR 97116-1797
Fax: (503) 352-2975
E-mail: JohnHarn@pacificu.edu
Phone: (503) 352-2851

**Paier College of Art**
www.paiercollegeofart.edu
Admissions Secretary
20 Gorham Avenue
Hamden, CT 06514-3902
Fax: (203) 287-3021
E-mail: paier.admission@snet.net
Phone: (203) 287-3031

**Paine College**
www.paine.edu
Office of Admissions
1235 15th Street
Augusta, GA 30901
Fax: (706) 821-8648
E-mail: ffenner@paine.edu
Phone: (706) 821-8320

**Palm Beach Atlantic University**
www.pba.edu
Undergraduate Admissions
901 South Flagler Drive
P.O. Box 24708
West Palm Beach, FL 33416-4708
Fax: (561) 803-2115
E-mail: brittany_henson@pba.edu
Phone: (561) 803-2111

**Palm Beach State College**
www.palmbeachstate.edu
International Student Admissions Office
4200 Congress Avenue
Lake Worth, FL 33461
Fax: (561) 868-3605
E-mail: labordef@palmbeachstate.edu
Phone: (561) 868-3031

**Palo Verde College**
www.paloverde.edu
Admissions & Records
One College Drive
Blythe, CA 92225
Fax: (760) 921-5570
E-mail: shamilton@paloverde.edu
Phone: (760) 921-5483

**Palomar College**
www.palomar.edu
International Edcuation Office
1140 West Mission Road
San Marcos, CA 92069-1487
Fax: (760) 761-3592
E-mail: yoneill@palomar.edu
Phone: (760) 744-1150 ext. 2167

**Pamlico Community College**
www.pamlicocc.edu
PO Box 185
Grantsboro, NC 28529
Fax: (252) 249-2377
E-mail: cwarner@pamlicocc.edu
Phone: (252) 249-1851

**Panola College**
www.panola.edu
Testing Coordinator/Advisor/International Student Coordinator
1109 West Panola Street
Carthage, TX 75633
Fax: (903) 693-2031
E-mail: sgee@panola.edu
Phone: (903) 693-2046

**Paradise Valley Community College**
www.pvc.maricopa.edu
18401 North 32nd Street
Phoenix, AZ 85032
Fax: (602) 787-6625
Phone: (602) 787-7020

**Paralegal Institute**
www.theparalegalinstitute.edu
7332 East Butherus Drive, Suite 102
Scottsdale, AZ 85260
Fax: (602) 212-0502
E-mail: blaing@theparalegalinstitute.edu
Phone: (800) 354-1254

**Paris Junior College**
www.parisjc.edu
International Student Adviser
2400 Clarksville Street
Paris, TX 75460
Fax: (903) 782-0427
E-mail: nwhitaker@parisjc.edu
Phone: (903) 782-0430

**Park University**
www.park.edu
International Student Office
8700 NW River Park Drive
Parkville, MO 64152
Fax: (816) 505-5443
E-mail: enrollmentservices@park.edu
Phone: (816) 584-6379

**Parkland College**
www.parkland.edu
International Education
2400 West Bradley Avenue
Admissions and Records, Parkland College
Champaign, IL 61821-1899
Fax: (217) 353-2640
E-mail: intlinfo@parkland.edu
Phone: (217) 351-2890

**Parsons The New School for Design**
www.newschool.edu
Office of Admissions
79 Fifth Avenue, Floor 5
New York, NY 10003
Fax: (212) 229-8975
E-mail: thinkparsons@newschool.edu
Phone: (212) 229-8989

**Pasadena City College**
www.pasadena.edu
International Students Office
1570 East Colorado Boulevard
Pasadena, CA 91106
Fax: (626) 585-7915
Phone: (818) 585-7391

**Pasco-Hernando State College**
www.phsc.edu
Director Admissions and Student Records
10230 Ridge Road
New Port Richey, FL 34654-5199
Fax: (727) 816-3389
E-mail: carrioe@phsc.edu
Phone: (727) 816-3261

**Passaic County Community College**
www.pccc.edu
Admissions Office
One College Boulevard
Paterson, NJ 07505-1179
Fax: (973) 684-6778
E-mail: mdavila@pccc.edu
Phone: (973) 684-6307

**Patrick Henry College**
www.phc.edu
10 Patrick Henry Circle
Purcellville, VA 20132-3197
Fax: (540) 441-8119
E-mail: admissions@phc.edu
Phone: (540) 441-8110

**Patrick Henry Community College**
www.patrickhenry.edu
International Student Advisor
645 Patriot Avenue
Martinsville, VA 24112
Fax: (276) 656-0352
E-mail: ecrehan@patrickhenry.edu
Phone: (276) 656-0200 ext. 473

**Patten University**
www.patten.edu
Admissions
2433 Coolidge Avenue
Oakland, CA 94601-2699
Fax: (510) 534-4344
E-mail: chogeboom@patten.edu
Phone: (510) 261-8500 ext. 7764

**Paul D. Camp Community College**
www.pdc.edu
Admissions and Records
100 North College Drive
PO Box 737
Franklin, VA 23851-0737
Fax: (757) 569-6795
E-mail: tjones@pdc.edu
Phone: (757) 569-6700

**Paul Quinn College**
www.pqc.edu
Office of Enrollment Management
3837 Simpson Stuart Road
Dallas, TX 75241
Fax: (214) 379-5448
E-mail: jlara@pqc.edu
Phone: (214) 379-5449

**Paul Smith's College**
www.paulsmiths.edu
Admissions
PO Box 265, Routes 30 & 86
Paul Smiths, NY 12970-0265
Fax: (518) 327-6862
E-mail: atuthill@paulsmiths.edu
Phone: (800) 421-2605

**Peirce College**
www.peirce.edu
Admissions
1420 Pine Street
Philadelphia, PA 19102-4699
Fax: (215) 670-9366
E-mail: info@peirce.edu
Phone: (888) 467-3472 ext. 9214

**Pellissippi State Community College**
www.pstcc.edu
International Admissions and Records
Box 22990
Knoxville, TN 37933-0990
Fax: (865) 539-7217
E-mail: latouzeau@pstcc.edu
Phone: (865) 539-7013

**Peninsula College**
www.pencol.edu
International Coordinator Students
1502 East Lauridsen Boulevard
Port Angeles, WA 98362
Fax: (360) 417-6482
E-mail: gyl@pcadmin.ctc.edu
Phone: (360) 417-6491

**Penn Commercial Business and Technical School**
www.penncommercial.edu
Admissions
242 Oak Spring Road
Washington, PA 15301
Fax: (724) 222-4722
E-mail: jtuite@penncommercial.edu
Phone: (724) 222-5330 ext. 227

**Penn Foster College**
www.pennfostercollege.edu
14300 North Northsight Boulevard, Suite 125
Scottsdale, AZ 85260
E-mail: Robert.Gaffey@pennfoster.edu
Phone: (800) 800-3232

**Penn State Abington**
www.abington.psu.edu
Admissions
1600 Woodland Road
Abington, PA 19001
Fax: (814) 863-7590
E-mail: admissions@psu.edu
Phone: (814) 865-5471

**Penn State Altoona**
www.altoona.psu.edu
Admissions
3000 Ivyside Park
Altoona, PA 16801
Fax: (814) 863-7590
E-mail: admissions@psu.edu
Phone: (814) 865-5471

**Penn State Beaver**
www.br.psu.edu
Admissions
100 University Drive
113 Student Union
Monaca, PA 15061
Fax: (814) 863-7590
E-mail: admissions@psu.edu
Phone: (814) 865-5471

**Penn State Berks**
www.bk.psu.edu
Admissions
Tulpehocken Road
PO Box 7009, Perkins Student Center, Room 14
Reading, PA 19610
Fax: (814) 863-7590
E-mail: admissions@psu.edu
Phone: (814) 865-5471

**Penn State Brandywine**
www.brandywine.psu.edu
Admissions
25 Yearsley Mill Road
Media, PA 19063
Fax: (814) 863-7590
E-mail: admissions@psu.edu
Phone: (814) 865-5471

**Penn State DuBois**
http://dubois.psu.edu
Admissions
1 College Place
Hochrein House
DuBois, PA 15801
Fax: (814) 863-7590
E-mail: admissions@psu.edu
Phone: (814) 865-5471

**Penn State Erie, The Behrend College**
http://psbehrend.psu.edu
Director for Undergraduate Admissions
Metzgar Admissions & Alumni Center
4851 College Drive
Erie, PA 16563
Fax: (814) 898-6044
E-mail: admissions@psu.edu
Phone: (814) 865-5471

**Penn State Fayette, The Eberly Campus**
www.fe.psu.edu
Admissions
110 Eberly Building
2201 University Drive
Lemont Furnace, PA 15456
Fax: (814) 863-7590
E-mail: admissions@psu.edu
Phone: (814) 865-5471

**Penn State Greater Allegheny**
http://ga.psu.edu
Admissions
123 Frable Building
4000 University Drive
McKeesport, PA 15132
Fax: (814) 863-7590
E-mail: admissions@psu.edu
Phone: (814) 865-5471

**Penn State Harrisburg**
www.hbg.psu.edu
Admissions
Swatara Building
777 West Harrisburg Pike
Middletown, PA 17057
Fax: (814) 863-7590
E-mail: admissions@psu.edu
Phone: (814) 865-5471

**Penn State Hazleton**
http://hazleton.psu.edu/
Admissions
110 Schiavo Hall
76 University Drive
University Park, PA 18202
Fax: (814) 863-7590
E-mail: admissions@psu.edu
Phone: (814) 865-5471

**Penn State Lehigh Valley**
www.lv.psu.edu
Admissions
2809 Saucon Valley Road
Center Vally, PA 18034
Fax: (814) 863-7590
E-mail: admissions@psu.edu
Phone: (814) 865-5471

**Penn State Mont Alto**
www.ma.psu.edu
Director for Undergraduate Admissions
1 Campus Drive
Mont Alto, PA 17237
Fax: (814) 863-7590
E-mail: admissions@psu.edu
Phone: (814) 865-5471

**Penn State New Kensington**
www.nk.psu.edu
Admissions
3550 Seventh Street Road
New Kensington, PA 15068
Fax: (814) 863-7590
E-mail: admissions@psu.edu
Phone: (814) 865-5471

**Penn State Schuylkill**
www.sl.psu.edu
Admissions
102 Administration Building
200 University Drive
Schuylkill Haven, PA 17972
Fax: (814) 863-7590
E-mail: admissions@psu.edu
Phone: (814) 865-5471

**Penn State Shenango**
www.shenango.psu.edu
Admissions
147 Shenango Avenue
Sharon Hall
Sharon, PA 16146
Fax: (814) 863-7590
E-mail: admissions@psu.edu
Phone: (814) 865-5471

**Penn State University Park**
www.psu.edu
Admissions
201 Shields Building
University Park, PA 16802
Fax: (814) 863-7590
E-mail: admissions@psu.edu
Phone: (814) 865-5471

**Penn State Wilkes-Barre**
www.wb.psu.edu
Admissions
Hayfield House 101
Lehman, PA 18627
Fax: (814) 863-7590
E-mail: admissions@psu.edu
Phone: (814) 865-5471

**Penn State Worthington Scranton**
www.sn.psu.edu
Admissions
Dawson Building, Room 5, 120 Ridge View
Drive
Dunmore, PA 18512
Fax: (814) 863-7590
E-mail: admissions@psu.edu
Phone: (814) 865-5471

**Penn State York**
www.yk.psu.edu
Admissions
Room 139, Main Classroom Building, 1031
Edgecomb Avenue
York, PA 17403
Fax: (814) 863-7590
E-mail: admissions@psu.edu
Phone: (814) 865-5471

**Pennco Tech**
www.penncotech.edu
3815 Otter Street
Bristol, PA 19007
E-mail: admissions@penncotech.com
Phone: (215) 824-3200

**Pennsylvania Academy of the Fine Arts**
www.pafa.edu
Office of Admissions
128 North Broad Street
Philadelphia, PA 19102
Fax: (215) 972-0839
E-mail: admissions@pafa.edu
Phone: (215) 972-7625

**Pennsylvania College of Art and Design**
www.pcad.edu
Admissions Department
PO Box 59
204 North Prince Street
Lancaster, PA 17608-0059
Fax: (717) 396-1339
E-mail: radey@pcad.edu
Phone: (717) 396-7833 ext. 1001

**Pennsylvania College of Health Sciences**
www.pacollege.edu
850 Greenfield Road
Lancaster, PA 17601
E-mail: admission@pacollege.edu
Phone: (800) 622-5443

**Pennsylvania College of Technology**
www.pct.edu
Director of Admissions
One College Avenue
DIF #119
Williamsport, PA 17701-5799
Fax: (570) 321-5551
E-mail: admissions@pct.edu
Phone: (570) 327-4761

**Pennsylvania Highlands Community
College**
www.pennhighlands.edu
Director of Admissions
101 Community College Way
Johnstown, PA 15904
Fax: (814) 262-6420
E-mail: jmaul@pennhighlands.edu
Phone: (814) 262-6431

**Pennsylvania Institute of Health and
Technology**
www.piht.edu
Route 119 North and Mount Braddock Road
Mount Braddock, PA 15465
Fax: (724) 437-6053
E-mail: admissions@piht.edu
Phone: (724) 437-4600

**Pensacola State College**
www.pensacolastate.edu
Registrar
1000 College Boulevard
Pensacola, FL 32504-8998
Fax: (850) 484-1829
E-mail: sdesbrow@pensacolastate.edu
Phone: (850) 484-1605

**Pepperdine University**
www.pepperdine.edu
International Student Services
24255 Pacific Coast Highway
Malibu, CA 90263-4392
Fax: (310) 506-7403
E-mail: oiss@pepperdine.edu
Phone: (310) 506-4246

**Peru State College**
www.peru.edu
Admissions
P.O. Box 10
Peru, NE 68421-0010
Fax: (402) 872-2296
E-mail: admissions@peru.edu
Phone: (402) 872-2221

**Pfeiffer University**
www.pfeiffer.edu
Director of Admissions
PO Box 960
Misenheimer, NC 28109
Fax: (704) 463-1363
E-mail: emily.carella@pfeiffer.edu
Phone: (704) 463-3047

**Philadelphia University**
www.PhilaU.edu
Admissions Office
4201 Henry Avenue
Philadelphia, PA 19144
Fax: (215) 951-2907
E-mail: Regerj@philau.edu
Phone: (215) 951-2800

**Philander Smith College**
www.philander.edu
Assistant Dean of Recruitment & Admissions/
Registrar
900 West Daisy Bates Drive
Little Rock, AR 72202-3718
Fax: (501) 370-5225
E-mail: bowens@philander.edu
Phone: (501) 370-5215

**Phillips School of Nursing at Mount Sinai
Beth Israel**
www.pson.edu
Admissions
776 Sixth Avenue, Fourth Floor
New York, NY 10001
Fax: (212) 614-6109
E-mail: bstern@chpnet.org
Phone: (212) 614-6176

**Phoenix College**
www.phoenixcollege.edu
International Student Office
1202 West Thomas Road
Phoenix, AZ 85013
Fax: (602) 285-7813
E-mail: nellie.torres@phoenixcollege.edu
Phone: (602) 285-7664

**Piedmont College**
www.piedmont.edu
Admissions
1021 Central Avenue
PO Box 10
Demorest, GA 30535-0010
Fax: (706) 776-0103
E-mail: bboonstra@piedmont.edu
Phone: (800) 277-7020

**Piedmont Community College**
www.piedmontcc.edu
Director
1715 College Drive
PO Box 1197
Roxboro, NC 27573
Fax: (336) 598-9283
E-mail: patricia.hatchett@piedmontcc.edu
Phone: (336) 599-1181 ext. 2153

**Piedmont International University**
www.piedmontu.edu
Admissions
420 South Boad Street
Winston-Salem, NC 27101-5133
Fax: (336) 725-5522
E-mail: hoovera@piedmontu.edu
Phone: (336) 725-8344 ext. 7927

**Piedmont Technical College**
www.ptc.edu
Admissions
620 North Emerald Road
Greenwood, SC 29646
Fax: (864) 941-8357
E-mail: Frazier.R@ptc.edu
Phone: (864) 941-8369

**Piedmont Virginia Community College**
www.pvcc.edu
Office of Admissions
501 College Drive
Charlottesville, VA 22902-7589
Fax: (434) 961-5425
E-mail: mwalsh@pvcc.edu
Phone: (434) 961-6540

**Pierce College**
www.pierce.ctc.edu
International Education
9401 Farwest Drive SW
Lakewood, WA 98498-1999
Fax: (253) 964-6256
E-mail: intledu@pierce.ctc.edu
Phone: (253) 964-7327

**Pierpont Community and Technical College**
www.pierpont.edu
1201 Locust Avenue
Fairmont, WV 26554
E-mail: admit@pierpont.edu
Phone: (304) 333-3684

**Pikes Peak Community College**
www.ppcc.edu
Admissions
5675 South Academy Boulevard
Colorado Springs, CO 80906-5498
E-mail: Michelle.Freeburger@ppcc.edu
Phone: (719) 502-2230

**Pillar College**
www.pillar.edu
60 Park Place, Suite 701
Newark, NJ 07102
Fax: (973) 230-3220
E-mail: info@pillar.edu
Phone: (973) 803-5000

**Pine Manor College**
www.pmc.edu
Admissions
400 Heath Street
Chestnut Hill, MA 02467
Fax: (617) 731-7102
E-mail: admission@pmc.edu
Phone: (617) 731-7011

**Pine Technical & Community College**
www.pine.edu
Director of Admission
900 Fourth Street SE
Pine City, MN 55063
Fax: (320) 629-5101
E-mail: schelinder@pine.edu
Phone: (320) 629-5114

**Pinnacle Career Institute: Kansas City**
www.pcitraining.edu
1001 East 101st Terrace, Suite 325
Kansas City, MO 64131-3367
Fax: (816) 331-2026
E-mail: bricks@pcitraining.edu
Phone: (816) 331-5700

**Pittsburg State University**
www.pittstate.edu
Asst. Director, International Undergraduate
Admission & Recruitment
1701 South Broadway
Pittsburg, KS 66762
Fax: (620) 235-4962
E-mail: ahurt@pittstate.edu
Phone: (620) 235-4093

**Pittsburgh Institute of Aeronautics**
www.pia.edu
Director of Admissions
PO Box 10897
Pittsburgh, PA 15236-0897
Fax: (412) 466-0513
E-mail: ssabold@pia.edu
Phone: (412) 346-2100

**Pittsburgh Institute of Mortuary Science**
www.pims.edu
5808 Baum Boulevard
Pittsburgh, PA 15206-3706
Fax: (412) 362-1684
E-mail: krocco@pims.edu
Phone: (412) 362-8500

**Pitzer College**
www.pitzer.edu
International Programs Office
1050 North Mills Avenue
Claremont, CA 91711-6101
Fax: (909) 621-0518
E-mail: todd_sasaki@pitzer.edu
Phone: (909) 621-8308

**Platt College: Los Angeles**
www.plattcollege.edu
Admissions
1000 South Fremont Avenue A9W
Alhambra, CA 91803
Fax: (626) 300-3978
E-mail: jboylan@plattcollege.edu
Phone: (626) 300-5444

**Platt College: Moore**
www.plattcolleges.edu
201 North Eastern
Moore, OK 73160
Phone: (405) 912-3260

**Platt College: Oklahoma City Central**
www.plattcolleges.edu
309 South Ann Arbor
Oklahoma City, OK 73128
Fax: (405) 943-2150
E-mail: klamb@plattcollege.org
Phone: (405) 946-7799

**Platt College: Ontario**
www.plattcollege.edu
Admissions
3700 Inland Empire Boulevard
Ontario, CA 91764
Fax: (909) 941-9660
E-mail: cconceicao@plattcollege.edu
Phone: (909) 941-9410

**Platt College: San Diego**
www.platt.edu
6250 El Cajon Boulevard
San Diego, CA 92115
Fax: (619) 308-0570
E-mail: info@platt.edu
Phone: (619) 265-0107 ext. 33

**Platt College: Tulsa**
www.plattcolleges.edu
3801 South Sheridan
Tulsa, OK 74145-1132
Fax: (918) 622-1240
E-mail: stephanieh@plattcollege.org
Phone: (918) 663-9000

**Plymouth State University**
www.plymouth.edu
Admission Office
17 High Street MSC 52
Plymouth, NH 03264-1595
Fax: (603) 535-2594
E-mail: plymouthadmit@plymouth.edu
Phone: (800) 842-6900

**Point Loma Nazarene University**
www.pointloma.edu
Admissions
3900 Lomaland Drive
Admissions
San Diego, CA 92106-2899
Fax: (619) 849-2601
E-mail: admissions@pointloma.edu
Phone: (619) 849-2541

**Point Park University**
www.pointpark.edu
International Student Services and Enrollment
201 Wood Street
Pittsburgh, PA 15222-1984
Fax: (412) 392-4792
E-mail: iss@pointpark.edu
Phone: (412) 392-4775

**Point University**
www.point.edu
Admission Office
507 West 10th Street
West Point, GA 31833
Fax: (706) 645-9473
E-mail: rusty.hassell@point.edu
Phone: (706) 385-1503

**Polk State College**
www.polk.edu
Enrollment Management, Winter Haven
Campus
999 Avenue H NE
Winter Haven, FL 33881-4299
Fax: (863) 297-1060
E-mail: mwestgate@polk.edu
Phone: (863) 297-1010 ext. 5201

**Pomona College**
www.pomona.edu
Admissions Office
333 North College Way
Claremont, CA 91711-6312
Fax: (909) 621-8952
E-mail: admissions@pomona.edu
Phone: (909) 621-8134

**Ponce Paramedical College**
www.popac.edu
Calle Acacia 1213, Urb. Villa Flores
PO Box 800106
Ponce, PR 00780-0106
E-mail: admisiones@popac.edu
Phone: (787) 848-1589 ext. 413

**Pontifical Catholic University of Puerto Rico**
www.pucpr.edu
Admissions
2250 Las Americas Avenue, Suite 284
Ponce, PR 00717-9777
Fax: (787) 651-2044
E-mail: rene_marrero@pucpr.edu
Phone: (787) 841-2000 ext. 1000

**Porterville College**
www.portervillecollege.edu
Admissions and Records Office
100 East College Avenue
Porterville, CA 93257
Fax: (209) 791-2349
Phone: (209) 791-2222

**Portland Community College**
www.pcc.edu
International Student Education
12000 SW 49th Avenue
Portland, OR 97219-7132
Fax: (971) 722-7170
E-mail: jeandarc.campbell@pcc.edu
Phone: (971) 722-7148

**Portland State University**
www.pdx.edu
International Admissions
PO Box 751-ADM
Portland, OR 97207-0751
Fax: (503) 725-5525
E-mail: intladm@pdx.edu
Phone: (503) 725-5503

**Post University**
www.post.edu
Assistant Director, International Admissions
800 Country Club Road
PO Box 2540
Waterbury, CT 06723-2540
Fax: (203) 841-1163
E-mail: bstadler@post.edu
Phone: (203) 591-5234

**Potomac State College of West Virginia University**
www.potomacstatecollege.edu
Enrollment Services
75 Arnold Street
Keyser, WV 26726
Fax: (304) 788-6939
E-mail: BELittle@mail.wvu.edu
Phone: (304) 788-6820

**PowerSport Institute**
www.ohiotech.edu
Admissions
21210 Emery Road
North Randall, OH 44128
Fax: (216) 881-9145
E-mail: jcolosi@ohiotech.edu
Phone: (216) 881-1700 ext. 142

**Prairie State College**
www.prairiestate.edu
Career and Transfer Center
202 South Halsted Street
Chicago Heights, IL 60411
Fax: (708) 755-2587
Phone: (708) 709-3512

**Prairie View A&M University**
www.pvamu.edu
Office of Admissions
PO Box 519, MS 1009
Prairie View, TX 77446-0519
E-mail: ntwoods@pvamu.edu
Phone: (936) 261-1067

**Pratt Community College**
www.prattcc.edu
Director of Admissions
348 Northeast State Route 61
Pratt, KS 67124-8317
Fax: (620) 672-5288
E-mail: lynnp@prattcc.edu
Phone: (620) 450-2222

**Pratt Institute**
www.pratt.edu
International Admissions Office
200 Willoughby Avenue
Brooklyn, NY 11205-3817
Fax: (718) 636-3670
E-mail: admissions@pratt.edu
Phone: (718) 636-3514

**Presbyterian College**
www.presby.edu
Admissions
503 South Broad Street
Clinton, SC 29325-2865
Fax: (864) 833-8195
E-mail: spetrusch@presby.edu
Phone: (864) 833-8194

**Prescott College**
www.prescott.edu
Admissions
220 Grove Avenue
Prescott, AZ 86301
Fax: (928) 776-5242
E-mail: admissions@prescott.edu
Phone: (877) 350-2100

**Presentation College**
www.presentation.edu
Vice President for Student Enrollment
1500 North Main Street
Aberdeen, SD 57401
Fax: (605) 229-8332
E-mail: joellen.lindner@presentation.edu
Phone: (605) 229-8424

**Prince George's Community College**
www.pgcc.edu
Admissions and Records
301 Largo Road
Largo, MD 20774
Fax: (301) 322-0119
E-mail: enrollmentservices@pgcc.edu
Phone: (301) 322-0863

**Princeton University**
www.princeton.edu
Princeton University
Box 430
Princeton, NJ 08542-0430
Fax: (609) 258-6743
E-mail: uaoffice@princeton.edu
Phone: (609) 258-3060

**Professional Golfers Career College**
www.golfcollege.edu
26109 Ynez Road
Temecula, CA 92591
Fax: (951) 719-1643
E-mail: pattipaulsen@golfcollege.edu
Phone: (800) 877-4380

**Professional Golfers Career College: Orlando**
www.golfcollege.edu
Temecula
PO Box 892319
Temecula, CA 92589-2319
Fax: (951) 719-1643
E-mail: patti.paulsen@golfcollege.edu
Phone: (800) 877-4380

**Providence Christian College**
www.providencecc.edu
Admissions
1539 East Howard Street
Pasadena, CA 91104
Fax: (626) 696-4040
E-mail: admission@providencecc.edu
Phone: (626) 696-4014

**Providence College**
www.providence.edu
Admissions
Harkins Hall 103, 1 Cunningham Square
Providence, RI 02918-0001
Fax: (401) 865-2826
E-mail: rfonts@providence.edu
Phone: (401) 865-2754

**Provo College**
www.provocollege.edu
1450 West 820 North
Provo, UT 84601
Fax: (801) 375-9728
E-mail: admissions@provocollege.edu
Phone: (801) 375-1861

**Pueblo Community College**
www.pueblocc.edu
Admissions
900 West Orman Avenue
Pueblo, CO 81004-1499
Fax: (719) 549-3012
E-mail: laura.lucero@pueblocc.edu
Phone: (719) 549-3015

**Pulaski Technical College**
www.pulaskitech.edu
Student Services
3000 West Scenic Drive
North Little Rock, AR 72118-3347
Fax: (501) 812-2316
E-mail: rhudson@pulaskitech.edu
Phone: (501) 812-2734

**Purdue University**
www.purdue.edu
Office of International Students and Scholars
475 Stadium Mall Drive
West Lafayette, IN 47907-2050
Fax: (765) 494-6340
E-mail: intl-admissions@purdue.edu
Phone: (765) 494-0380

**Purdue University North Central**
www.pnc.edu
Director of School Partnerships
1401 South US Highway 421
Westville, IN 46391-9542
Fax: (219) 785-5538
E-mail: swilson@pnc.edu
Phone: (219) 785-5236

**Purdue University Northwest**
https://www.pnw.edu
International Programs Office
2200 169th Street
Hammond, IN 46323-2094
Fax: (219) 989-8302
E-mail: iadmissions@purduecal.edu
Phone: (219) 989-2053

**Queens University of Charlotte**
www.queens.edu
Traditional Undergradute Office of Admissions
1900 Selwyn Avenue
Harris Welcome Center - MSC 1428
Charlotte, NC 28274-0001
Fax: (704) 337-2403
E-mail: simsj@queens.edu
Phone: (704) 688-2751

**Quincy College**
www.quincycollege.edu
International Student Office
1250 Hancock Street
Quincy, MA 02169
Fax: (617) 984-1794
E-mail: lstack@quincycollege.edu
Phone: (617) 984-1663

**Quincy University**
www.quincy.edu
Admissions Office
1800 College Avenue
Quincy, IL 62301-2699
Fax: (217) 228-5479
E-mail: admissions@quincy.edu
Phone: (217) 228-5210

**Quinnipiac University**
www.qu.edu
Undergraduate or Graduate Admissions
275 Mount Carmel Avenue
Hamden, CT 06518-1908
Fax: (582) 582-8906
E-mail: admissions@quinnipiac.edu
Phone: (582) 582-8600

**Quinsigamond Community College**
www.qcc.edu
Admissions
670 West Boylston Street
Worcester, MA 01606
Fax: (508) 854-7525
E-mail: admissions@qcc.mass.edu
Phone: (508) 854-4576

**Rabbi Jacob Joseph School**
One Plainfield Avenue
Edison, NJ 08817
Phone: (732) 985-6533

**Rabbinical Academy Mesivta Rabbi Chaim Berlin**
1593 Coney Island Avenue
Brooklyn, NY 11230
Phone: (718) 377-0777

**Rabbinical College Beth Shraga**
PO Box 412
Monsey, NY 10952
Phone: (845) 356-1980

**Rabbinical College Bobover Yeshiva B'nei Zion**
http://rabbinicalcollegeboboveryeshiva.edu/
1577 48th Street
Brooklyn, NY 11219
Phone: (718) 438-2018

**Rabbinical College Ch'san Sofer of New York**
1876 50th Street
Brooklyn, NY 11204
Phone: (718) 236-1171

**Rabbinical College of America**
www.rca.edu
226 Sussex Avenue, CN 1996
Morristown, NJ 07962-1996
Fax: (973) 267-5208
Phone: (973) 267-9404

**Rabbinical College of Long Island**
205 West Beech Street
Long Beach, NY 11561
Phone: (516) 431-7414

**Rabbinical College of Ohr Shimon Yisroel**
215-217 Hewes Street
Brooklyn, NY 11211
Phone: (718) 855-4092

**Rabbinical College of Telshe**
28400 Euclid Avenue
Wickliffe, OH 44092-2584
Fax: (440) 943-5303
Phone: (440) 943-5300 ext. 17

**Rabbinical Seminary of America**
76-01 147th Street
Flushing, NY 11367
Fax: (718) 268-4684
E-mail: registrar@rabbinical.org
Phone: (718) 268-4700

**Radford University**
www.radford.edu
Admissions Office
PO Box 6903
Radford, VA 24142
Fax: (540) 831-5038
E-mail: admissions@radford.edu
Phone: (540) 831-5371

**Rainy River Community College**
www.rainyriver.edu
Admissions
1501 Highway 71
International Falls, MN 56649
Fax: (218) 285-2314
E-mail: berta.hagen@rainyriver.edu
Phone: (218) 285-2207

**Ramapo College of New Jersey**
www.ramapo.edu
Admissions
505 Ramapo Valley Road
Admissions- McBride Building
Mahwah, NJ 07430-1680
Fax: (201) 684-7964
E-mail: rleshowi@ramapo.edu
Phone: (201) 684-1440

**Randolph College**
www.randolphcollege.edu
Admissions Office
2500 Rivermont Avenue
Lynchburg, VA 24503-1555
Fax: (434) 947-8996
E-mail: admissions@randolphcollege.edu
Phone: (434) 947-8100

**Randolph-Macon College**
www.rmc.edu
Admissions
PO Box 5005
Ashland, VA 23005-5505
Fax: (804) 752-4707
E-mail: admissions@rmc.edu
Phone: (804) 752-7305

**Ranger College**
www.rangercollege.edu
Registrar
1100 College Circle
Ranger, TX 76470
Fax: (254) 647-3739
E-mail: registrar@rangercollege.edu
Phone: (254) 647-3234

**Ranken Technical College**
www.ranken.edu
Admissions
4431 Finney Avenue
St. Louis, MO 63113
Fax: (314) 286-3309
E-mail: admissions@ranken.edu
Phone: (314) 286-4809

**Rappahannock Community College**
www.rappahannock.edu
Registrar
12745 College Drive
Glenns, VA 23149-2616
Fax: (804) 758-3852
E-mail: fpackett@rappahannock.edu
Phone: (804) 333-6741

**Raritan Valley Community College**
www.raritanval.edu
Advising and Counseling
118 Lamington Road
Lower Floor of the Library Building
Branchburg, NJ 08876-1265
Fax: (908) 253-6691
E-mail: elizabeth.sullivan@raritanval.edu
Phone: (908) 526-1200 ext. 8452

**Rasmussen College: Appleton**
www.rasmussen.edu
3500 East Destination Drive
Appleton, WI 54915
Phone: (920) 750-5900

**Rasmussen College: Aurora**
www.rasmussen.edu
2363 Sequoia Drive, Suite 131
Aurora, IL 60506
Phone: (630) 888-3500

**Rasmussen College: Bismarck**
www.rasmussen.edu
Admissions
1701 East Century Avenue
Bismarck, ND 58503
Fax: (701) 530-9604
E-mail: mike.heitkamp@rasmussen.edu
Phone: (701) 530-9600

**Rasmussen College: Blaine**
www.rasmussen.edu
3629 95th Avenue NE
Blaine, MN 55014
Phone: (763) 795-4720

**Rasmussen College: Bloomington**
www.rasmussen.edu
Admissions
4400 West 78th Street
Bloomington, MN 55435
Phone: (952) 545-2000

**Rasmussen College: Brooklyn Park**
www.rasmussen.edu
Admissions
8301 93rd Avenue North
Brooklyn Park, MN 55445
Phone: (763) 493-4500

**Rasmussen College: Eagan**
www.rasmussen.edu
Admissions
3500 Federal Drive
Eagan, MN 55122
Fax: (651) 687-0507
E-mail: jon.peterson@rasmussen.edu
Phone: (651) 687-9000

**Rasmussen College: Fargo**
www.rasmussen.edu
4012 19th Avenue SW
Fargo, ND 58103
Fax: (701) 277-5604
Phone: (701) 277-3889

**Rasmussen College: Fort Myers**
www.rasmussen.edu
9160 Forum Corporate Parkway, Suite 100
Fort Myers, FL 33905-7805
Phone: (239) 477-2100

**Rasmussen College: Green Bay**
www.rasmussen.edu
904 South Taylor Street, Suite 100
Green Bay, WI 54303-2349
Phone: (920) 593-8400

**Rasmussen College: Lake Elmo/Woodbury**
www.rasmussen.edu
8565 Eagle Point Circle
Lake Elmo, MN 55042-8637
Fax: (651) 259-6601
Phone: (651) 259-6600

**Rasmussen College: Mankato**
www.rasmussen.edu
Admissions
130 Saint Andrews Drive
Mankato, MN 56001
Fax: (507) 625-6557
Phone: (507) 625-6556

**Rasmussen College: Mokena/Tinley Park**
www.rasmussen.edu
8650 West Spring Lake Road
Mokena, IL 60448
Phone: (815) 534-3300

**Rasmussen College: Moorhead**
www.rasmussen.edu
1250 29th Avenue South
Moorhead, MN 56560
Fax: (218) 304-6201
Phone: (218) 304-6200

**Rasmussen College: New Port Richey**
www.rasmussen.edu
Financial Aid
8661 Citizens Drive
New Port Richey, FL 34654
Fax: (727) 938-5709
E-mail: susan.hammerstrom@rasmussen.edu
Phone: (727) 942-0069

**Rasmussen College: Ocala**
www.rasmussen.edu
Admissions
2221 Southwest 46th Court
Ocala, FL 34474
Fax: (352) 629-0926
E-mail: susan.hammerstrom@rasmussen.edu
Phone: (352) 629-1941

**Rasmussen College: Pasco/Land O'Lakes**
www.rasmussen.edu
18600 Fernview Street
Land O' Lakes, FL 34638

**Rasmussen College: Rockford**
www.rasmussen.edu
6000 East State Street, Fourth Floor
Rockford, IL 61108-2513
Phone: (815) 316-4800

**Rasmussen College: Romeoville/Joliet**
www.rasmussen.edu
400 West Normantown Road
Romeoville, IL 60446
Phone: (815) 306-2600

**Rasmussen College: St. Cloud**
www.rasmussen.edu
Admissions
226 Park Avenue South
St. Cloud, MN 56301-3713
Fax: (320) 251-3702
Phone: (320) 251-5600

**Rasmussen College: Tampa/Brandon**
www.rasmussen.edu
4042 Park Oak Boulevard
Tampa, FL 33610
Phone: (813) 246-7600

**Rasmussen College: Wausau**
www.rasmussen.edu
1101 Westwood Drive
Wausau, WI 54401
E-mail: susan.hammerstrom@rasmussen.edu
Phone: (715) 841-8000

**Reading Area Community College**
www.racc.edu
Enrollment Services Office
10 South Second Street
PO Box 1706
Reading, PA 19603-1706
Fax: (610) 607-6257
E-mail: jmelones@racc.edu
Phone: (610) 607-6224

**Red Rocks Community College**
www.rrcc.edu
Office of English Language/Intercultural
Services
13300 West Sixth Avenue
Box 5
Lakewood, CO 80228-1255
Fax: (303) 314-6716
E-mail: international@rrcc.edu
Phone: (303) 914-6416

**Redlands Community College**
www.redlandscc.edu
Student Services
1300 South Country Club Road
El Reno, OK 73036
Fax: (405) 422-1239
E-mail: jennifer.hardaway@redlandscc.edu
Phone: (405) 422-6202

**Redstone College**
www.redstone.edu
10851 West 120th Avenue
Broomfield, CO 80021-3401
Fax: (303) 469-3797
Phone: (303) 466-1714

**Reed College**
www.reed.edu
Admission
3203 SE Woodstock Boulevard
Portland, OR 97202-8199
Fax: (503) 777-7553
E-mail: admission@reed.edu
Phone: (503) 777-7511

**Reedley College**
www.reedleycollege.edu
Admissions and Records
995 North Reed Avenue
Reedley, CA 93654
Fax: (559) 638-5040
E-mail: veronica.jury@reedleycollege.edu
Phone: (559) 638-0323

**Refrigeration School**
www.refrigerationschool.com
4210 East Washington Street
Phoenix, AZ 85034-1816
Fax: (602) 267-4805
Phone: (602) 275-7133

**Regent University**
www.regent.edu
Assistant VP of Enrollment Management
1000 Regent University Drive
LIB 102
Virginia Beach, VA 23464-9800
Fax: (757) 352-4452
E-mail: intladmissions@regent.edu
Phone: (757) 352-4127

**Regis College**
www.regiscollege.edu
Admission
235 Wellesley Street
Weston, MA 02493-1571
Fax: (781) 768-7071
E-mail: paul.vaccaro@regiscollege.edu
Phone: (781) 768-7100

**Regis University**
www.regis.edu
Office of Admissions
3333 Regis Boulevard, Mail Code A12
Denver, CO 80221-1099
Fax: (303) 964-5534
E-mail: sengel@regis.edu
Phone: (303) 458-4900

**Reinhardt University**
www.reinhardt.edu
Admissions
7300 Reinhardt Circle
Waleska, GA 30183-2981
Fax: (770) 720-5899
E-mail: jcf@reinhardt.edu
Phone: (770) 720-5527

**Remington College of Nursing**
www.remingtoncollege.edu
660 Century Point
Lake Mary, FL 32746
E-mail: admissions@remingtoncollege.edu

**Remington College: Baton Rouge**
http://baton-rouge.remingtoncollege.edu
10551 Coursey Boulevard
Baton Rouge, LA 70816
Phone: (225) 240-7049

**Remington College: Cleveland**
http://cleveland.remingtoncollege.edu
Director of Recruitment
14445 Broadway Avenue
Cleveland, OH 44125
Fax: (216) 475-6055
E-mail: admissions@remingtoncollege.edu
Phone: (216) 475-7520

**Remington College: Columbia**
www.remingtoncollege.edu/columbia/
607 Bush River Road
Columbia, SC 29210
E-mail: admissions@remingtoncollege.edu

**Remington College: Dallas**
www.remingtoncollege.edu/dallas
1800 Eastgate Drive
Garland, TX 75041
E-mail: admissions@remingtoncollege.edu
Phone: (972) 268-6506

**Remington College: Fort Worth**
http://fort-worth.remingtoncollege.edu
300 East Loop 820
Fort Worth, TX 76112
Fax: (817) 496-1257
E-mail: marcia.kline@remingtoncollege.edu
Phone: (817) 451-0017

**Remington College: Greenspoint Campus**
http://greenspoint.remingtoncollege.edu
11310 Greens Crossing, Suite 300
Houston, TX 77067
E-mail: admissions@remingtoncollege.edu
Phone: (832) 699-2221

**Remington College: Honolulu**
http://honolulu.remingtoncollege.edu
Admissions Office
1111 Bishop Street, Suite 400
Honolulu, HI 96813-2811
Fax: (808) 533-3064
Phone: (808) 942-1000

**Remington College: Lafayette**
http://lafayette.remingtoncollege.edu
Director of Admissions
303 Rue Louis XIV
Lafayette, LA 70508
Fax: (337) 983-7130
E-mail: admissions@remingtoncollege.edu
Phone: (337) 981-4010

**Remington College: Little Rock**
http://little-rock.remingtoncollege.edu
19 Remington Drive
Little Rock, AR 72204
E-mail: admissions@remingtoncollege.edu
Phone: (501) 303-4385

**Remington College: Memphis**
www.memphis.remingtoncollege.edu
2710 Nonconnah Boulevard
Memphis, TN 38132
E-mail: admissions@remingtoncollege.edu
Phone: (901) 389-5302

**Remington College: Mobile**
http://mobile.remingtoncollege.edu
Registrar
828 Downtowner Loop West
Mobile, AL 36609-5404
Fax: (251) 343-0577
E-mail: admissions@remingtoncollege.edu
Phone: (251) 343-8200

**Remington College: Nashville**
http://nashville.remingtoncollege.edu
441 Donelson Pike, Suite 150
Nashville, TN 37214
E-mail: admissions@remingtoncollege.edu
Phone: (615) 229-6057

**Remington College: Shreveport**
http://shreveport.remingtoncollege.edu
2106 W Bert Kouns Industrial Loop
Shreveport, LA 71118
E-mail: admissions@remingtoncollege.edu
Phone: (318) 239-4309

**Remington College: Tampa**
www.tampa.remingtoncollege.edu
International Department
6302 East Dr. Martin Luther King Jr.
Boulevard
Ste 400
Tampa, FL 33619
Fax: (813) 935-7415
E-mail: gary.schwartz@remingtoncollege.edu
Phone: (813) 935-5700

**Remington College: Webster Campus**
http://webster.remingtoncollege.edu
20985 Interstate 45 South
Webster, TX 77598
Phone: (713) 581-9000

**Remington College: Westchase Campus**
http://houston.remingtoncollege.edu
Admissions
3110 Hayes Road, Suite 380
Houston, TX 77082
Fax: (281) 597-8466
E-mail:
kevin.wilkinson@remingtoncollege.edu
Phone: (281) 899-1240

**Rensselaer Polytechnic Institute**
www.rpi.edu
Admissions Office
110 Eighth Street
Troy, NY 12180-3590
Fax: (518) 276-4072
E-mail: rosatn@rpi.edu
Phone: (518) 276-6216

**Renton Technical College**
www.RTC.edu
3000 NE Fourth Street
Renton, WA 98056-4195
Fax: (425) 235-7832
E-mail: pbrown@rtc.edu
Phone: (425) 235-5840

**Research College of Nursing**
www.researchcollege.edu
Admission Office
2525 East Meyer Boulevard
Kansas City, MO 64132-1199
Fax: (816) 995-2813
E-mail: mitch.nelson@rockhurst.edu
Phone: (816) 501-4000

**Restaurant School at Walnut Hill College**
www.walnuthillcollege.edu
Admissions and Financial Aid
4207 Walnut Street
Philadelphia, PA 19104
Fax: (215) 222-2811
E-mail: info@walnuthillcollege.edu
Phone: (215) 222-4200 ext. 3053

**Resurrection University**
www.resu.edu
1431 North Claremont Avenue
Chicago, IL 60622
Fax: (773) 227-3838
E-mail: admissions@resu.edu
Phone: (773) 252-6464

**Rhode Island College**
www.ric.edu
Admissions Office
600 Mount Pleasant Avenue
Forman Center
Providence, RI 02908
Fax: (401) 456-8817
E-mail: internationals@ric.edu
Phone: (401) 456-8234

**Rhode Island School of Design**
www.risd.edu
Admissions
2 College Street
Providence, RI 02903-2784
Fax: (401) 454-6309
E-mail: admissions@risd.edu
Phone: (401) 454-6300

**Rhodes College**
www.rhodes.edu
Associate Director of Admissions
2000 North Parkway
Memphis, TN 38112
Fax: (901) 843-3631
E-mail: SEFTONL@rhodes.edu
Phone: (901) 843-3700

**Rice University**
www.rice.edu
Admission Office
6100 Main Street
Office of Admission MS-17 PO Box 1892
Houston, TX 77251-1892
Fax: (713) 348-5323
E-mail: admission@rice.edu
Phone: (713) 348-7423

**Richard Bland College**
www.rbc.edu
Division of Enrollment Services
11301 Johnson Road
South Prince George, VA 23805
Fax: (804) 862-6490
E-mail: apply@rbc.edu
Phone: (804) 862-6249

**Richland College**
www.richlandcollege.edu
Multicultural Center
12800 Abrams Road
Dallas, TX 75243-2199
Fax: (972) 682-6165
E-mail: tadams@dcccd.edu
Phone: (972) 238-6903

**Richland Community College**
www.richland.edu
Director, Admissions
One College Park
Decatur, IL 62521
Fax: (217) 875-7783
E-mail: csebok@richland.edu
Phone: (217) 875-7200 ext. 558

**Richmond Community College**
www.richmondcc.edu
Registrar
Box 1189
Hamlet, NC 28345
Fax: (910) 582-7102
Phone: (910) 410-1737

**Rider University**
www.rider.edu
Undergraduate Admissions
2083 Lawrenceville Road
Box 3001
Lawrenceville, NJ 08648-3099
Fax: (609) 895-6645
E-mail: admissions@rider.edu
Phone: (609) 895-5635

**Ridgewater College**
www.ridgewater.edu
Admissions Office
2101 15th Avenue Northwest
Willmar, MN 56201
Fax: (320) 222-5216
E-mail: sally.kerfeld@ridgewater.edu
Phone: (320) 222-5977

**Ringling College of Art and Design**
www.ringling.edu
Admissions
2700 North Tamiami Trail
Sarasota, FL 34234-5895
Fax: (941) 359-7517
E-mail: afischer@ringling.edu
Phone: (941) 351-5100

**Rio Hondo College**
www.riohondo.edu
3600 Workman Mill Road
Whittier, CA 90601-1699
Fax: (562) 692-8318
E-mail: agonzalez@riohondo.edu
Phone: (562) 463-7643

**Rio Salado College**
www.riosalado.edu
Registration and Records
2323 West 14th Street
Tempe, AZ 85281
Fax: (480) 377-4689
E-mail: admissions.standards@riosalado.edu
Phone: (480) 517-8152

**River Valley Community College**
www.rivervalley.edu
Admissions
One College Drive
Claremont, NH 03743-9707
Fax: (603) 543-1844
E-mail: ckusselow@ccsnh.edu
Phone: (603) 542-7744

**Riverland Community College**
www.riverland.edu
1900 Eighth Avenue, NW
Austin, MN 55912-1407
Fax: (507) 433-0515
E-mail: mmorem@river.cc.mn.us
Phone: (507) 433-0600

**Riverside City College**
www.rcc.edu
Center for International Students and
Programs
4800 Magnolia Avenue
Riverside, CA 92506
Fax: (951) 222-8376
E-mail: internationalcenter@rcc.edu
Phone: (951) 222-8160

**Rivier University**
www.rivier.edu
Admissions Office
420 South Main Street
Nashua, NH 03060-5086
Fax: (603) 891-1799
E-mail: admissions@rivier.edu
Phone: (603) 897-8516

**Roane State Community College**
www.roanestate.edu
Recruitment Office
276 Patton Lane
Harriman, TN 37748
Fax: (865) 882-4585
E-mail: gonzalesmr@roanestate.edu
Phone: (865) 882-4628

**Roanoke College**
www.roanoke.edu
Admissions
221 College Lane
Salem, VA 24153-3794
Fax: (540) 375-2267
E-mail: admissions@roanoke.edu
Phone: (540) 375-2270

**Roanoke-Chowan Community College**
www.roanokechowan.edu
Student Services
109 Community College Road
Ahoskie, NC 27910-9522
Fax: (252) 862-1355
E-mail: afwiggins7415@roanokehowan.edu
Phone: (252) 862-1200

**Robert B. Miller College**
www.millercollege.edu
450 North Avenue
Battle Creek, MI 49017
E-mail: danielsonc@millercollege.edu
Phone: (269) 660-8021 ext. 2933

**Robert Morris University**
www.rmu.edu
Office of International Admissions
6001 University Boulevard
Moon Township, PA 15108-1189
Fax: (412) 397-2425
E-mail: admissionsoffice@rmu.edu
Phone: (800) 762-0097

**Robert Morris University: Chicago**
www.robertmorris.edu
Student Information
401South State Street
Chicago, IL 60605
Fax: (312) 935-4177
E-mail: studentrecords@robertmorris.edu
Phone: (312) 935-4180

**Roberts Wesleyan College**
www.roberts.edu
Associate VP of Undergraduate Admissions
2301 Westside Drive
Rochester, NY 14624-1997
Fax: (585) 594-6371
E-mail: admissions@roberts.edu
Phone: (585) 594-6411

**Robeson Community College**
www.robeson.edu
PO Box 1420
5160 Fayetteville Road
Lumberton, NC 28359
Fax: (910) 618-5686
E-mail: rlocklear@robeson.edu
Phone: (910) 272-3347

**Rochester College**
www.rc.edu
Enrollment Services
800 West Avon Road
Rochester Hills, MI 48307
Fax: (248) 218-2035
E-mail: admissions@rc.edu
Phone: (248) 218-2031

**Rochester Community and Technical College**
www.rctc.edu
International Admissions Office
Admissions and Records Office (Box 7)
851 30th Avenue SE
Rochester, MN 55904-4999
Fax: (507) 285-7496
E-mail: Glen.Saponari@rctc.edu
Phone: (507) 280-5511

**Rochester Institute of Technology**
www.rit.edu
Undergraduate Admissions Office
60 Lomb Memorial Drive
Rochester, NY 14623-5604
Fax: (585) 475-7424
E-mail: admissions@rit.edu
Phone: (585) 475-6631

**Rock Valley College**
www.rockvalleycollege.edu
Enrollment Services
3301 North Mulford Road
Rockford, IL 61114-5699
Fax: (815) 921-4269
E-mail: m.foreman@rockvalleycollege.edu
Phone: (815) 921-4251

**Rockford University**
www.rockford.edu
Office of Undergraduate Admission
5050 East State Street
Rockford, IL 61108-2311
Fax: (818) 226-2822
E-mail: admissions@rockford.edu
Phone: (815) 226-4050

**Rockhurst University**
www.rockhurst.edu
Associate Director of Admission
1100 Rockhurst Road
Kansas City, MO 64110-2561
Fax: (816) 501-4142
E-mail: mitch.nelson@rockhurst.edu
Phone: (816) 501-4538

**Rockingham Community College**
www.rockinghamcc.edu
Box 38
Wentworth, NC 27375-0038
Fax: (336) 342-1809
E-mail: admissions@rockinghamcc.edu
Phone: (336) 342-4261 ext. 2333

**Rockland Community College**
www.sunyrockland.edu
International Student Services
145 College Road
Suffern, NY 10901-3699
Fax: (845) 574-4433
E-mail: cspring2@sunyrockland.edu
Phone: (845) 574-4193

**Rocky Mountain College**
www.rocky.edu
International Programs
1511 Poly Drive
Billings, MT 59102-1796
Fax: (406) 259-9751
E-mail: amber.westmartin@rocky.edu
Phone: (406) 657-1107

**Rocky Mountain College of Art & Design**
www.rmcad.edu
Admissions
1600 Pierce Street
Denver, CO 80214
Fax: (303) 567-7281
E-mail: kjohnson2@rmcad.edu
Phone: (303) 225-8585

**Roger Williams University**
www.rwu.edu
Office of Admission
1 Old Ferry Road
Bristol, RI 02809-2921
Fax: (401) 254-3557
E-mail: admit@rwu.edu
Phone: (401) 254-3500

**Rogers State University**
www.rsu.edu
Office of Admissions
1701 West Will Rogers Boulevard
Office of Admissions
Claremore, OK 74017-3252
Fax: (918) 343-7595
E-mail: aschmidt@rsu.edu
Phone: (918) 343-7546

**Rogue Community College**
www.roguecc.edu
Enrollment Services
3345 Redwood Highway
Grants Pass, OR 97527-9291
E-mail: jduarte@roguecc.edu
Phone: (541) 956-7176

**Rollins College**
www.rollins.edu
Admission
1000 Holt Avenue, Campus Box 2720
Winter Park, FL 32789
Fax: (407) 646-1502
E-mail: admission@rollins.edu
Phone: (407) 646-2161

**Roosevelt University**
www.roosevelt.edu
Office of International Porgrams
430 S Michigan Ave
Chicago, IL 60605-1394
Fax: (312) 341-6377
E-mail: dhougland@roosevelt.edu
Phone: (312) 341-6464

**Rose State College**
www.rose.edu
Admissions
6420 SE 15th Street
Midwest City, OK 73110-2799
Fax: (405) 736-0309
E-mail: dsorrell@rose.edu
Phone: (405) 736-0203

**Rose-Hulman Institute of Technology**
www.rose-hulman.edu
Assistant Director of Graduate and
International Admissions
Office of Admissions
5500 Wabash Avenue, CM 1
Terre Haute, IN 47803-3999
Fax: (812) 877-8941
E-mail: goulding@rose-hulman.edu
Phone: (800) 248-7448

**Rosedale Technical College**
www.rosedaletech.org
215 Beecham Drive
Suite 2
Pittsburgh, PA 15205-9791
Fax: (412) 521-2520
E-mail: admissions@rosedaletech.org
Phone: (412) 521-6200

**Roseman University of Health Sciences**
www.roseman.edu
Registrar and Director of Student Services
11 Sunset Way
Henderson, NV 89014-2333
Fax: (702) 968-2097
E-mail: abigby@roseman.edu
Phone: (702) 968-2046

**Rosemont College**
www.rosemont.edu
Undergraduate College Admissions
1400 Montgomery Avenue
Rosemont, PA 19010-1699
Fax: (610) 520-4399
E-mail: sean.fisher@rosemont.edu
Phone: (610) 527-0200 ext. 2608

**Rowan College at Burlington County**
www.rcbc.edu
Office of International Student Services
900 College Circle
Mt. Laurel, NJ 08054
Fax: (856) 439-1205
E-mail: international@rcbc.edu
Phone: (856) 222-9311 ext. 2232

**Rowan College at Gloucester**
www.rcgc.edu
Admissions
1400 Tanyard Road
Sewell, NJ 08080-4222
Fax: (856) 468-8498
E-mail: ckulisek@rcgc.edu
Phone: (856) 468-5000 ext. 6273

**Rowan University**
www.rowan.edu
International Center
Savitz Hall, 201 Mullica Hill Road
Glassboro, NJ 08028-1701
Fax: (856) 256-5676
E-mail: mccafferty@rowan.edu
Phone: (856) 256-4105

**Roxbury Community College**
www.rcc.mass.edu
Admissions
1234 Columbus Avenue
Roxbury Crossing, MA 02120-3400
Fax: (617) 541-5316
E-mail: msamuels@rcc.mass.edu
Phone: (617) 541-5310

**Rush University**
www.rushu.rush.edu
International Affairs
College Admissions
600 South Paulina Street, Suite 440
Chicago, IL 60612
Fax: (312) 942-7773
E-mail: helen_lavelle@rush.edu
Phone: (312) 942-2030

**Rust College**
www.rustcollege.edu
Registrar's Office
150 Rust Avenue
Holly Springs, MS 38635-2328
Fax: (662) 252-2258
E-mail: csmith@rustcollege.edu
Phone: (662) 252-8000 ext. 4056

**Rutgers, The State University of New Jersey: Camden Campus**
www.camden.rutgers.edu
Assistant Dean, International Students
406 Penn Street
Camden, NJ 08102
Fax: (856) 225-6579
E-mail: ois@camden.rutgers.edu
Phone: (856) 225-2521

**Rutgers, The State University of New Jersey: New Brunswick/Piscataway Campus**
www.newbrunswick.rutgers.edu
65 Davidson Road, Room 202
Piscataway, NJ 08854-8097
Fax: (732) 445-0237
E-mail:
RUInternational@admissions.rutgers.edu
Phone: (848) 445-3624

**Rutgers, The State University of New Jersey: Newark Campus**
www.newark.rutgers.edu
Office of International Student and Scholar
Services
249 University Avenue
Newark, NJ 07102-1896
Fax: (973) 353-5577
E-mail: oiss@andromeda.rutgers.edu
Phone: (973) 353-1427

**Sacramento City College**
www.scc.losrios.edu
International Student Office
3835 Freeport Boulevard
Sacramento, CA 95822
Fax: (916) 558-2490
E-mail: sccaeinfo@scc.losrios.edu
Phone: (916) 558-2486

**Sacred Heart Major Seminary**
www.shms.edu
Office of the Vice Rector
2701 Chicago Boulevard
Detroit, MI 48206-1799
Fax: (313) 883-8659
E-mail: Forrester.Linda@shms.edu
Phone: (313) 883-8563

**Sacred Heart University**
www.sacredheart.edu
Office of International Admissions
5151 Park Avenue
Fairfield, CT 06825
Fax: (203) 365-7607
E-mail: neversc@sacredheart.edu
Phone: (203) 767-0386

**Saddleback College**
www.saddleback.edu
International Education Office
28000 Marguerite Parkway
Mission Viejo, CA 92692
Fax: (949) 582-4800
E-mail: sc-iso@saddleback.edu
Phone: (949) 582-4637

**The Sage Colleges**
www.sage.edu
Admission
65 1st Street
Troy, NY 12180-4115
Fax: (518) 244-6880
E-mail: robere@sage.edu
Phone: (518) 244-2217

**Saginaw Chippewa Tribal College**
www.sagchip.edu
2274 Enterprise Drive
Mount Pleasant, MI 48858
Fax: (989) 775-4528
E-mail: flaugher.amanda@sagchip.edu
Phone: (989) 775-4123

**Saginaw Valley State University**
www.svsu.edu
International Programs
7400 Bay Road
University Center, MI 48710
Fax: (989) 790-0180
E-mail: intadmit@svsu.edu
Phone: (989) 964-4473

**St. Ambrose University**
www.sau.edu
International Admissions
518 West Locust Street
Davenport, IA 52803-2898
Fax: (563) 333-6038
E-mail: RogalskiMatthewE@sau.edu
Phone: (563) 333-5724

**St. Andrews University**
www.sa.edu
Assistant Director of Admissions
1700 Dogwood Mile
Laurinburg, NC 28352
Fax: (910) 277-5087
E-mail: taylorsm@sa.edu
Phone: (910) 277-5555 ext. 3974

**Saint Anselm College**
www.anselm.edu
Admission
100 Saint Anselm Drive
Manchester, NH 03102-1310
Fax: (603) 641-7550
E-mail: ksimenson@anselm.edu
Phone: (603) 641-7246

**St. Augustine College**
www.staugustine.edu
1345 West Argyle
Chicago, IL 60640-3501
Fax: (773) 878-0937
Phone: (773) 878-8756

**Saint Augustine's University**
www.st-aug.edu
Admissions
1315 Oakwood Avenue
Raleigh, NC 27610-2298
Fax: (919) 516-5804
E-mail: admissions@st-aug.edu
Phone: (919) 516-4014

**Saint Bonaventure University**
www.sbu.edu
Admissions
Box D
St. Bonaventure, NY 14778
Fax: (716) 375-4005
E-mail: shanson@sbu.edu
Phone: (716) 375-2033

**St. Catharine College**
www.sccky.edu
Admissions
2735 Bardstown Road
St. Catharine, KY 40061
Fax: (859) 336-5031
E-mail: ticha.chikuni@sccky.edu
Phone: (859) 336-5082 ext. 1313

**St. Catherine University**
www.stkate.edu
Assistant Director International Admission
2004 Randolph Avenue #F-02
St. Paul, MN 55105
Fax: (651) 690-8824
E-mail: aethostenson@stkate.edu
Phone: (651) 690-6029

**St. Clair County Community College**
www.sc4.edu
Enrollment Services
323 Erie Street
Box 5015
Port Huron, MI 48061-5015
Fax: (810) 984-4730
E-mail: enrollment@sc4.edu
Phone: (810) 989-5500

**Saint Cloud State University**
www.stcloudstate.edu
Center for International Studies
720 Fourth Avenue South, AS 115
St. Cloud, MN 56301
Fax: (320) 308-4223
E-mail: international@stcloudstate.edu
Phone: (320) 308-4224

**St. Cloud Technical and Community College**
www.sctcc.edu
Admissions
1540 Northway Drive
St. Cloud, MN 56303
Fax: (320) 308-5087
E-mail: jelness@sctcc.edu
Phone: (800) 222-1009

**St. Edward's University**
https://www.stedwards.edu
Dean of International Admission
3001 South Congress Avenue
Austin, TX 78704-6489
Fax: (512) 464-8877
E-mail: amyk@stedwards.edu
Phone: (800) 555-0164

**St. Elizabeth College of Nursing**
www.secon.edu
Director of Finance & Enrollment
2215 Genesee Street
Utica, NY 13501
Fax: (315) 801-8271
E-mail: swojnas@secon.edu
Phone: (315) 801-8206

**St. Francis College**
www.sfc.edu
Student Services
180 Remsen Street
Brooklyn Heights, NY 11201-9902
Fax: (718) 802-0453
E-mail: clectura@sfc.edu
Phone: (718) 489-3486

**St. Francis University**
www.francis.edu
Office of International Admissions and
Student Services
Box 600
117 Evergreen Drive
Loretto, PA 15940
Fax: (814) 472-3335
E-mail: intl@francis.edu
Phone: (800) 472-3100

**St. Gregory's University**
www.stgregorys.edu
International Office
1900 West MacArthur Drive
Shawnee, OK 74804
Fax: (405) 878-5198
E-mail: int-admissions@stgregorys.edu
Phone: (405) 878-5177

**St. John Fisher College**
www.sjfc.edu
Office of Freshman Admissions
3690 East Avenue
Rochester, NY 14618-3597
Fax: (585) 385-8386
E-mail: valfieri@sjfc.edu
Phone: (585) 385-8064

**St. John's College**
www.sjc.edu
Admissions
60 College Avenue
Annapolis, MD 21401
Fax: (410) 269-7916
E-mail: amanda.stevens@sjc.edu
Phone: (410) 626-2524

**St. John's College**
www.sjc.edu
Admissions Office, Undergraduate
1160 Camino Cruz Blanca
Santa Fe, NM 87505
Fax: (505) 984-6162
E-mail: SantaFe.Admissions@sjc.edu
Phone: (505) 984-6060

**St. John's University**
www.csbsju.edu
Admissions
College of St Benedict/St John's University
PO Box 7155
Collegeville, MN 56321-7155
Fax: (320) 363-3206
E-mail: aschleper@csbsju.edu
Phone: (320) 363-2263

**St. John's University**
www.stjohns.edu
Office of Undergraduate Admission
8000 Utopia Parkway
Queens, NY 11439
Fax: (718) 990-8220
E-mail: intladm@stjohns.edu
Phone: (718) 990-2000

**St. Joseph Seminary College**
www.sjasc.edu
Registrar
75376 River Road
St. Benedict, LA 70457-9990
Fax: (985) 327-1085
E-mail: registrar@sjasc.edu
Phone: (985) 867-2273

**Saint Joseph's College**
www.saintjoe.edu
Admissions
Box 890
Rensselaer, IN 47978-0890
Fax: (219) 866-6170
E-mail: lisag@saintjoe.edu
Phone: (800) 447-8781

**St. Joseph's College New York: Suffolk Campus**
www.sjcny.edu
Admissions
155 West Roe Boulevard
Patchogue, NY 11772-2325
Fax: (631) 447-3601
E-mail: glamens@sjcny.edu
Phone: (718) 940-5800

**Saint Joseph's College of Maine**
www.sjcme.edu
Admissions Office
278 Whites Bridge Road
Standish, ME 04084-5236
Fax: (207) 893-7862
E-mail: nray@sjcme.edu
Phone: (207) 893-7670

**St. Joseph's College, New York**
www.sjcny.edu
Undergraduate Admissions
245 Clinton Avenue
Brooklyn, NY 11205-3602
Fax: (718) 636-8303
E-mail: bkadmissions@sjcny.edu
Phone: (718) 940-5800

**Saint Joseph's University**
www.sju.edu
Undergraduate Admissions
5600 City Avenue
Philadelphia, PA 19131
Fax: (610) 660-1314
E-mail: madekoya@sju.edu
Phone: (610) 660-1300

**St. Lawrence University**
www.stlawu.edu
Admissions
Payson Hall
Canton, NY 13617
Fax: (315) 229-5818
E-mail: admissions@stlawu.edu
Phone: (315) 229-5261

**Saint Leo University**
www.saintleo.edu
Office of Admission
Box 6665 MC2008
Saint Leo, FL 33574-6665
Fax: (352) 588-8257
E-mail: admissions@saintleo.edu
Phone: (352) 588-8283

**St. Louis Community College at Florissant Valley**
www.stlcc.edu
3400 Pershall Road
St. Louis, MO 63135
Fax: (314) 513-4724
Phone: (314) 513-4244

**Saint Louis University**
www.slu.edu
Division of Enrollment Management
One North Grand Boulevard
DuBourg Hall
St. Louis, MO 63103
Fax: (314) 977-3412
E-mail: icadmit@slu.edu
Phone: (314) 977-2318

**St. Luke's College**
www.stlukescollege.edu
2800 Pierce Street Suite 410
Sioux City, IA 51104
Fax: (712) 233-8017
E-mail: sherry.mccarthy@stlukescollege.edu
Phone: (712) 279-3158

**Saint Martin's University**
www.stmartin.edu
Office of International Programs and Development
5000 Abbey Way SE
Lacey, WA 98503-3200
Fax: (360) 438-4359
E-mail: jyung@stmartin.edu
Phone: (360) 438-4504

**St. Mary-of-the-Woods College**
www.smwc.edu
1 St Mary of Woods Coll
Saint Mary of the Woods, IN 47876-1099
Fax: (812) 535-5010
E-mail: admission@smwc.edu
Phone: (812) 535-5106

**Saint Mary's College**
www.saintmarys.edu
Admission Office
122 Le Mans Hall
Notre Dame, IN 46556-5001
Fax: (574) 284-4841
E-mail: rpiontek@saintmarys.edu
Phone: (574) 284-4763

**St. Mary's College of California**
www.stmarys-ca.edu
Dean of Admissions
1928 Saint Mary's Road
P.M.B. 4800
Moraga, CA 94575
Fax: (925) 376-7193
E-mail: international@stmarys-ca.edu
Phone: (925) 631-4552

**St. Mary's College of Maryland**
www.smcm.edu
Vice President of Enrollment Management
47645 College Drive
St. Mary's City, MD 20686-3001
Fax: (240) 895-5001
E-mail: admissions@smcm.edu
Phone: (240) 895-5000

**St. Mary's University**
www.stmarytx.edu
Director of Undergraduate Admission
One Camino Santa Maria
San Antonio, TX 78228-8504
Fax: (210) 431-6742
E-mail: uadm@stmarytx.edu
Phone: (210) 436-3126

**St. Mary's University of Minnesota**
www.smumn.edu
700 Terrace Heights #2
Winona, MN 55987-1399
Fax: (507) 457-1722
E-mail: tharing@smumn.edu
Phone: (507) 457-6962

**Saint Michael's College**
www.smcvt.edu
Office of Admission
One Winooski Park
Box 7
Colchester, VT 05439
Fax: (802) 654-2357
E-mail: kspensley@smcvt.edu
Phone: (802) 654-3000

**St. Norbert College**
www.snc.edu
Admissions
100 Grant Street
De Pere, WI 54115-2099
Fax: (920) 403-4072
E-mail: admit@snc.edu
Phone: (920) 403-3005

**St. Olaf College**
www.stolaf.edu
Admissions
1520 St. Olaf Avenue
Northfield, MN 55057
Fax: (507) 786-3832
E-mail: howensti@stolaf.edu
Phone: (507) 786-3813

**Saint Peter's University**
www.saintpeters.edu
Dean of International Enrollment
2641 Kennedy Boulevard
Jersey City, NJ 07306
Fax: (201) 761-7105
E-mail: lcardenas@saintpeters.edu
Phone: (201) 761-7115

**St. Petersburg College**
www.spcollege.edu
International Student Studies
Box 13489
St. Petersburg, FL 33733-3489
Fax: (727) 499-4613
E-mail: InternationalCenter@spcollege.edu
Phone: (727) 341-4370

**St. Philip's College**
www.alamo.edu/spc
International Student Services
1801 Martin Luther King Drive
San Antonio, TX 78203
Fax: (210) 486-2604
E-mail: pballard4@alamo.edu
Phone: (210) 486-2876

**St. Thomas Aquinas College**
www.stac.edu
Admissions Office
125 Route 340
Sparkill, NY 10976-1050
Fax: (845) 398-4372
E-mail: sbazile@stac.edu
Phone: (845) 398-4104

**Saint Thomas University**
www.stu.edu
VP for Enrollment
16401 Northwest 37th Avenue
Miami Gardens, FL 33054-6459
Fax: (305) 628-6591
E-mail: cabrown@stu.edu
Phone: (305) 474-6034

**St. Vincent College**
www.stvincent.edu
Admission
300 Fraser Purchase Road
Latrobe, PA 15650-2690
Fax: (724) 537-5069
E-mail: admission@stvincent.edu
Phone: (724) 805-2500

**Saint Xavier University**
www.sxu.edu
Recruitment & Admission Enrollment
3700 West 103rd Street
Chicago, IL 60655
Fax: (773) 298-3076
E-mail: admission@sxu.edu
Phone: (773) 298-3096

**Salem College**
www.salem.edu
Admissions Counselor
601 South Church Street
Winston-Salem, NC 27108
Fax: (336) 917-5972
E-mail: tricia.rybak@salem.edu
Phone: (336) 917-5567

**Salem Community College**
www.salemcc.edu
Admissions
460 Hollywood Avenue
Carneys Point, NJ 08069-2799
Fax: (856) 299-9193
E-mail: kmcshay@salemcc.edu
Phone: (856) 351-2919

**Salem International University**
www.salemu.edu
Admissions
223 West Main Street
Box 500
Salem, WV 26426
Fax: (304) 326-1592
E-mail: lningi@salemu.edu
Phone: (304) 326-1518

**Salem State University**
www.salemstate.edu
Assistant Dean of Undergraduate Admissions
352 Lafayette Street
Salem, MA 01970-5353
Fax: (978) 542-6893
E-mail: admissions@salemstate.edu
Phone: (978) 542-6200

**Salisbury University**
www.salisbury.edu
Center for International Education
1101 Camden Avenue
Salisbury, MD 21801
Fax: (410) 219-2853
E-mail: axliszkowska@salisbury.edu
Phone: (410) 677-5495

**Salish Kootenai College**
www.skc.edu
PO Box 70
Pablo, MT 59855
Fax: (406) 275-4801
E-mail: raelyn_dumontier@skc.edu
Phone: (406) 275-4855

**Salt Lake Community College**
www.slcc.edu
International Students Office
4600 South Redwood Road
Box 30808
Salt Lake City, UT 84130-0808
Fax: (801) 957-4432
E-mail: nancy.fillat@slcc.edu
Phone: (801) 957-4528

**Salve Regina University**
www.salve.edu
Office of International Recruitment and
Admissions
100 Ochre Point Avenue
Newport, RI 02840-4192
Fax: (401) 848-2823
E-mail: ronn.beck@salve.edu
Phone: (401) 341-2908

**Sam Houston State University**
www.shsu.edu
Office of International Programs
SHSU Campus Box 2418
Huntsville, TX 77341-2418
Fax: (936) 294-4620
E-mail: grad.intl@shsu.edu
Phone: (936) 294-4455

**Samford University**
www.samford.edu
Admissions
800 Lakeshore Drive
Birmingham, AL 35229
Fax: (205) 726-2171
E-mail: kgriem@samford.edu
Phone: (205) 726-4637

**Samuel Merritt University**
www.samuelmerritt.edu
Office of Admission
370 Hawthorne Avenue
Oakland, CA 94609-9954
Fax: (510) 869-6525
E-mail: admission@samuelmerritt.edu
Phone: (510) 869-6610

**San Antonio College**
www.alamo.edu/sac
International Students Office
1300 San Pedro Avenue
San Antonio, TX 78212-4299
Fax: (210) 486-9229
E-mail: sac-iso@alamo.edu
Phone: (210) 486-0116

**San Bernardino Valley College**
www.valleycollege.edu
Foreign Student Adviser Counseling Office
701 South Mount Vernon Avenue
San Bernardino, CA 92410
E-mail: admissions@valleycollege.edu
Phone: (909) 384-4401

**San Diego Christian College**
www.sdcc.edu
Admissions
200 Riverview Parkway
Santee, CA 92071-5822
Fax: (619) 201-8749
E-mail: kncamarillo@sdcc.edu
Phone: (619) 201-8739

**San Diego City College**
www.sdcity.edu
International Student Admissions
1313 Park Boulevard
San Diego, CA 92101-4787
Fax: (619) 388-3505
E-mail: dmeza@sdccd.edu
Phone: (619) 388-3476

**San Diego Mesa College**
www.sdmesa.edu
International Admissions
7250 Mesa College Drive
San Diego, CA 92111
Fax: (619) 388-2960
E-mail: csawyer@sdccd.edu
Phone: (619) 388-2717

**San Diego Miramar College**
www.sdmiramar.edu
International Student Advisor
10440 Black Mountain Road
San Diego, CA 92126-2999
Fax: (619) 388-7915
E-mail: kgsllagh@sdccd.edu
Phone: (619) 388-7840

**San Diego State University**
www.sdsu.edu
Office of Admissions
5500 Campanile Drive
San Diego, CA 92182-7455
E-mail: intladmission@sdsu.edu
Phone: (619) 594-1847

**San Francisco Art Institute**
www.sfai.edu
Office of Admissions
SFAI - Admissions Office
800 Chestnut Street
San Francisco, CA 94133
Fax: (415) 749-4592
E-mail: admissions@sfai.edu
Phone: (415) 749-4500

**San Francisco Conservatory of Music**
www.sfcm.edu
Director of Admission
50 Oak Street
San Francisco, CA 94102
Fax: (415) 503-6299
E-mail: mcocco@sfcm.edu
Phone: (415) 503-6207

**San Francisco State University**
www.sfsu.edu
Office of International Programs
1600 Holloway Avenue
San Francisco, CA 94132
Fax: (415) 338-6234
E-mail: oip@sfsu.edu
Phone: (415) 338-1293

**San Jacinto College**
www.sanjac.edu
Call Center
8060 Spencer Highway
Pasadena, TX 77505-5999
Fax: (281) 478-2720
E-mail: information@sjcd.edu
Phone: (281) 998-6150

**San Joaquin Delta College**
www.deltacollege.edu
International Student Program Specialist
5151 Pacific Avenue
Stockton, CA 95207-6370
Fax: (209) 954-5769
E-mail: mblack@deltacollege.edu
Phone: (209) 954-6126

**San Joaquin Valley College**
www.sjvc.edu
8400 West Mineral King Avenue
Visalia, CA 93291-9283
Fax: (559) 651-0574
Phone: (559) 651-2500

**San Jose City College**
www.sjcc.edu
International Student Counselor
2100 Moorpark Avenue
San Jose, CA 95128-2798
Fax: (408) 298-1935
E-mail: doriann.tran@sjcc.edu
Phone: (408) 298-2181 ext. 3751

**San Jose State University**
www.sjsu.edu
International Programs & Services
One Washington Square
San Jose, CA 95192-0014
Fax: (408) 924-5976
E-mail: leann.cherkaskymakhni@sjsu.edu
Phone: (408) 924-6750

**San Juan College**
www.sanjuancollege.edu
Admissions
4601 College Boulevard
Farmington, NM 87402-4699
Fax: (505) 566-3500
E-mail: admissions@sanjuancollege.edu
Phone: (505) 566-3545

**Sandhills Community College**
www.sandhills.edu
Admissions
3395 Airport Road
Pinehurst, NC 28374
Fax: (910) 695-3981
E-mail: mcallisterr@sandhills.edu
Phone: (910) 878-5804

**Santa Ana College**
www.sac.edu
International Students Office
1530 West 17th Street
Santa Ana, CA 92706
Fax: (714) 667-0751
E-mail: gitonga_kanana@rsccd.edu
Phone: (714) 564-6047

**Santa Barbara Business College**
www.sbbcollege.edu
Language Programs
506 Chapala Street
Santa Barbara, CA 93101
Fax: (805) 967-4248
E-mail: Angela.Cunningham@sbbcollege.edu
Phone: (805) 967-9677 ext. 1185

**Santa Barbara Business College: Bakersfield**
www.sbbcollege.edu
5300 California Avenue
Bakersfield, CA 93304
Phone: (866) 749-7222

**Santa Barbara Business College: Rancho Mirage**
www.sbbcollege.edu
Language Programs
34275 Monterey Avenue
Rancho Mirage, CA 92270
E-mail: Fysal.Safieh@sbbcollege.edu
Phone: (760) 341-2602 ext. 1345

**Santa Barbara Business College: Santa Maria**
www.sbbcollege.edu
303 East Plaza Drive
Santa Maria, CA 93454
Fax: (805) 346-1862
E-mail: Fysal.Safieh@sbbcollege.edu
Phone: (805) 339-6370 ext. 1345

**Santa Barbara Business College: Ventura**
www.sbbcollege.edu
4839 Market Street
Ventura, CA 93003
Fax: (805) 339-2994
E-mail: infodesk@sbbcollege.edu
Phone: (866) 749-7222

**Santa Barbara City College**
www.sbcc.edu
International Student Office
721 Cliff Drive
Santa Barbara, CA 93109-2394
Fax: (805) 965-0781
E-mail: smithc@sbcc.edu
Phone: (805) 965-0581 ext. 2243

**Santa Clara University**
www.scu.edu
Undergraduate Admissions
500 El Camino Real
Santa Clara, CA 95053
Fax: (408) 554-5255
E-mail: rkonowicz@scu.edu
Phone: (408) 554-4700

**Santa Fe College**
www.sfcollege.edu
International Student Services
3000 NW 83rd Street, R-01
Gainesville, FL 32606-6210
Fax: (352) 395-4484
E-mail: christine.frank@sfcollege.edu
Phone: (352) 395-5504

**Santa Fe Community College**
www.sfcc.edu
Admissions
6401 Richards Avenue
Santa Fe, NM 87508-4887
Fax: (505) 428-1237
E-mail: anna.tupler@sfcc.edu
Phone: (505) 428-1273

**Santa Fe University of Art and Design**
www.santafeuniversity.edu
Office of Admissions
1600 Saint Michael's Drive
Santa Fe, NM 87505-7634
Fax: (505) 473-6133
E-mail: international@santafeuniversity.edu
Phone: (505) 473-6937

**Santa Monica College**
www.smc.edu
International Students Center
1900 Pico Boulevard
Santa Monica, CA 90405-1628
Fax: (310) 434-3645
E-mail: Admissions@smc.edu
Phone: (310) 434-3465

**Santa Rosa Junior College**
www.santarosa.edu
International Admissions
1501 Mendocino Avenue
Santa Rosa, CA 95401-4395
Fax: (707) 527-4791
E-mail: khunt@santarosa.edu
Phone: (707) 524-1751

**Santiago Canyon College**
www.sccollege.edu
International Students
8045 East Chapman Avenue
Orange, CA 92869
Fax: (714) 667-0751
E-mail: gitonga_kanana@sac.edu
Phone: (714) 564-6047

**Sarah Lawrence College**
www.sarahlawrence.edu
Undergraduate Admissions
1 Mead Way
Bronxville, NY 10708-5999
Fax: (914) 395-2515
E-mail: slcadmit@slc.edu
Phone: (914) 395-2510

**Sauk Valley Community College**
www.svcc.edu
Academic Advisor
173 Illinois Route 2
Dixon, IL 61021-9112
Fax: (815) 288-3190
E-mail: mandy.m.aldridge@svcc.edu
Phone: (815) 835-6390

**Savannah College of Art and Design**
www.scad.edu
Office of Admission
PO Box 2072
Savannah, GA 31402-2072
Fax: (404) 253-3280
E-mail: admission@scad.edu
Phone: (912) 525-5100

**Savannah State University**
www.savannahstate.edu
Admissions
Office of Admissions and Recruitment
Box 20209
Savannah, GA 31404
Fax: (912) 356-2256
E-mail: admissions@savannahstate.edu
Phone: (912) 356-2181

**Savannah Technical College**
www.savannahtech.edu
Admissions
5717 White Bluff Road
Savannah, GA 31401-5521
Fax: (912) 443-5705
E-mail: mstump@savannahtech.edu
Phone: (912) 443-5706

**Schenectady County Community College**
www.sunysccc.edu
Admissions Office
78 Washington Avenue
Schenectady, NY 12305
Fax: (518) 836-2799
E-mail: sampsodg@gw.sunysccc.edu
Phone: (518) 381-1366

**Schiller International University**
www.schiller.edu
Admissions Office
8560 Ulmerton Road
Largo, FL 33771
Fax: (727) 736-3920
E-mail: admissions@schiller.edu
Phone: (877) 748-4338 ext. 410

**School of Advertising Art**
www.saa.edu
President
1725 East David Road
Kettering, OH 45440-1612
Fax: (937) 294-5869
E-mail: admissions@saa.edu
Phone: (877) 300-9866

**School of the Art Institute of Chicago**
www.saic.edu
Office of Admissions
36 South Wabash Avenue
Chicago, IL 60603
Fax: (312) 629-6101
E-mail: dmurray@saic.edu
Phone: (312) 629-6100

**School of the Museum of Fine Arts**
www.smfa.edu
Admissions Office
230 The Fenway
Boston, MA 02115
Fax: (617) 369-4264
E-mail: admissions@smfa.edu
Phone: (617) 369-3626

**School of Visual Arts**
www.sva.edu
Admissions Office
209 East 23rd Street
New York, NY 10010-3994
Fax: (212) 592-2242
E-mail: admissions@sva.edu
Phone: (212) 592-2100

**Schoolcraft College**
www.schoolcraft.edu
International Coordinator/Senior Academic
Advisor
18600 Haggerty Road
Livonia, MI 48152-2696
E-mail: admissions@schoolcraft.edu
Phone: (734) 462-4429

**Schreiner University**
www.schreiner.edu
Admissions
2100 Memorial Boulevard
Kerrville, TX 78028-5697
Fax: (830) 792-7226
E-mail: admissions@schreiner.edu
Phone: (830) 792-7217

**Scott Community College**
www.eicc.edu
Admissions
500 Belmont Road
Bettendorf, IA 52722-6804
Fax: (563) 441-4101
E-mail: sbergren@eicc.edu
Phone: (563) 441-4004

**Scottsdale Community College**
www.scottsdalecc.edu
Center for Civic and Global Engagement
9000 East Chaparral Road
Scottsdale, AZ 85256-2626
Fax: (480) 423-6099
E-mail: therese.tendick@scottsdalecc.edu
Phone: (480) 423-6590

**Scripps College**
www.scrippscollege.edu
Admissions
1030 Columbia Avenue
Claremont, CA 91711-3905
Fax: (909) 607-7508
E-mail: Jjohnsto@Scrippscollege.edu
Phone: (909) 621-8149

**Seattle Central College**
www.seattlecentral.edu
International Education Programs
1701 Broadway
2BE 1104
Seattle, WA 98122
Fax: (206) 934-3868
E-mail: david.roseberry@seattlecolleges.edu
Phone: (206) 934-3893

**Seattle Pacific University**
www.spu.edu
Admissions
3307 Third Avenue West, Suite 115
Seattle, WA 98119-1997
Fax: (206) 281-2544
E-mail: international@spu.edu
Phone: (800) 366-3344

**Seattle University**
www.seattleu.edu
Assistant Director of International Admissions
901 12th Avenue
Box 222000
Seattle, WA 98122-4340
Fax: (206) 296-5656
E-mail: birdw@seattleu.edu
Phone: (206) 296-5808

**Selma University**
www.selmauniversity.org
1501 Lapsley Street
Selma, AL 36701
Fax: (334) 872-7746
E-mail: info@selmauniversity.org
Phone: (334) 872-2533 ext. 18

**Seminole State College**
www.sscok.edu
Corey Quiett
PO Box 351
2701 Boren Boulevard
Seminole, OK 74818-0351
Fax: (405) 382-9524
E-mail: c.quiett@sscok.edu
Phone: (405) 382-9501

**Seminole State College of Florida**
www.seminolestate.edu
Office of Admissions
100 Weldon Boulevard
Sanford, FL 32773-6199
Fax: (407) 708-2395
E-mail: smitha@seminolestate.edu
Phone: (407) 708-2041

**Sessions College for Professional Design**
www.sessions.edu
51 West Third St, Suite E-301
Tempe, AZ 85281
E-mail: admissions@sessions.edu
Phone: (480) 212-1704

**Seton Hall University**
www.shu.edu
Office of Undergraduate Admissions
400 South Orange Avenue
Admissions Office
South Orange, NJ 07079-2680
Fax: (973) 275-2321
E-mail: thehall@shu.edu
Phone: (800) 843-4255

**Seton Hill University**
www.setonhill.edu
Office of Admissions
1 Seton Hill Drive
Greensburg, PA 15601
Fax: (724) 830-1294
E-mail: admit@setonhill.edu
Phone: (724) 838-4255

**Sewanee: The University of the South**
www.sewanee.edu
Office of Admissions
Office of Admission
735 University Avenue
Sewanee, TN 37383-1000
Fax: (931) 598-3248
E-mail: international@sewanee.edu
Phone: (931) 598-1436

**Seward County Community College**
www.sccc.edu
Assistant Registrar
1801 North Kansas Avenue
PO Box 1137
Liberal, KS 67905-1137
Fax: (620) 417-1079
E-mail: krystal.zimmerman@sccc.edu
Phone: (620) 417-1062

**Shasta Bible College and Graduate School**
www.shasta.edu
Registrar
2951 Goodwater Avenue
Redding, CA 96002
Fax: (530) 221-6929
E-mail: registrar@shasta.edu
Phone: (530) 221-4275 ext. 26

**Shasta College**
www.shastacollege.edu
Admissions and Records
Box 496006
Redding, CA 96049-6006
Fax: (530) 225-4995
E-mail: cprice@shastacollege.edu
Phone: (530) 242-7665

**Shaw University**
www.shawu.edu
Office of Admissions
118 East South Street
Raleigh, NC 27601
Fax: (919) 546-8271
E-mail: ssowell@shawu.edu
Phone: (919) 719-1996

**Shawnee State University**
www.shawnee.edu
Admissions
940 Second Street
Portsmouth, OH 45662
Fax: (740) 351-3111
E-mail: ameans@shawnee.edu
Phone: (740) 351-3576

**Shenandoah University**
www.su.edu
International Admissions
Office of Admissions
1460 University Drive
Winchester, VA 22601-5195
Fax: (540) 665-4627
E-mail: tmielke@su.edu
Phone: (540) 665-4766

**Shepherd University**
www.shepherd.edu
Admissions
PO Box 5000
Shepherdstown, WV 25443-5000
Fax: (304) 876-5165
E-mail: kturnbul@shepherd.edu
Phone: (304) 876-5212

**Sheridan College**
www.sheridan.edu
Executive Director of Admissions Services
PO Box 1500
Sheridan, WY 82801-1500
Fax: (307) 674-3373
E-mail: jbmueller@sheridan.edu
Phone: (307) 674-6446 ext. 2007

**Shiloh University**
www.shilohuniversity.edu
Admissions Office
100 Shiloh Drive
Kalona, IA 52247
Fax: (319) 656-2448
E-mail: admissions@shilohuniversity.edu
Phone: (319) 656-2447

**Shimer College**
www.shimer.edu
Office of Admissions
3424 South State Street
Chicago, IL 60616
Fax: (888) 808-3133
E-mail: admissions@shimer.edu
Phone: (847) 623-8400

**Shippensburg University of Pennsylvania**
www.ship.edu
Assistant Dean of Admissions
1871 Old Main Drive
Old Main 105
Shippensburg, PA 17257-2299
Fax: (717) 477-4016
E-mail: jaluna@ship.edu
Phone: (717) 477-1231

**Shor Yoshuv Rabbinical College**
www.shoryoshuv.org
One Cedar Lawn Avenue
Lawrence, NY 11559
E-mail: info@shoryoshuv.org
Phone: (516) 239-9002

**Shoreline Community College**
www.shoreline.edu
International Student Office
16101 Greenwood Avenue North
Seattle, WA 98133
Fax: (206) 546-7854
E-mail: isp@shoreline.edu
Phone: (206) 546-6940

**Shorter University**
www.shorter.edu
Admissions
315 Shorter Avenue
Rome, GA 30165
Fax: (706) 233-7224
E-mail: lpalumbo@shorter.edu
Phone: (706) 233-7409

**Siena College**
www.siena.edu
Associate Director of International Programs
515 Loudon Road
Loudonville, NY 12211-1462
Fax: (518) 783-4950
E-mail: international@siena.edu
Phone: (518) 786-5047

**Siena Heights University**
www.sienaheights.edu
1247 East Siena Heights Drive
Adrian, MI 49221-1796
Fax: (517) 264-7745
E-mail: dmorris@sienaheights.edu
Phone: (517) 264-7001

**Sierra College**
www.sierracollege.edu
International Students Office
5000 Rocklin Road
Rocklin, CA 95677-3397
Fax: (916) 630-4522
E-mail:
internationalstudents@sierracollege.edu
Phone: (916) 660-7374

**Sierra Nevada College**
www.sierranevada.edu
Admissions Office
999 Tahoe Boulevard
Incline Village, NV 89451-4269
Fax: (775) 831-6223
E-mail: admissions@sierranevada.edu
Phone: (866) 412-4636

**Silicon Valley University**
www.svuca.edu
Student Affairs Officer
2160 Lundy Avenue Suite #110
San Jose, CA 95131
Fax: (408) 955-0887
E-mail: gary@svuca.edu
Phone: (408) 435-8989

**Silver Lake College of the Holy Family**
www.sl.edu
Admissions
2406 South Alverno Road
Manitowoc, WI 54220
Fax: (920) 686-6322
E-mail: admissions@sl.edu
Phone: (920) 686-6175

**Simmons College**
www.simmons.edu
Undergraduate Admissions
300 The Fenway
Boston, MA 02115-5898
Fax: (617) 521-3190
E-mail: heather.zeman@simmons.edu
Phone: (617) 521-2052

**Simpson College**
www.simpson.edu
Office of Admissions
701 North C Street
Indianola, IA 50125
Fax: (515) 961-1870
E-mail: michael.norris@simpson.edu
Phone: (515) 961-1624

**Simpson University**
www.simpsonu.edu
Admissions
2211 College View Drive
Redding, CA 96003-8606
Fax: (530) 226-4861
E-mail: admissions@simpsonu.edu
Phone: (530) 226-4606

**Sinclair Community College**
www.sinclair.edu
International Education Office
444 West Third Street
Dayton, OH 45402-1460
Fax: (937) 512-2125
E-mail: intladm@sinclair.edu
Phone: (937) 512-3999

**Sinte Gleska University**
www.sintegleska.edu
Box 105
Mission, SD 57555
Fax: (605) 747-4258
Phone: (605) 747-2263

**Sisseton Wahpeton College**
www.swc.tc
BIA 700, Box 689
Sisseton, SD 57262-0689
Fax: (605) 698-3132
E-mail: dredday@swc.tc
Phone: (605) 698-3966 ext. 1101

**Skagit Valley College**
www.skagit.edu
International Programs
2405 East College Way
Mount Vernon, WA 98273
Fax: (360) 416-7868
E-mail: ganeson@skagit.ctc.edu
Phone: (360) 416-7734

**Skidmore College**
www.skidmore.edu
Admissions
815 North Broadway
Saratoga Springs, NY 12866
Fax: (518) 580-5584
E-mail: admissions@skidmore.edu
Phone: (518) 580-5570

**Skyline College**
www.skylinecollege.edu
International Students
3300 College Drive
San Bruno, CA 94066-1662
Fax: (650) 738-7140
E-mail: skyinternational@smccd.edu
Phone: (650) 738-4430

**Slippery Rock University of Pennsylvania**
www.sru.edu
Global Engagement
1 Morrow Way
North Hall Welcome Center
Slippery Rock, PA 16057-1383
Fax: (724) 738-2289
E-mail: genevieve.bordogna@sru.edu
Phone: (724) 738-2603

**Smith College**
www.smith.edu
Admission
7 College Lane
Northampton, MA 01063
Fax: (413) 585-2527
E-mail: kkristof@smith.edu
Phone: (413) 585-2500

**Snow College**
www.snow.edu
International Students Admissions
150 East College Avenue
Ephraim, UT 84627
Fax: (435) 283-7438
E-mail: alex.peterson@snow.edu
Phone: (435) 283-7430

**Soka University of America**
www.soka.edu
Office of International Student Services
1 University Drive
Aliso Viejo, CA 92656-8081
Fax: (949) 480-4151
E-mail: mkasahara@soka.edu
Phone: (949) 480-4135

**Solano Community College**
www.solano.edu
4000 Suisun Valley Road
Fairfield, CA 94534-3197
Fax: (707) 646-2053
E-mail: admissions@solano.edu
Phone: (707) 864-7171

**Somerset Community College**
www.somerset.kctcs.edu
Student Affairs Admissions
808 Monticello Street
Somerset, KY 42501
Fax: (606) 679-4369
E-mail: tina.whitaker@kctcs.edu
Phone: (606) 451-6636

**Sonoma State University**
www.sonoma.edu
Academic Records Specialist/Evaluator
1801 East Cotati Avenue
Rohnert Park, CA 94928-3609
Fax: (707) 664-2060
E-mail: inquiryi@sonoma.edu
Phone: (707) 664-3030

**South Arkansas Community College**
www.southark.edu
Enrollment Services
Box 7010
El Dorado, AR 71731-7010
Fax: (870) 864-7137
E-mail: dinman@southark.edu
Phone: (870) 862-8131

**South Carolina State University**
www.scsu.edu
Admissions and Recruitment
300 College Street NE
PO Box 7127
Orangeburg, SC 29117
Fax: (803) 536-8990
E-mail: awrigh22@scsu.edu
Phone: (803) 536-7186

**South Central College**
www.southcentral.edu
Admissions
1920 Lee Boulevard
PO Box 1920
North Mankato, MN 56003
Fax: (507) 388-9951
E-mail: admissions@southcentral.edu
Phone: (507) 389-7444

**South Coast College**
www.southcoastcollege.com
2011 West Chapman Avenue
Orange, CA 92868
E-mail: requestinfo@southcoastcollege.com
Phone: (714) 867-5009

**South College**
www.southcollegetn.edu
Admissions
3904 Lonas Drive
Knoxville, TN 37909
Fax: (865) 470-8737
E-mail: admissions@southcollegetn.edu
Phone: (865) 251-1800

**South Dakota School of Mines and Technology**
www.sdsmt.edu
Ivanhoe International Student Center
501 East St. Joseph Street
Rapid City, SD 57701
Fax: (605) 394-6883
E-mail: susan.aadland@sdsmt.edu
Phone: (605) 394-6884

**South Dakota State University**
www.sdstate.edu
Office of International Affairs & Outreach
Box 2201 SAD 200
Brookings, SD 57007-0649
Fax: (605) 688-6540
E-mail: sdsu.intlstud@sdstate.edu
Phone: (605) 688-4122

**South Florida State College**
www.southflorida.edu
Dean of Student Services
600 West College Drive
Avon Park, FL 33825
Fax: (863) 784-7235
E-mail: timothy.wise@southflorida.edu
Phone: (863) 453-6661 ext. 7104

**South Georgia State College**
www.sgsc.edu
Admissions office
100 West College Park Drive
Douglas, GA 31533-5098
Fax: (912) 260-4441
E-mail: angie.evans@sgsc.edu
Phone: (912) 260-4206

**South Louisiana Community College**
www.solacc.edu
Admissions
1101 Bertrand Dr.
Lafayette, LA 70506-4124
Fax: (337) 262-2101
E-mail: rachel.alexander@solacc.edu
Phone: (337) 521-8943

**South Mountain Community College**
www.southmountaincc.edu
7050 South 24th Street
Phoenix, AZ 85042
Fax: (602) 243-8199
E-mail: della.garcia@southmountaincc.edu
Phone: (602) 243-8124

**South Plains College**
www.southplainscollege.edu
Admissions
1401 South College Ave
Levelland, TX 79336
Fax: (806) 897-3167
E-mail: aruiz@southplainscollege.edu
Phone: (806) 894-9611 ext. 2371

## South Puget Sound Community College
www.spscc.edu
International Student Programs Office
2011 Mottman Road, SW
Olympia, WA 98512-6218
Fax: (360) 664-0780
E-mail: hlukashin@spscc.edu
Phone: (360) 596-5247

## South Seattle College
www.southseattle.edu
International Programs Office
6000 16th Avenue, SW
Seattle, WA 98106-1499
Fax: (206) 934-5836
E-mail: ip@seattlecolleges.edu
Phone: (206) 934-5360

## South Texas College
www.southtexascollege.edu
Admissions
3201 West Pecan Boulevard
McAllen, TX 78502
Fax: (956) 872-8321
E-mail: romerol@southtexascollege.edu
Phone: (956) 872-2250

## South University: Savannah
www.southuniversity.edu
Admissions office
709 Mall Boulevard
Savannah, GA 31406
Fax: (912) 201-8070
E-mail: dmaddox@southuniversity.edu
Phone: (912) 201-8018

## Southeast Arkansas College
www.seark.edu
Admissions
1900 Hazel Street
Pine Bluff, AR 71603
Fax: (870) 543-5956
E-mail: bdunn@seark.edu
Phone: (870) 543-5957

## Southeast Kentucky Community and Technical College
www.southeast.kctcs.edu
Admissions
700 College Road
Cumberland, KY 40823
Fax: (606) 589-5423
E-mail: cookie.baldwin@kctcs.net
Phone: (606) 589-2145

## Southeast Missouri Hospital College of Nursing and Health Sciences
www.sehcollege.edu
2001 William Street
Cape Girardeau, MO 63703
Fax: (573) 339-7805
E-mail: dhowey@sehcollege.edu
Phone: (573) 334-6825 ext. 2215

## Southeast Missouri State University
www.semo.edu
Office of International Education and Services
One University Plaza MS 3550
Cape Girardeau, MO 63701
Fax: (573) 986-6866
E-mail: intadmit@semo.edu
Phone: (573) 986-6863

## Southeastern Baptist College
www.southeasternbaptist.edu
Academic Dean
4229 Highway 15 North
Laurel, MS 39440
Fax: (601) 426-6347
E-mail: aparker@southeasternbaptist.edu
Phone: (601) 426-6346

## Southeastern College: Greenacres
www.sec.edu
6812 Forest Hill Boulevard
Greenacres, FL 33413
Phone: (561) 433-2330

## Southeastern College: Miami Lakes
www.sec.edu
17395 NW 59th Avenue
Miami Lakes, FL 33015
Phone: (305) 820-5003

## Southeastern Community College
www.scciowa.edu
Enrollment Services
1500 West Agency Road
PO Box 180
West Burlington, IA 52655-0605
Fax: (319) 758-6725
E-mail: kthorarinsdottir@scciowa.edu
Phone: (319) 752-2731 ext. 5026

## Southeastern Community College
www.sccnc.edu
Admissions Office
4564 Chadbourn Highway
PO Box 151
Whiteville, NC 28472-0151
Fax: (910) 642-5658
E-mail: jfowler@sccnc.edu
Phone: (910) 642-7141 ext. 265

## Southeastern Illinois College
www.sic.edu
Academic Advising
3575 College Road
Harrisburg, IL 62946
Fax: (618) 252-3062
E-mail: tyler.billman@sic.edu
Phone: (618) 252-5400 ext. 2430

## Southeastern Louisiana University
www.southeastern.edu
Office of Admissions
SLU 10752
Hammond, LA 70402
Fax: (985) 549-5882
E-mail: admissions@southeastern.edu
Phone: (985) 549-2360

## Southeastern Oklahoma State University
www.se.edu
Office of Admissions and Enrollment Services
1405 North Fourth Avenue, PMB 4225
Durant, OK 74701-0607
Fax: (580) 745-7502
E-mail: admissions@se.edu
Phone: (580) 745-2061

## Southeastern Technical College
www.southeasterntech.edu
Admissions
3001 East First Street
Vidalia, GA 30474
Fax: (912) 538-3156
E-mail: amcrae@southeasterntech.edu
Phone: (478) 289-2259

## Southeastern University
www.seu.edu
Admission
1000 Longfellow Boulevard
Lakeland, FL 33801-6034
Fax: (863) 667-5200
E-mail: admission@seu.edu
Phone: (863) 667-5150

## Southern Adventist University
www.southern.edu
International Enrollment Advisor
PO Box 370
Collegedale, TN 37315-0370
Fax: (423) 236-1835
E-mail: karobert@southern.edu
Phone: (423) 236-2808

## Southern Arkansas University
www.saumag.edu
International Student Admissions
Box 9382
Magnolia, AR 71754-9382
Fax: (870) 235-5096
E-mail: pjsitumeang@saumag.edu
Phone: (870) 235-4146

## Southern Arkansas University Tech
www.sautech.edu
Vice Chancellor for Student Services
PO Box 3499
6415 Spellman Road
Camden, AR 71711-1599
Fax: (870) 574-4478
E-mail: dmcleane@sautech.edu
Phone: (870) 574-4504

## Southern Baptist Theological Seminary
www.sbts.edu
2825 Lexington Road
Louisville, KY 40280
E-mail: admissions@sbts.edu
Phone: (502) 897-4200

## Southern California Institute of Architecture
www.sciarc.edu
Admissions
960 E 3rd Street
Los Angeles, CA 90013
Fax: (213) 613-2260
E-mail: rachel_wagmaister@sciarc.edu
Phone: (213) 356-5373

## Southern California Institute of Technology
www.scitech.edu
School Director
525 North Muller Street
Anaheim, CA 92801
Fax: (714) 300-0310
E-mail: pshams@scitech.edu
Phone: (714) 300-0300

**Southern California Seminary**
www.socalsem.edu
International Admissions
2075 East Madison Avenue
El Cajon, CA 92019
Fax: (619) 201-8975
E-mail: dmullen@socalsem.edu
Phone: (619) 590-2140

**Southern Connecticut State University**
www.southernct.edu
Admissions
131 Farnham Avenue
New Haven, CT 06515-1202
Fax: (203) 392-5727
E-mail: belchert1@southernct.edu
Phone: (203) 392-5726

**Southern Crescent Technical College**
www.sctech.edu
501 Varsity Road
Griffin, GA 30223
Fax: (770) 229-3227
E-mail: admissions@sctech.edu
Phone: (770) 228-7348

**Southern Illinois University Carbondale**
www.siu.edu
Center for International Education
Undergraduate Admissions, Mailcode 4710
Carbondale, IL 62901
Fax: (618) 453-7660
E-mail: issinfo@siu.edu
Phone: (618) 453-5774

**Southern Illinois University Edwardsville**
www.siue.edu
Office of Graduate and International
Admissions
Rendleman Hall, Rm 2120
Campus Box 1600
Edwardsville, IL 62026-1600
Fax: (618) 650-5013
E-mail: jmonaha@siue.edu
Phone: (618) 650-2756

**Southern Maine Community College**
www.smccme.edu
Enrollment Services
2 Fort Road
South Portland, ME 04106-1611
Fax: (207) 741-5760
E-mail: jlane@smccme.edu
Phone: (207) 741-5880

**Southern Methodist University**
www.smu.edu
Interim Dean of Undergraduate Admission
PO Box 750181
Dallas, TX 75275-0181
Fax: (214) 768-0103
E-mail: ugadmission@smu.edu
Phone: (214) 768-2058

**Southern Nazarene University**
www.snu.edu
International Student Services
6729 NW 39th Expressway
Bethany, OK 73008
Fax: (405) 491-6320
E-mail: lcantwel@snu.edu
Phone: (405) 491-6324

**Southern New Hampshire University**
www.snhu.edu
International Student Admission
2500 North River Road
Manchester, NH 03106-1045
Fax: (603) 626-9100
E-mail: s.call@snhu.edu
Phone: (603) 645-9629

**Southern Oregon University**
www.sou.edu
Admissions
1250 Siskiyou Boulevard
Ashland, OR 97520-5032
Fax: (541) 552-8403
E-mail: admissions@sou.edu
Phone: (541) 552-6411

**Southern Regional Technical College**
www.southernregional.edu
15689 US Highway 19 North
Thomasville, GA 31792-9960
Fax: (229) 227-2666
Phone: (229) 225-5060

**Southern Technical College**
www.southerntech.edu
1685 Medical Lane
Ft. Myers, FL 33907-1108
Fax: (239) 936-4040
E-mail: cwallace@swfc.edu
Phone: (239) 939-4766

**Southern Union State Community College**
www.suscc.edu
Admissions
750 Roberts Street
PO Box 1000
Wadley, AL 36276
Fax: (256) 395-2215
E-mail: cstringfellow@suscc.edu
Phone: (256) 395-2211

**Southern University and Agricultural and Mechanical College**
www.subr.edu
Center for International Affairs and University
Outreach
T.H. Harris Hall
PO Box 9231
Baton Rouge, LA 70813
Fax: (225) 771-2654
E-mail: barbara_carpenter@subr.edu
Phone: (225) 771-2613

**Southern University at New Orleans**
www.suno.edu
Admissions
6400 Press Drive
New Orleans, LA 70126
Fax: (504) 284-5481
E-mail: svinnett@suno.edu
Phone: (504) 286-5314

**Southern University at Shreveport**
www.susla.edu
Admissions
3050 Martin Luther King, Jr. Drive
Shreveport, LA 71107
Fax: (318) 670-6483
E-mail: danderson@susla.edu
Phone: (318) 670-9211

**Southern Utah University**
www.suu.edu
Amissions Office
351 West University Boulevard
Cedar City, UT 84720
Fax: (435) 865-8223
E-mail: lauramcaneney@suu.edu
Phone: (435) 586-7744

**Southern Vermont College**
www.svc.edu
Admissions
982 Mansion Drive
Bennington, VT 05201-6002
Fax: (802) 681-2868
E-mail: admissions@svc.edu
Phone: (802) 447-6300

**Southern Virginia University**
www.svu.edu
Admissions Office
One University Hill Drive
Buena Vista, VA 24416-3097
Fax: (540) 261-8559
E-mail: brett.garcia@svu.edu
Phone: (540) 261-4503

**Southern Wesleyan University**
www.swu.edu
Admissions
PO Box 1020
Central, SC 29630-1020
Fax: (864) 644-5972
E-mail: ayoung@swu.edu
Phone: (864) 644-5550

**Southwest Baptist University**
www.sbuniv.edu
Admissions
1600 University Avenue
Bolivar, MO 65613-2597
Fax: (417) 328-1808
E-mail: cstandley@sbuniv.edu
Phone: (417) 328-1810

**Southwest Florida College: Tampa**
www.swfc.edu
3910 Riga Boulevard
Tampa, FL 33619
Phone: (813) 630-4401

**Southwest Minnesota State University**
www.smsu.edu
Admissions
1501 State Street
Marshall, MN 56258-1598
Fax: (507) 537-7154
E-mail: allan.vogel@smsu.edu
Phone: (507) 537-6286

**Southwest Tennessee Community College**
www.southwest.tn.edu
PO Box 780
Memphis, TN 38101-0780
Fax: (901) 333-4523
E-mail: lmbrooks4@southwest.tn.edu
Phone: (901) 333-4399

**Southwest Texas Junior College**
www.swtjc.edu
2401 Garner Field Road
Uvalde, TX 78801
Fax: (830) 591-7396
E-mail: admoffice@swtjc.edu
Phone: (830) 278-4401 ext. 7255

**Southwest University**
www.southwest.edu
Office of Admissions
2200 Veterans Memorial Boulevard
Kenner, LA 70062-4005
Fax: (504) 468-3213
E-mail: admissions@southwest.edu
Phone: (800) 433-5923

**Southwest University of Visual Arts**
www.suva.edu
Admissions Office
2525 North Country Club Road
Tucson, AZ 85716
Fax: (520) 325-5535
E-mail: admissions@suva.edu
Phone: (520) 325-0123

**Southwest Virginia Community College**
www.sw.edu
Admissions
PO Box SVCC
Richlands, VA 24641-1101
Fax: (276) 964-7716
E-mail: dionne.cook@sw.edu
Phone: (276) 964-7301

**Southwest Wisconsin Technical College**
www.swtc.edu
Dean of Students
1800 Bronson Boulevard
Fennimore, WI 53809
Fax: (608) 822-6019
E-mail: hmiller@swtc.edu
Phone: (608) 822-2352

**Southwestern Adventist University**
www.swau.edu
International Admissions
Box 567
Keene, TX 76059
Fax: (817) 202-6753
E-mail: rahneeka@swau.edu
Phone: (817) 202-6733

**Southwestern Assemblies of God University**
www.sagu.edu
Admissions
1200 Sycamore Street
Waxahachie, TX 75165
Fax: (972) 937-0006
E-mail: pthompson@sagu.edu
Phone: (972) 937-4010 ext. 1229

**Southwestern Baptist Theological Seminary**
www.swbts.edu
Director of International Student Office
PO Box 22000
Fort Worth, TX 76122
E-mail: amorris@swbts.edu
Phone: (817) 923-1921

**Southwestern Christian College**
www.swcc.edu
Admissions
PO Box 10
200 Bowser Circle
Terrell, TX 75160
Fax: (972) 563-7133
E-mail: swccadmissions@yahoo.com
Phone: (972) 524-3341 ext. 161

**Southwestern Christian University**
www.swcu.edu
Academic Affairs
Box 340
Bethany, OK 73008
Fax: (405) 495-0078
E-mail: chad.pugh@swcu.edu
Phone: (405) 789-7661 ext. 3442

**Southwestern College**
www.swccd.edu
Admissions Center Evening Lead
900 Otay Lakes Road
Chula Vista, CA 91910-7297
Fax: (619) 482-6489
E-mail: amora@swccd.edu
Phone: (619) 482-6584

**Southwestern College**
www.sckans.edu
Admissions
100 College Street
Winfield, KS 67156
Fax: (620) 229-6344
E-mail: micah.mitchell@sckans.edu
Phone: (620) 229-6269

**Southwestern Community College**
www.swcciowa.edu
Admissions Coordinator
1501 West Townline Street
Creston, IA 50801
Fax: (641) 782-3312
E-mail: carstens@swcciowa.edu
Phone: (641) 782-7081 ext. 453

**Southwestern Community College**
www.southwesterncc.edu
Student Services
447 College Drive
Sylva, NC 28779
E-mail: admissions@southwesterncc.edu
Phone: (800) 447-4091

**Southwestern Illinois College**
www.swic.edu
Admissions
2500 Carlyle Avenue
Belleville, IL 62221-5899
Fax: (618) 222-9768
E-mail: sonia.fischer@swic.edu
Phone: (618) 235-2700 ext. 5664

**Southwestern Michigan College**
www.swmich.edu
58900 Cherry Grove Road
Dowagiac, MI 49047-9793
Fax: (269) 783-2162
E-mail: enrollment@swmich.edu
Phone: (269) 782-1499

**Southwestern Oklahoma State University**
www.swosu.edu
International Student Affairs
100 Campus Drive
Weatherford, OK 73096
Fax: (580) 774-7165
E-mail: randy.beckloff@swosu.edu
Phone: (580) 774-6172

**Southwestern Oregon Community College**
www.socc.edu
International Student Services
1988 Newmark Avenue
Coos Bay, OR 97420-2956
Fax: (541) 888-7247
E-mail: chockman@socc.edu
Phone: (541) 888-7185

**Southwestern University**
www.southwestern.edu
Admission
PO Box 770
Georgetown, TX 78627-0770
Fax: (512) 863-9601
E-mail: bowmanc@southwestern.edu
Phone: (512) 863-1200

**Spalding University**
www.spalding.edu
Dean of Enrollment Management
845 S Third Street
Louisville, KY 40203
Fax: (502) 992-2418
E-mail: chart@spalding.edu
Phone: (502) 873-4179

**Spartan College of Aeronautics and Technology**
www.spartan.edu
8820 East Pine Street
PO Box 582833
Tulsa, OK 74158-2833
Fax: (918) 831-5234
E-mail: spartan@mail.spartan.edu
Phone: (918) 836-6886 ext. 228

**Spartanburg Community College**
www.sccsc.edu
Admissions
Box 4386
Spartanburg, SC 29305-4386
Fax: (864) 592-4642
E-mail: dalel@sccsc.edu
Phone: (864) 592-4800

**Spartanburg Methodist College**
www.smcsc.edu
Admissions
1000 Powell Mill Road
Spartanburg, SC 29301-5899
Fax: (864) 587-4355
E-mail: hidalgoa@smcsc.edu
Phone: (864) 699-4647

**Spelman College**
www.spelman.edu
International Student Services Coordinator
350 Spelman Lane SW, Campus Box 277
Atlanta, GA 30314-4395
Fax: (404) 270-5539
E-mail: lbackum@spelman.edu
Phone: (404) 681-3643 ext. 5681

**Spencerian College**
www.spencerian.edu
Admissions
4627 Dixie Highway
Louisville, KY 40216
Fax: (502) 447-4574
Phone: (502) 447-1000

**Spencerian College: Lexington**
www.spencerian.edu
Admissions
2355 Harrodsburg Rd
Lexington, KY 40504
Fax: (859) 224-7744
E-mail: cdouglas@spencerian.edu
Phone: (859) 223-9608

**Spokane Community College**
www.scc.spokane.edu
Program Coordinator
1810 North Greene Street
Spokane, WA 99217-5399
Fax: (509) 533-8181
E-mail: TAllen@scc.spokane.edu
Phone: (509) 533-8659

**Spokane Falls Community College**
www.spokanefalls.edu
Program Coordinator
3410 West Fort George Wright Drive
Admissions MS 3011
Spokane, WA 99224
Fax: (509) 533-3237
E-mail: KatherineT@spokanefalls.edu
Phone: (509) 533-3242

**Spoon River College**
www.src.edu
Student Advisor
23235 North County Road 22
Canton, IL 61520
Fax: (309) 833-6062
E-mail: patrick.denecke@src.edu
Phone: (309) 833-6022

**Spring Arbor University**
www.arbor.edu
Admissions
106 East Main Street
Spring Arbor, MI 49283-9799
Fax: (517) 750-6620
E-mail: hfoster@arbor.edu
Phone: (517) 750-6471

**Spring Hill College**
www.shc.edu
Admissions Office
4000 Dauphin Street
Mobile, AL 36608-1791
Fax: (251) 460-2186
E-mail: admit@shc.edu
Phone: (251) 380-3030

**Springfield College**
www.springfieldcollege.edu
International Center
263 Alden Street
Springfield, MA 01109
Fax: (413) 731-1681
E-mail: dalm@springfieldcollege.edu
Phone: (413) 748-3215

**Springfield Technical Community College**
www.stcc.edu
Admissions
One Armory Square
PO Box 9000, Suite 1
Springfield, MA 01102-9000
Fax: (413) 755-6344
E-mail: admissions@stcc.edu
Phone: (413) 755-3333

**Stanbridge University**
www.stanbridge.edu
Admissions
2041 Business Center Drive, Suite 107
Irvine, CA 92612
Fax: (949) 794-9094
E-mail: eriepma@stanbridge.edu
Phone: (949) 794-9090 ext. 5116

**Stanford University**
www.stanford.edu
Undergraduate Admission
Montag Hall
355 Galvez Street
Stanford, CA 94305-6106
Fax: (650) 723-6050
E-mail: admission@stanford.edu
Phone: (650) 723-2091

**Stark State College**
www.starkstate.edu
Admissions
6200 Frank Avenue NW
North Canton, OH 44720
Fax: (330) 497-6313
E-mail: jcooney@starkstate.edu
Phone: (330) 494-6170

**State College of Florida, Manatee-Sarasota**
www.scf.edu
Box 1849
Bradenton, FL 34206-1849
Fax: (941) 727-6179
E-mail: admissions@scf.edu
Phone: (941) 752-5418

**State Fair Community College**
www.sfccmo.edu
Admissions and Outreach
3201 West 16th Street
Sedalia, MO 65301-2199
E-mail: astoecklein1@sfccmo.edu
Phone: (660) 596-7379

**State Technical College of Missouri**
www.statetechmo.edu
Office of Admissions
One Technology Drive
Linn, MO 65051-3203
Fax: (573) 897-5026
E-mail: jordon.deeken@statetechmo.edu
Phone: (573) 897-5282

**Stenotype Institute: Jacksonville**
www.stenotype.edu
3563 Phillips Highway, Building E, #501
Jacksonville, FL 32207
Fax: (904) 398-7878
E-mail: info@thestenotypeinstitute.com
Phone: (904) 398-4141

**Stephen F. Austin State University**
www.sfasu.edu
International Studies and Programs
Box 13051, SFA Station
Nacogdoches, TX 75962-3051
Fax: (936) 468-7215
E-mail: international@sfasu.edu
Phone: (936) 468-3927

**Stephens College**
www.stephens.edu
Admissions
1200 East Broadway
Box 2121
Columbia, MO 65215
Fax: (573) 876-7237
E-mail: apply@stephens.edu
Phone: (800) 876-7207

**Sterling College**
www.sterling.edu
Admissions
125 West Cooper
Sterling, KS 67579
Fax: (620) 278-4416
E-mail: admissions@sterling.edu
Phone: (620) 278-4275

**Sterling College**
www.sterlingcollege.edu
Director of Admissions
PO Box 72
Craftsbury Common, VT 05827-0072
Fax: (802) 586-2596
E-mail: tpatterson@sterlingcollege.edu
Phone: (802) 586-7711 ext. 124

**Stetson University**
www.stetson.edu
Admissions
Campus Box 8378
DeLand, FL 32723
Fax: (386) 822-7112
E-mail: admissions@stetson.edu
Phone: (386) 822-7100

**Stevens Institute of Business & Arts**
www.siba.edu
Admissions
1521 Washington Avenue
St. Louis, MO 63103
Fax: (314) 421-0304
E-mail: admissions@siba.edu
Phone: (314) 421-0949 ext. 1118

**Stevens Institute of Technology**
www.stevens.edu
Undergraduate Admissions
1 Castle Point Terrace
Ruesterholz Admissions Center
Hoboken, NJ 07030-5991
Fax: (201) 216-8348
E-mail: Jackie.Williams@stevens.edu
Phone: (201) 216-5207

**Stevens-Henager College: Boise**
www.stevenshenager.edu
Campus Director
1444 S Entertainment Avenue
Boise, ID 83709
Fax: (208) 345-6999
E-mail: shane.reeder@stevenshenager.edu
Phone: (208) 383-4540

**Stevens-Henager College: Logan**
www.stevenshenager.edu
755 South Main
Logan, UT 84321
Fax: (435) 755-7611
E-mail: clay.buttars@stevenshenager.edu
Phone: (435) 792-6970 ext. 5002

**Stevens-Henager College: Murray**
www.stevenshenager.edu
383 West Vine Street
Salt Lake City, UT 84123
Fax: (801) 262-7660
Phone: (800) 622-2640

**Stevens-Henager College: Ogden**
www.stevenshenager.edu
1890 South 1350 West
Ogden, UT 84401
Fax: (801) 621-0853
Phone: (801) 394-7791

**Stevens-Henager College: Orem**
www.stevenshenager.edu
Salt Lake Campus International Students
1476 South Sand Hill Road
Orem, UT 84058
Fax: (801) 375-9836
E-mail: jesse.hafen@stevenshenager.edu
Phone: (800) 233-9762

**Stevenson University**
www.stevenson.edu
Admissions Office
1525 Greenspring Valley Road
Stevenson, MD 21153-0641
Fax: (443) 352-4440
E-mail: admissions@stevenson.edu
Phone: (443) 352-4410

**Stillman College**
www.stillman.edu
Admissions
3601 Stillman Boulevard
PO Box 1430
Tuscaloosa, AL 35403
Fax: (205) 247-8156
E-mail: mfinch@stillman.edu
Phone: (205) 366-8814

**Stockton University**
www.stockton.edu
Admissions Office
101 Vera King Farris Drive
Galloway, NJ 08205
Fax: (609) 748-5541
E-mail: admissions@stockton.edu
Phone: (609) 652-4261

**Stone Child College**
www.stonechild.edu
8294 Upper Box Elder Road
Box Elder, MT 59521
Fax: (406) 395-4836
Phone: (406) 395-4875 ext. 262

**Stonehill College**
www.stonehill.edu
Office of Admission
320 Washington Street
Easton, MA 02357-0100
Fax: (508) 565-1545
E-mail: jpepin1@stonehill.edu
Phone: (508) 565-1373

**Stratford University: Falls Church**
www.stratford.edu
International Student Office
7777 Leesburg Pike Suite 1LN
Falls Church, VA 22043
Fax: (703) 539-6960
E-mail: isoua@stratford.edu
Phone: (703) 539-6890

**Stratford University: Woodbridge**
www.stratford.edu
International Student Office
14349 Gideon Drive
Woodbridge, VA 22192
E-mail: isoua@stratford.edu
Phone: (703) 539-6890

**Strayer University**
www.strayer.edu
1133 15th Sreet NW
Washington, DC 20005
Fax: (202) 419-1425
E-mail: washington@strayer.edu
Phone: (202) 408-2400

**Suffolk County Community College**
www.sunysuffolk.edu
Central Admissions
533 College Road
Selden, NY 11784
Fax: (631) 451-4415
E-mail: spagnoe@sunysuffolk.edu
Phone: (631) 451-4000

**Suffolk University**
www.suffolk.edu
Undergraduate Admissions
8 Ashburton Place
Boston, MA 02108
Fax: (617) 557-1574
E-mail: admission@suffolk.edu
Phone: (617) 573-8460

**Sul Ross State University**
www.sulross.edu
Center for Enrollment Services
PO Box C-2
Alpine, TX 79832
Fax: (432) 837-8431
E-mail: kstubblefield@sulross.edu
Phone: (432) 837-8050

**Sullivan College of Technology and Design**
www.sctd.edu
Admissions
3901 Atkinson Square Drive
Louisville, KY 40218-4524
Fax: (502) 456-2341
E-mail: hcunningham@sctd.edu
Phone: (502) 456-6509

**Sullivan County Community College**
www.sunysullivan.edu
Office of the Dean of Community Outreach
112 College Road
Loch Sheldrake, NY 12759-5151
Fax: (845) 434-0923
E-mail: salhona@sunysullivan.edu
Phone: (845) 434-5750 ext. 4356

**Sullivan University**
www.sullivan.edu
Admissions Office
3101 Bardstown Road
Louisville, KY 40205
Fax: (502) 456-0040
E-mail: admissions@sullivan.edu
Phone: (502) 456-6505

**SUM Bible College & Theological Seminary**
www.sum.edu
Academic Dean
735 105th Avenue
Oakland, CA 94603
Fax: (510) 568-1024
E-mail: lbartley@sum.edu
Phone: (510) 567-6174

**SUNY College at Brockport**
www.brockport.edu
International Education
350 New Campus Drive
Brockport, NY 14420-2915
Fax: (585) 637-3218
E-mail: applyint@brockport.edu
Phone: (585) 395-2119

**SUNY College at Buffalo**
www.buffalostate.edu
International Student Affairs
1300 Elmwood Avenue, Moot Hall
Buffalo, NY 14222-1095
Fax: (716) 878-6100
E-mail: burnhasl@BuffaloState.edu
Phone: (716) 878-5522

**SUNY College at Cortland**
www2.cortland.edu/home
Admissions
PO Box 2000
Cortland, NY 13045-0900
Fax: (607) 753-5998
E-mail: admissions@cortland.edu
Phone: (607) 753-4711

**SUNY College at Fredonia**
www.fredonia.edu
Office of Admissions
280 Central Avenue, Fenner House
Fredonia, NY 14063-1136
Fax: (716) 673-3249
E-mail: admissions@fredonia.edu
Phone: (716) 673-3251

**SUNY College at Geneseo**
www.geneseo.edu
International Student and Scholar Services
1 College Circle
Geneseo, NY 14454-1401
Fax: (585) 245-5405
E-mail: hope@geneseo.edu
Phone: (585) 245-5404

**SUNY College at New Paltz**
www.newpaltz.edu
Center for International Programs
100 Hawk Drive
New Paltz, NY 12561-2443
Fax: (845) 257-3608
E-mail: intadmissions@newpaltz.edu
Phone: (845) 257-3595

**SUNY College at Old Westbury**
www.oldwestbury.edu
Enrollment Services
Box 307
Old Westbury, NY 11568-0307
Fax: (516) 876-3307
E-mail: enroll@oldwestbury.edu
Phone: (516) 876-3073

**SUNY College at Oneonta**
www.oneonta.edu/home/default.asp
Office of International Education
Admissions Office, 116 Alumni Hall
State University College
Oneonta, NY 13820-4016
Fax: (607) 436-2475
E-mail: savannah.bao@oneonta.edu
Phone: (607) 436-3369

**SUNY College at Oswego**
www.oswego.edu
Office of Admissions
229 Sheldon Hall
Oswego, NY 13126-3599
Fax: (315) 312-3260
E-mail: oberst@oswego.edu
Phone: (315) 312-2250

**SUNY College at Plattsburgh**
www.plattsburgh.edu
Global Education Office
Kehoe Administration Building
Plattsburgh, NY 12901
Fax: (518) 564-3292
E-mail: geo@plattsburgh.edu
Phone: (518) 564-3287

**SUNY College at Potsdam**
www.potsdam.edu
Office of Admissions
44 Pierrepont Avenue
Potsdam, NY 13676
Fax: (315) 267-2163
E-mail: admint@potsdam.edu
Phone: (315) 267-2180

**SUNY College at Purchase**
www.purchase.edu
Admissions Office
735 Anderson Hill Road
Purchase, NY 10577-1400
Fax: (914) 251-6314
E-mail: barbaraw@purchase.edu
Phone: (914) 251-6300

**SUNY College of Agriculture and Technology at Cobleskill**
www.cobleskill.edu
International Programs
Knapp Hall
Cobleskill, NY 12043
Fax: (518) 255-5113
E-mail: jagends@cobleskill.edu
Phone: (518) 255-5558

**SUNY College of Agriculture and Technology at Morrisville**
www.morrisville.edu
Admissions Office
PO Box 901
Morrisville, NY 13408-0901
Fax: (315) 684-6427
E-mail: longoer@morrisville.edu
Phone: (315) 684-6046

**SUNY College of Environmental Science and Forestry**
www.esf.edu
Undergraduate Admissions
Gateway Center
One Forestry Drive
Syracuse, NY 13210
Fax: (315) 470-6933
E-mail: esfinfo@esf.edu
Phone: (315) 470-6600

**SUNY College of Technology at Alfred**
www.alfredstate.edu
International Education
Huntington Administration Building
10 Upper College Drive
Alfred, NY 14802-1196
Fax: (607) 587-4299
E-mail: hollanmr@alfredstate.edu
Phone: (607) 587-4215

**SUNY College of Technology at Canton**
www.canton.edu
Admissions
34 Cornell Drive
Canton, NY 13617-1098
Fax: (315) 386-7929
E-mail: admissions@canton.edu
Phone: (315) 386-7123

**SUNY College of Technology at Delhi**
www.delhi.edu
Admissions
2 Main Street
Delhi, NY 13753-1190
Fax: (607) 746-4104
E-mail: enroll@delhi.edu
Phone: (607) 746-4546

**SUNY Empire State College**
www.esc.edu
Center for International Programs
1 Union Avenue
Saratoga Springs, NY 12866
Fax: (518) 580-0287
E-mail: erin.barrett@esc.edu
Phone: (518) 587-2100 ext. 2231

**SUNY Farmingdale State College**
www.farmingdale.edu
International Education
2350 Broadhollow Road
Laffin Hall
Farmingdale, NY 11735-1021
Fax: (631) 420-2780
E-mail: international@farmingdale.edu
Phone: (631) 420-2460

**SUNY Maritime College**
www.sunymaritime.edu
6 Pennyfield Avenue
Throggs Neck, NY 10465
E-mail: ineil@sunymaritime.edu
Phone: (718) 409-7221

**SUNY Polytechnic Institute**
www.sunypoly.edu
Office of International Admissions & Student Services
100 Seymour Road
Utica, NY 13502
Fax: (315) 792-7221
E-mail: international@sunyit.edu
Phone: (315) 792-7219

**SUNY University at Albany**
www.albany.edu
Office of International Admissions
Office of Undergraduate Admissions,
University Hall
1400 Washington Avenue
Albany, NY 12222
Fax: (518) 442-5383
E-mail: ugadmissions@albany.edu
Phone: (518) 442-5435

**SUNY University at Binghamton**
www.binghamton.edu
Undergraduate Admissions
PO Box 6001
Binghamton, NY 13902-6001
Fax: (607) 777-4445
E-mail: intlbu@binghamton.edu
Phone: (607) 777-2171

**SUNY University at Buffalo**
www.buffalo.edu
International Admissions
12 Capen Hall
Buffalo, NY 14260-1660
Fax: (716) 645-6411
E-mail: intladmit@buffalo.edu
Phone: (716) 645-6900

**SUNY University at Stony Brook**
www.stonybrook.edu
International Admissions
118 Administration Building
Stony Brook, NY 11794-1901
Fax: (631) 632-9898
E-mail: enrollintl@stonybrook.edu
Phone: (631) 632-6868

**SUNY Upstate Medical University**
www.upstate.edu
International Student Advisor
766 Irving Avenue
Syracuse, NY 13210
Fax: (315) 464-8857
E-mail: abbottj@upstate.edu
Phone: (315) 464-8817

**Susquehanna University**
www.susqu.edu
Office of Admissions
514 University Avenue
Selinsgrove, PA 17870-1164
Fax: (570) 372-2722
E-mail: suadmiss@susqu.edu
Phone: (570) 372-4260

**Sussex County Community College**
www.sussex.edu
Dean of Student Affairs
One College Hill Road
Newton, NJ 07860
Fax: (973) 579-5226
E-mail: dmcfadden@sussex.edu
Phone: (973) 300-2201

**Swarthmore College**
www.swarthmore.edu
Admissions Office
500 College Avenue
Swarthmore, PA 19081
Fax: (610) 328-8580
E-mail: jbock2@swarthmore.edu
Phone: (610) 328-8300

**Swedish Institute**
www.swedishinstitute.edu
151 West 26th Street
New York, NY 10001
E-mail: admissions@swedishinstitute.edu
Phone: (212) 924-5900 ext. 199

**Sweet Briar College**
www.sbc.edu
Admissions
PO Box 1052
Sweet Briar, VA 24595-1502
Fax: (434) 381-6152
E-mail: admissions@sbc.edu
Phone: (434) 381-6142

**Syracuse University**
www.syr.edu
Office of Admissions
900 South Crouse Avenue
100 Crouse-Hinds Hall
Syracuse, NY 13244-5040
Fax: (315) 443-4226
E-mail: orange@syr.edu
Phone: (315) 443-3611

**Tabor College**
www.tabor.edu
Admissions
400 South Jefferson
Hillsboro, KS 67063-7135
Fax: (620) 947-6276
E-mail: admissions@tabor.edu
Phone: (620) 947-3121 ext. 1727

**Tacoma Community College**
www.tacomacc.edu
International Student Office
6501 South 19th Street
Tacoma, WA 98466-9971
Fax: (253) 566-6027
E-mail: admit@tacomacc.edu
Phone: (253) 566-5166

**Taft College**
www.taftcollege.edu
Admissions
29 Cougar Court
Taft, CA 93268
Fax: (661) 763-7758
E-mail: admissions@taftcollege.edu
Phone: (661) 763-7741

**Talladega College**
www.talladega.edu
Admissions
627 West Battle Street
Talladega, AL 35160
Fax: (256) 362-0274
E-mail: Karemu@talladega.edu
Phone: (256) 761-6175

**Tallahassee Community College**
www.tcc.fl.edu
International Student Services
444 Appleyard Drive
Tallahassee, FL 32304-2895
Fax: (850) 201-8474
E-mail: jensenb@tcc.fl.edu
Phone: (850) 201-6200

**Talmudic University**
www.talmudicu.edu
Office of Admissions
4000 Alton Road
Miami Beach, FL 33140
Fax: (305) 534-8444
E-mail: plw@talmudicu.edu
Phone: (305) 534-7050

**Talmudical Academy of New Jersey**
Route 524, PO Box 7
Adelphia, NJ 07710
Phone: (732) 431-1600

**Talmudical Institute of Upstate New York**
www.tiuny.org
769 Park Avenue
Rochester, NY 14607
Fax: (585) 442-0417
Phone: (585) 473-2810

**Talmudical Seminary Oholei Torah**
www.tsot.edu
667 Eastern Parkway
Brooklyn, NY 11213-3397
Phone: (718) 774-5215

**Tarleton State University**
www.tarleton.edu
International Academic Programs
Box T-0030
Stephenville, TX 76402
Fax: (254) 968-9618
E-mail: iap@tarleton.edu
Phone: (254) 968-9632

**Tarrant County College**
www.tccd.edu
International Admissions Services
300 Trinity Campus Circle
Fort Worth, TX 76102-1964
Fax: (817) 515-0624
E-mail: nichole.mancone@tccd.edu
Phone: (817) 515-1580

**Taylor Business Institute**
www.tbiil.edu
318 West Adams Street, 5th Floor
Chicago, IL 60606
Phone: (312) 658-5100

**Taylor University**
www.taylor.edu
Admissions Office
236 West Reade Avenue
Upland, IN 46989-1001
Fax: (765) 998-4925
E-mail: drkamwesa@taylor.edu
Phone: (765) 998-4612

**Technical Career Institutes**
www.tcicollege.edu
Student Affairs
320 West 31st Street
New York, NY 10001
Fax: (212) 629-3937
E-mail: admissions@tcicollege.edu
Phone: (212) 594-4000

**Telshe Yeshiva-Chicago**
3535 West Foster Avenue
Chicago, IL 60625
Fax: (773) 463-2894
Phone: (773) 463-7738

**Temple University**
www.temple.edu
Undergraduate International Admissions
103 Conwell Hall
1801 North Broad Street
Philadelphia, PA 19122-6096
Fax: (215) 204-4990
E-mail: international.admissions@temple.edu
Phone: (215) 204-4900

**Tennessee State University**
www.tnstate.edu
Foreign Student Adviser
3500 John A. Merritt Boulevard
Nashville, TN 37209-1561
Fax: (615) 963-7219
E-mail: recruitment@tnstate.edu
Phone: (615) 963-7371

**Tennessee Technological University**
www.tntech.edu
Office of Admissions
Box 5006
Cookeville, TN 38505-0001
Fax: (931) 372-6111
E-mail: cwilkerson@tntech.edu
Phone: (931) 372-3634

**Tennessee Wesleyan College**
www.tnwesleyan.edu
Vice President for Admissions
204 East College Street
Athens, TN 37303
Fax: (423) 744-9968
E-mail: jlanders@tnwesleyan.edu
Phone: (423) 746-5279

**Terra State Community College**
www.terra.edu
Admissions Office
2830 Napoleon Road
Fremont, OH 43420-9600
Fax: (419) 334-9035
E-mail: ktaylor01@terra.edu
Phone: (419) 559-2350

**Texas A&M International University**
www.tamiu.edu
Admissions Office
5201 University Boulevard
Laredo, TX 78041-1900
Fax: (956) 326-2199
E-mail: adms@tamiu.edu
Phone: (956) 326-2200

**Texas A&M University**
www.tamu.edu
Office of Admissions
750 Agronomy Road, Suite 1601
0200 TAMU
College Station, TX 77843-0200
Fax: (979) 845-8737
E-mail: lbarnes@tamu.edu
Phone: (979) 458-0971

**Texas A&M University-Commerce**
www.tamuc.edu
International Student Services
Box 3011
Commerce, TX 75429-3011
Fax: (903) 468-3200
E-mail: John.Jones@tamuc.edu
Phone: (903) 468-8144

**Texas A&M University-Corpus Christi**
www.tamucc.edu
Admissions
6300 Ocean Drive, Unit 5774
Corpus Christi, TX 78412-5774
Fax: (361) 825-5887
E-mail: karin.griffith@tamucc.edu
Phone: (361) 825-2624

**Texas A&M University-Kingsville**
www.tamuk.edu
Office of Admission
MSC 128
700 University Boulevard
Kingsville, TX 78363-8202
Fax: (361) 593-5509
E-mail: admissions@tamuk.edu
Phone: (361) 593-4885

**Texas A&M University-Texarkana**
www.tamut.edu
Student Services
7101 University Avenue
Texarkana, TX 75503
Fax: (903) 223-3118
E-mail: carl.greig@tamut.edu
Phone: (903) 223-3062

**Texas Christian University**
www.tcu.edu
International Admissions
TCU Box 297013
Fort Worth, TX 76129
Fax: (817) 257-5256
E-mail: frogworld@tcu.edu
Phone: (817) 257-7871

**Texas College**
www.texascollege.edu
Office of Enrollment Services
2404 North Grand Avenue
PO Box 4500
Tyler, TX 75712-4500
Fax: (903) 593-6551
E-mail: jroberts@texascollege.edu
Phone: (903) 593-8311 ext. 2251

**Texas County Technical College**
www.texascountytech.edu
Admissions
6915 South Highway 63
P.O. Box 314
Houston, MO 65483
Fax: (417) 967-4604
E-mail: ccasebeer@texascountytech.edu
Phone: (417) 967-5466

**Texas Lutheran University**
www.tlu.edu
Enrollment Services
1000 West Court Street
Seguin, TX 78155-5999
Fax: (830) 372-8096
E-mail: anavarro-jusino@tlu.edu
Phone: (830) 372-8057

**Texas Southern University**
www.tsu.edu
International Student Affairs
3100 Cleburne Street
Bell Building 225
Houston, TX 77004
Fax: (713) 313-1878
E-mail: luckettph@tsu.edu
Phone: (713) 313-7930

**Texas State Technical College**
www.tstc.edu
Admissions and Records
3801 Campus Drive
Waco, TX 76705
Fax: (254) 867-2250
E-mail: carolyn.plant@tstc.edu
Phone: (254) 867-2362

**Texas State University**
www.txstate.edu
International Undergraduate Admissions
Center
429 North Guadalupe Street
San Marcos, TX 78666-5709
Fax: (512) 245-8264
E-mail: admissions@txstate.edu
Phone: (512) 245-7966

**Texas Tech University**
www.ttu.edu
Office of International Affairs
Box 45005
Lubbock, TX 79409-5005
Fax: (806) 742-0062
E-mail: alexa.smith@ttu.edu
Phone: (806) 742-3667

**Texas Tech University Health Sciences
Center**
www.ttuhsc.edu
3601 Fourth Street
Lubbock, TX 79430
Phone: (806) 743-2300

**Texas Wesleyan University**
www.txwes.edu
International Programs
1201 Wesleyan Street
Fort Worth, TX 76105-1536
Fax: (817) 531-4980
E-mail: aharris@txwes.edu
Phone: (817) 531-5868

**Texas Woman's University**
www.twu.edu
International Education
Box 425589
Denton, TX 76204-5589
Fax: (940) 898-2048
E-mail: intloffice@twu.edu
Phone: (940) 898-3338

**Theological University of the Caribbean**
www.utcpr.edu
PO Box 901
Saint Just, PR 00978-0901
E-mail: admisiones@utcpr.edu
Phone: (787) 761-0808 ext. 246

**Thiel College**
www.thiel.edu
Admissions
75 College Avenue
Greenville, PA 16125-2181
Fax: (724) 289-2013
E-mail: admissions@thiel.edu
Phone: (724) 589-2345

**Thomas Aquinas College**
www.thomasaquinas.edu
Admissions Office
10000 Ojai Road
Santa Paula, CA 93060-9621
Fax: (805) 421-5905
E-mail: admissions@thomasaquinas.edu
Phone: (805) 525-4417

**Thomas College**
www.thomas.edu
Admissions
180 West River Road
Waterville, ME 04901
Fax: (207) 859-1114
E-mail: kentj@thomas.edu
Phone: (207) 859-1101

**Thomas Edison State University**
www.tesu.edu
Admissions
111 West State Street
Trenton, NJ 08608-1176
Fax: (609) 984-8447
E-mail: admissions@tesc.edu
Phone: (888) 442-8372

**Thomas Jefferson University**
www.jefferson.edu
Office of Admissions
130 South Ninth Street, Edison Building,
Suite 100
Philadelphia, PA 19107
Fax: (215) 503-7241
E-mail: erin.finn@jefferson.edu
Phone: (215) 503-8890

**Thomas More College**
www.thomasmore.edu
Admissions Office
333 Thomas More Parkway
Crestview Hills, KY 41017-3495
Fax: (859) 344-4444
E-mail: admissions@thomasmore.edu
Phone: (859) 344-3332

**Thomas More College of Liberal Arts**
www.thomasmorecollege.edu
Admissions
Six Manchester Street
Merrimack, NH 03054-4818
Fax: (603) 880-9280
E-mail: admissions@thomasmorecollege.edu
Phone: (800) 880-8308

**Thomas Nelson Community College**
www.tncc.edu
Admissions and Records
PO Box 9407
Hampton, VA 23670
Fax: (757) 825-2763
E-mail: admissions@tncc.edu
Phone: (757) 825-2800

**Thomas University**
www.thomasu.edu
Director of Marketing
1501 Millpond Road
Thomasville, GA 31792-7499
Fax: (229) 227-6919
E-mail: rgagliano@thomasu.edu
Phone: (229) 226-1621 ext. 214

**Three Rivers Community College**
www.trcc.edu
Admissions
2080 Three Rivers Boulevard
Poplar Bluff, MO 63901-1308
Fax: (573) 840-9058
E-mail: mfields@trcc.edu
Phone: (573) 840-9675 ext. 675

**Tidewater Community College**
www.tcc.edu
International Student Services
300 Granby Street
Norfolk, VA 23510
Fax: (757) 822-7544
E-mail: iss@tcc.edu
Phone: (757) 822-7342

**Tiffin University**
www.tiffin.edu
International Admissions
155 Miami Street
Tiffin, OH 44883
Fax: (419) 443-5006
E-mail: admissions@tiffin.edu
Phone: (800) 968-6446 ext. 3332

**Tillamook Bay Community College**
www.tbcc.cc.or.us
4301 Third Street
Tillamook, OR 97141
E-mail: StudentServices@tillamookbay.cc
Phone: (503) 842-8222 ext. 1100

**Toccoa Falls College**
www.tfc.edu
Admissions
PO Box 899
Toccoa Falls, GA 30598
Fax: (706) 282-6012
E-mail: rstewart@tfc.edu
Phone: (888) 785-5624 ext. 5381

**Tohono O'odham Community College**
www.tocc.edu
PO Box 3129
Sells, AZ 85634-3129
Fax: (520) 383-0029
E-mail: lluna@tocc.edu
Phone: (520) 383-8401 ext. 35

**Tompkins Cortland Community College**
www.TC3.edu
Enrollment Services Center
170 North Street
Box 139
Dryden, NY 13053-0139
Fax: (607) 844-6541
E-mail: armstrc@tompkinscortland.edu
Phone: (607) 844-6580 ext. 4320

**Torah Temimah Talmudical Seminary**
507 Ocean Parkway
Brooklyn, NY 11218
Phone: (718) 853-8500

**Tougaloo College**
www.tougaloo.edu
Office of Admissions
500 West County Line Road
Tougaloo, MS 39174
Fax: (601) 977-4501
E-mail: jjacobs@tougaloo.edu
Phone: (601) 977-7768

**Touro College**
www.touro.edu
Registrar
27 West 23rd Street
New York, NY 10010
Fax: (212) 627-9542
E-mail: eddies@touro.edu
Phone: (212) 463-0400 ext. 607

**Touro University Worldwide**
www.tuw.edu
Admission Office
10601 Calle Lee, #179
Los Alamitos, CA 90720
Fax: (818) 688-3244
E-mail: online@tuw.edu
Phone: (877) 868-7690

**Towson University**
www.towson.edu
International Admissions
8000 York Road
Towson, MD 21252-0001
Fax: (410) 704-3030
E-mail: intladm@towson.edu
Phone: (410) 704-6069

**Transylvania University**
www.transy.edu
Associate Dean for Diversity & International
Student Experience
300 North Broadway
Lexington, KY 40508-1797
Fax: (859) 233-8797
E-mail: swright@transy.edu
Phone: (859) 233-8805

**Treasure Valley Community College**
www.tvcc.cc
Academic Advising Coordinator / Advisor
650 College Boulevard
Ontario, OR 97914-3423
Fax: (541) 881-5520
E-mail: cbuttice@tvcc.cc
Phone: (541) 881-5801

**Trevecca Nazarene University**
www.trevecca.edu
Office of Admissions
333 Murfreesboro Road
Nashville, TN 37210
Fax: (615) 248-7406
E-mail: admissions_und@trevecca.edu
Phone: (615) 248-1320

**Tri-County Technical College**
www.tctc.edu
Admissions
PO Box 587
Pendleton, SC 29670
Fax: (864) 646-1890
E-mail: info@tctc.edu
Phone: (864) 646-1550

**Triangle Tech: Bethlehem**
www.triangle-tech.edu
3184 Airport Road
Bethlehem, PA 18017
Fax: (610) 266-2911
Phone: (610) 266-2910

**Triangle Tech: Greensburg**
www.triangle-tech.edu
222 East Pittsburgh Street, Suite A
Greensburg, PA 15601-3304
Fax: (724) 834-0325
Phone: (724) 832-1050

**Trident Technical College**
www.tridenttech.edu
International Admissions Coordinator
PO.Box 118067, AM-M
Charleston, SC 29423-8067
Fax: (843) 574-6483
E-mail: paula.talbot@tridenttech.edu
Phone: (843) 574-6921

**Trident University International**
www.trident.edu
Admissions
Attn: Office of the Registrar
5757 Plaza Drive, Suite 100
Cypress, CA 90630
Fax: (800) 403-9024
E-mail: admissions@trident.edu
Phone: (800) 579-3170

**Trine University**
www.trine.edu
Admissions
One University Avenue
Angola, IN 46703
Fax: (260) 665-4578
E-mail: admit@trine.edu
Phone: (260) 665-4149

**Trinidad State Junior College**
www.trinidadstate.edu
Admissions
600 Prospect Street
Trinidad, CO 81082
Fax: (719) 846-5620
E-mail: bernadine.degarbo@trinidadstate.edu
Phone: (719) 846-5621

**Trinity Baptist College**
www.tbc.edu
800 Hammond Boulevard
Jacksonville, FL 32221
Fax: (904) 596-2309
E-mail: admissions@tbc.edu
Phone: (800) 786-2206

**Trinity Christian College**
www.trnty.edu
Registrar
6601 West College Drive
Palos Heights, IL 60463
Fax: (708) 239-3969
E-mail: Jaynn.Tobias-Johnson@trnty.edu
Phone: (708) 239-4759

**Trinity College**
www.trincoll.edu
Admissions
300 Summit Street
Hartford, CT 06106
Fax: (860) 297-2287
E-mail: mandi.haines@trincoll.edu
Phone: (860) 297-2551

**Trinity College of Florida**
www.trinitycollege.edu
Office of Admissions
2430 Welbilt Boulevard
Trinity, FL 34655-4401
Fax: (727) 569-1411
E-mail: admissions@trinitycollege.edu
Phone: (727) 376-6911 ext. 306

**Trinity International University**
www.tiu.edu
Undergraduate Admissions
2065 Half Day Road
Deerfield, IL 60015
Fax: (847) 317-8097
E-mail: admissions@tiu.edu
Phone: (847) 317-7000

**Trinity University**
www.trinity.edu
Admissions
One Trinity Place
San Antonio, TX 78212-7200
Fax: (210) 999-8164
E-mail: eric.maloof@trinity.edu
Phone: (210) 999-7207

**Trinity Valley Community College**
www.tvcc.edu
Student Affairs
100 Cardinal Drive
Athens, TX 75751
Fax: (903) 675-6209
E-mail: ccurran@tvcc.edu
Phone: (903) 670-2648

**Trinity Washington University**
www.trinitydc.edu
Admissions
125 Michigan Avenue, NE
Washington, DC 20017
Fax: (202) 884-9403
E-mail: admissions@trinitydc.edu
Phone: (202) 884-9400

**Triton College**
www.triton.edu
Records Evaluator
2000 North Fifth Avenue
River Grove, IL 60171
Fax: (708) 583-3147
E-mail: veronicahoward@triton.edu
Phone: (708) 456-0300 ext. 3444

**Trocaire College**
www.trocaire.edu
Admissions
360 Choate Avenue
Buffalo, NY 14220
Fax: (716) 828-6107
E-mail: lesinskic@trocaire.edu
Phone: (716) 826-1200 ext. 1218

**Troy University**
www.troy.edu
Dean of International Students
University Avenue, Adams Administration
111
Troy, AL 36082
Fax: (334) 670-3735
E-mail: dstewart@troy.edu
Phone: (334) 670-3335

**Truckee Meadows Community College**
www.tmcc.edu
Admissions and Records
7000 Dandini Boulevard
MS RDMT 319
Reno, NV 89512
Fax: (775) 673-7028
E-mail: international@tmcc.edu
Phone: (775) 674-7699

**Truett McConnell University**
www.truett.edu
Admissions
100 Alumni Drive
Cleveland, GA 30528
Fax: (706) 865-3110
E-mail: agailey@truett.edu
Phone: (706) 865-2134 ext. 4301

**Truman State University**
www.truman.edu
Center for International Students (CIS)
100 East Normal Avenue
Kirksville, MO 63501
Fax: (660) 785-5395
E-mail: intladmit@truman.edu
Phone: (660) 785-4215

**Tufts University**
www.tufts.edu
Undergraduate Admissions
Bendetson Hall
Medford, MA 02155
Fax: (617) 627-3860
E-mail: undergraduate.admissions@tufts.edu
Phone: (617) 627-3170

**Tulane University**
www.tulane.edu
Undergraduate Admissions
6823 St. Charles Avenue
New Orleans, LA 70118-5680
Fax: (504) 862-8715
E-mail: undergrad.admission@tulane.edu
Phone: (504) 865-5731

**Tulsa Community College**
www.tulsacc.edu
Northeast Campus - Global Learning
6111 East Skelly Drive
Tulsa, OK 74135-6198
Fax: (918) 595-7598
E-mail: nathan.bryson@tulsacc.edu
Phone: (918) 595-7533

**Tulsa Welding School**
www.weldingschool.com
Admissions
2545 East 11th Street
Tulsa, OK 74104-3909
Fax: (918) 295-6821
E-mail: monte.schaich@twsweld.com
Phone: (918) 587-6789

**Tunxis Community College**
www.tunxis.edu
Admissions
271 Scott Swamp Road
Farmington, CT 06032-3187
Fax: (860) 255-3559
E-mail: amccarthy@txcc.commnet.edu
Phone: (860) 255-3556

**Turabo University**
www.ut.suagm.edu
Director of Admissions
PO Box 3030
Gurabo, PR 00778
E-mail: dyrodriguez@suagm.edu
Phone: (787) 743-7979 ext. 4453

**Turtle Mountain Community College**
www.tm.edu
PO Box 340
Belcourt, ND 58316
Fax: (701) 477-7892
E-mail: jlafontaine@tm.edu
Phone: (701) 477-7862

**Tusculum College**
www.tusculum.edu
International Student Admissions Counselor
60 Shiloh Road
Box 5097
Greeneville, TN 37743
Fax: (423) 798-1622
E-mail: mripley@tusculum.edu
Phone: (423) 636-7300 ext. 5374

**Tuskegee University**
www.tuskegee.edu
Margaret Murray Washington Hall
1st floor - Admissions
Tuskegee, AL 36088
Fax: (334) 727-5750
E-mail: thevines@mytu.tuskegee.edu
Phone: (334) 727-8390

**U.T.A. Mesivta-Kiryas Joel**
48 Bakertown Road, Suite 501
Monroe, NY 10950-2169
Phone: (845) 783-9901

**Ulster County Community College**
www.sunyulster.edu
Admissions
Cottekill Road
Stone Ridge, NY 12484
Fax: (845) 687-5090
E-mail: greenm@sunyulster.edu
Phone: (845) 688-1568

**Umpqua Community College**
www.umpqua.edu
Student Services
1140 Umpqua College Road
PO Box 967
Roseburg, OR 97470-0226
Fax: (541) 440-7713
E-mail: LaVera.Noland@umpqua.edu
Phone: (541) 440-7743

**Union College**
www.unionky.edu
Admission
310 College Street, Box 005
Barbourville, KY 40906
Fax: (606) 546-1667
E-mail: cgrooms@unionky.edu
Phone: (606) 546-1221

**Union College**
www.ucollege.edu
Enrollment Services
3800 South 48th Street
Lincoln, NE 68506-4300
Fax: (402) 486-2566
E-mail: keericks@ucollege.edu
Phone: (402) 486-2504

**Union College**
www.union.edu
Office of Admissions
Grant Hall, 807 Union Street
Schenectady, NY 12308-3107
Fax: (518) 388-6986
E-mail: admissions@union.edu
Phone: (518) 388-6112

**Union County College**
www.ucc.edu
Admissions, Records and Registration
1033 Springfield Avenue
Cranford, NJ 07016-1528
Fax: (908) 709-7070
E-mail: pbelmonte@ucc.edu
Phone: (908) 709-7000

**Union Institute & University**
www.myunion.edu
Registrar's Office
440 East McMillan Street
Cincinnati, OH 45206
Fax: (513) 861-3218
E-mail: chris.mcnay@myunion.edu
Phone: (513) 861-6400 ext. 1277

**Union University**
www.uu.edu
Enrollment Counselor
1050 Union University Drive
Jackson, TN 38305-3697
Fax: (731) 661-5017
E-mail: smooberry@uu.edu
Phone: (731) 661-5010

**United States Coast Guard Academy**
www.uscga.edu
Admissions
31 Mohegan Avenue
New London, CT 06320
Fax: (860) 701-6700
E-mail: Chris.A.McMunn@uscga.edu
Phone: (860) 701-6778

**United States Merchant Marine Academy**
www.usmma.edu
Admissions
300 Steamboat Road, Admissions Center
Kings Point, NY 11024-1699
Fax: (516) 773-5390
E-mail: admissions@usmma.edu
Phone: (516) 726-5642

**United States Naval Academy**
www.usna.edu
Naval Attache in the United States Embassy
of home country
52 King George Street
United States Naval Academy
Annapolis, MD 21402-1318
Fax: (410) 293-4348
E-mail: webmail@usna.edu
Phone: (410) 293-1858

**United States Sports Academy**
www.ussa.edu
One Academy Drive
Daphne, AL 36526
Fax: (251) 625-1035
E-mail: admissions@ussa.edu
Phone: (251) 626-3303

**United Talmudical Seminary**
191 Rodney Street
Brooklyn, NY 11211
Phone: (718) 963-9770

**United Tribes Technical College**
www.uttc.edu
Admission Department
3315 University Drive
Bismarck, ND 58504
Fax: (701) 530-0640
E-mail: vgillette@uttc.edu
Phone: (701) 255-3285 ext. 1334

**Unity College**
www.unity.edu
Admissions
PO 532
Unity, ME 04988-0532
Fax: (207) 512-1212
E-mail: jsalty@unity.edu
Phone: (207) 509-7205

**Universal Technical Institute**
www.uti.edu/Phoenix
Campus Admissions
10695 West Pierce Street
Avondale, AZ 85323
Fax: (623) 245-4605
E-mail: info@uticorp.com
Phone: (623) 245-4600

**Universal Technology College of Puerto Rico**
www.unitecpr.edu
Apartado 1955, Victoria Station
Aguadilla, PR 00605
E-mail: admisiones@unitecpr.net
Phone: (787) 882-2065 ext. 308

**Universidad Adventista de las Antillas**
www.uaa.edu
Student Affairs Office
PO Box 118
Mayaguez, PR 00681-0118
Fax: (787) 834-9597
E-mail: jlopez@uaa.edu
Phone: (787) 834-9595 ext. 2213

**Universidad Central del Caribe**
www.uccaribe.edu
Decanato de Admisiones y Asuntos
Estudiantiles
PO Box 60327
Bayamon, PR 00960-6032
Fax: (787) 269-7550
E-mail: icordero@uccaribe.edu
Phone: (787) 740-1611

**Universidad del Este**
www.suagm.edu/une
PO Box 2010
Carolina, PR 00984-2010
Fax: (787) 257-8601
E-mail: ue_rfuentes@suagm.edu
Phone: (787) 257-7373 ext. 3332

**Universidad Metropolitana**
www.suagm.edu/umet
Director of Admissions
Apartado 21150
San Juan, PR 00928
Fax: (787) 751-0992
E-mail: yrivera@suagm.edu
Phone: (787) 766-1717 ext. 6683

**Universidad Pentecostal Mizpa**
www.mizpa.edu
Dean of Students Affairs
RR 16 Box 4800
San Juan, PR 00926
Fax: (787) 720-2012
E-mail: decanatoestudiantes@mizpa.edu
Phone: (787) 720-4476 ext. 228

**Universidad Politecnica de Puerto Rico**
www.pupr.edu
Admissions Office
PO Box 192017
San Juan, PR 00919-2017
Fax: (787) 764-8712
E-mail: tcardona@pupr.edu
Phone: (787) 622-8000 ext. 309

**University College of San Juan**
www.cunisanjuan.edu
Admissions Office
180 Jose R. Oliver Avenue
San Juan, PR 00918
Fax: (787) 274-1388
E-mail: sanrivera@sanjuancapital.com
Phone: (787) 480-2424 ext. 2396

**University of Advancing Technology**
www.uat.edu
Manager of International Recruitment
2625 West Baseline Road
Tempe, AZ 85283-1056
Fax: (602) 383-8228
E-mail: bstadheim@uat.edu
Phone: (800) 658-5744

**University of Akron**
www.uakron.edu
International Programs
Simmons Hall
302 Buchtel Common
Akron, OH 44325-2001
Fax: (330) 972-8604
E-mail: international@uakron.edu
Phone: (330) 972-6349

**University of Akron: Wayne College**
www.wayne.uakron.edu
1901 Smucker Road
Orrville, OH 44667-9758
Fax: (330) 684-8989
E-mail: wayneadmissions@uakron.edu
Phone: (330) 683-2010

**University of Alabama**
www.ua.edu
Undergraduate Admissions
Box 870132
Tuscaloosa, AL 35487-0132
Fax: (205) 348-9046
E-mail: international.admissions@ua.edu
Phone: (205) 348-5924

**University of Alabama at Birmingham**
www.uab.edu
Undergraduate Admissions
1720 2nd Avenue South
Birmingham, AL 35294-4600
Fax: (205) 934-8664
E-mail: cpcrowe@uab.edu
Phone: (205) 934-3328

**University of Alabama in Huntsville**
www.uah.edu
Office of International Engagement
UAH Office of Undergraduate Admissions
301 Sparkman Drive
Huntsville, AL 35899
Fax: (256) 824-4515
E-mail: Sabrina.Williams@uah.edu
Phone: (256) 824-2744

**University of Alaska Anchorage**
www.uaa.alaska.edu
International Student Services
PO Box 141629
3901 Old Seward Highway
Anchorage, AK 99514-1629
Fax: (907) 786-4888
E-mail: dracki@alaska.edu
Phone: (907) 786-1573

**University of Alaska Fairbanks**
www.uaf.edu
Office of International Programs and
Initiatives
PO Box 757480
Fairbanks, AK 99775-7480
Fax: (907) 474-5979
E-mail: uaf-internationalprograms@alaska.edu
Phone: (907) 474-5327

**University of Alaska Southeast**
www.uas.alaska.edu
Admissions
11120 Glacier Highway
Juneau, AK 99801-8681
Fax: (907) 796-6365
E-mail: joe.nelson@uas.alaska.edu
Phone: (907) 796-6100

**University of Antelope Valley**
www.uav.edu
Admissions
44055 Sierra Highway
Lancaster, CA 93534
Fax: (661) 341-3707
E-mail: araceli.jimenez@uav.edu
Phone: (661) 726-1911

**University of Arizona**
www.arizona.edu
Director, International Admissions
1428 East University Boulevard
PO Box 210073
Tucson, AZ 85721-0040
Fax: (520) 621-9799
E-mail: rabeech@email.arizona.edu
Phone: (520) 621-6123

**University of Arkansas**
www.uark.edu
International Admissions
232 Silas H. Hunt Hall
Fayetteville, AR 72701
Fax: (479) 575-5055
E-mail: mosesso@uark.edu
Phone: (479) 575-6246

**University of Arkansas at Fort Smith**
www.uafs.edu
Admissions
PO Box 3649
Smith-Pendergraft Campus Center 219
Fort Smith, AR 72913-3649
Fax: (479) 788-7402
E-mail: kelly.dewitt@uafs.edu
Phone: (479) 788-7106

**University of Arkansas at Little Rock**
www.ualr.edu
Office of International Services
2801 South University Avenue
Student Services Center, Room 219
Little Rock, AR 72204-1099
Fax: (501) 683-7567
E-mail: prgerman@ualr.edu
Phone: (501) 683-7566

**University of Arkansas at Monticello**
www.uamont.edu
Admissions
Box 3600
Monticello, AR 71656
Fax: (870) 460-1926
E-mail: whitingm@uamont.edu
Phone: (870) 460-1026

**University of Arkansas at Pine Bluff**
www.uapb.edu
International Program Adviser/Admissions
Officer
1200 North University Drive, Mail Slot 4981
Pine Bluff, AR 71601-2799
Fax: (870) 575-4607
E-mail: owasoyop@uapb.edu
Phone: (870) 575-8732

**University of Arkansas for Medical
Sciences**
www.uams.edu
4301 West Markham Street
Little Rock, AR 72205
Phone: (501) 686-5000

**University of the Arts**
www.uarts.edu
Office of Admissions
320 South Broad Street
Philadelphia, PA 19102
Fax: (215) 717-6045
E-mail: abrown@uarts.edu
Phone: (215) 717-6037

**University of Baltimore**
www.ubalt.edu
Admission
1420 North Charles Street
Baltimore, MD 21201-5779
Fax: (410) 837-4793
E-mail: admission@ubalt.edu
Phone: (410) 837-1962

**University of Bridgeport**
www.bridgeport.edu
International Admissions
126 Park Avenue
Bridgeport, CT 06604
Fax: (203) 576-4941
E-mail: admit@bridgeport.edu
Phone: (203) 576-4552

**University of California: Berkeley**
www.berkeley.edu
110 Sproul Hall, #5800
Berkeley, CA 94720-5800
Phone: (510) 642-6000

**University of California: Davis**
www.ucdavis.edu
178 Mrak Hall, One Shields Ave
Davis, CA 95616
Fax: (530) 752-1280
E-mail: undergraduateadmissions@ucdavis.edu
Phone: (530) 752-2971

**University of California: Irvine**
www.uci.edu
Principal Admissions Evaluator
260 Aldrich Hall
Irvine, CA 92697-1075
Fax: (949) 824-2591
E-mail: kerry.lekutai@uci.edu
Phone: (949) 824-9344

**University of California: Los Angeles**
www.ucla.edu
UCLA Undergraduate Admissions
1147 Murphy Hall
Box 951436
Los Angeles, CA 90095-1436
Fax: (310) 206-1206
E-mail: ugadm@saonet.ucla.edu
Phone: (310) 825-3101

**University of California: Merced**
www.ucmerced.edu
Admissions & Outreach
5200 North Lake Road
Merced, CA 95343-5603
Fax: (209) 228-4244
E-mail: admissions@ucmerced.edu
Phone: (209) 228-6995

**University of California: Riverside**
www.ucr.edu
Office of Undergraduate Admissions
Undergraduate Admissions
3106 Student Services Building
Riverside, CA 92521
Fax: (951) 827-6344
E-mail: internationalinfo@ucr.edu
Phone: (951) 827-3411

**University of California: San Diego**
www.ucsd.edu
International Admissions, 0021
9500 Gilman Drive, 0021
La Jolla, CA 92093-0021
Fax: (858) 534-5629
E-mail: admissionsreply@ucsd.edu
Phone: (858) 534-4831

**University of California: Santa Barbara**
www.ucsb.edu
Associate Director of Admissions
1210 Cheadle Hall
Santa Barbara, CA 93106-2014
Fax: (805) 893-2676
E-mail: donna.coyne@sa.ucsb.edu
Phone: (805) 893-8551

**University of California: Santa Cruz**
www.ucsc.edu
Admissions
Cook House, 1156 High Street
Santa Cruz, CA 95064
Fax: (831) 459-4163
E-mail: internationaladmissions@ucsc.edu
Phone: (831) 459-2131

**University of Central Arkansas**
www.uca.edu
Office of International Engagement
201 Donaghey Avenue
Bernard 101
Conway, AR 72035
Fax: (501) 450-5095
E-mail: internationaladmission@uca.edu
Phone: (501) 450-5098

**University of Central Florida**
www.ucf.edu
International Student Services
Box 160111
Orlando, FL 32816-0111
Fax: (407) 823-2526
E-mail: admission@ucf.edu
Phone: (407) 823-1850

**University of Central Missouri**
www.ucmo.edu
Office of International Programs
WDE 1400
Warrensburg, MO 64093
Fax: (660) 543-4201
E-mail: intladmit@ucmo.edu
Phone: (660) 543-8502

**University of Central Oklahoma**
www.uco.edu
Office of Global Affairs
100 North University Drive
NUC 116, Box 151
Edmond, OK 73034-0151
Fax: (405) 974-3842
E-mail: ddunham1@uco.edu
Phone: (405) 974-2390

**University of Charleston**
www.ucwv.edu
Admissions
2300 MacCorkle Avenue, SE
Charleston, WV 25304
Fax: (304) 357-4781
E-mail: admissions@ucwv.edu
Phone: (304) 357-4758

**University of Chicago**
www.uchicago.edu
1101 East 58th Street
Rosenwald Hall, Suite 105
Chicago, IL 60637
Fax: (773) 702-4199
E-mail: mhetlage@uchicago.edu
Phone: (773) 702-8658

**University of Cincinnati**
www.uc.edu
Admissions Office
PO Box 210091
Cincinnati, OH 45221-0091
Fax: (513) 556-1105
E-mail: international.admissions@uc.edu
Phone: (513) 556-1100

**University of Cincinnati: Blue Ash College**
www.ucblueash.edu
Office of Admissions
9555 Plainfield Road
Muntz Hall 150
Blue Ash, OH 45236-1007
Fax: (513) 745-5768
E-mail: admissions@ucblueash.edu
Phone: (513) 745-5700

**University of Cincinnati: Clermont College**
www.ucclermont.edu
Director of International Services
4200 Clermont College Drive
Batavia, OH 45103
Fax: (513) 556-2990
E-mail: international.students@uc.edu
Phone: (513) 556-4278

**University of Colorado Boulder**
www.colorado.edu
Office of Admissions
Regent Administrative Center 125
University of Colorado, 552 UCB
Boulder, CO 80309-0552
Fax: (303) 492-7115
E-mail: intladm@colorado.edu
Phone: (303) 492-6301

**University of Colorado Colorado Springs**
www.uccs.edu
International Services Specialist
1420 Austin Bluffs Parkway
Colorado Springs, CO 80918
Fax: (719) 255-3116
E-mail: wchao@uccs.edu
Phone: (719) 255-7526

**University of Colorado Denver**
www.ucdenver.edu
International Affairs
Box 173364, Campus Box 167
Denver, CO 80217-3364
Fax: (303) 315-2610
E-mail: george.kacenga@ucdenver.edu
Phone: (303) 315-2384

**University of Connecticut**
www.uconn.edu
Office of Undergraduate Admissions
2131 Hillside Road, Unit 3088
Storrs, CT 06269-3088
Fax: (860) 486-1476
E-mail: beahusky@uconn.edu
Phone: (860) 486-3137

**University of the Cumberlands**
www.ucumberlands.edu
Office of Admissions
6178 College Station Drive
Williamsburg, KY 40769
Fax: (606) 539-4303
E-mail: jerry.jackson@ucumberlands.edu
Phone: (606) 539-4225

**University of Dallas**
www.udallas.edu
Office of Undergraduate Admission
1845 East Northgate Drive
Irving, TX 75062-4736
Fax: (972) 721-5017
E-mail: crusader@udallas.edu
Phone: (972) 721-5266

**University of Dayton**
www.udayton.edu
International Admission
300 College Park
Dayton, OH 45469-1602
Fax: (937) 229-4729
E-mail: goglobal@udayton.edu
Phone: (937) 229-1850

**University of Delaware**
www.udel.edu
Admissions Officer
210 South College Avenue
Newark, DE 19716
Fax: (302) 831-6905
E-mail: ehinson@udel.edu
Phone: (302) 831-8123

**University of Denver**
www.du.edu
Office of International Admission
2197 South University Boulevard
Denver, CO 80208
Fax: (303) 871-3522
E-mail: intladm@du.edu
Phone: (303) 871-2790

**University of Detroit Mercy**
www.udmercy.edu
Admissions Office
4001 West McNichols Road
Detroit, MI 48221-3038
Fax: (313) 993-3326
E-mail: moorec@udmercy.edu
Phone: (313) 993-1592

**University of the District of Columbia**
www.udc.edu
Office of International Students
4200 Connecticut Avenue NW
Washington, DC 20008
Fax: (202) 274-6180
E-mail: dantoine@udc.edu
Phone: (202) 274-5933

**University of Dubuque**
www.dbq.edu
Admissions
2000 University Avenue
Dubuque, IA 52001-5099
Fax: (563) 589-3490
E-mail: bbroshou@dbq.edu
Phone: (563) 589-3199

**University of Evansville**
www.evansville.edu
Office of International Admission
1800 Lincoln Avenue
Evansville, IN 47722
Fax: (812) 488-6389
E-mail: bf28@evansville.edu
Phone: (812) 488-2146

**University of Findlay**
www.findlay.edu
Director, International Admissions and
Services
1000 North Main Street
Findlay, OH 45840-3653
Fax: (419) 434-5507
E-mail: bennett@findlay.edu
Phone: (419) 434-4730

**University of Florida**
www.ufl.edu
Office of Admissions
201 Criser Hall-PO Box 114000
Gainesville, FL 32611-4000
Fax: (352) 392-2115
E-mail: cmitche@ufl.edu
Phone: (352) 392-1365

**University of Georgia**
www.uga.edu
Office of Undergraduate Admission
Terrell Hall
210 South Jackson Street
Athens, GA 30602-1633
Fax: (706) 542-1466
E-mail: admintl@uga.edu
Phone: (706) 542-2112

**University of Great Falls**
www.ugf.edu
Assistant Director of Admissions
1301 20th Street South
Great Falls, MT 59405
Fax: (406) 791-5209
E-mail: aclutter01@ugf.edu
Phone: (406) 791-5200

**University of Hartford**
www.hartford.edu
International Admission
Bates House
200 Bloomfield Avenue
West Hartford, CT 06117-1599
Fax: (860) 768-4961
E-mail: skinner@hartford.edu
Phone: (860) 768-4839

**University of Hawaii at Hilo**
www.hilo.hawaii.edu
Admissions
200 West Kawili Street
Hilo, HI 96720-4091
Fax: (808) 932-7459
E-mail: pgrossma@hawaii.edu
Phone: (808) 932-7446

**University of Hawaii at Manoa**
www.manoa.hawaii.edu
Admissions
2600 Campus Road, QLCSS 001
Honolulu, HI 96822
Fax: (808) 956-4148
E-mail: manoa.admissions@hawaii.edu
Phone: (808) 956-8975

**University of Hawaii: Hawaii Community College**
www.hawaii.hawaii.edu
Counseling and Student Support Services
1175 Manono Street
Hilo, HI 96720-5096
Fax: (808) 934-2501
E-mail: cdamate@hawaii.edu
Phone: (808) 934-2720

**University of Hawaii: Honolulu Community College**
www2.honolulu.hawaii.edu
Admissions
874 Dillingham Boulevard
Honolulu, HI 96817
Fax: (808) 847-9872
E-mail: admissions@hcc.hawaii.edu
Phone: (808) 845-9129

**University of Hawaii: Kapiolani Community College**
www.kcc.hawaii.edu
4303 Diamond Head Road
Honolulu, HI 96816-4421
Fax: (808) 734-9896
E-mail: liantmei@hawaii.edu
Phone: (808) 734-9312

**University of Hawaii: Kauai Community College**
www.kauai.hawaii.edu
Admissions and Records Office
3-1901 Kaumualii Highway
Lihue, HI 96766-9500
Fax: (808) 245-8297
E-mail: loride@hawaii.edu
Phone: (808) 245-8225

**University of Hawaii: Leeward Community College**
www.lcc.hawaii.edu
International Programs
96-045 Ala Ike
Pearl City, HI 96782
Fax: (808) 455-0568
E-mail: lccintl@hawaii.edu
Phone: (808) 455-0519

**University of Hawaii: Maui College**
www.maui.hawaii.edu
Student Services
310 West Kaahumanu Avenue
Kahului, HI 96732-1617
Fax: (808) 984-3287
Phone: (808) 984-3514

**University of Hawaii: West Oahu**
www.uhwo.hawaii.edu
Admissions Specialist
91-1001 Farrington Highway
Kapolei, HI 96707
Fax: (808) 453-6075
E-mail: ralynnn@hawaii.edu
Phone: (808) 454-4700

**University of Hawaii: Windward Community College**
www.wcc.hawaii.edu
Admissions and Records
45-720 Kea'ahala Road
Kaneohe, HI 96744
Fax: (808) 235-9148
E-mail: wccinfo@hawaii.edu
Phone: (808) 235-7432

**University of Holy Cross**
www.olhcc.edu
Enrollment Services
4123 Woodland Drive
New Orleans, LA 70131-7399
Fax: (504) 391-2421
E-mail: kkopecky@olhcc.edu
Phone: (504) 394-7744 ext. 175

**University of Houston**
www.uh.edu
International Admissions
Office of Admission
4400 University Drive
Houston, TX 77004
Fax: (713) 743-7542
E-mail: admissions@uh.edu
Phone: (713) 743-1010

**University of Houston-Clear Lake**
www.uhcl.edu
International Admissions
2700 Bay Area Boulevard
Houston, TX 77058-1098
Fax: (281) 226-7038
E-mail: OIAP@UHCL.edu
Phone: (281) 283-2740

**University of Houston-Downtown**
www.uhd.edu
International Admissions
One Main Street, Suite S350
Houston, TX 77002
Fax: (713) 223-7984
E-mail: internationaladmissions@uhd.edu
Phone: (713) 221-8910

**University of Houston-Victoria**
www.uhv.edu
Admissions/Enrollment Services
3007 North Ben Wilson
Victoria, TX 77901-4450
Fax: (361) 580-5500
E-mail: kraatze@uhv.edu
Phone: (361) 570-4112

**University of Idaho**
www.uidaho.edu
Undergraduate Admissions
875 Perimeter Drive MS 4264
Moscow, ID 83844-4264
Fax: (208) 885-9119
E-mail: admissions@idaho.edu
Phone: (208) 885-6326

**University of Illinois at Chicago**
www.uic.edu
Admissions and Records
Office of Admissions and Records, UIC, PO
Box 5220
Chicago, IL 60607-5220
Fax: (312) 413-7628
E-mail: uicadmit@uic.edu
Phone: (312) 996-4350

**University of Illinois at Urbana-Champaign**
http://illinois.edu
International Admissions
901 West Illinois
Urbana, IL 61801-3028
Fax: (217) 244-4614
E-mail: admissions@illinois.edu
Phone: (217) 333-0302

**University of Illinois: Springfield**
www.uis.edu
Admissions
One University Plaza, MS UHB 1080
Springfield, IL 62703-5407
Fax: (217) 206-6620
E-mail: admissions@uis.edu
Phone: (217) 206-4847

**University of the Incarnate Word**
www.uiw.edu
International Admissions
4301 Broadway
CPO 285
San Antonio, TX 78209-6397
Fax: (210) 805-5701
E-mail: adestefa@uiwtx.edu
Phone: (210) 805-5707

**University of Indianapolis**
www.uindy.edu
International Student Admissions
1400 East Hanna Avenue
Indianapolis, IN 46227-3697
Fax: (317) 788-3300
E-mail: kgunyon@uindy.edu
Phone: (317) 788-3600

**University of Iowa**
www.uiowa.edu
Admissions
107 Calvin Hall
Iowa City, IA 52242-1396
Fax: (319) 335-1535
E-mail: rebecca-hanson@uiowa.edu
Phone: (319) 335-3847

**University of Jamestown**
www.uj.edu
Admissions
6081 College Lane
Jamestown, ND 58405
Fax: (701) 253-4318
E-mail: dgibson@uj.edu
Phone: (701) 252-3467 ext. 5505

**University of Kansas**
www.ku.edu
International Recruitment and Undergraduate
Admissions
1502 Iowa Street
Lawrence, KS 66045-7576
Fax: (785) 864-5017
E-mail: world@ku.edu
Phone: (785) 864-2616

**University of Kansas Medical Center**
www.kumc.edu
Varies by academic school
KUMC Office of Admissions, Mail Stop 4005
3901 Rainbow Boulevard
Kansas City, KS 66160
E-mail: kumcadmissions@kumc.edu
Phone: (913) 945-7347

**University of Kentucky**
www.uky.edu
100 Funkhouser Building
Lexington, KY 40506-0054
Fax: (859) 257-3823
E-mail: mlkrin0@uky.edu
Phone: (859) 257-4708

**University of La Verne**
www.laverne.edu
Undergraduate Admissions
1950 Third Street
La Verne, CA 91750
Fax: (909) 392-2714
E-mail: awu@laverne.edu
Phone: (909) 448-4032

**University of Louisiana at Lafayette**
www.louisiana.edu
Director of Admissions
Box 41210
Lafayette, LA 70504-1210
Fax: (337) 482-1317
E-mail: admissions@louisiana.edu
Phone: (337) 482-6473

**University of Louisiana at Monroe**
www.ulm.edu
International Student Programs and Services
700 University Avenue
Monroe, LA 71209-1160
Fax: (318) 342-1915
E-mail: saowens@ulm.edu
Phone: (318) 342-1885

**University of Louisville**
www.louisville.edu
Admissions
2211 South Brook Street
Louisville, KY 40292
Fax: (502) 852-6526
E-mail: admitme@louisville.edu
Phone: (502) 852-4957

**University of Maine**
www.umaine.edu
Office of International Programs
5713 Chadbourne Hall
Orono, ME 04469-5713
Fax: (207) 581-2920
E-mail: internationaladm@maine.edu
Phone: (207) 581-2905

**University of Maine at Augusta**
www.uma.edu
Admissions
46 University Drive
Augusta, ME 04330
Fax: (207) 621-3333
E-mail: trask@maine.edu
Phone: (207) 621-3140

**University of Maine at Farmington**
www.umf.maine.edu
Office of Admission
246 Main Street
Farmington, ME 04938
Fax: (207) 778-8182
E-mail: umfadmit@maine.edu
Phone: (207) 778-7050

**University of Maine at Fort Kent**
www.umfk.maine.edu
Admissions
23 University Drive
Fort Kent, ME 04743
Fax: (207) 834-7609
E-mail: jillb@maine.edu
Phone: (207) 834-7602

**University of Maine at Machias**
www.umm.maine.edu
Admissions Office
116 O'Brien Avenue
Machias, ME 04654-1397
Fax: (207) 255-1363
E-mail: mahmoud.sowe@maine.edu
Phone: (207) 255-1332

**University of Maine at Presque Isle**
www.umpi.edu
Admissions
181 Main Street
Presque Isle, ME 04769
Fax: (207) 768-9450
E-mail: bethany.lord@maine.edu
Phone: (207) 768-9536

**University of Management and Technology**
www.umtweb.edu
1901 Fort Myer Drive, Suite 700
Arlington, VA 22209-1609
Fax: (703) 516-0985
E-mail: info@umtweb.edu
Phone: (703) 516-0035

**University of Mary**
www.umary.edu
Enrollment Services
7500 University Drive
Bismarck, ND 58504-9652
Fax: (701) 255-7687
E-mail: mcheitkamp@umary.edu
Phone: (701) 355-8190

**University of Mary Hardin-Baylor**
www.umhb.edu
Office of International Student Services
900 College Street
UMHB Box 8004
Belton, TX 76513
Fax: (254) 295-4535
E-mail: etanaka@umhb.edu
Phone: (254) 295-4949

**University of Mary Washington**
www.umw.edu
Admissions
1301 College Avenue
Fredericksburg, VA 22401-5300
Fax: (540) 654-1857
E-mail: admit@umw.edu
Phone: (540) 654-2000

**University of Maryland: Baltimore**
www.umaryland.edu
University Registrar
220 Arch Street
Baltimore, MD 21201
Fax: (410) 706-4053
E-mail: rholtz@umaryland.edu
Phone: (410) 706-7480

**University of Maryland: Baltimore County**
www.umbc.edu
Office of Undergraduate Admissions
1000 Hilltop Circle
Baltimore, MD 21250
Fax: (410) 455-1094
E-mail: massey@umbc.edu
Phone: (410) 455-6705

**University of Maryland: College Park**
www.maryland.edu
Office of International Student and Scholar
Services
Mitchell Building
College Park, MD 20742-5235
Fax: (301) 314-3280
E-mail: internationalservices@umd.edu
Phone: (301) 314-1713

**University of Maryland: Eastern Shore**
www.umes.edu
Student Development Center, Suite 1140
Princess Anne, MD 21853
Fax: (410) 651-8386
E-mail: lskhoza@umes.edu
Phone: (410) 651-6079

**University of Maryland: University College**
www.umuc.edu
Admission Office
1616 McCormick Drive
Largo, MD 20774
Fax: (240) 684-2153
E-mail: admissions@umuc.edu
Phone: (800) 888-8682

**University of Massachusetts Amherst**
www.umass.edu
Undergraduate Admissions Office
University Admissions Center
37 Mather Drive
Amherst, MA 01003-9291
Fax: (413) 545-4312
E-mail: mail@admissions.umass.edu
Phone: (413) 545-0222

**University of Massachusetts Boston**
www.umb.edu
Undergraduate Admissions
100 Morrissey Boulevard
Boston, MA 02125-3393
Fax: (617) 287-5999
E-mail: enrollment.info@umb.edu
Phone: (617) 287-6000

**University of Massachusetts Dartmouth**
www.umassd.edu
Undergraduate Admissions Office
285 Old Westport Road
Dartmouth, MA 02747-2300
Fax: (508) 999-8633
E-mail: jkarppinen@umassd.edu
Phone: (508) 910-6972

**University of Massachusetts Lowell**
www.uml.edu
Admissions Office
University Crossing, Suite 420, 220 Pawtucket
Street
Lowell, MA 01854-2874
Fax: (978) 934-3086
E-mail: admissions@uml.edu
Phone: (978) 934-3931

**University of Memphis**
www.memphis.edu
Office of Admissions
101 Wilder Tower
Memphis, TN 38152
Fax: (901) 678-3053
E-mail: dwelch@memphis.edu
Phone: (901) 678-2111

**University of Miami**
www.miami.edu
Office of International Admission
PO Box 248025
Coral Gables, FL 33124-4616
Fax: (305) 284-6811
E-mail: mreid@miami.edu
Phone: (305) 284-2271

**University of Michigan**
http://umich.edu/
Office of Undergraduate Admissions
1220 Student Activities Building
515 East Jefferson Street
Ann Arbor, MI 48109-1316
Fax: (734) 936-0740
E-mail: yale@umich.edu
Phone: (734) 764-7433

**University of Michigan: Dearborn**
www.umdearborn.edu
Admissions
4901 Evergreen Road, 1145 UC
Dearborn, MI 48128-1491
Fax: (313) 436-9167
E-mail: urana@umich.edu
Phone: (313) 593-5100

**University of Michigan: Flint**
www.umflint.edu
International Center
303 East Kearsley Street
245 University Pavilion
Flint, MI 48502-1950
Fax: (810) 762-0006
E-mail: dadams@umflint.edu
Phone: (810) 762-0867

**University of Minnesota: Crookston**
www.crk.umn.edu
International Programs Office
2900 University Avenue
Suite A Owen Hall
Crookston, MN 56716-5001
Fax: (218) 281-8588
E-mail: gillette@umn.edu
Phone: (218) 281-8442

**University of Minnesota: Duluth**
www.d.umn.edu
Office of Admissions
Solon Campus Center 25
1117 University Drive
Duluth, MN 55812-3000
Fax: (218) 726-6394
E-mail: besselst@d.umn.edu
Phone: (218) 726-7171

**University of Minnesota: Morris**
www.morris.umn.edu
Office of Admissions
600 East Fourth Street
Morris, MN 56267
Fax: (320) 589-6051
E-mail: krudney@morris.umn.edu
Phone: (320) 589-6045

**University of Minnesota: Rochester**
http://r.umn.edu
Admissions
111 South Broadway, Suite 300
Rochester, MN 55904
Fax: (507) 258-8021
E-mail: applyumr@r.umn.edu
Phone: (507) 258-8087

**University of Minnesota: Twin Cities**
http://twin-cities.umn.edu/
Admissions
240 Williamson Hall
231 Pillsbury Drive S.E.
Minneapolis, MN 55455-0213
Fax: (612) 626-1693
Phone: (800) 752-1000

**University of Mississippi**
www.olemiss.edu
Office of International Programs
145 Martindale
PO BOX 1848
University, MS 38677-1848
Fax: (662) 915-7486
E-mail: intladmu@olemiss.edu
Phone: (662) 915-7404

**University of Missouri: Columbia**
www.missouri.edu
International Student Admissions
230 Jesse Hall
Columbia, MO 65211
Fax: (573) 882-7887
E-mail: inter@missouri.edu
Phone: (573) 882-3754

**University of Missouri: Kansas City**
www.umkc.edu
International Student Affairs Office
5100 Rockhill Road, AC120
Kansas City, MO 64110-2499
Fax: (816) 235-6502
E-mail: gaults@umkc.edu
Phone: (816) 235-6234

**University of Missouri: St. Louis**
www.umsl.edu
International Student and Scholar Services
One University Boulevard
351 Millennium Student Center
St. Louis, MO 63121-4400
Fax: (314) 516-5636
E-mail: westdav@umsl.edu
Phone: (314) 516-5525

**University of Mobile**
www.umobile.edu
Admissions
5735 College Parkway
Mobile, AL 36613-2842
Fax: (251) 442-2498
E-mail: ksanders@umobile.edu
Phone: (251) 442-2222

**University of Montana**
http://umt.edu
International Students and Scholars Global
Engagement Office
Lommasson Center 101
Missoula, MT 59812
Fax: (406) 243-6115
E-mail: effie.koehn@umontana.edu
Phone: (406) 243-5580

**University of Montana: Western**
www.umwestern.edu
Admissions
710 South Atlantic Street
Dillon, MT 59725
Fax: (406) 683-7493
E-mail: janet.jones@umwestern.edu
Phone: (406) 683-7331

**University of Montevallo**
www.montevallo.edu
Admissions
Palmer Hall, Station 6030
University of Montevallo
Montevallo, AL 35115-6000
Fax: (205) 665-6032
E-mail: admissions@montevallo.edu
Phone: (205) 665-6030

**University of Mount Olive**
www.mou.edu
Office of Admissions
634 Henderson Street
Mount Olive, NC 28365
Fax: (919) 658-9816
E-mail: mkistler@moc.edu
Phone: (919) 299-4942

**University of Mount Union**
www.mountunion.edu
International Admissions
1972 Clark Avenue
Alliance, OH 44601-3929
Fax: (330) 823-5097
E-mail: hajecki@mountunion.edu
Phone: (330) 823-2590

**University of Nebraska - Kearney**
www.unk.edu
International Education Admissions
905 West 25th
Kearney, NE 68849
Fax: (308) 865-8160
E-mail: intladmin@unk.edu
Phone: (308) 865-8953

**University of Nebraska - Lincoln**
www.unl.edu
Admissions
1410 Q Street
Box 880417
Lincoln, NE 68588-0417
Fax: (402) 472-0670
E-mail: admissions@unl.edu
Phone: (402) 472-2023

**University of Nebraska - Omaha**
www.unomaha.edu
International Admissions
6001 Dodge Street
Omaha, NE 68182-0005
Fax: (402) 554-2949
E-mail: emaloley@mail.unomaha.edu
Phone: (402) 554-2293

**University of Nevada: Las Vegas**
www.unlv.edu
4505 Maryland Parkway, Box 451021
Las Vegas, NV 89154-1021
Fax: (702) 895-0155
E-mail: internationaladmissions@unlv.edu
Phone: (702) 774-2914

**University of Nevada: Reno**
www.unr.edu
Office of International Students and Scholars
Mail Stop 120
Reno, NV 89557
Fax: (775) 327-5843
E-mail: psa@unr.edu
Phone: (775) 682-7508

**University of New England**
www.une.edu
Admissions
11 Hills Beach Road
Biddeford, ME 04005
Fax: (207) 221-4898
E-mail: admissions@une.edu
Phone: (800) 477-4863

**University of New Hampshire**
www.unh.edu
Admissions Office
3 Garrison Avenue
Durham, NH 03824
Fax: (603) 862-0077
E-mail: admissions@unh.edu
Phone: (603) 862-1360

**University of New Hampshire at Manchester**
www.manchester.unh.edu
Admissions
88 Commercial Street
Manchester, NH 03101-1113
Fax: (603) 641-4342
E-mail: unhm.admissions@unh.edu
Phone: (603) 641-4150

**University of New Haven**
www.newhaven.edu
Office of International Admissions
300 Boston Post Road
West Haven, CT 06516-1916
Fax: (203) 932-7137
E-mail: IntUGadm@newhaven.edu
Phone: (203) 932-7320

**University of New Mexico**
www.unm.edu
Global Education Office
Office of Admissions
PO Box 4895
Albuquerque, NM 87196-4895
Fax: (505) 277-1867
E-mail: geo@unm.edu
Phone: (505) 277-4032

**University of New Orleans**
www.uno.edu
International Admissions and Recruitment
University of New Orleans, 105 Earl K. Long Library
New Orleans, LA 70148
Fax: (504) 280-7317
E-mail: jfranco@uno.edu
Phone: (504) 280-7263

**University of North Alabama**
www.una.edu
Office of International Affairs
One Harrison Plaza, UNA Box 5011
Florence, AL 35632-0001
Fax: (256) 765-4960
E-mail: czhang@una.edu
Phone: (256) 765-4626

**University of North Carolina at Asheville**
www.unca.edu
Admissions
CPO#1320, UNCA
One University Heights
Asheville, NC 28804-8502
Fax: (828) 251-6482
E-mail: admissions@unca.edu
Phone: (828) 251-6481

**University of North Carolina at Chapel Hill**
www.unc.edu
Undergraduate Admissions
Jackson Hall
CB# 2200
Chapel Hill, NC 27599-2200
Fax: (919) 962-3045
E-mail: pbaum@admissions.unc.edu
Phone: (919) 966-6546

**University of North Carolina at Charlotte**
www.uncc.edu
Undergraduate Admissions
Undergraduate Admissions- Cato Hall
9201 University Boulevard
Charlotte, NC 28223-0001
Fax: (704) 687-1664
E-mail: intl.admissions@uncc.edu
Phone: (704) 687-5507

**University of North Carolina at Greensboro**
www.uncg.edu
Undergraduate Admissions
PO Box 26170
Greensboro, NC 27402-6170
Fax: (336) 334-4180
E-mail: admissions@uncg.edu
Phone: (336) 334-5243

**University of North Carolina at Pembroke**
www.uncp.edu
Associate Director for International
Recruitment
Box 1510
One University Drive
Pembroke, NC 28372
Fax: (910) 521-6497
E-mail: christine.bell@uncp.edu
Phone: (910) 521-6262

**University of North Carolina at Wilmington**
www.uncw.edu
Assistant Director
601 South College Road
Wilmington, NC 28403-5904
Fax: (910) 962-3038
E-mail: hornej@uncw.edu
Phone: (910) 962-4096

**University of North Carolina School of the Arts**
www.uncsa.edu/
Admissions
1533 South Main Street
Winston-Salem, NC 27127-2738
Fax: (336) 770-3370
E-mail: lawsons@uncsa.edu
Phone: (336) 770-3290

**University of North Dakota**
www.und.edu
Assistant Director
2901 University Avenue Stop 8264
Grand Forks, ND 58202-8264
Fax: (701) 777-2721
E-mail: UND.admissions@UND.edu
Phone: (701) 777-3000

**University of North Florida**
www.unf.edu
International Center
1 UNF Drive
Jacksonville, FL 32224-7699
Fax: (904) 620-3925
E-mail: trobinso@unf.edu
Phone: (904) 620-2768

**University of North Georgia**
www.ung.edu
Admissions
82 College Circle
Dahlonega, GA 30597
Fax: (706) 864-1478
E-mail: molly.potts@ung.edu
Phone: (706) 864-1800

**University of North Texas**
www.unt.edu
UNT International
1401 West Prairie Suite 309
1155 Union Circle #311277
Denton, TX 76203-5017
Fax: (940) 565-4822
E-mail: dotty@unt.edu
Phone: (940) 565-2195

**University of North Texas at Dallas**
www.untdallas.edu
7300 University HIlls Boulevard
Admin (B1) 100
Dallas, TX 76039
E-mail: admissions@untdallas.edu
Phone: (972) 780-3642

**University of Northern Colorado**
www.unco.edu
International Admissions
501 20th Street, Campus Box 10
Greeley, CO 80639
Fax: (970) 351-2371
E-mail: international@unco.edu
Phone: (970) 351-2831

**University of Northern Iowa**
www.uni.edu
Admissions
1227 West 27th Street
Cedar Falls, IA 50614-0018
Fax: (319) 273-2885
E-mail: kristi.marchesani@uni.edu
Phone: (319) 273-2281

**University of Northwestern - St. Paul**
www.unwsp.edu
Admissions Office
3003 Snelling Avenue North
Saint Paul, MN 55113-1598
Fax: (651) 631-5680
E-mail: admissions@nwc.edu
Phone: (651) 631-5209

**University of Northwestern Ohio**
www.unoh.edu
200 Building
1441 North Cable Road
Lima, OH 45805
Fax: (419) 998-3139
E-mail: info@unoh.edu
Phone: (419) 998-8843

**University of Notre Dame**
www.nd.edu
Admissions
220 Main Building
Notre Dame, IN 46556
Fax: (574) 631-8865
E-mail: jmoloney2@nd.edu
Phone: (574) 631-7505

**University of Oklahoma**
www.ou.edu
Office of Admissions & Recruitment
1000 Asp Avenue, Room 127
Norman, OK 73019-4076
Fax: (405) 325-7124
E-mail: admrec@ou.edu
Phone: (405) 325-2251

**University of Oregon**
www.uoregon.edu
International Affairs
1217 University of Oregon
Eugene, OR 97403-1217
Fax: (541) 346-1232
E-mail: intl@uoregon.edu
Phone: (541) 346-3206

**University of the Ozarks**
www.ozarks.edu
415 North College Avenue
Clarksville, AR 72830-2880
Fax: (479) 979-1417
E-mail: flebois@ozarks.edu
Phone: (479) 979-1443

**University of the Pacific**
www.pacific.edu
Assistant Director of Admission
3601 Pacific Avenue
Stockton, CA 95211-0197
Fax: (209) 946-2413
E-mail: ksanpei@pacific.edu
Phone: (209) 346-2211

**University of Pennsylvania**
www.upenn.edu
The Office of Undergraduate Admissions
1 College Hall
Room 100
Philadelphia, PA 19104-6376
Fax: (215) 898-9670
E-mail: info@admissions.upenn.edu
Phone: (215) 898-7507

**University of Phoenix: Atlanta**
www.phoenix.edu
1625 W. Fountainhead Pkwy
Tempe, AZ 85282

**University of Phoenix: Augusta**
www.phoenix.edu
1625 West Fountainhead Parkway
Tempe, AZ 85282

**University of Phoenix: Austin**
www.phoenix.edu
10801 North MoPac
Austin, TX 78759-5459

**University of Phoenix: Baton Rouge**
www.phoenix.edu
2431 South Acadian Thruway
Baton Rouge, LA 70808-2300

**University of Phoenix: Bay Area**
www.phoenix.edu
3590 North First Street
San Jose, CA 95134-1805

**University of Phoenix: Birmingham**
www.phoenix.edu
100 Corporate Drive
Birmingham, AL 35242

**University of Phoenix: Boston**
www.phoenix.edu
19 Granite Street
Braintree, MA 02184-1744

**University of Phoenix: Central Florida**
www.phoenix.edu
8325 South Park Circle
Orlando, FL 32819

**University of Phoenix: Central Valley**
www.phoenix.edu
45 River Park Place West
Fresno, CA 93720-1552

**University of Phoenix: Charlotte**
www.phoenix.edu
3800 Arco Corporate Drive
Charlotte, NC 28273-3409

**University of Phoenix: Chicago**
www.phoenix.edu
1625 W. Fountainhead Pkwy
Tempe, AZ 85282

**University of Phoenix: Cleveland**
www.phoenix.edu
3401 Enterprise Parkway
Beachwood, OH 44122-7343

**University of Phoenix: Columbia**
www.phoenix.edu
1001 Pinnacle Point Drive
Columbia, SC 29223-5727

**University of Phoenix: Columbus**
www.phoenix.edu
7200 North Lake Drive
Columbus, GA 31909

**University of Phoenix: Dallas Fort Worth**
www.phoenix.edu
12400 Coit Road
Dallas, TX 75251-2004

**University of Phoenix: Denver**
www.phoenix.edu
10004 Park Meadows Drive
Lone Tree, CO 80124-5453

**University of Phoenix: Des Moines**
www.phoenix.edu
1625 West Fountainhead Parkway
Tempe, AZ 85282

**University of Phoenix: Harrisburg**
www.phoenix.edu
1625 West Fountainhead Parkway
Tempe, AZ 85282

**University of Phoenix: Hawaii**
www.phoenix.edu
745 Fort Street
Honolulu, HI 96813

**University of Phoenix: Houston Westside**
www.phoenix.edu
11451 Katy Freeway
Houston, TX 77079-2004

**University of Phoenix: Idaho**
www.phoenix.edu
1422 South Tech Lane
Meridian, ID 83642-5114

**University of Phoenix: Indianapolis**
www.phoenix.edu
1625 West Fountainhead Parkway
Tempe, AZ 85282

**University of Phoenix: Jackson**
www.phoenix.edu
1625 W. Fountainhead Pkwy
Tempe, AZ 85282

**University of Phoenix: Jersey City**
www.phoenix.edu
100 Town Square Place
Jersey City, NJ 07310-1756

**University of Phoenix: Kansas City**
www.phoenix.edu
1625 W. Fountainhead Parkway
Tempe, AZ 85282

**University of Phoenix: Knoxville**
www.phoenix.edu
10133 Sherrill Boulevard
Knoxville, TN 37932-3347

**University of Phoenix: Las Vegas**
www.phoenix.edu
3755 Breakthrough Way
Las Vegas, NV 89135-3047

**University of Phoenix: Little Rock**
www.phoenix.edu
10800 Financial Center Parkway
Little Rock, AR 72211-3552

**University of Phoenix: Louisiana**
www.phoenix.edu
One Galleria Boulevard, Suite 725
Metairie, LA 70001-2082

**University of Phoenix: Louisville**
www.phoenix.edu
10400 Linn Station Road
Louisville, KY 40223-3839

**University of Phoenix: Maryland**
www.phoenix.edu
8830 Stanford Boulevard
Columbia, MD 21045

**University of Phoenix: Memphis**
www.phoenix.edu
65 Germantown Court
Cordova, TN 38018-7290

**University of Phoenix: Metro Detroit**
www.phoenix.edu
26261 Evergreen Road
Southfield, MI 48076-4400

**University of Phoenix: Milwaukee**
www.phoenix.edu
10850 West Park Place
Milwaukee, WI 53224-3606

**University of Phoenix: Minneapolis-St. Paul**
www.phoenix.edu
435 Ford Road
Saint Louis Park, MN 55426

**University of Phoenix: Nashville**
www.phoenix.edu
616 Marriott Drive
Nashville, TN 37214-5048

**University of Phoenix: New Mexico**
www.phoenix.edu
5700 Pasadena Avenue NE
Albuquerque, NM 87113-1570

**University of Phoenix: North Florida**
www.phoenix.edu
4500 Salisbury Road
Jacksonville, FL 32216

**University of Phoenix: Northern Nevada**
www.phoenix.edu
10345 Professional Circle
Reno, NV 89521-5862

**University of Phoenix: Northern Virginia**
www.phoenix.edu
11730 Plaza America Drive
Reston, VA 20190-4750

**University of Phoenix: Northwest Arkansas**
www.phoenix.edu
1625 West Fountainhead Parkway
Tempe, AZ 85282

**University of Phoenix: Oklahoma City**
www.phoenix.edu
1625 West Fountainhead Parkway
Tempe, AZ 85282

**University of Phoenix: Oregon**
www.phoenix.edu
13221 Southwest 68th Parkway
Tigard, OR 97223-8328

**University of Phoenix: Philadelphia**
www.phoenix.edu
1625 West Fountainhead Parkway
Tempe, AZ 85282

**University of Phoenix: Phoenix-Hohokam**
www.phoenix.edu
1625 West Fountainhead Parkway
Tempe, AZ 85282-2371

**University of Phoenix: Pittsburgh**
www.phoenix.edu
1625 West Fountainhead Parkway
Tempe, AZ 85282

**University of Phoenix: Puerto Rico**
www.phoenix.edu
1625 W. Fountainhead Pkwy
Tempe, AZ 85282

**University of Phoenix: Raleigh**
www.phoenix.edu
5511 Capital Center Drive, Suite 390
Raleigh, NC 27606-3380

**University of Phoenix: Richmond**
www.phoenix.edu
9750 West Broad Street
Glen Allen, VA 23060-4169

**University of Phoenix: Sacramento Valley**
www.phoenix.edu
2860 Gateway Oaks Drive
Sacramento, CA 95833-4334

**University of Phoenix: San Antonio**
www.phoenix.edu
8200 IH010 West
San Antonio, TX 78230-3876

**University of Phoenix: San Diego**
www.phoenix.edu
9645 Granite Ridge Drive
San Diego, CA 92123-2658

**University of Phoenix: Savannah**
www.phoenix.edu
1625 West Fountainhead Parkway
Tempe, AZ 85282

**University of Phoenix: Shreveport**
www.phoenix.edu
350 Plaza Loop Drive
Bossier City, LA 71111-4390

**University of Phoenix: South Florida**
www.phoenix.edu
2400 SW 145th Street
Miramar, FL 33027-4145

**University of Phoenix: Southern Arizona**
www.phoenix.edu
300 South Craycroft Road
Tucson, AZ 85711-4574

**University of Phoenix: Southern California**
www.phoenix.edu
3100 Bristol Street
Costa Mesa, CA 92626-3099

**University of Phoenix: Southern Colorado**
www.phoenix.edu
5725 Mark Dabling Boulevard
Colorado Springs, CO 80919-2221

**University of Phoenix: St. Louis**
www.phoenix.edu
13801 Riverport Drive
St. Louis, MO 63043-4828

**University of Phoenix: Tulsa**
www.phoenix.edu
1625 West Fountainhead Parkway
Tempe, AZ 85282

**University of Phoenix: Utah**
www.phoenix.edu
5373 South Green Street
Salt Lake City, UT 84123-4642

**University of Phoenix: Washington DC**
www.phoenix.edu
25 Massachusetts Avenue NW
Washington, DC 20001-1431

**University of Phoenix: West Florida**
www.phoenix.edu
12802 Tampa Oaks Boulevard
Temple Terrace, FL 33637-1920

**University of Phoenix: West Michigan**
www.phoenix.edu
318 River Ridge Drive NW
Walker, MI 49544-1683

**University of Phoenix: Western Washington**
www.phoenix.edu
1625 West Fountainhead Parkway
Tempe, AZ 85282

**University of Pikeville**
www.upike.edu
International Student and Scholar Services
147 Sycamore Street
Pikeville, KY 41501-1194
Fax: (606) 218-5255
E-mail: DiannWhitter@upike.edu
Phone: (606) 218-5741

**University of Pittsburgh**
www.pitt.edu
Admissions and Financial Aid
4227 Fifth Avenue, 1st Floor, Alumni Hall
Pittsburgh, PA 15260
Fax: (412) 624-8184
E-mail: intladm@pitt.edu
Phone: (412) 624-7488

**University of Pittsburgh at Bradford**
www.upb.pitt.edu
Associate Vice President Enrollment
Management
300 Campus Drive
Bradford, PA 16701
Fax: (814) 362-5150
E-mail: admissions@upb.pitt.edu
Phone: (814) 362-7555

**University of Pittsburgh at Greensburg**
www.greensburg.pitt.edu
Office of Admissions
150 Finoli Drive
Greensburg, PA 15601
Fax: (724) 836-7471
E-mail: upgadmit@pitt.edu
Phone: (724) 836-9885

**University of Pittsburgh at Johnstown**
www.upj.pitt.edu
Office of International Services
450 Schoolhouse Road, 157 Blackington Hall
Johnstown, PA 15904-1200
Fax: (814) 269-7044
E-mail: jskist@pitt.edu
Phone: (814) 269-7049

**University of Pittsburgh at Titusville**
www.upt.pitt.edu
Office of Admissions and Student Aid
UPT Admissions Office
504 East Main Street
Titusville, PA 16354-0287
Fax: (412) 624-7105
E-mail: uptadm@pitt.edu
Phone: (412) 624-7125

**University of Portland**
www.up.edu
Office of Admissions
5000 North Willamette Boulevard
Portland, OR 97203-5798
Fax: (503) 943-7315
E-mail: mcdonaja@up.edu
Phone: (503) 943-7147

**University of the Potomac**
www.potomac.edu
Admissions
4000 Chesapeake Street NW
Washington, DC 20016
Fax: (703) 709-8972
E-mail: danny.carrasco@potomac.edu
Phone: (703) 442-3555

**University of the Potomac**
www.potomac.edu
International Student Services
2070 Chain Bridge Road
Vienna, VA 22182
Fax: (703) 709-8972
E-mail: omega.barrow@potomac.edu
Phone: (202) 521-1298

**University of Puerto Rico: Aguadilla**
www.uprag.edu
Admissions Office
Box 6150
Aguadilla, PR 00604-6150
Fax: (787) 890-4543
E-mail: melba.serrano@upr.edu
Phone: (787) 890-2681 ext. 2280

**University of Puerto Rico: Arecibo**
www.upra.edu
PO Box 4010
Arecibo, PR 00614-4010
Fax: (787) 817-3461
E-mail: magaly.mendez@upr.edu
Phone: (787) 815-0000 ext. 4101

**University of Puerto Rico: Bayamon University College**
www.uprb.edu
174 Street #170 Minillas Industrial Park
Bayamon, PR 00959-1919
Fax: (787) 993-8929
E-mail: cmontes@uprb.edu
Phone: (787) 993-8952

**University of Puerto Rico: Carolina Regional College**
www.uprc.edu
Admissions Office
PO Box 4800
Carolina, PR 00984-4800
Fax: (787) 750-7940
E-mail: celia.mendez@upr.edu
Phone: (787) 757-1485

**University of Puerto Rico: Cayey University College**
www.cayey.upr.edu
Admissions Office
Universidad de Puerto Rico en Cayey Oficina de Admisiones
PO Box 372230
Cayey, PR 00737-2230
Fax: (787) 738-5633
E-mail: arturo.collado@upr.edu
Phone: (787) 738-2161 ext. 2233

**University of Puerto Rico: Humacao**
www.uprh.edu
Director of Admissions
Call Box 860
Humacao, PR 00792
Fax: (787) 850-9428
E-mail: milagros.alvarez@upr.edu
Phone: (787) 850-9301

**University of Puerto Rico: Mayaguez**
www.uprm.edu
International Students Office
Admissions Office
PO Box 9000
Mayaguez, PR 00681-9000
Fax: (787) 265-5432
E-mail: gildreth@uprm.edu
Phone: (787) 265-3896

**University of Puerto Rico: Medical Sciences**
www.rcm.upr.edu
PO Box 365067
San Juan, PR 00936-5067
Fax: (787) 282-7117
E-mail: maribel.ortiz5@upr.edu
Phone: (787) 758-2525 ext. 5211

**University of Puerto Rico: Ponce**
www.uprp.edu
Director of Admissions
Box 7186
Ponce, PR 00732
Fax: (787) 840-8108
E-mail: avelazquez@uprp.edu
Phone: (787) 844-8181 ext. 2530

**University of Puerto Rico: Rio Piedras**
www.uprrp.edu
Box 21907
San Juan, PR 00931-1907
Fax: (787) 763-5733
E-mail: luis.irizarry9@upr.edu
Phone: (787) 764-0000 ext. 86200

**University of Puerto Rico: Utuado**
uprutuado.edu
Admissions
PO Box 2500
Utuado, PR 00641
Fax: (787) 894-2891
E-mail: maria.robles4@upr.edu
Phone: (787) 894-2828 ext. 2212

**University of Puget Sound**
www.pugetsound.edu
Assistant Director of Admission
1500 North Warner Street
CMB #1062
Tacoma, WA 98416-1062
Fax: (253) 879-3993
E-mail: admission@pugetsound.edu
Phone: (253) 879-3211

**University of Redlands**
www.redlands.edu
Associate Dean, Director of International Recruitment
1200 East Colton Avenue
PO Box 3080
Redlands, CA 92373-0999
Fax: (909) 335-4089
E-mail: admissions@redlands.edu
Phone: (909) 748-8074

**University of Rhode Island**
www.uri.edu
Office of Admission
Newman Hall
14 Upper College Road
Kingston, RI 02881-1322
Fax: (401) 874-5523
E-mail: internationaladmission@uri.edu
Phone: (401) 874-7100

**University of Richmond**
www.richmond.edu
Queally Center for Admissions and Career Services
30 UR Drive
University of Richmond, VA 23173
Fax: (804) 287-6535
E-mail: intladm@richmond.edu
Phone: (804) 289-8640

**University of Rio Grande**
www.rio.edu
Student Services
218 North College Avenue
Box F-30
Rio Grande, OH 45674
Fax: (749) 245-7341
E-mail: aquinn@rio.edu
Phone: (740) 245-7126

**University of Rochester**
www.rochester.edu
Admissions
300 Wilson Boulevard
Box 270251
Rochester, NY 14627-0251
Fax: (585) 461-4595
E-mail: international@ur.rochester.edu
Phone: (585) 275-3221

**University of Saint Francis**
www.sf.edu
Admissions
2701 Spring Street
Fort Wayne, IN 46808
Fax: (260) 399-8152
E-mail: srobinson@sf.edu
Phone: (260) 399-7700 ext. 6309

**University of Saint Joseph**
www.usj.edu
Admissions
1678 Asylum Avenue
West Hartford, CT 06117
Fax: (860) 231-5744
E-mail: admissions@usj.edu
Phone: (860) 231-5216

**University of San Diego**
www.sandiego.edu
Admissions Office
5998 Alcala Park
San Diego, CA 92110-2492
Fax: (619) 260-6836
E-mail: msmalloy@sandiego.edu
Phone: (619) 260-4506

**University of San Francisco**
www.usfca.edu
Director, International Admission
2130 Fulton Street
San Francisco, CA 94117-1080
Fax: (415) 422-5172
E-mail: admission@usfca.edu
Phone: (415) 422-4172

**University of Science and Arts of Oklahoma**
www.usao.edu
Office of Admissions
1727 West Alabama
Chickasha, OK 73018-5322
Fax: (405) 574-1220
E-mail: usao-admissions@usao.edu
Phone: (405) 574-1357

**University of the Sciences**
www.usciences.edu
Student Affairs
600 South 43rd Street
Philadelphia, PA 19104-4495
Fax: (215) 895-1100
E-mail: w.perry@usciences.edu
Phone: (215) 596-8890

**University of Scranton**
www.scranton.edu
Admissions Office
800 Linden Street
The Estate
Scranton, PA 18510-4699
Fax: (570) 941-5995
E-mail: caitlyn.hollingshead@scranton.edu
Phone: (570) 941-4416

**University of Sioux Falls**
www.usiouxfalls.edu
Admissions Office
1101 West 22nd Street
Sioux Falls, SD 57105-1699
Fax: (605) 331-6615
E-mail: admissions@usiouxfalls.edu
Phone: (800) 888-1047

**University of South Alabama**
www.southalabama.edu
Office of International Services
Meisler Hall, Suite 2500
307 University Boulevard North
Mobile, AL 36688-0002
Fax: (251) 414-8213
E-mail:
internationalservices@southalabama.edu
Phone: (251) 460-6050

**University of South Carolina: Aiken**
http://web.usca.edu/
Admissions Office
471 University Parkway
Aiken, SC 29801-6399
Fax: (803) 641-3727
E-mail: admit@usca.edu
Phone: (803) 641-3366

**University of South Carolina: Beaufort**
www.uscb.edu
Admissions Office
One University Boulevard
Bluffton, SC 29909
Fax: (843) 208-8290
E-mail: mrwilli5@uscb.edu
Phone: (843) 208-8112

**University of South Carolina: Columbia**
www.sc.edu
Undergraduate Admissions Office
Office of Undergraduate Admissions
902 Sumter St Access/Lieber College
Columbia, SC 29208
Fax: (803) 777-0101
E-mail: MCCLARYF@mailbox.sc.edu
Phone: (803) 777-7700

**University of South Carolina: Lancaster**
usclancaster.sc.edu
Admissions
PO Box 889
Lancaster, SC 29721
Fax: (803) 313-7116
E-mail: jpjones1@mailbox.sc.edu
Phone: (803) 313-7073

**University of South Carolina: Sumter**
www.uscsumter.edu
Admissions
200 Miller Road
Sumter, SC 29150-2498
Fax: (803) 938-3901
E-mail: kbritton@uscsumter.edu
Phone: (803) 938-3882

**University of South Carolina: Union**
uscunion.sc.edu
PO Drawer 729
Union, SC 29379
Fax: (864) 424-8085
Phone: (864) 429-8728

**University of South Carolina: Upstate**
www.uscupstate.edu
Admissions
800 University Way
Spartanburg, SC 29303
Fax: (864) 503-5727
E-mail: dstewart@uscupstate.edu
Phone: (864) 503-5280

**University of South Dakota**
www.usd.edu
International Student Services
414 East Clark Street
Vermillion, SD 57069-2390
Fax: (605) 677-4260
E-mail: isso@usd.edu
Phone: (605) 677-6061

**University of South Florida**
www.usf.edu
International Admissions
4202 East Fowler Avenue, SVC 1036
Tampa, FL 33620-9951
Fax: (813) 974-2662
E-mail: international@usf.edu
Phone: (813) 974-8884

**University of South Florida: Saint Petersburg**
www.usfsp.edu
140 Seventh Avenue South
St. Petersburg, FL 33701
E-mail: admissions@usfsp.edu
Phone: (727) 873-4142

**University of South Florida: Sarasota-Manatee**
www.usfsm.edu
Global Engagement Office
8350 North Tamiami Trail
SMC107
Sarasota, FL 34243
Fax: (941) 359-4585
E-mail: amela@usf.edu
Phone: (941) 359-4314

**University of Southern California**
www.usc.edu
Dean of Admission
Office of Admission
University Park
Los Angeles, CA 90089-0911
Fax: (213) 740-1556
E-mail: admdean@usc.edu
Phone: (213) 740-6753

**University of Southern Indiana**
www.usi.edu
Center for International Programs
8600 University Boulevard
Evansville, IN 47712
Fax: (812) 465-7154
E-mail: gahan@usi.edu
Phone: (812) 465-1248

**University of Southern Maine**
www.usm.maine.edu
Office of International Programs
PO Box 9300
Portland, ME 04104
Fax: (207) 780-4933
E-mail: ksink@usm.maine.edu
Phone: (207) 780-4550

**University of Southern Mississippi**
www.usm.edu
Office of International Student and Scholar Services
118 College Drive #5166
Hattiesburg, MS 39406-0001
Fax: (601) 266-4898
E-mail: isss@usm.edu
Phone: (601) 266-4841

**University of the Southwest**
www.usw.edu
Office of Enrollment Management
6610 North Lovington Highway, #506
Hobbs, NM 88240
Fax: (575) 392-6006
E-mail: mgoar@usw.edu
Phone: (575) 492-2161

**University of St. Francis**
www.stfrancis.edu
Admissions
500 Wilcox Street
Joliet, IL 60435-6169
Fax: (815) 740-4282
E-mail: rmorley@stfrancis.edu
Phone: (800) 735-7500

**University of St. Mary**
www.stmary.edu
Office of Admission
4100 South Fourth Street Trafficway
Leavenworth, KS 66048
Fax: (913) 758-6307
E-mail: admiss@stmary.edu
Phone: (800) 752-7043

**University of St. Thomas**
www.stthomas.edu
2115 Summit Avenue, Mail 5017
Saint Paul, MN 55105
Fax: (651) 962-6160
E-mail: international@stthomas.edu
Phone: (651) 962-6150

**University of St. Thomas**
www.stthom.edu
Director of International Student and Scholar Services
3800 Montrose Boulevard
Houston, TX 77006-4626
Fax: (713) 525-3896
E-mail: isss@stthom.edu
Phone: (713) 525-3503

**University of Tampa**
www.ut.edu
Office of Admissions
401 West Kennedy Boulevard
Tampa, FL 33606-1490
Fax: (813) 258-7398
E-mail: admissions@ut.edu
Phone: (813) 253-6211

**University of Tennessee: Chattanooga**
www.utc.edu
International Student Services
615 McCallie Avenue
University Center #101, Dept 5105
Chattanooga, TN 37403
Fax: (423) 425-4081
E-mail: Eunice-Davis@utc.edu
Phone: (423) 425-2110

**University of Tennessee: Knoxville**
www.utk.edu
Office of Undergraduate Admissions
320 Student Services Building, Circle Park
Knoxville, TN 37996-0230
E-mail: broadhea@utk.edu
Phone: (865) 974-1151

**University of Tennessee: Martin**
www.utm.edu
International Programs Office
201 Administration Building
Martin, TN 38238
Fax: (731) 881-7322
E-mail: afenning@utm.edu
Phone: (731) 881-7353

**University of Texas at Arlington**
www.uta.edu
Admissions
UTA Box 19088
Arlington, TX 76019
Fax: (817) 272-5114
E-mail: jrussel@uta.edu
Phone: (817) 272-3252

**University of Texas at Austin**
www.utexas.edu
Graduate and International Admission Center
PO Box 8058
Austin, TX 78713-8058
Fax: (512) 475-7395
E-mail: pat.ellison@austin.utexas.edu
Phone: (512) 475-7398

**University of Texas at Dallas**
www.utdallas.edu
Enrollment Services
Admission and Enrollment Services
800 West Campbell Road
Richardson, TX 75080-3021
Fax: (972) 883-2599
E-mail: interest@utdallas.edu
Phone: (972) 883-2270

**University of Texas at El Paso**
www.utep.edu
Office of International Programs
500 West University Avenue
El Paso, TX 79968
Fax: (915) 747-8893
E-mail: oip@utep.edu
Phone: (915) 747-5664

**University of Texas at San Antonio**
www.utsa.edu
International Programs
One UTSA Circle
San Antonio, TX 78249-0617
Fax: (210) 458-7222
E-mail: internationalprograms@utsa.edu
Phone: (210) 458-7995

**University of Texas at Tyler**
www.uttyler.edu
Admissions
3900 University Boulevard
Tyler, TX 75799
Fax: (903) 566-7068
E-mail: admrequest@uttyler.edu
Phone: (903) 566-7080

**University of Texas Health Science Center at Houston**
www.uth.tmc.edu
Office of International Affairs
Box 20036
Houston, TX 77225
Fax: (713) 500-3189
E-mail: admissions@uth.tmc.edu
Phone: (713) 500-3176

**University of Texas Medical Branch at Galveston**
www.utmb.edu
301 University Boulevard
Galveston, TX 77555-1305
Fax: (409) 772-4466
E-mail: enrollment.services@utmb.edu
Phone: (409) 772-1215

**University of Texas of the Permian Basin**
www.utpb.edu
Admissions
4901 East University
Odessa, TX 79762
Fax: (432) 552-3605
E-mail: admissions@utpb.edu
Phone: (432) 552-2605

**University Of Texas Rio Grande Valley**
www.utrgv.edu
International Admissions and Student Services
Office of Global Engagement
1201 West University Drive
Edinburg, TX 78539
Fax: (856) 665-2687
E-mail: Jessica.Cantu@utrgv.edu
Phone: (956) 882-8298

**University of Toledo**
www.utoledo.edu
Office of Undergraduate Admissions
2801 West Bancroft Street
Toledo, OH 43606-3390
Fax: (419) 530-5713
E-mail: mark.schroeder5@utoledo.edu
Phone: (419) 530-1213

**University of Tulsa**
utulsa.edu
International Student Services
Office of Admission
800 South Tucker Drive
Tulsa, OK 74104-3189
Fax: (918) 631-3322
E-mail: inst@utulsa.edu
Phone: (918) 631-2329

**University of Utah**
www.utah.edu
Admissions Office
201 South 1460 East
Room 250 S
Salt Lake City, UT 84112-9057
Fax: (801) 585-7864
E-mail: iao@sa.utah.edu
Phone: (801) 581-8761

**University of Valley Forge**
www.valleyforge.edu
Admissions
1401 Charlestown Road
Phoenixville, PA 19460-2373
Fax: (610) 917-2069
E-mail: mscernero@valleyforge.edu
Phone: (800) 432-8322

**University of Vermont**
www.uvm.edu
Admissions
194 South Prospect Street
Burlington, VT 05401-3596
Fax: (802) 656-8611
E-mail: admissions@uvm.edu
Phone: (802) 656-4620

**University of Virginia**
www.virginia.edu
Office of Undergraduate Admission
Box 433160
Charlottesville, VA 22904-4160
Fax: (434) 924-3587
E-mail: undergradadmission@virginia.edu
Phone: (434) 982-3200

**University of Virginia's College at Wise**
www.uvawise.edu
Chancellor for Enrollment Management
1 College Avenue
Wise, VA 24293-4412
Fax: (276) 328-0251
E-mail: rdn2f@uvawise.edu
Phone: (276) 328-0104

**University of Washington**
www.washington.edu
Office of Admissions
1410 Northeast Campus Parkway, Box 355852
Seattle, WA 98195-5852
Fax: (206) 543-9772
E-mail: intladm@u.washington.edu
Phone: (206) 616-3867

**University of Washington Bothell**
www.uwb.edu
Director of Admissions
Box 358500, Enrollment Management
Bothell, WA 98011
Fax: (425) 352-5455
E-mail: uwbintl@uw.edu
Phone: (425) 352-5000

**University of Washington Tacoma**
www.tacoma.uw.edu
International Student Services
Campus Box 358430
1900 Commerce Street
Tacoma, WA 98402-3100
Fax: (253) 692-4414
E-mail: uwtiss@uw.edu
Phone: (253) 692-4695

**University of the West**
www.uwest.edu
Office of Admissions
1409 North Walnut Grove Avenue
Rosemead, CA 91770
Fax: (626) 571-1413
E-mail: admission@uwest.edu
Phone: (626) 656-2120

**University of West Alabama**
www.uwa.edu
Director of International Programs
Station 4
Livingston, AL 35470
Fax: (205) 652-5510
E-mail: mdavis@uwa.edu
Phone: (205) 652-3570

**University of West Florida**
www.uwf.edu
Office of Admissions
11000 University Parkway
Pensacola, FL 32514-5750
Fax: (850) 474-3360
E-mail: admissions@uwf.edu
Phone: (850) 474-2115

**University of West Georgia**
www.westga.edu
International Student Admissions & Programs
1601 Maple Street
Carrollton, GA 30118
Fax: (678) 839-5509
E-mail: isp@westga.edu
Phone: (678) 839-4780

**University of Wisconsin-Baraboo/Sauk County**
www.baraboo.uwc.edu
Associate Registrar
1006 Connie Road
Baraboo, WI 53913-1098
Fax: (608) 356-0752
E-mail: lori.turner@uwc.edu
Phone: (608) 356-8351 ext. 255

**University of Wisconsin-Barron County**
www.barron.uwc.edu
Associate Registrar
1800 College Drive
Rice Lake, WI 54868
Fax: (715) 234-8024
E-mail: lori.turner@uwc.edu
Phone: (715) 234-8176

**University of Wisconsin-Eau Claire**
www.uwec.edu
Center for International Education
111 Schofield Hall
Eau Claire, WI 54701
Fax: (715) 836-4948
E-mail: marchwcc@uwec.edu
Phone: (715) 836-4411

**University of Wisconsin-Fox Valley**
www.uwfox.uwc.edu
1478 Midway Road
Menasha, WI 54952-2850
Fax: (920) 832-2850
Phone: (920) 832-2620

**University of Wisconsin-Green Bay**
www.uwgb.edu
Office of International Student Services
2420 Nicolet Drive
Green Bay, WI 54311-7001
Fax: (920) 465-2949
E-mail: oie@uwgb.edu
Phone: (920) 465-2889

**University of Wisconsin-La Crosse**
www.uwlax.edu
Office of International Education
1725 State Street, Cleary Center
La Crosse, WI 54601
Fax: (608) 785-8923
E-mail: uwlworld@uwlax.edu
Phone: (608) 785-8922

**University of Wisconsin-Madison**
www.wisc.edu
Office of Undergraduate Admissions and Recruitment
702 West Johnson Street, Suite 1101
Madison, WI 53715-1007
Fax: (608) 262-7706
E-mail: onwisconsin@admissions.wisc.edu
Phone: (608) 262-3961

**University of Wisconsin-Marathon County**
www.uwmc.uwc.edu
Associate Registrar
518 South Seventh Avenue
Wausau, WI 54401-5396
Fax: (715) 261-6331
E-mail: lori.turner@uwc.edu
Phone: (715) 261-6100

**University of Wisconsin-Marinette**
www.marinette.uwc.edu
Associate Registrar
750 West Bay Shore Street
Marinette, WI 54143
Fax: (715) 735-4304
E-mail: lori.turner@uwc.edu
Phone: (715) 735-4301

**University of Wisconsin-Marshfield/Wood County**
www.marshfield.uwc.edu
Associate Registrar
2000 West Fifth Street
Marshfield, WI 54449
Fax: (608) 265-9473
E-mail: lori.turner@uwc.edu
Phone: (608) 262-9652

**University of Wisconsin-Milwaukee**
www.uwm.edu
International Admissions
P.O. Box 413
Milwaukee, WI 53201
Fax: (414) 229-0521
E-mail: isss@uwm.edu
Phone: (414) 229-2276

**University of Wisconsin-Oshkosh**
www.uwosh.edu
Dean of Students
800 Algoma Boulevard
Oshkosh, WI 54901-8602
Fax: (920) 424-1207
E-mail: jgraf@uwosh.edu
Phone: (920) 424-3100

**University of Wisconsin-Parkside**
www.uwp.edu
Admissions
PO Box 2000
Kenosha, WI 53141-2000
Fax: (262) 595-2008
E-mail: moldenht@uwp.edu
Phone: (262) 595-2355

**University of Wisconsin-Platteville**
www.uwplatt.edu
Office of Admission
One University Plaza
Platteville, WI 53818
Fax: (608) 342-1122
E-mail: admit@uwplatt.edu
Phone: (608) 342-1125

**University of Wisconsin-Richland**
www.richland.uwc.edu
Coordinator of International Education
1200 Highway 14 West
Richland Center, WI 53581
Fax: (608) 647-2275
E-mail: emery.sanchez@uwc.edu
Phone: (608) 647-6186 ext. 246

**University of Wisconsin-River Falls**
www.uwrf.edu
Director of Admissions
410 South 3rd Street
112 South Hall
River Falls, WI 54022-5001
Fax: (715) 425-0676
E-mail: sarah.r.egerstrom@uwrf.edu
Phone: (715) 425-3500

**University of Wisconsin-Rock County**
www.rock.uwc.edu
Associate Registrar
2909 Kellogg Avenue
Janesville, WI 53546-5699
Fax: (608) 758-6579
E-mail: lori.turner@uwc.edu
Phone: (608) 262-9652

**University of Wisconsin-Sheboygan**
www.sheboygan.uwc.edu
Student Affairs
One University Drive
Sheboygan, WI 53081
Fax: (920) 459-6602
E-mail: bryan.bain@uwc.edu
Phone: (920) 459-6633

**University of Wisconsin-Stevens Point**
www.uwsp.edu
International Students and Scholars Office
Student Services Center
1108 Fremont Street Room 102
Stevens Point, WI 54481
Fax: (715) 346-3819
E-mail: isso@uwsp.edu
Phone: (715) 346-3849

**University of Wisconsin-Stout**
www.uwstout.edu
International Education
1 Clocktower Plaza
Menomonie, WI 54751
Fax: (715) 232-2500
E-mail: kuesterv@uwstout.edu
Phone: (715) 232-2132

**University of Wisconsin-Superior**
www.uwsuper.edu
Director
Belknap and Catlin
PO Box 2000
Superior, WI 54880
Fax: (715) 394-8363
E-mail: mmaclean@uwsuper.edu
Phone: (715) 394-8052

**University of Wisconsin-Washington County**
www.washington.uwc.edu
Associate Registrar
400 University Drive
West Bend, WI 53095
Fax: (262) 335-5274
E-mail: jessica.cole@uwc.edu
Phone: (608) 970-0

**University of Wisconsin-Waukesha**
www.waukesha.uwc.edu
Director of International Education
1500 North University Drive
Waukesha, WI 53188
Fax: (262) 521-5530
E-mail: tim.urbonya@uwc.edu
Phone: (608) 263-9676

**University of Wisconsin-Whitewater**
www.uww.edu
International Education and Programs
800 West Main Street
Whitewater, WI 53190-1790
Fax: (262) 472-1491
E-mail: chenowec@uww.edu
Phone: (262) 472-5759

**University of Wyoming**
www.uwyo.edu
International Students and Scholars Office
Dept 3435
1000 East University Avenue
Laramie, WY 82071
Fax: (307) 766-4053
E-mail: uwglobal@uwyo.edu
Phone: (307) 766-5193

**Upper Iowa University**
www.uiu.edu
Center for International Education
Parker Fox Hall
PO Box 1859
Fayette, IA 52142
Fax: (563) 425-5833
E-mail: international@uiu.edu
Phone: (563) 425-5884

**Urbana University**
www.urbana.edu
Director of the International Office
579 College Way
Urbana, OH 43078
Fax: (937) 652-6871
E-mail: rschumacher@urbana.edu
Phone: (937) 652-6809

**Ursinus College**
www.ursinus.edu
Admissions
PO Box 1000
601 East Main Street
Collegeville, PA 19426-1000
Fax: (610) 409-3197
E-mail: admission@ursinus.edu
Phone: (610) 409-3200

**Ursuline College**
www.ursuline.edu
Admission
2550 Lander Road
Pepper Pike, OH 44124-4398
Fax: (440) 684-6114
E-mail: stephanie.ratkovich@ursuline.edu
Phone: (440) 449-4203

**Utah State University**
www.usu.edu
Office of Global Engagement
0160 Old Main Hill
Logan, UT 84322-0160
Fax: (435) 797-0136
E-mail: usuintl@usu.edu
Phone: (435) 797-1124

**Utah Valley University**
www.uvu.edu
International Admissions
800 West University Parkway
Orem, UT 84058-5999
Fax: (801) 225-4677
E-mail: whaleyco@uvu.edu
Phone: (801) 863-8466 ext. 8475

**Utica College**
www.utica.edu
Dean of International Education
1600 Burrstone Road
Utica, NY 13502-4892
Fax: (315) 792-3003
E-mail: dmlewis1@utica.edu
Phone: (315) 792-3340

**Utica School of Commerce**
www.uscny.edu
201 Bleecker Street
Utica, NY 13501
Fax: (315) 733-9281
E-mail: admissions@uscny.edu
Phone: (315) 733-2307

**Valdosta State University**
www.valdosta.edu
International Programs
1500 North Patterson Street
Valdosta, GA 31698-0170
Fax: (229) 245-3849
E-mail: inikolov@valdosta.edu
Phone: (229) 333-7410

**Valencia College**
www.valenciacollege.edu
Admissions and Records
PO Box 3028
Orlando, FL 32802-3028
Fax: (407) 582-1403
E-mail: Lherlocker@valenciacollege.edu
Phone: (407) 582-1506

**Valley City State University**
www.vcsu.edu
Enrollment Services
101 College Street SW
Valley City, ND 58072-4098
Fax: (701) 845-7299
E-mail: jessica.oday@vcsu.edu
Phone: (701) 845-7112

**Valley Forge Military College**
www.vfmac.edu
1001 Eagle Road
Wayne, PA 19087
Fax: (610) 688-1545
E-mail: ddreese@vfmac.edu
Phone: (610) 989-1307

**Valparaiso University**
www.valpo.edu
Office of Undergraduate Admission
Kretzmann Hall, 1700 Chapel Drive
Valparaiso, IN 46383-6493
Fax: (219) 464-6898
E-mail: Laura.Coleman@valpo.edu
Phone: (219) 464-5011

**Vance-Granville Community College**
www.vgcc.edu
Registrar
Box 917
Henderson, NC 27536
Fax: (252) 430-0460
E-mail: edwardsl@vgcc.edu
Phone: (252) 492-2061

**Vanderbilt University**
www.vanderbilt.edu
Undergraduate Admissions
2305 West End Avenue
Nashville, TN 37203-1727
Fax: (615) 343-8326
E-mail: admissions@vanderbilt.edu
Phone: (615) 936-2811

**VanderCook College of Music**
www.vandercook.edu
Admissions
3140 South Federal Street
Chicago, IL 60616-3731
Fax: (312) 225-5211
E-mail: admissions@vandercook.edu
Phone: (312) 788-1120

**Vanguard University of Southern California**
www.vanguard.edu
Undergraduate Admissions
55 Fair Drive
Costa Mesa, CA 92626-9601
Fax: (714) 966-5471
E-mail: nichole.wike@vanguard.edu
Phone: (714) 556-3610

**Vassar College**
www.vassar.edu
Office of Admissions
Box 10, 124 Raymond Avenue
Poughkeepsie, NY 12604-0077
Fax: (845) 437-7063
E-mail: admissions@vassar.edu
Phone: (845) 437-7300

**Vatterott College: Berkeley**
www.vatterott-college.edu
8580 Evans Avenue
Berkeley, MO 63134
Fax: (314) 522-6174
E-mail: adm@vatterot-college.edu
Phone: (314) 264-1040

**Vatterott College: Cleveland**
www.vatterott-college.edu
5025 East Royalton Road
Broadview Heights, OH 44147
Fax: (440) 526-1933
E-mail: cleveland@vatterott-college.edu
Phone: (440) 526-1660

**Vatterott College: Des Moines**
www.vatterott-college.edu
7000 Fleur Drive
Des Moines, IA 50321
Fax: (515) 309-0366
E-mail: desmoines@vatterott-college.edu
Phone: (515) 309-9000

**Vatterott College: Joplin**
www.vatterott.edu
809 Illinois Avenue
Joplin, MO 64801
Phone: (417) 781-5633

**Vatterott College: Kansas City**
www.vatterott.edu
8955 East 38th Terrace
Kansas City, MO 64129
Fax: (816) 861-1400
E-mail: kc@vatterott-college.edu
Phone: (816) 861-1000

**Vatterott College: Memphis**
www.vatterott.edu
2655 Dividend Drive
Memphis, TN 38132
Fax: (901) 763-2897
E-mail: paulette.thomas@vatterott-college.edu
Phone: (901) 761-5730

**Vatterott College: O'Fallon**
www.vatterott-college.edu
3350 West Clay Street
St. Charles, MO 63301
Fax: (636) 978-5121
E-mail: ofallon@vatterott-college.edu
Phone: (636) 978-7488

**Vatterott College: Oklahoma City**
www.vatterott.edu
5537 Northwest Expressway
Oklahoma City, OK 73132
Fax: (405) 945-0788
Phone: (405) 945-0088

**Vatterott College: Quincy**
www.vatterott.edu
3609 North Marx Drive
Quincy, IL 62305
Fax: (217) 223-6771
Phone: (217) 224-0600

**Vatterott College: Sunset Hills**
www.vatterott.edu
12900 Maurer Industrial Drive
Sunset Hills, MO 63127
E-mail: jessalyn.mckeown@vatterott-college.edu
Phone: (314) 843-4200

**Vatterott College: Tulsa**
www.vatterott.edu
4343 South 118th East Avenue
Tulsa, OK 74146
Fax: (918) 836-9698
E-mail: tulsa@vatterott-college.edu
Phone: (918) 835-8288

**Vaughn College of Aeronautics and Technology**
www.vaughn.edu
International Student Admissions
8601 23rd Avenue
Flushing, NY 11369
Fax: (718) 779-2231
E-mail: david.griffey@vaughn.edu
Phone: (718) 429-6600 ext. 117

**Ventura College**
www.venturacollege.edu
Admissions & Records
4667 Telegraph Road
Ventura, CA 93003
Fax: (805) 654-6357
E-mail: sbricker@vcccd.edu
Phone: (805) 654-6457

**Vet Tech Institute**
www.vettechinstitute.edu
125 Seventh Street
Pittsburgh, PA 15222-3400
Fax: (412) 232-4348
E-mail: admissions@vettechinstitute.edu
Phone: (412) 391-7021

**Vet Tech Institute of Houston**
www.bradfordschools.com
4669 Southwest Freeway
Houston, TX 77027
E-mail: mortiz@bradfordschoolhouston.edu
Phone: (713) 629-1500

**Victor Valley College**
www.vvc.edu
Admissions and Records
18422 Bear Valley Road
Victorville, CA 92392-5850
Fax: (760) 843-7707
E-mail: millenb@vvc.edu
Phone: (760) 245-4271 ext. 2668

**Victoria College**
www.victoriacollege.edu
Director of Enrollment Services
2200 East Red River
Victoria, TX 77901
Fax: (361) 582-2525
E-mail: edrel.stoneham@victoriacollege.edu
Phone: (361) 572-6407

**Villa Maria College of Buffalo**
www.villa.edu
Admissions
240 Pine Ridge Road
Buffalo, NY 14225-3999
Fax: (716) 896-0705
E-mail: admissions@villa.edu
Phone: (716) 896-0700 ext. 1870

**Villanova University**
www.villanova.edu
Admission
Austin Hall, 800 Lancaster Avenue
Villanova, PA 19085-1672
Fax: (610) 519-6450
E-mail: gotovu@villanova.edu
Phone: (610) 519-4000

**Vincennes University**
www.vinu.edu
Admissions
1002 North First Street
Vincennes, IN 47591
Fax: (812) 888-5707
E-mail: intstudent@vinu.edu
Phone: (812) 888-4319

**Virginia College in Augusta**
www.vc.edu/campus/augusta-georgia-college.cfm
2807 Wylds Road
Augusta, GA 30909
Fax: (706) 288-2599
E-mail: augusta.info@vc.edu
Phone: (706) 288-2500

**Virginia College in Austin**
www.vc.edu/campus/austin-texas-college.cfm
6301 E. Highway 290
Austin, TX 78723
Fax: (512) 371-3502
Phone: (512) 371-3500

**Virginia College in Baton Rouge**
www.vc.edu/campus/baton-rouge-louisiana-college.cfm
9501 Cortana Place
Baton Rouge, LA 70815
Fax: (225) 236-3999
E-mail: batonrouge.info@vc.edu
Phone: (225) 236-3900

**Virginia College in Biloxi**
www.vc.edu/college/biloxi-colleges-mississippi.cfm
920 Cedar Lake Road
Biloxi, MS 39532
Fax: (228) 392-2039
Phone: (228) 392-2994

**Virginia College in Birmingham**
www.vc.edu/campus/birmingham-alabama-college.cfm
488 Palisades Boulevard
Birmingham, AL 35209
Fax: (205) 271-8225
Phone: (205) 802-1200

**Virginia College in Charleston**
www.vc.edu/college/charleston-colleges.cfm
6185 Rivers Avenue
North Charleston, SC 29406
E-mail: charleston.info@vc.edu
Phone: (843) 614-4300

**Virginia College in Columbia**
www.vc.edu/college/columbia-colleges.cfm
7201 Two Notch Road
Columbia, SC 29223
E-mail: columbia.info@vc.edu
Phone: (803) 509-7100

**Virginia College in Columbus**
www.vc.edu/college/columbus-georgia-colleges.cfm
5601 Veterans Parkway
Columbus, GA 31904
E-mail: columbus.info@vc.edu
Phone: (762) 207-1600

**Virginia College in Florence**
www.vc.edu/florence
2400 David H. McLeod Boulevard
Florence, SC 29501
E-mail: florence.info@vc.edu
Phone: (843) 407-2200

**Virginia College in Greensboro**
www.vc.edu/greensboro
3740 S. Holden Road
Greensboro, NC 27406
E-mail: greensboro.info@vc.edu
Phone: (336) 398-5400

**Virginia College in Greenville**
www.vc.edu/campus/greenville-south-carolina-college.cfm
78 Global Drive
Greenville, SC 29607
E-mail: greenville.info@vc.edu
Phone: (864) 679-4900

**Virginia College in Jackson**
www.vc.edu
4795 Interstate 55 North
Jackson, MS 39206
Fax: (601) 977-2719
E-mail: mtlittle@vc.edu
Phone: (601) 977-0960

**Virginia College in Jacksonville**
www.jacksonville.vc.edu
5940 Beach Boulevard
Jacksonville, FL 32207
E-mail: jacksonville.info@vc.edu
Phone: (904) 520-7400

**Virginia College in Macon**
www.vc.edu/campus/macon-georgia-college.cfm
1901 Paul Walsh Drive
Macon, GA 31206
E-mail: macon.info@vc.edu
Phone: (478) 803-4600

**Virginia College in Mobile**
www.vc.edu
3725 Airport Boulevard, Suite 165
Mobile, AL 36608
Fax: (251) 343-7287
Phone: (251) 343-7227

**Virginia College in Montgomery**
www.vc.edu
6200 Atlanta Highway
Montgomery, AL 36117
Phone: (334) 277-3390

**Virginia College in Pensacola**
www.vc.edu/pensacola
19 West Garden Street
Pensacola, FL 32502
Fax: (850) 436-4838
E-mail: melanie.parlier@vc.edu
Phone: (850) 436-8444

**Virginia College in Richmond**
www.richmond.vc.edu
7200 Midlothian Turnpike
Richmond, VA 23225
E-mail: richmond.info@vc.edu
Phone: (804) 977-5100

**Virginia College in Savannah**
www.vc.edu/campus/savannah-georgia-college.cfm
14045 Abercorn Street, Suite 1503
Savannah, GA 31419
E-mail: savannah.info@vc.edu
Phone: (912) 721-5600

**Virginia College in Shreveport**
www.vc.edu/shreveport
2950 East Texas Street, Suite C
Bossier City, LA 71111
E-mail: shreveport.info@vc.edu

**Virginia College in Spartanburg**
www.spartanburg.vc.edu
8150 Warren H. Abernathy Highway
Spartanburg, SC 29301
E-mail: spartanburg.info@vc.edu
Phone: (864) 504-3200

**Virginia College in Tulsa**
www.vc.edu/college/tulsa-oklahoma-colleges.cfm
5124 South Peoria Avenue
Tulsa, OK 74105
E-mail: tulsa.info@vc.edu

**Virginia College School of Business and Health in Chattanooga**
www.chattanooga.vc.edu
721 Eastgate Loop
Chattanooga, TN 37411
E-mail: chattanooga.info@vc.edu

**Virginia College School of Business and Health in Knoxville**
www.vc.edu/knoxville
5003 North Broadway Street
Knoxville, TN 37918
E-mail: knoxville.info@vc.edu
Phone: (865) 745-4500

**Virginia Commonwealth University**
www.vcu.edu
Office of International Admissions
Box 842526
Richmond, VA 23284-2526
Fax: (804) 828-1829
E-mail: vcuia@vcu.edu
Phone: (804) 828-6016

**Virginia Marti College of Art and Design**
www.vmcad.edu
Admissions
11724 Detroit Avenue
Lakewood, OH 44107
Fax: (216) 221-2311
E-mail: mmiller@vmcad.edu
Phone: (216) 221-8584

**Virginia Military Institute**
www.vmi.edu
Admissions
VMI Office of Admissions
319 Letcher Avenue
Lexington, VA 24450-9967
Fax: (540) 464-7746
E-mail: admissions@vmi.edu
Phone: (540) 464-7211

**Virginia Polytechnic Institute and State University**
www.vt.edu
925 Prices Fork Road
Blacksburg, VA 24061
Fax: (540) 231-3242
E-mail: admissions@vt.edu
Phone: (540) 231-6267

**Virginia State University**
www.vsu.edu
International Education
1 Hayden Drive
PO Box 9018
Petersburg, VA 23806
Fax: (804) 524-5466
E-mail: fmarshall@vsu.edu
Phone: (804) 524-5928

**Virginia Union University**
www.vuu.edu
Office of Admissions
1500 North Lombardy Street
Richmond, VA 23220
Fax: (804) 342-3511
E-mail: admissions@vuu.edu
Phone: (804) 342-3571

**Virginia University of Lynchburg**
www.vul.edu
Registrar
2058 Garfield Avenue
Lynchburg, VA 24501-6417
Fax: (434) 528-2705
E-mail: dsmith@vul.edu
Phone: (434) 528-5276 ext. 102

**Virginia Wesleyan College**
www.vwc.edu
Admissions Office
1584 Wesleyan Drive
Norfolk, VA 23502-5599
Fax: (757) 461-5238
E-mail: admissions@vwc.edu
Phone: (757) 455-3208

**Virginia Western Community College**
www.virginiawestern.edu
Student Services
3094 Colonial Avenue
Roanoke, VA 24013
Fax: (540) 857-6163
E-mail: smeixner@virginiawestern.edu
Phone: (540) 857-6711

**Visible Music College**
www.visible.edu
200 Madison Avenue
Memphis, TN 38103
Fax: (901) 377-0544
E-mail: seeyourself@visible.edu
Phone: (901) 377-2991

**Vista College: Online**
www.vistacollege.edu
1785 E. 1450 S. Suite 300
Clearfield, UT 84015
E-mail: admissions@vistacollege.edu
Phone: (801) 774-9900

**Viterbo University**
www.viterbo.edu
Admissions
900 Viterbo Drive
La Crosse, WI 54601-8804
Fax: (608) 796-3020
E-mail: krfelts@viterbo.edu
Phone: (608) 796-3171

**Volunteer State Community College**
www.volstate.edu
Assistant Director of Records & Registration
1480 Nashville Pike
Gallatin, TN 37066-3188
Fax: (615) 230-3645
E-mail: pam.carey@volstate.edu
Phone: (615) 452-8600 ext. 3558

**Voorhees College**
www.voorhees.edu
Office of Admissions
213 Wiggins Road
PO Box 678
Denmark, SC 29042
Fax: (803) 780-1444
E-mail: williej@voorhees.edu
Phone: (803) 780-1049

**W.L. Bonner Bible College**
www.wlbc.edu
4430 Argent Court
Columbia, SC 29203
Fax: (803) 333-9349
Phone: (803) 726-3496

**Wabash College**
www.wabash.edu
Coordinator of International Admissions
PO Box 352
Crawfordsville, IN 47933
Fax: (765) 361-6437
E-mail: weira@wabash.edu
Phone: (765) 361-6254

**Wade College**
www.wadecollege.edu
Director of Financial Services
1950 North Stemmons Freeway, Suite 4080
LB #562
Dallas, TX 75207
Fax: (214) 637-0827
E-mail: lhoover@wadecollege.edu
Phone: (214) 637-3530

**Wagner College**
www.wagner.edu
Admissions
One Campus Road
Pape Admissions Building
Staten Island, NY 10301
Fax: (718) 390-3105
E-mail: allen.koehler@wagner.edu
Phone: (718) 420-4526

**Wake Forest University**
www.wfu.edu
Associate Dean of Admissions
PO Box 7305
Winston-Salem, NC 27109-7305
Fax: (336) 758-3227
E-mail: bridgelm@wfu.edu
Phone: (336) 758-4621

**Wake Technical Community College**
www.waketech.edu
International Student Coordinator
9101 Fayetteville Road
Raleigh, NC 27603
Fax: (919) 661-0117
E-mail: pmsolomon@waketech.edu
Phone: (919) 866-5426

**Walden University**
www.waldenu.edu
Admissions
100 Washington Avenue South, Suite 900
Minneapolis, MN 55401
E-mail: peter.scanlan@mail.waldenu.edu
Phone: (410) 206-9015

**Waldorf University**
www.waldorf.edu
Admissions
106 South Sixth Street
Forest City, IA 50436-1713
Fax: (641) 585-8125
E-mail: international@waldorf.edu
Phone: (641) 585-8117

**Walla Walla Community College**
www.wwcc.edu
Admissions and Records
500 Tausick Way
Walla Walla, WA 99362-9972
Fax: (509) 527-3661
E-mail: carlos.delgadillo@wwcc.edu
Phone: (509) 527-4282

**Walla Walla University**
www.wallawalla.edu
Admissions
204 South College Avenue
College Place, WA 99324-3000
Fax: (509) 527-2397
E-mail: dallas.weis@wallawalla.edu
Phone: (800) 541-8900 ext. 2608

**Wallace State Community College at Hanceville**
www.wallacestate.edu
Admissions
801 Main Street NW/PO Box 2000
Hanceville, AL 35077-2000
Fax: (256) 352-8129
E-mail: jim.milligan@wallacestate.edu
Phone: (256) 352-8256

**Walsh College of Accountancy and Business Administration**
www.walshcollege.edu
Coordinator, International Students
PO Box 7006
Troy, MI 48007-7006
Fax: (248) 823-1611
E-mail: admissions@walshcollege.edu
Phone: (248) 823-1235

**Walsh University**
www.walsh.edu
Admissions
2020 East Maple Street
North Canton, OH 44720-3396
Fax: (330) 490-7165
E-mail: admissions@walsh.edu
Phone: (330) 490-7172

**Walters State Community College**
www.ws.edu
Enrollment Development
500 South Davy Crockett Parkway
Morristown, TN 37813-6899
Fax: (423) 585-6786
E-mail: sherry.watson@ws.edu
Phone: (423) 585-2691

**Warner Pacific College**
www.warnerpacific.edu
Vice President for Enrollment and Marketing
2219 SE 68th Avenue
Portland, OR 97215-4026
Fax: (503) 517-1352
E-mail: dseipp@warnerpacific.edu
Phone: (503) 517-1020

**Warner University**
www.warner.edu
Admissions
13895 Highway 27
Lake Wales, FL 33859
Fax: (863) 638-7290
E-mail: jason.roe@warner.edu
Phone: (863) 638-7213

**Warren Wilson College**
www.warren-wilson.edu
Office of Admission
PO Box 9000
Asheville, NC 28815-9000
Fax: (828) 298-1440
E-mail: slytle@warren-wilson.edu
Phone: (828) 771-2075

**Wartburg College**
www.wartburg.edu
Office of Admissions
100 Wartburg Boulevard, PO Box 1003
Waverly, IA 50677-0903
Fax: (319) 352-8579
E-mail: global.admissions@wartburg.edu
Phone: (319) 352-8511

**Washburn University**
www.washburn.edu
International Student Services
1700 SW College Avenue, Morgan 100
Topeka, KS 66621
Fax: (785) 670-1067
E-mail: heidi.staerkel@washburn.edu
Phone: (785) 670-2087

**Washington & Jefferson College**
www.washjeff.edu
Admission Office
60 South Lincoln Street
Washington, PA 15301
Fax: (724) 223-6534
E-mail: kcrosby@washjeff.edu
Phone: (724) 503-1001 ext. 6025

**Washington Adventist University**
www.wau.edu
Director of Admissions
7600 Flower Avenue
Takoma Park, MD 20912
Fax: (301) 891-4563
E-mail: enroll@wau.edu
Phone: (301) 891-4080

**Washington and Lee University**
www.wlu.edu
Admissions
204 West Washington Street
Lexington, VA 24450-2116
Fax: (540) 458-8062
E-mail: admissions@wlu.edu
Phone: (540) 458-8710

**Washington College**
www.washcoll.edu
300 Washington Avenue
Chestertown, MD 21620-1197
Fax: (410) 778-7287
E-mail: tlittlefield2@washcoll.edu
Phone: (410) 778-7700

**Washington County Community College**
www.wccc.me.edu
Admissions
One College Drive
Calais, ME 04619
Fax: (207) 454-1092
E-mail: smingo@wccc.me.edu
Phone: (207) 454-1000

**Washington State Community College**
www.wscc.edu
710 Colegate Drive
Marietta, OH 45750
Fax: (740) 373-7496
E-mail: admissions@wscc.edu
Phone: (740) 568-1900

**Washington State University**
www.wsu.edu
International Programs, Admissions
370 Lighty Student Services Bldg
PO Box 641067
Pullman, WA 99164-1067
Fax: (509) 335-2373
E-mail: international@wsu.edu
Phone: (509) 335-3188

**Washington University in St. Louis**
https://www.wustl.edu
Office of Undergraduate Admissions
Campus Box 1089, One Brookings Drive
St. Louis, MO 63130-4899
Fax: (314) 935-4290
E-mail: admissions@wustl.edu
Phone: (314) 935-6000

**Washtenaw Community College**
www.wccnet.edu
Enrollment Services
4800 East Huron River Drive
Ann Arbor, MI 48105-4800
Fax: (734) 677-5414
E-mail: laeilts@wccnet.edu
Phone: (734) 973-3315

**Watkins College of Art, Design & Film**
www.watkins.edu
Admissions Office
2298 Rosa L. Parks Boulevard
Nashville, TN 37228
Fax: (615) 383-4849
E-mail: admissions@watkins.edu
Phone: (615) 383-4848 ext. 7458

**Wayland Baptist University**
www.wbu.edu
Admissions
1900 West Seventh Street, CMB #1294
Plainview, TX 79072
Fax: (806) 291-1960
E-mail: admityou@wbu.edu
Phone: (806) 291-3500

**Wayne County Community College**
www.wcccd.edu
International Programs/Global Partnerships
801 West Fort Street
Detroit, MI 48226
Fax: (313) 962-0324
E-mail: IPGP@wcccd.edu
Phone: (313) 496-2756

**Wayne State College**
www.wsc.edu
Admissions Office
1111 Main Street
Wayne, NE 68787
Fax: (402) 375-7204
E-mail: admit1@wsc.edu
Phone: (402) 375-7234

**Wayne State University**
www.wayne.edu
Office of Admissions
PO Box 02759
Detroit, MI 48202-0759
Fax: (313) 577-7536
E-mail: admissions@wayne.edu
Phone: (313) 577-3577

**Waynesburg University**
www.waynesburg.edu
Admission Counselor
51 West College Street
Waynesburg, PA 15370-1222
Fax: (724) 627-8124
E-mail: rdbarnha@waynesburg.edu
Phone: (724) 852-3346

**Weatherford College**
www.wc.edu
225 College Park Drive
Weatherford, TX 76086
Fax: (817) 598-6205
E-mail: lhines@wc.edu
Phone: (817) 598-6468

**Webber International University**
www.webber.edu
Admissions
1201 North Scenic Highway
PO Box 96
Babson Park, FL 33827-0096
Fax: (863) 638-1591
E-mail: picardRP@webber.edu
Phone: (863) 638-2910

**Weber State University**
https://www.weber.edu
Director of International Student Services
1137 University Circle
Ogden, UT 84408-1137
Fax: (801) 626-7693
E-mail: memami@weber.edu
Phone: (801) 626-7534

**Webster University**
www.webster.edu
International Recruitment and International
Services
470 East Lockwood Avenue
St. Louis, MO 63119-3194
Fax: (314) 246-7122
E-mail: intlstudy@webster.edu
Phone: (314) 246-7860

**Welch College**
www.welch.edu
Enrollment Services
3606 West End Avenue
Nashville, TN 37205-2403
Fax: (615) 269-6028
E-mail: jketteman@welch.edu
Phone: (615) 844-5214

**Wellesley College**
www.wellesley.edu
Admissions Office
106 Central Street
Wellesley, MA 02481-8203
Fax: (781) 283-3678
E-mail: mmareva@wellesley.edu
Phone: (781) 283-2270

**Wells College**
www.wells.edu
Admissions
170 Main Street
Aurora, NY 13026
Fax: (315) 364-3227
E-mail: admissions@wells.edu
Phone: (315) 364-3264

**Wentworth Institute of Technology**
www.wit.edu
Admissions Office
550 Huntington Avenue
Boston, MA 02115
Fax: (617) 989-4010
E-mail: macdonaldt1@wit.edu
Phone: (617) 989-4006

**Wentworth Military Junior College**
www.wma.edu
1880 Washington Avenue
Lexington, MO 64067-1799
Fax: (660) 259-3395
E-mail: admissions@wma1880.org
Phone: (660) 259-2221 ext. 517

**Wesley College**
www.wesley.edu
120 North State Street
Dover, DE 19901-3875
Fax: (302) 736-2382
E-mail: rebecca.miller2@wesley.edu
Phone: (302) 736-2411

**Wesleyan College**
www.wesleyancollege.edu
Admissions
4760 Forsyth Road
Macon, GA 31210-4462
Fax: (478) 757-4030
E-mail: admission@wesleyancollege.edu
Phone: (478) 757-5206

**Wesleyan University**
www.wesleyan.edu
Office of Admission
70 Wyllys Avenue
Middletown, CT 06459-0260
Fax: (860) 685-3001
E-mail: toverton@wesleyan.edu
Phone: (860) 685-3000

**West Chester University of Pennsylvania**
www.wcupa.edu
Assistant Director of International Admissions
Emil H. Messikomer Hall
100 West Rosedale Avenue
West Chester, PA 19383
Fax: (610) 436-2436
E-mail: international@wcupa.edu
Phone: (610) 436-6963

**West Hills College: Coalinga**
www.westhillscollege.com
300 Cherry Lane
Coalinga, CA 93210
Fax: (559) 934-2852
E-mail: danieltamayo@whccd.edu
Phone: (559) 934-2432

**West Hills College: Lemoore**
www.westhillscollege.com
Daniel Tamayo
555 College Avenue
Lemoore, CA 93245
Fax: (559) 925-3837
E-mail: danieltamayo@whccd.edu
Phone: (559) 934-2000 ext. 2432

**West Liberty University**
www.westliberty.edu
208 University Drive
West Liberty, WV 26074
Fax: (304) 336-8403
E-mail: admissions@westliberty.edu
Phone: (304) 336-8076

**West Los Angeles College**
www.wlac.edu
Dean
9000 Overland Avenue
Culver City, CA 90230
Fax: (310) 287-4327
E-mail: IchonE@wlac.edu
Phone: (310) 287-4305

**West Tennessee Business College**
www.wtbc.edu
1186 Highway 45 Bypass
Jackson, TN 38301
E-mail: sheree.bradford@wtbc.edu
Phone: (731) 668-7240

**West Texas A&M University**
www.wtamu.edu
International Student Office
WTAMU Box 60907
Canyon, TX 79016-0001
Fax: (806) 651-2071
E-mail: kcombs@mail.wtamu.edu
Phone: (806) 651-2073

**West Valley College**
www.westvalley.edu
Counseling Center - Foreign Student Adviser
14000 Fruitvale Avenue
Saratoga, CA 95070-5698
Fax: (408) 867-5033
E-mail: Sara_Patterson@wvm.edu
Phone: (408) 741-2009

**West Virginia Junior College: Bridgeport**
www.wvjc.edu
176 Thompson Drive
Bridgeport, WV 26330
Fax: (304) 842-8191
E-mail: admissions@wvjcinfo.net
Phone: (304) 842-4007 ext. 110

**West Virginia Northern Community College**
www.wvncc.edu
Dean of Enrollments Management
1704 Market Street
Wheeling, WV 26003
Fax: (304) 232-8187
E-mail: jfike@northern.wvnet.edu
Phone: (304) 233-5900 ext. 4363

**West Virginia State University**
www.wvstateu.edu
Assistant Director International Affairs
124 Ferrell Hall
PO Box 1000
Institute, WV 25112-1000
Fax: (304) 766-3097
E-mail: mnorman@wvstateu.edu
Phone: (304) 204-3097

**West Virginia University**
www.wvu.edu
International Admissions
Office of Admissions
PO Box 6009
Morgantown, WV 26506-6009
Fax: (304) 293-8832
E-mail: internationaladmissions@mail.wvu.edu
Phone: (304) 293-2121

**West Virginia University at Parkersburg**
www.wvup.edu
Enrollment Management
300 Campus Drive
Parkersburg, WV 26104-8647
Fax: (304) 424-8332
E-mail: Christine.Post@mail.wvu.edu
Phone: (304) 424-8221

**West Virginia University Institute of Technology**
www.wvutech.edu
Director of Admissions
405 Fayette Pike
Montgomery, WV 25136-2436
Fax: (304) 442-3097
E-mail: tech-admissions@mail.wvu.edu
Phone: (304) 442-3146

**West Virginia Wesleyan College**
www.wvwc.edu
Admission
59 College Avenue
Buckhannon, WV 26201-2998
Fax: (304) 473-8108
E-mail: admission@wvwc.edu
Phone: (304) 473-8510

**Westchester Community College**
www.sunywcc.edu
International and Immigrant Student Affairs
75 Grasslands Road
Valhalla, NY 10595
Fax: (914) 606-5629
E-mail: Anne.Verini@sunywcc.edu
Phone: (914) 606-8567

**Western Carolina University**
www.wcu.edu
International Programs and Services
102 Camp Building
Cullowhee, NC 28723
Fax: (828) 227-7080
E-mail: lmwaniki@email.wcu.edu
Phone: (828) 227-7494

**Western Connecticut State University**
www.wcsu.edu
Undergraduate Admissions
181 White Street
Danbury, CT 06810-6826
Fax: (203) 837-8338
E-mail: admissions@wcsu.edu
Phone: (203) 837-9000

**Western Dakota Technical Institute**
www.wdt.edu
800 Mickelson Drive
Rapid City, SD 57703
Fax: (605) 394-2204
E-mail: admissions@wdt.edu
Phone: (605) 718-2411

**Western Illinois University**
www.wiu.edu
Center for International Studies
1 University Circle
115 Sherman Hall
Macomb, IL 61455-1390
Fax: (309) 298-2245
E-mail: international-ed@wiu.edu
Phone: (309) 298-2426

**Western Iowa Tech Community College**
www.witcc.edu
Global Education
Box 5199
Sioux City, IA 51102-5199
Fax: (712) 274-6412
E-mail: terry.yi@witcc.edu
Phone: (712) 274-8733 ext. 1820

**Western Kentucky University**
www.wku.edu
International Admissions
1906 College Heights Boulevard #11020
Bowling Green, KY 42101
Fax: (270) 745-6133
E-mail: iem@wku.edu
Phone: (270) 745-4857

**Western Michigan University**
https://wmich.edu/
International Admissions and Services
1903 West Michigan Avenue
Kalamazoo, MI 49008-5211
Fax: (269) 387-5899
E-mail: juan.tavares@wmich.edu
Phone: (269) 387-5866

**Western Nebraska Community College**
www.wncc.edu
Student Services
1601 East 27th Street
Scottsbluff, NE 69361
Fax: (308) 635-6732
E-mail: international@wncc.edu
Phone: (308) 635-6026

**Western Nevada College**
www.wnc.edu
Admission and Records
2201 West College Parkway
Carson City, NV 89703-7399
Fax: (775) 445-1347
E-mail: Dianne.Hilliard@wnc.edu
Phone: (775) 445-3288

**Western New England University**
www.wne.edu
Admissions
1215 Wilbraham Road
Springfield, MA 01119-2684
Fax: (413) 782-1777
E-mail: learn@wne.edu
Phone: (413) 782-1321

**Western New Mexico University**
www.wnmu.edu
Admissions
Castorena 106
Box 680
Silver City, NM 88062
Fax: (575) 538-6127
E-mail: laram@wnmu.edu
Phone: (575) 538-6000

**Western Oklahoma State College**
www.wosc.edu
2801 North Main Street
Altus, OK 73521
Fax: (580) 477-7723
E-mail: lana.scott@wosc.edu
Phone: (580) 477-7720

**Western Oregon University**
www.wou.edu
International Students and Scholar Affairs
345 North Monmouth Avenue
Monmouth, OR 97361
Fax: (503) 838-8425
E-mail: yangn@wou.edu
Phone: (503) 838-8590

**Western State Colorado University**
www.western.edu
International Student Programs
600 North Adams Street
Gunnison, CO 81231
Fax: (970) 943-2702
E-mail: kwheaton@western.edu
Phone: (970) 943-3216

**Western Technical College**
www.westerntech.edu
9624 Plaza Circle
El Paso, TX 79927
Fax: (915) 532-6946
Phone: (915) 532-3737

**Western Technical College**
www.westerntc.edu
Counseling Center
400 Seventh Street North
La Crosse, WI 54601
Fax: (608) 785-9094
E-mail: EnrollServices@westerntc.edu
Phone: (608) 785-9575

**Western Technical College: Diana Drive**
www.westerntech.edu
9451 Diana Drive
El Paso, TX 79924
Fax: (915) 565-9903
Phone: (915) 566-9621

**Western Texas College**
www.wtc.edu
Director of International Student Services
6200 College Avenue
Snyder, TX 79549
Fax: (866) 265-9240
E-mail: mdoucette@wtc.edu
Phone: (325) 574-7650

**Western Washington University**
www.wwu.edu
Office of Admissions
516 High Street
Bellingham, WA 98225-9009
Fax: (360) 650-7369
E-mail: admit@wwu.edu
Phone: (360) 650-3966

**Western Wyoming Community College**
www.westernwyoming.edu
Admissions
Box 428
Rock Springs, WY 82902-0428
Fax: (307) 382-1636
E-mail: admissions@wwcc.wy.edu
Phone: (307) 382-1648

**Westfield State University**
www.westfield.ma.edu
Office of Admissions
577 Western Avenue
PO Box 1630
Westfield, MA 01086-1630
Fax: (413) 572-0520
E-mail:
internationaladmission@westfield.ma.edu
Phone: (413) 572-5218

**Westminster College**
www.westminster-mo.edu
Office of Off-Campus and International
Programs
501 Westminster Avenue
Fulton, MO 65251-1299
Fax: (573) 592-5251
E-mail: robert.anderson@westminster-mo.edu
Phone: (573) 592-5147

**Westminster College**
www.westminster.edu
Office of Admissions
Remick Hall, Westminster College
319 South Market Street
New Wilmington, PA 16172-0001
Fax: (724) 946-7171
E-mail: chapmadm@westminster.edu
Phone: (724) 946-6125

**Westminster College**
www.westminstercollege.edu
Admissions Office
1840 South 1300 East
Salt Lake City, UT 84105
Fax: (801) 832-3101
E-mail: admission@westminstercollege.edu
Phone: (801) 832-2200

**Westmont College**
www.westmont.edu
Assistant Director of Admissions and
Admissions Counselor for Transfers and
International Students
955 La Paz Road
Santa Barbara, CA 93108-1089
Fax: (805) 565-6234
E-mail: mmckinniss@westmont.edu
Phone: (805) 565-6819

**Westmoreland County Community College**
www.wccc.edu
Admissions
145 Pavilion Lane
Youngwood, PA 15697
Fax: (724) 925-4292
E-mail: littles@wccc.edu
Phone: (724) 925-4064

**Westwood College: Denver North**
www.westwood.edu/locations/colorado/denver-
north-campus
International Admissions
7350 North Broadway
Denver, CO 80221
Fax: (303) 487-0214
E-mail: krushak@westwood.edu
Phone: (303) 975-5003

**Wharton County Junior College**
www.wcjc.edu
Admissions Office
911 Boling Highway
Wharton, TX 77488-0080
Fax: (979) 532-6494
E-mail: maryanng@wcjc.edu
Phone: (979) 532-6454

**Whatcom Community College**
www.whatcom.ctc.edu
International Programs Office
237 West Kellogg Road
Bellingham, WA 98226
Fax: (360) 383-3241
E-mail: international@whatcom.ctc.edu
Phone: (360) 383-3245

**Wheaton College**
www.wheaton.edu
Undergraduate Admissions
501 College Avenue
Wheaton, IL 60187-5593
Fax: (630) 752-5285
E-mail: becky.wilson@wheaton.edu
Phone: (630) 752-5011

**Wheaton College**
www.wheatoncollege.edu
Office of Admission
26 East Main Street
Norton, MA 02766
Fax: (508) 286-8271
E-mail: admission@wheatoncollege.edu
Phone: (508) 286-3781

**Wheeling Jesuit University**
www.wju.edu
International Student Advisor's Office
316 Washington Avenue
Wheeling, WV 26003-6295
Fax: (304) 243-2243
E-mail: eileenv@wju.edu
Phone: (800) 624-6992 ext. 2346

**Wheelock College**
www.wheelock.edu
Office of Admission
200 The Riverway
Boston, MA 02215-4104
Fax: (617) 879-2449
E-mail: undergrad@wheelock.edu
Phone: (617) 879-2209

**White Earth Tribal and Community
College**
www.wetcc.edu
PO Box 478
Mahnomen, MN 56557
Fax: (218) 936-5736
E-mail: amber.fox@wetcc.edu
Phone: (218) 935-0417 ext. 322

**Whitman College**
www.whitman.edu
Admission
345 Boyer Avenue
Walla Walla, WA 99362-2046
Fax: (509) 527-4967
E-mail: leej@whitman.edu
Phone: (323) 346-6196

**Whittier College**
www.whittier.edu
Admissions
13406 East Philadelphia Street
Whittier, CA 90608-0634
Fax: (562) 907-4870
E-mail: larenste@whittier.edu
Phone: (562) 907-4238

**Whitworth University**
www.whitworth.edu
Undergraduate Admissions
300 West Hawthorne Road
Spokane, WA 99251-2515
Fax: (509) 466-3758
E-mail: mwhalen@whitworth.edu
Phone: (509) 777-4571

**Wichita Area Technical College**
www.watc.edu
Admissions
4004 North Webb Road, Suite 100
Wichita, KS 67226
Fax: (316) 677-9555
E-mail: amcfayden@watc.edu
Phone: (316) 677-9400

**Wichita State University**
www.wichita.edu
Office of International Education
1845 Fairmount, Box 124
Wichita, KS 67260-0124
Fax: (316) 978-3777
E-mail: international@wichita.edu
Phone: (316) 978-3232

**Widener University**
www.widener.edu
Office of Admissions
One University Place
Chester, PA 19013
Fax: (610) 499-4676
E-mail: jbyoung1@widener.edu
Phone: (888) 943-3637

**Wilberforce University**
www.wilberforce.edu
Admissions
1055 North Bickett Road
PO Box 1001
Wilberforce, OH 45384-1001
Fax: (937) 376-4751
E-mail: ddriscoll@wilberforce.edu
Phone: (937) 708-5556

**Wiley College**
www.wileyc.edu
711 Wiley Avenue
Marshall, TX 75670
Fax: (903) 927-3366
E-mail: gemitchel@wileyc.edu
Phone: (903) 927-3218 ext. 3218

**Wilkes Community College**
www.wilkescc.edu
1328 South Collegiate Drive
PO Box 120
Wilkesboro, NC 28697-0120
Fax: (336) 838-6547
E-mail: elisabeth.blevins@wilkescc.edu
Phone: (336) 838-6135

**Willamette University**
www.willamette.edu
Office of Admission
900 State Street
Salem, OR 97301-3922
Fax: (503) 375-5363
E-mail: eyandall@willamette.edu
Phone: (844) 232-7228

**William Carey University**
www.wmcarey.edu
Admissions
498 Tuscan Avenue
WCC Box 13
Hattiesburg, MS 39401
Fax: (601) 318-6765
E-mail: bdillon@wmcarey.edu
Phone: (601) 318-6103 ext. 6104

**William Jessup University**
www.jessup.edu
Director of Admissions
2121 University Ave
Rocklin, CA 95765
Fax: (916) 577-2220
E-mail: admissions@jessup.edu
Phone: (916) 577-2222

**William Jewell College**
www.jewell.edu
Office of Admission
500 College Hill
Liberty, MO 64068
Fax: (816) 415-5040
E-mail: parsonsm@william.jewell.edu
Phone: (816) 415-7577

**William Paterson University of New Jersey**
www.wpunj.edu
Admissions
300 Pompton Road
Wayne, NJ 07470
Fax: (973) 720-2910
E-mail: admissions@wpunj.edu
Phone: (973) 720-2125

**William Penn University**
www.wmpenn.edu
Admissions Office
201 Trueblood Avenue
Oskaloosa, IA 52577
Fax: (641) 673-2113
E-mail: strongk@wmpenn.edu
Phone: (641) 673-1012

**William Woods University**
www.williamwoods.edu
Office of Admissions
One University Avenue
Fulton, MO 65251-2388
Fax: (573) 592-1146
E-mail: admissions@williamwoods.edu
Phone: (573) 592-4421

**Williams Baptist College**
www.wbcoll.edu
International Programs
PO Box 3665
Walnut Ridge, AR 72476
Fax: (870) 759-4163
E-mail: awatson@wbcoll.edu
Phone: (870) 759-4120

**Williams College**
www.williams.edu
Admission Office
995 Main Street
Williamstown, MA 01267
Fax: (413) 597-4052
E-mail: admission@williams.edu
Phone: (413) 597-2211

**Williamson College**
www.williamsoncc.edu
274 Mallory Station Road
Franklin, TN 37067
Fax: (615) 771-7810
E-mail: susan@williamsoncc.edu
Phone: (615) 771-7821

**Williston State College**
www.willistonstate.edu
Enrollment Services Office
1410 University Avenue
Williston, ND 58801
Fax: (701) 774-4211
E-mail: leah.windnagle@willistonstate.edu
Phone: (701) 774-4220

**Wilmington College**
www.wilmington.edu
Student Life
Box 1325 Pyle Center
Wilmington, OH 45177
Fax: (937) 382-7077
E-mail: mark_denniston@wilmington.edu
Phone: (937) 382-6661 ext. 264

**Wilson College**
www.wilson.edu
Admissions
1015 Philadelphia Avenue
Chambersburg, PA 17201-1285
Fax: (717) 262-2546
E-mail: kelsey.winton@wilson.edu
Phone: (717) 262-2002

**Wilson Community College**
www.wilsoncc.edu
Student Services
Box 4305
902 Herring Avenue
Wilson, NC 27893-0305
Fax: (252) 246-1384
E-mail: slackner@wilsoncc.edu
Phone: (252) 246-1435

**Wingate University**
https://www.wingate.edu/
Admissions Counselor
220 N. Camden Drive
Wingate, NC 28174-0157
Fax: (704) 233-8110
E-mail: victoria@wingate.edu
Phone: (704) 233-8207

**Winona State University**
www.winona.edu
Office of International Services
Office of Admissions
PO Box 5838
Winona, MN 55987
Fax: (507) 457-2474
E-mail: is@winona.edu
Phone: (507) 457-5303

**Winston-Salem State University**
www.wssu.edu
International Student Affairs
601 Martin Luther King Jr Drive
206 Thompson Center
Winston-Salem, NC 27110
Fax: (336) 750-2079
E-mail: admissions@wssu.edu
Phone: (336) 750-2306

**Winthrop University**
www.winthrop.edu
701 Oakland Avenue
Office of Admissions
Rock Hill, SC 29733
Fax: (803) 323-2340
E-mail: poolela@winthrop.edu
Phone: (803) 323-3441

**Wiregrass Georgia Technical College**
www.wiregrass.edu
Admissions
4089 Val Tech Road
Valdosta, GA 31602
Fax: (229) 333-2153
E-mail: nicole.west@wiregrass.edu
Phone: (229) 333-2100 ext. 4836

**Wisconsin Indianhead Technical College**
www.witc.edu
Registrar
505 Pine Ridge Drive
Shell Lake, WI 54871
Fax: (715) 468-2819
E-mail: shane.evenson@witc.edu
Phone: (715) 468-2815 ext. 2280

**Wisconsin Lutheran College**
www.wlc.edu
8800 West Bluemound Road
Milwaukee, WI 53226-4699
Fax: (414) 443-8547
E-mail: admissions@wlc.edu
Phone: (414) 443-8811

**Wittenberg University**
www.wittenberg.edu
Admission Office
Ward Street and North Wittenberg
PO Box 720
Springfield, OH 45501-0720
Fax: (937) 327-6345
E-mail:
internationaladmission@wittenberg.edu
Phone: (877) 206-0332

**Wofford College**
www.wofford.edu
Admission
429 North Church Street
Spartanburg, SC 29303-3663
Fax: (864) 597-4147
E-mail: admission@wofford.edu
Phone: (864) 597-4168

**Wood Tobe-Coburn School**
www.woodtobecoburn.edu
8 East 40th Street
New York, NY 10016-0190
Fax: (212) 686-9171
Phone: (212) 686-9040

**Woodbury University**
www.woodbury.edu
Admissions
7500 Glenoaks Boulevard
Burbank, CA 91504-1052
Fax: (818) 767-7520
E-mail: admissions@woodbury.edu
Phone: (800) 784-9663

**Woodland Community College**
http://wcc.yccd.edu
2300 East Gibson Road, Building 700
Woodland, CA 95776
E-mail: WCCAdmissionsinfo@yccd.edu
Phone: (530) 661-5700

**Worcester Polytechnic Institute**
www.wpi.edu
Admissions
100 Institute Road
Worcester, MA 01609-2280
Fax: (508) 831-5875
E-mail: intl_admissions@wpi.edu
Phone: (508) 831-5286

**Worcester State University**
www.worcester.edu
Associate Director of Admissions
Office of Undergraduate Admission
486 Chandler Street
Worcester, MA 01602-2597
Fax: (508) 929-8183
E-mail: kdonis@worcester.edu
Phone: (508) 929-8041

**The Workforce Institute's City College**
http://www.citycollege-careers.org/
1231 North Broad Street
Philadelphia, PA 19122
Fax: (267) 592-4189
Phone: (267) 516-0168

**World Mission University**
www.wmu.edu
Admissions Department
500 Shatto Place
Los Angeles, CA 90020
Fax: (213) 385-2332
E-mail: wmuoffice@gmail.com
Phone: (213) 385-2322

**Wright State University**
www.wright.edu
University Center for International Education
3640 Colonel Glenn Highway, 108 SU
Dayton, OH 45435
Fax: (937) 775-3242
E-mail: international-admissions@wright.edu
Phone: (937) 775-4400

**Wright State University: Lake Campus**
http://lake.wright.edu/
University Center for International Education
7600 Lake Campus Drive, State Route 703
Celina, OH 45822-2952
Fax: (937) 775-3242
E-mail: international-admissions@wright.edu
Phone: (937) 775-4400

**Xavier University**
www.xavier.edu
Office of Admission
3800 Victory Parkway
Cincinnati, OH 45207-5311
Fax: (513) 745-4319
E-mail: augustine1@xavier.edu
Phone: (513) 745-3197

**Xavier University of Louisiana**
www.xula.edu
Dean of Admissions
One Drexel Drive
New Orleans, LA 70125-1098
Fax: (504) 520-7920
E-mail: wbrown@xula.edu
Phone: (504) 520-7587

**Yakima Valley Community College**
www.yvcc.edu
Manager, Housing and International Students
PO Box 22520
Yakima, WA 98907-2520
Fax: (509) 574-4882
E-mail: bmugleston@yvcc.edu
Phone: (509) 574-4880

**Yale University**
www.yale.edu
International Admissions
Yale Undergraduate Admissions
Box 208234
New Haven, CT 06520-8234
Fax: (203) 432-9392
E-mail: student.questions@yale.edu
Phone: (203) 432-9300

**Yavapai College**
www.yc.edu
Registration
1100 East Sheldon Street
Prescott, AZ 86301
Fax: (928) 776-2151
E-mail: Marianne.Doyle@yc.edu
Phone: (928) 776-2144

**Yeshiva and Kolel Bais Medrash Elyon**
73 Main Street
Monsey, NY 10952
Phone: (845) 356-7064

**Yeshiva and Kollel Harbotzas Torah**
1049 East 15th Street
Brooklyn, NY 11230
Phone: (718) 692-0208

**Yeshiva Beth Yehuda-Yeshiva Gedolah of Greater Detroit**
24600 Greenfield Road
Oak Park, MI 48237
Fax: (248) 968-8613
Phone: (248) 968-3360

**Yeshiva College of the Nations Capital**
1216 Arcola Avenue
Silver Spring, MD 20902
Phone: (301) 593-2534

**Yeshiva Derech Chaim**
1573 39th Street
Brooklyn, NY 11218-4413
Phone: (718) 438-3070

**Yeshiva D'Monsey Rabbinical College**
2 Roman Boulevard
Monsey, NY 10952
Phone: (845) 352-5852

**Yeshiva Gedolah Imrei Yosef D'Spinka**
1466 56th Street
Brooklyn, NY 11219
Phone: (718) 851-8721 ext. 2103

**Yeshiva Gedolah Rabbinical College**
1140 Alton Road
Miami Beach, FL 33139
Phone: (305) 673-5664

**Yeshiva Gedolah Zichron Moshe**
84 Laurel Park Road
Box 580
South Fallsburg, NY 12779
Fax: (845) 434-1009
Phone: (845) 434-5240

**Yeshiva Karlin Stolin**
1818 54th Street
Brooklyn, NY 11204-1545
Phone: (718) 232-7800

**Yeshiva of Nitra**
www.yeshivaofnitra.org
Pines Bridge Road
Mount Kisco, NY 10549
Phone: (718) 387-0423

**Yeshiva of the Telshe Alumni**
4904 Independence Avenue
Riverdale, NY 10471
Phone: (718) 601-3523

**Yeshiva Shaar Hatorah**
www.shaarhatorah.edu
117-06 84th Avenue
Kew Gardens, NY 11418
Phone: (718) 846-1940

**Yeshiva Shaarei Torah of Rockland**
www.yst.edu
91 West Carlton Road
Suffern, NY 10901
Phone: (845) 352-3431

**Yeshivas Novominsk**
1690 60th Street
Brooklyn, NY 11204
Phone: (718) 438-2727

**Yeshivat Mikdash Melech**
www.mikdashmelech.net
1326 Ocean Parkway
Brooklyn, NY 11230-9963
Fax: (718) 998-9321
E-mail: mikdashmelech@verizon.net
Phone: (718) 339-1090

**Yeshivath Beth Moshe**
930 Hickory Street
Scranton, PA 18505
Fax: (717) 346-2251
Phone: (717) 346-1747

**Yeshivath Viznitz**
25 Phyllis Terrace
Monsey, NY 10952
Phone: (845) 731-3700

**York College**
www.york.edu
1125 East 8th Street
York, NE 68467
Fax: (402) 363-5623
E-mail: dodom@york.edu
Phone: (402) 363-5620

**York College of Pennsylvania**
www.ycp.edu
Admissions
441 Country Club Road
York, PA 17403-3651
Fax: (717) 849-1672
E-mail: iramirez@ycp.edu
Phone: (717) 849-1786

**York County Community College**
www.yccc.edu
Director of Admissions
112 College Drive
Wells, ME 04090
Fax: (207) 641-0837
E-mail: fquistgard@yccc.edu
Phone: (207) 216-4406

**Young Harris College**
www.yhc.edu
Admissions
PO Box 116
Young Harris, GA 30582-0116
Fax: (706) 379-3108
E-mail: nmaddox@yhc.edu
Phone: (706) 379-3111 ext. 5254

**Youngstown State University**
www.ysu.edu
The Center for International Studies and Programs
One University Plaza
Youngstown, OH 44555-0001
Fax: (330) 941-2338
E-mail: cisp@ysu.edu
Phone: (330) 941-2336

**YTI Career Institute: Altoona**
www.yti.edu
2900 Fairway Drive
Altoona, PA 16602
Fax: (814) 944-5309
E-mail: altoonaadmission@yti.edu
Phone: (814) 944-5643

**Yuba College**
http://yc.yccd.edu
Director, Admissions and Enrollment Services
2088 North Beale Road
Marysville, CA 95901
Fax: (530) 741-6872
E-mail: shorn@yccd.edu
Phone: (530) 741-6989

# EducationUSA Advising Centers

NOTE: For the most up to date list of centers, please visit: educationusa.state.gov

## Afghanistan

*Kabul*
KEAC
Sarak Bazar-e Karte 4
International School of Kabul (ISK)
Kabul, Afghanistan
Tel: +93 (0) 795 240 089

*Kabul*
Public Affairs Section, US Embassy
EducationUSA Afghanistan
The Great Massoud Road
Kabul, Afghanistan
Tel: +93 (0) 795 240 089

## Albania

*Tirana*
EducationUSA Advising Center
US Embassy
Universiteti Marin Barleti, Rr. Sami
Frasheri, Nr. 41
Tirana, Albania
Tel: 355 692084436
Web: http://www.educationusa.al

## Algeria

*Algiers*
US Embassy
Educational Advising Center
05 Chemin Cheikh Bachir Ibrahimi
Algiers 16030, Algeria
Tel: 213-770-082-000 ext.2295
Web: //algiers.usembassy.gov/
edu_training.html

## Angola

*Luanda*
EducationUSA Advising Center
Rua Houari Boumedienne, 32,
Miramar, Luanda 6484, Angola
Tel: 244-222-641122
Web: //angola.usembassy.gov/
study_usa.html

## Anguilla, British West Indies

*The Valley*
Anguilla Library Service
The Valley
Anguilla, Leeward Islands
Tel: 264-497-2441

## Antigua and Barbuda

*St. John's*
Antigua State College
Golden Grove
St John's, Antigua and Barbuda
Tel: 268 728 6540

## Argentina

*Buenos Aires*
ICANA-Instituto Cultural
Argentino Norteamericano
Sede Central:
Maipu 672
Buenos Aires
Argentina
Tel: 54-11-5382-1526
Web: www.icana.org.ar

*Buenos Aires*
Fulbright Commission
Educational Adviser
Viamonte 1653, 2 piso
Buenos Aires
Argentina
Tel: 54-11-4814-3561
Web: www.fulbright.edu.arz

*Cordoba*
Instituto de Intercambio Cultural
Argentino Norteamericano
IICANA Dept de Orientacion
Educacional
Dean Funes 454
Cordoba 5000, Argentina
Tel: 54-351-4236396
Web: www.iicana.org/asesoria.html

*Mendoza*
Asociacion Mendocina de
Intercambio Cultural
Argentino Norteamericano
(AMICANA)
Chile 987
Mendoza 5500, Argentina
Tel: 54-261-4236271
Web: www.educationusa.org.ar

*Rosario*
Asociacion Rosarina de
Intercambio Cultural
Argentino Norteamericano
(ARICANA)
Buenos Aires 934
Rosario S2000CEQ, Argentina
Tel: 54-341-4217664
Web: www.educationusa.org.ar

## Armenia

*Yerevan*
EducationUSA Armenia
Advising Center
Yerevan American Councils
4/7 Amiryan Street
Yerevan, Armenia
Tel: 374-10-544-012
Web: www.americancouncils.am

## Australia

*Brisbane*
EducationUSA "Festival Towers"
108 Albert St
Brisbane QLD, Australia
Tel: 61-7-3832-5112

*Melbourne VIC*
EducationUSA - Melbourne
U.S. Consulate General Level 6/
553 St. Kilda Road
Melbourne VIC 3004, Australia
Tel: 61-414-413-416

*Perth WA*
EducationUSA Perth
U.S. Consulate General
16 St. Georges Terrace, Level 4
Perth WA 6000, Australia
Tel: 61-8-9225-6839

*Sydney NSW*
EducationUSA Advising Center
US Consulate General
Level 59, MLC Center
19-29 Martin Place
Sydney NSW 2000, Australia
Tel: 61-2-9373-9226

## Austria

*Vienna (Wien)*
EducationUSA at The Centre International
Universitaire
OeAD International Testing Services
1010 Wien Ebendorferstraße 6, Austria
Tel: 43 (0)1 533 65 33
Web: www.ciu.at

*Vienna (Wien)*
Fulbright Vienna
quartier21/MQ
Museumsplatz 1
1070 Vienna, Austria
Tel: 43-1-236 7878 0
Web: www.fulbright.at/studying -in-the-us/
us-universities-colleges.html

## Azerbaijan

*Baku*
American Councils Azerbaijan
Caspian Business Center
40 J. Jabbarli Street, 2nd Floor
1065 Baku, Azerbaijan
Tel: 994-12-436-75-31
Web: www.americancouncils.az

# EducationUSA Advising Centers

## Bahamas

*Nassau*
EducationUSA advising center at CR2
College Ready Bahamas, Town Center Mall
Baillou Hill Road
Nassau, Bahamas
Tel: (242) 328-8113
Web: www.collegereadybah.com

## Bahrain

*Manama*
US Embassy
Bldg 979, Road 3119, Block 331
Manama, Bahrain
Tel: 973-17-242767
Web: //bahrain.usembassy.gov/resources/
    education-advising.html

## Bangladesh

*Chittagong*
EducationUSA at American Corner,
Chittagong Independent University,
Minhaj Complex,
12 Jamal Khan Road,
Chittagong 4000, Bangladesh
Tel: (88) 031-611262, 031-638464 ext. 123

*Dhaka*
EMK
Midas Center 9th Floor
No. 5, Road 27 (old), Dhanmondi
Dhaka 1209, Bangladesh
Tel: +880-2-9119776

*Dhaka*
EducationUSA at The American Center
U.S. Embassy Dhaka, Progati Sharani, Plot
    No. 1, J Block,
Dhaka 1212, Bangladesh
Tel: 88-02-5566 ext 2000
Web: //dhaka.usembassy.gov/ advising.html

## Barbados

*St. Michael (Bridgetown)*
Counselling and Placement Centre
Barbados Community College
"Eyrie" Howell's Cross Road
BB11058
St. Michael, Barbados
Tel: 246-426-2858 ext. 5254
Web: www.bcc.edu.bb/

## Belarus

*All cities*
European Humanities University
Valakupių g. 5 LT-
10101 Vilnius, Lithuania
Tel: 370 5 274 0622
Web: //belarus-eac.org

## Belgium

*Brussels*
Fulbright Brussels
Boulevard de l'Empereur, 4
Keizerslaan
B-1000, Brussels, Belgium
Tel: 32-2-519.57.72
Web: www.fulbright.be/General_Info/
    Advising_Center.htm

## Belize

*Belize City*
EducationUSA Advising Center
Leo Bradley Library
Princess Margaret Drive
Belize City, Belize
Tel: +1(501)223-4248

## Benin

*Cotonou*
Centre Culturel Americain
Boulevard de France
Pres du Conseil de l'Entente
Cotonou, Benin
Tel: 229-21-30 03 12
Web: //cotonou.usembassy.gov/
    advising_office.html

## Bermuda

EducationUSA Advising Center
Counselling and Career Centre
2nd Level Library Building, Bermuda
    College
Paget PG 04, Bermuda
Tel: 441 239-4018

## Bolivia

*Cochabamba*
EducationUSA Advising Center, CBA
    Cochabamba Centro Boliviano
    Americano,
Asesoramiento Educativo
Calle 25 de Mayo N-0365
Cochabamba, Bolivia
Tel: 591-4-422-9934
Web: www.cbacoch.org/

*La Paz*
Centro de Asesoramiento Educativo
EducationUSA Centro Boliviano Americano
Avenida Arce-Parque Zenon
Iturralde No.121
La Paz, Bolivia
Tel: 591-2-2430998
Web: www.educationusabolivia.org

*Santa Cruz de la Sierra*
EducationUSA, Centro Boliviano
    Americano - Santa Cruz
Calle Potosí #78 Santa Cruz
Bolivia
Tel: 591-3-3342299 ext.103
Web: www.cba.com.bo

*Sucre, Chuquisaca*
Centro de Asesoramiento Educativo
    EducationUSA
Centro Boliviano Americano-Sucre
Calle Calvo #301
Sucre, Bolivia
Tel: 591-4-644-1608
Web: www.cbasucre.org/

*Tarija*
Centro Boliviano Americano-Tarija
Calle Suipacha 738 Barrio La Pampa
(Zona Central)
Tarija, Bolivia
Tel: 591-4-6113612

## Bosnia & Herzegovina

*Banja Luka*
National and University Library of the RS
Carice Milice 1a
(Dvorana Obilićevo/Mejdan)
78000 Banja Luka
Bosnia & Herzegovina
Tel: 387 51 46 69 93

*Sarajevo*
EducationUSA at American Councils
Vrbanja 6, Sarajevo
Bosnia & Herzegovina
Tel: 387 33 838 262
Web: www.educationusa.ba

## Botswana

*Gaborone*
EducationUSA Advising Center - Gaborone
Embassy Drive, Government Enclave
Gaborone, Botswana
Tel: 267 395-3982
Web: http://botswana.usembassy.gov

## Brazil

*Anápolis, Goiás*
UniEvangelica - Anápolis
Av. Universitária Km. 3,5
Cidade Universitária
Anápolis - Goiás
75083-515, Brazil
Tel: 55 62 3310 6823

*Belem PA*
Centro Cultural Brasil-Estados
Unidos (CCBEU)
Travessa Padre Eutiquio, 1309
Belém - Pará
66023-710, Brazil
Tel: 55 91 3221 6113
Web: www.ccbeu.com.br

*Belo Horizonte MG*
EducationUSA - PUC Minas
Avenida Dom José Gaspar, 500,
Prédio 43 - 6º andar
Coração Eucarístico
Belo Horizonte - Minas Gerais
30535-901, Brazil
Tel: 55 31 3319 4716

*Boa Vista*
SENAC - Boa Vista
Avenida Capitão Júlio Bezerra, 1772-1
Nossa Senhora Aparecida
Boa Vista - Roraima
69.306-025, Brazil
Tel: 55 95 3224 1988

*Brasilia DF*
Casa Thomas Jefferson
CTJ - Brasília
SGAN 606-bloco B
Brasilia DF 70840-060, Brazil
Tel: 55-61-3442.5599
Web: www.thomas.org.br

*Campinas SP*
CCBEU - Campinas
Av. Julio de Mesquita, 606
Campinas SP 13025-061, Brazil
Tel: 55-19-3794-9700
Web: www.ccbeuc.com.br

*Ribeirão Preto, SP*
UNAERP - Ribeirão Preto
Av. Costábile Romano, 2.201
Ribeirania
Ribeirão Preto - São Paulo
14096-900, Brazil
Tel: 55 16 3703 6737

*Curitiba, Parana*
Interamericano - Curitiba
Av. Munhoz da Rocha, 490, Cabral
Curitiba PR 80035-000, Brazil
Tel: 55-41-3352-8693

*Curitiba, Parana*
FAE Centro Universitário - Curitiba
Rua 24 de Maio, 135 80.230-080
Curitiba, Parana
Brazil
Tel: 55-41-2105-4844
Web: www.fae.edu/educationusa

*Fortaleza, Ceara*
UNIFOR / EducationUSA Vice-
Reitoria de Extensão e Comunidade
Universitária Prédio da Reitoria
Av. Washington Soares, 1321
Bairro Edson Queiroz Fortaleza CE
60811-905, Brazil
Tel: 55-85-3477.3481
Web: www.unifor.br

*Fortaleza, Ceara*
IBEU
Rua Nogueira Acioly, 891
Fortaleza, CE 60110-140, Brazil
Tel: 55 85 4006.9941
Web: www.ibeuce.com.br

*Franca, SP*
CCBEU - Franca
Av. Major Nicácio, 1907, Cidade Nova
Franca-SP-Brazil 14401135.
Tel: 55-16-3724-4300

*Goiania, Goias*
Centro Cultural Brasil-Estados
Unidos (CCBEU) - Goiania
Rua C-243, QD 557, LT. 5, 6 Jardim America
Goiana
Goiania, Goias 74015-050
Brazil
Tel: 55-62-30961234

*Joinville SC*
Centro Cultural Brasil-Estados
Unidos- Joinville
Rua Tijucas, 370
Joinville SC 89204-020, Brazil
Tel: 55-47-3433-4110
Web: www.ccbeuj.com.br

*Londrina PR*
Instituto Cultural Brasil Estados Unidos
ICBEU - Londrina
Rua Professor Joao Candido, 1114
Londrina PR 86010-001, Brazil
Tel: 55 43 3375 9999

*Manaus, Amazonas*
ICBEU - Manaus
Av. Joaquim Nabuco, 1286
Manaus AM 69020-030, Brazil
Tel: 55-92-3232-5919

*Natal*
Universidade Potiguar - Natal
Av. Roberto Freire, 1684 Capim
Macio Natal, Rio Grande do Norte
59082-902 – Brasil
Tel: 55-84.3216.8640

*Porto Alegre RS*
Instituto Cultural Brasileiro Norte-
Americano ICBNA
Rua Riachuelo, #1257 2nd floor
Porto Alegre RS 90010-271
Brazil
Tel: 55-51-3025-0618
Web: www.cultural.org.br

*Recife, Pernambuco*
Associacao Brasil-America (ABA)
Servicos de Orientacao
Av. Rosa e Silva,1510-Aflitos
Recife, Pernambuco 52050-220
Brazil
Tel: 55-81-3427-8821

*Ribeirão Preto, SP*
UNAERP - Ribeirão Preto
Av. Costábile Romano, 2.201
Ribeirania
Ribeirão Preto - São Paulo
14096-900, Brazil
Tel: 55 16 3703 6737

*Rio de Janeiro RJ*
EducationUSA Center,
PUC Rio
Rua Marques de Sao Vicente, 225
Ed. Pe. Leonel Franca, sala 55,
Gavea
Rio de Janeiro RJ 22451-041
Brazil
Tel: 55-21-3527-1457
Web: www.educationusa.org.br

*Rio de Janeiro RJ*
Instituto Brasil-Estados Unidos-
IBEU/BNC
Av. Nossa Senhora de
Copacabana, 690 - 80 andar
Rio de Janeiro RJ 22050-001
Brazil
Tel: 55-21-3816-9468
Web: www.ibeu.org.br

*Salvador, Bahia*
ACBEU-Bahia
Av. Prof. Magalhaes Netto, 1520 -
Stiep
Salvador, Bahia 41820-140, Brazil
Tel: 55-71-3340-5400
Web: www.acbeubahia.org.br

*Sao Jose dos Campos SP*
ICBEU Sao Jose dos Campos
Av. Dr. Adhemar de Barros, 464
Vila Ady'Anna
Sao Jose dos Campos 12243-010 SP Brazil
Tel: 55-12-3203-1000
Web: www.icbeusjc.com.br

*Sao Paulo SP*
Associacao Alumni
Rua George Eastman 98
Morumbi
Sao Paulo - São Paulo
05690.000, Brazil
Tel: 55 11 3759 3216
Web: www.alumni.org.br

*Sao Paulo SP*
Uniao Cultural Brasil Estados Unidos
Rua Teixeira da Silvia 560
Sao Paulo SP 04002-032, Brazil
Tel: 55-11-2148-2921
Web: www.uniaocultural.com.br

*Sao Paulo SP*
Centro Universitário Senac -
Sao Paulo
Av. Engenheiro Eusébio Stevaux,
823 Prédio Acadêmico 2
Jurubatuba São Paulo - SP
Brazil 04696-000
Tel: 55-11-5682-7457
Web: www.sp.senac.br

*Sorocaba*
EducationUSA CCBEU Sorocaba
Rua Cesario Mota, 517
Sorocaba-SP 18035-200, Brazil
Tel: 55-15-33881515
Web: www.ccbeusorocaba.com.br

*Uberaba*
ICBEU - Uberaba
Rua Pedro Floro, 230
Estados Unidos
Uberaba-MG - Minas Gerais
38015-380, Brazil
Tel: 55 34 3332 3161

*Vila Velha*
IBEUV - Vila Velha
R. Sete de Setembro 135
Centro
Vila Velha - Espírito Santo
29100-301, Brazil
Tel: 55 27 3089 1300

## Brunei

*Bandar Seri Begawan*
EducationUSA Brunei
Simpang 336-52-16-9, Jalan
Duta, Bandar Seri Begawan
Brunei
Tel: 673-2384616
Web: http://brunei.usembassy.gov/
studyusa.html

## Bulgaria

*Plovdiv*
American Space Plovdiv
Library Ivan Vazov
ul. "Avksentiy Veleshki" 17
Plovdiv, Bulgaria
Web: amspace@libplovdiv.com

*Sofia*
Fulbright Sofia
17, Alex. Stamboliiski Boulevard
Sofia, Bulgaria
Tel: 359-2-981 6830
Web: www.fulbright.bg

## Burkina Faso

*Ouagadougou*
EducationUSA
U.S Embassy Ouagadougou Avenue
    Sembene Ousmane Rue 15.873
Ouagadougou, Burkina Faso
Tel: 226-50-49-53-00 Ext 5579
Web: //ouagadougou.usembassy. gov/
    educationusa_advising_center.html

## Burma (Myanmar)

*Mandalay*
Tel: 95-1-223140
Web: //burma.usembassy.gov/
    educational_exchange.html

*Rangoon (Yangon)*
EducationUSA Burma
The American Center
14, Tawwin Road
Dagon Township
Yangon, Burma (Myanmar)
Tel: 95-1-223140 ext. 323

## Burundi

*Bujumbura*
EducationUSA Advising Center -
    Bujumbura
U.S. Embassy Av. des Etats -Unis, Kigobe
Bujumbura, Burundi
Tel: 257 22 207 051

## Cambodia

*Phnom Penh*
University of Phnom Penh
Rm 103 Phnom Penh,
Cambodia
Tel: 855-23-884-320
Web: www.camedusa.com

*Phnom Penh*
PUC - Phnom Penh
No. 184, Norodom Blvd.,
Phnom Penh, Cambodia
Tel: 855-23-993 957
Web: http://www.puc.edu.kh/index.php/
    institutes-centers/educationusa-
    advising-center

## Cameroon

*Yaoundé*
EducationUSA Yaoundé
6.050 Avenue Rosa Parks
Yaounde, Cameroon
Tel: 237-220-1500 ext 4009
Web: http://yaounde.usembassy.gov/
    educational_advising.html

## Canada

*Ottawa*
EducationUSA Advising Center at Canada-
    U.S. Fulbright Commission
Virtual Advising
Web: //canada.usembassy.gov/
    educationusacanada.html

## Cape Verde

*Praia*
EducationUSA Praia
Rua Abilio Macedo 6
Praia, Cape Verde
Tel: 238-260-8900
Web: //praia.usembassy.gov/
    resources/academic-advising.html

## Chad

*N'Djamena*
EducationUSA Ndjamena US Embassy,
Avenue Felix Eboue
Ndjaména, Chad
Tel: 235 2251 7009
Web: //ndjamena.usembassy.gov/
    educational_advising.html

## Chile

*Antofagasta*
Instituto Chileno Norteamericano
    (Antofagasta) Educational Adviser
Carrera 1445
Antofagasta, Chile
Tel: 56-55-644401

*Chillan*
Instituto Chileno Norteamericano Chillan
18 de Septiembre 253
Chillan, Chile
Tel: 56-42-221-414

*Concepcion*
Instituto Chileno Norteamericano Concepcion
Caupolican 315
Concepcion, Chile
Tel: 56-41-222-5506 ext. 8
Web: www.ichnc.cl

*Curico*
Instituto Chileno Norteamericano
Estado 563
Curico, Chile
Tel: 56-75-311129

*La Serena*
Instituto Chileno Norteamericano La Serena
Cisternas 2281
La Serena, Chile 1700000
Tel: 56 51 522687
Web: www.norteamericanolaserena.cl

*Santiago*
EducationUSA
Granaderos 1150
Providencia Santiago
Chile
Tel: 56 22 518 9972
Web: www.fulbright.cl

*Santiago*
Comisión Fulbright
Av. Providencia 2331, oficina 901,
Providencia, Santiago, Chile
Tel: 56 2 963 8304
Web: www.educationusa.cl

*Temuco*
Universidad Católica de Temuco
Facultad de Educación (Edificio A)
Manuel Montt 56
Temuco, Chile
Tel: 56-94556638

*Valparaiso*
Instituto Chileno Norteamericano
    de Cultura de Valparaiso
Esmeralda 1069,
Valparaiso, Chile
Tel: 56-32-2450400 ext. 17
Web: http://www.chilenonorteamericano.cl/
    cursos_disponibles/requisitos-de-ingreso/

## China

*Beijing*
EducationUSA China
Suite 2801 Jing Guang Center
Hu Jia Lou, Chaoyang District
Beijing 13100020, China
Tel: 86-10- 6597-3242

## Colombia

*Armenia, Quindio*
EducationUSA BNC Colombo Americano -
    Armenia
Avenida Bolivar 1-55
Armenia, Quindio, Colombia
Tel: 576-746-3717 Ext 16
Web: www.educationusacolombia.info/
    educationusa

*Barranquilla, Atlantico*
EducationUSA at Centro Cultural Colombo
    Americano Barranquilla
Calle 52 No. 43 esquina
Barranquilla, Colombia
Tel: 575-3854444 ext 130
Web: www.colomboamericano.org/

*BNC Cartagena*
Centro, Calle de la Factoria
# 36-27
Cartagena BOL, Colombia
Tel: (575) 6641714

*Bogota*
Centro Colombo Americano
Bogotá - Educational Advising Center
Calle 19 No. 2A-49
Bogota CUN, Colombia
Tel: 571-3347640 ext 1243 or 1202
Web: www.colombobogota.edu.co

*Bogota*
COLFUTURO
Carrera 15 No. 37-15
Bogota, Colombia
Tel: 57-1-340-5394 ext 124
Web: www.colfuturo.org

*Bogota*
Centro de Consejeria Educativa - Fulbright
   Colombia
Casa Fulbright
Calle 37 # 15-73
Bogota, Colombia
Tel: 571-232-4326 ext.15
Web: www.fulbright.edu.co/consejeria

*Bucaramanga*
BNC Bucaramanga
Carrera 22 No. 37-74
Bucaramanga, Colombia
Tel: 57 7 6343300 ext. 102
Web: www.colombobucaramanga.edu.co

*Cali, Valle*
Centro Cultural Colombo
Americano Cali
Calle 13 Norte, # 8-45
Cali, Colombia
Tel: 57-2-687-5800 ext 114/134
Web: www.colomboamericano.edu.co

*Manizales, Caldas*
Centro Colombo Americano
   Manizales
Carrera 24 B No. 61A-50
Manizales, Colombia
Tel: 57-6-881-1525
Web:www.colombomanizales.com/
   educationusa

*Medellin, Antioquia*
Centro Colombo Americano Medellin
Carrera 45 No. 53-24 Oficina 901
Medellin, Colombia
Tel: 57-4-513 4444 ext. 159

*Pereira, Risaralda*
Centro Colombo Americano
Pereira
Carrera 6 # 22-12
Pereira, Colombia
Tel: 57-6-325-4032 ext 128
Web: www.colombopereira.com

## Comoros

*Moroni*
American Corner,
IFERE Building, Hamramba
Moroni, Comoros
Tel: 269-336 48 55/763 16 40

## Congo, Rep. (Brazzaville)

*Brazzaville*
US Embassy
Brazzaville, Congo
Tel: 242 6122 181
Web: brazzaville.usembassy.gov/

## Congo, Democratic Republic

*Kinshasa*
Congo American Language Institute
Complex Utexafrica
Avenue Colonel Mondjiba
Kinshasa, Dem. Republic of Congo
Tel: 243-81-7152350

## Costa Rica

*San José*
EducationUSA advising center Centro
   Cultural Costarricense-
Norteamericano
150 metros norte de Gasolinera La Favorita,
   los Yoses
San Pedro, Costa Rica
Tel: (506) 2207-7592
Web: www.centrocultural.cr

## Côte d'Ivoire

*Abidjan*
EducationUSA Abidjan
U.S. Embassy Riviera Golf rue des
   Ambassades
Abidjan, Ivory Coast
Tel: 225-22-49 41 45
Web: //abidjan.usembassy.gov/
   study_in_the_us.html

## Croatia

*Zagreb*
Institute for the Development of Education
Trg Nikole Subica Zrinskog 9
HR-10000 Zagreb, Croatia
Tel: 385-1-4817-195

## Cuba

*Havana*
Tel: 537 839-4169

## Cyprus

*Nicosia*
J.W. Fulbright Center
Marcos Drakou Street
1102 Nicosia, CYPRUS
Tel: 357-2-22 669757
Web: www.studyusa.com.cy

## Czech Republic

*Prague*
Fulbright Prague
Karmelitska 17, Praha 1
Prague 11800, Czech Republic
Tel: 420-222718452
Web: www.fulbright.cz

## Denmark

*Copenhagen*
Fulbright Copenhagen
Nørregade 7A, 1. tv
1165 Copenhagen, Denmark
Tel: 45 3318 1000
Web: www.wemakeithappen.dk

## Djibouti

*Djibouti*
EducationUSA Advising Center
American Embassy, Djibouti Lot 350-B
   Haramouss B.P. 185
Djibouti, Djibouti
Tel: 253 2145 3000 ext. 3064
Web: //djibouti.usembassy.gov/
   educational_advising_center.html

## Dominica, Commonwealth

*Roseau*
EducationUSA advising centre at the
   Dominica Public Library
Victoria Street
Roseau
Commonwealth of Dominica
Tel: 767-266-3341

## Dominican Republic

*Santiago de los Caballeros*
Centro Cultural Dominico-Americano
Avda. Salvador Estrella Sahdala 101
Santiago
Dominican Republic
Tel: 809-582-1244

*Santo Domingo*
Instituto Cultural Dominico-Americano
Educational Counseling Office
Ave. Abraham Lincoln #21, Sector
Mata Hambre
Santo Domingo 10102
Dominican Republic
Tel: 809-535-0665 ext. 3120
Web: www.icda.edu.do/espanol/eco

## East Timor (Timor-Leste)

*Dili*
American Studies Center
Embaixada EUA
Avenida de Portugal Praia dos Coqueiros
Dili, Timor-Leste

## Ecuador

*Cuenca*
EducationUSA, CEDEI
Gran Colombia 11-02 y General Torres
Tel: 072839003 ext. 105
Web: www.educationusa.cedei.org

*Guayaquil*
ESPOL Campus Las Peñas
   (cerca de la Oficina de Admisiones)
Malecón 100 y Loja
Guayaquil, Ecuador
Tel: 593-4-253-0277
Web: www.educationusa.espol.edu.ec

*Quito*
Comision Fulbright del Ecuador
Centro de Asesoria Academica
EducationUSA
Almagro N25-41 y Av. Colon
Quito, Ecuador
Tel: 593-2-222-2104
Web: www.fulbright.org.ec/educationusa/
   estudiantes

## Egypt

*Alexandria*
AMIDEAST
15 Abdel Hamid El Abady Street.
RoshdyAlexandria, Egypt
Tel: 20-3-54 613 57
Web: www.amideast.org

*Cairo (Giza)*
AMIDEAST
38 Mohie El Din Abul Ezz Street.
Dokki, Giza, Egypt
Tel: 20-2-3332-0411
Web: www.educationusa.info/cairo

## El Salvador

*San Salvador*
Centro Cultural Salvadoreno
Student Advising Office
Avenida los Sisimiles, Costado
norte de Metrocentro
San Salvador, El Salvador
Tel: 503 2239-8073
Web: www.ccsa.edu.sv/23.php

## Eritrea

*Asmara*
American Center, US Embassy
Public Affairs Section
Ala Street, #179
Asmara, Eritrea
Tel: 291-1-12-00-04
Web: //eritrea.usembassy.gov/
   educational_advising.html

## Estonia

*Tallinn*
EducationUSA Advising Center
Tallinn University of Technology
Ehitajate tee 5, Room III-208
Tallinn 19086, Estonia
Tel: 372-2-620 3543
Web: www.eac.ttu.ee

*Tartu*
EducationUSA Advising Center
Tartu University Library
W. Struve 1-325
Tartu 50091, Estonia
Tel: 372-737 5714
Web: www.ut.ee/ameerika

## Ethiopia

*Addis Ababa*
US Embassy, Public Affairs Section
Entoto Street
Woreda 11, Kebele 10
Addis Ababa, Ethiopia
Tel: 011-307944

## Fiji

*Suva*
U.S. Embassy Public Affairs
31 Loftus Street
Suva, Fiji
Tel: 679-3314466 ext. 8204
Web: //suva.usembassy.gov/
   educational_exchange.html

*Lautoka*
Western Regional Library

## Finland

*Helsinki*
Fulbright Helsinki
Hakaniemenranta 6
Helsinki 00530, Finland
Tel: 358 44 5535 286
Web: www.fulbright.fi

## France

*Paris*
Fulbright Paris
9, rue Chardin
Paris 75016, France
Tel: 33 (0)1 44 14 53 61
Web: www.fulbright-france.org/

## Gabon

*Libreville*
U.S. Embassy
Libreville, Gabon
Tel: 241-76-2003

## Gambia, The

*Banjul*
US Embassy
Kairaba Avenue, Fajara
Gambia
Tel: 220-439-2856 ext 2166
Web: //banjul.usembassy.gov/news/
   education/educational-system-of-the-
   gambia.html

## Georgia

*Akhaltsikhe*
Center for International Education
65 Rustaveli Str.
0800 Akhaltsikhe, Georgia
Tel: 995-93 44 14 12
Web: www.cie.ge

*Batumi*
Center for International Education
Gorgiladze St. 91, 2nd floor
Batumi 6010, Georgia
Tel: 995-222-75817/7-40-13

*Kutaisi*
Kutaisi Center For International Education
Akaki Tsereteli State University Building I,
   Floor II
59 Tamar Mepe str.
Kutaisi, Georgia
Web: http://www.cie.ge

*Tbilisi*
Center for International Education
Chovelidze,10
0108 Tbilisi, Georgia
Tel: 995-32-252615
Web: www.cie.ge

*Telavi*
Center for International Education
Telavi State University
Qartuli universiteti street #1, bldg 1
Telavi 2200, Georgia
Tel: 995-350-7-31-39
Web: www.cie.ge

## Germany

*Berlin/all cities*
US Mission Germany
Pariser Platz 2
10117 Berlin, Germany
Tel: 49 30 8305 2154
Web: www.educationusa.de

*Freiburg*
German-American Institute Freiburg
Eisenbahnstrasse 62
Freiburg 79098
Germany
Tel: 49-761-55652716
Web: www.carl-schurz-haus.de

*Hamburg*
Amerikazentrum Hamburg
Am Sandtorkai 5
Hamburg 20457, Germany
Tel: 49-40-70 38 36 98
Web: www.amerikazentrum.de

*Heidelberg*
German American Institute
Sofienstrasse 12
Heidelberg 69115, Germany
Tel: 49-6221-607315
Web: www.dai-heidelberg.de

*Kiel*
Kennedy Infozentrum Kiel
Olshausenstrasse 10
Kiel 24118, Germany
Tel: 49-431-586 999 3
Web: www.amerika-gesellschaft.de

*Leipzig*
American Corner Leipzig
Leipzig 04107, Germany
Tel: 49-341-213 84 65
Web: http://www.americanspace-leipzig.de/

*Munich*
Amerika Haus Munich
Bavarian Center for Transatlantic Relations
   Dept. Education & Exchange
Karolinenplatz 3
Munich 80333, Germany
Web: www.amerikahaus.de/exchange.html

*Nürnberg*
GAI Nurnberg
Gleissbuhlstrasse 9
90402 Nuernberg, Germany
Tel: 49-911-2306912
Web: www.dai-nuernberg.de/
   DAIFrameStudy.htm

*Stuttgart*
Deutsch-Amerikanisches Zentrum
James-F.-Byrnes Institut e.V.
Charlottenplatz 17
Stuttgart 70173, Germany
Tel: 49-711-22 81 80
Web: www.daz.org

*Tübingen*
German American Institute
Karlstrasse 3
Tuebingen 72072, Germany
Tel: 49-7071-795-2616
Web: www.dai-tuebingen.de

## Ghana

*Accra*
EducationUSA Accra
US Embassy
No. 24, Fourth Circular Road
Cantonments-Accra
Accra, Ghana
Tel: 233-302-741 531
Web: //ghana.usembassy.gov/
   educational_advising.html

*Kumasi*
EducationUSA
ACE Consult Ltd.
3rd FL Top Martin's Complex,
Asokwa
Kumasi, Ghana
Tel: 233-244-369027
Web: http://www.aceconsultghana.com

## Greece

*Athens*
Fulbright Athens
6 Vassilissis Sophias Avenue
Athens 10674, Greece
Tel: 30 210 724181 Ext. 204
Web: www.fulbright.gr/

## Grenada

*St. Georges*
EducationUSA Advising Center at
   T.A. Marryshow Community College
Ross Building, Carenage St. Georges,
   Grenada
Tel: 473 456-0731

## Guatemala

*Guatemala City*
EducationUSA Advising Center
Instituto Guatemalteco Americano - IGA
Ruta 1, 4-05, Zona 4, 1st Fl, Of.108
Guatemala City 01004, Guatemala
Tel: 502 2422-5590
Web: www.iga.edu/educationusa

## Guinea

*Conakry*
EducationUSA Conakry
Centre d'Etudes de la Langue
Anglaise CELA
Universite GLC de Sonfonia
Route Donka
Conakry, Guinea
Tel: 224-60-26 19 67
Web: //conakry.usembassy.gov/
   study_in_the_us1.html

## Guyana

*Georgetown*
EducationUSA Advising Center United
   States Embassy
99-100 Young and Duke Streets
Kingston
Georgetown, Guyana
Tel: 1(592)225-4900 Ext 4018
Web: //georgetown.usembassy.gov

## Haiti

*Port au Prince*
EducationUSA Advising Center
US Embassy
Port au Prince, Haiti

## Honduras

*San Pedro Sula*
EducationUSA Advising Center
Centro Cultural Sampedrano
Barrio Guamilito 3 Calle, 3-4
Avenida, N.O.
San Pedro Sula Cortés, Honduras
Tel: 504-553-3911
Web: www.centrocultural-sps.com

*Tegucigalpa*
EducationUSA Advising Center Instituto
   Hondureno de Cultura Interamericana
Blvd. Morazan 1/2 cuadra antes
   del Mall El Dorado
Florencia Norte Edificio Tovar y Asociados
   Segunda Planta
Tegucigalpa Francisco Morazán, Honduras
Tel: (504) 221-3128
Web: www.ihcihn.org

## Hong Kong & Macau

*Hong Kong*
U.S. Consulate PAS - Hong Kong
Public Affairs Section
U.S. Consulate General
26 Garden Road Central,
Hong Kong SAR, Hong Kong
Tel: 852-2841-2402
Web: http://educationusa.hk/

## Hungary

*Budapest*
Fulbright Budapest
Baross u. 62
Budapest 1082, Hungary
Tel: 36-1-462-8050
Web: http://www.fulbright.hu/educationusa

*Debrecen*
American Corner Debrecen
Méliusz Juhász Péter Könyvtár H-4026
Debrecen Bem tér 19, Hungary
Tel: 36 52 531 982
Web: //americancorner.hu/htmls/
   ac_debrecen.html

*Pecs*
American Corner
Zsolnay Kulturalis Negyed, Pécs Building
   No. 8.
Pecs 7630, Hungary
Tel: 36-72-500.386
Web: //pecs.americancorner.hu/htmls/
   study_in_the_usa.html

*Szeged*
University of Szeged, Library
AFIK Ady ter 10
Szeged 6722, Hungary
Tel: 36-62-546-625
Web: www.bibl.u-szeged.hu/afik/

*Veszprem*
American Corner
H-8200 Veszprem
Komakut ter 3.
Veszprem, Hungary
Tel: 36-88-560-600
Web: www.americancorner.hu

## Iceland

*Reykjavik*
Fulbright Reykjavik
Laugavegur 59, 3rd floor
IS-101 Reykjavik, Iceland
Tel: 354-551-0860
Web: www.fulbright.is

## India

*Ahmedabad*
EducationUSA at IAES, Ahmedabad
Fifth Fl, 502/503, Akik Tower,
Near Pakwan Restaurant, S. G
Road, Ahmedabad 380054,
Gujarat, India
Tel: 91-79-26872826
Web: www.iaesgujarat.org

*Bangalore*
EducationUSA @ Yashna Trust
102 Park View Complex
40 Haines Road, Fraser Town
Bangalore KA 560005, India
Tel: 91-80-4125-1922
Web: www.yashnatrust.org

*Chennai*
EducationUSA at USIEF, Chennai
American Consulate Building,
Anna Salai
Chennai TN 600006, India
Tel: 91-44-28574423

*Hyderabad*
U.S. Consulate General
Paigah Palace1-8-323,
Chiran Fort Lane
Begumpet, Secunderabad 500003
India
Tel: +91-40-4033 8438
Web: http://www.usief.org.in/Study-in-the-
   US/Hyderabad.aspx

*Kolkata (Calcutta)*
EducationUSA at USIEF, Kolkata
American Center
38A, Jawaharlal Nehru Road
Kolkata WB 700 071
India
Tel: 91-33-3984-6310
Web: www.usief.org.in/

*Mumbai (Bombay)*
EducationUSA at USIEF, Mumbai
Maker Bhavan 1, Floor 2, New
Marine Lines, Churchgate
Mumbai 400020, India
Tel: 91-22-2262-4603
Web: www.usief.org.in/

*New Delhi*
EducationUSA at USIEF, New Delhi
Fulbright House
12 Hailey Road
New Delhi 110001, India
Tel: 91-011-42090977
Web: www.usief.org.in/

## Indonesia

*Jakarta*
U.S. Embassy Jakarta Public Affairs
Jl. Medan Merdeka Selatan No. 3 - 5
10110 Jakarta, Indonesia

*Jakarta*
@america
EducationUSA at @america
The Pacific Place 3rd Floor
#325 Jl. Jend. Sudirman Kav. 52-53
Jakarta 12190, Indonesia

*Malang*
EducationUSA Malang
Universitas Muhammadiyah
Gedung Perpustakaan, 3rd FL
Jl. Raya Tlogomas no. 246
Malang 65144, Indonesia
Tel: 62-341-463 345
Web: www.educationusa.or.id

*Medan*
EducationUSA Medan
Jalan R.A. Kartini No. 32
20152 Medan, Indonesia
Tel: 62-61 4562647

*Surabaya*
AMINEF/EducationUSA
International Village 2nd Floor
Universitas Surabaya
Jl. Raya Kalirungkut
Surabaya, DC 60293, Indonesia
Tel: 62.81.833.5156
Web: www.educationusa.or.id

## Iran

*All cities*
EducationUSA Iran Virtual Advising Center
Web: www.educationusairan.com

## Iraq

*Baghdad*
U.S. Embassy Iraq
Web: iraq.usembassy.gov/studyintheusa.html

*Erbil*
U.S. Consulate General Erbil
Ankawa District
Erbil, Iraqi Kurdistan,
Iraq
Tel: 964 770 443 4403
Web: http://erbil.usconsulate.gov/studyusa.html

## Ireland

*Dublin*
Fulbright Dublin
Brooklawn House, Crampton Avenue
Dublin 4, Ireland
Tel: 353-1-660 7670
Web: www.fulbright.ie

## Israel

*Tel Aviv*
U.S. Israel Educational Foundation
Fulbright
1 Ben Yehuda Street, 10th Fl
Tel Aviv 61261, Israel
Tel: 972-3-517-2131 ext 207
Web: www.fulbright.org.il

## Italy

*Naples (Napoli)*
Fulbright Naples
Public Affairs Section
Piazza della Repubblica, 2
Naples 80122, Italy
Tel: 39-81-681487
Web: www.fulbright.it

*Rome*
Fulbright Rome
Via Castelfidardo, 8
Rome 00185, Italy
Tel: 39-6-4888.211
Web: www.fulbright.it

## Jamaica

*Kingston*
EducationUSA Advising Center
US Embassy
142 Old Hope Road
Kingston 6, Jamaica, W.I.
Web: //kingston.usembassy.gov/

## Japan

*Fukuoka*
Fukuoka American Center
Solaria Parkside Bldg, 8th fl.
2-2-67-8F, Tenjin, Chuo-ku
Fukuoka 810-0001, Japan
Tel: 81-92-733-0246
Web: /http://fukuoka.usconsulate.gov/
  fukuoka/e/f-fac-about.html

*Nagoya*
U.S. Consulate Nagoya
Nagoya Kokusai Center Bldg. 6F 1-47-1
Nagono, Nakamura-ku
Nagoya, 450-0001
Japan
Tel: 81-(0)52-581-8633
Web: http://japanese.nagoya.usconsulate.gov/

*Okinawa*
US Consulate
901-2104 Okinawa
Urasoe
2-1-1 Toyama, Japan
Tel: 098-876-4211

*Osaka*
U.S. Consulate Osaka, Kansai American Center
2-11-5 Nishitenma, Kita-ku,
Osaka 530-8543, Japan
Tel: 06-6315-5970
Web: http://osaka.usconsulate.gov/

*Tokyo*
American Center Japan
107-0052 Tokyo
1-1-14 Akasaka, Japan
Tel: 81(0)3-3224-5247
Web: http://connectusa.jp/study/index.html

*Tokyo*
Japan-U.S. Educational Commission
  (Fulbright Japan)
Sanno Grand Bldg. #207,
2-14-2, Nagata-cho, Chiyoda-ku
Tokyo 100-0014, Japan
Tel: 81-(0)3-3580-1339
Web: http://www.fulbright.jp/eng/study/
  index.html

*Tokyo*
U.S. Consulate Sapporo
064-0821 Hokkaido
Sapporo Kita 1, Nishi 28, Chuo-ku, Japan
Tel: 81 (0) 11-641-1861
Web: http://japanese.sapporo.usconsulate.
  gov/ja/index.html

## Jordan

*Amman*
U.S. Embassy Jordan
Al Umawiyeen Street 32
Amman 11118, Jordan
Tel: 962-6-552-3901

## Kazakhstan

*Aktobe*
EducationUSA Aktobe AKEAC
6-A, 101-oi Strelkovoi Brigady Street
Aktobe 030000, Kazakhstan
Tel: 7-3132-514 331
Web: www.akeac.org

*Almaty*
EducationUSA Almaty
American Councils
20A Kazibek Bi St., 4th floor Almaty
  050010, Kazakhstan
Tel: 7 (727) 291 9226
Web: //americancouncils-kz.com/

*Astana*
EducationUSA Astana, American Councils
Syganak Street 29, Office 1522
Astana, Kazakhstan 010000
Tel: 7-7172-91 00 68

*Karaganda*
EducationUSA Karaganda, Bilim EAC
20 Bukhar Zhyrau Avenue
office 228-230
Karaganda 100000, Kazakhstan
Tel: 7-7212-42 0761

*Shymkent*
EducationUSA Shymkent
2A Tauke Khan Ave.
160012
Shymkent, Kazakhstan
Tel: +7 702 748 16 52

## Kenya

*Nairobi*
EducationUSA Advising Center
Embassy of the United States
United Nations Avenue
P.O. Box 606 Village Market
Nairobi 00621, Kenya
Tel: +254203636583
Web: http://nairobi.usembassy.gov/edusa.html

## Korea, South (ROK)

*Seoul*
American Center Korea
10 Namyoung-dong, Yongsan-gu,
Seoul, South Korea 140-160
Tel : (02)397- 4647, 4789, 4713

*Seoul*
Korean-American Educational Commission
(Fulbright)
U.S. Education Center
Fulbright Building 23, Baekbeom-ro 28-gil,
Mapo-gu Seoul 121-874, South Korea
Tel: 02-3275-4000
Web: http://www.fulbright.or.kr/xe/index_
educationusa

## Kosovo

*Prishtina*
American Advising Center-Kosova
American School of Kosova
Rr. Luan Haradinaj n.n. (Pallati i
Rinise-Sportit)
Prishtina 10000, Kosovo
Tel: 381-38-227277; 228288 ext107
Web: www.aacks.org

## Kuwait

*Sharq, Kuwait City*
U.S. Embassy Kuwait
Masjid Al Aqsa Street
Kuwait
Tel: 965-2-259-1001
Web: http://kuwait.usembassy.gov/
exchange2.html

## Kyrgyzstan

*Bishkek*
EducationUSA Center at
Bayalinov Youth And Children's Library
3rd floor
Ogonbaev str. 242
Bishkek 720040, Kyrgyzstan
Tel: (996) 550-95-01-12
Web: http://www.americancouncils.kg

## Laos

*Vientiane*
US Embassy
Information Resource Center
Rue Bartholonie
That Dam, Vientiane, Laos
Tel: 856-21-267089
Web: http://laos.usembassy.gov/eduadv.html

## Latvia

*Daugavpils*
Info USA Daugavpils
Latgale Central Library
Rīgas 22a
Daugavpils LV-5401, Latvia
Tel: 371 6542 2483
Web: www.lcb.lv/asvinfo/

*Riga*
EducationUSA at RTU Riga Business School
Skolas Street 11
Riga LV-1010, Latvia
Tel: 371-670 89808
Web: www.educationusa.lv

## Lebanon

*Beirut*
AMIDEAST
Bazerkan Building, 1st fl,
Nijmeh Square
Beirut 2011 5601, Lebanon
Tel: 961-1-989901 ext 161
Web: www.amideast.orglebanon/

## Lesotho

*Maseru*
EducationUSA Advising Center - Maseru
254 Kingsway Ave.
Maseru 100, Lesotho
Tel: 266-22-312-666
Web: //maseru.usembassy.gov

## Liberia

*Monrovia*
EducationUSA Advising Center
US Embassy
Monrovia, Liberia
Tel: 0777207296
Web://monrovia.usembassy.gov/
informationandadvising.html

## Libya

*Tripoli*
EducationUSA Virtual Advising Office
United States Embassy
Public Affairs Section
Jaraba Street-Ben Ashoor area
Tripoli, Libya
Tel: 218-91-954-4548
Web:
//libya.usembassy.gov/edu_advising.html

## Lithuania

*Kaunas*
Youth Career and Advising Center
S.Daukanto 27-310
Kaunas LT-44249, Lithuania
Tel: 370-37-228151
Web: www.karjeroscentras.eu

*Vilnius*
Vilnius Educational Advising Center
Sauletekio 9
VU ITTC, 107 kabinetas
Vilnius 10222, Lithuania
Tel: 370 686 14555

*Vilnius*
American Center Vilnius
Akmenu gatve 7
Vilnius 03106, Lithuania
Tel: 370-5-266-543
Web: //vilnius.usembassy.gov/resources/
educational-exchanges2/
fulbright-graduate-student-program.html

## Luxembourg

*Luxembourg*
Public Affairs Section, U.S. Embassy,
Luxembourg
211, route d'Esch
Luxembourg L-1471, Luxembourg
Tel: 352-478-8650
Web: http://www.cedies.public.lu/fr/index.html

## Macedonia

*Bitola*
American Corner Bitola
Center for Culture
Marshal Tito bb
Bitola 7000, Macedonia
Tel: 389-47-203-326
Web: http://www.acmacedonia.org/

*Skopje*
National and University Library
Blvd. Goce Delchev 6
1000 Skopje, Macedonia
Tel: 389-02-3120-020
Web: http://www.acmacedonia.org/

*Tetovo*
American Corner Tetovo
Blvd "Iliria" - bb, House of Culture,
1200 Tetovo, Macedonia
Tel: 389 44 332 183

## Madagascar

*Antananarivo*
EducationUSA Advising Center
22, Làlana Rainitovo Antsahavola
Antananarivo 105, Madagascar
Tel: 261-32 02 275 59
Web: www.antananarivo.usembassy.gov/

## Malawi

*Lilongwe*
Education USA Advising Center - Lilongwe
Public Affairs Section, US Embassy
Old Mutual Building
Robert Mugabe Crescent
Lilongwe, Malawi
Tel: 265-1-772222 ext 5213
Web: //lilongwe.usembassy.gov/
advising_services.html

## Malaysia

*Kuala Lumpur*
Malaysian-American Commission
on Educational Exchange
MACEE 18th Floor, Menara
Yayasan Tun Razak
200, Jalan Bukit Bintang
Kuala Lumpur 50200, Malaysia
Tel: 60-3-21668878
Web: www.macee.org.my

*Penang*
EducationUSA Penang SEBERANG JAYA:
Penang Public
Library Corporation JKR 2118,
Jalan Perpustakaan Seberang Jaya,
13700 Perai,
Penang, Malaysia
Tel: (6-04) 019-611-2463
GEORGE TOWN: Penang Public
Library George Town Branch JKR 2936,
Jalan Scotland 10450,
Penang, Malaysia
Tel: 60-4-229-3555
Coord. Tel: 60-4-019-611-2463
Web: www.macee.org.my

## Mali

*Bamako*
EducationUSA Bamako
US Embassy
ACI 2000
Bamako, Mali
Tel: 223-270-2419

## Malta

*Msida*
Reference Department
University of Malta, Valetta
Msida, MSD 2080, Malta
Tel: 356-2340-2050
Web: www.lib.um.edu.mt

## Marshall Islands

*Majuro*
College of the Marshall Islands
Tilmaake Resource & Career Center
   (TRACC)
Majuro, MH 96960

*Majuro*
U.S. Embassy Majuro
Tel: 692-247-4011 ext 228

## Mauritania

*Nouakchott*
EducationUSA American Embassy
   Nouakchott 288,
rue 42-100 (Rue Abdallaye) BP: 222
Nouakchott, Mauritania
Tel: 222-525-2660 ext 4733
Web: http://mauritania.usembassy.gov

## Mauritius

*Port Louis*
EducationUSA Advising Center - Port Louis
   4th Floor Rogers House
John Kennedy Street
Port Louis, Mauritius
Tel: 230-202-4445
Web: http://mauritius.usembassy.gov/

## Mexico

*Chihuahua, Chihuahua*
EducationUSA Advising Center At Esquina
   Benjamin Franklin, Mediateca
Municipal Ave. Teófilo Borunda El Palomar
   Chihuahua 1617, Mexico
Tel: 52 (614) 4154097

*Cuernavaca*
UAEM Cuernavaca Casa de la Ciencia de la
   UAEM
Av. Morelos #275 Col. Centro
62000 Cuernavaca, Morelos, Mexico
Tel: 777-318-36-07

*Guadalajara, Jalisco*
EducationUSA Advising Center Instituto
   Cultural Mexicano
Norteamericano De Jalisco A.C.
Enrique Diaz de Leon Sur 300
Colonia Moderna
Guadalajara 44170, Mexico
Tel: 52-33-3825-5838 ext. 110;
Web: www.institutocultural.com.mx

*Hermosillo*
EducationUSA SEC SONORA
Subsecretaría de Educación Media y
   Superior del Estado de Sonora
Calle Guerrero #39 entre Calle Sonora y
Luis Donaldo Colosio, Colonia Centro
Hermosillo - Mexico
Tel: 52(662)2-89-76-00 ext. 2317

*Merida, Yucatan*
Universidad Autonoma de Yucatan
   Coordinacion de General de Cooperacion
   e Internacionalizacion
Biblioteca del Area de Ciencias
Sociales 3er piso Km. 1 Carretera
Tizimin, tramo Cholul,
97305 Merida, Yucatan
Tel: 52+999 927-2811 ext. 1359
Web: http://bit.ly/UADY_Global_EdUSA

*Mexico D.F*
EducationUSA Advising Center At COMEXUS
Liverpool 31 (entre Berlin y Dinamarca)
Mexico D.F. 06600, Mexico
Tel: 52 (55)-5703-0167

*Monterrey, Nuevo Leon*
EducationUSA Advising Center At
   Biblioteca Benjamin Franklin de
   Monterrey, ABP/Relaciones Culturales
Porfirio Diaz 949 Sur entre Hidalgo y
   Ocampo Col. Centro o Hidalgo
#768 Pte. entre Serafin Peña y Porfirio Diaz
   Col. Centro
Monterrey, Mexico
Tel: 52-81-8343-3907
Web: www.relacionesculturales.edu.mx/bbf/

*Morelia, Michoacan*
EducationUSA Advising Center At
   Universidad Vasco De Quiroga
555 Av. Juan Pablo II Santa Marìa de Guido
Morelia 58090, Michoacán, Mexico
Tel: 52-443-323-5171 Ext. 2181
Web: www.uvaq.edu.mx

*Oaxaca, Oaxaca*
EducationUSA Advising Center at Oaxaca
   Outreach Center
Oaxaca, Mexico
Tel: 521(951)280-0774
Web: www.iielatinamerica.org

*Saltillo, Coahuila*
EducationUSA Advising Center At IMARC
   Saltillo Instituto Mexicano
Norteamericano de Relaciones
Culturales
Av. Presidente Cardenas 840
Zona Centro
Saltillo, Coahuila 25000, Mexico
Tel: 52-844-414 8422

*San Luis Potosi SLP*
EducationUSA San Luis Potosi Universidad
   Autonoma de San Luis Potosi
Centro de Asesoria Educativa,
Centro de Idiomas
Zaragoza 505
San Luis Potosi 78000, Mexico
Web: //cidiomas.uaslp.mx

*Zacatecas*
EducationUSA Zacatecas At Biblioteca
Maurício Magdaleno Calzada Cerro
   del Grillo
No. 100 Centro Urbano Quebradilla Zona
   Centro Zacatecas
Zacatecas 98000
Mexico
Tel:52(492)924-0562

## Micronesia FSM

*Palikir, Pohnpei*
College of Micronesia
Palikir, Micronesia
Tel: 691-320-2481

## Moldova

*Chisinau*
Chisinau EAC
16 Puskin St.
Chisinau MD 2012, Moldova
Tel: 373-22-22 11 72
Web: www.eac.md

## Mongolia

*Khovd*
Educational Advising Center American
   Corner Hovd
Public Library, Khovd, Mongolia
Tel: 97699112790

*Ulaanbaatar*
Educational Advising Resource
   Center - Mongolia
MKM 24th Building, 1st Floor
8th khoroo Student's Street,
Sukhbaatar district
Ulaanbaatar, Mongolia
Tel: 976-11-319016
Web: www.earcmn.org

## Morocco

*Casablanca*
EducationUSA Casablanca
AMIDEAST
3 Boulevard Al Massira Al Khadra
Maarif, Casablanca, Morocco
Tel: 212-522-25-93-93

*Rabat*
AMIDEAST - Rabat
35, Zanqat, Rue Oukaimeden
Agdal, Rabat- Morocco
Tel: 212-5-37-67-5075
Web: www.amideast.org/morocco

## Mozambique

*Maputo*
EducationUSA Advising Center - Maputo
Av. Mao Tse Tung, 542
Maputo, Mozambique
Tel: 258 21 355412
Web: //maputo.usembassy.gov/

## Namibia

*Windhoek*
EducationUSA Advising Center - Windhoek
Independence Avenue
3rd Floor, Sanlam
Windhoek, Namibia
Tel: 264-61-229801
Web: //windhoek.usembassy.gov

## Nepal

*Kathmandu*
US Educational Foundation in
  Nepal (USEF-Nepal)
Fulbright Commission
Gyaneshwor
Kathmandu, Nepal
Tel: 977-1-4414598
Web: www.fulbrightnepal.org.np

## Netherlands

*Amsterdam*
Fulbright Center
Westerdoksdijk 215 Amsterdam 1013 CA,
  Netherlands
Tel: 31-20-5315930
Web: www.fulbright.nl

## New Zealand

*Auckland*
EducationUSA NZ
3rd Floor, Citigroup Centre
23 Customs St. East Auckland CBD
Private Bag 92022
Auckland, New Zealand
Tel: 64-9-303 2724 ext.2832
Web: http://newzealand.usembassy.gov

*Wellington*
Fulbright New Zealand
Level 8, 120 Featherston Street
Wellington 6011, New Zealand
Tel: 64 4 494 1504
Web: www.fulbright.org.nz

## Nicaragua

*Managua*
EducationUSA Advising Center Centro
  Cultural Nicaraguense
Norteamericano
Semáforos de la UCA 700 metros al Norte,
  100 metros al Oeste.
Managua, Nicaragua
Tel: (505) 2278-1288
Web: www.ccnn.org.ni/

## Niger

*Niamey*
EducationUSA Niamey Centre Culturel
  Americain
US Embassy
Niamey, Niger
Tel: 227-20-73-41-07
Web: //niamey.usembassy.gov/niger/
  educational_advising3.html

## Nigeria

*Abuja*
EducationUSA Abuja
U.S. Embassy Plot 1075, Diplomatic Drive
Business District
Abuja, Nigeria
Tel: 234-9-4614251
Web: //nigeria.usembassy.gov/
  educational_advising.html

*Lagos*
EducationUSA Lagos, US Consulate
Public Affairs Section
2 Walter Carrington Crescent,
Victoria Island Lagos, Nigeria
Tel: 234-1-460-3801
Web: //nigeria.usembassy.gov/
  educational_advising.html

## Norway

*Oslo*
Fulbright Oslo
Arbinsgate 2
Oslo 0253, Norway
Tel: 47-22 01 40 12
Web: www.fulbright.no

*Oslo*
EducationUSA
US Embassy Public Affairs
Henrik Ibsensgate 48
0244 Oslo, Norway
Tel: 47-21 30 89 26
Web: //norway.usembassy.gov/
  educational_exchange.html

## Oman

*Muscat*
AMIDEAST Muscat
Al Jama'a Al Akhbar Street Building 93
Airport Heights, Muscat, Oman
Tel: +968-2459-0309
Web: www.amideast.org/oman/

## Pakistan

*Islamabad*
US Educational Foundation in Pakistan
Islamabad, Pakistan
Tel: 92-51-8431508
Web: www.usefpakistan.org

*Karachi*
The U.S. Educational Foundation USEF
  Pakistan Karachi Center
Tel: 92-21-3-5810671-3
Web: www.usefpakistan.org

*Lahore*
US Consulate General Lahore
Lahore 54000, Pakistan
Tel: 92-42-36034256
Web: lahore.usconsulate.gov

*Lahore*
USEF Pakistan Lahore Center
Lahore, Pakistan
Tel: 92-42-35762467
Web: www.usefpakistan.org

## Palau

Palau Community College

## Palestine Territories

*El-Bireh, Ramallah*
AMIDEAST West Bank
Al-Watanieh Towers, 1st Floor
34 El-Bireh Municipality St.
El-Bireh, Ramallah District
Palestinian Territories
Tel: 972-2-240-8023 ext.103
Web: http://www.amideast.org/west-bank-
  gaza/advising/advising-services-west-bank

*Gaza*
AMIDEAST Gaza
Al Jondi Al Majhool Square Martyr Raja
  Street, #8/704,
Bseiso Building, 8th Floor
Rimal, Gaza
Palestinian Territory
Tel: 972-8-2824635
Web: www.amideast.org

## Panama

*Panama City*
EducationUSA Advising Center
Cromos Building, Via España
Panama City, Panama
Tel: 507 380-2200 ext. 2202

## Papua New Guinea

*Port Moresby*
University of Papua New Guinea
U.S. Embassy Douglas Street Port Moresby
Papua New Guinea
Tel: 675.3267585
Web: //portmoresby.usembassy.gov

## Paraguay

*Asuncion*
Centro Cultural Paraguayo Americano
Espana 352 e/ Brasil y EEUU
Asuncion, Paraguay
Tel: 595-21-224-831
Web: www.ccpa.edu.py

## Peru

*Arequipa*
EducationUSA- Centro Cultural Peruano
  Norteamericano
calle Melgar 109, Cercado
Arequipa, Peru
Tel: 51-54-391020, ext.290
Web: www.educationusa-peru.info

*Chiclayo*
Instituto Cultural Peruano
Norteamericano de Chiclayo-Asesoria
  Educativa
Manuel Maria Izaga 807
Chiclayo, Peru
Tel: 51-74-231241
Web: www.icpnachi.edu.pe

*Cusco*
Instituto Cultural Peruano
Norteamericano de Cusco
Av. Los Incas 1504, Wanchaq
5to. Piso
Cusco, Peru
Tel: 0051-84-224112 ext.526
Web: www.icpnacusco.org

*Huancayo*
EducationUSA ICPNA
Jr. Ayacucho 169, First Floor
Huancayo, Peru
Tel: 51-64-211873, ext. 219
Web: http://www.icpnarc.edu.pe

*Ilo*
Centro Cultural Peruano
Norteamericano
Urb. Villa del Mar D-1,
Ilo, Peru
Tel: 51-53-484102
Web: www.cultural.edu.pe

*Lima*
Instituto Cultural Peruano
    Norteamericano- Lima
Av. Angamos Oeste 120
Lima 18, Peru
Tel: 51-1-7067000 ext.9065
Web: www.icpna.edu.pe

*Lima*
Centro De Asesoria EducationUSA,
    Comision Fulbright, Lima
Juan Romero Hidalgo 444
San Borja, Lima 41, Peru
Tel: 51-1-476-0666
Web: www.educationusa-peru.info

*Piura*
BNC Piura
Apúrimac 447
Piura, Peru
Tel: 51-073-309102
Web: http://www.icpna.edu.pe/education-
    usa/education-usa/

*Puno*
Puno BNC
Jr. Luis N. Chevarría N° 128
Tel: +(51)(51)365988 ext 24
Web: http://www.cultural.edu.pe

*Tacna*
BNC Tacna
Coronel Bustios 146
Tacna, Peru
Tel: 51-52-24 44 06
Web: www.educationusa-peru.info

*Trujillo*
Centro Peruano Americano
Trujillo
Av. Venezuela 125 Urb. El Recreo
Trujillo, Peru
Tel: 51-44-232512. ext.112
Web: www.elcultural.com.pe

## Philippines

*Bacolod City*
University of St. La Salle
American Studies Resource Ctr, La Salle Ave.
Bacolod City 6100, Philippines
Web: http://www.fulbright.org.ph

*Baguio City*
St. Louis University
Web: http://www.fulbright.org.ph

*Batac, Ilocos Norte*
Mariano Marcos State University
American Studies Resource Ctr,
Batac 2906, Ilocos Norte
Philippines
Web: http://www.fulbright.org.ph

*Davao City*
Ateneo de Davao University
American Studies Resource Ctr,
E. Jacinto ST
Davao City 8000, Philippines
Web: www.fulbright.org.ph

*Dumaguete City*
American Studies Resource Center
Silliman University
Hibbard Avenue
Dumaguete City 6200, Negros
Oriental, Philippines
Tel: 63-35-422-6002 ext. 361
Web: www.fulbright.org.ph

*Ilo-ilo City*
Vice President for Academic Affairs
Central Philippine University
Lopez Jaena ST, Jaro
Iloilo City 5000, Philippines
Web: http://www.fulbright.org.ph

*Makati, Manila*
Philippine-American Educational
    Foundation (PAEF)
10/F Ayala Life FGU Center
6811 Ayala Avenue
Makati City 1226, Philippines
Tel: 63-2-812-0945
Web: www.fulbright.org.ph

*Zamboanga City*
Ateneo de Zamboanga University,
La Purisima Street
Zamboanga City 7000, Philippines
Web: www.fulbright.org.ph

## Poland

*Krakow*
US Consulate General Krakow
Public Affairs
ul. Stolarska 9
Krakow 31-043, Poland
Tel: 48-12-424 5140
Web: //krakow.usconsulate.gov/krakow/
    studyus.html

*Warsaw*
Polish-U.S. Fulbright Commission
Educational Advising Center
ul. K.I. Gałczyńskiego 4
Warsaw 00-362, Poland
Tel: 48 22 10 10 040
Web: www.fulbright.edu.pl

*Warsaw*
US Embassy Public Affairs IRC
ul. Piekna 14a
Warsaw 00-540, Poland
Tel: 48 22 504 23 91
Web: //poland.usembassy.gov/poland/
    programs/education-advising-center.html

## Portugal

*Lisbon*
Fulbright Information Center
Avenida D. Carlos I, n.º126 - 4º andar
1249-074 Lisbon, Portugal
Tel: 351 217 996 390
Web: www.fulbright.pt

## Qatar

*Doha*
US Embassy Public Affairs Section
22 February Road
Doha, Qatar
Tel: 974-4496-6749
Web: //qatar.usembassy.gov/education

## Romania

*Bucharest*
Fulbright Commission
2, Ing. N Costinescu St
Bucharest 011878, Romania
Tel: (4021) 2319016
Web: www.fulbright.ro/
    educational-advising-center.html

## Russia

*Moscow*
EducationUSA Advising Center
Library of Foreign Literature
1 Nikoloyamskaya, 3rd Floor
Moscow 109189, Russia
Tel: 7 (495) 926-4554 ext 2

*Novosibirsk*
EducationUSA Advising Center
Novosibirsk, Russia

*St. Petersburg*
EducationUSA Advising Center
St. Petersburg, Russia
Web: www.educationusarussia.org

*Vladivostok*
Vladivostok EducationUSA Center
Posyetskaya, 45, office 309
Vladivostok 690091, Russia
Tel: 7-423-2508653

*Voronezh*
Voronezh Regional Educational Advising
    Center
Ulitsa Nikitinskaya 52 A, Office 55
Voronezh 394018, Russia
Tel: 7-951 552 3163

## Rwanda

*Kigali*
US Embassy-EducationUSA Advising Center
2657 Avenue de la Gendarmerie
P.O.BOX 28
Kigali, Rwanda
Tel: 250 252 596689
Web: //rwanda.usembassy.gov/

## Saudi Arabia

*Dhahran*
US Consulate General Dhahran
Public Affairs Section
next to KFUPM
Dhahran 31942, Saudi Arabia
Tel: 966-3-330-3200 ext 3044
Web: //dhahran.usconsulate.gov/dhahran/
    resources.html

*Jeddah*
US Consulate General Jeddah
Public Affairs Section
Falasteen Street, Al Ruwais District
Jeddah, Saudi Arabia
Tel: 966-2-667-0080 ext 4151
Web: //jeddah.usconsulate.gov/
    educational-advising.html

*Riyadh*
Education Advising Office
US Embassy-Riyadh
Diplomatic Quarter
Riyadh 11693, Saudi Arabia
Tel: 966-1-488 3800 ext 4505
Web: //riyadh.usembassy.gov

## Senegal

*Dakar*
US Embassy Public Affairs
Route des Almadies Almadies
Dakar, Senegal
Tel: 221 33 879 4273
Web: //dakar.usembassy.gov/resources/
    education-advising-service.html

## Serbia

*Belgrade*
International Academic Center
Decanska 12, 1st Floor
Belgrade 11000, Serbia
Tel: 381 11 334 9639
Web: www.iacbg.org

## Sierra Leone

*Freetown*
EducationUSA Advising Center
US Embassy Public Affairs
Southridge-Hill Station
Freetown, Sierra Leone
Tel: 232 76-515-363
Web: //freetown.usembassy.gov/
    educational_advising_services.html

## Singapore

*Singapore*
EducationUSA Advising Center
1 Woodleigh Lane, Singapore 357684
Tel: 65 6709 4838

## Slovakia

*Banska Bystrica*
SAIA EducationUSA Advising Center
Tajovskeho 51
Banska Bystrica 974 00, Slovakia
Tel: 421-48-4137810
Web: www.saia.sk

*Bratislava*
Fulbright Commission
Levicka 3
Bratislava 821 08, Slovakia
Web: www.fulbright.sk

*Kosice*
InfoUSA Center Kosice
Hlavna 10
Kosice 042 30, Slovakia
Tel: 421 918 245 863
Web: //www.svkk.sk/usinfo

## Slovenia

*Ljubljana*
Slovene Human Resources Development &
    Scholarship Fund
Dunajska 22, 6th FL
1000 Ljubljana, Slovenia
Tel: 386-1-434 10 88
Web: http://www.sklad-kadri.si/si/
    izobrazevanje-v-tujini/svetovalnica-za-
    izobrazevanje-v-tujini/educationusa/

## South Africa

*Cape Town*
US Consulate General
EducationUSA Advising Center
2 Reddam Ave.
Cape Town, Western Cape
Tokai 7945, South Africa
Tel: 27-21-702-7362
Web: //southafrica.usembassy.gov/
    educational-advising.html

*Durban*
EducationUSA Advising Center
30th Fl, 303 Dr. Pixley Kaseme Street
Old Mutual Bldg
Durban 4001, South Africa
Tel: 27-31-305-7600 ext.3135
Web: //southafrica.usembassy.gov/

*Johannesburg*
US Consulate General
EducationUSA Advising Center
1 Sandton Drive
Johannesburg 2196, South Africa
Tel: 27 11 290 3108
Web: //southafrica.usembassy.gov/
    educational-advising.html

## South Sudan

*Juba*
EducationUSA Advising Center
American Corner, University of Juba
Juba, South Sudan
Tel: 211 912138622

## Spain

*Madrid*
Fulbright Commission
Calle General Oráa, 55
28006 Madrid, Spain
Tel: 34 91 702 7002
Web: //fulbright.es/ver/estudiar-en-eeuu

## Sri Lanka

*Colombo*
US-Sri Lanka Fulbright Commission
EducationUSA Advising Center
55, Abdul Caffoor Mawatha
Colombo 03, Sri Lanka
Tel: 94-11-256 4176
Web: www.fulbrightsrilanka.com/

## St. Kitts and Nevis

*Charlestown*
Nevis Public Library
EducationUSA Advising Center
Prince William Street
Charlestown, St. Kitts and Nevis
Tel: (869) 469 0421

## St. Lucia, West Indies

*Castries*
Students Services Centre
Sir Arthur Lewis Community College
Morne Fortune
Castries, St. Lucia, West Indies
Tel: 758-457-7300
Web: www.salcc.edu.lc

## St. Vincent & Grenadines

*Kingstown*
EducationUSA Advising Center
National Public Library, Richmond Hill
Kingstown
St. Vincent & the Grenadines
Tel: 784-456-1689

## Sudan

*Khartoum*
EducationUSA Advising Center
U.S. Embassy Khartoum
Kilo 10, Soba Khartoum, Sudan
Tel: 249-187-022-851
Web: //sudan.usembassy.gov/
    publicaffairssection/educationusa/

## Suriname

*Paramaribo*
Business Education Resource Center,
US Embassy
Dr. Sophie Redmondstraat 129
Paramaribo, Suriname
Tel: 597-472900 ext.2267
Web: //suriname.usembassy.gov/

## Swaziland

*Mbabane*
EducationUSA Advising Center
American Compound
Ryan House, Cnr Sir Robert Croydon
    Avenue & Jubela Street
Mbabane, Swaziland
Tel: 268-2-404-2059 ext 3241
Web: //swaziland.usembassy.gov

## Sweden

*Malmö*
Malmö Borgarskola
EducationUSA Advising Center
Regementsgatan 36
211 42 Malmö, Sweden
Tel: 46-40-34 70 20
Web: www.malmo.se/borgarskolan

*Stockholm*
Fulbright Commission
Vasagatan 15-17, 4th floor
Stockholm 111 20, Sweden
Tel: 46-8-534 818 80
Web: www.fulbright.se/

## Switzerland

*Bern*
US Embassy
Public Affairs Section
Sulgeneckstrasse 19
3007 Bern, Switzerland
Tel: 41-31-357-7011
Web: //bern.usembassy.gov/study_usa.html

## Syria

*Damascus*
EducationUSA
Virtual Advising Office
Damascus, Syria
Web://damascus.usembassy.gov/eato2.html

## Taiwan

*Taipei*
AIT American Center
Suite 2101, 21F,
No. 333 Keelung
Road - Section 1
Taipei 110, Taiwan
Tel: 886-2-2723-3959 x233
Web: www.educationusa.org.tw

*Taipei*
Foundation for Scholarly Exchange
Fulbright Office
3F, 45 Yanping S. Road
Taipei 10043, Taiwan
Tel: 886-2-2388-7600 x142
Web: www.educationusa.tw/

## Tajikistan

*Dushanbe*
American Councils for
International Education:
EducationUSA Advising Center
86 Tolstoy Street
Dushanbe 734003, Tajikistan
Tel: 992-37-221 2103
Web: www.americancouncils-tj.org

## Tanzania

*Dar es Salaam*
US Embassy-Office Public Affairs
   EducationUSA Advising Center
686 Old Bagamoyo Road, Msasani
Dar es Salaam, Tanzania
Tel: 255-22-2294192
Web: //tanzania.usembassy.gov/
   educational_advising.html

## Thailand

*Bangkok*
Office of the Civil Service Commission
Pitsanuloke Road, Dusit,
   Bangkok 10300, Thailand
Tel: 6622820876
Web: www.ocsc.go.th

*Bangkok*
American University Alumni (AUA)
179 Rajdamri Road, Lumpini,
Pathumwan
Bangkok 10330, Thailand
Tel: 66-2383933-4 ext4006
Web: www.auathailand.org/

*Bangkok*
Public Affairs Section
U.S. Embassy
GPF Wittayu Tower
Tower A 10th Floor 93/1
Bangkok 10330, Thailand
Tel: 66-2-205-4596
Web: //bangkok.usembassy.gov/

*Chiang Mai*
ACE! Academy for EducationUSA
21 Soi 9 Nimmanhaemin Road
Chiang Mai 50200, Thailand
Tel: 66.81.8840203; 66.53.895699
Web: //acethai.weebly.com/

## Timor-Leste

*Dili*
American Embassy
Public Affairs Section
EducationUSA
Dili, Timor-Leste

## Togo

*Lomé*
US Embassy-Public Affairs Section
EducationUSA Advising Center
4332, BLVD Eyadema Cité OUA
Lomé, Togo
Tel: 228 2261 54 70
Web: //togo.usembassy.gov/
   educational_advising.html

## Tonga

*Nuku'alofa*
EducationUSA Tonga
Tupou Tertiary Institute
Lavinia Rd, Fasi moe Afi,
Nuku'alofa Tonga
Tel: 676-862-8890

## Trinidad & Tobago, WI

*Port of Spain*
US Embassy Public Affairs
Information Resource Center
15 Queen's Park West
Port of Spain,
Trinidad & Tobago, WI
Tel: (868) 822-5582
Web: //trinidad.usembassy.gov

## Tunisia

*Tunis*
AMIDEAST Tunis
22 Rue Al Amine Al Abassi
Cite Jardins, Belvedere
1002 Tunis, Tunisia
Tel: 216-7-114-5716; 216-7-114-5700
Web: www.amideast.org/tunisia/advising/
   educationusa-services

## Turkey

*Ankara*
Fulbright Commission
Eskisehir Yolu, 9.Km Tepe Prime Is Merkezi
   B Blok No: 124
06800 Cankaya 06
Ankara, Turkey
Tel: 90-312-4284824
Web: www.fulbright.org.tr

*Istanbul*
Fulbright Istanbul Ofisi
Dumen Sokak 3/11, Gumussuyu
Taksim-Beyoglu
Istanbul 34437, Turkey
Tel: 90-212-244 1105
Web: www.fulbright.org.tr

*Izmir*
EducationUSA Advising Center
Talatpaşa Blv., 1439 Sk., no. 25
TÖMER Binası, 6. Kat Alsancak
Alsancak, Konak, Turkey
Tel: 90-543-531 5283

## Turkmenistan

*Ashgabat*
EducationUSA Advising Center
American Councils
Gerogly 48/A, 2nd floor
Ashgabat 744036
Turkmenistan
Tel: 993-12-97-10-16
Web: //americancouncilstm.org

*Dashoguz*
Dashoguz American Corner
Turkmenbashy str. 7/2
Dashoguz, Turkmenistan
Tel: 993 322 60773
Web: //americancornerstm.org

*Mary*
Mary American Corner
42a Agziberlik Avenue
Mary 745400, Turkmenistan
Tel: 993-522-7-38-65
Web: //americancornerstm.org/

*Turkmenabat*
Turkmenabat American Corner
3rd floor, Shatlyk Building
33 Pushkina Street
Turkmenabat, Turkmenistan
Tel: 993-422-3 37 71
Web: //americancornerstm.org

## Uganda

*Kampala*
EducationUSA Advising Center
Plot 1577 Ggaba Road
Nsambya-Kampala, Uganda
Tel: 256-414-306-315
Web: //kampala.usembassy.gov/
educational_exchange.html

## Ukraine

*Dnipropetrovsk*
"Osvita" Educational Information and
Advising Center
Prospekt Karla Marksa 60, rm.75
Dnipropetrovsk 49000, Ukraine
Tel: 380987759847
Web: www.center-osvita.dp.ua

*Kharkiv*
Kharkiv "Osvita" Educational
Advising Center
13 Chernyshevskogo Str,
office 701 Kharkiv 61057,
Ukraine
Tel: 380-57- 756-7562
Web: www.osvita.kharkiv.org

*Kyiv*
EducationUSA Advising Center
American Councils for International
Education
vul. Esplanadna 20, (6th floor)
Kyiv 01001, Ukraine
Tel: 380- 44-289-3952
Web: www.americancouncils.org.ua

*Lviv*
Osvita Educational Advising Center
prospekt Chornolova, 4, room 1
Lviv 79019, Ukraine
Tel: 380-94 99-33-053; 380-50 570-1100
Web: www.osvita.org/

## United Arab Emirates

*Abu Dhabi*
US Embassy Public Affairs
Airport Road at Rabdan
Embassies District 29th Street
Abu Dhabi, United Arab Emirates
Tel: 971-2-414 2245
Web: //abudhabi.usembassy.gov

*Dubai*
EducationUSA Advising Center
US Consulate General
bin Zayed Road
Dubai, United Arab Emirates
Tel: 971-43094142

## United Kingdom

*London, England*
US-UK Fulbright Commission
Unit 302, 3rd Floor, Camelford House
89 Albert Embankment
London SE1 7TP, United Kingdom
Tel: 44 0207 498 4010
Web: www.fulbright.org.uk

## Uruguay

*Montevideo*
Alianza Cultural Uruguay
EducationUSA Advisor
Montevideo 1217, Uruguay
Tel: 598 2902 51 60

*Montevideo*
EducationUSA Advising Center
U.S. Embassy Montevideo
Lauro Muller 1776 CP
Montevideo 11200 Uruguay
Tel: 598 2 1770 2166

## Uzbekistan

*Tashkent*
US Embassy
EducationUSA Advising Center
3 Moyqorghon Street, 5th Block
Yunusobod District
100093 Tashkent, Uzbekistan
Tel: 998-71-140-24-47
Web: //uzbekistan.usembassy.gov/advising

## Venezuela

*Caracas*
Asociacion Venezolano Americana de
Amistad
Av. Francisco de Miranda, Edif.
Centro Empresarial Miranda Piso
1, Ofic. 1-C y Los Ruices,
Caracas 1071, Venezuela
Tel: 58-0212-2335-7821 Ext. 104
Web: www.avaa.org

*Caracas*
EducationUSA Advising Center
United States Embassy
Caracas, Venezuela
Tel: 58 212 9078496
Web: www.caracas.usembassy.gov

*Maracaibo*
Centro Venezolano Americano de Zulia
(CEVAZ) Maraciabo
Calle 63, #3E-60, Sector Las Mercedes
Maracaibo 4001, Venezuela
Tel: 58-261-7934517
Web: www.cevaz.org/

*Merida*
Centro Venezolano Americano de Merida
Urbanizacion El Encanto Prolongacion
Avenida 2 (Lora) Esquina Calle 43
No. 1-55
Merida 5101, Venezuela
Tel: 58-274-2631362
Web: www.cevam.org

## Vietnam

*Hanoi*
EducationUSA Advising Center
US Embassy
3rd Floor, Rose Garden Tower, 170
Ngoc Khanh, Ba Dinh District
Hanoi, Vietnam
Tel: 84-4-3850-5000
Web: vietnam.usembassy.gov/
educationusa.html

*Ho Chi Minh City*
EducationUSA

US Consulate General
Diamond Plaza 8th Floor,
34 Le Duan, District 1
Ho Chi Minh City, Vietnam
Tel: 84-8-3520-4610
Web: //hochiminh.usconsulate.gov/

## Yemen

*Aden*
AMIDEAST Aden
142 Hadaiq Al-Andalus Street
Al-Safarat District
Khormaksar Aden, Yemen
Tel: 967-2-235-069 / 070 / 071 x105
Web: www.amideast.org/yemen

*Sana'a*
AMIDEAST Sana'a
Off Algiers Street
Behind Tunisian Embassy
Sana'a, Yemen
Tel: +1-240-565-5131
Web: www.amideast.org/yemen

## Zambia

*Lusaka*
EducationUSA Advising Center
Embassy of the United States of America
Subdivision 694 /Stand 100
Kabulonga District Lusaka 10101, Zambia
Tel: 260 211 357279

## Zimbabwe

*Bulawayo*
EducationUSA Advising Center
Bulawayo Public Library
100 Fort Street & 8th Avenue
Bulawayo, Zimbabwe
Tel: 263-9-882989
Web: //harare.usembassy.gov

*Gweru*
EducationUSA Advising Center &
American Center
Gweru Memorial Library
50 Cnr 8th Street & Lobengula Ave
Gweru, Zimbabwe
Tel: 263 54 222 628

*Harare*
EducationUSA Advising Center
Eastgate Building, 7th Floor
Goldbridge, Crn 3rd and R. Mugabe
Harare, Zimbabwe
Tel: 263-4-758800/1/5
Web: //harare.usembassy.gov/
educational_advising.html

*Mutare*
EducationUSA Multare Center
1 Queensway st Civic Centre Complex
Mutare, Zimbabwe
Tel: 263 020 68173
Web: //harare.usembassy.gov

# Take learning to new heights.

With 38 courses in everything from Computer Science to Art History, AP® gives high school students the opportunity to earn college credit and stand out on college applications.

collegeboard.org/ap

**AP®** CollegeBoard

# Get credit for knowing.

CLEP® exams help you earn college credit for what you already know, for a fraction of the cost of a college course. CLEP offers 33 exams that cover what's taught in introductory college courses, saving you time and money toward a degree.

clep.org

© 2017 The College Board.

# Show up ready on test day.

Now, the best way to get ready for the SAT is free for everyone. The College Board partnered with Khan Academy® to create Official SAT® Practice. It's free, personalized, and the only online practice tool from the makers of the test. It's simply the best way to prepare. Sign up today.

satpractice.org

# Registered and ready?

The SAT® tests what students are already learning in class. Preparing for it is easier than ever with free, personalized practice on Khan Academy®. Encourage your students to register today.

sat.org

SAT® | CollegeBoard